Sensorimotor Control and Learning

Sensorimotor Control and Learning

An introduction to the behavioral neuroscience of action

James Tresilian
University of Warwick

palgrave
macmillan

First published 2012 by
PALGRAVE MACMILLAN

Palgrave Macmillan in the UK is an imprint of Macmillan Publishers Limited, registered in England, company number 785998, of Houndmills, Basingstoke, Hampshire RG21 6XS.

Palgrave Macmillan in the US is a division of St Martin's Press LLC, 175 Fifth Avenue, New York, NY 10010.

Palgrave Macmillan is the global academic imprint of the above companies and has companies and representatives throughout the world.

Palgrave® and Macmillan® are registered trademarks in the United States, the United Kingdom, Europe and other countries

ISBN: 978-0-230-37105-7

This book is printed on paper suitable for recycling and made from fully managed and sustained forest sources. Logging, pulping and manufacturing processes are expected to conform to the environmental regulations of the country of origin.

A catalogue record for this book is available from the British Library.

A catalog record for this book is available from the Library of Congress.

10 9 8 7 6 5 4 3 2 1
21 20 19 18 17 16 15 14 13 12

Printed in China

In memory of my father

Short contents

Contents

Figures and tables

Figures

Tables

Preface

Everyone said that it couldn't be done,
But he, with a grin, replied
That he'd never be one to say it couldn't be done
Leastways, not 'til he'd tried.
So he buckled right in with that same little grin,
By Golly! He went right to it,
He tackled the thing that couldn't be done
And he, um ...

... couldn't do it.

Anon[1]

This book provides a tutorial introduction to sensorimotor behavior and learning. It is written to be used as a primary text for teaching at the upper undergraduate and beginning graduate levels in kinesiology and psychology. The breadth and depth of coverage is likely to make it useful to research students and to undergraduates in other disciplines such as human factors, biomedical engineering, physiotherapy, and the neurosciences. I have made an effort to use real-world examples throughout; I have not attempted to cover applications. There are many texts that emphasize applications in physical education and sports (e.g., Edwards, 2010; Magill, 2010; Schmidt and Lee, 2011), ergonomics and human factors engineering (e.g., Wickens *et al.*, 2003), and movement therapy and rehabilitation (e.g., Shumway-Cook and Woollacott, 2011); this book is not intended to be an alternative to these. Its purpose is to provide an advanced-level introduction to the scientific study and understanding of sensorimotor behavior.

The book has a self-explanatory structure (see Contents) and is designed to support many different courses of study (I have never attempted to teach more than about four chapters' worth of material in any single-semester course). I have made the book as modular as possible so that it can be used in a flexible manner: the material has been used to support teaching at all levels of undergraduate study in the UK by judicious selection of sections and subsections. The material seems to have gone down surprisingly well with psychology students; the only negative comments have been occasional statements to the effect that 'this isn't psychology' and 'too much science'. Depending upon one's point of view, comments of this sort are not necessarily bad.

The original idea was to present a comprehensive, up-to-date, balanced, and accessible introduction to the field. I hope that what I have managed to produce is balanced, accessible, and up-to-date. I freely confess, however, that it is not comprehensive. I, um ... couldn't do it: there weren't enough hours in the day or days in the week, and no sensible publisher could have justified production of a book with the number of words and figures that would have been needed. If anyone doubts my claim that there weren't enough hours in the day, consider the following. The book has about 650 numbered figures, many with multiple diagrams. In

---

[1] This is a parody of a poem by Edgar Guest as recounted to me by my father when I was a small boy. The original may be found in Guest (1947).

fact, there are more than 1000 individual diagrams all drawn by the author. The average time taken to prepare a diagram (including captions and labelling) was about 2 hours, which makes a total of a little over 2000 hours or 50 weeks of full time work (5 days a week, 9 am to 5 pm). This had to come from the author's spare time (I have a full-time job), which gives an idea of the magnitude of the task. The result is that the book has numerous sins of omission, some of which I was very reluctant to commit. The treatment of learning is particularly thin: I have only been able to scrape the surface of the vast literature relevant to sensorimotor learning and memory. My decisions concerning what to cover and what to leave out were guided by:

(1)   The courses I teach and have taught.

(2)   My interests (which are narrow) and my prejudices (which range widely).

(3)   What is most commonly taught in courses on motor control and learning. Different people teach different topics, of course, and different textbooks cover different material. I looked at the latest editions of existing textbooks and at course outlines from various universities around the world to determine the most frequent topics.

(4)   Accessibility: the research literature in sensorimotor control and learning is replete with models and methods that involve the use of advanced mathematical techniques and/or complex concepts from engineering and physics. In my experience, the average undergraduate student of kinesiology or psychology lacks the background necessary to be able to gain any useful understanding of these techniques and concepts without studying them formally. Intuitive presentations of the simpler ideas is important, but I remain to be persuaded that this is true for many of the more advanced and complex ideas. Intuitive descriptions of dynamical systems theory, for example, have a tendency to befuddle the reader, or worse, imbue them with the illusion of understanding[2]. Thus, I have not attempted to provide intuitive discussions of more complex mathematical ideas.

If, as a result of my decisions, I have left out your favorite topic, theory, or experiment, then I can only apologize. Please feel free to write to me with a request that it be included in the next edition (but beware, there may never be one).

JAMES TRESILIAN

---

[2] A more rigorous approach would be to start with a book like Blanchard, Devaney, Hall (2011).

Author's acknowledgments

My thanks to the many reviewers (all anonymous with the exception of Florian Kagerer) who took the time to make helpful and encouraging comments, either on selected chapters or on the text as a whole. I acted on almost all suggestions for improvement, with the exception of one or two with which I disagreed. Unfortunately, I was forced to ignore most of the requests for additional content – I simply didn't have enough time or space to squeeze anything more in.

Thanks to Richard Carson and Mark Mon-Williams for encouraging me to persevere with this project, to Jaime Marshall at Palgrave Macmillan for his relentless but good-humored insistence that I get on with it, to Anna Plooy for pedagogical advice and helpful tips for drawing in Word, and to Friedericke Schlaghecken for welcome doses of common sense and coffee. I lay the blame for my interest in the lambda equilibrium point hypothesis (described at length in Chapter 6) on Randy Flanagan, though he may disagree with my continuing conviction that it is a valuable (if misunderstood) contribution to our understanding of neuromuscular control.

The hard work of Aléta Bezuidenhout and her team on the book's design is greatly appreciated. With one or two exceptions, I drew the diagrams using Word drawing tools. Some are based on figures from elsewhere; in such cases I have acknowledged sources, and I sought permission from copyright holders when that seemed necessary. I hope that cases where it didn't seem necessary are similarly interpreted by the relevant copyright holders and their teams of ruthless, high-powered lawyers. Last, but not least, my heartfelt thanks to Nico – who had to put up with a lot, bore it stoically and never ceased to be encouraging (perhaps because she thought that would be the quickest way to bring the ghastly torment to an end!) – and to Thomas, who also had to put up with a lot (but luckily for me he won't remember a thing about it).

Permissions

The author and publisher wish to thank[1] the following for permission to reproduce or adapt copyright material:

Figure 1.4A. The Musée d'Art et d'Histoire, Neuchâtel, Switzerland: photo of *Le Dessinateur* (The Draughtsman) by S. Iori.

Figure 1.4B. *The History of Computing Project* (Ed.,T. Stahl), www.thocp.net/reference/robotics/robotics.html.

Figure 3.33. Adapted from *Trends in Neurosciences*, 6 (12), R.S. Johansson and A.B. Vallbo, Tactile sensory coding in the glabrous skin of the human hand, pp. 588-594. Copyright 1983, with permission of Elsevier.

Figure 3.53. Adapted from Figure 1 in Walsh, L.D., Moseley, G.L., Taylor, J.L., Gandevia, S.C. (2011) Proprioceptive signals contribute to the sense of body ownership. *Journal of Physiology (London)*, 589, 3009-3021. With permission of John Wiley & Sons Ltd.

Figure 3.58. Adapted from Solomon, H.Y., Turvey, M.T. (1988) Haptically perceiving the distances reachable with hand-held rods. *Journal of Experimental Psychology: Human Perception & Performance*, 14, 404-427. With permission of the American Psychological Association.

Figure 4.9. Adapted from *Vision Research*, 12, A. Hughes, A schematic eye for the rabbit. Pp. 123-138. Copyright 1972, with permission of Elsevier.

Figure 5.29. Adapted from *Brain Research Reviews*, 57, J. Schouenborg, Action-based sensory encoding in spinal sensorimotor circuits, 111-117. Copyright 2008, with permission of Elsevier.

Figure 6.12. Adapted from *Vision Research*, 12, D.A. Robinson, Eye movements evoked by collicular stimulation in the alert monkey, pp. 1795–1808. Copyright 1972, with permission of Elsevier.

Figure 7.50. Reproduced from *Gait & Posture*, 3, D.A. Winter, Human posture and balance during standing and walking, pp. 193-214. Copyright 1995, with permission of Elsevier.

Figures 7.61 and 7.63. Adapted from Horak, F.B., Nashner, L.M. (1986) Central programming of postural movements: adaptation to altered support-surface configurations. *Journal of Neurophysiology*, 55, 1369-1381. With permission of the American Physiological Society.

Figure 9.4. Panel B with kind permission from Springer Science+Business Media, *Experimental Brain Research*, Interaction of the body, head and eyes during walking and turning, 136, 2001, 1-18, T. Imai, S.T. Moore, T. Raphan & B. Cohen.

Figure 9.6. Panel B adapted from Thomson, J.A. (1983) Is continuous visual monitoring necessary in visually guided locomotion? *Journal of Experimental Psychology: Human Perception & Performance*, 9, 427-443. With permission of the American Psychological Association.

Figures 9.11, 9.12 and 9.13 adapted from Warren, W.H. (1984) Perceiving affordances: visual guidance of stair climbing. *Journal of Experimental Psychology: Human Perception & Performance*, 10, 683-703. With permission of the American Psychological Association.

Figures 9.15 and 9.16 adapted from Warren, W.H., Whang, S. (1987) Visual guidance of walking through apertures: body-scaled information for affordances. *Journal of Experimental Psychology: Human Perception & Performance*, 13, 371-383. With permission of the American Psychological Association.

Figure 10.17. Adapted from from Warren, W.H., Morris, M., Kalish, M.L. (1988) Perception of translational heading from optical flow. *Journal of Experimental Psychology: Human Perception & Performance*, 14, 646-660. With permission of the American Psychological Association.

Figure 10.19. Reproduced from Warren, W.H., Morris, M., Kalish, M.L. (1988) Perception of translational heading from optical flow. *Journal of Experimental Psychology: Human Perception & Performance*, 14, 646-660. With permission of the American Psychological Association.

Figure 10.34 from Duchon, A.P., Warren, W.H. *Psychological Science*, 13 (3), pp. 272-278, copyright © 2002, Association for Psychological Science. Reprinted with permission of SAGE Publications.

Figure 11.15. Adapted, with kind permission from Springer Science+Business Media, from *Experimental Brain Research*, Spatial control of arm movements. 42, 1981, 223–227, P. Morasso.

Figure 12.14. Panels B and C adapted from Schmidt, R.A., Zelaznik, H., Hawkins, B., Frank, J., Quinn, J.T. (1979) Motor-output variability: A theory for the accuracy of rapid motor acts. *Psychological Review*, 86, 415-451. With permission of the American Psychological Society.

Figures 12.17 and 12.18. Adapted from Fitts, P.M. (1954) The information capacity of the human motor system in controlling the amplitude of movement. *Journal of Experimental Psychology*, 47, 381-391. With permission of the American Psychological Society.

Figures 12.33 and 12.34. Adapted from *Neuroscience*, 49, T.E. Milner, A model for the generation of movements requiring endpoint precision, pp. 487-496. Copyright 1992, with permission of Elsevier

Figures 12.48 and 12.50. Panels B with kind permission from Springer Science+Business Media, *Experimental Brain Research*, Systematic changes in the duration and precision of interception in response to variations of amplitude and effector size. 171, 2006, 421-435, J.R. Tresilian & A.M. Plooy.

Figure 12.51. Panel B with kind permission from Springer Science+Business Media, *Experimental Brain Research*, Constraints on the spatio-temporal accuracy of interceptive action: effects of target size on hitting a moving target. 155, 2004, 509-526 J.R. Tresilian, A.M. Plooy & T.J. Carroll.

Figure 13.5. Panel B reprinted from *Neuroscience*, 5, C.A. Terzuolo & P. Viviani, Determinants and characteristics of motor patterns used for typing, pp.1085-1103. Copyright 1980, with permission of Elsevier.

Figure 13.8. Panel B reprinted from *Current Biology*, 12, G. Wallis, A. Chatziastros & H. Bulthoff, An unexpected role for visual feedback in vehicle steering control, pp. 295-299. Copyright 2002, with permission of Elsevier.

Figure 13.9. Adapted from Guenther, F.H. (1995) Speech sound acquisition, coarticulation, and rate effects in a neural network model of speech production. *Psychological Review*, 102, 594-621. With permission of the American Psychological Association.

---

[1] The author's thanks go to those copyright holders who gave permission free of charge.

Figure 13.24. Adapted from *Neuroscience*, 10, P. Viviani & G. McCollum, The relationship between linear extent and velocity in drawing movements, pp. 211-218. Copyright 1983, with permission of Elsevier.

Figure 13.25. Adapted from *Acta Psychologica*, 82, C.E. Wright, Evaluating the special role of time in the control of handwriting, pp. 5-52. Copyright 1993, with permission of Elsevier.

Figure 13.26. Adpated from *Acta Psychologica*, 54, F. Lacquaniti, C.A. Terzuolo & P. Viviani, The law relating the kinematic and figural aspects of drawing movements, pp. 115-130. Copyright 1983, with permission of Elsevier.

Figure 3.27. Adapted from Viviani, P., Cenzato, M. (1985) Segmentation and coupling in complex movements. *Journal of Experimental Psychology: Human Perception & Performance*, 6, 828–845. With permission of the American Psychological Association.

Figure 14.3 Panel B adapted from Tranel, D., Damasio, A.R., Damasio, H., Brandt, J.P. (1994) Sensorimotor skill learning in amnesia: additional evidence for the neural basis of nondeclarative memory. *Learning & Memory*, 1, 165-179. With permission of Cold Spring Harbor Laboratory Press.

Figure 14.5. Panel B adapted from Bourne, L.E., Archer, E.J. (1956) Time continuously on target as a function of distribution of practice. *Journal of Experimental Psychology*, 51, 25-33. With permission of the American Psychological Association.

Figure 14.6. Panel B adapted from Kimble, G.A., Shatel, R.B. (1952) The relationship between two kinds of inhibition and the amount of practice. *Journal of Experimental Psychology*, 44, 355-359. With permission of the American Psychological Association.

Figure 14.7. Panel B adapted from Bahrick, H.P., Fitts, P.M., Briggs, G.E. (1957) Learning curves – facts or artefacts? *Psychological Bulletin*, 54, 256-268. With permission of the American Psychological Association.

Figure 14.13. Panel B adapted from Leaton, R.N. (1976) Long-term retention of the habituation of lick suppression and startle response produced by a single auditory stimulus. *Journal of Experimental Psychology: Animal Behavior Processes*, 2, 248-259. With permission of the American Psychological Association.

Figure 14.24. Panel B adapted from Schneiderman, N., Gormezano, I. (1964) Conditioning of the nictitating membrane of the rabbit as a function of the CS-US interval. *Journal of Comparative & Physiological Psychology*, 57, 188-195. With permission of the American Psychological Association.

Figure 14.25. Reproduced from Smith, M.C., Coleman, S.R., Gormezano, I. (1969) Classical conditioning of the rabbit's nictitating membrane response at backward, simultaneous, and forward CS-US intervals. *Journal of Comparative & Physiological Psychology*, 69, 226-231. With permission of the American Psychological Association.

Figure 15.4. Panel B reproduced from *Trends in Neurosciences*, 20, J.R. Wolpaw, The complex structure of a simple memory, pp. 588–594. Copyright 1997, with permission of Elsevier.

Figures 15.8 and 15.9B. Adapted from Winstein, C.J, Schmidt, R.A. (1990) Reduced frequency of knowledge of results enhances motor skill learning. *Journal of Experimental Psychology: Learning Memory & Cognition*, 16, 677-691. With permission of the American Psychological Association.

Every effort has been made to trace rights holders, but if any have been inadvertently overlooked the publisher would be pleased to make the necessary arrangements at the first opportunity.

FUNDAMENTALS

CHAPTER 1

Motor Behavior and Control

1.1 Goal-Directed Motor Behavior

1.1.1 Introduction

Animals and people do things: birds sing, spiders spin webs, dogs run to fetch sticks, cats catch mice. These things are instances of **motor behavior**: behavior that involves exerting muscular forces that affect the limbs or other body parts. According to this definition, motor behavior is produced by the contraction of muscles[1]. This means that not moving can count as motor behavior, providing that it involves muscular contraction. Maintaining a static posture of a body part – keeping the head in a fixed position while you watch television, for instance – may not involve any observable movement of the body, but it is motor behavior nonetheless.

Most animal motor behavior is complex and adaptive; even the execution of routine tasks can be remarkably flexible and elaborate, as the following quotation illustrates:

> ... a wild rat digs a burrow ... Its movements are bafflingly complex ... The precise form of these movements varies constantly. These variations are not random. They are almost always functionally appropriate. The variations enable the rat to overcome obstacles to its continued tunneling. They adapt the digging pattern to the fluctuating conditions with which it must cope[2].

Animal motor behavior is not machine-like, with a fixed, stereotypical form; rather the movements vary so as to produce a particular outcome (such as a burrow) despite the presence of obstructions and changing conditions. The behavior is said to be *outcome-directed* or **goal-directed**. Intuitively, we see goal-directed motor behavior as behavior performed in order to do something, to achieve a specific outcome[3] (the goal). This contrasts with the movement of most robots[4], notably those used for industrial purposes such as spray-painting vehicle bodywork. These machines generate rigidly fixed patterns of movement, and so will only produce a particular outcome (e.g., painted bodywork) if the conditions are just right: change the conditions or throw in an obstruction, and the outcome may be completely different.

In this first part of the chapter, we will consider the distinction between behavior that is *goal-directed* and behavior that is not. We will define and illustrate the use of a number of terms that are used when discussing goal-directed motor behavior, and we will try to clarify its key features. Later in the chapter we will discuss mechanistic concepts from control engineering that can help us to understand goal-directed behavior in people and animals[5]. These concepts are central to almost all theoretical accounts of how human and animal movement is generated and controlled[6]; they will be used extensively in later chapters.

1.1.2 If you bring about a goal outcome by means of motor behavior, you have performed a motor action

Motor behavior is a general term that could be used to refer to all the motor activity that you get up to over some period of time. It is useful to have a term that refers to the particular motor behavior that leads to a specific outcome: the movements made in order to tie shoelaces, for instance. A term that is widely used is **goal-directed motor action**, or simply **motor action**. The word 'action' is used in a variety of different ways in everyday language: the Merriam-Webster online dictionary, for example, lists ten different meanings for the word. Two pertinent dictionary definitions are these[7]:

(1)   A thing done by something or an effect produced by something
(2)   The process of doing something to achieve an aim.

The term 'motor action' indicates that the outcome (thing done) is carried out by means of motor behavior. If you have brought about an outcome by means of motor behavior then you have performed a (goal-directed) motor action. For instance, if you go and shut the door, you have performed a door-closing action. If you accidentally bump into the door and it closes as a consequence, you have performed an action, but it was accidental, not goal-directed.

It is often useful to think of a motor action as the solution to a problem posed by a motor task. A task is a specification of something – the *task objective* – that a person is required to do, wants to do or needs to do: wash the dishes, close the door, hit the ball, avoid the hole. A **motor task** specifies an objective that can be done by means of motor behavior:

> **MOTOR TASK:** The specification of something, such as a particular state of affairs (the **task objective**), that can be brought about by means of motor behavior.

Some motor tasks involve simpler, component motor tasks, sometimes called **sub-tasks**. For example, the task of making a cup of tea is likely to include the following sub-tasks: (1) boil water; (2) get a cup from the cupboard; (3) get a tea-bag from the box; (4) put the tea-bag in the cup; (5) pour boiling water into the cup. Some of these sub-tasks can themselves be analyzed into more elementary sub-tasks (see next section for further discussion).

A person attempting a motor task faces a **motor problem**: how to achieve the task objective by means of motor behavior. How should the body be moved and the muscles contracted in order to achieve the objective? If your task is to tie your shoelaces, your motor problem is how to move so that the shoelaces get tied; actually tying them (the motor action) is your solution.

1.1.3 An elemental motor action is one that cannot be resolved into component actions

There is an intuitive distinction between goal-directed actions that involve a number of component actions and those that do not. The example discussed in the previous section was making a cup of tea: the tea is made by executing a sequence of simpler actions. It may be possible to break these component actions up into still simpler components, but at some point this is no longer possible. A goal-directed action that cannot be resolved into simpler goal-directed components can be called an *elemental goal-directed motor action* or **elemental action** for short[8]:

> **ELEMENTAL ACTION:** A motor action in which the goal outcome is achieved by executing just one goal-directed action (as opposed to two or more goal-directed actions in combination).

An example might be hitting a baseball. A person hitting a ball pitched at them does not do so by performing a sequence of component actions, each directed at achieving some intermediate goal: the hitting action cannot be broken down into component actions[9]. The idea of an elemental action seems simple enough, but it is not always easy to say whether a particular action is elemental or not. The difficulties involved will be discussed further in Chapter 13, where we will also discuss how elemental actions can be combined together to form more complex actions. Elemental actions are like building blocks from which more complex actions can be constructed.

The execution of an elemental action will usually involve an identifiable start point and an identifiable end point. That is, the movements and muscle contractions involved in executing the action begin and end at identifiable times. In the ball-hitting example, execution begins when the bat starts to swing toward the location at which the impact takes place; execution ends once the swing is complete, and this includes any follow-through after the ball has been struck. For this reason, elemental actions are usually **discrete actions**[10]:

> **DISCRETE ACTION:** A motor action whose execution has clearly identifiable start and end points.

1.1.4 Action and movement are different things

An action is not the same as a set of movements or of muscular contractions. Consider closing an open door. You could do this in several different ways: you might grasp the door handle with your hand and push the door closed; you might kick the door closed with your foot, shove it closed with your shoulder, or even butt it with your head. In each case the same motor action is performed, but the details of the actual motor behavior involved are different. It doesn't matter what movements you make or what muscles you contract in order to perform an action; the motor action is the same if the outcome is the same. Thus, a motor action is not the same thing as making particular movements or contracting particular muscles.

Even if an action is performed by the same means on different occasions, the exact movements and muscle activations involved are extremely unlikely to be the same for any two performances. This is because the circumstances in which you perform an action will be slightly different each time, and the movements you make need to be right for the particular conditions. When picking up a pen, for instance, the arm movements and muscle activations required to move your hand to the pen will depend on where the pen is located. Examples of this kind illustrate a general principle: in order to achieve the same outcome in different circumstances, different movements and/or muscle activations will be required. This important principle has no accepted name, so we will have to invent one, *the principle of motor fit*:

> **PRINCIPLE OF MOTOR FIT:** Achieving the same outcome in different circumstances will generally require different motor behavior (e.g., different body movements and/ or muscle contractions): the behavior must fit with the particular circumstances.

An animal that is able to fit its behavior to the circumstances demonstrates motor **adaptability**. An **adaptable** animal is one that changes its behavior in order to achieve a particular outcome in different circumstances; it adapts its behavior to the circumstances. Here is a suitable definition of (motor) adaptability that follows standard dictionary definitions:

> **(MOTOR) ADAPTABILITY:** The capacity to adjust or alter motor behavior in new conditions (or in response to changes to the prevailing conditions) so that a goal outcome (or task objective) is achieved.

Closely connected to the principle of motor fit and adaptability is the notion of **motor equivalence**[11]. Different movements and muscle contractions that produce the same outcome are said to be *motor equivalent*:

> **MOTOR EQUIVALENCE:** Equality of outcome of two or more movements, movement patterns or muscle contractions that may be different in other respects.

Motor equivalence is illustrated in Figure 1.1. On the left is a list of five different patterns of motor behavior (sets of movements/muscle contractions/exerted forces). The first three of these lead to the same overall outcome (outcome 1) and so are motor equivalent. The last two (4 and 5) lead to a different outcome (outcome 2), and are motor equivalent to each other but not to the first three. The ability to perform a particular action in different ways is essential for adaptability: if a behavior can only be performed in one way, then performance cannot be changed to deal with different circumstances.

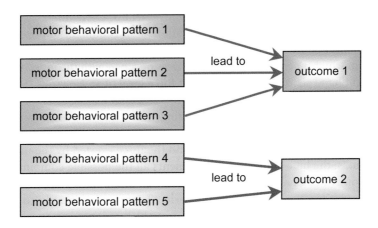

Figure 1.1: *Different motor patterns that produce the same outcome are motor equivalent.*

1.1.5 Repetitions of the same action do not necessarily involve repeating the same movements or forces

It may sometimes seem that repetitions of a particular action are performed in exactly the same way: the outcome is achieved in the same way, so the concept of motor equivalence is not needed. However, subjective impressions of this sort are misleading; it is always the case that different performances in a sequence of repetitions differ from one another, even though the differences may sometimes be quite small. This was recognized early in the study of human motor behavior, as illustrated by the following quotation, dating from 1932:

> Suppose I am making a stroke in a quick game, such as tennis or cricket ... When I make the stroke I do not, as a matter of fact, produce something absolutely new, and I never merely repeat something old ... I may think that I reproduce exactly a series of text-book movements, but demonstrably I do not[12].

One of the earliest empirical studies of this phenomenon was conducted in the 1920s by the Russian physiologist Nicolai Bernstein, and examined repetitive hammering of a chisel by highly skilled blacksmiths[13]. Figure 1.2 shows three consecutive frames of someone hammering; the swing of the hammer involves movement about the shoulder, elbow, and wrist joints. Bernstein found that the trajectory of the hammer-head was fairly consistent from one swing to the next, and led to error-free striking of the chisel. However, movements about the individual joints were much less consistent: different strikes in the sequence of repetitions involved different arm movements. Thus, there was motor equivalence: the same outcome (hammer-head trajectory and striking the chisel) was achieved using (slightly) different movements of the limb segments each time.

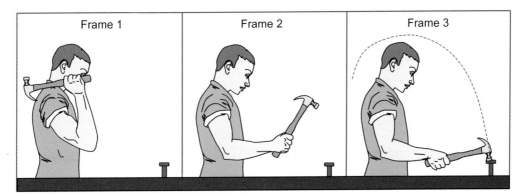

Figure 1.2: *A sequence of three frames in a cartoon of a person striking a drill or cold chisel. The path of the hammer-head is indicated by a dotted line in frame 3.*

A natural question to ask is: how can the same movement of the hammer-head be achieved if the movements of the limb segments are all different? It is difficult to provide a complete answer at this point, so we will consider a simpler example that illustrates the basic idea. Imagine a task in which a person is required to press on a pad with the index and middle fingers of their right hand so as to produce a target force level of 30 Newtons (Figure 1.3, panel A)[14]. The person could produce 30 Newtons by pressing with a force of 10 Newtons with the index finger and 20 Newtons with the middle finger, or using any other combination that adds up to 30. This is represented graphically in panel B of Figure 1.3. The force exerted by the index finger is plotted on the vertical axis and the force exerted by the middle finger on the horizontal axis: the blue diagonal line represents all the possible combinations that add up to 30 Newtons (index finger force + middle finger force = 30N). Suppose that the person repeats the task ten times and performs perfectly, producing exactly 30 Newtons each time. Panel C of Figure 1.3 shows how the force might have been produced on each trial: the white circles are data points that represent the forces produced on the ten trials. All the points lie on the 30-Newton line, but the forces produced by the two fingers are different each time. This example provides a simple illustration of how the same outcome (a total force of 30N) can be produced by different forces of the individual fingers involved. Likewise, we can imagine that the same trajectory of the hammer-head can be produced by different motions of the limb segments (for detailed discussion of similar cases see Chapter 11).

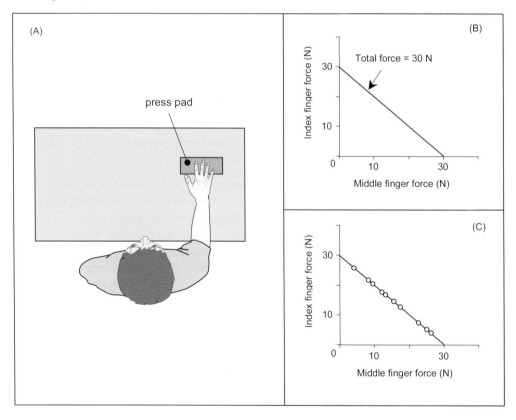

Figure 1.3: *A force-production task that requires pressing on a pad with the index and middle fingers to produce a total force of 30 Newtons. (See text for details.)*

1.1.6 Voluntary behavior is goal-directed by definition

Much of our daily motor activity is voluntary, which means that we intend or choose to do it, or at least we think we do. Any definition of voluntary behavior must appeal to our intuitions concerning intention and choice. One thing seems uncontroversial, voluntary behavior is goal-directed: we perform voluntary behavior in order to achieve outcomes. The following intuitive definition of voluntary behavior applies to human beings and will be sufficient for the requirements of this text:

> **VOLUNTARY BEHAVIOR:** Goal-directed behavior that is performed deliberately and with the conscious intention to achieve the goal. The performer is aware of having the choice of whether or not to carry it out.

This means that voluntary behavior is goal-directed by definition – it is done with the conscious intention of achieving an outcome. The definition does not necessarily imply that conscious intentions are causal in the production of voluntary behaviors; it merely says that voluntary behavior is associated with such intentions. Conscious intentions may or may not be causal, animals may or may not have conscious intentions – we may never know. Such matters are best left to philosophers[15], though some authors have argued that the question of whether conscious intentions are causal in voluntary action is amenable to empirical investigation[16].

Note that voluntary behavior is not the same as behavior carried out freely, without coercion. For behavior to count as voluntary you only need be aware of having the choice to do it or not: behavior that you do because you were ordered to do it or coerced into doing it still counts as voluntary. Behavior that is not voluntary is called **involuntary behavior**. This type of behavior is performed without conscious intention, and the person is not aware of having a choice about whether it is produced or not. An example is the reflexive response of the pupils to changes in the light level: constriction of the pupils in bright light and dilation of the pupils in dim light (the pupiliary light reflex).

It is not immediately clear whether or not involuntary behavior is goal-directed. Some pathological involuntary motor behavior is not goal-directed, such as the tremors and jerks that characterize neurological disorders like Parkinson's and Huntington's diseases (see Chapter 2 for more detail). These pathological behaviors lack purpose, but other involuntary behavior does serve a purpose. The pupiliary light reflex response is an example: it regulates the amount of light entering the eye so that you have enough to see by but not so much that your sensitive retinas are damaged.

Is purposive, involuntary behavior goal-directed or not? It might seem as though the lack of a conscious intent to achieve a goal means that these behaviors are not goal-directed. This possibility appears paradoxical, since it means that a behavior can serve a purpose but not be goal-directed. In the next section we will discuss this conundrum and consider what criteria might be used to determine empirically whether or not a behavior is goal-directed.

1.1.7 How can we tell whether motor behavior is goal-directed or not?

How can behavior serve a purpose, yet not be goal-directed? We will consider two types of example to show how this can be possible: (1) the behavior of clockwork automata, and (2) animal behaviors that have no obvious goals.

Clockwork automata are machines designed to mimic particular behaviors of either people or animals. Many clever examples were made in Europe in the 17th and 18th centuries, notably by the Swiss watchmaker Pierre Jacquet-Droz and his son, Henri. One of their most famous creations is 'The Draughtsman,' which still works today (Figure 1.4, panel A). This remarkable mechanical device is constructed from thousands of cogs, cams, wheels, rods, and joints. It is able to draw four different pictures (panel B) and follows the movements of the pencil with its eyes while doing so; it even blows on the paper to remove excess pencil dust.

The draughtsman is constructed in such a way that the sequence of movements it makes when drawing one of the pictures is always the same: the same movements in the same order. It will make the same movements regardless of whether there is any lead in the pencil or any paper on the desk, or whether the pencil is correctly positioned in its hand. Clearly, if there is no pencil or no paper, then no picture will be drawn, but the automaton continues to move regardless. Thus, its movements are not directed towards achieving an outcome (the drawn picture). We can consider the automaton's behavior to have a purpose (to draw the picture), since this is what it was designed to do. However, the behavior is not directed at achieving the outcome it was designed to produce.

(A) The Draughtsman

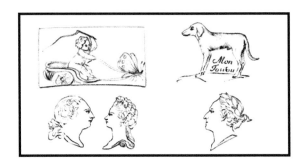

(B) The four pictures

Figure 1.4: *The Draughtsman and the pictures he creates. Image (A) courtesy of the* Musée d'Art et d'Histoire, Neuchâtel (photo: S. Iori). *Image (B) courtesy of The History of Computing Project.*

Can something similar arise in animal behavior? Is it possible for the behavior of an animal to have a purpose but not be goal-directed? Consider an example of an animal behavior that does not have an immediately obvious goal: the claw-waving behavior of male fiddler crabs[17] (Figure 1.5). Why do male fiddler crabs do this? What purpose does it serve? On the face of it, the crab would seem to be putting himself at risk, as claw-waving may attract predators; it must have some benefits that outweigh its costs. When biologists talk about costs and benefits, they are usually talking about effects on the survival and reproductive success of an animal. Something that improves an animal's chances of surviving and producing offspring is beneficial; something that has an adverse effect on these chances is a cost. How might claw-waving benefit a crab? There are two possibilities: (1) it intimidates other males and keeps them off his territory; (2) it attracts female crabs. Of course, it could do both these things – what intimidates a rival may attract a mate. There is some evidence to suggest that males wave at females almost exclusively, indicating that the main benefit of waving is that it attracts females and improves the males' chances of reproducing[18]. A biologist would then say that the function of claw-waving is to attract mating partners.

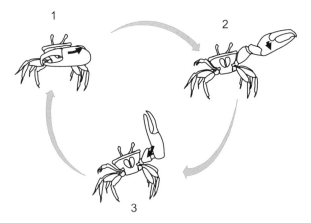

Figure 1.5: *Male mudflat fiddler crab (*Uca rapax*) 'waving' his major claw. Starting from position 1, he moves the claw outward to position 2, returns to position 1 via position 3, and repeats. (Based on an unnumbered figure in Chapter 1 of Dixon, 1981.)*

Is it possible that the function of claw-waving is to attract females, but that the claw-waving movements are not directed at achieving this goal? In order for this possibility to be plausible, the function needs to have been established by something external to the animal. In the case of behaviors that are inherited and have a genetic basis, this external thing is the process of evolution by natural selection. According to the theory of evolution, organisms have the (heritable) characteristics that they do because these enabled the organism's ancestors to survive and reproduce and to do so more successfully than their competitors; as a result, the genes responsible were passed from generation to generation. Thus, male fiddler crabs that waved their claws attracted more mates and had greater reproductive success than males that did not. The claw-waving males passed on their claw-waving genes until eventually they completely out-competed the non-wavers and none were left. Claw-waving need only have the effect of attracting females in order for the claw-waving males to have a reproductive advantage; it need not be directed at the goal of attracting females.

How can we determine whether or not a behavior like claw-waving is directed at attracting females or not? More generally, how can we determine whether a behavior is goal-directed or not? The Draughtsman's behavior suggests some answers. As we discussed earlier, the Draughtsman produces the same movements regardless of the circumstances and so will only successfully draw if the circumstances are just right. It cannot achieve the same outcome (a drawn picture) in different conditions. Furthermore, the Draughtsman does not do anything if it fails to draw a picture; it has no concept of failure and no means for determining whether it has failed or not. Human goal-directed behavior is quite different: we alter what we do – the movements we make, the limbs we move, the muscles we contract – in order to achieve an outcome under different conditions, and we may try and try again to achieve an outcome if we fail[19]. Of course, trying again may sometimes be impossible because the opportunity for achieving an outcome has passed: for example, if you attempt to hit a ball with a racket or bat and you miss, then the moment has passed – you can't try to hit the same ball again.

The above discussion suggests that there are at least two characteristics of goal-directed behavior that can allow us to determine empirically whether any given behavior is goal-directed or not[20]:

> (1) **ADAPTABILITY:** The same outcome can be achieved in different conditions using different motor behavior. (Includes adjustments to ongoing behavior in response to changes in circumstances that occur after execution has begun.)
>
> (2) **PERSISTENCE IN RESPONSE TO FAILURE:** When possible, if an outcome is not achieved on the first attempt, further attempts may be made until the outcome is achieved.

If behavior clearly displays these characteristics, then we can consider it to be goal-directed. If it displays neither of them, then we cannot consider it goal-directed.

Other criteria for goal-directedness are sometimes used. One derives from studies of learning in animals. A frequently used technique for training animals to perform some simple behavior is to give them food (a 'reward') whenever they perform the behavior. Many experiments conducted in the 1940s and 50s involved giving rats food rewards for pressing a lever[21], with the result that the rats came to press the lever, sometimes at high rates. There could be two types of goal-directedness involved. There is the intrinsic goal-directedness of the lever-pressing act itself: the rat contracts muscles and moves its body in order to press the lever (to qualify as being directed at pressing the lever, the two defining criteria listed above would have to be met). There is also the 'higher-level' goal of getting food, which the rat can achieve by pressing the lever. If this is the goal of lever-pressing, then we would expect that a rat that has not been fed for some time (a hungry animal) would press the lever at a high rate, but one that has been fed until it no longer eats (a satiated animal) would either not press the lever or press at a very low rate[22]. If a satiated animal persists in pressing the lever at a high rate, it may be concluded that the lever-pressing is not directed at a goal of getting food. In this case, the behavior is said to be a *habit* and not goal-directed[23]. However, we cannot conclude from the mere fact of persistent lever-pressing in a satiated animal that the lever presses lack the intrinsic goal-directedness described earlier. It might be that habitual lever presses are intrinsically goal-directed in the sense that they are *directed at* pressing the lever, but they are not *directed by* the goal of getting food. The idea of being directed by (rather than at) a particular goal is expressed in the following quotation: '[o]ur conception of goal directedness ... requires that the outcome of the action should be represented as a goal for the agent at the time of performance'[24]. The behavior is one that is regulated by or guided by some kind of internal representation of the goal. This is briefly discussed next.

1.1.8 Does 'directed at' imply 'directed by'?

Our experience suggests that voluntary behavior is not only *directed at* achieving a goal, but is also *directed by* some internal representation of the goal. We usually have an idea in our heads of the outcome we want, and this idea serves as a sort of reference that we can use to judge whether or not we have achieved our goal. These kinds of intuitions lead to the notion that behavior that is directed at achieving a goal is also directed by some internal representation of the goal. In other words, there is information within the nervous system that specifies the goal and that contributes in an essential way to the generation of motor behavior used to achieve the goal. The goal-related information might be supplied by the sensory systems, or it might be stored within the nervous system. This basic idea underlies the automatic mechanisms designed by engineers to control such things as the heaters and air conditioners that keep interior temperatures comfortable. In these mechanisms, goals are not encoded as mental constructs (ideas, mental images, intentions); they are encoded by the states of various components or sometimes by the way in which mechanical parts are put together (see section 1.2.9 for an example). The principles by which these mechanisms operate are discussed later in the chapter. In Part II of the book we will discuss how these principles can be applied to human and animal motor behaviors and aid in understanding how muscles and limbs are controlled.

It seems that goal-directedness requires that there be some kind of internal information about the goal itself that contributes to the generation of behavior. However, it is not always clear that this is the case. For example, consider a spider spinning a web or a colony of termites building a mound. It is implausible to suggest that the spider has an internal representation of a web against which it can compare its ongoing effort, or that each termite has a set of mound blueprints encoded into its nervous system. In these cases, it seems as if something other than an internal representation of the eventual outcome (the web or the mound) is governing behavior[25].

A simple example of a case in which an internal representation of the outcome of behavior is not guiding the behavior is provided by the common rough woodlouse (*Porcellio scaber*, Figure 1.6). These little crustaceans are often found in dark, damp places: they will dry out and die if their surroundings are insufficiently moist. If you put them in a dry place, they will run around until they find another sufficiently moist place. At first glance it may look as if their behavior is directed toward moist places – perhaps they detect moisture and head toward it. This turns out not to be the case. What actually happens is that they move around in a more or less random fashion in a manner that depends on the humidity: the less humid it is, the more actively they move around[26]. If they by chance happen to arrive at a location where the humidity is high enough, they slow down and may become completely inactive. More often than not, this behavior gets a woodlouse to a humid place and it survives. Examples of this kind show that it is not always obvious how a goal is represented in the nervous system of an animal or how it guides behavior[27]. In particular, it is not necessarily the case that the outcome is explicitly represented and used as a reference against which current achievement can be compared[28].

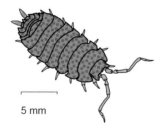

5 mm

Figure 1.6: *Common rough woodlouse,* Porcellio scaber.

1.1.9 Goal-directed motor behavior is sensorimotor behavior

The most interesting question concerning goal-directed behavior is not 'is such and such a behavior goal-directed or not?' Answering this question is just a first step to addressing more interesting questions such as 'how is it possible to produce goal-directed behavior?' and 'what is it that makes goal-directed behavior goal-directed?' We will consider these and related questions in more detail later on in this chapter and in some subsequent chapters.

One important point can now be made: sensory perception is necessary for the production of goal-directed motor behavior. In fact, this is so fundamental that we will elevate it to the status of a principle and call it the *sensorimotor principle*:

> **SENSORIMOTOR PRINCIPLE:** Sensory perception is necessary for goal-directedness. It is sensory perception that makes it possible for motor behavior to be goal-directed.

What is the reasoning behind this principle? As we saw in section 1.1.7 above, the two key defining characteristics of goal-directed behavior are adaptability and persistence in response to failure. Both require that the animal performing the behavior be able to obtain information about what is going on in the world. For instance, you cannot pick up a pen if you don't have information about where the pen is. Persistence in response to failure requires that failure be recognized – if an animal did not have the information that it had failed, then it could not persist in response to that failure.

The only way to obtain information about whether or not a goal has been achieved or what the environmental conditions are like is through sensory perception. This might be visual: you might look and see that the goal has been achieved or see what the environment is like. Whatever the sensory system involved, the basic fact remains: the information needed to adapt behavior to the conditions or to respond to failure can only be obtained through the senses. Thus, sensory perception is fundamental to the goal-directedness of behavior: goal-directed motor behavior is *sensorimotor* behavior.

1.2 Principles of Error-Correcting Feedback Control

1.2.1 Introduction: what is control?

Having control over something means being able to make it behave in a way that meets our requirements rather than following its own inclinations. This is achieved by doing things to it that will make it behave in the required manner. Thus, we may state the principal objective of control:

> **PRINCIPAL OBJECTIVE OF CONTROL:** to make a system's behavior meet a specific set of requirements by doing things to it.

The term 'system' refers to anything that is composed of linked, interacting parts.

Having control over a motor vehicle would typically mean being able to make it go in the direction you want at the speed you want. In order to achieve these requirements, you do things to the vehicle – turn the steering wheel and move the brake and accelerator pedals.

Of course, you need to move the pedals and steering wheel in the 'correct' way. For instance, if you want to get your car to go to the right so as to follow a bend in the road (Figure 1.7A), then you need to turn the steering wheel in the correct direction (clockwise) by the correct amount – not too much and not too little. If you turn the wheel counterclockwise your vehicle will turn in the wrong direction (left). If you turn the wheel clockwise but too much, then your vehicle will turn in the correct direction but may leave the road on the inside of the curve (oversteer, Figure 1.7B). If you turn the wheel clockwise but not far enough, you risk leaving the road on the outside of the curve (understeer, Figure 1.7C). This example illustrates the fundamental problem – in order to achieve a control objective, you need to determine the correct things to do:

> **FUNDAMENTAL PROBLEM OF CONTROL:** To determine what you need to do in order to make a system's behavior meet a specific set of requirements.

Notice that the requirements can be considered to be goals, and so successful control involves goal-directedness in an essential way. In this part of the chapter, we will provide an informal description of how feedback can be used to solve the fundamental control problem. We will also look at the circumstances in which the solution provided is adequate and those in which it is inadequate.

The ideas and concepts that will be described in what follows are quite general in their applicability. The system that needs to be controlled might be mechanical, hydraulic, electrical, thermodynamic, chemical or financial – the same set of ideas can be applied to all of them, regardless of their physical makeup. We can, in fact, use these ideas to understand control in biological systems[29], and they have become fundamental in the explanation of motor behavior. This part of the chapter provides an informal introduction to control concepts using everyday examples[30].

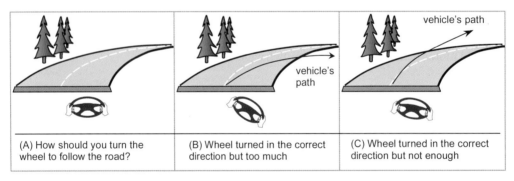

Figure 1.7: *Steering around a bend.*

1.2.2 A block diagram represents a system as something that produces outputs in response to inputs

A device like a microphone transforms something into something else: a microphone transforms sound into electrical signals. We normally say that it transforms an **input** into an **output**. The term *input* suggests some physical thing that is put into something else, like putting cheese into the refrigerator. The more general conception is of something that can be done to a system to stimulate it, move it or change its behavior in some way. Here is a definition:

> **INPUT:** Anything that can be done to a system to alter its behavior in some way. A force, a stimulus, an excitation are all examples of inputs.

Likewise, the term *output* is not used only to refer to something material that comes out. It can also mean something that a system does, or some measurable property of a system that can change. Thus, the temperature of a system could be an output – it is a measurable quantity that can take different values. In this book, the types of outputs we will encounter are variables like force, position and speed. Here is a definition:

> **OUTPUT:** Anything that a system does (any system behavior) or any measurable quality of the system that can vary. An output is only very rarely something material that comes out of a system.

Anything that receives an input and changes its output in response can be represented using a simple type of schematic diagram in which a system is represented by a box, also called a **block**. The input and output are represented by arrows going in and coming out:

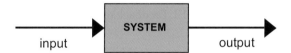

This kind of diagram is called a **block diagram**. It does not represent anything about the construction of the system (what's inside it), and it tells us nothing about how the transformation from input to output is actually achieved. If we drew a block diagram of a microphone, for example, we might label the block with the word 'microphone' and label the input 'sound' and the output 'electrical signal'. Note that sound is not the only quantity that can influence the behavior of a microphone, and the electrical signal it generates is not the only quantity that describes its behavior. For example, we could push the microphone so that it moves: the pushing force is an input and the movement is an output. We could also heat the microphone up by, for example, bombarding it with microwave radiation. In this case, the microwave radiation is the input, the temperature of the microphone is the output. Normally, of course, when we use a block diagram representation, only the inputs and outputs that are of interest are included.

The convenient thing about block diagrams is that they allow us to produce easily understood pictorial representations of systems that are constructed from individual components (subsystems) coupled together. This physical coupling means that the output of one forms the input to another like this:

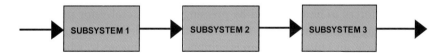

These three blocks are connected together to form a chain: the blocks are said to be connected in **series**. Series connectivity means that the first block in the chain does its job first, then the second block does its job, then the third and so on: a system with serially organized components does one thing at a time. Another fundamental type of connectivity is called **parallel** connectivity. Panel A of Figure 1.8 shows an example in which the output of block 1 is divided to form the input to blocks 2 and 3, which are connected in parallel. A system with components connected in parallel can do more than one thing at the same time: in Panel A, block 2 would be doing its job at the same time as block 3 was doing its job.

A block can also be connected to itself in the manner shown in panel B of Figure 1.8: the output of the block forms its input. This is called **feedback** because the output is 'fed back' to the input, forming a loop called a **feedback loop**. The term feedback is used in a number of different contexts in slightly different ways, but in each case some aspect of the system output is fed back as an input. For example, a familiar type of feedback is the sort that a student receives about their written work. The work the student submits for assessment is

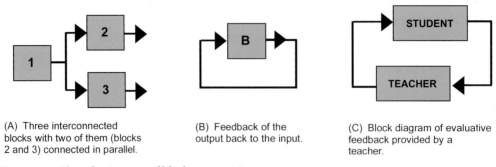

(A) Three interconnected blocks with two of them (blocks 2 and 3) connected in parallel.

(B) Feedback of the output back to the input.

(C) Block diagram of evaluative feedback provided by a teacher.

Figure 1.8: *Three basic types of block connectivity.*

their output. A teacher assesses the work and gives the student information about its quality. This information is a kind of feedback usually called **evaluative feedback**. A block diagram of the situation is shown in panel C of Figure 1.8. Evaluative feedback is important in learning, and we will encounter it again in Part III. Feedback of output to input is critical for control as discussed in what follows.

1.2.3 Controlling a system output requires adjustment of relevant inputs

If we want a system to produce a particular output, we must be able to apply inputs that influence that output. For instance, if we want to control the speed with which something moves, we need to be able to apply forces that increase or decrease the speed. Consider the everyday example of driving a motor vehicle. When driving, you need to control what your vehicle does: you might want it to go at a particular speed or go in a particular direction. Vehicle speed and direction of travel are both variable output quantities that you can control. Quantities of this sort are called **controlled variables**:

> **CONTROLLED VARIABLE:** A system output quantity whose value can be influenced (and so controlled) by applying particular types of input to the system.

The driver of the vehicle does not directly apply the forces that actually increase the speed or alter its direction of travel: these forces are developed by the engine, the brakes and the interaction of the tires and the road surface. What the driver does is interact with systems that cause these forces to be developed by pressing on the accelerator pedal or the brake pedal, or by turning the steering wheel. These systems are called **actuating systems**.

In a motor vehicle, an actuating system is equipped with a means by which the driver can interact with it: the accelerator pedal, the steering wheel and the brake pedal are examples. These are called **controls**. When the driver moves a control, the actuating system causes a force to develop that will alter an associated controlled variable. For example, moving the brake pedal causes frictional forces to develop between the wheel and brake pads, which slows the vehicle down.

When a driver moves a control, the control changes its position. For instance, when the steering wheel is moved, its angular position changes. The position of a control device is obviously a variable quantity. In this case, it is a variable that the driver can alter in order to control the vehicle. A variable like this is called a **control variable**:

> **CONTROL VARIABLE:** An input to a controlled system (or actuating device) that can be altered in order to make an associated controlled variable take the value(s) required.

1.2.4 A control system is a set of components that work together to achieve control

In the previous subsection we saw that the task of controlling a system can be expressed in terms of adjusting control variables in order to bring about required changes in controlled variables. In the driving example, three component systems contribute to the process of control: the driver, the actuating system(s) and the rest of the vehicle. A block diagram showing how these components are linked together is shown in panel A of Figure 1.9. This diagram shows the general set-up for control: one system (the driver) applies inputs to another system (the vehicle) by means of intermediary systems (actuating systems). The system that is being controlled – the vehicle in our example – is called the **controlled system**[31]:

> **CONTROLLED SYSTEM:** A system that is being controlled (having inputs applied to it) in order to make it behave in a way that meets a requirement or set of requirements.

The driver is the **controller** – the system that determines what to do (how to adjust the control variables) in order to meet the control objectives:

> **CONTROLLER:** A system that generates the control inputs that affect the behavior of the controlled system, usually via intermediary devices (actuating systems).

In general, therefore, the basic scheme for control can be represented using a block diagram like that shown in panel B of Figure 1.9. In this diagram the control input is a change of the control variable (e.g., change in the position of a steering wheel) which causes a change in the actuating input (e.g., change in the position of the front wheels), and the output of interest is the controlled variable (e.g., the direction of travel). The actuating system can sometimes be thought of as a component of the controlled system itself. For example, we usually think of the steering system or braking system as part of the vehicle. This allows us to simplify the diagram by absorbing the actuating device block into the controlled system block to give us the diagram in panel C of Figure 1.9.

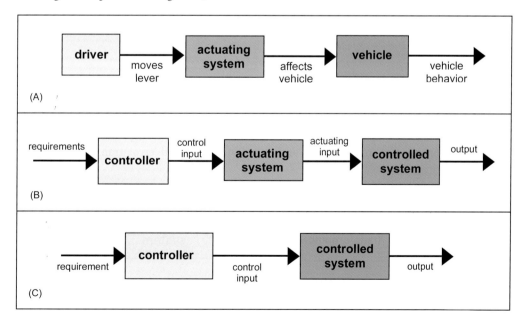

Figure 1.9: *Block diagrams showing the connection between controller and the controlled system.*

A system that is comprised of a controller, a controlled system, and possibly other components that work together to achieve some required behavior is called a **control system**. The controller is not necessarily a person; it may be a completely automatic device. When it is a person, the system is called a **manual control system**. When the controller is an artificial device, the system is called an **automatic control system**.

1.2.5 Feedback provides a means for achieving control objectives

Consider the vehicle speed control example again. The control problem is to determine how the accelerator pedal should be moved so that the vehicle travels at the required speed. If the vehicle is already traveling at the right speed, then there is no need to change anything: the driver will keep the accelerator pedal in the same position. If the vehicle is not traveling at the right speed, then there is a speed error equal to the difference between the actual speed and the required speed. For example, if the required speed were 90 km/h and the actual speed were 80 km/h, then the error would be 90 − 80 = +10 km/h. To go at the required speed requires adjusting the position of the accelerator pedal to correct for this error. The control process involved in this example is an instance of what is called **negative feedback control** or **error-correcting feedback control** (a common alternative term is *closed loop control*). The fundamental objective of this type of control can be stated as follows:

> **FUNDAMENTAL OBJECTIVE OF (ERROR-CORRECTING) FEEDBACK CONTROL:** To reduce errors to zero, or as close to zero as makes no practical difference.

The process involves feedback, because an output variable of the control system (vehicle speed) is fed back to the controller (driver). In the example, the vehicle speed is measured by a tachometer and displayed to the driver on the dashboard. The feedback is referred to as *negative* because the fed-back value is *subtracted* from the required value to give the error: error equals required value minus fed-back value. We can state the basic idea of feedback control as follows:

> **BASIC IDEA OF (ERROR-CORRECTIVE) FEEDBACK CONTROL:** Observe/measure what the controlled system is actually doing, and use the difference between what you require and what you observe (i.e., the error) to determine what needs to be done to eliminate the error.

Note that the value of the controlled variable is fed back to the controller via a measuring device or **sensor**. This is the tachometer in the case of vehicle speed. Thus, there is an essential sensory or observational component to feedback control. Figure 1.10 shows a block diagram of a generic error corrective (negative) feedback control system. The controller has been resolved into two subcomponents: a comparator (⊗) and a component labeled 'error transformation' that

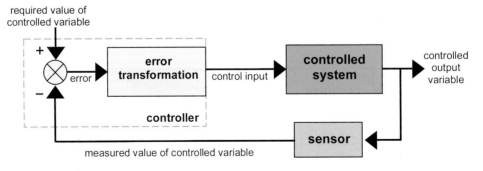

Figure 1.10: *Block diagram of a negative feedback control system.*

transforms the error signal into an input to the controlled system (labeled 'control input'). The comparator is simply a block that subtracts the measured value of the controlled variable from the required value to form the error. When it is possible for errors to arise, feedback is essential for control: without feedback it would be impossible for the controller to determine what the controlled system is doing, and thus impossible to detect errors. Possible sources of error are discussed next.

1.2.6 Errors arise for three basic reasons: disturbances, mistakes by the controller and changes in the requirements

Why do errors arise? One cause of errors is a change in any of the external conditions that can affect a system's behavior. For example, a vehicle's speed can be affected by a hill – it will tend to slow down when going up and speed up when going down – or by a headwind or a tailwind. A vehicle's direction of travel can be affected by a sidewind, a pothole or a change in the camber of the road. These things disturb system behavior and are therefore called **disturbances**.

A second cause of errors is mistakes by the controller. It is easy to imagine a person making mistakes if they are acting as the controller. A driver, for example, could generate an error by accidently pressing on the accelerator or turning the steering wheel. It is also possible to make the wrong correction for an error when one arises: a driver could turn the steering wheel too far and oversteer (Figure 1.7B) or not turn it enough and understeer (Figure 1.7C).

A third cause of error is a change in the requirements. If a system output meets one set of requirements and the requirements change, then the output will not meet the new requirements and there will be an error. For example, a vehicle may enter a section of road with a lower speed limit, and the driver may revise down the required speed. Thus, there are three basic sources of error as follows:

(1) **Disturbances:** Inputs external to the control system could affect the controlled variable(s) and so produce errors.

(2) **Controller mistakes:** The controller could make a change in the control variable when it is not needed, or respond to an error with an inappropriate change of the control variable.

(3) **Changes to the requirements:** If the required value of the controlled variable changes, an error is likely to be created.

Note that a feedback controller needs no information about what caused the error to occur in the first place in order to produce a corrective response. In most automatic control systems the controller is blind to the cause of the error; the controller simply transforms the error into a change in the control variable.

If the required value of the controlled variable does not change for long periods of time, the value is referred to as the **set-point**. An everyday example is the thermostat setting on a home central-heating system: this system is a feedback control system for maintaining temperature in the home at the value set on the thermostat, which typically remains constant for long periods. Here is a definition:

> **SET-POINT:** The name given to the required value of the controlled variable when this (required) value remains fixed for extended periods of time.

The control problem in this case is to find control inputs that will bring the value of the controlled variable to the set-point in the first place and that will restore it to the set-point should there be a disturbance or mistake that moves it away. This problem is usually called a **regulation problem**:

> **REGULATION PROBLEM:** The control problem that exists when the control objective is to bring a controlled variable to a specific, fixed value (set-point) and maintain that value in the face of disturbances.

In some cases the required value of the controlled variable may change over time, possibly continuously. For example, when steering a vehicle along a winding road, the required value for the vehicle's direction of travel is the direction of the road, which is changing continuously. In such cases, the control objective is to make the controlled variable follow the changing required value. The control problem involved is called a **tracking problem**:

> **TRACKING PROBLEM:** The control problem that exists when the control objective is to make the controlled variable follow (track) changes in the required value.

Both regulation and tracking problems can be solved using feedback control. In both cases, the control system is organized as in Figure 1.10 and the controller must transform the error into an appropriate control input. This transformation is clearly a vital part of the feedback control process and is discussed next.

1.2.7 A feedback controller transforms the error into changes in the control variable

A driver who is attempting to maintain a specific speed can use feedback control to adjust the position of the accelerator pedal to correct detected errors in speed. According to the block diagram in Figure 1.10, the error needs to be transformed into a change in accelerator-pedal position that will eliminate it. If the error is positive, the vehicle is going slower than required, so the driver needs to push the pedal further down. If the error is negative, the vehicle is going too fast, so the driver needs to let the pedal up, which results in engine braking that slows the vehicle down. Regardless of whether the vehicle is going too fast or too slow, the size of the error determines how far to move the pedal: the bigger the error, the further the pedal needs to be moved. This example illustrates two things about how the error is transformed into changes in the control variable in feedback control: *the sign of the error determines the direction (or sign) of the change in the control variable; and the size of the error determines the size of change in the control variable.*

To illustrate how this principle works, we will examine a simplified version of the speed control problem, in which the brakes are not used. Imagine that the vehicle is traveling along a completely flat road and that a change in accelerator pedal position leads to a proportional change in vehicle speed[32]. This means that if you change the pedal position by some amount, say 3 cm, the change in vehicle speed (in km/h) will be some number times 3; the number is called the constant of proportionality (denoted by 'B'). So we have the following relationship between changes in pedal position (in cm) and changes in speed (in km/h):

Change in vehicle speed = B × (change in accelerator pedal position)   **(1.1)**

If this is true, then the error can be transformed into a corrective change in the accelerator pedal position. The error is the change in speed you require to reach the required speed. For instance, if the required speed is 90 km/h and the actual speed displayed on the dashboard is 80 km/h, then you need to change speed by +10 km/h to reach the required speed, and this is exactly the error. From the above relationship (equation 1.1), a 10 km/h increase in speed can be brought about by pushing the accelerator pedal 10÷B cm further towards the floor. Thus, if you know the value of B, then you can produce the right change in pedal position. For example, if you knew that B happened to have a value of 5, then you could correct a speed error of +10 km/h by pushing the pedal 2 cm further to the floor.

The rule for turning an error into a change in the control variable is called a **feedback control law**; it is the rule by which the error transformation block in Figure 1.10 operates:

> **FEEDBACK CONTROL LAW:** The rule or procedure that determines how to transform the error signal into the control variable. For example, such a rule may state how to transform a value of the error into a change in the control variable.

The simplest and most widely used control law is one in which the change in the control variable is directly proportional to the error. This is called a **proportional feedback control law**. The rule discussed above for changing accelerator position to control vehicle speed is an example. When control is continuous (see section 1.2.8 for a definition), a proportional law can be written in shorthand using the following notation: let C be the control variable and E be the error, then

$$C = g_p E + b \qquad\qquad (1.2)$$

at all instants of time. There are two constants in this equation, g_p and b, which are referred to as **control law parameters**. The constant of proportionality, g_p, is called the **gain** of the feedback controller. The other constant, b, is the value of the control variable when the error is zero: when there is no error, the control variable stays fixed at this value (which could be zero). In order for the control system to work – that is, in order for it to meet the objective of reducing the error to as near to zero as makes no difference – the parameters need to have appropriate values. We discuss what these values might be in section 1.2.9.

1.2.8 Feedback can be used continuously or intermittently

The feedback control process continues over time, and the corrective adjustments to the control variable can be made continuously or intermittently over time. We will say that a feedback controller either operates in the **continuous control mode** or in the **intermittent control mode**.

The intermittent mode is probably more intuitive, as it corresponds more closely with a person's experience of acting as the controller in a feedback loop[33]. Consider being the driver of a vehicle and attempting to maintain a particular speed. The process of control is intermittent: you briefly look at the speed display on the dashboard, and if it differs from the speed you want to go, you make an accelerator adjustment. You check the speed display again after making the adjustment; if there is still an error, you make another adjustment. You repeat this process until the speed takes the value you want. Whether people actually adjust the accelerator in exactly this manner is unknown, but it is intuitively plausible and could certainly be one way of doing it. Moreover, we could easily design an automatic cruise control system for a vehicle that works this way. Such a system would follow a sequence of four steps, which seems almost obvious:

STEP 1: Observe the speed signaled by the tachometer to get a measure of the speed at some point in time (call the first measurement V1, the next V2 and so on).

STEP 2: Compare the measured speed (e.g., V1) with the required speed (call it V*) to give the error (e.g., V* − V1 = E1).

STEP 3: Based on the error calculated in step 2, use the control law to determine the appropriate adjustment of the accelerator (e.g., if equation 1.1 applied, then the appropriate adjustment would be error÷B cm).

STEP 4: Make the corrective accelerator adjustment determined in step 3 and then return to step 1.

Repeatedly following these steps produces a temporal sequence of corrective adjustments to accelerator position:

measurement   error   adjustment

V1 ⟶ E1 ⟶ E1÷B ---- V2 ⟶ E2 ⟶ E2÷B   and so on …

The sequence of adjustments (E₁÷B, E₂÷B, etc.) continues until the error is zero, at which point no correction is necessary until either the speed is disturbed or the required value changes.

In the continuous mode, the sensory measurements of the controlled variable and the corrective adjustments to the control variable occur continuously in time with no breaks. The continuous control mode is frequently encountered in artificial feedback control devices, but may not be as intuitive as the intermittent mode because it does not correspond to people's conscious experience of acting as the controller in a feedback control system. Nevertheless, certain continuous feedback control systems are familiar to many people; one such example is described next.

1.2.9 In continuous feedback control, the control variable follows variations in the error

A simple, easily understood example of continuous feedback control is provided by the system for regulating the water level in tanks used in some flush toilets. Figure 1.11 shows a schematic of a tank with its components. The tank is filled through the in-pipe and emptied through the out-pipe. The float-valve system acts to maintain the water level in the tank. The float balloon follows the water level, so when some water is let out (when the toilet is flushed) and the level drops, the float moves down. The float is connected to the in-pipe valve by a linking rod, so that as the float moves up or down, the linkage rod presses down on the valve plunger that closes or opens the valve. When the tank is at the full level (L_{full}), the valve aperture is completely closed and no water enters the tank. When the tank is empty, the valve aperture is completely open and water flows in at the maximum rate. At intermediate levels the valve aperture is partially open: the lower the level, the more the valve plunger is pressed down and the more open the aperture. The system automatically refills the tank after water has been let out of it.

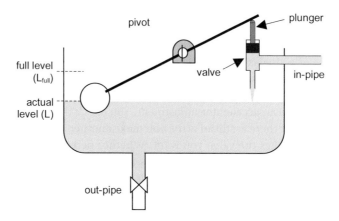

Figure 1.11: *Water tank and components that regulate water level.*

The tank system can be considered to be a feedback control system in which the controlled variable is the level of water in the tank, the required level is L_{full} and the control variable is the valve position[34]. A block diagram of the system is shown in Figure 1.12. In this system the valve is an actuator and the balloon float acts as a sensor for the water level (L). The full level can be set by adjusting the distance of the float from the pivot by sliding it along the connecting rod: the further the float from the pivot, the higher the full level. If there is an error (the tank is not full), then the valve plunger is depressed by one of the connecting rods to a degree that depends on the size of the error (see Figure 1.12). The degree to which the plunger is depressed determines the size of the valve aperture and hence the rate at which water flows into the tank. Notice how the set-point is 'represented' within the system: it is encoded in the mechanical linkage between the float and the pivot.

In this system, the feedback of water level via the float continuously regulates the valve aperture and hence the flow of water into the tank. As the float moves, the connecting rods move, and so the extent to which the valve plunger is depressed follows the position of the float without interruption. Note that the tank level control system only works when the error is positive, that is, when the actual level in the tank is less than the full level; once the tank is full, the valve closes and that is that[35]. Since the control process only acts when errors are to one side (the positive side) of zero, it can be called **one-sided control**. As we will see later, there are biological examples of one-sided negative feedback systems; one of these is the muscle stretch reflex (see Chapters 5 and 6).

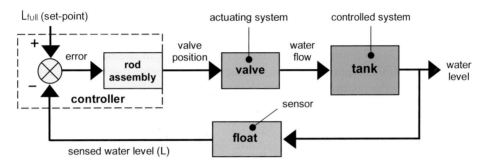

Figure 1.12: *Block diagram of water tank control system.*

1.2.10 Control law parameters need to be matched to the controlled system

In order for a feedback control system to work properly, the control law parameters need to be appropriately matched to the system under control (the controlled system itself and any actuating systems involved). We have already encountered an example of this in the simplified discussion of vehicle speed control presented earlier. In that example, the change in vehicle speed was equal to B times the change in accelerator position. The gain of the intermittent feedback controller was equal to 1/B. The constant B is a property of the vehicle, so the appropriate value for the controller gain depends on that system. This is an instance of a general principle that applies to all types of feedback control law:

> **CONTROL LAW PARAMETERS DEPEND ON THE CONTROLLED SYSTEM:** The parameters of feedback control laws must be properly matched to the properties of the controlled system (and actuating systems) in order to successfully meet the control objectives.

This principle is sometimes expressed by saying that the control law parameters represent a kind of *model* of the controlled system. In the case of proportional control, the model is implicit in the values of the parameters (g_p and b in equation 1.2) since these values depend on the controlled system. In general, the model is of a kind known as an **inverse model**[36]. To get an idea about what this means, recall that in the speed-control example, the vehicle was considered to be described by the constant B. The gain of the feedback control was 1/B, the inverse of B.

1.3 Feedback Control Is Not All About Correcting Errors

1.3.1 Introduction: control objectives extend beyond error correction

Feedback control is not limited to the correction of errors; it can also be used to control what is called the **dynamic response** of the controlled system. Roughly speaking, this refers to the manner in which the controlled variable changes as the error is reduced: feedback can be used to control how the controlled variable changes as the required value is approached. This kind of control allows us to expand the notion of a control objective beyond simply eliminating or reducing errors.

Figure 1.13 presents in graphical form two examples of how the controlled variable might change over time following a change in the required value in a feedback control system. The graph shows the controlled variable (measured up the vertical axis) plotted against time. At time zero the controlled variable is being held close to an initial required value R1. After 2 seconds the required value changes to R2. The solid line shows a slow response to this change; the dashed line shows a much faster response.

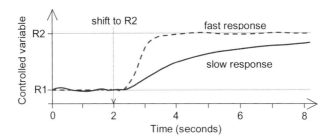

Figure 1.13: *Fast and slow changes of controlled variable in response to a shift in the required value (set-point).*

There are clearly situations in which we want to eliminate an error quickly: suppose you enter a section of road with a lower speed than the section you have just left, and the lower-speed section is equipped with speed cameras. You would want to reduce your speed quickly to avoid a speeding fine. Merely taking your foot off the accelerator and allowing the vehicle to slow down under the action of air resistance and engine braking will probably take too long.

A rough rule of thumb is that when the controller uses a proportional control law, the response to a particular error will be faster when the value of the gain (g_p in equation 1.2) is larger. If the gain is large, the controller will output a large change in the control variable in response to the error, since the size of this change is just the gain multiplied by the error. Although a larger gain will tend to produce a faster response, it also tends to produce a more forceful response, and the result of this can be **overshoot**. An illustration of

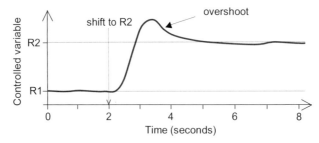

Figure 1.14: *Overshoot in system response.*

this is shown in Figure 1.14. As in the previous example, the required value is shifted from R1 to R2 two seconds after time zero. In the figure, the value of the controlled variable goes past (overshoots) the new required value (R2). Overshoot can be undesirable: for example, if you are reaching for a glass of wine, you want your hand to slow to a stop as it reaches the glass; if it overshoots, you risk knocking the glass over.

A high gain can also result in the value of the controlled variable overshooting one way, then the other way and so on so that it **oscillates** back and forth across the required value (Figure 1.15). The oscillation shown in the figure gradually decreases in amplitude and so the controlled variable deviates less and less from the required value. Oscillation can also be undesirable: if you are controlling the movement of your arm and hand to pick up an object, you don't want your hand to oscillate back and forth.

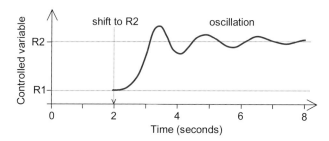

Figure 1.15: *Oscillation in system response.*

These examples show that we often require more from a feedback control system than elimination of an error. In some cases we might require that the controlled system's behavior be as good as possible with respect to some specific criterion. For instance, we might want the error to be reduced in the shortest possible time or in the most energy-efficient way. This is usually expressed by saying that we want the behavior to be **optimal** with respect to the criterion. A control law that produces behavior that is optimal with respect to some criterion is called an **optimal control law**.

To achieve additional objectives, the control law parameters need to have the right values. However, a proportional control law will typically be unable to accomplish all of the control objectives simultaneously, regardless of the values of its parameters. As already noted, increasing the gain of the controller may speed up the response, but is also likely to lead to overshoots and oscillations. If a fast response without oscillation or significant overshoot is required, a more complex control law is likely to be necessary. An example of a control law that can be effective at reducing overshoots and oscillations is the proportional-derivative (or PD) control law. The PD control law can be usefully illuminated by drawing an analogy with springs, which we do next.

1.3.2 Feedback control systems are analogous to springs

Some important insights into feedback control systems can be gained by drawing an analogy with a spring. A spring is not only a very familiar thing, but as we will see in the next chapter, muscles are like springs in some respects and their spring-like characteristics are important in determining how they behave. Thus, springs have a wider significance in understanding motor behavior.

Springs come in a variety of forms, of which the coil spring is the most familiar (Figure 1.16). The thing about springs is that when you pull on them they stretch (Figure 1.16, diagram 1); when you push on them they compress (diagram 3). When you neither pull nor push, they adopt an intermediate length called the **resting length** (denoted ℓ_o, diagram 2).

Whenever the spring is longer than its resting length (extended) or shorter than its resting length (compressed) it develops a force that resists the change in length. The force acts to move the spring back towards the resting length. For this reason, the force is often called a **restoring force**. A spring that resists changes in length with a large restoring force

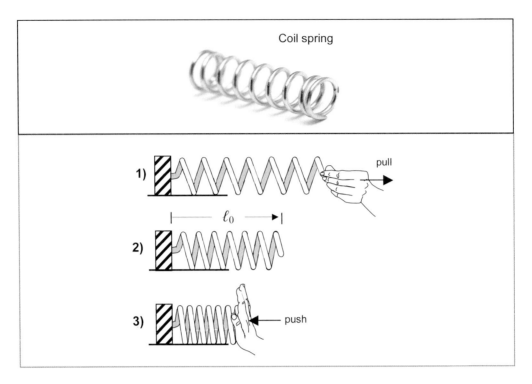

Figure 1.16: *Coil spring.*

is called a stiff spring; one that resists length changes with only a small force is called a soft spring. It's hard to stretch a stiff spring, but easy to stretch a soft one.

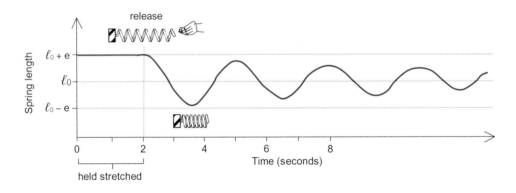

Figure 1.17: *Graph of the oscillation of a coil spring following release.*

What happens when you stretch or compress a spring and then release it? The answer to this question depends on how much resistance to the spring's movement is present. If the spring is submerged in water or syrup, then there may be quite a lot of resistance. If the spring is hanging freely and not rubbing against anything, there will be very little. Consider first the case in which there is very little resistance and the spring is released from a stretch. Once released, it will move back and forth for some time before coming to a stop at its resting length. This kind of behavior is illustrated in Figure 1.17, which shows a graph of the spring's length as a function of time. At first, the spring is stretched so that it is a small amount (e) longer than its resting length (ℓ_0). Then it is released when time = 2 seconds. After release, the spring oscillates so that it is alternately longer and shorter than the resting length.

Now consider a case in which there is a substantial amount of resistance: the spring is submerged in syrup, for example. When it is released from a stretch it does not oscillate: it is restored to the resting length without overshooting. This kind of behavior is illustrated in Figure 1.18. The resistance acts to prevent the spring from oscillating and is referred to as

damping for this reason – it dampens out oscillations. If a spring had absolutely no damping at all – which never happens in the real world – it would continue to oscillate indefinitely with no decrease in the amplitude of its oscillations.

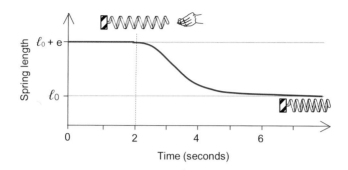

Figure 1.18: *Graph of length as function of time for a damped spring.*

The similarities between the behavior of springs and continuous feedback control systems allow us to draw an analogy[37] between the two types of system that will aid in understanding some aspects of feedback control function, proportional-derivative control laws in particular. We explore this analogy next.

1.3.3 Proportional-derivative control is analogous to a spring and damper

As we saw in the last section, a spring that is disturbed from its resting length (i.e., stretched or compressed) develops a force that acts to restore the spring to that length once the disturbance is over. When you are holding a spring at a stretched length you are pulling on the spring and the spring is pulling back on you with an equal force. In the diagram in Figure 1.19 the spring has been stretched to a length L and is being held stationary at that length, which means that the pulling force and the restoring force are equal but act in opposite directions, one to the left and the other to the right. The spring is longer than its resting length, ℓ_o, by an amount equal to $(L - \ell_o)$.

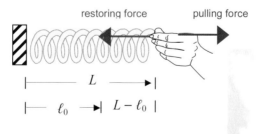

Figure 1.19: *Forces acting on a stretched spring.*

Many springs obey something called Hooke's law, which simply states that the restoring force is proportional to the amount the spring is stretched (or compressed). If we name the restoring force T, then Hooke's law can be written in shorthand either as $T = -k(L - \ell_o)$, or equivalently,

$$T = k(\ell_o - L) \tag{1.3}$$

where k is the constant of proportionality. The constant of proportionality is a measure of the strength of the spring and is called the **stiffness coefficient** (or just *stiffness*). If k has a large value, the spring is stiff; if k has a small value, the spring is soft.

Notice the similarity between Hooke's law for a spring (equation 1.3) and the equation describing the proportional feedback control law (equation 1.2). If the value of b in equation

1.2 is zero (there is no control input when there is no error), then the proportional law can be written:

$$C = g_p(R - M) \tag{1.4}$$

where R is the required value and M the measured value of the controlled variable. We can see from the similarity of the two expressions 1.3 and 1.4 that $(\ell_o - L)$ in the expression for Hooke's law is like the error (R − M) in the feedback control law, with ℓ_o playing the role of the required value (R). So we can think of the difference between the spring's resting length and its actual length as an error that the restoring force acts to eliminate.

It should now be somewhat clearer why the behavior of a proportional feedback control system resembles the behavior of a spring. The spring generates a force that tends to restore its length to the resting value (ℓ_o); the proportional feedback controller generates a control signal that tends to bring the controlled variable to a required value (R). Of course, the *mechanisms* in the two cases are quite different – in the feedback control system there is a sensor and a controller, but in a spring there are no such things.

How does what we have discussed so far aid in understanding the proportional-derivative control law? The answer lies with damping. A spring without damping will oscillate. This oscillation can be reduced or eliminated by adding damping – you could attach a damper in parallel with the spring, as is done in vehicle suspensions, or you could immerse the spring in syrup. In a feedback control system, you can do the same thing by adding derivative control.

A damper introduces a force that is proportional not to the length of the spring but to how quickly the spring is moving (lengthening or shortening). Thus, a damper only produces a force when the spring is moving. This force is a resistance to movement. A simple type of damping is where the resistive damping force (call it *D*) is proportional to the speed (call it *v*) at which the spring lengthens or shortens. A shorthand expression for this type of damping is simply,

$$D = \beta \times v \tag{1.5}$$

where 'β' is the constant of proportionality called the **damping coefficient**. The value of the damping coefficient would be larger for thick syrup than for water. The speed at which a spring lengthens or shortens is also referred to as the spring's *rate of change of length over time* or as the *time derivative* of the spring's length. So if you see the phrase 'the time derivative of length' it means exactly the same as 'the speed of lengthening or shortening'.

A damping effect can be produced by a feedback control law that generates a control signal proportional either to the rate of change of the controlled variable (analogous to the rate of change of a spring's length) or the rate of change of the error. Such a control law is called a *derivative law* because the term 'derivative' means the same 'rate of change'. We will consider the first type, in which the control signal is proportional to the derivative of the controlled variable[38]. The law can be written as follows:

$$C = g_d \times (\text{derivative of controlled variable}) \tag{1.6}$$

where C is the control variable and g_d is the gain of the derivative control process. Note the similar form of equations 1.6 and 1.5.

Derivative control added to proportional control produces proportional-derivative control. The purpose of adding the derivative control is to increase the effective damping in the control system and so be able to meet control objectives that require the elimination of overshoot or oscillation. We can think of derivative control as damping that is implemented using the mechanism of feedback control.

A block diagram of proportional-derivative control is shown in Figure 1.20. In both cases the control signal produced by the proportional controller (P-control law block output) and the signal produced by the derivative controller (g_d block output) are combined by the central summing block so that the controlled variable (C) is given by the combination of equations 1.2 and 1.6. This defines the proportional-derivative control law as follows:

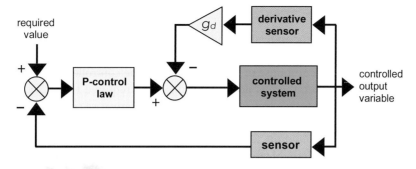

Figure 1.20: *Block diagram of one variant of proportional-derivative control.*

$$C = \underbrace{g_p \times (\text{error}) + b}_{\text{Proportional part}} - \underbrace{g_d \times (\text{derivative of controlled variable})}_{\text{Derivative part}}$$

The effect of changing the gain (g_d) in the derivative control loop is essentially the same as the effect of changing the value of the damping coefficient (β) in a spring-damper system. This is summarized in Figure 1.21. On the left of the figure is a spring and damper system, on the right a proportional-derivative feedback control system. The graphs in the figure show the behavior of the two types of system following a stretch and release (spring system) or a shift to a new required value (from R1 to R2) for different values of the damping coefficient or derivative gain. At small values, the system output (spring length or controlled variable) oscillates (graph 1). The oscillations die away more quickly when the β or g_d is larger (graph 2). For large enough values, there is no overshoot. For very large values there is no overshoot, but the output takes a longer time to reach a steady value (either ℓ_o or R2). It is clear from Figure 1.21 that derivative feedback can be used to control the way in which the controlled variable reaches the required value.

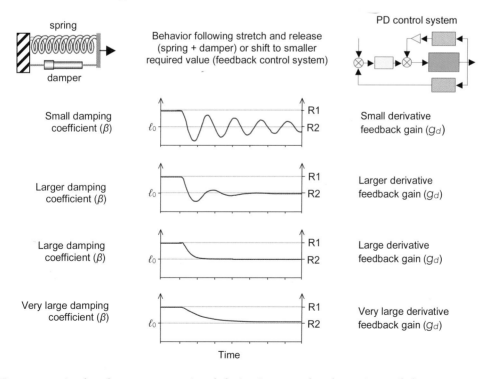

Figure 1.21: *Analogy between proportional-derivative control and a spring-and-damper system.*

1.3.4 Derivative feedback does not correct errors

One thing that distinguishes the derivative control law from the proportional law is that there is no subtraction of a measured value from a required value. Derivative control is about controlling the dynamic response of the system so that the controlled variable follows a desirable trajectory. However, there is no comparison of the required trajectory with the actual, measured trajectory to form a trajectory error. In short, derivative control is not about correcting errors and so is not an example of error-corrective feedback control. Although error correction can be considered the fundamental objective of feedback control, feedback can also be used to achieve a desirable dynamic response. This important point can be summarized as follows:

> **FEEDBACK CONTROL OBJECTIVES:** Feedback can be used to achieve two sorts of objective: (1) elimination of error (error-corrective feedback control); (2) a desirable dynamic response (e.g., suppression of oscillations or overshoot).

As we have seen, the effect of derivative control is to generate damping forces that oppose change in the controlled variable. As there are always damping forces present in all real systems, the controlled variable will eventually end up at some unchanging value unless there is something to keep it moving. Derivative control introduces additional damping that speeds up the process. Once the controlled variable is unchanging, the derivative controller does nothing (the derivative control input is zero). The value of the controlled variable at which this happens is irrelevant to the derivative controller. This means that derivative control cannot be used to make a controlled variable go to a specific set-point and maintain it there. Normally, we would want the controlled variable to reach a specific value (set-point); since derivative control cannot achieve this[39], proportional control is needed. Thus, derivative control is not used on its own, but in combination with proportional control.

1.4 Alternatives and Extensions to Feedback Control

1.4.1 Introduction: feedback control has limitations

Feedback control has certain drawbacks that can limit its use in the control of human and animal motor behavior. One drawback is that the simple feedback control processes are typically inadequate for meeting control objectives when it takes a significant length of time for signals to travel around the feedback loop. The time actually taken depends on two things: (1) how signals are transmitted from one component to the next, and (2) the processes involved in producing an output in response to an input in each of the components. If signal transmission and process operation are very fast, the time delays involved can be negligibly small and do not cause problems. In biological systems, however, time delays are not negligible. This can make simple control types like proportional and proportional-derivative control ineffective.

A second drawback is that feedback control is fundamentally an error corrective process and so errors must first arise before they can be corrected. Feedback control is therefore essentially *reactive* – it reacts to errors once they have occurred. Sometimes it is desirable or necessary to avoid errors developing in the first place. In this part of the chapter we discuss these two drawbacks of feedback control and consider ways in which they can be overcome or avoided altogether.

1.4.2 Feedback control can be ineffective when there are time delays

The time taken for signals to travel around a feedback loop can lead to undesirable behavior. A sufficiently long time delay can result in sustained oscillations that cannot be effectively removed by the addition of derivative feedback. In some circumstances the oscillations can increase in amplitude over time, effectively amplifying the error – the exact opposite of what is required.

Taking a shower provides a familiar situation in which oscillations due to a time delay can sometimes be produced. A person in the shower tries to adjust the temperature of the water to a comfortable level, but a common result is that the water is alternately too hot and too cold, with only brief periods at a comfortable level. The water oscillates between scalding and freezing with frustrating regularity. Why does this happen? Imagine you are under the shower and the water is too cold. You turn the faucet to provide more hot water. Your adjustment has no immediate effect, due to a time delay of several seconds between turning the faucet and a change in water temperature. A few seconds pass and nothing seems to be happening, so you turn the faucet some more. The water temperature starts to rise and soon reaches a comfortable level. Unfortunately it continues to rise, and the water is soon too hot: you turned the faucet too far. You adjust the faucet to provide more cold, but the temperature continues to rise, so you turn the faucet further. After a while the temperature decreases and the water is comfortably warm again, but annoyingly, it continues to fall and soon becomes too cold. Once again you turned the faucet too far, and now you are back where you started. This sequence of adjustments and the trajectory of the water temperature is shown in Figure 1.22. Once you are back where you started, doing the same as before will simply repeat the cycle, producing an oscillation between too hot and too cold.

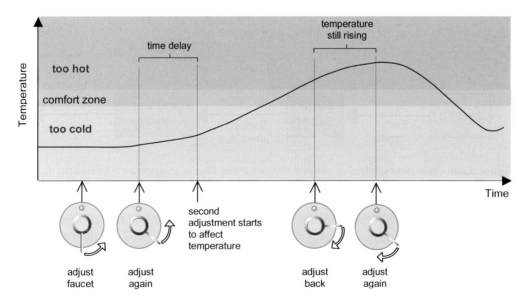

Figure 1.22: *Attempting to adjust a faucet so as to achieve a comfortable water temperature.*

In the shower example, corrective adjustments are made before the effects of the previous adjustment have had time to affect the control variable. In Figure 1.22 the second adjustment is made before the temperature has risen due to the first. This means that the second adjustment is not correcting for the error that exists when it has its effect, but for an error that existed in the past. Thus, by the time the feedback-based adjustment has its effects on the controlled variable, it is out of date – the system has moved on. We will briefly consider how to overcome this difficulty in the next section.

1.4.3 In the absence of disturbances, control may be possible without using feedback

A person who persists in trying to correct for errors in water temperature using a strategy like that illustrated in Figure 1.22 is doomed to be alternately scalded and frozen for as long as they stay under the shower. However, people do not always persist in applying a strategy that isn't working; we have the capacity to change and to try out new things. One obvious thing to do in the shower situation is to make an adjustment and wait until it has had its effect before making any further adjustment. This will work well in the shower because the only thing that is likely to affect the water temperature is the adjustment you make to the faucet, which means that it is easy to tell when the effect of the adjustment has occurred – the water reaches a higher, steady temperature. Indeed, if there are no disturbances, then it is possible to operate without feedback. To see why, suppose you knew in advance exactly how far to turn the faucet to achieve a comfortable water temperature. With this knowledge, you could just turn the faucet to the correct position and you would be done. Knowing how much to turn the faucet to get a desired water temperature amounts to having a properly calibrated mixer faucet that displays a temperature scale so that the faucet can be moved to the position associated with a particular temperature, as shown at the top of Figure 1.23.

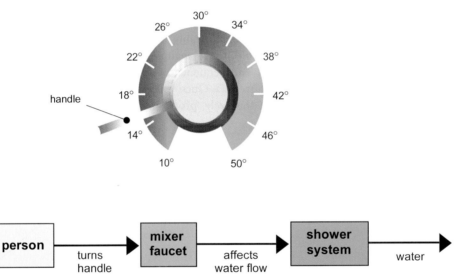

Figure 1.23: *Open-loop control of shower temperature. Top: a temperature-calibrated faucet. Bottom: block diagram of manual control system that uses a calibrated faucet.*

With a calibrated faucet of this kind, the knowledge of where to position the faucet to get the desired temperature is contained in the scale. We could also imagine having a shower that we have used so many times that we know where to position the faucet in order to get the temperature we want without the aid of a scale. In this case the knowledge would be 'in the head'.

The control system formed by the person, the faucet and the shower system without feedback control has a block diagram like that shown at the bottom of Figure 1.23. There is no feedback loop because any feedback the person receives is not used for control. For this reason, control of this sort is called **open-loop control**:

> **OPEN-LOOP CONTROL:** A style of control in which the output of the controlled system is not fed back to the controller. What the controlled system is actually doing has no effect on the control inputs supplied by the controller.

When feedback does determine the control inputs, the feedback loop is said to be *closed*, hence the term *closed-loop control* as an alternative name for feedback control.

1.4.4 Open-loop control requires detailed knowledge about the controlled system

In the previous subsection we saw that knowledge about the controlled system was required in order to make open-loop control of shower temperature possible. This is a fundamental to open-loop control in general, so it can be elevated to the status of a principle:

> **PRINCIPLE OF OPEN-LOOP CONTROL:** To achieve a control objective, control inputs are determined from the objectives together with prior knowledge about the controlled system (or controlled system + actuating system).

We have already seen that a similar principle applies to feedback (closed-loop) control as well, but in open-loop control the knowledge required is generally much more precise and its necessity is more obvious (in feedback control the knowledge is 'hidden' in the values of the control law parameters). Earlier in the chapter we noted that the knowledge of the controlled system contained in the value of the proportional control law gain can be conceived of as a kind of crude 'inverse model'. The knowledge required for open-loop control can be conceived in a similar way, as shown next using a very simple example.

Imagine that the system we want to control is a very elementary kind of device that simply increases the magnitude of its input 7.75 times to produce an output. In other words, the output is just an amplified version of the input, where the amplification factor – the gain – is equal to 7.75. The control problem is to find the value of the input (control variable) that produces the required value of the output (controlled variable). Since the system output is 7.75 times the input, the input-output transformation of the system can be written like this:

$$\text{output} = 7.75 \times \text{input} \tag{1.7}$$

or drawn as a block diagram like this:

$$\text{input} \longrightarrow \boxed{7.75} \longrightarrow \text{output}$$

The control problem is easy to solve: if we want some value of the output – call the value O – then the input needed to produce it is just $O \div 7.75$. This is the inverse transformation, which can be written,

$$\text{input} = \text{output} \div 7.75 \tag{1.8}$$

Obviously, we can use this inverse transformation to find the value of the input needed to produce any output value we might want. Thus, a suitable controller is one that performs the inverse transformation given by equation (1.8). The block diagram looks like this:

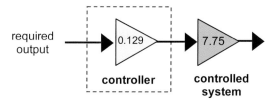

where 0.129 = 1 ÷ 7.75; so the value of the gain (0.129) represents knowledge about the controlled system. This arrangement clearly works. For example, if we wanted an output of 3.30, this would be input to the controller, which would output a signal of magnitude 3.30 × 0.129 = 0.426. The controlled system would then output a signal of magnitude 0.426 × 7.75 = 3.30, as required.

When a controller's transformation of its inputs (required values) into its outputs is the inverse of the controlled system's input-output transformation, it is said to implement an **inverse model** of the controlled system. It is clear that the accuracy of this kind of control depends on the accuracy of the inverse model. In the example given above, if the inverse were slightly inaccurate – say 0.125 instead of 0.129 – then the controlled system's output would be inaccurate – 3.2 rather than 3.3. For this simple system, the size of the inaccuracies in the inverse model lead to correspondingly sized discrepancies between the actual output and the required output. Thus, more precise open-loop control requires a more accurate model[40].

1.4.5 The drawbacks of open-loop control can sometimes be avoided by adding feedback control

Open-loop control processes do not, by definition, have any mechanism for correcting any errors that do arise. Errors in open-loop systems can arise for two basic reasons:

(1) Disturbances that cannot be taken into account in the formation of the control signals.
(2) Incompleteness or inaccuracy in the knowledge (or model) of the controlled system that is being used to determine the control signals.

One obvious way to avoid these difficulties is to add a feedback loop that can correct any errors that arise. Errors due to model inaccuracy and/or incompleteness can be quite small, in which case the open-loop controller is able to get the controlled system to behave nearly as required. The role of the feedback controller is then to correct for any small residual errors. To get such a system to work well, the feedback process should only become active after the open-loop control signals have had a chance to bring the controlled variable close to the required value. The block diagram of a control system of this sort is shown in Figure 1.24, with the interconnections of the open-loop part shown as solid black lines and those of the feedback part as dotted blue lines. In the arrangement shown, the open-loop and feedback controllers are in parallel, and the control signals they produce are combined to form the input to the controlled system. If the feedback control part were removed, the open-loop part would still function in its normal way.

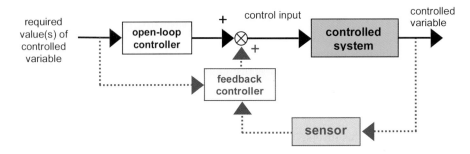

Figure 1.24: *Combined open- and closed-loop system.*

1.4.6 Feedback control is reactive

The second problem with feedback control is that it is reactive – an error must exist before it can be corrected. In some cases, it is desirable to avoid errors altogether. As an example, consider a film camera and a human eye. The amount of light entering the eye is determined by the size of the pupil (Figure 1.25), which is regulated by a feedback control mechanism (for details see Chapter 4). The amount of light entering an eye and reaching the retina needs to be kept within limits: too much and the retina could be irreversibly damaged, too little and it's not possible to see properly. The amount of light reaching the retina is the controlled variable; it is measured by retinal photoreceptors (light-sensitive cells). The signals generated by these cells are fed via nerve circuits to muscles in the iris that cause changes in the pupil size. If the amount of light reaching the retinal sensory cells is more than desirable, then there is an error. The response is pupil constriction, which reduces the amount of light entering the eye (Figure 1.25, top). If too little light reaches the retinal sensors, the pupil dilates (Figure 1.25, bottom), allowing more light to enter. This system keeps the light reaching the retina within acceptable limits.

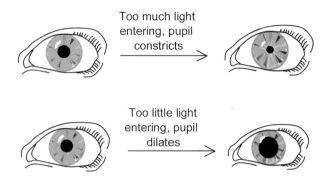

Figure 1.25: *Action of the pupiliary light reflex.*

In a film camera, the amount of light reaching the film needs to be controlled so that it is within acceptable limits: if too much light reaches the film, the photograph will be over-exposed and appear bleached out; if too little reaches the film, the photograph will be under-exposed and be too dark. The amount of light reaching the film depends on the size of the camera aperture (Figure 1.26). However, you can't measure the amount of light reaching the film and adjust the aperture so that the photograph is properly exposed, because as soon as the light reaches the film the photograph is exposed and that's that. The aperture needs to be adjusted to the right size before the light reaches the film. The way this is done is to estimate the amount of light likely to reach the film before it is exposed, and use the estimate to adjust the aperture in advance. This is an anticipatory, open-loop process because feedback about the actual exposure of the film is not used to adjust the control variable (aperture size).

Figure 1.26: *Different apertures in a camera.*

There are many other cases in which waiting for feedback would be inappropriate, particularly if an error could result in damage or injury. In order to prevent unacceptable errors from developing, it is necessary to anticipate or predict their occurrence and take pre-emptive action. Pre-emptive action might involve doing something that avoids or blocks the disturbance so that it cannot affect the system; alternatively it may involve doing something that does not avoid the disturbance but that cancels out its effect. Avoiding a disturbance is more intuitive, and we will encounter plenty of examples in later chapters. Doing something to cancel the effect of a disturbance is less obvious. This will be discussed in more detail next.

1.4.7 Sensory feedforward control makes pre-emptive adjustments to cancel the effects of disturbances

The method used to avoid incorrectly exposing film in a camera is closely related to a more general control strategy known as **(sensory) feedforward control**. The basic idea is to detect a potential disturbance before it has had a chance to affect the controlled system, and to make pre-emptive adjustments to the control variable. These adjustments do not avoid the disturbance; they have the effect of canceling out its effect.

A block diagram of a sensory feedforward control system is shown in Figure 1.27. As the diagram makes clear, there is no feedback of the controlled system output. A sensory device is needed in order to detect that there is a disturbance likely to affect the controlled system and then feed this information to the controller, as shown in the figure. The controller uses this information to generate a control signal that compensates for the disturbance so that it does not affect the controlled variable, which remains at its required value.

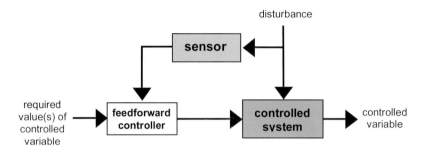

Figure 1.27: *Block diagram of sensory feedforward control.*

Like other types of open-loop control, sensory feedforward control requires knowledge of the controlled system. In this case, the knowledge is needed so that the feedforward control signals will affect the controlled system in a way that compensates for the disturbance. This style of control also requires that disturbances can be detected and measured in advance. Not all disturbances can be anticipated in this way, and so this mode of control is limited. These limitations can be overcome to some extent by adding feedback control.

In biological motor control systems, feedforward is usually found in conjunction with feedback mechanisms. One example that we will discuss in detail later (see Chapters 4 and 5) is found in the control of the direction in which the eyes are looking. When you are looking at something, you need to keep your eyes pointed in the direction of that thing. Various factors can disturb this desirable state of affairs: your head might move, as it does when you are walking or being jiggled around when driving along a rough road. A reflexive mechanism known as the vestibulo-ocular reflex is a sensory feedforward control mechanism that works to keep the eyes pointing at a fixed location despite movements of the head. The mechanism works by sensing motion of the head before it has a chance to have any significant effect on where the eyes are looking – the vestibular organs are the sensors involved (for details see Chapter 5).

References & Notes

[1] This definition excludes active movements produced by some single-celled organisms.

[2] Gallistel (1980), p. 1.

[3] Motor behavior can have outcomes other than that intended (the goal). Striking your thumb when hammering a nail is a behavioral outcome but not the one intended.

[4] But not all: notable exceptions are robots developed by the Boston Dynamics company (http://www.bostondynamics.com/).

[5] These ideas have even been used as the basis for an entire theory of human psychology (Powers, 1973).

[6] Some authors have attempted to avoid the use of control theory (CT) altogether by using dynamical systems theory, DST (Kugler, Turvey, 1987). DST is a mathematical theory used for developing models of physical processes. Control theory is a sub-theory of DST, so the two are not incommensurate (Kalman, Falb, Arbib, 1969; Rosen, 1985).

[7] Definitions adapted from the Concise Oxford Dictionary of Current English online (http://oxforddictionaries.com) and the Merriam-Webster online dictionary (http://www.merriam-webster.com/dictionary/).

[8] Also called basic actions (Reed, 1982a, 1985).

[9] Some authors have attempted to define an elemental component of action as 'a movement entity that cannot be intentionally stopped before its completion' (Polyakov et al., 2009a). This restricts motor elements to very briefly executed acts or movements, since those of longer duration can typically be halted during execution. We do not adopt this as part of our definition, since many acts that can be stopped before completion cannot be meaningfully decomposed into sub-components.

[10] For a discussion of the distinction between discrete and continuous (rhythmic) behavior, see Hogan and Sternad (2007).

[11] Lashley (1930).

[12] Bartlett (1932), pp. 201–202.

[13] See Latash (2008a, b).

[14] Based on an example due to Latash (2008a; Latash et al. 2001).

[15] See Searle (1983).

[16] See Libet (1985), who concluded that intention is not causal, though his interpretation of the data is questionable.

[17] How, Zeil, Hemmi (2009).

[18] Pope (2000).

[19] Tolman (1925).

[20] Watson (2005).

[21] See Domjan (2010).

[22] Ashby, Turner, Horvitz (2010).

[23] Yin, Knowlton (2006).

[24] Dickinson, Balleine (1994), p. 1.

[25] Kugler, Turvey (1987). Another nice illustration of the goal-directedness of invertebrate behavior is Reed's (1982b) analysis of Charles Darwin's earthworm studies.

[26] Fraenkel, Gunn (1940).

[27] Powers (1973) describes some examples in human behavior.

[28] This has led some authors to question whether internal representation of a goal is a valid explanatory concept: see Kugler, Kelso, Turvey (1982); Kugler, Turvey (1987).

[29] As recognized early in this field of study (Wiener, 1948/1961).

[30] For formal introductions see Dorf, Bishop (2008); Goodwin, Graebe, Salgado (2006).

[31] A commonly used alternative name is **plant**.

[32] The relationship given here is clearly oversimplified: the basic idea is that the accelerator pedal position determines the torque developed by the motor.

[33] For a recent account of intermittent feedback control mechanisms in human behavior, see Gawthrop et al. (2011).

[34] Coury (1999).

[35] This is adequate provided water can only get into the tank through the open valve.

[36] Goodwin Graebe, Salgado (2006); Jordan (1996).

[37] The analogy can be made a formal, mathematical one (Rosen, 1985).

[38] This version of derivative control is not quite equivalent to the version in which the derivative of the error is used.

[39] Note that derivative control is not the same as controlling speed, since speed control does not mean reducing the speed to zero.

[40] There are certain systems where a more accurate inverse model does not lead to more accurate control (see Rosen, 1985).

CHAPTER 2

Neuromechanical Foundations

2.1 Neurons

2.1.1 Introduction: cells, tissues and organs

Animals' bodies are made up of enormous numbers of individual, microscopic cells. A cell is like a little bag of fluid with various structures suspended in it, which include the cell nucleus and mitochondria. Cells come in a number of different types that differ in their physiological properties and perform different functions. With a few exceptions, cells of a particular type are found grouped together in the body to form **tissues**. There are four fundamental types of tissue in the human body and the bodies of other large animals:

(1)   **Epithelial tissue:** this is tissue formed of cells packed together into continuous sheets. It forms the membranes that line the mouth, nasal passages, stomach, and other structures within the body.
(2)   **Connective tissue:** this comes in a variety of forms including bone, fat and blood. Connective tissues that hold body structures together and provide support include bone, tendon, ligament and cartilage.
(3)   **Muscle tissue:** this is tissue that contracts; we will have a lot more to say about this type in section 3 of this chapter.
(4)   **Nervous tissue:** this is the tissue type that forms the brain.

The **organs** of the body are functional structures composed of two or more types of tissue. Muscles are organs composed mainly of muscle tissue, but they also contain connective and epithelial tissues. **Organ systems** are groupings of several organs – these organs work together to achieve particular functions. The organ systems that we will be concerned with in this chapter are the **skeletal system** (composed of bones, cartilage, tendons and ligaments), the **muscular system**, and the **nervous system** (comprising all the nervous tissue in the body). The nervous system has two major divisions:

(1)   The **central nervous system (CNS)**, comprising those parts that are surrounded and protected by bone: the **brain**, contained within the skull cavity, and the **spinal cord** that passes through the vertebrae.
(2)   The **peripheral nervous system (PNS)**, comprising the parts that are not surrounded by bone; it includes nerves (bundles of axons) and groups of neurons called **ganglia** (plural of *ganglion*).

The vast majority of all neurons are located in the CNS, and most of these are in the brain. The nervous system is responsible for many things, from the regulation of basic physiological processes to thought and consciousness. In this chapter we will be concerned with its role in the control and coordination of body movements and exerted forces. In this first part we will describe the properties of nerve cells.

2.1.2 Nervous tissue is composed of neurons and glial cells

Nervous tissue is composed of two specialized cell types: the **nerve cells** or **neurons**, and **glial cells**. Neurons are the basic functional elements of the nervous system – it is through the activity of these cells that movements of the body are controlled, that perception of the outside world is possible, that thought and language are produced. Glial cells are less familiar but are the more numerous cell type in nervous tissue. Glial cells have a variety of known functions[1]: they provide nutrient   neurons, insulate neurons from the extracellular fluid and provide structural sup   vous tissue.

Both neurons and glial c   rne in a variety of shapes and sizes, with many of these differences in form being associated with differences in the precise function the cells perform.

Our focus will be on neurons; we will have very little to say about glial cells. Neurons are the most elaborately and intricately shaped cells in existence. Most cells in the body have smooth contours and simple shapes. They may be long and thin like muscle cells, disc-shaped like red blood cells, or ovoid (egg-shaped) like kidney cells; the shapes are often irregular because cells are squeezed in among numerous other cells. Neurons are very different; their shapes are impossible to properly describe in words, except to say that many of them resemble leaf-less bushes or trees. There is no such thing as a typically shaped neuron; they come in nearly as many different shapes as do trees and bushes. Figure 2.1 shows a two-dimensional picture of a type of neuron found in the brain (a Purkinje cell from the cerebellum) that illustrates the complex and intricate shape of many neurons (a real neuron is three-dimensional, of course). The branches and twigs of the neuron's tree-like structure are tubular processes called **neurites**. These sprout from the **cell body** of the neuron, the bulbous part of the cell in Figure 2.1 that contains the nucleus. The whole of the complex structure is contained within a single, continuous cell membrane.

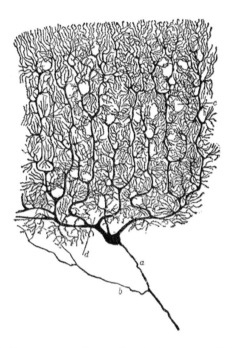

Figure 2.1: *Type of cerebellar neuron. From* Gray's Anatomy of the Human Body *(1918, Fig. 628).*

Although many neurons in the human nervous system have a complex form that is a variant of the one shown in Figure 2.1, there are some neurons that have a simpler form. Some neurons do not possess a bushy mass of neurites sprouting from their cell bodies. An example in which only one neurite sprouts from the cell body is shown in panel A of Figure 2.2. This is a **unipolar** neuron[2]. A neuron that has two neurites sprouting from its cell body is called a **bipolar** neuron (Figure 2.2, panel B). Thus the polarity of a neuron refers to the number of neurites sprouting from its cell body. Neurons like the one shown in Figure 2.1 are called **multipolar neurons**; panel C of Figure 2.2 shows another example.

The great variety in the shapes and sizes of neurons reflects the great variety of functions that they serve. As a general rule, neurons that perform different functions have different shapes and/or sizes, and we will encounter numerous examples in this and later chapters. Although there are numerous specialized functions that neurons perform, they can be divided into three basic classes:

(1)　**Sensory neurons:** neurons specialized to respond to stimuli impinging on them from sources outside the nervous system, such as light, sound or mechanical pressure. These are the input neurons of the nervous system.

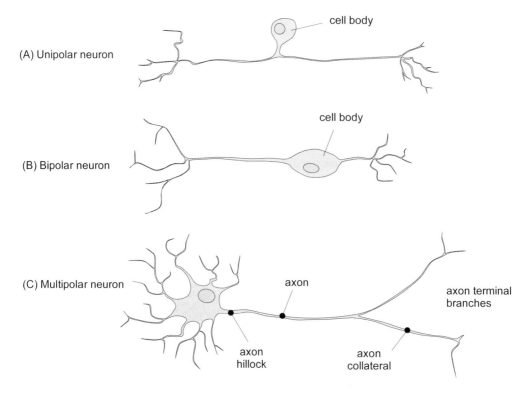

(A) Unipolar neuron — cell body

(B) Bipolar neuron — cell body

(C) Multipolar neuron — axon — axon terminal branches — axon hillock — axon collateral

Figure 2.2: *Three basic forms exhibited by mammalian neurons (illustrative).*

(2)   **Motoneurons** (contracted form of **motor neuron**): neurons that send signals to cells outside the nervous system, including muscle cells and the cells of certain glands. These are the means by which the nervous system controls behavior: they are the output neurons.

(3)   **Interneurons:** neurons that are neither sensory nor motoneurons, and which receive signals only from other neurons and send signals only to other neurons. The vast majority of neurons are interneurons of one sort or another.

This simple classification is universal and important to remember, and can be elevated to the status of a principle:

> **NEURON CLASSES:** Any neuron falls into one and only one of three basic classes: it is a sensory neuron, or an interneuron or a motoneuron.

2.1.3 Most neurons in the mammalian nervous system are multipolar

The vast majority of neurons in the nervous systems of people and other mammals are found in the brain and spinal cord. Most of these neurons are of the multipolar kind. Figure 2.2C shows a representative multipolar neuron with various parts named. All but one of the neurites sprouting from the neuron are **dendrites** (a word derived from the Greek word *dendron*, meaning 'tree'). The dendrites are the input lines of the neuron: they receive signals from other neurons (we will see what this means in the following subsections). All the dendrites of a neuron form a bushy structure called the **dendritic tree**.

There is one neurite that sprouts from the cell body that is not a dendrite. This neurite is the **axon**[3], and there is only ever one of these, a fact known as the **single axon rule**:

> **SINGLE AXON RULE:** If a neuron has an axon, then it has only one.

The axon is the output line of the neuron: signals are transmitted to other neurons along the axon. There is typically a marked thickening where the axon sprouts from the cell body, which is identified in Figure 2.2C as the **axon hillock**. An axon typically splits to form collaterals and terminal branches. The very tips of the terminal braches often have a slightly bulbous appearance and are referred to as **terminal buttons**. Axons of different neurons vary in length; some are very short (much less than a millimeter), while others can be very long: the longest axons in the human nervous system can be a meter or more in length. Neurons are the longest cells in the animal kingdom.

2.1.4 Neurons make connections with one another at synapses

Every neuron in the nervous system is connected to at least one other neuron. Through its connections, a neuron receives inputs from some neurons and sends outputs to others. Typically an individual neuron connects with many more than one other neuron – in some cases a single neuron may be directly connected to more than 100,000 others. The vast majority of the connections are made by the terminal buttons of one neuron at small, localized sites on the cell membrane of either the dendrites or the cell body of the other neuron. These junctions are called **synapses**. Synapses located at sites on the dendrites are sometimes called **axo-dendritic** synapses to distinguish them from synapses located on the cell body, which are called **axo-somatic** synapses. Synapses are so tiny that they are not visible except through the most powerful microscopes; there may be tens of thousands of them on a single neuron. This means that synapses are very, very small compared to the cell as a whole.

There are two basic types of synapse. In one type, the membranes of the two neurons making the connection are physically connected to one another at *gap junction channels* that allow electrically charged particles (ions) to pass from one cell directly into the other. A synapse of this type is called an *electrical synapse*. Panel A of Figure 2.3 shows an idealized cross-section through an electrical synapse formed by two neurons; only small regions of the cells in the location of the synapse are shown. Electrical synapses are rare in the human nervous system and we will not need to know anything more about them.

The other type of synapses involves no physical contact between the two neurons, which are separated by a fluid-filled gap called the **synaptic cleft** that is about 20 millionths of a millimeter across. A synapse of this sort is called a **chemical synapse** because one neuron is able to influence the other by means of chemical substances released into the synaptic cleft. These substances are called **neurotransmitters**. An idealized cross-section through a chemical synapse is shown in panel B of Figure 2.3. One of the two neurons contains small ovoid or spherical structures called **synaptic vesicles**; these contain the neurotransmitter. Only

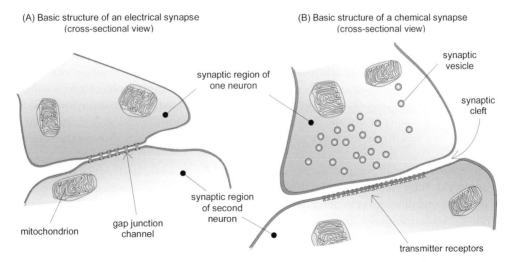

Figure 2.3: *Two types of synapse.*

the neuron containing the vesicles releases neurotransmitter molecules into the synaptic cleft; it is referred to as the **presynaptic neuron**. Neurotransmitter molecules diffuse across the synaptic cleft and bind to specialized receptor molecules within the membrane of the other neuron, which is called the **postsynaptic neuron**. This binding causes a change in the electrical potential difference that exists across the membrane of the postsynaptic neuron (see section 2.1.5). Thus, the release of neurotransmitters by the presynaptic neuron leads to a response (change in membrane potential) in the postsynaptic neuron. This is the way in which signals are transmitted from one neuron to another.

2.1.5 An electrical potential exists across a neuron's cell membrane

When a neuron is neither receiving nor transmitting signals, there is always a small electrical potential difference across its membrane. If this potential remains relatively constant over time, in the absence of any external stimulus, it is called the **resting membrane potential** and the neuron is said to be in a state of rest, usually referred to as a **resting state**. For some neuron types, such as motoneurons, the notion of a resting membrane potential is a valid one; for other types it is not (see section 2.1.16)

An electrical potential difference is created when positive and negative electrical charges are separated. Opposite charges attract – they exert a force on one another that acts to draw them together. When they are prevented from moving together, they are said to possess electrical potential energy: they have the potential to move together because of the attractive electrical force. The electrical potential at some location, such as the outside of a neuron, is equal to the electrical potential energy that would be possessed by a unit of electrical charge if it were placed at that location. All this is exactly analogous to saying that something held above the Earth's surface has gravitational potential energy: it has the potential to move (fall to the Earth), because of the gravitational attractive force, but is prevented from doing so (it's being held up). The gravitational potential at some location above the Earth's surface is equal to the gravitational potential energy possessed by a unit of mass held at that location.

The electrical potential inside a neuron is different from the electrical potential outside, and so we say that there is a **potential difference** across the membrane. A potential difference exists when the neuron is in the resting state, because the fluid just outside the cell contains more positive charges than negative charges; inside the cell it's the other way around – there are more negative than positive charges. The result is a force of attraction between the excess positive charge outside and the excess negative charge inside, but the membrane prevents the excess charges from moving together. Active metabolic processes are needed to maintain this difference in electrical charge.

Positive charge is carried mainly by atoms of sodium (chemical symbol, Na) and potassium chemical symbol, K) that have been stripped of an electron. Atoms and molecules that carry a charge are called **ions**: a sodium ion has one positive charge (denoted Na^+), and a potassium ion also has one charge (K^+). Negative charge is carried by chlorine atoms with an extra electron – chloride ions, Cl^- – and by a number of organic molecular ions such as aspartate ions. Inside the cell, the positive charge is carried mainly by potassium ions and the negative charge mainly by organic ions. Outside the cell, the positive charge is carried mainly by sodium ions and the negative charge mainly by chloride ions. This is shown schematically in Figure 2.4.

The standard units of potential energy are joules and the standard units of electrical charge are *coulombs*. Since electrical potential is energy per unit charge, the standard units of electrical potential and differences in potential are *joules per coulomb*, which are usually called *volts* (1 volt = 1 joule/coulomb). The resting membrane potentials of most neurons lie between about −40 and −90 millivolts (thousandths of a volt). The value is negative because the inside of the cell is negatively charged relative to the outside.

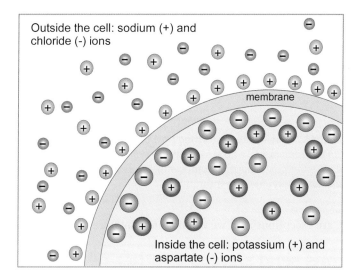

Figure 2.4: *Distribution of charges across a cell membrane.*

2.1.6 Inputs from other neurons depolarize or hyperpolarize the cell membrane

Consider two neurons connected together at a chemical synapse – one of them is the presynaptic neuron, the other is the postsynaptic neuron. As mentioned in section 2.1.4, when neurotransmitter molecules are released by the presynaptic neuron, they diffuse across the synaptic cleft and bind to receptors in the postsynaptic neuron's membrane. The presynaptic neuron is said to provide a synaptic *input* to the postsynaptic neuron. The input produces a change in the membrane potential of the postsynaptic neuron at the location of the synapse. The change to the postsynaptic neuron's membrane potential can be of two types:

(1)   The potential becomes more positive (increases). This is called **depolarization**.
(2)   The potential becomes more negative (decreases). This is called **hyperpolarization**.

For reasons discussed later, a synapse with a depolarizing effect is known as an **excitatory synapse** and the associated change in membrane potential is called an **excitatory postsynaptic potential**. A synapse with a hyperpolarizing effect is known as an **inhibitory synapse** and the associated change in membrane potential is called an **inhibitory postsynaptic potential**.

As mentioned earlier, when two neurons connect to one another, they do not do so at just one synaptic site, but at a very large number – typically thousands of synaptic connections are made between two neurons, most of them on the dendrites (axo-dendritic synapses). The presynaptic terminals of all the synaptic connections between two neurons release the same type of neurotransmitter substance. In most cases only one type of neurotransmitter substance is released, though there are exceptions. This brings us to our first neurophysiological rule of thumb, known as *Dale's Principle*, which can be stated as follows:

> **DALE'S PRINCIPLE:** Any neuron that forms chemical synapses with other neurons releases the same neurotransmitter substance (or small set of substances) at all of its synapses.

Although there are some known exceptions to this principle[4], it nevertheless holds for a large number of different types of neuron, and we will not have cause to deal with any of the exceptions in this text.

A particular neurotransmitter substance typically has the same type of effect on the membrane potential of postsynaptic neurons: it either has a depolarizing (excitatory) effect or it has a hyperpolarizing (inhibitory) effect, but it does not have a depolarizing effect on some neurons and a hyperpolarizing effect on others. This means that Dale's Principle has the consequence that if a neuron makes connections with more than one other neuron, its synaptic inputs will have the same effect on all of them: either all will be excitatory, or all will be inhibitory. This brings us to our second rule of thumb, which we will call Dale's Corollary:

> **DALE'S COROLLARY:** The synapses formed by a particular neuron with other (postsynaptic) neurons are all of the same type: either all are excitatory (synaptic inputs depolarize the postsynaptic membrane), or all are inhibitory (synaptic inputs hyperpolarize the postsynaptic membrane).

Once again, there are exceptions[5], but we will not encounter any of them in this text.

2.1.7 Neurons send signals to other neurons via their axons

A neuron sends signals to other neurons via its axon. The axon can be thought of as a cable along which a neuron transmits signals. The signals are electrical in nature and are transmitted in two different ways:

(1) **Passive conduction:** this is similar to the process by which electrical currents are conducted along wires in household electric appliances. Charged particles move so as to equalize potential differences, and unless they are prevented from moving they will continue to do so as long as a potential difference exists.

(2) **Active propagation:** this is a process that requires metabolic energy (hence it is active). It involves specialized mechanisms, called voltage gated ion channels, which are present in the cell membrane of neurons that use this method of transmission. Signals are transmitted as localized membrane potential depolarizations called **action potentials**; they are also known as **nerve impulses** or **spikes**. These travel along the axon membrane and spread to all the axon terminals and terminal buttons, where they stimulate the release of neurotransmitters into the synaptic cleft.

An individual neuron uses either one or the other of these methods to transmit signals along axons, but never both. As we will see in section 2.1.9, passive conduction is the means by which excitatory and inhibitory postsynaptic potentials are transmitted to the cell body along dendrites. However, it is relatively rare as a mode of transmitting signals along axons. The main reason for this is that passively conducted potentials die away as they travel away from the site at which they were initiated. This decline of amplitude with distance means that passive conduction cannot be used to transmit potential changes over large distances. The nervous system uses action potentials to transmit electrical signals over significant distances (more than about a millimeter). Transmission by action potentials is the only method we will consider.

An action potential is a localized membrane depolarization that travels along an axon and along its terminal branches. It can be likened either to the burning part of a fuse which travels along the fuse wire, or to a single wave traveling along a water channel. Like a wave or a burning fuse, the action potential travels in a constant direction – it never turns back on itself to go back the way it came. The mechanisms that produce action potentials are quite well understood; details can be found in most neurobiology texts[6].

An action potential can be measured using electrodes placed in suitable locations. One method involves inserting one very fine electrode, called a **microelectrode**, into the axon, and positioning another outside the axon. The microelectrode inserted into the cell is referred to as an **intracellular electrode**. Such an arrangement results in an electrical potential difference between the two electrodes that is equal to the potential difference across the axon's membrane. This potential difference can be measured using a voltmeter or amplified and displayed on a screen.

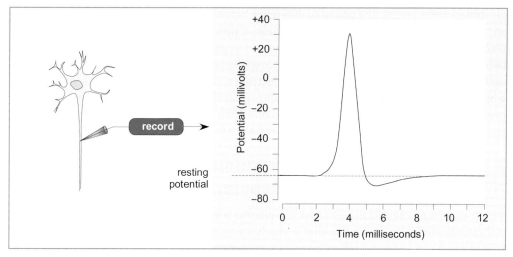

Figure 2.5: *Intracellular recording of an action potential (illustrative).*

When no action potentials are travelling along the axon, the potential difference between the electrodes is just the resting membrane potential of the neuron. When an action potential passes the point at which the electrode is inserted into the axon, the membrane potential changes, and this change is displayed on the screen. When plotted as a graph of membrane potential against time, the action potential takes the form shown in Figure 2.5. As the graph shows, the action potential lasts a very short time, only a few milliseconds, and involves a very rapid depolarization of the membrane. The depolarization reverses the sign of the membrane potential: the resting potential is negative, but the action potential briefly changes the sign to positive. The peak of the action potential shown in Figure 2.5 is about +30 mV; the precise value depends on the type of neuron and the species of animal involved. Following the peak of the spike, the membrane potential declines rapidly and for a brief period drops to below (more negative than) the resting level: during this period the membrane is hyperpolarized. The period of hyperpolarization is called the **afterpotential**.

An alternative method for recording action potentials is to have the two electrodes positioned along the axon, but both outside of it. This method is called **extracellular** recording, and is an important technique in the study of sensorimotor behavior. The technique cannot be used to measure resting potential, because when the axon is resting, there is no potential difference between two extracellular electrodes (they are both at the same potential). However, when an action potential propagating down the axon passes beneath first one electrode and then the other, a potential difference between the electrodes can be recorded. This is

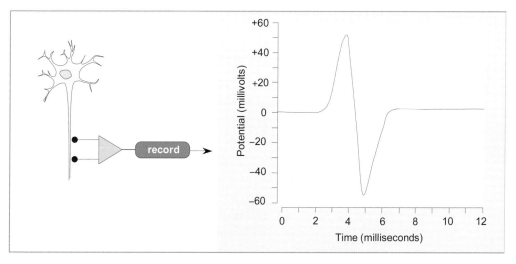

Figure 2.6: *Extracellular recording of an action potential (illustrative).*

illustrated in Figure 2.6. The potential difference between the electrodes is initially zero; when an action potential reaches the first electrode, a potential difference between electrodes is recorded. This drops to zero again when the action potential is exactly half way between the two electrodes. The action potential then passes beneath the second electrode, and there is again a potential difference between the electrodes, but opposite in sign. The result is that a biphasic action potential is recorded, as shown on the right of Figure 2.6. The value of the peak potential difference recorded depends on where the electrodes are positioned (how far from the axon, for example) and how thick the axon is.

2.1.8 Action potentials are generated when the cell membrane is sufficiently depolarized

When an action potential is generated, the neuron is said to **fire**. A neuron will fire only if its cell membrane is depolarized so that it reaches a specific value. If the membrane potential fails to reach this value, no action potentials are generated; if it reaches or exceeds this value, at least one action potential will be generated. This value is called the **firing threshold** and is typically at least 15–20 mV above (more positive than) the resting potential, though different neurons can have very different firing thresholds[7].

The membrane can be depolarized either by synaptic inputs or by artificial electrical stimulation[8]. We will consider how synaptic inputs lead to the generation of action potentials in the next section. Here we will consider the slightly simpler case in which stimulating microelectrodes are used to apply electric shocks that depolarize the cell membrane. The fact that electric shocks can make neurons fire means that neurons can be stimulated artificially with precisely controllable stimuli, which is useful in experimental studies.

Suppose that brief shocks are applied to the axon by a stimulator, and recorded using an intracellular microelectrode inserted slightly further down the axon, as shown on the left of Figure 2.7. The top right of the figure shows a graph of the shocks as voltage plotted against time. There are three shocks, each of which lasts only a few milliseconds, but they are of different strengths: the first is a weak shock, the second slightly stronger, the third is the strongest. The responses of the axon to the shocks as measured by the recording electrodes are shown plotted on the bottom right of the figure. The first shock causes a membrane depolarization that lasts a few milliseconds – various mechanisms ensure that the resting membrane potential is quickly restored. The shock does not result in the generation of an action potential, because the depolarization it evokes is below the firing threshold: it is **subthreshold**. The second shock causes a slightly greater depolarization, but it is still subthreshold, and so no action potential is generated. The third shock depolarizes the membrane to the firing threshold level, and an action potential is generated.

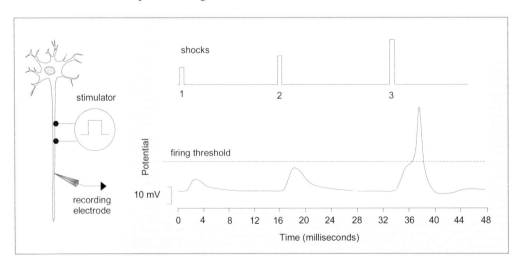

Figure 2.7: *Response of a neuron to electric shocks of various strengths (illustrative).*

If the magnitude of the shock is increased beyond the level of the third shock in Figure 2.7, the magnitude of the action potential does not change. In fact, the action potentials produced by a particular neuron in response to a depolarizing stimulus are all very similar to one another, regardless of the nature of the stimulus that caused their production. In particular, the maximum (positive) value of the membrane potential is virtually the same for all action potentials produced by a particular neuron. This fact is the basis of what is often called the **all-or-nothing law**, which can be stated as follows:

> **ALL-OR-NOTHING LAW:** The action potentials produced in a particular neuron all reach (almost) exactly the same maximum value. Thus, they are either generated as a whole (all) or they are not generated at all (nothing).

There are some exceptions to this law, and there can be small variations in both the duration and amplitude of the action potential generated by a given neuron, but these variations are not involved in the transmission of information[9].

2.1.9 Neurons produce action potentials in response to excitatory synaptic inputs

Neurons normally produce action potentials in response to synaptic inputs from other neurons (though many sensory neurons produce them in response to sensory stimulation). When one neuron makes synaptic connections with another, the number of individual synapses is typically in the thousands. According to Dale's corollary, these synapses are of the same type – all excitatory or all inhibitory. If the synapses are excitatory, then the postsynaptic neuron may produce one or more action potentials in response to synaptic inputs. This is the reason for referring to such synapses as excitatory: when a neuron is excited it may produce action potentials; when it is inhibited it will not.

Synaptic inputs are produced when an action potential in the presynaptic axon reaches the terminal buttons and causes the release of a neurotransmitter. At an excitatory synapse the neurotransmitter causes a small depolarization of the postsynaptic membrane at the synaptic site (an *excitatory postsynaptic potential*) due to a flow of positive ions into the cell at that location. This same process happens almost simultaneously at all the individual synaptic connections between the two neurons. The inflow of ions at an individual synapse does not cause an action potential to be generated. The positive ions that flow in at all the synaptic sites are passively conducted towards the cell body. The individual postsynaptic potentials thus contribute to the depolarization of the cell membrane at the cell body – they are combined together[10]. This combination of multiple postsynaptic potentials is referred to as **spatial summation**. The term 'spatial' is used because the process involves the combination of postsynaptic potentials produced simultaneously at different spatial locations. The word 'summation' is used because the combination process originally appeared to simply involve adding together all the individual potentials. More recent work has shown that the process is typically much more complex than this, but the word summation is still used.

Action potentials are normally initiated at the axon hillock, though in some cases initiation takes place further down the axon. From the initiation site, they propagate down the axon to its terminal buttons. In some cases, action potentials initiated in the axon hillock also propagate towards the cell body and along the dendrites[11]. We will consider only the propagation of action potentials down the axon. In order for an action potential to be generated, the cell membrane potential at the location of the axon hillock must be depolarized to the firing threshold.

The synaptic inputs from a single action potential arriving at all the terminal buttons of the presynaptic neuron are seldom sufficient to cause an action potential to be produced at the axon hillock. How does a neuron generate an action potential if the synaptic inputs resulting from an action potential in the presynaptic neuron are unable to depolarize it to threshold? The answer is that the depolarizing effects of more than one action potential must be combined. The combination can be of action potentials that arrive simultaneously from two or more presynaptic neurons, which is an example of spatial summation in which the combination involves the synaptic inputs from two or more presynaptic neurons.

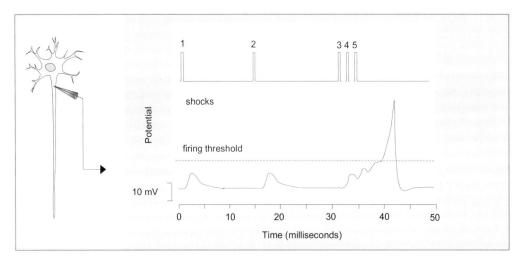

Figure 2.8: *Temporal summation of subthreshold stimuli (illustrative).*

An alternative type of combination involves two or more action potentials that arrive one after the other along the same presynaptic axon. As before, the depolarization due to any one of these action potentials at the axon hillock location is subthreshold, but their combination reaches threshold. This type of combination is called **temporal summation**. The idea of temporal summation is illustrated in Figure 2.8. The left of the figure shows a neuron with a microelectrode inserted into the axon hillock region, which records the membrane potential at that location. The right side of the figure shows the recorded responses to a series of stimuli that individually produce subthreshold depolarizations – these could either be action potentials in the presynapatic axon or brief electric shocks applied artificially (as in Figure 2.7). Stimuli 1 and 2 produce subthreshold depolarizations that have died away before the next stimulus is applied. In contrast, stimuli 3, 4 and 5 are applied in quick succession and the depolarizations do not have time to die away; the result is that they add together. In combination, they are able to bring the membrane potential to threshold and so evoke an action potential.

As a final point, a neuron may receive excitatory (depolarizing) synaptic input from some presynaptic neurons and inhibitory (hyperpolarizing) input from others. If we think of spatial summation of depolarizations as approximately an addition, we can view the spatial summation of hyperpolarizations as approximately a subtraction. The spatial summation of both is roughly the sum of the depolarizations minus the sum of the hyperpolarizations. A similar argument applies roughly to temporal summation also. Thus, inhibitory synaptic inputs can cancel out the effects of excitatory synaptic inputs, and so prevent a neuron from firing.

2.1.10 Synapses can have different strengths

How large is the postsynaptic potential that is produced in response to an action potential arriving at the presynaptic terminal? The answer to this question is that it depends. The size of the postsynaptic potential is influenced by a number of factors, such as the amount of neurotransmitter released and the number of receptors in the postsynaptic membrane. Thus, the size of the postsynaptic potential may be different at different synapses. This leads to a notion of synaptic *efficacy*, usually referred to as **synaptic strength**. A strong synaptic connection between two neurons means that the magnitude of the postsynaptic potential induced by an action potential arriving at the presynaptic terminal will be relatively large. If the connection is a weak one, the magnitude of the postsynaptic potential will be smaller. The strength of a synapse is not something that is fixed: a synapse can get stronger or weaker depending upon a number of factors. As we will see in part III, change in synaptic strength is one of the major neural mechanisms of learning and memory.

2.1.11 Different axons transmit action potentials at different speeds

How quickly do action potentials travel along axons? It turns out that different axons propagate action potentials at different speeds. In mammalian nervous systems, the slowest speeds are around 0.5 m/s, which is about the speed of a slow, ambling walk. The fastest speeds are around 120 m/s (432 km/h), which is just over one-third of the speed of sound in air (330 m/s).

In the nervous system of any animal, two factors are largely responsible for differences in propagation speed; these are:

(1)   Whether the axon is myelinated or not
(2)   The thickness of the axon

A **myelinated axon** is one that is sheathed along its length by a sequence of specialized glial cells that each wrap their membranes several times around the axon to form what is called the **myelin sheath**. True myelin is found only in vertebrate nervous systems. Figure 2.9 shows how the myelin sheath is formed in the central nervous system: specialized glial cells called **oligodendrocytes** wrap their membranes around axons, like you might wrap a bandage around a limb. This wrapping, the myelin sheath, insulates the axon from the extracellular fluid. Between one wrapping and the next, there is a small, unwrapped gap where the axon membrane is exposed. These gaps are called **nodes of Ranvier**. The axon membrane cannot propagate action potentials along the insulated segments; only at the nodes can an action potential be developed. Ions are rapidly conducted along the insulated segments through the intracellular fluid, and the action potentials appear to 'jump' from one node to the next[12] – a process called **saltatory conduction**. Other things being equal, a myelinated axon will conduct action potentials at least twice as fast as one that is unmyelinated. In the peripheral nervous system, myelin is formed by a different kind of glial cell called a **Schwann cell**.

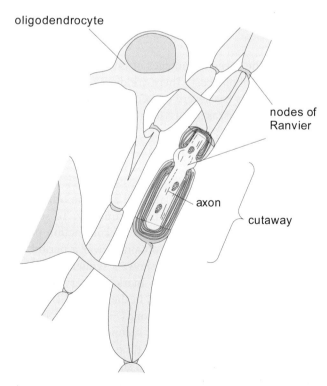

Figure 2.9: *Oligodendrocytes form myelin sheaths within the central nervous system (roughly based on Fig. 2-6 in Delcomyn, 1998).*

The second factor that affects speed of action potential propagation is the thickness of the axon. The general rule is that the thicker the axon, the faster the propagation speed. The thickness of the axon of a single neuron will typically vary – axons are often thicker near to the cell body and thinner further away, though this difference can be negligible or absent in long, unbranching lengths of axon. The axons of different neurons may have very different thicknesses: in the mammalian nervous system, the diameter of an axonal cross-section ranges from less than half a micrometer or micron (μm, one millionth of a meter) to more than 20 microns.

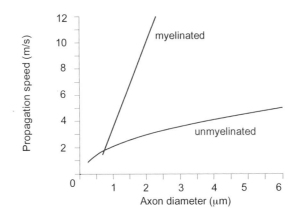

Figure 2.10: *Spike propagation speed as a function of axon diameter.*

Figure 2.10 shows how propagation speed varies with axon diameter for myelinated and unmyelinated axons in mammalian nervous systems. Unmyelinated axons thicker than about 2 microns are very unusual, as are myelinated axons thinner than 1 micron. The speed in unmyelinated axons varies roughly as the square root of the axon diameter. In myelinated axons, the speed is directly proportional to the axon diameter. If speed is measured in meters per second and diameter is measured in microns, the propagation speed (V) is roughly six times the axon diameter (D):

$$V \approx 6D$$

(V in m/s and D in μm). The speed advantages of myelinization are considerable, and they even come at a reduced metabolic cost. There are diseases, such as multiple sclerosis, that selectively destroy myelin. This has severe consequences for motor control, which relies on fast-conducting myelinated axons, as discussed later.

2.1.12 The firing rate is the number of spikes transmitted per second

A neuron can develop many action potentials, one after the other. The rate at which they are generated is called the **firing rate** or **firing frequency**. To see how this quantity can be measured, suppose a microelectrode is used to record action potentials as they pass a particular point along the axon. The record obtained over a period of half a second or so might be as shown in Figure 2.11. The figure shows a sequence of action potentials, which is sometimes called a **spike train**, with two marked intervals of 0.1 seconds duration. There are four spikes in the first interval and 15 in the second. The average firing rate in the first interval is calculated as 4 spikes ÷ 0.1 seconds = 40 spikes per second. In the second interval the average firing rate is 150 spikes per second. From this example, we see that the average firing rate (r) over a specific period of time is calculated as the number of spikes (N) divided by the duration of the interval (T). In shorthand, this calculation can be written as follows:

$$r = N/T$$

Average firing rates are typically given in units of Hertz (Hz = 1/seconds). Notice that the calculated value of the firing rate will depend on the length of the time interval over which it is calculated, as well as on where the interval starts from. In Figure 2.11, for example, if an interval duration of 200 milliseconds were used, then the average firing rate in an interval starting at the same time as the first interval shown would be 16 spikes ÷ 0.2 seconds = 80 Hz.

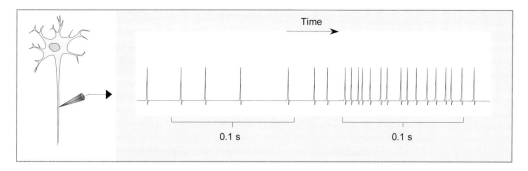

Figure 2.11: *Spike train recorded from an axon (illustrative).*

It is typically found that the firing rate is greater when the depolarizing input is greater. If the input depolarizes the membrane to the firing threshold, increasing the input results in an increase in the firing rate[13]. Information can be transmitted from one neuron to another as variations in the firing rate. We will discuss this idea further in Chapter 3, where we consider the transmission of sensory signals from sensory neurons to interneurons.

The minimum firing rate is, of course, zero. The maximum firing rate is limited by the fact that the membrane cannot propagate two action potentials at the same location on the cell membrane at the same time. In fact, a spike is followed by a very brief period during which it is first impossible and subsequently very difficult to elicit a second spike. This period, which lasts only a few milliseconds, is called the **refractory period**. As noted earlier, transmission of an action potential along an axon is in some respects rather like the burning part of a fuse travelling along a fuse wire. A fuse clearly cannot conduct two burning parts at the same place and time: if it is to conduct a second, the flammable material (gunpowder) must be replenished. Once an action potential has been propagated, active cellular processes restore the axon's ability to conduct another.

The refractoriness of neural membranes limits the maximum firing rate – the most rapid firing rates that have been evoked in axons are a little more than 800 Hz. Axons in the nervous system seldom transmit action potentials at the maximum rate, and if they do it is only in brief bursts. Firing rates during normal nervous system activity tend to be quite low, probably because transmitting at high rates uses a lot of metabolic energy[14].

2.1.13 Neural circuit diagrams are drawn using simple conventions

We have seen that neurons have complex shapes and connect to one another at many thousands of individual synapses. This is impossible to draw, and so if we are to produce diagrams showing how neurons are interconnected, it will be necessary to make some substantial simplifications. It follows from Dale's Corollary, together with the principle of spatial summation, that all the individual synaptic connections between a pre- and postsynaptic neuron behave in the same way as would a single large synapse. For this reason, when we draw neural circuit diagrams we represent the connection between two neurons as one large synapse. Whenever the synaptic connection is excitatory, we will use a triangle (◁) to represent the terminal part (terminal button) of an axon. When the synaptic connection is inhibitory, we will used a filled circle (●). These circuit diagram conventions are shown in panel A of Figure 2.12, where the cell body is represented as a circle and the axon as a straight line. This is a convenient simplification when drawing complicated circuits. The presynaptic neurons (1) are also shown in a different color to the postsynaptic neurons (2). Real neurons have barely any color at all, but appear gray when packed together in sufficiently large numbers. However, when drawing circuits it is often convenient to use different colors for different types of neuron.

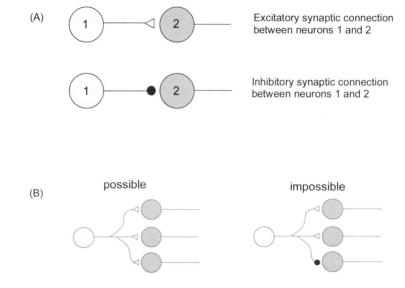

Figure 2.12: *Circuit diagram conventions.*

Using these conventions for drawing circuit diagrams, the simple circuit shown on the left of panel B in Figure 2.12 is possible since it conforms to Dale's Corollary: the synaptic connections are all excitatory. The circuit shown on the right of panel B is not possible according to Dale's Corollary, because the presynaptic neuron makes excitatory synaptic connections with two neurons and an inhibitory connection with another. We will never encounter a circuit that violates Dale's Corollary.

2.1.14 There are basic patterns of neural connectivity

Neurons are connected together to form circuits and pathways that can be enormously complex and dense, given the vast numbers of individual neurons involved and the extent of their connectivity – a single neuron may send signals directly to many hundreds or thousands of other neurons and may receive inputs from similar numbers of neurons. Despite this complexity, it is possible to identify basic patterns of connectivity that are found in many different parts of the nervous system. Some of these will be described here, using the diagrammatic conventions introduced earlier.

Neurons can be connected directly to each other or connected via other neurons. When two neurons are directly connected, as in panel A of Figure 2.12, their connectivity is said to be **monosynaptic**. When two neurons are connected via an intermediate neuron, their connectivity is said to be **disynaptic**; disynaptic connectivity between neurons labeled P and Q is shown in panel A of Figure 2.13. If there are two intermediate neurons, then the connectivity is said to be **trisynaptic**. This is as far as 'numbering' is typically taken: if there are more than two intermediate neurons, the connectivity is said to be **polysynaptic** (meaning many synapses).

Within the nervous system, different populations of neurons connect to other populations via pathways that often have connectivities of the sort just described; specific examples will be encountered later in this chapter and elsewhere. In such cases there can be what is termed **convergence** in the pathway, or there can be **divergence**. In a convergent pathway, a number of neurons in the source population connect to a smaller number in the target population, as illustrated in panel B of Figure 2.13. A divergent pathway shows the opposite pattern, with fewer neurons in the source population connecting to a larger number in the target population, as shown in panel C of the figure.

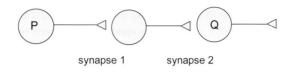

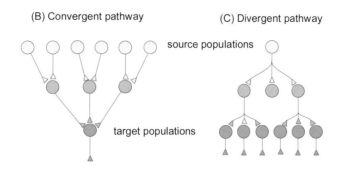

Figure 2.13: *Patterns of neural interconnectivity.*

The patterns of connectivity just described all act to transmit signals from one place (neuron A or source population) to another (neuron B or target population): they are all examples of *feedforward* connectivity. Feedback connectivity is also found throughout animal nervous systems. Two basic kinds of feedback connectivity[15] are found in nervous systems and are shown in Figure 2.14: feedback excitation in panel A and feedback inhibition in panel B (two alternative ways of drawing each type are shown). Feedback inhibition with the disynaptic connectivity shown in panel B is known as **recurrent inhibition**. In both examples shown, the feedback connectivity is disynaptic, but trisynaptic and polysynaptic feedback connectivities are possible.

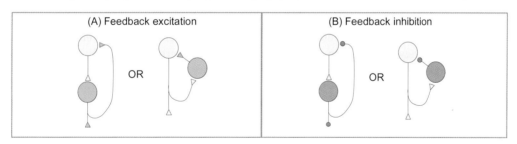

Figure 2.14: *Local feedback connectivity.*

2.1.15 Behavior of some neurons can be captured in a simple model

Neurons are very elaborate devices, and the full complexity of their behavior is only beginning to be unraveled. So far, we have presented some simple generalizations that are able to provide an approximate description of the behavior of some neuron types found in mammalian nervous systems. In the chapters that follow, it will often be sufficient to assume that neurons behave in this way. These generalizations can be summarized by the following propositions:

(1) **Dale's Corollary:** all individual synaptic junctions between one neuron and another are of the same type and behave as if they were a single, large synapse.

(2) **Resting potential:** in the absence of synaptic inputs, a neuron's membrane potential assumes a constant value called the resting potential. Synaptic inputs change the value:

excitatory inputs increase its value (make it more positive); inhibitory inputs decrease its value (make it more negative).

(3) **Firing threshold:** if the membrane potential at the axon hillock reaches a specific value that is more positive than the resting potential – called the firing threshold – it generates at least one action potential or spike. The quantity 'membrane potential at the axon hillock' is equal to the sum of the synaptic inputs to the neuron from all presynaptic neurons. Excitatory inputs contribute positively (add) to this sum, and inhibitory inputs contribute negatively (subtract).

(4) **All-or-nothing principle:** all spikes produced by particular neurons are the same (they are all or nothing) – there is no such thing as a half-sized spike or a double-sized spike. Thus, greater synaptic input does not change the spikes themselves, it changes the number of spikes generated per unit time (the firing rate). More excitatory input produces a higher firing rate.

(5) **Neural output:** spikes propagate down the axon to terminals that make synaptic connections with other neurons. Thus, spikes can be considered to be the outputs of a neuron.

(6) **Synaptic strength:** a single spike in a given (presynaptic) neuron can deliver a larger or smaller synaptic input to another (postsynaptic) neuron according to the strength of the synaptic connection between the two.

These properties specify what amounts to a model or idealized neuron. Many of the neurons that we will encounter in later chapters possess these properties and so conform closely to the model. However, no neuron possesses a truly constant resting potential (property 2): in many neurons, fluctuations in the membrane potential can be large enough to reach the cell's firing threshold. Some examples are described next.

2.1.16 Most neurons do not possess a constant resting potential

Most neurons in the mammalian nervous system possess membrane properties that lead to fluctuations of the membrane potential in the absence of synaptic inputs, fluctuations that sometimes reach the firing threshold. When this happens the cell will generate one or more action potentials. Fluctuations in membrane potential can be either random or periodic. If they are random, then the cell generates action potentials more or less randomly, and the firing rate of the cell is called its **resting firing rate**. Here is a definition:

> **RESTING FIRING RATE:** the firing rate of a neuron when it is not receiving any synaptic input, with the condition that the action potentials occur at random intervals (or at least are non-periodic).

In most cells the resting firing rate is quite low, with only a few action potentials per second, or less.

If the fluctuations in a cell's membrane potential are not random but rise and fall periodically, then the cell may generate action potentials periodically, either singly or in bursts. A cell generating periodic bursts of action potentials is shown in panel A of Figure 2.15: the interval of time between the start of one burst and the start of the next is approximately one second in this example. A cell that generates bursts like this in the absence of synaptic input is called an **autonomous bursting neuron**. Another type of bursting neuron is one that generates bursts when subjected to constant input, either in the form of tonic synaptic input or by a constant artificial stimulus. Such a cell could be called a **non-autonomous bursting neuron**.

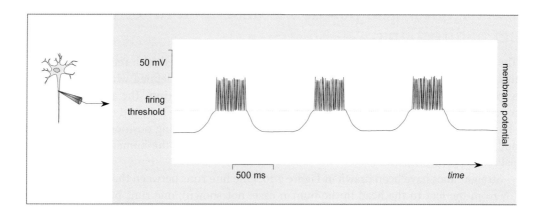

Figure 2.15: *Bursting behavior in neurons.*

Bursting neurons, and other neurons that fire periodically, play a role in generating a number of fundamental types of rhythmic behavior in animals and people. Such behavior includes breathing, chewing, peristalsis (rhythmic contractions of the smooth muscles of the gut), and circadian cycles such as the daily sleep-wake cycle. Periodically firing neurons that contribute to rhythmical behavior are called **pacemaker neurons**:

> **PACEMAKER NEURON:** a neuron that is able to fire periodically (either autonomously or in response to tonic input) and contribute to the generation of rhythmic or periodic patterns of behavior.

2.2 Motor Components of the Central Nervous System

2.2.1 Introduction

Mammalian nervous systems are interconnected, such that none of the nervous tissue is completely separate from the rest. Despite this interconnectedness, the nervous system divides up rather naturally into anatomically distinct components. We have already encountered the division between the central nervous system (CNS) and the peripheral nervous system (PNS). The latter can itself be divided into two parts: an **autonomic** part and a **somatic** part. The autonomic part is concerned with the regulation of basic bodily processes such as respiration, digestion, blood supply, excretion and temperature control. We will have very little to do with the autonomic nervous system and will not describe it any further in this chapter. The somatic part of the PNS is comprised of the dorsal root ganglia and the cranial ganglia, together with the axons of sensory and motoneurons. These axons are bundled together into nerves. We will discuss the peripheral nervous system in more detail in the next part of this chapter and in Chapter 3. In this part of the chapter we will describe the functional anatomy of the CNS, with an emphasis on those parts particularly involved in sensorimotor control.

2.2.2 Anatomical position is described in terms of a set of directions

The positions of structures within an animal's body are described with reference to a set of intrinsic cardinal directions. These directions are most simply defined when the body is in a specific straight posture called the (**standard**) **anatomic position**. The anatomic position for a typical quadrupedal mammal is shown in panel A of Figure 2.16, and that of a person is shown in panel B. These positions correspond to normal standing positions of quadrupeds and humans (with the exception of the lower arm position in the human case, where the palms face the front).

Straight lines have been drawn in Figure 2.16. One line runs between the tail and the head (or from the feet to the head in the human case, not shown), one runs between the abdomen and the back, and one runs from side to side (not shown for the dog). Consider the line joining the head and tail of the dog: we might consider this line to be pointing from head to tail or from tail to head, as indicated by the arrows. The head-to-tail direction is called the **caudal** direction (from the Latin *caudum*, meaning 'tail'); the tail-to-head direction is called the **rostral** direction (from the Latin *rostrum*, meaning 'beak'). (There are alternative names for these directions, as discussed below.) Something that is nearer the head than something else is said to be rostral to it. Thus, the lungs are rostral to the intestines. Something that is nearer the tail (or the feet in humans) than something else is said to be caudal to it. Thus, the intestines are caudal to the lungs.

The line that runs between the belly and the back can also point in two directions. The belly-to-back direction is called the **dorsal** direction (from the Latin *dorsum*, meaning 'back'). The opposite direction (back-to-belly) is called the **ventral** direction (from the Latin *ventrum*, meaning 'abdomen'). Something that is further in the direction of the belly than something else is said to be **ventral** to it. Thus, the navel is ventral to the spine. Something that is further towards the back than something else is said to be **dorsal** to it. Thus, the spine is dorsal to the navel.

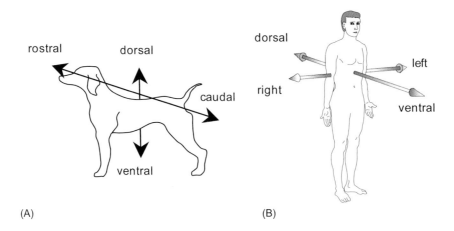

(A)   (B)

Figure 2.16: *Cardinal directions.*

The line that runs from side to side can point either to the right or to the left. However, it is anatomically more useful to think of it as pointing away from the middle of the body or towards the middle of the body, irrespective of the side of the body concerned. The direction can be considered to be either from the side towards the middle, or from the middle towards the side. The middle-to-side direction is called the **lateral** direction; the side-to-middle direction is the **medial** direction. On either the right or left of the body, something that is further from the middle of the animal than something else is said to be lateral to it. For example, an ear is further to the side than an eye, so the right ear is lateral to the right eye. Something that is closer to the middle of the body than something else is said to be medial to it. Thus the right eye is medial to the right ear.

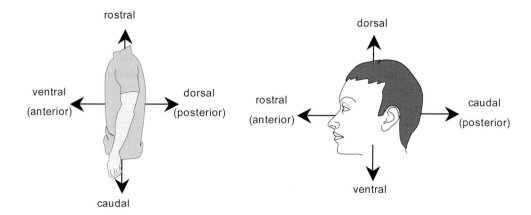

Figure 2.17: *Distinctions between rostral-caudal and anterior-posterior directions in the human body.*

So far everything is clear enough, but there are some potential sources of confusion intro-duced because of the differences between the standard anatomic position of most mammals and that of humans. The directions towards an animal's front and rear are sometimes called the *anterior* and *posterior* directions rather than the rostral and caudal directions. This applies to people too, but the front and rear of a quadruped are not anatomically the same as the front and rear of a person: a person's belly is at the front, but a dog's belly is not. For a quadruped, the rostral and anterior directions are the same, and the caudal and posterior directions are the same. This is not the case for a person: the anterior and posterior directions of the human trunk are the same as the ventral and dorsal directions, respectively (Figure 2.17, left). For the human head, however, the anterior-posterior and dorsal-ventral directions correspond to those of other mammals, as the head is oriented similarly. Thus, the nose is anterior (rostral) to the ears and the top of the head is dorsal to the jaw (Figure 2.17, right).

2.2.3 The three bodily axes define a set of anatomical planes

The lines drawn in Figure 2.16 form, in effect, axes at right angles to one another. The axis that passes longitudinally through the middle of the body is a **rostrocaudal** axis; the axis that

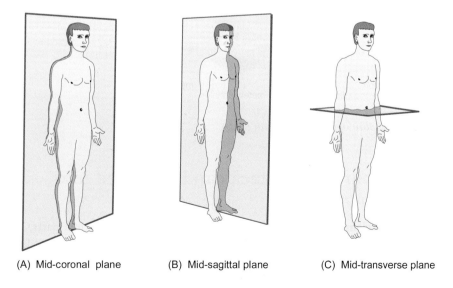

(A) Mid-coronal plane   (B) Mid-sagittal plane   (C) Mid-transverse plane

Figure 2.18: *Cardinal planes.*

passes through the front and back of the body is a **dorsoventral** axis (also called an *antero-posterior* axis); the axis that passes through the sides of the body is a **mediolateral** axis.

Rostrocaudal and dorsoventral axes span a plane called a **sagittal** plane; rostrocaudal and mediolateral axes span a plane called a **coronal** plane (sometimes called a *frontal* plane); mediolateral and dorsoventral axes span a plane called a **transverse** plane (Figure 2.18). The sagittal plane shown in panel B of Figure 2.18 is often called the *mid-sagittal* plane because it passes through the middle of the body, dividing it into a left half and a right half. The coronal plane in panel A divides the body into a front half and back half (the *mid-coronal* plane); the transverse plane in panel C divides the body into a top half and a bottom half (the *mid-transverse* plane). Any plane that passes through the body parallel to the mid-coronal plane is another coronal plane (and similarly for the other planes in Figure 2.18).

Slicing through the body reveals its internal structures. If a body part is sliced through in a coronal plane, we get a coronal cross-section – or **coronal section** – of that body part. Slices in sagittal and transverse planes yield sagittal and transverse sections, respectively. We will encounter plenty of examples of sectional views later in this part of the chapter.

2.2.4 The CNS is divided into a stack of parts

The mammalian central nervous system is divided by anatomists into a sequence of parts or segments that are stacked from the caudal end to the rostral end. These parts can be identified in all mammalian brains, and are evident early in the development of the fetus. Figure 2.19 shows a simple schematic plan of the mammalian nervous system (mid-sagittal slice), with the sequence of parts identified with different colors. The spinal cord is at the caudal end and merges with the **hindbrain**. The caudal part of the hindbrain is called the **myelencephalon**, the rostral part is called the **metencephalon**. The metencephalon merges with the **midbrain**, also called the **mesencephalon**. The hindbrain and midbrain together form the **brainstem**. The rostral midbrain merges into the **forebrain**. The caudal part of the forebrain is called the **diencephalon** and the rostral part is called the **telencephalon**. There is a network of interconnected chambers and canals within the nervous tissue that is filled with fluid (cerebrospinal fluid).

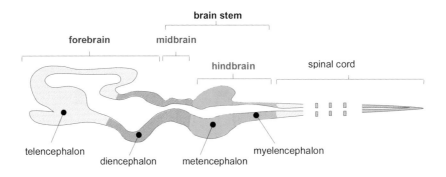

Figure 2.19: *Basic plan of the mammalian brain.*

2.2.5 Each part of the stack can be divided into several elements

Each of the seven elements shown in Figure 2.19 consists of visibly distinct parts. The most obvious distinction is between **gray matter** and **white matter:** the gray matter is nervous tissue that consists primarily of neural cell bodies, their dendrites, unmeyelinated axons, and glial cells; the white matter is nervous tissue that consists of myelinated axons. Both white and gray matter is found in all the elements of the stack.

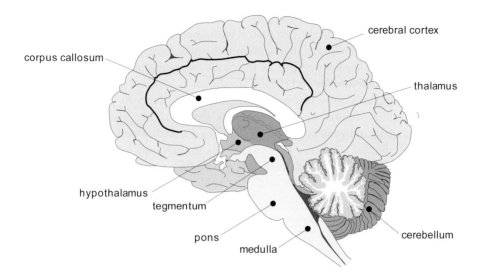

Figure 2.20: *Mid-sagittal section through a human brain.*

In the brain, gray matter is found either in lumps or in sheets. A well-defined lump is called a **nucleus**; a sheet is called a **cortex**. Figure 2.20 shows a mid-sagittal section of the human brain that identifies some of the larger anatomical structures. The hindbrain structures identified are the medulla, the pons and the cerebellum; each of these structures consists of substructures at a finer grain, as we will see later. The midbrain structure identified in the figure is the tegmentum. The diencephalic part of the forebrain includes the thalamus and the hypothalamus. The telencephalic part consists of the cerebral cortex and various nuclei, together with a large amount of white matter (including the corpus callosum shown in the figure). The cerebral cortex is what you would see if you removed the top of the skull and stripped away the brain's protective membranes. It has two halves (see below), and each is a folded, wrinkly sheet of gray matter about 2 to 4 millimeters thick in the human case. The clefts and fissures formed by the folds are called **sulci** (singular: *sulcus*) and the lumps between them are called **gyri** (singular: *gyrus*). In some mammals, such as the rat, the cortex is not folded and so appears smooth. The cerebellum also consists mainly of a folded sheet of gray matter – the cerebellar cortex – which is thinner and more tightly folded than the cerebral cortex.

All elements of the stack have components directly involved in sensory, motor or sensori-motor functions. Those components with mainly sensory functions will be described in the next two chapters. In this chapter we will describe the components that are known to be involved in motor control. These include the spinal cord, nuclei in the medulla, pons and midbrain, the cerebellum, the superior and inferior colliculi, regions of the cerebral cortex and several forebrain nuclei.

2.2.6 CNS has approximate bilateral symmetry: structures present on left side are also present on right side

A mid-sagittal section divides the mammalian central nervous system into two halves that are very nearly mirror images of each other: the gross anatomy of the right half is the mirror image of the gross anatomy of the left half. There are some differences in the details, but these are not very obvious. Since the mammalian brain is mirror-symmetric in the mid-sagittal plane, it is said to have bilateral symmetry.

Some CNS structures straddle the midline. Examples include the corpus callosum, the gray matter of the spinal cord and the pineal gland. The mid-sagittal plane cuts these structures into nearly equal halves. Other structures are not cut by the mid-sagittal plane. In these cases, there are two of each structure, one on the right side and one on the left side. Examples include the superior colliculi, the inferior colliculi and the forebrain nuclei. Figure 2.21 shows a coronal section of the human brain, just rostral to the pons, that illustrates the approximate bilateral symmetry of the forebrain (the section only cuts through the forebrain; midbrain and hindbrain structures are not present). In the figure, white matter is shown in white, open spaces within the brain (ventricles and canals) are shown in blue and gray matter is shown in gray or purple. Several structures can be seen duplicated on the right and left sides: the left and right caudate nucleus, putamen, globus pallidus, thalamus, hypothalamus and mammillary body. The caudate and putamen are actually joined together and form a large nucleus called the *striatum*, but we will often refer to them as though they were distinct nuclei. The thalamus is a closely packed group of nuclei that are important in sensory processing, as we will see in Chapter 3.

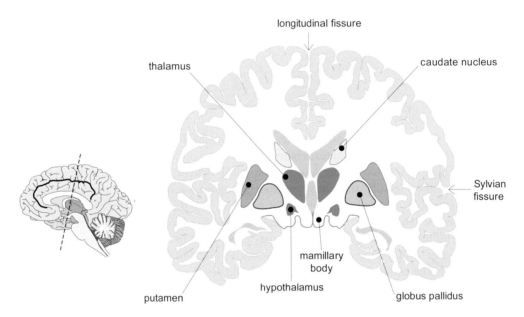

Figure 2.21: *Coronal section of a human brain.*

The cerebral cortex also comes in two halves, since the cortical gray matter is not continuous across the midline – there is a sheet on the left and a sheet on the right. These folded sheets wrap around the rest of the forebrain to form the cerebral hemispheres. The two halves of the cortex are connected together by a large bundle of myelinated axons – a fiber tract – called the **corpus callosum**. The rest of the white matter is made up largely of fiber tracts that connect one region of gray matter to another. Figure 2.21 also shows that each half of the cerebral cortex forms a kind of skin that contains other nervous tissue – the white matter and the forebrain nuclei. On each side, the cortical skin together with the forebrain structures it contains is known as a cerebral hemisphere.

Notice that the left and right sides of the brain shown in Figure 2.21 are not exactly the same: the differences lie in the details, not in the overall structure. These asymmetries may or may not be of functional significance – they may arise, for instance, as the result of asymmetric growth of the skull.

2.2.7 How can the functions of brain regions be determined?

It is a fact universally acknowledged that different parts of the brain are specialized for different functions – different parts do different things. This concept is called **localization of function**. The different parts work together to implement the overall functional operations of the brain. The concept of functional localization can tempt people into making three types of assumption without evidence: we will refer to these as the *localization assumption*, the *structure = function assumption* and the *fixed function assumption*.

(1)   **Localization assumption:** if there is a neural mechanism that controls or produces some behavioral attribute, then that mechanism is localized to some specific region or structure in the brain. This assumption cannot be made without evidence, since there is no reason to suppose that a functional mechanism is localized in a particular structure: the mechanism could be distributed over several regions or structures.

(2)   **Structure = function assumption:** an anatomically identifiable component of the nervous system (structural component) is also a functional component (it has one or more identifiable functions). There is no *a priori* reason to suppose that this is generally true (it might be true, or it might not be). This assumption probably arises due to our familiarity with artificial machines and devices that are constructed from parts, each of which serves a particular purpose. If you take a motor vehicle apart, for example, you end up with a large number of individual components, each of which has a particular function.

(3)   **Fixed function assumption:** any neural structure or identifiable region that has a particular function (or set of functions) always performs this function (or set of functions) when it is active. There is no reason to suppose that neural structures are like this (some might be, others might not be). It is possible that anatomically identifiable structures do different things at different times. Once again, this assumption probably arises because we are familiar with the workings of artificial mechanical and electronic devices that are made of distinct parts that have particular, fixed functions. For instance, most automobiles are equipped with spark plugs; their purpose is to ignite the fuel in the cylinders. This is all that they do; they do not sometimes function as brakes and at other times as engine coolers.

Of course, it might be the case that a function is localized, that an anatomical structure has a particular function and that its function is fixed. To determine whether it is the case requires careful evaluation based on empirical evidence. Three basic types of empirical method are used to determine what the different structures and regions of the brain do: *lesion methods*, *recording methods* and *stimulation methods*. The basic idea of the lesion method is to observe how damage to circumscribed regions of nervous tissue alters behavior: inferences about the function of the lesioned tissue are then drawn from changes in behavior that can be attributed to the lesion. Recording methods are more diverse, but the basic idea is to measure activity in particular areas of the brain and determine whether variations in activity is associated either with the performance of some behavior or with attributes of sensory stimulation. Finally, stimulation methods involve directly stimulating neural tissue at particular locations, usually electrically or magnetically, and observing the responses evoked by the stimuli. These responses can sometimes provide information about the normal functional role of the stimulated structures. These three methods are briefly discussed in the following sections.

2.2.8 Lesion methods can be either destructive or non-destructive

Experimental lesion methods involve removing or deactivating a circumscribed region of nervous tissue. The behavior of lesioned individuals (the experimental group) can then be compared with behavior of unlesioned individuals (the control group). Alternatively, the behavior of individuals before and after the lesion can be compared. The observed differences in behavior provide insight into the functional role of the lesioned tissue.

Lesions can be made destructively by cutting or removing tissue with a knife or by using a chemical agent. Destructive lesioning is irreversible and can only be used on experimental animals: it was once widely used, but is less common today. Non-destructive lesion techniques are also possible, and have the advantage that they can be used in experiments with human participants. These techniques involve temporarily rendering a region of nervous tissue inactive, and are reversible. Deactivating nervous tissue can be done by cooling, using a thermal probe inserted into or close to the region to be deactivated: if neurons are cooled sufficiently, they become incapable of transmitting signals. Another way to render a region of tissue inactive is to stimulate the tissue repetitively with a high-strength, pulsed magnetic field: the field is turned on for a brief period, then off, then on again, and so on. Stimulation by a briefly pulsed magnetic field is called **magnetic stimulation**; stimulation by a train of four or more pulses is called **repetitive magnetic stimulation**. We will discuss magnetic stimulation in more detail in section 2.2.11. Temporarily deactivating regions of nervous tissue, by repetitive magnetic stimulation or by cooling, is referred to as the **virtual lesion** technique, to emphasize the non-destructive, reversible nature of the effects produced[16].

Lesion methods involve the production of 'lesions' in specific locations. Lesions may also be produced as the result of accidents or of neurological disease. The locations and extent of the lesions produced by accidents and pathologies can usually be established using one or other of the structural brain-scanning methods available, such as MRI (magnetic resonance imaging) scans. People unfortunate enough to have been the victims of accidents or to suffer from neurological disease show various symptoms and behavioral patterns that provide clues to the function of the damaged tissue. In general, tissue damage in naturally occurring lesions is not confined to particular circumscribed regions or structures. In such circumstances, it is very difficult to draw any conclusions regarding the function of the damaged regions from observations of behavior. However, there are cases in which the lesions are localized to particular structures or regions. Such cases can provide insights into the function of the damaged tissue; we will encounter several examples later in this chapter and in the two chapters that follow. Table 2.1 summarizes the different lesion types and the methods by which they are produced.

Table 2.1: *Different types of lesion.*

Lesion type	Destructive	Non-destructive (virtual)
Produced by experimenter	Removing or cutting tissue, destroying tissue with chemical agents or heat	Cooling tissue, applying repetitive magnetic stimulation
Naturally occuring	Death of cells due to loss of blood supply (e.g., stroke), mechanical damage or disease processes	May not exist

Lesions to nervous tissue may lead to changes in motor behavior that reduce the quality of performance, make it impossible to perform certain behaviors, or produce non-functional behavioral effects that interfere with performance of goal-directed action. Such detrimental changes are referred to as *deficits*, and a lesion may produce one or more of them. It is clear that lesioned neural tissue is associated in some way with the deficits produced by lesioning it, but it is seldom clear what the relationship is. For example, if the abililty to perform a behavior is lost following a lesion, then it is tempting to conclude that the nervous tissue at the site of the lesion normally functions to produce that behavior. However, such conclusions are not logically valid because although the lesioned tissue is necessary for production of the behavior, it is not necessarily the site of production: it might, for instance, be a region that is needed to activate the primary site of production. Consider the following example: it has been found that lesions to the heart can result in loss of consciousness; can you conclude from this that the heart is the organ of consciousness? You can hypothesize that the heart is the organ of consciousness based on the observation that removing it eliminates consciousness, but you clearly cannot conclude that it is.

A second kind of error is to conclude that the function of the lesioned tissue is to produce or control the deficient aspects of the behavior. For example, if you found that a lesion leads to movements that are too slow, it would not be legitimate to conclude that the lesioned tissue is a movement speed controller. One well-known example illustrates the fallacy of drawing such conclusions: an electronic component, such as a resistor, is removed from the circuitry of a radio receiver; as a result of the removal, the radio emits a high-pitched whistling noise[17]. It cannot be concluded from this that the component was a whistle suppressor.

2.2.9 Electromagnetic activity can be recorded from living brains

There are two types of activity that can be recorded from nervous tissue: electromagnetic activity and metabolic-related activity. Both types can provide measures of the functional activity of the tissue. When neural tissue is engaged in functional processing, neurons are generating action potentials and transmitting signals to one another (electromagnetic activity). This requires energy, so the metabolic activity of the nervous tissue is greater when neurons are electrically active. Living nervous tissue is never electrically or metabolically inactive. This means that experimenters do not simply look for activity; they either look for differences in activity between experimental conditions, or they look for variations in activity that are correlated with variations in sensory stimulation, or correlated with variables associated with performance (such as muscle force or direction of limb movement).

In section 1 of this chapter we saw how electrical activity of individual neurons can be recorded using microelectrodes. When such recordings are made from neurons in living brains, the method is called *single cell recording*. The method can be used to determine how single neurons in particular regions of the brains of experimental animals respond to sensory stimuli, or to determine how their activity is related to the performance of motor tasks. Thus, single cell recording can provide useful information concerning the functional role of brain regions in sensorimotor behavior, but it is not a method that can be used with people. Activity in human brains must be recorded using less invasive methods: two such methods that record the electromagnetic activity are briefly outlined next.

The electrical activity of neurons in the brain generates changing electrical fields that penetrate through the skull; as a result, small variations in electrical potential can be recorded using electrodes placed on the scalp. This is the basis for a method called **electroencephalography (EEG)**. The electrodes used in EEG are typically disk- or cup-shaped and a few millimeters in diameter. Such an electrode placed on the scalp is exposed to a changing electrical field that results from the combined activity in a very large number of neurons: those neurons that lie within brain tissue sufficiently close to the electrode to make non-negligible contributions to the electric field at the electrode site. EEG recording involves measuring differences in electrical potential between two electrodes. The simplest configuration would be to have just two electrodes, one on the scalp (the recording electrode) and another placed at a location where electrical fluctuations are minimal, such as on the ear (the reference electrode). A recording of the potential difference (voltage) between the two electrodes over a period of time is called a raw **EEG signal**: the signal can be thought of as a measure of neural activity in the region of cortex in the vicinity of the scalp electrode, which may contain as many as a billion neurons. It is believed that the primary contribution to EEG signals derives from electrical currents (movement of ions) in the dendrites of cortical neurons produced in response to synaptic inputs, and not from the propagation of action potentials[18].

EEG signals can be used to obtain useful information about how cortical activity changes from moment to moment: EEG methods are said to have good *temporal resolution*, which essentially means that moment-to-moment changes in the signal give an indication of moment-to-moment changes in activity in the tissue that contributes to the signal. However, EEG methods have poor spatial resolution: tissue over quite a large area in the vicinity of a scalp electrode can contribute to the signal, and it is impossible to know exactly how far the region extends – a signal could reflect a large amount of activity further away from the electrode site, or a small amount of activity nearby, or some combination. Thus, EEG methods can provide only limited information about those cortical regions that are particularly active during performance of a motor task or processing of a sensory stimulus. Deployment of a large number of electrodes, 256 being the typical maximum, set out in a regular array over the scalp, can be used to better localize the sources of recorded electrical brain activity, when combined with sophisticated data processing methods[19].

The precision of locating sources of activity in the cortex can be improved by recording the variations in the magnetic field produced by the electrical activity (whenever an electrical current flows, a magnetic field is generated). Thus, variations in electrical brain activity produce varying magnetic fields. These fields are extremely weak, but can be measured using highly sensitive detectors[20], provided that these can be shielded from variations in environmental magnetic fields, which are typically much stronger. Special shielded rooms must be constructed to achieve this, and within these rooms arrays of magnetic detectors placed over the scalp can record variations in the brain's magnetic field at different scalp locations. This method is called **magnetoencephalography (MEG)** (the same mechanisms are responsible for the EEG signals and MEG signals). MEG can provide better spatial resolution than EEG. Two limitations of MEG are cost (MEG is extremely expensive, whereas EEG is relatively cheap) and the fact that only the magnetic fields generated within cortical tissue in the sulci of the cortex can be recorded from outside the scalp – the fields generated by activity in gyral tissue are virtually undetectable and are almost completely absent from MEG recordings.

2.2.10 Metabolic activity can be recorded from living brains

An indirect way of measuring the functional activity of nervous tissue is to measure its metabolic demand; there are several ways of doing this, but we will describe only one method. The more active the neurons are (the higher their firing rates, for example), the greater their requirement for food and oxygen (metabolic demand). This increased demand leads to measureable changes in the tissue. One of these is an increase in the flow of oxygenated blood into the active region: metabolically active cells produce chemical compounds that signal a requirement for oxygenated blood to the vascular system, which responds accordingly. The result is that more active regions of nervous tissue have a higher proportion of oxygenated blood in them.

It has been discovered that the ratio of oxygenated blood to deoxygenated blood in a region of tissue can be measured if the tissue is placed within a very powerful magnetic field and then exposed to pulses of radio waves. Nuclei of atoms in the tissue first absorb the radio waves and then re-emit them, a process known as *nuclear magnetic resonance*. There is a difference between the emission characteristics of oxygenated blood and deoxygenated blood: it is this difference that underlies **functional magnetic resonance imaging (fMRI)**. The principles underlying this imaging technique and the details of how it works are too complex to be described here[21]. The following gives a rough idea of what is going on when the human brain is imaged using this method[22]. The person's head is placed within the magnetic field generated by a large and very powerful electromagnet (on the order of 100,000 times stronger than the Earth's magnetic field, 1000 times stronger than an average fridge magnet). The fMRI machine emits pulses of radio waves and picks up the radio waves emitted in response from small volumes of tissue. These are called *voxels* (short for *volumetric picture element*) and are typically about 3 mm^3 in size[23]. From the radio waves received, a blood-oxygen level dependent (BOLD) signal is derived that is a measure of the ratio of oxygenated to deoxygenated blood[24] in each voxel. The BOLD signal is an indirect measure of the relative level of neural activity in each voxel. From these signals, a picture is typically produced that shows the voxels that are more active than the baseline level. The active voxels are shown in bright colors and superimposed on a gray image of the brain. In such a picture, the active areas appear lit up in different colors, which is why people say that brain regions 'light up' when they are active.

The advantage of fMRI over the EEG and MEG techniques is that it has much better spatial resolution: the location of active regions can be determined more precisely, being limited primarily by voxel size. The disadvantage is that fMRI has relatively poor temporal resolution, since it depends on measuring the vascular response to variations in neural activity. The vascular response to changes in activity develops over several seconds and produces measurable changes in the BOLD signal after a period of between 1 and 5 seconds. The actual changes in neural activity to which the vascular system is responding may occur on a timescale of tens of milliseconds. Thus, fMRI can give us a fairly precise picture of where things are happening, but only a crude picture of when they happened.

2.2.11 The brain can be stimulated through the scalp

Stimulation of the nervous system can provide useful information concerning the role of a stimulated region in the production of behavior. The two types of stimulation that we will encounter are electrical stimulation and magnetic stimulation. Electrical stimulation applied to nervous tissue can excite large numbers of neurons simultaneously (those neurons close to the stimulating electrodes). One way to apply electrical stimulation is to bring electrodes directly into contact with nervous tissue. This was the method used in the famous experiments of Wilder Penfield in which the motor cortices of people undergoing brain surgery were electrically stimulated (see section 2.2.13). It is also possible to apply electrical stimuli to a person's brain using electrodes placed on the scalp, a method called **transcranial electrical stimulation (TES)**. As this requires quite large currents, it can be painful, and may produce uncomfortable contractions in the muscles of the head. These unpleasant side effects of TES can be largely avoided by using **transcranial magnetic stimulation (TMS)**.

A suitable magnetic stimulus is produced by passing a very brief pulse of powerful electrical current through tightly wound coils of wire, either a single coil shaped like a bagel or two coils next to each other in a figure-eight configuration, as shown in panel A of Figure 2.22. The figure-eight coil configuration is the most commonly used because it provides a more localized, focal stimulus; the position of the focus is beneath the location indicated in the figure. When the pulse of electrical current flows through the coil, a transient but intense magnetic field is generated that very quickly rises in strength to a peak (in about a tenth of a millisecond) and dies away again, as shown in panel B of Figure 2.22. A changing magnetic field causes electrical current to flow in any conducting material through which it passes, a phenomenon called electromagnetic induction. During its rise to a peak, which takes about ten microseconds, the magnetic field is changing very rapidly, rapidly enough to induce electrical currents in nervous tissue large enough to cause neurons to fire. If the coil is held close to a person's scalp as shown in panel A of Figure 2.22, induced currents depolarize neurons in the cortical tissue exposed to the changing magnetic field and cause them to fire.

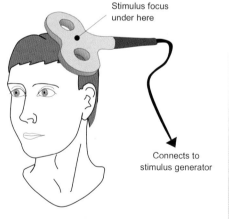

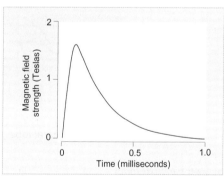

(A) Figure of 8 coil positioned against the scalp   (B) Magnetic field strength over time at the focus

Figure 2.22: *Transcranial magnetic stimulation.*

2.2.12 The cerebral cortex has a number of regions involved in the production of motor behavior

Anatomists divide the cortex of each hemisphere of the human brain into four lobes as shown in Figure 2.23: the occipital lobe, the parietal lobe, the temporal lobe and the frontal lobe. The central sulcus divides the frontal and parietal lobes. This division is not based on the functions performed by the different brain regions. However, each lobe does differ from the others in the functions it is involved in, though there is considerable overlap. As we will discuss further in Chapter 3, inputs from the different sensory systems arrive in different lobes. The occipital lobe receives visual inputs, and is primarily involved in the processing of visual information. The temporal lobe receives auditory and olfactory sensory inputs: parts of it are involved in the processing of acoustic information, other parts in the processing of olfactory information. However, it is also involved in many other functional processes including the processing of language (in humans), the visual recognition of objects and faces, and in navigation and spatial orientation. The parietal lobe receives inputs from sensory receptors in the skin, muscles, joints and associated connective tissues, tongue (taste information) and from the vestibular system; it is also involved in sensory and sensorimotor integration, and in the ability to direct attention to particular tasks. The sensory speech area (Wernicke's area) straddles the parietal and temporal lobes – damage to this area leads to a disorder called sensory aphasia characterized by a loss of the ability to understand spoken language.

The frontal lobes are involved in a number of complex mental functions, but they also contain a cluster of neighboring regions that are fundamental in voluntary motor control and in deciding and planning what actions to perform. The major areas are as follows:

▸ **Primary motor cortex**, also denoted **M1** (short for motor area 1)
▸ **Premotor cortex**
▸ **Supplementary motor area** (SMA)
▸ **Pre-SMA** (immediately rostral to the SMA)
▸ **Cingulate motor area** (CMA)
▸ **Broca's area** or motor speech area
▸ **Frontal eye field** (FEF, at the rostral border of the premotor cortex[25])

The approximate locations of most of these regions in the human cerebral cortex are identified for one hemisphere in Figure 2.24 (the picture is the same for the other hemisphere, with the exception of Broca's area).

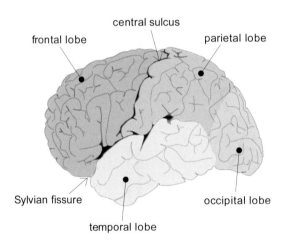

Figure 2.23: *Cortical lobes.*

Given these many areas, the obvious question to ask is: what are they all doing? What is their function? This is an impossible question to answer without first knowing what it is that needs to be done in order to produce motor behavior, as we discussed in Chapter 1. Thus it is not really appropriate to try to describe the functions of these areas at this stage. However, what we can say is that despite substantial investigation into the function of these areas using the methods described in section 2.2.7, it is very difficult to say very much at all about their precise functions. The premotor cortex, SMA, pre-SMA and CMA are involved in a wide variety of different types of motor behavior, but their precise functions are particularly unclear and controversial. In contrast, the eye fields and Broca's area (the motor speech area) appear to be involved mainly in very particular types of behavior. The frontal eye fields are involved in the voluntary control of eye movements; we will discuss their role in more detail in Chapter 6. Broca's area is involved in the production of speech, as its alternative name –

the motor speech area – suggests. However, its role in language production is not restricted to speech, as it also plays a role in the production of written language; there is also evidence to suggest that it may be involved in some aspects of language comprehension. It seems to be the case that language production is lateralized, that is, that Broca's area is located either in the right hemisphere or the left – usually the left – but not both. The corresponding area in the other hemisphere is not critical for language production, though it appears to retain language-related functions.

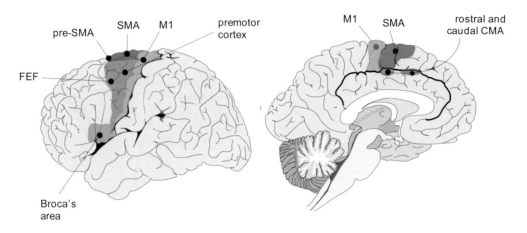

Figure 2.24: *Motor areas of the human cerebral cortex.*

If Broca's area is damaged, the person concerned suffers from serious impairments to the ability to express themselves verbally using both spoken and written language – it is usually still possible for them to make speech sounds, to write individual letters, to utter individual words and to sing. Thus, the ability to produce the movements and muscle contractions needed to make speech sounds or write words is preserved, but the ability to communicate is lost. The impairment appears to be in the formulation of communicative acts and the planning of spoken and written language, not in controlling the actual movements involved in making speech sounds or writing words and letters. The distinction between planning and decision-making functions and the process of producing the necessary movements and muscle contractions is associated with the rostral-caudal location of cortical regions. The more caudal regions, M1 in particular, are usually thought of as being involved in the production of movement and force; the more rostral regions are involved in planning and decision-making processes. Thus, we have a general picture of the cortical motor areas in which the rostral-to-caudal direction is associated with a transition from abstract to concrete processes of behavioral production. This picture serves as a general rule of thumb: the details of what each area does and whether or not they are really functionally separable are unclear. In the following sections we will discuss the functional organization of M1 and consider the sense in which it can be considered to be involved in more concrete functions than the rostral regions.

2.2.13 The primary motor cortex (M1) has a somatotopic organization

It has been known since the 19th century that brief, focal stimulation of the region now known as the primary motor cortex (M1) in dogs, cats and monkeys produces brief movements of particular body parts: stimulation at different locations produces movement of different parts. These observations were later repeated in humans with similar results. The most famous human studies were carried out by Wilder Penfield on patients whose brains were exposed for surgery[26]. Penfield applied focal electrical stimulation to different points on the surface of the exposed cortex. The results were summarized using a dramatic visual representation dubbed a *homunculus* (Latin for 'little man'): stimulation of M1 at different locations gave rise to the *motor homunculus*, a version of which is shown in Figure 2.25. Similar pictures can be drawn for other mammals: in the monkey the picture is called a *simiusculus* and in the rat it is a *ratunculus*.

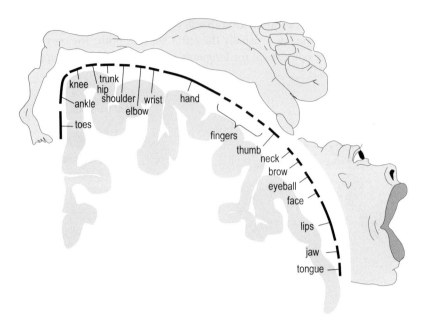

Figure 2.25: *The motor homunculus, based on Penfield and Rasmussen (1950).*

The motor homunculus shows pictorially which parts of the body move when stimuli are applied to regions of M1. Different body parts are associated with different sized areas of M1. For instance, stimulation of locations over a relatively large area of M1 evokes movement of the hand, whereas movements of the trunk can only be evoked from a much smaller region. The different sizes of the cortical regions associated with particular body parts is represented by the size of the body part in the homunculus – the size of the hand in Figure 2.25 is much larger than the trunk. Notice that body parts that make small, precisely controlled movements, such as the hands and the face, are associated with larger cortical areas than body parts that do not make such movements, such as the trunk.

The kind of neural tissue organization in which parts of the body are associated with particular areas of a cortical region, with adjacent cortical regions being associated with adjacent parts, is called **somatotopy**. Thus, M1 has a *somatotopic organization*. The physiological basis for the observed somatotopy of M1 is that the axons of output neurons within a region associated with a particular body part project to the motoneurons that innervate muscles that move that body part. These output neurons are sometimes called *upper motoneurons*; their axons project down through the midbrain and from there either to the cranial motor nuclei or into the spinal cord (see 2.2.25).

2.2.14 The somatotopic organization of M1 is overlapping and complex

It used to be thought that regions of M1 associated with a particular body part might be resolved into smaller regions associated with the individual muscles responsible for moving that part. For example, the region associated with movements of the face might be resolved into a number of smaller regions each associated with one of the many individual muscles responsible for facial movements. If this were the case, then M1 could be likened to a sort of motor keyboard: activating a specific region would cause a contraction of a specific muscle and performing an action involving a properly timed pattern of muscle activation would be like playing a melody on this keyboard. Although some early investigations lent support for this view[27], more recent work has shown that it is wrong. The current picture is that the somatotopy of M1 is overlapping and fuzzy, and does not involve specific regions devoted to individual muscles or joints.

The relationship between particular regions of M1 and parts of the body is much less clear-cut than the homunculus picture might suggest. In fact, Penfield himself warned his readers not to take the picture too literally, stating that it 'cannot give an accurate indication of the specific joints in which movement takes place, for in most cases movement appears at more than one joint simultaneously ... [the homunculus] is a cartoon ... in which scientific accuracy is impossible'[28]. Penfield's original work actually showed that there was considerable overlap of the different regions. For instance, there was overlap of the regions from which movements of the different fingers could be evoked, and there was overlap of the hand and finger regions with the arm region. These findings could have been the result of the rather crude stimulation techniques that Penfield used: the effects of the stimulation would have likely spread over quite significant regions of the cortex. However, subsequent work with monkeys using much more precise stimulation techniques has confirmed that the regions of M1 from which movements of particular body parts can be evoked overlap significantly. It has also become clear that resolution into regions that are associated with individual muscles is not possible. Stimulation of particular cortical sites almost always results in the activation of many muscles, and particular muscles can typically be activated by stimulation over relatively large cortical regions rather than at specific, highly localized sites[29].

Part of the physiological basis for the overlapping somatotopy in M1 appears to be the widespread distribution of the cortical output neurons that make connections with the motoneurons that innervate a particular muscle (see section 2.3 for more about motoneurons). It has recently been demonstrated in macaque monkeys that there are M1 output neurons that make monosynaptic connections with the motoneurons innervating thumb and finger muscles not only throughout the classic hand and finger areas but also within the arm and shoulder areas[30]; the latter were not previously associated with muscles of the thumb or fingers. Overall, the pathway from M1 to the muscles has been found to be both <u>divergent</u> *motor equivalence* (the same cortical neuron projects to motoneurons of multiple muscles) and <u>convergent</u> (motoneurons of the same muscle receive inputs from cortical neurons located in different areas of the classical picture)[31].

Lateral connectivity between neurons in M1 also contributes to its overlapping somatotopy. There is evidence of relatively long-range lateral connections between M1 neurons, such that those within one area of the classical picture are linked to those in other areas.

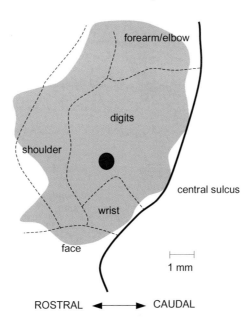

Figure 2.26: *Lateral connectivity in M1. Based on results reported in Huntley & Jones (1991).*

Figure 2.26 shows an example from the monkey motor cortex. A region of the surface of a monkey's M1 has been mapped using the standard micro-stimulation techniques into regions associated with particular body parts (labeled). Anatomical techniques revealed that neurons in the small area of the digit region marked as a red circle connected laterally with neurons throughout the whole pink region.

What does this complex picture tell us about the functional role of M1 in the production of motor behavior? First, it tells us that the naïve idea that M1 is like a motor keyboard that is played on by the higher levels of the motor production process is not correct. If you press a single key on a piano keyboard, you produce a single note. 'Pressing' on a single location on M1 is likely to evoke responses in many muscles and movement at several joints – it would be like pressing a single key on a piano and producing a whole chord. In fact, the reality seems to be even more complex than this, as described next.

2.2.15 Sustained stimulation of M1 can elicit complex movement patterns

The kind of movements evoked by stimulating M1 depends upon the duration of the stimulation. Very brief stimuli, lasting less than about 50 ms, evoke very brief twitches and jerks that seldom resemble the movements made when performing goal-directed actions. Stimulation of longer duration does not merely evoke similar movements of longer duration; rather, it tends to produce movement patterns that resemble those involved in the performance of particular actions. The stimulation in Penfield's original experiments was somewhat sustained and often coordinated motions of body parts were evoked, rather than a brief jerk of a single joint or limb. For instance, stimulation of the hand area evoked extension of all the fingers of one hand or closure of the fingers and thumb together with wrist flexion[32].

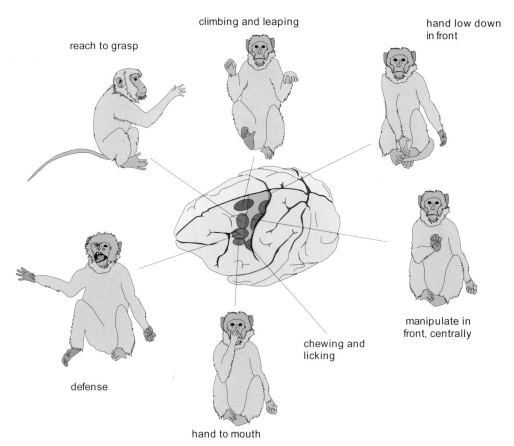

Figure 2.27: *Action zones in the motor cortex (adapted from a diagrammatic concept published in various forms by M.S.A. Graziano, with permission).*

More recent and systematic studies of the effects of sustained stimulation of M1 (½ second or more) in the monkey have found that quite complex, coordinated movement patterns can be evoked[33]. The patterns appear the same as those normally produced when the animal performs goal-directed actions from its behavioral repertoire. These include chewing and licking, leaping and/or climbing, defensive behavior, reaching and grasping, placing in the mouth, and manipulating with the hand. The type of movement pattern evoked depends upon the location at which the stimulation is applied. Figure 2.27 summarizes the results of several experiments. The figure shows the monkey cortex with various regions of the left hemisphere identified: M1 is shown in green, together with seven dark gray regions that lie either partially or wholly within the boundary of M1. The latter are regions from which various movement types can be evoked by sustained stimulation: these regions have been called **action zones**, since they are associated with movement patterns appropriate for the performance of particular goal-directed actions[34]. In the figure, each action zone is linked to a cartoon of the monkey in the type of final posture the animal would move to when the cortex was stimulated in the associated location.

2.2.16 What is the functional role of M1?

The traditional picture of M1 ascribes to it a clear functional role: it is the output region of the cortex that allows the brain to communicate with individual muscles and joints. Small, circumscribed areas are connected to individual muscles or joints. Signals output from these small areas cause contractions in only one muscle or movement in a single joint, leading to a keyboard analogy for M1. The more rostral motor areas of the frontal lobes appear to deal with decisions about what to do, what body parts to use and what movement patterns to produce. These more abstract characterizations of performance are then resolved into commands for individual muscles or joints that are 'played out' on the M1 keyboard. Thus, the traditional view supposes that M1 requires that actions are coded in terms of individual muscle contractions or individual joint motions. More rostral areas produce such codes and these play out over M1 to produce behavior.

The previous sections have shown that the traditional picture is largely mistaken. Small regions of M1 are not connected to individual muscles or joints but to many muscles and joints. Output signals from localized areas of M1 can produce coordinated patterns of movement and muscle contraction, patterns that are characteristic of goal-directed actions. This picture of M1 has suggested that it is involved with the organization of coordinated patterns of movements and muscle contractions. As we will describe in detail a little later, M1 is not the only region that has output neurons that connect with spinal interneurons and motoneurons: such connections also exist throughout the more caudal regions of premotor cortex and SMA. Taken together, the findings suggest that M1 is not a distinct output region, but rather part of a larger output zone that extends into the premotor cortex and the SMA[35]. Nevertheless, the overall organization of the motor areas conforms fundamentally to the scheme described at the end of section 2.2.7, in which the rostral areas are involved in abstract processes and the caudal areas are more closely related to actual motor behavior.

2.2.17 An interconnected network of forebrain and midbrain nuclei is important in voluntary motor control

Several of the forebrain nuclei have been directly implicated in the control and production of motor behavior: the *caudate nucleus*, the *putamen* and the *globus pallidus*. These three nuclei are densely interconnected; indeed the caudate nucleus and the putamen are considered to be parts of a single structure called the *striatum*. Together with two other nuclei they form a group known as the **basal ganglia**[36]. The other nuclei of the basal ganglia are the *subthalamic nucleus*, which lies at the junction of the forebrain and the midbrain, and the *substantia nigra*, which lies completely within the midbrain. The anatomical locations of some of these nuclei in a coronal section of the human brain were shown in Figure 2.21. Part of a similar coronal section through one hemisphere, showing the approximate relative anatomical locations of the five nuclei, is shown in Figure 2.28.

The primary source of evidence demonstrating an important role for the basal ganglia in the control of voluntary movement[37] comes from observations of patients with pathological changes in one or more of the component nuclei. Parkinson's disease, hemiballism and Huntington's disease are the result of pathological degeneration in parts of the basal ganglia. They are characterized by rather diverse impairments of motor performance that can be severe in the later stages of the disease process.

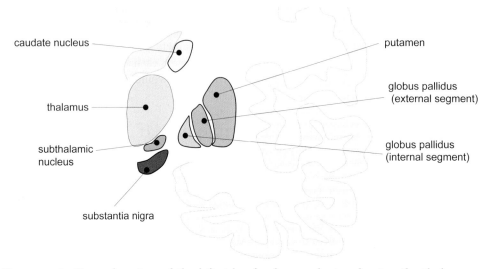

Figure 2.28: *Coronal section of the left side of a human brain, showing the thalamus and component nuclei of the basal ganglia.*

The primary pathological changes in Parkinson's disease take place in the substantia nigra, where neurons die in large numbers. The effects on motor behavior increase in severity as the disease progresses. The earliest signs are often observed in the control of upright posture: the patient has an increased likelihood of falling, adopts a slightly stooped posture and walks with a shuffling gait. The most characteristic symptoms include a characteristic tremor in the upper limbs when they are not engaged in active movement (at rest), which can sometimes also be observed in the head and legs. This resting tremor is usually most evident in the hands and forearms and has a frequency of about 5 Hz. Other characteristic symptoms include the following:

▶ Slowness of voluntary movements (*bradykinesia*)
▶ Increased muscle tone that gives the patient's limbs a resistance to being moved by an external force, even when they are asked to relax and not resist (*hypertonia*)
▶ Difficulty in voluntarily getting a movement started, which can develop into a complete inability to voluntarily initiate movement (*akinesia*)
▶ A tendency for voluntary movements to be of inadequate amplitude: for example, not moving the hand far enough to make contact with an object being reached for (*hypometria*)

The symptoms of Huntington's disease and hemiballism are somewhat similar to each other and very different from those characteristic of Parkinson's disease. Both disorders are characterized by excessive involuntary motor activity, and so differ dramatically from Parkinsonism, which is characterized by a lack of movement. The involuntary movements are known as dyskinesias. In hemiballism, the majority of dyskinetic movements take the form of quick, large-amplitude, often violent movements of the limbs on one side of the body (hence 'hemiballism'). The movements are primarily driven by muscles close to the body, such as the shoulder muscles, and so will involve the whole limb.

In Huntington's disease the dyskinetic movements are less violent and of smaller amplitude, and take the form of jerky, random movements and contortions of the limbs and face.

The movements are known as choreic movements from the Greek word for dance, hence the alternative name for the disease, Huntington's chorea. The limb movements are primarily driven by muscles further from the body, such as those in the forearms and hands or calves and feet. Thus the choreic movements of the upper limbs tend to be in the fingers, hand and forearms.

In the next two sections we will see how the basic patterns of connectivity within the basal ganglia, and between the basal ganglia and other structures, can explain some of the symptomatology of Parkinson's disease and hemiballism.

2.2.18 The basal ganglia receive inputs from the cortex and send outputs to the thalamus and pons

The nuclei of the basal ganglia are interconnected, but they are also connected to other structures in the brain: primarily to the thalamus, the motor areas of frontal cortex, and the pons. Figure 2.29 shows the main interconnections for one hemisphere in block diagram form: excitatory and inhibitory connections are distinguished using the convention introduced in section 2.1.14. Output fibers from the basal ganglia leave via the globus pallidus (internal segment) and input fibers come from the frontal cortex to the putamen and the subthalamic nucleus (STN). The output fibers project to the thalamus and to the pons (the pedunculo-pontine nucleus[38], PPN); there are no direct outputs to the spinal cord. Outputs to the thalamus are relayed to the frontal cortex and there is thus a loop: cortex → putamen → globus pallidus → thalamus → cortex. This is the basal ganglia-thalamocortical circuit. There are two pathways through the putamen and globus pallidus; they are shown in pink and blue in Figure 2.29. The pathway in pink is called the **direct pathway** as it leads directly through to the outputs. The other pathway (blue) is called the **indirect pathway** and leads to the subthalamic nucleus (STN).

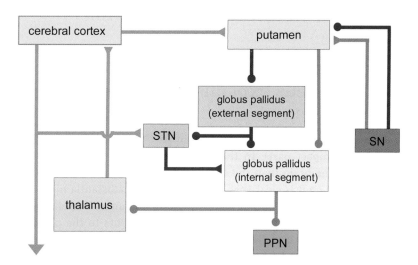

Figure 2.29: *Block diagram showing the basic interconnectivity between nuclei of the basal ganglia on one side of the brain and their connections to other important, ipsilateral structures (cortex, thalamus and pedunculopontine nucleus, PPN).*

The block diagram shown in Figure 2.29 makes it easy to see which structures affect which others and whether the effects are excitatory or inhibitory. This can help us to understand how changes due to a disease produce particular symptoms. Here we will consider a disorder called hemiballism that can result from lesions of the subthalamic nucleus (STN) caused by small strokes (though the same symptoms can be produced by other causes[39]). These typically occur in one of the subthalamic nuclei, not both, so the symptoms are confined to one side of the body. The lesions lead to a decrease in the normal activity in the STN and, as a result, output to the internal segment of the globus pallidus (abbreviated GPi) is reduced.

This output is excitatory and, if it decreases, the level of activity in the neurons of the GPi decreases. Low activity in the GPi leads to a reduction in output activity to target structures outside the basal ganglia. Since these outputs are inhibitory, when their activity is reduced, the target structures are disinhibited and become abnormally active. The pattern of changes is illustrated in Figure 2.30, where decreased activity in a pathway is shown as thinner, paler, dotted lines and increased activity by fatter, darker lines. It is the abnormally high activity in the motor areas of the cortex and in the pontine nuclei that give rise to the involuntary, aimless movements that characterize hemiballism. Thus, hemiballism is caused by abnormally low activity in the globus pallidus (internal segment) leading to increased activity in the cortex and pons. Almost the opposite happens in Parkinson's disease, as described next.

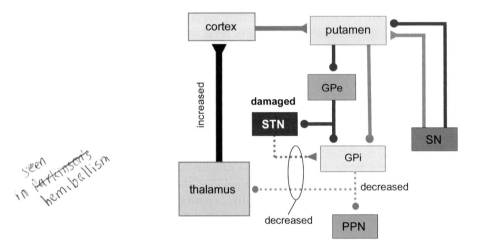

Figure 2.30: *Primary effects of damage to the subthalamic nucleus (STN).*

2.2.19 Overactivity in the globus pallidus and subthalamic nucleus explains the motor symptoms of Parkinson's disease

Parkinson's disease involves the loss of neurons in part of the substantia nigra called the *pars compacta* (the compact part). In the early stages of the disease the loss is usually greater on one side of the brain than the other, so the symptoms are worse on one side of the body. From Figure 2.29 it is clear that neural loss in the substantia nigra (SN) will lead to a decrease in the activity of its output pathways to the putamen. The effects on the direct pathway (pink) are easiest to understand. The excitatory inputs to the putamen from the substantia nigra will be decreased. This reduction of excitation leads to reduced activity of neurons in the putamen that inhibit the internal segment of the globus pallidus. The result is that the globus pallidus neurons become more active, since their inhibition has been reduced (disinhibition), and so the output from the internal segment of the globus pallidus is increased. The figure shows that this output is inhibitory, so the structures to which the outputs are sent will be more inhibited than normal. The effects on the indirect pathway are a little more involved, but the overall effect is the same – increased output from the internal segment of the globus pallidus. The pattern of changes is illustrated in Figure 2.31: as in Figure 2.30, decreased activity in a pathway is indicated by thinner, paler lines, and increases by fatter, darker lines. As can be seen, there is a decreased inhibition (disinhibition) of the internal segment of the globus pallidus via the direct pathway, and an increased excitation of the internal segment via the indirect pathway. Thus, loss of neurons in the substantia nigra leads to excessive activity in the internal segment of the globus pallidus, due to both disinhibition and increased excitation.

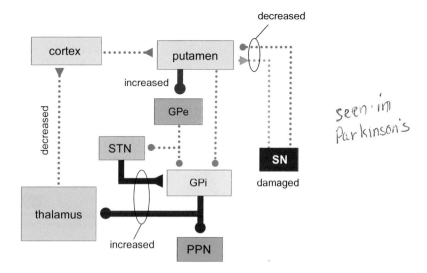

Figure 2.31: *Primary effects of damage to the substantia nigra (SN).*

The abnormally high activity in the internal segment of the globus pallidus is the primary reason for the motor symptoms of Parkinson's disease. This structure provides the outputs from the basal ganglia to other part of the nervous system. These outputs are inhibitory and so, if they increase, then the activity in their targets will be reduced. It is a reduction of activity in motor cortical areas that seems to be responsible for the lack of voluntary movement in Parkinson's disease – bradykinesia, akinesia and hypometria. Thus, we see that the basal ganglia damage in Parkinson's disease leads to an effect that is the opposite of that in hemiballism. Parkinson's disease results in an abnormally high level of activity in the GPi and a corresponding reduction in the activity in the pons and motor areas of the cortex; hemiballism results in an abnormally low level of activity in the GPi and a correspondingly high level of activity in the cortex and pons.

2.2.20 The brainstem contains many components that have motor functions

Within the brainstem there is white matter (fiber tracts) as well as many nuclei and other structures that have motor functions of one sort or another. The midbrain contains numerous nuclei that are involved in motor control, including the **red nucleus** and two that we encountered in the description of the basal ganglia – the *substantia nigra* and the *subthalamic nucleus*. A number of midbrain nuclei and other structures are important in the control of the eyes, including the **oculomotor** and **trochlear nuclei**, the **superior colliculi**, the *interstitial nuclei* and several others including the **accessory optic nuclei** (or Edinger-Westphal nuclei). The latter are involved in the response of the pupil to light and adjustment of the focus of the eye. Eye movement control also involves the **abducens nuclei** and other pontine nuclei, as we will see in later chapters. Some of these structures are identified in Figure 2.32, which shows a posterior (dorsal) view of the brainstem with the cerebellum removed (left side of figure). A series of three transverse sections through the brainstem at the marked locations (①, ②, ③) are shown on the right of the figure: the dorsal side of each cross section is at the top.

Extending through the core of the medulla and pons and into the midbrain, but not identified specifically in Figure 2.32, is the so-called **reticular formation**. To early anatomists this appeared to be a relatively undifferentiated mass with a web-like or net-like internal structure (*reticulum* is the Latin word for net). Closer examination has revealed that this structure is differentiated into numerous, often densely interconnected clusters of neurons that could be considered to be individual nuclei. Many of these clusters lack any visible anatomical boundaries even under the microscope, but can be differentiated based on their cell types. It is known that some cell clusters of the reticular formation are involved in motor functions such as eye movement control, the generation of the rhythmic patterns involved in breathing and chewing, and the generation of movement patterns involved in swallowing, hiccupping, coughing and sneezing.

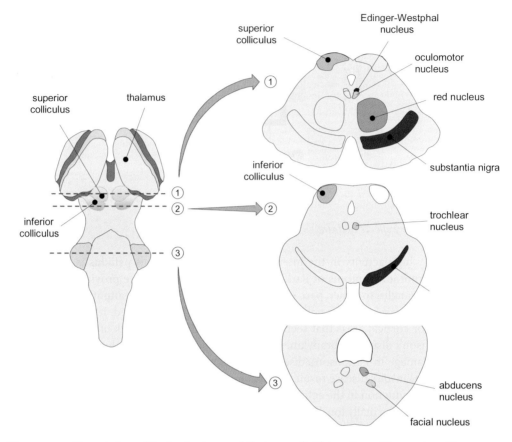

Figure 2.32: *Dorsal view of the brainstem and thalamus (left) together with a series of transverse sections (right).*

2.2.21 Brainstem nuclei contain motoneurons that innervate the skeletal muscles of the head, eyes, mouth and throat

A number of brainstem nuclei contain the motoneurons that innervate the skeletal muscles of the head, which include muscles of the face, eyes, mouth and jaw. All these nuclei come in pairs – one on the left side of the brainstem and one on the right side. The nuclei on the left innervate muscles on the left side of the body; nuclei on the right innervate muscles on the right. The *oculomotor nuclei*, *trochlear nuclei* and *abducens nuclei* contain motoneurons that innervate the muscles that move the eyes. The **facial motor nucleus** contains the motoneurons that innervate the skeletal muscles of the face – the muscles used for making facial expressions. The **trigeminal motor nucleus** contains the motoneurons that innervate the muscles involved in chewing. The **hypoglossal nucleus** contains motoneurons that innervate the intrinsic muscles of the tongue. The **nucleus ambiguus** contains motoneurons that innervate the skeletal muscles of the larynx and pharynx that are used in generating speech.

2.2.22 The cerebellum has multiple inputs and outputs

By far the largest and most obvious structure at the brainstem level is the **cerebellum**, which means *little brain*. It sits at the back of the pons, as can be seen in Figure 2.20. Although relatively small, it has been estimated to contain at least as many neurons as the whole of the rest of the brain. It resembles the forebrain in that it is formed of a bilaterally symmetrical, tightly folded sheet of gray matter – the cerebellar cortex – which surrounds an inner core of white matter and nuclei. There are three pairs of nuclei: the *dentate*, the *fastigial* and the *interposed* nuclei. Unlike the cerebral cortex, the cerebellar cortex is a single sheet, and the clefts are called **fissures** (not sulci). Many of these fissures run almost in parallel laterally across the dorsal cerebellar cortex from one side to the other, giving it a striped appearance. The folds of cortex between the fissures are called **folia** (not gyri).

The cerebellum receives inputs and sends outputs via three pairs of tracts containing numerous axons: one of each pair lies to the left of the midline, the other lies to the right. These tracts are the cerebellar peduncles – the superior peduncle, the middle peduncle and the inferior peduncle – and they connect the cerebellum to the brainstem. The superior peduncle carries most of the output fibers from the cerebellum. These fibers project primarily to targets in the thalamus, the red nucleus and the vestibular nuclei. There are also some outputs to the reticular formation (RF) via the fastigial nuclei. All the output fibers originate from cells in the cerebellar nuclei, with the exception of some from a small region of the cerebellar cortex – the flocculonodular (FN) lobe – that project directly to the vestibular nuclei. Figure 2.33 shows the primary output pathways for the right half of the cerebellum in block diagram form (the left half is the mirror image). Note that the output fibers from the cerebellar nuclei cross the midline and project to targets on the left side of the brain. The flocculonodular lobe projects to ipsilateral vestibular nuclei. The figure shows that the outputs from the cerebellar cortex have primarily inhibitory effects on their targets, whereas outputs from the cerebellar nuclei have primarily excitatory effects.

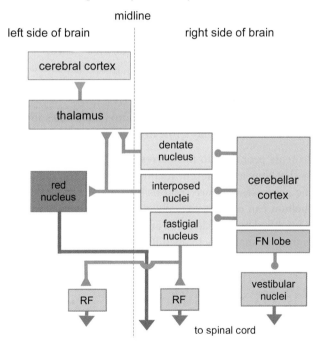

Figure 2.33: *Block diagram of the basic connectivity of the components of the right cerebellum.*

The cerebellum receives substantial input from sensory systems, particularly the vestibular and somatosensory systems, but also from the visual system and the auditory system. Much of the sensory information sent to the cerebellum seems to be about how the body is moving and how it is oriented in space. The cerebellum also receives signals from spinal interneurons and from the motor cortex: these signals appear to carry information about motor commands sent to motorneurons that innervate skeletal muscles. Thus, the cerebellum receives sensory information about what movements and forces were actually produced, and also receives information about what commands were issued (the intended pattern of movement). Thus, it is in a position to compare what actually happened with what was intended to happen, and use the resulting information to assist with motor control and learning.

2.2.23 The cerebellum is a critical structure in the production of coordinated motor behavior

Damage to or loss of cerebellar tissue does not lead to paralysis; rather, it leads to diverse deficits in control and coordination. These include the following:

▸ Abnormalities of voluntary motor behavior commonly referred to as **ataxia** (lack of coordination). This is characterized by jerky movements and a difficulty coordinating movement of several limb segments, either concurrently or as a smoothly integrated sequence. For example, when reaching for something, a normal person will move the shoulder and elbow joints at the same time; a person with cerebellar damage may move first the shoulder and then the elbow joint producing an unnaturally clumsy motion of the arm. This symptom is sometimes called *decomposition of movement.*

▸ Impaired ability to make accurate voluntary movements. For instance, when reaching for something, the hand may not move in the correct direction or the correct distance, going either too far or not far enough to make contact with the object being reached for. This is called **dysmetria**.

▸ **Tremor**: cerebellar damage can lead to both static and kinetic tremor. The static tremor appears when the person is actively producing muscle force to keep a body part in a fixed position or posture. This differs from the tremor in Parkinson's disease, which is present when muscles are not being actively used to produce force.

▸ Inability to maintain a rhythm in voluntary repetitive movements or actions, a deficit referred to as **dysdiacochokinesia**.

▸ Impaired ability to maintain balance when standing upright and walking or running. When standing still, people with cerebellar damage often sway backwards and forwards much more than normal people, and they produce exaggerated responses when their posture is disturbed. These effects are more pronounced with the eyes closed.

▸ **Hypotonia**: a decrease in the resistance offered by joints to passive movement; muscles become flaccid and tire easily.

▸ Impairments of eye movement control.

▸ Impairments to sensorimotor learning. Given the previous entries in this list, it would be surprising if the cerebellum did not play a role in learning.

These diverse impairments probably do not correspond to diverse functions of the cerebellum. It is more likely that they are different manifestations of the failure of just a few functional elements of the processes that are responsible for the production of motor behavior. Damage to the cerebellum can disrupt virtually all types of sensorimotor behavior and can also disrupt how it is modified by experience (learning). This could be because the cerebellum carries out functions that are shared by many different types of behavior.

2.2.24 Signals from the brain are sent to motoneurons via descending fiber tracts

We have seen that axons arising from cell bodies in various parts of the brain (source structures) project either directly (monosynaptically) or indirectly (via local interneurons) to motoneurons that innervate the skeletal muscles. The axons arising from a particular source structure are bunched together and form anatomically distinct tracts that extend to the target neurons. Tracts whose axons arise from cell bodies in source structures more rostral than their targets are called **descending tracts**[40]:

> **DESCENDING TRACT:** A bundled group of myelinated axons that arise from cell bodies in a source structure that is more rostral than the target structure. The latter is either the spinal cord or the brainstem motor nuclei.

The descending tracts comprise the pathways via which the brain communicates with the skeletal muscles. Descending tracts arise from the cerebral cortex (**pyramidal tracts**), the red nuclei (**rubrospinal tracts**), the superior colliculi (**tectospinal tracts**), the vestibular nuclei (**vestibulospinal tracts**), and the reticular formation (**reticulospinal tracts**).

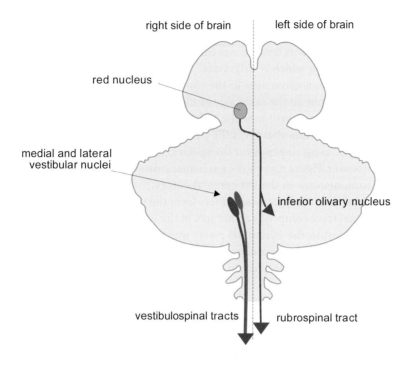

Figure 2.34: *Vestibulospinal and rubrospinal tracts (originating from right side only).*

Figure 2.34 shows the rubrospinal tract that arises from the red nucleus on the right side of the brain: it crosses the midline within the brainstem and continues down the contralateral (left) side. The rubrospinal tracts have not been much studied in humans, but in other mammals such as cats and monkeys they project to target neurons in the olivary nuclei in the medulla and down the spinal cord, where the axons synapse with spinal interneurons. Also shown in the figure are the medial and lateral vestibulospinal tracts that arise from the right vestibular nuclei in blue (similar on the left): the right medial tract arises from the ipsilateral medial vestibular nucleus, and the right lateral tract arises from the lateral vestibular nucleus (also called Dieter's nucleus). The figure does not show the reticulospinal tracts: there are two of these on each side of the brain (medial and lateral tracts) that travel ipsilaterally down the length of the spinal cord. The tectospinal tracts are not shown either: these tracts cross the midline and descend contralaterally into the cervical spinal cord (the neck), but no further.

2.2.25 The pyramidal tract contains axons from cortical neurons and divides to form the corticospinal and corticobulbar tracts

The pyramidal tract is a descending tract that consists of myelinated axons that arise from cell bodies within the cerebral cortex. These cell bodies are located close to the inner surface of the cortex over a large area that extends from the parietal lobes to the premotor areas of the frontal lobes. In monkeys, about 60% of the axons within the tract arise from cell bodies in M1, the premotor areas and the SMA. It is the pyramidal tract that carries all the output axons from M1 to the motoneurons. The remaining 40% of the axons arise from cell bodies in the parietal lobe, particularly the primary somatosensory cortex (see Chapter 3). The situation in humans is similar.

Some axons in the pyramidal tract descend into the spinal cord; others project to the motor nuclei in the brainstem. The axons that project to brainstem nuclei form the corticobulbar division of the pyramidal tract – the **corticobulbar tract**. In humans, axons in the cortico-bulbar tract project to the trigeminal, facial and hypoglossal nuclei, where many make monosynaptic connections with motoneurons. They do not project to the nuclei containing the motoneurons that innervate the eye muscles.

The axons that project into the spinal cord form the corticospinal division of the pyramidal tract – the **corticospinal tract**. This tract passes through the midbrain and pons ipsilaterally to the cortical cell bodies from which it originates. In humans, when the tract reaches the medulla, about 80% of the axons cross over to the contralateral side and pass into the spinal cord; the remaining 20% remain on the same side of the midline. A crossing over of this kind is called a **decussation**: the decussation of the corticospinal tract occurs at the medullary pyramids (the anatomical structure that gives the pyramidal tract its name). The proportion of corticospinal axons that cross depends on the species: in the domestic dog, for example, 100% of the axons cross over. Figure 2.35 shows a schematic diagram of the human corticospinal tract that arises from neurons in the left cerebral cortex. The fibers that cross over form the **lateral corticospinal tract**, the uncrossed fibers form the **ventral corticospinal tract**. In humans, the corticospinal tract comprises about 30% of the white matter of the spinal cord.

Some axons that descend in the pyramidal tracts make monosynaptic connections with motoneurons. Such connectivity is extremely rare and possibly absent in some mammals such as rats, but is abundant in monkeys and humans. Monosynaptic connections are particularly abundant between M1 output neurons and the motoneurons of muscles involved in making precise and controlled movements, such as those that move the fingers, hands and face. Monosynaptic connections with the motoneurons of arm and leg muscles are less common; they may be absent altogether for muscles of the trunk and muscles with a predominantly postural role. The following rule of thumb applies:

> **CORTICO-MOTONEURONAL CONNECTIONS:** In mammals with monosynaptic M1–motoneuronal connections, these connections exist in larger numbers for muscles involved in more precise, controlled movements, and are absent for the postural muscles of the trunk and legs.

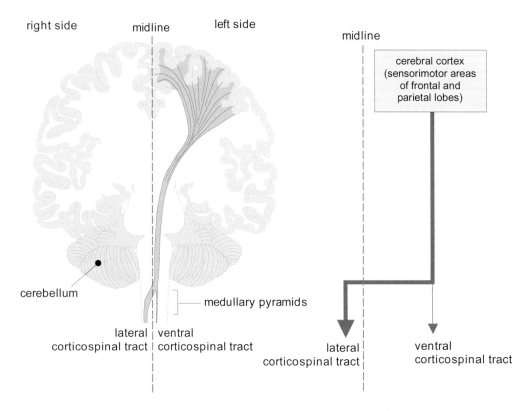

Figure 2.35: *Corticospinal tract originating from neurons in the left cerebral cortex.*

2.2.26 The spinal cord consists of both white and gray matter

The spinal cord consists of myelinated axons (spinal white matter) and neural cell bodies (spinal gray matter), with the white matter on the outside and the gray matter on the inside. The distribution of white and gray matter is clearly seen when you slice horizontally through the cord. Figure 2.36 shows two transverse sections through the human spinal cord. The gray matter is shaped somewhat like the letter H or a butterfly's wings. The exact shape depends upon where the cross-section is made: the section on the left of the figure is typical for the thoracic level; that on the right is typical for the lower cervical level. The gray matter contains the cell bodies of motoneurons and a large number of interneurons (it contains no sensory neuron cell bodies); it forms a more or less continuous mass from the bottom to the top of the cord, without the obviously distinct substructures that characterize the brain. The dorsal lobes of the gray matter are called the **dorsal horns**, and the ventral lobes are called the **ventral horns**. The motoneurons innervate skeletal muscles and are located in the ventral horns of the cord.

The axons within the white matter originate from a variety of sources. A proportion of the white matter is formed by the descending tracts described earlier. The remaining white matter is formed by **ascending tracts** and **propriospinal tracts**. The latter are discussed later (section 2.2.29). The ascending tracts carry sensory information, derived from sensory receptors in the body's tissues, to the brain; they carry signals 'upwards' (in standing humans, at least). An ascending tract can be defined as follows:

> **ASCENDING TRACT:** A bundled group of axons that arise from cell bodies in a source structure that is more caudal than the target structure. The former is usually the spinal cord gray matter, and the latter structures lie within the brain.

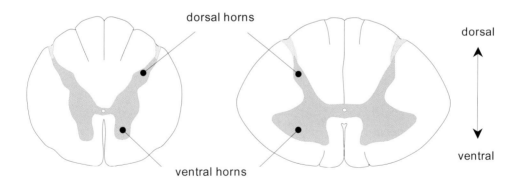

Figure 2.36: *Transverse sections through the human spinal cord at the thoracic level (left) and the cervical level (right).*

2.2.27 Motoneuron cell bodies are grouped into clusters

As already mentioned, the cell bodies of motoneurons that innervate the skeletal muscles of the body (excluding the head and throat) are found in the ventral horn of the spinal cord. The motoneurons that innervate an individual muscle form the muscle's **motoneuron pool**. This is an important concept that can be defined as follows:

> **MOTONEURON POOL:** All the motoneurons that innervate a particular skeletal muscle. These motoneurons are grouped together into clusters, which are separate from the motoneurons of other muscles (motoneurons associated with two different muscles are not found together in the same cluster).

The clusters are small and localized. They consist not only of motoneurons but also interca-lated interneurons, similar to the motor nuclei of the brainstem; indeed, these clusters can be considered to be individual motor nuclei. Strictly speaking, the motoneuron pool itself does not include the interneurons, just the motoneurons in the cluster.

The motoneuron pools of different muscles are found in different places within the ventral horns. Most obviously, the motoneuron pools of the muscles on the left side of the body are found in the left side of the spinal cord; those of the muscles on the right are found in the right side of the cord. On a particular side, the motoneuron pools of muscles closer to the middle of the body are found closer to the middle of the spinal cord; the motoneuron pools of extensor muscles are located more dorsally, and those of flexor muscles are more ventral. The axons of the motoneurons exit the spinal cord via the ventral roots of the spinal cord, as described in section 2.2.28.

2.2.28 The spinal cord has a segmental organization

The spinal cord has a structure that is referred to as *segmental*. Each segment is defined by a pair of nerves, one on each side (Figure 2.37); there are 30 pairs of nerves in total along the human spinal cord. The pairs of nerves, and therefore the spinal segments, are divided into four groups:

(1)   The cervical group: eight pairs of nerves exit the spinal cord at the level of the neck (Latin: *cervix* = neck). The associated spinal segments are numbered C1, C2, … , C8.

(2)   The thoracic group: twelve pairs exit the spinal cord at the level of the chest. The asso-ciated spinal segments are numbered T1, T2, … , T12.

(3)   The lumbar group: five pairs exit the spinal cord at the upper abdominal level. The associated spinal segments are numbered L1, L2, … , L5.

(4)   The sacral group: five pairs exit the spinal cord at the lower abdominal level and pass out through the sacrum. The associated spinal segments are numbered S1, S2, … , S5.

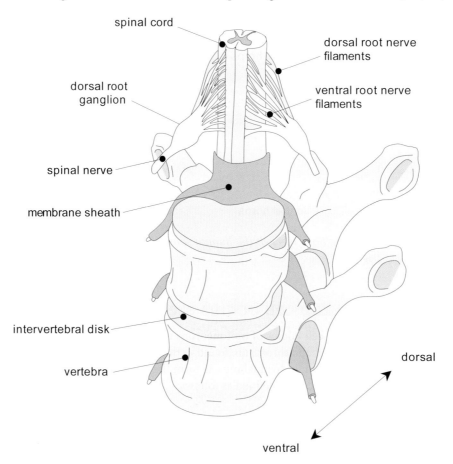

Figure 2.37: *Spinal cord and vertebrae of the spinal column.*

Each nerve has a sensory part and a motor part. The motor part of a nerve consists of the axons of motoneurons, which exit the cord through the nerve's ventral root. The sensory branch contains axons of sensory neurons, and these enter the cord almost exclusively through the dorsal roots, though there are a few that enter through the ventral roots. The cell bodies of the sensory neurons are located outside the spinal cord in the dorsal root ganglia.

Figure 2.37 shows four neighboring segments of the spinal cord: the lower two segments are shown encased within vertebrae, the top two segments are exposed. The sheath of membrane that surrounds the cord has been cut away from the top segment to reveal the structure of the roots. Several motor nerve filaments exit from different positions along the ventral aspect of a segment, and form the ventral root of the spinal nerve. Each bulge near to where the motor nerve filaments meet is a dorsal root ganglion that contains sensory neuron cell bodies. Axons of sensory neurons leave the ganglion in groups that form sensory nerve filaments; these form the dorsal root of the spinal nerve and enter the spinal cord at different positions along the dorsal aspect of a segment (not visible in the figure). As we will describe in more detail in Chapter 3, the sensory part of a spinal nerve innervates a well-defined region of the body, meaning that the receptive endings of the sensory neurons are all located within this region. Something similar is true for motor nerves, though because some muscles are large structures that extend for significant distances, the innervated regions are overlapping and much less clear cut.

The gray matter of each segment contains the motoneuron pools of those muscles innervated by the axons that travel along its ventral nerve root. Also within the segmental gray matter are various interneurons, including the intercalated interneurons within the motor nuclei and the interneurons of the dorsal horns. Some of these interneurons have neurites that project only within their own segment or short distances into a neighboring segment. Others project to more distant segments along myelinated axons. These are called **propriospinal neurons** as their axons travel in the propriospinal tracts. These neurons are briefly discussed next.

2.2.29 Descending propriospinal axons relay signals from corticospinal neurons to upper limb motoneurons

Propriospinal tracts are confined to the spinal cord. Axons arising from interneuronal cell bodies in one part of the cord travel along these tracts to make connections with neurons in other parts of the cord. Some propriospinal axons ascend from more caudal regions of the spinal gray matter to more rostral regions (ascending fibers); others descend from more rostral regions to more caudal regions (descending fibers).

Some of the axons that descend into the spinal cord along the corticospinal tracts do not make monosynaptic connections with motoneurons or with nearby segmental interneurons. These axons make synaptic connections with propriospinal neurons in more rostral segments of the cord. The axons of these propriospinal neurons project to motoneurons and interneurons in more caudal segments[41]. Figure 2.38 shows a simplified schematic of some of the connectivity believed to be involved in the cervical propriospinal system that relays signals descending primarily along corticospinal axons[42] (axons from other descending tracts also make synaptic connections with propriospinal neurons). The propriospinal neurons themselves are located in higher cervical segments (C3 and C4), and their axons descend to motoneuron pools in more caudal segments (C5 to C8), where they make connections with motoneurons innervating muscles of the hands, arms and shoulders, and with segmental interneurons. In Figure 2.38, a propriospinal neuron (PN) makes synaptic connections with several motoneurons (MNs) within a single pool located in an ipsilateral cervical segment lower down the cord (C7). Propriospinal neurons also receive signals from sensory neurons located in more caudal segments, either directly or via local interneurons. These sensory signals derive primarily from stimulation of receptors in muscles, joints and skin of the upper limbs. As shown in the figure, monosynaptic connections between sensory neurons and propriospinal neurons are excitatory, whereas those via local interneurons may be inhibitory (feedback inhibitory interneurons).

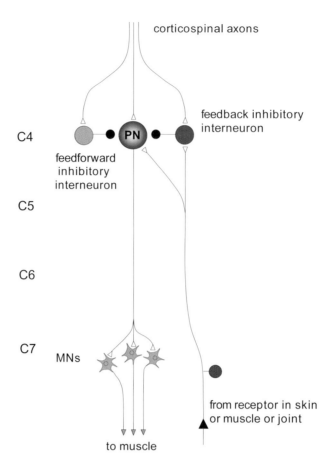

Figure 2.38: *Basic connectivity of propriospinal neurons in the cervical propriospinal system.*

The connectivity shown in Figure 2.38 means that the cervical propriospinal relay system provides a circuitry that can integrate the descending signals from the cortex with sensory information from receptors in the muscles, skin and joints. This integration occurs before the descending signals reach the motoneuron pools themselves, and so is somewhat independent of them. The reason for organizing the system for transmitting signals from the brain to the muscles in this way is not certain, though a variety of possibilities have been proposed[43].

2.3 Nerve and Muscle

2.3.1 Introduction

Motor behavior is produced by contracting **skeletal muscles**. There are about six hundred skeletal muscles in the human body, and these vary enormously in size, strength and structure. Many of them are attached to bones by connective tissue at both their 'ends' (though the term 'end' may not always be very descriptive; see Figure 2.39). The attachment closer to the midline of the body – the proximal attachment – is called the **origin** of the muscle. The other, distal, attachment is called the **insertion** of the muscle. Both the origin and insertion of a muscle may be on bones, but in some cases the muscle may attach to some other tissue – the muscles that move the eye, for example, insert on the eye ball. In this part of the chapter we will describe the basic structure and behavior of skeletal muscles.

2.3.2 Skeletal muscles are made up of bundles of long, thin cells called muscle fibers

Skeletal muscle cells are long, thin, fiber-like cells that are usually referred to as **muscle fibers**. Each fiber is a kind of 'super cell' that is formed by the fusion of many hundreds of individual stem cells early in development (adults cannot grow new muscle fibers). As a result, muscle cells have many nuclei, unlike other cells that have just one. In humans and other primates, muscle fibers typically run in parallel from the origin of the muscle to its insertion[44]. A number of different variations of this basic scheme can be found: four common arrangements are shown in Figure 2.39, where the tendon is shown in gray, the muscle in red, and the direction of the muscle fibers is indicated by black lines.

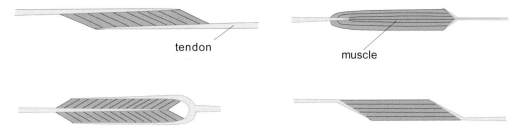

Figure 2.39: *Different arrangements of muscle fibers (based on Figure 365 in Gray, 1918).*

The length of muscle fibers varies substantially between muscles. Very short muscles have correspondingly short fibers: the *stapedius* muscle, located in the inner ear, is the shortest muscle in the human body, and its fibers are only about 1 millimeter long. Other muscles have fibers that may be several centimeters long. The *sartorius* muscle is the longest in the human body; it is a thin, ribbon-like muscle that runs in a lateral-to-medial direction across the front of the thigh from the hip to the knee and may contain some muscle fibers over 50 cm in length[45] (the exact length will depend on how long the person's legs are).

Long muscles have long fibers; thick muscles may have thick fibers and/or more fibers. When someone trains a muscle by pushing heavy weights, the muscle thickens over time not because it gains more fibers, but because the thickness of the existing fibers increases. The number of fibers in human muscles ranges from a few hundred in the smallest to about two million in the largest; the number in a particular muscle varies between individuals. Some examples are given in Table 2.2.

Table 2.2: *Number of fibers in a selection of different muscles.*

Muscle	Number of fibers
tensor tympani (muscle of the inner ear)	1100
lateral rectus (extraocular muscle)	22,000
first dorsal interosseus (intrinsic muscle of the hand)	40,500
sartorius (thigh muscle, see text)	128,150
biceps brachii (upper arm muscle)	580,000
masseter (jaw muscle)	929,000
medial gastrocnemius (calf muscle)	1,120,000

Source: Table 6.4 in Enoka (2008) and from Table 1.1 in MacIntosh, Gardiner, McComas (2006).

Skeletal muscles are made up of both muscle fibers and connective tissue. The individual fibers are sheathed in membranous connective tissue (*endomysium*). Individual fibers within a muscle are grouped together into bundles by sheaths of connective tissue (*perimysium*), rather like spaghetti in a packet. These bundles are called **fascicles**. The whole muscle is made up of a number of fascicles and is itself sheathed in connective tissue (*epimysium*). Thus, the muscle is made up of a number of parallel fascicles that are themselves composed of many parallel muscle fibers.

Muscles are connected to bones via tough, collagen-rich connective tissue. This tissue comes in ropelike form called *tendon* and in sheets or ribbons called *aponeuroses*. Some tendons can be easily seen beneath the skin: the long tendons of the muscles that extend the fingers can be seen on the back of the hand, and two long tendons of the muscles that flex the fingers can be seen on the inside of the wrist. Aponeuroses are less familiar but are often associated with tendons. At the junction with a muscle, for example, tendons often flatten out to form aponeuroses.

2.3.3 Muscle fibers are innervated by motoneurons and conduct action potentials

Motoneuron axons terminals make synaptic connections with muscle fibers. These are chemical synapses referred to as **neuromuscular junctions**. In all vertebrate species, *acetylcholine* (ACh) is the neurotransmitter released into the synaptic cleft by the motoneuron terminals.

When an action potential causes ACh to be released from the presynaptic membrane of the neuromuscular junction, the substance diffuses quickly across the synaptic cleft and binds to the muscle cell membrane, causing it to depolarize. Thus, an action potential arriving at the neuromuscular junction along the axon terminals of a motoneuron produces an excitatory postsynaptic potential in the muscle fiber. Typically, a single action potential arriving at the motoneuron terminals is sufficient to evoke an action potential in the muscle fiber. This is the only known example in the mammalian nervous system of a single action potential in the presynaptic cell resulting in the generation of an action potential in the postsynaptic cell.

Action potentials evoked in a muscle fiber propagate relatively slowly along the cell membrane – between about 3 and 5 meters/second in mammalian muscles – and in both directions along the fiber away from the location of the neuromuscular junctions. It is the propagation of action potentials along the muscle cell membrane that initiates the process of muscle contraction. Some characteristics of the process and the muscle contraction that results are briefly described in the sections below.

2.3.4 Motoneurons are classified into three basic kinds

Motoneurons that innervate skeletal muscles are classified as alpha (α), beta (β) and gamma (γ) motoneurons, according to the type of muscle fiber that they innervate. The muscle fibers that we have described already are those responsible for the production of muscular force, but there is another type of muscle fiber found in virtually all mammalian skeletal muscles that does not contribute to force development. This is the type of fiber found within sensory organs called *muscle spindles*. Relative to the main fibers of the muscle, these spindle fibers – called **intrafusal fibers** – are very small. The main fibers of the muscle are sometimes referred to as **extrafusal fibers**. We will describe intrafusal fibers in more detail in Chapter 3. The three types of motoneuron innervate different types of fiber:

▸ Alpha-motoneurons (α-MNs) innervate only extrafusal muscle fibers.
▸ Beta-motoneurons (β-MNs) innervate both extrafusal and intrafusal fibers.
▸ Gamma-motoneurons (γ-MNs) innervate only intrafusal fibers.

In a very young animal, muscle fibers may be innervated by the axons of several different motoneurons, but during development these connections die off until the fiber is innervated by only one motoneuron. This yields the following principle:

> **SINGLE MOTONEURON INNERVATION RULE:** in a mature animal, any given skeletal muscle fiber is innervated by one and only one motoneuron.

Extrafusal fibers are predominantly innervated by α-motoneurons, and we will focus on these for the remainder of this part of the chapter.

2.3.5 When stimulated, a muscle fiber generates a contractile force

When a muscle fiber membrane conducts action potentials, it generates force that acts to shorten it – a **contractile force** (*contract* means to shorten or shrink). The effect of neural excitation is always the generation of a contractile force. A muscle never generates a force that acts to lengthen it; forces that lengthen a muscle are always forces produced by something external to the muscle.

It is frequently the case that when a muscle fiber generates a contractile force, it shortens (contracts); but this does not always happen. If there is another, external force acting on the fiber that is greater than the force of contraction, then the fiber will lengthen. Although the word *contract* means *shrink* or shorten, the term *muscle contraction* is used to refer to the muscle's state when it is generating a contractile force, regardless of whether it actually contracts (shortens) or not. This means that three basic types of muscle contraction can be distinguished, depending upon whether muscle fibers shorten, lengthen or remain the same length. These are defined as follows:

(1) CONCENTRIC CONTRACTION (OR CONTRACTION): Generation of contractile force that is accompanied by a decrease in the length (shortening) of the muscle or muscle fiber.
(2) ECCENTRIC CONTRACTION: Generation of contractile force that is accompanied by an increase in the length of the muscle or muscle fiber, due to the presence of an external force on the muscle that has a greater magnitude than the contractile force and acts in the opposite direction.
(3) ISOMETRIC CONTRACTION: Generation of contractile force that is accompanied by no change in the length of the muscle or muscle fiber, due to the presence of an opposing external force equal to the contractile force.

As an action potential travels along a muscle cell membrane, it sets in motion the electrochemical process that leads to the generation of a contractile force; the process is referred to as **excitation-contraction coupling**. The molecular mechanisms of this process are well understood, but the details go beyond the scope of the present discussion (many excellent accounts can be found elsewhere[46]). Briefly, the process involves several steps that lead to the production of molecular links, called **cross-bridges**, that form between filaments of protein. These cross-bridges develop tiny forces that pull the protein filaments together: the forces of many millions of cross-bridges combine to produce the contractile force developed by an individual muscle fiber.

2.3.6 A single action potential produces a twitch contraction; a train of action potentials can produce a tetanic contraction

When a single action potential propagates along a muscle fiber it sets in motion the process that culminates in cross-bridge formation and contraction. However, since the action potential itself lasts only a short period of time, the contraction it produces is also quite brief – the muscle fiber generates a contractile force for a short time and then relaxes. This is called a **twitch contraction**.

The active force developed by a muscle fiber during an isometric twitch contraction increases from zero to a peak as the muscle develops contractile force, and then declines back to zero as the muscle relaxes again. This pattern is illustrated in Figure 2.40. The muscle force starts to rise a short time after the action potential is initiated; the delay is due to the time it takes for the action potential to propagate along the fiber and initiate the formation of cross-bridges. It is common to refer to this as the **electromechanical delay**. The length of this delay depends upon the length and type (see section 2.3.8) of the muscle fibers involved.

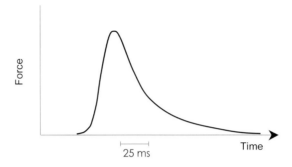

Figure 2.40: *A single twitch contraction.*

The peak force reached and the duration of the twitch contraction can vary between fibers from different muscles, but also between individual muscle fibers from the same muscle. This is because different muscle fibers may not only be of different length and thickness, but they may also have different physiological properties that determine the amount of force that they can develop (see section 2.3.8).

If two action potentials are propagated along the muscle fiber membrane in quick succession, then the twitch induced by the second may be initiated while the twitch induced by the first is still ongoing. In this case, the force of the second twitch adds to the force of the first. If a train of many action potentials propagate along the fiber at a high enough frequency, then their individual twitches combine to produce a kind of contraction called a **tetanic contraction**. In a tetanic contraction, the force developed by a muscle fiber is continuously above zero, but may still show up-and-down variation due to the individual twitches. If such variation is present, the tetanic contraction is called **unfused**. If the action potential frequency is high enough, the variation in force disappears and the tetanic contraction is said to be **fused**. These possibilities are shown in Figure 2.41. In panel A, the time between action potentials is

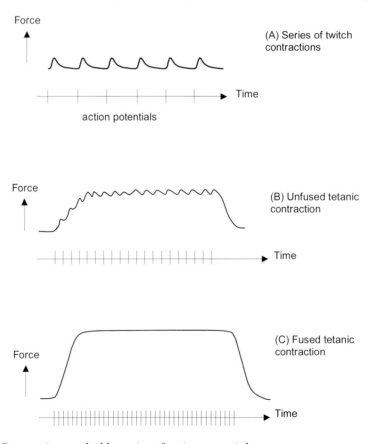

Figure 2.41: *Contractions evoked by trains of action potentials.*

too great for the twitches to add together – one twitch is over before the next begins. In panel B, the action potential frequency is higher than in A, and the level of force generated by the fiber is greater, but the twitch responses are still visible in the force profile (unfused tetanus). In panel C, the stimuli are delivered at a high rate and the individual twitches are no longer evident in the force developed by the fiber (fused tetanus).

Figure 2.41 also illustrated the finding that as the firing frequency of the muscle fiber increases, the force it develops increases. In fused tetanus, the force developed by the fiber is at a maximum: any further increase in action potential frequency does not produce any increase in force. The force developed during smooth, fused tetanic contractions can be as much as ten times greater than the peak force developed during a single twitch.

2.3.7 An alpha-motoneuron and the muscle fibers it innervates comprise a motor unit

Each α-motoneuron in a muscle's motoneuron pool innervates several muscle fibers. This means that the nervous system cannot determine the excitation delivered to one muscle fiber independent of the rest. Rather, the excitation is delivered to groups of muscle fibers – those innervated by individual α-motoneurons. This is the smallest unit of force development that the central nervous system can exert control over, and it is called the **motor unit** (abbreviated MU). Here is a definition:

> **MOTOR UNIT (MU):** The whole α-motoneuron (cell body and neurites) together with all the extrafusal muscle fibers that it innervates.

The α-motoneurons within a muscle's motoneuron pool come in different sizes; there are smaller ones and larger ones; large motoneurons innervate more muscle fibers than small ones (Figure 2.42). Thus, we can talk of the sizes of a muscle's motor units: a large motor unit has a large motoneuron and a large number of muscle fibers; a small motor unit has a small motoneuron and a small number of fibers. Note that large α-MNs have the thickest axons, while smaller α-MNs have correspondingly thinner axons. This means that the largest motor units are associated with axons with the fastest conduction speed, as thicker axons conduct action potentials at greater speed. Conduction speed in mammalian α-motoneuron axons ranges from between about 30 and 40 m/s to over 100 m/s.

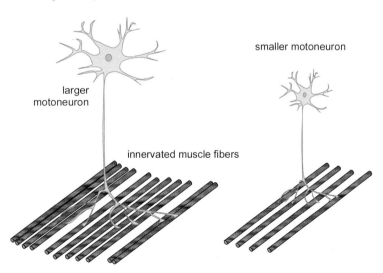

Figure 2.42: *A larger motor unit (left) and a smaller one (right).*

For a given muscle, the average number of fibers in a motor unit is referred to as the muscle's **innervation ratio**; it is calculated as the number of fibers in the muscle divided by the number of α-motoneurons innervating it. For example, the human medial gastocnemius has an innervation ratio of about 2000 fibers/MU, whereas the lateral rectus has an innervation ratio of 5 fibers/MU. In order to be able to make a muscle produce precisely controlled forces, motor units with very few fibers are needed. The muscles that move the eyes, such as lateral rectus, possess many such units, some with as few as two or three fibers. A muscle such as gastrocnemius is not used to produce very precise forces, and possesses no motor units with as few as five fibers – the smallest motor units in gastrocnemius have several hundred fibers.

2.3.8 Motor units are divided into different types

Not only do MUs have different sizes, they have different contractile properties as well. Two contractile characteristics are normally used to discriminate different types of motor unit in mammalian muscles: the rapidity of the motor unit's twitch contraction, and how the unit fatigues. The rapidity of a twitch is usually quantified by the **contraction time** – the time from the onset of force production to the peak force generated during a twitch. Figure 2.43 shows the twitch contractions produced by two different motor units that have different contraction times. The unit with the shorter contraction time is called a **fast-twitch motor unit**; the unit with the longer contraction time is a **slow-twitch motor unit**. Motor units either have short contraction times and are classified as fast-twitch, or they have longer contraction times and are classified as slow-twitch.

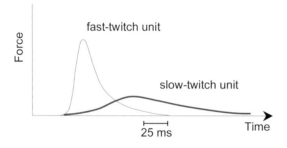

Figure 2.43: *Force-time profiles of fast- and slow-twitch motor units (illustrative).*

If a motor unit contracts again and again, the amount of force it is able to produce will gradually decline – it exhibits fatigue. Given the same stimulation, the rate of decline in force production differs between motor units: in some the decline is quicker than it is in others. Motor units that show a slow decline are said to be more resistant to fatigue than those in which the decline is faster. Using suitable measures of the fatigability of motor units[47], it has been found that motor units tend to fall into two relatively well-defined groups: units that are relatively quick to fatigue and units that fatigue relatively slowly.

In most mammals, the motor units making up a given muscle fall into three roughly defined groups based on their fatigability and contraction time, and these groups are called 'types'. The three types of motor unit are as follows:

(1)   Fatigue-resistant, slow-twitch motor units (**S units**). These are the smallest type of unit and develop the least force.

(2)   Fatigue-resistant, fast-twitch motor units (**FR units**). These are larger than the slow-twitch units in the same muscle and develop more force.

(3)   Quick to fatigue, fast-twitch motor units (**FF units**). These are the largest type of unit and develop more force than either the FR or S units in the same muscle.

Many muscles will contain units of all three types, though some may lack FF units. Those lacking FF units tend to be postural muscles, which are not used to develop large forces very quickly, but which need to sustain force production for long periods and so need to be fatigue resistant. The cellular and molecular characteristics of the muscle fibers in the different types of unit are responsible for the different contractile properties. A discussion of these properties is beyond the scope of this text[48].

This classification scheme for motor units is not as clear cut in humans as it is in the cat, for example. We do possess both fast- and slow-twitch units, but the smallest, weakest units do not always have the shortest contraction time. There are some fast-twitch units that are smaller and weaker than many of the slow-twitch units[49].

2.3.9 Smaller motor units tend to be activated before larger ones

When a muscle is used to develop force during performance of a motor task, its motoneuron pool is excited by input from elsewhere in the nervous system. The excitation causes some motoneurons to fire, and it is typically found that the smaller motoneurons fire before the larger ones. The number of motoneurons that actually fire will depend upon the amount of excitatory input that the pool receives. If only a small amount is received, then a small number of the smaller motoneurons will fire.

Experiments have shown that motoneurons begin firing in response to excitatory input in strict order of their size. If a person gradually and voluntarily increases the force developed by a muscle up to the maximum that they are able to produce, a gradually increasing excitatory input to its motoneuron pool arrives via the corticospinal tract. In response to the excitation, the smallest motoneurons fire first, and then slightly larger ones, and so on until the largest ones fire (see below). When a motoneuron fires, the associated motor unit is said to be recruited. Thus, as excitation of the motoneuron pool increases, the motor units are recruited in order of size. This is called the **size principle**[50] for motor unit recruitment:

> **SIZE PRINCIPLE FOR MOTOR UNIT RECRUITMENT:** The order in which the motor units of a muscle are recruited into force production is determined by the size of the associated motoneuron: small units are recruited first and larger ones later, in strict order of size.

As with the other principles that we have encountered in this chapter, there are exceptions to the size principle[51].

As might be expected, when the excitation of a motoneuron pool decreases, the largest motoneurons stop firing first and the smaller ones later, as the excitation reaches lower levels. This means that the fatigue-resistant units in a muscle are recruited first (they are the smaller ones), and they tend to be active for longer than the fatigable units (the larger ones). When performing a task in which muscles generate only small amounts of contractile force, only the small, fatigue-resistant motor units will be active. The larger, fatigable units only become active in tasks that require greater force. Thus, the fatigable units are likely to be inactive for much of the time, held in reserve for use in tasks that require rapid production of large forces, such as escaping from a predator.

2.3.10 Force developed by muscle depends on the number of active motor units and their firing frequencies

The contractile force developed by a muscle depends upon several factors: two of the more important are these (others will be described in sections 2.3.16–18):

(1) *The number of active motor units.* The forces developed by individual motor units add together to produce the force developed by the muscle as a whole, so the more of them are active and developing contractile force, the greater the total muscle force.

(2)   *The firing rate of the active units.* As we saw in section 2.3.7, the force developed by muscle fibers depends on the firing frequency as the force produced by individual twitch contractions add together (up to the maximum, which is achieved during smooth tetanus).

As the force developed by a muscle increases, more units become active, and the firing rates of those already active increases[52].

Different motor units do not usually fire their action potentials at the same time (synchronously); rather; they fire at different times (asynchronously) – an action potential in one unit will often occur in the time between action potentials in other units. This means that although individual units often do not produce fused tetanic contractions (fused tetanus is rarely observed in normal activity), the sum of many asynchronous unfused contractions results in a fairly smooth overall muscle contraction. Some degree of synchrony of motor unit firing is not uncommon, but in some cases a high degree of synchronization can occur – when a muscle is very fatigued, for example – and this can produce oscillatory contractions of the whole muscle (tremor).

2.3.11 Motor unit activity in a muscle can be recorded using electrodes placed on the skin: electromyography

The fact that action potentials propagate along muscle fibers during a contraction means that electrical signals can be recorded by electrodes placed sufficiently near to the muscle (extracellular electrodes). The principle is exactly the same as for making extracellular recordings from neurons (section 2.1.7). A typical method involves placing two small, circular electrodes a few millimeters in diameter on the surface of the skin directly over the muscle of interest. It is possible to use just one, but a two-electrode arrangement is preferred and is referred to as a **bipolar** configuration. The two electrodes are separated by a few millimeters and placed so that they lie along the line of the fibers in the underlying muscle. A third electrode is normally placed at some convenient location on the body surface and connected to the earth. This earthed electrode is needed in order that the recording electrodes selectively respond to voltage changes due to electrical activity in the muscle – without the earthed electrode, these changes are contaminated with irrelevant electrical activity (called noise). It is important that the earthed electrode not be placed over a muscle.

The electrical signal recorded from electrodes on the skin surface is a combination of the action potentials being propagated by all the underlying muscle fibers that are sufficiently close to the electrodes for their activity to be detected. This is typically a very large number of fibers and so the signal recorded at the skin surface is the sum of a very large number of action potentials. The potentials propagating along more superficial muscle fibers closer to the electrodes contribute more to the sum than fibers deeper in the muscle. The amplitude of the electrical signal is very small: peak amplitudes seldom exceed a few tens of millivolts (mV, a thousandth of a volt) and are usually in the order of hundreds of microvolts (µV, a millionth of a volt). This signal is known as an **electromyographic signal**, usually abbreviated to EMG signal, and a signal record is often called an electromyogram. The process of recording electromyographic signals is called **electromyography**.

The typical form of an EMG signal recorded from the skin surface during a muscle contraction is shown in Figure 2.44: the figure shows the signal produced when the muscle is initially relaxed, then contracts, then relaxes again. The signal is both negative and positive because the action potentials are recorded by extracellular electrodes (section 2.1.7). The amplitude of the signal depends upon the number of motor units that are actively firing and how close the fibers are to the electrodes: the more units that are firing and the closer the muscle fibers to the electrodes, the larger the signal. Where the amplitude is greatest, a large number of motor units are firing and many superficial muscle fibers will also be contributing to the signal. Where the amplitude is small, relatively few units are firing.

Figure 2.44: *Typical appearance of a raw (unprocessed) electromyogram (illustrative).*

2.3.12 Activity in a single muscle can be more precisely differentiated by inserting the recording electrodes into it

When electrodes are placed on the skin overlying a muscle, they are able to respond to action potentials conducted along any sufficiently nearby muscle fibers. For a muscle like biceps brachii, all the fibers sufficiently near to the electrodes to contribute to the recorded EMG signal are likely to be fibers of the biceps. It is not always possible, however, to be certain that electrodes on the skin surface are responding only to activity in the muscle of interest. Most muscles lie in very close proximity to other muscles, as can easily be appreciated by inspecting textbooks of muscular anatomy. Electromyographic activity in these nearby muscles can contribute to the EMG signal recorded from electrodes placed on the skin overlying a muscle of interest. If it is necessary to record selectively from a specific muscle, then contamination by activity in nearby muscles must be avoided. This can be done using wire electrodes that are inserted into the muscle of interest, a technique known as **intramuscular** or **fine-wire electromyography**. This technique can also be used for recording electromyographic activity from deep muscles that lie beneath other, more superficial muscles, but the user needs to be sufficiently skilled to be able to insert the electrode into the deep muscle and not into something else or into some other muscle.

Fine-wire electromyography involves inserting one or two very thin wires into a muscle using a hollow needle such as the syringe needles used for delivering injections. When the needle is withdrawn, one end of the wire is left within the muscle; the other end is connected to an amplifier. The wire is covered by a thin coating of insulation, except for the last one or two millimeters where the metal is exposed. It is from these exposed ends of the wires that recordings are actually made, and so these must lie within the muscle of interest. As with surface recordings, the surface of the body is earthed through an electrode attached to the skin surface over a bony part of the body. Electromyographic signals from muscle fibers in the vicinity of the uninsulated tips of the wires can then be recorded. These signals will come from muscle fibers close to the electrode tips. The number of motor units that contribute to the signal depends on the placement of the wire, the distribution of the fibers of individual units within the muscle and the length of the exposed portion of the wire – the more of the wire that is exposed, the greater the number of units that will contribute. Depending upon the number of contributing units, a fine-wire EMG signal can be much simpler in form than that recorded using surface electrodes, as far fewer motor units contribute. It may be possible to resolve the activity of the individual motor units themselves, something that is normally impossible with surface electrodes.

2.3.13 Processed EMG signals can be used to obtain measures of muscle activity

Obtaining good electromyographic signals from muscles using either surface or intramuscular electrodes is something of an art; details of how to develop and apply this art can be found elsewhere[53]. Multiple factors can affect the signal, including the particular motor units that contribute to the recorded signal, the quality of the connection between the skin and the electrode, the quality of the connection to earth, the presence of electromagnetic noise in the recording environment, the size of the muscle being recorded from (which depends upon the individual person or animal), and the thickness of subcutaneous fat.

Provided a good signal can be obtained, EMG can be used to make a variety of measures of muscle activity. For example, it can be used to determine when a muscle starts to be active, when its activity changes, when it becomes inactive, how long it is active for, and how its level of activity depends on different conditions. Such measurements are most reliable when made with surface electrodes: these sample the activity of a large number of motor units and so are likely to detect the firing of the first motor units recruited. Intramuscular EMG electrodes sample far fewer units and may not detect activity in the first recruited units, which means that they will not detect the start or finish of activity in the muscle as a whole, but only in motor units that are recorded from.

Raw EMG signals are usually not suitable for reliably deriving measures of the kind described in the last paragraph, as they are far too noisy. To obtain more reliable measures, the raw EMG signals are processed in various ways. Typically the signal is first rectified, which means made all positive. There are two ways to do this: (1) remove all the negative values to leave only the positive ones (half-wave rectification); (2) make the negative values positive (full-wave rectification). Panels A and B of Figure 2.45 show the results of performing these operations on the EMG signal of Figure 2.44. Following rectification, the signal is then usually low pass filtered, which means removing the rapid variations in the signal to produce a smoothed-out version. Panel C of Figure 2.45 shows a low pass filtered version of the full-wave rectified signal in panel B.

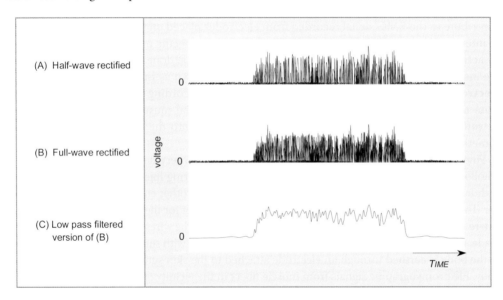

Figure 2.45: *Electromyogram from Figure 2.44 rectified and filtered (illustrative).*

2.3.14 Elastic material stretches when you pull on it

All biological tissues, including bone, are elastic or 'springy' to some degree. Muscles and associated connective tissues are good examples of elastic tissues: when you pull on them, they stretch, and when you release the pull, they quickly return to their original length. In this respect, muscle and connective tissue are very similar to other elastic material like rubber. It is useful to consider something familiar like a rubber band, as an understanding of its properties will be very helpful for understanding the properties of muscles and tendons.

Imagine that you have a length of rubber band that is attached to something solid at one end. If you don't pull on the unattached end, the band will be floppy and possibly have loops or kinks in it, as shown in Figure 2.46A. A gentle pull on the free end will straighten out the loops and kinks – it can be held like this without applying force to the free end (Figure 2.46B). In order to increase the length of the band any further it is necessary to pull. The length of the band beyond which it cannot be lengthened without pulling is called the **resting length**, denoted ℓ_o (see Chapter 1). If a pulling force (F_{pull}) is applied, as in panel C of the figure, the band increases in length (stretches) to a new length, and as it does so it develops a force that resists the stretch: a **restoring force** (denoted T for tension; see Chapter 1, section 1.3.2). The band will stop lengthening when the pulling force and restoring force are equal in magnitude but in opposite directions, written $T = - F_{pull}$. Thus the forces add up to zero ($T + F_{pull} = 0$), which is what it means to say that they are in equilibrium.

As panel C of Figure 2.46 illustrates, when the forces are in equilibrium, the band is stretched to a length which remains constant as long as the pulling force remains constant. If the pulling force is increased, the band will stretch further. If it is decreased, the band will shorten. An obvious question to ask is, *what is the relationship between the length of the band and the pulling force applied to the end?* We address this question next.

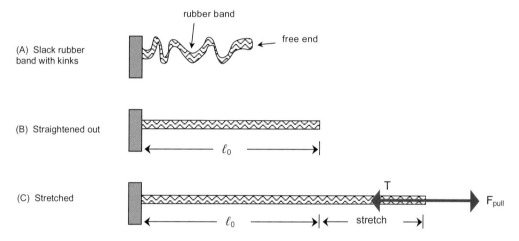

Figure 2.46: *Stretching a piece of rubber band.*

2.3.15 Elastic things can be described by their force-length characteristics

It is relatively easy to discover what the relationship is between the force with which you pull and the length at which the band stops stretching (the equilibrium length). Imagine that we can apply forces of 1, 2, 3, 4 and 5 Newtons to the free end of a band with a resting length of 10 cm, and that it stretches to lengths of 12, 14, 16, 18 and 20 centimeters (at equilibrium) when these forces are applied. These results can be plotted on a graph with force along the vertical axis and length along the horizontal, as shown in Figure 2.47. This is a graphical portrayal of

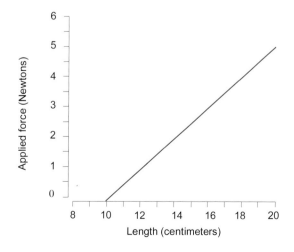

Figure 2.47: *Force-length characteristic.*

the relationship between the applied force and the band's length; a relationship of this type is called a **force-length characteristic**.

When the force-length characteristic is a straight line, the elastic object obeys **Hooke's law**. As described in Chapter 1, Hooke's law states that an elastic object develops a restoring force that is proportional to the amount of stretch (the restoring force minus the stretching force). The amount of stretch is just the length at equilibrium (L) minus the resting length (ℓ_o). Thus, Hooke's law can be written in shorthand as $T = -k(L - \ell_o)$ (see Chapter 1, equation 1.3). The constant of proportionality k is called the **stiffness** and is equal to the slope of the line in Figure 2.47. A steep slope (high stiffness) would mean that the band was very resistant to being stretched and a large pulling force would be needed for a relatively small increase in length. A shallow slope (low stiffness) would mean that the band was not very resistant to being stretched. For our purposes it will be sufficient to define stiffness as follows[54]:

> **STIFFNESS:** A quantity that characterizes the resistance of an object or piece of material to increases in its length (stretch). It is equal to the slope of the force-length characteristic of the object, and is measured in units of force (Newtons) per unit length of stretch (meters), Newtons/meter.

Not all pieces of elastic material obey Hooke's law: muscles, tendons and ligaments are examples. The force-length characteristics of muscles are discussed in the next section.

2.3.16 A muscle's force-length characteristic depends on its activity

If a similar procedure that we imagined being used to produce the graph in Figure 2.47 were applied to a muscle, its force-length characteristic could be measured. You can imagine doing this when the muscle is completely relaxed (no motor units are firing) and when it is actively contracting. If the measurements are made when no motor units are firing, then you obtain the muscle's **passive** force-length characteristic. The passive force is primarily due to stretch of the connective tissues (see section 2.3.2).

Figure 2.48 shows the typical form of a passive force-length characteristic. The range of lengths within the region labeled *physiological range* in the figure corresponds to the muscle length within the extremes of the normal range of motion of the body part that the muscle moves. Within this range, muscles typically produce very little passive force, as is the case in the figure. Thus, muscles offer very little passive resistance to stretch in normal circumstances. Outside the physiological range, the muscle passively resists stretch much more strongly and can develop quite large forces.

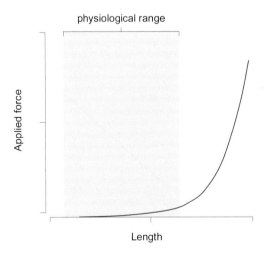

Figure 2.48: *Passive force-length characteristic (illustrative).*

When a muscle is actively generating a contractile force, it resists stretch much more strongly. However, it behaves very differently depending upon whether or not the muscle stretch reflex pathways are intact and can contribute to force development. We will deal with muscle stretch reflexes in Chapters 5 and 6. For the moment, we will consider a muscle without reflexes. A way of measuring the force-length characteristics of active muscle without reflexes is to cut the sensory nerves innervating the muscle, and then excite it artificially by electrical stimulation of the intact motor nerve. The amount of stimulation that the muscle receives can then be kept constant at any desired value. If the stimulation is constant, then the muscle activity is maintained at a relatively constant level and the force-length characteristic obtained is called an **isoactivation characteristic**. Typical force-length characteristics of a muscle without reflexes measured under isoactivation conditions are shown in Figure 2.49: these look very different from the passive characteristic shown in Figure 2.48. The shape can be explained in terms of the molecular mechanisms of contraction[55].

The precise shape of the force-length characteristic of active muscle depends on what muscle it is – different muscles have slightly different characteristics[56] – and on how stimulated it is (how many motor units are active). Figure 2.49 shows force-length characteristics at different levels of activation[57]. If the activation is low, the muscle develops less force at any given length – which is what you would expect, since only a few motor units will be contributing.

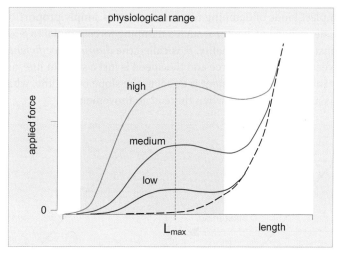

Figure 2.49: *Illustrative force-length characteristics of active muscle without reflexes (solid lines) at three levels of activation (high, medium, low); the dashed line is the passive characteristic.*

A curvilinear force-length characteristic means that the stiffness of the muscle is not a constant: the slope of the curve depends upon where you are on the curve. For the passive characteristic (Figure 2.48), the slope is very shallow at the start (low stiffness), but very steep outside the physiological range (high stiffness). The isoactivation characteristic is more complex and has a slope of zero where it reaches its peak (at length L_{max} in Figure 2.49) and is actually negative over a small range of lengths greater than L_{max}. A zero slope means that the muscle force does not change as it is stretched (it does not resist further stretching); a negative slope means that the muscle force decreases as the muscle is stretched. Thus, if sufficient force is applied to the muscle for it to stretch to L_{max}, then any further pull, however small, will cause the muscle to lengthen rapidly without any further resistance. Such behavior is referred to as *yielding*: a muscle with the force-length characteristic of Figure 2.49 yields when stretched beyond L_{max}. In the figure, the muscle can yield within its physiological range. One behavioral effect of such yielding could be that a person who is quite capable of holding a load with a limb in any posture where the muscle length is less than L_{max}, finds themselves unable to support it when the limb is in a posture where the length is greater than L_{max} – the muscle would seem to give way (yield) and the limb would quickly move to the extreme of its range of motion. This rarely happens in reality, because muscles are equipped with special mechanisms (stretch reflexes) which counteract the yielding tendency (see Chapter 6).

2.3.17 The force developed by elastic objects usually depends on the speed of lengthening or shortening

We have seen that the force developed by a piece of elastic material, like a rubber band or a muscle, depends upon the length to which it is stretched. This applies in static conditions when the force and resisting force are in equilibrium. It is natural to ask what happens while length is changing.

When something is moving, it is always subject to resistive forces: when something moves through the air, it encounters air resistance that slows it down; when something slides over the ground, it encounters friction that slows it down. Forces of this sort frequently depend on the speed with which something moves, being greater when it moves faster; when it stops moving, they disappear altogether. Air and fluid resistance, for example, are greater at greater speeds. You can appreciate this when you move your hand through water – the faster you try to move, the more resistance you encounter.

When a piece of elastic material is in the process of lengthening or shortening, we would expect forces to develop that resist the movement, and that the resistance will be greater at higher speeds. In this context, the resistive forces are usually called *damping forces* because they act to dampen down oscillations: oscillations arise in elastic materials when they are stretched and released, as we discussed in detail earlier (Chapter 1, section 1.3.2).

One of the simplest kinds of damping force is one that is simply proportional to the speed of movement. As described in Chapter 1, such a damping force is equal to $\beta \times v$, where v is the speed and the constant of proportionality, β, is called the *damping coefficient*. A graph of this relationship between the damping force and the speed is just a straight line, as shown in panel A of Figure 2.50. The damping coefficient is equal to the slope of the line, which goes through zero since there is no damping force when there is no movement.

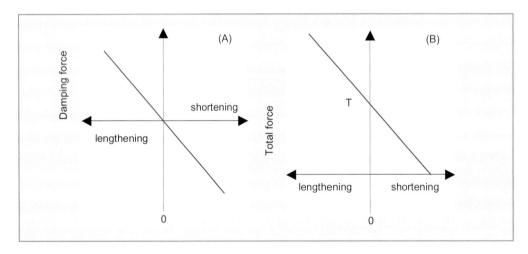

Figure 2.50: *Relationship between force and velocity at a single length. (A) Damping force. (B) Total force (damping force + elastic restoring force).*

The total force produced by a damped, elastic object is the sum of two forces[58]: (1) the force produced due to the amount of stretch (restoring force), and (2) the force produced due to the speed with which the object's length is changing (damping force). If we imagine conducting an experiment in which we measure the total force generated when the object is at a particular length but is in the process of lengthening or shortening, then we end up with a graph like that shown in panel B of Figure 2.50 (damping force = $\beta \times v$). There is a force (labeled T) generated when the speed is zero: this is the elastic restoring force. The kind of graph shown in panel B is called a **force-velocity relationship** and has been measured experimentally for skeletal muscles, as described next.

2.3.18 A muscle's contractile force depends on speed as well as length

Force-length characteristics are measured when the muscle force and the applied force are in equilibrium and the muscle is neither lengthening nor shortening. If the force is measured while an active muscle is either shortening or lengthening, it is found to vary with the speed of shortening or lengthening. The result of such measurements can be presented on a graph as shown in Figure 2.51. The graph shows the force developed by a muscle with a constant level of activation when it is shortening, lengthening and not changing length (muscle speed = 0). The graph shows the muscle's (isoactivation) *force-velocity relationship*.

As can be seen from the graph, when the muscle is lengthening while generating contractile force (eccentric contraction), it generates more force than it does when it is not changing length (muscle velocity = 0). Conversely, the muscle generates less force when it is shortening (concentric contraction) and drops to zero when the shortening speed is sufficiently fast. This is the maximum active shortening speed of the muscle (denoted vmax in the figure). Notice that the form of the graph in Figure 2.51 shows that muscles generate force in a manner that tends to resist both lengthening and shortening. If the muscle is lengthening, then the force increases in opposition to lengthening. If the muscle is shortening, then the force – which is acting to shorten the muscle – decreases. In effect, the force-velocity relationship describes the intrinsic damping properties of the muscle: the relationship is clearly not as simple as the straight line relationship shown in Figure 2.50B. The form of the relationship can be largely explained in terms of how cross-bridges are formed and broken when the muscle is lengthening and shortening[59]. Thus, the physical mechanisms responsible for the force-velocity relationship in skeletal muscles are not the same as the mechanisms responsible for air and fluid resistance. There will, of course, be resistance to muscle lengthening and shortening that are passive (not due to cross-bridges), but the contribution of these passive resistive forces to the force-velocity relationship are small relative to the contribution of the cross-bridges. However, passive damping forces can make a substantial contribution during actual movements of body parts. An example is movements of the eyes in their sockets, where the passive damping forces produced when the eye moves are alone sufficient to prevent significant oscillations. These passive forces come from tissues rubbing together.

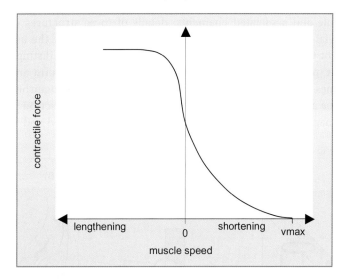

Figure 2.51: *Form of the force-velocity relationship (illustrative).*

2.4 Joint Movements and Muscles

2.4.1 Introduction

The scientific study of motor behavior is founded on the description and measurement of that behavior. There are many ways of describing motor behavior: we can describe it in terms of its outcome(s), in terms of the movement of a tool or particular part of the body such as a finger or a foot, in terms of the rotations about joints of the different body segments involved, or in terms of the forces developed by contributing muscles. We need to define what quantities are needed in order to provide the chosen description, and we need a means for measuring these quantities.

In this part of the chapter we will begin by looking at how body segments are jointed together and how they rotate about these joints. The study and description of movement without consideration of the forces that cause the movement is called **kinematics**. Kinematic descriptions involve quantities such as position, displacement, distance, speed, velocity and acceleration. The study and description of the causal processes that produce movement is called **dynamics** (or sometimes *kinetics*); quantities such as force and torque appear in dynamic descriptions of phenomena. We will present an informal (i.e., non-mathematical) account of the kinematic and dynamic concepts needed for a full understanding of material in later chapters.

2.4.2 There are six basic types of synovial joint

Joints are the junctions between bones that hold them together. Many but not all joints allow movement: the bony segments of the skull, for example, are held together by tough, fibrous connective tissue, and active movement of these joints is not possible. Joints made of cartilaginous connective tissue allow some movement, but it is only the **synovial joint** that allows free movement of the connected body segments.

Synovial joints are structured so as to hold bones together and allow them to move smoothly without becoming separated (dislocated). The structures that achieve this include the joint capsule and associated ligaments: details of these structures can be found elsewhere[60]. Synovial joints can be classified based on the shapes of the articulating surfaces and how they fit together. Six basic types of synovial joint can be distinguished in humans: the **hinge joint, pivot joint, saddle joint, condylar joint, plane joint** and **ball-and-socket joint**. Sometimes a seventh type called the *ellipsoid joint* is distinguished, but it is usually considered to be a subtype of the ball-and-socket joint. We will describe a hinge joint in this section, and imagine that one of the jointed segments is held fixed and the other is free to move.

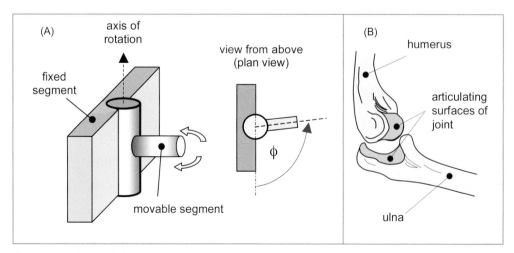

Figure 2.52: *Hinge joints.*

Figure 2.52A shows an idealized hinge joint. The joint only allows rotation of the movable segment in the manner indicated by the curved arrows. Examples of hinge joints in the human body include the interphalangeal joints of the fingers and the articulation of the humerus (upper arm bone) and the ulnar (forearm bone) at the elbow. Panel B of the figure shows how the humerus and ulnar fit together at the elbow to form a hinge joint. The movable segment of a hinge joint can only move back and forth in a single plane. This means that the position of the movable segment with respect to the fixed segment can be specified by a single number – the **joint angle**. This is the angle formed between the long axes of the two segments, and is denoted ϕ in the figure. It is measured from the fixed segment to the movable one, as indicated by the arrow head. In the body, the angle is measured from the proximal segment to the distal segment, as described next.

2.4.3 Movement of a hinge joint is either a flexion or an extension

In the human body, the angle of a hinge joint can be measured either internally or externally, as shown in Figure 2.53 for the articulation of the humerus and ulnar at the elbow joint. The angle of a hinge joint is always measured from the long axis of the proximal segment (upper arm in the figure) to that of the distal segment (forearm). If the elbow joint angle is measured from the upper arm to the forearm, it is called an **internal joint angle**. If it is measured 'upwards' to the forearm, it is called an **external joint angle**.

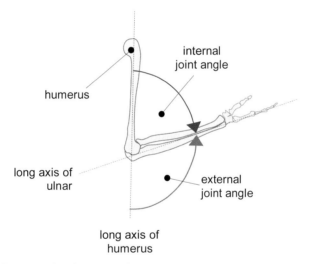

Figure 2.53: *Elbow (humeroulnar) joint angles.*

When the internal angle is 180°, the external angle is zero and the elbow is fully extended. A movement towards the fully extended position is an **elbow extension movement**, or simply an *elbow extension*. A movement in the opposite direction brings the two segments of the arm together into a more flexed posture. This movement is called an **elbow flexion movement**, or just an *elbow flexion*. The elbow is fully flexed when the internal angle is about 10°.

Due to the fact that the humeroulnar articulation at the elbow can only flex and extend, it is said to have a single **degree-of-freedom** of movement. Any movable thing that needs just one number to completely specify its position has one degree-of-freedom of movement.

2.4.4 Pivot joints have one degree-of-freedom of movement

Panel A of Figure 2.54 shows an idealized pivot joint in which a movable segment (the pivot) is free to swivel within a circular hole in the fixed segment (the ring). If the roles of the two segments are reversed, then the ring is the movable segment and it rotates about a fixed pivot: a wheel and axle form such an arrangement. Examples in the human body include the articulation of the radius and the ulnar at the elbow (described later), and the articulation of the two vertebra beneath the skull: the atlanto-axial articulation (the atlas is the vertebra immediately beneath the skull, the axis is the vertebra beneath the atlas). The atlanto-axial articulation allows the head to turn to the left and right on the neck, but it is not a pure pivot joint, as it also allows some rotation forwards and backwards.

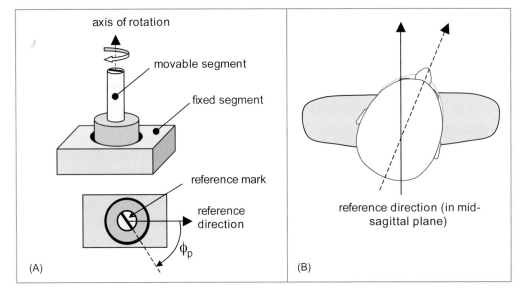

Figure 2.54: *Pivot joint.*

The pure pivot joint has a single degree-of-freedom of movement as shown in Figure 2.54: to completely specify the angular position of the movable segment requires a single joint angle. This requires a reference direction from which to measure the angle of turn, and a feature on the movable segment that allows its position to be defined. In Figure 2.54, the reference direction lies parallel to the long axis of the fixed segment, and the feature on the movable segment is a line on its end (reference mark). The angular position of the movable segment is specified by the joint angle, ϕ_p. If we wanted to measure the angular position of the head in

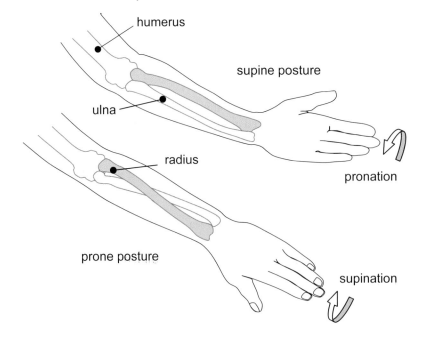

Figure 2.55: *Pronation-supination.*

the transverse plane as it rotates about the atlanto-axial joint, the angle could be defined by a reference direction fixed to the mid-sagittal plane, and a suitable anatomical landmark, such as the nose, as shown in Figure 2.54B.

The articulation of the radius and ulnar (forearm bones) at the elbow – the proximal radio-ulnar joint – is a pivot joint: the radius is the pivot, and the ring is formed by ligaments and a notch in the ulnar. Rotation about this joint allows the forearm to rotate along its long axis, a movement that occurs when turning a handle grasped in the hand. This axial rotation is called either a **pronation** or a **supination**, depending upon the direction, as shown in Figure 2.55. The forearm is in a supine posture when the palm of the hand faces upwards and in a prone posture when the palm faces downwards. As the figure shows, pronation turns the hand towards the prone position and supination turns the hand towards the supine position.

2.4.5 Condylar and saddle joints have two degrees-of-freedom

The condylar joint and the saddle joint both allow two degrees-of-freedom of movement. The knuckles (metacarpophalangeal joints) are condylar and allow flexion-extension movements (one degree-of-freedom) and abduction-adduction movements (second degree-of-freedom), as illustrated in Figure 2.56. An abduction movement of the finger rotates it away from the midline of the hand (to abduct is to take away). An adduction movement of the finger rotates it towards the midline. The saddle joint is so called because of the saddle-like shape of the articulating surfaces. The carpometacarpal joint of the thumb is the only true saddle joint in the human body. It permits both flexion-extension and abduction-adduction of the thumb as a whole.

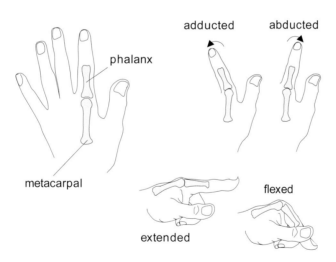

Figure 2.56: *Movements of the index finger about the metacarpophalangeal joint.*

2.4.6 Ball-and-socket joints have three degrees-of-freedom

The ball-and-socket joint is, as you might guess, comprised of one segment with a ball at one end that fits into a hole (the socket) in the other segment. An idealized ball-and-socket joint, with the socket segment considered fixed and the ball segment considered movable, is shown in Figure 2.57A. In principle such a joint has three degrees-of-freedom of movement, as it allows rotation about the three axes that are drawn in the figure (V, H and A). These three degrees-of-freedom are shown separately in panel B. Rotation of the movable segment about the vertical axis, V, moves the segment forwards and backwards (black arrows): the angular position can be specified using the angle φ (panel B, top). Rotation about the horizontal axis, *H*, moves the segment up and down (blue arrows); the angular position can be specified using the angle θ (panel B, middle). Finally, the movable segment can be rotated about its long axis (*A*), which twists the movable segment around: the angular position is specified by the angle ψ (panel B, bottom). Thus, three numbers are required (φ, θ and ψ) to completely specify the angular position of one segment of a ball-and-socket joint relative to the other.

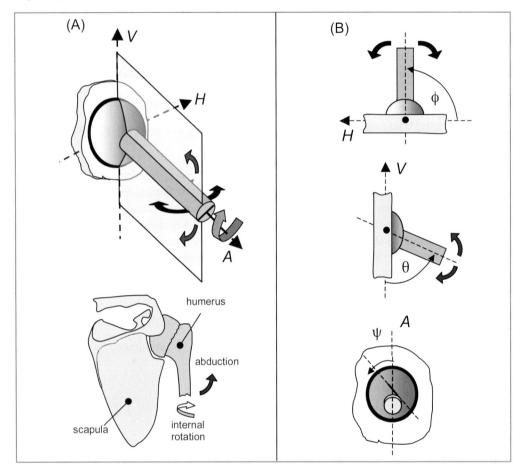

Figure 2.57: *Degrees-of-freedom of a ball-and-socket joint.*

The hip and shoulder joints provide examples of the ball-and-socket type. At the shoulder, the ball is formed by the head of the humerus, and the socket by the glenoid cavity of the scapula (shoulder blade) – the bones are shown at the bottom of panel A in Figure 2.57. The humerus is held in place by ligaments and the connective tissue of the joint capsule. The forward-backward rotations of the upper arm about the shoulder joint are called flexion-extension of the shoulder joint; the up-and-down rotations are called abduction-adduction; the axial rotation is called internal-external rotation.

2.4.7 The number of degrees-of-freedom of several linked segments is equal to the sum of the degrees-of-freedom of the individual joints

Provided there are no additional constraints, the number of degrees-of-freedom (d.o.f.s) of a combination of several jointed segments is equal to the number of d.o.f.s of each of the joints. The limbs are, of course, formed from several jointed segments, and so each limb has a total number of d.o.f.s equal to the sum of the d.o.f.s at each joint. For example, ignoring the fingers and thumb, the arm has three d.o.f.s at the shoulder, two at the elbow, and two at the wrist, giving a total of seven d.o.f.s. To specify a particular postural configuration of the arm requires seven numbers, a value for each of the seven joint angles. Thus, without the finger and thumb joints, the postural description will consist of the degree of abduction-adduction, flexion-extension and internal-external of the shoulder; the degree of flexion-extension and pronation-supination of the forearm; and the degree of flexion-extension and radioulnar deviation of the wrist. Figure 2.58 illustrates radioulnar deviation of the wrist: ulnar deviation rotates the hand towards the ulna, radial deviation rotates it towards the radius. If the fingers and thumb are included, then twenty more d.o.f.s are added[61].

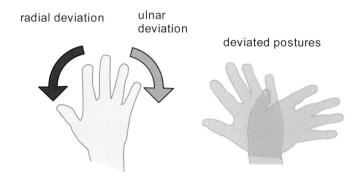

Figure 2.58: *Radioulnar deviation of the wrist.*

A constraint is something that prevents or restricts movement in some way. An example would be a plaster cast that is used to prevent movement at a joint while a broken bone heals. If a person wears a plaster cast that prevents motion at the elbow joint, then the arm loses two degrees-of-freedom: rotation about the humeroulnar joint is no longer possible (elbow flexion-extension), and neither is rotation about the proximal radioulnar joint (pronation-supination). A constraint may also prevent independent movement at two or more joints, which also has the effect of reducing the degrees-of-freedom of a linked system of segments.

What we have said so far about the degrees-of-freedom of individual joints and systems of jointed segments (such as limbs) leads to the following definition for the d.o.f.s of a jointed system of rigid segments:

> **DEGREES-OF-FREEDOM (D.O.F.S) OF A SYSTEM OF RIGID, JOINTED SEGMENTS:**
> the number of independent parameters (e.g., joint angles) that are needed to completely specify the configuration (posture) of the whole linkage.

2.4.8 Movement at a single joint can be described in terms of angular velocity

A single degree-of-freedom movement at a joint, such as a flexion or extension movement about the elbow, can be described in terms of the angular velocity and acceleration. Figure 2.59 shows the right forearm bones in two positions, before (blue) and after (green) an elbow flexion movement through 75°. Elbow flexion rotates the forearm in the counterclockwise direction, which is considered to be positive by convention, so the forearm in Figure 2.59 has been moved through an **angular displacement** of +75°.

The joint's **angular velocity** describes how fast the joint angle is changing and the direction in which the change is taking place. The quantity **angular speed** is a measure of how fast the angle is changing without reference to the direction. Thus, angular speed can only be positive, whereas angular velocity is positive if the movement is in the counterclockwise direction and negative if it is in the clockwise direction[62]. Suppose that the arm in Figure 2.59 makes the 75° extension movement from 45° to 120° in 0.8 seconds. In this case, the average angular speed over the whole movement is equal to the angular distance travelled (75°) divided by the time taken (0.8 s), which is 93.75° per second. The average angular velocity would have the same magnitude but be negative, because it is in the clockwise direction (−93.75°/s). Of course, during the movement the angular speed (or velocity) will almost always be different from

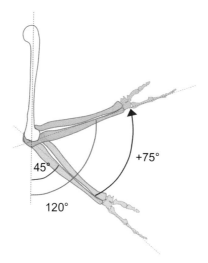

Figure 2.59: *Angular displacement of the forearm through +75°.*

93.75°/s. To see why, imagine driving a car from one place to another, say from home to work. The speed at the beginning and the end will be zero (stopped) and might be zero in between (when you stop at the traffic lights, for instance); it will be faster along clear, straight sections, and slower when going around bends – in short, your speed will vary from moment to moment during the drive. You can calculate your average speed as the distance you have driven divided by the time you took, but you will have been going at different speeds for most of your journey.

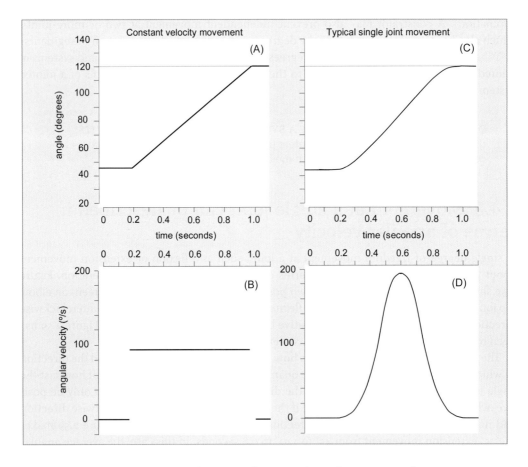

Figure 2.60: *Angle and angular velocity as a function of time for two types of movement.*

When a person makes an elbow flexion or extension movement from one stationary position to another, their angular velocity changes continuously. The difference between the kind of movement a person would make and a constant velocity movement is illustrated in Figure 2.60. Panels A and B show two graphs that represent a constant angular velocity movement in the counterclockwise direction from an initial angle of 45° to a final angle of 120°. The movement starts at a time of 0.2 seconds from the start of the measurement and lasts for 0.8 seconds. Panel A shows the angle plotted against time during the course of the movement; the slope of the plot is constant and equal to the angular velocity. Panel B shows the angular velocity plotted against time for the movement. Panels C and D show two graphs that are characteristic of the type of movements people make when flexing or extending the elbow joint[63]. Panel C shows the external joint angle plotted against time, panel D shows the angular velocity plotted against time[64].

In panel D of Figure 2.60, the magnitude of the angular velocity – the angular speed – is different at every instant of time: it starts from zero, increases to a peak, and then decreases back to zero. The value of the angular speed at an instant of time is called the **instantaneous angular speed**. Since the curve is always above zero, the direction of the velocity is constant. The angular velocity at an instant of time is the **instantaneous angular velocity**. It is often convenient to leave out the word 'instantaneous' and just talk of the angular speed or velocity.

2.4.9 Angular acceleration is the rate of change of angular velocity

Angular acceleration describes how fast angular velocity is changing over time – it is the rate of change of angular velocity. In all the cases we will encounter, the angular acceleration is equal to the slope of the graph of angular velocity against time. If angular velocity is constant, then the acceleration is zero, which accounts for the zero slope of the angular velocity graph in panel B of Figure 2.60. If the angular acceleration for the movement shown in panels C and D of Figure 2.60 is plotted against time, we obtain a graph like that shown in panel B of Figure 2.61: panel A reproduces the angular velocity plot from Figure 2.60D. Notice that the value of the

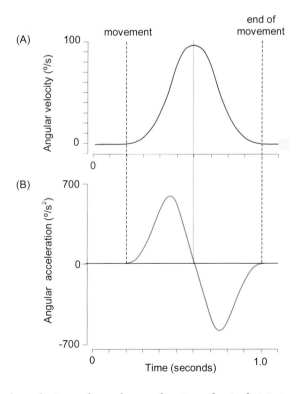

Figure 2.61: *Angular velocity and angular acceleration of a single joint movement (illustrative).*

angular acceleration for the flexion movement is not constant but changes continuously during the movement, starting from and finishing at zero (limb not moving). Thus, at every instant of time, the angular acceleration has a particular value, the **instantaneous angular acceleration**.

Like angular velocity, angular acceleration has both magnitude and direction, but there is no special name for the magnitude of acceleration like there is for the magnitude of velocity. Figure 2.61 shows that the angular acceleration changes direction about half way through the movement. During the first half of the movement, the angular velocity is positive and increasing to its peak: the limb is accelerating in the counterclockwise direction, and so the angular acceleration is positive. During the second half of the movement after the peak in the velocity curve, the angular velocity is still positive but the speed is decreasing. The limb is now accelerating in the opposite (clockwise) direction and the result is that the limb slows down. When acceleration is manifested as a decrease in speed, it is often called **deceleration**. Thus, if the acceleration is in the same direction as the velocity, the speed increases (the normal understanding of acceleration). If the acceleration is in the opposite direction to the velocity, the speed decreases (deceleration).

2.4.10 Most actions involve multi-joint movements

So far we have focused on a particularly simple sort of movement – movement of a single joint about a single axis of rotation (a single degree-of-freedom movement). Such movements are very unlikely to ever occur alone during the execution of a goal-directed action. Even actions as simple as reaching out and picking something up involve movements of several joints simultaneously: as you reach, you may concurrently flex at the shoulder, extend at the elbow, and extend the finger and thumb joints so as to open the hand in preparation for grasping. Other motions may also be involved, such as flexion or extension of the wrist, and pronation or supination of the forearm. Movements comprising simultaneous motion at several joints are referred to as **multi-joint movements**:

> **MULTI-JOINT MOVEMENT:** a movement of the body that involves simultaneous movement of body segments at two or more joints.

The fact that goal-directed actions almost always involve motions at many joints means that a complete description of the movement will require a description of the movement of all the joints involved, some of which may involve two or more degrees-of-freedom. Such a description is very cumbersome indeed, even for an apparently simple action like reaching out to pick something up. If you wanted to determine whether the performance of an action was influenced by some feature of the task situation, such as the size of the object to be grasped or the distance the hand had to be moved to grasp it, a description of the movements at all the joints could be used. With such a description you would be able to determine the effects of the task feature on how the movements at all the joints were executed. However, such elaborate and detailed descriptive investigations are rarely attempted; researchers restrict their attention to just a few key joint motions, or use simple measures such as **movement time** (the time between the start and end of a movement).

2.4.11 Execution of an action often involves a body part or tool that is directly involved in goal achievement

Actions like grasping objects, turning faucets, pressing switches, and so on, involve making contact with these things with a particular part of the body – usually the hand. This is the part of the body that is directly involved in achieving a goal. For example, when reaching to grasp something, the arm and hand are involved, but the hand is the part that directly achieves the goal – grasps the thing; the arm moves the hand into a position where the hand can grasp it.

The term **end-effector** is often used to refer to the body part that is directly involved in goal achievement. This term originates in robotics, where it refers to the device at the end of a robotic arm through which the robot interacts with its environment. Thus, both robotic and human hands are end-effectors. The other parts of the body that are involved in performance of an action are often called **effectors**. An end-effector does not have to be a body part; it could be a tool of some sort. For example, when writing on a piece of paper, the pen or pencil you are writing with is the end-effector; in ball sports like tennis and baseball, the end effector is the racket or bat used to hit the ball. Thus, an end-effector may be a biological body part, or it may be a grasped tool, or a prosthesis.

In tasks like writing or hammering, there is one location on the end-effector that actually makes contact with the writing surface or the nail: the point of the pen and the head of the hammer. It is often useful to distinguish this part of the end-effector – the end of the end-effector, as it were – from the rest of it. The term **working point** is used to refer to this part of the end-effector[65]. The term is also conveniently used for computer-based tasks in which a person moves a cursor of some kind over a computer screen or within a computer-generated, virtual environment. In such tasks, the cursor is the working point.

2.4.12 Performance can be described in terms of the motion of the working point

Performance of an action can be described in terms of the motion of the end-effector or the working point, rather than in terms of the motions of all the different joints; this can vastly simplify the kinematic description. Description of the motion of a working point does not normally involve the angular variables used for describing motion about joints; it involves more familiar translational variables. Drawing lines on a piece of paper or a board provides a simple, familiar task situation that illustrates the basic ideas.

Imagine drawing a line on a flat piece of paper between two points – a starting point and a finishing point. Figure 2.62 shows an example: a person draws a straight line with a pen between two locations marked with filled circles. The hand holding the pen is shown at its starting position (pink) and at its finishing position (blue). At any moment in time while the line is being drawn, the hand is somewhere between the start and finish points (one such position is shown in the figure). A movement like this is called a **translational movement**, since something – the pen in our example – is being translated from one location to another. The line that is drawn is a record of the **path** that the pen-point followed as it was moved across the paper. The line itself does not tell us anything much about the speed of the pen-point as it moved along its path, or about its acceleration. After all, you can follow the same path in many different ways – you can make stops on the way or not stop at all; you can slow down and speed up periodically or randomly, or even backtrack a bit before going forward again. The motion of the pen-point as it moves along the line can be described in terms of the speed with which it moves along the line and its acceleration. This is ordinary, **translational speed**, the kind of speed that is shown on the speedometer when you drive a motor vehicle (measured in kilometers/hour or meters/second). We will define the translational velocity and acceleration in the following sections.

Since the path itself does not specify how the working point moved along it, it is useful to have a terminological distinction between the path and the movement through space. We will use the term **path** to refer only to the route taken to travel from one point to another; it is a line or curve that runs between the two points. The term **trajectory** refers to the motion of a thing through space – the thing's path, together with where it is on the path at any given time. A path is a curved line (a curve), a trajectory is a time-parameterized curve. Thus, the line drawn using a pen is the path the pen followed, not its trajectory.

It seems quite natural to describe performance of a line-drawing task in terms of the movement of the pen-point (the working point), rather than in terms of the motion of all the joints involved in moving the pen. When a person draws a straight line from a start position to a target position, they typically keep moving without back-tracking: they move continuously towards the target position. The kind of movement involved is discussed fully in Chapters 11 and 12.

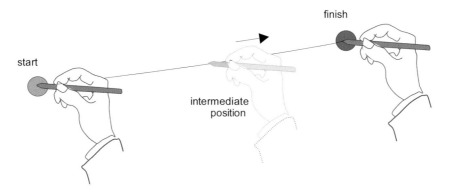

Figure 2.62: *Drawing a straight line.*

2.4.13 The velocity of a working point is a vector

Translational motion along a straight line can be treated as one-dimensional, since the direction of movement never changes. In one-dimensional (1-D) motion there are only two possible directions, and so the vector nature of velocity and acceleration reduces to a simple matter of sign: positive for motion in one direction, negative for the other. Thus, we do not need to worry about vectors in 1-D motion. However, when the trajectory is curved, the vector character of velocity and acceleration is important.

Although there are circumstances in which movement of a working point is a straight line, there are many others in which it is not. When drawing and writing, for example, the pen-point is more likely to be used to draw a curved or wiggly line than a straight one. When the working point follows a curved line, at every instant of time it is moving with a particular speed (the instantaneous speed) in a particular direction (the instantaneous direction). The instantaneous speed is the magnitude of the velocity vector at an instant of time, and the instantaneous direction is the direction of the velocity vector. For our purposes, a vector may be defined to be a quantity that has magnitude and direction in space.

A vector quantity can be represented pictorially as a directed straight-line segment or 'arrow': the segment lies in the direction of the vector, and the arrow head indicates which way movement is going along this line. The length of the segment represents the magnitude of the vector. Figure 2.63 illustrates the idea. A person draws a blue, wiggly line on a piece of paper; at any moment of time, the pen has a particular velocity. The figure shows the location of the pen along its path at three instants of time (1, 2, and 3); the velocity of the pen-point at each instant is represented by an arrow (directed line segment) that points in the direction of movement at that instant. The line segment representing the velocity vector touches the

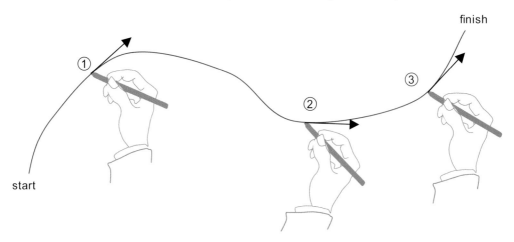

Figure 2.63: *Drawing a curved line. The velocity vector (arrow) is shown at three different times.*

pen's path at a single point (the point where the pen-point is at that instant) but does not intersect the pen's path. A line that touches a curve in this way is said to be *tangent* to the curve and is called a *tangent line*. For this reason, the velocity of the working point is called the **tangential velocity**, and the magnitude is called the **tangential speed**. The tangential speed is just the speed with which the path is being traversed: if you were driving along a path in a vehicle, then the speedometer would display the tangential speed.

In the research literature, it is common to describe movement of a working point in terms of the tangential speed together with a sign (plus or minus), to indicate whether the direction of motion is towards the finish point (positive) or back towards the starting point (negative). There is no special name for this quantity, but it is sometimes referred to as the *tangential velocity*, though it contains no information about the direction of the velocity vector.

2.4.14 Translational acceleration is a vector

When travelling in one dimension, the translational acceleration is a vector, but its vector character can be captured by sign: a positive acceleration is an increase in speed in one direction along the line; a negative acceleration is an increase in speed in the other direction (or a decrease in speed in the first direction). This case is relatively easy to understand. In two or three dimensions, things become a little more complicated. A discussion of the 2-D case will be sufficient for later chapters.

Figure 2.64 shows three examples in which a ball is accelerating in different ways. In panel A, we have a situation that is essentially one-dimensional, since motion is along a straight line (dashed). The ball is shown at three different moments, and its speed is increasing, since the length of the velocity vector is getting longer as the motion proceeds from the top of the figure to the bottom. The direction of the vector is unchanging. In this case, the acceleration is the rate at which speed is increasing, and it is increasing along the path of motion, so the acceleration vector points in the same direction as the velocity vector.

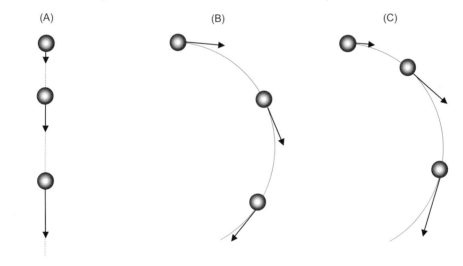

Figure 2.64: *Translational acceleration (arrows represent velocity vectors).*

In panel B of Figure 2.64, motion is in a circle, and the velocity vector at an instant of time is tangent to the circle (tangential velocity). The length of the velocity vector does not change as motion proceeds, but the direction of the vector does change. In this case, the acceleration is the rate at which the direction of the velocity vector is changing: even though the speed is unchanging, there is acceleration. If you drive a car at constant speed around in a circle, the speedometer has the same reading all the way around, but you are nevertheless accelerating because your velocity is changing. Thus, contrary to the everyday usage of the term acceleration, it is possible to be accelerating but not to be speeding up or slowing down. In Figure 2.64(B), the direction of the acceleration is towards the center of the circle; it is called the **centripetal acceleration** (which means 'center-seeking' acceleration).

In panel C of Figure 2.64, motion is in a circle, but it differs from panel B in that the length of the velocity vector is increasing, so both the direction and magnitude of the velocity vector are changing. If you were driving a car around the circle in this fashion, the speedometer would show the speed increasing as you drove. In this case, the acceleration can be considered to have two components. One component is the centripetal acceleration, and it points towards the center of the circle. The other component is the acceleration along the path. If the speed is increasing, this acceleration component points in the same direction as the (tangential) velocity vector; if the speed is decreasing, it points in the opposite direction. Since this vector is, like the velocity vector, tangential to the path, it is called the **tangential acceleration**.

2.4.15 Mechanical force is the cause of movement

Mechanical forces can be intuitively understood as pushes or pulls. When you push or pull on something that is stationary, it will start to move unless it is being held in place. In everyday life, objects do not move unless there is a force acting that causes them to move. So if you push on something that is resting on flat ground, it will move over the ground surface; if you stop pushing, it will eventually stop moving. It stops because there are frictional forces that stop it. If you pushed on an object to start it moving and then stopped pushing, it would continue moving for ever if there were no forces acting on it. This fact is a fundamental mechanical law discovered by Isaac Newton, and can be stated as follows:

> **NEWTON'S FIRST LAW OF MOTION:** an object on which no external forces act will remain at rest (stationary) or continue to move at constant velocity.

For translational motion, constant velocity means in a straight line (constant direction) at an unchanging speed. For rotational motion, it means rotation in the same plane in the same direction (constant direction of the angular velocity vector) at an unchanging angular speed.

If an external force does act on an object, it will either start moving (if it was initially at rest) or its velocity will change (if it was initially moving). Thus, the effect of a force is to change the state of motion of an object. A changing state of motion occurs when the object's velocity is not constant, in other words, when the object is accelerating: the effect of a force is to produce acceleration. This forms the basis of another fundamental mechanical law discovered by Newton; a statement of this law for *translational* motion is as follows:

> **NEWTON'S SECOND LAW OF MOTION:** if there is a resultant force acting on an object, then the object will accelerate in the direction of the force. The magnitude of the acceleration will be proportional to the magnitude of the force.

The term 'resultant force' is used because if there are several forces acting, they may sum to zero, in which case there is no resultant force (the result of the sum) and consequently no acceleration. The same basic law applies to rotational motion, but requires the concept of torque, defined in the next section. Newton's second law is the key to understanding how force and movement are related, because it tells us how changes in a thing's state of motion are related to the impressed forces.

Newton's second law is familiar to many people when written as an equation, F = ma. This equation applies to translational motion along one dimension: F stands for the value of the resultant force acting on the object, a is the value of the object's acceleration, and m is the mass of the object. Note that if the units of mass are kilograms (kg) and the units of acceleration are meters/second/second (m/s^2), then the units of force are kg × m/s^2 (kg m/s^2) and called Newtons in honour of Isaac Newton (1 Newton = 1 kg m/s^2).

In two or three dimensions, the vector nature of force must be taken into account. A force has strength (magnitude) and also acts in a particular direction, so like a velocity it is represented in pictures as a directed line segment. We will encounter examples in the next section.

2.4.16 Skeletal muscles exert torques about joints

As described in section 2.3, skeletal muscles generate contractile force when activated. In order for muscle force to cause movement about a joint, it is necessary that it attaches to two different bones on either side of the joint. The brachialis muscle, for example, attaches to the humerus (its origin) and the ulna (its insertion), and so crosses the humeroulnar joint of the elbow. When brachialis contracts, it tends to flex the elbow joint.

When a force causes a rotational movement, it is said to produce a **torque** about the axis of rotation. Torque can be conceived of as *turning force*, since it plays the same role in rotational motion that force plays in translational motion. In translational motion, force changes velocity (causes acceleration); in rotational motion, torque changes angular velocity (causes angular acceleration). Thus, Newton's second law holds for rotational motion:

> **NEWTON'S SECOND LAW OF MOTION (ROTATIONAL):** if there is a resultant torque acting on an object about some axis of rotation, then there will be an angular acceleration of the object in the direction of the torque. The magnitude of the angular acceleration will be proportional to the magnitude of the torque.

The constant of proportionality is called the **moment of inertia**, which is the rotational version of mass. Mass is a measure of how difficult it is to get something moving – something with a large mass is hard to get moving. Moment of inertia is a measure of how difficult it is to get something rotating – something with a large moment of inertia is hard to get spinning. The torque produced by a force depends on where that force is applied, not just on its magnitude and direction. This is obvious if you think of pushing on a door: if you push with the same force (strength and direction) at different locations, the tendency of the door to rotate (open or close) will be different. If you push on the door very close to the hinge, it is difficult to move; if you push with the same force close to the handle (which is far from the hinge), it is easier to move. The magnitude of the torque produced by a force about an axis of rotation is equal to the magnitude of the force multiplied by the shortest distance between the axis and the line along which the force acts. The shortest distance is called the **moment arm**. Thus, if the force has magnitude F Newtons and the moment arm is d meters, the torque has magnitude F × d (units: Newton meters). A greater torque can be produced either by applying a greater force in the same place, or by applying the same force further from the axis of rotation.

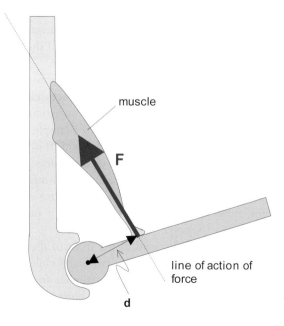

Figure 2.65: *Muscle force acts at a distance (d) from the axis of rotation.*

Figure 2.65 shows a schematic of a hinge joint actuated by a single muscle that pulls on two rigid segments (bones). The muscle is shown pulling on the green segment with a force, F (thick blue arrow), that has a line of action lying in the plane of the page (shown as a dashed line). The shortest distance from the line of action to the joint's axis of rotation is the distance labeled d (the moment arm). Thus, the magnitude of the torque exerted by the muscle about the axis of rotation of the joint is F × d. Due to the fact that the muscle insertion point is fixed on the bone, the value of the moment arm depends upon the joint angle (d is smaller when the joint is more extended).

2.4.17 Muscles can be classified on the basis of their mechanical action

The type of movement produced as a direct result of a muscle generating contractile force is called a **mechanical action** of that muscle or, more simply, a **muscle action**.

> **MECHANICAL ACTION OF A MUSCLE (MUSCLE ACTION):** the type of joint rotation that results from the torque produced about the joint's axis of rotation by the contractile force developed by the muscle.

For example, contraction of brachialis produces torque about the elbow that causes flexion of the joint. Thus elbow flexion is a mechanical action of brachialis. For this reason, brachialis is classed as an **elbow flexor** muscle. It is not the only elbow flexor; both *biceps brachii* and *brachioradialis* are elbow flexors. *Triceps brachii* is an elbow extensor, and the first palmar interosseous is an index finger adductor. In some cases, the name of the muscle describes its mechanical action. Examples include *flexor pollicus longus*, which is a thumb flexor (*pollex* is the Latin for thumb), and *pronator teres*, which pronates the forearm.

Although classification and naming of muscles based on their mechanical action seems sensible, it is complicated by the fact that many muscles have more than one mechanical action, as described in the next subsection. In addition, the mechanical actions of some muscles can change with the position of a joint.

2.4.18 Some muscles cross one joint, others cross two or more joints

Brachialis is a muscle that crosses one joint (the elbow) – its origin lies on one of the bones jointed at the elbow (the humerus), and it inserts on another of the jointed bones (the ulna). A muscle that crosses one joint is called a **uniarticular muscle**.

Some uniarticular muscles generate force that leads to movement in one degree-of-freedom only. The brachialis is such a muscle – it produces elbow flexion only, and so can be functionally described as an elbow flexor. Other uniarticular muscles may produce movement along two or three degrees-of-freedom. An example is *brachioradialis*, a uniarticular muscle that, like brachialis, crosses the elbow joint. It originates on the lower half of the humerus and inserts on the styloid process of the radius, as shown in Figure 2.66. Contraction of brachioradialis produces elbow flexion as you might expect, but it can also produce pronation or supination, depending upon the posture of the arm. Thus brachioradialis is, like brachialis, functionally an elbow flexor, but it has a pronation-supination action as well.

The largest muscle crossing the elbow joint at the front of the arm is the *biceps brachii* (usually just called *biceps*). This muscle consists of two parts called 'heads': the word *biceps* comes from the Latin for 'two heads'. The muscle originates in two places on the scapula (shoulder blade) as if it were two separate muscles, but both parts connect at the distal end to the same tendon, which attaches to the radius. Thus, the biceps muscle crosses two joints, the shoulder and the elbow joints. A muscle that crosses two joints is called a **biarticular muscle**. Biarticular muscles are common in the human body.

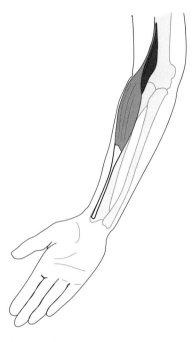

Figure 2.66: *The brachioradialis muscle.*

Contraction of the biceps muscle produces torque about both the elbow and shoulder joints and acts to flex both joints. The torque about the shoulder joint is relatively small compared with the torque produced about the humeroulnar articulation at the elbow, so the biceps is usually thought of as an elbow flexor. However, contraction of biceps can also produce shoulder flexion and supination of the forearm (due to the way it inserts onto the radius). Thus, biceps can produce elbow flexion, shoulder flexion and supination of the forearm. A muscle that has several mechanical actions is called a **multifunctional muscle**.

Muscles that cross three joints are called **triarticular**, and those that cross more than three are called **multiarticular**. Examples of multiarticular muscles are the finger flexors: the muscle fibers are located in the forearm, and long tendons insert on the distal phalanges of the fingers and so cross several joints. When a finger flexor muscle contracts, it will typically cause all the joints of the finger to flex.

2.4.19 Muscles can act together or in opposition to one another

There are three muscles that cross the front of the elbow: brachialis, brachioradialis and biceps brachii. These three muscles form a group that can produce torque about the axis of rotation of the humeroulnar joint in the elbow flexion direction. They form a group of elbow flexors, and performance of an elbow flexion movement may involve a contribution from all three.

Muscles that act to produce torque about the same axis of rotation in the same direction are called **mechanical synergists**; they have the same mechanical action:

> **MECHANICAL SYNERGISTS:** two different muscles are mechanical synergists if their contraction produces torque about the same axis of rotation of a joint in the same direction (clockwise or counterclockwise). The muscles are synergists with respect to this axis of rotation, but not necessarily any others.

Note that biceps brachii and brachialis are mechanical synergists only with respect to elbow flexion torque: biceps brachii also produces supination torque and shoulder flexion torque, but brachialis produces neither, and so does not act synergistically with biceps with respect to shoulder flexion or supination of the forearm.

Muscles that produce opposing torques about the same axis of rotation are said to have an **antagonistic relationship** or to be **antagonists**:

> **ANTAGONISTIC RELATIONSHIP:** two different muscles have an antagonistic relationship if their contraction produces torque about the same axis of rotation but in opposite directions: one clockwise, the other counterclockwise. The muscles are antagonists with respect to this axis of rotation, but not necessarily with respect to any others.

Figure 2.67 shows an antagonistic pair of muscles that cross the elbow joint: brachialis and triceps brachii. Both muscles produce torque about the axis of rotation of the humeroulnar joint: contraction of brachialis produces flexion torque; contraction of triceps produces extension torque. These torques are in opposite directions and oppose one another, so the two muscles are antagonists. When one direction of movement is being considered for an antagonistic pair of muscles, then the muscle with a mechanical action in that direction is called the **agonist** for that movement and the other muscle is called the **antagonist**. For movement in the flexion direction at the humeroulnar joint, brachialis is an agonist, and triceps brachii an antagonist. For movement in the extension direction, triceps is an agonist and brachialis an antagonist.

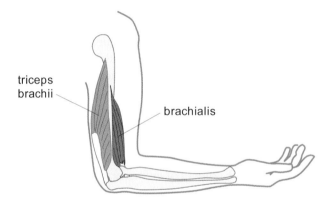

Figure 2.67: *Triceps brachii and brachialis are antagonists.*

The antagonistic relationships of multifunctional muscles can be quite complicated. Biceps, for example, produce torque about the glenohumeral (shoulder) joint, the humeroulnar joint of the elbow, and the radioulnar joint of the elbow. It has an antagonistic relationship with triceps brachii at the humeroulnar joint and at the glenohumeral joint. At the radioulnar joint, biceps has an antagonistic relationship with a muscle called pronator teres, which exerts torque in the pronation direction opposing the supination torque produced by biceps (triceps does not produce torque about this joint).

2.4.20 Simultaneous contraction of antagonistic muscles is called co-contraction

If a pair of muscles that have an antagonistic relationship about the axis of rotation of a joint contract simultaneously, then the torque produced by one will oppose the torque produced by the other. This is called **co-contraction**. The resultant muscle torque is the sum of the torques of the two muscles, and determines the direction in which a segment will move about the joint.

As a simple example, imagine the humeroulnar joint being actuated by just two antagonistic muscles, triceps and biceps. If the biceps torque is greater in magnitude than the triceps torque, there will be a resultant flexion torque, and the joint will flex. In this case we would say that the biceps is the agonist (since it is the flexor), and triceps is the antagonist. If the torques produced by the two opposing muscles are equal in magnitude, then the resultant torque is zero (biceps torque + triceps torque = 0) and there will be no movement.

It is easy to co-contract the flexors and extensors at the elbow joint so that the resultant torque is zero. When a bodybuilder holds the arm in a flexed posture to show off the biceps, they are co-contracting the elbow flexors and extensors in this way: the arm is held in a stationary posture and so there is no resultant torque, but the muscles are highly contracted and generating a lot of force.

Imagine trying to maintain a particular elbow joint angle while someone else tries to flex your arm or extend it. In order to prevent the arm from changing position when the other person pushes or pulls on it, the natural thing to do is to co-contract the flexors and extensors: the flexors resist extension of the joint and the extensors resist flexion, making it difficult for the other person to change your elbow joint angle. The result of co-contraction is to stiffen the elbow joint. Just like a stiff spring strongly resists any change in its length, a stiff joint strongly resists any change in its position. We will return to joint stiffness and how it is controlled in Chapter 6.

References & Notes

[1] Glial cells may also play some role in nervous system functions usually attributed only to neurons.

[2] The type of unipolar neuron shown here has a neurite with two distinct branches. This type is often referred to as a *pseudounipolar* neuron.

[3] Not all neurons possess an axon.

[4] Mammalian motoneurons are an exception; they release only acetylcholine at the neuromuscular synapse, but release acetylcholine and glutamate at their central synapses (Nishamaru *et al.*, 2005).

[5] Synapses have been found in some organisms that have a dual action and are capable of producing either excitatory or inhibitory effects on the postsynaptic neuron, depending on the circumstances. Some examples of neurons that have excitatory effects on some of the neurons they are connected to and inhibitory effects on others have also been discovered. See Kandel *et al.* (2000) for a textbook account.

[6] Squire *et al.* (2008); Kandel *et al.* (2000).

[7] The firing threshold is not a fixed property of a neuron, and it does not appear to be associated with a specific physical mechanism (see Izhikevich, 2007).

[8] Some neurons generate action potentials in response to the termination of inhibitory synaptic input, a phenomenon known as *rebound spiking*.

[9] Most of the exceptions to the all-or-nothing law do not appear to carry information. However, some may carry information, such as the complex spikes generated by the Purkinje cells of the cerebellum.

[10] The contribution of an individual postsynaptic potential to the depolarization at the cell body depends, in part, on how far it had to travel to get there. There is some evidence that the strength of synapses further from the cell body is greater than that of those nearer to it, so the postsynaptic potentials at the more distant synapses are larger. This compensates to some extent for the greater distance to be travelled; see Carpenter (2003).

[11] Stuart *et al.* (1997).

[12] A single action potential is actually distributed over an extended length of axon that may include several nodes of Ranvier. The following example is given in Chapter 5 of Squire *et al.* (2008): in an axon that conducts spikes of 1 millisecond duration at a speed of 120 m/s, the spike itself is spread out over a length of about 120 mm, which contains over 100 nodes.

[13] This is as much as we will need to know in this book. There are some subtleties that we have not discussed. Carpenter (2003) presents an accessible discussion.

[14] Attwell, Laughlin (2001).

[15] It is also possible to imagine that a neuron makes synaptic connections with itself, but such connectivity does not appear to be present in mammalian nervous systems.

[16] Pascual-Leone, Walsh, Rothwell (2000); Zieman (2010).

[17] This example is due to R.L. Gregory.

[18] For a tutorial review see Purves *et al.* (2008). More detail is provided by Nidermeyer and Lopes da Silva (2005).

[19] For overview see Nunez (2002).

[20] The detectors used today are superconducting quantum interference devices (SQUIDs); see Clarke (1994).

[21] For non-mathematical introductions see Hashemi, Bradley, Lisanti (2010) and Ward (2010). Ashby (2011) provides an overview of fMRI data and methods of analysis.

[22] There is another MRI functional imaging technique called diffusion tensor imaging that is not described here (see Mori 2007).

[23] The voxel size is dependent on the strength of the magnetic field: stronger fields permit smaller-sized voxels.

[24] More precisely, the ratio of oxygenated hemoglobin to deoxygenated hemoglobin in the blood.

[25] Lobel *et al.* (2001).

[26] Penfield, Boldrey (1937).

[27] Asanuma (1981).

[28] Penfield, Rasmussen (1950).

[29] Schieber (2001).

[30] Rathelot, Strick (2006).

[31] Schieber (2001).

[32] See Schieber (2001).

[33] Graziano (2006, 2010).

[34] Graziano (2010).

[35] Graziano, Aflalo (2007).

[36] The elements are nuclei, not ganglia.

[37] For a review of the roles of the basal ganglia in movement control, see Turner and Desmurget (2010).

[38] The fact that the PPN is not included as one of the basal ganglia nuclei is somewhat arbitrary (Mena-Segovia, Bolam, Magill, 2004).

[39] Postuma, Lang (2003).

[40] For a review of descending motor tracts, see Lemon (2008).

[41] Evidence in humans is indirect (Pierrot-Deseilligny, Burke, 2005).

[42] Figure 2.38 is based on figures that appear in Chapter 10 of Pierrot-Deseilligny, Burke (2005).

[43] See Pierrot-Deseilligny, Burke (2005).

[44] In other mammals, this is not necessarily the case: short muscle fibers are often arranged in series to form a long muscle (Paul, 2001).

[45] Harris *et al.* (2005).

[46] Enoka (2008); Kandel *et al.* (2000).

[47] Burke *et al.* (1973).

[48] See Enoka (2008).

[49] See Enoka (2008).

[50] Henneman (1979).

[51] See Enoka (2008).

[52] Monster, Chan (1977).

[53] E.g., Basmajian, DeLuca (1985); Loeb, Gans (1986).

[54] This intuitive definition applies in one dimension. In three dimensions, stiffness is not a single number but a table of numbers with three rows and three columns (the stiffness tensor).

[55] See Enoka (2008).

[56] E.g., Baratta *et al.* (1993).

[57] For experimental details and example data, see Rack, Westbury (1969).

[58] Assuming that the two forces are independent.

[59] See Enoka (2008).

[60] E.g., Enoka (2008); Levangie, Norkin (2001).

[61] Jones, Lederman (2006).

[62] Angular velocity is a vector quantity. Its magnitude is the angular speed, and its direction is the orientation of the axis of rotation.

[63] E.g., Gottlieb, Corcos, Agarwal (1989a).

[64] The plots shown in the figure are characteristic of movements that do not require accuracy (see Chapter 12).

[65] Latash (2008a).

CHAPTER 3

Sensorimotor Foundations

3.1 General Principles

3.1.1 Introduction

All sensory processes are based on specialized elements that absorb energy from their surroundings and produce an output of some kind in response. These elements are called **sensory receptors**; they are classified into different kinds according to the type of energy to which they primarily respond in natural conditions. For instance, some receptors respond to light energy and do not respond to any other type of energy during their normal operation: these light-sensitive receptors are called **photoreceptors**.

Energy that can evoke a response from a sensory receptor is said to **stimulate** the receptor. It is the stimulation of sensory receptors that provides an animal with the information needed for goal-directed motor activity. However, the stimulation of individual receptors provides, in itself, very little useful information. Light stimulating a photoreceptor only carries the information that there is light in the surroundings, and a change in the strength of the stimulation only carries the information that something happened to cause the change, not what that thing was. Most useful information is present in the variations in the composition and strength of the stimulating energy, from place to place and moment to moment. These variations form spatial and temporal patterns, and large numbers of receptors are needed to obtain information from these patterns. For example, light energy varies in both intensity and wavelength composition from place to place and from moment to moment. The human eye projects this pattern as an image onto an array of millions of photoreceptors. In much the same way, a digital camera projects an image onto an array of millions of photosensitive elements: an eight-megapixel camera has eight million such elements. This is where the resemblance between an eye and a camera ends. The electronic circuitry that processes the responses of the individual photosensitive elements in a digital camera is not concerned with obtaining information from images. A digital camera is merely a device that converts patterned energy from one form (light) to another (electrical signals) and back again, so that the images can be viewed on a screen. In contrast, the neural circuitry that processes the responses of photoreceptors is concerned with obtaining information about the environment – there is no screen and there is no viewer. Obtaining information from sensory stimulation is an essential part of what is called **sensory perception**.

In this first part of the chapter, we will discuss general characteristics of sensory receptors and perceptual processes. The specifics of the sensory systems important in human motor behavior are discussed in subsequent parts.

3.1.2 Sensory receptors respond to stimulation

Different types of sensory receptor are primarily responsive to different kinds of energy. Those found in the human body respond to four basic kinds: light energy, mechanical energy, chemical energy, and thermal energy[1]. Different names are given to these different types of receptor:

(1) **Photoreceptor:** primarily responsive to light.
(2) **Mechanoreceptor:** primarily responsive to mechanical energy (e.g., vestibular and touch receptors).
(3) **Chemoreceptor:** primarily responsive to certain chemical substances (e.g., taste and smell receptors).
(4) **Thermoreceptor:** primarily responsive to thermal energy.

Only pain receptors (**nociceptors**) do not fit clearly into one of these categories, as many of them respond in a similar way to more than one type of energy. Each of the four basic types of receptor comes in a number of different varieties, defined by the characteristics of the stimulation to which they are particularly sensitive. For example, there are several different types of mechanoreceptor in the skin that respond to different characteristics of the stimulation produced when the skin comes in contact with objects in the environment (see section 3.3). The human eye has not one but four different kinds of photoreceptor[2].

3.1.3 Biological sensory receptors can be classified based on the origin of the stimulation to which they primarily respond

Sensory receptors are located in different places in the body. Photoreceptors are located within the eyes; auditory mechanoreceptors are located within the inner ear, while other mechanoreceptors are located in the skin, the muscles, tendons, joints and deep tissues; chemoreceptors and thermoreceptors are located at various places throughout the superficial and deep tissues of the body.

The location of a sensory receptor strongly influences the kind of stimulation that it is normally exposed to. For example, photoreceptors are located where they are normally only stimulated by light; auditory mechanoreceptors are normally only stimulated by sound; mechanoreceptors in the arterial walls are normally only stimulated by changes in blood pressure. These examples illustrate the fact that some receptors are stimulated by energy that enters from outside the animal (such as light and sound), while others are stimulated by energy that exists within the bodily tissues. This led C.S. Sherrington to propose a threefold classification of sensory receptors according to the origin of the stimuli to which they primarily respond:

(1) **Exteroceptors:** respond to mechanical, chemical, thermal or electromagnetic contact with the external environment. Examples include mechanoreceptors in the skin, photoreceptors and olfactory chemoreceptors.

(2) **Interoceptors:** respond to stimulation produced by physiological processes within the body. They include thermoreceptors within deep tissues that respond to the internal temperature of the body, mechanoreceptors in arterial walls, mechanoreceptors in the gut wall and a variety of internal chemoreceptors.

(3) **Proprioceptors:** respond to mechanical stimulation associated with the angular position of joints, movements of joints, the orientation of body segments, tensions in ligaments, tendons and other connective tissues, muscle length and changes in muscle length.

Not all sensory receptors fall exclusively into a single category; there are some that fit into two (none fit into all three). For example, mechanoreceptors in the skin respond when the skin is deformed by contact with external objects; they can therefore be classified as exteroceptors. However, those located in the skin around joints also respond when the skin is deformed (stretched or compressed) due to movement about the joint[3], so they can also be classified as proprioceptors.

3.1.4 Biological sensory receptors are specialized cellular structures that produce a receptor potential in response to stimulation

Biological sensory receptors are structures formed from specialized cells or cellular components, sometimes in conjunction with other tissue in which they are encased or encapsulated. The specialized cells from which sensory receptors are formed are called **receptor cells**. When stimulated, the membrane potential in the sensitive region of a receptor cell changes. This response is called a **receptor potential**. The mechanisms responsible for the production of a receptor potential differ in different types of receptor – the mechanisms of light transduction in photoreceptors is different from the mechanism of chemical transduction in olfactory (smell) receptors – but, in all cases, stimulation is transduced into a receptor potential. Receptor potentials are subsequently converted into action potentials in afferent axons that transmit information from the receptors to the central nervous system (see next section).

Examples of different sensory receptors found in the human body are shown in Figure 3.1. Panel A shows a receptor called a *pacinian corpuscle*, a kind of mechanoreceptor involved in touch. It is formed from an axon terminal of a neuron (the sensory ending) encased in a laminated capsule. Receptor potentials are evoked in the sensory ending when the capsule is squeezed (see section 3.3). Panel B shows a gustatory (taste) receptor cell, a type of chemoreceptor found in the taste buds of the tongue. The receptive structures of these cells are terminal cellular processes (microvilli) that are able to come into contact with chemical substances. These microvilli are examples of **sensory endings**. Panel C shows a type I vestibular receptor cell, a kind of mechanoreceptor found in the inner ear. Deflection of the sensory hairs evokes a receptor potential (see section 3.2). Panel D shows two kinds of photoreceptor (a cone and a rod). These receptors possess a light-sensitive part at one end called the *outer segment*, which contains chemical substances that absorb light energy.

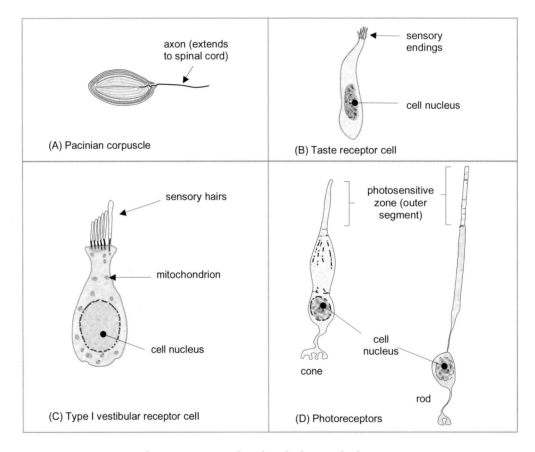

Figure 3.1: *Four types of sensory receptor found in the human body.*

3.1.5 Receptor potentials are converted into action potentials and transmitted to central nervous system

The second stage in the processing of sensory signals is the conversion of receptor potentials into action potentials. Some sensory receptor cells generate action potentials in response to receptor potentials evoked in their sensory endings. These include the sensory neurons that innervate the skin, muscles, tendons and joints – **somatosensory neurons**. The cell bodies of these (pseudo)unipolar neurons are located in dorsal root ganglia and cranial ganglia. The receptor potential evoked in the sensory endings initiates action potentials at a location close to the endings called the **spike initiation zone**. The impulses propagate along the axon, which projects into the central nervous system (see section 3.3). Photoreceptor cells are neurons that do not generate action potentials. Receptor potentials evoked by absorption of light energy propagate passively to the cells' neurites, which make synaptic connections with other neurons in the retina (see Chapter 4).

Taste receptor cells and vestibular receptor cells are not neurons (they are specialized epithelial cells); they do not generate action potentials and do not have dendrites or axons. However, they do make synaptic connections with afferent neurons (as shown in Figure 3.2), and they release neurotransmitter at these synapses. The vestibular receptor cell in Figure 3.2 is surrounded by a dendritic terminal that forms a kind of shell called a *nerve calyx* (which means 'cup'). Receptor potentials evoked by deflection of the sensory hairs propagate passively along the cell membrane to the synaptic sites. If the receptor potential is a depolarization, there is an increase in the release of neurotransmitter into the synaptic cleft. If the receptor potential is hyperpolarizing, the release of neurotransmitter is reduced. Neurotransmitter released by the receptor cell can initiate action potentials in the afferent axon, and these propagate along the axon to the central nervous system.

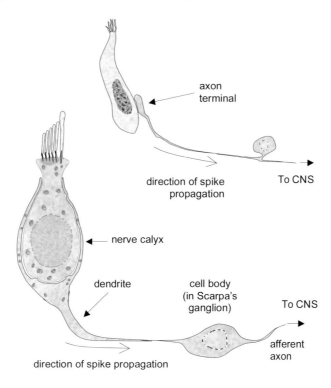

Figure 3.2: *Taste (top) and vestibular (bottom) receptor cells connect to afferent neurons.*

3.1.6 Receptor potentials are greater and afferent firing rates higher when the stimulation is stronger

A basic characteristic of sensory receptors is that the more strongly they are stimulated, the greater the receptor potential. Figure 3.3 shows the relationship between the amplitude of the stimulation and the amplitude of the receptor potential for a vertebrate muscle stretch receptor (more details about muscle stretch receptors is given in section 3.3). As the figure shows, stronger stimulation (greater stretch) causes a larger receptor potential.

If the receptor potential in a stretch receptor is sufficiently large it will cause the initiation of action potentials in the spike initiation zone of the axon. The greater the receptor potential, the more frequently spikes will be initiated, and so the firing rate of the axon will be greater. Figure 3.4 shows the relationship between stimulation strength and firing rate in the afferent axon for a type of mechanoreceptor found in the skin of a monkey's hand. This receptor is stimulated when a small probe is pressed against the skin to produce a sustained indentation (it is slow adapting; see next section). Stimulation strength is measured as the depth of indentation (in millimeters). Stronger stimulation produces a greater firing rate in the afferent axon. For the receptor type shown, the relationship is linear. The form of the relationship tends to be slightly different for different types of receptor: in some types it has a logarithmic form, similar to that shown in Figure 3.3.

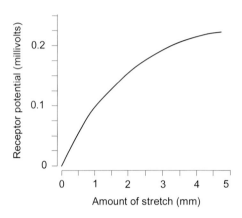

Figure 3.3: *Receptor potential as a function of stimulus strength (stretch). Based on data reported by Katz (1950).*

A consistent relationship between stimulation strength and afferent firing rate like that shown in Figure 3.4 means that firing rate carries information about the strength of receptor stimulation. This fact is usually expressed by saying that the afferent firing rate **encodes** the strength of the stimulation. The way in which information is coded in the firing rate is called a **rate code**.

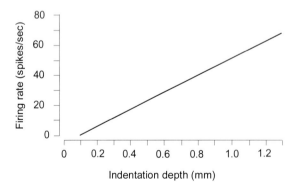

Figure 3.4: *Firing rate of a cutaneous mechanoreceptor afferent as a function of stimulus strength. Based on data presented by Mountcastle, Talbot and Kornhuber (1966).*

3.1.7 The response of a sensory neuron declines when the level of stimulation does not change

Receptor potentials and the firing rates of sensory neurons tend to decline over time if the strength of the stimulation that evokes the response remains constant. Such declines are examples of a phenomenon called **sensory adaptation**. If the decline is slow, the sensory receptor is called a **slow adapting receptor**. If the decline is fast, it is called a **fast adapting receptor**.

The left side of Figure 3.5 shows an idealized representation of the response to sustained pressure of a fast adapting mechanoreceptor found in the skin (a **cutaneous mechanoreceptor**) and the associated afferent axon. The right side of the figure shows the idealized response of a slow adapting cutaneous mechanoreceptor. The fast adapting receptor generates a response (receptor potential) when the stimulation is initially applied (stimulation onset), but this response quickly dies away once the stimulation reaches its sustained level. When the stimulation is removed (offset), the receptor generates another response that quickly dies away. The slow adapting receptor starts to respond at the onset of stimulation, but the response declines very slowly and is maintained throughout the period during which the stimulation is present. The firing rates of the associated afferent axon closely follow the receptor potential.

In principle, the speed with which a receptor response declines can take any value from very fast to so slow that there seems to be no decline at all. However, the rates of decline observed in sensory receptors can be classified into two groups – the fast and slow adapting receptors. Each group cover a range of different rates.

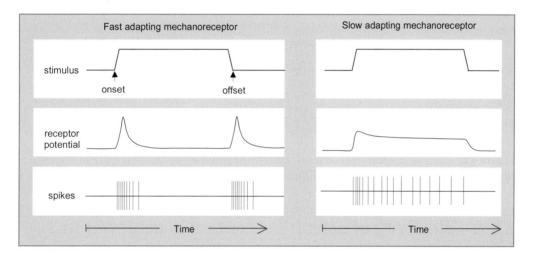

Figure 3.5: *Response of fast (left) and slow (right) adapting sensory receptors (illustrative). Top: stimulus applied to the receptor. Middle: receptor potential recorded from the receptor. Bottom: firing rate of the associated afferent axon.*

Figure 3.5 indicates that the slow adapting mechanoreceptor can provide information about the strength of sustained stimulation. The firing rate of the associated afferent axon is sustained while the stimulation is present and is greater when the stimulus is stronger (e.g., Figure 3.4). In contrast, the fast adapting mechanoreceptor only responds when the stimulus comes on or goes off: as there is no response while the stimulus is sustained, so no information is conveyed about the strength of the stimulation.

The fast adapting mechanoreceptor in the figure does not respond to the strength of the stimulation per se, but to the rate at which the stimulus strength is changing. The stimulus strength changes quickly when it comes on and goes off, but does not change during the period in between. A fast adapting receptor that responds to the rate of change of stimulus strength functions as a speed sensor. An example of how this works is shown in Figure 3.6. The figure shows the firing pattern in the afferent axon associated with a fast adapting cutaneous mechanoreceptor in response to pressure stimulation applied at three different, constant speeds (measured in millimeters of skin indentation per second, mm/s). In each case, the slope of the stimulation profile corresponds to the speed of skin indentation. The figure indicates that the afferent firing rate depends on the speed at which the indentation occurs, not on the amount of indentation (which reaches the same constant level in each case). Thus, we can say that the stimulation to which this receptor is sensitive is the speed of indentation, not indentation per se[4].

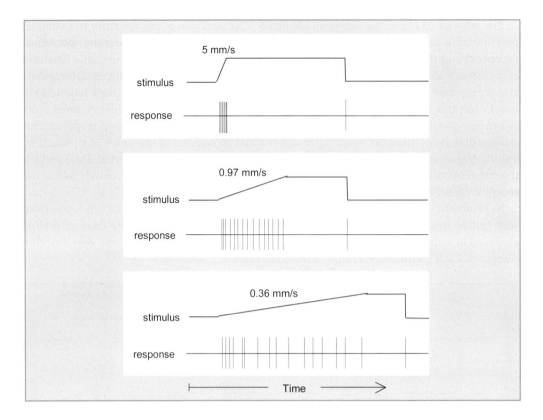

Figure 3.6: *Firing in afferent axon of a fast adapting cutaneous mechanoreceptor in response to different rates of skin indendation (stimulus). Based on data presented in Talbot* et al. *(1968).*

3.1.8 Selectivity of sensory receptors is achieved in two ways

Sensory receptors are selective; they respond to some things and not others. This is essential if a receptor is to contribute useful information. Imagine you wanted to know how fast you are going when driving a motor vehicle. To do this, you need a system that measures the speed of the vehicle and presents you with the result. In most vehicles, the system comprises a speed measuring device (a tachometer) and a dashboard display. Ideally, you want the tachometer response to depend only on vehicle speed; you don't want it to respond to anything else, such as the temperature or the amount of light falling on it. In short, a tachometer must be selective for speed; how can this be achieved? There are two basic methods:

(1) **Structure:** make a sensor in such a way that it responds selectively to the required type of stimulation.

(2) **Shielding** or **placement:** prevent the sensor from responding to unwanted types of stimulation, either by shielding it or placing it in a location where it will not be affected by them.

The sensory systems of humans and other animals employ both methods. Photoreceptors, mechanoreceptors, chemoreceptors, and thermoreceptors have a physiology that makes them selective for particular types of stimulation, but none are completely selective. For example, all biological receptors will respond to sufficiently strong electrical stimulation, and photoreceptors also respond to mechanical stimulation. You can easily demonstrate the latter by closing your eyes and pressing gently on the eyelid with a finger tip. The best place to press is just next to the nose with your eyes 'looking' straight ahead. The pressure stimulates photoreceptors and as a result you can see a dim spot in the periphery of your vision opposite to where you press.

In natural conditions, it is highly unlikely that a receptor response would be evoked by anything other than the specific type of stimulation for which it is selective. This means that responses of different types of receptors carry information about stimulation type, and so receptor type serves as a kind of code for the type of stimulation. This kind of code is called a **labeled line code**: the axon or pathway along which signals from a receptor type are transmitted is the 'line', and it is 'labeled' in the sense that the nervous system 'knows' from which receptor type the line derives. As a result, the nervous system treats the responses of particular receptors as if they arose from particular types of stimulation (but see section 3.1.18 for exceptions). This is demonstrated by the fact that a person will have a particular type of sensory experience when a certain type of receptor is stimulated, regardless of the nature of the stimulation involved. For example, if a group of photoreceptors in a small region of the retina is briefly stimulated, a person will experience a flash of light coming from a direction that depends on the retinal location stimulated. The flash will be experienced regardless of the type of stimulation: the nervous system always treats responses from photoreceptors as if they were evoked by light stimulation.

3.1.9 Invidual receptor responses provide information about the strength, timing, type and location of stimulation

From what was said in the last two sections, we can infer that receptor responses can provide information about the strength and duration of stimulation, the type of stimulation, and where the stimulation was received. Thus, responses of individual sensory receptors may carry four different kinds of information about their stimulation:

(1)   **Information about stimulus STRENGTH.** The size of the receptor potential (and consequently the firing rate in the afferent axon) carries information about the strength of the stimulation applied to the receptor.

(2)   **Information about the TIMING of stimulation.** The length of time for which the receptor responds carries information about the length of time for which stimulation is present. The time of response onset and offset carries information about when stimulation begins and ends.

(3)   **Information about stimulus TYPE.** By virtue of its selectivity for a particular type of stimulation, when a receptor responds, its response carries the information that that type of stimulation is present.

(4)   **Information about stimulus LOCATION.** A particular receptor is located at a particular place and responds to stimulation applied at that location. Thus, if a receptor responds, stimulation must exist at its location.

Information about stimulation is not useful in itself; it is useful because it can tell us something about what is present in the environment, what is happening there, and what is happening within our bodies. If our sensory receptors are stimulated, then something caused that stimulation. Sound is produced when things happen in the environment; light reaches us from luminous sources and by reflection from solid surfaces; chemical stimulants in the air are released by food, by other animals, and by unpalatable plants and substances; mechanical deformation of the skin is produced by contact with physical objects. Thus, information about the stimulation – its strength, duration, type and location – is useful because it may also carry information about the cause of the stimulation. The stimulation itself is often referred to as the proximal stimulus, and the cause of the stimulation as the distal stimulus, as discussed next.

3.1.10 The term 'stimulus' is used in two different ways

A *sensory stimulus* is something that evokes a response from an organism's sensory receptors. However, the term *stimulus* is not always used in this way: it is sometimes used to mean an object or event in the environment that is the source of the energy that stimulates an organism. For example, an object might be brought into contact with the skin, causing the cutaneous receptors to be stimulated. The object itself is often described as the stimulus, although it is the deformation of the skin tissue that results from contact with the object that actually stimulates the receptors. To avoid confusion between the two meanings of the term *stimulus*, the words *proximal* and *distal* are usually added to yield the terms **proximal stimulus** and **distal stimulus**. Here is a definition of the second term:

> **DISTAL STIMULUS:** An object or event in the environment that is the source or cause of sensory stimulation.

Thus, in visual perception, distal stimuli are objects and events that you see – tables, chairs, trees, people are all distal stimuli. The term *proximal stimulus* can be defined as follows:

> **PROXIMAL STIMULUS:** Physical energy (electromagnetic, mechanical, acoustic, chemical) that impinges on sensory receptors and evokes a change in the membrane potential (produces a receptor potential).

Thus, an individual proximal stimulus would be the sensory stimulation produced by a particular distal stimulus (i.e., a particular object or event).

3.1.11 Receptor responses can be used to control simple behavior

In some instances, sensory receptors respond directly to things that the animal needs information about. For example, taste receptors respond directly to chemical substances that enter an animal's mouth, and cutaneous receptors respond to contact with the skin. The raw (i.e., unprocessed) responses of these receptors can be used for the control of behavior.

The kinds of behavior that can be controlled using the raw responses of sensory receptors include only the most low-level, automatic and regulatory kinds, like the pupiliary light reflex and the regulation of body temperature. We will discuss several other examples in Chapter 5. Most motor behavior requires more information than can be provided by the responses of individual receptors. For example, when we reach for an object to pick it up, we need information about the object's identity, its size, its shape and its location relative to us. Individual sensory receptors cannot provide this kind of information – we do not have receptors that respond to the size of an object, to its shape, identity or location. In order to obtain information about these kinds of things, the responses of many sensory receptors need to be combined and processed, as discussed next.

3.1.12 Most useful information is carried in the patterns of responses in large numbers of receptors

Information about the outside world is usually needed to produce goal-directed behavior, and it is obvious that our sensory systems provide us with this information. When we open our eyes we don't see only light: we see objects and surfaces laid out in three dimensions; we see stationary things and moving things, their shapes, sizes and textures. The problem, therefore, is to understand how information about the external environment is obtained from receptor responses. The answer has to do with the fact that information about the environment is present in patterns of stimulation, patterns that are distributed over areas much larger than the small regions occupied by sensory receptors – they are spatially extended patterns. Not only are they spatially extended, they are extended in time as well – they are spatio-temporal patterns. The most obvious examples come from vision. Visual stimulation takes the form of light patterns projected onto the retinae of the eyes – retinal images. These images contain information about the external environment, but this information is spatially extended over regions of the image, and so is not present in the response of any individual photoreceptor. The patterns are transduced into patterns of response in large numbers of photoreceptors. It is the spatio-temporal response pattern across an array of closely packed photoreceptors that carries information about the environment.

3.1.13 Perception is a process of obtaining information from sensory stimulation and making it available for action

Our ability to determine the identity, location, size, motion and shape of objects and surfaces in our environment from the responses of our sensory receptors is part of what is called **sensory perception**. Using the proximal/distal terminology, sensory perception can be described as a process that extracts information about distal stimuli from proximal stimuli. Visual perception, for example, is the process by which information about objects and events in the environment (distal stimuli) are extracted from retinal images (proximal stimuli).

It is helpful to keep the notions of perception and perceiving distinct from the notions of sensation and sensing. Sensing is what sensory receptors do: transduce stimulus energy into electrical signals. *Sensation* is a term that usually refers to the conscious feeling associated with sensing. Stimulation of sensory receptors may evoke a conscious experience in a person; the qualities of the experience are called *sensations*. For instance, when a photoreceptor is stimulated, a person is likely to have a visual experience with the qualities of brightness and color. These qualities are sensations[5].

Perception is not about the experiencing of sensations; it is about obtaining useful information from sensory stimulation. However, not only must the information be extracted, it must also be made available in a form suitable for the various uses to which it is put: for deciding on appropriate courses of action, for planning and initiating actions, for communicating about the world to others, for committing to memory. Thus, perception is essentially the process of obtaining information from sensory stimulation and making it available in a useful form, which leads to the following, rough definition:

> **SENSORY PERCEPTION:** The process of obtaining information (about the surroundings and the body) from sensory stimulation and making it available for decision making, planning and controlling motor actions, reasoning, memorizing and communicating.

Notice that this definition makes no reference to conscious awareness. The reason conscious awareness does not appear is that the term *perception* is routinely used in circumstances where (i) conscious awareness is absent and (ii) it is impossible to say whether awareness is present or not. Conscious awareness is absent in so-called **subliminal perception**, where stimulation is so weak that the person exposed to it is quite unaware of anything, yet their behavior is affected by information contained in the stimulation[6]. It is impossible to know whether or not animals have conscious perceptual awareness. According to our definition, animals perceive irrespective of whether they have any conscious experiences.

3.1.14 Perception involves the processing of receptor responses

Sensory perception begins with the transduction of stimulating energy into the responses of sensory receptors. These responses are transmitted along axons to interneurons, where they are combined with signals from other receptors and sometimes with signals from other parts of the nervous system. These interneurons generate signals that are, in turn, sent to other interneurons that carry out further operations – combining and integrating signals from a variety of sources. Whenever such integrative operations are carried out, we say that signals are being **processed**. Thus, the nervous system is engaged in the processing of the receptor responses. As we will see later in the chapter, in animal brains there are vast numbers of neurons devoted to the processing of sensory signals. In some species of primate, as much as 30 per cent of the cerebral cortex seems to be devoted solely to the processing of visual information.

The neural machinery that is involved in processing signals from sensory receptors is engaged in obtaining information about the environment and the body, and making it available for use. In other words, it is the machinery or mechanism of perception. Exactly how information is obtained and made available – how the mechanisms of perception work – is far from being fully understood. For example, it is not clear to what extent perception is based on information present in patterns of stimulation. Some theorists have proposed that in most real-world situations, perception is based entirely on information present in stimulation[7]. Others have proposed that perception always involves information additional to that present in stimulation, because there is never enough information in the stimulus. This additional information is usually thought to be information derived from past experience, though it could be inherited information that is manifested in the wiring of the nervous system as it is laid down during development. It is also possible to imagine a middle ground, in which some perceptions are based completely on stimulus information, whereas others incorporate information from sources internal to the nervous system. A treatment of these matters and the details of how sensory signals are processed goes beyond the scope of this text; the interested reader can consult the numerous books devoted to these topics[8]. In what follows in this chapter and the next, we will introduce only as much as is needed for understanding the principles of sensorimotor control.

3.1.15 Perception is an active process that involves motor behavior

Voluntary behavior requires information about the environment, but the information cannot usually be obtained simply by waiting for the right stimulation. It is necessary to obtain the information in an active way. For example, if you want to walk from one place to another over obstacle-strewn terrain, you need to obtain information about the location, size and shape of the obstacles in advance so that you can take appropriate action to avoid them. If you simply waited to be stimulated by the obstacles, you would have a very uncomfortable journey.

People and animals use their sensory organs as instruments for obtaining the information they need in order to carry out motor tasks. To obtain visual information, people and animals engage in activity usually called **looking**, which involves movements of the eyes and the head and sometimes of the body as a whole (see Chapter 4). Obtaining auditory information is called listening; obtaining tactile information is called feeling; obtaining olfactory information is called sniffing or smelling. In each case, active bodily movement is involved – the head, and in some animals the ears, are turned and tilted when listening; the hands are moved when feeling; the head is moved when sniffing, and muscles of the chest are used to move air past the sensory cells in the nasal cavities. Thus, motor processes are an essential part of perceiving: animals do not simply perceive in order to move, they move in order to perceive[9].

If we view perception as the process of obtaining information, then the activities involved in looking, listening, smelling and feeling are part of perception. The processing of receptor responses, together with the orienting and moving of sensory organs to obtain stimulation, constitute the perceptual process. We explore this idea further in the next section.

3.1.16 Perception involves sensory intruments and sets of motor procedures for using them

The examples in the previous section show that we use our sensory organs in much the same way as we use measuring instruments. For example, if you want to measure the temperature of something with a thermometer, you need to move the thermometer so that it is in an appropriate location, either within or on the thing of interest. To obtain useful information from a measuring instrument like a thermometer, ruler or voltmeter requires that it be used in the correct way. To use a ruler you must lay it straight between the points to be measured; to use a voltmeter you must position its terminals at the two points between which you want to determine the potential difference. Thus, obtaining a measurement involves two things: the instrument itself and a set of procedures for using it. Sensory perception can also be considered to involve two components: a part that responds to and processes stimulation – the sensory instrument – and a part that directs and controls the operations of this instrument. The second part involves moving the sensory organs so as to obtain the required information: moving the hands over objects, moving the head and eyes to look in different directions or from different vantage points[10]. These movements constitute a set of procedures or routines for using the sensory organs to obtain information. As we will see later in this chapter (section 3.4.13) and in Chapter 4, these motor procedures have a consistent form: they display similar characteristics each time they are performed.

A sensory instrument together with the motor systems that generate the procedures for using it comprise what the psychologist J.J. Gibson called a **perceptual system**[11]: a system that obtains useful information and makes it available for action. As we will see in what follows, there is more to using a sensory instrument than positioning and orienting it; the processes of obtaining information are also subject to control.

3.1.17 The sensitivity of some sensory receptors is regulated by efferent signals

The sensitivity of some sensory receptors to stimulation is influenced by efferent signals. In humans, the receptors of the auditory and vestibular systems are innervated by efferent neurons. Panel A of Figure 3.7 shows a type II vestibular receptor cell that makes synaptic connections with an afferent neuron and an efferent neuron: the synaptic terminal of an afferent neuron is shown in brown, and the terminal of the efferent neuron is shown in green. The cell bodies of the efferent neurons lie in the brainstem, close to the abucens nuclei. The sensitivity of sensory receptors embedded in skeletal muscles (muscle spindle receptors) is also influenced by efferent signals. The fact that these receptors can be affected by efferent signals from the central nervous system means that their responsiveness can be regulated. The regulation of the sensitivity of vestibular receptors is not properly understood[12] and we will not consider it any further; we note only that regulation takes place. The regulation of muscle spindle sensitivity is much better understood (see section 3.3.9).

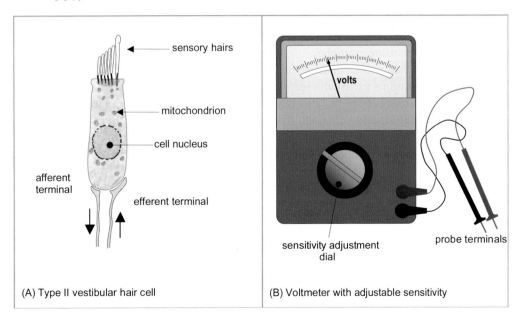

(A) Type II vestibular hair cell

(B) Voltmeter with adjustable sensitivity

Figure 3.7: *Sensory instruments.*

The analogy with measuring instruments may assist in grasping some of what is going on. Imagine a measuring instrument like a voltmeter that is used to measure voltages in electrical circuits and systems. A typical voltmeter is shown in panel B of Figure 3.7: it consists of a box with a display and a dial for adjusting sensitivity, and a pair of probe terminals. Using the meter involves positioning the terminals at appropriate locations, and turning the dial so that the sensitivity of the meter is suitable for the voltage being measured. Moving the terminals to appropriate locations is analogous to moving and orienting a sensory organ; adjusting the dial is analogous to adjusting the sensitivity of receptors by efferent signals.

We have now seen that the perceptual process typically involves the active movement of sensory organs and in some cases the efferent tuning of receptor sensitivities. Thus, the central nervous system has a powerful influence over what stimulation the receptors are exposed to and, in some cases, how the receptors respond to that stimulation. This does not exhaust the ways in which the process of obtaining information from stimulation is regulated and controlled, as discussed next.

3.1.18 Perception is multimodal

The manner in which the senses are introduced to children and spoken about in everyday life tends to suggest to people that they are separate things. Every schoolchild is introduced at an early age to the five senses – sight, hearing, touch, smell and taste – in a way that emphasizes their distinctness and independence. We learn that each sense has its own sensory organ(s): the eyes are for seeing, the ears are for hearing, the skin is for touching and feeling, the nose is for smelling and the tongue is for tasting. Thus, the different senses are viewed as being concerned with different kinds of information and as having their own particular kinds of sensory qualities: color is a uniquely visual quality and loudness a uniquely auditory one, for example. Of course, our perceptual experience is unitary. For example, the experience of a campfire involves sight, hearing, smell and the cutaneous feelings of warmth. The individual senses are integrated and coordinated to produce a unified perceptual experience of the fire as a single crackling, burning, smoking, warming thing, located in a particular place and occurring over a particular period of time. Information provided by the different senses is put together by the nervous system to create a single, integrated experience. In this example, the overall perceptual experience is unitary, with the different sensory systems making distinct, individual contributions – the contributions are initially separate, and the nervous system needs to coordinate them to produce the unified percept. All this conforms to a naïve view of the sensory systems as modules that operate independently. However, sensory systems do not process stimulus input separately from one another, and so do not function as independent processing modules[13]. In addition, they are not restricted to extracting particular kinds of information and to producing unique qualities of sensory experience. These two points will be discussed in turn, using examples.

To illustrate the first point, consider the visual perception of the spatial location of things. When we look around us we usually see objects of various sorts lying in different directions and at different distances from us. This is an essential part of visual perception, but it is not entirely based on information obtained from visual stimulation (stimulation of photoreceptors). To see why, imagine being in a completely dark room in which the only visible thing is a small luminous spot on one of the walls. This spot will be perceived as being spatially localized: it will be seen in a particular direction relative to you (its egocentric direction) and be seen to be a particular distance away (these perceptions will typically correspond quite closely with the spot's actual location within the room). If you turn your head or move your eyes, the perceived egocentric direction of the spot does not change. This means that the position of the eyes in their sockets and the position of the head on the shoulders is contributing to the perception of direction, but information about these positions is not obtained by the visual system (it's completely dark). The perception of egocentric direction involves visual information about the location of the spot's image on the retinas, and proprioceptive information about eye and head position[14]. The perception of the spot's distance away also depends on non-visual information, as the spot's retinal images carry no information about its distance.

The only information about the spot's distance comes from the angle of convergence of the two eyes when the spot is fixated[15] (see Figures 4.59–4.61). Thus, the visual experience of a spot lying at a particular distance is not determined by visual information. This example shows that visual perception of spatial location depends not only on visual stimulation but also on information from proprioceptive modalities as well[16] – it is *multimodal*.

The second point is illustrated by the phenomenon of sensory substitution, in which a perceptual function normally carried out by one sense is carried out by another that does not normally carry it out. For example, we usually think of the perception of where objects are in the environment as being a visual function: we look around us and see where things are. We think of the sense of touch as telling us about the properties of objects and surfaces that we make contact with. Tactile-visual sensory substitution turns this around: it involves a device that coverts images (patterns of light intensity focused onto the detector array of a video camera) into vibrotactile or electrotactile stimulation[17]. Vibrotactile stimulation is applied to the skin (usually on the back) using an array of small stimulators laid out in a grid. In the early studies there were 400 vibrotactile stimulators in a 20 × 20 grid ten inches square; each one stimulated the skin with the end of a small rod (1 mm diameter), which moved in and out and pressed against the skin[18]. The image recorded by a video camera is divided into an array of pixels laid out in a grid that matches the stimulator grid, so that each pixel in the image is wired up to a corresponding stimulator. In this way, the pattern of light and dark in the image is converted into a pattern of vibrotactile stimulation on the skin. When people first experience this kind of vibrotactile stimulation, they feel tickling sensations over the stimulated skin surface, as would be expected. However, provided that they are able to hold the video camera and move it around, the experience gradually changes over several hours of use into something very different. The tactile perception experienced initially is replaced by an experience of the scene imaged by the camera: objects of different shapes and sizes laid out in three-dimensional space. The acquired perceptual experience is of the external world and seems to share many of the spatial characteristics of visual perception (reported by both sighted and congenitally blind study participants). Moreover, participants in the studies were able to perform tasks usually associated with vision such as recognizing faces and hitting moving objects with a bat[19]. These findings demonstrate that, given the right experience, the tactile system is capable of carrying out some of the perceptual functions of vision if it is provided with the right information.

3.2 The Vestibular System

3.2.1 Introduction: the vestibular labyrinth is part of the inner ear

The innermost part of the ear is a complex structure consisting of a network of interconnected membranous tubes and chambers (the *membranous labyrinth*) that lie within a system of passages and cavities in the bones of the skull. These passages have a lining of laminar bone called the *bony labyrinth*. Figure 3.8 shows a cutaway of the human ear in which the inner surface of the bony labyrinth is exposed and shown shaded dark gray. It has two easily recognizable parts: a coiled tube that resembles a snail shell (the **cochlea**) and a part that is distinguished by three part-circular tubes that lie in different planes (the **vestibular labyrinth**).

Although they are both parts of the inner ear, the cochlea and the vestibular labyrinth are associated with very different sensory functions. The cochlea contains the sensory organs of hearing. The vestibular labyrinth comprises a set of sensory organs that are often described as mediating a 'sense of balance' This description is somewhat misleading, since it suggests that the role of the vestibular sensory system is to inform about whether we are falling over or at risk of falling. Although the vestibular system does play an important role in maintaining

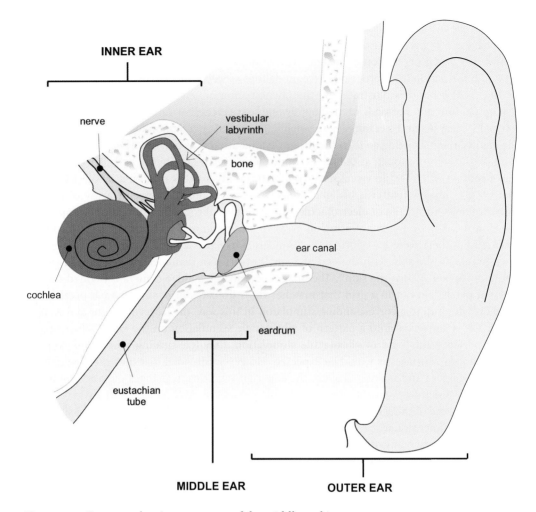

Figure 3.8: *Cutaway showing structures of the middle and inner ear.*

the body in an upright posture (see Chapters 6 and 7), there are two reasons why it can be misleading to say that it mediates a sense of balance:

(1)   The vestibular system is not the only sensory system that underlies our sense of balance and the maintenance of postural equilibrium. The 'sense of balance' and the control of postural equilibrium are multisensory abilities to which the vestibular system is a contributor.

(2)   The vestibular system contributes not just to balance but to other things as well, such as our sense of movement through the environment, the control of eye movements and motion sickness.

In this part of the chapter we will describe the vestibular sensory organs, the stimulation to which they respond and the parts of the central nervous system that receive vestibular signals.

3.2.2 The vestibular labyrinth houses five sensory organs: three semicircular canals and two otolith organs

Figure 3.9 shows a membranous vestibular labyrinth from one side of the head – it is the network of fluid-filled tubes and chambers formed of connective and other tissue that lies within the bony labyrinth. The figure shows that the labyrinth has several components. There are three part-circular tubes called **semicircular canals**: the *anterior canal*, the *posterior canal* and the *horizontal canal*. These tubes are very thin: in human beings the diameter of a cross-section is about 0.3 mm, only about three times thicker than an average human hair.

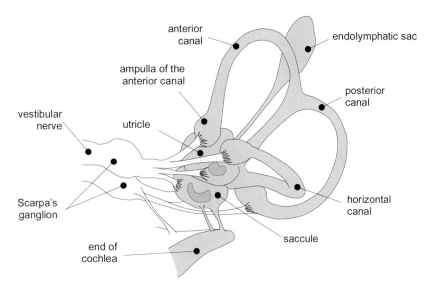

Figure 3.9: *The (left) membranous vestibular labyrinth (about 10 times real size, based on Figure 925 in the 1918 edition of* Gray's Anatomy*).*

The canals connect to a chamber called the **utricle** which is connected to another chamber that lies under it, the **saccule**. The utricle and saccule together are known as the **otolith organs**. The three semicircular canals and the two otolith organs are the five sensory organs of the vestibular system. The whole structure is filled with fluid called **endolymph**. The semicircular canals interconnect with the utricle, and each has a swelling called an **ampulla** at one of their junctions with the utricle. The ampullae contain sensory hair cells, the receptor cells of the vestibular system. These come in two types: flask-shaped type I cells (Figures 3.1 and 3.2) and the more cyclindrical type II cells (Figure 3.7)[20]. The hair cells are clustered together in a ridge of epithelium called the **crista**, and their hairs project into a gelatinous diaphragm called the **cupula**. The sensory hair cells of the otolith organs are found clustered in layers of epithelial tissue called **maculae**. The sensory hair cells are innervated by bipolar sensory neurons whose cell bodies are located in a bipartate ganglion called **Scarpa's ganglion**. Nerves from Scarpa's ganglion branch to innervate the cristae of the canals and the maculae of the otolith organs, as shown in Figure 3.9.

3.2.3 Hair cells respond when their hairs are deflected

A change in their membrane potential (receptor potential) is evoked in sensory hair cells when their hairs are deflected. Figure 3.10 gives an intuitive explanation of what deflection means. Panel A shows a cross-section of a type II hair cell with the hairs in the undeflected orientation. One of the cell's hairs is thicker than the others and has a slight bulge at its top – this hair is called the **kinocilium**, and the others are called **stereocilia**. In panel B the hairs have been deflected – the stereocilia are deflected towards the kinocilium, which is deflected away from the cell's midline. In panel C the hairs are deflected in the opposite direction, with the kinocilium deflected towards the midline.

When the hairs are undeflected, the hair cell has a resting membrane potential and releases excitatory neurotransmitter at its synapses with afferent fibers. This causes the afferents to fire at a constant rate called the **resting firing rate** that may be as high as 100 spikes/s. When the hairs are deflected in the direction shown in panel B of Figure 3.10, the cell depolarizes, which results in an increase in the amount of neurotransmitter released at the afferent synapses. The firing rate of the afferent fibers increases as a result. When the hairs are deflected as shown in panel C of Figure 3.10, the cell is hyperpolarized, which results in a decrease in neurotransmitter release and a corresponding reduction in the afferent firing rate. These facts are summarized diagrammatically in Figure 3.11.

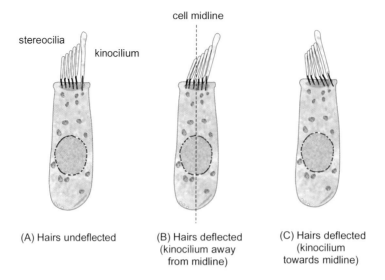

Figure 3.10: *Deflection of hairs of a vestibular hair cell.*

We have only considered deflection of the hairs such that the stereocilia are deflected towards or away from the kinocilium. This deflection is in the plane of the page in Figures 3.10 and 3.11, but it is also possible for hairs to be deflected at right angles to the plane of the page. Figure 3.12 shows the arrangement of the hairs when looking down on the cell from above. Each dot represents a hair: the smaller dots are stereocilia and there is an array of these – the number varies from about 20 to over 100, depending on the type of hair cell. The large dot is the kinocilium; there is only one of these. Four directions of deflection are indicated by arrows: (A) kinocilium deflected away from cell midline and away from the stereocilia (as Figure 3.10B); (B) kinocilium deflected towards cell midline and towards the stereocilia (as Figure 3.10C); (C) and (D) stereocilia deflected neither towards nor away from the kinocilium. In the latter two cases, the deflection has no effect on the membrane potential of the cell. Thus, the cell only responds if there is deflection to left or right as in Figure 3.12; we say that the hair cells are **polarized** or **directionally selective**. This selectivity is usually represented by an arrow pointing in the direction of the deflection that depolarizes (excites) the cell (the arrow shown in Figure 3.12A).

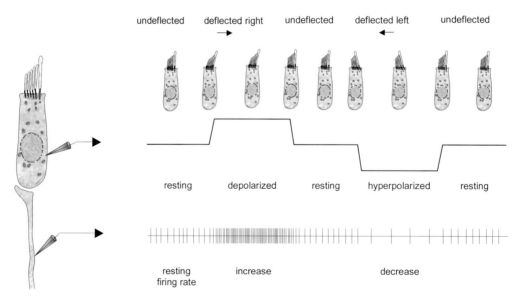

Figure 3.11: *Effects of deflecting the sensory hairs on the cell membrane potential and the afferent firing rate.*

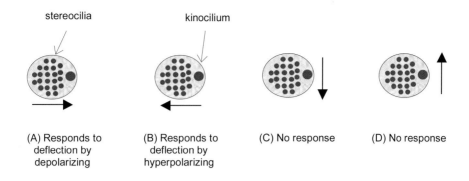

(A) Responds to deflection by depolarizing

(B) Responds to deflection by hyperpolarizing

(C) No response

(D) No response

Figure 3.12: *Deflection of sensory hairs in different directions.*

3.2.4 Semicircular canal hair cells are deflected during angular accelerations of the head

Each semicircular canal can be thought of as being a roughly circular, fluid-filled tube with a flexible membrane (the cupula) sealing the bore at one location so that the fluid cannot flow past it. Figure 3.13 shows the arrangement: the tube has a thickened part (ampulla) that houses the cupula. At the base of the cupula is the sensory epithelium of the canal (the crista), which contains approximately seven thousand hair cells in humans. The figure shows a single hair cell with its hairs projecting into the cupula.

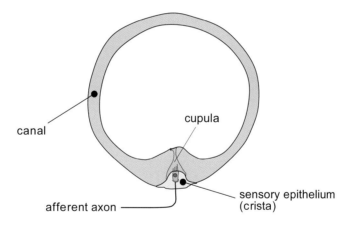

Figure 3.13: *Schematic of the anatomy of a semi-circular canal.*

If you start to turn a fluid-filled tube like that shown in Figure 3.13 about an axis perpendicular to the page (i.e., to the left or right), the tube itself will start to move, but the fluid within it will tend to stay where it is. This is because you are applying a turning force to the tube and not to the fluid. The result is that the fluid and tube move relative to one another. The cupula is attached to the canal and so moves with it, but it meets resistance from the stationary fluid. This resistance causes the cupula to be deformed, and this deflects the hairs embedded within it.

When the tube begins to be turned, it is being rotationally accelerated. If the acceleration stops and the tube is kept turning at a constant angular velocity, the fluid will soon come to be moving at the same velocity, due mainly to frictional drag between the fluid and the walls of the tube. When the tube and fluid are moving together at the same velocity, the cupula no longer experiences any resistance and is restored to its undeformed position in which the hairs are undeflected. These events are illustrated in Figure 3.14. At the top of the figure is a plot of the angular velocity of the canal over time. The velocity is zero for a period of time, then the canal is accelerated (velocity increases), held at a constant velocity for a period and finally decelerated back to zero again. Below the angular velocity plot are snapshots of the canal during each period, showing the deflection of the sensory hairs. These are not deflected when the canal is stationary or when it is rotating at constant speed. When the canal speeds up (acceleration) the fluid moves relative to the canal in a direction opposite to the acceleration; the cupula is deformed, and the hairs are deflected away from the cell midline (magnified in the inset). While the canal is slowing down (deceleration), the fluid keeps on moving and the sensory hairs are deflected, but in a direction opposite to that during the acceleration period (inset). The bottom of the figure shows the spikes recorded from the sensory afferent fiber during the movement: the firing rate follows the deflection of the hairs, as described in section 3.2.3. Thus, the hairs are deflected and the afferent firing rate changes when the canal is rotationally accelerated. To put it another way, the sensory hair cells are stimulated by angular accelerations of the canal.

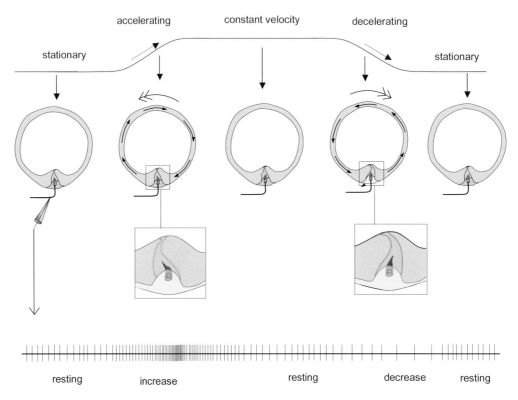

Figure 3.14: *Stimulus and response for a semicircular canal. Top: angular velocity of the canal (and head). Middle: cupula deflection and relative motion of fluid in canal at five moments in time. Bottom: Firing of afferent axon.*

The only way in which a semicircular canal can be moved in natural circumstances is by moving the head. If the head turns, then the semicircular canals turn with it. Thus, angular accelerations of the head cause deflections of the hair cells and changes in the firing rates of the associated afferent fibers. Although angular accelerations are what stimulate the sensory cells of the canals, the semicircular canals do not function as angular acceleration detectors. Their signaling characteristics are discussed next.

3.2.5 The firing rate of semicircular canal afferents is proportional to angular velocity

The facts represented in Figure 3.14 suggest that the canals might be sensory devices that measure angular accelerations of the head, i.e., angular accelerometers. In fact, within the range of head accelerations encountered in natural circumstances, the canals function as angular velocity detectors due to their mechanical properties[21].

Consider again the situation shown in Figure 3.14: a canal is turned in its own plane such that its angular velocity first increases from zero (acceleration), then the angular velocity is held constant for a period, before a deceleration back to zero. As shown at the bottom of Figure 3.14, the firing rate of afferent fibers of the canal increases above the resting rate during the period of acceleration and decreases below the resting rate during deceleration. A continuous estimate of the afferent firing rate is shown in Figure 3.15, together with the angular velocity profile. The figure shows that during the periods of acceleration and deceleration, the firing rate follows the angular velocity. When the acceleration or deceleration stops, the firing rate slowly returns to the resting level. Thus, during periods of angular acceleration or deceleration, the canal afferent firing rate changes in proportion to the angular velocity.

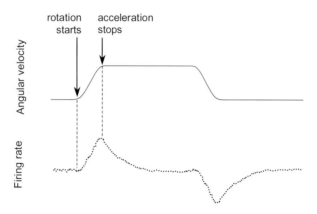

Figure 3.15: *Firing rate of canal afferents follows the angular velocity during acceleration and deceleration. (Based on data reported by Goldberg and Fernandez, 1971.)*

3.2.6 The three semicircular canals lie in mutually perpendicular planes

Figures 3.8 and 3.9 show that the three semicircular canals lie in different planes. In fact, the planes are approximately at right angles to one another, as shown in panel A of Figure 3.16: the anterior canal lies in the unshaded plane, the horizontal canal in the darker shaded plane. Panel B shows how the canals are oriented within the head: the horizontal canals lie approximately in the plane of the page (transverse plane of the head), so they are close to horizontal when the head is in an upright position[22]. The anterior and posterior canals lie in planes perpendicular to the page, and so both are approximately vertical when the head is upright. The orientations of the anterior and posterior canals are indicated by the dashed/dotted lines: they meet the mid-sagittal plane of the head at 45°.

Panel B of Figure 3.16 also shows that the labyrinths on the two sides of the head are mirror images of one another (reflection in the mid-sagittal plane). As a result, the left anterior canal lies in a plane parallel to the right posterior canal (dashed lines) and the left posterior canal and the right anterior canal lie in parallel planes (dotted lines). The functional significance of this anatomical fact is discussed later (section 3.2.8). The mutually perpendicular arrangement of the semicircular canals means that their receptors are stimulated by angular accelerations of the head about different axes of rotation. The horizontal canal receptors are stimulated when the head rotates about a vertical axis (turns of the head to the left or right). The receptors of the other canals are stimulated by rotations about two perpendicular axes that lie in the horizontal plane, as shown in Figure 3.17 for the canals on the left side of the head.

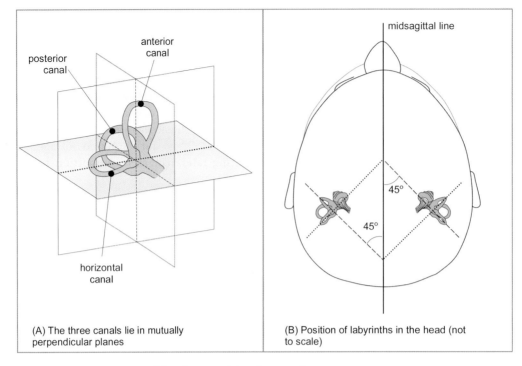

(A) The three canals lie in mutually perpendicular planes

(B) Position of labyrinths in the head (not to scale)

Figure 3.16: *Orientation of the three semicircular canals.*

The arrangement means that nodding the head (rotation about a horizontal axis that runs from ear to ear) stimulates receptors in both the anterior and posterior canals on both sides of the head, but does not stimulate receptors in the horizontal canals. Rolling the head from side to side ear to shoulder (rotation about a horizontal axis that runs from front to back) also stimulates receptors in the anterior and posterior canals but not the horizontal canals. These axes are shown in Figure 3.18 together with the vertical axis.

3.2.7 Vestibular afferent axons project to the vestibular nuclei in the brainstem

As briefly mentioned earlier, the sensory hair cells of the vestibular labyrinths are innervated by bipolar sensory neurons with cell bodies in Scarpa's ganglia (Figure 3.9). The dendrites of these neurons innervate the hair cells and the proximal axons project to various parts of the brain. The majority project to the ipsilateral **vestibular nuclei** in the brainstem, but some project to the cerebellum and the reticular formation[23].

The vestibular nuclei are clusters of four component nuclei, one cluster on each side of the brain, as shown in panel A of Figure 3.19. The figure shows a dorsal (rear) view of the brainstem, with the cerebellum removed and the vestibular nuclear clusters exposed and shaded pink. The

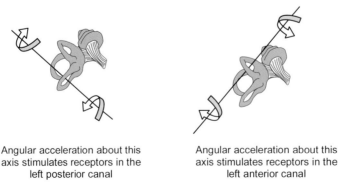

Angular acceleration about this axis stimulates receptors in the left posterior canal

Angular acceleration about this axis stimulates receptors in the left anterior canal

Figure 3.17: *Acceleration about different axes of rotation stimulates different canals (left labyrinth, viewed from above).*

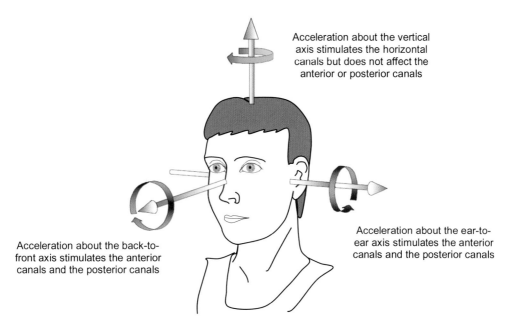

Figure 3.18: *Three cardinal axes of head rotation.*

nuclei are named for their relative positions in the brainstem: the inferior, medial, lateral and superior vestibular nuclei. Panel B of the figure shows that the anterior and horizontal canals (shaded blue) project primarily to the ipsilateral superior and medial vestibular nuclei, where they make excitatory synaptic connections with interneurons. The posterior canal (shaded brown) not only projects to the superior and medial nuclei but also to the lateral nucleus.

The axons of the sensory neurons that innervate the sensory hair cells of the otolith organs also project to the ipsilateral vestibular nuclei, but unlike the canal afferents, they make very few connections with neurons in the superior vestibular nuclei. As shown in Figure 3.20, sensory afferent axons from both the utricle and the saccule project primarily to the medial, inferior and lateral nuclei.

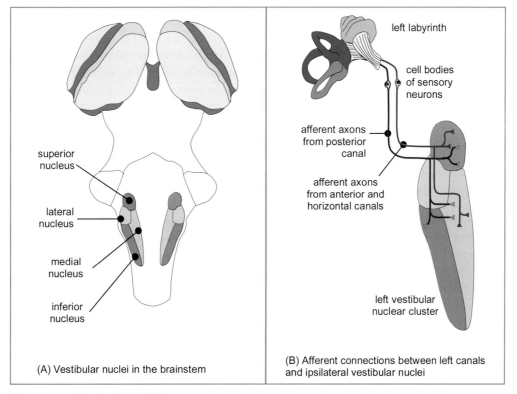

Figure 3.19: *Vestibular nuclei.*

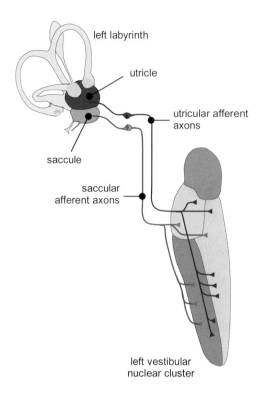

left labyrinth

utricle

utricular afferent
axons

saccule

saccular
afferent axons

left vestibular
nuclear cluster

Figure 3.20: *Afferent connections between left otoliths and ipsilateral vestibular nuclei.*

3.2.8 Pairs of canals work together in a push-pull fashion

As described in section 3.2.6, pairs of canals on the two sides of the head are stimulated by angular accelerations about the same axis. There are three such pairs. One pair is formed by the two horizontal canals that are stimulated by acceleration about the vertical axis. A second pair is formed by the left posterior canal and the right anterior canal that are stimulated by acceleration about a horizontal axis at 45° to the mid-sagittal line. The third pair is formed by the left anterior canal and the right posterior canal that are stimulated by acceleration about a horizontal axis at right angles to the one that defines the second pair. In what follows, we will use the horizontal pair as an example (the same principles apply to the other pairs).

Figure 3.21 shows how the horizontal pair of canals work together in the case of a turn of the head to the left (counterclockwise). The two canals are shown at the top: as the head accelerates to the left, the fluid in the canals tends to remain stationary, and so moves clockwise relative to the walls of the canal as indicated. The motion of the fluid relative to the canal deforms the cupulae and deflects the hair cells. Note that the hair cells deflect away from the midline of the hair cell in the left canal and towards the midline of the cell in the right canal. The result is an increase in the firing rate of the sensory afferent axons in the left vestibular nerve and a decrease in the firing rate in the right vestibular nerve, as shown in the middle of the figure. This is called a **push-pull relationship**: the hair cells of the two canals respond in opposite ways to the same angular acceleration.

The bottom of Figure 3.21 summarizes part of the initial neural connectivity within the vestibular nuclei. The sensory axons from the hair cells make direct, excitatory synaptic connections with neurons in the ipsilateral vestibular nuclei; these are called **first order interneurons (INs)**. The axons of some first order INs project across the midline. These **commissural first order interneurons** make excitatory synaptic connections with inhibitory interneurons in the contralateral vestibular nuclei. These inhibitory neurons make synaptic connections with first order INs on the same side. This circuitry establishes an antagonistic relationship between the two canals: the non-commissural first order INs receive excitatory input from the ipsilateral canal and inhibitory input from the contralateral canal. These first order INs can be thought of as calculating the difference between the signals from the left and right canals. If the signals from the left and right canals are denoted S_L and S_R respectively, then the INs on the left calculate $S_L - S_R$ and those on the right calculate $S_R - S_L$.

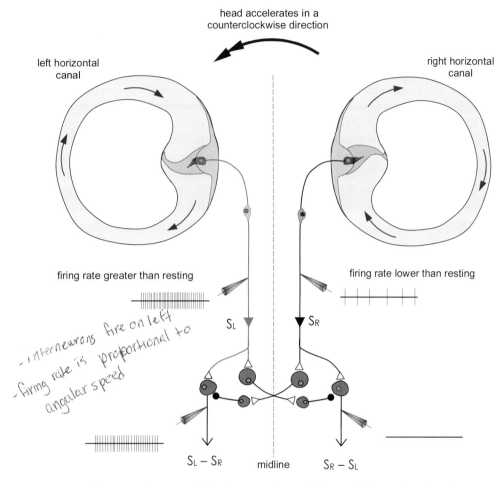

Figure 3.21: *Schematic diagram of the horizontal canals (viewed from above) and associated circuitry illustrating their push-pull arrangement.*

The effect of this arrangement is that the output of non-commissural first order interneurons signals the direction in which the head is accelerating and its angular speed. If the head is not accelerating, then the afferent input to both sides is equal (resting firing rate in both canals) and the excitation and inhibition of the interneurons cancels out ($S_R - S_L = 0 = S_L - S_R$). In this case the interneurons do not fire, which signals no acceleration. If the head is accelerating, then the afferent input is unequal. Consider the example in Figure 3.21: the firing rate is higher on the left than on the right. The result is that interneurons on the right side receive greater contralateral inhibition than ipsilateral excitation, and so they do not fire. Conversely, on the left, the ipsilateral excitation is greater than the inhibition, and the interneurons fire ($S_L - S_R > 0$). Thus, when the head accelerates to the left, the interneurons on the left fire but those on the right do not, which means that the side which is firing signals the direction of the acceleration. In the figure, the interneuron on the right is not firing, while that of the left is firing, indicating that the acceleration is to the left. The firing rate of the interneurons is proportional to the angular speed of the head, for reasons discussed in section 3.2.5. So, for example, a low firing rate of interneurons on the left means that the head is accelerating to the left and is moving at a low angular speed.

3.2.9 The maculae of the otolith organs are patches of epithelium containing hair cells that project into a gelatinous membrane

The utricle and the saccule are small, egg-shaped chambers filled with fluid and interconnected with the semicircular canals (Figure 3.9). In both otolith organs there is a specialized patch of epithelium that contains the sensory hair cells. These patches are the **sensory maculae**, and each covers a small region on the inner surface of its otolith organ: the saccular macula lies in the medial wall of the saccule, and the utricular macula lies on the inferior wall of the utricle. There are about 30,000 hair cells in the human utricular macula, and about half as many in the saccular macula. The hairs project into a gelatinous sheet called the **otolithic membrane**. Adhering to the top of this membrane is a fused mass of calcium carbonate crystals called **otoliths**, which literally means 'ear-stones' – the word is derived from the ancient Greek words for ear (*otos*) and stone (*lithos*)[24]. A common name for these crystals is **otoconia**. Figure 3.22 shows the basic structure of the maculae of the otolith organs. Panel A shows a small rectangular patch of macula from which the otolithic membrane has been peeled away except for the right third. Several hair cells, the otolithic membrane and otoconia are visible. Panel B shows the same small patch from above, with the otolithic membrane removed to show how the hair cells are oriented; the arrows indicate the directional polarization of each cell (see section 3.2.3).

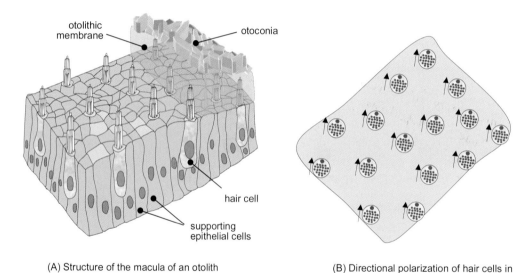

(A) Structure of the macula of an otolith

(B) Directional polarization of hair cells in small patch of macula

Figure 3.22: *Small segment of the macula of an otolith.*

On a very small piece of macula like that shown in the figure, all the hair cells will typically be oriented in the same direction (all the arrows point the same way). When the whole of the macula is considered, the directions of hair cell polarization form a rather more complex, fan-like pattern, as shown in Figure 3.23. The maculae of both the utricle and the saccule are divided into two parts by a **striola**, a curved, thread-like indentation that runs across the macula. The hair cells on the two sides of the striola are polarized in opposite directions, as shown in the figure. In the macula of the utricle, the hairs are polarized such that they 'point' towards the striola. In the macula of the saccule, the cells are polarized such that they point away from it. The figure also shows that the maculae lie in different planes that are close to perpendicular. The macula of the saccule almost lies in a sagittal plane of the head, and so is close to vertical when the head is in an upright posture. The macula of the utricle lies in a plane that is almost perpendicular to the sagittal plane and tilted between 20° and 30° to the horizontal when the head is in an upright posture. In humans and many other mammals, the utricle seems to be a much more important sensory organ than the saccule. We will focus on the utricle in what follows.

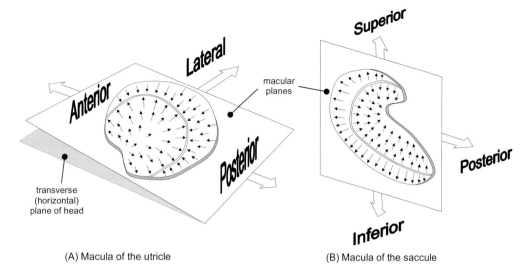

(A) Macula of the utricle   (B) Macula of the saccule

Figure 3.23: *The otolithic maculae, showing the striolae and the polarization patterns of the hair cells.*

3.2.10 Hair cells in the otolith organs are deflected when the fused mass of the otoconia is displaced

The otoconia form a dense, solid and relatively heavy mass that adheres to the top of the lighter, flexible otolithic membrane. When an otolith organ is tilted, the force of gravity pulling on the otoconia causes them to move relative to the macular surface, because the jelly-like otolithic membrane deforms. The result, of course, is that the sensory hairs embedded in the membrane are deflected, and an associated change in the afferent firing rate is produced. Figure 3.24 shows the effect of tilting the utricle on a small patch of macula. Three situations

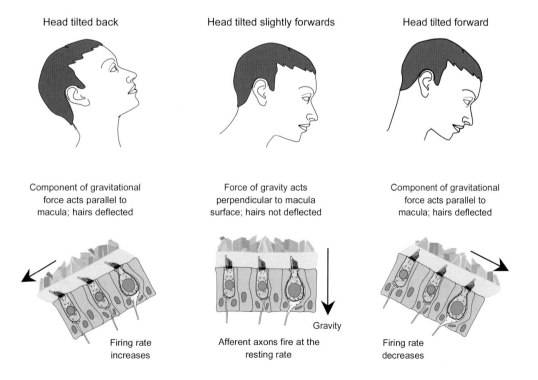

Figure 3.24: *Effects of head tilt on the utricular maculae.*

are shown: in the center of the figure, the utricle is oriented horizontally (head tilted slightly forward) and the sensory hairs are not deflected. On the right of the figure, the head is tilted further forward. The mass of otoconia is now on a slope, and gravity pulls on it so that it moves into a new position in which the sensory hairs are deflected. For the hair cells shown, a forward tilt deflects the hairs towards the midline of the cells, which results in a decrease in the firing rate of the associated afferent axons. The left of the figure shows that the hair cells are deflected away from the midline when the head is tilted back. The firing rate will therefore increase for the patch of macula when the head is tilted backwards.

As you can imagine from looking at the radial pattern of utricular hair cell polarization in Figure 3.23A, the effect of a tilt forwards or backwards (anterior-posterior tilts) on the hair cells will vary across the macula. In some places, the hairs will be deflected as shown in Figure 3.24; in other places the hairs will be deflected perpendicular to their polarization axes, and so the firing rates of their afferents will not change. Thus, the pattern of changes in afferent firing rates produced by a tilt of the head carries information about the direction of the tilt: a tilt forwards or backwards produces a pattern of firing different from a side-to-side tilt, and a diagonal tilt produces a firing pattern that is a combination of the patterns produced by forwards-backwards and side-to-side tilts.

3.2.11 Utricular hair cells are deflected by linear accelerations of the head

If the head accelerates forwards or backwards, the walls of the utricle and the hair cell bodies will accelerate with the rest of the head, as they are firmly attached to it. The otoconia, however, are attached to the utricular wall by the flexible otolithic membrane, and will tend to stay where they are due to their inertia. The result is that when the head accelerates forwards or backwards, the otoconia are displaced backwards or forwards relative to the macula surface and the hair cells are deflected accordingly. This is illustrated in Figure 3.25 for the same small segment of utricular macula that appears in Figure 3.24. In the center, the head is not accelerating and the otoconia are not displaced. On the left of the figure, the head accelerates forwards carrying the utricle with it. The otoconia tend to stay where they are because they are not rigidly attached to the rest of the utricle, which results in them moving relative to the macular surface in a direction opposite to the acceleration. The hair cells are deflected

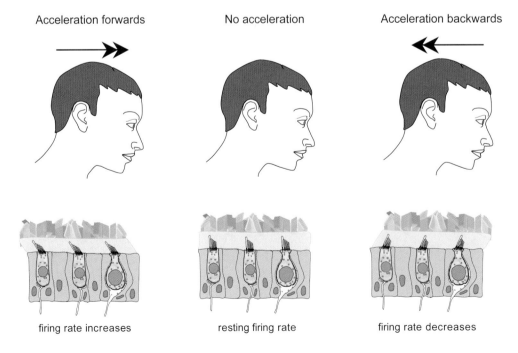

Figure 3.25: *Effect of translational acceleration of the head on the utricular maculae.*

and for those shown, the deflection causes an increase in the firing rate of the associated afferent axons. On the right, the head is accelerating backwards: the person might be in an accelerating train in a seat facing opposite to the direction of travel; alternatively they could be facing the direction of travel and decelerating. The result, once again, is that the otoconia move relative to the macular surface in a direction opposite to the acceleration. This time, the deflection of the hairs causes a decrease in the firing rate of the associated afferent axons.

3.2.12 Afferent signals from the otolith organs are inherently ambiguous

Comparison of Figures 3.24 and 3.25 shows that the hairs of the utricular maculae can be deflected by translational accelerations of the head in the same way as they are by tilts of the head. A forwards translational acceleration deflects the hairs in the same way as a tilt backwards (left side of the figures), and a backwards translational acceleration (or equivalently, a slowing of forward speed) deflects the hairs in the same way as a tilt forwards. This is true not only for the hair cells in the small patch of macula shown in the figures, but for all hair cells in the two utricular maculae. As a consequence, for any tilt of the head there is a translational acceleration that will produce exactly the same response from the utricles. The same is true for the saccules. Thus, the afferent signals from the otolith organs are inherently ambiguous: any given signal could have been produced by a head tilt or by a translational acceleration. This should not be viewed a design flaw: if there were a flaw in the design of the otoliths, we could be fairly sure that evolution would have eradicated it. As described in Chapter 7, the otoliths are able provide useful information about the orientation of the head relative to something called the *gravitoinertial force vector*, in which context their inability to discriminate between head tilts and accelerations is irrelevant (see section 7.2).

[handwritten margin note: This is assuming we are the most evolved there will ever be]

Of course, head tilts and linear accelerations will have different effects on other sensory organs. For example, during a tilt the head will be angularly accelerating, which will stimulate the anterior and posterior semicircular canals. Translational accelerations do not stimulate the canals, so only tilts are accompanied by signals from the canals. In addition, if the neck bends to tilt the head, proprioceptors in the muscles, tendons and joints of the neck will be stimulated. The stimulation of these proprioceptors will be very different during translational accelerations. Finally, it will often be possible to see whether your head is tilted or whether you are translationally accelerating. Thus, in almost all circumstances that are likely to arise naturally, there is sensory information available that will enable you to distinguish between head tilts and translational accelerations. The neural mechanisms underlying the disambiguation of vestibular signals are beginning to be uncovered[25].

3.2.13 Vestibular sensory information is sent from the vestibular nuclei to several different locations in the CNS

Neurons in the vestibular nuclei project to several different target regions in the central nervous system. These projections are summarized in Figure 3.26. Panel A shows an anatomical representation of the projections: projections to various motor nuclei are shown originating from the left vestibular nuclear cluster, projections to the cerebellum and cerebral cortex are shown for the right cluster. Of course, both clusters project to all targets. Panel B summarizes in block diagram form the ipsilateral projections from the vestibular nuclei (as shown in panel A); also shown are feedback connections from the cerebellum and cerebral cortex (not shown in A).

The projections to motor nuclei are as follows. There are projections via the medial lemniscus to the motor nuclei that innervate the muscles that move the eyes – the abducens, trochlear and oculomotor nuclei. These projections mediate the *vestibulo-ocular reflexes*, a group of reflexes that stabilize the eyes, described in Chapters 4 and 5. There are projections via the medial vestibulospinal tract to motor nuclei in the cervical spinal cord that innervate the muscles of the neck. These projections are involved in the *vestibulocollic reflexes*, a group of reflexes that maintain a stable posture of the head, described in Chapter 6. Finally, there are projections via the lateral vestibulospinal tracts to motor nuclei and interneuron in the thoracic and lumbar spinal cord. The motor nuclei innervate the muscles of the trunk and limbs. These projections are involved in a number of reflexes that stabilize upright posture.

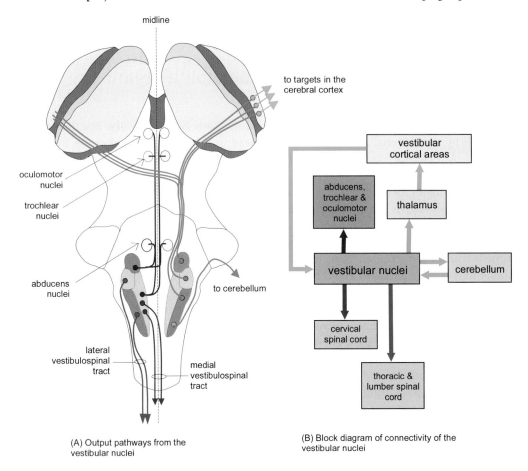

Figure 3.26: *Connectivity of the vestibular nuclei.*

The projections to the cerebral cortex go via several nuclei in the thalamus (including the ventro-posterior group of nuclei) to targets in various regions of the cortex. At least four tar-get regions have been identified in monkeys: (1) the parieto-insular vestibular cortex (PIVC); (2) a region at the junction of the parietal and temporal lobes (region T3); (3) a small region

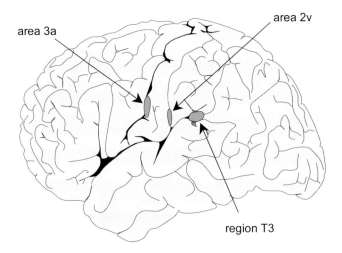

Figure 3.27: *Approximate locations of the cortical regions that receive vestibular information via the thalamus.*

of the postcentral gyrus (somatosensory cortex, area 2v); (4) a region at the junction of the primary motor cortex and the somatosensory cortex (area 3a)[26]. These regions have analogs in the human cortex[27]. Figure 3.27 shows the approximate locations of areas 2v, 3a, and T3; all three of these areas are enfolded in deep sulci. The insular cortex is found at the bottom of the Sylvian fissure; the PIVC is located within the insular cortex close to region T3 in the figure. The various cortical areas that contain neurons that respond to vestibular stimulation form a network, with PIVC at its focus and with all other regions projecting to it[28].

3.3 The Somatosensory System

3.3.1 Introduction

Sensory receptors of various sorts are distributed throughout almost all the tissues of the body, nervous tissue being a notable exception – there are no sensory receptors in the brain. There are receptors in the skin, in the muscles, in tendons and ligaments, in the joints, in lymph nodes, in the walls of blood vessels, in the ureter and urinary bladder, in the lungs, in the walls and lining of the gastrointestinal tract and in other abdominal viscera. Some of these receptors belong to the autonomic division of the nervous system, we will not be concerned with these. The others belong to the somatic division: the mechanoreceptors, thermoreceptors, and nociceptors (pain receptors) found in skin, muscles, joints, tendons and ligaments. These are called **somatosensory receptors**:

> **SOMATOSENSORY RECEPTOR:** Any mechanoreceptor, thermoreceptor or nociceptor found embedded in the skin, fatty tissue beneath the skin, muscle tissue or musculoskeletal connective tissue (tendon, ligament or other joint capsule tissue).

Stimulation of thermoreceptors and nociceptors is associated with sensations of hot, cold and pain. Such stimulation can contribute to the perception of object properties by touch and can elicit skeletomotor and autonomic reactions in an involuntary, reflexive manner. Such reactions include withdrawal of the hand from a hot surface, constriction of peripheral blood vessels and the production of goose-pimples in cold weather. We will have little further to say about either thermoreceptors or nociceptors. The focus of this part of the chapter will be on the somatosensory mechanoreceptors that provide sensory information for touch, for the perception of bodily posture and movement, and for the perception of physical effort and exertion of force.

3.3.2 Somatosensory mechanoreceptors incorporate the endings of thick, myelinated axons

Somatosensory receptors are formed from the endings of sensory axons which arise from cell bodies located in the dorsal root ganglia or, in the case of most receptors in the head and throat, the sensory ganglia of cranial nerves. Some sensory axons are myelinated and others are unmyelinated, and they vary considerably in thickness, ranging between 0.2 micrometers (μm) to about 20 μm in diameter, the very thinnest being unmyelinated. Four groups of sensory afferent axon are distinguished based on thickness and myelinization. The myelinated axons fall into three groups based on their thickness: a thick group (13 to 20 μm in diameter), a medium thick group (6-12 μm) and a thin group (1 to 5 μm). The unmyelinated fibers (0.2 to 1.5 μm) form the fourth group. There are two different nomenclatures that are commonly used to denote these groupings: a numerical nomenclature and an alphabetical

---

nomenclature. The alphabetical nomenclature originally derived from conduction speeds and the numerical one from fiber diameter. Since fiber diameter and conduction speed have a simple, one-to-one relationship for myelinated fibers as described in Chapter 2, the two nomenclatures are equivalent. The alphabetical nomenclature is commonly used for afferent fibers that innervate the skin[29], while the numerical one is commonly used for the fibers that innervate muscles, joints and associated connective tissue. In the alphabetical nomenclature, the capital letter 'A' is used for myelinated fibers and 'C' for unmyelinated fibers. The three thickness groupings for myelinated fibers are denoted by letters from the Greek alphabet (α, β, δ), so the three types of myelinated fibers are denoted Aα, Aβ and Aδ. The numerical nomenclature simply uses the Roman numerals I to IV. These facts are summarized in Table 3.1.

Table 3.1: *Somatosensory afferent fiber groupings.*

Fiber group (muscle/joint)	Fiber group (cutaneous)	Characteristic	Diameter (μm)	Conduction speed (m/s)
I	Aα	Large myelinated	13 – 20	80 – 120
II	Aβ	Medium myelinated	6 – 12	35 – 75
III	Aδ	Small myelinated	1 – 5	5 – 30
IV	C	Unmyelinated	0.2 – 1.5	0.5 – 2

The variation in conduction speed means that the time taken to transmit signals from the innervated tissue to the spinal cord can vary more than a hundredfold. For example, the axons of receptors in the skin of the toes are approximately one meter in length: it would take two seconds for action potentials transmitted along a 0.2 μm type C fiber to reach the spinal cord, but only 20 milliseconds for action potentials transmitted along a type Aβ fiber that conducts at 50 m/s.

Non-nociceptive, somatosensory mechanoreceptor fibers are of the two thickest types (I/Aα and II/Aβ): these fibers and their associated receptors comprise the input end of the **large-fibered afferent system**[30]. The other two fiber types are associated with thermoreceptors and nociceptors and comprise the input end of the **small-fibered afferent system**. In what follows, we will be concerned exclusively with the large-fibered afferent system.

3.3.3 There are five types of mechanoreceptor found close to the surface of human skin

Five basic types of mechanoreceptor are found in human external skin and in the layers of fatty and connective tissue immediately beneath it[31]. Table 3.2 lists the five types together with small diagrams showing their gross anatomical structure and a rough indication of their size[32]. These receptors are referred to as **cutaneous mechanoreceptors**, meaning that they are located in the skin, though the Ruffini end organs and Pacinian corpuscles are also found beneath the skin in the subcutaneous layers. Merkel disc receptors, Meissner corpuscles, Ruffini end organs and Pacinian corpuscles are found in hairless (glabrous) skin, which is found on the hands, the soles of the feet and the lips[33]. Hairy skin contains all these types, with the exception of Meissner corpuscles, and also contains hair follicle receptors[34].

Each mechanoreceptor is a tiny sensory organ formed of the sensory endings of a single axon that innervate other tissue structures, as shown in the diagrams in Table 3.2. Each organ is innervated by the axon terminals of a sensory neuron[35]. In some cases, the axon terminals innervate only one sensory organ. In other cases, the axon terminals branch out to several sensory organs. For example, a single axon may branch to form as many as one hundred Merkel disc receptors, which are each formed from a single Merkel cell. Since these numerous individual receptors are innervated by a single axon, they can be considered to form a single, distributed sensory organ.

Table 3.2: *Cutaneous mechanoreceptor organs.*

Receptor	Merkel disk receptors	Meissner corpuscle	Ruffini end organ	Pacinian corpuscle	Hair follicle receptor
Diagram	0.01 mm Merkel cell axon terminal	0.05 mm axon terminals	0.5 mm	0.75 mm	skin surface hair axon terminal
Fiber group	Aβ	Aβ	Aβ	Aβ	Aβ
Adaptation characteristic	Slow adapting	Fast adapting	Slow adapting	Fast adapting	Fast adapting
Skin type	Glabrous & hairy	Glabrous & hairy	Glabrous & hairy	Glabrous & hairy	Hairy

3.3.4 Different cutaneous mechanoreceptors respond to different characteristics of stimulation

The various types of cutaneous mechanoreceptor are stimulated by contact between the surface of the skin and a physical object or a substance that may be solid, liquid or gaseous. When a solid object rests on the palm of your hand, for example, its weight compresses the skin and subcutaneous tissues: this stimulates various mechanoreceptors. When the object is first placed on the palm, the compression builds up very quickly and then is sustained at a constant level for as long as the object remains stationary in the palm. If the object is removed, the compression very quickly disappears. The compression of the skin would then follow a stimulation profile similar to that shown in Figure 3.5. Pacinian corpuscles and Merkel disk receptors are particularly sensitive to compression of the skin (skin pressure). The firing rates recorded from afferent fibers of the Pacinian corpuscles in the palm would show a pattern like that on the left of Figure 3.5: a volley of action potentials is transmitted along the fiber when the object is first placed on the palm and again when it is removed, but not while it is resting there. The firing rates recorded from the afferent fibers of the slowly adapting Merkel disc receptors would show a pattern like that on the right of Figure 3.5: the afferent fibers begin firing when an object is placed on the palm, and continue firing until the object is removed.

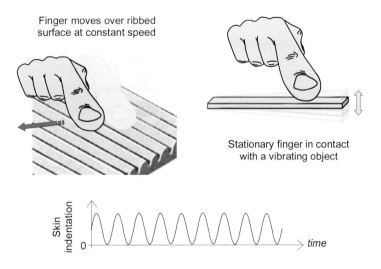

Figure 3.28: *Two ways of producing a cyclical pattern of skin indentation.*

A different kind of stimulation results when the surface of the hand is rubbed over a ribbed surface or when it comes into contact with a vibrating object. If you run your finger tip over a ribbed surface, the skin is briefly compressed as it passes over each rib, while there is no compression as the skin passes over the troughs between the ribs. If the finger moves over the surface at constant speed as suggested by the cartoon at the top left of Figure 3.28, a cyclical pattern of skin indentation is the result, as shown at the bottom of the figure. A similar kind of pattern could be produced when a stationary finger is held against a surface that is vibrating and so moving backwards and forwards, periodically compressing the skin and then allowing it to relax during each cycle of the vibration (top right of Figure 3.28). A cyclically varying skin indentation of the sort shown in Figure 3.28 will stimulate fast adapting mechano-receptors but will not provide a good stimulus for the slow adapting receptors.

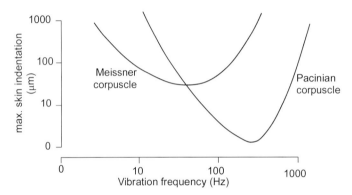

Figure 3.29: *Threshold level of skin indentation for Meissner and Pacinian corpuscles (logarithmic scales on both axes, based on data from Mountcastle* et al., *1972).*

Pacinian and Meissner corpuscles are both fast adapting receptors that will respond to the type of cyclical skin compression shown in Figure 3.28. Figure 3.29 shows how the sensitivity of Pacinian and Meissner corpuscles varies with the frequency of skin indentation produced with a vibrating probe. Points on each curve represent the smallest skin indentation (at the peak of the vibration cycle) that can reliably evoke a change of firing rate in the afferent fiber that innervates the corpuscle: this is the threshold of the receptor[36]. The smaller the threshold, the more sensitive the receptor is to the stimulation. As the graphs show, Pacinian corpuscles are most sensitive when the frequency of vibration is in the region of 250 Hz (the lowest point on the curve). At this frequency, the sensory endings will reliably respond to skin indentations of only a few thousandths of a millimeter. Meissner corpuscles are most sensitive when the frequency is between about 30 and 50 Hz, though they are never as sensitive as Pacinian corpuscles (the lowest point in the curve is much higher). Being fast adapting, neither type of receptor responds to vibrations of very low frequency (below two or three cycles per second) or to sustained compression of the skin.

Table 3.3: *Somatosensory afferent fiber groupings.*

Mechanoreceptor	Effective stimulation
Merkel discs	Sustained skin contact and pressure, slowly changing skin deformations (frequencies less than ~5 Hz)
Meissner corpuscles	Lateral movement, vibration and fairly rapid changes in skin deformation (~5–50 Hz)
Ruffini end organs	Sustained and slow changes in skin stretch or tension
Pacinian corpuscles	High frequency vibration (~40–400 Hz), contact events and rapid skin deformations

The slow adapting Ruffini end organ receptors are insensitive to pressure on the skin but respond strongly to skin stretch. Being slow adapting, they respond to the amount of skin stretch rather than the speed at which it is stretching – they are skin stretch sensors. Finally, the hair follicle receptors respond when the hairs are moved. Being fast adapting, these receptors respond while the hair is moving, but do not respond to sustained deflections of the hair. Table 3.3 lists the characteristics of skin stimulation to which the cutaneous mechanoreceptors are thought most likely to be responsive. We will discuss the information carried by cutaneous mechanoreceptor responses in more detail later (section 3.4).

3.3.5 Different types of cutaneous mechanoreceptive afferents have different receptive fields

A mechanoreceptive afferent fiber will only shows a response to stimulation applied to a particular region of the skin surface. This region of skin surface is called the **receptive field** of the afferent fiber. For somatosensory afferents in general, the concept of a receptive field can be defined as follows:

> **RECEPTIVE FIELD (OF A SOMATOSENSORY AFFERENT FIBER):** The total area of the skin surface within which suitable stimulation will evoke a response (change in the firing rate) in the afferent fiber.

Notice that the receptive field is defined for an afferent fiber and not for a specific mechanoreceptive organ. In some cases, it would make no real difference whether the receptive field were defined for the fiber or the receptor, but in cases where a single afferent fiber innervates more than one mechanoreceptive organ, there would be a difference.

Examples of the receptive fields of the afferent fibers innervating the four kinds of mechanoreceptors found in the glabrous skin of the hand are shown in Figure 3.30. The hand at the top of the figure shows ten receptive fields of afferents that innervate Meissner corpuscles shaded in green (on the index finger, thumb, and palm) and five receptive fields of afferents that innervate Merkel disk receptors shaded in gray (on the middle finger, ring finger and palm). These receptive fields are small (a few millimeters across) and have quite well-defined borders. If the receptive fields of all such afferents were shown, they would overlap with one another and cover almost the entire surface of the hand. The receptive field of one of the Merkel disk afferents is shown enlarged to reveal its internal structure in the form of a contour map. The different shaded regions represent different sensitivities – the darker the shading, the more sensitive the afferent is to stimulation in that region of skin. The darkest regions correspond to the positions where the Merkel disk receptors innervated by the afferent fiber are actually located (recall that a single afferent innervates numerous individual Merkel discs)[37].

The hand shown at the bottom of Figure 3.30 shows two receptive fields of afferents innervating Pacinian corpuscles (on the middle finger and the left side of the palm) and two receptive fields of afferents innervating Ruffini end organs (on the index and ring fingers). These receptive fields are large and have indistinct, fuzzy borders. They are large because suitable stimulation (e.g., vibration) anywhere in the region is transmitted by the tissues of the hand to the receptor organ itself. The areas of skin where the afferents are most sensitive are shown as dark spots: the receptor organ itself is located within these regions (each afferent fiber innervates only one Pacinian corpuscle or Ruffini organ). The sensitive region for one of the Pacinian corpuscle afferents is shown enlarged, and reveals that there is a very small region that is particularly sensitive – this is likely to be directly over the Pacinian corpuscle.

Ruffini end organs are sensitive to skin stretch: in the figure, the direction of stretch that evokes a response in the afferent fiber is indicated by an arrow (stretch in the opposite direction evokes no response). The afferent that innervates a Ruffini ending in the index finger is stimulated by stretch in one direction in the part of the receptive field towards the tip of the finger, and by stretch in the opposite direction in the part towards the base of the finger.

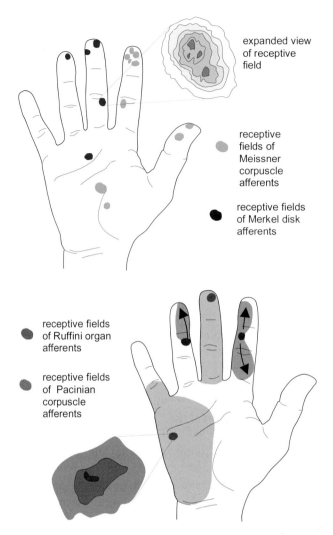

Figure 3.30: *Receptive fields of selected afferents in the human hand. Based on figures presented in Johansson & Vallbo (1983).*

3.3.6 Five types of mechanoreceptive organ are found in the musculoskeletal system

The musculoskeletal system of humans and other mammals contains five basic types of mechanoreceptor organ that belong to the large fiber system: **muscle spindles**, **golgi tendon organs**, **Ruffini type receptors**, **Paciniform receptors** and **Golgi endings**. All these mechanoreceptive organs are usually classified as proprioceptors, though they also contribute to the perception of the properties of felt and wielded objects (i.e., they serve an exteroceptive function, see section 3.4). They are found in the various soft tissues of the musculoskeletal system as follows:

(1) **Skeletal muscle:** with the exception of the perioral muscles that move the lips and the muscles of the inner ear, all the skeletal muscles in the human body contain muscle spindles; they are found distributed throughout the belly of the muscle. Some muscles have also been found to have Paciniform and Ruffini type receptors in their connective tissues; these are essentially the same as the corpuscles found in the skin, but little is known about their function.

(2) **Tendon:** Golgi tendon organs (GTOs) are located at the junction between the muscle fibers and the tendinous tissue that attaches the muscle to the bone. They are found in most but not all muscles[38]. Paciniform receptors are also found in tendons.

(3) **Joints and ligaments:** the mechanoreceptors found in ligaments and the soft tissues of joints are collectively referred to as **joint receptors**. There are three varieties: Ruffini type receptors (similar to cutaneous Ruffini end organs), Paciniform receptors (similar to cutaneous Pacinian corpuscles but much smaller) and Golgi endings, which resemble GTOs and are only found in ligaments.

3.3.7 Muscle spindles are complex sensory organs with both afferent and efferent innervation

The muscle spindle is a complex structure comprising a group of small, specialized skeletal muscle fibers that are sheathed in a capsule of connective tissue, as shown in Figure 3.31. They are called spindles because their shape is reminiscent of the old-fashioned spindles used in spinning thread. There are about 28,000 spindles in the human body, and they have a particularly high density in the muscles of the hand and neck. They vary in length from about two or three millimeters to about one centimeter long. The muscle fibers within the capsule are called **intrafusal muscle fibers**, the word '*intrafusal*' meaning 'inside the spindle' (from the Latin *fusus*, meaning spindle). The number of fibers in a spindle varies from as few as three or four up to as many as eighteen. The ends of the intrafusal fibers are attached to connective tissue within the body of the muscle; they do not contribute to the contractile force developed by the main fibers of the muscle, which are often referred to as **extrafusal fibers** (outside the spindle). An extrafusal fiber can typically generate thirty to forty times as much force as an intrafusal fiber.

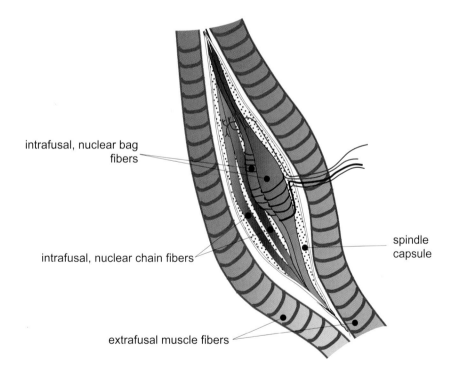

intrafusal, nuclear bag fibers

intrafusal, nuclear chain fibers

spindle capsule

extrafusal muscle fibers

Figure 3.31: *Structure of a muscle spindle.*

Figure 3.31 shows a spindle with four intrafusal fibers. Two are relatively thick and swollen in the middle; the swelling contains the nuclei of the fiber. These fibers are called **nuclear bag fibers**. The other fibers are thinner and lack the central swelling. The nuclei in these fibers are spread out along the length of the fiber; for this reason they are called **nuclear chain fibers**.

Each intrafusal fiber is innervated by an efferent fiber and one or more afferent fibers. The efferent fibers are the axons of gamma motoneurons (γ-MNs), of which there are two types (see below). The afferent fibers are of type I and type II; the type I afferent fibers that innervate spindles are called **type Ia afferents**. Figure 3.32 shows the innervation pattern of the four intrafusal fibers of Figure 3.31. A type Ia afferent axon innervates all four muscle fibers; a type II afferent axon innervates the nuclear chain fibers and one of the nuclear bag fibers.

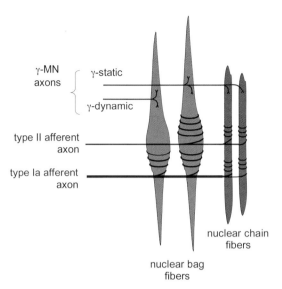

Figure 3.32: *Innervation of intrafusal fibers.*

The axon of one type of γ-MN called a **gamma static** MN innervates the nuclear chain fibers and one of the nuclear bag fibers. This bag fiber is called a **static nuclear bag fiber**. A second type of γ-MN called a **gamma dynamic** MN innervates the other nuclear bag fiber. This bag fiber is called a **dynamic nuclear bag fiber**. A muscle spindle will usually contain at least two nuclear bag fibers, one of each type, and a variable number of nuclear chain fibers.

3.3.8 Muscle spindle afferent endings are sensitive to muscle length and speed of muscle lengthening

The muscle spindle is elastic, and is lengthened (stretched) or shortened as the muscle in which it is embedded lengthens or shortens. When the intrafusal muscle fibers are stretched, the sensory endings entwined about them are mechanically stimulated, and the firing rate of the associated afferent fibers increases. When the intrafusal fibers shorten, stimulation of the afferent endings is reduced and the afferent firing rate decreases. For this reason, muscle spindles are often described as *muscle stretch receptors*.

A muscle stretch has two important characteristics: (1) the amount of stretch, and (2) the speed at which the stretch occurs[39]. Figure 3.33 shows two afferent responses to two different stretches. The stretch stimulus is shown at the top of each panel (muscle length against time). The muscle is stretched to the same length in each panel, but the speed of stretching is different: fast in panel A, slow in B (speed of lengthening is plotted as a function of time in the second row of the figure). The effect of these stretches on the firing rate of muscle spindle afferents is shown in the bottom two rows: the third row shows the firing of a type Ia afferent, the bottom row shows the firing of a type II afferent. Both afferents fire at a relatively low rate while the muscle is held at its initial (shorter) length. During the period for which the muscle is lengthening (shown shaded), the firing rate of the Ia afferent increases and is greater for the faster stretch. When the muscle is held at the longer, stretched length, the firing rate of the Ia afferent drops but is higher than at the initial length. In contrast, the firing rate of the type II afferent only shows a small increase in firing rate during the period of lengthening, but shows a substantially greater firing rate that is sustained for the time that the muscle is held at the the longer length. Thus, the type II afferents are slow adapting, whereas type Ia afferents have both fast adapting and slow adapting characteristics.

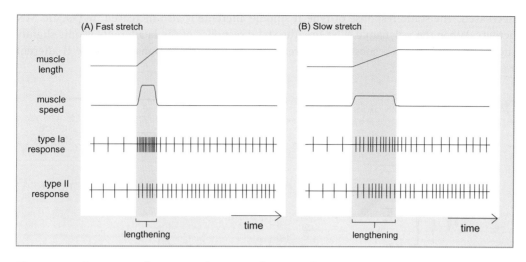

Figure 3.33: *Responses of type Ia and type II afferents to fast and slow stretches (illustrative).*

The pattern of behavior shown in Figure 3.33 demonstrates that the type Ia afferent is sensitive to muscle length and to the speed at which the muscle is lengthening. The type II afferent is sensitive to muscle length, but relatively insensitive to the speed at which the muscle lengthens. In sum, we can think of type II afferent endings as muscle length sensors (or more strictly, spindle length sensors) and type Ia afferents as muscle velocity sensors that also have some length sensitivity. A pure muscle velocity sensor could be formed by subtracting the (weighted) response of the type II afferent from that of the type Ia afferent.

3.3.9 Efferent signals influence the response of muscle spindle afferents

Spikes transmitted along the γ-MN axons cause the innervated intrafusal fibers to contract; this affects the sensitivity of the spindle afferent endings to muscle stretch. Figure 3.34 illustrates the effects of electrically stimulating γ-MN axons on the stretch responses of type Ia and type II afferents. The left side of the figure shows the stimulation and recording set-up. The right side shows the stretch stimulus to which the muscle is subjected (top, panel A), the firing rates recorded from the afferent fibers, and the period for which the electrical stimulus was applied ('on'). Panel A shows the firing rates recorded in the absence of efferent activity (no electrical stimulation). Panel B shows the afferent firing rates recorded when the γ-static MN axon was stimulated. Panel C record shows the afferent firing rates recorded when the γ-dynamic MN axon was stimulated. The stretch applied in panels B and C was as shown in panel A.

The firing recorded from the afferents in response to muscle stretch only (panel A) is similar to that shown in Figure 3.33 but plotted as a graph rather than as a spike train. There is a burst of activity (dynamic response) in the Ia afferent response during the period of stretching; no such burst is evident in the type II afferent response. Stimulation of the γ-static MN axon (panel B) causes the intrafusal chain and static bag fibers to contract. This has two effects on the firing of the Ia afferent: (1) during the periods when the muscle is not changing length, the firing rate is raised relative to its level when the MN axon is not stimulated (increased static response). (2) During the period of stretching, the dynamic response of the Ia afferent is reduced (reduced dynamic response). The type II afferent response is similar to the first effect on the Ia afferent response. Stimulation of the gamma dynamic MN axon (panel C) only causes the dynamic nuclear bag fiber(s) to contract. This affects the type Ia afferent response: there is a small effect on the static response, but a large effect on the dynamic response, which is increased relative to the other conditions shown in panels A and B. There is no effect on the type II afferent response (response is the same in panels A and C).

In sum, when the γ-static MNs fire, the Ia afferent response to a change in length (static response) is increased, but the response to the rate of lengthening (dynamic response) is decreased. The static response of type II spindle afferents is also increased by γ-static MN activity. When the γ-dynamic MNs fire, the static response of the Ia afferents is only slightly increased, but there is a substantial increase in the dynamic response (the type II afferent response is unaffected).

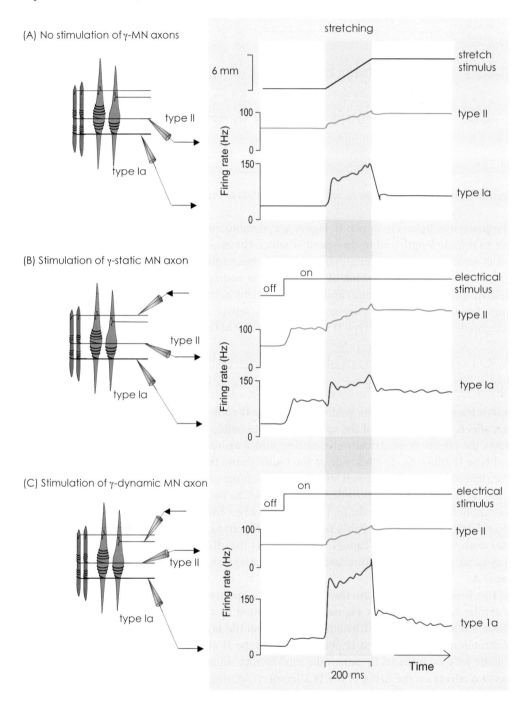

Figure 3.34: *Effect of γ-MN stimulation on the response of spindle afferents to stretch. Based on data from Crowe and Matthews (1964) and Prochazka (1996).*

3.3.10 Golgi tendon organs are muscle force sensors

The Golgi tendon organ (GTO) is an encapsulated bundle of collagen strands innervated by afferent axons that branch into numerous fine terminals within the organ capsule and intermesh with the collagen strands. They range in length between about 0.2 and 1 millimeter, and are about five or ten times thinner than they are long (a 1 mm long organ will be about 0.1 to 0.2 mm across at the widest point). As shown in Figure 3.35, tendon organs are actually located not within tendons but at the junctions between muscle and tendon: they are attached to several extrafusal muscle fibers at one end, and to tendon at the other. The number of attached muscle fibers varies, but is typically between 10 and 20. The afferent axons innervating tendon organs are large diameter, myelinated fibers referred to as **type Ib afferents**.

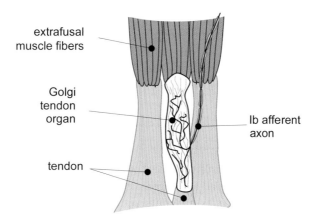

Figure 3.35: *Golgi tendon organ.*

When a force is applied across a GTO, the collagen strands within it are stretched slightly, and this causes them to squeeze on the enmeshed axon terminals. This squeezing of the terminals depolarizes them and the Ib afferent fiber generates action potentials. The greater the force across a tendon organ, the more the afferent terminals are squeezed and the greater their depolarization. The result is that the firing rate of the afferent fiber increases with the force across the tendon organ. Some studies have found that over quite a wide range of forces (from about 0.5 to 25 Newtons) the Ib afferent firing rate increases in direct proportion to the force[40]. These results suggest that tendon organs function as force sensors.

Given that tendons organs are attached to muscle at one end and tendon at the other, a force will only be applied across them in normal conditions when the muscle fibers are actively developing force. This makes tendon organs suitable for the sensing of forces developed by active muscle rather than to forces imposed passively on inactive muscle. In inactive muscle, passive forces are transmitted mainly in the connective tissues of the muscle, not by the muscle fibers connected to the tendon organs. Individual GTOs have been found to be exquisitely sensitive to forces developed by active muscles and can respond to forces between 30 and 90 microNewtons (a force equivalent to a weight of less than one hundredth of a gram)[41]. When forces are applied to passive, inactive muscle, they need to be nearly 100,000 times greater in order to evoke a response from a tendon organ. The receptor endings are relatively slow adapting, resembling type II spindle afferents, and their firing rate tends to follow the level of active force generated by the muscle[42]. Thus, GTOs function most effectively as sensors that continuously signal the active muscle force transmitted to the tendon. Note that tendon length can be obtained from these signals, since the force and length of a tendon have a one-to-one relationship, so that if you know the force and the relationship, you can derive the length[43].

3.3.11 Joint receptors may function as limit detectors

The three types of mechanoreceptor found in the connective tissue surrounding joints – the Golgi endings, Ruffini receptors and Paciniform receptors – are innervated by afferent fibers of similar types to those that innervate their cutaneous or musculo-tendinous counterparts. They also have similar adaptation characteristics: Golgi endings and Ruffini receptors are slow adapting, Paciniform receptors are fast adapting. The Golgi endings are found in ligaments; Ruffini and Paciniform receptors are found in the tissue of the joint capsule.

Joint receptors respond when the connective tissues of a joint are deformed (stretched or twisted), which occurs due to forces applied to the tissue. Deformation of the joint capsule stimulates the Paciniform and Ruffini receptors; stretch of the ligaments stimulates Golgi endings. Recordings from joint receptor afferent fibers in cats showed that the majority of receptors only responded at the extremes of joint position (e.g., around full extension and full flexion); only a minority responded at intermediate joint positions[44]. These results suggest that joint receptors are involved in signaling that an extreme joint position is being approached, leading to the view that joint receptors are limit detectors[45]. However, studies of human joint receptors show that they do carry at least some information throughout the full range of joint motion[46] and so could make a contribution to the perception of the position and movement of joints. We discuss this later in the chapter (section 3.4.3).

3.3.12 Somatosensory information is transmitted to the brain along six different groups of fiber tracts

The cell bodies of somatosensory neurons are located in the dorsal root ganglia of the spinal cord or, in the case of those in the head and throat, in the ganglia of the cranial nerves. The peripheral branch of the afferent axon transmits action potentials evoked at the sensory endings to the sensory ganglia, and from there they are transmitted into the spinal cord or brainstem by the axon's central branch.

The central branches of both the small and large somatosensory afferent fibers enter the spinal cord via the dorsal roots. Within the gray matter of the cord they branch into numerous terminals and make synaptic connections with spinal interneurons and, in the case of Ia afferent axons, with motoneurons. Many of these connections form part of the spinal circuitry involved in reflexes, as described in detail later (Chapters 5 and 6). Somatosensory information is also transmitted to various regions of the brain along myelinated fibers that ascend up the spinal cord. Most of these ascending fibers are the axons of spinal interneurons with which the central branches of afferent fibers make synaptic connections, but some of them are main branches of large diameter afferent axons (Figure 3.36).

There are six groups of ascending fiber tracts along which the axons of the large-fibered afferent system travel up to the brain. The axons of the sensory neurons themselves travel along two fiber tracts at the back of the cord called the **dorsal columns**, and terminate in the dorsal column nuclei of the medulla. The location of the dorsal columns is shown in Figure 3.36, along with an example sensory axon (in blue) that enters the right side of the spinal cord and projects to one of the dorsal column nuclei. As the figure shows, the sensory axons project ipsilaterally to these nuclei. The majority of axons of neurons in the dorsal column nuclei cross to the other (contralateral) side of the brain and project to the thalamus along fiber tracts called the *medial lemnisci* (one medial lemniscus on the left and one on the right). In the thalamus they make synaptic connections with neurons that project to the cerebral cortex. Some neurons in the dorsal column nuclei transmit somatosensory information to the cerebellum along the *cuneocerebellar tracts* (see below). Axons travel from the dorsal column nuclei to the thalamus along the medial lemniscus. This route up the spinal cord to the cortex is called the **dorsal column-medial lemniscal pathway**.

The five other groups of ascending fiber tracts carry the axons of spinal interneurons with which somatosensory axons make synaptic connections. These tracts are named for the target structures where the ascending axons terminate: the **spinothalamic tracts** (axons terminate in the thalamus), the **spinocerebellar tracts** (axons terminate in the cerebellum), the **spino-olivary tracts** (axons terminate in the inferior olivary nuclei of the medulla), the **spinotectal tracts** (axons terminate in the superior colliculi), and the **spinoreticular tracts** (axons terminate in the reticular formation).

The spinothalamic tracts on each side have two components: the ventral spinothalamic tract and the lateral spinothalamic tract. Only the ventral spinothalamic tracts carry information from the large-fibered somatosensory afferents; the lateral tracts carry information derived from the small-fibered afferents (the spinoreticular tracts carry information derived from both large- and small-fibered afferents). Figure 3.36 also shows the path followed by sensory information carried up the right ventral spinothalamic tract (in green). As the figure shows, the tract on the right side carries sensory information from sensory afferents that enter the spinal cord on the left (contralateral) side and have sensory endings in the left side of the body.

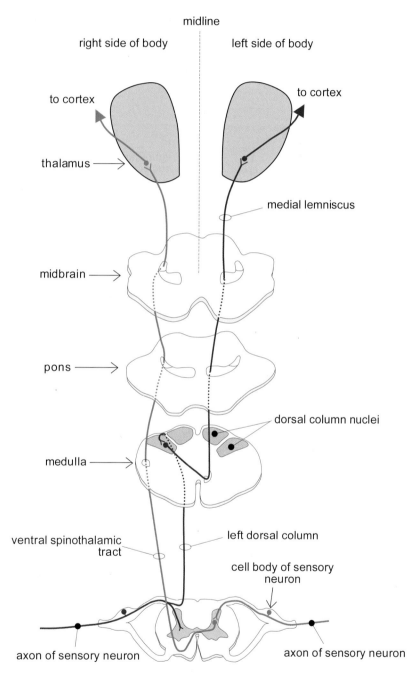

Figure 3.36: *Somatosensory pathways to the cerebral cortex.*

The group of tracts that relay somatosensory information to the cerebellum include the dorsal and ventral spinocerebellar tracts, the cuneocerebellar tract, and the spino-olivary tracts. Figure 3.37 shows the path followed by the majority of axons in the right dorsal spinocerebellar tract, which carries sensory information from the right (ipsilateral) side of the body (the leg and lower part of the trunk) to the cerebellum. The axons in the tract derive from cell bodies in Clarke's nucleus, which stretches down through most of the lumbar spinal segments.

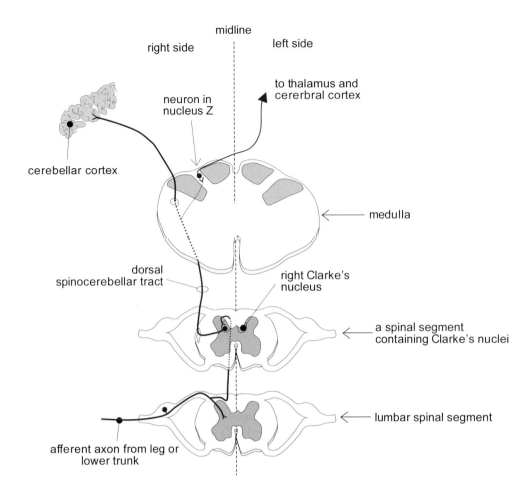

Figure 3.37: *Dorsal spinocerebellar tract.*

As the figure shows, some fibers in the dorsal spinocerebellar tract branch off and make connections to neurons in nucleus Z of the medulla. These neurons project to the thalamus from where signals are relayed to the cortex. Sensory information from the upper part of the trunk is carried in the dorsal spinocerebellar tracts, and information from the upper limbs is carried in the cuneocerebellar tracts. Table 3.4 summarizes the pathways by which somatosensory information is transmitted to the brain in the large-fibered afferent system; it includes the main kinds of mechanoreceptors from which the information carried along each pathway is derived.

Table 3.4: *Pathways that carry somatosensory information to the brain.*

Tracts	Fibers	Target structures of tracts	End of pathway	Receptors (large-fibered)
Dorsal columns	Mainly the axons of sensory neurons	Ipsilateral dorsal column nuclei in the medulla	Cerebral cortex (via medial lemniscus & thalamus); Cerebellar cortex (via cuneocerebellar tract)	Cutaneous, muscles and joints
Ventral spinothalamic	Spinal interneurons	Contralateral thalamus (ventro-posterior nuclei)	Cerebral cortex	Cutaneous
Spinocerebellar	Spinal interneurons	Ipsilateral cerebellar cortex	Cerebellar cortex + some to thalamus	Mainly muscles and joints
Spino-olivary	Spinal interneurons	Contralateral olivary nucleus	Cerebellar cortex	Mainly muscles and joints
Spinotectal	Spinal interneurons	Contralateral superior colliculus	Superior colliculi	Cutaneous
Spinoreticular	Spinal interneurons	Contralateral reticular formation	Various	Cutaneous

3.3.13 Somatosensory information is transmitted from the thalamus to three regions in the parietal lobe

Neurons in the thalamic nuclei that receive somatosensory inputs via the medial lemniscus, the spinothalamic tracts and the spinocerebellar tracts project to three regions of the parietal lobe. These areas are shown in Figure 3.38: the **primary somatosensory area (SI)** that occupies the post-central gyrus, the **secondary somatosensory area (SII)** and the **posterior parietal area** (also known as the *posterior parietal lobule*). SII starts from the most inferior part of the post-central gyrus and continues along the upper bank of the lateral sulcus, as shown on the left of the figure[47] (the section on the left was made by slicing a brain along the dashed line shown on the right). These areas are crucial for the conscious experiences of touch, the perception of felt objects and surfaces, and the perception of limb position and movement in the absence of vision.

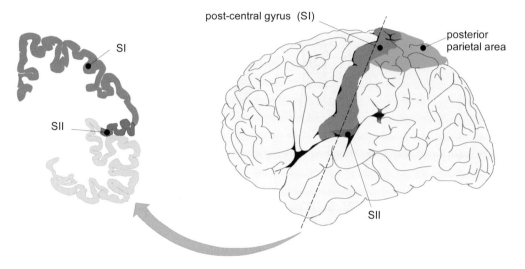

Figure 3.38: *Somatosensory areas of the human cerebral cortex.*

Figure 3.39 shows a schematic block diagram representation of the somatosensory projections from the thalamus to the three cortical areas. As the figure shows, SI has four sub-areas (distinguished based on their cellular anatomy). These are areas 1, 2, 3a and 3b, which all run down the whole length of the SI like a series of stripes: area 2 is the most caudal and lies in the

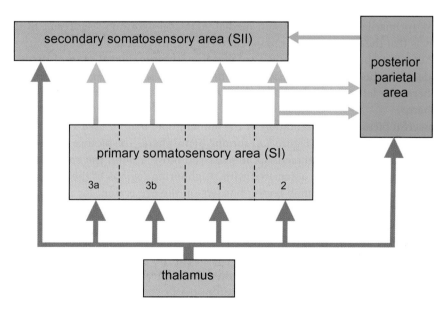

Figure 3.39: *Thalamocortical projections.*

intraparietal sulcus, area 1 forms the crown of the post-central gyrus, and areas 3b and 3a are the most rostral and lie in the central sulcus.

Figure 3.40 shows a cross-section through the post-central gyrus and shows the regions occupied by the four sub-areas. These areas receive information from different groups of mechanoreceptors: areas 2 and 3a receive information from muscle and joint afferents, with area 2 also receiving information from cutaneous mechanoreceptors. Areas 1 and 3b receive information primarily from cutaneous receptors. The secondary somatosensory cortex (SII) has a more uniform cellular architecture and receives signals from all the sub-areas of SI, as well as from the thalamus. The thalamic projection to this area carries signals that derive mainly from cutaneous mechanoreceptors.

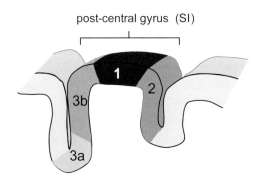

Figure 3.40: *Sagittal section through S1 showing division into sub-areas.*

3.3.14 The primary somatosensory cortex is somatotopically organized

The somatosensory system is topographically organized, with neural cell bodies and axons associated with nearby regions of the body being found grouped close together. When found in the somatosensory system, topographic organization is referred to as **somatotopy**. This concept will be illustrated using the example of the primary somatosensory cortex (SI).

As shown in Figure 3.40, SI comprises four sub-regions – areas 3a, 3b, 1 and 2. The figure shows that the surface of the gyrus that is visible on an exposed brain is largely occupied by area 1. Area 1 receives sensory input almost exclusively from cutaneous somatosensory receptors. This region is somatotopically organized such that afferents that innervate nearby regions of skin are connected to nearby neurons in the cortex via the ascending pathways (primarily the dorsal column-medial lemniscal pathway). The result of this connectivity is that the body surface is mapped to the surface of area 1 of the primary somatosensory cortex to produce what is known as a **somatotopic neural map** of the body. The right side of the body surface is mapped to the primary somatosensory cortex of the left hemisphere; the left side of the body is mapped to the corresponding area of the right hemisphere.

A powerful pictorial representation of the somatotopic map in area 1 of SI is Penfield's homunculus[48], reproduced in Figure 3.41 for one hemisphere. The picture clearly shows two characteristics of the somatotopic map: first, as you move around the cortex, neighboring regions of cortical tissues are associated with neighboring regions of the skin surface with only a few exceptions (the thumb region borders on the eye region, for instance). Second, equally sized regions of body surface do not generally map to equally sized regions of the cortex: some small areas of the skin map to disproportionately large areas of cortex and some large areas of skin map to disproportionately small areas of cortex. The thumb, for example, maps to an area of cortex similar in size to the area to which the whole leg is mapped. This is often expressed by saying that the **cortical representation** of the thumb is similar in size to the cortical representation of the leg. Inspection of the figure suggests that the cortical representation of the lips is larger than the cortical representation of the whole arm.

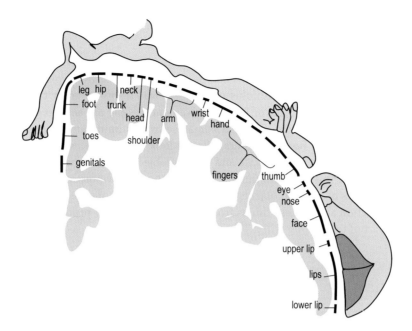

Figure 3.41: *Cortical representation of the body surface over SI. (Based on Penfield and Rasmussen, 1951.)*

There is a simple reason for the differences in the sizes of cortical representations: those parts of the body where the skin is densely populated by mechanoreceptors have large cortical representations, those parts where the skin is more sparsely populated have smaller cortical representations. The fingers and lips have particularly dense populations of mechanoreceptors and large cortical representations; they are also exquisitely sensitive to tactile stimulation.

It should be noted that the size of the receptive fields of the afferent fibers innervating the mechanoreceptors is an important determinant of tactile sensitivity. The large-fiber afferents innervating regions of the skin that are sparsely populated with mechanoreceptors typically have larger receptive fields than those innervating regions that are densely populated. In the hand, for example, the receptive fields of afferent fibers that innervate Merkel disk mechanoreceptors are only a few millimeters across (see section 3.3.4). The receptive fields of Merkel disc afferents in the skin of the trunk may be one hundred times larger. The sizes of the receptive fields limits the accuracy with which tactile stimuli can be localized.

3.4 Proprioceptive Afference and Kinesthesis

3.4.1 Introduction: somatosensory stimulation contains information about the body and about material objects

The mechanoreceptors of the large-fibered afferent system are stimulated when the tissues in which they are embedded are distorted by mechanical forces. As we saw in the last part of the chapter, different mechanoreceptors respond to different characteristics of tissue distortion: some respond to stretch, some to compression, some respond to sustained distortions (slow adapting receptors), some to rapid changes (fast adapting receptors). These tissue distortions are caused by various things: skin deformation can be caused by mechanical contact with objects; muscle length changes can be caused by muscle contractions or by external forces applied to the body segments. It is not possible to tell from the response of an individual afferent fiber what caused the firing.

Individual large-fiber afferents carry information about tissue distortion in the locality of their sensory endings. These distortions can be considered to be the proximal stimuli for the mechanoreceptors. The distal stimulus is whatever was responsible for the local tissue distortion, such as a physical object or a limb movement. People are able to determine the nature of these distal stimuli from proximal somatosensory stimulation – we are aware of the relative positions of our body segments without looking at them, we can feel how our limbs are moving, we can feel the shapes and sizes of objects that are held in our hands or are pressing against us. This indicates that information about body position, body movement and the characteristics of physical objects is present in proximal somatosensory stimulation. Extracting information about these things from the stimulation they produce is a perceptual problem. This part of the chapter will discuss this type of perception.

3.4.2 Kinesthesis is the perception of body movement and position from proprioceptive afference

A receptor that responds to stimulation produced by contact with the external environment is an *exteroceptor*. The afferent signals generated by exteroceptors in response to the external stimulation is **exteroceptive afference**. Exteroceptive afference contains information about external objects, substances and events. A mechanoreceptor that responds to stimulation produced by body position, movement and muscular contraction is a proprioceptor. In this case, the afferent signals produced in response to stimulation is **proprioceptive afference:**

> **PROPRIOCEPTIVE AFFERENCE:** Afferent signals generated by somatosensory mechanoreceptors in response to stimulation that is produced as a consequence of the positions and movements of body parts and tensions in muscles and joints.

Proprioceptive afference is transmitted to a number of regions within the central nervous system and is used for a variety of purposes. It is transmitted to motoneurons either directly or via spinal interneurons, and so can have a very immediate effect on muscular activity: these effects are described as reflexive, and are discussed in Chapters 5 and 6. It is transmitted to the brainstem and cerebellum mainly via the spinocerebellar tracts and the cuneocerebellar tracts: these proprioceptive signals are used in various ways to control and organize motor behavior outside of conscious awareness. It is transmitted to somatosensory areas of the cerebral cortex via the dorsal column-medial lemniscal pathway, where it contributes to cortical sensorimotor control processes and to perceptual awareness – it contributes to perception of the heaviness of objects, and also to the perception of the positions of body parts in relation to one another and of their movements. The perception of body position and movement from proprioceptive afference is called **kinesthetic perception** or **kinesthesis**[49]:

> **KINESTHETIC PERCEPTION (KINESTHESIS):** The process of obtaining information about the angular positions of joints, and the relative spatial locations, orientations and movements of limbs and other body parts, from proprioceptive afference.

The term derives from the same Greek root as *kinematic*, which refers to the position and motion of things without reference to the forces involved. We have defined kinesthesis similarly: perception of position and motion, but not of force. The feel of our limbs moving or of the degree to which a joint is flexed or extended are instances of kinesthetic perception. Kinesthesis provides us with information about where our limbs and body parts are. Imagine being in complete darkness with your left hand held out somewhere in front of you: you would find it easy to reach with your right index finger and touch any part of your left arm that you want – the left elbow, the wrist or the thumb. Without kinesthesis this would not be possible, as you would have no sensory information about where your arm was.

Another term that is often encountered in the literature is **proprioception**, which is a general term for perception based on proprioceptive afference and includes the perception of muscular force and effort. We will use the following definition:

> **PROPRIOCEPTION:** A kind of sensory perception in which the only sensory source of information is proprioceptive afference (non-sensory sources may also be involved). Any perception based on information obtained from proprioceptors and no other type of sensory receptor is an instance of proprioception.

According to the definitions given here, kinesthesis is a kind of proprioception that does not include perception of force and effort. It is important to be aware that *proprioception* is not used consistently in the literature: some authors use it to mean the same as *proprioceptive afference*. Some authors restrict it to conscious 'sensations', whereas others include unconscious perceptual functions. For some authors the term encompasses the perceptual functions of the vestibular system, but others exclude them. According to the definition given here, proprioception does not include perception based on vestibular afference, and is not restricted to conscious sensory experience. It can be used interchangeably with kinesthesis, but it is a broader term since it can include perceptions of effort and force.

3.4.3 Kinesthetic perceptual abilities can be assessed using matching or discrimination tasks

The accuracy with which the position or motion of a joint or a limb segment can be perceived is often assessed in experiments using **matching tasks**. In a matching task, a person tries to match the position or movement of a body segment (called the **target**) with something else, which can either be another body segment or a moveable device of some sort. The match may be attempted while the target is present (**simultaneous** matching task), or alternatively the target is presented and the match is attempted after the target has been removed (**successive** matching task). The successive version of the task is sometimes referred to as **memory guided**, because the person has to remember the target position.

Figure 3.42 shows a set-up used for a simultaneous matching task in which the participant attempts to match a target elbow joint angle of the left arm with their right arm[50]. In this set-up the forearms are strapped to hinged boards that can rotate about a hinge at the base. The experimenter sets the angle of the left elbow joint by moving the left board to a chosen position. The blindfolded participant then attempts to match the set position of his left elbow joint by flexing and/or extending his right elbow until he feels that the two angles are the same. Performance in this task is scored as the difference between the target joint angle and the person's attempted match.

There are many possible variants of the type of matching task, in which the participant attempts to match a target angle or posture of one limb using the other limb. In the example shown in Figure 3.42, the participant attempts to match a single joint angle, which in the case shown is the same as matching the orientation of the forearm segments. Matching segment orientations is not always equivalent to matching joint angles, however. For example, imagine holding your right forearm perpendicular to your upper arm and then internally rotating the shoulder joint so that the forearm is at an angle to the vertical, as the stick figure on the left of Figure 3.43 shows. If the task is to match the angle of internal rotation of the right shoulder with the left shoulder, with the limbs in similar postures, then the left arm should mirror the right arm (middle of Figure 3.43). If the task is to match the orientation of the left forearm, then the right arm should adopt the position shown on the right of Figure 3.43[51].

Experimenter positions
this board to set the left
elbow joint angle

Participant flexes and/or extends
the right elbow until the two
elbow angles feel the same

Figure 3.42: *Kinesthetic matching task (based on Allen and Proske, 2006).*

A successive version of the task shown in Figure 3.42 would typically involve the use of just one limb (though this is not necessary). The experimenter would first move one elbow to a target angle. Next the elbow would be moved to some other angle and then the participant flexes or extends the elbow in an attempt to restore it to the target angle previously experienced. This type of task requires the participant to remember the target angle. Performance is scored in the same way as the simultaneous version of the task. Successive versions of the tasks shown in Figure 3.43 follow the same kind of procedure[52].

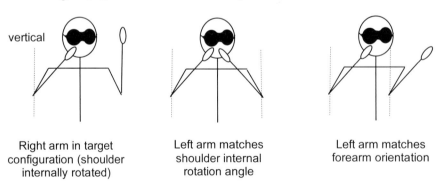

vertical

Right arm in target
configuration (shoulder
internally rotated)

Left arm matches
shoulder internal
rotation angle

Left arm matches
forearm orientation

Figure 3.43: *Kinesthetic matching task in which the person attempts to match the posture of the right arm with the left arm.*

The advantage of the successive version of the matching task is that a left and a right limb are not needed (so it can be used to study head orientation perception). An alternative task that shares this advantage involves using a movable device to match the angle of a joint or the orientation of a limb segment. An example is shown in Figure 3.44, where perception of the angular position of the right wrist joint is being assessed. In the task shown in the figure, the right hand is held between two plates, with the finger and thumb joints extended. The experimenter can move the wrist into different degrees of flexion or extension (examples shown on the right of the figure). The participant's task is to move a pointer that lies directly over the right hand so that it is aligned with the direction of the hand (angular position of the pointer matches the wrist joint angle). In this task the participant is not blindfolded and so is able to see where the pointer is (but not the hand); in effect they match the seen position of the pointer to the felt position of the hand (a **visual-kinesthetic match**). Performance is scored as the difference between the angular positions of the wrist and the pointer.

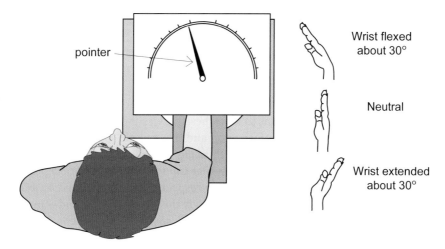

Figure 3.44: *Task involving a visual-kinesthetic match. Based on Figure 4 in Proske & Gandevia (2009).*

Matching tasks involve processes other than purely perceptual processes. Simultaneous matching tasks involve the person actively moving the matching limb (a motor process) and some sort of process that decides whether or not the two angles, segment orientations, or limb configurations are the same. The task shown in Figure 3.44 requires a comparison across perceptual modalities: the person has to decide whether the pointer (angular position perceived visually) is the same as the angular position of the wrist joint (perceived kinesthetically). As mentioned above, participants make a visual-kinesthetic match in this task. Successive matching tasks additionally involve memory processes. These other processes are likely to contribute to performance in a matching task, so the scores that are recorded depend on kinesthetic perception and the other processes. Thus, when these tasks are used to assess kinesthetic perception, performance of the task should be compared between conditions that affect kinesthesis but do not affect the other processes. For example, you might be interested in determining whether the accuracy of kinesthetic perception is affected by anesthetizing a joint. If you used the task shown in Figure 3.44, you would compare performance without anesthetic with performance with the wrist joint anesthetized. Anesthetizing the joint does not affect visual perception of the pointer or the process that decides whether or not the visually perceived pointer angle matches the kinesthetically perceived joint position. Thus, the difference between the two conditions only reflects differences in kinesthesis.

An alternative to matching tasks is the **discrimination task**. In such a task, the participant attempts to tell the difference between two or more situations. Similar set-ups to those used in matching tasks can be used, but the protocol is different. For example, a discrimination task using the set-up shown in Figure 3.42 could be as follows. The experimenter first sets joints angles for both the right and left elbow, and then asks the participant to judge whether the left elbow is more flexed (or more extended) than the right elbow. This method can be used to determine the smallest difference in the two joint angles that can be reliably discriminated. This difference is called the **discrimination threshold**.

3.4.4 Muscle, joint and cutaneous mechanoreceptors contribute to kinesthesis

The sensory information for kinesthesis comes from proprioceptive afference, but which mechanoreceptors actually contribute? In principle, any of the somatosensory mechanoreceptors that are stimulated when a joint or body part moves or is held in a fixed position can contribute kinesthetic information. These include joint receptors, GTOs, muscle spindles and cutaneous mechanoreceptors. We have already seen that the variations in the stretch of the skin around a joint produced when the joint moves stimulate Ruffini end organs; these receptors can therefore generate proprioceptive afference. It has also been found that when the finger and thumb joints are flexed and extended, all the different classes of cutaneous mechanoreceptors in the glabrous skin of the hand are stimulated to some degree, and so all have the potential to contribute to kinesthetic perceptions of digit movement and posture[53]. Do all these different kinds of mechanoreceptor contribute to kinesthesis, or only a few of them?

It was once thought that cutaneous mechanoreceptors were purely exteroceptors mediating the sense of touch, but irrelevant to kinesthesis. It was thought that joint receptors were the primary source of kinesthetic information and that muscle spindles provided little or no information. We now know that this early thinking was mistaken, and that all the different groups of somatosensory mechanoreceptors that can function as proprioceptors are able to contribute to kinesthesis to some degree. With respect to the roles played by joint receptors and muscle spindles, early thinking was completely the wrong way around – muscle spindles have turned out to be the most important sensory source of kinesthetic information, and joint receptors have been found to contribute little.

An ingenious set of experiments conducted on the distal interphalangeal joint (terminal joint) of the middle finger provides a nice illustration of how the contributions of different mechanoreceptors to kinesthesis can be evaluated[54]. The participant held their hand in one of the two postures shown in Figure 3.45: all fingers extended (panel A) or all fingers extended except the middle finger which was flexed at the first interphalangeal joint (panel B). The terminal joint was moved by the experimenter (passive movement) from a flexed starting position; the movement either flexed the joint further or extended it. The participant's task was to indicate whether the joint had been moved in the flexion direction or in the extension direction (a discrimination task).

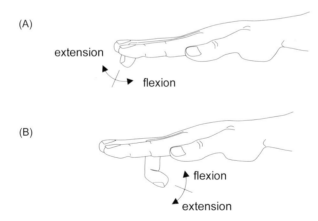

Figure 3.45: *Two postures of the hand used in the study of kinesthetic perception of movement of the distal interphalangeal joint of the middle finger.*

In the extended finger posture shown in Figure 3.45A, the muscles that flex the finger will move the terminal segment and conversely, movement imposed on the terminal segment will stretch the flexor muscles. In the panel B posture (middle finger flexed), the flexor muscles are 'disengaged', and movement of the terminal segment does not affect them. Thus, when the task is performed with the middle finger in an extended posture, muscle proprioceptors (spindles and tendon organs) can contribute, but they cannot contribute when the middle finger is in the flexed posture. Joint receptors and cutaneous mechanoreceptors can contribute in both postures.

To summarize, in the middle finger extended posture (Figure 3.45A) all types of mechanoreceptor can potentially contribute to performance of the discrimination task; in the middle finger flexed posture (Figure 3.45B), only joint and cutaneous receptors can contribute.

Afferent signals from joint and cutaneous receptors can be 'knocked out' by applying a suitable local anesthetic to the sensory nerves innervating the finger. If this is done in the middle finger extended posture, then only the muscle proprioceptors can contribute. Finally, if anesthetic is injected into the joint capsule, afference from joint receptors can be blocked without affecting afference from cutaneous receptors. These procedures yield five different experimental conditions:

(1)   Middle finger extended (Fig. 3.45A), unanesthetized: cutaneous, joint and muscle mechanoreceptors can contribute.
(2)   Middle finger extended, finger anesthetized: only muscle mechanoreceptors can contribute.
(3)   Middle finger extended, joint anesthetized: cutaneous and muscle mechanoreceptors can contribute.
(4)   Middle finger flexed (Fig. 3.45B), unanesthetized: cutaneous and joint mechanoreceptors can contribute.
(5)   Middle finger flexed (Fig. 3.45B), joint anesthetized: only cutaneous mechanoreceptors can contribute.

It was found that kinesthetic performance was best (the direction in which the terminal joint had been moved was most often correctly identified) in condition 1, in which all the different types of mechanoreceptor could contribute. Performance was degraded somewhat in condition 2. Performance in condition 3 was similar to that in condition 2. Disengaging the muscles (condition 4) led to a more substantial degradation of performance, and when only cutaneous receptors could contribute performance was at its worst (condition 5). The pattern of results obtained is shown in Figure 3.46. As the figure shows, performance was assessed when moving the terminal segment at different speeds, and degradation of performance in conditions 1–5 was greatest at slower speeds.

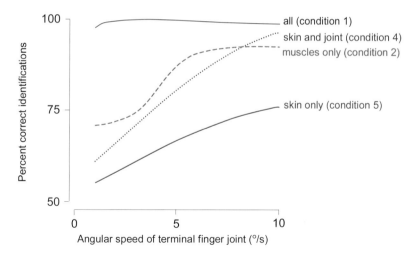

Figure 3.46: *Discrimination of motion of the distal interphalangeal joint of the middle finger under various conditions. Summary of data reported in Gandevia and Burke (1992) and Gandevia* et al. *(1983).*

These results demonstrate that all the different types of mechanoreceptors can function as proprioceptors and contribute to kinesthetic perception. The results from condition 2 show that muscle and tendon proprioceptors contribute to kinesthesis (evidence that muscle spindles can contribute is discussed in the next section); the results from condition 5 show that cutaneous proprioceptors can contribute. Better performance in condition 4 (joint + cutaneous receptors) than condition 5 (cutaneous only) demonstrates that joint receptors can contribute. The finding that performance in conditions 2 (muscle receptors only) and 3 (muscle + joint receptors) were the same indicates that joint receptors do not provide any information additional to that provided by muscle proprioceptors. The latter result is consistent with studies showing that replacing a joint with an artificial one has little or no discernible effect on kinesthesis[55].

Similar results to those described here have been obtained for other joints, though the contributions of different receptor types does differ between joints[56]. For example, skin and joint anesthesia has no discernible effect on kinesthetic acuity in the knee and ankle joints[57], but does have an effect in the finger joints (Figure 3.46).

3.4.5 Tendon vibration selectively stimulates type Ia spindle afferents and produces kinesthetic illusions

Placing a vibrating probe against a tendon can deflect the tendon as shown in Figure 3.47. The shaft of the probe moves a small distance (may be less than a millimeter) in and out of a sheath in a repetitive fashion (this is the vibration). The tip of the probe is held against the tendon and deflects it as it moves out of the sheath. The tendon deflection stretches the muscle very slightly, but does so quite rapidly (the speed of stretching depends on the frequency of vibration – the higher the frequency, the more rapid the stretch). The amount of muscle stretch produced is too small to stimulate the type II spindle afferent endings, but the speed of stretching can be sufficient to stimulate the type Ia endings, provided that the frequency is high enough: from about 20 to 100 Hz is effective. Thus, tendon vibration selectively stimulates the type Ia endings. The Ia spindle afferents fire action potentials during each deflection, and if the deflections occur many times a second, the afferents are firing almost continuously.

Tendon vibration has been found to evoke illusory perceptions of joint movement if the person cannot see the joint[58]. For example, if a vibrating probe is held against the biceps tendon at the elbow joint with the arm stationary, a person will experience the illusory perception that the elbow is extending, provided that they cannot see their arm. If the probe is held against the triceps tendon, the perception is one of elbow flexion. Thus, the direction of the illusory joint movement is consistent with the muscle lengthening: extension is associated with biceps lengthening, flexion is associated with triceps lengthening. The illusory percepts are predominantly of joint movement, though there is a perceived change in the position of the joint both during and after vibration.

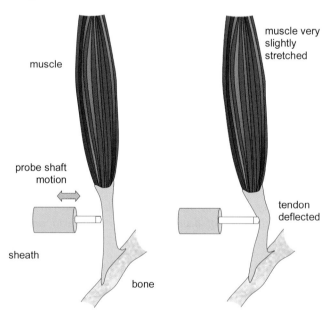

Figure 3.47: *Mechanical effect of holding a vibrating probe against a tendon.*

Illusions evoked by tendon vibration are frequently powerful and compelling and can be of quite complex motions: vibration applied to tendons at the wrist while a person holds a pen can evoke illusory drawing movements[59], for example. In some situations, tendon vibration can lead to perceptions of anatomically impossible joint positions, including hyperextension (bending backwards) at the elbow joint[60]. An interesting variation on the theme of impossible positions is the *Pinocchio illusion*, which is evoked by vibration of the biceps tendon while the fingers of the vibrated arm touch or grasp the nose[61]. Vibration of the biceps tendon produces an illusion that the elbow is extending, so moving the hand away from the face. Since the fingers are in contact with the nose throughout the period of vibration, there is tactile information that signals the contact. Thus, the brain is in receipt of two pieces of information during the period of vibration: (1) the hand is moving away from the face, and (2) the fingers are continuously in contact with the nose. The person perceives that the nose is growing as the hand moves (Figure 3.48), hence the name given to the illusion[62].

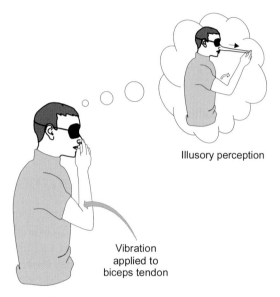

Illusory perception

Vibration applied to biceps tendon

Figure 3.48: *The Pinocchio illusion.*

These kinesthetic illusions have been established as being due to the stimulation of type Ia spindle afferents, and so demonstrate that these afferents have a substantial effect on kinesthetic perception (see next section). Other experiments have demonstrated that type II spindle afferents also contribute to kinesthesis[63].

3.4.6 Spindle information dominates information supplied by other proprioceptors, and vision dominates kinesthesis

Kinesthetic illusions evoked by tendon vibration suggest that information supplied by spindle receptors overrides the information provided by other proprioceptors. Tendon vibration selectively stimulates the type Ia spindle afferents and has very little or no effect on the other proprioceptors – skin stretch receptors, joint receptors and GTOs[64]. These receptors are therefore signaling that there is no movement of the joint or change in its position. The experience of powerful kinesthetic illusions suggests that the nervous system is using the information provided by the spindle afferents to determine how the limb is moving, and ignoring the conflicting signals from the other proprioceptors[65]. Resolution of a conflict between different sources of sensory information about a single perceived quantity by using one source and ignoring the others is referred to as **sensory dominance**. In the kinesthetic illusion example, the spindle afferent signals constitute a source of information that dominates the other available sources (signals transmitted by other proprioceptive afferents).

There is another example of sensory dominance that relates to kinesthetic illusions. As noted earlier, in order for a person to experience illusory motion of a joint or limb, they must not be able to see it. If a person looks at the limb or joint, no kinesthetic illusion is experienced. Being able to see that the limb is not moving completely overrides the effect of the proprioceptive stimulation produced by vibration. In effect, the nervous system ignores the kinesthetic information and relies on the visual information. This is a case of vision dominating kinesthesis.

The two example of dominance that we have considered differ: the dominance of spindle afferent signals over other proprioceptive signals occurs within a sensory modality (the kinesthetic modality), whereas the dominance of vision over kinesthesis occurs between two different modalities. The basic principle is the same in both cases, however, and may be stated as follows:

> **SENSORY DOMINANCE:** when two (or more) sources of sensory information about the same quantity (e.g., the position of a joint) *conflict* with one another, the perception of that quantity may be largely or completely determined by only one of the sources (the others do not contribute). When this happens, the source that determines the perception is said to dominate the other sources.

Vision is often found to dominate other sensory modalities[66]. In such cases a phenomenon known as *visual capture* can occur; some illustrative examples of this phenomenon are discussed next.

3.4.7 A limb can be felt where it is seen, not where it actually is

A striking effect of visual dominance over kinesthesis was discovered in the 1930s and is relatively easy to demonstrate if you happen to have access to a good-quality model finger that looks like the real thing[67]. With their limbs screened from view, a person moves their hand to a location where they think one finger should be visible, poking out from under the screen. In reality, they cannot see their own finger: what they see is a realistic model finger protruding from under the screen. In these conditions, a person can experience feeling their finger to be in the place where the model finger is seen to be, even though their real finger may be some distance away. The person has the compelling impression that the model finger is actually their own finger. Kinesthetic awareness of the finger is referred to the visually seen location, so that the finger's felt position coincides with the seen position of the model finger. This effect is called **visual capture** and vision is said to *capture* kinesthesis.

There are a number of interesting examples of visual capture. Ventriloquism provides one that is well known. The ventriloquist speaks so that their lip movements are not visible to the audience while simultaneously moving the mouth of the dummy: the voice then seems to come from the dummy's mouth, not the ventriloquist's. In a typical ventriloquism show, the ventriloquist and dummy are close together, but the phenomenon can be observed even when the actual source of a voice is some distance from the moving mouth[68]. Visual capture of sound is a very widespread phenomenon: when we watch a movie on the television or in a theatre, our experience is of the voices of the actors coming from their mouths and the sounds of motor vehicles coming from their locations on the screen. These sounds are actually emitted by loud-speakers that may be some distance from the screen, and if you close your eyes in a movie theater it can be difficult to be certain about which direction the sounds are coming from.

An interesting recent variant on visual capture of kinesthesis by a model body part is the so-called *rubber hand illusion*[69], which involves touch as well as vision and kinesthesis. The illusion is typically evoked as follows (see Figure 3.49): a person (the subject) sits with one (unseen) hand lying flat on a table under a screen. Lying on top of the screen and visible to the subject is a realistic model hand in a similar posture; it doesn't have to be made of rubber, but its posture and orientation need to be similar to that of the subject's own hand[70]. A second person (the illusionist) repetitively strokes both the subject's unseen hand and the visible model hand, taking care that each stroke occurs simultaneously on the real and model hands (if the strokes are not synchronous, the illusion is not evoked). After the stroking has continued for a short period of time (less than a minute in most cases), the subject develops the compelling impression that the model hand is their own hand: they feel their hand to be where they can see the model hand (visual capture of kinesthesis) and refer their feeling of stroking to the model hand (visual capture of touch).

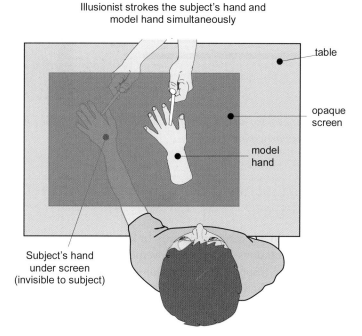

Illusionist strokes the subject's hand and model hand simultaneously

table

opaque screen

model hand

Subject's hand under screen (invisible to subject)

Figure 3.49: *Set-up for evoking the rubber hand illusion.*

In this illusion, the illusionist does not initially make any attempt to fool the subject into thinking that the model hand is their own hand: it is the simultaneous stroking of the two hands that produces this impression. This illusion can be evoked in most people, and the experience is reported as being vivid and compelling. The strength of the illusion is further evidenced by the finding that while people are experiencing the illusion, they will flinch if a threat is made to injure the model hand by striking it; such physical threats are associated with increased skin sweating and increased activation of areas of the brain associated with pain and arousal[71]. A number of dramatic variants of the rubber hand type illusion have recently been reported involving a person's whole body, not just a single part: people report having the experience of occupying a different body – a kind of out-of-body experience[72]. It has also been demonstrated that the illusion can be evoked by movement as well as by touch, and that tactile stimulation is not necessary to experience the illusion[73]. The technique used is shown in Figure 3.50. As in Figure 3.49, the participant's arm is lying on a table above which is another (upper) table, on which rests the false hand (in this case, only a model finger is visible). The distal part of the participant's index finger is inserted into a tube that is coupled to the false finger above, such that when the model finger is rotated about its proximal interphalangeal joint, the movement is transmitted to the participant's finger and it moves in the same way. In the experiment, the experimenter gripped the tip of the model finger and moved it so that it rotated about its interphalangeal joint. This was done with participants' fingers anesthetized and unanesthetized. The anesthetic eliminated sensory signals from the finger itself, but did not affect the muscle or tendon organ afferents. An illusion of model finger ownership was induced by model finger movement in both conditions. This result demonstrates that tactile stimulation is not necessary for the illusion to occur, and that muscle proprioceptors can contribute to the sense of body ownership.

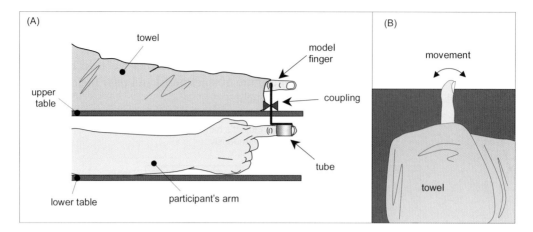

Figure 3.50: *(A) Set-up for evoking an illusion of ownership of a model finger, based on Figure 1 in Walsh* et al. *(2011). (B) The participant's view.*

3.4.8 How is kinesthetic information obtained from proprioceptors?

Individual proprioceptors do not respond directly to kinesthetically perceived variables like joint angles, segment orientations and limb movements. The relationship between these variables and proprioceptor responses is often quite complex. This raises the question of how information about kinesthetically perceived variables is extracted from proprioceptive afference. Here we will briefly outline some of the complexities associated with obtaining kinesthetic information from the response of different proprioceptors:

▸ **Muscle spindle receptors:** these proprioceptors respond to muscle length and speed of lengthening, and so can provide information about these quantities. There are three main reasons[74] why spindle afference cannot inform directly about joint position and movement:

(1) Joint position and motion depends not on the length and lengthening/shortening of muscles but on the length and rate of change of length of muscle + tendon. As a result, a joint can be in different positions but the length of the muscle can be the same, and conversely, the joint can be in the same position but the muscle can have different lengths. The obvious example is where a muscle contracts with the joint held in a fixed position (pseudo-isometric contractions): the muscle can shorten in these conditions because the tendon stretches.

(2) Many muscles cross more than one joint: the length of such a muscle is affected by the position of all the joints it crosses. As a result, for a given muscle length, there are a potentially infinite number of possible combinations of joint positions. A changing muscle length may be due to movement at only one joint, or some combination of movements at all of them.

(3) Spindle receptor responses depend not only on muscle length or speed of lengthening, but also on the gamma-efferent signals to the intrafusal fibers (see section 3.3.9): a change in the efferent signal can cause a change in the afferent signals without any change in muscle length or speed.

▸ **Cutaneous stretch receptors:** Skin stretch receptor responses can be influenced by joint position and motion. However, anything that pulls on the skin will stretch it and stimulate skin stretch receptors. Thus, the response is ambiguous: the stretch might be due to changes in joint position or to something pulling on the skin.

▸ **Joint receptors:** These respond to deformation of the joint capsule by forces acting at the joint. These forces may be affected by joint position, muscle forces, and external loads. Thus, there can be changes in the activity of joint receptors in the absence of any changes in joint position. For example, an increase in muscle force in isometric conditions will cause a change in the magnitude of the forces acting to compress the joint capsule, and change the receptor responses. This makes a joint receptor response ambiguous: it may be due to a change in joint position, or to an increase in force, or to some combination of the two[75].

These examples show that the responses of proprioceptors are *ambiguous* concerning the causes of the stimulation: the response could have been due to any one of a number of different things, or to some combination of them. In order to obtain reliable and accurate information about joint position or motion, the signals from different types of proprioceptors must be combined. As an example, consider the perception of finger posture. Muscle spindle receptors cannot provide accurate information about finger posture because (1) joint position depends on muscle + tendon length; (2) the finger muscle tendons cross all three finger joints; (3) a spindle's afferent response depends on the gamma-efferent signal it receives. An estimate of the tendon length can be derived from GTO responses (as described in section 3.3.10), and so the muscle + tendon length can be obtained from a combination of GTO responses, spindle responses and internal information about the muscle length associated with the gamma-efferent signal. To obtain an estimate of finger posture (three joint angles), information from cutaneous and joint receptors can provide additional information about individual angles[76].

3.4.9 Efference and afference contribute to proprioception

We have seen that muscle spindle afference is a major contributor to kinesthesis. As noted in the last section, spindle afferent signals depend on the level of the gamma-efferent activity. This implies that information about muscle length and/or joint position can only be obtained from spindle afferent signals if the process of extracting the information somehow takes into account the efferent signals as well. The nature of the processes by which efferent signals are taken into account has not been firmly established. We will briefly discuss how motor commands may contribute to proprioception, and refer the reader to the literature for details[77].

One way in which motor command processes have been proposed to contribute to kinesthesia is by establishing a frame of reference for the interpretation of proprioceptive afference[78]. A simple example illustrates the basic idea: in general, measurement of length or position requires a zero point, a calibrated scale and (in more than one dimension) a set of directions (see Figure 3.53). Measurements of muscle length or joint angular position are one-dimensional and so require a zero point and a scale. It has been proposed that the zero point and scale used for the measurement of muscle length and/or joint position are provided by the level of central command[79]. According to this idea, internal information about the commanded muscle length (or joint angle) plays an essential role in kinesthesis, but it is not necessarily able to generate kinesthetic perceptions in the absence of proprioceptive afference[80].

Recent work has shown that the generation of voluntary motor commands can produce kinesthetic perceptions[81]. This was done by temporarily paralyzing and anesthetizing the right forearms of experimental participants, who were therefore unable to either move or feel their arms from the elbow down. Under these conditions, the paralyzed right arm was hidden from view and the wrist was moved into six different positions of flexion and extension (Figure 3.51). In each position, participants indicated the perceived orientation of their right wrist by moving a pointer with their left hand (a matching task like that shown in Figure 3.44). This was done under three conditions: (1) No attempt to contract the muscles that flex and extend the right wrist, (2) an attempt to flex the wrist with 30% of maximum voluntary effort, and (3) an attempt to extend the wrist with 30% of maximum voluntary effort. Figure 3.51 shows the results. The actual position of the right wrist had no effect on its perceived position (i.e., the position indicated using the pointer), which would be expected given that all sensation in the right hand and forearm was blocked. However, the perceived position was strongly influenced by the voluntary effort to move the wrist into flexion or extension: when the flexion effort was made, the wrist was perceived to be flexed by about 40°, and when the extension effort was made it was perceived to be extended by about 15° to 20°, regardless of its actual position. The data clearly show that the voluntary effort had a strong effect on the wrist's perceived position in the absence of any afferent feedback from the limb. Thus, voluntary motor commands can affect limb position perception: the position of a paralyzed limb is perceived to change in the direction of the voluntary command in the complete absence of sensory feedback.

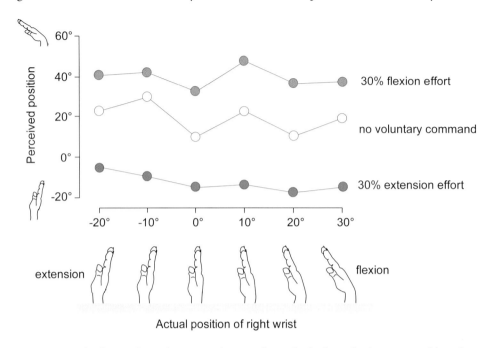

Figure 3.51: *Results from a kinesthetic matching task in which the right forearm and hand were paralyzed and anesthetized. Data from Gandevia* et al. *(2006), Figure 3.*

The results described in the previous paragraph show that voluntary motor command can contribute to kinesthetic perception. It has also been demonstrated that it can contribute to perceptions of exerted force and of heaviness[82]. Another kind of proprioceptive percept to which the motor command contributes is the *sense of effort* or *sense of exertion* that accompanies voluntary action. This percept is self-explanatory, but the degree to which afference and motor commands contribute to it has been a source of controversy since the nineteenth century[83]. There are two extreme views concerning the perception of effort and exertion: (1) it is determined entirely by somatosensory feedback; (2) it is determined entirely by the motor command. Figure 3.52 shows simplified representations of these two views. Although it might seem hard to imagine that a perception of effort is produced without any contribution from afferent feedback, there is a large body of evidence that supports the view that the sense of effort depends only on central command generation[84]. Indeed, the phrase 'sense of effort'

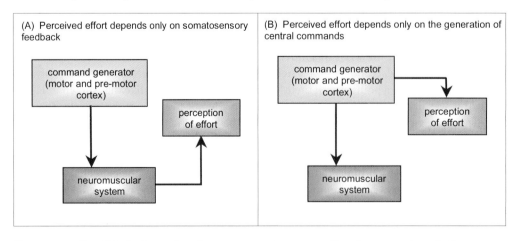

Figure 3.52: *Simplified schematics of two extreme views regarding the perception of effort.*

is often used to refer to perceptions that arise due to the production of voluntary motor commands independently of any sensory feedback[85] (i.e., the perceived motor command). However, a role for somatosensory afference in the perception of effort and exertion has not been ruled out, and it seems likely that it can contribute[86].

3.4.10 Kinesthetic information about the location of a body part is represented using a system of coordinates

So far in this part of the chapter we have focused on the kinesthetic perception of the position or motion of a single joint or limb segment. We can also perceive the configuration of a whole limb, and we are able to feel where particular parts of it are: a finger tip, for example. The ability to perceive the location of a body part based on proprioceptive afference is usually called **kinesthetic localization**.

The notion of spatial location – where something is – is a relative one: a thing is located some distance away from something else and in some direction relative to it. Specifying spatial location requires a **coordinate system**, comprised of an origin together with a set of reference directions or axes that are fixed to that origin. The origin is the location relative to which all others are specified. The most frequently encountered coordinate system is the Cartesian system, that comprises an origin and three mutually perpendicular axes that are usually labeled X, Y and Z. Panel A of Figure 3.53 shows a Cartesian system centered at an origin, O. The location of a point p is specified as the distances you need to move along each of the three axes to get from O to p: in the figure these distances are p_x along the X-axis, p_y along the Y-axis, and p_z along the Z-axis. The three numbers (p_x, p_y, p_z) are called the *Cartesian coordinates* of the point; they implicitly specify both the distance and direction of the point relative to the origin (you can calculate the distance and direction from these numbers if you know the right formulae). The distance and direction can be specified explicitly using **polar coordinates**.

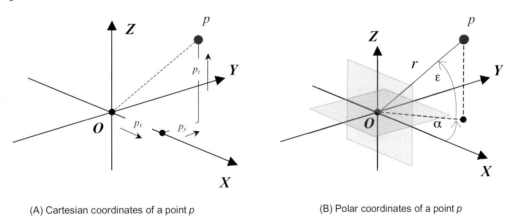

(A) Cartesian coordinates of a point p (B) Polar coordinates of a point p

Figure 3.53: *Different types of coordinate system.*

A polar coordinate system consists of an origin and two perpendicular reference planes centered on the origin. Panel B shows a system in which one plane contains the X and Z axes of the Cartesian system in panel A ('vertical' plane), and the other plane contains the X and Y axes ('horizontal' plane). The location of the point p is given in terms of the length of the straight line from O to p – the radial distance (r) of p from O – and the two angles labeled α and ε. The angle α, called the azimuth, is the angle through which the vertical (X-Z) plane must be rotated to reach the point p. The angle ε, called the elevation, is the angle through which the horizontal (X-Y) plane must be rotated to reach p. The three numbers (r, α, ε) are called the *polar coordinates* of the point p.

Polar coordinates provide a more natural way of specifying the location of a body part relative to a fixed origin somewhere in the body. An example is shown in Figure 3.54. In panel A a person's finger tip is at a location in front of them and the arm segments lie in a horizontal plane. A possible origin for a coordinate system is shown as white circle: it is high in the chest at shoulder level in the same plane as the arm, lying approximately on the midline of the body[87] (a schematic of the geometry is shown in panel B). The location of the finger tip in the horizontal plane can be expressed in polar coordinates as the distance of the finger tip from the origin (r_t) and the angle (θ) made with the mid-sagittal (vertical) plane of the body indicated by the dashed line. In this illustrative example, the elevation angle is zero because the finger and origin lie in the same plane.

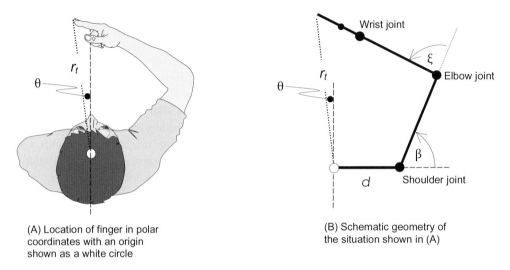

(A) Location of finger in polar coordinates with an origin shown as a white circle

(B) Schematic geometry of the situation shown in (A)

Figure 3.54: *Polar coordinate representation of finger tip location.*

The brain must represent the location of perceived objects in some kind of coordinate system, possibly like the one shown in Figure 3.54. The origin of such a coordinate system is called a **perceptual egocenter**[88]:

> **PERCEPTUAL EGOCENTER:** the origin (center) of the system of coordinates in which perceptual information about the location of something (an object in the environment, a body part) is represented by the nervous system.

Thus, the origin of a set of coordinates in which kinesthetic information about the location of body parts is represented is called a **kinesthetic egocenter**. If the white circle in Figure 3.54 is a kinesthetic egocenter, then the position of the finger tip could be represented by the brain as the distance r_t and the angle θ. The coordinate system that the brain uses to represent spatial locations is not something that can be determined without careful empirical investigation, and is not yet fully understood. There is evidence that the brain uses a polar-coordinate-type representation of limb orientation and hand position[89]; the location of the kinesthetic egocenter has been found to depend what task a person undertakes and the body parts involved[90]. We will return to the topic of spatial representation later (Chapter 11).

3.4.11 Kinesthetic perception of the location of a body part requires information from many muscles and joints

How can a person use proprioceptive afference to obtain explicit information about the location of a finger tip in a system of coordinates centered on a kinesthetic egocenter? In Figure 3.54, this would be the problem of obtaining information about the distance of the finger from the egocenter, and its angle relative to the mid-sagittal plane, from the responses of proprioceptors in the hand, arm and shoulder. As described earlier, people are able to use proprioceptive afference to determine the position of individual joints. If the angles of all the joints in the arm are known (the shoulder, elbow, wrist and finger joint angles), then it is a relatively simple geometrical problem to compute the distance (r_t) and direction (θ) of the finger tip in the body-centered coordinate system shown in the figure. Panel B of Figure 3.54 shows a schematic of the geometry of the situation shown in panel A. The shoulder and elbow joint angles are labeled β and ξ respectively; the wrist and finger joints lie along a line and are all zero in this example. The finger tip's distance and direction can be found if the joint angles are known (derived from proprioceptive afference) and if all the body segment lengths are known, including the distance from the egocenter to the shoulder joint (d in the figure). When the arm is held stationary there is no proprioceptive information about body segment lengths, but these lengths are constant in adults, and knowledge of them derived from previous experience can be used. In short, it is possible to perceive the spatial location of a body part within a kinesthetic frame of reference using information obtained from proprioceptive afference and previous experience.

It might be expected that people would be better at making judgments of the position and orientation of single joints or body segments than they are at kinesthetic localization tasks. This expectation arises because it appears that the latter might be complex perceptions built from the former, since they involve integration of information from several joints. However, this has not been supported in experiments, where it has been found that performance on localization tasks requiring integration of information from several joints can be more precise than performance on single-joint tasks[91]. This is probably because kinesthetic localization tasks have functional relevance (we may need to know where the hand or finger is), but knowing the angle of a single joint has little use in the real world. Our nervous systems are practiced at making information about the location of body parts in space available, but not at making joint angle information available.

3.4.12 How well can people kinesthetically localize a body part?

Kinesthetic localization is studied using a type of task that requires the participant to place a body part, usually a finger, in a particular target location. Figure 3.55 shows a simple example of such a task that resembles touching your finger tips together with your eyes closed. The participant is shown blindfolded, and a target position is defined by the index finger of the right hand, which is placed on top of a solid surface (table top); the participant attempts to position the index finger of the left hand directly underneath the right index finger. This kind of task will be called a **localization task**. The version of the task shown in the figure is a simultaneous task – the target position is present while the localizing movement is executed. Successive (memory guided) versions of the task have also been used[92].

Figure 3.55: *An example of a kinesthetic localization task.*

People's ability to kinesthetically localize the position of their hand or finger turns out to depend on a number of factors that include (1) where the body part is in space, (2) what body parts are involved[93] and (3) whether the target position is achieved by the experimenter moving the participant's limb passively or by the participant moving actively[94]. The results of a simple experiment that illustrates these dependencies are shown in Figure 3.56. The experiment employed a task like that shown in Figure 3.55, except that the participants held a stylus in each hand, and attempted to move the position of the tip of the stylus held in one hand to a target defined by the tip of the stylus held in the other. There were nine possible target locations arranged in a line along the table top (these locations are indicated by squares in Figure 3.56), and localization was performed with both the left hand and the right hand, with the other hand being moved to the target location either passively by the experimenter or actively by the participant. This yielded four experimental conditions: (1) left hand moved passively to target, localized with right hand; (2) left hand moved actively to target, localized with right hand; (3) right passive, localized with left; (4) right active, localized with left.

The data points in the figure show the average positions to which participants moved the localizing stylus tip – the distance between a data point and the corresponding target represents the average error of localization[95]. The green diamond data points are for conditions in which the left hand was used to define the target location (conditions 1 and 2); the blue circle data points are for conditions in which the right hand defined the target location (conditions 3 and 4). The open symbols and dashed lines are for conditions in which the target was acquired actively (2 and 4); the filled circles and solid lines are passive conditions (1 and 3).

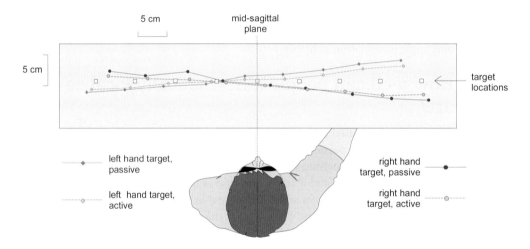

Figure 3.56: *Results from a kinesthetic localization task. Data from Haggard* et al. *(2000), Figure 8.*

The results show that the error in participants' localizations of the target depends on all factors: the hand used for localizing, the position of the target, and whether the target was initially acquired passively or actively. One feature of the results is that in the forwards-backwards direction, the localization error is larger for the passive condition than the active one (there is no marked difference in the left-right direction). This result has been obtained in many other kinesthetic localization tasks[96], and is likely due to the fact that participants have access to more information about target location when they move actively. The other features of the results shown in Figure 3.56 cannot be interpreted as being entirely a consequence of kinesthetic perception, since performance may be affected not only by perceptual localization but also by how well a person is able to perform the localization response (moving to the target). The influence of other, non-perceptual factors can be avoided by making comparisons between conditions in which these factors (such as the hand used, the direction, or the distance that needs to be moved to reach the target) are the same (see section 3.4.3). This allows any differences between conditions to be interpreted as due to perceptual factors.

3.4.13 People can judge the lengths of hand-held rods by wielding them

People are not only able to judge how far one body part is from another without looking, they are also able to tell how far the end of a hand-held rod or pole is simply by wielding it. In other words, by holding a rod and moving it around, people are able to get a perceptual impression of the rod's length and to spatially localize its end[97]. Simply holding a rod in the hand without moving it is sufficient to get an impression of its length[98]. It is easy to get an idea of your ability to do this: firmly grasp a rod of some kind with one hand; with your eyes closed and without changing the position of your grip, move the rod around by means of motions of the hand about the wrist joint. From these motions you develop perceptual impressions of the rod's length and where the end of it is located; doing the same thing with different objects yields different impressions. Perception of this kind is not kinesthesis, because it is perception of an environmental object, but at least some of the information on which perception is based is supplied by proprioceptive afference. When an object is held and wielded, cutaneous receptors are stimulated by the object's contact with the skin and the manner in which the skin is compressed and stretched as the object is moved. The cutaneous mechanoreceptors generate exteroceptive afference in response to this stimulation. Proprioceptors in the muscles and joints of the arm are also stimulated as muscular forces are produced to hold the object against gravity and to move it around. Thus, both exteroceptive and proprioceptive afference contribute to the non-visual perception of the held object, a combination of tactile and kinesthetic information.

There are various names for the perception of environmental objects based on information obtained from both tactile and proprioceptive stimulation, including *kinesthetic touch*[99] and *active touch*[100]. An alternative term that we will use in what follows is **active haptic perception**[101], where use of the word 'active' emphasizes the role of active movement. The term *haptic perception* refers to the perception of the environment based on information obtained from somatosensory receptors, both those classified as exteroceptors and those classified as proprioceptors. It is more or less equivalent to perception by touching and feeling, and includes 'feeling' by hefting and wielding.

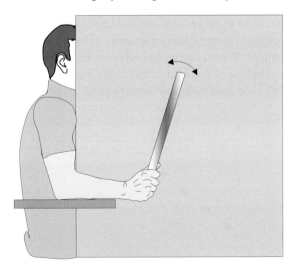

(A) Participant wields an unseen rod by radio-ulnar deviation of the wrist

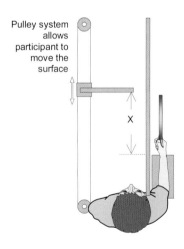

Pulley system allows participant to move the surface

(B) Participant adjusts the position of a sheet to the maximum distance away that is reachable with the rod

Figure 3.57: *Experimental task for studying the haptic perception of length.*

A type of experimental task used to study people's ability to haptically perceive the lengths of wielded rods is shown in Figure 3.57[102]. The experimental participant sits to one side of a screen or curtain, with one arm out of view on the other side (panel A). They grasp the base of a rigid rod in the unseen hand; they have no prior information about the rod's length. They are free to wield the rod about the wrist, primarily by means of radioulnar deviations, so that the rod moves in the vertical plane; flexion-extension movements are restricted, so that the person does not contact the screen. The participant uses the other hand to position a vertical flat sheet (Figure 3.57, panel B) at the maximum distance reachable by the tip of the rod (a kind of matching task). The participant can see the sheet and so they are, in effect, attempting to move the sheet to a visually perceived distance that coincides with the haptically perceived location of the rod's tip when held horizontally.

Accurate performance in such a task demonstrates that a person is able to obtain information about the length of the rod from the stimulation produced as a consequence of wielding it. Figure 3.58 shows the type of results that have been obtained. The graph plots the distance of the wrist to the surface (X, in Figure 3.57B) against the actual length of the rod. The distance (X) of the wrist to the surface is a measure of the perceived length of the rod: if the person is able to perceive the length accurately, this distance should be almost the same as the rod length. Seven different rod lengths were used in this experiment, ranging between 30.5 cm and 122 cm. The graph shows a close correspondence between the perceived length and the actual length of the rod, with a tendency to underestimate the length of the longer rods.

The results shown in Figure 3.58 pose the following question: what information is there about the length of a rod within the pattern of proprioceptive and tactile stimulation produced while holding and wielding it? The stimulation patterns depend on the forces and torques that act on the hand, wrist and other joints that may be involved. These include both the forces and torques due to the object, and the forces and torques developed by muscles. When holding a rod, for example, the weight of the rod exerts a torque about the wrist. When wielding a rod, the rod resists changes in its angular speed and direction of rotation in a manner that depends on its moment of inertia about the axis of rotation. Both the torque exerted by the weight of the rod and the rod's moments of inertia depend on its length as well as its mass. Thus, the muscle torques needed to turn the rod and to hold it steady depend on the length and mass of the rod. In principle, therefore, there is some information about the rod's length in the proprioceptive afference produced when holding and wielding it. Exactly what information this is, and to what extent it depends on the moments of inertia and the torque exerted by the weight, is controversial[103]. Whatever the exact nature of the information and the contribution of the weight torque and moments of inertia, the same information could be used to perceive the length of limb segments, since these are also wielded about joints (when the segment is moved) and held in static positions (when holding postures): a firmly held rod behaves in many ways like an extra body segment. There is empirical evidence to suggest that kinesthetic localization of body parts and perception of segment orientations depends on the same quantities as perception of the length of hand-held rods and other objects[104].

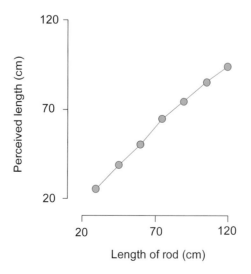

Figure 3.58: *Results from an experiment using the task shown in Figure 3.60 (average data from Experiment 1 of Solomon and Turvey, 1988).*

3.4.14 Active haptic perception involves motor procedures

Haptic perception normally involves active manipulation. The hands can be used as perceptual instruments, and they engage in a variety of subtle activities to obtain sensory information: they prod, grope, press, twist, shake, squeeze, rub, enclose, heft and wield. These activities allow us to obtain information about the following characteristics of objects and surfaces without looking:

(1) Geometrical properties including shape and size
(2) Surface properties such as texture, smoothness (or roughness) and stickiness
(3) Material properties such as heaviness, rigidity and hardness
(4) Structural properties such as distribution of mass, bendiness and the existence of linked or jointed parts.

J.J. Gibson[105] referred to the activities that we use to obtain information about these properties as **exploratory**, to distinguish them from the *performatory* manipulative activities that we engage in to execute manual tasks like writing and typing, using hand tools, picking things up, and the vast array of other things that we do with our hands.

Everyday experience tells us that we perform particular types of motor activity in order to obtain particular types of information: we do different things to obtain information about different properties. For example, if we want to determine the temperature of a surface, we might press the palm of one hand against it for a period of time; if we want to determine the texture of a surface, then we rub our fingers over it. A variety of such activities have been indentified and are usually referred to as **exploratory procedures**[106]; these are motor routines used in the haptic perception of different properties of objects and surfaces. Those that have received the most empirical study are shown in Figure 3.59, together with an explanation of their characteristics. Several others could be added to the list, including the type of wielding activity described in section 3.4.13 (which can be used to obtain information about heaviness and mass distribution as well as length), the application of bending forces and twisting forces (such as when you hold an object in both hands and try to twist it or snap it), and the kinds of things we do to determine if an object has loose or moveable parts. Each procedure is best suited for obtaining certain types of information, but may also provide other types of information. For example, the contour-following procedure shown in Figure 3.59 is used to obtain shape information, but will also provide some information about the object's surface texture. Note also that the procedures are not mutually exclusive, as it is possible to execute some of them concurrently. For example, enclosure and unsupported holding can be executed at the same time, and you can press on something at the same time as rubbing it.

With the exception of static contact, all the exploratory procedures shown in Figure 3.59 involve bodily movements, postures or exerted forces that provide information about the physical characteristics of the object. Cutaneous receptors in the skin that comes into contact with the object will be stimulated and convey information about the location of contact, the sharpness of edges, surface textures and pressure. Proprioceptors in the muscles and joints will carry information about the postures of the fingers and hands, the speed of finger and joint movements and the muscular forces developed to support or compress the object. As a result, they will carry information about the size, volume and shape of the object. For example, when an object is enclosed by the fingers, the posture of the fingers provides information about the size of the object and the shape of the contours to which the fingers are molded. Thus, both tactile and kinesthetic information is needed for the perception of object properties, and must be combined to form coherent haptic percepts of manipulated objects.

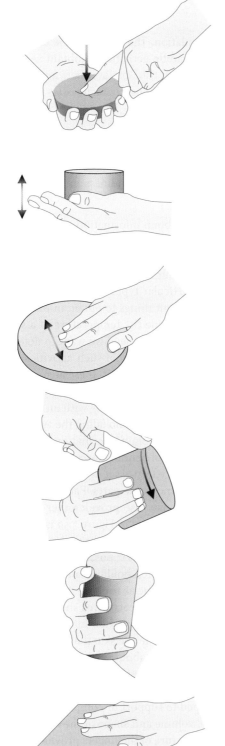

PRESSURE

Behavior: pressing or squeezing an object while holding it steady

Information: hardness

UNSUPPORTED HOLDING

Behavior: object is held without any external support for the limb; the hand is usually raised and lowered repetitively (hefting)

Information: heaviness of the object (weight)

LATERAL MOTION

Behavior: fingers are moved over the surface with little pressure, often in a back-and-forth or circular motion (rubbing)

Information: surface texture

CONTOUR FOLLOWING

Behavior: Fingers (or other body part) follow the edges or internal contours of an object or surface

Information: details of the shape of an object or surface

ENCLOSURE

Behavior: fingers and hand(s) are molded to the object surface and maintain contact for periods of time; patterns of enclosure may be periodically changed by shifts of the object in the hand(s)

Information: overall shape, volume, size

STATIC CONTACT

Behavior: a large area of the skin surface, such as that on the fingers and palm, rest on a surface without pressing on it or actively molding to its contours

Information: Temperature

Figure 3.59: *Exploratory procedures for haptic perception. Based on diagrams in Lederman and Klatzky (1987).*

References & Notes

1 Some animals have receptors that respond to magnetic field energy and electrical field energy.

2 There may be five types (see Chapter 4).

3 Edin, Johansson (1995).

4 This means, in effect, that a speed sensor is a fast adapting position sensor. For a discussion of the functions of adaptation, see Wark, Lundstrom, Fairhall (2007).

5 This led philosophers to propose theories in which sensations are the building blocks from which perceptions are constructed, a point of view that cannot be properly justified. We could, perhaps, view sensory qualities (sensations) as the media in which information is represented (or presented) in consciousness.

6 E.g., Eimer, Schlaghecken (1998).

7 See Gibson (1979).

8 E.g., Wolfe *et al.* (2011).

9 For review see Schroeder *et al.* (2010).

10 The movements involved in extracting visual information can be rather subtle; see Schreiber *et al.* (2001) for one example.

11 Gibson (1966).

12 For a recent investigation, see Sadeghi *et al.* (2009).

13 Shimojo, Shams (2001).

14 Ebenholtz (2003) and Howard (1982).

15 First suggested by René Descartes in the 17th century. Later experiments confirmed that the vergence angle of the eyes could play a significant role in determining the perceived distance of visual objects (Foley, 1980; Tresilian *et al.*, 1999). The accommodative state of the eye has also been suggested to be an extra-visual source of information, though there is little evidence to support this conjecture (Mon-Williams, Tresilian, 2000).

16 See Ebenholtz (2003).

17 Bach-y-Rita (2004).

18 White *et al.* (1970).

19 Bach-y-Rita (1972, 2004).

20 The two types of afferent may carry different types of information; see Sadeghi *et al.* (2007).

21 Wilson, Melvill Jones (1979).

22 The horizontal canals are actually tilted backwards by between 20° and 30° when the head is upright.

23 The findings described here come mainly from studies of monkeys and cats.

24 The term *statolith* (from *statos*, 'to place') is also used (Schone, 1984).

25 Green, Angelaki (2010b).

26 Fukushima (1997).

27 Dieterich, Brandt (2008); Fasold *et al.* (2002).

28 Guldin, Grusser (1998).

29 A third nomenclature for cutaneous afferents was developed in the context of human microneurography and based on receptive field size (I = small, II = large) and adaptation characteristics (SA and FA), so a Pacinian corpuscle afferent is of type FAII (fast adapting, large receptive field). This nomenclature is often used for cutaneous afferents in people (Johansson, Flanagan, 2009).

30 Mountcastle (2005).

31 Several of the receptors found in the external skin are also found in the skin of the tongue, the inside of the mouth and the nasal cavities.

32 The sizes of the receptors can vary substantially. Pacinian corpuscles, for example, vary in size from about 0.2 mm to over 4 mm in diameter.

33 The lips appear to lack Pacinian corpuscles, but possess a related type of mechanoreceptor called *Krause bulbs*.

34 Subtypes of the five basic types exist.

35 It has been found that many Meissener corpuscles are innervated not only by a type II afferent fiber, but also by one or more type IV fibers (Mountcastle, 2005).

36 Defined for a vibration as the smallest amplitude of vibration that can evoke at least one spike per cycle.

37 Johansson, Flanagan (2009).

38 Some skeletal muscles do not possess GTOs. These include the extraocular muscles (Ruskell, 1999).

39 See Matthews (1981).

40 Crago, Houk, Rymer (1982).

41 Binder *et al.* (1977).

42 The firing rate of Golgi tendon organ afferents tends to follow the EMG activity of the muscle, and EMG co-varies with active force (Al-Falahe, Nagaoka, Vallbo, 1997).

43 The principle can be illustrated using Hooke's law (the relationship between length

and tension). If you measure the force (T) and know that $T = -k(L - \ell_0)$, then L is given by $\ell_0 - T/k$.

44 Results of this sort have been obtained from cats and other mammals (Burgess, Clark, 1969).

45 Proske, Gandevia (2009).

46 Burke, Gandevia, Macefield (1988).

47 These areas have been identified in both monkeys and humans. Brain imaging studies have shown that the cortical organization of somatosensory processes is very similar in monkeys and humans (Burton, 2002).

48 Penfield, Rasmussen (1950).

49 This definition follows modern usage (Proske, Gandevia, 2009).

50 E.g., Allen, Proske (2006).

51 Several studies have examined the difference between matching joint angles and matching segment orientations (Soechting, 1982; Worringham, Stelmach, Martin, 1987; Darling, Hondzinski, 1999).

52 E.g., Darling (1991).

53 E.g., Burke *et al.* (1988).

54 Gandevia, McCloskey (1976); Ferrell, Gandevia, McCloskey (1987).

55 Grigg, Finerman, Riley (1973); Kelso, Holt, Flatt (1980); Wada *et al.* (2002).

56 Gandevia (1996).

57 Clark *et al.* (1979, 1985); though cutaneous information can support kinesthetic perception of knee and elbow joint position and motion (Collins *et al.*, 2005; Edin, 2001).

58 Goodwin, McCloskey, Matthews (1972); Jones (1988).

59 Roll *et al.* (1996, 2009).

60 Craske (1977).

61 Lackner (1988).

62 Pinocchio is a fictional character whose nose grew longer whenever he told lies.

63 See Proske, Gandevia (2009).

64 Roll, Vedel, Ribot (1989).

65 This is not completely certain. The nervous system may be combining the signals from all the different proprioceptors, such that a signal of 'substantial movement' from the spindles combined with a signal of 'no movement' from the other proprioceptors yields an overall signal that indicates 'some movement'.

66 See Howard (1982).

67 Tastevin (1937).

68 See Woods, Reganzone (2004).

69 Botvinick, Cohen (1998).

70 Pavani, Spence, Driver (2000).

71 Armel, Ramachandran (2003); Ehrsson *et al.* (2007).

72 Petkova, Ehrsson (2008, 2010).

73 Walsh *et al.* (2011).

74 Muscle spindle responses have also been found to be dependent on the recent history of muscle contraction (Proske, Morgan, Gregory, 1993).

75 Gandevia (1996).

76 Sturnieks, Wright, Fitzpatrick (2007).

77 See Proske, Gandevia (2009); Feldman, Latash (1982).

78 Feldman, Latash (1982); Feldman, Levin (1995).

79 Feldman, Latash (1982); McCloskey, Torda (1975).

80 Gandevia (1987).

81 Gandevia *et al.* (2006); Smith *et al.* (2009).

82 Carson, Riek, Shahbazpour (2002); Gandevia, McCloskey (1977); McCloskey *et al.* (1974).

83 See Waller (1891).

84 Marcora (2009).

85 E.g., Proske, Gandevia (2009).

86 See commentaries on Marcora (2009).

87 The midline is thought to define a primary axis for the representation of spatial information (Jeannerod, 1988).

88 Howard (1982).

89 Soechting, Ross (1984); Helms Tillery, Flanders, Soechting (1991); Baud-Bovy, Viviani (1998).

90 Shimono, Higashiyama, Tam (2001).

91 Fuentes, Bastian (2010).

92 These typically involve placing the participant's finger at a target location, moving it away, and then have the participant attempt to localize the target (Helms Tillery *et al.*, 1991; Baud-Bovy, Viviani, 1998).

93 Paillard (1991).

94 Paillard, Brouchon (1968).

95 This is the *constant error* (see Chapter 12 for details).

96 E.g., Paillard, Brouchon (1968).

[97] Carello, Fitzpatrick, Turvey (1992).

[98] Burton, Turvey (1990); Chan (1994).

[99] Loomis, Lederman (1986).

[100] Gibson (1962). Other terms such as dynamic touch are also used (Turvey, 1996).

[101] For a review of haptic perception generally, see Lederman and Klatzky (2009).

[102] Solomon, Turvey (1988).

[103] Kingma, Van der Langenberg, Beek (2004); Lederman, Ganeshan, Ellis (1996).

[104] Turvey, Carello (1995); Van der Langenberg, Kingma, Beek (2008).

[105] Gibson (1966).

[106] Lederman, Klatzky (1987) .

CHAPTER 4

Visuomotor Foundations

4.1 Eyes and Images

4.1.1 Introduction

Our visual systems are what allow us to see, but what does it mean, to see? The following provides a starting point:

> The plain man's answer … would be, to know what is where by looking. In other words, vision is the process of discovering from images what is present in the world and where it is[1].

This answer conforms to our general definition of sensory perception given in Chapter 3: visual perception is the process by which information is obtained from stimulation (images) in a form that can be used for performing whatever task requires it.

Visual perception results from the integrated activity of multiple component systems: there are the neural mechanisms that receive stimulation and process it to extract information, there are motor mechanisms that regulate the process of image formation (the pupilary reflex and the accommodative reflex); motor mechanisms that coordinate the movements of the two eyes so that we do not suffer from 'double vision'; mechanisms that move the eyes to look in different directions; mechanisms by which the eyes are kept stable so that we can fix our gaze on objects of interest; selective mechanisms which affect the processing of visual information so that we obtain the information we need to perform a task, in a form that is uncontaminated by irrelevant information. In this part of the chapter we will discuss the nature of visual stimulation and how an eye forms an image.

4.1.2 Light travels in straight lines (rays) and is reflected by the surfaces in the environment

The starting point of visual perception is the stimulation of photoreceptors by light energy. Light is curious stuff: it is neither wave nor particle, it possesses no mass, it only exists in motion (you cannot have stationary light), and it moves at an incredible speed that is the same relative to any observer. Luckily we will not need to worry about the quirky physics of light. All we will need to know is that light can be considered to travel in straight lines called **rays**, and that it comes in different wavelengths. We can only see light with wavelengths from a little under 400 nanometers to nearly 750 nanometers (nm; 1 nanometer = 10^{-9} meters). This range of wavelengths is called the **visible spectrum**.

When light in the visible range strikes an opaque surface, some proportion of it is reflected back and some proportion is absorbed. If a small proportion is reflected, the surface appears dark – a black surface may absorb 90% or more of the visible light that falls on it. If a large proportion is reflected, the surface appears light – a white surface may reflect as much as 90% of the visible light that falls on it. The color, or more precisely the hue, of a surface depends on the degree to which the surface reflects different wavelengths. A white, black or gray surface is said to be achromatic, which means it is without color or hue. Such a surface reflects all visible wavelengths in roughly equal proportion. Colored surfaces reflect different wavelengths to different degrees. Perfectly matt surfaces reflect light in all directions equally and have no shine or luster. Perfectly mirrored surfaces reflect a ray of light back in only one direction (the angle at which it is incident is equal to the angle of reflection). Surfaces in the world have characteristics of both perfectly matt and perfectly mirrored surfaces; they are in between these two extremes. However, most are more matt than they are mirrored.

4.1.3 Light reaches points of observation from all directions

When the sun is up, the world is filled with light: light rays reach points in the open air from all directions. Some rays may reach such a point from the sun, some from the sky and others from reflective surfaces. Light is said to be **ambient** at a point in the open air because light rays will converge on it from all directions: the point is completely surrounded or enclosed by light. These points are locations where an eye or a camera could potentially be placed, and are sometimes referred to as (potential) **points of observation** for this reason. Rays reflected from some surfaces reach a particular point of observation, but rays from other surfaces do not. The surfaces from which rays reach the point are **visible** from that point.

The light arriving at a point of observation from different directions will have different characteristics. There will be less light arriving from dark surfaces than from bright surfaces or from the sun and sky, so the light reaching a point of observation will be more intense from some directions than from others. Different wavelengths are reflected in different amounts from differently colored surfaces, so light from different directions will contain different wavelengths. In short, the structure of the environment that surrounds a point of observation gives a structure to the light that reaches that point. This structure is a pattern of intensity variation and wavelength composition across the different directions.

The psychologist J.J. Gibson invented the term **(ambient) optic array** to refer to the light reaching a point of observation in the environment[2]:

> **(AMBIENT) OPTIC ARRAY** (at a point of observation): The spatial pattern of light (variation in intensity and wavelength composition) reaching a particular point of observation from its surroundings.

The word 'array' is used because the light has an arrangement or structure[3]. The array represents the potential visual stimulation that exists at any point where an eye could be located. It is often visualized in terms of a spherical surface centered on the point of observation, since all directions from a point 'fill' a spherical surface in the sense that associated with each direction there is a unique point on the surface. The array is the intensity and wavelength composition of the light in all directions, and so can be visualized to be a pattern of light on the surface of this imaginary spherical surface. Cameras and most eyes work by projecting a portion of the optic array onto a light-sensitive surface to form an image, as described next.

4.1.4 Vertebrate eyes use converging lenses to form sharp images

The eyes of vertebrate animals project a segment of the optic array onto a surface at the back of the eye – the retina – to form an image called a **retinal image**. The retinal surfaces onto which images are projected contain arrays of densely packed photoreceptors. Thus, it is the retinal image that constitutes the proximal visual stimulation, not the optic array. In this section and the next we will briefly consider some of the essentials of image formation.

Both eyes and cameras are light-proof chambers (*camera* is the Latin for 'chamber') with a hole through which light can enter (the aperture or pupil). The simplest form is the pin-hole camera, which is just a light-proof chamber with a very small hole in it (Figure 4.1, panel A). This is sufficient to form an image, and the eyes of some invertebrate animals have this design; the eyes of cephalopod molluscs of the nautilus family provide examples. The problem with using little holes to form images is that the hole must be very small to form a sharply focused image, but a small hole lets in very little light, and so the image is very dim. A larger hole lets in more light, but does not form a sharp image. Both cameras and the eyes of vertebrate animals overcome this problem by using a system of lenses to focus the image.

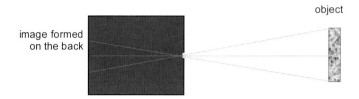

(A) Pinhole camera: light rays from objects pass through a small hole in the front and form an image on the back

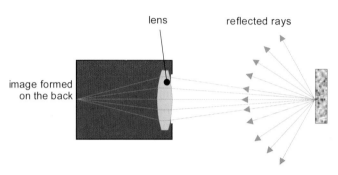

(B) Camera with converging lens

Figure 4.1: *Basic structure of two kinds of camera.*

A converging lens is a lens that focuses rays of light in the manner shown in panel B of Figure 4.1. Rays are reflected in many directions from a point on a surface and some of them reach the lens. The refractive characteristics of the lens bend these rays so that they converge to a single point on an imaging surface. Thus, the lens collects light from a range of different directions and can form a brighter image than a pin-hole. If a lens focuses light rays from a single point in the environment to a single point in the image (as shown in the figure), then the image is sharp. If the rays are focused onto an area in the image, then the image is blurred. No lens can form a perfectly sharp image; there will always be some blur. The optics of an animal's eye form images that are sharp enough for the animal to be able to obtain the information it needs.

The human eye possesses two converging lenses. One of these is the cornea, the transparent film of cells that lies directly in front of the iris and pupil. The other lens lies behind the pupil and is simply called the *lens*. Both are shown in the cross-section of the eye in Figure 4.2. These two lenses are responsible for collecting light and focusing an image on the retina at the back of the eye. The cornea does a substantial part of the focusing; the lens is a fine-tuning device (see next section).

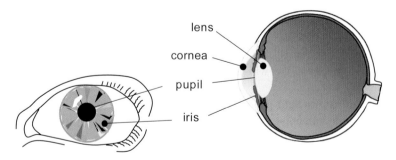

Figure 4.2: *Human eye: the cross-section on the right shows the location of the lens.*

As briefly alluded to above, it is tempting to think of an image formed by a pinhole or by a system of lenses as being like a picture of the surroundings. However, it is misleading to think in this way when trying to understand visual perception, because a picture is something to be looked at, whereas the image formed on the back of the eye is not. The retinal image is the stimulation applied to an array of photoreceptors. The brain does not look at these images, nor does it convert them into electrical signal so that they can be looked at by a little man in the head. The brain extracts information from them by processing the photoreceptor responses. The temptation to think of a retinal image as a picture that is looked at by something is an obstacle to the understanding of visual perception: there is nothing looking at the images.

4.1.5 Human eyes have adjustable aperture and focus

Cameras and vertebrate eyes both have holes to let the light in, and systems of lenses to focus an image onto a light sensitive surface. Although the details of their designs are obviously different, both have adjustable apertures and adjustable focus that allow them to operate properly over a range of different light levels, and to focus sharp images of objects at different distances. In both eyes and modern cameras, the adjustment processes work automatically (the 'user' does not have to think about them). We have already discussed the automatic process that adjusts pupil size for different light levels (Chapter 1, Figure 1.25); it is called the pupiliary light reflex. The eye also possesses an automatic mechanism for adjusting focus, like the autofocus of a camera; it is called the **accommodative reflex**.

Figure 4.3 provides a simplified explanation for why an adjustable focusing mechanism is needed. A lens with a particular shape bends rays of light in a particular way, so that it forms an image some distance away that depends on the angles of the rays that it collects. Rays from nearby objects enter the lens at sharper angles (Figure 4.3A) than rays from more distant objects (Figure 4.3B). Since the lens bends the rays through the same angles in each case, the image of a nearby object is focused further from the lens than the image of a more distant object. A camera adjusts for this by moving the lens nearer to or further from the imaging plane, depending on the distance to the object. The eye's autofocus works differently. The lens does not move, but changes its shape so that the curvature of the lens increases or descreases. The more curved the surface of a lens, the greater its refractive power: a highly curved converging lens bends light more (has greater refractive power) than a flatter one.

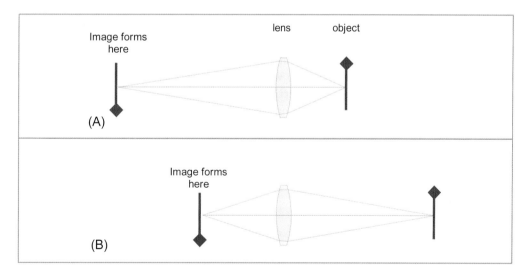

Figure 4.3: *Images of more distant objects are focused closer to the lens.*

The curvature of the lens in the eye changes as a result of contracting and relaxing the ciliary muscle – a smooth muscle located within the eyeball. This muscle is attached to the lens by the suspensory ligament, such that when the muscle relaxes, the ligament pulls on the lens. This stretches the lens, making it slightly less curved. When the muscle contracts, the pull on the lens decreases and it becomes fatter and more curved. To form a sharp image of a near object requires more refractive power, and so the lens needs to be thicker and more curved, as shown in panel A of Figure 4.4. To form a sharp image of a distant object requires less refractive power, and so the lens needs to be less curved (panel B of Figure 4.4). The accommodative reflex is a feedback control mechanism that works (very roughly[4]) by detecting how blurry the image is and causing the ciliary muscle to contract or relax accordingly – the lens changes shape, and this brings the image into sharp focus. Image blur is the controlled variable. The brain is able to measure the blur in the image from the responses of photoreceptors: the perceptual estimate of blur serves as an error signal that is used to regulate the curvature of the lens so as to eliminate the blur and bring the image into sharp focus.

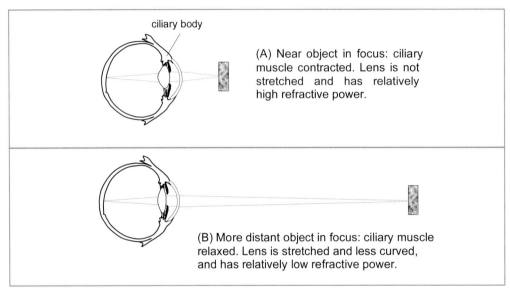

Figure 4.4: *Focusing action of the accommodative reflex.*

4.1.6 Light enters the eye from almost a hemisphere of directions

Light enters the human eye from almost the full hemisphere of directions. Panels A and B of Figure 4.5 show a vertical and horizontal cross-section through this hemisphere: light rays can enter the eye from any direction within the shaded segments. The angular extent of this vertical section (θ) is called the **vertical angle of view** of the eye and is nearly 180°. The angular extent of the horizontal section (ϕ) is the **horizontal angle of view** and is also nearly 180°.

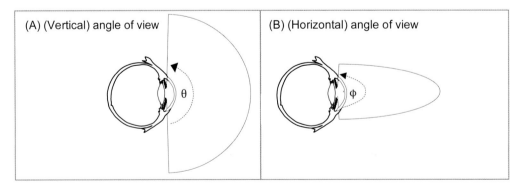

Figure 4.5: *Angle of view of an eye.*

The angle of view is closely related to the concept of an eye's **field of view** (also called the **visual field**[5]). This is the region of the external surroundings from which light can enter a stationary eye and stimulate photoreceptors. It does not include light entering from the visible parts of the orbit of the eye or the nose, so the angular extent of the field of view is generally slightly less than the angle of view. Here is a definition:

> **FIELD OF VIEW** (of a single eye): The total region of the surroundings of a stationary eye (excluding the orbit and nose) from which rays of light can enter it and reach the photoreceptors. Also called the **visual field**.

Figure 4.6 illustrates the concept in two dimensions (transverse plane). The field of view is shown shaded. In panel A, the eye is looking straight ahead, and the white triangle, blue circle gray circle and orange square are within the eye's field of view. In panel B the eye has turned to the right, and now only the blue and gray circles are within the field of view. Notice that because of the position of the nose, the angular extent of the field of view is greater in panel A than in panel B.

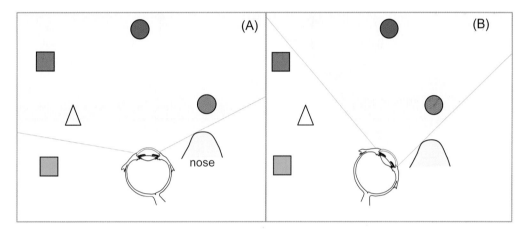

Figure 4.6: *Field of view of an eye in the transverse (horizontal) plane.*

The light that enters an eye from its field of view is a segment of an optic array. It is this segment that is projected onto the back of the eye to form the retinal image. However, the field of view is not normally defined in terms of the optic array, for reasons given in section 4.1.9.

4.1.7 An object in the field of view subtends a visual angle at the eye

Imagine straight lines joining points in the field of view to the locations where their images fall on the back of the eye (Figure 4.7A shows some examples). These lines all meet at a single point called the **nodal point** of the eye[6], which lies directly behind the pupil near the back of the lens, about 17 mm from the retina, as shown in Figure 4.7A. The nodal point can be considered to coincide with the point of observation occupied by the eye.

If straight lines are drawn from the nodal point to the boundaries of an object within the eye's field of view, the angle at which they meet is called the **visual angle**, subtended by the object at the eye. In panel B of Figure 4.7, the vertical extent of an object subtends a visual angle α. The visual angle subtended by an object depends on the object's distance from the eye. Panel C shows the same object at two different distances from the eye. At the nearer distance the object subtends a visual angle of about 45°; at the further distance the angle is only about 15° (labelled β). More generally, if an object of height H is a distance D from the nodal point of the eye and subtends an angle β, then the three quantities are related to one another by the following equation:

$$\tan(\beta/2) = H/2D$$

It is also clear from panel C that the image of an object is larger when the object is closer to the eye. When the object is a distance D from the eye and subtends a visual angle β, the height of the image is approximately equal to nβ, which is the distance (n) from the nodal point to the back of the eye multiplied by visual angle (H ≈ nβ).

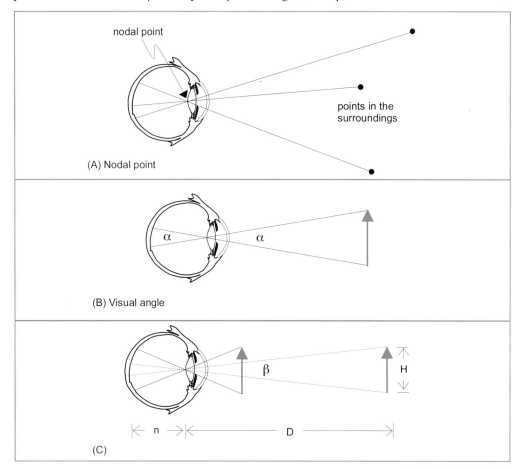

Figure 4.7: *Nodal points and visual angles.*

4.1.8 The binocular field of view is formed by the overlapping segments of the fields of view of the two eyes

Vertebrate animals have two eyes, and their fields of view overlap to some extent. Many mammal and bird species have eyes located on the sides of the head, so that one eye faces to the left and the other to the right – cows, horses, deer, rabbits and ducks are all examples.

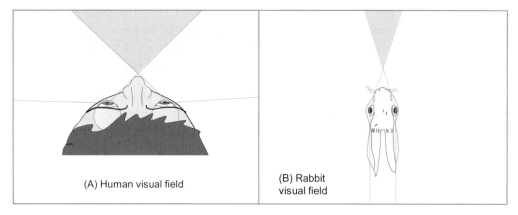

Figure 4.8: *Extent of the visual fields in the transverse plane of the head. The binocular overlap is shaded darker.*

In these animals the fields of view of the eyes have a relatively small region of overlap. Human beings and some other animals, including primates, cats and owls, have eyes in the front of their heads so that both face forwards. This results in a much larger overlap of the visual fields. The degree of overlap in the horizontal plane of the head is shown in Figure 4.8 for a person (panel A) and a rabbit (panel B). In both panels of the figure, the overlap of the fields of view is shown shaded darker. This overlapping region is called the **binocular field of view** (or *binocular visual field*) and is defined to be the total area of the visual surroundings from which rays of light can enter both eyes and reach the photoreceptors (with both eyes stationary). The horizontal angular extent of the binocular field of view is over 100° in human beings; in rabbits it is about 30°.

To emphasize the distinction between the binocular field of view and the fields of view of the individual eyes, the latter are sometimes called **monocular fields of view**. The total field of view (or just the field of view) is the sum of the two monocular fields of view (the total shaded regions in panels A and B of Figure 4.8). The total field of view and the binocular field of view are not segments of an optic array, and so cannot be defined in these terms. This is the reason that the field of view is defined in terms of the visual surroundings and not in terms of the optic array.

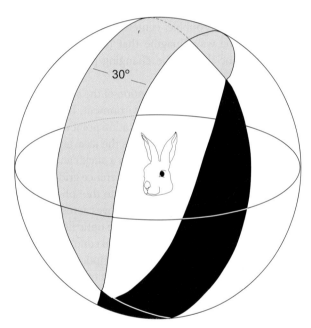

Figure 4.9: *Field of view of the rabbit (based on Hughes, 1972).*

As Figure 4.8 shows, the total field of view is much larger in the rabbit than in human beings. In animals with eyes on the side of the head, the total field of view can extend through nearly the full 360° in a horizontal (transverse) plane through the eyes. Such large, panoramic fields of view are often found in herbivorous animals that live in open areas with few trees. This allows these animals to detect predators approaching from any direction without having to move their heads around. Figure 4.9 shows a complete picture of the rabbit's field of view. The unshaded regions represent the exclusively monocular segments of the field of view; the binocular field of view is the segment shaded pale brown. The region shaded dark brown is not part of the rabbit's field of view – light cannot reach the rabbit's eyes from this region. As the figure shows, above the transverse plane through the eyes (upper hemisphere) the rabbit can see all around (full 360°), and within this hemisphere part of the binocular field extends behind the animal's head. The rabbit's panoramic field of view makes it very difficult for a predator to creep up on it undetected.

4.1.9 The optic flow is the available stimulation at a moving point of observation

Animals frequently move their heads, up and down, from side to side, and from place to place. As the head moves, the eyes move with it, such that they occupy different points of observation over time. The optic array is different at each point of observation, which means that as an eye moves through space and occupies a succession of observation points, so the optic array changes. The continuous change in the light reaching a moving point of observation is called the optic flow. Where the optic array is the visual stimulation potentially available at a stationary point of observation, the optic flow is the visual stimulation available at a moving point of observation. Here is a rough definition:

> **OPTIC FLOW** (at a moving point of observation): The continuous change over time of the spatial pattern of light (variation in intensity and wavelength composition) reaching a point as it moves through its surroundings.
> relative to surroundings

The optic flow is a difficult concept, but it can be visualized in a similar way to the optic array. Recall that in section 4.1.3 the optic array was visualized as the pattern of light playing on an imaginary spherical surface, like a soap bubble, centered on the point of observation. We can visualize the optic flow in the same way. Imagine that the sphere is carried along with the moving observation point: the optic flow is the changing pattern of light on the surface of this moving sphere.

The dominant characteristic of optic flow is the motion of the abrupt changes in light intensity that correspond to boundaries and features in the environment. If we think of the flow as light pattern playing on a spherical surface, then as the observation point moves, the optical boundaries and contours on this surface move. Figure 4.10 illustrates the idea: a point of observation is moving through the environment past an object (blue ball on a stick!) and is shown at three instants of time in the three frames. The imaginary sphere has a reference grid drawn on it. The light from the object incident at the point of observation projects onto the sphere to form a kind of image. As the observation point moves, this 'image' changes: it moves across the sphere, changes in size (gets larger from frame 1 to 3), and changes shape. Thus, the optic flow involves motion of optical boundaries and changes in the shape (deformation) of optical contours. There is more to the optic flow than this[7], but we will not need a more complete description. As we will see later (sections 4.1.12 and 4.1.13), the optic flow contains a substantial amount of information about the surroundings and about how the observation point is moving through the surroundings.

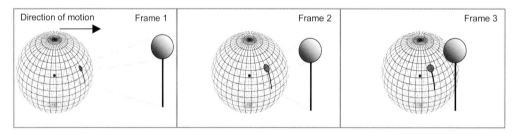

Figure 4.10: *Cartoon illustration of the concept of optic flow.*

When an animal moves through its environment, segments of the optic flow are projected onto the back of its eyes, giving rising to image motion that is known as **image flow**. Image flow is described next.

4.1.10 Projection of the optic flow onto the back of the eye forms an image flow

When an eye is stationary, the retinal image is a projection of a segment of the optic array. When an animal moves so that its eyes are travelling through the environment, then a segment of the optic flow is projected onto the back of each eye to form a moving image.

The projection of the optic flow on the back of one eye forms an image flow. When an eye moves through the environment without turning in the socket, the image flow is simply a projection of the optic flow; we will consider this case first.

Imagine that a person is travelling in a straight line through their surroundings, with each eye pointing straight ahead, so that the pupil lies in the direction of travel. For simplicity, we will assume that the surroundings themselves are stationary – it is a still day, and nothing is moving in the scene. A vertical cross-section of this kind of situation is shown in Figure 4.11 for a single eye. The person's eye is moving in the plane of the page over flat ground towards a gate in front of a small tree. Light rays will reach the eye from every point in its field of view, but only four are shown. As the eye moves towards the tree, the direction of these points from the eye change, and their images move over the back of the eye as shown in the inset: the arrows indicate the direction in which the image points move, the length of the arrows indicates the speed with which the image points move. The image flow comprises the motion of all visible points[8].

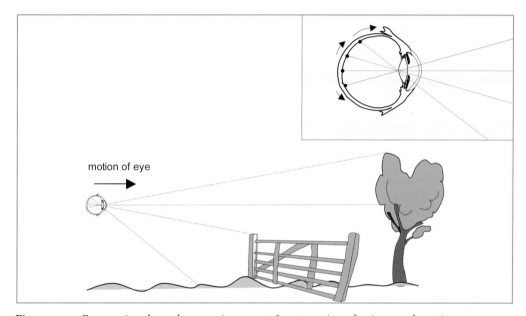

Figure 4.11: *Eye moving through an environment. Inset, motion of points on the retina.*

Notice that the four points shown imaged in Figure 4.11 do not move across the retina at the same speed: some move quicker than others, and one point is not moving at all. This stationary image point corresponds to the point in the field of view that the eye is moving directly towards. The direction of this point does not change as the eye moves, and so its image remains in the same place. Image points close to this stationary point move slowly, whereas points further away move more quickly. The result is a pattern of motion across the image that seems to flow out from a stationary center (see Figure 4.12). It is also the case that images of objects closer to the eye move faster than the images of more distant objects.

Thus, there are two factors that determine how image points move as the eye moves through its surroundings: (1) the speed and direction of the eye's movement through the surroundings, and (2) the distances from the eye to the points in the surroundings that are imaged on the retina. Let us briefly consider the first of these factors (the second is discussed in section 4.1.13). To keep things simple, imagine that the eye moves in a straight line through stationary surroundings. A particularly simple flow pattern is produced if the eye is traveling directly towards a flat, vertical surface. Figure 4.12 shows the image flow pattern for this case represented in the form of *streamlines*: as time passes and points move across the image, the streamlines are the paths followed by points for a short period of time. The longer the streamline, the further a point has moved during the time period. Since points that are moving faster travel further, the longer streamlines are associated with faster-moving points in the image. The streamline pattern shown in Figure 4.12 can be described as a radial outflow pattern: the flow originates from a stationary point in the image and moves radially outwards.

The point from which the flow seems to originate is called the **focus of radial outflow** (an alternative term is the *focus of expansion*[9]).

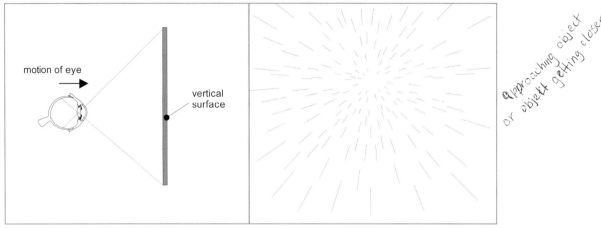

(A) Eye moving towards a vertical surface   (B) A pattern of radial outflow in the image

Figure 4.12: *Radial outflow pattern is produced when an eye moves towards a surface without rotation.*

In the case we have been considering – an eye moving through the surroundings in a straight line without turning – the image flow pattern is the same as the optic flow pattern (the difference is that the image flow is left-right reversed and upside down relative to the optic flow). In other words, the image flow is a projection of that portion of the optic flow that is contained within the eye's field of view[10]. If the eye does turn in its socket, then there will be image motion due to the turning of the eye, and this motion is not part of the optic flow. In fact, when a stationary eye turns, there is image flow but no optic flow.

4.1.11 The image flow comprises two components

When the head is stationary and an eye rotates in its socket, then the image moves relative to the retina – there is image motion. The whole image sweeps across the back of the eye so the motion is said to be *whole field* – it is an example of an image flow. Figure 4.13 illustrates what happens when an eye rotates in the plane of the page, and shows the flow pattern produced. Panel A shows a cross-section through an eye together with rays from five points in the surroundings. The eye rotates in the direction indicated by the large curved arrow about an axis of rotation perpendicular to the page that passes close to the center of the eye. Images of the points in the surroundings move relative to the retina as the eye rotates: their motions are indicated by the small arrows. Panel B shows a hemisphere representing the back of the eye; the motions of image points relative to the hemisphere are indicated by curved blue arrows. This pattern of arrows represents the image flow due to eye rotation.

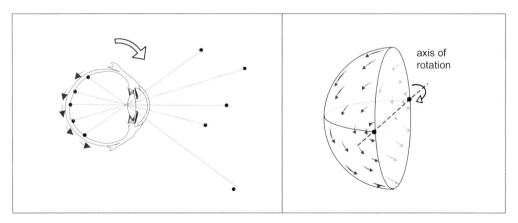

Figure 4.13: *Image flow due to eye rotation.*

If an eye moves through the environment and the eye turns in its socket at the same time, then there will be an image flow that is composed of two parts: the projection of the optic flow due to the movement of the eye through the environment, and the flow due to the turning of the eye. The projection of the optic flow is usually called the **translational component of the image flow**, because it is due to translation of the eye through its surroundings. The flow due to the eye turning is called the **rotational component of the image flow**, because it is due to rotation of the eye within the environment. We are now in a position to define what is meant by retinal image flow:

> **RETINAL IMAGE FLOW:** The continuous change over time of an image formed on the back of the eye (the retina) that arises as a consequence of the translation of the eye through its surroundings and/or rotation of the eye within its socket. In general, the image flow will be due to both types of motion: the sum of a *translational component* (flow due to translation, a projection of the optic flow) and a *rotational component* (flow due to eye rotation).

A simple and everyday situation in which the image flow is the sum of a translational component and a rotational component occurs when you gaze out of the side window of a moving vehicle to look at an object that interests you. As you pass by, your eyes rotate in their sockets so that you stay looking at the object. The image of the object being looked at does not move across the retina – that's part of what it means to look at something – but the images of things not being looked at do move across the retina. This case is described in more detail in Chapter 10.

The translational component of the image flow contains information about the layout of the visible surroundings and about how the eye is moving through the surroundings (described below). The rotational component contains no information about the surroundings, but it does contain information about the eye rotation that produced it.

4.1.12 The translational component of the image flow contains useful information about the layout of the visible surroundings

The translational component of the image flow depends not only on the motion of the eye through the surroundings but also on the distances of the visible points. The images of points near to the eye tend to move faster than the images of more distant points. This conforms to everyday experience: if you look out of the side window of a moving vehicle, nearby things whiz past, whereas things further away appear to move past much more slowly. Differences in the speeds of images of points that lie at different distances is called **motion parallax**. The fact that the images of nearby things move faster than the images of more distant things means that there is information in the translational component of the image flow about the *relative distances* of the visible points. You cannot determine exactly how far away any object is from you using motion parallax, but you can tell how far away objects are relative to each other – which are nearer to you and which are further away.

When you look out of the window of a moving vehicle at a particular object, the pattern of relative motion in the image becomes complicated by the addition of a rotational flow component, due to turning of the eye. The image of the object being looked at does not move on the retina; images of points in the scene further away from you than the object move in one direction, while images of points closer than the point you are looking at move in the other direction. It is clear, however, that information about the relative distances of points in the scene is still present in the image flow. In this case, you can tell whether things in the scene are closer or further than the object being looked at, because the images of closer things move in one direction whereas images of more distant things move in the opposite direction.

Although there is information present in motion parallax about the relative distances of things in the surroundings, it is not necessarily the case that people or other animals are able to extract this information and use it. Hermann von Helmholtz, one of the early pioneers in the study of vision, gave a nice description of the sort of experience that suggests that we can perceive relative distances from motion parallax. Helmholtz asks us to imagine a man standing motionless in a woodland, looking at a dense tangle of branches and foliage some distance away. While motionless, the man has no clear perception of how the branches and foliage are laid out in depth; however, 'the moment he begins to move forward, everything disentangles itself and immediately he gets a [perception] of the material contents of the woods and their relations to each other in space'[11]. Conclusive experimental evidence showing that motion parallax can be used was provided much later[12]. The basic idea of the experiments is illustrated in Figure 4.14. Panel A shows an artificially constructed scene with two flat panels, one in front of the other, being viewed by a person who is looking with one eye only (the other is patched). The visible surfaces of the panels are carefully painted with a random pattern, so that the one in front is camouflaged and cannot be distinguished from the one behind if the eye remains in a fixed position[13]. Panel B shows what the scene looks like when viewed from the position shown in panel A without moving the head: it looks like a flat surface covered with a random texture, and it is impossible to see that there are two objects separated in depth. However, when the person moves their head from side to side, they are able to see quite clearly that there is a smaller square object in front of the other, as suggested in panel C. This is because when the head moves, the retinal images of the dots on the nearer surface move faster than the retinal images of the dots on the more distant surface: head movement creates motion parallax, and this carries information about the relative distances of the two surfaces.

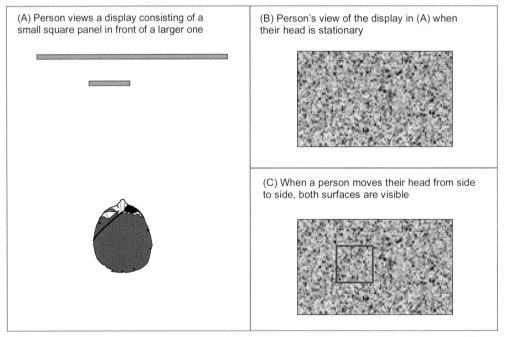

Figure 4.14: *The idea behind experiments demonstrating that people can use motion parallax to perceive the layout of visible surfaces.*

Mathematical analysis of the translational component of the image flow has shown that it contains information not only about relative distances of objects but also about their shapes and orientations, and about the slopes of surfaces. Experimental studies that exploit the same basic idea as described above with reference to Figure 4.14 have demonstrated that people are able to extract all this information[14].

4.1.13 The translational component contains information about movement through the environment

The translational component of the image flow is caused by the eye undergoing translational motion through its surroundings. As a result, the translational component carries some information about the eye's translational motion relative to the surroundings. Importantly, it carries information about the direction in which the eye is moving. In particular, the focus of radial outflow (see section 4.1.10 and Figure 4.12B) coincides with the image of the point in the surroundings towards which the eye is moving. Thus, the translational component of the flow provides information about where in the surroundings the eye is going: it is headed towards the point that is imaged at the location of the focus of radial outflow. We will discuss the use of this information in Chapter 10; in the next section, we consider the kind of perceptual experiences produced by image flow.

4.1.14 Artificially generated image flows evoke perceptions of self-motion

Image flow is caused by an eye's motion in the environment, and hence carries information about how the eye is moving. For this reason we might expect that image flows give rise to the perception that we are moving through the environment – perceptions of **self-motion**. With this in mind, consider the following two situations: (1) A person moves in a straight line through an environment; (2) A person stands still and the environment is moved straight past them. These two situations create the same image flow and so cannot be distinguished purely on the basis of the visual stimulation. Of course, the second situation never occurs in the natural world – the whole environment never moves past you while you are standing still. However, such situations can be created artificially, which raises the question, *what do people perceive when they are stationary and the environment is moved past them*? There are two possible answers:

(i) They correctly perceive themselves to be stationary and the environment to be moving past them.

(ii) They incorrectly perceive themselves to be moving through a stationary environment.

It turns out that the second answer describes people's perception. Such perceptions are frequently experienced while sitting in a stationary train carriage when a train standing at the neighboring platform pulls out of the station: people often feel that their train is moving and that it is the neighboring one that is stationary (the *train illusion*). Fairground and amusement parks have exploited the phenomenon since the late 19th century, when an attraction called the 'haunted swing' was invented. This attraction was described by a visitor as follows[15]: '[o]n entering the building we found ourselves in a spacious cubical room, furnished with a sofa, table, chairs, etc., ... But the most conspicuous object was the huge swing, capable of holding forty or more persons, which hung in the center, suspended from an iron cylinder which passed through the center of the room.' The 'swing' was an open, boat-shaped carriage with rows of seats suspended as described. Once the visitors were seated, the room would be moved in a swinging motion, but the carriage would remain stationary. The perceptual experience was one of being swung forwards and backwards in a stationary room. The same type of experience is produced in some modern amusement parks using computer generated movies that are projected onto wide-angle screens, similar to those used in IMAX cinemas. The visitors are seated in a carriage, and their impression of moving through the scene is often completely compelling and is enhanced by vibration and tilting of the carriage.

Perceptions of apparent self-motion induced by movement of the visual field is called **vection**[16]. Perceptions of motion in a straight line is called **linear vection**; perception of rotating about a vertical axis is called **circular vection** (see section 4.3.12); and perception of rotating about horizontal axes is either **roll vection** (rotation in the coronal plane) or **pitch vection** (rotation in the sagittal plane)[17]. It has been found that stimulation of the peripheral retinas is important for producing the effect[18]. This is not surprising, since merely watching a movie, in which only the central regions of the retinas are stimulated, produces little if any impression of self-motion. When the entire visual field moves, a strong feeling of self-motion is evoked, which is not significantly reduced by masking out a circular region in the center of as much as 60 degrees across[19]. In addition, motion of the background is more important for producing the effect than motion of the foreground[20]. This corresponds with the train illusion described earlier: objects in the foreground, in the train car where the person is sitting, do not move; only the train on the neighboring track (the background) moves. As discussed in Chapter 7, motions of the whole visual field not only induce vection, they also evoke postural reactions. The mechanisms underlying these two effects are different, since the postural reactions can be elicited in the absence of vection and have a short latency (100 to 150 ms, see Chapter 7), which is much shorter than the time it takes to experience vection[21].

4.2 Pathways and Processes

4.2.1 Introduction

The eye itself does not see. The eye forms an image that is transduced into electrical signals by the retina. These signals are transmitted along the optic nerves to the brain, and it is the brain that does the 'seeing'. In this part of the chapter we will describe (1) the structure and function of the retina, (2) the pathways that carry the retinal output signals to the brain and (3) what the brain does with these signals. We will have little to say about how the signals are processed in order to extract useful information from them; this is a matter for specialized texts that deal with visual perception[22].

4.2.2 Images projected onto the retina stimulate an array of photoreceptors

The surface of the back of vertebrate eyes is covered with a thin skin of tissue less than 0.5 mm thick, the **retina**. It is formed from layers of neurons and associated glial cells, and contains the photoreceptors – the rod and cone cells. The human retina contains about 120 million rods and about seven million cones arrayed side by side. Figure 4.15 shows how most of the retina is structured. The photoreceptors lie at the back of the retina, furthest from the pupil, and so light must pass through several layers of cells before reaching the receptors. In front of the photoreceptors, nearer to the pupil, are several layers containing different types of neuron. The photoreceptors make synaptic connections with neighboring photoreceptors and with two types of neurons: horizontal cells and bipolar cells. Horizontal cells have neurites that spread across the retina and make synaptic connections with a number of photoreceptors. Bipolar cells carry signals from the photoreceptors and from horizontal cells to more superficial neurons: the amacrine cells and the retinal ganglion cells. The ganglion cells are the output neurons of the retina; their axons travel out of the eye to the brain.

The region of retina shown in Figure 4.15 is typical of the structure that covers almost all the back of the eye (with the exception of the fovea): there are relatively few cones, but large numbers of rods, and layers of neurons lie over these receptors. The rods are only responsive at low light levels, and do not function at the light levels encountered during normal daylight hours. Cones, in contrast, are less sensitive to light, and contribute to vision only when light levels are sufficiently high. At night the cones do not function, and so only the rods contribute to vision. The term **scotopic vision** is the technical term for vision in low light levels when only the rods are contributing – often called *night vision* in everyday language. The term **photopic vision** is the technical term for vision in high light levels where only the cones are contributing. At intermediate light levels, both rods and cones contribute; the technical term for this is **mesopic vision**.

Although much of the human retina and that of other mammals has a structure similar to that shown in Figure 4.15, it is not entirely uniform, and there are some areas that are structured very differently. These are described next.

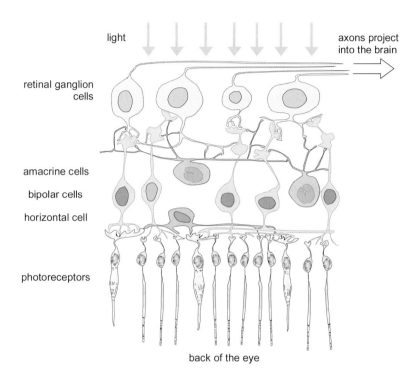

Figure 4.15: *Structure of the primate retina outside the central (foveal) area.*

4.2.3 The human retina has a small blind region and a small acute region

The sheet of photoreceptors that covers the back of the human eye has a hole in it – there is a small region where there are no photoreceptors. This region is called the **optic disc** or the **blind spot**. At this location, ganglion cell axons from all parts of the retina converge and pass out through the back of the eye to form the optic nerve. It is also the place where blood vessels enter and leave the eye. Figure 4.16 shows a horizontal cross-section through the human eye showing the location of the optic nerve and the optic disc, together with the part of the visual field that is 'missing'. The size of this blind spot varies between individuals, but is typically about 5° or 6° across in the cross-section shown in the figure.

There is another small spot on the retina that is visible through an ophthalmoscope, called the **macula**. It is located quite close to the optic disc, as indicated in Figure 4.16. The optic disc is on the nasal side of the macula in both eyes, so the eye in Figure 4.16 must be a right eye. As the center of the macula there is a small, roughly circular depression called the **fovea** (fovea is the Latin word for 'pit'). The pit is formed because the layers of cells and blood vessels that cover the photoreceptors elsewhere in the retina are not present in the foveal region. The fovea has no blood vessels, and the neurons within the more superficial retinal layers lie at the sides of the pit, so that the photoreceptors are more directly exposed to light. The fovea itself is very small, about one to one and a half millimeters across, which corresponds to about 3° or 4° of the visual field (1° corresponds to about 0.3 mm across the retina). The bottom of the pit – the *foveola* – is smaller still, less than 0.5 mm across.

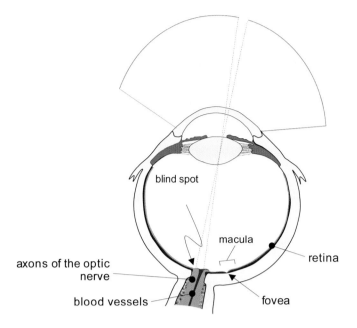

Figure 4.16: *Cross-section of the eye showing the optic disc (blind spot) and the fovea.*

Within the foveola there are no rods at all, only cones, which are very densely packed: counts have revealed that there are about 50,000 cones in the foveola (a density of 200,000/mm²). Since cones are only active when light levels are sufficiently high (photopic vision), the foveola is effectively blind when light levels are very low. As shown in Figure 4.17A, cone density drops off very rapidly outside the fovea: about 10° from the foveal center cone, density is down to about 20,000/mm². Beyond about 20° the cone density levels off to less than

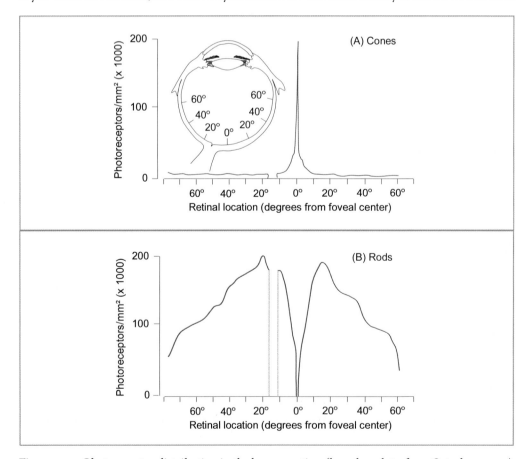

Figure 4.17: *Photoreceptor distribution in the human retina (based on data from Osterberg, 1935).*

5000/mm². Rod density is rather different. As already noted, rods are completely absent from the foveola, and the fovea as a whole contains very few. Outside the fovea they are present in large numbers. Figure 4.17B shows how the rods are distributed across the human retina: there are none in the foveola or the optic disc, but elsewhere they are found in large numbers, with a peak density of about 200,000/mm² (similar to cone density in the fovea) about 20° from the foveal center.

The difference in cone density across the retina is one of the reasons why, in well illuminated conditions, we have very acute, clear vision in the center of our visual fields, but are able to see much less clearly outside this central region (though this is far from being the whole story; see section 4.2.5). The central region, where the fine details of objects and surfaces can be seen, is only a very small part of the whole visual field, as discussed next.

4.2.4 Foveal vision has high acuity; peripheral vision has low acuity

Very fine details can only be discriminated in the central part of the visual field, where vision is mediated by the fovea. In this region, vision is said to have high **acuity**, which is another way of saying that it is possible to discriminate fine details and see small objects. Outside the central region, visual acuity drops off and fine details cannot be discriminated. The graph in Figure 4.18 shows how visual acuity varies with retinal position. Acuity is shown as a percentage of the highest level of acuity (the relative acuity): at the center of the fovea, where vision has the highest acuity, the relative acuity is 100%. Vision mediated by the fovea is called **foveal vision** or **focal vision** and comprises only the central 3° or 4° of the visual field. Vision is acute throughout this small region, as Figure 4.18 shows.

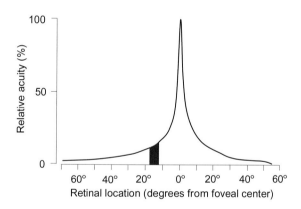

Figure 4.18: *Visual acuity across the retina (based on Wertheim, 1894).*

The macula is a spot about 10° across; the vastly larger part of the retina (about 95% of the total retinal area) that lies outside the macular region is called the **peripheral retina** (identified in the cross-section through the eye shown in Figure 4.19). Vision mediated by the peripheral retina is called **peripheral vision**, and comprises all of the visual field outside the central 10° (±5° from the center)[23]. Acuity is low in peripheral vision, dropping from 30% of maximum acuity in the near periphery to 2% in the far periphery. The part of the retina between the fovea and the peripheral retina is usually called the parafoveal retina, so the central 10° of the retina comprises the fovea and the parafoveal retina (Figure 4.19).

Since the foveola contains no rods and the rest of the fovea very few, focal vision is effectively night-blind. In contrast, the parafoveal and peripheral retina contains both rods and cones, so peripheral vision works well at night. Given that the peripheral retina contains many more rods than cones, it might be expected that peripheral vision would have better acuity at night than during the day. However, the acuity of peripheral vision is similar regardless of the light level. This is because it is not the number of photoreceptors in a given region of the retina that really matters. What matters for acuity is the number of output fibers that travel from a given retinal region to the brain. We will discuss this further in section 4.2.5.

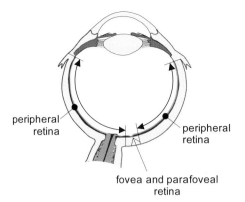

peripheral
retina

peripheral
retina

fovea and parafoveal
retina

Figure 4.19: *Divisions of the retina.*

Although fine details cannot be resolved in peripheral vision, it would be wrong to imagine that peripheral vision is worse than focal vision in all respects. Peripheral vision covers the vast majority of the visual field, and is useful for detecting things that happen outside of the central few degrees: we often detect movement 'out of the corner' of our eyes. It is perhaps not surprising, therefore, to discover that peripheral vision is at least as good and sometimes better than focal vision at detecting moving and flickering stimuli[24]. However, the motion and flicker sensitivity of the peripheral retina merely alerts us that there is something there; to find out what it is will usually require focal vision.

When we look at an object in the world, its image or part of its image falls on the foveas. Movements of the eyes are essential for looking and seeing: they allow us to bring the images of interesting things into focal vision. Eye movements will be discussed in detail in the next part of the chapter. At this point we will merely note that a major reason for moving the eyes is to bring images of interesting objects or surface regions into focal vision. In fact, eye movements go hand in hand with foveas – eyes with foveas must be moved around in order to see the fine details of things of interest in the visual field.

4.2.5 Visual acuity depends on the size of receptive fields

It was noted earlier that the high density of cones in the fovea contributes to the acuity of foveal vision and the low density of cones in the peripheral retina contributes to the low acuity of peripheral vision. However, there is more to differences in acuity than differences in photoreceptor density. That this is the case is indicated by the acuity of peripheral vision in high and low light levels. In high light levels, peripheral vision is mediated only by the cones in the peripheral retina (photopic peripheral vision); in low light levels it is mediated only by the rods (scotopic peripheral vision). Cone density is low in the periphery, whereas rod density is very high (Figure 4.17), so we might expect scotopic peripheral vision to have much better acuity than photopic peripheral vision. But this is not the case: the acuity of peripheral vision is much the same in different light levels. Factors other than photoreceptor density must also contribute to acuity. One major additional factor is the convergent pathway from photoreceptors to ganglion cells within the retina itself.

We have seen that the retinal ganglion cells are the output neurons of the retina: their axons form the optic nerve that passes out of the back of the eye and carries signals to the brain. There are many more photoreceptors in the retina than there are ganglion cells: about 120 million rods, seven million cones and fewer than two million ganglion cells. This indicates that many photoreceptors converge onto single ganglion cells via intermediate neurons, particularly the bipolar and horizontal cells. It turns out that the firing rate of most ganglion cells in the retinas of primates is affected by photoreceptors from roughly circular or oval regions of the photoreceptor array. Panel A of Figure 4.20 gives a rough illustration of the idea: a group of neighboring photoreceptors that occupy a roughly circular region of the retina (shaded orange) are connected via intermediate cells to a single ganglion cell.

The firing rate of the ganglion cell is affected by stimulation reaching any of the photorecep-tors that are connected to it, i.e., photoreceptors within the circular region. This region of the photoreceptor array is called the **receptive field** of the ganglion cell. In principle, a receptive field can be specified for any neuron in the visual pathway that is affected by the activity of photoreceptors, such as neurons in the brain that are further along the visual pathway. Here is an intuitive definition[25]:

> **RECEPTIVE FIELD (OF A NEURON IN THE VISUAL PATHWAY):** The region (or regions) of the photoreceptor array which when stimulated can affect the activity of the neuron.

The receptive fields of retinal ganglion cells overlap one another, so that a particular region of retina may be part of the receptive fields of several different ganglion cells, as shown in panel B of Figure 4.20. The figure shows how circular receptive fields might overlap with one another.

Receptive fields come in different sizes; some cover a large area of the photoreceptor array, others only a small area. Large receptive fields incorporate a large number of photorecep-tors, whereas small receptive fields incorporate fewer. It is the size of the receptive fields that limits visual acuity: small receptive fields are needed to resolve small details. In the peripheral retina, ganglion cells have relatively large receptive fields, and so fine details cannot be seen. In the fovea, ganglion cells have receptive fields of relatively small size; some are very small, incorporating only a few cones and making high acuity vision possible.

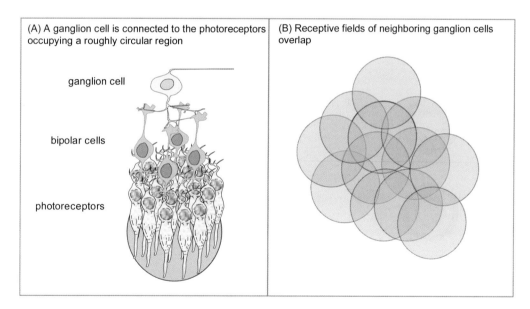

Figure 4.20: *Receptive fields of retinal ganglion cells.*

Receptive fields of ganglion cells do not simply represent a compression of activity from a large number of photoreceptors into a single signal; there is also some processing of the stimulation going on, as described next.

4.2.6 Processing of visual stimulation begins in the retina

If photoreceptors within a neuron's receptive field are stimulated, the effect on the neuron may be excitatory or inhibitory. There are a number of different types of ganglion cell in the retinas of humans and other primates. Two types are particularly numerous, together mak-ing up nearly 90% of all ganglion cells in each retina: these are the smaller **midget ganglion**

cells, also called *parvo* (small) cells, and the larger **parasol ganglion cells**, also called *magno* (large) cells. The receptive fields of these two types of cell are divided into two parts. Stimulation of photoreceptors in one part excites the ganglion cell; stimulation of photoreceptors in the other part inhibits the ganglion cell. This is called **spatial opponency**, because different spatial regions of the receptive field have *opposing* effects on the cell. A discussion of the neural mechanisms responsible for spatially opponent receptive fields is beyond the scope of this text.

In midget and parasol retinal ganglion cells, the two opponent regions of the receptive field are organized in a concentric fashion, with one part forming the center of the receptive field and the other part the region of the receptive field surrounding it. This is shown in Figure 4.21 and is called a **center-surround** arrangement, for obvious reasons. Some ganglion cells have center-surround receptive fields in which stimulation of the center excites the ganglion cell and stimulation of the surround inhibits it. These are called *on-center, off-surround* ganglion cells. The receptive fields of other ganglion cells are the other way around, so that stimulation of the center inhibits the cell and stimulation of the surround excites it. These are called *off-center, on-surround* cells. Figure 4.21 shows how these types of ganglion cell respond when the different parts of their receptive fields are stimulated by light. In each case, the excitatory part of the receptive field is shaded in a light color and the inhibitory part is shaded in a dark color.

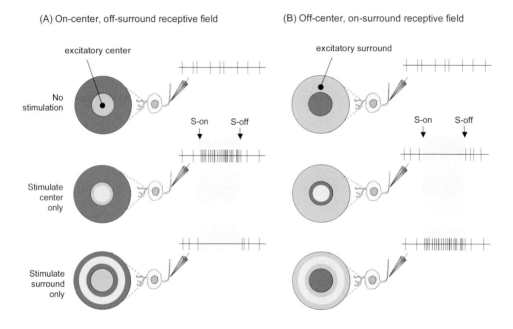

Figure 4.21: *Ganglion cell receptive fields and their responses to stimulation. A) On-center, off-surround receptive field: fires sporadically in the absence of stimulation (resting rate), firing rate increases when light falls on the center only (excitatory effect on ganglion cell) and decreases when light falls on the surround only (inhibitory effect on cell). B) Same as A), but for off-center, on-surround field. (Illustrative.)*

The excitatory and inhibitory effects in the center and surround are balanced, so that if the whole receptive field is uniformly stimulated, the excitation and inhibition cancel one another out and the ganglion cell does not respond. This means that the ganglion cell does not respond to light, per se: stimulation of its receptive field by light is not sufficient to make the cell respond. In order that the ganglion cell respond, it is necessary that there be a difference in the stimulation of the center and the surround of its receptive field. For example, if the part of the retinal image that falls on the receptive field is such that more light falls on the surround than on the center, then an off-center, on-surround cell will increase its firing rate. This is illustrated in Figure 4.21.

The signals transmitted to the brain along the axons of retinal ganglion cells with spatially opponent receptive fields do not carry information about the amount of light reaching the retina; they carry information about structure in the image and how the structure changes over time. This is exactly the sort of information that forms the basis for perceiving what is where and what it is doing. Further details are beyond the scope of this text, but can be found in the many texts dealing with visual perception[26]. A small proportion of retinal ganglion cells do not have spatially opponent receptive fields, and are capable of transmitting information about the amount of light reaching them. The significance of these cells is described further later in the chapter.

4.2.7 Information from the left and right halves of the two retinas is transmitted to the corresponding side of the brain

The retina of the human eye can be regarded as being divided roughly into two halves by an imaginary line (or *meridian*) running vertically from the top to the bottom of the eye through the center of the fovea[27]. The retina is divided into a left half and a right half by this meridian. Within each optic nerve, axons from ganglion cells in the left half of the retina are clustered together, and axons from cells in the right half of the retina are clustered together. The two optic nerves meet at the **optic chiasm**: at this point, the axons from the left halves of the two retinas form the left **optic tract** and the axons from the right halves of the retinas form the right optic tract. Thus, the ganglion cell axons form the optic nerves that run from the retinas to the optic chiasm; beyond the chiasm these axons form the optic tracts. The arrangement is shown in Figures 4.22 and 4.23, which both show that axons from the left halves of the two retinas (shaded in blue) project to the left side of the brain, and axons from the right halves of the retinas (shaded in red) project to the right side of the brain.

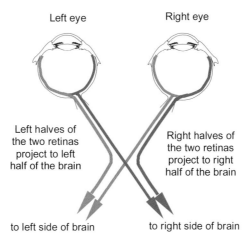

Left eye   Right eye

Left halves of the two retinas project to left half of the brain

Right halves of the two retinas project to right half of the brain

to left side of brain   to right side of brain

Figure 4.22: *Axons from the left and right hemiretinae project to corresponding sides of the brain.*

A consequence of the arrangement shown in Figure 4.22 is that the visual field is also divided into two halves: the left half of the visual field is imaged on the right halves of the two retinas, and the right half of the visual field is imaged on the left halves, as shown in Figure 4.23. Since the left and right halves of the retinas project to different sides of the brain, information from the right half of the visual field is sent to the left side of the brain and information from the left half of the field is sent to the right half of the brain. This is true everywhere except along the dividing line itself, where the situation is a little fuzzy: the boundary between the left and right halves of the retinas is not perfectly sharp, but is blurred and overlapping.

As you might imagine, not all ganglion cell bodies will sit neatly on one side or the other of the imaginary meridian that divides the retinas into two halves; some will be crossed by it. The receptive fields of these ganglion cells and of others just to the left or right of the dividing meridian will be partly in the left side of the retina and partly in the right side. As a result, stimulation of some photoreceptors near the dividing meridian in the left half of each retina affects ganglion cells with axons that project to the right side of the brain. Likewise, stimulation of some photoreceptors near the dividing meridian in the right half of the retina affects ganglion cells with axons that project to the left side of the brain. Thus, there is a thin strip of retina along the dividing meridian that is connected to both sides of the brain – all the rest of the retina is connected to one side or the other. The strip is about 1° wide in the peripheral retina and slightly wider in the fovea[28].

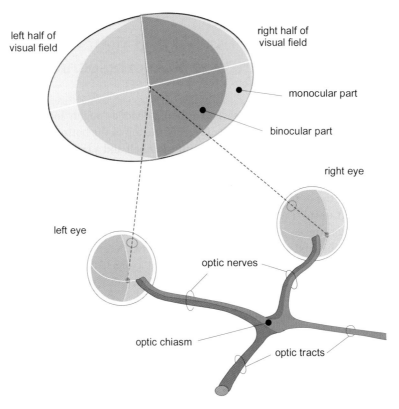

Figure 4.23: *Left and right halves of the visual field are sent to structures in the left and right sides of the brain, respectively.*

4.2.8 Ganglion cell axons project to several different nuclei

The axons of retinal ganglion cells project to a number of different nuclei in the brain. A large proportion project to the lateral geniculate nucleus of the thalamus; a smaller proportion project to other nuclei. Some project to the pulvinar nucleus (also part of the thalamus), some to the suprachiasmic and paraventricular nuclei in the hypothalamus, and some to the midbrain. Of those that project to the midbrain, most terminate in the superior colliculi, but a few terminate in nuclei of the pretectum, and others terminate in several small nuclei in the tegmentum. Figure 4.24 shows a block diagram summary of the different projections on one side of the brain (the other side is the same).

The thickness of the arrows in Figure 4.24 crudely represents the proportion of axons in the different projections: the thicker the arrow, the greater the number of axons. In humans and primates, very few project to the hypothalamus, tegmentum, pretectum and pulvinar (only one or two percent in total); about 10% project to the superior colliculus, but the vast majority (nearly 90%) project to the lateral geniculate nucleus.

Projections of retinal ganglion cell axons to the pretectum form part of the neural pathway of the pupilary light reflex. A substantial proportion of the axons that project to the pretectum are of the ganglion cell types that do not have spatially opponent receptive fields. This is to be expected, since the pupilary light reflex requires information about the amount of light reaching the retinas: the responses of cells with spatially opponent receptive fields do not provide this information (see section 4.2.6). The suprachiasmic and paraventricular nuclei are important in setting the daily rhythms of sleep and wakefulness so that they match the day-night cycle. Like the pupilary reflex, this requires information about the amount of light, and the ganglion cells that project to these hypothalamic nuclei are also of the types that do not have spatially opponent receptive fields[29].

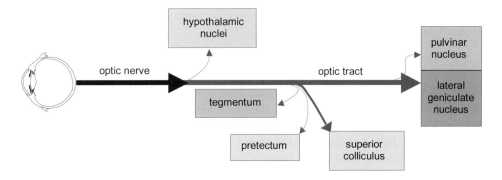

Figure 4.24: *Projections of retinal ganglion cell axons to nuclei in the brain.*

Projections to the pulvinar and tegmentum have long been known to exist in humans, but their functional roles are not completely understood. The projections to the tegmental nuclei are formed by the axons of motion sensitive ganglion cells that do not have spatially opponent receptive fields. These projections form what is called the *accessory optic system*, which plays a role in postural control and stabilization of the head and eyes[30]. It is thought that the pulvinar may also play a role in eye movement control[31].

The large projection to the lateral geniculate nuclei of the thalamus consists mainly of the axons of midget and parasol cells mentioned in section 4.2.6. This projection forms the initial part of the **geniculostriate pathway** that is described further in the sections that follow. The projection to the superior colliculi in the midbrain is often called the **retinotectal pathway**. This pathway is important for visual orienting: moving the head and eyes so that images of important or interesting objects and events in the environment are projected onto the foveas. We will encounter the superior colliculi again in Chapter 5.

4.2.9 The geniculostriate pathway carries visual information from the retinas to the cerebral cortex

Figure 4.25 shows the route taken by retinal ganglion cell axons along the optic nerves and optic tracts to the superior colliculi and to the lateral geniculate nuclei of the thalamus. The geniculostriate pathway goes from the retinas to the lateral geniculate nuclei and from there to the cerebral cortex, via arrays of axons called the **optic radiations**. The ganglion cell axons terminate in the lateral geniculate nuclei; the axons of the optic radiations are those of neurons within the lateral geniculate nuclei.

Axons of the optic radiations terminate on neurons in the occipital lobe of the cerebral hemispheres: the left optic radiation terminates in the left hemisphere, the right optic radiation terminates in the right hemisphere. This means that information from the left half of the visual field (blue in Figure 4.25) is transmitted to the left hemisphere, and information from the right half of the visual field (red in the figure) is transmitted to the right hemisphere. The axons make synaptic connections with neurons in a circumscribed region of the occipital lobe that is known by several names, including **striate cortex** (which accounts for the name *geniculostriate* given to the pathway) and **visual area 1** (or **V1**). V1 is where the cortical processing of visual information begins[32].

Without the geniculostriate pathway, there is no conscious vision: damage to the pathway leads to loss of conscious vision in part or all of the visual field, even if all the other pathways from the retina to the brain are intact and functioning normally. The other pathways mediate visual functions that do not lead to visual awareness of the world around us. This leads to a phenomenon known as *blindsight* in people with damage to the geniculostriate pathway. Such people are blind in parts of their visual field, in the sense that they are not aware of seeing anything in these regions – there is no conscious vision. However, they are able to perform certain visual tasks within the blind parts of the field, such as determining whether or not there is an object present within the blind field, and obtaining some rudimentary information about its shape. The person's experience in such tasks is that they are merely guessing, since they cannot 'see' anything. It seems likely that the perceptual abilities are mediated by the other visual pathways[33].

4.2.10 Visual area 1 has a retinotopic organization

The letters A to I are shown across the visual field at the top of Figure 4.25. The eyes are pointed at the letter E, which is imaged on the foveal area; B to H fall in the binocular visual field; A and I fall in monocular parts of the visual field. The ordering of the numbers in the left and right halves of the visual field is shown preserved in V1. This illustrates the fact that information from neighboring locations in the two halves of the visual field is transmitted along

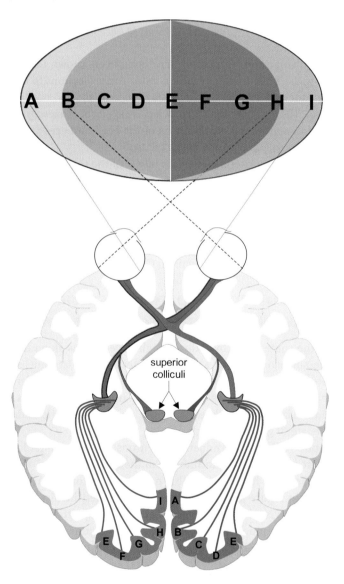

Figure 4.25: *Visual pathways from the retinas to the superior colliculi and V1.*

the geniculostriate pathway to neighboring locations in V1. Signals derived from neighboring locations on the retina are transmitted along the axons of ganglion cells with neighboring or overlapping receptive fields. The axons of neighboring ganglion cells project to neighboring neurons (or groups of neurons) in the lateral geniculate nucleus (LGN). Neighboring output neurons in the LGN project to neighboring groups of neurons in V1. A simplified schematic of the basic arrangement is shown in Figure 4.26. **Topographic organization** is the general term for this kind of spatial arrangement. This term can be applied to any structure or stage in any sensory pathway that exhibits it – the somatotopic organization of the somatosensory system described in Chapter 3 is an example. The topographic organization within the geniculostriate pathway is said to be **retinotopic** because neighboring locations in each retina project to neighboring locations in each lateral geniculate nucleus (LGN) and in area V1.

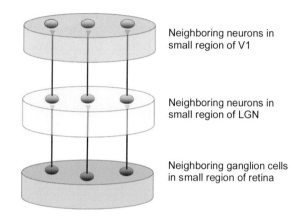

Neighboring neurons in
small region of V1

Neighboring neurons in
small region of LGN

Neighboring ganglion cells
in small region of retina

Figure 4.26: *Retinotopic organization of the visual pathway.*

The retinotopic projection from retina to cortex keeps neighboring points together, but it does not preserve the relative sizes of different regions of the retina – it has a distorting effect similar to that already described in the somatosensory system. The retinotopic map is distorted such that neighboring locations in the retina are next to one another in V1 (retinotopy) but the relative sizes of different retinal regions are not preserved in V1. For example, the foveal region of each retina is about 0.1% of the total retinal area, but projects to a region of V1 amounting to about 10% of the total. Thus, more sensitive regions of the retina are associated with larger regions of the cortex (similar to the somatosensory system).

One way to think about the way the retina projects to V1 is to consider the distance across the cortical surface of V1 that is associated with each degree across the retina. At the fovea, one degree across the retina is associated with about 11.5 mm across the cortical surface; outside the fovea but within the macula, 1° projects to about 4 mm of cortex[34]. In the peripheral retina, the cortical distance progressively drops off and is about 0.5 mm per degree of retina at an eccentricity of 25°; it is even less in the far periphery. The number of millimeters of cortex that are devoted to each degree across the retina is called the **cortical magnification factor** (CMF): the CMF is about 11.5 mm/deg in the fovea, and drops to 0.1 mm/deg in the far periphery. It is clear that retinal regions of higher acuity are associated with larger regions of V1 than parts of the retina with lower acuity[35].

Figure 4.27 illustrates how different parts of the visual field that are imaged on different regions of the retina are represented in V1. An oval segment of the visual field is shown at the top of the figure, divided into quadrants and three concentric regions. The central region is imaged on the fovea (quadrants 1 to 4). The occipital lobes of the cerebral hemispheres are shown in the lower part of the figure, split apart to reveal visual area 1 (V1) in the left and right hemispheres. The regions of V1 to which the numbered segments in the visual field project are shown: the foveal quadrants of the visual field are represented by larger areas of cortex than the more peripheral segments.

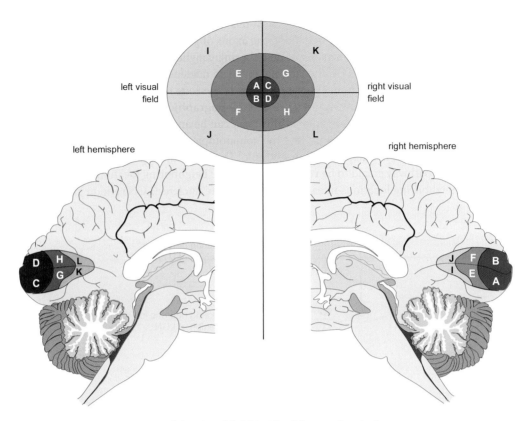

Figure 4.27: *Representation of the visual field in V1 of the two hemispheres.*

4.2.11 Cortical processing of visual information proceeds along two primary streams

V1 is the region of cortex that receives the visual information that underlies our conscious visual perception of the surroundings. Much of this information is also used in the planning and control of voluntary actions, though we may not be directly aware that it is being used for these purposes. V1 is part of a larger area of the posterior cortex that is primarily devoted to the processing of visual information. This whole area is usually called **visual cortex** and is largely confined to the occipital lobes in the human brain. The region of visual cortex outside of V1 is referred to as **extrastriate** visual cortex.

Research on the brains of monkeys and other mammals has shown that extrastriate visual cortex is itself composed of many individual areas distinguished by the type of visual information to which they primarily respond. Imaging studies of the human brain have revealed a similar picture[36]. V1 is a multipurpose area that has neurons for processing many different types of visual information; neurons in the extrastriate areas are often primarily concerned with one type of information. For example, cells in visual area 4 (V4) are primarily involved with the processing of color information, and those in visual area 5 (V5, also known as MT) are primarily involved with processing motion information. More than 40 distinct areas have already been identified in the primate brain, and it seems likely that still finer divisions will be made as research progresses. These areas are interconnected in complex ways, each one making connections with many others: more than three hundred neural projections between visual areas have been identified[37]. The connections are both feedforward and feedback: an area that receives input from another area (feedforward connection) may project back to that same area (feedback connection).

The extrastriate cortex, with its densely interconnected component regions, is far too complex to describe here. Fortunately, there is an important and influential simplifying scheme that divides the processing of visual information in the cortex into two principal streams or pathways[38]. One of these streams runs ventrally into the lower part of the temporal lobe, while the other runs dorsally into the parietal lobe, as shown in Figure 4.28: they are referred to as the **ventral stream** and **dorsal stream**. These streams are not formed by linear sequences of interlinked areas but by complex networks of interacting regions of cortex. Moreover, although they are anatomically distinguishable beyond visual area 2 (V2), it is nevertheless the case that they are overlapping and interconnected. Despite the overlap, these two streams appear to have somewhat different functions, as described next.

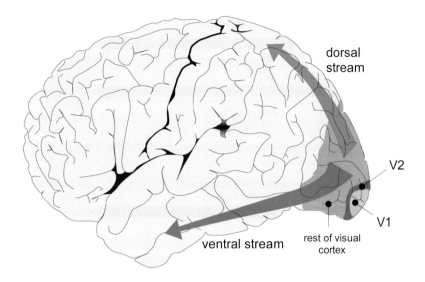

Figure 4.28: *The dorsal and ventral streams of visual processing.*

4.2.12 What are the functions of the two visual streams?

It was initially proposed that the dorsal and ventral streams are involved in processing different kinds of information[39]. The data available at the time strongly suggested that the dorsal stream was involved with the processing of information about the layout of the visible surroundings, with the animal or person's movement through them, and with the directions, distances and motions of objects. The ventral stream, in contrast, seemed to be involved with processing information about the shape, color and identity of objects and surfaces rather than with their locations and motions. This early proposal is usually summarized by saying that the dorsal stream is concerned with extracting information about *where* things are and where they are moving – the *'where' pathway* – while the ventral stream is concerned with extracting information about *what* things are – the *'what' pathway*. More recent research has shown that a simple division between 'what' and 'where' is not really appropriate: information about object identity is processed in the dorsal stream and information about spatial layout is processed in the ventral stream[40].

An influential alternative account[41], proposed in the early 1990s, can accommodate the fact that both streams process information about location and identity, as well as other data inconsistent with a strict division between 'what' and 'where'. This account proposes that the two streams are not distinguished so much by the type of information that they are involved in processing – though there may be some differences – but by the use to which the information is put. The new theory proposes that the ventral stream underlies what we normally think of as seeing – conscious visual awareness of our surroundings that we get when our eyes are open – whereas the dorsal stream underlies the visual control of voluntary action.

The newer proposal is often summarized by saying that the dorsal stream is concerned with **vision-for-action**, whereas the ventral stream is concerned with **vision-for-perception**. Here the term 'perception' is used rather loosely to refer to conscious visual experience of the surroundings. Block diagram representations of the two theories are shown in Figure 4.29.

In both theories, there are initial stages of visual information processing from which both streams emerge, though these stages are not necessarily the same in the two theories. There are also interactions between the streams themselves. The most obvious difference in the diagrams lies in where the streams project. The original 'what' and 'where' theory supposed that both streams contribute to control of action and both contribute to conscious visual perception, via some integrated post-stream processing stages. The newer theory proposes that the streams project to separate processes, as shown in panel B of the figure.

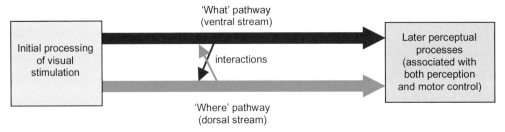

(A) Block diagram of the 'what' vs 'where' theory of visual stream function

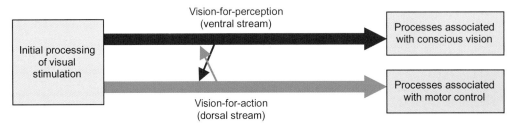

(B) Block diagram of the vision-for-action/vision-for-perception theory of visual stream function

Figure 4.29: *Different conceptions of the functions of the two visual streams.*

The functional distinction between vision-for-action and vision-for-perception in the newer theory does not imply that only the dorsal stream contributes to the production of motor behavior. Rather, the type of contribution made by the two streams is different. The ventral stream is involved with making conscious decisions about what to do and planning courses of action to achieve an overall goal. Thus, conscious vision can have an effect on motor control processes, as indicated in the block diagram shown in Figure 4.30, where there is a route to motor control via the ventral stream. Any action or change to a course of action that is made using consciously available visual information will involve this indirect, ventral stream route. Visual information processed along the dorsal stream influences the production of motor behavior more directly, without consciousness being involved.

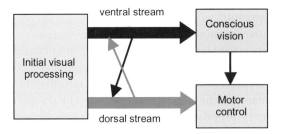

Figure 4.30: *Conscious visual process can affect motor control.*

Although this new theory is undoubtedly a simplification and cannot be regarded as more than an approximation[42], it does provide a simple framework for thinking about the visual processing involved in different types of task. It also helps to understand how visual information can be used to control voluntary actions without awareness, as discussed next.

4.2.13 Vision can affect voluntary action without awareness

A major feature of the vision-for-action/vision-for-perception theory of the two visual streams is that it provides a mechanism by which voluntary motor behavior can be guided or directed by visual information without conscious awareness. Notable cases where this happens in everyday life occur when playing racket sports like tennis or badminton. In these sports it sometimes happens that a player makes a quick return of a smash without being aware of quite how they did it. Return shots of this sort are often described as being reflexive, precisely because they are executed without any apparent volition (though they are not reflexes in the technical sense, as we will see in Chapter 5). It is clear that the shots must be under visual guidance, since it is impossible to hit a ball that you cannot see. The fact that they are executed without any conscious volition can be easily accommodated by the theory: visual information affects motor control in these actions via the dorsal stream[43].

A circumstance in which visual information has been shown to affect the performance of voluntarily initiated motor actions in the absence of conscious awareness is in cases of blindsight, a phenomenon briefly discussed in section 4.2.9. In one such case, a male patient (known by his initials, DB) had undergone surgical removal of a large part of his right occipital lobe and was missing almost all of V1 on that side[44]. As a consequence, he had no conscious vision in most of his left visual field – he felt himself to be blind in this region. Nevertheless, he was able to direct his hand accurately towards the locations of visual targets in his blind field and so point at them, though he insisted that he was simply guessing the location of the targets, which he could not see. His pointing movements must have been guided by visual information about the location of visual targets obtained from non-conscious perceptual processes. This observation can be accommodated by the theory when the additional projections into the dorsal stream from subcortical regions are taken into account. Figure 4.28 shows the stream as being fed from the extrastriate cortex, which itself receives visual information from V1. However, there are projections into the dorsal stream from subcortical visual regions, including the superior colliculi and the pulvinar nuclei[45] of the thalamus, and so visual information can get to the motor control processes via the dorsal stream route in the absence of V1. Figure 4.31 shows a schematic block diagram that includes the relevant connectivity: it clearly shows that if V1 is damaged, visual information from the pulvinar and superior colliculus can still enter the dorsal stream. It is visual information reaching the dorsal stream from these sources that is thought to explain DB's ability to point accurately at visual targets that he could not 'see'[46].

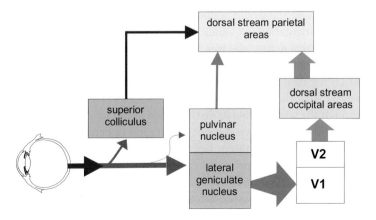

Figure 4.31: *Projections from the retina to the dorsal stream.*

Performance of skilled voluntary actions often appears to be guided by visual information without a person being aware that vision is playing a role. It is frequently the case in everyday life that we execute visually guided actions without thinking about their execution – we just do things and they are automatically regulated by visual information, without our having to think about it.

4.2.14 Brain damage can impair conscious vision but leave visuomotor skill intact

It is possible, at least in principle, to damage the brain in such a way that just one of the two streams is affected. According to the vision-for-action/vision-for-perception theory, damage to one stream will have very different effects from damage of the other. Consider damage to the ventral stream that leaves the dorsal stream intact. This would be expected to have an effect on conscious visual perception, but leave the visual control of voluntary actions unaffected. Conversely, if the dorsal stream is damaged but the ventral stream intact, then visual control of action will be affected, but conscious perception will not be. It is not possible to damage someone's brain in order to discover whether these predictions hold true. However, a few individuals have suffered brain damage due to unfortunate accidents and been left with deficits consistent with the predictions of the theory. One of these, known by her initials (DF), suffered diffuse, bilateral damage to cortical regions at the boundary between the occipital lobes and the inferior temporal lobes as a result of carbon monoxide poisoning, but V1 and her dorsal stream were left largely intact[47]. The site of the damage was largely confined to the early stages of the ventral stream.

According to the vision-for-action/vision-for-perception theory, the damage suffered by DF would be expected to have effects on conscious visual perception but to leave the visual guidance of voluntary action unaffected[48]. The effects of the brain damage on DF's behavior were found to be consistent with the theory. Although not consciously blind, she was found to be unable to accurately report the sizes, shapes, orientations and identities of many objects presented to her visually, and had difficulty with many other visual discriminations that require conscious seeing. Thus, although she reported being aware of visual stimulation, her consciousness did not seem to have access to the information needed for performing visual tasks like reporting the sizes of things and recognizing objects. People with perceptual deficits of this sort are said to suffer from **visual form agnosia**.

Despite her difficulties with seeing, DF was found to have no apparent problems with visually guided motor actions, even when their successful performance required the same kind of information that she was unable to access consciously. For example, in one test she was required both to report on the orientation of a slot positioned in the center of a board (perceptual task) and to push a card through the slot (visuomotor task). She repeated these two tasks a number of times with the slot in different orientations. It was found that her conscious perceptual judgments of the slot's orientation were seriously impaired: her reports were usually incorrect, and she would sometimes indicate an orientation as much as ninety degrees from the true orientation (e.g., indicate a horizontally orientated slot as being vertically oriented). Despite this deficit, she was able to push a card through the slot without difficulty, in a manner indistinguishable from that of normal people. Pushing the card through clearly requires that the card be moved so that its orientation matches the orientation of the slot. DF was able to match the card's orientation to the slot's orientation while in the process of inserting it, though she was not able to do this when asked to indicate the slot's orientation by turning a hand-held card to match the slot orientation (a perceptual task). These findings indicate that DF's motor control system had access to information about slot orientation, presumably via her intact dorsal stream, but she was unable to access this information consciously – she was unable to accurately 'see' the slot's orientation.

DF's case provides compelling evidence that visual information can reach the motor system via a different route from that by which visual information is transmitted to the processes that underlie conscious perception. The site of her lesion indicates that this route to the motor system is the dorsal stream[49]. However, the picture provided by DF's case is incomplete. According to the vision-for-action/vision-for-perception theory, it should also be possible to damage the dorsal stream without damaging the ventral stream, which would result in impaired visuomotor performance but conscious visual perception would be unaffected. There are cases in which this has been observed, as described next.

4.2.15 Brain damage can impair visuomotor skill but leave conscious vision intact

People who suffer from a neurological disorder called **optic ataxia** often have impairments that are almost the reverse of those of patient DF described in section 4.2.14. Optic ataxic patients have no difficulties recognizing objects, or describing their shapes and sizes: their conscious visual perception appears to be normal. What they suffer from are impairments to visually guided motor behavior. The most commonly reported problem is an inability to accurately direct voluntary movement towards visible objects, as when reaching for something or turning the head and eyes to look at something. This is not simply a general problem of sensorimotor control, as patients can accurately direct movements towards targets defined by non-visual sensory information. For example, they are able to accurately direct limb movements towards other body parts, such as bringing the finger tips of the left and right hands together.

Optic ataxic patients who have difficulty using visual information to guide movements towards visible targets, but who are unimpaired on perceptual tasks like reporting the shape, location or identity of an object, have been found to have lesions to the parietal lobes in areas considered part of the dorsal stream[50]. These cases complement the case of DF to support the vision-for-action/vision-for-perception theory. DF, who has damage to the ventral stream, shows impaired vision-for-perception but largely intact vision-for-action. Optic ataxics who have damage to the dorsal stream show impaired vision-for-action, but intact vision-for-perception.

The pattern of impairment shown by DF and optic ataxic patients provides strong support for the idea that the dorsal and ventral streams support vision-for-action and vision-for-perception respectively. However, it would be wrong to think that the dorsal stream makes no contribution to conscious visual perception or that the ventral stream makes no contribution to visuomotor control. As shown in Figure 4.30, the two streams interact with one another, so that information is transferred between them, and conscious visual perception can influence motor behavior in a number of ways. This makes the functional roles of the two streams less clear cut than a naïve interpretation of the vision-for-action/vision-for-perception distinction might suggest[51]. Nevertheless, guidance of voluntary movement execution can occur without awareness, and this appears to rely on the dorsal stream. In addition, our ability to consciously see and identify objects is known to depend on regions of the temporal lobes that are fed information by the ventral stream.

4.3 Moving the Eyes and Head

4.3.1 Introduction: looking involves movements of the head and eyes

The activity of looking almost invariably involves active, coordinated movement of both the head and the eyes. The eyes are not rigidly fixed to the head like the ears; they are free to swivel around within their sockets, and these rotations can occur independently of head movement. A rotation of an eye within its socket is called an *eye movement*:

EYE MOVEMENT: a rotation of an eye within its socket.

When the head moves, the eye moves with it, but if there is no rotation of the eye in its socket then we don't call it an eye movement.

Active eye movements are produced by contractions of small skeletal muscles called **extraocular muscles** that insert onto the globe of the eye. These muscles are arranged so that it is possible to produce almost any eye movement you can think of by contracting the muscles in different combinations. These muscles are continuously active day and night throughout our lives, yet they seldom seem to fatigue and are capable of producing rapid, precise and subtle eye movements over and over again for extended periods of time. Why does such a precise mechanism for movement exist? The basic answer, of course, is that eye movements help us to see clearly, and so clear vision requires precise control of these movements. In what follows, we will describe the different types of eye movements that people produce and how they contribute to clear vision. Although the focus will be eye movements, the head normally moves as well, and we will see how both head and eye movements are involved in seeing.

4.3.2 The direction an eye points is called the direction of gaze

The human eye is a foveate eye – it possesses a fovea. When we point our eyes at an object so that we can look at it, we orient the eyes so that the image of the object falls on the foveas. When this happens we can imagine a ray of light from the object that passes through the nodal point of the eye and reaches the very center of the fovea. The path of this ray of light is a straight line called the **visual axis** and is shown in Figure 4.32.

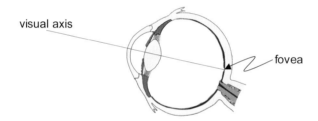

Figure 4.32: *The visual axis.*

The visual axis defines the direction in which the eye is looking. Thus, the direction of the visual axis relative to the environment is called the **direction of gaze** of the eye. The measure of the direction of gaze is the **gaze angle** – the angle between the visual axis and an immobile reference direction fixed to the surroundings. Panel A of Figure 4.33 shows how a gaze angle can be defined in the horizontal plane: an eye is looking at a stationary object. The reference direction is shown fixed to this object, but it could equally well be fixed to some other immobile object. The horizontal gaze angle is the angle (labeled θ) between the visual axis and the reference direction; a *vertical gaze angle* can be defined in a similar way in the vertical plane. In general, the horizontal and vertical gaze angles together define the direction of gaze.

The angular position of the eye in its socket can be defined as the angle between the visual axis and a reference direction fixed to the head, which is clearly different from the gaze angle. Panel B of Figure 4.33 shows how the angular position of the eye can be defined in the horizontal plane. The reference line passes through the axis of rotation of the head perpendicular to the coronal plane. The angular position of the eye in the head is the angle labeled ϕ (phi): when the eye is looking straight ahead (with visual axis parallel to the reference line) the angle ϕ is zero. An eye movement, as defined in the previous section, is a change in the eye's angular position. It is clear from panels A and B of Figure 4.33 that the gaze angle is equal to the angular position of the eye in the head plus the angular position of the head relative to the environment. Note that the gaze direction can be changed either by making an eye movement and keeping the head still, or by moving the head without making an eye movement (i.e., without changing the eye's position in its socket).

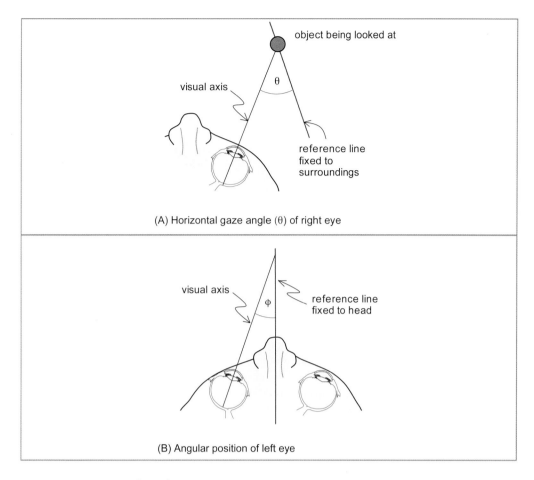

Figure 4.33: *Gaze angle and eye position.*

4.3.3 The eye has three degrees-of-freedom of movement

Human eyes and those of many other vertebrate animals are free to rotate within a bony socket called the *orbit*. In effect, the eye and the orbit form a ball-and-socket joint, though unlike other joints of this kind there is no segment attached to the ball. An eye is free to rotate up and down, left and right, and also around the visual axis[52]: the different motions are shown in Figure 4.34. In the figure, the eye starts looking straight ahead with the visual axis pointing out of the page (top row). Panels A, B and C show rotation about three axes of rotation, each of which passes through the center of the globe; the axes are assumed not to move as the eye rotates about them. In common with most joints in the human body, an eye's axes of rotation are not quite fixed, but move around a little as the eye moves. This movement is very small, however, and can safely be ignored. Panel A of Figure 4.34 shows a rotation of the eye upwards towards the eyebrow and a downward rotation towards the cheek, about a horizontally oriented axis. Upward movement is called **elevation**; downward movement is called **depression**. Panel B shows a leftward rotation of the eye towards the nose and a rightward rotation of the eye towards the temple about a vertically oriented axis. Movement towards the nose is an **adduction**; movement towards the temple is an **abduction**. Panel C shows rotations about the visual axis (out of the page); a vertical line has been drawn across the iris to indicate the effects of such rotations, which are called **torsional** rotations. A rotation to the left tilts the eye inwards towards the nose and is referred to as **intorsion**; a rotation towards the right tilts the eye outwards and is referred to as **extorsion**. Elevation-depression, adduction-abduction and intorsion-extorsion comprise the three degrees-of-freedom of rotational movement possessed by the human eye.

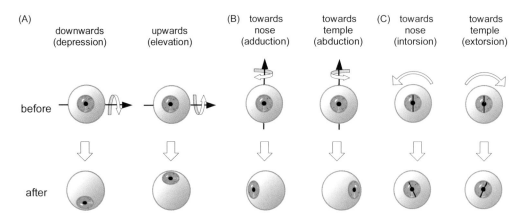

Figure 4.34: *An eye's three degrees-of-freedom of movement.*

4.3.4 There are two basic types of coordinated movement of the two eyes

Some animals, such as the chameleon, are capable of moving their eyes independently of one another. Most vertebrate animals, including ourselves, cannot produce genuinely independent movements of the eyes. As a general rule, people move both their eyes simultaneously, either in the same direction or in opposite directions. In the latter case, we can only move our eyes in opposite directions either simultaneously inwards towards the nose or simultaneously outwards towards the central position. We cannot move the eyes outwards from the central position nor can we voluntarily move one eye upwards while the other moves downwards or vice-versa. Movements in which the two eyes move together in the same direction are referred to as **conjugate eye movements** or sometimes as *version eye movements*:

> **CONJUGATE (OR VERSION) EYE MOVEMENT:** a coordinated movement of the two eyes in which both eyes move in the same direction at the same time through the same angle.

Figure 4.35, panel A shows an example of a conjugate movement in which both eyes rotate simultaneously to their right: the positions of the eyes before the movement are shown at the top, and their positions afterwards are shown at the bottom. Panel B shows an example of a movement in which the eyes move in opposite directions (simultaneous adduction of both eyes). Such a movement is referred to as a **convergence** of the eyes; an opposite, outward movement is referred to as a **divergence** of the eyes. Divergence is only possible from an initially converged posture outwards towards the central position; diverging outwards from the central position is impossible. Convergent and divergent movements involve simultaneous movements of the two eyes in opposite directions. They are called **disconjugate eye movements,** but the more common name is **vergence eye movements**:

> **DISCONJUGATE OR VERGENCE EYE MOVEMENT:** a coordinated movement of the two eyes in which the eyes move in opposite directions at the same time through the same angle.

Coordinated torsional eye movements also occur: both conjugate and disconjugate torsional movements are observed. Disconjugate torsional movements are called *cyclovergence* movements. A simultaneous pure intorsion in the two eyes is an *incyclovergence*. A simultaneous extorsion movement is an *excyclovergence*. Involuntary disconjugate eye movements in which one eye is slightly elevated and one slightly depressed are also possible[53] (*vertical vergence* movements). We will have little more to say about vertical vergence or cyclo-vergence movements[54].

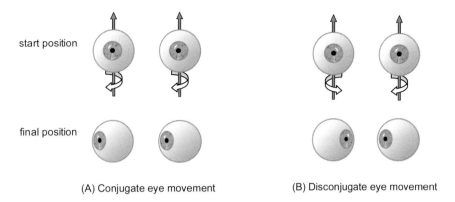

Figure 4.35: *Two types of eye movement.*

4.3.5 The human eye is moved by six extraocular muscles

There are a total of six extraocular muscles that act to move a human eye around in its socket. Figure 4.36 shows two cutaway views of a human eye in its bony orbit: a view from the temporal side and a view from above. All muscles insert onto the surface of the eyeball, and all except the inferior oblique originate from a ring of tendon – the annulus of Zinn – that surrounds the optic nerve and is attached to the bone of the orbit. Note that the superior oblique originates from the annulus and has a tendinous end that passes through a small loop of cartilaginous tissue at the margin of the orbit called the *trochlea* before inserting on the globe. The trochlea acts like a little pulley by changing the direction of the superior oblique tendon, thereby allowing contractions of the muscle to produce intorsional eye movements. In recent years it has become clear that more subtle, pulley-like connective tissue structures also exist for the other extraocular muscles[55]. These structures have significant effects on how the muscles act, but a discussion is beyond the scope of this text[56].

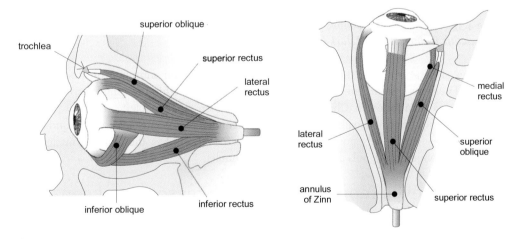

Figure 4.36: *The extraocular musculature (based on Figures 776 and 889 of the 1918 edition of Gray's Anatomy).*

The mechanical actions of the extraocular muscles depend somewhat on the position of the eye in the orbit[57]. We will simplify things by considering the actions of the muscles when the eye is in its **central position**[58]: the eye centered in the orbit and looking straight ahead, such that the visual axis is perpendicular to the coronal plane of the head. Figure 4.37 illustrates the movements of the eyeball from the central position produced by contraction of each of the six extraocular muscles. In each case, a dark line has been drawn across the iris and pupil to indicate the torsional position of the eye, and the contracting muscle is shown shaded darker than the others.

Figure 4.37 shows that the extraocular muscles of each eye form three antagonistic pairs. The lateral rectus and the medial rectus have opposing actions (abduction-adduction) in the horizontal direction (inwards and outwards). The superior and inferior recti have opposing primary actions (elevation-depression) in the vertical direction (up and down). The superior and inferior obliques have opposing primary actions (intorsion-extorsion) along the gaze direction. Thus, to a first approximation, the three antagonist pairs rotate the eye in its three degrees-of-freedom of movement.

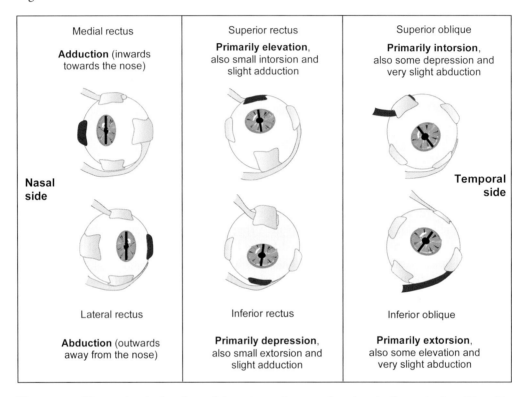

Figure 4.37: *The mechanical actions of the extraocular muscles when in the central position. The muscle acting is shown shaded dark red (based on Moses, 1975).*

Like other skeletal muscles, the extraocular muscles have their motoneuron pools within the central nervous system. The motoneuron pools do not lie within the spinal cord but in the brain stem, as mentioned in Chapter 2. The pools form small nuclei[59]: the MN pools of the inferior oblique and of the inferior, superior and medial rectus muscles are all found in the oculomotor nuclei; the MN pools of the lateral recti are found in the abucens nuclei; and the superior oblique MN pools are in the trochlear nuclei.

4.3.6 The eyes move for two basic reasons: to keep them steady and to bring images onto the foveas

One of the two reasons for moving the eyes is **to keep the image, as a whole, steady on the retina**. This is important because our ability to extract useful information from an image is impaired if the image moves around, particularly in focal vision, where perceptual clarity is impaired if the amplitude of the image motion exceeds about ½° and has a speed of more than about 5° per second. You can roughly demonstrate to yourself the difficulty of seeing in the presence of image motion by holding a book in your hands and jiggling it around while trying to read it: small-amplitude, rapid jiggling makes it impossible to see the words clearly.

The head jiggles around continuously during our waking hours, and is a major cause of unsteadiness of the retinal images. The head jiggles when we are standing still as a result of breathing, blood being pumped through the vessels, postural activity and motor noise. When we walk or run, it rocks from side to side and tilts backwards and forwards. Even when seated with the head supported, the blood pulsing through the arteries of the head and neck causes tiny vibrations of the head, which lead to jiggling of the retinal images sufficient to interfere with clear vision[60]. Without mechanisms for making eye movements that counteract the jiggling of the head, the eyes would jiggle around as the head moves, and so the retinal images would be jiggling around as well.

In Figure 4.38, panel A shows a person who is trying to stand perfectly still and is looking straight ahead at a wall in front of them with a laser pointer glued to their head. They have been instructed to gaze intently at a specific point on the wall and not to move their eyes to look at anything else. When a person gazes at a stationary point in their surroundings in this way, the point is imaged on the foveas, and the person is said to be **fixating** the point. Although the head and eyes do not seem to move when someone is fixating, they are nevertheless moving around a little; it's just that these movements are so small that they are hardly noticeable. Thus, the spot that the laser pointer projects on the wall moves around a little bit. The path traced out by the moving spot provides a record of the head movement (Figure 4.38, panel B, left). In the example shown in which the person is trying to stand as still as possible, the path traced out by the laser dot on a wall two meters away fits inside a circle of roughly 3½ centimeters in diameter, which corresponds to a maximum angular deviation of the head of about one degree as indicated in the figure. The path traced out on the wall by the visual axis of one eye is shown on the right of panel B (if a thin beam of light were emitted from the center of the fovea, it would trace out this path). The path of the visual axis fits inside a circle with a diameter of about ½°. The movement of the eye is therefore substantially less than the movement of the head. This means that there must be mechanisms that are generating eye movements which compensate for the head movements. These mechanisms are discussed in the next section.

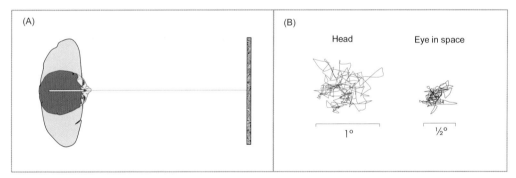

Figure 4.38: *Head and eye motions relative to the environment when standing and fixating. (Illustrative, based on data presented in Skavenski et al., 1979.)*

The second reason for moving the eyes applies to eyes with foveas or equivalent sensitive regions. As already mentioned in section 4.1, in order to see the finer details of objects and surfaces, their images need to be focused on the foveas and kept there as long as necessary. If the image of something of interest is not projected onto the foveas, then the eyes must be moved. Thus, the second reason for moving the eyes is **to bring images onto the foveas and hold them there**. Human voluntary eye movements are all made for this reason, as will be discussed in section 4.4. The remainder of this part of the chapter will deal with movements that keep images stable.

4.3.7 Two eye movement systems keep images stable when the head moves

There are two functional systems that act to keep the eyes steady when the head moves. Both systems produce only conjugate eye movements. One is the **vestibular/cervical reflex system**, which acts to keep the retinal image as a whole stable when the head moves. This system comprises two component subsystems: the **vestibulo-ocular reflex (VOR) system** and the **cervico-ocular reflex (COR) system**. Both these subsystems are themselves composed of several subsystems: the VOR system, for example, has two major sub-components called the **rotational vestibulo-ocular reflex**[61] (*rotational-VOR*) and the **translational vestibulo-ocular reflex**. The VOR system generates eye movements in response to stimulation of the vestibular organs; in the case of the rotational-VOR, it is stimulation of the semicircular canals that evokes the reflex response. The COR system generates eye movements in response to stimulation of somatosensory proprioceptors embedded in the muscles, skin and connective tissues of the neck. It turns out that in human beings the cervico-ocular reflexes are present, but make very little contribution to stabilizing eye movements in normal circumstances; it only becomes important when the vestibular system is damaged or lost. For this reason we will concentrate on the eye movements generated by the VOR system. How the neural mechanisms of the VOR actually work to produce eye movements is described in Chapter 5. The second system is the **optokinetic reflex system**, which functions to keep the image stable during smooth, sustained movements of the head. This reflex system generates eye movements in response to image flow stimulation.

Almost all animal species that have moveable eyes possess vestibular/cervical reflex systems and optokinetic systems, regardless of whether or not their eyes have foveas – only a small number of species have foveate eyes. In animals that have foveas, the reflex systems will not only keep the images stable on the retinas but also keep the gaze direction steady during head movements. In the following sections these two reflex systems are discussed in turn. The chart below provides a summary for ease of reference:

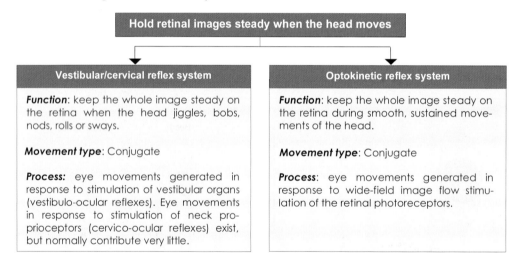

4.3.8 The VOR system generates counter-rotational eye movements

During normal everyday activities like walking, watching a movie, or traveling in a vehicle, the head is being jiggled around. These jiggling head movements involve continuous changes in the speed of the head and repetitive changes in direction: the head may roll from side to side, turn left and right, pitch forwards and backwards with a nodding motion, or move with some combination of these motions. In order to keep the retinal images stable on the retinae during these head movements, rotations of the eyes in the opposite direction to the head movements are needed: these are called **counter-rotational eye-movements**. In people it is the vestibulo-ocular reflex system that is responsible for generating these movements. Figure 4.39 shows the kind of horizontal (left-right) rotational motion of the head that occurs when someone walks along. The graph plots the horizontal angular velocity of the head as a function of time for a period of about two seconds. During this time the person completes nearly five steps. Each step with the right leg rotates the body and the head to the left; each step with the left leg rotates the head to the right. Each head rotation reaches a maximum speed of about 15°/second; the corresponding maximum change in the head's angular position in either direction is about 2°.

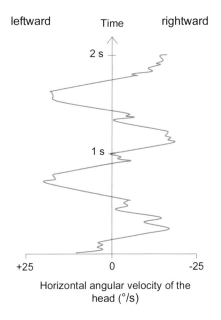

Figure 4.39: *Angular velocity of the head while walking. Based on data from Grossman* et al. *(1989).*

If the walker made no compensatory eye movements, the eyes would rotate with the head. This would result in the eyes deviating to the left and right by roughly 2°, and the image would move as a whole across the retinas with speeds of up to 15°/s. Such image motion would make clear vision impossible, but it does not occur, because the vestibulo-ocular reflex system produces counter-rotational eye movements that keep the eyes steady. Figure 4.40 shows the horizontal angular velocity of the *eyes relative to the head* (blue trace) together with the head rotations relative to the surroundings as shown in Figure 4.39 (green trace). The eye movements are in the opposite direction to the head movements and of approximately equal amplitude. The result is that the eye movements compensate for the head movements, so that the eyes remain steady with respect to the surroundings. The black trace in the figure shows the angular velocity of the eyes relative to the environment (gaze velocity). The gaze velocity never exceeds 2.5°/s, which is within the 5°/s limit above which clear vision is significantly impaired.

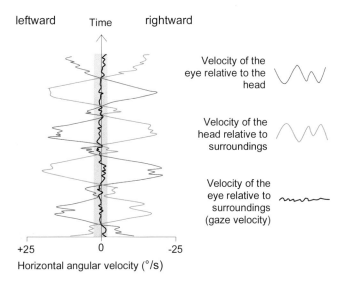

Figure 4.40: *Counter-rotational eye movements keep gaze steady when walking. Based on data from Grossman* et al. *(1989).*

You can observe yourself making eye movements that compensate for head rotations by fixating your image in a mirror and turning your head from side to side. The eyes will be seen to swivel in their sockets so as to remain almost stationary with respect to the surroundings as the head turns, which maintains the direction of gaze. The eyes swivel together from left to right, and so the movements are conjugate adductions and abductions of the two eyes. The situation is shown in Figure 4.41: when the head turns to the left, the eyes counter-rotate to the right; when the head turns to the right, the eyes counter-rotate to the left.

The counter-rotational eye movements shown in Figure 4.41 are movements in the horizontal plane and compensate for rotations of the head about a vertical axis. For this reason, the part of the VOR system that generates these eye movements is known as the *horizontal* component of the rotational-VOR.

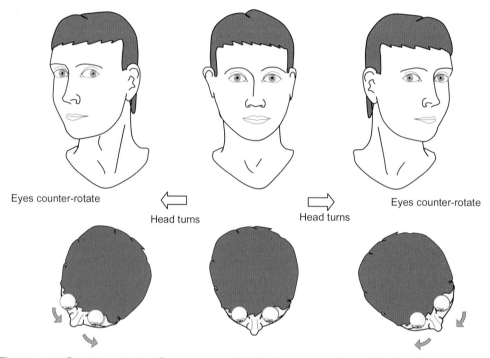

Figure 4.41: *Counter-rotational eye movement in the transverse plane of the head.*

4.3.9 The VOR generates counter-rotational eye movements that keep the images steady when the head rotates about any axis

The horizontal component of the rotational-VOR system generates counter-rotational eye movements that keep the eyes steady during left-to-right rotations of the head about a vertical axis. Of course, the head may also rotate forwards and backwards or from side to side, and counter-rotational eye movements are also generated in these cases. Panel A of Figure 4.42 indicates how the eyes counter-rotate up when the head is tilted forwards. The axis of rotation is oriented horizontally and runs through the head from right to left (perpendicular to the plane of the page in Figure 4.42A). When the head rotates forwards and backwards about this axis, conjugate, counter-rotational elevations and depressions of the eyes are generated. The component of the VOR-system that generates these eye movements is known as the *vertical* component of the rotational-VOR.

Panel B of Figure 4.42 shows how the eyes counter-rotate when the head rolls to one side. The movement is a conjugate torsion. Here the axis of rotation lies horizontally and passes through the head from the back to the front (perpendicular to the page). Black lines have been drawn across the irises to indicate the orientation of the eyes: the counter-torsional movements maintain the eyes' orientation. The component of the VOR system that generates these eye movements is known as the *torsional* component of the rotational-VOR. The dynamic response of this component is mainly mediated by the semicircular canals[62], primarily the posterior canals. However, when the head is held stationary and tilted to one side, the semicircular canals are not stimulated. In these conditions a tonic component of the VOR-system produces a small amount of steady counter-torsion that persists as long as the head is held in a tilted position. This response is mediated by the otoliths, and is called the static otolith-ocular reflex.

You can observe your own eyes counter-rotating in response to head rotations about any of the three axes mentioned so far, using the method described in section 4.3.8: look in a mirror, fixate the bridge of your nose, and then either turn the head from left to right (Figure 4.41), nod it up and down (Figure 4.42A) or roll it from side to side (Figure 4.42B). During regular everyday activities when the head is jiggling around, it is likely to be rotating in all three dimensions simultaneously. In these circumstances, the eyes counter-rotate in all three dimensions simultaneously to hold the images steady.

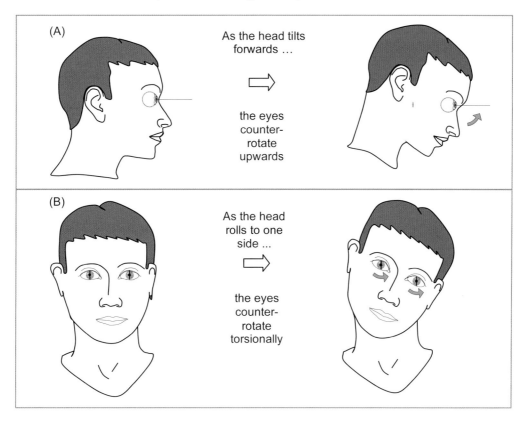

Figure 4.42: *Vertical and torsional counter-rotational eye movements.*

4.3.10 The gain of the VOR provides a measure of its effectiveness

In order for the rotational-VOR to keep the retinal images steady during head rotations, it is not enough that the eyes counter-rotate; they must do so fast enough and far enough to compensate for the head movement. Consider rotation of the head about a vertical axis as in Figure 4.41, and imagine that the head is being repeatedly turned to the left and right in an oscillating fashion while the person looks into the distance. Figure 4.43 shows the angular velocity of the head during such an oscillatory movement (green line) in which the head turns through an angle of about 80° (40° left and right). The positions of the head shown on the left of the figure are when its speed is momentarily zero (the extreme left and right positions) and when its speed is maximum (the straight-ahead position). If the eyes are to remain steady in the environment so that gaze direction remains constant and the images do not move, then they should counter-rotate at the same time and with an equal velocity to the head. Panel B of Figure 4.43 shows the angular velocity of the eyes that keeps the gaze direction perfectly constant when the head moves as shown in panel A: at each moment in time, the eye velocity is equal to the head velocity but in the opposite direction (counter-rotation).

In the ideal case shown in Figure 4.43, in which the head and eye velocities are equal and opposite at every moment of time, the ratio of the negative of the angular velocity of the eyes to the angular velocity of the head is equal to one. This ratio is the **gain** of the process responsible for generating the counter-rotational eye movements, which we are assuming to be the rotational-VOR (but see below). Gain is usually calculated as[63]:

$$\text{Gain} = \frac{\text{Peak angular velocity of the eyes}}{\text{Peak angular velocity of the head}}$$

A gain of one means that the angular velocities are equal and opposite. A gain less than one but greater than zero means that the eyes counter-rotate, but not enough to keep gaze direction constant: the closer the gain is to zero, the less effective the eye movements are[64]. If the gain is negative, it means that the eyes are not counter-rotating, they are rotating in the same direction as the head.

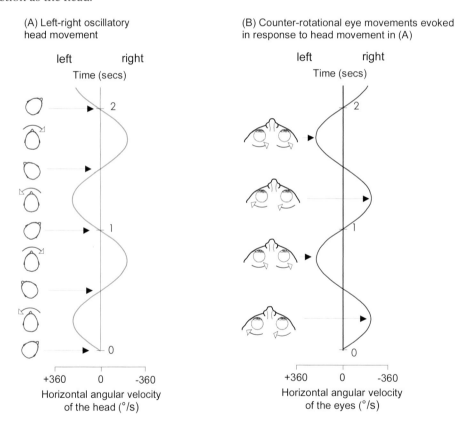

(A) Left-right oscillatory head movement

left   right
Time (secs)

+360   0   -360
Horizontal angular velocity of the head (°/s)

(B) Counter-rotational eye movements evoked in response to head movement in (A)

left   right
Time (secs)

+360   0   -360
Horizontal angular velocity of the eyes (°/s)

Figure 4.43: *Oscillatory motion of the head and counter-rotational eye movements.*

When the process that generates the counter-rotational eye movements is the rotational-VOR, then the equation gives the gain of the VOR. However, if there is visual stimulation present, then it is possible that the optokinetic reflex makes a contribution to the eye movements, particularly if the frequency of oscillation is low. If the head turns on the shoulders stimulating neck proprioceptors, then the COR may also make a small contribution. For these reasons, the gain of the VOR is usually measured with the person in the dark (no visual stimulation) while being turned on a chair (head not turning on the shoulders).

Measurements of the gain of the horizontal component of the rotational-VOR in people have yielded a variety of different values. Overall, it appears that its gain is substantially less than 1.0 at very low frequencies, being about 0.5 at 0.1 cycles/second. At higher frequencies the gain gets closer to 1.0, and it is very close to 1.0 in the range 0.5 to 5.0 cycles/second. Frequencies of head motion in this range are common when walking and running[65]. This pattern is summarized in the graph shown in Figure 4.44, which plots the gain of the horizontal component of the rotational-VOR as a function of the frequency of sinusoidal head oscillation. The vertical component of the rotational-VOR is similar, but the maximum gain of the torsional component seldom exceeds 0.5, and so never fully compensates for head roll.

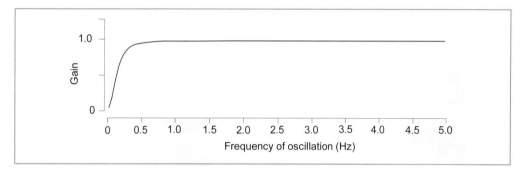

Figure 4.44: *Gain of the horizontal rotational-VOR (illustrative).*

4.3.11 Part of the VOR system generates counter-rotational eye movements that keep images steady as the head translates

We have seen that the rotational-VOR subsystem generates counter-rotational eye movements that keep the retinal images stable during pure rotations of the head. There is another component of the system that generates counter-rotational eye movements that keep images stable during brief and cyclical *translations* of the head. This is the *translational vestibulo-ocular reflex* (*translational-VOR*) and it is mediated by the otolith organs[66].

Walking and running not only causes cyclical rotations of the head, but also cyclical translations: the head bobs up and down (vertical translation or 'bobbing') and shifts from side to side (lateral translation or 'weaving') a little, as shown at the top of Figure 4.45[67]. The left of panel A shows the position of a stick representation of a person walking at five moments in time; the right leg is shaded blue and the left leg green. The head bobs up and down in a cyclical fashion as the person walks. The right of panel A shows the walking person's head viewed from above at moments 1, 3 and 5. Both feet are on the ground at these moments; the right foot's position is shaded blue, the left is shaded green. As the person walks, the head shifts cyclically to the left and right.

During the head's bobbing and weaving motion, its speed is continuously changing: the head is accelerating and decelerating vertically as it bobs and laterally as it weaves. If there were no counter-rotational eye movements, these accelerations would cause the eyes to jiggle around in their sockets. Thus, the cyclical head translations during walking not only translate the eyes up and down and side to side, they cause them to jiggle around as well. The counter-rotational eye movements generated by the translational-VOR perform two functions: they prevent the images from jiggling around as the head translates, and they prevent the eyes from losing fixation as they are moved up and down and from side to side. The latter function is illustrated in panel B of Figure 4.45: during a bobbing motion (left) as the head moves up, the eyes counter-rotate down so that the same point is fixated[68]. During a weaving motion as the eyes move to the left, the eyes counter-rotate to the right such that gaze is stabilized and fixation preserved. These counter-rotational eye movements do not eliminate image motion, since translations of the eye generate motion parallax (section 4.2.12): the images of points at different distances move over the retina at different speeds[69]. No eye movement can cancel out the image motions produced by eye translation (the translational image flow).

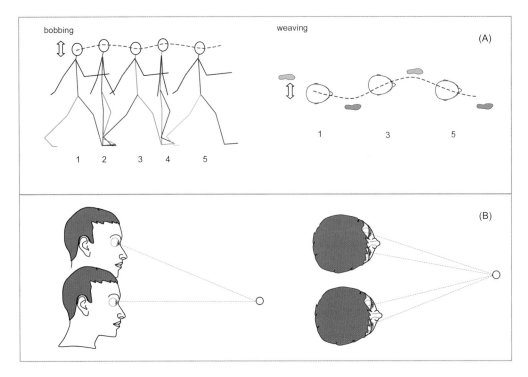

Figure 4.45: *(A) Translational motion of the head (bobbing and weaving) while walking. (B) Counter-rotational eye movements preserve gaze direction during head translations.*

4.3.12 The optokinetic reflex system

When the head rotates at constant velocity or translates at constant velocity, the VOR system does not function, because the vestibular system is not stimulated during such motion – the vestibular system is stimulated when the head velocity changes (head acceleration; see section 3.3). This means that the VOR system is unable to keep retinal images steady on the retinas during constant velocity rotations and translations of the head. It is also ineffective during slow, low-frequency rotations where it has a low gain. It is potentially useful to counter-

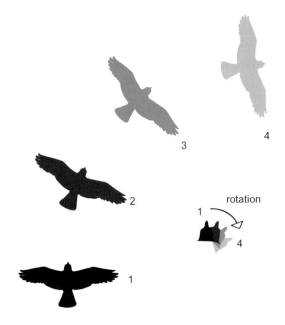

Figure 4.46: *As a bird flies along a curved path, its head and eyes rotate relative to the environment.*

rotate the eyes to prevent the images moving during smooth, sustained rotations of the head. Nature has provided many animals with a mechanism for doing this, which is mediated by visual stimulation, the optokinetic reflex (OKR) system[70]. This system supplements the VOR and takes over in conditions in which the VOR cannot effectively stabilize the retinal images.

Sustained, smooth rotations of the head occur when an animal travels along a curved path, as illustrated in Figure 4.46 for a bird flying. The bird is shown in a sequence of four positions along a curved flight path, and its head changes its orientation with respect to the surroundings (the page) from one position to the next. Thus, the head rotates with respect to the surroundings as the bird moves along the curve, as indicated in the center of the figure. As the head rotates, so do the eyes, and this generates a rotational image flow (section 4.2.11) that could lead to blurred vision. The image flow can be cancelled out with a suitable counter-rotational eye movement. The optokinetic reflex system generates compensatory eye movements in response to the visual stimulation produced by rotational image flows.

It is quite difficult to study the eye movements of people and animals when they are traversing curved paths. For this reason, the OKR is usually studied experimentally by placing a stationary subject in a rotating environment. This can be done using wide-angle computer graphic displays, but the early experiments were conducted by physically moving the visible surroundings so that they rotated about the subject. A simple apparatus for doing this is a large cylinder mounted on a bearing so that it can rotate about a vertical axis. The experimental participant sits or stands inside the cylinder, which is called an *optokinetic drum*. The inner surface of the cylinder is usually painted with vertical stripes as shown in Figure 4.47. The visual motion stimulation produced by rotating the optokinetic drum not only evokes eye movements (see below), it also produces a perception of self-motion called *circular vection* (as mentioned in section 4.1.14): the person develops the perception of turning around and around within a stationary environment. This perception does not develop immediately: initially a person veridically perceives the drum to be turning around them, but over a period of about 30 seconds they develop the impression that they are turning inside a stationary drum[71].

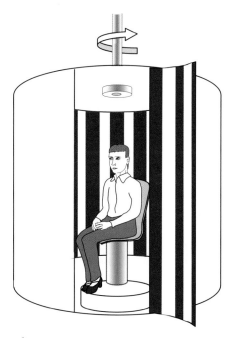

Figure 4.47: *The optokinetic drum.*

A person or animal placed in an optokinetic drum starts to produce compensatory eye movements shortly after the drum starts to rotate. If only the eyes are permitted to move, they do so with a characteristic pattern called **nystagmus**. The eyes follow the motion of the drum through an angle of 20° or so, then quickly flick back to a roughly central position and begin following again. The movement that follows the drum's motion is relatively slow compared to the movement that returns the eyes to a central position. For this reason, the motion-following movements are referred to as the **slow phase** of nystagmus and the return movements as the **quick phase**. The quick phase movements are examples of *saccadic eye movements*; the characteristics of saccadic movements are discussed in more detail in section 4.4.3. Figure 4.48 shows the basic features of the nystagmic eye movements evoked in a rotating optokinetic drum (**optokinetic nystagmus, OKN**): the repeating pattern of a slow phase followed by a quick phase is very clear, as it produces a characteristic saw-tooth waveform. When the drum rotates at a constant speed or oscillates at very low frequencies, the slow phase moves the eyes at the speed required to keep the image stationary on the retinas (eliminating the retinal image flow), provided that the rotational speed is not too great. The OKR effectively eliminates retinal flow at stimulus speeds of up to about 30°/s, but is less effective at higher speeds, and breaks down completely when the stimulus speed reaches 100°/s.

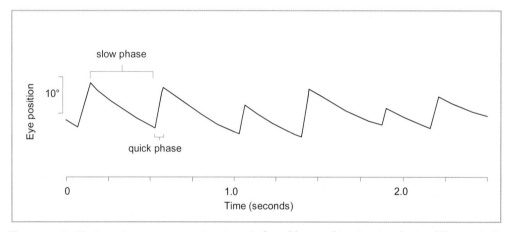

Figure 4.48: *Nystagmic eye movement pattern induced by optokinetic stimulation (illustrative).*

In many animals, the OKR can be easily evoked by immersion in an optokinetic drum, and the compensatory eye movements are pure OKR responses, uncontaminated by responses produced by other systems. In people and other primates, however, the OKR is invariably contaminated by movements generated by the smooth pursuit system[72] (see section 4.4.6), which is often a major contributor to the eye movements observed when a person is placed in an optokinetic drum[73]. The OKR does not appear to be particularly important in people: we make voluntary eye movements almost continually, and the performance of these movements often demands that the OKR is suppressed. The reasons that OKR suppression is needed are described in the next part of the chapter.

4.4 Bringing Images onto the Foveas

4.4.1 Introduction: voluntary and involuntary eye movements

The VOR and OKR systems are reflexive: they produce eye movements involuntarily in response to stimulation (see Chapter 5 for further discussion of the nature of reflexes). The compensatory eye movements generated by these systems require sensory stimulation for their production and cannot occur in the absence of such stimulation. The eye movements that are made to bring the images of interesting objects onto the foveas are different: they can be evoked voluntarily (in response to an internal decision to move) as well as involuntarily (in response to eliciting stimulation), and in some cases they can be produced in the absence of any sensory stimulation. These are the eye movements that we make when looking, and they are often accompanied by head movements; in some instances the head movement may be much more significant than the eye movement. The eye and head movement that bring images onto the foveas are described in this part of the chapter.

4.4.2 Animals with foveate eyes possess four systems for bringing images onto the foveas and holding them there

Human beings and other animals with foveate eyes possess systems that work to bring the images of interesting or important objects onto the foveas and to keep them there. The following four systems are distinguished:

(1) **Saccadic system:** Acts to rapidly shift gaze from one direction to another. When you look around your surroundings, you make a series of brief fixations as you look at one location in the surroundings and then another. The transition between these fixations is effected by very rapid conjugate eye movements; head turns are usually involved as well. When only the eyes move, the rapid transitions between fixations are examples of saccadic eye movements, and are simply called **saccades**. The term 'saccade' comes from the French noun *saccade* meaning a jerk or a jolt: the term was adopted because these movements, particularly the eye movements, appear as rapid jerks.

   Saccadic movements can occur in any direction within the eye sockets. Saccades that move the eyes to the left or right are called **horizontal saccades**, those that move the eyes up and down are called **vertical saccades**, and those that move the eyes diagonally are called **oblique saccades**. We will restrict attention to horizontal saccades; the other directions are basically similar. When a rapid shift in gaze involves coordinated, concurrent head and eye movement, it is called an **eye-head saccade**.

(2) **Fixation system:** Acts to hold the eyes steady during the brief periods of fixation between saccades, but is distinct from the image stabilization systems already discussed (the VOR and OKR systems). When there is no VOR or OKN activity, fixation requires continuous contraction of the eye muscles to keep the eye in position, and even then the eyes are making continuous miniature movements.

(3) **Smooth pursuit system:** When you look at an object that is moving relative to you, you need to keep the image of the object on the foveas as it moves. This requires that the eyes move to follow the object. If an object moves smoothly and not too quickly, then the eyes move smoothly to follow it. Conjugate eye movements of this kind are called **smooth pursuit** eye movements; they are generated by the smooth pursuit system. Head movements are often involved as well as eye movements. There is some controversy about the extent to which the pursuit and fixation systems can be considered distinct, since both systems act to keep the images of an object on the retinas. This controversy is beyond the scope of our discussion[74].

(4) **Vergence system:** When you want to change fixation so as to look from a far-off object to one nearby, your eyes converge so that the nearby object is imaged on the two foveas. The vergence system is responsible for generating convergent eye movements when gaze is shifted to look at nearer objects, and divergent movements when gaze is shifted to look at objects further away. It also generates such movements when looking at an object that moves towards you or recedes away from you (vergence pursuit movements). There are other types of vergence movements (cyclovergence and vertical vergence; see section 4.3.4) but we will not discuss these.

In the sections that follow, the types of movement generated by these systems are discussed in turn. The chart overleaf provides a summary for ease of reference:

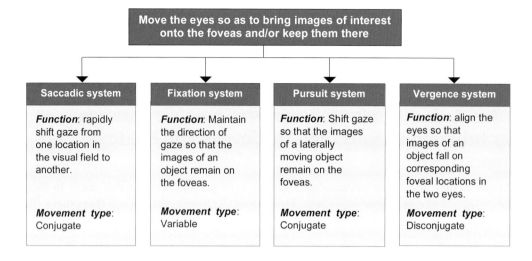

4.4.3 The form of saccadic eye movements is always much the same

In this section we will be concerned with saccadic eye movements; eye-head saccades are discussed further in section 4.4.4. While performing everyday tasks like making coffee, watching the television, or reading, our eyes are continually making saccades. A typical rate for tasks like reading and coffee-making is three or four saccades every second[75]. The saccades that we make when carrying out tasks like these occur without conscious decisions: they occur automatically as part of executing the task, without us having to think about making them.

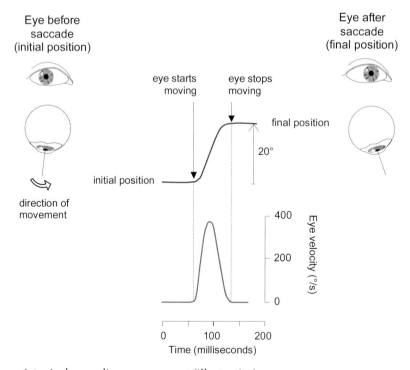

Figure 4.49: *A typical saccadic eye movement (illustrative).*

Saccades may differ from one another in amplitude and direction: the eyes may rotate through a large or a small angle, they may move left, right, up, down or obliquely. Despite these differences, the eyes always move in a very similar way. Figure 4.49 shows a typical saccadic movement that moves the eye horizontally from one fixation to another. The movement is a smooth, continuous progression of the eye from the initial to the final position as shown in the graph of eye position against time (upper graph). The *amplitude* of the saccade is the angular distance through which the eye travels between the two fixation positions – 20° in the example shown in Figure 4.49. The lower graph in the figure shows the eye's angular velocity as a function of time: during the saccade, the eye accelerates smoothly to a peak velocity and then decelerates to a stop at the new fixation position. The movement is quick: the eye reaches a maximum speed of nearly 400°/s and the movement lasts about 75 milliseconds.

The form of the graphs of eye position and eye velocity against time shown in Figure 4.49 are characteristic of saccades regardless of amplitude or direction. Thus, the way the eye moves when making a saccade is rather stereotyped. Furthermore, if a person makes several saccades from the same starting position to the same terminal position, one saccade will be almost exactly the same as the others. The saccades will all have a similar duration and reach a similar peak velocity, and their position and velocity profiles will all have the form shown in Figure 4.49. In other words, the amplitude of a saccade determines its duration and peak speed – we cannot choose to make faster saccades or slower saccades. Panel A of Figure 4.50 shows the relationship between saccade amplitude and peak velocity. The eyes reach greater peak velocities when executing saccades of larger amplitude. The largest possible saccade is one from the extreme nasal position of the eye to the extreme temporal position – about 100° in amplitude. These saccades reach the highest peak velocities, which varies somewhat between individuals, but is typically about 700°/s. Panel B of Figure 4.50 shows the relationship between saccade amplitude and saccade duration (movement time), and shows that duration increases in direct proportion to amplitude[76].

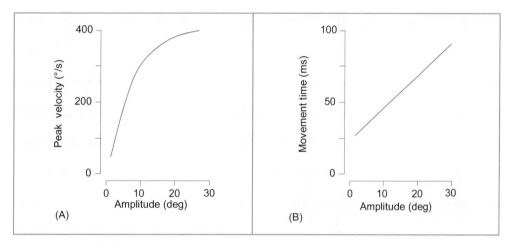

Figure 4.50: *Peak velocity (A) and movement time (B) of saccadic eye movements as a function of amplitude. Based on data presented by Zee and Robinson (1979).*

Saccades with amplitudes greater than about 40° are almost never observed in natural conditions. People can easily produce such saccades in laboratory experiments, but rarely, if ever, produce them in everyday life. In everyday tasks, saccadic amplitude is typically less than 10°; larger movements of 20° or 30° are occasionally observed[77]. Reading, for example, involves sequences of saccades that average about 2° in amplitude, as the eyes move between words on the same line of text, and larger saccades of about 20° that move the eyes from the end of one line to the beginning of the next[78]. When a large gaze shift is required, an eye-head saccade is usually made, as described next.

4.4.4 Large shifts of gaze direction combine eye and head movements

The eyes cannot move to the right or left of the central position by more than about 50°; to shift gaze by more than this requires movement of the head. In fact, gaze shifts greater than about 15° usually involve head movements, and sometimes the head is moved when making smaller amplitude gaze shifts[79]. Very large angle gaze shifts will involve movements of the trunk as well as the head and eyes[80] – turning to look at something behind you, for instance.

In some cases, when both the head and eyes are involved in moving to fixate an object, the eyes move first and the object is foveated before the head has moved very much. Figure 4.51 shows such a gaze shift in which the eyes move horizontally[81]: gaze is initially directed about 30° to the person's right, and the person turns their head and eyes to their left so that gaze is shifted by 60°. After the shift of gaze is complete, the eyes are centrally positioned in their orbits (total shift of 60° = eye movement of 30° + head movement of 30°). The graphs on the right side of the figure show the horizontal position of an eye in its socket during the gaze shift (top), the angular position of the head relative to the surroundings during the shift (middle) and the direction of one of the visual axes relative to the surroundings (gaze direction). The gaze direction is simply the sum of the eye's position in its socket and the head position relative to the surroundings. From the graphs it is clear that the gaze shift is largely accomplished by an initial saccadic eye movement, which is nearly complete by the time the head begins to move. The head moves smoothly from its initial position to its final position and during this movement the eyes counter-rotate in their sockets so that gaze is held steady as the head moves. This counter-rotation is produced by the vestibulo-ocular reflex.

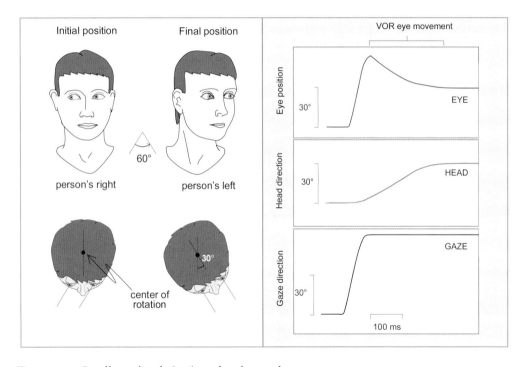

Figure 4.51: *Small amplitude (60°) eye-head saccade.*

The pattern of head and eye movement shown in Figure 4.51 is characteristic of gaze shifts of up to about 60° in amplitude to unexpected targets. The eyes and head move in sequence: the saccadic eye movement is almost complete before the head begins to move. In a typical experiment, the participant initially fixates some visible location, and they are told that when a target stimulus appears in their peripheral vision, they should turn to look at it as quickly as they can. The target appears at a time and location that the person cannot anticipate. Somewhat different patterns of movement are observed when the gaze shifts are of large amplitude, and also when the person knows in advance where gaze will be shifted to[82].

Figure 4.52 shows the eye, head and gaze movements typical of a very large gaze shift (205°) in which the head rotates through 174°. In this case the head and eyes move concurrently to produce the gaze shift. The way in which the gaze moves (bottom graph) during the coordinated head and eye movement closely resembles the way in which the eyes move during a saccadic eye movement. This gaze movement is what we referred to as an eye-head

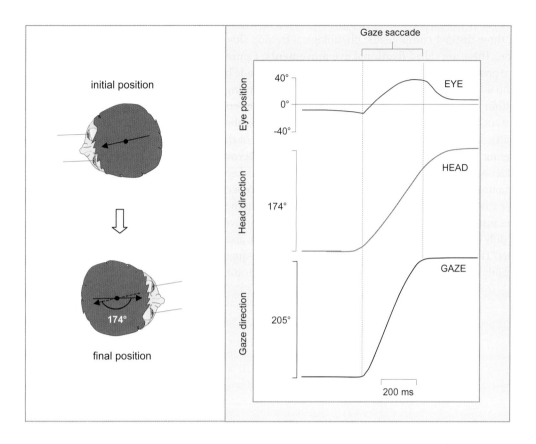

Figure 4.52: *Eye, head and gaze movement during a large amplitude (205°) eye-head (gaze) saccade. Based on data presented in Laurutis and Robinson (1986).*

saccade in section 4.4.2. An alternative term is **gaze saccade**, which can also be applied to shifts of gaze that involve the head, eyes and trunk.

During head turns, the rotational-VOR will normally produce counter-rotational eye movements. If this happened during an eye-head saccade like that shown in Figure 4.51, the VOR would act to move the eyes in the opposite direction to the head's movement and keep the gaze direction constant. This is clearly not what is happening in the figure: the head and eyes move together in the same direction, and the gaze direction changes. This means that the VOR must be suppressed while gaze is shifting during an eye-head saccade[83]. Once the gaze has reached the target, the VOR is reactivated, and counter-rotational eye movements are produced that maintain gaze direction as indicated in the figure. Note that in the sequential pattern of head-eye movement shown in Figure 4.51, the head hardly moves during the saccadic eye movement, so the VOR does not need to be suppressed.

4.4.5 Fixation involves tiny eye movements

When looking at a single object, we shift fixation frequently from one location on the object to another. The individual fixations themselves are normally rather brief: each one may last only ¼ second or less. Staring intently so that fixation is maintained on a single point for extended periods requires a great deal of conscious effort, and is not something that occurs in natural circumstances. Long duration fixations that last for seconds are rarely executed except when a person is instructed to fixate for the purposes of laboratory experiments[84]. Figure 4.38 shows that the eyes move much less than the head when a person is standing still and fixating intently; the vestibular/cervical reflex system is compensating for the head movements. However, the visual axis is still not completely motionless – it moves around within a region about ½° in diameter. If the head is fixed so that it cannot move, the eyes still jiggle around[85] with a maximum amplitude of between ¼° and ½°. Thus, even when the head is completely motionless during a fixation, the eyes are in continual motion.

Precise measurement of eye position during fixations reveals that its movement is composed of three distinct components: physiological tremor, slow drifts, and small, rapid jumps in position. These are called **fixational eye movements**. Figure 4.53 shows what a record of horizontal eye position might look like during a long fixation made by someone whose head is held fixed and who is instructed to stare intently at a fixed point. During the fixation, the gaze direction remains within a range of about ¼°. The plot shows the three sorts of movement just mentioned: there are sudden changes in position where the trace steps abruptly, more gradual changes (positional drift), and very rapid, very small wiggles in the line of the trace itself, which is the physiological tremor. The rapid changes in position are called **microsaccades**. Microsaccades vary in amplitude: some may shift gaze direction by nearly ½°, others shift gaze by less than a tenth of this amount; their average amplitude is about 0.1°. Microsaccades sometimes occur to reposition the eye when it has drifted too far away from the optimum fixation position, but they also occur in the absence of drift[86]. The physiological tremor has an average amplitude of less than 0.01°, which is only enough to move the image over the retina by about the width of one or two photoreceptors. Tremor appears to be a consequence of high frequency noise in the oculomotor system, due mainly to randomness inherent in the firing of the motor units of the extraocular muscles.

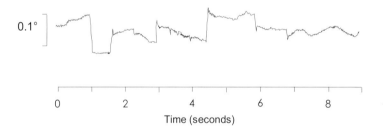

Figure 4.53: *Horizontal eye position as a function of time during a sustained fixation (illustrative).*

It was once thought that the primary purpose of drift and microsaccades was to maintain slight movement of the image and so prevent it from remaining stationary on the retina. If the image does not move at all, vision of our surroundings starts to fade within a few seconds, and eventually disappears altogether. However, the time taken for vision to start to fade is far longer than the typical dwell time of fixations made during natural viewing (about ¼ second). Moreover, if the purpose of microsaccades and drift were to prevent fading, then it might reasonably be expected that such movements would increase in frequency when vision starts to fade, or during long fixations when the risk of fading is greatest. However, neither expectation has been confirmed[87]; in fact, it has been found that the frequency of microsaccades can decrease during tasks that involve extended fixations, such as threading a needle[88]. Of course, any drifts and microsaccades that do occur during long fixations will serve to prevent fading, but long-drawn-out fixations are the exception rather than the rule. Recent evidence has demonstrated that vision does not fade during the short dwell times characteristic of normal fixations, and indicates that the main reason for making microsaccades is to enhance the brain's ability to extract information about fine details from the image[89].

4.4.6 Pursuit eye movements are used to follow a moving object

Imagine keeping your gaze directed at a moving object that travels past you from left to right or from right to left, such as a passing motor vehicle or a bird in flight. If you attempt this with your head held still so that only your eyes move, then the eye movements you make are usually of the **smooth pursuit** type. These movements are somewhat similar to those used to follow a moving object with a movie camera: the camera operator smoothly turns the camera to follow a moving object, so that its image is kept in the same position within the frame.

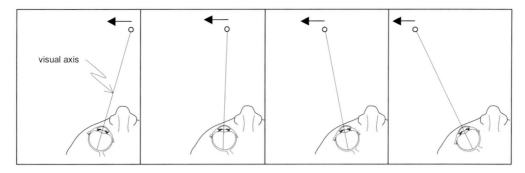

Figure 4.54: *An eye pursues a moving object.*

Figure 4.54 shows a sequence of four frames of a cartoon movie of an eye making a pursuit movement. The head is stationary and the left eye rotates to follow a target that moves from right to left across the page. In each frame the target lies on the eye's visual axis, and so the target's image is kept on the fovea. The effectiveness with which a pursuit process keeps the image stationary on the fovea can be quantified using the gain. Like the gain of the VOR (see section 4.3.10), the gain of the pursuit process is obtained by dividing the angular velocity of the eyes by the angular velocity of the target:

$$\text{Gain} = \frac{\text{Angular velocity of the eyes}}{\text{Angular velocity of the target}}$$

The angular velocity of the target is measured relative to a reference line fixed to the middle of the eye socket. This line coincides with the visual axis when the eye is in the central position, as shown in Figure 4.55. Measured as shown, the angular velocity of the target relative to the head[90] is the rate of change of the angle labeled β, which is equal in magnitude to the speed with which the target's image moves across the retina if the eye is stationary.

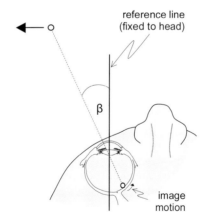

Figure 4.55: *The angular velocity of the target relative to the head is the rate of change of β.*

When the gain is equal to one, the eyes and target are moving with the same angular velocity, which means that the image of the target is being held stationary on the retina. When the gain is less than one but greater than zero, the target is moving faster than the eyes and so its image will be moving away from the fovea. The gain is zero when the eyes are stationary, and negative when they move in the opposite direction to the target; in these cases there is no pursuit. The gain of pursuit depends on a large number of factors, too numerous to discuss here[91]. One significant finding[92] is that when pursuing a target that moves with constant angular velocity relative to the head, the gain is close to one for speeds up to about 100°/s. This is about the fastest that the eyes are able to move during smooth pursuit of constant velocity targets, and so even if the target moves faster, the speed of the eyes does not exceed 100°/s. If you were watching a motor race standing about 25 meters from the track, and a race car passed you traveling at about 150 km/hr, then its angular velocity at your eyes would be roughly 100°/s.

Figure 4.56 illustrates what happens when a person makes a pursuit eye movement to follow a constant velocity target with a gain very close to one. The dotted line plots the angular position of the target over time; the blue solid line plots the angular position of the eye. The target is initially stationary and is being fixated. After a short time the target starts to move at constant angular velocity (about 15°/s in the example shown). After the target has started to move the eye remains stationary for a short period (about 200 ms in the figure) and then makes an initial saccade to catch up with the target[93]. The eye then immediately begins to make a pursuit movement and follows the target very closely thereafter.

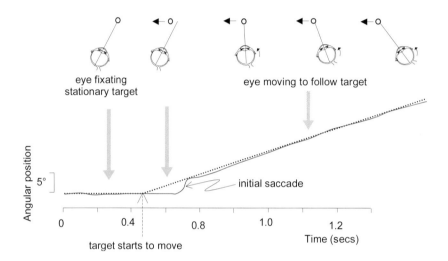

Figure 4.56: *Eye's angular position during pursuit of a constant velocity target (illustrative).*

If the pursuit gain is less than one, the eye is not moving fast enough to keep up with the target, and its image will drift away from the fovea during the pursuit movement. When this happens, saccadic eye movements are made to re-foveate the image; these are called *catch-up saccades*. It is common to see periods of slow, smooth pursuit interspersed with small catch-up saccades, particularly for faster moving targets and targets that oscillate back and forth. Figure 4.57 shows the position of a target over time and the position of the pursuing eye when the pursuit gain is less than one, so that catch-up saccades are needed to re-foveate the target's image. The speed of the eye (slope of the blue line) is less than the speed of the target (dotted line), and so the eye does not keep up with the target during pursuit.

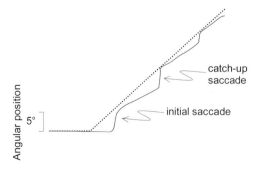

Figure 4.57: *Pursuit movement with catch-up saccades (illustrative).*

4.4.7 Stimulation is important for the generation of pursuit movement

A moving object does not normally involuntarily elicit pursuit eye movement[94]. An internal decision to pursue the object is needed to activate the pursuit process. In the presence of many things in motion – many cars on the road or people in a busy town center – a person must also select which of them to pursue. The requirements for internal activation and target selection have led to pursuit eye movements being classified as voluntary eye movements. Nevertheless, people cannot generate pursuit eye movements in the absence of a moving stimulus. The stimulus does not have to be visual, however. For example, many people are able to produce smooth pursuit eye movements to follow their unseen finger as they move it in darkness. The generation of pursuit involves a complex interplay of voluntary and involuntary processes that cannot be discussed here[95]; a general description of the way voluntary and reflexive processes interact is presented in Chapter 6.

Notice that when the eye moves to pursue a moving object, only the image of this object remains approximately stationary on the fovea. The images of other things in the surroundings all move across the retina because the eye rotation produces a retinal image flow as described in section 4.1.10. Such a rotational image flow would normally be the stimulus for the optokinetic reflex (OKR), since it is identical to the image flow that would be produced if the environment rotated as a whole about an axis through the eye. If the OKR were evoked by the image flow produced by a pursuit eye movement, then the OKR response would be in the opposite direction to the pursuit movement and would seriously interfere with it. This means that the OKR normally needs to be suppressed during voluntary pursuit.

4.4.8 People usually move their heads to watch a moving target

Following a moving target with pursuit eye movements is a behavior seldom observed for significant periods of time outside the laboratory. In everyday life, people normally move their heads when they look at moving objects as they pass by. The spectators at tennis matches provide a classic example. As the players hit the ball across the net, the spectators turn their heads to watch the ball – the heads turn one way and then the other as the players rally the ball. Visual tracking of a moving target that involves head movement can be referred to either as **eye-head pursuit** or **gaze pursuit**. As with saccadic movements, the term *gaze pursuit* is more general, since a person may also turn their body as they watch a moving object.

In principle, gaze pursuit could be achieved without moving the eyes within their sockets: the head could turn to follow the target and the eyes could remain stationary within the head. This type of behavior is not typically observed, however. Both the eye and head movements are usually found to contribute to gaze pursuit[96]. Figure 4.58 shows how the head, eyes and gaze move when following a target that moves repeatedly from left to right and back again in an oscillatory fashion (the frequency is 0.16 Hz). Gaze (bottom graph) closely follows the moving target (top graph) with a gain very close to one[97]. The gaze is the sum of the head movement (second graph) and eye movement (third graph). The behavior shown in the figure resembles the kind of behavior shown by spectators at a tennis match who pursue the ball as the players rally it back and forth.

The oscillatory motion of the head shown in Figure 4.58 would normally be expected to be a stimulus for the rotational-VOR and to elicit counter-rotational eye movements that keep gaze direction steady. This clearly conflicts with the goal of pursuit, which requires that gaze follow the moving target. Thus, in order to produce gaze pursuit, the rotational-VOR needs to be suppressed or otherwise prevented from producing counter-rotational eye movements. We return to the question of how this is achieved in Chapter 5. In general, therefore, generation of effective gaze pursuit requires that both the rotational-VOR and the OKR be prevented from generating counter-rotational eye movements in response to the vestibular and image flow stimulation produced by the pursuit movements.

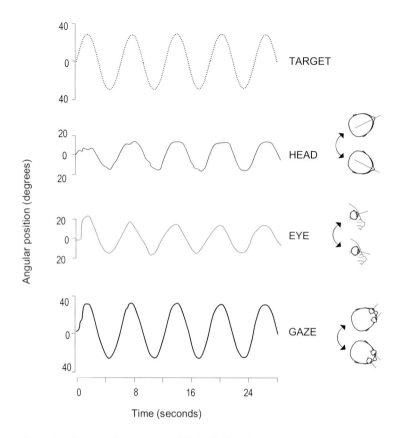

Figure 4.58: *Pursuit of a moving target with both head and eye movements. Based on data reported by Collins and Barnes (1999).*

4.4.9 Vergence movements shift gaze between objects at different distances

When we fixate an object we do so with both eyes – **binocular fixation** – so that the image of the object falls on both foveas. If the object is closer than about five or six meters away, the eyes need to be converged in order that the image fall on both foveas. When you look at something nearby such as a finger held about 25 centimeters from your face (Figure 4.59, panel A), the two eyes must adopt a significantly converged position. If you look at a more distance object, such as a clock on the wall about two meters away (Figure 4.59, panel B), the eyes do not need to adopt such a converged posture. The angle between the two visual axes, labeled γ in the figure, is called the **vergence angle**. A vergence angle of zero (visual axes parallel) means that the eyes are not converged at all; the greater the vergence angle, the more converged the eyes. The visual axes are very close to parallel when you binocularly fixate an object four meters away: the vergence angle is about one degree. The visual axes are typically parallel (zero convergence) when looking at something more than six meters distant.

If the images of an object do not fall on the same retinal locations in the two eyes, double vision (**diplopia**) can be the result. This is also illustrated in Figure 4.59. In panel A, the fixated finger is about 25 cm from the viewer and there is a clock on the wall behind that is 2 meters away. What the viewer sees in this situation is shown at the bottom of panel A. The finger and hand is seen singly because the images fall on corresponding foveal locations on the two retinas (the location of the image is the same in the two eyes[98]). A double image of the clock is seen (diplopia) because the clock does not fall on corresponding locations on the two retinas. In panel B, the person is fixating the clock. In this case, the view is of a single clock but the finger and hand are seen double.

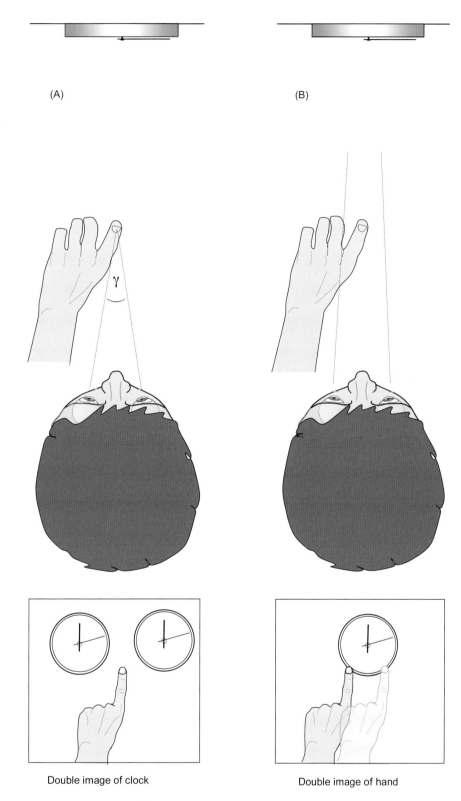

(A)　　　　　　　　　　　　　　(B)

Double image of clock　　　　　　　　Double image of hand

Figure 4.59: *Convergence and diplopia.*

If the person is initially fixating their finger (Figure 4.59A) and wants to look at the clock, then they would make a divergent movement that rotates both eyes away from the nose and closer to the central position. Conversely, if a person is initially looking at the clock and wants to inspect their finger, they would make a convergent movement that rotates the eyes inwards towards the nose. Movements of this sort are produced by the vergence eye movement system. Pure vergence movements are those in which the eyes move through the same angle but in opposite directions. This occurs when shifting gaze between two visible points that lie in a transverse plane through the eyes along a line that passes exactly half-way between them, as shown in Figure 4.60.

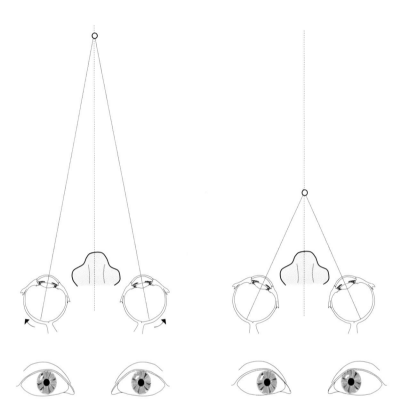

Figure 4.60: *Pure convergence along the mid-sagittal plane.*

Vergence movements that shift fixation between objects at different distances are the vergence equivalent of conjugate saccades. However, these vergence movements are not properly described as saccadic, since they are relatively slow – many times slower than conjugate saccades of the same amplitude[99]. For example, a conjugate saccade in which each eye moves through 5° would typically take about 30 milliseconds, and the eyes would reach a peak speed of about 200°/s. A convergent shift of fixation in which both eyes move through 5° – roughly the movement involved when shifting fixation from the clock to the finger in Figure 4.59 – would take 400 milliseconds or more, and the eyes would reach a peak speed of less than 50°/s. Divergent shifts have been found to be even slower than convergent shifts[100]. The maximum speed that can be reached by the eyes during pure vergence movements is in the region of 100°/s.

4.4.10 Stimulation is important for generating vergence eye movements

Vergence eye movements may occur automatically as reflexive responses to stimulation, but they can also be produced voluntarily. The stimulus situation that produces diplopia drives vergence movements that act to eliminate the diplopia and so produce a single percept of an object. Diplopia is produced when the image of an object falls on different retinal locations in the two eyes; the difference in the retinal locations is called **binocular disparity**. Thus, binocular disparity is a stimulus that drives vergence movements. Movements driven by disparity are referred to as **fusional vergence** movements because they act to fuse a diplopic percept into a single one. A single, fused percept of an object will often contain small, residual disparities that cannot be eliminated by vergence but do not interfere with single vision.

These disparities contribute to the percept of three-dimensionality of the viewed object – they provide information about the relative distances between different parts of the object. The perception of solid, three-dimensional objects based on the information provided by binocular disparities is called **binocular stereopsis**; the term *stereopsis* derives from ancient Greek and literally means 'solid vision' (*stereos* is the ancient Greek word for 'solid').

A negative feedback control process drives fusional vergence movements in an automatic, reflexive fashion. Voluntary shifts of gaze from far to near or vice-versa require that this fusional vergence mechanism be activated volitionally, and usually also require that a particular object be selected volitionally from the numerous objects that lie within the visual field. Thus, like pursuit, the production of vergence involves an interplay of volitional and stimulus-driven, automatic processes.

Binocular disparity is not the only type of stimulus that can drive vergence eye-movements. Blurred images can also drive vergence via a signal derived from the accommodative reflex system. Vergence driven in this way is called **accommodative vergence**; the mechanism is briefly discussed in Chapter 5. Other visual information about the distance of an object can also drive vergence, and so can the felt location of a finger in darkness[101]. In the next section we will see how motion of an object towards or away from a viewer drives the vergence equivalent of pursuit movements.

4.4.11 The vergence system produces movements that allow tracking of an object that moves in depth

When an object moves towards or away from you it is said to move in **depth**. If an object moves in depth along the line joining two fixation points, then binocular fixation can be maintained by a vergence movement in which the two eyes both follow the moving target. This is the vergence equivalent of smooth pursuit, which can be referred to as **vergence pursuit**. When a person views an object more than about 5 or 6 meters away, the eyes do not need to be converged in order to maintain binocular fixation. Thus, it is only when an object is closer than this that vergence pursuit becomes relevant.

People are only able to accurately follow relatively slowly moving objects with vergence pursuit eye movements. Vergence pursuit movements can keep the images of approaching or receding objects on the foveas[102] provided the eyes rotate at angular speeds of less than about 15°/s (the gain of vergence pursuit is close to one at these speeds). This corresponds to a target that approaches or recedes from the viewer at a speed less than about 3 m/s. Eye movements of up to 50°/s during vergence tracking of moving targets have been reported, but tracking is quite inaccurate[103]. This means that accurate vergence tracking of objects that move as fast as a baseball approaching a batter (up to 40 m/s) is not possible. It has been found that batters do not try to pursue the ball; rather, they fixate the pitcher and then refixate to a point much closer[104].

Like conjugate pursuit eye movements, people are only able to generate vergence pursuit in the presence of suitable stimulation. Visual stimulation is important – people are very poor at generating vergence pursuit to follow a moving finger in darkness, for example[105]. Visual stimuli that have been found to be effective at driving vergence pursuit include changing binocular disparity and changing image size[106]. That changing image size should evoke vergence movements makes sense when you consider that as an object gets nearer, its retinal image gets larger, and when the object moves further away, its image gets smaller. Although changing size and changing disparity are able to drive vergence pursuit when presented on their own, in normal conditions they are both present together, and it is in such circumstances that vergence pursuit is most effective.

4.4.12 Many eye movements require that the eyes rotate through different angles

Purely conjugate eye movements occur when there is no need for any change in vergence. Changes in vergence are not needed in two situations: (1) when objects are too far away for convergence to be required; (2) when two fixation locations require equal convergence.

The latter situation is illustrated in panel A of Figure 4.61 for points in the horizontal plane through the two eyes. Any point on the circular arc requires that the eyes are converged to the same extent: in the example shown in the figure, the vergence angle (γ) for all points on the arc is about 30°. This means that a shift in binocular fixation from point P to point Q can be achieved with a purely conjugate movement. If an object moves along the circle from P to Q, the eyes can follow it with a purely conjugate pursuit movement. Other circular arcs can be drawn for different vergence angles – ones of larger radius for smaller vergence angles, of smaller radius for larger angles. These constant vergence circular arcs are called **Veith-Müller circles**.

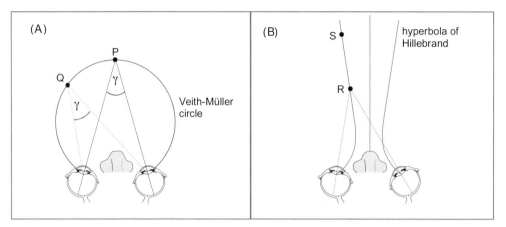

Figure 4.61: *(A) Vergence angle is the same for all points on a Veith-Müller circle. (B) Only vergence changes between points on Hillebrand hyperbolas.*

Pure vergence eye movements occur when binocular fixation is shifted between two points that require no change in the direction of gaze, and hence no conjugate eye movement. An example is shown in Figure 4.60, where fixation is shifted between two points that lie on a line half way between the two eyes. This is called a *line of constant version* or a **hyperbola of Hillebrand**. Two other such lines are shown in panel B of Figure 4.61. A shift in gaze from point R to point S (or vice versa) involves a pure change in vergence but no conjugate movement.

It will often be the case that a person wants to shift fixation between two points that both lie neither on a Veith-Müller circle nor on a Hillebrand hyperbola. An example is shown in Figure 4.62, where the eyes are initially fixating a nearby point, A, and a shift in fixation to point B is required. The shift requires that the two eyes rotate in the same direction (leftward) through different angles: the right eye must rotate through about 25° (α in Figure 4.62) and the left eye must rotate through about 55° (β). Such a movement is neither a conjugate movement nor a vergence movement. It seems to be a kind of movement that we have not yet described; the nature of these eye movements is discussed in what follows.

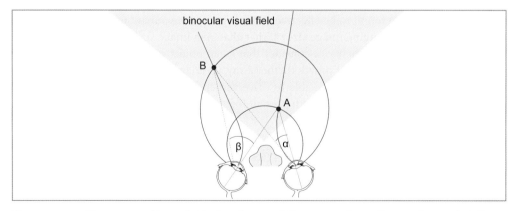

Figure 4.62: *Two points (A and B) that lie on different Veith-Muller circles and different Hillebrand hyperbolas.*

4.4.13 How many types of binocular eye movement are there?

In section 4.3.4 we noted that there are two basic types of binocular eye movement: the eyes move together at the same time through the same angle either in the same direction (conjugate movements), or in opposite directions (vergence movements). In the 19th century, Edwald Hering proposed that these are the only types of eye movement that people are normally able to produce. He wrote as follows:

> The movements of both eyes are to such an extent united with each other that the one will not move independently of the other; on the contrary, the musculature of both eyes reacts simultaneously from one and the same effort of the will. Accordingly we are in general not capable of elevating or depressing one eye without the other, but both eyes are raised or lowered at the same time and in equal extent[107].

At first glance, this statement seems incompatible with the sort of movement needed to shift fixation between A and B in Figure 4.62. However, this incompatibility is merely superficial: Hering was well aware that people make eye movements in which the two eyes move through different angles or in which one eye moves and the other remains almost stationary. Figure 4.63 shows a situation in which the latter is observed: a person shifts fixation between two points C and D that both lie on the visual axis of the left eye. To shift fixation, only the right eye needs to move.

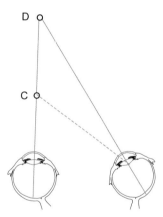

Figure 4.63: *Only the right eye need move to shift fixation from C to D.*

What Hering actually proposed was that all eye movements are a combination of a vergence movement and a conjugate movement executed at almost the same time. That the movement from A to B in Figure 4.62 can be accomplished by a vergence component and a conjugate component is demonstrated in Figure 4.64: a pure divergence movement of about 15° in each eye (panel A) and a pure conjugate movement through about 40° (panel B). If these two movements are executed simultaneously, then the right eye will move 25° left (40° left + 15° right = 25° left) and the left eye will move 55° left. A similar account can be given for the situation shown in Figure 4.63, in which the vergence and conjugate movements in the left eye are equal in size but opposite in direction and so cancel one another out. The result is that the left eye remains stationary; in practice, however, it often moves slightly, indicating that the movements are not executed simultaneously.

Thus, Hering proposed that there are only two types of binocular eye movement – vergence and conjugate movements – and that all movements can be understood as a combination of these two basic types. This means that we need to understand how two such movements are actually combined. We look at this question next.

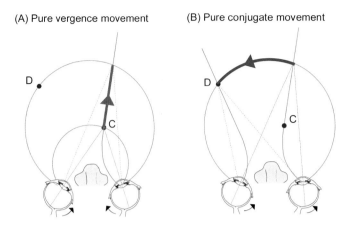

Figure 4.64: *Shifting fixation from C to D by making a vergence movement (A), then a conjugate movement (B).*

4.4.14 Hering's law describes how vergence and conjugate movements can be combined

Figure 4.65 shows the two eyes, the four muscles that move them in the transverse plane of the head (horizontally), and the nuclei that contain the muscles' motoneuron pools. The muscles of the left and right eyes work together in pairs to produce either conjugate or vergence movements. For example, equal and simultaneous contractions of the lateral rectus of the left eye and the medial rectus of the right eye will act to move both eyes to the left (conjugate movement). Equal, simultaneous contractions of both medial recti will act to move the eyes inwards towards the nose (convergence). These pairs of agonist muscles (one in each eye) are called **yoked pairs**. If we interpret Hering's single 'effort of will' as meaning a single command signal, then we arrive at the idea that a pure vergence or conjugate eye movement is produced by a single command signal that is sent to a yoked pair of muscles, so that the two contract equally and simultaneously. Thus, the two eyes are controlled as a single unit. This idea is known as **Hering's law of equal innervation**, because the agonist muscles involved receive equal neural input:

> **HERING'S LAW OF EQUAL INNERVATION:** A conjugate or vergence eye movement is generated by a single control signal sent to the muscles of a yoked pair so that they both contract equally and at the same time.

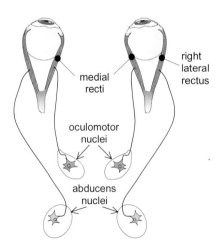

Figure 4.65: *Muscles and motoneuron pools involved in horizontal eye movements.*

A pictorial representation of the law is probably a better way of thinking about it than a verbal statement. Figure 4.66 shows two processes in the nervous system: one generates command signals for vergence movements, the other generates command signals for conjugate movements. Panel A shows the conjugate process generating a single command signal that is split into two equal parts that activate the left lateral rectus and the right medial rectus (the yoked pair for leftward conjugate eye movements). Panel B shows the vergence process generating a single command signal for a convergent movement that splits into two equal parts and activates the motoneuron pools of the two medial recti (the yoked pair for convergence). The figure merely provides a pictorial representation of Hering's law; it does not attempt to accurately portray the anatomical pathways that are likely to be involved (for details of these see Chapters 5 and 6).

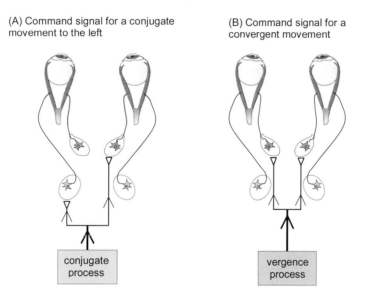

(A) Command signal for a conjugate movement to the left

(B) Command signal for a convergent movement

conjugate process

vergence process

Figure 4.66: *Diagrammatic representation of Hering's law.*

Hering's law can be used to understand how a conjugate and vergence movement can be combined to change fixation between the two points in Figures 4.63 and 4.64. Consider, for example, the change in fixation from C to D in Figure 4.63, in which only the right eye moves. According to Hering's law, such a change in fixation is the result of a vergence command signal and a conjugate command signal that act on the muscles of the left eye so that no movement is produced, and on the muscles of the right eye to produce a leftward rotation through an angle of about 30°. This could be achieved by combining a vergence movement in which both eyes rotate inwards through 15°, and a conjugate movement in which both eyes move leftward by 15°. According to Figure 4.66, the right medial rectus motoneuron pool (right oculomotor nucleus) receives a vergence command signal and a conjugate command signal. These add together to produce an overall excitation of the motoneurons that produces an inward rotation of 30°. The left eye's medial rectus motoneuron pool receives only the vergence command signal and the left eye's lateral rectus pool receives only the conjugate signal. These command signals are equal, and so the two muscles contract equally, but since they are antagonists the contractile forces cancel one another out and the eye does not move[108].

Note that the left eye in the example just given only remains immobile if the vergence and conjugate commands arrive simultaneously at the motoneuron pools of the two antagonistic muscles and last for exactly the same length of time. Research has shown that this seldom happens and so changes in fixation between two points like A and B in Figure 4.62 will often involve movements of both eyes. Such cases are described next.

4.4.15 The effects of vergence and conjugate commands are not quite simultaneous: evidence for Hering's law

Suppose a person shifts fixation between points such as A and B in Figure 4.62 or C and D in Figure 4.64, but issues the vergence and conjugate commands such that they do not reach the motoneuron pools simultaneously. What will happen? Consider the case in which the vergence signal arrives slightly in advance of the conjugate signal. If this happens a vergence movement will begin first, and a conjugate movement shortly afterwards. Experiments have shown that the vergence movement does begin slightly before the conjugate movement, and that the two are of different speeds. Figure 4.67 shows two examples. In panel A, fixation shifts from point C to point D, and the path followed by the intersection of the visual axes of the two eyes – the **binocular gaze point** – is shown as a solid blue line. The movement consists of three segments. The first segment is a pure convergent movement that is relatively slow. The second segment is a more rapid conjugate saccade superimposed on the on-going vergence movement. The third segment is the completion of the slow convergent movement after the saccade has ended. In panel B, fixation is shifted from point E to point F and the path of the binocular gaze point is again shown as a solid blue line. As in panel A, the eyes begin by making a pure vergence movement and after a short time a conjugate saccade occurs which moves the gaze point to the left. If the left eye remained immobile during the shift in fixation, the path of the gaze point would coincide with the visual axis of the left eye (the line that intersects points E and F in the figure).

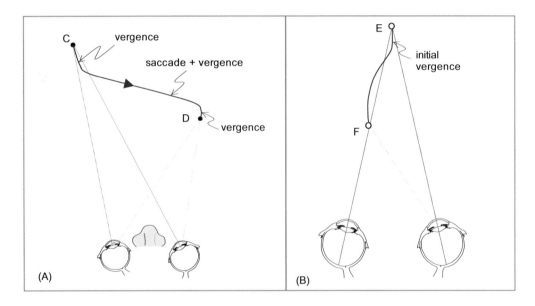

Figure 4.67: *Changes in fixation that require both vergence and conjugate movements (based on data reviewed by Ono, 1983).*

Results of the kind illustrated in Figure 4.67 are consistent with Hering's law because they indicate that fixation shifts are a combination of vergence and conjugate components. Also consistent with the law are neurophysiological findings showing that vergence and conjugate movements are generated by different neural systems[109]. However, the evidence in favor of Hering's law is not decisive, since it is possible that commands are generated separately for the two eyes. Situations in which Hering's law appear to fail have been reported from time to time[110], and the results have been interpreted as supporting the alternative view that the two eyes are controlled independently[111]. Others have disputed the apparent failures and argued that the available data are compatible with Hering's law when properly interpreted[112]. The arguments are too involved and subtle to be discussed here; we simply note that Hering's law remains the most plausible account of eye movement control.

References & Notes

1 Marr (1982).

2 Gibson (1966).

3 Of course, in certain circumstances there may be no light reaching a point of observation from some directions – there are 'holes' in the array. If present, these holes could be considered to be parts of the array (i.e., parts where the light intensity is zero).

4 The process is actually quite complex and only partially understood (see Fincham, 1951; Gambra et al., 2010).

5 Sometimes the two terms are used to mean slightly different things (Smythies, 1996).

6 The eye actually has two nodal points that are very close together (Howard, 1982).

7 See Gibson (1979); Koenderink (1986).

8 It also includes motion of shadows, specularities and reflections, and so is more than simply the projection of a set of (moving) points.

9 Also *center of outflow* (Gibson, 1979). *Focus of radial outflow* is the most descriptive term (Warren et al., 1988).

10 Unclear definitions lead to pointless arguments (Regan, Beverley, 1982; Priest, Cutting, 1985; Torrey, 1985).

11 Helmholtz (1925), p. 296.

12 Rogers, Graham (1979).

13 The scene was generated by a computer in the experiments.

14 Regan, Gray (2000).

15 Wood (1895), p. 277.

16 After Fischer and Kornmüller (1930), cited by Howard (1982).

17 Schöne (1984).

18 Brandt, Dichgans, Koenig (1973); Johansson (1977).

19 Brandt, Dichgans, Koenig (1973).

20 Brandt, Wist, Dichgans (1975).

21 Nashner, Berthoz (1978).

22 E.g., Bruce, Green, Georgeson (2003); Wolfe et al. (2011).

23 Findlay, Gilchrist (2003).

24 Baker, Braddick (1985).

25 The receptive field of a visual neuron can be defined in terms of the visual field rather than the photoreceptor array: roughly speaking, it is that part of the visual field to which the neuron responds. These definitions are equivalent.

26 Wolfe et al. (2011); Findlay, Gilchrist (2003).

27 Roughly speaking, a vertical meridian through the foveal center is perpendicular to a meridian that passes through the middle of the retina and the center of the optic disc.

28 Reinhard, Trauzettel-Klosinski (2003).

29 The ganglion cells that project to the suprachiasmic nuclei have been found to be intrinsically photosensitive and can be considered to be another type of photosensor. For discussion of their properties and connectivity see Berson (2003); Dacey et al. (2005).

30 Fredericks et al. (1988); Masseck, Hoffman (2009).

31 Glaser (1999).

32 There is evidence to suggest that a small minority of axons from the lateral geniculate nuclei project not to V1 but to other regions of the occipital lobe (Sincich et al., 2004).

33 There is some controversy concerning the correct interpretation of blindsight phenomena (Cowey, 2009, 2010).

34 See Anstis (1998).

35 For a discussion of the relationship between acuity and cortical representation see Azzopardi, Cowey (1993).

36 For a review of early work see Tootell et al. (1998).

37 Van Essen (2005).

38 Ungerleider, Mishkin (1982).

39 Ungerleider, Mishkin (1982).

40 Milner, Goodale (2006).

41 Goodale, Milner (1992).

42 Mcintosh, Schenk (2010).

43 See Tresilian (1995).

44 Weiskrantz et al. (1974).

45 Kaas, Lyon (2007).

46 Milner, Goodale (2006).

47 James et al. (2003).

48 Goodale et al. (1991).

49 For a more recent case with a more focal lesion than DF see Karnath et al. (2009).

50 Jeannerod, Decety, Michel (1994); Karnath, Perenin (2005).

[51] Pisella *et al.* (2009); Mcintosh, Schenk (2010).

[52] Translations of the eyeball within the orbit are negligible.

[53] Vertical vergence movements are evoked in response to vertical binocular disparity – the image of an object on one retina is slightly higher (or lower) than its image on the other. The eye movements produced are of very small amplitude (less than 2°). See Maxwell, Schor (2006).

[54] See Leigh, Zee (2006).

[55] These pulley structures resemble sleeves through which the muscles pass. Smooth muscle fibers in the sleeves allow active regulation of their stiffness (Kono, Poukens, Demer 2002).

[56] For review see Miller (2007).

[57] The exact manner in which the action of a muscle depends on gaze direction is determined in part by the soft tissue pulley structures (Miller, 2007).

[58] Leigh, Zee (2006).

[59] Unlike other skeletal muscles, the extraocular muscles contain a small proportion (about 15%) of muscle fibers that do not propagate action potentials and that produce graded contractions rather than twitch contractions (Leigh, Zee, 2006).

[60] Crawford (1952).

[61] Alternatively, *angular-VOR*.

[62] There is evidence that the otoliths contribute to the torsional and vertical components of the rotational-VOR (Bockisch, Straumann, Haslwanter, 2005).

[63] Leigh, Zee (2006).

[64] Here we are assuming that the eyes are looking into the distance. A gain of slightly less than 1.0 is appropriate if the eyes are converged to look at a nearby object.

[65] Grossman *et al.* (1988).

[66] See Angelaki (2004).

[67] The faster a person walks (or runs), the greater the amplitude and frequency of these head translations (Hirasaki *et al.*, 1999).

[68] Moore *et al.* (1999).

[69] It has been proposed that the translational-VOR may act to optimize the extraction of motion parallax information from retinal images (Liao *et al.*, 2009).

[70] See Masseck, Hoffman (2009).

[71] Brandt, Dichgans, Koenig (1973); Wong, Frost (1978).

[72] Miles (1998).

[73] For this reason, a phenomenon called *optokinetic after nystagmus* is often used to study the characteristics of the human optokinetic system (Leigh, Zee, 2006).

[74] See Leigh, Zee (2006).

[75] See Findlay, Gilchrist (2003).

[76] The data can be well described by the following equation: T = 2.2 A + 21, where T is saccade duration in milliseconds and A is saccadic amplitude in degrees (Carpenter, 1998).

[77] Bahill, Adler, Stark (1975); Land, Mennie, Rusted (1999).

[78] For review see Findlay, Gilchrist (2003).

[79] The tendency to make eye-head saccades rather than saccadic eye movements for smaller-amplitude gaze shifts varies between individuals (Fuller, 1992).

[80] Land (2004).

[81] Based on data presented in Becker (1991).

[82] See Leigh, Zee (2006).

[83] Pelisson, Prablanc, Urquizar (1988); Roy, Cullen (1998).

[84] See Howard (1982).

[85] Findlay, Gilchrist (2003).

[86] Drift seems to be actively controlled by a slow-acting, correctional process called the *field-holding reflex* (Leigh, Zee, 2006).

[87] Cornsweet (1956); for review see Collewijn, Kowler (2008).

[88] Winterson, Collewijn (1976).

[89] Rucci *et al.* (2007).

[90] Note that if the target is moving in a straight line, then its velocity through space is not constant if its angular velocity at the eye is constant. This subtlety is ignored in the text.

[91] See Leigh, Zee (2006).

[92] Meyer, Lasker, Robinson (1985).

[93] There is usually some initial pursuit that occurs within about 120 ms of the onset of target motion and before the initial saccade (Barnes, 2008).

[94] Though there is evidence that moving objects can elicit pursuit movements reflexively in certain circumstances (Barnes, 2008).

[95] See Leigh, Zee (2006).

[96] Collins, Barnes (1999); Dubrovsky, Cullen (2002).

[97] No phase lag is evident at low frequencies; at higher frequencies there is phase lag (Barnes, 2008).

[98] For a technical definition see Howard, Rogers (2008).

[99] Erkelens, Steinman, Collewijn (1989a); Yang, Le, Kapoula (2009).

[100] Hung *et al.* (1994) found that in some cases the peak speed of convergent movements could be double that of divergent movements.

[101] Purely volitional vergence appears to occur when a person goes cross-eyed, particularly if they do so in the dark. However, movements of this type appear to be driven through the accommodation system (Ebenholtz, 2003).

[102] With a vergence error of less than 2° (1° in each eye); Erkelens *et al.* (1989b).

[103] Erkelens *et al.* (1989b).

[104] Watts, Bahill (2000).

[105] Erkelens *et al.* (1989b).

[106] Erkelens, Regan (1986).

[107] Ebenholtz (2003), p. 32.

[108] A complete account must also include reciprocal inhibition (see Chapter 5).

[109] Moschovakis (1995).

[110] Bahill et al. (1976); Enright (1996); Zhou, King (1998).

[111] King, Zhou (2000).

[112] Hung, Ciuffreda (2002); Semmlow, Yuan, Alvarez (1998).

PART **II**

SENSORIMOTOR CONTROL

Stimulus-Elicited Behavior

5.1 Different Types of Stimulus-Elicited Behavior

5.1.1 Introduction: what is stimulus-elicited behavior?

All creatures, from the simplest to the most complex, react to events that occur in their environments. If a hawk appears in the sky above a flock of chickens, the chickens dash for cover. If a loud noise unexpectedly occurs, a person may jump or flinch (a startle reaction). If you step on a sharp stone, you quickly withdraw your foot. In each of these examples there is a behavior that occurs as a reaction to something that stimulates sensory receptors: light reflected from the hawk stimulates the chickens' retinas, the noise stimulates receptors in the ear, the stone stimulates cutaneous receptors in the foot. Such cases can all be represented using a simple schematic diagram:

object or event $\xrightarrow{\text{stimulates}}$ animal $\xrightarrow{\text{produces}}$ behavior

A behavior that is produced as a reaction to sensory stimulation is called the **behavioral response**. A behavior that occurs as a direct, involuntary response to a stimulus is called a **stimulus-elicited behavior**; here is a definition:

> **STIMULUS-ELICITED BEHAVIOR:** behavior that is produced as an involuntary and relatively immediate consequence of sensory stimulation: the behavior is an *involuntary response* to the stimulation.

Reflex actions are the most familiar examples of stimulus-elicited behaviors. Jumping or flinching in response to a loud noise is one example; it is called the *acoustic startle reflex*. Reflexes will be discussed in detail later.

Clearly, a particular behavior is not produced in response to just any old stimulus: the sight or sound of a fly will not prompt a chicken into making a dash for cover; contact of the foot with a smooth, flat surface does not elicit withdrawal. For any given stimulus-elicited behavior, it is possible to identify a number of stimuli that are capable of eliciting the behavioral response and a number that are not. For example, withdrawal can be elicited by contact with any sufficiently hot object or any sufficiently sharp object, but not by cooler or blunter objects. A stimulus that is able to elicit a particular response is called an **eliciting stimulus** (for that response):

> **ELICITING STIMULUS:** Any stimulus that is effective at eliciting a particular behavioral response. Such a stimulus is then an eliciting stimulus for that particular behavior.

It is possible for a stimulus to be an eliciting stimulus for more than one type of behavior. For example, stepping on a sharp object might elicit withdrawal of the foot, but it might also elicit pain-related responses such as vocalizations (ouch!). Thus, we cannot completely describe an eliciting stimulus without specifying the particular behavior that it is the eliciting stimulus for. Conversely, we cannot completely describe a stimulus-elicited behavior without specifying the stimulation that elicits it.

5.1.2 How can we demonstrate that a behavior is stimulus-elicited?

Imagine that a stimulus event occurs and an animal then executes a behavior. If you observed this happening, you might suppose that the stimulus elicited the behavior. This is certainly a possibility, but there are at least two others:

(1)   The execution of the behavior following the stimulus event was a chance occurrence; the behavior was not elicited by the stimulus.

(2)   The behavior may have been a voluntary response to the stimulus. In this case, the stimulus did not elicit the response; the response was initiated by a voluntary decision process.

To draw the conclusion that a behavior was executed in response to a stimulus, we need to be able to rule out these other alternatives. Consider the first: it states that the occurrence of the behavior after the stimulus was a chance happening, an unlikely unique event. If a stimulus is an eliciting stimulus for a behavior, then the behavior should follow the stimulus on other occasions; it should be *repeatable*. However, it is not necessary that the behavior *always* follow the stimulus. As we will see later, it is normally the case that following some presentations of the stimulus the behavior does not occur.

Consider the second alternative: how can we distinguish a stimulus-elicited behavioral response from a voluntary one? One way is to use the fact that a stimulus-elicited response follows soon after the stimulus – only a short period of time elapses between stimulus and response. If a behavior began a minute or more after a stimulus, we could not claim that the behavior was elicited by that stimulus. Furthermore, a person can delay a voluntary response to a stimulus if they are asked to, whereas they cannot do the same if the response is stimulus-elicited. Thus, the time between stimulus and response must be short and not modifiable in accordance with instructions. The period of time between a stimulus and the response is called the **reaction time (RT)** if the behavior is voluntary; if it is stimulus-elicited, the period is called the **response latency**:

> **RESPONSE LATENCY:** the period of time that elapses between the onset of the stimulus and the onset of the (involuntary) response it elicits

Consider an example: if a puff of air is directed at an open eye, most animals will blink in response. This is called the air-puff eye-blink reflex and it has been used extensively in the study of learning processes, as we will see in Chapter 14. Figure 5.1 shows how the blink response is typically elicited. If air is puffed into the eye, how can we be sure that any subsequent blink was a response to the puff and not just a spontaneous blink? After all, animals blink spontaneously from time to time – people blink their eyes at least once every few seconds. To qualify as a stimulus-elicited (reflex) blink, the blink must occur during an appropriate interval of time following the stimulus. It takes between fifty and one hundred milliseconds[1] for signals to be transmitted from the receptors that detect the puff to the muscle that closes the eyelid (*m. orbicularis oculi*) and then a little more time is needed for the muscle to contract. Thus, if a blink begins less than about 100 ms after an air puff stimulus, it

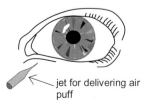 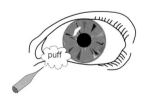 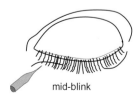

jet for delivering air puff

puff

mid-blink

Figure 5.1: *Eliciting a blink using a puff of air.*

is unlikely to have been elicited by the puff, since it occurred too soon – it was probably just a spontaneous blink that happened to occur after the stimulus. Any blink occurring more than 200 ms after the puff could be a voluntary blink, since people are able to make voluntary reactions to cutaneous stimuli in about 180 to 200 ms. Thus, if the blink occurs more than 100 ms but less than 200 ms after the air puff, it is a candidate reflex blink.

To summarize, the observation that a behavior was executed after presentation of a stimulus is not sufficient to conclude that the behavior was elicited by the stimulus. To be a candidate for a stimulus-elicited response requires that (1) the response reliably follows the stimulus (repeatability), (2) the time between the stimulus and response is within an appropriate range (neither too short nor too long).

5.1.3 Four types of stimulus-elicited behavior

Four different types of stimulus-elicited behavior can be distinguished. Perhaps the most familiar of these are *reflex behaviors* such as the air-puff eye-blink reflex. Reflexes are the main topic of the rest of this chapter and Chapter 6.

There are some stimulus-elicited behaviors that are often called reflexes in everyday language. For example, in racket sports like tennis and badminton, very quick shots like volleys and returns of smashes are often referred to as reflex shots. The reason for using the term *reflex* is that there appears to be too little time for the player to have been able to play the shot voluntarily. However, it is important to recognize that these sorts of actions are not reflexes in the scientific sense. As we will see in Chapter 12, shots in racket sports can be considered to be stimulus-elicited, but involve processes rather different from those involved in reflexes.

A third type of stimulus-elicited behavior involves fast adjustments to voluntary movements that are made following the sensory detection of a disturbance to the movement or an error in its execution. People can make such adjustments without ever being aware that they have made them. This, together with the fact that the latency of such adjustments can be much shorter than the voluntary reaction time, suggest that they are involuntary. This qualifies them as stimulus-elicited actions. Behavior of this kind will be discussed in later chapters, particularly Chapters 11 and 12.

A fourth type of stimulus-elicited behavior has been identified by researchers who study animal behavior. Many animal species exhibit distinctive behaviors, often quite elaborate ones, that are elicited by very specific kinds of stimuli. The courtship displays elicited in male birds by the sight of a female of the species provide examples of such behaviors. Another classic example is egg-retrieval behavior exhibited by several species of ground-nesting birds, such as the herring gull and the graylag goose (Figure 5.2)[2]. When brooding, these birds will pull into their nests eggs that they see just outside the nest. Visual detection of the egg elicits the retrieval response as illustrated in the figure. The bird reaches out to the egg (frame 1), it then pulls the egg into the nest with its bill (frame 2), and finally it tucks the egg under its body and into the nest (frame 3). These stimulus-elicited behaviors are known as **modal action patterns**[3]. This term is preferred over the original term *fixed action pattern*[4], which erroneously suggests that the movements are always the same (i.e., fixed). In fact, the movements made are adapted to suit the conditions of execution. For example, egg retrieval requires that the bird reach in the right direction (towards the egg!) and the right distance. In addition, if the egg starts to slip away as it is pulled back towards the nest, the bird makes corrective side-to-side movements of its head to prevent the egg slipping away.

Notice that a modal action pattern is not elicited merely as the direct result of proximal stimulation. The animal must also identify the distal stimulus: the male bird must identify a female bird of his species, the goose must identify an egg. This requirement for recognition and identification is something that distinguishes modal action patterns from reflexes. Note that it is also a difference between reflexes and the other two types of elicited behavior described above.

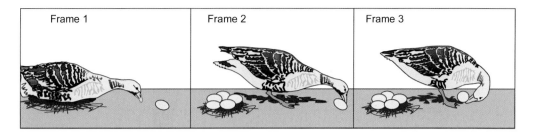

Figure 5.2: *A sequence of three frames of a movie showing a graylag goose retrieving an egg. Based on Lorenz and Tinbergen (1938).*

5.1.4 Some types of stimulus-elicited behavior are genetically determined

Reflex-type elicited behaviors are sometimes said to be hard-wired into the nervous system. This means that the circuits responsible are laid down during the early development of the nervous system under genetic control. Stimulus-elicited behaviors of this kind are said to be **genetically determined** (defined below). This must not be taken to mean that the environment plays no role in the development of these behaviors: all characteristics of animals are the result of an interaction between genes and the environments in which they are expressed. Genes are in a sense analogous to instructions that are carried out by a machine: the 'machine' is the environment (including the organism itself), which is governed by the laws of chemistry and physics.

Modal action patterns like courtship displays and egg-retrieval are different from reflexes in that they tend to be different in different species. Different species have very different courtship displays, and birds that nest in trees do not exhibit a retrieval response, whereas many reflexes such as the pupiliary light reflex and the muscle stretch reflex are similar in a large number of quite different species. Behaviors exhibited by only one species or a small group of related species are said to be **species specific** (though they might only be exhibited by one sex, e.g., males in the case of courtship displays). Elicited behaviors of this kind can often be elicited from an animal without it ever having to learn how to perform them or having to practice them. In such cases, the behaviors are often said to be instinctive, which is just another way of saying that they are genetically determined:

> **GENETICALLY DETERMINED BEHAVIOR** (also instinctive behavior): behavior that develops without being practiced and without any other obvious, performance-relevant experience. It appears complete and functional on its first performance.

Genetically determined does not necessarily mean that no experience of any kind is necessary for it to be performed, nor does it mean that the behavior cannot be influenced by experience and learning. We return to these matters in Part III.

5.1.5 The response may be driven by the eliciting stimulus

How does a stimulus actually elicit a behavioral response? Two possibilities can be distinguished: in one the stimulus *drives* the response, in the other, the stimulus releases the response. We will discuss the first in this section.

Figure 5.3 shows a neural pathway that links a receptor to a muscle. If the receptor is stimulated, action potentials will be evoked in the sensory axon and transmitted along the pathway to the muscle, which will contract. The muscle contraction is a response to the stimulus, a simple kind of stimulus-elicited behavior. In this situation, the stimulus evokes the action

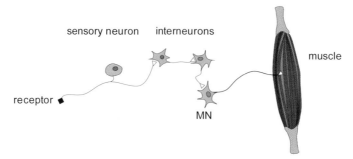

Figure 5.3: *Neural pathway from receptor to muscle.*

potentials that are transmitted to the muscle, and cause it to contract. This is what is meant by the statement that the eliciting stimulus 'drives' the response. Here is a definition:

> **STIMULUS-DRIVEN RESPONSE:** A stimulus-elicited behavior in which the neural activity that causes the muscle contractions derives directly from that evoked by the eliciting stimulus in the axons of sensory neurons.

It is clear that a stimulus-driven response will have characteristics that are determined by the stimulus. For example, a stimulus that persists for a long time may continue to evoke action potentials in the afferents for as long as it lasts. Thus, the contractile response will be sustained for as long as the action potentials continue to reach the muscle. A stimulus of short duration will evoke neural activity for a shorter time and so evoke a shorter-duration contraction.

Stimulus-elicited behaviors in which the response is driven by the stimulus often turn out to be the behavioral manifestations of either negative feedback control mechanisms or, in a few cases, sensory feedforward control mechanisms. We will encounter examples later in the chapter and in Chapter 6.

5.1.6 The response may be released by the eliciting stimulus

Not all stimulus-elicited behaviors can be understood in terms of pathways that transmit stimulus-evoked activity directly from the sensory receptors to the muscles. For example, a brief glimpse of a hawk overhead will send chickens dashing for a hiding place – a response that will likely be sustained for as long as it takes a bird to reach a safe location, however brief the eliciting stimulus. In this case, a brief stimulus elicits a sustained response. The stimulus-evoked neural activity dies away quickly once stimulation has ceased, so the activation that sustains the response cannot be directly evoked by the stimulus. To understand what is going on in these cases, we must suppose that there is a source of activity within the animal's nervous system that drives the response and that this activity is released by the eliciting stimulus.

The idea can be explained by making use of the fluid analogy[5]. Imagine a large tank full of water, with an outlet pipe with a spring-loaded valve as shown in Figure 5.4. The spring holds the valve closed until it is opened by pulling on the attached rod. The latch holds the valve open after the pull has stopped. When the valve is open, the water in the tank can flow out through the outlet pipe; water will continue to flow out as long as the latch holds the valve open. Think of a pull on the rod as analogous to a stimulus. Water flowing from the outlet pipe can then be thought of as a response elicited by this stimulus. In this case the pull (stimulus) simply *allows* the water to flow out (response): it releases the water from the tank. In an analogous way, we can think of a sensory stimulus as releasing neural activity stored in some sort of reservoir. Of course, action potentials themselves cannot be stored, so the idea is that of a neural mechanism that generates action potentials when it receives a signal to do so.

This signal derives from the eliciting stimulus. Thus, a glimpse of a hawk elicits the chicken's dash for cover, but continuous viewing of the hawk is not needed to sustain the dash. Many modal action patterns (section 5.1.3) are released by their eliciting stimuli. When an eliciting stimulus acts in this way it is sometimes called a *releasing stimulus*.

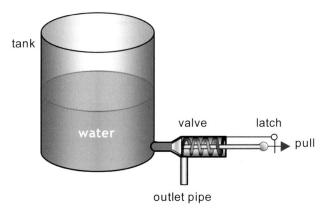

Figure 5.4: *Water tank with spring-loaded valve on the outlet.*

To summarize, here is a definition of a response released by the eliciting stimulus:

> **STIMULUS-RELEASED RESPONSE:** A stimulus-elicited behavior where the neural activity that causes the muscle contractions does not derive from the eliciting stimulus. The activity is produced by a response-generating mechanism that generates it when it receives a signal derived from the eliciting stimulus.

The characteristics of stimulus-released responses do not depend on the eliciting stimulus like stimulus-driven responses do. The response characteristics depend on the activity produced by the response-generating mechanism. The stimulus merely provides the signal that triggers the mechanism into generating neural activity. This means that not only is the response largely independent of the strength of the eliciting stimulus, it is also independent of the duration of the eliciting stimulus. Once the response has been triggered, it will be executed to completion regardless of whether the eliciting stimulus persists or not. The response is said to be **all-or-nothing**: egg-retrieval is an example (see section 5.1.8).

Having now made the distinction between stimulus-driven responses and stimulus-released responses, it is important to be aware that it is not necessarily a case of either one or the other. There are stimulus-elicited behaviors that cannot be easily classified as being stimulus-driven or as stimulus-released, since they have characteristics of both types.

5.1.7 The basic differences between driven and released responses

To summarize the previous sections, stimulus-driven responses differ from stimulus-released responses as follows:

▶ The characteristics of a stimulus-driven response depend on the characteristics of the (proximal) stimulation that drives it. (The nervous system transforms stimulus-evoked activity into efferent activity.)

▶ The characteristics of a (purely) stimulus-released response are independent of the characteristics of the stimulus that released it. (The nervous system does not transform stimulus-evoked activity into efferent activity.)

Is there functional significance to this difference that makes stimulus release appropriate for some behaviors and stimulus drive appropriate for others? The answer is yes, and some examples will explain why.

A stimulus-driven response will be more forceful, faster and/or of greater amplitude when the eliciting stimulus is stronger, and will be of longer duration when the stimulus lasts for longer. These characteristics are important for responses like the pupiliary light reflex response: a greater change in light intensity should produce a larger change in pupil size, and the pupil should remain at an appropriate size for as long as the light remains at any given intensity. The same is true for any reflex that is a manifestation of negative feedback control (see Chapter 6) or of sensory feedforward control (e.g., the vestibulo-ocular reflex; see section 5.4.3).

The forcefulness, speed and/or amplitude of a (purely) stimulus-released response are unaffected by the strength of the releasing stimulus. This is important for a response such as a gaze saccade (a rapid turn of the head, the eyes, and possibly also the body that reorients the direction you are looking; see Chapter 4). Saccades can be elicited reflexively by various stimuli, including auditory and visual stimuli. For example, a flash of light in peripheral vision can elicit a reflexive turn of the eyes and head so as to look in the direction of the flash. To achieve this, the turn needs to be of the right amplitude – turn too far or not far enough, and your eyes won't be looking in the direction of the stimulus. In short, the amplitude of the saccadic gaze shift needs to be independent of the intensity of the flash and other characteristics of the flash, such as its color. To be effective, the shift amplitude should depend only on the location of the flash on the retina and be independent of the characteristics of the flash itself. Chapter 6 gives more details concerning how reflex saccades are generated.

In summary, to be effective at achieving an appropriate outcome, some elicited responses need to depend on (proximal) stimulus characteristics, while others should be independent of stimulus characteristics. The stimulus-driven mode is appropriate for the former, the stimulus-released mode for the latter. Most modal action patterns are stimulus-released responses, as briefly discussed next.

5.1.8 What are the characteristics of modal action patterns?

The egg-retrieval response (Figure 5.2) is an example of a stimulus-released response. As such, its execution is expected to be independent of the strength and duration of the eliciting stimulus. The latter is straightforward to demonstrate: if the egg is taken away after the bird has started the response, the response does not stop. The bird performs the whole behavior to completion, but without the egg. It is not so clear how to demonstrate that the response is independent of stimulus strength, since the eliciting stimulus is an egg, and there is no obvious way to define the strength of an egg stimulus.

An egg is a distal stimulus (an object in the environment), not a proximal stimulus. In order for the retrieval response to be released, the bird must identify that there is an egg to be retrieved, so that it doesn't waste time and effort trying to 'retrieve' other things such as small rocks and stones. How egg-like does something have to be in order for the bird to retrieve it? The answer to this question will help us to understand what stimulus strength means in this context.

A brooding bird will retrieve one of its own eggs, but it will also retrieve objects that closely resemble its eggs. What is surprising is that it may retrieve objects that seem to us not to resemble eggs at all: a herring gull, for example, will retrieve rectangular blocks and doorknobs. However, a real egg is better at releasing the response than is a rectangular block. This can be demonstrated by giving a bird a choice of an egg and another object and then seeing which one it goes for. In one experimental study with herring gulls[6], brooding birds were presented with a choice between two dummy 'eggs' which could be one of two different shapes (egg-shaped or block-shaped), be one of two different colors (brown or green), and be speckled or plain. Real gull eggs are pale brown with speckles. When faced with various choices, the egg that the bird retrieved was recorded. Each choice pair was presented several times. If a choice was presented ten times and the bird chose one of the objects more than five times, then the bird is said to prefer that object over the other one. If both are chosen five out of ten times, then the bird shows no preference. A stimulus object that is preferred over another is said to have a higher **releasing value**, which constitutes a measure of the strength of the stimulus.

A preference chart can be constructed from a bird's choices to show pictorially which eggs are preferred over others. Figure 5.5 shows a selection from such a chart. It shows that plain green eggs are preferred over brown speckled eggs of the same size – they have the same releasing value as brown speckled eggs about two sizes larger (sizes are numbered 5 to 16). Green speckled eggs have the highest releasing value of all. A size 11 green speckled egg, for example, has about the same releasing value as a size 15 brown speckled egg. These results are surprising, because real gull eggs are brown and speckled with an average size of about 10: a gull would preferentially retrieve a larger, plain green dummy egg over a real egg of its own. A stimulus that is more effective at eliciting a behavior than the natural object of the behavior is called a *supernormal stimulus*.

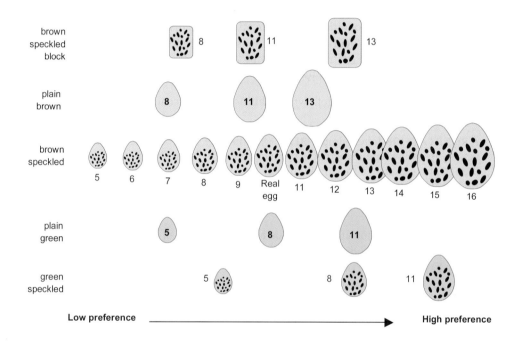

Figure 5.5: *Partial preference chart for egg retrieval, see text for details. (Based on data reported in Baerends, Blokzijl, Kruijt, 1982.)*

The releasing value determines which of two stimuli is preferred and also whether a response is released or not. The releasing value could be zero, meaning that the stimulus does not elicit the response at all; in general, the higher the releasing value, the more likely it is to elicit the response. However, the vigor and amplitude of the response are independent of releasing value: a bird does not reach further and pull more vigorously on an egg with a high releasing value. The distance reached depends on the location of the stimulus, not on its releasing value. Thus, stimulus characteristics such as size, color, texture and brightness do not affect response vigor.

5.2 Reflexes

5.2.1 Introduction: a reflex is a kind of stimulus-elicited behavior

Many stimulus-elicited behaviors are examples of what are typically called *reflex actions* (or simply *reflexes*). Reflexes are distinguished from other types of stimulus-elicited behavior by two key characteristics:

▸ The response to a discrete stimulus is a discrete action, such as an eye blink or, in some cases, a sustained period of activity that may be cyclical or repetitive (e.g., scratching).
▸ Elicitation occurs as a direct consequence of the proximal stimulation of a specific group of sensory receptors. No recognition or identification of the distal stimulus is involved – the proximal stimulus evokes neural activity in sensory afferents and this activity evokes the behavioral response. A startle response will be elicited by a loud noise without a person needing to identify what sort of noise it was.

These considerations suggest the following definition of a reflex action:

> **A REFLEX ACTION (often simply 'REFLEX'):** a discrete action or a period of sustained activity (possibly repetitive) that is produced as a direct, involuntary and relatively immediate response to the stimulation of a specific population of sensory receptors. No identification of a *distal stimulus* is involved.

Notice that both a behavior and a stimulus are components of a reflex action. The names given to reflexes often include explicit references to both: the *air-puff eye-blink reflex* is an example we have already encountered. The reason for making explicit reference to the stimulus in this case is that there are other kinds of eye-blink reflexes. One of these is the acoustic startle eye-blink reflex, in which the eye-blink is produced in response to a sudden, loud noise. Although both reflexes involve an eye-blink response, the eliciting stimulus is different and so they are different reflexes.

5.2.2 There are skeletomotor and autonomic reflexes

Almost all examples of reflexes that will be discussed in this book are **skeletomotor reflexes** – reflexes in which the response is produced by the activity of skeletal muscles. Of course, there are reflexes that do not involve skeletal muscles. These are the **autonomic reflexes**: reflexes mediated by the autonomic nervous system. Autonomic reflex responses are produced by the activity of smooth muscles, cardiac muscle, and glands such as the salivary glands and the pancreas.

Two autonomic reflexes that we have already encountered are involved in seeing – the *pupiliary light reflex* and the *accommodation reflex* of the eye. The latter acts to bring a blurry retinal image into sharp focus: the eliciting stimulus is blurriness of the retinal image, and the response is a change in lens thickness produced by a change in the contractile state of the ciliary muscle (a smooth muscle). The pupiliary light reflex involves changes in the size of the pupil in response to variations in the amount of light reaching the eye. The purpose of this reflex is to regulate the amount of light reaching the retinas so that there is sufficient to see but not enough to damage the retinas. The reflex is effective, but it cannot cause the pupils to close completely. Light can sometimes become so intense that even the smallest pupils let in enough light to produce retinal damage. In such situations, skeletomotor reflex responses are elicited that prevent light reaching the retinas. These include closing of the eyelids, turning the head away from the light source and covering the eyes with a hand or arm.

As you can appreciate from the descriptions of the pupiliary and accommodation reflexes, their responses are very simple. However, this is not generally the case for skeletomotor reflexes, as we will see in the following sections.

5.2.3 Skeletomotor and autonomic reflex responses often occur in combination

Some autonomic reflex responses occur in combination with skeletomotor responses and are elicited by the same stimulus event. Consider, for example, the acoustic startle reflex: a sudden loud noise like a balloon pop elicits the skeletomotor startle response – a flinch or jump that involves skeletal muscles in the face and neck and also in the limbs (in the case of a jump). The same loud pop is also likely to elicit autonomic responses such as an increase in heart rate, release of adrenalin, and vasodilatory responses in peripheral blood vessels. These autonomic responses tend to provide support for skeletomotor activity. For example, vasodilation and increased heart rate result in an increase of blood flow to skeletal muscles. This is useful because whatever caused the startling stimulus might need to be run away from or engaged in battle ('flight or fight'): in either case the muscles will require more oxygen from the blood. Notice that the autonomic responses are elicited by the same stimulus that elicits the motor behavioral response: it is not the case that the autonomic responses are a reaction to the muscle activity produced by the motor behavioral response. This means that the autonomic responses are anticipatory, since they prepare the body for skeletomotor activity. Figure 5.6 shows a schematic representation of this situation, with the stimulus leading to activation of both the autonomic and the somatic nervous systems.

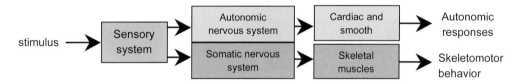

Figure 5.6: *A stimulus can elicit both autonomic and skeletomotor reflex responses.*

5.2.4 Skeletomotor reflex responses are seldom simple

Some reflex responses like eye-blinks and changes in pupil size are very simple. However, such examples give the erroneous impression that simplicity is a defining feature of reflex responses. Quite the opposite is actually the case: the vast majority of skeletomotor reflex responses are not simple. As an example, consider a sneeze. When people sneeze they may go 'ah, ah, ah, ah … TCHOOOO'. The 'ah, ah, ah...' part involves breathing in and is called the *inspiratory phase*. The 'TCHOOOO' part involves a forceful breathing out and is called the *expiratory phase*. The inspiratory phase is characterized by brief contractions of the diaphragm and of the external intercostal and abductor muscles of the upper airway, as well as neck extension and opening of the mouth using the orofacial and jaw muscles. The expiratory phase involves a relaxation of all inspiratory muscles, a glottal narrowing, flexion of the neck, closure of the eyes and changes in the activation of muscles of the mouth and jaw. The activation and relaxation of all these muscles needs to be properly coordinated if the sneeze is to be effectively executed.

Clearly, a sneeze is not a particularly simple sort of response, but involves the coordinated activation of a large number of muscles distributed throughout the body. Most reflex responses involve the coordinated contraction of a large number of muscles; many examples will be given later in the chapter. The simple part of a reflex action is not the response, but the way in which the response is elicited: neural activity evoked by stimulation of sensory receptors is transmitted directly to response production mechanisms.

5.2.5 Skeletomotor reflex responses are seldom stereotyped: they are goal-directed

Blinks are not just simple, they are also *stereotyped* actions. This means that they are always very much the same. This suggests that reflex responses might be stereotyped contractions in a specific muscle or set of muscles. However, this is not generally the case: most skeletomotor reflex responses do not involve stereotyped contractions of a fixed set of muscles. A particularly good illustration is provided by the wiping reflex of the frog.

When something irritates the skin of a frog, the animal typically responds by wiping a hind foot across the skin at the location of the irritation. Figure 5.7 shows how the response is executed[7]: in frame 1 the frog has moved its foot into a position under (caudal to) the irritating stimulus (small black diamond). In frame 2 the frog has begun to extend the leg, and the foot has moved closer to the stimulus. In frame 3, the frog has completed the leg extension that has wiped the stimulus from the skin. The function of this reflex is obvious – the wipe tends to remove the source of irritation. Successful removal requires that the foot is wiped across the skin at the location of the irritation. If the movements of the limb elicited by the irritating stimulus were always the same (stereotyped), then the foot would always be wiped over the same location on the skin, and irritants located anywhere else could never be removed. Of course, the foot is wiped over the skin at the location of the irritant, so the movements of the limb cannot possibly be the same every time the response is elicited.

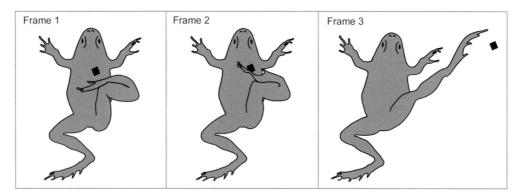

Figure 5.7: *Frog wiping reflex: the frog wipes off an irritating stimulus (diamond) with its right foot.*

Figure 5.8 shows the position of the foot prior to wiping irritating stimuli in two different locations, both different from that in Figure 5.7. The initial positioning of the foot is called the *aiming phase* of the reflex. Figure 5.8 shows the frog's leg in the postures reached at the end of the aiming phase. It is clear that the posture depends on the location of the stimulus, and so the aiming phase involves movements that are different depending on the location of the stimulus.

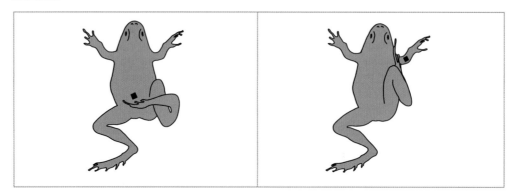

Figure 5.8: *Position of foot prior to wiping depends on the stimulus location.*

Much of the research into the frog's wiping reflex has been conducted on spinal preparations in which the frog's spinal cord is severed just rostral to the hindbrain, so the animal's brain can no longer communicate with its body. The wiping reflex is functionally intact in spinal frogs, which means that it is generated by neural circuits located entirely within the spinal cord[8]. The wiping reflex in the spinal frog shows a remarkable degree of adaptability to different circumstances, as illustrated by the following examples.

Example 1: In Figure 5.7, the stimulus is on the right side of the frog's body. As you might expect, if the stimulus is on the left side, the frog will use its left leg.

Example 2: In the right panel of Figure 5.8, the stimulus is located on the frog's foreleg. Clearly, the position the hind leg needs to adopt prior to wiping does not only depend on where on the skin of the foreleg the stimulus is located; it also depends on the posture of the foreleg. A spinal frog has no difficulty aiming the rear foot appropriately and wiping off the stimulus when the foreleg is in different postures. This shows that the frog's spinal cord is able to take the position of the foreleg into account in the production of the wiping movements of the hind leg.

Example 3: A surprising example of the ability of reflex mechanisms to take into account the posture of the body is demonstrated when a spinal frog is laid over a small object on a flat surface. This puts the frog in a humped posture, with its head and its hind legs lower than the middle of its body. In this posture the frog cannot reach the back of its head with either rear leg. What does it do to remove an irritant in this location? The answer is that it moves one hind leg into a suitable location while simultaneously inflating its throat to raise its head enough so that the subsequent leg extension will remove the irritant. A spinalized frog will do this spontaneously on the first attempt.

Example 4: If a spinal frog's normal hind leg movement is prevented by placing a cast on one of the joints of a leg so that the joint cannot flex or extend, the wiping reaction will still be effectively executed with this leg. The other joints that are free to move will compensate for the lack of movement in the cast joint. Moreover, the frog needs no practice to achieve this feat – it can remove the stimulus on the first attempt.

These findings show that even reflex reactions mediated by spinal circuits are not simply fixed patterns of contractions in particular groups of muscles, or fixed movements.

The ability to achieve the same outcome in different conditions by using different muscles and body segments is a defining characteristic of goal-directed behavior (Chapter 1). The frog's wiping reflex response can only be understood as a goal-directed action: the goal is to remove an irritating stimulus from the skin. Thus, the muscles, joints and movements involved in executing the response will depend on the conditions: the location of the stimulus, the posture of the body, and any restrictions imposed by such things as a limb cast.

5.2.6 Different types of skeletomotor reflex

In section 5.1 we drew a distinction between responses that are driven by the eliciting stimulus and responses that are released by the eliciting stimulus. The majority of reflexes can be understood in terms of the stimulus driving the response; exceptions include the frog's wiping reflex and the scratch reflex (see below). Since there are these two types of reflex, it will sometimes be useful to have a terminological means for distinguishing them. We will use the term **standard reflex** to designate those in which the stimulus drives the response:

> **STANDARD REFLEX:** a reflex in which the eliciting stimulus drives the response: the neural activation of the muscles (efference) is derived directly from neural activity evoked by the eliciting stimulus in sensory neurons (afference).

Thus, a standard reflex involves a direct *sensorimotor transformation* of afference into efference, and so variations in response execution (e.g., increases and decreases in amplitude) follow corresponding variations in the stimulus (e.g., increases and decreases in stimulus strength). Many standard reflexes are, in fact, the observable activity of negative feedback control systems, and so the terms *stimulus* and *response* are not necessarily very informative (see Chapter 6). A *non-standard reflex* is a reflex in which the response is not driven by eliciting stimulus, and so there can be variations in response execution that are independent of the stimulus.

Non-standard reflexes may involve the release of activity by the stimulus (see section 5.1.5), but this is not necessarily the case, as the example of the scratch reflex illustrates. The function of the scratch reflex is to remove skin irritants, and it is displayed by mammals and birds. Like the frog's wiping reflex, the scratch response involves an aiming phase that moves a limb into the right position. This is followed by a repeated cycle of movement that moves the foot, paw or hand back and forth across the skin (scratching); the two phases typically merge together. The aiming part of the response needs to be relatively independent of the eliciting stimulus strength, because its purpose is to move the foot or paw to a particular place. In contrast, the scratching movement is typically more vigorous when the stimulus is stronger. This is illustrated in Figure 5.9, which shows the type of results obtained by Sherrington using spinalized dogs[9]. Panel (A) shows the response to a weak stimulus, and panel (B) the response to a strong stimulus. The figure uses a standard diagrammatic convention for representing a stimulus that has constant characteristics during its delivery: the orange bar represents the time for which the stimulus is on.

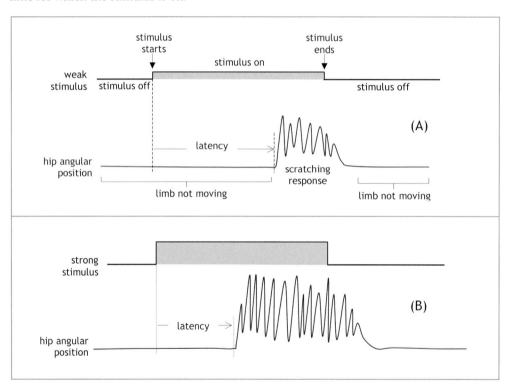

Figure 5.9: *Scratching response evoked by strong and weak stimulation. Based on data reported in Sherrington (1906/1947).*

Notice that stimulus strength has two effects on the response in Figure 5.9: the latency is shorter when the stimulus is stronger, and the amplitude of the response is greater (more vigorous) when the stimulus is stronger. As we will see later, these two features are characteristic of stimulus-driven responses. However, the response has two characteristics not exhibited by driven responses. First, the response movement cycles do not follow variations in the stimulus, which is sustained at a constant level. Second, the scratching movements continue for a short time after the stimulus has stopped. Partly on the basis of these features, Sherrington suggested that the scratching movements are produced by the activity of a spinal circuit that produces rhythmic bursts of activity when activated; these bursts are transmitted to the muscles to produce cyclical movements. The simplest such circuits are called (non-autonomous) **rhythm generators**:

> **RHYTHM GENERATOR (non-autonomous):** A simple neural circuit that produces rhythmic, repetitive bursts of activity when excited by a constant (tonic) activating signal.

A non-autonomous rhythm generator does not have its own store of activation. It needs a source of tonic activation to produce rhythmic output signals. In the case of the scratch reflex, this tonic activation is provided by a sustained eliciting stimulus. The afferent activity evoked by the stimulus powers the rhythm generator, which produces phasic bursts of efferent activity as illustrated in Figure 5.10. Rhythm generators are involved in a number of cyclical motor behaviors such as locomotion (walking and running; see Chapter 8).

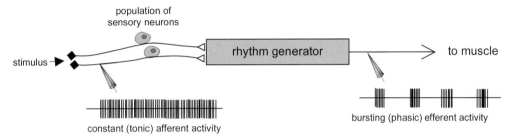

Figure 5.10: *A rhythm generator produces rhythmic bursts of action potentials (efferent activity) in response to a continuous train of action potentials (tonic afferent input).*

5.3 Elemental Reflexes: The Building Blocks of Reflex Action

5.3.1 Introduction: reflexes are built from multiple components

In the last section we saw that many reflex responses are not particularly simple – coughs, sneezes, wipes and scratches all involve coordinated activity in multiple muscles. Wipes and scratches are goal-directed actions that serve a useful purpose in the everyday life of a person or animal. How are such goal-directed responses generated? What kind of neural mechanisms are capable of generating coordinated patterns of movement in direct response to stimuli? These are questions that will be examined in the remainder of this chapter.

The basic approach to understanding how complex things work is to suppose that they are built of simpler component parts that can be easily understood. The first problem is to identify the components, and the second is to show how their combination explains the working of the original complex thing. Charles Sherrington was one of the first to adopt this **combinatorial approach** for the analysis of reflexes. Sherrington's idea was that natural, functional reflexes with complex responses are built of components that are themselves reflexes, but simpler ones. A complex reflex can then be understood in terms of the combined action of a number of these simple components. In this part of the chapter, we will develop the idea of *elemental reflexes* as the building blocks of standard reflexes[10].

5.3.2 Elemental reflexes are the components of natural reflexes

To understand a complex, goal-directed reflex in terms of simple components, the components themselves cannot have the characteristics that we want to explain or understand. Functional reflex responses involve coordination of multiple muscles, and which muscles are involved often depend on the circumstances. The reflex components can have neither of these characteristics; neither is possible if a reflex component involves only one muscle. In addition, the simplest and most fundamental elements of reflex action should not be further divisible into components that are reflexes. This implies that their responses should be unitary. What exactly this means will be illustrated later with examples; for the moment just think of a unitary response as one that cannot be meaningfully divided into parts. Thus, an elemental reflex can be defined as follows:

> **ELEMENTAL REFLEX:** a standard reflex in which the response is confined to a single, specific muscle and cannot be meaningfully divided into separate response components.

This definition means, of course, that if a reflex response involves multiple muscles it must involve the combined action of multiple elemental reflexes. Figure 5.11 shows a block diagram representation of a reflex mechanism that is composed of multiple elemental component mechanisms. An eliciting stimulus evokes a behavioral response from the natural reflex mechanism that is built from a number (N) of elemental reflex mechanisms that each consist of a reflex circuit connected to an individual muscle. Although somewhat simplified[11], this picture provides a visual impression of the basic idea. Next we consider the analysis of the stretch reflex into a set of elemental components.

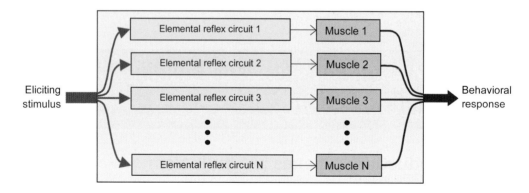

Figure 5.11: *A natural reflex mechanism is built from a number of elemental mechanisms.*

5.3.3 The autogenic stretch reflex has multiple components

When a muscle is stretched, it tends to reflexively contract in response. This is the **autogenic stretch reflex**:

> **AUTOGENIC STRETCH REFLEX:** the reflex for which the eliciting stimulus is a stretch of a particular muscle and the response is contraction of that same muscle.

The word *autogenic* simply means that the response is in the same muscle that was stretched (as we will see later, stretching a muscle can also elicit responses in other muscles). Since the stretch lengthens the muscle and a contraction shortens it, the reflex acts to counteract the stretch. In fact, as will be discussed in detail in the next chapter, the reflex has a negative feedback action.

Although the autogenic stretch reflex response is confined to a single muscle, the reflex is not elemental, because the response can be divided into several components. To illustrate this, consider a simple experiment in which the flexor muscles of the elbow are unexpectedly stretched by a forced extension of the elbow. Figure 5.12 (left) illustrates the situation: the elbow is forcibly and rapidly extended by about 20°, which stretches the flexor muscles. In the figure, EMG activity is being recorded from the biceps muscle, and so only the response of this one muscle is being examined. The right side of Figure 5.12 shows the muscle stretch as a function of time at the top and the EMG response (rectified, smoothed) recorded from the biceps at the bottom.

The response shows four peaks, suggesting that it is a compound of four components. These components are referred to as M1, M2, M3 and V (the peaks in Figure 5.12 are labeled accordingly). M1 occurs first; its latency depends on the muscle concerned, but typically lies between about 15 and 50 milliseconds. M2 occurs second, with a latency of between about 70 and 100 milliseconds; M3 follows about 20 to 30 milliseconds later. Finally the V occurs; its latency is typically between about 150 and 200 milliseconds. V is considered to be a voluntary reaction to the stretch. If a person is instructed not to respond to the stretch, V is typically absent. M1, M2 and M3 are reflex responses, though M2 and M3 are typically much reduced if a person is instructed not to respond.

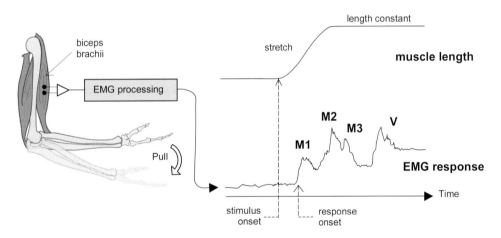

Figure 5.12: *Response components of the autogenic stretch reflex (illustrative).*

The three reflex components are mediated by different neural mechanisms. Spinalized animals – animals in which the spinal cord is surgically disconnected from the brain – possess the M1 component, but lack the other components in muscles below the neck. This demonstrates that the neural mechanism of M1 is confined to the spinal cord and peripheral nervous system – the brain is not involved in this reflex. A reflex of this sort is called a *spinal reflex*; here is a definition:

> **SPINAL REFLEX:** any reflex mediated by neural mechanisms that are confined to the peripheral nervous systems and spinal cord.

The absence of M2 and M3 in spinal animals suggests that they involve structures in the brain. For this reason, M2 and M3 are sometimes known as *long loop* reflex responses, because the neural mechanism involves a pathway that goes to the brain and back (a long loop). In the next section, the M1 response is discussed in more detail and shown to be a combination of the responses of two components.

5.3.4 The spinal autogenic stretch reflex has two components

Responses of the spinal autogenic stretch reflex to two types of stretch stimulus are shown in Figure 5.13. The stimulus in panel A is brief and impulsive – the muscle is stretched very quickly and then returns to its original length, all in just a few milliseconds. In panel B the muscle is rapidly lengthened and then held at the extended length (step stimulus). The responses to these stimuli are shown as EMG recordings (rectified and smoothed) from the stretched muscle. The response to the impulsive stimulus is a brief burst of activity that produces a brief muscle contraction. This is a **phasic** response. The response to the step stimulus is a little different. There is an initial burst, after which the muscle activity is sustained at a higher level than before the stretch. The sustained activity is a **tonic** response.

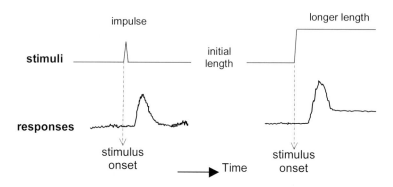

Figure 5.13: *EMG responses (rectified, smoothed) to impulsive and step stretch stimuli (illustrative).*

The phasic and tonic reflex responses are elicited by different aspects of the stretch stimulus. The phasic component is elicited by muscle lengthening. The tonic response is elicited by sustained stretch of the muscle: in an impulsive stimulus, the muscle stretch only lasts momentarily, not long enough to elicit a tonic response. Figure 5.14 illustrates further details of the phasic and tonic responses. Panel A reproduces the step stimulus of Figure 5.13: because the muscle is lengthened very quickly, this stimulus elicits a phasic response as well as a tonic response. In panel B the stretching takes place more slowly (ramp stimulus), and the phasic response is smaller in amplitude than in A. In panel C the stretching is very slow, and the response follows the stimulus: no phasic response is evident. In panel C, the speed of muscle lengthening is below the threshold necessary to elicit a phasic response, and only the tonic response is present.

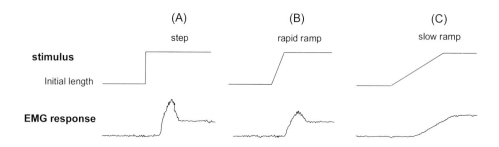

Figure 5.14: *EMG responses to step and ramp stretch stimuli (illustrative).*

Results like those shown in Figure 5.14 indicate that the spinal autogenic stretch reflex response is composed of two components elicited by different stimuli: a phasic component elicited by the speed of muscle lengthening, and a tonic component elicited by the amount of stretch. The two response components cannot be further subdivided; they are unitary responses. Thus, we can conclude that there are two elemental reflexes that contribute to the spinal autogenic stretch reflex[12]. These are called the (autogenic) **phasic stretch reflex** and the (autogenic) **tonic stretch reflex**:

> **(AUTOGENIC) PHASIC STRETCH REFLEX:** an elemental spinal reflex in which the eliciting stimulus is the speed of muscle stretching and the response is a phasic contraction of the stretched muscle.
>
> **(AUTOGENIC) TONIC STRETCH REFLEX:** an elemental spinal reflex in which the eliciting stimulus is the amount of muscle stretch and the response is a contraction of the stretched muscle that is sustained for as long as the stretch persists.

Since Ia spinal afferents respond to the speed of muscle lengthening, whereas type II afferents respond primarily to muscle length, you might imagine that Ia afferents are involved in the phasic reflex and type II afferents in the tonic reflex. This is partly true, as we will see later when we consider the neural mechanism underlying the phasic reflex.

5.3.5 The reflex arc is the simplest reflex mechanism

Figure 5.3 shows a neural circuit that connects a sensory receptor to a single muscle. Such pathways are the basic mechanistic elements of standard reflexes, and they are known as reflex arcs. Here is a definition:

> **(SKELETOMOTOR) REFLEX ARC:** a linked chain of individual neurons that connects a single sensory receptor to a single α-motoneuron.

Thus, a reflex arc always connects a sensory receptor to a single muscle. Two further examples are shown in panel A of Figure 5.15. The arc on the left has no interneurons: the sensory neuron makes synaptic connections directly with the motoneuron. This type of reflex arc is called a **monosynaptic arc** because it involves just one set of synaptic connections (those between the sensory neuron and the motoneuron). The arc on the right has one interneuron and is called a **disynaptic arc**. An arc with two interneurons is a **trisynaptic arc**. Arcs with more than two interneurons are usually simply called **polysynaptic arcs**.

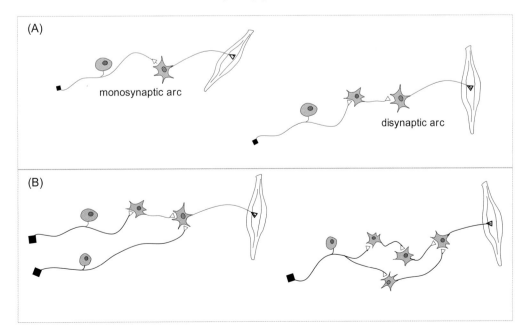

Figure 5.15: *Various reflex arcs.*

Panel B of Figure 5.15 shows arcs that share neurons. On the left are two arcs that share the same motoneuron: one arc is disynaptic, the other monosynaptic. On the right there are two arcs that share the same sensory neuron as well as the same motoneuron: one is disynaptic, the other trisynaptic.

Of course, a skeletal muscle is never innervated by just one motoneuron but by a whole population of them – the motoneuron pool (Chapter 2). Likewise, there is never just one sensory receptor of a particular type, but a whole population. Thus, there is never just one reflex arc, but a group of them connecting a population of sensory receptors to a population of motoneurons. Such a group of reflex arcs is the basic neural mechanism of an elemental reflex, and for this reason we will refer to it as an **elemental reflex pathway**.

5.3.6 The phasic stretch reflex has a monosynaptic pathway

The neural mechanism underlying the autogenic phasic stretch reflex is a monosynaptic reflex pathway[13]. The basic element of this pathway is the **monosynaptic stretch reflex arc**. Almost all the skeletal muscles in the human body are equipped with monosynaptic stretch reflex arcs. Only a very few skeletal muscles do not have them; these include the extraocular muscles[14]. Figure 5.16 shows one such arc where the muscle involved is the biceps. The arc connects the Ia afferent ending in a single muscle spindle embedded in the biceps to an α-motoneuron that innervates the muscle (a *homonymous* motoneuron).

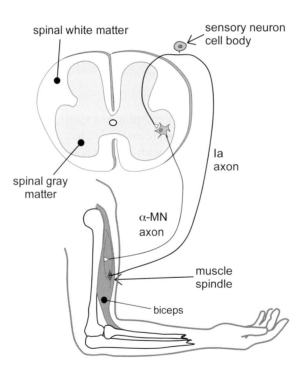

Figure 5.16: *Monosynaptic stretch reflex arc.*

The biceps monosynaptic stretch reflex pathway is comprised of all the elemental arcs of the sort shown in Figure 5.16, that is, all the arcs that connect the Ia endings in the whole population of muscle spindles to the α-motoneurons in the biceps motoneuron pool. Since the afferent endings are all type Ia, the eliciting stimulus for the reflex is speed of muscle lengthening, as described earlier (section 5.3.4).

5.3.7 The monosynaptic stretch reflex pathway is densely interconnected

The monosynaptic stretch reflex pathway is not simply a whole bunch of separate elemental reflex arcs of the sort shown in Figure 5.16. The arcs are interconnected and intermingled in an intricate way. For example, each Ia afferent typically synapses directly not just with one α-motoneuron but with a large number of them. Indeed, it has been reported that for certain muscles, a single Ia afferent may make monosynaptic connections with all the α-motoneurons in the pool[15]. Figure 5.17 shows a simplified representation of the monosynaptic connections made by a single Ia spindle afferent: the afferent axon branches to synapse with all five α-motoneurons in a pool. In real muscles, a single Ia fiber may synapse with several hundred motoneurons. Since each Ia afferent connects to most of the homonymous motoneurons, it follows that most individual motoneurons receive inputs from most of the Ia afferents. Thus, the monosynaptic reflex pathway comprises a densely interconnected system of monosynaptic arcs linking the population of Ia spindle afferents to the homonymous motoneuron pool.

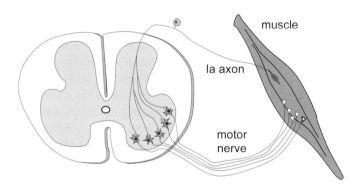

Figure 5.17: *A single Ia afferent makes connections with many α-MNs.*

5.3.8 Elemental reflex responses are almost impossible to elicit on their own

Functional reflex responses typically involve contributions from multiple elemental reflexes, but is it possible to elicit just the response of a single elemental reflex? It is extremely difficult to achieve this, as we will illustrate using *tendon-tap reflexes* as examples. The most famous tendon-tap reflex is usually called the *knee-jerk reflex*. The response is a brief extension of the knee joint (the knee 'jerk'), and it is elicited by a tap to the patellar tendon, as Figure 5.18 shows in cartoon form.

Figure 5.18: *Cartoon of the knee-jerk response to a tap on the patellar tendon.*

This reflex is actually a muscle stretch reflex. The effect of a tap to the patellar tendon is to produce an impulsive stretch of the quadriceps muscles that insert onto the knee cap (the patellar) and work to extend the knee joint. A stretch of these muscles elicits a reflex contraction resulting in the knee jerk. Similar responses can be elicited from other muscles by taps to their tendons. For example, a tap of the biceps tendon will elicit a brief contraction of the biceps resulting in a brief elbow flexion, an 'elbow jerk'.

The magnitude of the stretch produced by a tendon tap is very small (the muscle lengthens by about the thickness of a human hair), but because it occurs in such a short period of time – typically in a millisecond or so – the speed of muscle stretching is sufficient to excite the Ia afferent endings. For example, a stretch of 0.1 mm that takes 1 millisecond is likely to reach a peak speed that exceeds 20 cm/s, fast enough to evoke a response in the Ia afferent endings. Such a stimulus will elicit a phasic stretch reflex response and it is this that is primarily responsible for the jerk movement. However, other reflex mechanisms can be recruited and these can contribute to the observed movement. One of these is the **reciprocal Ia inhibition reflex pathway**, which causes the antagonist muscles to relax when a muscle is stretched. Also recruited are monosynaptic pathways that link Ia afferent endings in one muscle to the motoneuron pools of synergist muscles.

Figure 5.19 expands Figure 5.16 to include a reciprocal Ia inhibition arc and a monosynaptic arc involving a muscle that acts synergistically with biceps (*m. brachialis*). The three arcs shown in the figure share the same sensory neuron (the Ia afferent neuron that innervates a spindle in the biceps). The afferent axon splits into three branches, one for each arc. The branch in red is the autogenic monosynaptic stretch reflex arc. The orange branch connects to the α-motoneuron that innervates the brachialis. This is not an autogenic reflex arc; it is an example of a **heterogenic** arc. It has been reported that the Ia spindle afferents of one muscle can make monosynaptic connections with a large proportion of the α-motoneurons of synergist muscles[16]. The blue branch is part of the Ia reciprocal inhibition reflex arc. The afferent makes a connection with an inhibitory interneuron, which in turn makes a connection with an α-motoneuron that innervates the triceps muscle. The triceps acts antagonistically to the biceps and brachialis. The reciprocal inhibition arc is another example of a heterogenic arc.

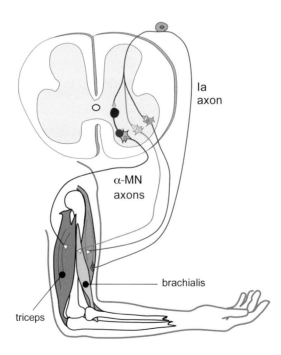

Figure 5.19: *Three different reflex arcs that share the same Ia afferent.*

When the biceps tendon is tapped, responses from all three reflex arcs shown in Figure 5.19 are elicited. The autogenic monosynaptic stretch reflex arc response is a brief contraction of biceps. The heterogenic monosynaptic stretch reflex arc response is a brief contraction of bra-chialis. The Ia reciprocal inhibition reflex arc response is a brief relaxation of the triceps. All these responses contribute to a flexion of the elbow joint (the elbow-jerk). It may be possible to observe an elemental reflex response independently of other responses by only recording EMG activity from a single muscle: only from the biceps, for example. However, even in this case, the response may be contaminated by heterogenic responses from synergists.

It is possible to directly observe the effects of reciprocal Ia inhibition using a very simple procedure[17]. If you want to try it, you will need a friend. Have your friend hold one arm in the posture shown in Figure 5.20A with their elbow flexors and extensors co-contracted (both muscles are tense, but the posture of the arm is held fixed). Gently squeeze your friend's biceps muscle: it will feel tense and hard. Now, while still gently squeezing the muscle, push up rapidly and quite hard on the wrist, as shown in Figure 5.20B. Make sure that your friend is not expecting this to happen (having them close their eyes will help). Following the push you should be able to feel the biceps relax. This is due to a reciprocal inhibition reflex in the biceps following a stretch of the triceps.

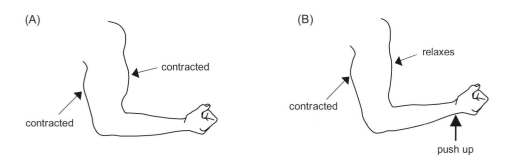

Figure 5.20: *Simple method for observing the effect of reciprocal Ia inhibition (see text for details).*

5.3.9 Elemental reflex responses are relatively easy to understand

Unlike natural, functional reflexes, elemental reflexes do have simple responses, since only one muscle is involved. Elemental reflexes are also standard reflexes – the response is driven by the stimulus via the reflex pathway. Thus, an elemental reflex response is a contraction of a single muscle with characteristics that are largely determined by the characteristics of the eliciting stimulus. This makes the characteristics of elemental reflexes quite simple to understand. We will consider the following characteristics:

(1) The relationship between the strength of the eliciting stimulus and the vigor of the response;

(2) The relationship between the duration of the eliciting stimulus and the duration of the response;

(3) The relationship between the strength of the eliciting stimulus and the response latency.

In the sections that follow, it will be explained in detail how each of these characteristics of elemental reflexes follow from the structure of their neural mechanisms.

5.3.10 The stronger the stimulus, the more vigorous the response

It seems reasonable to suppose that a strong stimulus will elicit a larger or more vigorous response than a weak stimulus. Indeed, such behavior seems to make good sense for many reflexes, especially those with a negative feedback action, as we will see in Chapter 6. It is certainly true for both components of the spinal autogenic stretch reflex. Figure 5.14 illustrates this for the phasic reflex: the slower the stretch, the weaker the stimulus for this reflex, and the smaller the phasic response. To see exactly why this happens for an elemental reflex, refer to Figure 5.21, which illustrates the situation using a monosynaptic arc. Suppose that the sensory receptor (left) is stimulated by a brief, strong stimulus. This will evoke a high-frequency volley of action potentials in the sensory afferent axon, which could be recorded using a microelectrode, as shown in the figure. This volley will be transmitted along the axon to the motoneuron, which responds in turn with a high-frequency volley that propagates down the motor nerve to the muscle. In the figure, a second microelectrode records from the motoneuron axon. The response in the muscle can be recorded as an EMG signal recorded by electrodes placed over the muscle as shown. The vigor of the response in Figure 5.21 could be measured in various ways. One obvious way is to measure the maximum reached in the EMG signal (the height of the signal above zero, labeled 'h' in the figure).

A weak stimulus evokes a lower-frequency volley, which is transmitted to the muscle and produces a smaller, less vigorous response. This is exactly what would be expected from a motor response that is driven by the neural activity evoked by the eliciting stimulus.

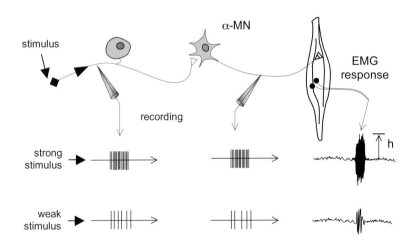

Figure 5.21: *Response vigor depends on stimulus strength (see text for explanation).*

Weak stimuli elicit weak responses, but there will come a point at which the stimulus is too weak to elicit any reflex response at all. Such stimuli are said to be below the **reflex threshold**:

> **REFLEX THRESHOLD:** the lowest strength of the eliciting stimulus that is capable of reliably eliciting the reflex response.

The reflex threshold does not correspond to the threshold of the sensory axon, i.e., the stimulus strength needed to evoke action potentials in the axon. This is because action potentials must be evoked at a frequency high enough to evoke action potentials from subsequent neurons in the reflex pathway and ultimately the α-MNs.

5.3.11 The longer the stimulus duration, the longer the response duration

Since an elemental reflex response is driven by the eliciting stimulus, we expect that when the stimulus ends, the response will terminate soon afterwards. This means that we expect the response duration to be similar to the stimulus duration. While this may seem obvious, it is important to be precise concerning what the eliciting stimulus is. For example, a loud noise can elicit an eye-blink response, but the duration of the noise has very little effect on the duration of the blink. Similarly, a fast stretch of a muscle may elicit a phasic stretch reflex response, but keeping the muscle stretched has no effect on the duration of this response.

The fact that the acoustic startle eye-blink response and the phasic stretch reflex response do not depend on the duration of the noise or the stretch seems to contradict the idea that the longer the stimulus duration, the longer the response duration. However, this apparent contradiction dissolves once we understand that these responses are not elicited by the noise and the stretch as such, but by specific features of these stimuli: it is the rate at which the noise or the stretch develops that serves as the eliciting stimulus. If a noise starts soft and gets progressively louder and louder, it does not startle us. In order to elicit a startle response, the sound must have a sudden, rapid onset, like a gunshot or a balloon pop.

As we saw earlier, the eliciting stimulus for the phasic stretch reflex is the speed of stretching rather than the amount of stretch. A very small change in muscle length can elicit a large phasic response provided that it occurs quickly enough. This is what happens when a muscle tendon is tapped: there is a very small but very rapid stretch. The graph at the top of Figure 5.22 shows a stretch stimulus in which the muscle is stretched very rapidly to a new, longer length and then held at that length (the stretch is sustained). Since the response is elicited by speed of stretching, only during the period of lengthening is there an eliciting stimulus for the phasic reflex. A sustained stretch does not elicit any response from the reflex. Thus, the phasic reflex response to such a stimulus is a brief contraction of the muscle. Panel (B) of the figure shows a graph of the speed of lengthening against time: the speed is zero except during the period of lengthening. This graph represents the eliciting stimulus for the phasic stretch reflex.

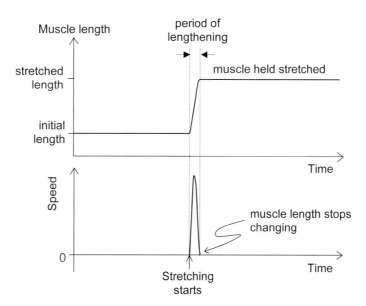

Figure 5.22: *Muscle stretch plotted as length against time (top) and as speed of lengthening against time (bottom).*

5.3.12 The stronger the eliciting stimulus, the shorter the latency

The latency of an elemental reflex will clearly depend on the anatomy of its neural mechanism. The longer the axons along which actions potentials are transmitted, and the more interneurons there are in the pathway, the longer the latency will be. This is straightforward, but if the anatomy of the reflex pathway were the only thing that mattered, then we would expect the latency to be much the same every time the response is elicited. However, the latency is not always the same, and so other factors must be involved.

One factor that affects latency is the strength of the eliciting stimulus: a basic finding is that the latency is shorter when the stimulus strength is greater. *Temporal summation* within the reflex pathway is the main reason for this effect. We can explain this using a monosynaptic reflex arc as an example. Figure 5.23 shows a monosynaptic arc at the top. (You could consider this to be the monosynaptic stretch reflex arc, but since it runs across the page in the diagram, you must imagine that the spindle has been removed from the muscle.) Micro-electrodes record action potentials from the afferent axon and from the axon hillock of the motoneuron. The recordings obtained from these electrodes are shown in the lower parts of the figure.

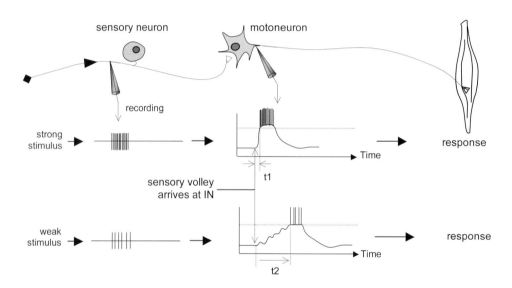

Figure 5.23: *Response latency depends on stimulus strength due to temporal summation (see text for explanation).*

A brief, strong stimulus applied to the sensory receptor will evoke a brief, high-frequency volley of action potentials in the afferent axon, as shown directly below it in the figure. The volley is transmitted down the afferent axon and arrives at the synapse between the sensory and motoneuron. The result is a rapid depolarization of the motoneuron, and it takes only a short time for the depolarization to reach the threshold at which action potentials are generated. This time is denoted t1.

The recordings obtained when the receptor is weakly stimulated are shown at the bottom of Figure 5.23. The volley of action potentials recorded from the sensory axon has a much lower frequency than that recorded when the stimulus was stronger. The time taken for this volley to depolarize the motoneuron to threshold t2 is much longer than for the more intense stimulus. This time contributes to the latency, and so the latency is greater when the stimulus is weaker.

5.3.13 Natural reflexes inherit the properties of their elemental components

In the previous three sections we described the following three relationships between the stimulus and the response that are expected to hold for elemental reflexes:

(1) Stronger stimulus → stronger response
(2) Longer duration stimulus → longer duration response
(3) Stronger stimulus → shorter response latency

These relationships have been found to hold, to some extent, in natural, functional reflexes. The scratch reflex is one example (see Figure 5.9). These relationships hold for natural reflexes for the same basic reasons that they hold for elemental reflexes. In the case of standard reflexes, these relationships are inherited from the elemental reflex mechanisms from which they are built.

5.4 The Combinatorial Approach to Functional Reflex Action

5.4.1 Introduction

Natural reflex responses all involve multiple muscles, and the muscles involved will typically be different when the response is executed in different conditions. According to the ideas presented in the previous part of the chapter, these reflexes are composed of multiple reflex components – the elemental reflexes. This raises two questions:

(1) The contractions and relaxations of contributing muscles must be properly coordinated to produce a functional outcome. Coordinated activity of the muscles requires coordinating the activity of the associated elemental reflexes; how is this achieved?
(2) The use of different muscles in different circumstances implies that different elemental reflexes are contributing. How are the required component reflexes selected?

This section of the chapter aims to provide preliminary answers to these questions by examining some important reflexes that involve multiple components, including the vestibulo-ocular reflex, the withdrawal reflex and the startle reflex.

5.4.2 The vestibular-ocular reflex involves coordinating the activity of the extraocular muscles in the two eyes

The rotational vestibulo-ocular reflex (rotational-VOR) described in Chapter 4 provides a good example of how the activity of multiple muscles is coordinated in a reflex response. The rotational-VOR generates conjugate eye movements (both eyes move in the same way). To produce such movements, the agonist muscles in the two eyes must be activated simultaneously and their antagonists relaxed. To see how this is achieved, we will consider the horizontal component of the rotational-VOR.

When the head turns to the right or left, the sensory receptors of the horizontal semicircular canals are stimulated. Neural activity evoked by this stimulation is transmitted along the pathways of the rotational-VOR to the muscles that move the eyes left and right – the medial and lateral recti. Figure 5.24 shows the basic circuitry responsible for counter-rotational eye movements to the left produced by a turn of the head to the right. These are driven by activity evoked in the horizontal semicircular canal on the right side of the head. The canal on the left does not contribute, so only the arcs connecting the right canal to the extraocular muscles are shown. The agonist muscles are the left lateral rectus and the right medial rectus. The other two muscles are antagonists.

The right canal is connected to the agonist muscles by excitatory reflex arcs that share an interneuron in the right vestibular nucleus. This arrangement means that the two agonist muscles are driven by the same sensory activity and are activated virtually simultaneously. As a result, the eyes will move together. Note that there are also reciprocal inhibitory arcs connecting the right canal to motoneurons of the antagonist muscles. These arcs result in relaxation of the antagonists in response to a turn of the head to the right. The relaxation occurs at the same time as the agonists contract. The overall effect is coordinated activity of the two agonists and their antagonists: a simultaneous contraction of the left lateral rectus and right medial rectus is accompanied by a simultaneous relaxation of their antagonists (the right lateral rectus and the left medial rectus). This ensures that both eyes move at the same time in the same direction – to the left in Figure 5.24.

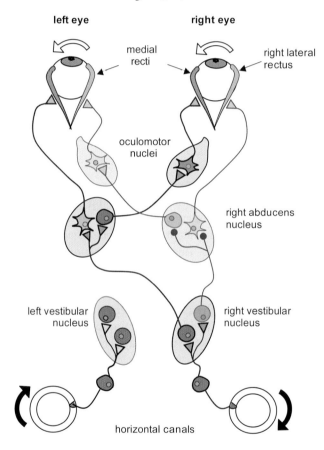

Figure 5.24: *Basic circuitry of the horizontal component of the rotational-VOR.*

The rotational-VOR illustrates how the coordination of multiple muscles (four in our example) can be achieved by wiring up the neural circuit in an appropriate way. The neural connectivity shown in Figure 5.24 yokes the left lateral rectus to the right medial rectus, so that these two muscles do the same things at the same time (either both contract or both relax, depending on the direction of eye-movement). It also yokes the right lateral rectus to the left medial rectus.

5.4.3 The rotational-VOR has phasic and tonic components

We saw in Chapter 3 that when the head is stationary, no activity is transmitted out of the vestibular nuclei, so there will be no response from the VOR circuitry shown in Figure 5.24.

Consider the following situation: the head is turned to the right and then stops in the turned position. What would the eyes do after the head has stopped, if the VOR no longer generates a response? The answer is that they would drift back to the central position, and so fixation would be lost. Of course, this does not happen: after the head turns, the eyes maintain fixation on the object of interest. The circuitry shown in Figure 5.24 cannot explain how fixation is maintained, since activity in the reflex arcs is only present while the head moves.

The maintenance of fixation is explained by a component of the rotational-VOR circuitry that is not shown in Figure 5.24. This component is called the **indirect pathway** *of the rotational-VOR* and is shown in Figure 5.25 on the left side only (the right side is similar). The circuit shown in Figure 5.24 is called the **direct pathway**. The indirect pathway goes from the vestibular nucleus to the *nucleus prepositus hypoglossi* in the medulla, and from there to the ipsilateral abducens nucleus.

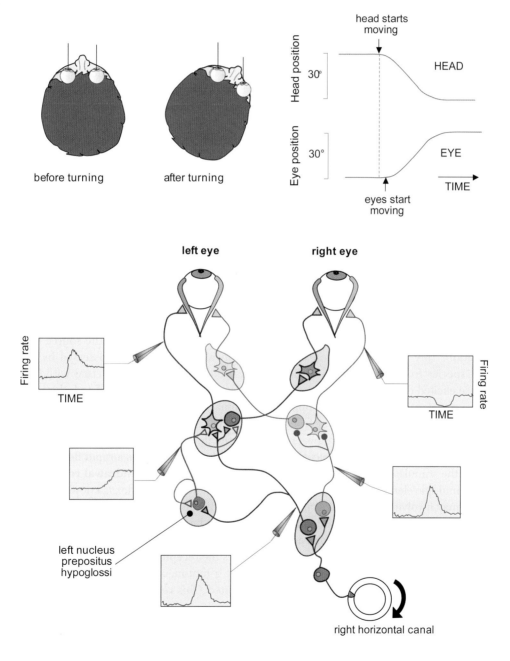

Figure 5.25: *The direct and indirect VOR pathways contribute phasic and tonic components of reflex action. The insets show the firing rates recording over time from different locations in the circuit (see text for explanation).*

The direct pathway generates a phasic response that is present during head acceleration and deceleration. The indirect pathway generates a tonic response. What this means, and how these responses combine to produce both the counter-rotational eye movements characteristic of the rotational-VOR and also preserve fixation when the head stops moving, is explained in Figure 5.25. The lower part of the figure shows the VOR circuitry that is responsible for counter-rotating the eyes to the left when the head makes a turn to the right. The top part of the figure shows the head before and after a turn to the right of approximately 30°. Plots of head and eye angular position as functions of time are shown in the top right of the figure. As indicated, the head starts to move slightly before the eyes: the difference in the two times corresponds to the latency of the rotational-VOR, which is less than 20 milliseconds in people.

The lower part of Figure 5.25 shows the rotational-VOR circuitry together with graphs that show the firing rate over time recorded at various points in the circuit. Immediately after the head begins turning, the vestibular afferent firing rate increases; it then decreases again as the head slows down to stop in the new position (a phasic response). The activity is transmitted from the vestibular nucleus to both abducens nuclei (direct pathway). It is also transmitted to the nucleus prepositus hypoglossi (indirect pathway), which responds by producing a signal that increases to a tonic level. This signal is transmitted to the left abducens nucleus, where it is combined with the phasic signal arriving along the direct pathway. The result is that a signal with both a tonic and a phasic component is transmitted to the muscles; the phasic part is responsible for the counter-rotation, and the tonic part for holding fixation when the head stops moving.

The rotational-VOR is an example of a sensory feedforward control system (see Chapter 1). The controlled variable is the direction of gaze (the direction of the eyes relative to the environment), but this variable is not measured and used for control as in the case of a negative feedback control system. Rather, head movement (which could disturb gaze direction) is measured, and the measurement is used to produce control signals that preserve gaze direction. It has been shown that for the feedforward control to be effective, it must incorporate an internal model (see Chapter 1) of the eye[18].

5.4.4 The flexor withdrawal reflex involves multiple elemental reflexes

When their skin is stimulated in a painful or otherwise aversive manner, most animals will quickly and automatically withdraw the stimulated part of the body from the source of the stimulation. This is a manifestation of the **withdrawal reflex**, a reflex possessed by most animal species from invertebrates to humans. As you can imagine, the actual withdrawal response elicited depends on the site of the stimulation. If the foot is stimulated, the animal withdraws its foot; if the head is stimulated, the animal withdraws its head. In each case, the stimulated body part is moved away from the location at which the stimulation was applied.

The most widely studied withdrawal response is the flexion of the leg that is elicited by an aversive stimulus applied to the sole of the foot: such a stimulus elicits a rapid flexion of the joints of the stimulated limb. This reflex is often called the **flexor withdrawal reflex**, and it involves multiple elementary reflex arcs. In rats, cats and dogs, this reflex is known to be spinal, and may involve excitatory trisynaptic reflex arcs that connect sensory receptors in the foot to flexor muscles in the leg; the same seems likely to be true in people as well[19]. One such arc together with an associated reciprocal inhibition arc is shown in Figure 5.26. An aversive stimulus is shown applied to the toes. This stimulates the receptors of the small fiber afferent system (nociceptors). When these are stimulated, the α-motoneurons of the flexor muscle are excited, and those of the extensor muscle are inhibited. This results in a contraction of the flexor and relaxation of the extensor, so the knee flexes.

Figure 5.26 shows just two reflex arcs associated with two elemental reflex pathways, but other elemental reflexes are also involved in withdrawal. Since there are seven muscles that flex the knee[20], there may be as many as seven excitatory elemental reflexes whose responses combine to produce knee flexion. Moreover, withdrawal of the foot does not only involve flexion of the knee: hip and ankle flexion are typically involved as well. This implies that elemental reflex pathways connecting the cutaneous afferents to these muscles contribute to the withdrawal reflex. Flexor withdrawal is clearly a multiple muscle response involving multiple elemental reflexes; we will return to this a little later (section 5.4.6).

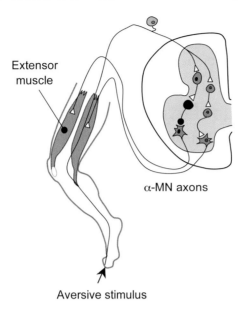

Figure 5.26: *Two reflex arcs that contribute to withdrawal of the foot.*

Flexor withdrawal is just one way of withdrawing, appropriate when the sole of the foot is aversively stimulated. Aversive stimulation of the skin on other parts of the body may elicit withdrawal that involves other types of muscles. After all, withdrawal is a goal-directed action – the goal is to withdraw from the aversive stimulation, and movements other than flexion are often needed to achieve this goal.

5.4.5 Multiple elemental reflexes provide a mechanism for reflex adaptability

A *flexor* withdrawal response is only functional if withdrawal from the stimulus can be achieved by flexing. Figure 5.27A shows a situation in which flexion of the joints of your arm would be effective at withdrawing the hand from the hot object. Compare this with panel (B) of the figure, in which a person touches the bottom of a hot object. Flexion of the arm in this case would force the hand into the source of the heat rather than remove the hand from it. In panel B, withdrawal requires *extension* of the arm. The fundamental point is that when you withdraw from the source of noxious cutaneous stimulation, you do so in a functional manner – you flex, extend, abduct, adduct, as required.

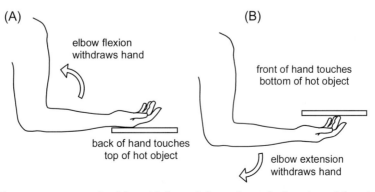

Figure 5.27: *The movement required for withdrawal depends on the location of the stimulation.*

These examples suggest that there are reflex arcs suitable for producing not only flexion but extension and abduction as well (and presumably any motion that a joint is capable of). The natural withdrawal reflex can thus be considered to comprise multiple elemental reflex pathways that activate flexors, extensors, abductors and so forth. The problem in any specific set of circumstances is to activate a subset of these pathways that are needed to produce the appropriate movement. How does the nervous system solve this problem? A partial answer is provided in the next two sections.

5.4.6 The elemental reflexes contributing to withdrawal have different receptive fields

Careful experimental studies of rats have established that the withdrawal reflex in these animals is a compound of multiple elemental reflexes[21]. Withdrawal in human beings and cats shows evidence of a similar organization[22]. In the rat experiments, aversive thermal stimuli were produced at very precise locations on the rats' feet using a laser. Figure 5.28 shows the bottom of a rat's foot with some of the typical sites stimulated (red circles).

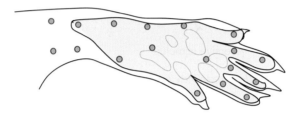

Figure 5.28: *Stimulation sites (red circles) on a rat's foot.*

The experimenters recorded the EMG activity evoked by these stimuli from a large number of different muscles. They found that those muscles that acted to move the skin away from something at the stimulus site were strongly activated by the stimulus, but those that did not were less strongly activated. This means that a given muscle may be strongly activated by stimuli presented at some skin sites, but only weakly activated, or not activated at all, by stimuli presented at others. The results can be described as an excitatory receptive field for the withdrawal reflex in each muscle. The receptive field for a cutaneous reflex, such as the withdrawal reflex, can be defined as follows:

> **(EXCITATORY) RECEPTIVE FIELD** (cutaneous reflex): the area of skin surface stimulation of which can elicit the reflex response in a specific muscle or limb.

Figure 5.29 shows examples of excitatory withdrawal reflex receptive fields (in shades of red) for two muscles, *m. tibialis anterior* and *m. gastrocnemius*. The darker the shade, the stronger the reflex activation of the muscle. The receptive fields directly reflect the mechanical action of the two muscles. Contraction of the gastrocnemius plantarflexes the foot: in a standing animal, this moves the heel away from the ground, as in the calf-raise exercise. Contraction of the tibialis anterior dorsiflexes the foot: contraction in a standing animal raises the toes off the ground, but not the heel. Stimuli to the base of the heel evoke strong contractions in gastrocnemius, but no contraction of tibialis anterior. Conversely, stimuli to the base of the toes evoke strong contractions of tibialis, but no contraction of gastrocnemius. Thus, to a good approximation, the receptive field is a region of skin which will be withdrawn from a stimulus presented within it when the muscle contracts.

Other muscles were also found to have withdrawal reflex receptive fields that matched their mechanical actions, and often the receptive field of one muscle overlapped with that of another. For example, the receptive field of biceps femoris (a knee flexor) covers the whole foot, and so overlaps with the receptive fields of all the other muscles involved in withdrawal. Thus, stimulation at a particular skin location activates all the muscles whose receptive fields include the stimulated site. Some muscles may be activated more strongly than others because different locations within their receptive fields lead to different response strengths, as indicated by the depth of shade in Figure 5.29.

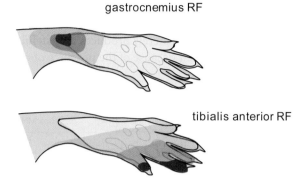

Figure 5.29: *Withdrawal reflex receptive fields (RF) of two muscles. Depth of color corresponds to strength of muscle response. Based on Schouenborg (2008).*

Figure 5.30 shows a schematic of the spinal reflex arcs that are believed to mediate the elemental reflex component of the rat's withdrawal reflex in tibialis anterior. The arcs connect a population of cutaneous afferents that innervate the receptive field with the motoneuron pool of tibialis anterior via trisynaptic arcs. The pathway involves the convergence of afferent signals from different regions of the receptive field onto secondary interneurons as shown. The strength of the connections with the secondary interneuron are indicated by the size of the synaptic terminal in the figure – the larger the terminal, the stronger the connection, and so the greater the response. Thus, stimulation of the dark red region of skin evokes the largest response, because this part of the pathway involves the strongest connection with the secondary interneuron.

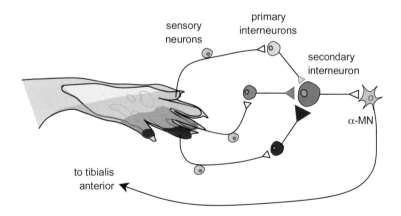

Figure 5.30: *Schematic of the reflex arcs involved in withdrawal of a rat's foot (see text for details).*

The rat's withdrawal reflex can involve a large number of muscles[23]. Each muscle has an associated elemental withdrawal reflex pathway that links cutaneous receptors in a specific region of skin (the receptive field) to the motoneuron pool. A stimulus at a specific site elicits responses from the group of muscles whose receptive fields contain that site. This provides an example of how reflex circuits can be organized so that functionally effective responses can be produced in different circumstances. We examine a more complex example in section 5.4.8.

5.4.7 Elemental reciprocal inhibition arcs in withdrawal

Experimental work on the rat's withdrawal reflex has also shown that some elemental reflexes can inhibit one another. For example, Figure 5.29 shows the excitatory receptive fields of the elemental withdrawal reflexes associated with gastrocnemius and tibialis anterior. The gastrocnemius plantarflexes the foot and the tibialis anterior dorsiflexes the foot; doing both at once is useless for withdrawal – it merely produces a wasteful co-contraction of the muscles. Such a waste of effort is avoided because of the presence of reciprocal inhibition, as shown schematically in Figure 5.31.

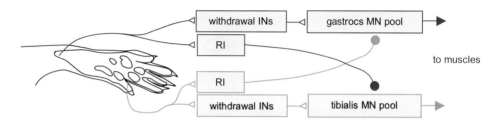

Figure 5.31: *Block diagram representation of the withdrawal circuits associated with the gastrocnemius and tibialis anterior muscles.*

As you can see in Figure 5.31, the elemental reflex pathway involving gastrocnemius (blue) is associated with a reciprocal inhibition (RI) pathway that inhibits the tibialis anterior motoneuron pool (green) and vice-versa. Suppose the receptive field of the gastrocnemius pathway is strongly stimulated, but the receptive field of the tibialis pathway is only weakly stimulated. The result will be a contraction of gastrocnemius and a relaxation of tibialis: the strong inhibition of the tibialis motoneuron pool will be much greater than the weak excitation. If both pathways are activated equally, then neither muscle will respond, as the excitation and inhibition of the motoneuron pools will cancel one another out[24]. If neither muscle responds, effort is not wasted co-contracting the muscles, but withdrawal will still occur, since the receptive field of biceps femoris (a knee flexor) covers the sole of the foot.

5.4.8 How can multiple elemental reflexes be organized to produce functional responses? A hypothetical example

Figure 5.32 expands on Figure 5.27 to show four different cases in which either the finger pads or the back of the hand are aversively stimulated. On the left of the illustration, the forearm is in a supine posture when the stimulus is applied; on the right, the forearm is in a prone posture. The figure shows that effective withdrawal is achieved by applying the following 'rules':

(1)   If the forearm is supinated, flex the elbow if stimulated on the back of the hand, extend if stimulated on the palm of the hand.

(2)   If the forearm is pronated, flex the elbow if stimulated on the palm of the hand, extend if stimulated on the back of the hand.

How could neural circuits be organized so that the withdrawal response obeys these rules? To withdraw using either flexion or extension, an arm requires a flexor withdrawal pathway and an extensor withdrawal pathway. For simplicity, the interneuronal circuits of these withdrawal pathways will be drawn as boxes with inputs from the cutaneous afferents and outputs to the relevant motoneuron pools. For example, the extension pathway can be drawn like this:

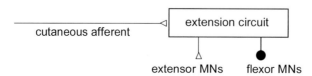

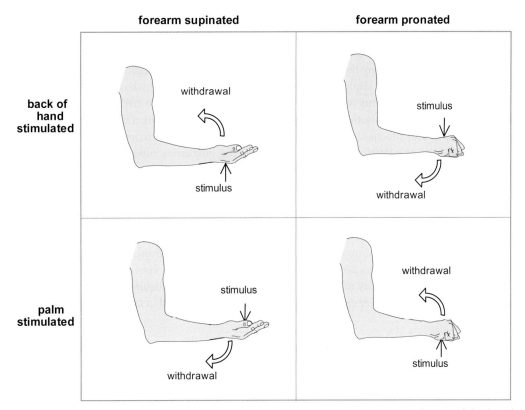

Figure 5.32: *Direction of withdrawal movement in response to aversive stimulation of the hand associated with supine and prone postures.*

Figure 5.33 shows the flexion and extension pathways drawn in this simplified way and organized so that their combination obeys rule (1): when the back of the hand is stimulated the elbow flexes, and when the finger pads are stimulated the elbow extends. This is appropriate when the forearm is in a supine posture as shown in the figures. When the forearm is prone, we want the opposite pattern of response (rule 2). How can this be achieved?

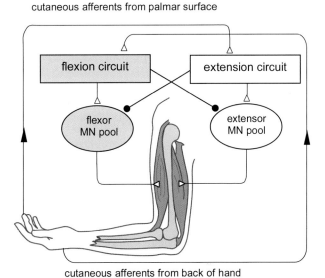

Figure 5.33: *Block diagram representation of hypothetical withdrawal reflex circuitry.*

To satisfy both rule (1) and rule (2), some additions need to be made to Figure 5.33. First, we need a way for afferents from the finger pads to activate the flexion circuit so that when the forearm is prone, aversive stimulation of the pads can elicit withdrawal. Second, we need a way for afferents from the back of the hand to activate the extension circuit when the forearm is prone. In addition, we need to add something that will prevent stimulation of the finger pads exciting the flexion circuit, and stimulation of the back of the hand exciting the extension circuit, when the forearm is supinated. Thus, information about the posture of the forearm (prone or supine) is needed. The required additions have been included in Figure 5.34. First, cutaneous afferents from the finger pads and the back of the hand make excitatory connections to both flexion and extension circuits. Second, a block has been added to represent neural mechanisms that determine forearm posture from kinesthetic sensory information from the limb's muscles and joints. If the posture is supine, cutaneous sensory signals from the palm are prevented from exciting the flexion circuit, and signals from the back of the hand are prevented from exciting the extension circuit, by presynaptic inhibition. In a prone posture, it is the other way around.

The hypothetical example described here illustrates how different elemental reflex pathways could be activated in different conditions. Here, the conditions could differ regarding the location of the stimulus and the posture of the body. The basic idea is that those pathways not relevant to the current circumstances are turned off (inhibited) and do not contribute to the response. Modulation of the excitability of reflex pathways is a fundamental feature of their organization, and we will encounter further examples of it later in this chapter and in subsequent chapters.

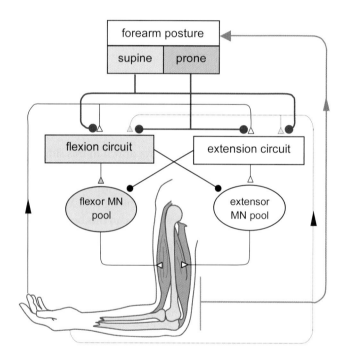

Figure 5.34: *Hypothetical withdrawal reflex circuitry of Figure 5.33 supplemented with a postural modulation circuit.*

5.4.9 Increased stimulus strength can lead to recruitment of more reflex arcs

For an elemental reflex, a stronger stimulus elicits a more vigorous response. When multiple elemental reflexes are involved, there is another mechanism that can contribute to response vigor. Imagine that a reflex involves a number of elemental reflex components which have different thresholds. A stimulus that is suprathreshold for all the components will elicit responses from all of them. A schematic illustration of such a situation is shown in Figure 5.35. A sensory receptor is connected to five different muscles via five disynaptic reflex arcs. The arcs are labeled (1) to (5). Each one of these arcs is part of an elemental reflex pathway. Assume that the thresholds increase, with arc (1) having the lowest threshold and arc (5) the highest. What kind of response will a stimulus then elicit from the circuitry in Figure 5.35? Consider two cases:

▶ **Case 1:** The stimulus is strong enough to elicit a response in the muscle of arc (5). This stimulus will also elicit responses from the other four muscles since arcs (1)–(4) have lower thresholds than (5). The response in muscle (1) will have the shortest latency and that in muscle (5) the longest latency, for two reasons: arc (5) has the longest axons and has the highest threshold.

▶ **Case 2:** The stimulus is only just strong enough to elicit a response in the muscle of arc (1). This stimulus is at about the threshold of arc (1) and so will not elicit responses in any of the other muscles, since the thresholds of arcs (2)–(5) are all higher than that of (1).

These cases illustrate that in a compound reflex, a strong stimulus not only elicits a more vigorous response from a single muscle, but may also recruit other muscles into the response. Many reflexes display this characteristic, including the withdrawal reflex, the stretch reflex, and the acoustic startle reflex[25]. Consider the latter. A noise is a strong startling stimulus if it has a sudden onset and reaches a high peak loudness: the more sudden the onset and the greater the peak loudness, the greater its strength as a startle stimulus. A gunshot is a very strong startle stimulus, because it reaches a very high intensity in a matter of a few microseconds. A strong stimulus can elicit a startle response involving muscles throughout the body from the head to the legs – a person startled by such a stimulus may literally jump in the air. A weaker stimulus not only elicits a less vigorous response, but the response may occur in fewer muscles. Sounds that reach a loudness of around 100dB may elicit only small responses in the muscles of the face and neck, the most notable being *m. orbicularis oculi*, the muscle involved in the acoustic startle eye-blink reflex described earlier[26].

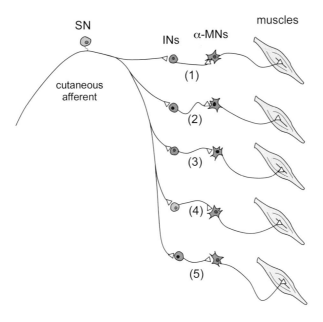

Figure 5.35: *Five different elemental reflex arcs that share the same afferent but have different thresholds (see text for explanation).*

5.4.10 Reflex modules are units intermediate between elemental reflexes and functional reflexes

It is convenient to identify a level of reflex organization more complex than an elemental reflex but simpler than the whole functional reflex. This is the level of the **reflex module**. Roughly speaking, a reflex module is a compound of a small number of elemental reflexes that work together as a single unit to produce a relatively simple functional response, such as a particular kind of movement.

We have already encountered an example of a reflex module in this chapter: the horizontal component of the rotational-VOR described in section 5.4.2. The rotational-VOR is usually considered to involve three different modules, each responsible for counter-rotating the eyes when the head moves in a specific way. The modules are usually called the horizontal rotational-VOR, the vertical rotational-VOR and the torsional rotational-VOR[27] (for details of the counter-rotational eye movements generated by these modules, see Chapter 4). As we saw in section 5.4.2, the horizontal rotational-VOR is driven by stimulation of the horizontal semicircular canals. The vertical rotational-VOR is driven primarily by stimulation of the posterior semicircular canals; the underlying circuitry has a structure similar to the circuitry that mediates the horizontal rotational-VOR, but involves different brainstem nuclei. The torsional rotational-VOR is driven by stimulation of the semicircular canals and the utricles[28].

The rotational-VOR example shows that a reflex module involves a group of elemental reflexes that combine to produce a particular kind of coordinated response in a set of muscles. Each module functions as a kind of unit. Other groupings of elemental reflexes that were discussed earlier in the chapter can also be considered to form reflex modules. One example is the group of elemental reflexes driven by stimulation of the Ia spindle afferents in a particular muscle, shown in Figure 5.19. In Figure 5.19 several elemental reflexes (the autogenic monosynaptic reflex, the heterogenic monosynaptic reflexes involving synergists, and the disynaptic reciprocal inhibition reflex) combine into a unit that acts to produce elbow flexion, analogous to the flexion circuit introduced in section 5.4.7. In these examples, the complete, functional reflex is considered to be composed of a number of elemental reflexes, but small groups of these elemental components work together as functional units called reflex modules. Thus, the natural, functional reflex can be considered as being composed of a relatively small number of reflex modules that are themselves groups of elemental reflexes.

5.4.11 Principles of elemental reflex combination

In this section of the chapter we have begun to see how elemental reflexes combine to form functional reflex mechanisms. The basic way in which such combination is achieved is that each of the elemental reflex pathways involved share sensory receptors. This was the case for all the examples discussed: the rotational-VOR, the withdrawal reflex and the acoustic startle reflex. Coordination of muscle activation in such combinations is a result of the structure of the elemental reflex pathways involved. If the pathways are similar in terms of axon lengths, thresholds and number of interneurons in the arcs, then the latency of their responses will be similar and muscles will be activated simultaneously. The composition of functional reflexes from elemental components can be represented using a block diagrammatic schema of the kind shown in Figure 5.11.

Combinations of elemental reflexes can explain how different combinations of muscles can contribute to a functional reflex response in different circumstances. We examined three mechanisms that contribute to this behavior. In the first, different elemental reflex pathways are associated with different populations of sensory receptors. As a result, a stimulus that excites the receptors in one population but not those in another will elicit a response from the elemental reflex pathway associated with the first population, but not from that associated with the second. The withdrawal reflex provides an example where the different receptor populations form the different receptive fields of the elemental reflexes (section 5.4.6). This basic idea can be represented in block diagram form as shown in Figure 5.36. In the figure, receptive fields (RFs) of the three reflex pathways overlap (1 overlaps with 2, and 2 overlaps with 3). So, for example, a stimulus (S) that is localized to the two receptors shown in orange can elicit a response from muscles 1 and 2, but not from muscle 3. Something similar happens in the rotational-VOR, but with the different modules: a left–right rotation of the head excites the sensory neurons of the horizontal canal but hardly affects the other canals, and so only the horizontal rotational-VOR module responds to such a stimulus. Head rotations that involve up-and-down tilts (nods) together with left and right turns (try it) will elicit responses from the horizontal and vertical rotational-VOR modules.

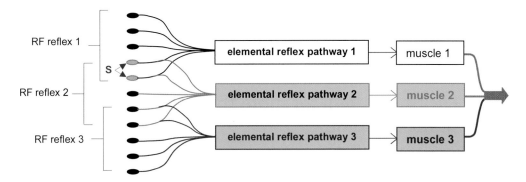

Figure 5.36: *Elemental reflex pathways with overlapping receptive fields (RFs). See text for explanation.*

In the second mechanism, postural context results in the *selective inhibition* of elemental reflex pathways, so that only some of them will respond when a stimulus is presented (section 5.4.8). The basic idea is illustrated in Figure 5.37, where the postural context block represents the process responsible for extracting postural information from kinesthetic stimulation. When the body is in the relevant posture, the posture block sends an inhibitory signal to the reflex pathway, which raises its threshold and may prevent it from producing a response at all.

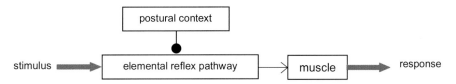

Figure 5.37: *Inhibition of elemental reflex by information about the postural context.*

In the third mechanism, stimulus strength determines the muscles that contribute to the reflex response. The basic result is that more muscles contribute when the stimulus is stronger, and it can be explained as a consequence of different elemental reflex pathways having different thresholds (section 5.4.9). Note that in all three cases, the elemental pathways that are recruited into the response are determined by sensory stimulation. In the first case, the location of the stimulation determines which receptive fields are stimulated, which in turn determines which muscles respond. In the second case, sensory information is used to determine the posture of the limb, which determines which of the elemental reflex pathways can be activated. In the third case, the strength of the stimulus determines which pathways are recruited.

5.5 Interactions Between Functional Reflexes

5.5.1 Introduction

When reflex circuitry is activated by a stimulus, the activity may have effects on other reflexes or it may not. If reflexes do not affect one another, we will say that they are *independent*. If they do affect one another, then they interact: in this part of the chapter, we will concentrate on interactions between natural, functional reflexes. We will look at how functional reflexes interact *concurrently* (i.e., when they are active at the same time) and *successively*. Successive interaction occurs when execution of one reflex response generates stimulation that elicits another response. The second response can be that of another reflex or of the same one again. The responses occur one after the other, which can result in a chain of responses, each response in the chain having been elicited by stimulation generated by the previous response (with the exception of the very first response). This is called the **reflex chaining principle** and was once believed to be the mechanism underlying the production of the repetitive movements involved in locomotion (see Chapter 8).

5.5.2 Eliciting stimuli for more than one reflex can occur at the same time

In the natural world it seldom happens that only one behavior-eliciting stimulus affects an animal at any given time. Nearly all the time, an animal will receive stimulation from a variety of different sources and some of this stimulation will be capable of eliciting reflex responses. As a result, concurrent elicitation of different reflex responses would be expected from time to time. In fact, when a skeletomotor reflex response is elicited, it is very likely that various autonomic responses will be being executed concurrently – autonomic reflexes are involved in the regulation of physiological processes, and this is happening nearly all the time. Moreover, as we saw in section 5.2.4, it is often the case that the stimulus that elicits a skeletomotor reflex response also elicits complementary autonomic responses. These autonomic responses prepare the animal or person for skeletomotor activity, as the cause of the eliciting stimulus might turn out to require fighting or fleeing (see section 5.2.4).

Sometimes different skeletomotor reflexes are elicited together and all act to produce the same outcome. For example, the vestibulo-ocular reflex (VOR) acts to keep the eyes steady when the head moves, but there are two other reflexes that have the same effect. These are the cervico-ocular reflex (COR) and the optokinetic reflex (OKN). As you can imagine, when the head and eyes move, it will typically be the case that there will be changes in the stimulation of the vestibular receptors, of the somatosensory receptors in the tissues of the neck, and of the retinas. The rotational-VOR response is elicited by vestibular stimulation, the COR response is elicited by stimulation of the somatosensory receptors, and the OKN is elicited by visual stimulation (see Chapter 4). All three reflexes work together as a system to keep the eyes steady. When a group of reflexes work together like the rotational-VOR, COR and OKN, they form a *reflex system*.

Of course, it is typically the case that different reflexes produce different outcomes – the withdrawal reflex produces an outcome different from that of the stretch reflex, for instance. In such cases, it is possible for reflex responses to get in each other's way if they are elicited concurrently. Such conflicts do not usually occur between autonomic and skeletomotor reflex responses, because they do not share any part of the structures and mechanisms involved in their execution. Autonomic and skeletomotor responses can be executed more or less independently of one another. This is not necessarily the case for skeletomotor reflex responses, as we will see in the next section.

5.5.3 Concurrent skeletomotor responses can conflict

There are some things that cannot be done at the same time. You obviously can't flex a joint and extend it at the same time – you have to do one or the other. Your parents probably told you that you cannot eat and speak at the same time. In these cases the two behaviors are said to be in *opposition* or to *conflict* with one another. As you can probably imagine, behaviors conflict when their execution demands different actions from the same structure(s) or mechanism(s). These might be anatomical structures such as muscles or joints. For example, one behavior could require that a joint be flexed, another that it be extended.

As an example, consider the following situation: you are holding your arm in a flexed posture with the forearm at about 90°. If something unexpectedly pushes up on your wrist, the elbow will flex, causing a stretch of the triceps muscle. The response is a reflex contraction of the triceps that acts to restore the arm to its original posture. Suppose, however, that the upward push was produced by a very hot object, sufficiently hot to elicit a withdrawal response. We now have a conflict between two reflex responses: a withdrawal response which involves a flexion at the elbow, and the stretch reflex response which involves extension. A simple picture of the basic reflex arcs involved is shown in Figure 5.38. Arcs associated with the stretch reflex are shown in blue; those associated with withdrawal are shown in red. The stretch excites the triceps motoneurons and reciprocally inhibits the biceps motoneurons. The heat excites cutaneous afferents, which results in excitation of the biceps motoneurons and reciprocal inhibition of the triceps motoneurons. So, what one reflex excites, the other inhibits – the responses are in direct opposition. What actually happens in this situation is discussed in the next section.

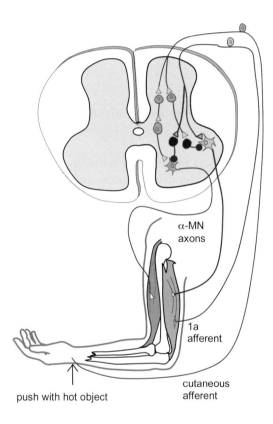

Figure 5.38: *Withdrawal and stretch reflex arcs that are in conflict (see text for explanation).*

Intermediate cases between direct opposition and complete independence of responses can occur. For instance, we might imagine two responses that involve many muscles, but only some of these are involved in both the responses. In such cases, concurrent execution of both behaviors may be possible, but execution of one could have a disruptive effect on execution of the other because of conflicting demands on the muscles the two have in common. This mutual disruption is called **interference**. The effect of interference is to reduce the efficacy of the behaviors affected. It is a matter of common experience that if we try to do two things at the same time, performance of both suffers.

5.5.4 What determines which reflex response is elicited?

Sherrington was one of the first to study how potentially conflicting reflex responses are expressed when their eliciting stimuli occur at the same time. He studied what happens when the scratch reflex and the flexor withdrawal reflex are elicited together in a spinalized dog[29]. A tickling stimulus applied to the dog's left flank elicits a scratching response by the left hind foot. This response can conflict with the withdrawal response elicited by an aversive stimulus to the left foot. Both reflexes are spinal: how does the spinal cord resolve the conflict when both eliciting stimuli occur together?

Figure 5.39 shows the type of scratch response obtained when a stimulus to the left flank (scratch stimulus) is applied together with a stimulus to the left foot (withdrawal stimulus). The scratch stimulus is turned on first and the dog soon begins to scratch. A little later a withdrawal stimulus is applied which is turned off before the scratch stimulus is turned off. Soon after the withdrawal stimulus is applied, the scratching stops. Once the withdrawal stimulus is turned off, the scratching quickly begins again.

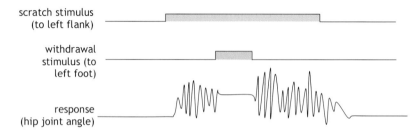

Figure 5.39: *Suppression of scratching during withdrawal. Based on results described by Sherrington (1906/1947).*

The behavior shown in Figure 5.39 makes good sense. In order to scratch the itch, the leg flexes so that the foot is close to the itchy location, and then the limb starts rhythmically scratching. In order to withdraw from the aversive stimulus, the limb must flex to move the foot away from it and hence away from the itchy location. Continuing to make scratching movements is then no longer useful, and so it makes sense to stop the scratching movement. The suppression of an on-going scratch reflex response when a withdrawal response is elicited suggests that the scratch reflex pathways are inhibited when withdrawal is elicited. This is shown in Figure 5.40: the circuitry that generates the scratch response and the circuitry that generates the flexor withdrawal response both make excitatory connections with the motoneuron pools of the flexor muscles. Activity evoked by the withdrawal stimulus reaches the withdrawal-generating circuits, and neurons within these circuits send inhibitory signals to the scratch-generating circuits. Thus, when withdrawal occurs, scratching stops, rather than the two occurring together.

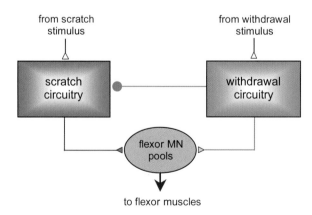

Figure 5.40: *Mechanism by which withdrawal can suppress scratching.*

The kind of mechanism shown in Figure 5.40 suggests that even a relatively weak withdrawal stimulus may be able to win out over a strongly itchy one. This is what Sherrington found: when the stimuli were presented in the order shown in Figure 5.40, even a weak withdrawal stimulus (alone sufficient to elicit only the weakest of withdrawal responses) was found to interrupt an ongoing scratching response to a stimulus sufficient to elicit a vigorous scratch. The withdrawal reflex wins out over the scratching reflex because of an inbuilt priority given to withdrawal implemented by the inhibitory input from flexion circuitry to scratching circuitry. Withdrawing from a potentially damaging stimulus is presumably more important than scratching an itchy one. Sherrington also found evidence to suggest that conflicting reflexes can **mutually inhibit** one another. Figure 5.41 shows the basic schematic for mutual inhibition between two reflex mechanisms.

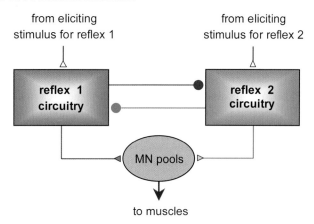

Figure 5.41: *Mutual inhibition between two reflex circuits.*

5.5.5 Skeletomotor and autonomic reflexes act in combination to achieve effective vision

As mentioned in section 5.5.2, several reflexes can act together to achieve a particular outcome. In such cases, reflexes can have excitatory effects on each other. To illustrate this kind of interaction we will look at how the accommodative reflex of the eye and the *fusional vergence* reflex influence one another.

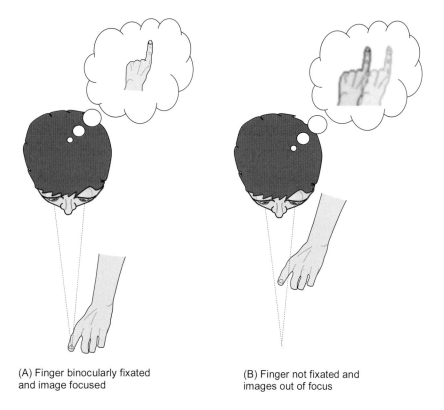

(A) Finger binocularly fixated and image focused

(B) Finger not fixated and images out of focus

Figure 5.42: *Binocular fixation, blur and diplopia (see text for explanation).*

Panel A of Figure 5.42 shows a person binocularly fixating their index finger. What the person sees is shown in the 'perceive' bubble: their index finger in sharp focus. In this situation, the retinal images are in focus and are in the same location on the retinas of the left and the right eyes (on the foveas). If the person's finger is unexpectedly moved closer to the person and their fixation does not follow it (remains at the original location of the finger), then their perception will be as shown in the 'perceive' bubble in panel B: a blurred double image of the finger. In the situation shown in panel B, the retinal images are out of focus and the locations of the finger on the two retinas is different. To restore the clarity of the percept, the eyes need to be brought into proper focus. This is achieved by the accommodative reflex: when the image is blurred, the accommodative reflex adjusts the thickness of the lens to bring the image into focus. To restore the singleness of the percept, the eyes need to converge so that the new location of the finger is fixated (i.e., so that the finger's image falls on the fovea in both eyes). This is achieved by the **fusional vergence reflex**: the eliciting stimuli for this reflex are differences in the locations of images in the two eyes (binocular disparities), and the response is a vergence eye movement that acts to eliminate the disparity (fuse the two images).

The accommodative and fusional vergence reflexes are crosslinked by mutually excitatory connections, which means that if the eliciting stimulus for one of them occurs but the eliciting stimulus for the other does not, both responses can nevertheless be elicited. For example, if an image of an object becomes blurred but the object's distance from the eyes does not change (e.g., you take off your glasses), then an accommodative response and a vergence response are elicited The latter response is called *accommodative vergence*. Conversely, if a fixated object moves closer, causing binocular disparity, but there is no change in the blurriness of its image (e.g., if it is part of a computer-generated binocular display), both a vergence and an accommodative response are elicited by the disparity stimulus. The accommodative response is called *vergence accommodation*. Figure 5.43 shows a block diagram representation of the two reflex mechanisms: the accommodative reflex mechanism at the top, and the fusional vergence reflex mechanism at the bottom. The accommodative mechanism is linked to the fusional mechanism by an excitatory connection called the *accommodative-vergence crosslink*. When the accommodation mechanism is activated by a blurry image stimulus, a response is elicited from the fusional mechanism via this crosslink. The fusional mechanism is linked to the accommodative mechanism by an excitatory connection called the *vergence-accommodation crosslink*, allowing binocular disparity to elicit an accommodative response.

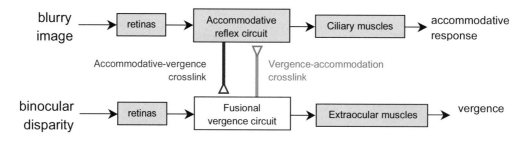

Figure 5.43: *The mechanisms of the fusional vergence and accommodation reflexes are crosslinked.*

5.5.6 Making a response affects sensory stimulation

Whenever a response is executed, sensory stimulation is changed as a result. For example, when a dog reflexively scratches itself, its foot makes contact with the flank and stimulates cutaneous sensory receptors. In fact, whenever the body moves somatosensory afferents in the muscles, joints and skin are stimulated; when the head moves, the vestibular organs are stimulated. If the body movements are part of an active response and not the result of externally imposed forces, then the stimulation is called *reafference* or *reafferent stimulation*.

The fact that making a response changes the stimulation that an animal receives can have three effects on responding: (1) it can have a feedback effect on the response that produced them; (2) it can have a feedforward effect on other responses (e.g., the rotational-VOR); (3) it can serve as an eliciting stimulus for another kind of response. We have encountered examples of the first type of effect several times already. Whenever a reflex mechanism acts as a feedback control system, the response changes the stimulation, which in turn changes the response. This is easy to see in the case of the pupiliary light reflex (section 5.1.7). The amount of light entering the eye is determined by the ambient illumination and the size of the pupil. If the pupil is dilated, a lot of light is able to enter and stimulate the retina. If the pupil is small (constricted), much less light can enter. Thus, any pupiliary response will change the amount of light that enters the eye and stimulates the retina.

When stimulation produced by one response elicits another response, two cases can be imagined: either the second response starts while the first is still on-going, or the second response starts at about the time the first ends. In the latter case, the two responses occur one after the other. This is the basis of the reflex chaining idea discussed next.

5.5.7 Stimulation due to making one response can elicit another: the chaining principle

Stimulation produced by the execution of one response can elicit a second response. Of course, execution of the second response will itself generate stimulation that could, in principle, elicit a third and so on. We could represent this process like this:

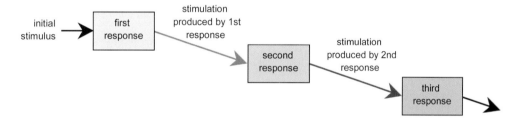

As you can see, if the stimulation produced by one response elicits another, a sequence or chain of responses can be produced. For this reason, generation of a sequence of response in this way is called **response chaining**; when the responses are reflex responses it is called **reflex chaining**. The principle underlying response chaining of this sort is usually called the *reflex chaining principle*.

The chaining principle was used in the late 19th century and the early 20th to explain behaviors that involved sequences of movements, including behaviors with repeated cycles of movement such as scratching, walking and running. In walking, for example, completion of one step was supposed to result in stimuli that elicited the next step, and so on. It has now been established that walking, swimming and other behaviors involving repeated movement cycles are not the result of reflex chaining (see Chapter 8).

Although reflex chaining is not the mechanism underlying cyclical behaviors, it does play a role in the production of some behavioral sequences. One example is provided by the consummatory sequence of predatory behavior in the cat[30]. A touch to the cheek of a predating cat elicits a turn of the head towards the source of the touch. The head turn tends to bring the touching object into contact with the cat's mouth. This contact elicits a jaw-opening response, allowing the object to contact the inner parts of the cat's mouth. Such contact elicits a vigorous bite: a snap-like closure of the jaws around the object. Other tearing or chewing responses may subsequently be elicited. The sequence – head turn, jaw opening, biting – results from later response elements being elicited by stimuli produced by the previous response: it is a chain of three elicited responses.

The terminal sequence in cat predatory behavior illustrates that chaining can operate as an organizing or coordinating principle. The response elements in the sequence occur in the correct order and at the correct time to ensure successful completion of the predatory act.

If an eliciting stimulus for one element does not occur, then the associated response will not be part of the sequence. For example, if the cat is facing the prey item, then it will not first touch the animal's cheek. This means that head turning, which is no longer required, will not be elicited. Thus, the chaining principle is a flexible way of producing sequences of elicited behaviors directed towards an overall goal. The actual behavioral response elements that occur in the sequence may be different on different occasions, because an element elicited in one set of circumstances may not be elicited in other circumstances. If the element that is not elicited is essential for elicitation of later elements in the sequence, then the sequence terminates (if the cat's mouth doesn't open, the terminal bite cannot occur). If the element is not essential, then it will simply be omitted from the sequence (if the cat's cheek isn't touched, it won't turn its head).

References & Notes

[1] The latency of blink responses to air puffs in people normally exceeds 100 ms (Reiter, Ison, 1977).

[2] Lorenz, Tinbergen (1939); Lorenz (1950).

[3] Barlow (1977).

[4] Lorenz (1950).

[5] Lorenz (1950).

[6] Baerends, Blokzijl, Kruijt (1982).

[7] Berkinblit, Feldman, Fukson (1986).

[8] See Berkinblit, Feldman, Fukson (1986); Bizzi *et al.* (2002).

[9] Sherrington (1906/1947).

[10] Sherrington called his components 'simple reflexes'. These seem to be more like the *reflex modules* to be introduced later (section 5.3.1) than elemental reflexes.

[11] No interconnections between elemental reflex mechanisms are shown.

[12] Liddell, Sherrington (1924).

[13] The phasic stretch reflex response includes small contributions from other reflex arcs, but the monosynaptic arc is the primary mechanism (Pierrot-Deseilligny, Burke, 2005).

[14] Primate extraocular muscles may lack stretch reflexes (Keller, Robinson, 1971). Intrinsic muscles of the human tongue and some orofacial muscles may also lack stretch reflexes (Neilson *et al.*, 1979).

[15] Mendell, Henneman (1971).

[16] Mendell and Henneman (1971) found that a single Ia afferent from the cat's gastrocnemius could make monosynaptic connections with up to 60% of the α-MNs of synergistic muscles.

[17] McMahon (1984), p. 253.

[18] See Green, Angelaki (2010b).

[19] Pierrot-Deseilligny, Burke (2005).

[20] *Semitendinosus, semimembranosus, biceps femoris, gracilis* and *sartorius* (thigh muscles), *gastrocnemius* and *popliteus* (calf muscles).

[21] Schouenborg (2002, 2008). Schouenborg uses the term 'reflex module' to include what are called here 'elemental reflexes'.

[22] Pierrot-Deseilligny, Burke (2005).

[23] Schouenborg (2002) reviews studies that investigated 15 different muscles.

[24] Assuming inhibitory interconnections of equal strength.

[25] Pierrot-Deseilligny, Burke (2005).

[26] Some authors consider that the eyeblink reflex has special characteristics that set it apart from the other components of the startle response (Brown *et al.*, 1991).

[27] There are many subtleties to the organization of the rotational-VOR that suggest that its division into three component modules may be an oversimplification. For a popular account see Tweed (2003).

[28] Bockisch, Straumann, Haslwanter (2005).

[29] Sherrington (1906/1947), Chapter IV.

[30] Flynn (1972).

6

Reflex Circuitry and Voluntary Motor Control

6.1 Central Processes Determine Reflex Excitability

6.1.1 Introduction

In Chapter 5 we examined reflex action and its neural mechanisms. These mechanisms are largely confined to lower levels of the nervous system – the spinal cord, brainstem and midbrain. We saw that these mechanisms can influence each other: activity in one reflex mechanism can affect that in another. Reflex mechanisms are not only affected by activity in the lower levels of the nervous system, but also by activity in higher levels of the brain descending into the brainstem and spinal cord. In particular, they are affected by such factors as mood, motivation and on-going voluntary motor activity.

6.1.2 Reflexes can be suppressed or potentiated by activity in the brain

As described in Chapter 2, axons of neurons in the cerebral cortex, the basal ganglia and the cerebellum descend into the midbrain, the brainstem, and in some cases down into the spinal cord. Many of these axons make synaptic connections with interneurons in reflex pathways. This means that they carry signals that can affect reflex action. The effects can be either excitatory or inhibitory, as illustrated in Figure 6.1, which shows a trisynaptic spinal reflex arc that is both excited and inhibited by neurons in the brain: the blue neuron has an inhibitory effect on the reflex arc, while the red neuron has an excitatory effect.

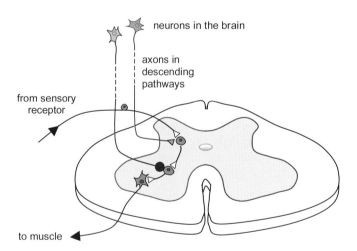

Figure 6.1: *Excitatory and inhibitory effects on reflex pathways by descending axons.*

If only the blue neuron is firing, the effect will be to make it more difficult for a stimulus to elicit a response from the arc – the threshold of the arc is raised, and the reflex is less excitable. This effect will be referred to as **reflex suppression**:

> **REFLEX SUPPRESSION:** the reduction of reflex excitability (raising the threshold) by inhibition that acts on the reflex circuits and originates from outside these circuits.

If only the red neuron in Figure 6.1 is firing, the first interneuron in the arc is excited, which can make it easier for a stimulus to elicit a response from the reflex arc. If this happens, then we will say that the reflex has been **potentiated**:

> **REFLEX POTENTIATION:** the increase in reflex excitability (lowering the threshold) by neural activity that arises from outside the reflex circuits themselves.

Excitation of the reflex pathway is one way of potentiating a reflex. If the reflex is being tonically suppressed, then there is another way: turning off the inhibition that is suppressing the reflex. This release from inhibition is called **disinhibition** and will clearly lower the threshold of the reflex. Thus, both excitation and disinhibition of reflex circuits are possible mechanisms of potentiation.

As a general rule, neurons in higher levels of the brain make numerous connections with the interneurons in reflex pathways, as well as with motoneurons. This means that reflexes can be suppressed or potentiated by central processes, such as those involved in generating voluntary behavior. What purpose does this suppression and potentiation serve? This is the basic question that will be addressed in this chapter.

6.1.3 Reflex action can interfere with voluntary behavior

We saw in Chapter 5 that reflex responses can sometimes conflict or interfere with one another. The same kind of conflicts can occur between reflex responses and voluntary actions. One example was described in Chapter 4: when your turn your head to look in a new direction, you do not want the VOR to produce counter-rotational eye movements that will keep you looking straight ahead. The VOR needs to be 'turned off' (suppressed) while the head and eyes turn to the left.

As another example, imagine that you want to flex your elbow. You might imagine that such a movement is produced by a voluntary command to the elbow flexors that causes them to contract. When the elbow begins to flex, the antagonist (triceps brachii) will be stretched. Stretch of the triceps could elicit a reflex contraction of that muscle, which would oppose the voluntary flexion movement. It could also elicit reflex inhibition of the flexors, which would also oppose the voluntary movement. Clearly, this kind of opposition does not occur, and so the activity of the stretch reflex in antagonistic muscles must be suppressed during voluntary movements. We will consider this situation in detail later in the chapter (section 6.4).

Reflex suppression in these two examples involves raising the reflex thresholds to an extent sufficient to prevent the responses being elicited. The mechanism is inhibition from higher regions of the brain (Figure 6.1, blue pathway), referred to as **descending inhibition**. The fact that these reflexes are turned off, but other reflexes are unaffected, means that the inhibition is targeted at just those reflexes that need to be suppressed – the inhibition is **selective**.

6.1.4 CNS damage provides evidence for descending inhibition

In a normal animal or person it is difficult to elicit large responses from the spinal tonic stretch reflex – such responses are typically small and difficult to record unambiguously. However, in spinalized animals, tonic stretch reflex responses are very much larger. In a spinalized animal the brain can no longer influence what is going on in the spinal cord. Therefore, the greater excitability of the spinal stretch reflexes suggests that disconnecting the spinal cord from the brain has prevented central inhibitory signals from reaching the stretch reflex circuits.

Sherrington found that several other reflexes are more excitable in spinal animals than in normal animals, suggesting that many different reflex pathways are normally subject to descending inhibition. Similar changes in reflex excitability occur in people who have suffered traumatic spinal injuries that prevent the brain from transmitting signals to spinal neurons below the site of the injury. One class of reflexes that can sometimes be released from inhibition by brain damage is the **tonic neck reflexes** (abbreviated TNR). The eliciting stimuli for TNRs are turns or tilts of the head away from the anatomic position (upright and facing to the front). Responses involve a pattern of sustained (tonic) activity in the flexor and/or extensor muscles of the limbs, which produces characteristic postures. Panel A of Figure 6.2 shows the postures produced in response to tilts of the head either backwards or forwards. These reflexes are called *symmetric TNRs* because all limbs do the same thing: either they extend (left side of figure) or they flex (right side of figure). Panel B of Figure 6.2 shows the postures produced in response to turns of the head to the left and right. In these cases, the limbs extend on the side of the body towards which the head is turned, and flex on the contralateral side. The pattern of response is asymmetrical – the limbs on the two sides of the body do different things – so these reflexes are called *asymmetrical TNRs*.

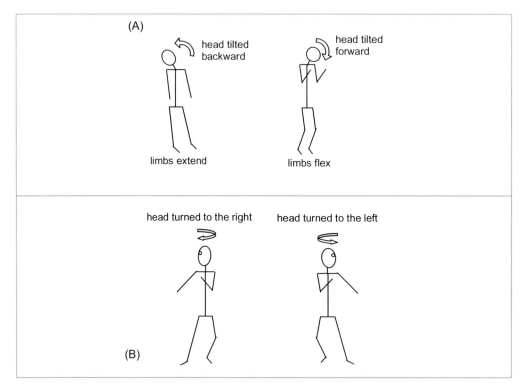

Figure 6.2: *Symmetric (A) and asymmetric (B) tonic neck reflex response postures.*

If someone's head is positioned as shown in Figure 6.2, they do not typically find themselves in one of the TNR postures. In fact, TNRs cannot normally be elicited from adults[1]. However, the postural responses can be elicited from newborn infants by moving their heads into the appropriate positions. As the infant gets older, it becomes more and more difficult to elicit a tonic neck reflex response, until by about eight weeks of age it is no longer possible (as in the adult). The reflexes are said to disappear. What has happened to them? The answer is that they have been suppressed by tonic descending inhibition. As the infant's nervous system matures, descending signals bring the TNR circuits under inhibitory control. Evidence for this is provided by the finding that certain types of damage to the brain can release the TNRs from inhibition, and the person who has suffered the damage will adopt the typical TNR postures when their head is positioned appropriately.

6.1.5 Reflex action can assist in voluntary behavior

You might be wondering why the TNRs exist at all: what is their purpose? It seems likely that in other mammals, the symmetric reflexes play a role in certain activities in which the postures are useful. For example, when jumping over an obstacle, an animal such as a dog or a horse extends the neck so as to look up, and forcibly extends the limbs to make the jump[2] –

the symmetric TNR on the left of Figure 6.2A shows this pattern. A four-legged animal that bends down to eat or drink may adopt a posture similar to that shown on the right of Figure 6.2A – the head tilts down and the limbs flex.

It is less clear that the reflex postures are useful for human beings, but there is evidence that they can be recruited to assist in certain types of behavior. Fukuda[3] made an extensive analysis of the postures adopted during the performance of athletic activities and dance. He found numerous instances of the characteristic tonic neck reflex postures during these activities. Figure 6.3 shows a classic example in which the asymmetric TNR posture is evident: a baseball fielder leaping to make a catch. Adoption of this posture could contribute to extension of the arm that moves the hand to the interception position, and to the dynamic balance of the body during the leap. It is possible that during performance of tasks in which the TNR postures could make useful contributions to performance, the descending inhibition that normally prevents the expression of the reflex is temporarily turned off. This means that the reflexes are potentiated during these tasks, so that when the athlete turns the head to look at the interception location, the reflex response is elicited. It should be noted that this suggested role for TNRs in dynamic tasks has not been rigorously tested, and so remains somewhat speculative.

Figure 6.3: *Baseball fielder leaping to make a catch.*

Another way in which TNR responses could contribute to performance in some tasks is illustrated by an experiment in which participants were required to repeatedly lift weights, either by means of wrist flexion or wrist extension[4]. The lifts were grouped into a series of bouts of 25 lifts each, with rest periods between bouts. The head was either turned towards the lifting limb (ipsilateral head turn) or away from the lifting limb (contralateral head turn). A measure of the total weight lifted during each bout was computed and then expressed as a percentage of the total lifted on the first bout. Figure 6.4 plots the results obtained for lifts made by flexing the wrist (panel A) and lifts made by extending the wrist (panel B).

For flexion lifts (panel A), more weight was lifted in bouts with the head turned away from the lifting limb (contralateral head turn). This is what would be expected were the asymmetric TNR providing additional drive to the flexor muscle motoneuron pools, since the reflex produces flexion in the limb away from which the head is turned (Figure 6.2B). For extension lifts (panel B), more weight was lifted in bouts with the head turned towards the lifting limb (ipsilateral head turn). This is again consistent with additional drive from the asymmetric TNR, since it produces extension in the limb towards which the head is turned.

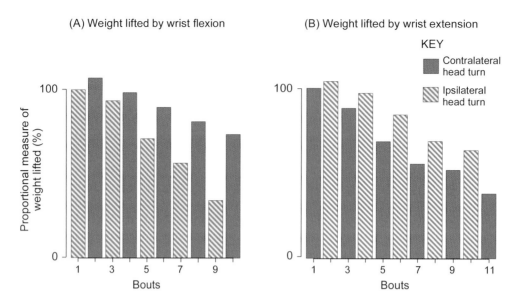

Figure 6.4: *Proportional measure of amount of weight lifted during successive bouts of lifting with the head in different positions on the shoulders. Data taken from Figure 3 in Hellebrandt et al. (1956).*

It is common to see fatigued runners in the closing stage of a race turning their heads to the right and left as they approach the finish line. Similarly, in gymnasiums, people pushing weights can often be observed moving their heads forwards and backwards or from right to left as they strain to lift the weight. Perhaps these twists and turns of the neck are recruiting a little extra muscle activity through the tonic neck reflex mechanisms[5]. Thus, in certain tasks the TNR responses may be able to play a useful role in performance. In such circumstances they may be potentiated by reducing or turning off the descending inhibition.

6.1.6 Voluntary behavior is accompanied by selective suppression and potentiation of skeletomotor reflexes

We have seen that reflexes can either interfere with voluntary action or, in some cases, assist voluntary action. When the reflex response is likely to interfere with voluntary action, it tends to be suppressed during performance of that action. The tonic neck reflexes are a little different: these reflexes are suppressed most of the time because they are either of no use or else are likely to interfere with ongoing behavior. When they may make a useful contribution, they can be released from inhibition.

Maintenance of an upright, standing posture is another behavior that is typically voluntary and supported by a number of reflexes. Many of these **postural reflexes** are potentiated when a person or animal is upright, and suppressed when they are sitting or lying down. An illustrative example will be given here. In Chapter 5, the flexor withdrawal reflex was described: the response is elicited when the sole of the foot is aversively stimulated, which could result from stepping on a sharp object. If you step on a sharp object, you are in an upright posture when it happens. When the stimulated leg is withdrawn, you are left standing on one leg. This leg must now provide all the postural support. To help achieve this, a reflex response is elicited in the support leg almost simultaneous with the withdrawal of the stimulated leg. This response is called the **crossed-extensor response**, and it enhances extension of the support leg.

The elemental neural circuitry that possibly mediates flexor withdrawal and crossed-extensor reflexes at the human knee joint[6] is shown in Figure 6.5. The crossed-extensor arcs involve the same cutaneous afferents as the withdrawal pathway, but affect the unstimulated leg. Notice that the responses in the knee flexors and extensors are opposite to those of the flexion response: the extensor motoneurons are excited and the flexor motoneurons are inhibited. The crossed-extensor response is only useful if a limb is stimulated while the

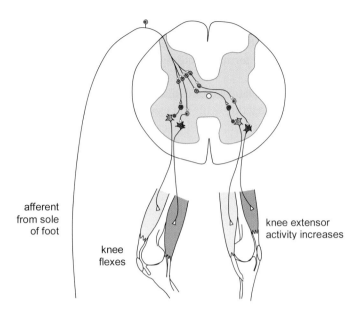

afferent
from sole
of foot

knee extensor
activity increases

knee
flexes

Figure 6.5: *Reflex arcs of the flexor withdrawal and crossed-extensor reflexes.*

person or animal is upright – if they were lying down or sitting, a crossed-extensor response would serve no purpose. It is perhaps not very surprising, therefore, to learn that if an aversive stimulus is applied to the foot of a sitting or lying person, the withdrawal response is typically elicited without the crossed-extensor response: people do not reflexively kick out with the unstimulated limb. Thus, the crossed-extensor circuitry in Figure 6.5 is suppressed when a person is lying or sitting, and potentiated when they are standing. By potentiating some reflexes and suppressing others, a person or animal is ready to respond in specific ways if particular stimuli occur. This can contribute significantly to the effectiveness of behavior: further examples are presented in the following sections.

6.1.7 Mood and motivation influence the excitablity of elicited behavior

Emotional and motivational states can act to potentiate or suppress reflexes. For example, when in a state of fear – an emotional state – a person or animal will tend to withdraw much more vigorously from aversive stimuli and be startled by much less intense stimuli than when in a calm, relaxed state. Motivational states like hunger and thirst have a similar type of effect.

When an animal or person is deprived of food, we say that a motivational state of hunger is established as a consequence of the deprivation. The animal is motivated to search for food, but is also disposed to respond to food-related stimuli in certain ways. For example, the sight of suitable food items will elicit approach and/or eating behaviors from a hungry animal, but may fail to elicit any such behavior from an animal that is not hungry. The overall behavioral goal of the hungry animal is to obtain food, and establishing a motivational state is equivalent to establishing this as the overall goal. The central motivating state directs the animal's behavior towards achieving this goal. This includes both the animal's spontaneous behavior (searching) and its elicited behavior. We have already discussed a related example: that of a cat in a predatory mood (see section 5.5.7), perhaps brought on by hunger. Tactile stimulation of the cat's 'face' when it is engaged in predatory behavior elicits responses associated with the biting and killing of prey: a touch to the cheek of a predating cat elicits a turn of the head towards the source of the touch; touching the outside of the mouth elicits jaw opening, and contact with the inner surfaces of the mouth elicits vigorous jaw closure (biting). The same stimuli will not elicit these responses from a cat that has just been fed. Indeed, they will typically elicit quite different reactions: a light touch to the side of the head is likely to elicit no response, and a cat will turn its head away from a firmer touch; a touch to the snout would elicit pursing of the lips and/or withdrawal[7]. Thus, when the cat is not in a 'predatory mood' it responds to these sensory stimuli in a way quite different from how it behaves when it is in such a mood. It appears that the reflexes elicited when the cat is predating are suppressed when the cat is engaged in other forms of activity. This example is considered further in the next section.

The example of a cat in a 'predatory mood' illustrates again that reflexes that serve a useful purpose are potentiated. Together with the examples presented in section 6.1.5, we see evidence of a general principle at work: it will be called the *principle of reflex set*:

> **PRINCIPLE OF REFLEX SET:** Voluntary behavior, and internally motivated behavior more generally, is accompanied by the potentiation of reflexes (and/or reflex systems) that can contribute positively to performance, and the suppression of reflexes (and/or reflex systems) that contribute negatively to performance.

6.1.8 Brain stimulation can affect motivation and hence reflex excitability

It has been found that electrical stimulation of specific, delimited locations in the brains of experimental animals can affect motivational state. For example, stimulation of a certain site in the hypothalamus causes rats to become thirsty. Of course, we do not know if rats experience thirst as such – what 'thirsty' means in this context is that the rat's behavior is affected such that it searches for water, and drinks when it has located it. Stimulation of the hypothalamic thirst center causes the animal to behave in this way – it motivates the animal to search and drink.

Experiments have demonstrated that a predatory mood can be established in the domestic cat by electrical stimulation of specific sites in the hypothalamus[8]. When such a site is stimulated, a cat will engage in predatory behavior. The stimulation was also found to potentiate the tactile reflexes described earlier: the responses could be elicited from the animal only when the brain stimulation was being applied to the correct locations. The brain stimulation itself did not elicit any of the reflex responses.

An interesting additional finding was also reported: exactly which reflexes were potentiated depended on the stimulation site in the hypothalamus. It was found that jaw opening could be elicited by two types of stimulus, tactile and visual. As a cat turns or lowers its head, the prey item may touch the snout and elicit the jaw-opening response (tactile jaw-opening reflex), or the prey may be seen by the cat (it provides a visual stimulus) which also elicits jaw-opening (visual jaw-opening reflex). Stimulation at some hypothalamic sites potentiated both types of reflex. Stimulation of other sites potentiated only the tactile reflex. One way this was demonstrated was as follows. Tactile sensory pathways from the cat's face were blocked (this can be achieved by anesthetic), preventing any responses being elicited by tactile stimuli anywhere on the face of the cat. Stimulation at appropriate hypothalamic sites would motivate the animal to engage in predatory behavior: it would stalk, pounce and pin a prey animal (rat or mouse). What happened next depended on the location of the stimulating electrodes. Two outcomes were reported. (1) When stimulation was applied at some sites, the cat would complete the sequence: it would lower its head, open its mouth and then bite the prey. (2) When stimulation was applied at certain other sites, the cat would lower its head and there the sequence would stop – the mouth would not open and so no bite would be made.

The second result (2) can be explained as follows. The hypothalamic stimulation potentiated only the tactile jaw-opening reflex. When the cat lowered its head, ensuing tactile stimuli were unable to elicit jaw-opening because the sensory nerves were blocked. The visual reflex was not potentiated, and as a consequence the jaw-opening response could not be elicited by visual stimulation. This selective facilitation of the tactile and not the visual reflex only occurred when stimulation was applied to particular sites. Stimulation at other sites would potentiate both reflexes, which explains the first observation.

6.2 The Contribution of Reflex Circuitry to Voluntary Movement

6.2.1 Introduction

Many actions can be elicited reflexively or produced voluntarily: you can blink voluntarily or blink reflexively, for instance. In this part of the chapter, we will consider whether the same mechanisms are involved irrespective of whether a behavior is stimulus-elicited or evoked voluntarily. We will focus on the example of saccadic eye movements, and we will see that both reflex and voluntary saccades are produced by activation of the *same neural mechanism*.

6.2.2 Reflex and voluntary eye movements use the same circuits in the brainstem

When someone looks from one object to another, the two eyes make a saccadic movement between fixations of the two objects (see Chapter 4). Saccades can be produced voluntarily – a person can decide to look from one thing to another. Saccades can also be elicited reflexively: the clearest example of reflex saccades are those elicited as part of the orienting reflex. This reflex involves moving so as to look at an unexpected stimulus event. In most cases, the response will involve head and trunk movement as well as eye movement. For the purposes of illustration will imagine that only a saccadic eye movement is involved. Panel A of Figure 6.6 shows a person looking straight ahead when a flash of light occurs to their left and can be seen out of the corner of their (left) eye. The flash elicits a reflex saccadic movement that moves the eyes so that they are looking in the direction of the flash, as shown in panel B. If a saccadic movement is evoked, it depends on the location of the stimulus but not on its strength: brighter flashes do not elicit more vigorous saccades.

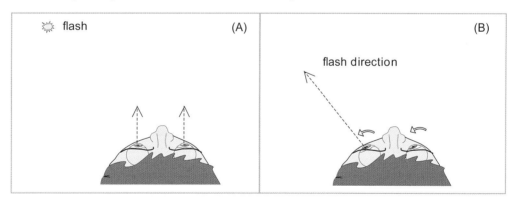

Figure 6.6: *A person is looking straight ahead when a flash of light appears to the left (A). A flash elicits a reflex saccade that moves the eyes so that gaze is directed in the direction of the flash (B).*

Regardless of whether the saccade is voluntary or reflexive, the same brainstem neural circuitry is involved. The circuits have been uncovered in experimental studies with animals[9]. Figure 6.7 (left) shows the basic circuitry involved in the production of leftward horizontal saccades (generation of rightward saccades involves a mirror-image circuit). The input end of the horizontal saccade circuit lies in two structures in the pons: the *paramedian pontine reticular formation* (PPRF), which contains *excitatory burst neurons* (EBNs), and the *nucleus raphe interpositus*, which straddles the midline and contains *omnipause neurons* (OPNs). The EBNs project to neurons in the *ipsilateral nucleus prepositus hypoglossi*, the ipsilateral *abducens nucleus* and to inhibitory burst neurons in the *ipsilateral nucleus paragigantocellularis dorsalis* (NPD). The approximate locations of some of these structures in the brainstem (with the exception of the raphe nucleus and the NPD, the latter lies just caudal to the abducens nucleus) are shown on the right of Figure 6.7. Vertical (up and down) saccades are produced by a different circuit, in which the *rostral interstitial nucleus* of the *medial longitudinal fasciculus* (riMLF) plays the role of the PPRF and the adjacent *rostral interstitial nucleus of Cajal* plays the role of the PPH. Oblique saccades involve simultaneous activity of both the horizontal and vertical saccade-generating circuitry.

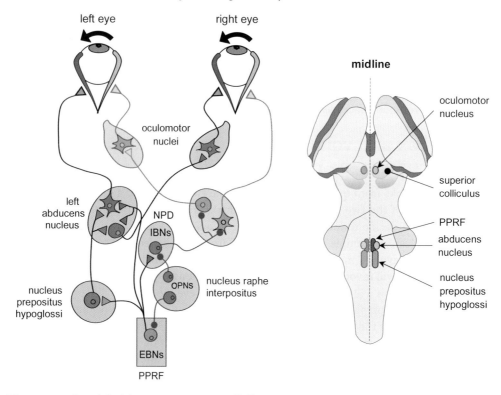

Figure 6.7: *Simplified brainstem circuitry (left) responsible for generating leftward, horizontal saccades and the approximate location of the nuclei involved (right). EBN/IBN = excitatory/ inhibitory burst neuron; OPN = omnipause neuron; PPRF = paramedian pontine reticular formation; NPD = nucleus paragigantocellularis dorsalis.*

Both reflex and volitional saccades are generated by sending command signals to the input end of brainstem saccade-generating circuitry (the PPRF and nucleus raphe interpositus in the case of horizontal saccades). Reflex and volitional saccades differ only in the origin of these signals. True reflexive saccades arise from sensory signals (these can be visual, auditory or tactile) transmitted to the superior colliculi and from there to the brainstem circuits[10]. For example, reflex saccades to unexpected visual stimuli can be evoked by signals that are transmitted directly from the retina to the superior colliculi via the retinotectal pathway[11]. The signals for volitional saccades arise in the frontal cortex and are sent to the superior colliculi and from there to the brainstem circuits; there are also direct pathways from the frontal eye fields to the PPRF and riMLF. This can be summarized as follows:

> *Reflex saccades (visual):* retina → superior colliculus → brainstem saccade circuits
> *Volitional saccades:* cortex (FEF) → superior colliculus → brainstem saccade circuits

It is possible to distinguish other types of saccades evoked in slightly different ways; details may be found in the literature[12].

Figure 6.8 shows a schematic of some of the main excitatory pathways involved in visually evoked reflex saccades and volitional saccades (an inhibitory pathway from the FEF via the basal ganglia to the superior colliculus is omitted, as is connectivity with the cerebellum and other subcortical structures)[13]. Pathways from three main cortical regions project to the nonsuperficial (deeper) layers of the superior colliculi – the frontal eye fields (FEF), the supplementary eye fields (SEF) and the parietal cortex (lateral intraparietal cortex, LIP, and posterior parietal cortex, PPC). These areas in the left hemisphere are shown in the figure. The outputs from the superior colliculi are transmitted to the contralateral brainstem saccade-generating circuits.

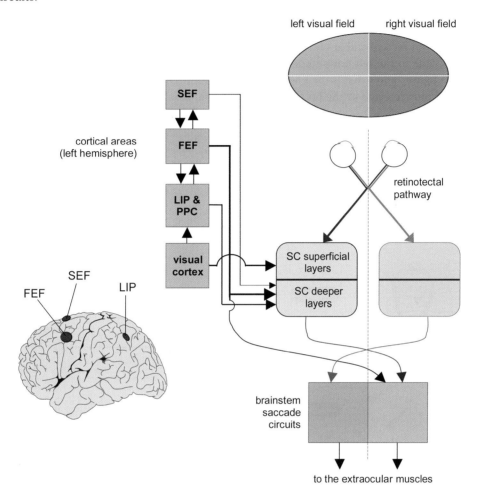

Figure 6.8: *Block diagram representation of the main excitatory pathways involved in volitional and visually evoked reflex saccadic eye movements. Only the left hemisphere cortical areas are shown (the right is similar); their approximate locations within the hemisphere are shown in the inset.*

6.2.3 Saccades are produced by pulse-step muscle commands

In what follows we will only discuss horizontal saccades, but saccades in other directions are basically similar. To produce a horizontal saccade, command signals are sent to the brainstem horizontal saccade-generating circuit (Figure 6.7 shows the circuit for leftward saccades). The command has two components. One component stops tonic activity in the inhibitory omni-pause neurons (OPNs); normally the OPNs are tonically active, and so they continuously inhibit the burst neurons unless a command shuts them off. The other command component excites the PPRF burst neurons and encodes information about the position to which the eyes are required to move so as to foveate the new target.

In response to the command inputs, the brainstem saccade circuits generate signals to the muscles (muscle commands) that cause the eyes to move saccadically to the target. Like the kinematic form of saccadic movements themselves (see Chapter 4), these muscle commands have a form that is rather stereotyped, being much the same regardless of the direction or amplitude of the saccade: a pulse-step command signal is issued to the agonist muscles, while the command signal to the antagonists shows an on-off-on pattern. The same patterns are observed in EMG activity recorded from the muscles. The pulse of activity in agonist MNs drives the eye rapidly to the new position, and the step acts to hold the eye in the new position. Figure 6.9 shows the pulse-step and on-and-off muscle command pattern in the agonist (lateral rectus) and antagonist (medial rectus) muscles of the left eye during a horizontal saccade to the left (amplitude ~ 20°). The movement of the left eye is shown at the top of the figure; below that is the EMG (rectified, smoothed) recorded from the agonist and antagonist muscles, and at the bottom is the firing pattern recorded from the motoneuron axons.

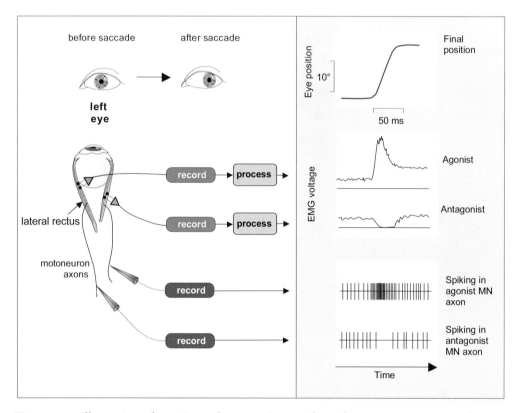

Figure 6.9: *Illustration of agonist and antagonist muscle and motoneuron activity during a leftward saccade. The EMG recorded from the muscles is rectified and filtered (by the 'process' block). (Not real data.)*

The pattern of muscle and motoneuron activity shown in Figure 6.9 is evoked from commands generated in the superior colliculus that shut off activity in the omnipause neurons and excite the burst neurons[14]. Figure 6.10 shows the activity (as continuous estimates of firing rates over time) in various parts of the brainstem circuitry that generates left horizontal saccades, which is evoked by commands from the superior colliculus to make a leftward saccade. The omnipause neurons (OPNs) are shut off for a brief period, during which time the burst neurons generate a burst of activity. The burst in the inhibitory burst neurons shuts down activity in the antagonist muscles. The burst in the excitatory neurons is transmitted to the agonist MNs, and the muscle contraction that is evoked is the driving force of the saccade. The burst is also transmitted to the nucleus prepositus hypoglossi, where it is integrated to form a tonic signal, which forms the step part of the muscle command and serves to hold the eye in its new position. How the process actually works is discussed next.

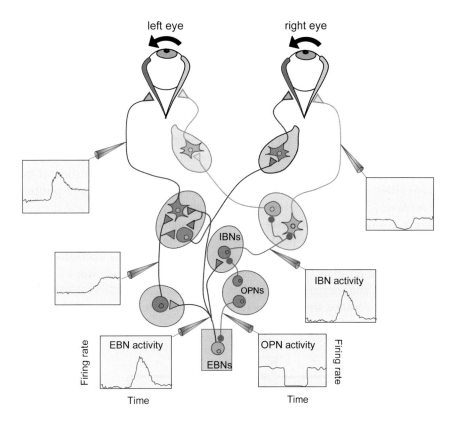

Figure 6.10: *Activity (firing rates) in various parts of the horizontal saccade-generating circuit shown in Figure 6.7 during the production of a saccade to the left (illustrative).*

6.2.4 How do the brainstem circuits generate horizontal saccades?

A detailed description of the functional components of the brainstem saccade-generating circuits has been pieced together over the last few decades. A number of different models have been proposed to explain exactly how the circuits work to generate the muscle commands. These models are too complex and varied to discuss here, and many issues remained un-resolved[15]: we will restrict attention to one particularly simple example as it applies to horizontal saccades, in order to illustrate some important concepts.

It used to be thought that saccadic eye movements are completely **ballistic**. This means that performance was thought to proceed in an open-loop fashion, generated by pre-structured motor commands that were run off without any contribution from information arising from their execution. Experimental work later showed this view to be untenable and that some kind of feedback information contributed to saccade generation[16]. This feedback cannot be sensory feedback, because there is insufficient time for such feedback to influence the execution of saccades[17]. Proprioceptive feedback from the extraocular muscles could potentially reach the saccade-generating circuits quickly enough to affect command generation, but complete elimination of such feedback has no detectable effect on saccade execution[18]. It was proposed that the feedback was internal feedback derived from within the saccade-generating circuits themselves[19], an idea that is incorporated in all contemporary models of saccade generation.

The first and simplest model[20] of the brainstem (horizontal) saccade-generating circuitry to incorporate internal feedback is shown in block diagram form in Figure 6.11[21]. The model proposes that the brainstem circuits receive two inputs from the superior colliculi (in accordance with the neurophysiological evidence; see previous section). One input encodes the required (horizontal) angular position of the eyes in the orbits, in which they would be pointed at the new target (required eye position signal). The other input is a *trigger* signal that initiates the saccade by briefly inhibiting the omnipause neurons (OPNs). The trigger is a brief volley of action potentials that transiently inhibits the OPNs, allowing the excitatory burst neurons (EBNs) to generate the pulse command that drives the saccade[22]. For the duration of the saccade, the OPNs are kept suppressed by input from inhibitory burst neurons (IBNs). The signal generated by the EBNs is sent to a neural integrator (∫) in the nucleus prepositus hypoglossi (NPH). Both these signals are fed to the motorneuron pools of the eye muscles (MNs). The output of the NPH carries information about the actual position of the eyes (assuming that the eyes obey the muscle command signal perfectly) – it can be used as an internal estimate of the actual eye position. It is fed back via a population of inhibitory interneurons (IINs) to the input, where it is subtracted from the required position signal (negative feedback). The difference between the required position signal and the estimate of the actual eye position provided by the NPH output signal is an error signal (motor error, ME) that encodes how far the eye has to move to reach the required position. It is this motor error that drives production of the pulse from the EBNs: when the estimated eye position reaches the required position, the motor error is zero and the process stops – the OPNs are no longer inhibited and they resume suppression of EBN activity. Thus, muscle commands are not prepared in advance, they are generated in response to a command that specifies the desired final position of the eye.

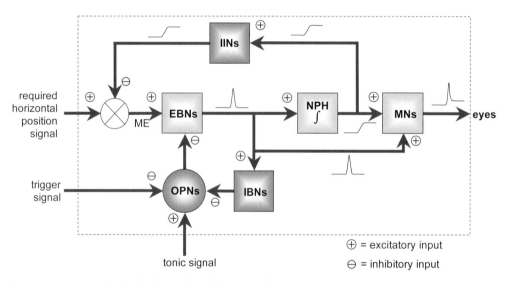

Figure 6.11: *Simple feedback model of horizontal saccade command generation by brainstem circuits: EBNs = excitatory bust neurons; IBNs = inhibitory burst neurons; IINs = inhibitory interneurons; ME = motor error; NPH = nucleus prepositus hypoglossi; OPNs = omnipause neurons.*

The model shown in Figure 6.11 is a feedback process for generating commands: it takes a specification of the required position of the eye as input, and generates commands for getting the eye to that position by a continuous feedback process that is entirely internal to the brainstem circuits (no sensory feedback is involved). The idea that the generation of saccadic muscle commands is an internal feedback process of the type present in the model shown in Figure 6.11 is now firmly established, but the original model shown in the figure has undergone a number of refinements and modifications since it was originally proposed[23]. One important modification was needed when it was discovered that the required position of the eye in the orbit is not the quantity encoded by the command inputs from the superior colliculi. The inputs encode the angular displacement of the eye required to move it so that it is pointing in the direction of the new target[24]: the command signal for a horizontal saccade encodes not where the eye has to move to, but how far it has to turn to get there. More generally, the commands to the saccade-generating circuits encode how far the eye needs to turn, and in which direction, to acquire a new target (angular displacement). Modern models, in which the command encodes displacement, are called **displacement models**; early models like that shown in Figure 6.11 are called **position models**[25].

6.2.5 How do the superior colliculi generate commands for the saccade-generating circuits?

The superior colliculi (SC) are the primary source of signals that tell the brainstem burst-generating circuits when and where the eyes need to move. Each colliculus is a nucleus comprising seven laminated sheets or layers[26]: the top three are the *superficial layers*, and the next four will be referred to as the *deeper layers*. The command signals to the brainstem saccade-generating circuits are transmitted via the axons of neurons found in the deeper layers; we will refer to these as *output neurons* of the SC[27].

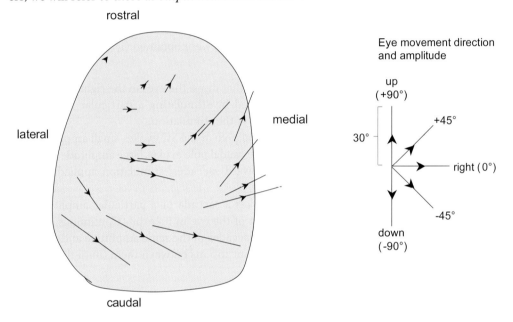

(A) Left superior colliculus with representation of saccades evoked from stimulation of different locations. Saccadic movements are represented as line segments centered on the stimulation site; the lines represent saccades according to the scheme on the right.

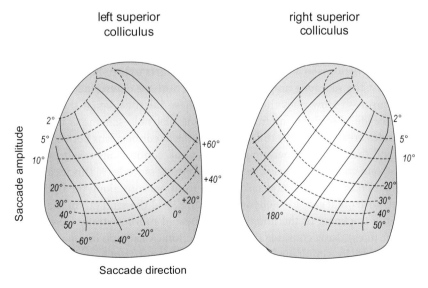

(B) Saccadic motor maps in the deeper layers of left and right superior colliculi.

Figure 6.12: *Microstimulation experiments reveal saccadic motor maps in the deeper layers of the monkey superior colliculi. Based on Robinson (1972).*

In monkeys, a high-frequency, vigorous burst of action potentials begins in the output neurons about 20 ms before the start of a saccade. The location of an output neuron in the layer determines the amplitude and direction of the saccade that is produced when it fires. This was first demonstrated indirectly by electrical microstimulation[28]: microelectrodes were inserted into the deeper layers of the SC of monkeys, and trains of 0.5-millisecond pulses of electrical current were delivered at different locations. It was found that if stimulation of sufficient strength (pulse amplitude) was delivered at a particular location, saccades of an amplitude and direction specific to that location were evoked. Increasing the strength of the current did not affect the amplitude, speed, direction or duration of the saccade. Some examples[29] are shown in panel A of Figure 6.12. The figure shows the left SC, with line segments representing the amplitude and direction of the saccades being evoked by microstimulation at the location of the arrow head. The lengths of the line segments indicate the amplitude of the eye movement; the angle of the line segment together with the arrow head indicates the direction of the movement, as shown at the top right of the illustration (horizontal lines represent horizontal saccades). The following findings were obtained (1, 3 and 4 are evident from Figure 6.12A):

(1)   Stimulation of the left SC evokes saccades that move the eyes to the right.
(2)   The characteristics of the saccades evoked by stimulating a particular location are largely independent of the characteristics of the stimulation.
(3)   Stimulation at locations close to the rostral pole of the SC evokes small amplitude saccades (short lines); stimulation close to the caudal pole evokes large amplitude saccades.
(4)   Stimulation applied medially evokes upward saccades; stimulation applied laterally evokes downward saccades.
(5)   Stimulation at a particular location evokes a saccade of a particular amplitude and direction, regardless of the start position of the eye in its orbit. Continuous stimulation over long periods evokes a series of saccades of the same amplitude and direction one after the other, with an interval of about 100 ms between them (until the limits of eye movement are reached).

These findings can be summarized by saying that the deeper layers of the SC embody a saccadic **motor map**, in which location in the map encodes saccade characteristics (a scheme sometimes referred to as a **place code**). Panel B of Figure 6.12 represents the map as a coordinate grid superimposed on the surface of the SC deeper layers (both left and right SC are shown; stimulation of the right SC evokes leftward saccades). The solid lines of the grid connect points from which saccades of the same direction can be evoked; the dashed lines connect points from which saccades of the same amplitude can be evoked.

Microstimulation of the deeper SC layers excites a localized population of output neurons that transmit signals to the brainstem saccade circuits. Recording studies have shown that a population of output neurons in a local region of the SC starts to fire shortly before a saccade, which suggests that the saccade's amplitude and direction are determined by this localized population of neurons[30]. How does the activity in these neurons signal the amplitude and direction of a saccade? Consider amplitude first. One plausible scheme is that saccades of different amplitudes are generated by different strengths of connections between output neurons in the SC and the saccade-generating circuits: weak connections result in small amplitude saccades, strong connections result in large amplitude saccades[31]. This idea is illustrated in panel A of Figure 6.13 for horizontal saccades. Output neurons along the 0° line in the SC only activate the horizontal saccade-generating circuits, and the strength of the connections is indicated by the thickness of the line: neurons located more rostrally have weaker connections (thinner lines). Now consider saccadic direction. A saccade in a particular oblique direction is produced by simultaneous activation of the horizontal and vertical saccade-generating circuits. For example, an oblique saccade that is 20° in amplitude, directed +40° to the horizontal (upwards to the right), is composed of a 15.3° horizontal saccade and a 12.9° vertical saccade (Figure 6.13B, left). Such a saccade can be generated by simultaneous activation of the vertical and horizontal generating circuits to the appropriate degree (the vertical circuits slightly less than the horizontal circuits: Figure 6.13B, right).

left superior colliculus

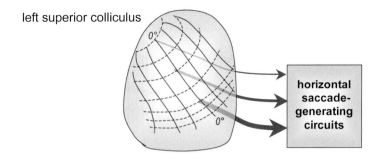

(A) Horizontal saccades of different amplitudes produced by different connection strengths between locations in the collicular motor map and the saccade-generating circuits.

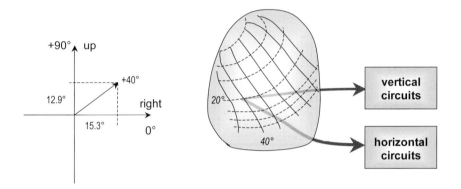

(B) Generation of a 20° oblique saccade directed upwards by 40° by simultaneous activation of the horizontal and vertical saccade-generating circuits.

Figure 6.13: *Scheme for generating saccades of different amplitudes and directions.*

6.2.6 The motor and visual maps in the superior colliculi overlay one another in close alignment

According to the scheme presented in the foregoing sections, production of a volitional or reflexive saccade requires that the appropriate location in the motor map of one or other superior colliculi (SC) be selectively activated. Thus, the question arises of how the appropriate location in the motor map is selectively activated. This is a complex issue[32]; here we will confine discussion to the visual, reflexive elicitation of saccades via the retinotectal pathway.

Retinal ganglion cell axons project via the retinotectal pathway to the superficial layers of the SC in such a way that neighboring locations on the retinas project to neighboring locations in the SC. The result is a retinotopic map in the SC, as shown in Figure 6.14 (similar to the retinotopic map in the visual cortex, Chapter 4)[33]. The figure shows a circular region of the visual field (top): the left field is shaded blue, the right field is shaded red, and a radial coordinate grid has been drawn so that it is possible to see where in the SC a given region of the visual field is mapped. The visual field is imaged on the retinas (middle) such that the center of the circular field falls on the foveas. Retinal ganglion cell axons project along the optic nerves and tracts to form a retinotopic map in the superficial layers of the SC, such that the right visual field is mapped to the left SC and the left visual field is mapped to the right SC. The figure shows that the central regions of the retinas are mapped to a relatively large area of the SC, so that the central 5° of the circular portion of the visual field (less than 1% of the total) is represented in a region occupying about 25% of the total area of the SC (*retinotopic magnification*; see Chapter 4). The fovea is represented in the rostral pole of each colliculus. A flash of light is shown at an eccentricity of about 25° from the center in the right visual field: it is imaged on both retinas, but only evokes a response in the left SC.

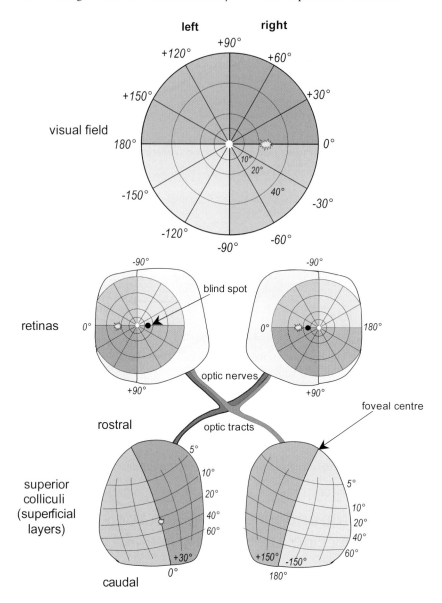

Figure 6.14: *Topographic projection of the visual field into the superior colliculi. Black spots mark the location of the blind spots in the retinas; the yellow star indicates the position of a flash of light in the right visual field (top), the retinas (middle) and the left superior colliculus (bottom).*

The retinotopic map of the visual field in the superficial SC layers lies directly above the motor map in the deeper layers and in close alignment with it[34]. This means that the retinal location in the visual map shown in Figure 6.14 lies directly above the location in the motor map (Figure 6.12) that codes for a saccade to that retinal location. The finding that the retinotopic and motor maps are aligned suggests a simple scheme for the reflexive elicitation of saccades to visual stimuli: signals evoked by a sufficiently 'important' visual event are transmitted from neurons of the retinotopic map layer to neurons immediately beneath them in the motor map layer (perhaps via neurons in intermediate layers)[35]. So, for example, the flash in Figure 6.14 evokes activity at the location shown in the retinotopic map, and is transmitted to the location beneath it in the motor map. Activity in this location of the motor map evokes a rightward horizontal saccade of about 25°, which brings the location of the flash onto the fovea. Although the necessary connections between the retinotopic map neurons and motor map neurons exist[36], the direct activation of motor map neurons by retinotopic map neurons does not explain the finding that activity in the superficial layers starts about 100 milliseconds before activity in the motor map[37]: transmission would be expected to take only a few milliseconds. It seems likely that the transmission of signals between the layers is regulated by other inputs, so that only important visual events are able to reflexively evoke saccades. It is not useful for an animal to be reflexively orienting to every event that occurs within its visual field: it needs some way of regulating responsiveness so that only the most important events evoke orienting reactions.

6.2.7 Spinal and brainstem circuits establish muscle synergies

The brainstem saccade-generating circuitry involves neural linkages between different muscles. The PPRF burst neurons send signals to the motoneurons of a muscle in one eye (e.g., the left lateral rectus in Figure 6.7) and to interneurons which relay the signal to the synergistic muscle in the other eye (e.g., the right medial rectus). This linkage means that the two muscles contract almost simultaneously in response to a signal from the burst neurons. The same linkage is involved in the rotational vestibulo-ocular reflex (see Chapter 5, Figure 5.24). Neural linkages of this sort mean that excitation of the linkage circuitry recruits two or more muscles almost simultaneously

The contractions and relaxations of a group of linked muscles are usually called *synergistic* motor patterns. In saccadic eye movements the contraction/relaxation patterns are very simple, since all the muscles respond nearly simultaneously. More complex patterns occur in which muscles contract and relax in sequences or cycles as well as simultaneously. A group of muscles that are neurally linked together such that they act together to produce a synergistic pattern is called a **muscle synergy**[38]:

> **MUSCLE SYNERGY:** a group of two or more muscles that are linked together by spinal or brainstem neural circuitry. When the circuitry is activated, the group of muscles contract and/or relax in a characteristic, coordinated pattern.

Muscle synergies are not the same as synergistic muscles (these are muscles that have the same mechanical action at a joint due to their anatomical arrangement; Chapter 2). Muscles in a synergy do not necessarily have the same mechanical action at a joint; in fact, two muscles in a synergy may be antagonists.

The saccadic eye-movement example shows that synergies are not necessarily specifically reflex or specifically voluntary, as they can often be recruited for either reflex or voluntary action. The fact that voluntary and reflex movements can involve the same synergy suggests that there is some advantage to directing voluntary command signals to the synergy circuits and not directly to the motoneuron pools of individual muscles. One possible advantage of this arrangement is described next.

6.2.8 Muscle synergies make voluntary control simpler

The brainstem saccade generator yokes the eyes together so that they automatically move together. Something similar is the case for the front two wheels of motor vehicles. The front wheels are yoked together by mechanical linkages so that they cannot be turned independently: when you turn the steering wheel, both wheels turn together.

Now imagine what it would be like to steer a motor vehicle if the front wheels were not yoked together, and instead of one steering wheel you had two, one for the left wheel and one for the right. This would make steering much more difficult: to make a turn you would have to rotate the two steering wheels by the same amount in the same direction at the same time. Instead of having to do just one thing, the driver now has to do two things, simultaneously and in a coordinated way. The advantage of a single steering wheel that turns a yoked pair of wheels is obvious. There is a similar advantage to be had from yoking the eyes together with neural linkages: a signal sent to the linkage mechanism will produce a coordinated movement of the two eyes. Instead of having to tell each muscle what to do, the controller need only send a command that says 'make a ten-degree saccade to the left' (but not in English, of course!). The saccade generator takes care of the details of the individual muscle activations needed to produce the movement.

The key thing to notice from this discussion is that the job of the controller is made easier by the linkages that make the wheels or the eyes move together: the controller does not need to control all the muscles individually, and so needs to send fewer command signals. This is a general advantage of sending signals to muscle synergy mechanisms rather than to individual muscles, and is often expressed by saying that the number of *degrees-of-freedom* to be controlled is reduced[39]. In this context, the degrees-of-freedom refer to the individual muscles that need to be controlled in order to execute the motor task, and there may be a large number of these. A controller that generates control signals for all the contributing muscles faces a difficult task: it must make sure that each muscle receives the right signal at the right time. This is an instance of the problem of controlling complex motor systems with many muscles and joints, called **the degrees-of-freedom problem**[40]:

> **THE DEGREES-OF-FREEDOM PROBLEM** (in motor control): How to generate control signals for the large number of individual degrees-of-freedom (e.g., individual muscles) that are involved in the execution of a motor task.

Most solutions to this problem propose that control is organized hierarchically, so that no individual level in the hierarchy is required to generate command signals for all the individual degrees-of-freedom. The highest levels of control are like a general in a military hierarchy: the general does not tell the individual soldiers what to do, and the voluntary motor control mechanisms do not tell the individual muscles what to do. The generals tell lower-level commanders like colonels and majors what to do, and they then decide how the soldiers should be deployed so as to achieve the general's orders. Likewise, voluntary motor control mechanisms influence lower-level synergy mechanisms, and these in turn determine how individual muscles will behave.

6.3 Reflexes and Feedback Control

6.3.1 Introduction: three roles for reflex mechanisms in voluntary action

So far we have seen two roles for reflex mechanisms in voluntary action: (1) they can be selectively potentiated (turned on) or suppressed (turned off) depending on whether they can make a positive or a negative contribution to voluntary behavior. (2) They can be recruited by voluntary control mechanisms for the production of movement: this can reduce the complexity of the control problem faced by the voluntary mechanisms. In the remainder of the chapter we will explore a third role.

In Chapter 1 we introduced the concept of negative feedback control, and in Chapter 4 we noted that some reflexes have a negative feedback control action. These include many autonomic reflexes such as the pupiliary light reflex and the accommodation reflex, as well as skeletomotor reflexes such as the autogenic stretch reflex. As stated in Chapter 1, the basic idea of using negative feedback to control something is to *observe what it is doing, and then use the difference between what you require it to do and what you observe (the error) to determine the action that needs to be taken to eliminate the difference*. Reflexes that have a negative feedback control action work in this way. As we will see, what is required of a reflex can change, and the changes can be made by voluntary mechanisms. In analogy with a climate control system that has a dial or keypad for setting the required temperature, the voluntary controller sets the required value by somehow 'turning the dial' of the reflex mechanism. In a climate control system, you do not have to actually turn on the heater or the air conditioner; you simply change the required temperature value using the dial or keypad, and the control system turns on the heater or air conditioner as required. In a similar way, the voluntary controller need not directly control the muscles: it sets the required value of the controlled variable, and the reflex mechanisms activate the muscles as required. This is the third role that reflex circuits can play in voluntary control. This part of the chapter presents a hypothetical example of how reflex circuits can be integrated into the voluntary control of head position.

6.3.2 Reflex action maintains the head in an upright posture

When people and animals are awake and alert, they normally keep their heads in an upright posture. People typically maintain their heads in an upright, face forward position on the shoulders. As detailed in the next chapter, the typical upright postures of the head and body are not mechanically stable in people and most animals. The mechanically unstable upright posture must be *actively stabilized* by the continuous modulation of activity in a number of muscles, mainly in the neck and shoulder girdle. Luckily, we don't have to think about doing this: keeping the head upright is normally an automatic process, based in significant part on the action of reflexive mechanisms.

Upright postures are maintained by complex reflex systems involving vestibular, somatosensory, and visual stimulation. We will focus on just one component of the system – the **vestibulocollic reflex (VCR)**[41]. Like many postural reflexes, the vestibulocollic reflex operates as a negative feedback control system, as detailed in what follows.

6.3.3 The vestibulocollic reflex (VCR) maintains head posture

If the muscles in your neck relaxed completely, your head would flop forwards, backwards, or perhaps to one side, due to the action of gravity and mechanical disturbances. The VCR is one of the mechanisms that prevent this happening – it helps resist and compensate for involuntary head movement. The name 'vestibulocollic' refers to the sensory and motor components of the reflex: it involves the vestibular system and muscles of the neck and shoulder girdle ('collic' comes from the Latin word for neck). Movements of the head stimulate the vestibular system, and the afferent signals produced cause changes in neck muscle activity that serve to restore head posture.

The VCR is a complex reflex with both phasic and tonic components that involves the semicircular canals, the utricles and the saccules, together with a large number of muscles – at least 23 of them – that act to move the head around. Like the vestibulo-ocular reflex, the VCR is usually subdivided into modules that produce responses in different planes[42]. For example, when the head tilts forwards and backwards (nose-down/nose-up), it moves in a sagittal plane; the VCR module that stabilizes the head in this plane is called the **sagittal-VCR**[43]. When the head rotates to the left and right, it moves in the horizontal plane, and the associated VCR module is called the **horizontal-VCR**. When the head tilts from side to side, it moves in a coronal plane, and the associated VCR module is called the **coronal-VCR**.

The complete VCR is far too complex to describe in detail here. In what follows, we will consider only the coronal-VCR, and we will simplify the account so as to illustrate the basic ideas. Tilts of the head to the left or right stimulate the utricles, the saccules and the semicircular canals (mainly the posterior canals). The neural mechanisms of the coronal-VCR transform the sensory responses to this stimulation into signals that activate the groups of muscles that laterally flex the neck. The next section presents a partial account of how utricular responses are converted into neck muscle activation.

6.3.4 The coronal-VCR involves conversion of utricular stimulation into neck muscle activity

As described in Chapter 3, the utricle is a relatively complex sensory device. Figure 6.15 reproduces the directional selectivity map of the sensory hair cells in the left utricle (panel A). Panel B shows a medio-lateral cross-section through the macula along the dashed line – a coronal section – with the head upright, so the afferents are firing at their resting rate (as indicated). Note that the hair cells to the left of the striola have the kinocilium (long hair) on their medial side, and those to the right have the kinocillium on their lateral side. This means that if the head tilts to the left (panel C), the firing rates of the afferents on the left of the striola decrease, and the firing rates of those to the right increase, as indicated in the figure.

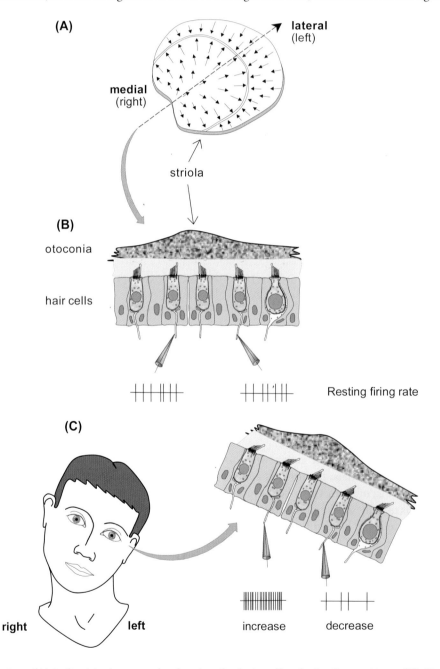

Figure 6.15: *(A) Left utricular macula showing the hair cell polarization pattern. (B) Medio-lateral cross-section through the macula in (A). Hairs are undeflected and the afferents fire at their resting rate. (C) Head tilted left, utricular hair cells are deflected, and the afferent firing rates change according to how the hairs are deflected.*

The coronal-VCR acts to resist tilts to the left and right and to restore the head to the upright position. In order for this to happen when the head is tilted down to the left, the lateral neck flexors on the right side of the head need to contract, because it is these muscles that pull the head upright. The lateral flexors on the left should relax, because these muscles act to pull the head to the left. Thus, the action of the reflex should be to decrease any excitation of the left lateral neck flexor motoneurons and increase excitation of the right flexor motoneurons. Part of the neural circuitry that achieves this effect is shown in Figure 6.16[44]. Utricular afferents synapse with interneurons in the ipsilateral vestibular nuclei, which are called **second order interneurons**. These interneurons synapse with inhibitory interneurons in the contralateral nucleus, which inhibit the second order interneurons on that side. Thus, the second order interneurons on the right inhibit those on the left (via the inhibitory interneurons), and vice-versa. The axons of the second order interneurons also synapse with the motoneurons of the neck muscles, and so afferent signals are transmitted to the neck muscles via neurons in the vestibular nucleus. In this way, the VCR circuits convert utricular stimulation into activation of the neck muscles. How this works to control head posture is discussed in the following sections[45].

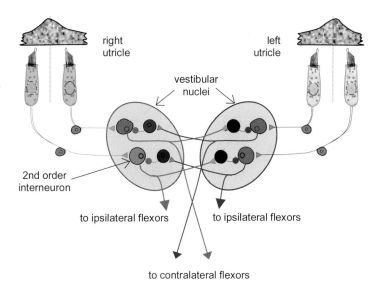

Figure 6.16: *Basic circuitry (reflex arcs) mediating the coronal vestibulocollic reflex.*

6.3.5 The coronal-VCR acts to restore the head to upright following a disturbance

The circuitry in Figure 6.16 looks quite cluttered. To simplify matters, we will exclude pathways to the ipsilateral flexors, since these pathways serve only to reduce the excitation of these muscles. The actual restoring movements are produced by the pathways to the contralateral flexors, so we will restrict attention to these pathways.

If the head is upright, the afference from both utricles is the same; due to their mutual inhibition, the firing rate of the second order interneurons is very low and is equal on both sides. As a result, the lateral flexors are activated equally by a small amount, so they are not completely relaxed – there is a slight co-contraction of these muscles. If the head is tilted to one side, the situation changes, because the utricular afference is no longer the same on both sides. Figure 6.17 shows the head tilted to the left, which results in an increased firing rate of afferents from the medial side of the striola in the left utricle (blue), and a decreased firing rate in the corresponding afferents from the right utricle (green).

The result of a change in afferent firing rates can be seen by following the course through the pathways in Figure 6.17. The increased afferent firing rate on the left and decreased firing rate on the right mean that the inhibition of the second order interneurons on the right (green) is greater than their afferent excitation: they no longer fire, and so the left lateral flexors relax. On the left, the afferent excitation of the second order interneurons is large, but there is no inhibition because the second order interneurons on the right are not firing. Thus, the increased excitatory activity is transmitted to the lateral neck flexor muscles on the right. The muscles contract more strongly and pull the head back upright. The VCR acts to make the upright head position into a stable equilibrium position, which is a consequence of its negative feedback control action, as described next.

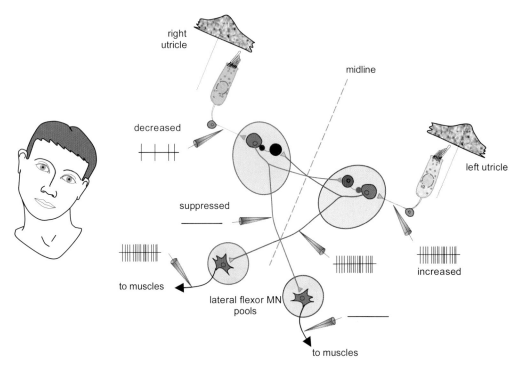

Figure 6.17: *Simplified coronal vestibulocollic reflex circuitry, and activity in various locations within it, during a tilt of the head to the left.*

6.3.6 The vestibulocollic reflex has a negative feedback control action

Negative feedback control involves determining the difference between what the system is required to do and what it is actually doing, and transforming this difference (the error) into control signals. These signals cause the system's behavior to change such that the error is eliminated. In the case of the coronal-VCR, there is an error if the head is tilted to the left or right. This error is signaled by a difference in the afference from the left and right utricles: if the afference differs, lateral flexor muscles on one side of the head contract and their antagonists on the other side relax, as described in section 6.3.5. The muscle contraction pulls the head back upright and so eliminates the error. This clearly corresponds to the action of a negative feedback control system, and it is possible to draw a classic negative feedback control block diagram to represent the VCR (see next section). The effect of the control action is to turn a mechanically unstable position of the head into a stable one.

Notice that the control action of the VCR, as described so far, poses a problem for voluntary head movement. Suppose that a person wants to tilt their head: as soon as the head is tilted, the VCR would be expected to try and restore the head to the upright. Clearly this does not happen: people and animals are perfectly capable of tilting their heads without encountering any reflex interference. How this is achieved is the topic of the next section.

6.3.7 Head tilts can be produced by central modulations of reflex circuits

The VCR does not normally interfere with head movements that are executed as components of other stimulus-elicited behaviors or voluntarily. One way to avoid any interference would be to suppress the reflex when voluntary or other head movements are made[46]. However, there is an alternative proposed by Erich von Holst[47] in which head movement can be achieved by modulation of the VCR reflex circuits.

As discussed in Chapter 1, there are two basic ways in which a response can be evoked from a feedback control system: (1) a disturbance affects the output (controlled variable), the change in the controlled variable is sensed, and a correction (response) is made. (2) There is a change in the desired value of the controlled variable; any difference between the new desired value and the sensed value evokes a corrective response.

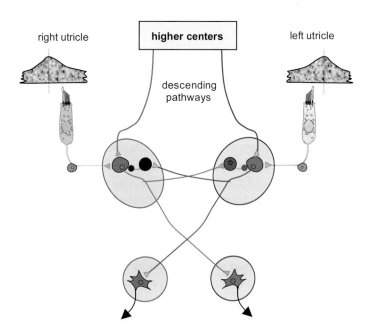

Figure 6.18: *Higher centers coupled to coronal-VCR circuits.*

In the above discussion of the coronal-VCR, we considered only the first of these ways of evoking a response – the head position is disturbed from its desired position by an external force. A response can also be evoked in the second way, as we will now demonstrate. Figure 6.18 reproduces those parts of the coronal-VCR circuitry shown in Figure 6.17, with an additional element – a 'higher centers' block that can excite the second order interneurons in either the left or the right vestibular nucleus (via the blue and green descending pathways, respectively). The effect of this excitation is to change the desired angle of head tilt. Suppose, for example, that the head is upright. If a tonic excitatory signal from the higher centers is then sent to the second order interneurons in the right vestibular nucleus (blue) their excitation will increase. This increased excitation will have two effects: (1) greater excitation of the left lateral neck flexor motoneurons, and (2) greater inhibition of the second order interneurons in the left vestibular nucleus. The result is decreased activation (relaxation) of the muscles on the right side, and increased activation of the muscles on the left side, which will cause the head to be pulled down to the left. As the head tilts to the left, the afferent firing rate on the left will increase, and that on the right will decrease. As a result, excitation of the second order neurons increases on the left but decreases on the right. At some point, there will be sufficient excitation on the left to activate the right lateral flexor muscles, while the muscles on the left will become progressively less active. The head will stop moving to the left and be held in a tilted posture when the muscle torque on the right is equal to the torques due to the muscles on the left and to the weight of the head (equilibrium). The head's angle of tilt when the equilibrium point is reached will depend on the amount of excitation descending from the higher centers: the greater the descending excitation, the greater the angle of tilt when equilibrium is reached.

From the example just presented, we see that the effect of central excitation of the second order interneurons is to change the balance of excitation between the left and right sides. When this happens, the reflex circuitry will cause the head to move to a tilted position that restores the balance. In effect, changes in the required level of excitation descending from higher centers is analogous to turns of the thermostat dial in a home heating system: they change the desired value of the controlled variable (room temperature and angle of head tilt, respectively). Thus, voluntary tilts of the head could be achieved by changing the level of descending excitation of the coronal-VCR circuits, rather than by activating the neck muscles directly. This has the advantage that the VCR is always active and will serve to make any desired head position into a stable equilibrium position, just as it does for the upright position. However, whether this mechanism is involved in human voluntary head movements is not known[48].

To complete our discussion of the coronal-VCR we will briefly discuss how to represent the circuit shown in Figure 6.18 as a negative feedback control block diagram. As mentioned in section 6.3.5, in the absence of any signals from higher centers, the coronal-VCR acts to restore the head to the upright position. This can be thought of as the zero angular position of the head: the desired head angle is zero (upright), and so no signal from the higher centers is needed. The antagonistic arrangement of the left and right utricles, in which signals from one side inhibit the other side via the cross-inhibitory interneurons, forms a head tilt angle sensor: the vestibular nucleus (left or right) that produces an output signals whether the head is tilted left or right, and the strength of the output signals how much the head is tilted. Figure 6.19 shows a block diagram representation of the coronal-VCR. The various functional blocks can be identified with different anatomical structures, except that there is no clear anatomical distinction between the head tilt sensor and the comparator. That is, there are no neurons that can be classed as implementing the comparator that are not also part of the sensor. Whether head movements away from the normal upright posture do involve modulation of the VCR, as described here, rather than VCR suppression, remains to be established[49].

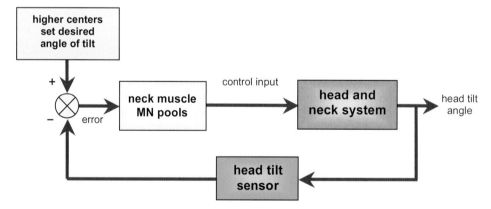

Figure 6.19: *Functional block diagram of the coronal-VCR.*

6.4 The Stretch Reflex and Voluntary Movement

6.4.1 Introduction: what's the autogenic stretch reflex for?

The autogenic stretch reflex was described in Chapter 5. Recall that the autogenic response is the response in the muscle that was stretched: it comprises both spinal and long-loop components. In this chapter, only the spinal components will be considered. The primary focus will be on the tonic stretch reflex. Birds, reptiles, mammals and fish all appear to possess stretch reflexes of this kind. In every case, the majority of the skeletal muscles in the animal's body are equipped with them. The ubiquity of these reflexes suggests that they are doing something important.

One possible function of the stretch reflex is to improve the mechanical characteristics of skeletal muscles so that they function more reliably and predictably. In Chapter 2 we saw that skeletal muscles behave like pieces of elastic – if you pull on them, they lengthen, but as they do so they produce a force that tends to oppose or resist that stretch. The passive elastic characteristics of skeletal muscles are largely irrelevant to most motor behavior. The characteristics of active muscle are far more important. As described in Chapter 2, muscles that lack reflex connections (e.g., deafferented muscles) resist stretch like a piece of elastic only up to a certain length; if they are stretched beyond this length, they yield (do not resist further stretch). The length at which a muscle yields typically occurs within the normal physiological range. This creates a potential problem: the muscle could yield during performance of a task and lead to a failure to achieve the task objectives. As will be described in the next sections, the stretch reflex counteracts the yielding behavior of skeletal muscle.

Another function of the stretch reflex relates to a possible role in movement control. The tonic stretch reflex has a negative feedback control action, with muscle length as the controlled variable. This suggests that control of limb position could be achieved by setting the desired value of muscle lengths and letting the reflex circuits drive the muscle to the desired length. In this section of the chapter, an introductory account of both these possible functions of the stretch reflex will be presented.

6.4.2 Muscles equipped with stretch reflexes do not yield

The concept of a (static) force-length characteristic was introduced in Chapter 2 and is critical for a full understanding of the remainder of this chapter. The force-length characteristic describes the relationship between the force that a muscle develops and its length. Figure 6.20 shows graphs of typical force-length characteristics for active muscle without reflexes (reflex-absent muscle), and for muscle with intact stretch reflexes (intact muscle). Panel A shows the characteristic for a reflex-absent muscle with electrical stimulation applied via a stimulator at a constant level, to maintain a constant level of muscle activity. Panel B shows the characteristic for an intact muscle with a constant level of excitation descending to the reflex circuitry from higher centers (the reason for a constant descending signal will become clear in later sections). The curve in panel A is clearly different from that in panel B. In panel A, the slope is positive to begin with (curve goes up), then zero (the curve reaches peak) and then negative (curve goes down) before becoming positive again. The yield point is the point where the slope is first zero. In panel B the slope is always positive (the curve is always going up), which means that to increase the muscle's length, you always have to pull harder: an intact muscle always resists stretching regardless of its length – it does not yield. In effect, the muscle behaves like a piece of elastic throughout its working range, whereas a reflex-absent muscle loses its elasticity beyond the yield point.

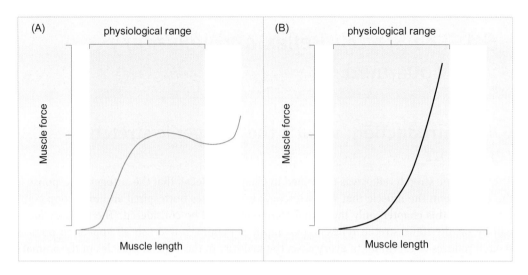

Figure 6.20: *Shape of force-length characteristics of reflex-absent muscle (A) and reflex-intact muscle (B) (illustrative).*

Without the reflex present, an active muscle does develop force that resists stretching, but only in part of the physiological range. With the reflex present, the ability of the muscle to resist stretch is present throughout its working range[50]. The stiffness of the intact muscle is always positive, whereas the stiffness of the reflex-absent muscle is zero at the yield point and then turns negative.

6.4.3 The force-length characteristic of an intact muscle is due to the action of the tonic stretch reflex

The force-length characteristic shown in panel B of Figure 6.20 is a result of the action of the tonic stretch reflex. Characteristics of this kind are obtained under conditions in which the inputs to the tonic stretch reflex pathways from elsewhere in the nervous system are either unchanging or absent altogether[51]. Under these conditions, increases in muscle activity when the muscle is stretched and held at the stretched length are due to the action of the tonic stretch reflex. The reflex response is an increase in the firing activity of the muscle's moto-neurons that is sustained for as long as the stretch persists. Figure 6.21 illustrates how the tonic stretch reflex contributes to muscle activity under the conditions just described. The left of the figure shows the force-length characteristic of a muscle: when the muscle is unstretched (length = L_0) it generates no active force[52], when it is stretched to length L_1 it generates force F_1, and when it is stretched to a longer length, L_2, it generates a larger force, F_2. The right side of the figure shows the EMG recorded from the muscle at each of the three lengths: no EMG is recorded when the muscle is unstretched; the EMG is greater when it is stretched to length L_1, and greater still when it is stretched to length L_2.

In Figure 6.21, the muscle is only active when it is longer than length L_0. As already stated, this activity is due to the action of the tonic stretch reflex. When the muscle is shorter than L_0, a reflex response is not elicited and the muscle is inactive. This means that L_0 corresponds to the *threshold of the tonic stretch reflex*: L_0 will be referred to as the muscle's **threshold length**.

We have seen that the tonic stretch reflex is primarily responsible for the force-length characteristic obtained for muscles with intact spinal reflex connections. The muscle behaves rather like a piece of elastic with a resting length of L_0. Since L_0 corresponds to the threshold of the tonic stretch reflex, it is not a fixed length – it depends on the level of excitation or inhibition of the stretch reflex circuitry, as discussed further in section 6.5.

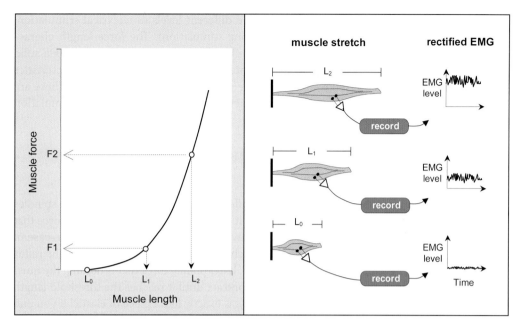

Figure 6.21: *A reflex intact muscle is more active the more it is stretched. It is inactive below a certain threshold length (L_o) and is more active at longer lengths (L_1 and L_2), as shown by recording EMG (illustrative).*

6.4.4 How are the force-length curves of muscles with and without reflexes related?

This section will attempt to explain the relationship between the force-length characteristics of intact and reflex-absent muscles. Recall that the force-length curve of an active reflex-absent muscle (Figure 6.20A) is obtained when the muscle has a *constant level of activity*. In Chapter 2 we saw that a different force-length curve is obtained from such a muscle for different levels of activation. In general, the greater the activation of a reflex-absent muscle, the greater the force it will develop at any given length.

The activity of a muscle with intact reflex connections increases as the muscle is lengthened (Figure 6.21). If the muscle's nerves were severed so that it was no longer connected to the nervous system (reflex-absent), then to get the same increase in activation, the muscle would have to be artificially stimulated more strongly as it was stretched to greater lengths. If this were done, then the reflex-absent muscle would be on a different constant activation force-length characteristic at each muscle length. The relationship between the two types of force-length characteristics[53] is shown in Figure 6.22. The figure shows the force-length

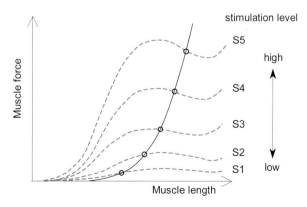

Figure 6.22: *Relationship between the force-length characteristics of reflex-intact (solid line) and reflex-absent (dashed lines) muscle.*

characteristics for a reflex-absent muscle with five different levels of electrical stimulation, increasing from S1 (weak stimulation) to S5 (strong stimulation). The force-length characteristic of the (same) muscle with the intact stretch reflex connections is shown as a solid curve. The points of intersection between the intact muscle's force-length characteristics and the characteristics of the reflex-absent muscle are marked with filled circles. These are points where the intact muscle's force-length characteristic is equal to the level of stimulation delivered to the reflex-absent muscle[54].

6.4.5 The tonic stretch reflex has a negative feedback control action

The (autogenic) stretch reflex circuits transform afferent feedback from the muscle spindles into efferent signals that excite the muscle, causing it to develop contractile force – a force that opposes or counteracts the stretch. This is a negative feedback control action. In the case of the tonic stretch reflex, when a muscle is held stretched beyond its threshold length, the reflex causes the muscle to develop a tonic opposing force. If the pulling force that is holding the muscle stretched is removed, the muscle will actively contract until it reaches the threshold length where it no longer generates a contractile force. This is exactly like a piece of elastic: if you pull on an elastic band, you can hold it stretched provided that you keep pulling; when the force is released, the band will rapidly shorten to its resting length (see Chapter 2). Although the reflex and the elastic behave in a similar way, there is of course no feedback control in the elastic.

Notice that the feedback control action of the stretch reflex is 'one-sided', in the sense that it opposes stretching of a muscle beyond the threshold length but does not oppose shortening – when a muscle is shorter than the threshold length, there is no reflex response. Other examples of one-sided control were discussed in Chapter 1.

The negative feedback action of the tonic stretch reflex suggests that it is a feedback control mechanism. Since the reflex opposes increases in length and tends to bring the muscle close to its threshold length, then the controlled variable is muscle length. The threshold length can be identified as the desired length of the muscle. This led to the hypothesis that the central nervous system controls movement not by directly determining a muscle's activation level, but by altering the threshold of the tonic stretch reflex[55]. The first complete version of this kind of idea was proposed in the 1950s by P.A. Merton[56], and will be referred to as **Merton's servo hypothesis**. Problems with this hypothesis emerged later on, and it was superseded by the so-called *lambda equilibrium point hypothesis* or **lambda hypothesis**. The lambda hypothesis will be described in some detail later (section 6.5). First, we will describe Merton's hypothesis and its problems.

6.4.6 Merton proposed that required length is specified by inputs to γ-motoneurons

When a limb is in a particular posture, the muscles in the limb all have particular lengths. This suggests that if you want to move the arm into a posture, you should arrange for your muscles to reach the lengths associated with that posture. To do this seems to require that the length of each individual muscle be controlled. Merton suggested how this could be done by considering the stretch reflex to be a negative feedback system for controlling muscle length. The basic idea was that descending signals from the brain determined the required muscle length, and the reflex would drive the muscle to that length.

A standard block diagram of a negative feedback system for controlling the length of a muscle is shown in Figure 6.23. To understand Merton's hypothesis, we need to explain how the sensor, comparator ($\otimes$) and gain (G) blocks correspond to the anatomical elements of the stretch reflex pathway. An important component of Merton's hypothesis is that the firing rate of the muscle spindle afferents signals the difference between the actual length of the muscle and the required length. Recall from Chapter 3 that a muscle spindle contains small muscle fibers – the intrafusal fibers – that are innervated by gamma (γ) motoneurons. In Merton's hypothesis, the firing rate of the γ-motoneurons specifies the required length of the muscle.

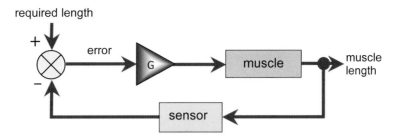

Figure 6.23: *Block diagram of a negative feedback control system for regulating muscle length.*

Firing of the γ-motoneurons causes the intrafusal fibers to become active. If there is no force resisting their contraction, they will shorten to a length that depends on the γ-motoneuron firing rate: this length corresponds to the required length of the muscle. The type II spindle afferents will fire as long as the muscle is longer than the required length: they fire at a rate that is approximately proportional to the difference between the actual length of the muscle and the required length – the 'error' in Figure 6.23 (for more details, refer back to Chapter 3).

The tonic stretch reflex pathway transmits this error signal via several interneurons to the α-motoneuron pool of the muscle. (Merton originally supposed that the monosynaptic pathway is the primary one involved, but this is implausible[57].) The α-motoneurons fire, causing the muscle to generate a contractile force that tends to shorten the muscle, bringing it closer to the required length. Thus, only when the actual length is greater than the required length does the reflex become active, which means that the required length corresponds to the reflex threshold, as described earlier.

It is instructive to illustrate the process of length control described in the last paragraph using schematic diagrams of the anatomical structures involved. The intrafusal and extrafusal muscle fibers and the associated neural circuits can be represented using the schematic shown in Figure 6.24. Since the number of interneurons in the tonic stretch reflex pathway is unknown, we simply represent them as a block. All the muscle fibers, both extrafusal and intrafusal, are shown fixed to the same structures at each end. Of course, this is not anatomically correct, since the intrafusal fibers are extremely short and attached to connective tissue within the bundle of extrafusal fibers. The representation in the figure does two things: it makes the intrafusals big enough to see in the diagram, and it reminds us that the length of the intrafusals just follows that of the extrafusals.

The basic idea is that a central signal to the γ-motoneurons causes the tonic reflex circuits to drive the muscle to the required length specified by that signal. Imagine that the muscle is initially completely relaxed so neither the α- nor the γ-motoneurons are firing. At some point in time, the person decides to move to a new position, which requires that the muscle shortens to a particular length (the new required length). The command to shorten to this length is a signal sent from the brain to the γ-motoneurons. This signal activates

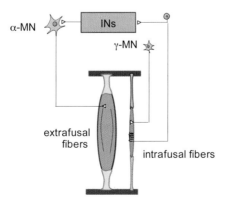

Figure 6.24: *Schematic diagram of a muscle together with its innervations by motoneurons and tonic stretch reflex connections.*

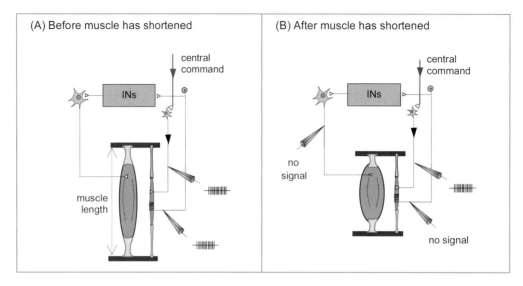

Figure 6.25: *Shortening (contraction) of muscle stretched beyond the reflex threshold (see text for explanation).*

the intrafusal fibers that then try to shorten, but they cannot, since they are held at their initial length by the extrafusal fibers. As a result, the spindle afferents start firing, signaling the difference between the required length and the actual length. If recordings were made from the γ-motoneuron axons and the afferent axons, we would obtain the kind of result illustrated in Figure 6.25A. The inter-neuronal pathway transmits the afferent signal to the α-motoneuron pool, and the result is muscle activation and contraction of the extrafusal fibers. Once the muscle has contracted to the required length, the error is zero and there is no longer any signal transmitted around the reflex pathway, as shown in Figure 6.25B.

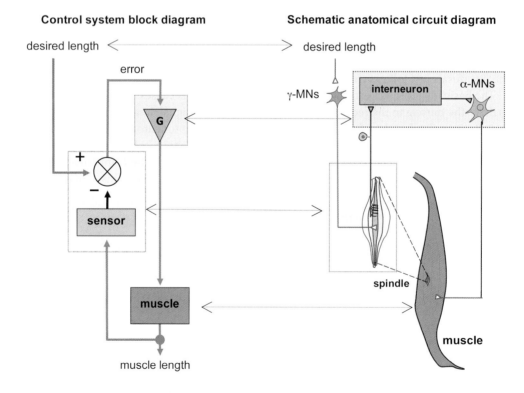

Figure 6.26: *Correspondence between the negative feedback control system block diagram (left) and the stretch reflex circuit components.*

How do the anatomical components shown in Figures 6.24 correspond to the blocks in the feedback control diagram (Figure 6.23)? Figure 6.26 shows the correspondence, and different colors are used to help identify corresponding elements. The sensor and comparator blocks together correspond to the spindle (orange/yellow); the muscle is the same in both (red); and the gain block corresponds to the interneurons and α-motoneurons in the reflex pathway (blue).

6.4.7 Empirical evidence shows that the descending signals can change the threshold of the tonic stretch reflex

According to Merton's servo hypothesis, the desired length of the muscle corresponds to the threshold of the tonic stretch reflex[58]. Thus, the effect of the central command is to change the reflex threshold. Experiments have shown that the tonic stretch reflex threshold can be changed by signals descending to the spinal arcs from higher levels of the CNS[59]. This was demonstrated directly in an experiment on domestic cats in which specific regions of the brainstem were electrically stimulated[60]. This stimulation resulted in action potentials propagating down axons in the animal's spinal cord to segmental reflex circuits. Several different, constant strengths of electrical stimulation were applied, and the force-length curves of the gastrocnemius muscle were measured at each stimulus strength. The result is presented in Figure 6.27. The effect of increasing the level of stimulation was to move the zero point of the force-length curve to the left along the muscle length axis – the zero point occurred at a shorter muscle length when the stimulation level was high. As described earlier, the zero point of the force-length characteristic of an intact muscle corresponds to the threshold of the tonic stretch reflex.

The force-length curves in Figure 6.27 are all similar in shape – the main difference between the curves is the location of the zero point on the length axis. Therefore, the main effect of the brain stimulation was to change the threshold of the tonic stretch reflex. This result is consistent with Merton's hypothesis, though, as discussed later (section 6.4.9), other empirical results contradict the hypothesis.

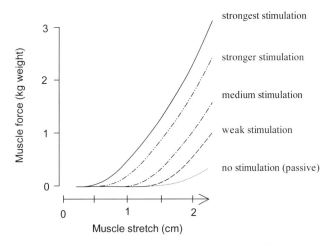

Figure 6.27: *The effect of electrical stimulation strength (of midbrain sites) on the force-length characteristics of reflex-intact muscle. (Based on data reported by Feldman and Orlovsky, 1972.)*

6.4.8 Merton's servo hypothesis only applies to slow movements

Merton's hypothesis implies that there will be a time delay between the arrival of a command at the γ-MNs and a contraction of the muscle. A command changes γ-MN activity first, with a change in the activation of the α-MNs following after signals have traversed the reflex arc.

The delay will be longer than the latency of the autogenic stretch reflex, because after the central command signal arrives at the γ-MNs it must be transmitted to the intrafusal fibers along the γ-MN axons before the stretch reflex circuit can respond.

Merton knew that α-MNs receive inputs from other parts of the central nervous system, including descending inputs from the brain. For the human distal musculature, these descending inputs include monosynaptic inputs from pyramidal output neurons in the motor cortex (Chapter 2). Merton supposed that the direct inputs to α-MNs were used for very urgent or rapid movements, when the time lag associated with use of the stretch reflex circuitry would slow down response time unacceptably. Thus, *Merton proposed two separate command systems: one for slow movements that sends signals to the γ-MNs, and one for urgent, rapid movements that sends signals directly to the α-MNs* (not shown in Figures 6.24–6.26). The advantage of the α-MN route is speed; the advantage of the γ-MN route is compensation for disturbances by the stretch reflex mechanism. Is Merton's proposal correct? This question is considered in the next section.

6.4.9 Other empirical evidence does not support Merton's hypothesis

Merton's servo hypothesis makes several predictions about what should be observed in experiments. First, according to Merton's theory, the sequence of events prior to a slow movement are as follows:

(1) The γ-MNs are activated by central commands, and action potentials are propagated along the γ-efferent axons to the intrafusal fibers.
(2) The spindle afferent stimulation changes in response to a change in intrafusal fiber tension, and action potentials are propagated along the afferent axons to the spinal cord.
(3) Afferent signals are transmitted to the α-MNs; these will fire and action potentials will be propagated along the α-efferent axons to the muscle.

This is not the sequence observed in experiments. During slow muscle contractions, it has been found that the firing rate of spindle afferents starts to change shortly after the start of changes in α-MN activity as measured from the muscle EMG signal, not before[61]. These results and those from many other studies have shown that central commands do not activate only the γ-MNs during slow movements. The general rule is that α-MNs and γ-MNs receive almost simultaneous descending inputs, a phenomenon referred to as **α–γ coactivation**. This appears to be true for both slow and fast movements.

A second problem for Merton's hypothesis is that muscles do not typically move to their threshold lengths (the length at which the muscle develops no force). In the presence of a sustained load, a muscle reaches a length at which the load force is balanced by the force developed by the muscle – the equilibrium length. This is the basis on which static force-length curves for muscles with reflexes are measured: a load force is applied to the muscle, which stretches it; the length at which the muscle stops stretching is where the muscle force is equal and opposite to the applied force. If we think in negative feedback control terms and suppose that the length of the muscle is the controlled variable, then the difference between the threshold length and the equilibrium length is a sustained error that the system cannot eliminate. In control theory, this is called the **steady-state error** of the control system. Steady-state error can be reduced by increasing the loop gain of the feedback system. However, increasing the loop gain can result in unstable behavior, especially when there are significant time delays in the loop (Chapter 1), as in the case of biological systems. It is not surprising, therefore, to find that the gain of the stretch reflex is quite low: far too low for control of muscle length to work in the manner proposed by Merton. The gain of the reflex refers to how much output the reflex circuits produce in response to a particular stimulus (input). The input might be measured as the amount the muscle is stretched beyond its threshold length (call this ΔL) and the output measured as the force developed in response to this stretch (call this ΔF). With input ΔL and output ΔF, the gain is given by $\Delta F/\Delta L$. The reflex gain determines the slope of the force-length characteristic, and hence the stiffness of the muscle – the higher the gain, the greater the stiffness.

Despite these problems, the basic idea behind Merton's servo-hypothesis – that voluntary control of muscle activity is achieved by controlling the threshold of the stretch reflex – is still a viable and important one. Merton's formulation of the idea does not quite fit the facts and requires the introduction of a different control scheme for fast, urgent movements. A reformulation that avoids these difficulties and has been developed into a much more complete account of movement control is the *lambda equilibrium point hypothesis*, described in the next section of the chapter.

6.5 An Introduction to the λ-Equilibrium Point Hypothesis

6.5.1 Introduction

The lambda (λ) equilibrium point hypothesis (**λ-hypothesis** for short) was formulated by A.G. Feldman and is a development of the ideas on which Merton's servo hypothesis is based. Like Merton's hypothesis, it supposes that central commands specify the threshold of the stretch reflex – specifically the tonic stretch reflex. The muscle's threshold length is denoted by the Greek letter lambda. Since central commands set the threshold length, the threshold is the *control variable* of the λ-hypothesis. This is the fundamental idea behind the hypothesis:

> **CONTROL VARIABLE IN THE λ-HYPOTHESIS:** the neuromuscular control variable is the threshold of the tonic stretch reflex (the muscle length at which tonic recruitment of α-motoneurons begins).

There are three crucial differences between the λ-hypothesis and Merton's servo hypothesis:

(1) The reflex threshold (λ) is centrally specified not only by signals to the γ-motoneurons but by any descending signals that influence the tonic stretch reflex pathway. This includes signals to the α-motoneurons and signals to interneurons in the pathway, which means that the λ-hypothesis is compatible with α–γ coactivation. We have already discussed how descending signals to interneurons in a reflex pathway can alter the threshold of a reflex (section 6.1.2) and the same principle applies when the signal descends to the α-MNs. Figure 6.28 illustrates the multiplicity of descending signals to neurons in the stretch reflex arcs.

(2) The mechanism of control is the same for both fast and slow movements, and the reflex loop delay does not contribute to the time between the arrival of the central command signal at the segmental reflex circuits and the initiation of a muscle contraction.

(3) The threshold length (λ) does not correspond to the length that the muscle is required to reach (it is not the *controlled* variable). Thus, there is no need for the reflex gain to be high to keep a steady-state error small: the difference between the threshold length and the actual length of the muscle is not an error.

If the threshold length is not the controlled variable, then what is? The λ-hypothesis provides a simple answer to this question: it is the equilibrium length of the muscle (or equilibrium position of a joint). Before explaining the exact meaning of this answer, it will be useful to consider how the lambda-hypothesis deals with the direct activation of α-motoneurons by descending signals.

6.5.2 Central commands cannot directly control muscle activity

There are direct (monosynaptic) corticospinal projections from the motor cortex (M1) to the α-MN pools of distal muscles of the upper limbs in humans and other primates (see Chapter 2). There are also indirect pathways from M1 to α-MNs that go via one or more spinal interneurons. Figure 6.28 shows both a direct and an indirect path by which central signals can reach the α-MNs. In Merton's hypothesis, these pathways would be used exclusively for fast, urgent movements; control signals descending to the γ-MNs are used for slow, careful movements.

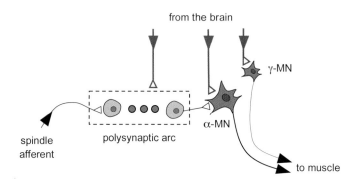

Figure 6.28: *Schematic illustration of some central connections with elements in the tonic stretch reflex arc.*

The problem with the direct control of muscle activity is that the firing rate of α-MNs does not depend only on the central command, but also on afferent signals received via the reflex pathways: in Figure 6.28, the α-MNs are affected by both descending signals and afferent signals. Thus, what an α-MN will actually do in response to a central command depends on the afferent signals it is receiving when the command arrives. In order for a command signal to control exactly what a muscle does, the firing rates of the α-MNs in the muscle's motoneuron pool must depend only on the command signal. This is not possible, since afferent signals will always make a contribution to the α-MN firing rates. In short, direct central commands to α-MN pools cannot specify the level of muscle activity and so cannot specify muscle force: both muscle activity and muscle force are co-determined by central commands and afferent feedback.

The distinction between direct and indirect control of muscle activity does not exist in the λ-hypothesis. In the λ-hypothesis, if a central command were sent only to the α-MNs, its effect would be described in the same way as for a command sent only to the γ-MNs: there would be a change in the threshold of the tonic stretch reflex. Even if a direct command were to cause α-MNs to fire and increase muscle activity, its effect is still describable as a change in the reflex threshold.

6.5.3 The muscle reaches an equilibrium length determined by the reflex threshold and the load

Recall that force-length characteristics are determined in experiments that involve applying particular stretching forces to the muscle (the loads) and measuring the steady lengths that the muscle adopts in each case once it has stopped stretching. At each steady length, the load and the muscle force are in equilibrium (equal in magnitude and acting in opposite directions); such a length is an **equilibrium length**.

The equilibrium length depends on both the load and the stretch reflex threshold. Figure 6.29 shows two different force-length characteristics associated with two different threshold lengths (λ_1, λ_2). If the load and muscle forces are equal in magnitude (call the magnitude F), then the equilibrium length of the muscle will be different when the thresholds are different:

in the figure, the equilibrium lengths are L_1 and L_2 respectively. In each case, the equilibrium length is longer than the threshold length – the muscle is stretched beyond the threshold, and the stretch reflex response is elicited. The amount of stretch is equal to the difference between the equilibrium length and the threshold, so in Figure 6.29 the stretches are equal to $(L_1 - \lambda_1)$ and $(L_2 - \lambda_2)$ for the orange and red cases respectively.

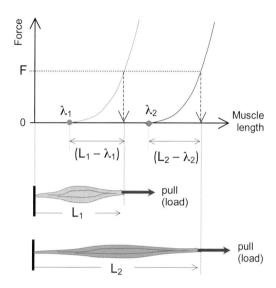

Figure 6.29: *The equilibrium length of a muscle subject to a particular load (pull) depends on the threshold length (λ).*

To summarize: when the load and the threshold length are constant, the muscle reaches an equilibrium length at which the load and muscle forces are equal and opposite. Thus, when loads are present, a muscle will not reach the threshold length – it will reach an equilibrium length that is greater than the threshold length. The presence of loads is the rule, not the exception. Whenever you hold something, or push or pull on something, or when something pushes or pulls on you, there are load forces that tend to stretch some of your muscles. In most circumstances, the weights of your limb segments act as loads on associated muscles. This means, of course, that the threshold length of a muscle cannot be the length that the neural control system requires the muscle to reach (the controlled variable), because the muscle will hardly ever be able to reach this length due to the action of loads.

6.5.4 The equilibrium length can be controlled only if the load is known

Suppose that the motor control centers in the nervous system require that a muscle reach a particular length. According to the λ-hypothesis, the control centers can only do this by setting the muscle's threshold length (λ). However, the length that the muscle will actually reach is determined not only by λ, but also by the load. For example, referring to Figure 6.30, if the length that the muscle is required to reach is L_1, the control centers need to set the threshold at the value λ_1, but this will only work if the load has the value F. If the load is different, the equilibrium length will be different. Figure 6.30 shows that the muscle will reach an equilibrium length of L_1 if the load has magnitude F, but a different length (L_1') if the load has magnitude F' (at equilibrium load and muscle force, magnitudes are equal). This means that in order to cause the muscle to reach a particular equilibrium length, the control centers need to know what the load is, so that the appropriate value of λ can be found. Thus, the control centers are doing the following: given a certain required muscle length and information about the load acting on the muscle, they determine the value of λ that will make the equilibrium length equal to the required length.

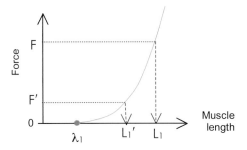

Figure 6.30: *If the threshold is constant, a muscle reaches different equilibrium lengths when the magnitude of the load force is different (illustrative).*

The major difference between the λ-hypothesis and Merton's servo hypothesis should now be clear. In Merton's hypothesis, the neuromuscular *control variable* (the quantity manipulated by the action of the central nervous system) and the *controlled variable* (the quantity that is required to reach a particular value) are one and the same: the threshold length of the muscle. In the λ-hypothesis, the control variable is still the threshold length, but the controlled variable is the equilibrium length of the muscle:

> **BASIC CONTROLLED VARIABLE IN THE λ-HYPOTHESIS:** for individual muscles, the controlled variable is the length at which equilibrium between the muscle force and the load force is reached.

It is now clear why the λ-equilibrium point hypothesis is so named: 'λ' refers to the control variable in the hypothesis, and 'equilibrium point' refers to the controlled variable.

The problem for Merton's hypothesis is that in the presence of loads, there will always be a steady-state error – a difference between the actual length of the muscle and the threshold length. This error is something that must either be avoided or at least kept very small, but this is only feasible if the gain of the reflex is high. High reflex gains are not physiologically plausible, nor have they been observed in experiments. In the λ-hypothesis, the difference between the actual length and the threshold length is not something to be avoided, and so a high reflex gain is not needed. However, there is a price to pay: in order to be able to control the equilibrium length, the central control mechanisms must be able to estimate the load acting on the muscle and use this information to determine the appropriate value for the threshold.

6.5.5 Shifts in lambda cause a muscle to move from one equilibrium to another

Consider Figure 6.30: if the load is initially F and then is changed to F', the muscle will shorten from an initial length of L_i to a final length of L_i'. This simply illustrates the fact that the length of a muscle will change if the load is changed (keeping the threshold length constant). Muscle length will also change if the load is kept constant and a central command changes lambda from one value to another – a shift in lambda. Such shifts are the mechanism of voluntary movement production according to the λ-hypothesis.

Figure 6.31 illustrates the effect of a shift in lambda. Panel A shows the initial situation: the current level of the central command is constant and specifies a threshold length $λ_i$ (i for initial), and the muscle has the force-length characteristic shown. The load has a particular magnitude (F), and the equilibrium length of the muscle under these conditions is L_i. The central command then shifts lambda from $λ_i$ to a new constant value, $λ_f$ (f for final). With lambda at the new value, L_i is no longer the equilibrium length – the equilibrium length has also shifted to a new value (L_f), as shown in panel B. The result is that the muscle will shorten from its initial length (L_i) to the new length (L_f).

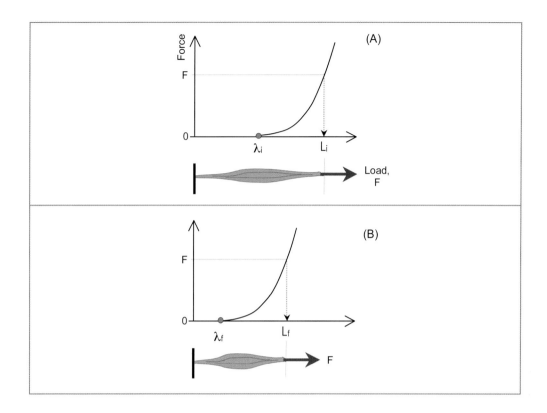

Figure 6.31: *Illustration of how a shift in the threshold (λ_i to λ_f) changes the equilibrium position (in constant load conditions).*

The simple example just presented illustrates the fact that in the λ-hypothesis, postures are associated with equilibria, and movements are the transitions from one equilibrium to another. The actual situation is rather more complex than the single muscle example that has been presented so far. Body movements and postures involve many muscles: it is the action of all of these that produce postures and movements of the limbs. In the sections that follow, we consider how antagonistic muscle groups acting at a single joint can be controlled to generate different movements and postures.

6.5.6 Antagonist muscles determine the equilibrium position of a single joint

When discussing limb movement and posture, we will stick to the familiar example of the elbow joint and flexion-extension movements. To keep things simple, we will suppose that the joint is actuated by just two muscles – a flexor muscle and an extensor muscle.

The position of a single joint is described by the joint angle, and in this context it makes better sense to consider the *torque-angle characteristic* of a muscle rather than its force-length characteristic. The two types of characteristic are very similar in shape, since each muscle length is associated with a particular joint angle, and a particular muscle force is associated with a particular torque (see Chapter 2). Since each length is associated with a particular angular position, the threshold length (λ) is associated with a **threshold joint angle**. We will normally use the Greek letter theta (θ) to denote joint angles, and the shorthand notation θ(λ) will be used to denote the threshold angle. This shorthand reminds us that the threshold angle is the joint's angular position (θ) when the muscle is at the threshold length (λ).

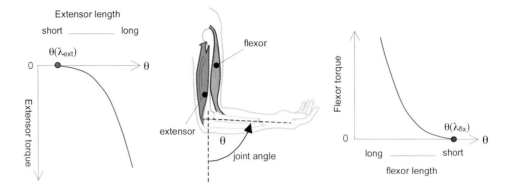

Figure 6.32: *Illustrative torque-angle characteristics of flexor and extensor muscles.*

Both the flexor and the extensor muscles have torque-angle characteristics; examples are shown in Figure 6.32. In the center of the figure is an arm with the elbow joint actuated by a flexor muscle and an extensor muscle. Sticking with convention, the elbow joint angle is defined externally, so that it increases in the flexion (counterclockwise) direction (see Chapter 2). The flexor muscle acts to increase the joint angle, and so it exerts a positive torque. As the joint angle increases, the length of the flexor decreases. This means that the flexor muscle force tends to be smaller when the angle is greater, and so the flexor torque is lower at greater angles. This accounts for why the flexor torque-angle characteristic (Figure 6.32, right) is the opposite way around to the force-length characteristics presented in earlier figures. The extensor muscle acts to decrease the joint angle (clockwise rotation in the figure) and so exerts a negative torque. As the joint angle increases, the length of the extensor increases. This accounts for why the extensor torque-angle characteristic is 'upside down' (Figure 6.32, left). The threshold lengths of the two muscles are denoted λ_{ext} (lambda extensor) and λ_{flx} (lambda flexor); the associated threshold angles are $\theta(\lambda_{ext})$ and $\theta(\lambda_{flx})$.

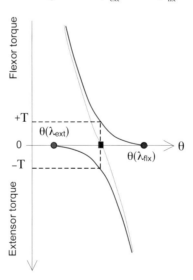

Figure 6.33: *Flexor and extensor torque-angle characteristics plotted on the same set of axes. The two muscle torques are equal when the joint angle has the value marked ■. The total torque (sum of the flexor and extensor torques) is represented by the dotted curve.*

It is convenient and instructive to put the two torque-angle characteristics together on a single graph, and this is done in Figure 6.33. It is clear that there is just one joint angle where the two muscle torques are equal in magnitude. This angle has been marked with a black square in the figure: the flexor torque is +T and the extensor torque is −T. Since these torques are equal and opposite, the angular position marked with a square is an equilibrium position of the joint. In effect, the torque developed by one muscle is acting as a load on the other.

Figure 6.33 also shows the total muscle torque as a function of joint angle (dotted curve). This is just the sum of the torques developed by the two muscles, and is clearly zero when the torques are equal and opposite. The dotted curve is called the **joint torque-angle characteristic**. This characteristic is useful for seeing what the equilibrium position will be when another load is present. As an example of such a load, suppose that the arm in Figure 6.32 were oriented vertically with respect to gravity. In this situation, the weight of the forearm segment produces a torque about the elbow that acts to extend the joint. The magnitude of this torque depends on the joint angle: it is equal to the weight multiplied by the sine of the joint angle, and so is zero at full extension (0°) and maximum at 90°. Figure 6.34 shows the magnitude of the load due to the weight of the forearm plotted as a function of joint angle, together with the joint torque-angle characteristic from Figure 6.33 (the torque is zero when the arm is extended with both segments oriented vertically). The load and muscle torques are equal and opposite at the point where the load force curve crosses the joint torque-angle characteristics (open circle). The equilibrium position of the limb is the angular position marked by the black square.

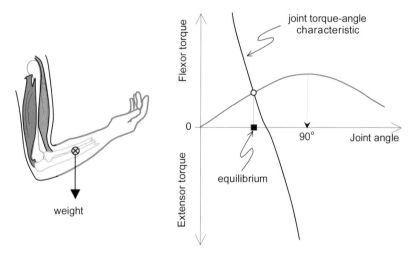

Figure 6.34: *The weight of the forearm exerts a torque at the elbow. The joint equilibrium angle (■) is where the weight torque is equal to the total joint torque.*

6.5.7 The equilibrium position of the joint can be controlled by shifting the threshold angles in the same direction

For simplicity, consider the situation in which there are no torques acting at the elbow other than the muscle torques. This can happens if the arm is held freely with both the upper arm and forearm in a horizontal plane. Figure 6.32 represents such a situation, since there are no torques other than the muscle torques. It should be clear from this diagram that if the threshold angles were both further to the right on the page, then the equilibrium position (■) would also be further to the right (at a larger joint angle). This is shown in Figure 6.35: the threshold angles have small values in 'A' and large values in 'B'.

Figure 6.35 shows that if the threshold angles of the flexor and extensor muscles are shifted together in the same angular direction (say from their locations in A to their locations in B), then the joint equilibrium position will also shift in that direction (black square in A to black square in B). A central command that shifted the flexor and extensor threshold lengths (λ_{flx}, λ_{ext}) to produce a shift of the threshold angles ($\theta(\lambda_{flx})$, $\theta(\lambda_{ext})$) in the same angular direction would have the effect of moving the joint equilibrium position. In Figure 6.35 a command that shifted the threshold lengths such that the threshold angles moved from their positions in A to those in B would cause the elbow to flex from the relatively extended posture shown on the left to the more flexed posture on the right. This simple example illustrates the control principle described by the title of this section: the equilibrium position of a joint can be controlled by a central command that shifts the threshold angles of the flexor and extensor muscles in the same angular direction (i.e., both to the left or both to the right on the joint angle axis of a torque-angle plot). More details are given in section 6.5.9.

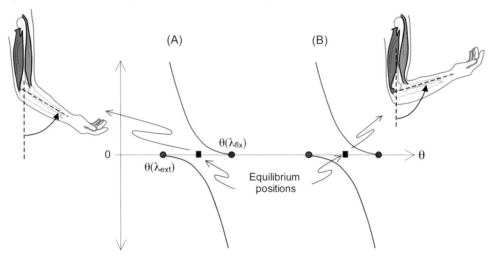

Figure 6.35: *Different threshold joint angles for the flexor and extensor muscles are associated with different equilibrium positions of the joint.*

6.5.8 The angular distance between threshold angles determines the level of antagonist co-contraction

In the situation illustrated in Figure 6.35, there are no external loads present, and the limb will adopt an equilibrium position in which both muscles are active and exerting equal and opposite torques at the elbow joint. This equilibrium is therefore a stable posture of the arm in which the antagonist muscles are co-contracted (see Chapter 2).

The muscles could be co-contracted and exerting relatively little torque (a low level of co-contraction) or they could be generating a lot of torque (a high level of co-contraction). The level of co-contraction depends on how far apart the threshold angles are, as illustrated in Figure 6.36. In this figure, the threshold angles are far apart in panel A, closer in B, and at the same position in C. The further apart the threshold angles are, the greater the level of co-contraction, provided that the flexor threshold angle is greater than the extensor threshold angle (panels A and B). If the thresholds coincide, there is no co-contraction and the muscles are relaxed (C). In this case, the threshold angle is the equilibrium position of the joint. If the flexor threshold angle is less than the extensor threshold angle (panel D), there is again no co-contraction, but now there is no unique equilibrium position: the muscles develop no active force at any point between the two thresholds (the relaxation zone).

In Figure 6.36, the equilibrium positions in panels A, B and C are all stable equilibria because small disturbances away from the equilibrium position result in muscle forces that bring the joint back to that position. These restoring forces are largest in A and smallest in C. This is not the case in panel D if the joint is at an angle between the two thresholds (in the relaxation zone) – small disturbances that move the joint within the relaxation zone do not result in restoring forces. All the joint positions between the two threshold angles are neutrally stable equilibrium points.

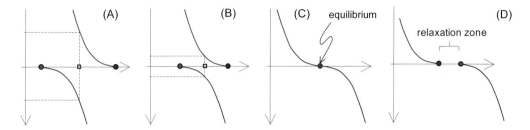

Figure 6.36: *The distance between the threshold joint angles for the flexor and extensor muscles determines the muscle torques at equilibrium.*

The observations made in the last paragraph can be usefully rephrased in terms of **joint stiffness**. This is the slope of the joint torque-angle characteristic (shown in Figure 6.33). The stiffness is greatest in panel A of Figure 6.36 and less in panel B (the joint characteristics are not shown). In panel C, the joint torque-angle characteristic is the same as the two muscle characteristics together, and the same is true in panel D; in other words, panels C and D show the joint torque-angle characteristics. Thus, it is clear from panel C that the joint stiffness is very low close to the equilibrium position, and panel D shows that the joint stiffness is zero in the relaxation zone.

6.5.9 Two different central commands for single joint control

A person can co-contract the muscles at a joint without moving (i.e., without changing the joint position): you can easily confirm this for yourself by simultaneously contracting the elbow flexors and extensors. It also seems intuitively likely that a person can move from one joint position to another without the level of co-contraction being different in the two positions. A series of experimental studies led Feldman[62] to propose that the central nervous system controls single joints using two independent commands:

(1) A **co-activation command** ('c-command' for short) that has the effect of co-activating the antagonist muscles without changing the joint angle at which the sum of the muscle torques is zero.

(2) A **reciprocal activation command** ('r-command' for short) that has the effect of changing the joint angle at which the muscle torques sum to zero but does not change the level of co-activation.

The c-command has the effect of shifting the threshold angles of the flexor and extensor muscles by the same amount in opposite directions along the joint angle axis (both thresholds are raised, or both are lowered). Notice that this means that the threshold lengths of the two muscles shift by the same amount in the same direction, either in the direction of shorter lengths or of longer ones. Thus, the c-command is simply a signal that causes the same shift in the threshold lengths of the flexor and extensor muscles.

If the c-command shift moves the threshold angles further apart (lowers both thresholds), the result is that the slope of the joint torque-angle characteristic increases (stiffness increases). If the shift moves the thresholds closer together (raises both thresholds), the result is that the slope of the joint torque-angle characteristic decreases (stiffness decreases). The first case is illustrated in Figure 6.37, in which only the joint torque-angle characteristics and threshold angles are shown. The thresholds are shifted by the same amount but in opposite directions, from an initial case shown in gray to a final case shown in green. The slope of the initial joint torque-angle characteristic (dashed gray curve) is less than the slope of the final characteristic (solid green curve), and so the joint stiffness has increased as a result of the shifts in the threshold angles. The black square marks the joint equilibrium angle. If you imagine that the green circles mark the initial threshold angles and the gray circles the final angles, then the figure would illustrate the second case.

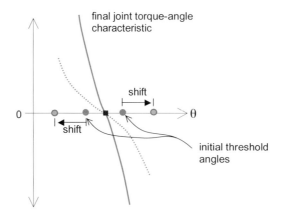

Figure 6.37: *A shift in the threshold angles in opposite directions changes the stiffness of the joint (slope of the joint torque-angle characteristic). See text for details.*

Notice that in Figure 6.37, the equilibrium angle (black square) is the same in the initial situation (gray) and the final situation (green). This means that when there are no other loads present (there are no loads in the figure), the shift of the thresholds does not change the position of the joint, only the joint stiffness.

The r-command has the effect of shifting the threshold angles of the flexor and extensor muscles by the same amount in the same directions along the joint angle axis. This is the situation shown in Figure 6.35, where the threshold shifts could be from initial locations in 'A' to final locations in 'B' or the other way around. A shift in the threshold angles in the same direction on the angle axis means that the threshold lengths of the two muscles shift in opposite directions along the length axis. Thus, the r-command is a signal that causes the same sized shift in the threshold lengths of the flexor and extensor muscles, but in opposite directions.

The effect of an r-command is a change in the joint equilibrium position with no change in the slope of the joint torque-angle characteristic. This means that the command causes a change in joint position (the limb moves to a new equilibrium position) but no change in joint stiffness. Of course, it is possible to issue a c-command and an r-command simultaneously, which would change the equilibrium position of the joint and the slope of the joint torque-angle characteristic at the same time.

The picture described in this section has a nice simplicity: changes in joint position are controlled by one type of central command, and changes in stiffness by another type. However, it is important to be aware that this simplicity is only apparent, as there are a number of subtleties involved. One of these relates to the fact that we have assumed that the torque-angle characteristics are exactly the same shape in the flexors and extensors, but exploration of this and other subtleties is beyond the scope of the present discussion[63].

6.5.10 How do the levels of the central commands change in the production of movement?

So far we have considered only the initial and final values of the thresholds and stated that a central command shifts the thresholds from the initial to the final values. We have not yet considered what type of shift is involved: is it sudden and immediate, or slow and progressive? An infinite number of possibilities exist for how the shift might take place, and it is likely to be different for different movements. Figure 6.38 shows three possible ways in which the r-command might shift from an initial value associated with the joint in one equilibrium position to a final value associated with the joint in a new equilibrium position: panel A is a step shift, panel B is a ramp, and panel C involves an overshoot of the final value of the command (similar possibilities can be imagined for the c-command). In the figure, the initial position is relatively extended and the final position relatively flexed. The r-command is considered to be a neural signal in which the firing rate determines the thresholds for both muscles in an antagonistic pair. In the case shown in Figure 6.38, the flexor is the prime mover, and so the r-command excites the reflex circuitry and lowers the threshold for this muscle. Conversely, the threshold for the extensor is raised, and so the r-command has an inhibitory effect on the extensor reflex circuitry. This is a reciprocal effect: when one threshold is raised, the other is lowered, which typically results in an increase in the activity of one muscle and a decrease in the activity of the other.

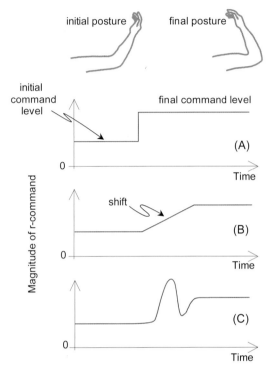

Figure 6.38: *Different ways in which the r-command could shift from an initial level to a final level to produce an elbow flexion movement from the initial posture to the final posture shown at the top.*

It is not yet possible to definitively say how the r- and c-commands must shift in order to produce movements like the ones that people actually make. There have been some plausible suggestions, but not enough of the necessary background material has been presented at this stage of the text for them to be discussed here (we return to this matter briefly in Chapter 11). The reader is referred to the research literature for complete discussions of how the central commands might be formulated in the λ-hypothesis and for how the hypothesis explains dynamic aspects of movement, such as the formation of limb trajectories and the evolution of EMG patterns over time[64].

6.5.11 Summary: two components of the λ-hypothesis

The λ-hypothesis is based on a set of fundamental ideas that have been described in the foregoing sections of this part of the chapter. These can be divided into two groups:

▸ **GROUP 1)** Ideas concerning the control and controlled variables. These ideas relate to the spinal and biomechanical mechanisms of movement control and execution.
▸ **GROUP 2)** Ideas concerning the organization and content of central commands. These ideas relate to the brain mechanisms of motor control.

We can say that group 1 relate to *peripheral* processes and group 2 to *central* processes. Figure 6.39 is an attempt to summarize in diagrammatic form the basic ideas and their division into these two groups. The example used is that of an elbow joint subject to an external load and actuated by a pair of antagonist muscles: a flexor in red and an extensor in blue. The segmental neural circuits associated with the autogenic stretch reflexes of these two muscles are represented as blocks with dials on them: the flexor circuits are shown in red, and the extensor circuits in blue. The dials represent the control variable – the threshold of the tonic stretch reflex. The threshold is manipulated by central command signals, as suggested by the schematic hands that turn the dials. The central commands themselves are formulated by command-generating circuits in the brain as r- and c-commands (coded gray and green respectively). At some point, these commands must be 'split' into separate command signals to the two muscles. This job is done by the distributor blocks in Figure 6.39, which may be located at a spinal level, as suggested in the figure. The c-command has a similar effect on the stretch reflex thresholds of the two muscles (it lowers or raises both). The r-command has a reciprocal effect on the thresholds: one threshold is raised (corresponding to a shorter muscle length), while the other is lowered (corresponding to a longer muscle length).

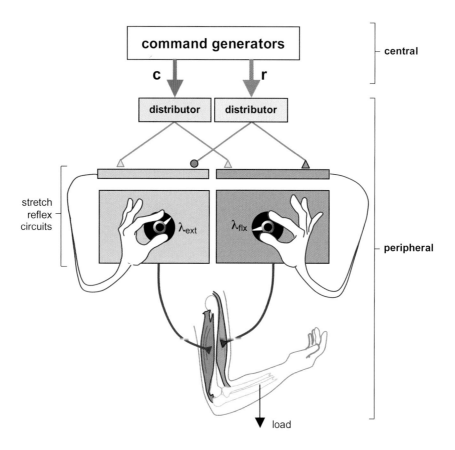

Figure 6.39: *Schematic representation of the elements of the λ-hypothesis divided into central (brain level) processes and peripheral (spinal and limb) level processes.*

6.5.12 Controversy

The λ-hypothesis is exactly what its name suggests: an hypothesis. As with all hypotheses, it has raised some controversy, and people disagree about whether it provides an adequate and/ or accurate description of neuromuscular control. No discussion of the hypothesis would be complete without some mention of the controversy surrounding it.

Two different types of objection can be distinguished: first, objections to the ideas that relate to peripheral processes (group 1 in section 6.5.11); second, objections to the ideas that relate to central processes (group 2 in section 6.5.11). It should be recognized that the two groups of ideas are to some extent independent, in the sense that those in group 2 could be in error but those in group 1 correct, or vice versa. The ideas in group 1 constitute the fundamentals of the λ-hypothesis. If these ideas are incorrect, then the λ-hypothesis must be abandoned, whereas if the ideas in group 2 are incorrect, the λ-hypothesis would still be viable, but new or better ideas concerning the organization of central commands would be needed. We will consider some of the ideas in group 2 in Chapter 11; here we will briefly consider two important objections[65] to the ideas in group 1, and a general objection that applies at both peripheral and central levels.

Objection 1: People and animals that have been deafferented are still capable of controlling movement. Although their skill is reduced, they are not completely incapacitated. This does not appear to be compatible with the idea that neuromuscular control is achieved by manipulating the threshold of the stretch reflex, since without afference there is no reflex.

Response: As we have seen, the central commands affect the excitability of segmental neurons, including α- and γ-motoneurons (section 6.5.1). These neurons are interconnected to form the circuitry of the autogenic stretch reflexes. When the nervous system is intact, the effect of the commands is to shift the threshold of the reflex. When the system is deafferented, such a description is no longer appropriate, since there is no reflex action. However, it is clear that the command mechanism remains intact and α-motoneurons can be still be activated, which means that voluntary (and involuntary) contraction of muscles is still possible. Thus, the λ-hypothesis is not incompatible with the possibility of controlling movement when deafferented, but in the deafferented preparation the threshold length for motoneuron recruitment cannot be altered and so is no longer the control variable. Thus, it is necessary for the animal to learn to use a different control variable – presumably just the level of muscle activation[66]. In effect, in a deafferented animal, λ is no longer the control variable, and so the λ-language becomes inappropriate. This may also be true for the control of extraocular muscles, which appear to lack stretch reflexes[67].

Objection 2: There is empirical evidence that not only can the threshold of the tonic stretch reflex be modified by central commands, but also its gain. The gain and threshold of the phasic stretch reflex also appear to be modifiable. How can these facts be reconciled with the λ-hypothesis, which supposes that control is based on the modification of the tonic reflex threshold only?

Response: It is clear that the CNS can modulate parameters other than the tonic stretch reflex threshold, and so the λ-hypothesis as described in this chapter can only be considered a first approximation to a more complete theory. We do not need to conclude that the λ-hypothesis as described here is wrong, merely that it is not complete. The hypothesis has been extended to include the phasic stretch reflex and possible modulation of its parameters, which is important for accounting for the generation of EMG patterns during movement[68]. This and other developments are highly technical, however, and beyond the scope of this text[69].

Objection 3: Proponents of the λ-hypothesis have claimed that internal models of limb geometry and dynamics are not necessary for the production of skilled motor behavior. However, recent empirical studies have made it clear that internal models of this sort are crucial. Does this not seriously undermine the plausibility of the λ-hypothesis?

Response: This is most likely a misunderstanding on the part of those who claim that internal models are not needed in the λ-hypothesis. It is impossible to control a dynamic system such as the musculoskeletal system without some kind of internal knowledge of the structure and/or dynamics of that system. As we saw in Chapter 1, knowledge concerning the controlled system that is used in the formation of control signals constitutes an internal model, and is essential for successful pre-programmed (open-loop) control, feedback control and sensory feedforward control. The λ-hypothesis is a hypothesis about the variable that the central nervous system uses to control muscles. Internal models are required regardless of the nature of the control variable.

References & Notes

[1] Very small changes in EMG consistent with the reflex responses have been reported (Tokizane *et al.*, 1951).

[2] Roberts (1978).

[3] Fukuda (1961).

[4] Hellebrandt *et al.* (1956).

[5] Similar results to those obtained at the wrist have been found in other limb muscles, such as the elbow flexors (Deutsch *et al.*, 1987).

[6] Based on animal work.

[7] Flynn (1972).

[8] Flynn (1972).

[9] The circuits have been determined in the monkey; human saccade generation appears to be similar (Moschovakis, Scudder, Highstein, 1996; Sparks, 2002; Scudder *et al.*, 2002).

[10] Maier, Groh (2009); Sparks (1986).

[11] There is also a pathway from the retina to V1 to the superior colliculi that may be involved in some reflex-like saccades (Isa, Sparks, 2006; Munoz, Schall, 2003).

[12] See Leigh, Zee (2006).

[13] The connectivity of the superior colliculus is more complex than can be described here; see Isa, Sparks (2006); Leigh, Zee (2006); Johnston, Everling (2008); McDowell *et al.* (2008).

[14] The account given here is somewhat simplified for the sake of clarity.

[15] See Leigh, Zee (2006); Scudder *et al.* (2002); Sparks (2002).

[16] Robinson (1975); Sparks (2002).

[17] See Sparks (2002).

[18] Guthrie, Porter, Sparks (1983).

[19] Robinson (1975); Zee *et al.* (1976).

[20] Robinson (1975).

[21] Figure based on figures in Sparks (2002) and Leigh, Zee (2006).

[22] There are actually two classes of excitatory burst neuron in the PPRF that play different roles in saccade generation: neurons in one class are just called EBNs, those in the other are called *long lead burst neurons* (LLBNs).

[23] See Gancarz, Grossberg (1998); Goossens, van Opstal (2006); Scudder *et al.* (2002).

[24] See references in notes 15 and 23 for details.

[25] Moschovakis, Scudder, Highstein, (1996); Sparks (2002).

[26] See Leigh, Zee (2006).

[27] There appear to be several different types of output neuron located in various places in the intermediate and deep layers. See Sparks (1986, 2002).

[28] Robinson (1972).

[29] Taken from data presented in Figure 4 in Robinson (1972).

[30] This is referred to as *population coding*. How the firing of a population determines the saccade characteristics is discussed in Sparks (2002), Gancarz, Grossberg (1998), Goossens, van Opstal (2006).

[31] Moschovakis *et al.* (1998).

[32] See Schall (2002), Sparks (2002).

[33] Figure based on first figure on page 275 in Rodieck (1998).

[34] Schiller, Stryker (1972).

[35] Robinson (1972); Schiller, Stryker (1972).

[36] At least in some species; see Isa, Sparks (2006); Lee *et al.* (1997).

[37] Sparks, Nelson (1987).

[38] The word 'synergy' has been used in a number of different ways in the literature. For discussion see Latash (2008b).

[39] There is some controversy concerning the role of muscle synergies in voluntary motor control; see Tresch, Jarc (2009).

[40] First identified by Nicolai Bernstein. The definition given here follows the discussion of Turvey, Fitch, Tuller (1982).

[41] Like the vestibuloocular reflex, the VCR has a rotational part and a translational part (Keshner, 2003). We discuss only the rotational part here.

[42] Wilson *et al.* (1992).

[43] Dutia, Hunter (1985).

[44] Figure 6.16 is a simplification of the circuitry hypothesized by Uchino and colleagues (Uchino, 2004).

[45] The circuits discussed here are not the only ones involved in the coronal VCR (Wilson, Schor, 1999). It seems likely that the disynaptic pathways mediate the phasic component of the VCR, not the tonic component. The phasic component probably acts primarily as a damping mechanism to reduce head oscillation (Goldberg, Cullen, 2011).

[46] Goldberg, Cullen (2011).

[47] Von Holst, Mittelstadt (1950/1973).

[48] The mechanism described in the text is probably only part of a more complex story. For instance, it has been reported that muscle activation patterns during reflex and 'voluntary' head movements in cats are different even when the movements themselves are indistinguishable (Keshner, Peterson, 1988). This suggests that voluntary movements involve more than can be provided by reflex mechanisms alone.

[49] Goldberg and Cullen (2011) describe findings from studies of single neuron recordings in the VCR pathway that lend some support to the hypothesis that the VCR is suppressed during active (voluntary) head movement in monkeys.

[50] Houk (1979).

[51] Matthews (1959a,b); Feldman, Orlovsky (1972).

[52] The muscle may develop a small passive force due to the intrinsic elasticity of the tissue itself. This small force is neglected in the discussion presented in the main text.

[53] Based on Windhorst (1994).

[54] For further discussion see Tresilian (1999a) and Windhorst (1994).

[55] Granit (1970).

[56] Merton (1953).

[57] The monosynaptic pathway mediates a response to muscle lengthening. For this reason, the mechanism in Merton's hypothesis is more appropriately identified with the tonic stretch reflex (Granit, 1970).

[58] In Granit's (1970) improved version of Merton's original proposal.

[59] Matthews (1959a,b); Feldman, Orlovsky (1972).

[60] Feldman, Orlovsky (1972).

[61] Valbo (1971).

[62] Feldman (1980a,b).

[63] It is known that flexor and extensor muscles typically have different strengths, sizes, tendon length and pennation pattern, and so are unlikely to possess torque-angle characteristics that are exactly the same shape. The only way to achieve a similar shaped torque-angle characteristic in muscles with different properties is to compensate for these differences with neural mechanisms. For a discussion see Tresilian (1999a).

[64] Feldman (1986) provides a good introduction to the application of the hypothesis in dynamic situations.

[65] A variety of objections to the ideas in group 1 have been raised, but many of these relate in one way or another to the two basic objections discussed in the text; see Bizzi et al. (1992), Feldman, Levin (1995, 2009), Feldman, Latash (2005).

[66] See Berkinblit et al. (1986).

[67] See Dancause et al. (2007); Tresilian (1999a).

[68] See Feldman et al. (1990).

[69] See, e.g., Feldman, Levin (1995, 2009)

CHAPTER 7

Orienting to the Environment and Controlling Upright Stance

7.1 Sensorimotor Orientation to the Gravitational Vertical

7.1.1 Introduction

We orient our bodies with respect to our environment in characteristic ways. When we stand, we normally adopt an upright orientation in which our feet are in contact with the ground and our legs, trunk and head are aligned more or less vertically. When we walk around, we hold our heads and trunks in somewhat similar vertically upright orientations. Most other animals also orient themselves in characteristic upright postures. Mammals, birds, lizards and fish all adopt upright body postures for most of their waking hours: Figure 7.1 shows a blue shark and a heron in characteristic upright orientations (the vertical direction is up the page).

Figure 7.1: *Blue shark and heron in 'upright' orientations (not drawn to scale!).*

Note that the shark is darker on its back (dorsal surface) than on its belly. This is called *countershading* and it is a characteristic that the shark shares with many other animals. It has been suggested that countershading makes animals more difficult to see, increasing the chances that a prey animal will not be seen by a predator or that an approaching predator, such as a shark, will not be seen by the prey – it is a form of camouflage[1]. Figure 7.2 reproduces one of the first photographic illustrations of the effectiveness of the camouflaging effect of countershading[2]: a grouse (a ground-nesting bird related to the chicken) with normal countershaded plumage is located within the scene in panel A, and with its countershading removed by dyeing the ventral plumage in panel B. Countershading will only work as camouflage if the animal orients itself with the dark side facing towards the light source and the pale side facing downwards towards the earth, as in the case of the grouse in panel A of Figure 7.2 and the shark in Figure 7.1.

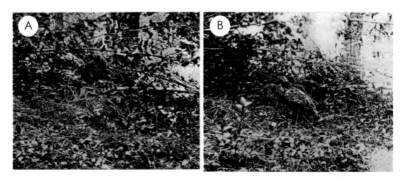

Figure 7.2: *A grouse with countershading (A) and without it (B). From Thayer (1896).*

How do people and animals achieve and maintain their characteristic upright postural orientations? To what exactly are they orienting themselves; how do they determine what is upright? In this part of the chapter we will look at the second question. We will look at the first question in subsequent parts of the chapter.

7.1.2 How should 'upright' and 'vertical' be defined?

We normally use the word upright to mean *vertically oriented* or 'placed in a vertical position'[3], which assumes that we already know the meaning of the term *vertical*. However, a clear and unambiguous definition of vertical seems hard to come by. For example, the Oxford English Dictionary defines *vertical* to mean 'at right angles to a horizontal plane; in a direction, or having an alignment, such that the top is directly above the bottom'[4]. Yes, certainly, but what does it mean for something to be 'directly above' something else, or to be horizontal? In order to provide a complete definition of vertical, we need a frame of reference within which a specific direction is defined to be the vertical direction.

The obvious way to define the vertical direction in natural environments is to identify it with the direction opposite to that of the Earth's gravitational pull. This is the **gravitational vertical**, often just referred to as *the vertical* since no other sorts of vertical are usually relevant:

> **GRAVITATIONAL VERTICAL** (at a particular location): the direction opposite to that of the Earth's gravitational force.

To say that an object is *upright with respect to the (gravitational) vertical* means that an important axis associated with the object is oriented so that it is parallel to the vertical direction, usually with the additional requirement that some part of the object identified as its 'top' be above the part identified as the 'bottom'. Figure 7.3 shows a bottle in an upright orientation: its longitudinal axis of symmetry is parallel to the vertical direction, and the top is directly above the bottom.

It is not quite so straightforward to define an upright orientation for an animal. The heron in Figure 7.1, for example, possesses no obvious axis that is oriented vertically. One basic feature of the vertically upright postures commonly adopted by both animals and people is that the sagittal plane of the trunk (abdomen and thorax) is vertically oriented. This alone is not sufficient; the animal must also be the right way up – feet at the bottom, head at the top, in the case of the heron or a person; dorsal surface up, ventral surface down, in the case of the shark. Of course, people are able to adopt standing postures in which no single body segment is oriented vertically (like the heron in Figure 7.1). As we will see in section 3 of this chapter, the requirement for a standing posture is that the center of gravity of the body (defined in section 7.3.2) lies vertically above the base of support (defined in section 7.3.6) formed by the feet. Thus, we can say that a standing posture for a person is one in which the feet are on the ground and the body's center of gravity is vertically above the base of support; an upright standing posture is one in which the sagittal plane of the trunk is vertically oriented.

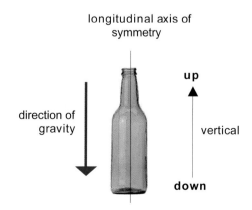

Figure 7.3: *An upright bottle.*

7.1.3 Information about the gravitational vertical can be obtained from the vestibular, somatosensory and visual systems

We naturally adopt upright postures of the body when standing and walking, and we can move a limb segment into a vertical or horizontal orientation. For instance, if you are asked to stretch out your arm horizontally (perpendicular to the gravitational vertical) as shown in Figure 7.4, you can do it quite easily (see section 7.1.4). In order to do these things, we need to obtain information about our orientation with respect to the gravitational vertical. This kind of information must be supplied by our sensory systems. Three sensory systems can provide relevant information: the vestibular system, the somatosensory system and the visual system.

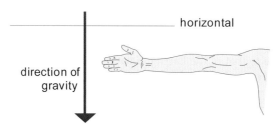

Figure 7.4: *Arm held out straight and horizontal.*

In Chapter 3, we saw how the otolith organs, particularly the utricles, are able to provide information about the orientation of the head with respect to the gravitational vertical (head tilt). In Chapter 6, we saw how the signals from the utricles can be used to maintain an upright orientation of the head with respect to gravity, via the mechanism of the vestibulo-collic reflex. If we can obtain information about how the head is oriented with respect to the vertical, then it is possible to obtain information about the orientation of any body part with respect to the vertical. For example, to determine the orientation of the trunk with respect to the vertical, we need to combine information about the head's orientation with information about the orientation of the head relative to the trunk. Figure 7.5 illustrates the idea: the head is oriented at an angle θ to gravity and the head is oriented at angle β relative to the trunk. Therefore, the trunk is oriented at an angle θ + β to the vertical: sensory information about the angle θ is obtained from the otoliths, while information about the angle β is obtained from proprioceptors in the neck.

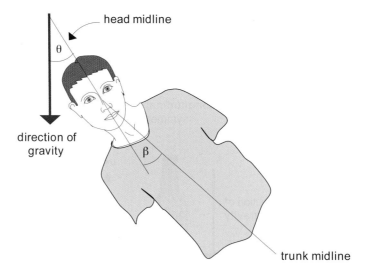

Figure 7.5: *A person leans so that the head and trunk are at different angles with respect to the gravitational vertical.*

Gravity pulls on all the parts of a person's body, which creates stresses and strains within the tissues that can stimulate somatosensory mechanoreceptors of various sorts. For example, joints between bones that support weight, such as the ankles, knees, hips and the intervertebral joints of the spine, are compressed by the weight they support, which deforms the soft tissues and stimulates joint receptors. Similarly, skin and subcutaneous tissues of the body parts that make contact with the surface of support will be compressed, and cutaneous mechanoreceptors will be stimulated. Finally, gravity will pull on tissues that are suspended from bones and other supporting structures; these tissues will be stretched, and mechanoreceptors embedded within them will be stimulated. Such tissues include muscles and their associated connective tissue, and also various internal organs such as the abdominal viscera, the large blood vessels of the trunk, and associated suspensory connective tissue. There is evidence that people are able to make use of information from all these different somatosensory sources, including information provided by visceral mechanoreceptors[5].

Finally, the visual system is also able to provide information about the body's orientation with respect to the gravitational vertical. Of course, gravity does not stimulate the photoreceptors in any way, but it does have an effect on the structure of the visible environment. This structure provides cues to the gravitational vertical. In the urban environment, most walls are vertical and floors horizontal; there are vertical edges to doors and windows, vertical lampposts, and various vertical supporting struts, legs and members. The natural environment also contains cues to the gravitational vertical: tree trunks and the woody stems of various plants are often vertical[6]; the horizon is horizontal, as are the surfaces of standing bodies of water.

7.1.4 Non-visual information contributes to orientation to the gravitational vertical

One way to investigate people's ability to use vestibular and somatosensory information about the direction of the gravitational vertical is to use kinesthetic or haptic orientation tasks[7]. These tasks involve blindfolding a person and having them try to position something so that it is oriented horizontally or vertically with respect to gravity (or possibly some other specified orientation). In a kinesthetic orientation task, the person attempts to move a body part, such as an arm or hand, so that its orientation matches the required orientation. The haptic orientation task is similar, except that the person attempts to move a hand-held rod into an orientation that matches the required orientation. The rods used in these experiments are normally gravity-neutral, in the sense that their weight does not provide information about their orientation relative to gravity. Figure 7.6 illustrates the two kinds of task for a person in a seated posture. Panel A shows a person engaged in a kinesthetic orientation task: they are attempting to move their arm into a horizontal orientation when seated upright (top) and when they are tilted backwards (bottom). This kind of tilt is called **pitch tilt**. Panel B shows a person engaged in a haptic orientation task: they are attempting to move a hand-held rod into a vertical orientation when seated upright (top) or tilted to their left (bottom). This kind of tilt is called **roll tilt**. People's ability to orient a limb segment or a rod to the vertical can be interpreted as a measure of their perception of the vertical. Thus, these tasks are frequently used to assess people's perception of the vertical direction.

Experiments have shown that people's performance in both kinesthetic and haptic orientation tasks is reasonably accurate over a wide range of both pitch and roll tilts. Example results from a haptic orientation task are shown in Figure 7.7. Participants in the experiment were strapped to a bed that could be pitched forwards and backwards or rolled side to side. They were held at different angles of pitch or roll, and their task was to indicate the perceived vertical using a gravity-neutral, hand-held rod. Panel A of Figure 7.7 shows the angle at which participants oriented the rod relative to their midlines (medians for the group) for different angles of pitch tilt (from 100° backwards to 80° forwards). The insert shows how the angles of tilt and rod orientation are defined. The angle of tilt is the angle between the gravitational vertical (blue line) and the midline of the person's head and trunk (dotted line); the rod angle is the angle between the midline and the rod's long axis (dashed line). Perfectly accurate

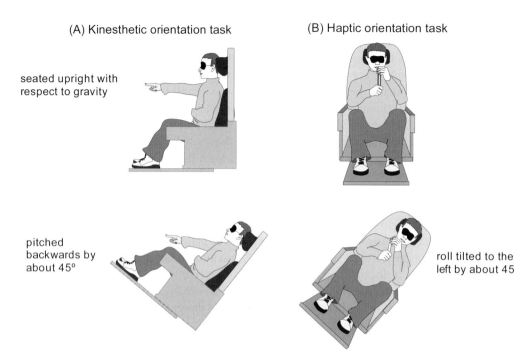

Figure 7.6: *Orientation tasks that involve orienting a body part (A) or an object (B) with respect to the vertical (based on Figure 3 of Carriot, DiZio, Nougier, 2008).*

performance is represented by the straight diagonal line in the graph (rod orientation angle equal to the angle of tilt). Panel A shows that participants were able to orient the rod to the vertical quite accurately. Panel B plots the data for variations in roll tilt (from 90° left to 90° right) and shows that performance is again quite accurate.

The data shown in the graphs in Figure 7.7 demonstrate that people are able to accurately perceive the vertical using information gained from the vestibular and somatosensory

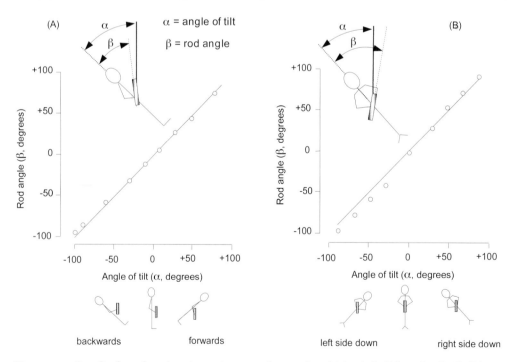

Figure 7.7: *Results from haptic orientation experiments in which pitch (A) and roll tilt (B) were varied. The rod angle (β) provides a measure of the perceived direction of the vertical. (Data from Bartolami et al., 2006a.)*

systems. Detailed experimental studies have shown that people are able to make use of all the different sources of information available, including information from the viscera[8], though it seems that the otoliths are a particularly important source of information[9]. Many of these studies have manipulated 'gravity' using centrifugation: we will discuss how this works later in the chapter.

Although performance in the kinds of tasks described here is often quite accurate, people have been found to show systematic biases in their perceptions of the vertical when their heads or bodies are tilted. There are two types of bias that are commonly observed; these are called *A-effects* and *E-effects*[10], which may be defined as follows:

(1)   **A-effect:** a bias to indicate that the vertical direction is tilted towards the midline of the body in the plane of the body's tilt (i.e., in the same direction as the body tilt). The stick figure insert at the top of panel A in Figure 7.7 is exhibiting an A-effect: the rod angle (β) is less than the angle of body tilt (α).

(2)   **E-effect:** a bias to indicate that the vertical is tilted away from the midline of the body in the plane of the body's tilt (i.e., in the direction opposite to the body's tilt). The stick figure insert at the top of panel B in Figure 7.7 is exhibiting an E-effect: the rod angle (β) is greater than the angle of body tilt (α).

The data shown in Figure 7.7 show evidence of both types of bias. In panel A there is evidence for a small A-effect ($<5°$) for large backward tilts ($>50°$); in panel B there is evidence of an E-effect (between $10°$ and $15°$) for tilts to the left, and a smaller E-effect ($<5°$) for tilts to the right greater than $50°$.

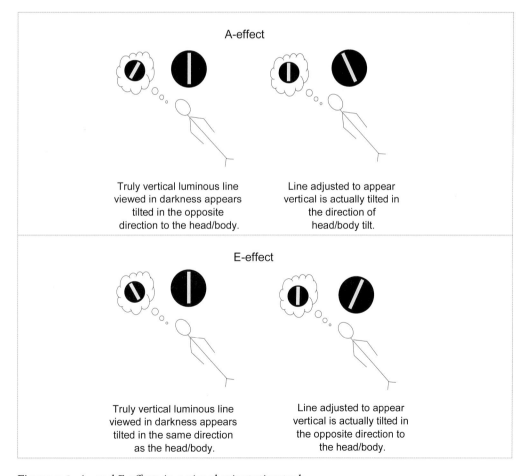

Figure 7.8: *A- and E-effects in a visual orientation task.*

Both these biases were originally discovered in tasks where people were tilted (either whole body tilts or head only) in complete darkness and asked to judge the orientation of a self-luminous line[11] (visual orientation task). If a line that is aligned with the gravitational vertical – a truly vertical line – appears to be tilted in the opposite direction to the tilt of the body, then there is an A-effect. This means that if a person adjusts the orientation of the line until it appears to be vertical, then it will be tilted in the same direction as the head or body, which corresponds to the definition of the A-effect given above. A pictorial illustration of both the A- and E-effects in a visual orientation task is presented in Figure 7.8.

A- and E-effects are typically larger and more consistent in visual orientation tasks than they are in haptic or kinesthetic orientation tasks[12]. In roll tilt, the effects in haptic and visual tasks are opposite: E-effects are observed in haptic tasks (Figure 7.7B), A-effects in visual tasks[13]. The reasons for these effects are not fully understood. One early suggestion was that they could be explained in terms of the variation in the responses of the utricles to different angles of body tilt[14]. The typical patterns of data were subsequently found to be inconsistent with this explanation[15], but consistent with the idea that the ratio of utricular and saccular responses contributes to the perception of the vertical[16]. However, this cannot be the complete explanation, since both E-effects and A-effects have been found to be present in people who have lost vestibular function[17], indicating a role for other sources of information. It is clear that the two effects could be interpreted as the results of a misperception of the tilt of the head and/or body. If a person underestimates their head/body tilt, they should experience an A-effect; if they overestimate their tilt, they should experience an E-effect. However, there is little evidence that people do systematically misperceive the orientation of their heads or bodies[18]. It has also been reported that an A-effect present in judgments of the vertical was accompanied not by an underestimation of body tilt, but by an overestimation[19], indicating that the effect is not due to a misperception of body position.

7.1.5 Visual information contributes to perception of and orientation to the vertical

As described in section 7.1.3, terrestrial environments typically contain numerous vertically and horizontally oriented contours that provide visually available information about the direction of gravity, and features such as the sky and the ground that establish what is up and what is down. These visible contours and features define a spatial frame of reference called the **visual frame of reference**. What does the visual frame of reference contribute to our ability to orient to the vertical?

We can easily stand upright without vision, and as described in the previous section, we are quite accurate at orienting body parts or hand-held objects in vertical or horizontal directions without vision. Thus, visual information is not necessary for successful performance of these tasks. However, there is no doubt that when visual information is available, it contributes to our perception of the vertical and to the performance of orientation tasks. One demonstration of this is provided by the tilted rooms sometimes found in amusement parks, science museums[20] and 'Mystery Spot' attractions[21]. The walls and furnishings of these rooms are all tilted by the same amount in the same direction; the ceilings and usually the floors are perpendicular to the tilted walls (Figure 7.9). The visible contours of the room establish a visual frame of reference in which the vertical direction (room vertical) is the direction from floor to ceiling parallel to the walls. In a tilted room, the visual frame of reference is not aligned with gravity, so the 'room vertical' differs from the gravitational vertical, as indicated in Figure 7.9.

If people use visual contours as information about the vertical direction, then they should show a tendency to orient themselves so that they are upright with respect to the room vertical, and they should perceive the vertical to be displaced from the gravitational vertical towards the room vertical. This is exactly what happens for modest angles of tilt (less than about 30°): upon entering such a room for the first time, people perceive themselves to be tilted and the room to be oriented in the normal way (i.e., vertically). They typically make adjustments to their postural orientation to compensate, leading to stumbling or falling over[22]. People can quickly learn to adapt their postural orientation so that their bodies are close enough to upright to prevent the loss of balance. However, the impression that they are

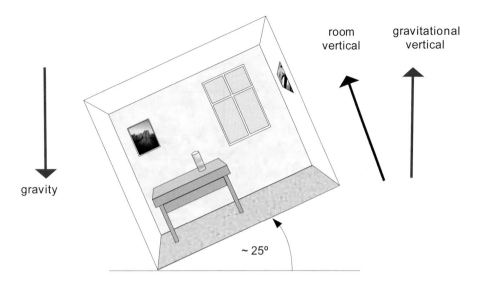

Figure 7.9: *A tilted room.*

in a room that is vertically oriented or close to vertical persists[23]. This leads to some curious visual perceptions that appear to defy the law of gravity: objects and people appear to lean at impossible angles, water can appear to flow uphill, and balls to roll uphill[24]. The reasons for these effects are explained in Figure 7.10. In each case, the perception of a person within the tilted room is shown on the left: the room is perceived to be vertical, or very nearly vertical. In panel A, another person standing on the table appears to lean over in a physically impossible fashion, in panel B, a ball appears to roll up an incline. The true situation is shown on the right: the person is actually standing upright with respect to the gravitational vertical, and the incline is actually a slight decline, so the ball is really rolling downhill.

Laboratory studies of the effects of the visual frame of reference on people's perception of the vertical have typically used either a tilted room, or an apparatus that resembles a tilted room to some degree. The simplest such apparatus consists only of a self-luminous rectangular or square frame viewed in complete darkness[25]. The general finding in these experiments is that the perceived vertical is affected by the extent of the visual field and the number of contours within it: the smaller the field of view and/or the fewer contours it contains, the less the perceived vertical deviates from the gravitational vertical[26]. For example, in one study participants looked into a small room (1.22 meters square) containing a table, a chair and a shelf with a book on it[27]. With the room tilted 22° to the left or right, participants perceived a visible test rod to be vertical when it was tilted 15° in the same direction as the room. In a second part of the study, participants saw only a self-luminous square frame. With the frame tilted 28° left or right, participants perceived a visible test rod to be vertical when tilted only 6° in the direction of room tilt, with some participants showing no effect of the frame. Results of this kind suggest that a larger number of contours distributed over a larger region of the visual field provide a more powerful cue to the vertical than a smaller number of contours within a smaller region of the visual field. This is what might be expected: reliable visual information about the vertical is not provided by just one or two contours or from within small regions of the visual field, because individual objects and surfaces are often tilted. For example, tree branches normally grow at an angle to the vertical; the trunks of some trees are not vertical; small regions of the ground surface are seldom horizontal; and the contours of many objects are neither vertical nor horizontal. Reliable visual information about the vertical can only be obtained as a kind of average over a number of different contours distributed over the whole visual field.

The effects and results described in this section imply that visual information is used in combination with other sources of information to determine people's perception of the vertical and their orientation to it. This combination is discussed next.

Situation as perceived by someone inside the room

Situation when viewed from outside

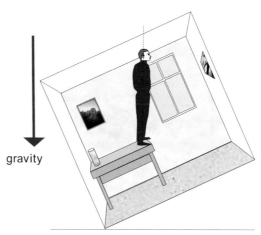

gravity

(A) A person standing on a table is seen to be leaning at an impossible angle (left), but in reality they are standing upright with respect to gravity (right).

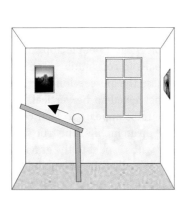
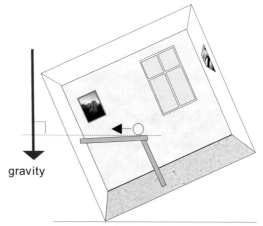

gravity

(B) A ball appears to spontaneously roll up a slope (left), but in reality it rolls down a slight slope (right).

Figure 7.10: *A person's perceptions within a tilted room (left) and the actual situation (right).*

7.1.6 Various sources of information are combined to determine the perceived vertical

Imagine the visual orientation task described at the end of section 7.1.4 (Figure 7.8). You can see nothing except a luminous line, and you have a clear, unambiguous perception of the line being in a particular location in space and having a particular orientation with respect to the vertical. You experience the line within a visual space with definite vertical and horizontal directions – a frame of reference with respect to which the orientation of the line is perceived. There is nothing visible to inform you about these directions, which means that they must be determined by other, non-visual sources of information about the vertical. As we have seen, such information is provided by the vestibular and somatosensory systems. Thus, we can conclude that the spatial frame of reference for visual perception of a self-luminous line is established by information provided by these other sensory systems[28]. In other words, what is described as a visual percept – the percept of the luminous line's orientation – is, in fact, a percept to which at least two different sensory systems are contributing.

In the previous section we saw that vision can contribute information about the vertical, and that the stronger the visual cues, the closer the perceived vertical will be to that specified by those cues. This means that the frame of reference with respect to which vertical judgments are made must be derived from two or more different sources of information about the vertical direction; the relative contributions of those sources depends on their availability and reliability. In the absence of visual information, information provided by the vestibular and somatosensory systems establishes the vertical direction for the frame of reference. It is generally agreed that the otoliths are the most important source of non-visual information about the gravitational vertical, but other information sources can make a contribution. As discussed earlier (section 7.1.3), somatosensory information is provided by muscle and joint proprioceptors, cutaneous mechanoreceptors and visceral mechano-receptors, and there is empirical evidence that all these sources can make a contribution to the perceived orientation of a luminous line viewed in darkness[29] and to the perceived orientation of the body in space[30].

7.1.7 Postural orientation and perception of the vertical can involve different information

From the description of people's experiences in tilted rooms given in section 7.1.5, it is apparent that after an initial period of disruption, people adjust their postural orientation so that they stand upright with respect to the gravitational vertical (if they did not do this, they would fall over). However, their visual perception of the room as vertical persists, and so their visually perceived vertical does not correspond to the postural upright. This suggests that postural control in a tilted room comes to be somewhat independent of static visual cues to the vertical. When a person initially enters the room and experiences postural disturbances (stumbling or falling), visual cues are presumably influencing postural orientation. When the person has been in the room long enough to be able to stand upright with respect to gravity without experiencing any disturbances, their postural orientation must be based on vestibular and somatosensory information about the vertical, which is unaffected by the room tilt.

Several empirical studies have found that when people are required to orient their bodies either vertically or horizontally, their orientations are very close to the veridical (gravitational) vertical or horizontal, whereas their perceptions may not be veridical[31]. For example, in one study, participants lay on their sides on a flat board and could adjust the orientation of the board by remote control[32]. In complete darkness (no vision) and starting from either a head-higher-than-the-feet position or head-lower-than-the-feet-position, participants were required to adjust the board so that they felt that they were lying in a horizontal position. They were found to be able to do this very accurately (to within a degree or two on average) and precisely (standard deviation of about 1.5° on average), but when asked to adjust a luminous line so that it appeared to be vertical, they showed a pronounced A-effect: their settings were biased towards their body orientation by about 10°. Results of this kind suggest that the information used for perception of the vertical can differ from that used for control of body orientation.

An obvious question to ask is why the visually perceived vertical does not always correspond to the true gravitational vertical, whereas postural orientation to the vertical or horizontal is close to veridical. The reason probably has to do with the different requirements of postural and perceptual tasks. The postural control system needs to have access to veridical information about the body's orientation to gravity in order to maintain balance: if the body is not properly oriented to the gravitational vertical when a person stands up, then they will fall over. Perceptual tasks appear to have different requirements. For example, if a picture on the wall is tilted to one side, then in order to look at it, we either turn it so that it is vertical or we tilt our heads into the same orientation as the picture. Tilting of the head is also commonly observed in tilted rooms: the body is oriented to the gravitational vertical, and the head is tilted so as to be more closely oriented to the room vertical[33]. This indicates that we prefer to perceptually orient ourselves to the visual frame of reference when we visually inspect our surroundings. We perceptually orient to the visual frame of reference and posturally orient to the gravitational frame of reference. Of course, the two frames are normally congruent – the vertical specified by visual cues is the same as the gravitational vertical – but in very unusual situations like tilted rooms, the two frames are different, and then a dissociation between visual and postural orientation can occur.

An interesting example of the power of the visual frame of reference to determine a person's perception of the vertical has been reported in the situation shown in Figure 7.11[34]. Experimental participants lay horizontal on a padded bed with their arms unsupported inside a room rotated through 90°. The room contained a variety of everyday objects fixed into their normal positions with respect to the room. In short, the room contained numerous visual cues to the vertical and horizontal directions. In these conditions people's perception of the vertical was largely determined by the visual information: they typically perceived themselves to be upright within a vertically oriented room, despite the fact that vestibular and somatosensory cues were in conflict with this interpretation. Thus, vision dominates the vestibular and somatosensory system. When participants held out their arms to their sides in an extended position and oriented horizontally with respect to gravity, they experienced what the authors of the study called a *levitation illusion*: they felt their arms to be weightless and floating in space. The reason for this experience was presumably due to the absence of gravity in the direction consistent with their perceived vertical orientation: gravity was not pulling the arms towards the floor of the room.

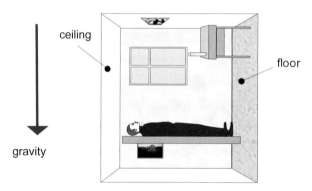

Figure 7.11: *Person in a room rotated through 90°.*

In the zero-gravity environments encountered in space, we would expect people's perception of the vertical to be determined by the visual frame of reference (if such a frame is present), given that no other sensory cues are present. Inside the cabin, visual cues to the vertical are provided by the horizontals and verticals of the walls and floor and by the orientations of instrument panels and furniture (if present). In cabins that lack a significant number of objects or features with obvious tops and bottoms, astronauts' perception of the vertical is strongly determined by the body's orientation within the cabin[35]: they tend to perceive the side of the cabin beneath their feet as the floor and the side above their head as the ceiling. Thus, if the astronaut turns through 180°, the vertical direction flips 180° as well – the floor becomes the ceiling and the ceiling becomes the floor. Such flips in the orientation of the vertical can also be induced if another astronaut enters the cabin upside down with respect to the first: the second crew member provides a strong visual cue to which direction is 'up', and the first astronaut's perception flips accordingly.

An astronaut is weightless within a spacecraft provided that the spacecraft is not accelerating. Once the craft accelerates, a kind of artificial gravity is produced. We consider the way in which accelerations can alter the force environment experienced by a person in the next part of the chapter.

7.2 Orientation to the Gravitoinertial Vertical

7.2.1 'Upright' can be defined with respect to the direction of an inertial force vector

If a spacecraft accelerates at a constant rate, then the direction of the acceleration vector can be used to define what is up and what is down. Inside the cabin, the acceleration produces what is called *pseudo-gravity*, which defines a 'pseudo' vertical – the direction parallel to the acceleration vector. Figure 7.12 helps to illustrate the idea. Panel A shows a spacecraft that is not accelerating; the side has been cut away so that we can see an astronaut inside. There is zero gravity, and the astronaut is shown floating freely in a position that is upright with respect to the cabin walls. If the drive rocket fires, the spacecraft will accelerate as indicated by the double-headed arrow in panel B. The spacecraft accelerates, but an astronaut who is not in contact with the cabin but floating within it does not accelerate. As a result, the shaded wall of the cabin accelerates towards the astronaut, who collides with it. From the astronaut's point of view, the floor accelerating towards him is indistinguishable from him accelerating towards the floor, as if he were being pulled by a gravitational force.

(A) No acceleration   (B) Capsule accelerating

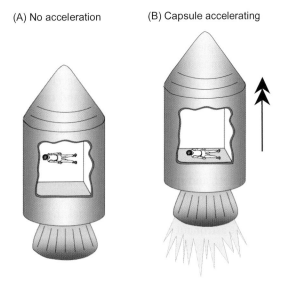

Figure 7.12: *A rocket capsule in space. (A) The astronaut floats freely in the cabin. (B) The capsule accelerates in the direction of the arrow.*

If a spacecraft accelerates at 9.81 m/s² (the normal gravitational acceleration at the Earth's surface), then the astronaut is unable to tell whether the craft is accelerating through space or sitting on the surface of the Earth unless s/he looks out of the cabin window. As first recognized by Albert Einstein[36], someone inside a windowless cabin has no way to distinguish between the situations shown in panels A and B of Figure 7.13: everything inside the cabin behaves in exactly the same way in the situation shown in panel A as it does in panel B. For example, if the astronaut in the accelerating cabin in Figure 7.13B holds an object in one hand and releases it, he will see it fall to the floor in exactly the same way as an object falls to the floor when it is dropped on Earth. The difference is that on Earth the object falls because it is attracted to the Earth by the force of gravity, whereas in the spacecraft it is the floor of the cabin that is accelerating up towards the object. Without looking outside, the astronaut cannot know for sure which situation he is actually in.

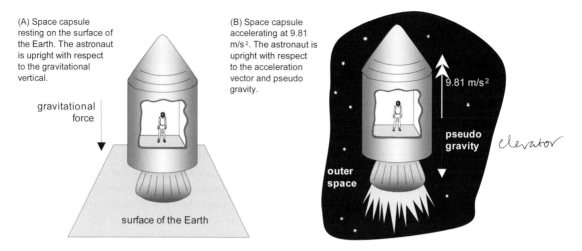

(A) Space capsule resting on the surface of the Earth. The astronaut is upright with respect to the gravitational vertical.

gravitational force

surface of the Earth

(B) Space capsule accelerating at 9.81 m/s². The astronaut is upright with respect to the acceleration vector and pseudo gravity.

9.81 m/s²

pseudo gravity

outer space

elevator

Figure 7.13: *To the astronaut inside the capsule, situations A and B are indistinguishable.*

From the foregoing discussion, we can see that an astronaut in a cabin accelerating through empty space at 9.81 m/s² experiences the situation exactly as does a person standing inside a stationary cabin sitting on the Earth. Consequently, from the astronaut's point of view, there is a gravitational force; because it is not a real gravitational force it is called **pseudo-gravity**. The astronaut in panel B of Figure 7.13 is in an upright position with respect to the direction of pseudo gravity.

Pseudo gravity is an example of what is called a **pseudo force** or an **inertial force** in physics, a concept that many people find difficult to understand. In the study of human and animal movement, the latter term is more generally used. Inertial forces are not 'real' forces (like gravity)[37] but arise because the frame of reference is accelerating. Within this frame of reference, a pseudo force behaves exactly like a real force and cannot be distinguished from a real force. Thus, gravity can be created artificially in a spacecraft simply by accelerating it. Accelerating in a straight line is not a very good way to create artificial gravity for a space station, because you have to keep accelerating, and so you move away from where you want to be at an ever increasing rate. Another way to produce artificial gravity is to make the spacecraft in the shape of a wheel, and spin it at a constant angular velocity.

An astronaut on the inside surface of the rim in a spinning space station is subjected to a real force applied to them by the rim itself. This force pushes the astronaut around in a circle (if the force were not there, the astronaut would move in a straight line; see Chapter 2, section 2.4.15). A force that acts to move something around in a circle is called a *centripetal force*, and it points towards the center of the circle. Although the centripetal force does not change the speed at which the astronaut is moving, it continuously changes his direction of motion, which is a kind of acceleration (a change in velocity) called the *centripetal acceleration*. This acceleration is also directed towards the center of the circle. Figure 7.14 shows an astronaut standing on the inner surface of the rim of a space station, with a double arrow representing the centripetal acceleration. From the astronaut's perspective, there seems to be a force pulling him directly towards the rim; its direction is opposite that of the centripetal acceleration – away from the center of the circle. This is an inertial force called the **centrifugal force**. To the astronaut on the rim, the centrifugal force provides artificial gravity[38]; the astronaut in Figure 7.14 is upright with respect to it[39].

The centrifugal force is not a real force; it arises due to the fact that the astronaut is in an accelerating frame of reference. It can also be experienced in more familiar terrestrial circumstances. When traveling in a car that turns a sharp left corner, you feel as if there is a force pushing you towards the door of the car. This is a centrifugal force. It arises because you are continuing to travel in the direction the car was going before it started to turn. As the car turns, you continue onward, and so find yourself heading towards the door or pressed up against it. In reality, there is no force pressing you against the door; it is simply that the door is preventing you from continuing to move in your original direction.

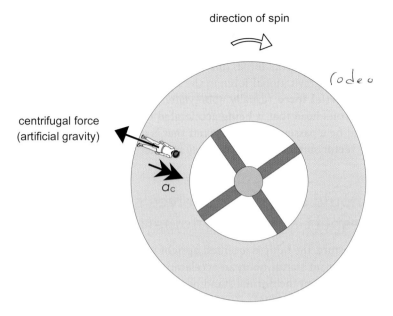

Figure 7.14: *Artificial gravity in a spinning space station is provided by the centrifugal force (a_c is the centripetal acceleration).*

To summarize, we have seen that an upright orientation can be defined not only with respect to gravity (the vertical) but also with respect to the direction of inertial forces (pseudo gravity) that exist within an accelerating frame of reference. You may be asking what this has to do with adopting an upright orientation in a terrestrial environment. We address this question next.

7.2.2 The gravitoinertial force is the sum of gravitational and inertial forces

Whenever you accelerate, you are subject to inertial forces. Whenever you drive a vehicle and push on the accelerator to speed up, you will experience an inertial force – a force that seems to be pushing you back into your seat. When you push the brake to slow down, you experience an inertial force – a force that seems to be throwing you forwards out of your seat. In both cases, the inertial forces are not real forces but are consequences of your being in an accelerating frame of reference (the vehicle), and your tendency to keep moving in the way you were before the accelerator or brakes were applied. These two examples of inertial forces are encountered when your speed changes but not your direction of motion, and so they are similar to the inertial force experienced by the astronaut in panel B of Figure 7.12.

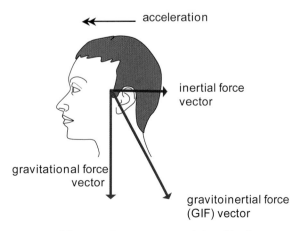

Figure 7.15: *The gravitoinertial force acting on a person's head is the vector sum of the gravitational and inertial forces.*

Centrifugal forces are experienced whenever you change direction, whether driving a car or motorcycle, or riding in a bus, a boat or an airplane. In each case, the vehicle is accelerating because its direction of motion is changing. Unlike the astronaut, a person in an accelerating vehicle is subject not only to the inertial forces due to the acceleration, but to gravity as well. The inertial force adds to the gravitational force in the normal way to produce a combined force called the **gravitoinertial force** (usually abbreviated GIF). Figure 7.15 illustrates the idea for the case of a person's head that is being accelerated forwards (to the left across the page) – the person might be a passenger in an aircraft that is accelerating along the runway prior to taking off. The vector sum of the gravitational and inertial forces yields the gravito-inertial force vector.

7.2.3 People should orient themselves so that they are upright with respect to the gravitoinertial force vector

In the normal standing posture, the body is oriented upright with respect to the gravitational force vector. When an astronaut stands up in an accelerating space vehicle or satellite when there is no true gravity, they adopt the normal standing posture, but are upright with respect to the inertial force vector (pseudo gravity).

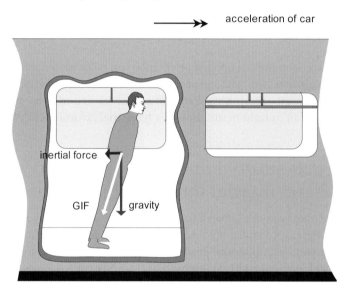

Figure 7.16: *Forces acting on a person's center of mass in an accelerating train car.*

In both true and pseudo gravity, if the standing posture were not upright with respect to the force vector, the person would topple over. When both gravity and inertial forces are present, a person must stand upright with respect to the gravitoinertial force vector to avoid toppling over. For example, if a person stands in a train carriage as the train accelerates forwards, then they need to lean forwards so as to be upright with respect to the gravitoinertial force (GIF) vector, as shown in Figure 7.16 (the GIF vector is represented by the white arrow). If they did not lean forwards, they would fall over backwards. Similarly, when standing on a train as it goes around a bend in the track, a person needs to adopt an upright orientation with respect to the GIF, which is the sum of gravity and the centrifugal force. This is easier to do in a tilt-train, because as the train negotiates a bend, the train cars tilt so that the floor is perpendicular to the GIF. Figure 7.17 shows a cross-sectional cutaway of a tilt-train carriage as it negotiates a curve: a person is shown standing upright with respect to the GIF. If the person tried to stand upright with respect to the gravitational vertical when the train was going around a curve, they would risk falling over – in Figure 7.17 they would fall towards the higher side of the carriage.

A particularly clear illustration of people orienting themselves to the gravitoinertial force vector and not to gravity can be observed in a velodrome. The velodrome arena contains a steeply banked circular or oval cycling track. A cyclist traveling around the track at high speed has a significant centripetal acceleration towards the center of the track and perpendicular to the direction of gravity. The cyclist is subject to gravity and a centrifugal force that sum to give the GIF shown in Figure 7.18. As the cyclists travel around the track, they orient themselves in the direction of the gravitoinertial force vector and may be quite tilted relative to gravity, as shown in the figure.

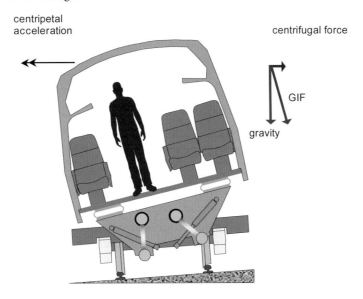

Figure 7.17: *Cross-section through the car of a tilt-train as it travels around a curved section of track.*

When traveling as a passenger in a tilt-train or in an aircraft you can usually tell when the train or plane starts to turn: your vestibular and somatosensory stimulation changes as the plane banks or the train tilts. Once the vehicle is traveling in a wide turn, however, you no longer have any vestibular or somatosensory information to tell you that you are going along a curved path. The cabin will be oriented to the gravitoinertial force vector, as in Figure 7.17 for the tilt-train: from the point of view of a person within the train car or airplane cabin, they are upright in an upright vehicle. If you looked out of the window of the train or plane, you might be able to see that the vehicle was actually tilted and traversing a curved path, but not necessarily: the plane might be in dense cloud, or it might be a pitch-black night outside. In such circumstances, it is impossible for a passenger to know whether they are traversing a curve or traveling in a straight line. The responses of the sensory systems in such conditions are the same as they would be if the person were traveling in a straight line, which is what they perceive to be the case.

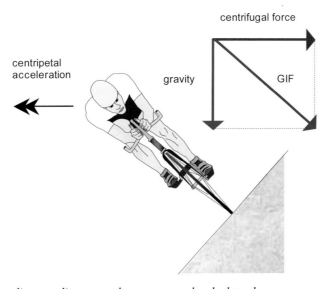

Figure 7.18: *A cyclist traveling around a curve on a banked track.*

It does not really matter whether a passenger in an aircraft can tell whether they are traversing an extended turn or traveling in a straight line, but it does matter for the pilot. If the pilot were to act on the perception of traveling in a straight line when the plane was actually traversing a turn, then the plane could end up seriously off course. To avoid problems of this kind, aircraft are equipped with various devices that inform the pilot about the vehicle's motion and orientation with respect to the Earth. Nevertheless, unless a pilot is properly trained and experienced, their perceptions may be so compelling that they act on them rather than on information from the instruments. In such situations, the pilot is said to be **spatially disoriented**. There are several situations in which spatial disorientation can have catastrophic consequences[40]; one example will be described later (section 7.2.7), but first we will describe some relevant results from studies of human centrifugation.

7.2.4 The effects of changing the gravitoinertial force vector can be studied using the human centrifuge

People's sensorimotor orientation to changes in the gravitoinertial force is often studied using a human centrifuge apparatus. This consists of a cabin mounted at the end of a beam that is spun around a central bearing by means of a large torque motor, as shown in Figure 7.19. The cabin moves around in a circle, and a person sitting in the cabin is subjected to gravity and to the centrifugal force produced by the spin. The person might sit facing the axis of rotation, as shown in panel A of Figure 7.19, or they might sit facing the instantaneous direction of travel, as shown in panel B. The centrifuge cabin in the figure has no windows, so the person cannot see out; in each panel of the figure, the side of the cabin has been cut away to reveal the person inside.

(A) Person in a 'human centrifuge' facing the axis of rotation.

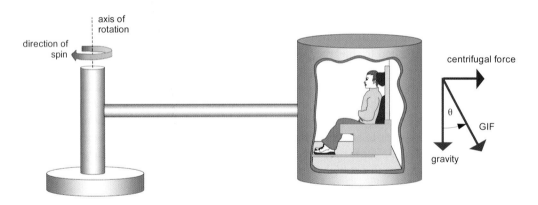

(B) Person in a 'human centrifuge' facing the instantaneous direction of travel (perpendicular to the axis of rotation).

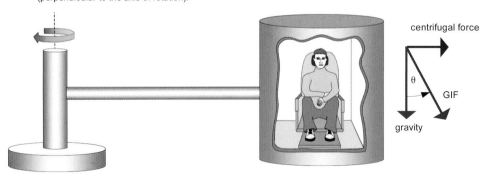

Figure 7.19: *The human centrifuge apparatus.*

Once the centrifuge is spinning at constant angular speed, the person in the cabin will be subjected to a gravitoinertial force vector that is not in line with gravity (as indicated in Figure 7.19). The angle between the GIF vector and gravity (θ in the figure) depends on the speed with which the centrifuge spins: the greater the speed, the larger the angle. Inside the frame of reference of the centrifuge cabin, the GIF vector is an artificial gravity (cabin gravity). In Figure 7.19 the person is not upright with respect to cabin gravity, but tilted through an angle θ: in panel A he is pitched backwards with respect to cabin gravity, whereas in panel B he is roll-tilted to his left. His vestibular and somatosensory systems will be signaling that he is tilted with respect to cabin gravity. Given that the cabin has no windows so the person cannot see outside, they should feel that they are tilted, particularly if the cabin is dark inside. This is exactly what has been reported in experimental studies of the effects of centrifugation[41]: people facing the axis of rotation feel pitched backwards; people facing the opposite direction feel pitched forwards. People facing the instantaneous direction of travel feel roll-tilted to their left; people facing the opposite direction feel tilted to the right. Panel A of Figure 7.20 shows the effect in cartoon form for a person facing the axis of rotation: the contents of the 'think bubble' indicate the person's perception of being tilted backwards. If the cabin is in darkness and the person's perception of the vertical (or horizontal) is assessed using a haptic, kinesthetic or visual orientation task (see section 7.1.4), then they indicate that the vertical is close to the direction of the GIF (horizontal perpendicular to it), and they typically show the same kind of A- and E-effects as they do when tilted in normal gravity[42]. Panel B shows the visual effect in cartoon form for a person being centrifuged in darkness and facing the instantaneous direction of motion: the person feels tilted to the left, and a luminous line that is vertical with respect to gravity is seen to be tilted in the opposite direction (to the right).

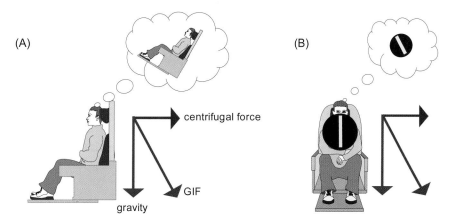

Figure 7.20: *Actual situation and the person's perception (in think bubble) during centrifugation.*

The perceptions of body tilt in accelerating frames of reference are usually referred to as **somatogravic illusions**[43]. The perception that the visual vertical is close to being in line with the GIF vector is usually referred to as an **oculogravic illusion**[44]. The reasons for calling these perceptions 'illusions' is that the perceived orientation does not correspond to the orientation with respect to 'true' gravity. Figure 7.20 makes this clear: what the person perceives does not correspond to their orientation with respect to gravity (panel A) or the line's orientation with respect to gravity (panel B). However, from the point of view of the person in the accelerating frame of reference, these perceptions are not illusions at all: the person *is* tilted with respect to the GIF (which for them is gravity), and the line *is* tilted with respect to the GIF. The person's perceptions are in a frame of reference in which the GIF defines the vertical: in this frame, their perceptions are close to veridical. Thus, to call these perceptions 'illusions' is 'misleading, since no sensory deception is involved'[45]. There can be illusory perceptions of tilt as we will see in the next section, but those described above are not illusory. Non-illusory perception of body tilt in an accelerating frame of reference is better described as a **somatogravic effect**, and the non-illusory perception of the visual vertical being in line with the GIF as an **oculogravic effect**[46].

7.2.5 When the magnitude of the gravitoinertial force exceeds gravity, people perceive themselves to be tilted backwards

In the centrifuge cabin, the effective gravity (cabin gravity) is provided by the gravitoinertial force. As we saw in the last section, a person upright with respect to Earth's gravity is tilted with respect to the GIF vector, and they perceive themselves to be tilted accordingly. If this were the only effect of centrifugation, then the human centrifuge would simply be a very expensive and elaborate apparatus for tilting people with respect to 'gravity'. However, centrifugation does have other effects[47], one of which is obvious from the force vector diagrams in Figures 7.15 to 7.20: the GIF vector is not only oriented in a different direction to the gravity vector, it is also longer. This means that the GIF is greater than the force of gravity: the human centrifuges used in the training of fighter pilots and astronauts are capable of subjecting a person to forces up to nine times the force of gravity. Thus, the centrifuge can be used to study the effects of increased gravity on a person.

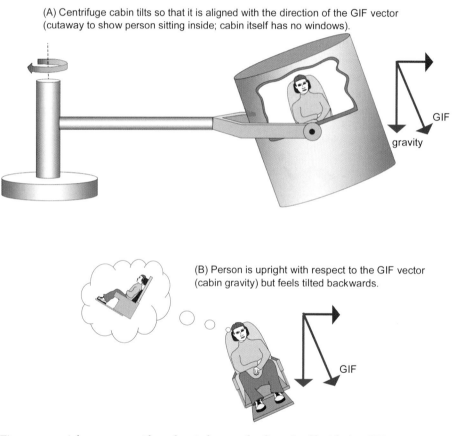

(A) Centrifuge cabin tilts so that it is aligned with the direction of the GIF vector (cutaway to show person sitting inside; cabin itself has no windows).

GIF

gravity

(B) Person is upright with respect to the GIF vector (cabin gravity) but feels tilted backwards.

GIF

Figure 7.21: *A human centrifuge that is free to tilt aligns itself with the GIF vector.*

The effects of increased 'gravity' can be studied independently of the effects of tilt with respect to the GIF, by using a centrifuge with a cabin that is free to rotate about a horizontal axis perpendicular to the radius of its circular path. A centrifuge of this sort is shown in panel A of Figure 7.21: as the cabin is spun around, it orients itself to the GIF, so the person seated inside is upright with respect to cabin gravity. Once the centrifuge is spinning at constant angular speed, a person in the cabin feels that they are tilted, and makes corresponding responses in orientation tasks even though they are upright with respect to cabin gravity. These perceptions of tilt are different from those experienced by a person spinning in a fixed-cabin centrifuge (Figures 7.19, 7.20). For example, a person facing the instantaneous direction of travel does not feel tilted to the left as they would in a fixed cabin centrifuge, but feels tilted backwards from an upright position, as indicated in panel B of Figure 7.21. If the person is free to move, they lean forwards with the head and trunk by between about 25° and 30° to compensate for the perceived tilt. Once they have leant forwards by this amount, they no longer perceive themselves to be tilted. If they lean forwards further, they feel that they are tilted forwards and lean backwards to compensate[48]. These perceptions can reasonably be called *somatogravic illusions* because when the person is actually sitting upright with respect to cabin gravity, they erroneously feel that they are tilted. When they are actually tilted forwards 25° to 30°, they erroneously perceive that they are upright. These illusory effects can all be accounted for in terms of the responses of the utricles to the increased cabin gravity, as described next[49].

7.2.6 The effects of centrifugation are largely due to altered vestibular stimulation

As described in Chapter 3, when a person's head is upright, gravity displaces the otoconia of the utricles, which deflects the hair cells and so determines the afferent signals that reach the brain. In the cabin of a centrifuge, it is the gravitoinertial force (cabin gravity) that displaces the otoconia. Since cabin gravity is greater than normal gravity, the otoconia are displaced more by cabin gravity, which deflects the hairs further. The greater displacement of the otoconia would be produced in normal gravity if the head were tilted backwards. This corresponds to the person's perception in a tilting centrifuge: a person seated with their head upright with respect to cabin gravity feels tilted backwards. Figure 7.22 presents a pictorial account. Panel A shows a person with head upright in normal gravity; their utricular maculae are tilted back by about 30° to the horizontal, and a component of the gravitational force (dotted blue arrow)

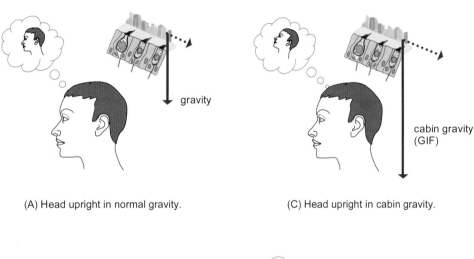

(A) Head upright in normal gravity.   (C) Head upright in cabin gravity.

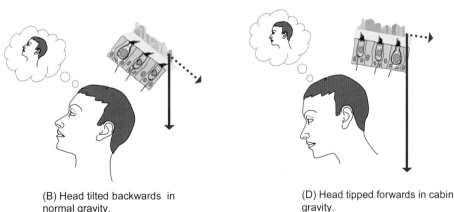

(B) Head tilted backwards in normal gravity.   (D) Head tipped forwards in cabin gravity.

Figure 7.22: *Actual situations and perceptions in normal gravity (left, panels A and B) and increased gravity (right, panels C and D).*

acts on the otoconia parallel to the macular surface, displacing them and deflecting the cilia of the hair cells. The afferent signal from the utricles specifies that the head is upright, which is what the person perceives. Panel B shows the person with their head tilted slightly backwards in normal gravity. The component of gravity acting on the otoconia (dotted arrow) is larger and they are displaced further. The afferent signal specifies that the head is tilted backwards, which is what the person perceives. The panels on the right of the figure show two situations in the centrifuge cabin. In panel C, the person's head is upright with respect to cabin gravity, and a component of the force acts on the otoconia (dotted arrow). This component has the same magnitude as the component of normal gravity that acts on the otoconia when the head is tilted backwards (the lengths of the dotted arrows are equal in panels B and C). Thus, the afferent signal from the utricles is the same in panels B and C, and the perception of head tilt is the same. This explains why a person feels tilted backwards in the centrifuge cabin of Figure 7.21.

Panel D of Figure 7.22 explains why a person feels upright in cabin gravity when they are actually leaning forwards. Leaning forwards reduces the magnitude of the component of cabin gravity acting on the otoconia parallel to the macular surface. This component has the same magnitude as the component of normal gravity that acts on the otoconia when the head is upright (the lengths of the dotted arrows are equal in panels A and D). Thus, the afferent signal from the utricles is the same in panels A and D, and the perception of head and body position is the same (upright). This assumes, of course, that the neural mechanisms that process utricular afference to generate estimates of head tilt are calibrated to normal gravity. In other words, these mechanisms associate a particular afferent signal with a particular head tilt that is appropriate provided gravity has the normal terrestrial value. If gravity is different, then the calibration is incorrect, and erroneous perceptions of tilt (somatogravic illusions) will result.

The effects described in this section can only be explained in terms of utricular stimulation; stimulation of other receptors that can contribute to perception of body orientation cannot explain them. The explanation in terms of utricular responses also predicts that the direction the person faces when sitting in the cabin of a centrifuge like that in Figure 7.21 should make no difference to their perceived body orientation: if the person sits upright, they should always feel tilted backwards, regardless of the direction they are facing. This is what is observed[50].

7.2.7 Inertial forces can disorient pilots: the case of illusory 'pitch-up' during low-visibility takeoffs

People living untechnological lives will seldom be exposed to inertial forces that are more than a few percent of the gravitational force, and will probably never be exposed to sustained inertial forces that persist for longer than a few seconds. For this reason, people in the past would never have experienced somatogravic and oculogravic effects and illusions[51]. This is no longer true: in our modern era of motorized travel, people can be subjected to large, sustained inertial forces. This is most extreme for astronauts and fighter pilots, who may be exposed to inertial forces many times the force of gravity. Much smaller but still significant inertial forces are routinely experienced by the occupants of commercial aircraft during takeoff and landing and while turning. These forces can lead to spatial disorientation, with potentially catastrophic consequences. Here we will consider one example: a somatogravic effect produced during takeoff and its influence on pilot behavior[52].

Figure 7.23 shows a plane traveling along a runway close to the point of taking off: the plane's engines are running at close to full power, so as to accelerate the plane to takeoff speed. The fact that the plane is accelerating means that the pilot is subjected to a sustained inertial force acting in the direction opposite to the acceleration, as shown in the inset. The pilot is tilted backwards with respect to the gravitoinertial force vector, and so is the cockpit, as shown in panel B. Under these conditions, there is the possibility that a pilot will feel that he or she is tilted backwards (a somatogravic effect), and consequently that the plane is tilted in a nose-high attitude. However, the pilot will be looking out of the cockpit windows and can see that the plane is traveling along the runway and is not tilted; the visual information dominates any somatogravic effects, and the pilot veridically perceives the plane's orientation with respect to the Earth.

When the plane leaves the ground the situation is slightly different, because the plane will be starting to climb, so it will have a small vertical component of acceleration[53]. However, the plane will still be accelerating forwards, and the pilot will still be tilted backwards with respect to the gravitoinertial force vector. As before, this does not result in the pilot perceiving the plane to be tilted more than is actually the case, because he or she can still see the horizon and other visible features such as trees and buildings, which permits a veridical perception of the plane's attitude. What we have described so far is the normal situation during a daytime takeoff, when the pilot can see how the plane is oriented with respect to the environment outside. Dark-night takeoffs or takeoffs into fog are a different matter, because the pilot may be unable to see anything outside. In this situation, the pilot has no sensory information about how the plane is oriented with respect to the outside environment.

(A) Pilot vertical with respect to gravity.

(B) Pilot and cockpit tilted backwards with respect to the gravitoinertial force vector.

GIF

GIF

acceleration

Figure 7.23: *When accelerating along the runway, the pilot is vertically oriented with respect to gravity, but tiltled backwards with respect to the GIF.*

Consider the dark-night takeoff situation in more detail. While the plane is traveling along the runway, the pilot will be able to see the runway lights, and so has visual information about the orientation of the plane relative to the ground. When the plane takes off, the runway lights quickly disappear from view: at this point the pilot may be unable to see anything outside the cockpit. If this happens, there is no longer any visual information to override the somatogravic effect: the pilot is tilted backwards with respect to the gravitoinertial force vector, and as a result feels tilted backwards more than is actually the case. Since the pilot is seated upright with respect to the cockpit, the pilot misperceives the plane to be tilted in a nose-high attitude. This can be classed as an illusion, because the plane is perceived to be more tilted than it really is; it is sometimes called the *pitch-up illusion*.

Figure 7.24 presents a pictorial illustration of the situation. The plane has just taken off, and the pilot cannot see anything outside the cockpit. He is tilted backwards with respect to the gravitoinertial force vector and so perceives himself to be tilted backwards (somato-gravic effect), which leads him to perceive that the plane is tilted backwards more than is actually the case (pitch-up illusion). This perception can be very strong. The pilot's natural tendency is to correct for the perceived excessive pitch-up of the plane by maneuvering the controls to bring the nose down. This is analogous to the leaning-forward response of people in the tilting centrifuge described in section 7.2.5. Bringing the nose down takes the

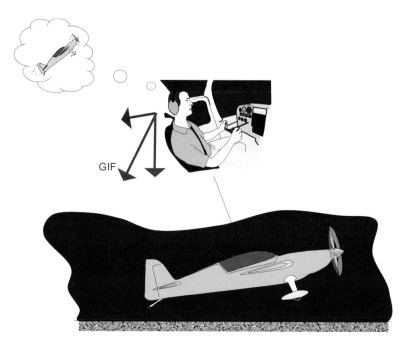

Figure 7.24: *The pitch-up illusion arises in dark-night takeoffs as a consequence of a somato-gravic effect (pilot feels tilted backwards).*

plane out of the climb, and the engine power goes into accelerating the plane forwards. The increase in forwards acceleration results in a greater inertial force, which increases the pitch-up illusion: so correcting for the perceived excessive tilt does not have the effect of eliminating it. If the pilot does not recognize that the perceived nose-up attitude of the aircraft is illusory, then further corrections will be made. These will quickly result in the plane plunging towards the ground. A cartoon representation of this sequence of events in shown in Figure 7.25.

The pitch-up illusion is clearly very dangerous, and a number of serious aircraft crashes are thought to have been a consequence of the pilot correcting for the illusory nose-up attitude during takeoffs when visibility was very poor[54]. The pilot can avoid such accidents by relying on the flight instruments rather than the 'seat of the pants' feel.

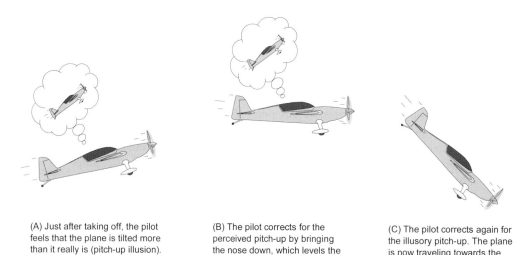

(A) Just after taking off, the pilot feels that the plane is tilted more than it really is (pitch-up illusion).

(B) The pilot corrects for the perceived pitch-up by bringing the nose down, which levels the plane out. This increases the horizontal acceleration and hence the illusion.

(C) The pilot corrects again for the illusory pitch-up. The plane is now traveling towards the ground under full climb power.

Figure 7.25: *Consequence of correcting for the pitch-up illusion.* Closed loop

7.3 Mechanics of Standing Posture

7.3.1 Introduction: gravity constrains posture

As mentioned in the previous parts of the chapter, a person needs to orient themselves to the gravitoinertial force vector in order to maintain a standing posture. In the remainder of the chapter we will consider only standing upright in normal gravity, but the same basic principles apply when inertial forces are present.

For large terrestrial animals like ourselves, the force of gravity has a major impact on motor activity generally and on postural orientation in particular. Gravity has a much greater effect on us than many of the other forces that we encounter, such as wind resistance, friction and liquid surface tension[55]. Our muscles work against gravity when we move our limbs, lift objects and maintain postures. Gravity constrains the kind of movements we can make, prevents us from lifting and carrying loads that are too heavy, and has a powerful effect on our ability to adopt and hold bodily postures. A person on the Earth's surface must use their muscles to maintain body posture unless there is external support. Some postures require so much muscular effort that they cannot be maintained for more than a few seconds; even holding an arm outstretched quickly becomes uncomfortable and is almost impossible to sustain for more than a few minutes. We prefer to adopt postures that require relatively little effort. Maintenance of these postures requires continuous, active, muscular control. In this part of the chapter we will discuss the mechanical effects of gravity on upright standing postures. We will provide intuitive, informal descriptions of concepts such as the center of gravity, stable and unstable equilibrium and *base of support*[56]. This will provide the foundation for understanding the control problems involved in achieving and maintaining upright posture.

7.3.2 The weight force acts at the center of gravity (CoG)

When the force of gravity pulls on a physical object, it pulls on all the individual atoms in the object, but behaves as if it pulls on a single point called the **center of gravity**. An object only has one center of gravity, and it is as if all the weight is concentrated at this single point. Here is a non-technical definition:

> **CENTER OF GRAVITY (CoG):** The single spatial location (point in space) associated with a physical object, where the Earth's force of gravity appears to act on the object.

Imagine a rod of uniform construction. Its center of gravity lies at the rod's center point: inside the rod and halfway along it, as indicated in panel A of Figure 7.26. The rod's **weight** is the force with which the Earth's gravity pulls on it. It is important to be clear that weight is a force: in everyday speech it is often used to refer to the amount of material substance (quantity of matter), but this is not the meaning of the term as used in physics. Being a force, weight has magnitude and direction and is indicated diagrammatically by a directed line segment (an arrow). The direction of the weight force is always the same – directly downwards towards the center of the Earth.

If you want to balance a rod horizontally on the tip of your finger, you need to position the finger directly beneath the rod's center of gravity as shown in panel B of Figure 7.26. If your finger is at a different position such as that shown in panel C, the rod will rotate as indicated. The rotation is produced because the weight force exerts a torque about the point where the finger and rod are in contact (the pivot point). The magnitude of the torque is calculated as the product of the magnitude of the force and the perpendicular distance between the pivot

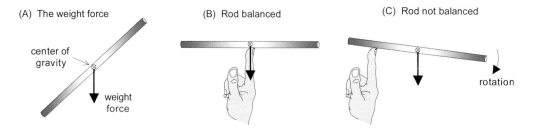

Figure 7.26: *The weight force acts at the center of gravity.*

point and the line of action of the force (more about this later). Thus the torque exerted by the weight is larger the further the finger is from the center of gravity.

A balanced position of the rod is called an **equilibrium position**, which means that there are no net forces or torques acting on it – all the acting forces and torques add up to zero. In panel B of Figure 7.26, the weight force acts downwards and a *reaction force* acts upwards at the point of contact between the rod and the finger. The sum of the weight force and reaction force is zero, so the rod is in equilibrium. We will return to reaction forces in section 7.3.8.

When the rod is balanced, as shown in Figure 7.26B, the configuration is somewhat **stable** in the plane of the page. This means that small, transient forces that disturb the rod up or down do not result in it falling off the finger tip[57]. It might wobble a little, but it will return to the configuration shown in the figure. Small disturbing forces might come from up or down movements of the hand, or trembling of the finger. A rod can also be balanced on one end, as shown in Figure 7.27. This configuration is unstable: very small, transient forces will cause the rod to topple over.

Figure 7.27: *Rod balanced vertically on a finger tip.*

The instability of a balanced rod makes it impossible to keep it balanced unless you can do something to stop it falling over when it's disturbed. In other words, keeping a rod balanced requires active control. As we will see in what follows, keeping the body in an upright posture poses a similar problem: the upright posture is unstable, and cannot be sustained without active control or external support.

7.3.3 The location of the center of gravity depends on the configuration of the body segments

In a uniform gravitational field, the center of gravity lies at the average position of all the mass of an object, a point called the **center of mass** (CoM). For all practical purposes, the CoM and the CoG can be considered to be the same point. The location of this point depends on how the mass of the object is distributed. The rods that we have considered so far were assumed to have their mass distributed uniformly along their length, which means that the average location of the mass is in the very center of the rod. Changing the distribution changes the average position: for example, a rod that is thick at one end and thin at the other, like a baseball bat, has more mass at the thick end, and so the CoG is closer to this end.

The distribution of mass in the human body depends on the relative positions of the body parts. When a body is in a symmetrical upright stance with the arms held at the sides, the CoG lies within the lower abdomen in the mid-sagittal plane (Figure 7.28, left). Exactly how high and how deep in the abdomen it is located depends on such things as the sex of the person and how much abdominal fat they have. The CoG of a young, slim, moderately athletic person typically lies inside the body at about 55–57% of the person's height (the vertical position of the CoG is indicated by the $\otimes$ symbol in Figure 7.28). Since the location of the CoG depends on the way in which the mass of the body is distributed, the CoG will be located in different positions when the body is in different configurations (postures). For example, if the person raises both arms above their head as shown (Figure 7.28, right) the mass of the arms is higher and the CoG is slightly higher.

Figure 7.28: *The position of the CoG depends on the position of the limb segments.*

It is possible for the body to be in a configuration that results in the CoG being located outside the body. One famous example of this occurs during the execution of a high jump, when the Fosbury flop technique is used. This technique derives its name from the American high-jumper Richard Fosbury, who won the gold medal in the 1968 Olympic games. The technique is now used by almost all competitive high-jumpers, and involves the athlete throwing him- or herself backwards over the bar so that they pass over the bar in a configuration like that shown in Figure 7.29. In this configuration, the body's CoG lies outside the body in roughly the position marked $\otimes$ in the figure. The effectiveness of the technique derives from the fact that it is possible to pass the CoG under the bar as the body goes over it.

Figure 7.29: *The Fosbury flop.*

7.3.4 A vertical inverted pendulum is in an unstable equilibrium position

Balancing a rod requires that its center of gravity is directly above where the rod makes contact with the support (the finger in Figure 7.26B and Figure 7.27), so that the line of action of the weight force passes through the region of contact. If a weight's line of action does not pass through the contact region, then it exerts a torque that acts to change the rod's angular position. Figure 7.30 illustrates how this is responsible for the instability of a rod balanced on

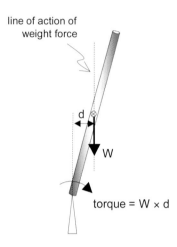

Figure 7.30: *The torque due to the weight topples the rod to the right.*

its end. The figure shows a rod perched on top of a pointed support and leaning to one side: the line of action of the weight force (dashed) does not pass through the point of contact, but is displaced a small distance to one side that is labeled 'd' in the figure. There is a torque about the contact point equal in magnitude to the weight, W, multiplied by the distance (torque = W × d). This torque causes the rod to turn about the contact point – it topples over. Clearly, a torque is produced whenever the distance d is greater than zero, so only a tiny disturbance is needed to start the rod toppling. Once it starts to topple, d increases, so the torque gets larger and larger. The upright, equilibrium position of the rod is said to be *unstable* because any disturbance, however small, will cause it to move away from this position.

Figure 7.31 shows a rod that is hinged at one end in two equilibrium positions. In panel A, the hinge joint is fixed to the ground, and the rod is upright in an unstable equilibrium position.

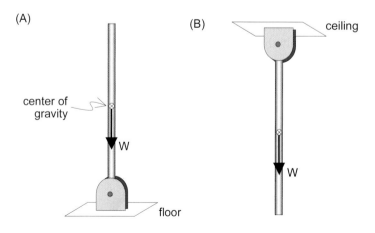

Figure 7.31: *Normal and inverted pendula (see text for explanation).*

In panel B, the rod is hanging vertically downwards from the hinge fixed to the ceiling. This is a stable equilibrium position: if the rod is disturbed away from the equilibrium, it will eventually return to it, possibly after swinging back and forth a few times. A rod that hangs down from a hinge like that shown in panel B of Figure 7.31 is an example of a **pendulum** – a body that is suspended from a fixed support in such a way that it swings freely under the influence of gravity. A body that is free to rotate about a support fixed to the ground, as in panel A of Figure 7.31, is called an **inverted pendulum**. The human body in an upright position is usually thought of as an inverted pendulum, albeit one that consists of several jointed segments (see section 7.3.9).

7.3.5 A helpful metaphor for thinking about stability

An intuitive way of thinking about stability is in terms of a landscape, with hills, valleys and basins, with a ball rolling around in it. This way of thinking is actually embodied in many mathematical models of physical systems, including pendulums[58]. Figure 7.32 shows some two-dimensional examples. A ball perched on top of a hill is in an unstable equilibrium position (panel A) – a small disturbance will send it careering down the hill. A ball at the bottom of a basin is in a stable equilibrium (panel B). If there is friction between the ball and the surface of the landscape, the ball will roll for a while after being disturbed and then come to a stop at the bottom. This kind of equilibrium position is said to be **asymptotically stable**. A ball on a flat surface (panel C) is in what is called a **neutrally stable** equilibrium position: a push will move the ball away from the initial equilibrium position to a new one nearby. How close the new equilibrium is to the original one depends on the size of the push and the friction between the ball and the surface. Only equilibrium positions can be stable – locations on the sides of hills, basins or valleys are unstable.

(A) Unstable equilibrium   (B) Stable equilibrium   (C) Neutrally stable equilibrium

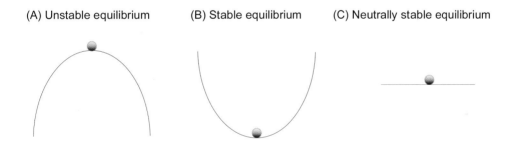

Figure 7.32: *Different types of equilibrium point (see text for explanation).*

We see intuitively that a neutrally stable equilibrium is less stable than an asymptotically stable one. More generally, the greater the size of the disturbance (force) needed to move something a specific distance from its (stable) equilibrium, the more stable that equilibrium. To put it another way, the harder it is to move something away from its equilibrium position,

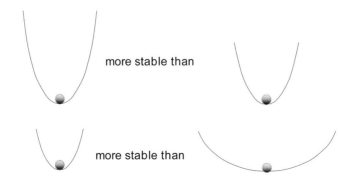

more stable than

more stable than

Figure 7.33: *Stable equilibria with differing degrees of stability.*

the more stable the equilibrium. In the landscape metaphor, the amount of force needed to move the ball from the bottom of a basin depends on the steepness of the basin's sides, so a ball at the bottom of a basin with steep side is in a more stable position than one at the bottom of a basin with gently sloping sides. It is also intuitive to suppose that a deep basin is more stable than a shallow one, even if the sides are equally steep, as it is more difficult to move a ball out of a steep basin than a shallow one. Thus, we can associate a notion of the degree of stability of an equilibrium with the depth of the basin in which it sits and the steepness of the basin's sides[59]. These ideas are summarized in Figure 7.33, where the two basins on the left are more stable than those on the right.

The examples in Figures 7.32 and 7.33 are shown in two dimensions, but remain the same in three. In three dimensions, other surface shapes are possible. An interesting one is the saddle shape shown in Figure 7.34, in which the equilibrium point where the ball is located is both at the top of a two-dimensional hill and at the bottom of a two dimensional bowl (indicated by dark lines on the surface). This corresponds to the stability of the rod balanced horizontally on the finger tip (Figure 7.26A) – it is stable if disturbances are in the plane of the figure (vertically up and down) but unstable if disturbances are perpendicular to the plane of the figure (horizontally back and forth).

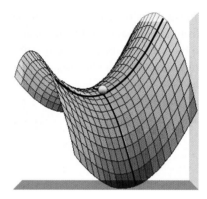

Figure 7.34: *A saddle point (see text for explanation).*

7.3.6 A larger base of support provides greater stability

A simple way to provide a rod or pole with more stability when it is upright is to provide it with support of some sort. It could be mounted on legs or on a flat disc (Figure 7.35). The effect of both these additions is to increase the size of the rod's **base of support**. The base of support is the region bounded by the points of contact with the ground. In panel A, the base of support is formed by the straight lines drawn between the three points where the legs make contact with the floor. In panel B, the base of support corresponds to the disc on which the rod is mounted, assuming that the floor and disc are smooth, flat and continuously in contact. Thus, base of support can be defined as follows:

> **BASE OF SUPPORT** (of an object standing on a support surface): the area of the support surface defined by straight lines drawn between the points where the object and the support surface make contact. If these points of contact form a continuous curve, they need not be joined by straight lines.

Consider a pole mounted on a disc base. A small push that tilts the pole only a few degrees from the upright is not sufficient to make it topple over, but a larger push can make it do so. The reason for this can be explained with the aid of Figure 7.36. Panel A shows the rod tilted about 10 degrees to the right. The rod and disc pivot about the contact point between the disc and the ground, and the center of gravity of the rod plus disc is to the left of this contact point. Thus, the torque exerted by the weight about the pivot point acts to rotate the rod to the left, restoring it to the upright position. Panel B shows the rod tilted further to the right, such that the center of gravity is to the right of the pivot point. The weight torque now acts to rotate the rod further to the right, and it falls over. Without the disc, the rod is like the ball on the top of a hill – any slight push will send it toppling over. In contrast, the disc-mounted rod is like a ball in a crater in the top of a hill, as shown in panel C. The disc-mounted rod is stable if pushes are small: a small push does not tilt the rod far enough to move the CoG beyond the boundary of the base of support, and so the gravitational torque rotates it back to the upright position.

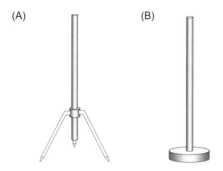

Figure 7.35: *A pole can be made more stable by mounting it on feet (left) or on a base (right).*

One last point should be noted concerning the addition of a disc or legs to the rod, as shown in Figure 7.35. The center of gravity (CoG) of the rod with additions is not half-way along the rod, but is closer to the end with the additions. This means that in the upright position, the CoG of the rod plus disc or legs is closer to the ground, which also increases the stability of the structure: it is clear from Figure 7.36 that the closer the CoG is to the ground, the further the rod must be tilted in order to move the CoG to a position outside the base of support. Note

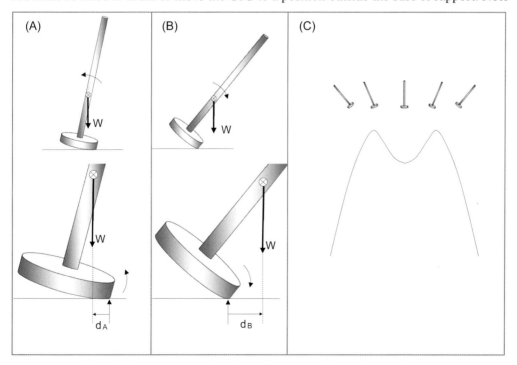

Figure 7.36: *(A) and (B) A pole on a disc-shaped base is stable in the upright position, provided that its CoG is not moved outside the base. (C) In landscape terms, this corresponds to a hill with a crater in the top.*

that the CoG of a standing person is relatively high – more than half-way up the body. The feet form the base of support (next section), but are relatively small and light. Large, heavy feet would provide more stability, but would be a handicap because they would be difficult to move when walking and running.

7.3.7 The feet define the base of support for an upright standing posture

When we stand on our feet, the area bounded by the points of contact between the feet (or the soles of the shoes) and the ground define the base of support for the body. Maintaining a steady, upright stance requires that our center of gravity be kept above this base. The size of the base of support depends on the placement of the feet. Three examples are shown in Figure 7.37: the base of support is shown shaded, its approximate boundary is indicated by a dashed line, and the horizontal position of the CoG is marked ⊗. In panel A of the figure, the feet are fairly close together. Standing with the feet further apart (panel B) increases the width of the base of support. The result is that CoG is further from the left and right boundaries of the base of support, which means that it will be harder to make the person topple over to the left or right, in the sense that a larger force will be required to topple them. We can say that the person's lateral stability is greater when their feet are further apart. Stability in the front–back direction is unaffected. Standing with one foot further forward, as shown in panel C, lengthens the base of support front-to-back and so increases stability in this direction, but narrows the base of support left-to-right and so reduces lateral stability. In general, the greater the horizontal distance of the CoG from the boundary of the base of support in a particular direction, the more stable a standing system is along that direction. Panel D of the figure shows how the base of support can be increased by using a stick: the person is leaning on a stick in front of them.

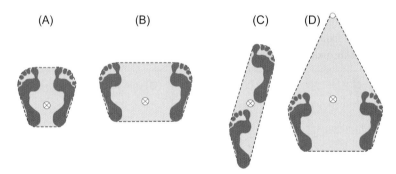

Figure 7.37: *The base of support (shaded) with the feet in different positions. The case on the right is for a person leaning forwards on a stick: ○ marks the location where the stick is in contact with the ground.*

7.3.8 The total vertical ground reaction force acts at a single point called the center of pressure (CoP)

When an object stands immobile on a firm supporting surface, the weight of the body presses it down onto the surface. The object does not penetrate into the surface or pass through it because the surface generates a force that resists such movement. This resisting force is equal and opposite to the object's weight force in both magnitude and direction: in effect, the surface pushes back on the body with a force equal to the force with which the body presses down on it. This is an instance of Newton's third law, which states that when an object A exerts a force on another object B, object B will exert an equal and opposite force on object A. The force with which B pushes back on A is called a **reaction force**.

When a person stands on the ground or on the floor, the reaction force with which the ground pushes back is called the **ground reaction force**. The total ground reaction force may be composed of as many as three components, depending on the forces that the feet exert on the ground. (1) If a foot presses vertically down on the ground, then the reaction from the ground is vertically upwards. (2) If a foot pushes forwards or backwards horizontally across the ground surface, then the reaction from the ground is a force on the foot in the opposite direction (backwards or forwards). This force is a frictional force: it is smaller for slippery surfaces, and only exists if the foot is pressing down on the ground at the same time as it pushes forwards or backwards. (3) If a foot pushes to the left or the right horizontally across the ground surface, then the reaction from the ground is a force on the foot in the opposite direction (right or left). This force is again a frictional force. From this description of the three components of the ground reaction force, we see that it is possible for there to be only a vertical component, but it is not possible for there to be a horizontal component in either direction unless there is also a vertical component.

Panel A of Figure 7.38 shows a person leaning on a stick that is in contact with the floor. At the contact point between the stick and the floor, there are two forces acting: the force applied by the stick to the floor that acts along the line of the stick (represented by the black arrow), and the ground reaction force that acts on the stick (represented by the blue arrow). Panel B shows the end of the stick in contact with the ground with each force resolved into a vertical component and a horizontal component. The horizontal component of the reaction force (blue arrow pointing to the right) is a frictional force. In this chapter, we will only need to consider the vertical components of the two forces.

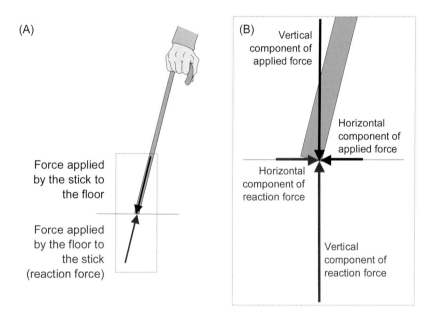

Figure 7.38: *Ground reaction force on a walking stick (see text for details).*

The force applied by a foot to the ground does not act at a single point but over the whole area of contact. Likewise, the reaction force of the ground on the foot is applied over this same area. When a force acts over an area it is called *pressure*, so we can think of the feet as applying pressure to the ground and the ground applying reaction pressure to the feet. Nevertheless, the forces behave as if they were applied at a single point. The point on the ground at which the vertical component of the ground reaction force acts is traditionally referred to as the **center of pressure** (CoP), a quantity that is often used as a dependent measure in the study of postural control. Here is a definition:

CENTER OF PRESSURE (CoP): The point where the sum of all the vertical ground reaction forces acting on an object (the resultant vertical ground reaction force) intersects the support surface. It is a spatial location.

Imagine a four-legged stool standing immobile on the floor: a vertical ground reaction force acts where each leg contacts the floor, as indicated in panel A of Figure 7.39. The total vertical ground reaction force acts at the central point of all four legs, directly beneath the middle of the seat, as shown in panel B. The CoP is the point where the total vertical ground reaction force vector intersects the surface of the floor. Note that this point is directly beneath the stool's center of gravity, which means that the CoP is also the point where the line of action of the weight force meets the floor (the projection of the CoG onto the support surface). It is important to note that the CoP is only directly beneath the CoG under static conditions. When a person stands upright, they are not motionless – people tend to sway slightly, even when trying to stand perfectly still. In these conditions, the CoP is not generally directly beneath the CoG. Thus, in human posture, the CoP does not typically coincide with the point where the line of action of the weight force meets the floor.

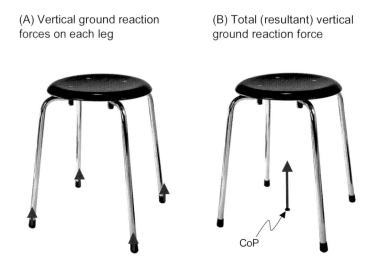

(A) Vertical ground reaction forces on each leg

(B) Total (resultant) vertical ground reaction force

CoP

Figure 7.39: *Ground reaction force on an object with four legs. CoP = center of pressure.*

7.3.9 The upright human body is an inverted compound pendulum

To maintain an upright stance, a person must keep their center of gravity above the base of support. The body is formed from a series of jointed segments that can rotate relative to one another. In upright stance, a series of jointed segments are balanced on top of one another: the lower legs above the feet, the upper legs above the lower legs, the trunk above the legs, and the head on top of the rest. An arrangement of this sort is referred to as an **inverted compound pendulum**, because it is an inverted pendulum composed of several linked segments. An example resembling an upright person is shown in Figure 7.40. It is simpler than a human mainly because the pendulum joints only permit rotation in the plane of the page (forwards–backwards rotation). The human neck, hip, spine and ankle all permit rotation from side to side as well as front to back.

As you can imagine, balancing an inverted compound pendulum in an upright position is far more difficult than balancing an inverted pendulum with a single segment. Each segment has its own center of gravity, which must be motionless above the base of support formed by the segment's contact with the one beneath it. This is achieved when the segments are oriented vertically, as shown in panel A of Figure 7.40. In this position, the CoG of all four segments combined is directly above the joint with the support (the 'ankle' joint). To achieve this balanced position is virtually impossible, as the slightest disturbance to any one of the segments will start it toppling, and all the others will follow: the pendulum will end up collapsed in a heap (panel B). In the human case, there is no passive, upright equilibrium position, due to the anatomical structure of the human skeleton: it is impossible to align all the bones so that the CoG of each segment is directly above the joint with the segment beneath. Whether there is a passive equilibrium or not makes no practical difference to the balancing problem: balancing a series of linked, jointed segments is practically impossible. Some mechanism for preventing the segments from rotating about the joints is needed.

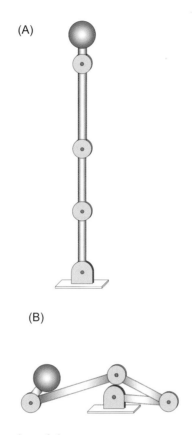

(A)

(B)

Figure 7.40: *A compound inverted pendulum.*

7.3.10 Muscular activity is essential for maintaining an upright standing posture

Standing supported only by the feet requires that body's center of gravity be located above the base of support, a requirement that can be met by infinitely many postures. Figure 7.41 shows four stick figures in standing postures that meet the requirement. In each posture, the mid-sagittal plane is in the plane of the page, and so the person can be considered to be upright with respect to gravity in all four postures. The posture that a person actually adopts will depend on what they are doing. For instance, a person might adopt posture 4 to look over the edge of a cliff, or posture 2 prior to lifting something heavy off the floor. When a person simply needs to stand, they spontaneously adopt the characteristic upright posture (posture 1).

It is easy to verify for yourself that postures 2, 3 and 4 in Figure 7.41 require significant muscular effort and are difficult to maintain for extended periods. This is particularly true for posture 2, which becomes quite tiring after only a few tens of seconds. Posture 1 is rather different, as people can maintain this posture for very long periods of time. When a person stands in posture 1 on flat, level ground, their CoG does not normally lie above a base of support defined by the ankle joint axes, but a few centimeters (typically less than 5 cm) in front of the ankle joints[60] (Figure 7.42). This means that there is a gravitational torque at the ankle joints that acts to topple the body forwards. To avoid falling forwards, an opposing torque must be generated. Some of this torque is produced by elasticity of the ankle joint connective tissues (ligaments and cartilage), some by static friction within the joint capsule, and some by active contraction of the calf muscles: the soleus muscle in particular is typically slightly active almost continuously in standing people[61].

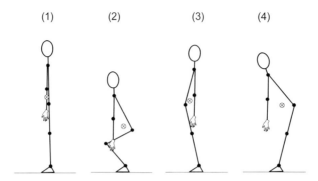

Figure 7.41: *Four different upright postures in which the CoG is above the base of support.*

Figure 7.42 also indicates that in a symmetrical, standing posture, the body's CoG does not lie above the knee or hip joint axes either: it lies very slightly in front of the knee joint axis and very slightly behind the axis of the hip joint. Thus, there is a gravitational torque about the knee joint that tends to rotate the femur forwards (extend the knee) and a gravitational torque about the hip that tends to rotate the pelvis backwards. These torques are small because the distance from the joint axis to the line of action of the weight force is small. Thus, only a small amount of opposing torque needs to be developed to balance the gravitational torques. At both the knee and the hip, a significant proportion of this opposing torque is developed passively by ligaments and other soft tissues around the joint[62]. Thus, very little muscle activity is needed in the knee flexors (hamstrings) or the hip flexors. The ongoing muscle activity that opposes gravitational torques and keeps the legs, trunk and head in alignment is referred to as **postural muscle tone**: many muscles in the neck, back, abdomen and legs possess a slight active tension (tone) while a person is standing (see section 7.4.3 for more details).

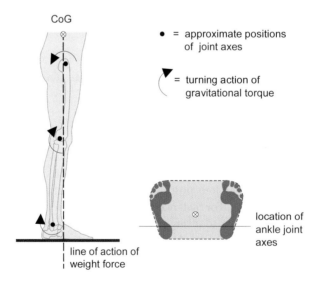

Figure 7.42: *Gravitational torques about the ankle, knee and hip joints when standing upright.*

Note that it is the action of the muscles that extends the base of support to the whole region bounded by the feet. As long as the CoG is above the base of support defined by the feet, it is possible for torques developed by the muscles to stop the body from toppling over. If the CoG moves outside the base of support, then the body will start to topple over, regardless of the size of the torques exerted by the muscles. If this happens, the only way to stop falling flat on the ground is to extend the base of support, either by moving the feet or grabbing on to something.

7.4 Quiet Standing and Postural Sway

7.4.1 Introduction

When we stand up, we move into a standing posture from a seated or recumbent posture and then remain standing for a period. We see intuitively that any act of standing involves two things: (1) moving into the particular standing posture from some other posture, and (2) actively maintaining the posture for some period of time (i.e., maintaining balance). Other kinds of postures involve the same two things: for example, to hold the arm stretched out horizontally, the arm must first be moved into the horizontal position, and then held there for however long is required.

To remain in a free standing posture it is both necessary and sufficient to keep the CoG directly above the base of support formed by the feet, but keeping it there is not the whole story. There are an infinite number of different postural configurations of the body in which CoG is above the base of support. The person must have some means of determining what postural configuration is appropriate for the task they are undertaking[63]. When the task is simply to stand still (quiet stance) the posture normally adopted is number 1 in Figure 7.41. The advantage of this posture is that it requires the least muscular effort to maintain. Other tasks may require more effortful postures in which major body segments are not oriented vertically: holding an unusual upright posture in gymnastics, or putting yourself into a position where you can reach an awkwardly located screw, can be very tiring.

What has been said so far can be summarized by saying that when we stand, not only do we keep our CoG above the base of the support, but we also maintain a specific postural configuration. Whenever a person stands up, they usually know where to place the feet so as to provide a suitable base of support, and they also know how the body segments need to be oriented for the task being undertaken. Thus, we can imagine that the nervous system has an internal representation of the desired postural configuration, and uses this in combination with knowledge of segment weights and lengths, and information about the gravitational vertical, to establish the levels of muscle activity needed to bring the body into the desired posture. It may be that bringing the body into a desired postural configuration involves processes that are different from those that maintain posture[64]. The main concern in this part of the chapter will be on the processes responsible for maintaining posture.

7.4.2 Negative feedback and other control mechanisms play a role in postural stabilization

Negative feedback control is a mode of control that acts primarily to stabilize system states that would be unstable without it. This suggests that it is particularly appropriate for the stabilization of upright posture, given that the upright position of the body is unstable[65]. We have already seen in Chapter 6 that negative feedback control can stabilize posture in the presence of disturbances with reference to the vestibulocollic reflex (section 6.3) and the stretch reflex (section 6.4).

Recall from Chapter 1 that standard negative feedback control involves a process that specifies the desired behavior (or output) of a system, which serves as a reference against which sensory feedback is compared to determine whether the actual behavior of the system matches the desired behavior. In postural control, a question arises concerning what the desired behavior is. As discussed in 7.3.10, there are two aspects to maintaining upright posture:

(1)   Keeping the body's CoG above the base of support.
(2)   Maintaining an alignment of the body segments (i.e., maintaining a particular configuration of the body).

Feedback control can be used to achieve both: the controlled 'variable' for (1) is the horizontal position of the CoG, while for (2) it is the configuration of the body. If the horizontal CoG position were the only controlled variable, then during standing we would expect that the CoG would (on average) remain close to a particular location (its desired location), whereas body configuration would be free to vary. If body configuration were the only controlled variable, then we would expect that the posture would remain close to a particular configuration (the desired configuration), and the CoG would remain close to a particular location. Note the difference between these two possibilities. Control of body configuration entails control of the position of the CoG, because if the body configuration is held constant then the position of the CoG does not change. In contrast, maintaining the same horizontal position of the CoG does not entail maintaining a postural configuration. This is because there are many different bodily configurations in which the CoG is in the same horizontal position. Thus, it appears likely that the postural control system acts to maintain a desired body configuration, a configuration that has two characteristics: (1) uses minimal muscular effort to maintain (segments are vertically aligned) and (2) places the CoG above the base of support. Although this seems most likely, it has not been firmly established empirically, and the system may involve some mechanisms that stablilize CoG position and others that stabilize body configuration[66].

Figure 7.43 shows a simplified negative feedback control block diagram that illustrates the basic idea. The 'postural planner' block represents the processes that generate a specification of the desired upright postural configuration (the orientation of segments with respect to the environment and to each other). The controller receives a specification of this desired posture from the planner, and information about the body's actual postural configuration from various sensory systems. The controller compares the desired posture with sensory feedback to determine whether the body is in the desired posture or not (the postural error) and generates control signals to the muscles accordingly. The mechanism will act to stabilize the reference postural configuration.

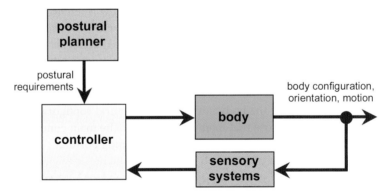

Figure 7.43: *Generic block diagram of feedback control for postural stabilization.*

The block diagram shown in Figure 7.43 is a simplified, overall representation of a mechanism that undoubtedly has a very complex internal structure. Each block is itself a complex system of component processes. For example, several sensory systems contribute to the control of upright posture: the visual system, the vestibular system, and the somatosensory system (including muscle and joint proprioceptors and cutaneous mechanoreceptors in the feet). Furthermore, a large number of different muscles contribute to postural maintenance, and so the controller needs to generate control signals to many muscles in a coordinated fashion.

Feedback control is not the only type of mechanism that can contribute to postural stabilization. As we will see, it is possible for the passive viscoelasticity of muscle and connective tissues to play a (small) role. In addition, sensory feedforward control is also potentially useful when an environmental disturbance can be anticipated – a person can make a postural adjustment in advance of the disturbance and so counteract its effects. Postural disturbances can also be produced by a person's own behavior, which can be anticipated and adjusted for (see next section and the next part of the chapter).

7.4.3 Perturbed and quiet standing

Maintaining an upright posture is complicated by the presence of disturbances that can occur almost continually. Many of these have the potential to topple a person over unless something is done to prevent this. Even a disturbance that is not sufficient to topple a person over can move the body's center of gravity closer to the boundary of the base of the support, making their position vulnerable to toppling by any further disturbances. Disturbances come from two sources: the environment and the person's own behavior. Environmental events that can disturb upright posture include gusts of wind, pushes or pulls applied to the body by another person or animal and movements of the support surface. The latter occur if you are standing in a bus or train and it starts to move, or if you are standing on a boat when the sea is choppy.

force pushes back on the shoulder (recoil)

force drives the bullet forwards

Figure 7.44: *Firing a gun in a standing posture.*

Behavioral sources of disturbance occur for two basic reasons. First, as we saw in section 7.3.3, changes in the positions of body segments change the position of the body's CoG. Thus, many movements that we make can produce shifts in the CoG that have a potentially disturbing effect on upright posture. Second, making a movement will typically produce reaction torques at numerous joints in the body (this is Newton's third law: 'to every action there is an equal and opposite reaction'), including those that need to be kept in alignment in order to maintain upright posture. As an example, imagine making a punch: the fist is thrust rapidly forwards and the force that pushes the fist forwards is associated with an equal and opposite force that pushes the body backwards. The same thing happens when firing a gun (Figure 7.44): explosion of the gunpowder produces a force that accelerates the projectile forwards and an equal and opposite force backwards, experienced as the recoil. The person throwing the punch or firing a projectile will stand with one foot in front of the other (as in Figure 7.44), so that the base of support is enlarged in the direction of the recoil. As a result of these disturbing effects, many of the movements that we make when executing everyday motor tasks have the potential to topple us over or move us into a precarious position.

Based on the different sources of disturbance and on whether or not they are present, it is usual to distinguish between three situations in the study of postural control:

(1)   **Quiet stance:** the person is standing still, is not subject to any disturbances from the environment, and does not perform any motor actions that disturb upright posture.

(2)   **Environmentally perturbed stance:** the standing person is subject to occasional disturbances from the environment.

(3)   **Action perturbed stance:** the standing person performs actions that involve movements that can potentially disturb the upright posture.

In this part of the chapter we will focus on quiet stance.

7.4.4 Quiet stance is a relaxed stance in which a person sways slightly

When simply standing upright, people will often adopt a posture in which the legs and arms are in a symmetrical configuration relative to the midline, the feet are slightly apart, and the segments of the legs are close to vertical, as are the trunk and head. This is a typical posture for quiet stance (though an asymmetrical posture in which one leg takes more of the weight is also very common). During quiet stance, people are normally quite relaxed and there is little on-going muscle activity. Nevertheless, some muscle groups need to be active to maintain the body segments in their approximately vertical orientation. Some of these are shown in panel A of Figure 7.45. Muscles that span the ankle joint act to maintain the orientation of the lower leg: these are the triceps surae group (the calf muscles: gastrocnemius and soleus) that plantarflexes the ankle, and the pretibial muscle group, primarily the tibialis anterior, that dorsiflexes the ankle.

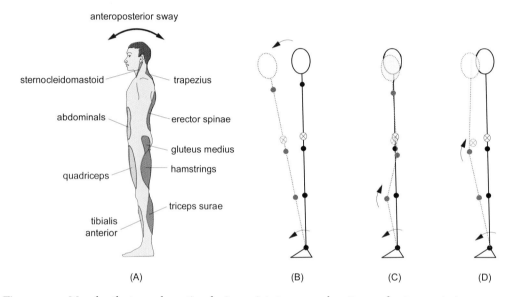

Figure 7.45: *Muscles that may be active during quiet stance, and patterns of anteroposterior sway.*

The triceps surae show almost continuous electromyographic activity during quiet stance, since the body's CoG is generally in front of the ankle joints (see section 7.3.10). However, the level of activity is quite low, only reaching a few percent of the maximum that can be achieved voluntarily[67]. Tibialis anterior typically becomes active if a disturbance pushes the body backwards, but may show periods of continuous activity, particularly if a person is trying to stand perfectly still. Muscles that span the knee maintain the orientation of the thigh: the hamstrings act to maintain an optimal alignment of the thigh, but the level of activity is typically very low. The quadriceps become active to prevent the knee flexing if the body moves backwards; otherwise they are usually inactive. Similar activity patterns are observed in muscles of the hip (gluteus medius and the iliopsoas group), trunk (abdominal and erector spinae groups) and neck (e.g., sternocleidomastoid and upper trapezius). The levels of EMG activity in all muscle groups is very low, indicating that little muscular effort is expended during periods of quiet standing – it is an energy-efficient activity. A person can remain standing for long periods without muscular fatigue. Any fatigue that is experienced appears to be fatigue due to pressure and tension in connective tissues and inadequacies of venous circulation.

During periods of quiet stance, a person may have the strong impression that the body is not moving at all, that they are truly standing still. Despite this impression, the body is actually swaying very slightly, both backwards and forwards and side to side. For much of the time, however, the amount of sway is so small that we may be unaware that we are moving[68]. Forward-backward sway is usually referred to as **anteroposterior sway**; side to side sway is referred to as **mediolateral sway**.

How exactly should sway be defined and quantified? The answer is not immediately obvious, because of the many different ways the body segments could rotate about the joints when a person stands. Figure 7.45 illustrates three possibilities for anteroposterior sway. If a person only sways about the ankle joints with all other joints held fairly rigid, then the body would be somewhat like a rigid pole pivoting about the ankle as indicated in panel B. The amplitude of the sway in panel B could be quantified in terms of the ankle joint angle or in terms of the distance moved by any point in or on the body, such as the CoG or a point on the shoulder or on the hip – any one measurement is equivalent to any other for the type of sway shown in panel B. However, if the higher joints are not held rigid, then different measurements are not equivalent. Consider the situation shown in panel C: here the lower leg has swayed forward through the same angle as in panel A (about 15°), but the knee has flexed such that the trunk and head hardly change their orientation. In this example, the sway at the ankle is not transmitted to the trunk because of the counter-rotation at the knee. In panel D, the trunk has rotated backwards by the same amount as the ankle has rotated forwards.

It turns out that in quiet stance, although anteroposterior sway often resembles the situation shown in panel B of Figure 7.45[69], there is motion at other joints, particularly the hip[70] (in the manner shown in panel D of Figure 7.45). A complete description of anteroposterior postural sway therefore requires a specification of motion about all the relevant joints; the same is true of mediolateral sway, as we will see later. In what follows, we will look at some of the basic characteristics of postural sway.

7.4.5 During quiet stance the amplitude of sway is small

The sway at the ankle is quite small: the range of motion at the ankle joint[71] is typically between about 1° and 2°. If ankle joint angle is plotted as a function of time over a period of quiet standing, it usually looks something like the graph shown in Figure 7.46: the joint moves in a repetitive, cyclical, but somewhat irregular manner. In the figure, the range of motion is 1.5° and indicated by the dashed lines. The ankle angle typically lies well within this range for most of the time, as it does in the figure. For this reason, the range of motion does not provide a very good measure of sway amplitude; a measure of the average deviation of the angle over time is preferable. The standard deviation of the angle is one such measure: typical values for the standard deviation of anteroposterior sway in quiet stance lie between about 0.1° and 0.5° (it's about 0.3° for the trace shown in the figure). The exact values of sway amplitude measures depend on a number of factors including a person's age, what they are standing on, the sensory information available, and what they are thinking about. Some of the factors that affect sway are discussed in the next section. The position of the feet can have a strong effect on sway[72]. Although a variety of different positions are possible, people usually place their feet side by side during periods of quiet stance. In this configuration, sway is affected by how far the feet are apart – the **stance width**. The feet are usually placed less than 30 to 40 cm apart, so that they lie within shoulder width. Variation in stance width within this range has very little effect on anteroposterior sway[73], but has a marked effect on mediolateral sway, as discussed below.

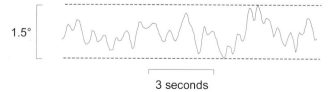

Figure 7.46: *Anteroposterior ankle joint angle (plantarflexion-dorsiflexion) during a period of quiet stance, with a peak-to-peak amplitude of 1.5° (not real data).*

Mediolateral sway in quiet stance is unlike anteroposterior sway because it normally involves the repetitive loading and unloading of the legs – one leg takes more of the weight of the body than the other, and then the load sharing is reversed. The shift in weight is quite small in quiet stance, typically within 2% or 3% of total body weight[74]. The loading-unloading process is easy to demonstrate to yourself: simply stand up with your feet about 30 cm apart and shift your weight from one side to the other. When you do this, it is possible to exhibit substantial mediolateral sway at the hips while keeping the head and shoulders relatively still, as indicated in cartoon form in panel A of Figure 7.47. If you stand with your feet together you will find that it is much more difficult to sway in this manner, but easier to sway about the ankle joint with the other joints held relatively rigid as shown in panel B of Figure 7.47. If you try to sway like this with the feet apart, you will find that one leg comes off the floor (Figure 7.47, panel C): you've transferred all your body weight to one leg.

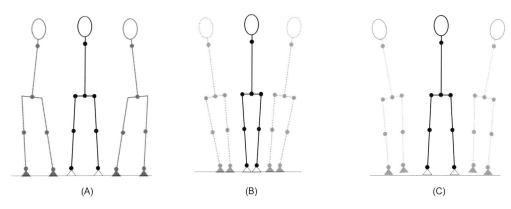

(A)   (B)   (C)

Figure 7.47: *Different patterns of mediolateral sway.*

Mediolateral sway is usually of smaller amplitude than anteroposterior sway, but is more affected by stance width. When standing with the feet apart, people sway more in the anteroposterior direction than mediolaterally, but when the feet are together, mediolateral sway increases substantially and may be greater in amplitude than anteroposterior sway[75]. Closing the eyes has also been found to have a greater effect on mediolateral sway than on anteroposterior sway[76]. The effect of closing the eyes on mediolateral sway is greatest when the feet are close together[77]. If you stand with your feet together and close your eyes, you will sway much more than you normally do. It is likely that you will be aware of swaying in these conditions.

Figure 7.48 presents some data for mediolateral sway for a person standing with their feet together (touching at the ankles) and eyes closed. The traces on the right of the figure show the horizontal position in the mediolateral direction of points at the level of the shoulders, hips, knees and ankles over a period of about 32 seconds. Movement at the shoulders, hips, knees and ankles follows an almost identical pattern, but the amplitude is smaller at locations closer to the ground. The range of motion is 24 mm for points at shoulder level and about 1 mm at the ankles (the angular range of motion is roughly 1.0° at the ankles). A similar pattern is observed for anteroposterior sway in quiet stance[78]. This pattern is what would be expected if the body swayed about the ankle joints in the manner shown in panel B of Figure 7.45 for anteroposterior sway and panel B of Figure 7.47 for mediolateral sway. If the knee, hip and spinal joints are held fairly rigid, then all points on the body sway in the same way, but move farther the higher they are above the ankles. However, it has been found that there is motion about other joints during quiet stance. The motion is particularly marked at the hip joint, where amplitude of motion can be similar to and sometimes greater than that at the ankle[79], but opposite in direction. Thus, anteroposterior sway will often involve motion of the type shown in panel D of Figure 7.45[80], and mediolateral sway often involves motion of the type shown in panel A of Figure 7.47. Even for the case shown in Figure 7.48 where the overall pattern is consistent with sway about the ankle joint only, more detailed analysis of the data showed that motion at other joints was also involved.

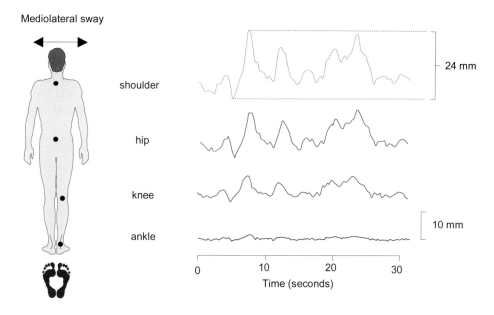

Figure 7.48: *Mediolateral sway during quiet stance. Based on data reported by Day* et al. *(1993).*

7.4.6 During quiet stance, the body's center of gravity moves slightly

If the body swayed rigidly as shown in panel B of Figures 7.45 and 7.47, then it is obvious that the CoG would move back and forth in both the anteroposterior direction and the mediolateral direction. However, since the body sway involves motions at other joints such as those shown in panel C of Figure 7.45 and panel A of Figure 7.47, it is conceivable that sway could involve little or no horizontal motion of the CoG. It turns out that the CoG does move in quiet stance, in both the anteroposterior and mediolateral directions. Figure 7.49 shows the horizontal motion of the CoG in the anteroposterior direction during a period of quiet stance lasting 40 seconds (eyes open, feet apart). It is not possible to directly measure the location of the CoG during stance, so its position must be obtained indirectly from other measurements. The data shown in Figure 7.49 were obtained by measuring the relative positions of all the body segments and then calculating the CoG based on estimates of the individual segment weights and dimensions[81]. The horizontal motion of the CoG is another possible measure of postural sway, but is not often used because of the difficulty of estimating it.

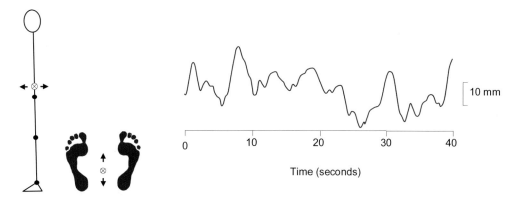

Figure 7.49: *Motion of the body's CoG in the anteroposterior direction during a period of quiet standing. (Data from Figure 1 of Winter* et al., *1998.)*

The range of horizontal motion of the CoG over the 40-second period shown in Figure 7.49 is about 30 mm. Typical values for the range lie between about 10 mm and 40 mm in quiet stance, with the standard deviation being between about one-quarter and one-fifth of the range. In the study from which the data presented in Figure 7.49 were obtained, the standard deviation of the horizontal motion of the CoG was about one-fifth of the range in both the anteroposterior and mediolateral directions. Where it has been measured, the horizontal motion of the CoG behaves in a similar manner to other measures of sway, such as ankle joint angle or horizontal position of locations on the body surface.

7.4.7 During quiet stance, the center of pressure moves slightly but it is not a measure of sway

The position of the center of pressure (CoP) is much easier to estimate than the position of the CoG, as it can be done using the measurements provided by a device called a **force platform**. The force platform is essentially a flat, rigid, instrumented plate that can be placed on or in the floor and is of sufficient area for a person to stand on it. Sometimes two platforms are used, one for each foot. Force-transducing devices built into the platform measure the ground reaction forces, and from these measurements the CoP can be computed using well-established techniques[82].

Given that the CoG lies directly above the CoP in static conditions (see in section 7.3.8), we might expect that when the CoG moves in the horizontal plane, the CoP will move as well. While this is true, it is not true that the CoP moves in the same way as the CoG. In fact, the horizontal motion of the CoG is different from the motion of the CoP, as shown in Figure 7.50. The figure shows the horizontal motion of the body's CoG (thin red line) and the motion of the CoP (thicker blue line) in the anteroposterior direction during a short period of quiet stance. The two are clearly not the same: the most obvious difference is that the CoP motion has a substantially greater amplitude (greater range and standard deviation) than the CoG motion, a pattern that is always obtained in quiet stance[83]. Since CoG motion is a measure of sway, results like those shown in Figure 7.50 show that CoP motion is not a measure of postural sway[84]. The CoP differs from the horizontal position of the CoG during sway due to the existence of muscular forces that are generated to keep the horizontal position of the CoG within the boundaries of the base of support. Thus, the motion of the CoP depends on the control processes that regulate upright stance; we return to these processes in subsequent sections.

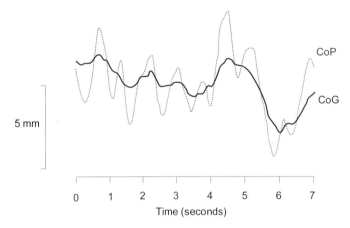

Figure 7.50: *Position of the center of pressure (blue) and the center of gravity (CoG, red) during a period of quiet stance. (Data from Figure 2 of Winter, 1995.)*

7.4.8 Postural sway is affected by a number of different factors

The amplitude of postural sway during quiet stance is affected by a wide variety of factors. These factors can be divided into the following groups:

(1) **Physical characteristics and condition of the individual.** Different people show different amounts of sway: younger children and elderly people sway more than working-age adults[85], for example. The same person may sway more in some circumstances than in others; they may sway more when they are tired, for instance, and women tend to sway more during the later stages of pregnancy[86].

(2) **Stance posture.** Quiet stance posture does not seem to vary very much, but the position of the feet does have a strong effect on sway as illustrated by findings described in section 7.4.5.

(3) **Support surface characteristics.** Physical characteristics of the support surface such as slipperiness, slope and compliance can affect sway. For example, people sway more when standing on soft, compliant surfaces than on firm, hard surfaces[87]; sway needs to be minimal on very slippery surfaces, otherwise you risk falling over.

(4) **Availability of sensory information.** Proprioceptive, vestibular and visual information are all relevant in postural control, but in natural conditions the only source that normally varies in its availability is visual information: in the dark or in dense fog there may be little or no useful visual information available. It is typically found that people sway more when they cannot see their surroundings[88]: early studies indicated that sway increases by as much as 50% with the eyes closed[89], and some subsequent studies have reported similar results[90]. However, this finding has not always been replicated: some studies have found little difference in postural sway between eyes-open and eyes-closed conditions[91].

(5) **Psychological factors.** What a person is thinking about and how they are feeling has been found to affect postural sway. For instance, if a person is anxious, they are likely to sway more[92]. Carrying out certain cognitive tasks such as memory tasks[93] and reasoning tasks can also lead to changes in the amount a person sways[94]. The perceived consequences of losing balance or falling also influences sway: when the consequences are perceived as potentially more damaging, such as occurs when standing on the edge of a cliff, people's sway changes – they may sway more or they may sway less[95].

We will have little further to say about factors in the first three groups (the references can be consulted for details), but we will explore some factors in groups (4) and (5).

The effects of psychological factors on postural sway during quiet stance are complex and difficult to summarize succinctly, due to the large number of often conflicting findings. For present purposes, it will be sufficient to note two things. First, adopting and maintaining a posture is a voluntary activity that involves some kind of mental (cognitive) activity. Second, sway is always present and cannot be eliminated. Although sway can sometimes be reduced by instructing a person to stand as still as possible[96], or instructing them to try to reduce the motion relative to the environment by attending to visible features[97], it is impossible for a person to eliminate sway altogether, even with extensive training[98].

Consider the first claim: that postural control involves cognitive activity. Everyday experience suggests that the maintenance of quiet stance occurs without any 'cognitive effort': we don't seem to need to think about maintaining stance while we are doing it. Despite this impression, postural-cognitive dual task studies have shown that maintaining upright stance does seem to require some kind of cognitive effort. In a postural-cognitive dual task situation, a person is required to maintain stance (the postural task) and to perform some mental task (the cognitive task) at the same time. The cognitive task might be to solve simple arithmetical problems (as suggested in cartoon form in Figure 7.51), or memorizing lists of words or a set of spatial locations. If performance of one task (task B) has a detrimental effect on the performance of the other (task A), we say that the task B **interferes** with task A. The difference between performance of task A when it is performed alone and when it is performed together with task B is called the **dual-task interference effect**. Such interference effects occur if performance of task A involves the use of some of the same mechanisms as performance of task B. Thus, if the volitional maintenance of upright posture involves the use of some of the same brain mechanisms that are involved in cognitive tasks, we would expect to see dual-task interference effects. Postural performance may be adversely affected by performance of the cognitive task. Conversely, if postural control does not make use of any of the mechanisms involved in cognitive task performance, then no interference effects would be expected.

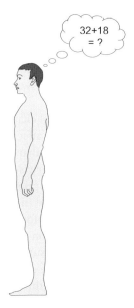

Figure 7.51: *Performing a cognitive task (mental arithmetic) during quiet stance.*

Postural-cognitive dual-task interference effects have been reported in quiet stance[99], though they are typically small and are often not observed at all unless the postural task is made more demanding by having someone stand on a narrow beam or with one foot in front of the other[100]. The effects are much more consistent in perturbed stance where disturbances from the environment occur[101]. These findings provide evidence that some kind of cognitive effort is involved in maintaining upright posture, and that this effort is greater when the postural task is more demanding or is subject to external disturbances.

7.4.9 Why do we sway in quiet stance?

We have seen that people cannot avoid swaying slightly when standing in quiet stance; what causes this sway? There are two possibilities, both of which probably contribute to sway. First, sway can be produced as a result of intrinsic disturbances to upright posture that are always present. Such sources of disturbance include rhythmical disturbances due to breathing[102], the beating of the heart[103], and small fluctuations in muscle force (physiological tremor). Tremor is generated by several different mechanisms, including random variations in firing rates within the neuromotor system[104]. Sway would then reflect the operation of a repeated disturbance-correction cycle: a disturbance moves the body's CoG in one direction, and a corrective response moves it in the opposite direction. The second mechanism that may contribute to sway is the normal operation of the postural control processes that maintain stance. If this mechanism contributes, as evidence suggests it does[105], then we would sway even if there were no disturbances at all.

Notice that these two reasons for swaying are not mutually exclusive alternatives: both may make a contribution to sway. There is no doubt that intrinsic disturbances are present during quiet stance and can contribute to sway. It is also becoming increasingly clear that there are control processes that produce sway as part of their normal operation. We will discuss these different contributions to sway in what follows.

7.4.10 The intrinsic elasticity of active muscles contributes to postural stability

In quiet stance there are small gravitational torques that must be balanced by opposing torques to prevent the body from toppling over. In section 7.3.10, we saw that a portion of the opposing torque at some joints is contributed by the passive connective tissue; the rest is contributed by active muscles. Once the muscles are generating sufficient torque to balance the gravitational torques, the intrinsic elasticity of the muscles provides a possible mechanism for restoring the position of a body segment to the balanced position if a small disturbance occurs. The idea is illustrated for a schematic inverted pendulum in Figure 7.52, which shows a pendulum being held at a slight angle by a length of elastic material attached to a hook in the floor. The weight of pendulum exerts a torque at the joint, and so does the tension in the elastic; when the elastic is holding the pendulum in position, the torques are equal in magnitude but in opposite directions (the weight torque acts clockwise, the tension torque acts counterclockwise). The pendulum's position is an equilibrium that is stable when subjected to small disturbances. A small, brief push to the left will move the pendulum towards the upright position and the weight torque will pull it back to the equilibrium position. A small push to the right will move the pendulum towards the floor, which stretches the elastic and increases the tension. The increase in tension provides sufficient torque to exceed the weight torque, and the pendulum is pulled back to the equilibrium position[106]. We will refer to the method for stabilizing the position of an inverted pendulum shown in Figure 7.52 as the **elastic holding mechanism**.

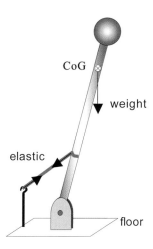

Figure 7.52: *Holding an inverted pendulum in an upright position using a piece of elastic.*

In principle, muscles can work to hold the body in an upright posture in a manner similar to the way in which the elastic holds the inverted pendulum. Once the nervous system has activated the relevant muscles to the degree needed to hold the body in an upright position, the intrinsic elasticity of active muscle will act to stabilize the body's position in the face of small disturbances, without any further neural activity. Active skeletal muscle behaves like a piece of elastic, so a stretch will result in an immediate increase in tension before any reflex mechanisms have had time to generate a response.

The elastic holding mechanism is active during quiet stance, since the muscles that hold the body segments in position are almost continuously active and so have significant stiffness. Since the muscles are only slightly active, the elastic forces that are generated when they are stretched will be relatively small. Nevertheless, the disturbances typically present during periods of quiet stance are small: in these periods, the elastic properties of the slightly active muscles may be sufficient to stabilize upright posture. Indeed, it has been proposed that this is the major reactive mechanism used to stabilize upright posture in quiet stance[107]. According to this idea, other reactive mechanisms (e.g., reflex mechanisms) that generate responses to sensed changes in body position and motion play only a secondary role during periods of quiet stance. The question of whether intrinsic muscle elasticity is the major contributor to the stability of quiet stance is considered next.

7.4.11 Is intrinsic muscle elasticity a major contributor to postural stability in quiet stance?

The idea that intrinsic muscle elasticity is the major contributor to postural stability in quiet stance is supported by two arguments. First, the observed in-phase relationship between the motion of the CoG and the CoP during quiet stance is what would be expected if the dominant stabilizing mechanism were provided by intrinsic muscle stiffness[108] (provided that the body pivots about the ankle joint, like the inverted simple pendulum shown in Figure 7.52). Second, for much of the time during quiet stance, the swaying movement is so slight that people are unaware of it. This suggests that the swaying motion may be too small to produce any significant changes in the responses of relevant sensory receptors, and therefore unlikely to be sufficient for making corrective adjustments to posture[109].

Controversy has arisen because neither argument is conclusive. Consider the second: it is possible for sensory stimulation to evoke responses from a person in the absence of conscious perceptual awareness (see Chapter 3). It has been shown that this is possible in postural control: reflex changes in plantarflexor activity in response to consciously imperceptible changes in body position have been observed during upright stance[110] (see section 7.4.14 for further examples). Thus, consciously imperceptible changes in position due to the disturbances encountered in quiet stance are capable of evoking corrective reflex responses. There is also evidence to suggest that when people closely attend to their sway, they are able to consciously detect its occurrence[111]. Under these conditions, people are capable of detecting angular changes at the ankle joints of between 0.06° and 0.12°, which is within the range of normal postural sway in quiet stance[112]. Thus, there is no evidence to suggest that quiet stance sway is too small to evoke sensory responses.

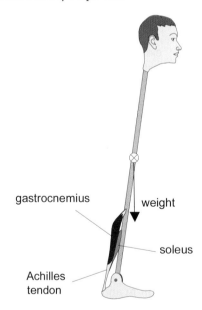

gastrocnemius

weight

soleus

Achilles
tendon

Figure 7.53: *Inverted pendulum model of a standing person.*

The argument based on the in-phase motion of the CoP and the CoG assumes that the body in quiet stance approximates the behavior of a simple inverted pendulum[113]. When this approximation holds, the body can be modeled as an inverted pendulum: the **inverted pendulum model** of human stance. In the anteroposterior direction – the only direction we will consider here[114] – the inverted pendulum model treats the body as a rigid pole that pivots about an ankle joint. Figure 7.53 shows a cartoon of the model. Since the CoG is slightly in front of the ankle, the plantarflexor muscles (triceps surae) are the most important, as they act to stop the body toppling forwards; they play the role of the elastic in Figure 7.52. If the CoG moves to a position behind the ankle joint, the tibialis anterior muscle (ankle dorsiflexor) acts to prevent the body toppling backwards. According to the model, the role of the muscles at other joints is simply to hold the body in position so that it behaves like a rigid pole. The model is formulated mathematically and is widely used for deriving quantitative predictions and conducting quantitative analysis[115], but the following verbal definition can be given:

> **INVERTED PENDULUM MODEL** (of the human body in the anteroposterior direction): An approximate, simplified mechanical model of upright posture in quiet stance, in which the legs, trunk and head are treated as a single rigid segment that pivots about an 'ankle' joint – the joint with a single rigid 'foot'. The body segment's CoG is a fixed distance from the ankle joint.

During periods of quiet stance, anteroposterior sway about the ankles closely approximates the motion of a simple inverted pendulum, especially at lower frequencies of oscillation[116], and produces the expected in-phase relationship between CoP and CoG motion. However, as noted earlier, (angular) motion about other joints such as the hip and neck joints is also observed, which is ignored in the inverted pendulum model. Moreover, it has been shown that when people are splinted so that motion at joints other than the ankle are not possible – they are constrained to move like an inverted pendulum – sway is greater than when movement at all joints is possible[117]. Thus, observations consistent with the model offer weak support for the idea that intrinsic muscle elasticity is the major contributor to postural stability in quiet stance.

Even in conditions in which the inverted pendulum model provides a reasonable description of the body, intrinsic tissue stiffness cannot be the only mechanism that stabilizes posture. Detailed studies have shown that the stiffness of the ankle musculature and associated connective tissue is not sufficient to stabilize upright posture[118]. It has also been shown that the lengths of the triceps surae muscles do not change in the manner expected if the muscle were simply behaving like a piece of elastic[119]. These findings imply that some additional stabilizing process is involved (see section 7.4.13).

To summarize, the intrinsic elastic properties of active postural muscles and associated connective tissues can contribute to the stabilization of upright posture, but there is no evidence to suggest that it is the main or most important mechanism. There must be other stabilizing mechanisms operative during quiet stance. What these mechanisms might be is addressed next.

7.4.12 The phasic stretch reflex does not contribute to postural stability in quiet stance

It was once thought that the stretch reflex was the major mechanism contributing to postural stability in both quiet and perturbed stance[120]. Sherrington's view seems to have been that the phasic stretch reflex played the major role in maintaining postural stability and controlling the sway of the body[121]. This is now known to be incorrect. As we saw in Chapter 6, the phasic reflex contributes to the damping of movement, not to stiffness, and so it cannot act to restore an equilibrium position (it can only slow down the swaying movement). Furthermore, during quiet stance, the speed of sway is likely to be too slow to stretch muscles quickly enough to evoke significant phasic responses[122]. Additional evidence that the phasic stretch reflex does not contribute significantly during quiet stance comes from patients with Charcot-Marie-Tooth disease, a neuropathy in which the large-diameter, peripheral axons are almost completely lost. Due to loss of type Ia afferents, these patients lack a phasic stretch reflex, but their postural sway during quiet stance appears to be unaffected[123].

In sum, it appears that during periods of quiet stance, the phasic stretch reflex will be making very little contribution to the control of sway when a person is standing on a firm, flat surface with the feet in a preferred position (side by side, slightly apart). In non-preferred positions, such as when the feet are together or one in front of the other, sway increases, and the phasic stretch reflex may make a contribution. In these conditions, the role of the phasic reflex is to increase damping of the joint motions, not to restore equilibrium following a disturbance.

The tonic stretch reflex (TSR) will contribute to the postural tone observed during standing (for reasons discussed in Chapter 6)[124] and so can be considered to contribute to postural orientation (problem 1 in section 7.4.2). Does this component of the stretch reflex also contribute to the stabilization of posture during quiet stance? The TSR acts to enhance the stiffness of skeletal muscle, so it could play a role in postural stabilization similar to that of the intrinsic muscle elasticity described earlier: when a muscle is stretched, the reflex causes the muscle to generate a contractile force that resists the stretch and acts to restore the body segment to its equilibrium orientation (see Chapter 6 for a general discussion of how the TSR contributes to the stability of body postures). The difference is that the force evoked reflexively in response to stretch is not developed immediately, but after a short time delay. However, the low gain of the TSR means that it may not have sufficient strength to provide all the additional stiffness needed to stop the body toppling over. This seems to be the case at the ankle joints[125], where there is little evidence of stretch–reflex-evoked muscle activity during quiet stance[126]. This suggests that there must be other stabilizing mechanisms operating during periods of quiet stance.

7.4.13 An active, intermittent control mechanism may contribute to postural stability and sway during quiet stance

We have now seen that the simple elastic holding mechanism is not alone sufficient for maintaining balance during quiet stance, due to low stiffness of the ankle joint. Exclusive use of this mechanism would require significantly greater activation of the triceps surae muscles than is actually observed. Two additional mechanisms have been implicated in control during quiet stance: (1) stabilizing adjustments made at joints other than the ankle (particularly the hip joint)[127] and (2) an active, intermittent modulation of ankle muscle activity[128].

The first of these is also important in perturbed stance, and will be discussed further in the next part of the chapter. Here we will give a brief, intuitive account of the second mechanism. The basic idea is illustrated in Figure 7.54: the aim is to stop the pendulum from falling over by giving it little pushes back towards the vertical position if it falls too far (the pushes are made with the index fingers in the figure). In frame 1, the pendulum is falling to the right; in frame 2, the index finger makes contact with the falling pendulum and exerts a force on it that stops its fall ('catches' the falling pendulum); in frame 3, the pendulum is moving back towards the vertical position following a little push from the finger. It is easy to verify that you can keep a pole from falling using this method, and it requires very little effort to do so, provided that the pole is not allowed to fall very far from the vertical.

In the application of the intermittent 'catch-and-push' mechanism to the maintenance of upright stance, the role of the finger in Figure 7.54 is taken by the triceps surae muscles, which develop torque at the ankle. The difference is that the muscles give a little pull towards the upright rather than a little push (muscles cannot push). Torque developed by triceps surae muscles can only stop the body falling forwards if the body's CoG is still within the base of support, so only very small angular motions of the ankle joint can occur before the muscles need to contract to 'catch' the fall.

There is evidence that such a mechanism is at work during quiet stance, and so postural sway is, at least in part, a consequence of repeated small falls followed by a catch and pull-up by the muscles[129]. This mechanism is able to explain the paradoxical muscle lengthening and shortening that has been observed using ultrasound measurements of muscle length during quiet stance[130]. As the body sways forward about the ankle, it would be expected that the triceps surae would lengthen, but a very slight shortening (between about 0.03 and 0.3 mm) can often be observed; likewise, the triceps surae would be expected to shorten as the body sways backward, but a small lengthening can often be observed. The triceps surae shortening during forward sway is active (a concentric contraction), since it is associated with an increase in EMG activity: the muscle is able to shorten because the Achilles tendon lengthens (the overall length of the muscle + tendon increases as the leg sways forwards). These observations cannot be explained by passive elastic mechanisms and are not consistent with the action of the stretch reflex; the catch and pull-up mechanism is able to account for it, though the details are too complex to describe here[131].

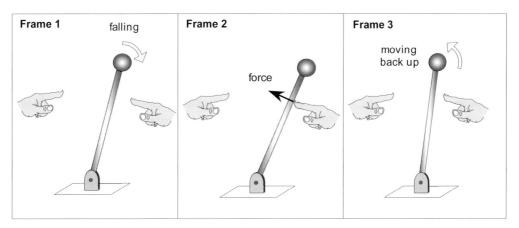

Figure 7.54: *Keeping a pendulum upright with intermittent pushes.*

7.4.14 Does vision play a role in the stabilization of quiet stance?

Postural sway in quiet stance tends to increase when people cannot see their surroundings. The increase can be very small: one study reported that people fall into two groups, those whose sway increased with eyes closed and those whose sway was unaffected[132]. Nevertheless, it seems that most people will show some increase in sway when they are unable to see their surroundings[133]. This suggests that when vision is available it makes a contribution to postural stabilization during quiet stance, but an increase of sway without vision does not establish a role for vision in the control of sway in quiet stance. A conclusive demonstration would be provided by showing that changes in visual stimulation that occur during quiet stance are capable of evoking postural responses.

The amplitude of sway during quiet stance is such that the maximum range of head displacement in either the anteroposterior or mediolateral directions will be in the region of 2 to 4 centimeters, but for much of the time the movement will be well within this range (e.g., Figure 7.48). Thus, if vision plays a role in stance stabilization, then it should be possible to observe postural responses to changes in visual stimulation that would be produced by head movements of less than 4 cm. Such changes in visual stimulation can be produced using two different methods. The first involves actually moving the visible environment the person is standing within (moving the environment 4 cm forwards in the anteroposterior direction is equivalent to the head moving backwards by 4 cm). The second involves use of a graphical projection: a person stands in a dark room in front of a large screen onto which a visible scene is projected – a virtual environment.

The first method typically involves the experimental participant standing with their head inside a large box that can be moved[134]. Several studies using this method suspended a large box by ropes attached to a high ceiling, which allowed the box to be moved by swinging it back and forth. The suspension point where the ropes are tied to the ceiling is far enough above the box that for small swinging movements, the box moves almost horizontally backwards and forwards. This is called the **swinging room** apparatus[135]. Figure 7.55 shows the set-up: the participant stands on a normal, stationary floor and the room is moved. In principle the room can be moved forwards and backwards (participant's anteroposterior direction in the figure) or side to side (mediolateral direction). A forward movement of the room produces retinal image motion the same as would be produced by a backward movement of the head in a stationary room; a leftward movement of the room produces image motion equivalent to a rightward movement of the head. If the room swings forwards and backwards, the visual stimulation is equivalent to a backwards-forwards swaying motion of the head. The brain interprets this stimulation as movement of the head in the environment, not as a movement of the environment with the head stationary. The reason for this interpretation is that in natural conditions the whole environment (or large segments of it) does not move, and so motions of the whole visual field (or large portions of it) are most likely to have arisen because the head moved.

Using either a real moving room (Figure 7.55) or a virtual moving room, it has been shown that moving the environment backwards and forwards in an oscillating fashion evokes compensatory postural sway[136]. The amount of scene displacement needed to evoke sway reactions is quite small. For example, forward-backward room displacements of 3 mm were sufficient to evoke anteroposterior sway when the visible surfaces were 30 cm from the observer[137], a 2 cm displacement[138] was sufficient at 1.1 m, and 2.5 cm was sufficient when the room surfaces were 2 meters from the person[139]. These displacements are so small that the movement is often not consciously perceived[140].

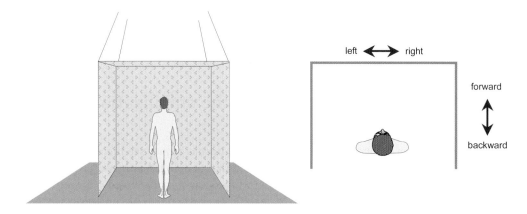

Figure 7.55: *The swinging room apparatus. Left: view into the room from behind the participant. Right: plan view showing the room walls and the participant from above.*

Provided that the oscillation of the visible scene has a low frequency (less than about 0.5 Hz), the body sways in phase with the scene movement: when the scene moves forwards, the person sways forwards, and when the scene moves backwards, the person sways backwards. Panel A of Figure 7.56 shows one type of experimental set-up that has been used to study how people's head motion depends upon the motion of the visible scene (stimulus)[141]. Participants stand in a darkened room and view a movie that simulates them moving relative to a simple stationary scene containing surfaces only a few metres away (in the figure the movie is back-projected onto a large screen that is parallel to the participant's coronal plane). Panel B shows a stimulus motion (dotted line) and the kind of head movement such motion has been found to evoke from participants (solid line). The stimulus motion is sinusoidal (frequency 0.2 Hz) and simulates a scene moving towards and away from the participant with an amplitude of 4 cm. In the figure, the participant's head moves back and forth almost in phase with the stimulus motion (the motion is mainly due to anteroposterior sway about the ankle joints). The head motion tends to reduce or eliminate the retinal image motion due to the movie and participants often report being unaware of any stimulus motion in such experiments. In a real swinging room (Figure 7.55), the participants' sway acts to reduce the relative motion between their heads and the walls of the room.

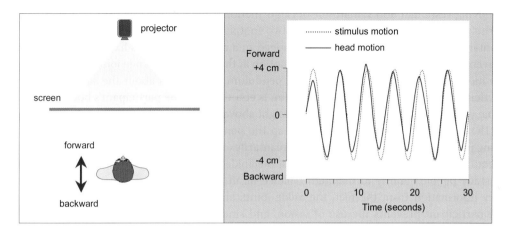

Figure 7.56: *Pattern of results obtained in experiments in which standing participants saw a stimulus that simulated sinusoidal relative motion between themselves and a vertical wall (frequency = 0.2 Hz). (Illustrative, based on the experiment reported by Dijkstra, Schöner, Gielen, 1994.)*

7.4.15 Balance can be achieved with limited sensory information

Swaying of the body can produce changes in the stimulation of several different sets of sensory receptors. Motions at the joints (primarily the ankles) will stimulate muscle and joint proprioceptors and cutaneous stretch receptors in the skin around the joint. This provides information about joint motion and position, and information from multiple joints can be combined to estimate the position and motion of the body's CoG. Motion of the head produces visual flow stimulation (see previous section) that provides information about how the head is moving relative to the environment. Head motion also stimulates the vestibular organs, which provide information about how the head is moving and about how it is oriented with respect to the gravitational frame of reference. Body sway also produces changes in the pressure distribution over the soles of the feet, which in turn changes the stimulation of pressure-sensitive cutaneous mechanoreceptors.

All of these sources of information could potentially contribute to postural stabilization during quiet stance. It appears, however, that none of them is absolutely necessary: removing any single source of information does not prevent a person from maintaining a quiet stance posture. As we saw in the last section, people can stand perfectly well without visual information, though sway is usually slightly increased. The same is true for the other sources of information. People who through disease or injury have lost their vestibular organs are able to maintain quiet stance after a period of adjustment following the loss, though sway may be greater than in people with intact vestibular systems, particularly with the eyes closed[142]. Likewise, people who have lost large-fiber somatosensory function in the lower limbs are able to maintain quiet stance on firm surfaces, provided that they are able to see their surroundings[143]. One particularly extreme example is provided by a patient known by the initials I.W. who has sensory neuronopathy[144], which has destroyed the large-fiber, myelinated afferents below his neck: he is unable to feel anything but pain and temperature from his shoulders to his feet. Although I.W. was initially incapacitated by his sensory loss, he gradually reacquired the ability to stand, walk, and live independently. In particular, he is able to maintain quiet stance provided that he is able to see the surroundings; without vision, he is unable to stand securely without external support[145].

In I.W.'s case and in cases of vestibular loss, an adjustment period of several days or weeks is needed before the person is able to stand unsupported. Studies with normal participants allow an assessment of how well people are able to stand without a particular source of information. This is easy to do with vision (just ask participants to shut their eyes), but more difficult in the case of vestibular or somatosensory information. One method of selectively removing vestibular and somatosensory information is shown in Figure 7.57, panel A[146]. The participant is upright with their feet on two footplates that can rotate, allowing the feet to plantarflex and dorsiflex. The body is strapped to a rigid board that is fixed to the floor. This prevents the body swaying and prevents motion at the neck, hip or knee joints. The footplates are mechanically coupled to an inverted pendulum that rotates about the same axis as the participant's ankles. The inverted pendulum is equivalent to the participant's body: it has the same weight, and its CoG is at the same height above the floor as the participant's.

The task in the experiment was to keep the pendulum balanced in an upright position using just the feet (contracting the ankle plantarflexor and dorsiflexor muscles), a task which is equivalent to standing upright using just the ankle muscles. Using this set-up, it is possible to study people's ability to maintain balance in an upright posture using only somatosensory information from the feet, the ankle joints and the associated muscles (blindfolding the participant prevents the use of vision, and since the head does not move, there is no vestibular stimulation). Inflation of pneumatic cuffs around the ankles creates a nerve block and anesthetizes the feet and ankles below the level of the cuff. A blindfolded participant with anesthetized feet can only use proprioceptive information from the muscles and their tendons. The graph in panel B of Figure 7.57 shows a root mean square (RMS) measure of average sway amplitude obtained when different sensory information was available. A condition in which people stood normally is shown for comparison. The graph shows that pendulum sway was a little greater than normal sway at the ankle joints when visual information about pendulum motion was available together with somatosensory information from the muscles, ankle joints and feet. Removal of somatosensory information from the ankles and feet resulted in only a very small increase in sway; removing vision had a much greater effect. When the only information available was from the muscles of the lower leg and their tendons, participants were still able to balance the body-equivalent pendulum. The sway was greatest in this condition, but still averaged less than 0.2°. They were able to balance the pendulum using only muscle and tendon information, 'without training and when distracted or engaged in conversation'[147].

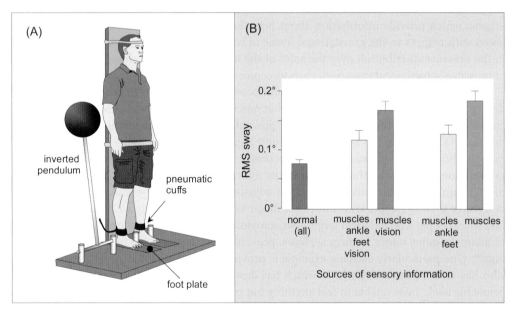

Figure 7.57: *Task set-up (A) and results (B) from a study in which people balanced a body-equivalent inverted pendulum by means of muscular torques exerted about the ankle joints; see text for details. Data taken from Fitzpatrick, Rogers, McCloskey (1994), Figure 3 (error bars show standard errors).*

Another finding shown in panel B of Figure 7.57 was that participants' sway was greater when they balanced the body-equivalent pendulum than in the control condition in which they stood normally. There are at least two possible factors that could contribute to this. First, vestibular information is available during normal standing, but is not available in the pendulum balancing task, since the head is fixed. Second, rotation about knee, hip and neck joints is possible in normal standing, but is not possible in the pendulum balancing task. A second part of the study provides some insight into which of these two possibilities is the more likely. The experimental set-up used is shown in panel A of Figure 7.58: participants stood strapped to a rigid, lightweight frame that prevented rotation at the knee, hip and neck joints but allowed rotation about the ankle joints. The participants' task was simply to stand quietly. Panel B of the figure shows some results using the same sway measure as before (Figure 7.57B). The solid gray bars are from the control condition, in which participants stood normally either with their eyes open or blindfolded (no vision). The striped gray bars are from the experimental condition in which participants were strapped to the splint. The green bars are data from the previous part of the experiment (Figure 7.57), included for comparison.

The data in Figure 7.58B show three things. (1) Sway is increased in normal quiet stance without vision (solid gray bars), which replicates previous research. (2) When people were strapped to the frame and only ankle joint motion was possible, their sway was greater than for normal standing, both with and without vision (striped gray bars). This suggests that the possibility of moving at the knees, hips and neck allows for better control of posture. (3) Performance when strapped to the frame was comparable to performance in the body-equivalent pendulum balancing task when the same sensory information was available (with the exception of vestibular information). This indicates that vestibular information makes little contribution to postural control during quiet stance: it is likely that head movement is too small to elicit corrective responses from the vestibular system[148]. Other work has shown that the vestibular system plays a less important role in generating corrective postural responses than other sensory systems[149], which goes against the traditional view that the vestibular system underlies our sense of balance. Nevertheless, the vestibular system may have a role to play in quiet stance, because it can provide information about the direction of gravity and so influence the reference configuration of the body[150].

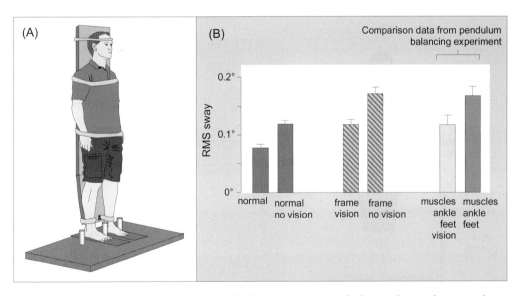

Figure 7.58: *Task set-up (A) and results (B) from a study in which people stood strapped to a lightweight fame to prevent motion at joints other than the ankles; see text for details. Data taken from Fitzpatrick, Rogers, McCloskey (1994), Figure 3 (error bars show standard errors).*

In summary, quiet stance can be maintained using information from different sensory systems: if one source of information is removed, people can still stand perfectly well, though their sway may increase slightly. How the different sources of information are combined and integrated during normal standing cannot be determined from the results described here, and is beyond the scope of this text[151]. Next we consider the role of tactile information in postural stabilization.

7.4.16 Light touch can contribute to the stablization of stance in some conditions

It is perhaps not surprising to learn that changes in the stimulation of cutaneous mechano-receptors in the soles of the feet can evoke stabilizing postural responses[152], though the role of this source of information in quiet stance is less clear. What is perhaps more surprising is that lightly touching something with the finger tip can act to stabilize stance.

It is clear that holding something or leaning against something can help a person stand upright. In many cases contact with things in the environment provides *mechanical support*: the person exerts force on whatever object they are holding on to or leaning against, and the reaction forces and torques applied to the person by the object provides postural support. However, it has been shown that it is not necessary that an object provide mechanical support in order for contact with it to have a stabilizing effect. Postural sway can be significantly reduced if the finger tip is in gentle contact with a fixed object. These effects can be observed if a person stands quietly with their feet positioned heel-to-toe or on one leg, postures in which sway is greater than when a person stands with their feet side by side. The first study[153] to demonstrate the effect used the task set-up shown in panel A of Figure 7.59. Participants stood on a firm, level surface in a heel-to-toe stance under three different conditions, with and without vision (eyes open and eyes closed):

(1)   *No contact*: participants' arms hung down at their sides, and only the soles of the feet were in contact with the environment.

(2)   *Light touch contact*: the tip of the right index finger lightly touched a bar fixed to the top of a rigid support. Participants were required to keep the force exerted on the bar below 1 Newton (100 grams weight force); the bar was instrumented with force transducers so that the force applied to it could be measured.

(3)   *Free contact*: the finger tip touched the bar and participants were free to exert as much force against it as they wanted to.

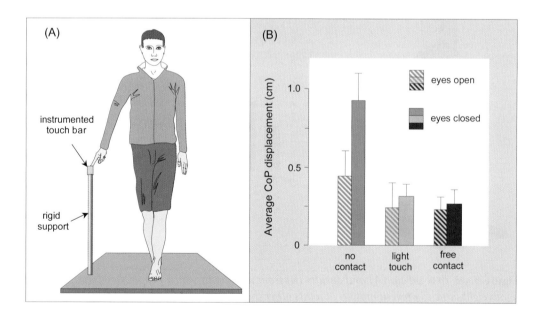

Figure 7.59: *Task set-up (A) and results (B) from a study in which people stood heel-to-toe and could touch a fixed bar with their index finger tip; see text for details. Data taken from Jeka, Lackner (1994), Figure 2.*

In each condition, participants maintained quiet stance for a period of 24 seconds, during which the position of the center of pressure (CoP) was recorded using a force plate mounted in the floor. The primary dependent measure was the average mediolateral (left-right) displacement of the CoP during the recording period. CoP displacement was closely correlated with postural sway, and so the average displacement can be considered to be a measure of sway[154]. Some basic results from the study are shown in panel B of Figure 7.59. In the no-contact condition, sway was greatest, and was about twice as large with the eyes closed as with eyes open. Sway in the contact conditions was about 50% or less of the sway in the no-contact condition, and was much less affected by the absence of vision. Sway was similar in the light-touch and free-touch conditions, though the force exerted on the bar was, on average, ten times greater in the free-touch condition.

The results in Figure 7.59B show that light touch reduced sway substantially and was able to compensate (to a large extent) for the absence of vision. It was estimated that the force applied by the finger tip in the light touch condition would only provide mechanical support sufficient to reduce the magnitude of the sway by about 2% to 3%. The fact that sway was reduced by 50% or more by light touch, and that more forceful touch made little difference, indicates that the touch was providing information about the body's movement relative to the environment, rather than mechanical support. Postural adjustments based on this information were made by muscles in the trunk and legs.

The body sways from side to side when people stand in a heel-to-toe posture. When the finger tip is in light-touch contact with a fixed object, as in Figure 7.59A, body sway will alternately press the finger tip slightly more firmly and slightly less firmly against the object. It is also possible that the finger tip may slip a little on the surface as the body sways, or the finger may pivot about the point of contact. Slips, pressure changes, and pivots will stimulate cutaneous mechanoreceptors in the finger tip, and so sensory information about sway-induced finger-tip motion is available to the person. Evidently people can use such information to reduce sway and stabilize posture[155].

7.5 Perturbed Stance

7.5.1 Introduction

In this part of the chapter we will discuss perturbed stance: both environmentally perturbed stance and action perturbed stance. Disturbances from the environment come in different 'sizes': someone giving you a push disturbs your upright posture; a hard shove is more disturbing than a little jostle. Similarly, if someone stands on the deck of a boat, the greater pitching and rolling of the boat in a rough sea disturbs posture more than the gentle pitch and roll in a calm sea. Different sized disturbances evoke different types of reaction that act to prevent a person from falling over. If the disturbance is large enough to move the horizontal position of the CoG outside of the base of support (*overbalancing*), then a person must enlarge the base of support to avoid falling over. There are two ways in which this can be achieved:

(1)   Moving one foot (stepping) so as to enlarge the base of support along the direction of the step (see Figure 7.37). To be effective, the step needs to be in the direction in which the CoG moves.

(2)   Reaching out with one or both hands so as to brace oneself against a support or grab hold of something that provides support, such as another person, or a grab-handle like those found in buses and trains.

In some circumstances, these reactions may not be possible: there may be nothing to brace against or hold onto, or there may be nothing to step onto. The latter occurs if someone is standing on the edge of a cliff when they are pushed from behind: if they step forward, they will fall off the cliff. In such circumstances, people don't attempt to stop themselves falling by stepping; they use a different method, in which the outstretched arms are swung around in circles (arm swinging). The muscular forces that accelerate the arm(s) also impart reaction forces to the trunk that act to oppose the tendency to fall forward. In order to be effective, the arm swinging must begin before the CoG has moved outside the base of support. Stepping, bracing, and arm swinging are referred to as **rescue reactions**[156].

Although rescue reactions are important for preventing falls, they have received relatively little study compared with reactions evoked by smaller disturbances, which do not involve movement of the feet or arms[157]. We will restrict attention to these better studied reactions that involve movement and muscle contractions at the ankles, knees, hips, and sometimes back and neck joints. We will also discuss the postural adjustments that accompany voluntary movements.

7.5.2 Small amplitude disturbances evoke characteristic postural reactions

People's responses to a variety of different types of postural disturbance have been studied experimentally. In a few studies, posture was disturbed by applying pushes or pulls to various parts of the body[158]; other studies have used platforms that can be moved while a person is standing on them[159]. People's responses to four basic types of platform movement have been studied: horizontal shifts of the platform, vertical shifts of the platform, platform tilts, and left-right turns of the platform. The platform movements can have different sizes, have different speeds, be applied to one or both feet, and be discrete (e.g., shift forwards and stop) or cyclical (e.g., oscillate backwards and forwards). Here we will restrict attention to discrete, forwards-backwards (anteroposterior) platform movements that unexpectedly disturb upright stance.

Consider first small-amplitude, forwards-backwards shifts of the platform that occur at unexpected times, so the participant in the experiment cannot anticipate exactly when a shift will occur (though participants were familiar with the nature of the shift itself, and practiced at responding to it). In one set of experiments[160], participants stood with the feet side by side and the platform shifts were either forwards or backwards at constant speed (13 cm/s) for a period of 250 ms, which produced a shift through about 3.25 cm. The effects of such shifts are illustrated on the left of Figure 7.60. In panel A the platform shifts backwards and the feet move with it, so the body sways forwards. In panel B the platform shifts forwards and the body sways backwards. The right side of the figure shows rectified and averaged EMG recordings from muscles that responded to the platform shift. The results from panel A show that the muscles which respond to a backward platform shift are those in the back (erector spinae) and the back of the legs (hamstrings and gastrocnemius). Muscles in the front of the body (abdominal muscles, quadriceps and tibialis anterior) showed little or no response to the shift. This pattern of muscle response acts to oppose the sway of the body and return it to the upright posture. The results from panel B show that the muscles in the front of the body respond to a forwards shift of the platform (there was little or no response in the muscles in the back of the body). This pattern acts to oppose the backward sway of the body and restore upright stance.

For both backward and forward platform shifts, the muscle responses show a distal to proximal pattern of onset: in panel A the gastrocnemius response occurs first and the erector spinae response last; in panel B, the tibialis anterior response starts first and the abdominal response last. The latency of the responses (between about 80 and 120 milliseconds) indicates that they are automatic, stimulus-elicited reactions to postural disturbances. At first glance, the patterns seem as though they might be due to the action of the stretch reflex: platform shifts move the feet but tend to leave the CoG where it is, so the ankle joints rotate, stretching the lower leg muscles first, with stretch of muscles spanning more proximal joints occurring slightly later. However, although the stretch reflex may contribute to the response (particularly in the lower leg muscles), there are several features of the responses that suggest that the response is not primarily due to the stretch reflex. First, the EMG responses begin with a strong burst of activity that would only be produced by stretch reflex mechanisms if the muscle were stretched very rapidly. However, the stretch would have been rather slow due to the slow speed (13 cm/s) at which the platform moved. Second, there would have been little stretch of the hamstrings given that the knees were almost at full extension in the starting posture. Third, the latency of the response in the lower leg muscles (about 80 to 90 ms) was also substantially longer than the latency of the stretch reflex (about 40 to 50 ms in these muscles). These considerations suggest that the pattern of muscle activation shown in Figure 7.60 is not simply the result of a proximal to distal recruitment of the stretch reflex. Further results suggested that the patterns are triggered as wholes in response to stimulation evoked by the platform shift. For example, it was found that tilts of the platform that stretched either the triceps surae (toes-up tilts) or the tibialis anterior (toes-down tilts), but without the associated forward or backwards sway produced by platform shifts, could evoke the same pattern of muscle activation[161].

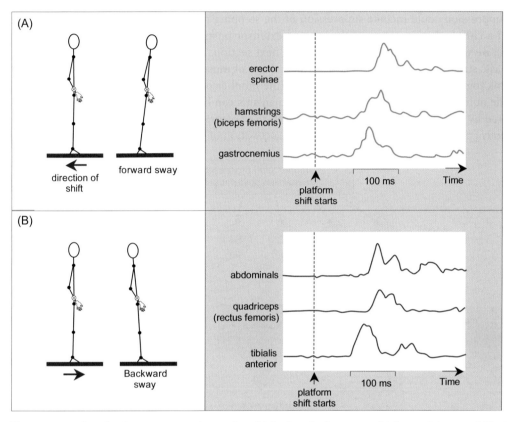

Figure 7.60: *Results from an experiment in which the platform on which participants shifted either backwards (A) or forwards (B). The graphs on the right plot the rectified, averaged EMG recordings from a group of 10 participants. (Adapted from Figure 2 of Horak, F.B, Nashner, L.M., (1986) Central programming of postural movements: Adaptation to altered support-surface configurations.* J. Neurophysiol., 55, 1369–1381.)

The findings we have described so far indicate that a coordinated pattern of activation in a group of muscles can be evoked as a unit. This suggests that the muscles are neurally linked together in much the same way that the muscles of the two eyes are linked together by the mechanisms that underlie production of conjugate saccadic eye-movements (see Chapter 6). As mentioned in Chapter 6, such neural linkages between groups of muscles are sometimes called *muscle synergies*, particularly in the context of postural control[162]. When recruited, a muscle synergy generates a specific kind of muscle activation pattern in a group of muscles. It has been proposed that the two patterns of muscle activation shown in Figure 7.60 are produced by muscle synergies[163] (the synergies concerned may involve more muscles than shown, but these were the only ones recorded from in the experiment).

A limited number of consistent patterns of muscle activation have been identified in human stance control, indicating that there exists a distinct set of muscle synergies that can be recruited to stabilize posture[164]. Each synergy generates a pattern of muscle activation that leads to a postural response that works to restore or preserve upright posture in some circumstances but not in others. For example, Figure 7.60 indicates that a synergy involving the gastrocnemius, hamstrings and erector spinae is recruited in response to disturbances that induced forward sway at the ankles; and a synergy involving tibialis anterior, the abdominals and quadriceps is recruited in response to disturbances that induce backward sway. In general, to respond appropriately to a particular disturbance, the correct synergy or combination of synergies needs to be recruited. There are two factors that can contribute to synergy selection. First, the nervous system must evaluate the sensory input so as to determine how the body is moving, and use this information to activate the appropriate synergies. Second, the environmental conditions and a person's postural goals can form a basis for the selective suppression or potentiation of synergies: a pattern of suppression and potentiation of different postural synergy mechanisms is sometimes referred to as **postural set**. Examples of selective suppression could include suppression of the stepping response when standing on the edge of a cliff, and suppression of the crossed-extensor postural response when sitting (Chapter 6); we will discuss further examples in the next section. Figure 7.61 shows a schematic of the basic structure of the ideas just described. A set of muscle synergy mechanisms (S1, S2, etc) link together different groups of muscles (the number of synergies, N, is much smaller than the number of muscles). The synergy mechanisms can be inhibited (suppressed) or potentiated by higher level processes that establish the postural set. Sensory information from the body can influence postural set, trigger the activation of synergies and regulate their activity.

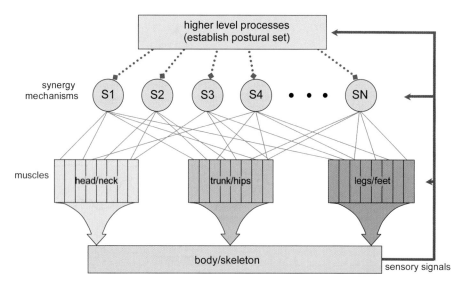

Figure 7.61: *Schematic representation of the idea that postural synergies underlie corrective reactions to disturbances to upright stance.*

7.5.3 Different postural reactions are recruited in different circumstances

The postural responses to forward-backward shifts of the support surface (platform) described in the previous section are adequate for maintaining stance when the disturbance is small and the surface is firm and not slippery. The disturbing effects of a platform shift depend both on the size of the displacement and the speed with which it occurs. The amplitude of the postural response has been found to increase when the displacement is larger (up to 12 cm)[165] and when it occurs faster[166]. These findings indicate that the postural responses are not simply stereotyped triggered reactions; rather, their amplitudes are adjusted so as to be appropriate for the size of the postural disturbance.

Not only was the amplitude of the synergistic responses shown in Figure 7.60 found to be larger when the platform shift was more disturbing, but there was also evidence for the recruitment of another pair of muscle activation patterns. These produce posture-preserving responses involving hip motion, which is different from the swaying motion about the ankles produced by the activation patterns shown in Figure 7.60. The difference in the body motions produced by the two different types of muscle activation pattern has led to them being referred to as the *ankle strategy* and the *hip strategy* for posture preservation, respectively[167]. Recruitment of the synergistic patterns shown in Figure 7.60 represents adoption of a pure ankle strategy for coping with the disturbance. Larger platform shifts lead to the recruitment of synergies underlying both the hip and ankle strategies, but under the support conditions in Figure 7.60 (a firm support platform much larger than the feet), a pure hip strategy has not been observed[168]. It has been observed when people stood on a small platform shorter than their feet (like standing on a beam)[169]. Figure 7.62 illustrates the task situation (left) and the results obtained (right). In panel A (left) the participant is shown standing on the short 'platform' (beam), which is shifted backwards at unexpected moments (the shift was the same as for the results shown in Figure 7.60). To stay standing upright on the beam, participants' responses involved hip flexion as indicated. The average pattern of muscle activity recorded in response to platform shifts is shown on the right: the response in the quadriceps and abdominals occurs first[170], with the erector spinae and hamstrings following 100 to 200 ms later. It is notable that there is little or no response in the lower leg muscles. Panel B shows the results for forwards shifts of the platform; in this case there is hip extension, and the erector spinae and hamstrings respond first. Once again, there is little or no response in the lower leg muscles.

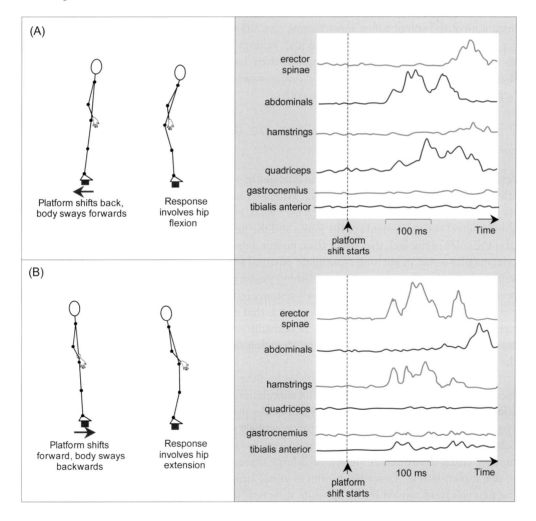

Figure 7.62: *Results from an experiment in which participants stood on a short (9 cm) 'platform' that shifted unexpectedly backwards (A) or forwards (B). The graphs on the right plot the rectified, averaged EMG recordings from a group of 10 participants. (Adapted from Figure 2 of Horak, F.B, Nashner, L.M., (1986) Central programming of postural movements: Adaptation to altered support-surface configurations.* J. Neurophysiol., 55, 1369–1381.)

The muscle activation patterns shown in Figure 7.62 are thought to reflect the activity of the muscle synergies that underlie the hip strategy. These synergies are appropriate for restoring posture following a disturbance when a person is standing on a beam or on a slippery surface, because they shift the position of the CoG without requiring significant torque at the ankles. The ankle strategy involves the development of posture restoring ankle torques, which requires a firm support surface with good traction. When conditions do not favor ankle torque development, observed postural behavior is consistent with suppression of the ankle strategy synergies so that they do not contribute to postural reactions (as in Figure 7.62). This may also be true in quiet stance on slippery or compliant surfaces[171].

The muscle synergies of the ankle and hip strategies act to preserve upright stance in the anteroposterior direction. A few others have been identified that act in different directions, but there is insufficient space to discuss them here[172]. These various synergies can be recruited individually or in combination, depending on the postural set and the type of disturbance. They are effective in restoring upright stance following disturbances that are not of a sufficient magnitude to move the CoG outside the base of support too quickly for it to be stopped by a corrective response. Thus, synergies represent a level of automatic (involuntary) protection against loss of balance that is intermediate between rescue reactions and the elastic mechanisms and spinal stretch reflexes that operate during quiet stance. These different sets of mechanisms form a series of lines of defense[173] against toppling over. Intrinsic elastic mechanisms offer only very limited resistance, but have the advantage of operating almost instantaneously; spinal reflex mechanisms also offer relatively little resistance (see section 7.4.12), but act quite quickly (within 50 ms); synergy mechanisms offer more resistance, and so can counteract larger disturbances, but their latency to activate the muscles is longer (between about 80 and 150 ms); finally, rescue reactions deal with disturbances that are too large for the other mechanisms to cope with.

7.5.4 Postural reactions can be evoked by changes to sensory stimulation

A real disturbance to the body results in changes in sensory stimulation; these changes evoke afferent signals that can activate postural synergies and so elicit corrective postural reactions. As we saw in the last part of the chapter, the visual, vestibular and somatosensory systems are able to detect the movements of the joints and the head, and changes in pressure distribution over the soles of the feet, that result from postural disturbances. Presumably all these sensory systems play a role in eliciting synergistic postural reactions, adjusting them so that they are suited to the circumstances, and establishing postural sets. It is very difficult to establish the precise roles played by different sensory systems in normal circumstances[174], and at present our understanding is limited. What is known is that changes in visual, vestibular, proprioceptive, and cutaneous stimulation can all individually evoke postural reactions in an involuntary manner. This has been demonstrated by changing one type of stimulation independently of the other types.

Disturbing posture by physically pushing/pulling a person or by moving the support surface will typically produce changes in the stimulation of all the sensory systems. To show that stimulation of a single sensory system can evoke postural responses requires that only that system is stimulated; techniques exist for selectively stimulating each of the sensory systems. Selective stimulation of the visual system can be achieved using the swinging room or a moving visual environment viewed on a large screen (see section 7.4.14). Moving the room in one direction (e.g., forwards) produces visual stimulation very similar to that produced if the person's head moved in the opposite direction (backwards). Such motion indicates that the person is toppling over and elicits a corrective postural response, even though the other sensory systems are signaling that the body is not moving[175]. The latency of such responses can be quite short, around 100 ms in some cases[176], indicating that they are of an automatic, involuntary nature. Of course, no postural correction is actually needed, and so producing one is destabilizing: in some cases, the postural response evoked is destabilizing enough to topple a person over[177].

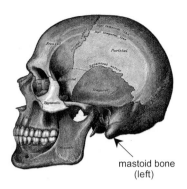

mastoid bone
(left)

Figure 7.63: *Location of the mastoid bone on the left side. Figure from the 20th edition of Gray's* Anatomy of the Human Body *(1918)*.

Selective stimulation of the vestibular system, at least as far as postural control is concerned, can be achieved by passing a weak, direct electric current through the head via electrodes placed on the two mastoid bones (these are skull processes located just behind the ears, identified in Figure 7.63). The usual method involves placing a positive electrode on the skin over one mastoid and a negative electrode over the other. The stimulation technique is called **galvanic vestibular stimulation (GVS)**. GVS applied to a standing person evokes postural responses that involve muscles throughout the body, from the neck to the feet; if the person is prevented from swaying or is seated, GVS evokes illusory perceptions of head and body motion[178]. The perception is typically of the head and trunk tilting or falling to the side on which the negative electrode is placed. The pattern of muscular activation evoked in a standing person causes them to sway in the direction opposite to the perceived movement. This suggests that GVS evokes a response from the vestibular system[179] which signals that the body is falling or swaying to one side, and a postural response is generated to correct for it. This is illustrated in panel A of Figure 7.64. The response is automatic and involuntary, since it has too short a latency to be voluntary. EMG recordings from the muscles involved have revealed two components to the response: a short latency component that begins about 50 to 60 milliseconds following the onset of GVS, and a longer latency component that begins about 100 to 120 milliseconds following GVS onset[180]. Thus, the postural reaction is not a response to the conscious feeling or perception of swaying or falling.

In Figure 7.64A, the GVS evokes a postural reaction that causes the body to sway mainly in the coronal plane towards the side on which the positive electrode is located. This direction of sway is evoked provided that the head is facing forwards. If the head is turned to one side, GVS evokes a postural reaction that causes the body to sway in the coronal plane of the head towards the positive electrode side[181]. Panel B of Figure 7.64 shows some results that illustrate this. The person stood with their head facing forwards (0° turn) and with it turned to the left or right through 22° and 45° (the different head positions are shown in the figure). GVS was applied with the head in these different positions, with the positive electrode on the left mastoid or on the right mastoid. The initial position of the head is marked by the gray square. The lines represent the sway response evoked by GVS; they are the paths of a point on the shoulders between the shoulder blades. These results show that the direction of body sway is strongly affected by the position of the head; the body sways in the coronal plane of the head towards the side of the positive electrode. In each case, GVS evokes a vestibular signal that indicates that the head is falling towards the negative electrode side. The nervous system interprets this as meaning that the body is toppling in this direction, and generates a sway in the opposite direction to correct for it. Thus, the evoked vestibular signal is not simply eliciting the same response irrespective of the head's position on the shoulders. The vestibular signal must be combined with sensory information about the head position to determine the appropriate response.

Finally, the somatosensory system can be selectively stimulated during postural tasks, either electrically or using vibration. As discussed in Chapter 3, vibrating a muscle's tendon selectively stimulates the spindle afferent endings of the muscle, which can evoke illusory sensations of movement. It has been found that vibration of the tendons of muscles that are playing a role in supporting body segments in upright stance (postural muscles) can produce illusory perceptions of body sway (with the eyes closed)[182] and evoke whole-body postural reactions[183]. The effects can be straightforward: vibrating the Achilles tendon, for example, signals lengthening of the triceps surae and hence that the body is falling forwards; a backwards sway response is evoked to compensate, and may cause the person to topple over backwards if the person's eyes are closed[184]. More subtle effects have also been observed: for example, vibration of the posterior neck muscles has been found to evoke responses in tibialis anterior (lower leg muscle that dorsiflexes the foot) within 70 to 100 milliseconds and produce a corresponding forward body sway[185]. It has also been found that localized vibration or cutaneous electrical stimulation of the soles of the feet in a standing person – stimulating cutaneous mechanoreceptors – evokes postural reactions with a latency of about 120 milliseconds[186].

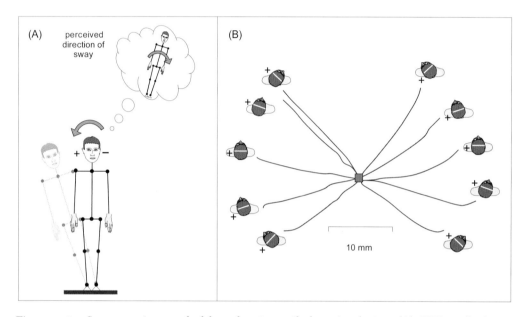

Figure 7.64: *Sway reactions evoked by galvanic vestibular stimulation. (A) GVS applied to a person standing as shown evokes the perception of sway to the negative electrode side and a postural reaction that moves them in the opposite direction (towards the positive electrode side). (B) Angular position of the head determines the direction of the sway ('+' indicates the side of the positive electrode). Data from Pastor, Day, Marsden (1993), Figure 2.*

In summary, selective stimulation of the visual, vestibular and somatosensory systems can elicit postural reactions from a standing person at a short latency (120 ms or less), indicating that the responses are elicited involuntarily. The same stimulation is often able to produce conscious perceptions of tilting or falling to one side, though the postural reactions are of too short a latency to be responses to the perceptions. In these cases, the postural reaction is in the opposite direction to the perceived tilt or fall, indicating that it is a reaction that corrects for the sway or tilt signaled by the afferent signals evoked by the stimulation.

7.5.5 Postural adjustments occur in advance of voluntary movement

Many disturbances to upright stance can be anticipated, and we can take pre-emptive action to avoid falling over or having to rely on reactive mechanisms to keep us upright. For example, if something is moving towards us on a collision course, we can anticipate that it will disturb our upright stance and brace ourselves for the impact. The impending collision object can be anticipated based on visual information available from the retinal images of the approaching object. As discussed in later chapters (9, 10 and 12), there is information to tell you not only that something is on a collision course but also when the collision will occur (time-to-collision information). Information about time-to-collision can allow a person to time pre-emptive posture-preserving actions to coincide with the moment of impact.

As noted earlier (section 7.4.3), a person's own actions will often be a source of postural disturbances, due to shifts in the position of the center of gravity, changes in the base of support and the development of reaction forces. The act of raising the left foot off the ground provides a simple example. Panel A of Figure 7.65 shows a person standing on two feet (left) and on the right foot only (right) after having raised the right foot by abducting the hip. The base of support in each case is shown at the bottom of the panel. When standing on two feet, the CoG lies between them, which means that if you simply lifted your right foot off the floor, the CoG would no longer be within the base of support, so you would immediately start to fall to the right. Leaning to the left so that the CoG is over the left foot prevents this from happening. Figure 7.65 panel B shows how the left shoulder, left hip and right ankle move when a person raises their right foot by abducting the hip. The important thing to note is that the left shoulder and hip start to move before the right foot (the left hip starts about 150 ms before the right foot). Thus, the person starts to shift their weight over what will be the support foot noticeably in advance of raising the other foot off the ground[187]. It looks like the lean to the left is part of the act of raising the right foot off the ground. In fact, it is almost impossible to lift the right foot off the ground unless you can lean over to the left (or otherwise support yourself). To experience this for yourself, stand next to a wall with your hands crossed in front of you and with your left ankle, hip, and shoulder in firm contact with the wall. Once in this position, attempt to raise your right foot off the floor, either by flexing the leg or by abducting the hip, but without losing contact with the wall: it is surprisingly hard to do, even for a moment.

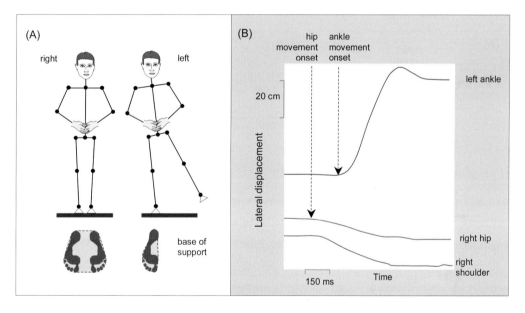

Figure 7.65: *Lifting the left leg (A) requires leaning to the right to keep the CoG over the base of support and avoid toppling over. (B) The rightward lean begins before the left foot starts to move; data from Tonolli* et al. *(2000), Figure 2.*

The leg-raising example shows that lifting one foot off the ground is not simply a matter of moving one leg – other movements are involved that shift weight over the support leg in preparation for lifting the foot. Preparatory muscle contractions and movements that adjust postural orientation or CoG position prior to or at the same time as making a voluntary movement are called **anticipatory postural adjustments (APAs)**. Many studies have shown that when people stand, unsupported APAs occur in postural muscles prior to the execution of voluntary movements of the upper body. The adjustments are functional[188] – that is, they counteract the disturbing effects of the voluntary movements – and are usually found to be larger when the voluntary movement itself is more perturbing (e.g., larger in amplitude or more forceful)[189] or when its effects are more perturbing[190] (e.g., pulling the trigger of a gun is a very small movement, but it results in a substantial disturbance).

It has been argued that postural preparations for a voluntary movement can be divided into two components or sets of components: early components that occur from about 400 to 700 milliseconds in advance of the voluntary movement, and later components that occur less than 200 milliseconds in advance of the movement[191]. It was suggested that the term *anticipatory postural adjustment* be used to refer to the later components and that the term **early postural adjustments** (**ERAs**) be used to refer to the earlier components. The early components do not occur in tasks in which a person is instructed to make an arm movement as soon as possible following an imperative stimulus – a *reaction time (RT) task* – since the voluntary movement in such tasks typically begins less than 300 milliseconds following the stimulus. In the next section, we focus on APAs, and in particular those that occur in RT tasks.

7.5.6 Anticipatory postural adjustments are context dependent

Almost any voluntary movement that a person executes while standing up will disturb upright stance to some extent, and so may be accompanied by anticipatory postural adjustments. Studies of these adjustments began in Russia in the 1960s, when it was discovered that the simple task of raising one arm in response to an imperative stimulus (RT task) while standing was accompanied by activity in the postural muscles of the legs and trunk that began about 50 milliseconds before activity in the muscles involved in raising the arm[192]. Figure 7.66 presents some characteristic results from a study in which participants were required to respond

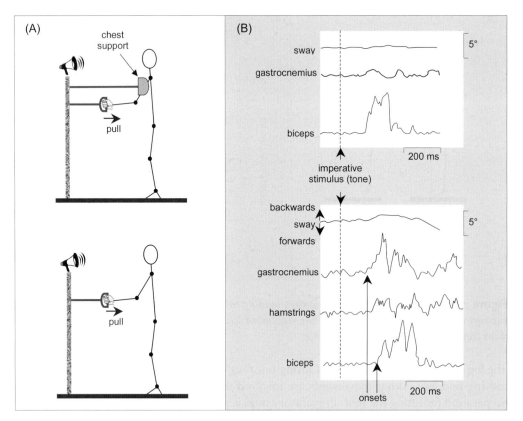

Figure 7.66: *Example results from an experiment in which participants pulled on a handle as soon as possible after they heard a tone (imperative stimulus). Data are records from typical single trials (taken from Figure 2 in Cordo, Nashner, 1982).*

as soon as possible following a tone (the imperative stimulus) by pulling on a handle with their right hand (panel A). The elbow flexors (e.g., biceps brachii) were prime movers for the pulling action. The handle resisted being pulled, and so the elbow flexion tended to pull the person towards the handle (forward sway). Two experimental conditions are shown in Figure 7.66, one in which the chest was supported (top), preventing forward sway when the handle was pulled, and another in which there was no chest support (bottom). In the experiment, body sway and EMG were recorded (from the right biceps brachii, gastrocnemius and hamstrings, primarily biceps femoris). The example records shown in panel B illustrate the basic findings. When the chest support was in place, preventing the body from swaying forwards, a burst of EMG activity in the biceps followed the imperative stimulus with a latency of about 130 ms (on average); there was little or no body sway or change in the EMG activity recorded from the leg muscles (only gastrocnemius is shown). Without the chest support, the latency of the biceps EMG burst was slightly longer (about 155 ms on average)[193], and there was activity in the leg muscles that onset at a shorter latency than that in the biceps (about 110 ms in gastrocnemius and 120 ms in hamstrings). There was also a small amount of body sway: a very slight backward sway (presumably produced by the early contraction of the leg muscles) followed by a small forward sway.

The preparatory activation in leg muscles prior to the activation of muscles involved in the voluntary response (Figure 7.66B) is an anticipatory postural adjustment that acts to reduce the forward sway that is produced by the voluntary response (though it does not completely eliminate it). The fact that no such adjustments were observed when the chest was supported indicates that APAs are not simply triggered automatically in preparation for the voluntary movements, but are only produced when their effects are needed. This can be interpreted in terms of the postural set concept. Experimental work suggests that the postural synergy mechanisms that underlie reactive postural responses to disturbances are also responsible for at least some APAs[194], and that in general APA mechanisms are separate from the mechanisms that generate motor commands for voluntary movements[195]. Thus, we can imagine a bank of postural synergy mechanisms that can be recruited either reactively, by sensory feedback signals evoked by postural disturbances, or by the control processes responsible for generating motor commands for voluntary movements. A simple version of this idea is shown in Figure 7.67: a bank of postural synergy mechanisms (circles labeled S1, S2, ... , SN) are responsible for the production of coordinated postural actions. The current postural goals and environmental conditions establish a pattern of suppression and potentiation of the synergy mechanisms (the postural set). They can be recruited either as reactions to postural disturbances by sensory signals, or as anticipatory adjustments by signals produced by the mechanisms responsible for generating the commands for voluntary action (voluntary command generators).

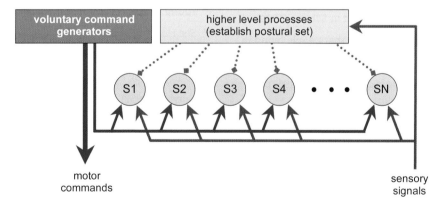

Figure 7.67: *Simple scheme for recruitment of postural synergy mechanisms (S1, ... , SN) either by sensory/perceptual signals or by signals from mechanisms that control voluntary action.*

References & Notes

[1] Though there is no direct empirical evidence for this interpretation (Ruxton, Speed, Kelly, 2004).

[2] Thayer (1896).

[3] Oxford Dictionary of English (2005), 2nd revised online edition, edited by C. Soanes, A. Stevenson.

[4] Oxford Dictionary of English (2005).

[5] Mittelstaedt (1996, 1998).

[6] The stems and trunks of individual plants and trees may deviate from the vertical, but the average orientation of a number of stems or trunks will typically be vertical.

[7] Other types of response are also used; see Carriot, DiZio, Nougier (2008).

[8] Mittelstaedt (1998).

[9] Bartolami et al. (2006b).

[10] For reviews see Howard (1982); Carriot, DiZio, Nougier (2008).

[11] See Howard (1982) or Schöne (1984).

[12] Young (2003).

[13] See Carriot, DiZio, Nougier (2008).

[14] Schöne (1964).

[15] Correia, Hixson, Niven (1968).

[16] Bartolami et al. (2006b).

[17] Miller, Fregly, Graybiel (1968).

[18] Young (2003); Mittelstaedt (1983).

[19] Jarchow, Mast (1999).

[20] Shimojo (2008).

[21] Banta (1995).

[22] H. Kleint (1936), cited in Schöne (1984).

[23] It has been reported that people living in buildings tilted 8° by an earthquake perceived the rooms to be vertical for the duration of their occupancy (Kitaharra, Uno, 1967).

[24] For discussion of other illusions, see Shimamura, Prinzmetal (1999).

[25] Witkin (1949).

[26] See Howard, Hu (2001).

[27] Asch, Witkin (1948).

[28] A possible additional factor is an intrinsic, non-sensory source of information (a kind of memory) about the orientation of the main axis of the body, called the *idiotropic vector* (Mittelstaedt, 1998). Alternatively, there may be prior information about the likelihood of being in particular orientations, which could affect perception (Laurens, Droulez, 2007).

[29] Trousselard et al. (2003); Trousselard et al. (2004).

[30] Mittelstaedt (1998).

[31] Carriot et al. (2008).

[32] Mittelstaedt (1983).

[33] Our ability to visually orient to a tilted object or tilted room by tilting our heads left or right is offset to some extent by the torsional counter-roll of the eyes produced by the vestibulo-ocular reflex (VOR) in response to head tilt. See Howard (1982).

[34] Howard, Hu (2001).

[35] Clément, Reschke (2008).

[36] Einstein (1920) provides a popular account.

[37] The physical equivalence of inertial and gravitational forces led Einstein to consider the possibility that gravity might be another kind of pseudo force that exists as a consequence of using a particular frame of reference. This idea led to the General Theory of Relativity. For a brief, introductory account, see Feynman, Leighton, Sands (1970).

[38] Artificial gravity in a rotating space station differs from Earth's gravity in that there is significant variation with the distance from the center of rotation (centrifugal force varies as the reciprocal of the radius). In addition, a person will be subject to significant *coriolis forces* when they move, which leads to some problematic perceptual effects and motion sickness (Young, 1999; Clément, Bukley, 2007).

[39] See Clément et al. (2001).

[40] Young (2003); Previc, Ercoline (2004).

[41] See Howard (1982).

[42] Carriot, DiZio, Nougier (2008).

[43] Young (2003); Previc, Ercoline (2004).

[44] Graybiel (1952).

[45] Schöne (1984), p. 114.

[46] Howard (1982).

[47] See Howard (1982).

[48] Wade, Schöne (1971); Schöne, Wade (1971).

[49] Increased gravity also affects saccular stimulation, but this does not appear to have a significant effect on people's perception of orientation (Bartolami et al., 2006b).

[50] Carriot, DiZio, Nougier (2008); Schöne (1984).

[51] These effects take time to develop and so can only be observed when inertial forces are sustained for many seconds or minutes. See Carriot, DiZio, Nougier (2008); Curtoys (1999); Howard (1982).

[52] Young (2003); Previc, Ercoline (2004).

[53] Any vertical component of acceleration will produce an inertial force in the same direction as gravity. We ignore this in the text.

[54] Previc, Ercoline (2004).

[55] These other forces are often more important than gravity for small, lightweight animals like insects and spiders; see Vogel (2003).

[56] For details see Roberts (1995).

[57] The rod is unstable perpendicular to the plane of the page.

[58] The ball-on-a-landscape way of thinking about mechanical systems is formalized by means of a quantity called the *potential energy* (PE). Roughly speaking, each position (or configuration) that the system can adopt is associated with a single value of the PE, which is therefore a function of the system's configuration. The graph of the PE resembles a landscape, and may have hills, valleys, basins, and so on. The tops of hills (local maxima of the PE) and the bottoms of basins (local minima) are the equilibrium positions of the system. The laws of motion that govern the system (e.g., Newton's laws) are such that the system moves towards configurations with minimum PE (bottoms of basins). A PE function cannot be defined for all systems, but the basic notion can often be extended by using more general mathematical constructions called Lyapounov functions.

[59] The ball will also return more quickly to the bottom of a steep basin than to the bottom of a shallow basin. Thus, time for equilibrium to be restored can serve as a measure of stability; see Kelso *et al.* (1987), Scholz, Kelso, Schöner (1987).

[60] Smith (1957).

[61] Horak, MacPherson (1996).

[62] It has been estimated that the passive tissues develop at least 70% of the torque needed to balance the gravitational torque at the knee: Smith (1957).

[63] Horak, MacPherson (1996).

[64] Gurfinkel *et al.* (1995).

[65] A number of feedback control models of human upright posture have been proposed, e.g., Alexandrov *et al.* (2005); Johansson, Magnusson (1991); Peterka (2002).

[66] Some authors have emphasized the control of body configuration, while others have emphasized control of CoG position; see Gurfinkel *et al.* (1995); Loram, Magnaris, Lakie (2005b); Massion (1998); Scholz *et al.* (2007).

[67] Basmajian, De Luca (1985).

[68] Winter *et al.* (1998).

[69] Winter *et al.* (1996).

[70] Aramaki *et al.* (2001); Creath *et al.* (2005); Gatev *et al.* (1999); Hsu *et al.* (2007); Pinter *et al.* (2008).

[71] Day *et al.* (1993); Gatev *et al.* (1999); Thomas, Whitney (1959).

[72] For reviews see e.g., Shumway-Cook, Woollacott (2011); Winter (1995).

[73] Day *et al.* (1993).

[74] Winter (1995).

[75] Day *et al.* (1993); Gatev *et al.* (1999).

[76] Winter *et al.* (1998).

[77] Day *et al.* (1993); Gatev *et al.* (1999).

[78] Gatev *et al.* (1999); Day *et al.* (1993).

[79] Day *et al.* (1993); Gatev *et al.* (1999); Aramaki *et al.* (2001).

[80] Creath *et al.* (2005); Zhang, Kiemel, Jeka (2007).

[81] See Winter (2009).

[82] Winter (2009).

[83] For reviews, see Winter (2009).

[84] Winter (2009).

[85] For a textbook review see Shumway-Cook, Woollacott (2011).

[86] Nagai *et al.* (2009).

[87] Creath *et al.* (2005).

[88] Day *et al.* (1993); Paulus, Staube, Brandt (1984); Riley *et al.* (1997).

[89] Travis (1945); Edwards (1946).

[90] Van Asten, Gielen, Denier van der Gon (1988).

[91] Winter *et al.* (1998).

[92] Wada, Sunaga, Nagai (2001).

[93] Ramenzoni *et al.* (2007).

[94] See Fraizer, Mitra (2008).

[95] Adkin *et al.* (2000).

[96] Though this instruction can sometimes lead to increased postural sway (Fraizer, Mitra, 2008).

[97] Wulf *et al.* (2004).

[98] Hamman *et al.* (1992).

[99] Fraizer, Mitra (2008).

[100] Kerr, Condon, McDonald (1985).

[101] See Fraizer, Mitra (2008).

[102] Hunter, Kearney (1981); Hodges *et al.* (2002).

[103] Sturm, Nigg, Koller (1980); Conforto *et al.* (2001).

[104] See Windhorst (2007).

[105] Loram, Magnaris, Lakie (2005b); Bottaro *et al.* (2005).

[106] A requirement for stability is that the torque due to the elastic tension is greater than the weight torque at angles larger in magnitude than the equilibrium angle.

[107] Winter *et al.* (1998); Winter *et al.* (2001).

[108] The idea is that since the response of elastic to stretch is immediate, the CoG and CoP should change together without delay (Winter *et al.*, 1998).

[109] Winter *et al.* (1998).

[110] Fitzpatrick, Taylor, McCloskey (1992).

[111] Fitzpatrick, McCloskey (1994).

[112] Fitzpatrick, McCloskey (1994).

[113] Gage *et al.* (2004).

[114] Winter *et al.* (1998) present an inverted pendulum model for the mediolateral direction.

[115] Winter (2009).

[116] Creath *et al.* (2005).

[117] Fitzpatrick, Rogers, McCloskey (1994).

[118] Morasso, Schieppati (1999); Casadio, Morasso, Sanguineti (2005); Loram, Lakie (2002).

[119] Loram *et al.* (2005a).

[120] Hellebrandt (1938).

[121] Fitzpatrick, Gandevia (2005).

[122] Kelton, Wright (1949); Nakazawa *et al.* (2003); Aniss *et al.* (1990).

[123] Nardone *et al.* (2000).

[124] According to the lambda equilibrium point hypothesis (Chapter 6), the central mechanisms that establish the upright postural orientation of the body would do so by setting the tonic stretch reflex threshold of the relevant postural muscles. The tonic level of muscle activity during quiet stance would then involve the stretch reflex.

[125] Arguments regarding the adequacy of ankle stiffness apply only if the inverted pendulum model is valid. Less stiffness may be required at the ankle if the body is modeled as a compound inverted pendulum (Rozendaal, van Soest, 2008).

[126] Loram *et al.* (2005b).

[127] Creath *et al.* (2005).

[128] Loram *et al.* (2005b).

[129] Loram *et al.* (2005b).

[130] Loram *et al.* (2005a).

[131] See Loram *et al.* (2005a,b). For an alternative intermittent negative feedback control model, see Bottaro *et al.* (2005) and Asai *et al.* (2009).

[132] Collins, De Luca (1995).

[133] Riley *et al.* (1997) found no evidence for a group of people who showed no increase in sway without vision.

[134] Witkin, Wapner (1950).

[135] Lee, Lishman (1975).

[136] Berthoz *et al.* (1979); Dijkstra, Schöner, Gielen (1994); Lee, Lishman (1975).

[137] Lee, Lishman (1975).

[138] Dijkstra, Gielen, Melis (1992).

[139] Stoffregen (1986).

[140] Dijkstra, Schöner, Gielen (1994).

[141] Dijkstra, Schöner, Gielen (1994).

[142] Horlings *et al.* (2009); Horak (2010).

[143] Horlings *et al.* (2009); Bloem *et al.* (2002).

[144] Cole, Sedgewick (1992).

[145] Day, Cole (2002).

[146] Fitzpatrick, Rogers, McCloskey (1994).

[147] Fitzpatrick *et al.* (1994), p. 401.

[148] Fitzpatrick, McCloskey (1994).

[149] Dietz, Trippel, Horstmann (1991); Horlings *et al.* (2009).

[150] Fitzpatrick, Rogers, McCloskey (1994). See also Horlings *et al.* (2009).

[151] See, e.g., Day, Guerraz (2007); Peterka, Loughlin (2004).

[152] Kavounoudias, Roll, Roll (1998, 2001).

[153] Jeka, Lackner (1994).

[154] Jeka (1997).

[155] Jeka (1997); Jeka *et al.* (1997); Lackner, Robin, DiZio (2001).

[156] Roberts (1978, 1995).

[157] Small disturbances that do not threaten overbalance can sometimes elicit stepping or

arm swinging, but experimental participants are usually instructed not to step or swing; see McIlroy, Maki (1993, 1999).

158 E.g., Roberts (1995).

159 Nashner (1977, 1983).

160 Horak, Nashner (1986).

161 Nashner (1977); Nashner, McCollum (1985).

162 The word 'synergy' has been used in a number of different ways in the literature; see Latash (2008b).

163 Shumway-Cook and Woollacott (2011) provide a more detailed textbook review.

164 Ting, McKay (2007); Torres-Oviedo, Ting (2007, 2010).

165 Diener, Horak, Nashner (1988).

166 Diener, Horak, Nashner (1988); Park, Horak, Kuo (2004); Runge *et al.* (1999).

167 Horak, Nashner (1986); Nashner, McCollum (1985).

168 Park, Horak, Kuo (2004); Runge *et al.* (1999).

169 Horak, Nashner (1986).

170 EMG activity was not recorded from the hip flexors.

171 Creath *et al.* (2005).

172 See Nashner, McCollum (1985); Ting, McKay (2007).

173 Latash (2008a,b).

174 See Oie, Kiemel, Jeka (2002); Peterka, Loughlin (2004).

175 For review see Wann, Mon-Williams, Rushton (1998).

176 Nashner, Berthoz (1978).

177 Lee, Aronson (1974); Wann *et al.* (1998).

178 For review see Fitzpatrick, Day (2004).

179 Recent evidence suggests that the signal that evokes the response derives from the semicircular canal afferents rather than the otolith afferents (Mian *et al.*, 2010).

180 Fitzpatrick, Day (2004).

181 Lund, Broberg (1983).

182 Lackner, Levine (1979).

183 Roll, Roll (1988).

184 Eklund (1972).

185 Andersson, Magnusson (2002).

186 Kavounoudias, Roll, Roll (1998, 2001).

187 Tonolli *et al.* (2000) found evidence in the center of pressure records to suggest that weight shift began as much as 500 or 600 milliseconds in advance of the leg raise.

188 Latash (2008b); Massion (1998).

189 Aruin, Latash (1996).

190 Aruin, Latash (1995).

191 Krishnan, Aruin, Latash (2011).

192 Belenkii, Gurfinkel, Paltsev (1967).

193 Cordo and Nashner (1982) attributed the longer latency in the unsupported condition as due to an active delay of the primary movement (elbow flexion) to allow time for the postural adjustments to take effect.

194 Cordo, Nashner (1982); Horak, McPherson (1996).

195 E.g., Aruin, Shiratori, Latash (2001).

CHAPTER 8

Locomotion
on Legs

8.1 Describing Locomotion on Legs

8.1.1 Introduction

Different animals get from one place to another by walking, running, jumping, hopping, swimming, flying, climbing, crawling, burrowing or slithering. This kind of movement is a defining characteristic of animals – if they didn't do it, they would be vegetables. The general term for actively changing location is **locomotion**:

> **LOCOMOTION:** the controlled act of moving the body as a whole from one place to another.

The important thing about locomotion is that it is controlled or guided by the individual animal or person concerned, not that it is powered by the animal. Downhill skiing is a form of locomotion that is powered by gravity.

When locomotion is self-propelled, three components of control can be distinguished:

(1)   **Control of the limb and body movements that generate propulsive forces.** In the case of human beings, these will usually be leg movements. Animals like snakes, worms and fish don't have limbs and move around using rather different kinds of body movements from those we use.

(2)   **Control of where you are going.** This includes the control of direction (steering), the control of speed (going faster, slowing down and stopping), the control of altitude and landing (if flying), and route finding.

(3)   **Control of posture and orientation.** The body must be kept properly oriented during locomotion; otherwise effective propulsion and control would be impossible.

In this chapter, the focus will be on the first of these. Chapters 9 and 10 will focus on the second. The third is beyond the scope of this text.

8.1.2 Locomotion involves repeated cycles of movement

Natural forms of legged locomotion almost always involve repeatedly executing particular movements of the legs. For each leg, these movements can be divided into two phases:

(1)   A propulsive phase, during which force is developed that propels the person or animal in a particular direction (usually forwards): this phase is sometimes called the **power-stroke**, particularly when people are swimming.

(2)   A phase that returns the limb to a position suitable for beginning another power-stroke – sometimes called the **return-stroke**.

Swimming, crawling, walking, running and flying all involve repeatedly executing these two phases – power-stroke, return-stroke, power-stroke, return-stroke, and so on. A power-stroke and a return-stroke together constitute a single locomotor movement cycle.

When a person walks or runs, each leg repeats a locomotor movement cycle in which the power-stroke is usually referred to as the **stance phase**:

> **STANCE PHASE:** the part of the locomotor movement cycle of one leg during which some part of the foot is in contact with the ground. Starts when the foot first contacts the ground, and ends the moment it breaks contact.

At the beginning of the stance phase, the leg supports the weight of the body, but little or no propulsive force is produced. Propulsive force is developed late in the stance phase, when the foot pushes back against the ground – the reaction force from the ground acts to propel the body forward. Due to the fact that the stance leg supports the weight of the body during this part of the movement cycle, it is sometimes referred to as the **support phase**. The return-stroke is called the **swing phase**:

> **SWING PHASE:** the part of the locomotor movement cycle of one leg during which no part of the foot is in contact with the ground. Starts when the foot breaks contact with the ground, and ends the moment it makes contact again.

During the swing phase, the foot is transferred from one point on the ground to another one where the next stance phase begins; for this reason it is sometimes referred to as the **return** or **transfer phase**.

A single movement cycle of one leg is usually called a **stride**:

> **STRIDE:** one movement cycle of a single leg, consisting of a stance phase and a swing phase.

A diagram makes the definitions more concrete. Figure 8.1 shows a temporal sequence of frames from a cartoon 'movie' of someone walking (legs only). From frame 1 to frame 7, the right leg (shown in blue) executes exactly one stride. The right heel is just making contact with the ground in frame 1 (right heel strike); the right foot is just breaking contact with the ground (toe off) in frame 5. Frame 7 is a repeat of frame 1 (right heel strike), marking the end of one stride and the beginning of the next.

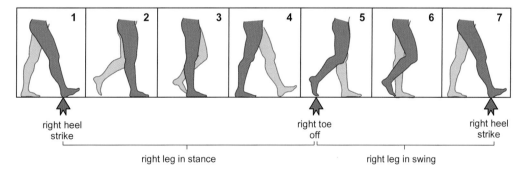

Figure 8.1: *Sequence of frames of legs walking.*

A useful way of showing the times for which two (or more) legs are in the stance and swing phases is the **stride pattern diagram** (also called a *gait pattern diagram*). A stride pattern diagram for the stride shown in Figure 8.1 is presented in Figure 8.2, where time runs from left to right across the page. Half a stride – from one heel strike to the next, say right heel strike to left heel strike – is usually called a **step**. Thus, when making a single stride with the right leg, a person takes two steps – first one with the left leg (right heel strike to left heel strike) and then one with the right (left heel strike to right heel strike).

The diagram in Figure 8.2 shows a **symmetrical** walking pattern, in which the movement cycles of the two legs are almost exactly the same. A symmetrical walking pattern is normal when walking in a straight line; asymmetrical walking patterns, in which there is a noticeable difference between the movements executed by the two legs, are characteristic of injury or of a neurological problem. A person with an asymmetrical walk is often said to be limping.

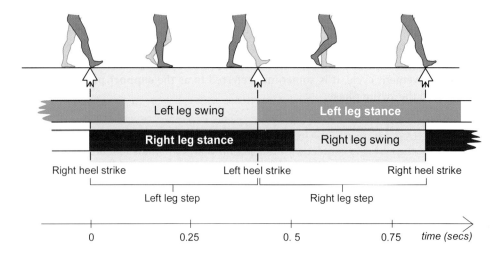

Figure 8.2: *Stride pattern for (symmetrical) human walking.*

From the stride pattern diagram we can see the following: (1) The two legs execute the same movement cycle, such that when the right leg is in stance, the left is in swing, and vice-versa. We say that the movement cycles of the two limbs are in **antiphase**. (2) The stance phase lasts longer than the swing phase. (3) The stance phases overlap – there is a short period of time for which both the right and left legs are in stance (both feet on the ground). This is called **double support**.

8.1.3 Walking and running are examples of different gaits

In Figures 8.1 and 8.2 the stance phase is of longer duration than the swing phase, and there is a period of double support. This permits a simple definition of a (bipedal) walk:

> **WALK (BIPEDAL):** a mode of legged locomotion in which the legs move in antiphase, one foot or the other is in contact with the ground at all times, and both feet are on the ground at the same time for a short period (double support).

Of course, walking is not the only form of locomotion that people engage in; we may also run, bound, hop, skip, or crawl. Different ways of moving the limbs in locomotion are called **gaits**. In the human running gait, both feet are never on the ground simultaneously (no double support), and there are times when both feet are off the ground at the same time – these times are called the **flight periods**. Figure 8.3 shows the stride pattern diagram for a person running at two different speeds: relatively slowly (panel A) and sprinting (B). The top of panel A shows a sequence of four movie frames of a person running: frame 3 occurs during the flight period.

Bipedal running can be defined as follows:

> **RUN (BIPEDAL):** a gait in which both legs move in antiphase. Both feet are never on the ground at the same time, but there are periods during which both feet are off the ground (flight periods).

Fast running (sprinting) differs from slow running (jogging) and walking in a way not yet mentioned. Human walking and jogging are normally **plantigrade** forms of locomotion, whereas sprinting is **digitigrade**. Digitigrade locomotion involves placing only the digits (toes) on the ground, whereas plantigrade locomotion involves placing the whole sole of the foot on the ground. The human foot is relatively unusual in the animal kingdom in that it is used for both forms of locomotion. The sole of the human foot extends from the heel bone – the calcaneus, one of the tarsals – to the distal phalanges (tips of the toes, Figure 8.4A). When walking, the heel strikes first and then the rest of the sole is placed progressively onto the ground – walking is therefore plantigrade. Walking on tip-toe is digitigrade.

(A) Slow run ≈ 3 m/s

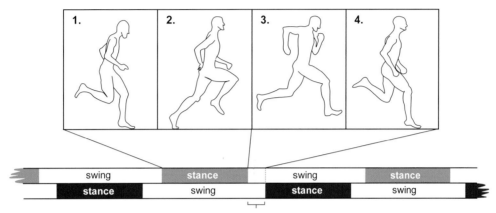

(B) Sprint ≈ 6 m/s

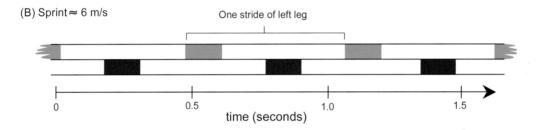

Figure 8.3: *Stride pattern diagrams of slow (A) and fast (B) running.*

A foot can be defined as the limb segment or segments that make contact with the ground during normal locomotion. In most terrestrial mammals, the hind foot does not include the tarsals, and typically does not even include the metatarsals. For example, a cat's paw includes only the phalanges (Figure 8.4B), and animals with hooves are effectively walking on the nail of a single toe. Normal locomotion in these animals is clearly digitigrade[1].

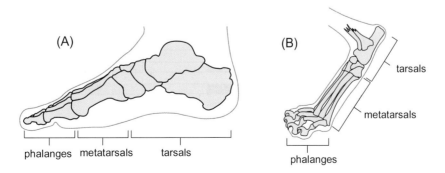

Figure 8.4: *Bones in the human foot (A) and the cat foot (B).*

8.1.4 Walking and running are not the only types of gait

The most common bipedal gaits are walking and running, but other gaits are also observed in nature. People and some birds sometimes use a skipping gait – children are especially fond of it – and animals such as kangaroos use a hopping or jumping gait. Panel A of Figure 8.5 shows a stride pattern diagram for a hopping kangaroo. Hopping differs from the other gaits described so far because the legs move **in phase**: both legs do the same thing at the same time.

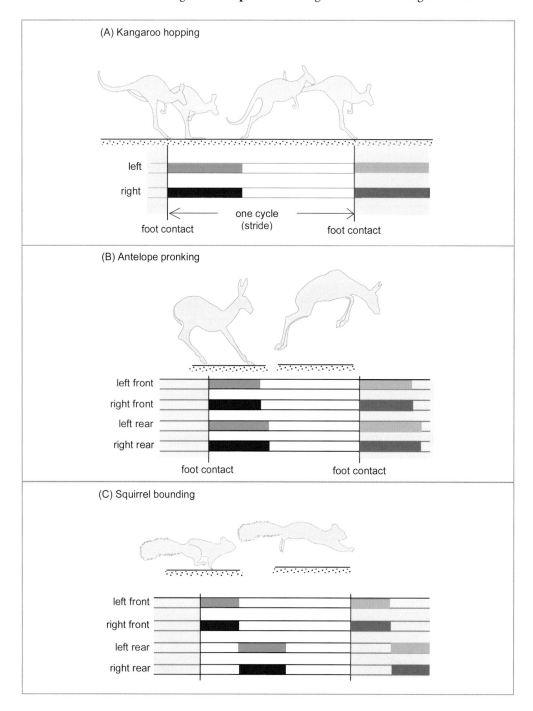

Figure 8.5: *Stride pattern diagrams for three quadrupedal gaits.*

Gaits in animals with four legs – *quadrupedal gaits* – are more complex than bipedal gaits, because there are two more legs to keep track of. The easiest quadrupedal gait to understand is the one in which all four legs move approximately in phase – all the legs do almost the same thing at the same time. This gait, called the pronk, is the four-legged version of the hop, and is relatively unusual. Some species of African antelope such as the springbok use a pronking gait when fleeing from predators. The gait pattern diagram is shown in panel B of Figure 8.5. The diagram shows that all four feet contact the ground at almost the same time, but the front feet leave the ground just before the rear feet.

Probably the next easiest gait to understand is the bound. When an animal bounds, the forelegs move in phase with each other and the hind legs move in phase with each other, but the forelegs and hind legs move in antiphase. What this means should be clear from the stride pattern diagram shown in panel C of Figure 8.5: when the forefeet are moving backwards relative to the body, the hind feet are moving forwards, and when the forefeet are moving forwards, the hind feet are moving backwards.

It is relatively easy to see what is going on in the pronk and the bound, because the two forelegs move in phase and the two hind legs move in phase. In other quadruped gaits, the forelegs, the hind legs, or both move out of phase. Examples include the four-legged walk, the trot, and the gallop. Gait pattern diagrams for the trot and the gallop are shown in Figure 8.6. In the trot (panel A), the left fore-leg moves in phase with the right hind leg and the right foreleg moves in phase with the left hind leg. However, the two hind legs move in antiphase and the two forelegs move in antiphase. If you look at only the forelegs in Figure 8.6A, or only at the hind legs, you will see that the gait pattern is the same as a bipedal slow run (Figure 8.3A). The gallop (Figure 8.6, panel B) is different, in that no two legs move in phase. In the figure, the footfalls are in the following sequence: left rear, right rear, left front, right front. This is followed by a flight period (all legs off the ground) before beginning again. The gallop used by the horse differs slightly from that used by the dog and cat when running at their fastest. These animals use a gallop with two flight periods when running very fast, though they may also use the horse-style gallop at slower speeds. We have not described all the quadrupedal gaits observed in nature. There are a number of others, including the pace, the canter, the half-bound and the amble.

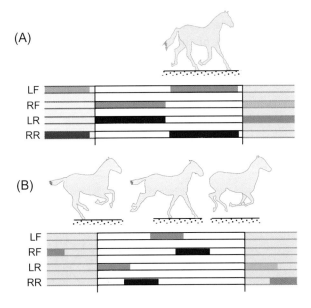

Figure 8.6: *Horse, (A) trotting, (B) galloping.*

8.1.5 How do the legs move during walking and running?

When a person walks, the joints in their legs and feet flex and extend in a rhythmical pattern. In this section we will look at the movements of the hip, knee and ankle joints. Figure 8.7 shows a sequence of frames, taken at equal intervals of time, of a stick leg taking two strides (right leg only). The stick leg is walking from left to right across the page, and the color of the leg identifies its position in the step cycle: stance is blue and swing is pink. The wavy horizontal lines are the paths taken by the hip (top, dotted), knee (middle, dashed), ankle (second from bottom, dashed) and toe (bottom, dotted). The figure shows that the hip, knee and toes do not move up and down very much during a stride. In contrast, the ankle is raised substantially early in the swing phase, and this helps to keep the foot clear of the ground.

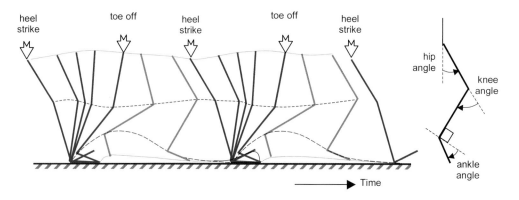

Figure 8.7: *Stick representation of one leg (right) taking two strides.*

The flexion-extension joint angles for the leg are shown on the right of Figure 8.7. Measurement of the joint angles during locomotion is often done to provide a quantitative description of gait. Such descriptions are particularly important for assessing the efficacy of clinical regimes for the rehabilitation of patients who have difficulty walking following injury, or due to neurological disorder. Figure 8.8 shows the knee joint angles as a function of time for a person walking in a straight line at a constant speed on a flat, level surface. For reference, the stride pattern diagram is included at the top of the figure, and a stick leg diagram at the bottom. The figure shows that the knee flexes slightly early in the stance phase, as the leg takes the weight of the body. The figure also brings out the antiphase pattern of joint movement in the two legs, with one leg flexing when the other is extended: the knee angle graphs for the two legs are very similar, but are out of phase by half a cycle.

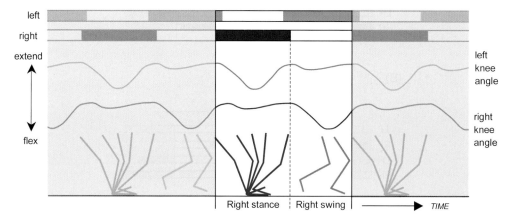

Figure 8.8: *Stride pattern diagram (top), knee joint angles of the two legs (middle) and stick diagram of right leg (bottom) over three strides of a walk (one stride of the right leg is highlighted).*

The flexion-extension movement pattern of the knee joint is similar in walking and running. This is shown in panel A of Figure 8.9, which shows the right knee joint angle over a single movement cycle (stride) of one leg. Time in this figure has been normalized so that it goes from zero to one hundred percent of the cycle duration. Panel A shows that the knee flexes more when running than walking. Panel B shows the ankle joint angles corresponding to the knee joint angle graphs shown in panel A.

The pattern of flexion-extension in multiple joints shows that walking and running involve relatively strict coordination of movement of the joints in each individual limb (**intra-limb coordination**). At the same time, movement of the different limbs involved must also be coordinated (**inter-limb coordination**), so that the limbs move, for example, in an antiphase pattern (Figure 8.2). Flexion-extension motions of the leg joints are the most obvious joint motions involved in legged locomotion, not only in people but in other animals as well. There are other joint motions involved in locomotion, and these are important for a full understanding of gait. The most important additional joint motions involved in human locomotion are discussed next.

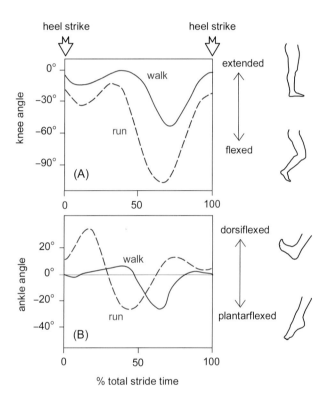

Figure 8.9: *Illustrative time normalized knee (A) and ankle (B) joint angles (in the sagittal plane) during a single stride of the right leg when walking and running (not sprinting, which displays a slightly different pattern, see Novacheck, 1998).*

8.1.6 What other joint motions are involved in human locomotion?

When people walk and run, other contributory motions are involved in addition to flexion-extensions of the leg joints. Most obvious are swinging motions of the arms. Of course, it is quite possible to walk and run without swinging the arms, but running is particularly uncomfortable if arm swings are prevented. People can run significantly faster with arm swinging than without. In this section we will concentrate on the motions of the pelvis.

When a person walks, the pelvis rotates and tilts in a characteristic manner[2]. Panel A of Figure 8.10 shows how the pelvis rotates about a vertical axis during normal walking. With pelvic rotation, the stride length is greater than it would be without it. Race walkers use a style of walking in which the amplitude of pelvic rotation is much greater than it is in normal walking. This permits a greater stride length than would otherwise be possible, and a greater walking speed. Panel B of Figure 8.10 shows how the pelvis tilts during normal walking: the tilt means that the hip of the swing leg drops slightly lower than the hip of the stance leg. This drop of the hip is particularly associated with flexion of the knee at the beginning of swing.

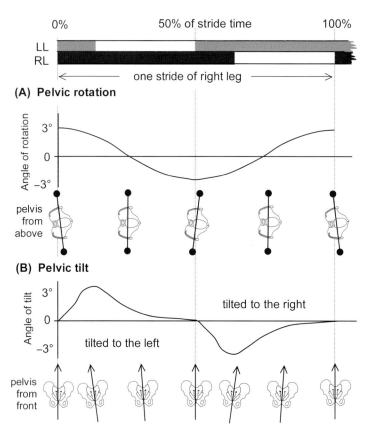

Figure 8.10: *Pelvic rotation and tilt during a single stride when walking (based on data reported by Saunders, Inman, Eberhart, 1953). Angles are exaggerated in the pictures of the pelvis for illustrative purposes.*

Figure 8.11 shows that another motion of the pelvis occurs during locomotion: a movement from side to side or *lateral displacement* of the pelvis. This motion occurs because the weight of the body is alternately transferred from one leg to the other. To keep the body from falling sideways, the center of gravity needs to be over the base of support (see Chapter 7): when only one leg is in stance, the base of support is provided by the stance foot, and this requires that the body move laterally, as first one leg and then the other are in stance. The extent of this motion will clearly depend on the lateral distance between the feet. This distance is called the **stride width**. The stride width in human beings would be wider were it not for the fact that the femur is tilted slightly inwards, as shown in Figure 8.11.

It is clear that a complex orchestration of motions in many different joints and parts of the body is involved. A complete description of the movements involved is laborious to obtain and difficult to interpret, though it is important for a complete understanding of the biomechanical processes involved and analysis of subtle gait abnormalities. Nevertheless, simpler descriptions are often useful and frequently desirable. A description using what are referred to as **gait parameters** provides this, and is considered in the following sections.

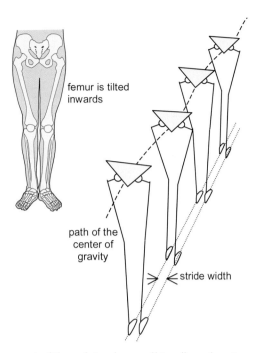

femur is tilted inwards

path of the center of gravity

stride width

Figure 8.11: *Lateral movement of the pelvis when walking (based on Inman, Ralston, Todd, 1981).*

8.1.7 Gait parameters provide simple quantitative descriptions of walking and running

There are several commonly used and very simple quantitative measures used to describe gaits that are taken from contacts between the feet and the ground. These are called **gait parameters**, the most important of which are stride length, step length, stride width, stride rate and stride time. Here these parameters are described for a biped (similar definitions can be applied to quadrupedal gaits).

▶ **Stride length** is the distance between a point on one foot at the beginning of a stride (first foot contact) and the same point on that foot when the next ground contact (footfall) occurs. It can be measured for the right leg and the left leg. The point used to measure stride length is normally the back of the heel, in which case stride length is defined as shown in Figure 8.12[3].

▶ **Step length** is the distance between subsequent footfalls, as shown in Figure 8.12: left step length is the distance between a right footfall and the subsequent left footfall, and vice-versa for right step length.

▶ **Stride width** is the lateral distance between the left and right feet during one stride, as shown in Figures 8.11 and 8.12.

▶ **Stride time** is the time taken to execute one stride, and can easily be measured as the time between one heel strike and the next heel strike by the same foot. It is usually measured in seconds.

▶ **Stride rate** is the number of strides per unit time. If the time unit is the second, then stride rate is measured in Hertz (number per second). A related measure that is sometimes used is the **cadence**, defined as the number of steps per unit time. Since there are two steps in every stride, cadence = 2 × stride rate.

When people walk or run, their stride lengths and stride times typically vary from one stride to the next. For this reason, the stride lengths and times are usually averaged over a sequence of strides. Stride rate is also computed for a sequence of strides, and is equal to [1 ÷ (average stride time)].

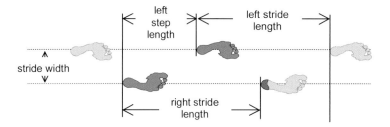

Figure 8.12: *Definition of stride length, stride width and step length.*

We can also measure **swing phase duration**, as the time for which the foot of one leg is off the ground, and the **stance phase duration** as the time for which the foot is on the ground. The stance phase duration expressed as a proportion of the stride time is a commonly calculated parameter called the **duty factor**, given by the following equation:

Duty factor = (stance phase duration) ÷ (stride time)

The duty factor is a number greater than zero but less than one. The duty factor for walking must always be greater than 0.5, and the duty factor for running must be less than 0.5.

8.1.8 As you go faster, the gait parameters change in predictable ways

The gait parameters are not always the same for a given gait, such as walking, but depend on several things such as the speed of locomotion, whether the person is going uphill or downhill, and whether the ground is hard or spongy. In this section, we will look at the effects of walking and running speed on the gait parameters.

Stride length and stride rate can both increase as a person walks faster – when you are walking quickly, your strides tend to be longer, and they are executed more quickly than when walking slowly. From the average stride length (in meters) and the stride rate (in Hertz) for a sequence of strides, it is possible to calculate the speed of locomotion in meters/second as follows:

Speed of locomotion = (average stride length) × (stride rate)

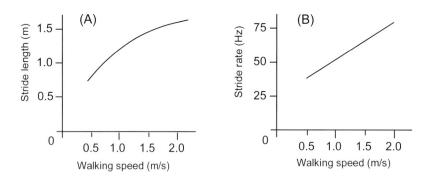

Figure 8.13: *Stride length and stride rate as a function of walking speed (illustrative).*

This relationship means that a person can increase their walking or running speed by increasing stride length, increasing stride rate, or some combination of both. Panel A of Figure 8.13 shows the typical relationship between walking speed and stride length for a person walking on a flat, level surface. Panel B shows the relationship between walking speed and stride rate. It is clear that greater speeds are associated with both greater stride lengths and greater stride rates. Note that most people find it very difficult to walk much faster than about

2 m/s to 2.5 m/s, and will spontaneously start to jog. Thus, the lines in Figure 8.13 do not extend much past 2.0 on the walking speed axis. The relationships between the gait parameters and speed shown in the figure are typical for treadmill and normal walking on a level surface. The relationships differ when people walk up or downhill. When walking uphill people find it quite difficult to increase their stride length, and prefer to increase speed mainly by changing stride rate. When walking downhill it is the other way around: people find it relatively easy to increase speed by taking longer strides, but not to increase the stride rate.

Since one stride of either leg comprises a swing phase and a stance phase, a change in stride rate could involve a change in the duration of the swing phase, of the stance phase, or both. In fact, there are changes in both, but the change in stance phase duration is much greater than that in swing phase duration. Figure 8.14 shows the swing and stance phase durations plotted as a function of walking speed for a person (panel A) and for the rear legs of a domestic cat (panel B). As the figure shows, the duration of the swing phase (dashed line) does not change very much as walking speed increases; in the cat it remains almost constant. One way to increase stride length is to swing the leg more forcefully, so that the foot moves further while it is off the ground. This would involve greater hip flexion during the swing phase, which raises the knee and foot higher and increases the distance moved by the foot during swing. Another contribution to increased stride length comes from pelvic rotation.

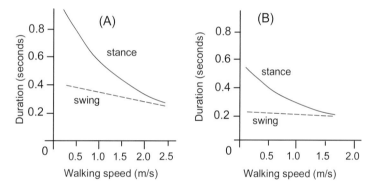

Figure 8.14: *Duration of stance and swing phases as a function of walking speed in humans (A) and cats (B).*

The relationships between running speed and the gait parameters differ slightly from those obtained for walking. Panel A of Figure 8.15 shows the relationships between running speed and both stride rate and stride length for trained runners on flat, level surfaces (the basic shape of the plots are similar for untrained runners[4]). Initial increases in speed are associated with relatively large changes in stride length, but small changes in stride rate. Above a certain speed (about 6 m/s), the pattern changes, and increases in speed are associated with increases in stride rate but no increase in stride length. Stride length actually begins to decrease slightly above about 7 m/s. The reason typically given for this pattern is that up to about 6 m/s, it takes less energy to increase stride length than it does to increase stride rate. A person will typically choose the less effortful course of action, and so prefers to increase stride length while keeping stride rate constant in order to run faster.

Panel B of Figure 8.15 shows the durations of the stance and swing phases plotted against running speed. As with walking, there is very little change in the duration of the swing phase, but there is a noticeable decrease in stance phase duration as speed increases. The figures also show the qualitative distinction between the swing-stance pattern in the two modes of locomotion: in walking, the stance phase curve is the higher of the two, since the stance phase is longer than the swing phase (Figure 8.14, duty factor > 0.5). The reverse is true for running (Figure 8.15, duty factor < 0.5).

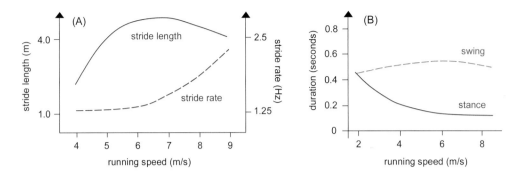

Figure 8.15: *Gait parameters as a function of running speed. (A) stride length and stride rate; (B) duration of swing and stance phases (illustrative, based on results of Cavanagh, Kram, 1989, and Nilsson, Thorstensson, Halbertsma, 1987).*

8.2 Muscles, Forces and Energetics

8.2.1 Introduction: during locomotion, muscles are activated in a rhythmic, cyclical pattern

Human locomotion involves cyclical movements of many different joints, and these are actuated by many muscles. The details of the muscle activations that contribute to locomotion depend on a number of things, including gait, whether the person is on the flat or going uphill or going downhill, whether they are carrying a heavy load, and whether they are going in a straight line or around a bend.

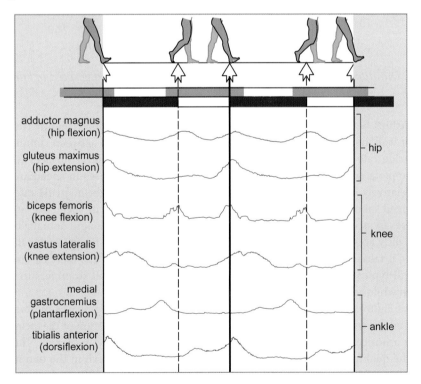

Figure 8.16: *Illustration of the pattern of EMG activity in the leg muscles during walking (illustrative).*

Figure 8.16 shows the basic characteristics of the pattern of (rectified, smoothed) electromyographic activity that can be recorded from leg muscles when a person walks in a straight line on a flat, horizontal surface (running produces a slightly different pattern). The exact pattern produced will vary from one person to another, but the basic features shown in the figure are common to healthy adults. Records from six different muscles of the right leg over two strides are shown (there are a number of others that are not shown). These muscles are involved in flexion-extension motions of the leg joints: gluteus maximus extends the hip, adductor magnus flexes and adducts the hip. Biceps femoris flexes the knee, vastus medialis extends it. The medial gastrocnemius plantarflexes the ankle, and tibialis anterior dorsiflexes it. Each muscle exhibits a bursting pattern of activity that is roughly repeated over strides[5]: people typically display some variation in activity of contributing muscles from one stride to the next[6], just as there is some variation in the movements of the legs.

Clearly, coordinating the contractions and relaxations of the large number of muscles involved in locomotion, and making sure that the movements produced are properly adapted to the terrain, is likely to require sophisticated and intricate neural machinery. The basic architecture of this machinery is discussed later (section 8.3). In this part of the chapter, we will consider how muscular activity is constrained by factors such as the biomechanical properties of the limbs and metabolic energy requirements.

8.2.2 What are the muscles doing during locomotion?

A complete understanding of what all the muscles are doing during the locomotor cycle in walking and running requires detailed understanding of the biomechanics and careful analysis of mathematical models[7]. The necessary biomechanics and mathematical techniques are beyond the scope of this text, and only a relatively simple, non-mathematical account can be attempted here (the references can be consulted for biomechanical details[8]).

Muscular activity in the legs and hips is needed for several purposes during locomotion; here is a partial list:

(1)   Providing the force needed for forward progression.
(2)   Supporting the weight of the body during stance[9].
(3)   Moving the leg from the one position on the ground to the next during the swing phase.
(4)   Keeping the foot clear of the ground during the swing phase.
(5)   Absorbing the force of impact at footfall.
(6)   Maintaining an upright posture throughout the movement cycle.

In the remainder of the chapter, we will mainly be concerned with (1), (3) and (4). Consider (1): propulsive force is provided by the reaction force from the ground that acts on the foot at the end of the stance phase. This force is produced in reaction to the leg pushing against the ground, and several muscles are likely to contribute to this push. Panel A of Figure 8.17 shows how the direction of the ground reaction force (GRF) vector changes during the stance phase.

The GRF vector can be decomposed into two components: a vertical component and a horizontal component, as shown in panel B of Figure 8.17. Panel C shows a typical graph of the two components of the GRF over the duration of the stance phase during walking on a level surface[10]. The vertical component is always positive (i.e., the vector always points upwards); the horizontal component is negative (points backwards) early in stance, zero at about mid-stance, and positive after that (points forwards).

The vertical component is a reaction to the vertical load the body applies to the ground. The horizontal component is a reaction to the horizontal force applied to the ground when the leg is pushing forwards (e.g., the leg's first position in the figure) or pushing backwards (e.g., the leg's last position in the figure). The reaction to the backwards push is the propulsive force – it acts to accelerate the person's center of gravity forwards – and it is created by friction. If there were no friction, there would be no horizontal component to the reaction force, and the foot would simply slide over the surface. Muscular activity is needed to generate the backward push that produces the forward reaction force. During walking on the flat, the muscles largely responsible for this push are the ankle plantar flexors, particularly the gastrocnemius; the knee extensors can also contribute. The activity of the medial grastrocnemius shown near the bottom of Figure 8.16 reflects this pushing action: it is inactive early in stance, but becomes active about mid-stance and reaches a peak shortly before toe-off. When walking uphill, the knee and hip extensors become more important in providing the push.

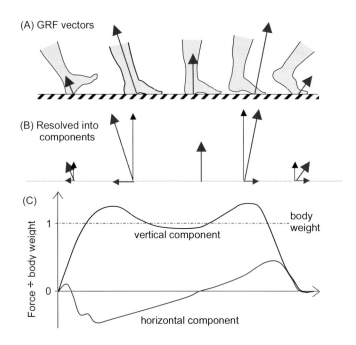

Figure 8.17: *Ground reaction force (GRF) during the stance phase of walking (illustrative).*

Now consider items (3) and (4) on the list of muscle actions given above: moving the leg during swing, and keeping the foot off the ground. Pushing off the ground with the stance foot begins the swing phase, and to lift the foot clear of the ground, the hip is flexed early in swing and the ankle is dorsiflexed later. Hip flexion raises the knee, which allows the shank to swing forwards, and ankle dorsiflexion keeps the foot up so that it does not drag on the ground. The activity of the hip flexors (adductor magnus in Figure 8.16) and the ankle dorsiflexors (tibialis anterior in Figure 8.16) reflects these actions: the hip flexors show a burst of activity early in the swing phase, which flexes the hip and raises the knee. The dorsiflexors become active shortly after the swing begins, and continue to be active throughout the swing phase, keeping the foot up all the way up to heel strike; they are relatively inactive during stance.

8.2.3 During locomotion, the legs behave like pendulums

If your foot is not touching the ground and your leg hangs down freely and relaxed from the hip joint, it will swing back and forth if pushed. If the push is applied to the thigh, the knee will bend as the leg swings, in a manner similar to the way the leg moves during the swing phase of walking. This is the natural, passive motion of a *compound pendulum* in response to an external push. This means that neuromuscular control is not required to drive the limb along its path, because the limb will swing that way under the action of gravity. The idea that this is what the leg does during the swing phase has a history that dates back over one hundred and fifty years[11].

 If the leg swings like a pendulum, then muscular activity is not needed throughout the swing phase to keep the leg moving; all that is needed is a 'push' at the beginning and some dorsiflexor activity to keep the foot up so it does not drag on the ground. As observed by Basmajian[12], 'very little electromyographic activity appears in any of the muscles during normal moderate-speed walking ... we need only small inputs of propulsive force and balancing mechanisms to maintain forward progress'. The lack of muscle activity during the swing phase is consistent with the swinging motion of the leg being largely passive when a person is walking at normal speeds, and is further supported by observations of swing phase duration. Swing phase duration is relatively constant over changes in walking speed and hence over changes in stride length (Figure 8.14): treating the leg as a compound pendulum can account quite well for this behavior[13].

Something that is attached to the ground, stands vertically upwards, and is free to swing about the attachment point is an *inverted pendulum* (see Chapter 7). During the stance phase of walking, the leg behaves like an inverted pendulum: it stays fairly straight and pivots about the ankle joint, as shown in Figure 8.18. The center of gravity moves up and down a little during each stride as a result. The motion of the stance leg is not exactly equivalent to an inverted pendulum, since it normally flexes slightly. This means that the up and down motion of the center of gravity is slightly less than it would be if the knee were locked in full extension throughout the stance phase. Although the stance leg is not completely straight, the approximation to an inverted pendulum is close enough that treating the leg in this way can provide important insights into human walking[14]. Simple models of walking based on the passive, pendulum-like characteristics of both the stance and swing legs have provided important insights into the nature of neural control[15]: some of these models and the insight that they have provided are discussed in the following sections.

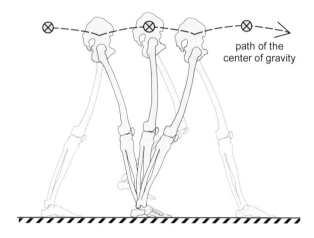

path of the
center of gravity

Figure 8.18: *Bones of the right leg and hip at three moments during the stance phase (start, middle and end), showing that the leg behaves rather like a rigid strut that pivots about the ankle.*

8.2.4 Walking speed is limited by mechanical factors

Treating the stance leg like an inverted pendulum can provide an understanding of why it is difficult to walk faster than a certain speed without adopting special techniques that can be tiring or difficult to master. For a typical adult person, it is difficult to walk at a speed much greater than about 2.5 m/s, and walking at speeds of 5 or 6 m/s is impossible. To understand these limitations, we will assume that the stance leg remains straight (Figure 8.18)[16]. To keep things simple, we will ignore any movement of the torso and arms, and assume that the mass of the walker is concentrated near the level of the hip (i.e., the center of gravity is in a position similar to that shown in Figure 8.18). We will also assume that the motion is confined to a plane (the plane of the page in Figure 8.18), so side-to-side motion is being ignored.

With the above assumptions, the center of gravity of the model walker follows a circular arc in the plane of the page. The center of the circle is the ankle joint, and the radius of the circle is almost exactly the length of the leg (L). When something moves in a circle or along a circular arc, it is accelerating towards the center of the circle. This acceleration is called the *centripetal acceleration* of the moving point. It is a fact of elementary Newtonian mechanics that the centripetal acceleration (a_c) is equal to the square of the speed (v) at which a point is moving along the circular arc, divided by the radius of the circle (L). This fact can be written in shorthand form as a_c = v²/L. The speed v is approximately equal to the speed at which the person is moving along – the walking speed. So the relationship a_c = v²/L can be interpreted as saying that for the model walker, the hip is accelerating towards the foot (a_c) at a rate equal to the square of the walking speed (v²) divided by the leg length (L).

How can this brief analysis just given help understand the maximum speed of the simple walker? The key is to appreciate that there is a constraint on the maximum value of the centripetal acceleration of the hip: it cannot be any greater than the acceleration due to gravity (g). This is because the hip can only fall towards the ground – it cannot be pulled, because the leg is straight and the feet are not fixed to the ground. If something falls freely, then its acceleration cannot be greater than the gravitational acceleration, which is about 9.8 m/s². The speed when a_c is equal to g is the maximum possible speed[17], which means that the maximum speed is equal to the square root of g × L.

To make this concrete, the leg of an adult male of average height is about 0.88 meters; therefore the maximum speed of walking should be about √[9.8 × 0.88], which comes out to about 2.9 m/s. This fits the facts quite well: adults find it very difficult to walk faster than 2.9 m/s. It also predicts that the maximum speed is greater for people with longer legs, again fitting the facts: taller adults can walk much faster than shorter children. Finally, the prediction is that maximum walking speed is slower when the gravitational field is weaker, which produces a smaller gravitational acceleration. On the moon, for example, the gravitational acceleration is about 1.6 m/s², so the maximum predicted walking speed is only about 1.2 m/s. Astronauts who landed on the moon confirmed that they could only walk very slowly, and so tended to adopt a kind of jumping gait which enabled them to get from one place to another much more quickly. More formal experimental tests have confirmed the prediction[18].

Notice that if the radius of the circular arc along which the center of gravity moves could be made greater, the maximum possible walking speed would also be greater. This can be achieved either by a bent-leg walking style, rather like that adopted by Groucho Marx, or using the chicken-walk style used by race walkers. People can certainly walk faster using these gaits, but it is not necessarily very comfortable to do so.

8.2.5 Bipedal locomotion is possible without motor control: passive dynamic walking

There are a number of old fashioned, bipedal children's toys that will walk down shallow slopes without requiring any internal power source; they walk using gravity alone. An example is shown in Figure 8.19. The legs are like two pendulums that are free to swing about the axle. To get it going, the toy needs a little sideways push or is started off leaning to one side. As it walks, it rocks to one side and then the other because of the curved shape of the 'soles' of its feet. When it rocks to one side – the left, for example (see figure) – the right leg is raised off the ground and swings forward under the action of gravity like a pendulum. As the right leg swings, the toy begins to rock to the right, which brings the foot back into contact with the ground. As the rightward rock continues, the left foot is raised off the ground and this leg swings forward, and so on. This walk is a natural, stable motion of the toy under the influence of gravity: it is clearly not a consequence of control, but rather of the toy's construction and the laws of physics. This type of walking is called **passive dynamic walking**[19]: 'passive' because it involves no active control, 'dynamic' because it depends on the dynamical properties of the walking device. It has inspired investigation into the extent to which animal and human locomotion can be understood as a natural form of motion that requires little in the way of complex motor control.

The gait of the toy shown in Figure 8.19 is rather comical and very different from that of any bipedal animal, partly because the toy's legs are completely rigid and straight – they lack jointed knees and ankles. More recently, however, passive dynamic bipedal walkers with knees have been constructed that walk with a surprisingly human-like gait[20]. In these walkers, the swing and stance legs behave as hanging and inverted pendulums respectively; they walk down shallow slopes with energy supplied by gravity alone. There are two crucial differences between these passive walkers and a real walking person. First, a person is not a passive walker[21]; muscle activations are involved when walking down slopes, and the pattern is not dissimilar to that observed when walking on the flat. Second, the passive walker's upright posture is mechanically stable, unlike a person's which is unstable and must be maintained by continuous control (see Chapter 7). Upright stability of passive walkers is usually achieved by giving them a low center of gravity and large feet, which provide a substantial base of support and so allow rocking to one side or the other without falling over.

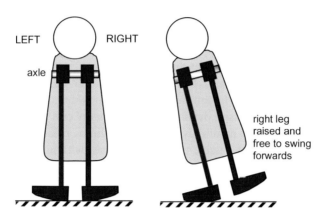

Figure 8.19: *The mechanism of operation of a walking toy (based on McMahon, 1984).*

Although a person is not a passive dynamic walker, the fact that bipedal walking with a human-like gait can be done by completely passive mechanisms shows that it is possible to walk without control and without using any internal energy source (at least for downhill walking, when gravity supplies the energy). The legs of the passive dynamic walkers described in this section work like pendulums[22]; as we saw earlier, when walking, a person's legs work like pendulums – the swing leg like a compound pendulum and the stance leg like an inverted pendulum. When a person walks, the muscles appear to act so as to inject energy into the movement cycle, since they are relatively inactive except at particular times (Figure 8.16). This suggests that the nervous system exploits the passive dynamic properties of the limbs to produce the walking action, rather than controlling the details of the movements of the limbs. The advantages of doing this are explored next.

8.2.6 Exploiting the natural dynamics of the legs simplifies control and keeps energy consumption low

Recent studies have extended the original work on passive dynamic walkers to walking on the flat or uphill, where gravity cannot supply the energy that is required[23]. In these situations, a passive walker requires actuators that can apply forces to the legs and so provide the energy needed. It has been shown that a force impulse applied to the stance leg immediately before toe-off is sufficient to sustain walking on the flat[24]. This force provides the push needed to keep going; subsequent movement of the legs is determined by their passive dynamics. The pattern observed in human walking is similar: the muscles involved in providing the push are active towards the end of stance and then become inactive. This suggests that human walking on the flat involves injecting energy into the step cycle at the end of the stance phase, and then letting the legs swing through in pendular fashion. This strategy of injecting energy to maintain the natural dynamic step cycle of a walker is called **active dynamic walking**. In some ways, it resembles the strategy used by a parent when pushing a child on a swing: to keep the swing swinging, energy is injected once per cycle – the parent gives the child a push.

Rather than keep a tight control over how the limbs move by having muscles actuate them continuously, the nervous system prefers to exploit the passive dynamics of the limbs. This simplifies the control problem – it is not necessary to determine what muscle activations are needed to develop the torques that would be required to drive the limbs along particular paths, it is only necessary to inject some energy into the step cycle at the right time. Not only does this reduce the demands on the controller, it also means that the amount of mechanical energy required to walk can be kept relatively small.

Energy used during locomotion is typically quantified either using the **rate of energy expenditure** (the energy used per unit time, measured in Watts) or a quantity called the **specific cost of transport** (c_T in shorthand), which is defined as follows:

$$c_T = \text{(energy expended)} \div \text{(weight} \times \text{distance traveled)}$$

where 'weight' is the total weight of the walker or runner. This quantity measures the energy expended moving a unit weight (e.g., one kilogram weight) over a unit distance (e.g., one meter). It is dimensionless, and so is useful for comparing the energy efficiency of animals of different weights or of movements over different distances. The specific cost of transport for people walking on the flat is similar to that of passive dynamic walkers that are equipped with actuators to provide the energy. In contrast, robot walkers that control the whole movement cycle and do not exploit the passive dynamics have an energy cost at least ten times as great[25].

In summary, exploiting the natural dynamics of the limbs means that movements can be produced partly as a result of passive physical processes without the need for detailed or continuous control. This active dynamic walking strategy not only reduces the demands on the controller, it also reduces the energy consumed when walking and running.

8.2.7 One of the goals in locomotion is to keep energy expenditure as low as possible

Keeping energy expenditure as low as possible has been proposed to be one of the principles that govern motor behavior: an animal is concerned not only with achieving a particular outcome, but also with doing so in a manner that uses as little energy as possible. We will call this the **principle of energy minimization**; it states that normal, mature, skilled motor behaviors are executed in such a way as to use as little energy as possible. Whether or not a given behavior actually conforms to this principle is an empirically testable hypothesis, and it has been tested most effectively for locomotion.

Empirical tests of the energy minimization principle in locomotion can be either direct or indirect. *Direct tests* are based on the idea that if animals and people are attempting to use as little energy as possible, then they will prefer to use a movement pattern that has the lowest energetic cost. The typical direct experiment involves estimating energy expenditure when people move in the preferred and non-preferred ways, and seeing if the energy cost is lower in the preferred case. *Indirect tests* involve using a mathematical model to determine what locomotor pattern minimizes energy expenditure, and then comparing actual performance against the minimum energy pattern determined from the model. Both types of test have led to the same basic conclusion: people and animals choose or prefer to adopt those patterns of locomotion that keep their energy expenditure close to the minimum. In this section we will concentrate on direct tests of the hypothesis[26].

Consider the hypothesis that people prefer to walk at a speed that minimizes their energy expenditure. To make a direct test of this hypothesis, we could measure energy expenditure when people walk at different speeds while all other relevant conditions, such as the temperature, the slope of the walking surface, and its slipperiness, are held constant. The energy a person expends while walking or running cannot be measured directly, but it can be estimated from measurements of their rates of oxygen consumption and carbon dioxide production using standard procedures[27]. To facilitate taking these measurements and keeping the conditions constant, this type of experiment usually involves the participants walking on a motorized treadmill in a laboratory. The participant walks at the speed of the treadmill, which is held constant while measurements are taken. Figure 8.20 shows the type of results that have been obtained in experiments of this sort. Results are shown for several different uphill slopes over a range of speeds. The specific cost of transport is plotted as a function of walking speed for the different slopes. For each slope there is a walking speed at which the energy cost is lowest, and this is different for the different slopes: the steeper the slope, the slower the speed at which the minimum occurs (about 0.6 m/s for the steepest slope and about 1.4 m/s for the shallowest). It has been found that people prefer to walk at the speed at which the energy cost is lowest, which conforms to the principle of energy minimization.

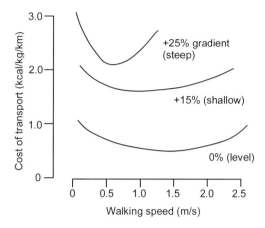

Figure 8.20: *Cost of transport for walking up different slopes as a function of speed (based on Margaria, 1938).*

Similar direct tests have been conducted for other characteristics of gait, such as stride rate, stride width, and stride length[28]. Consider stride rate: to achieve a particular walking speed, you can either take long strides at a slower rate, or short strides at a higher rate. Do people prefer to use the stride rate that minimizes their energy cost? In one experiment, participants walked on a treadmill at several different constant speeds; at each speed they were required to match their stride rate to the beat of a metronome[29]. A number of different stride rates were required, and the rate of energy expenditure was estimated from the rates of oxygen consumption and carbon dioxide production. The results were curves like that shown in Figure 8.21, which is for a speed of 1.5 m/s. At this speed, the minimum rate of energy expenditure, and hence the minimum energy cost, occurs at a stride rate of about 0.95 Hz. This corresponded to the stride rate that the person would spontaneously choose to walk at when not required to match the pace of a metronome. The same was true at all the different speeds tested: the stride rate at which energy cost was lowest corresponded closely to the spontaneously chosen rate. Similar results have been obtained for stride width. It has been found that people prefer to walk with a stride width of about 0.12 times their leg length, which corresponds very closely to the stride width at which energy costs are lowest[30].

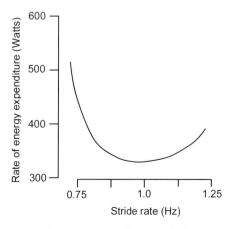

Figure 8.21: *Rate of energy expenditure when walking with different stride rates (based on data reported by Zarrugh and Radcliffe, 1978).*

It used to be thought that the energy costs of human walking were kept low by making movements that reduce the up and down motion of the center of gravity so that its path is flattened[31] (see Figure 8.18). The idea is that raising and lowering the center of gravity requires energy, and so avoiding doing so should reduce the energetic cost. Pelvic tilt, pelvic rotation and knee flexion can all contribute to a flattening of the path of the center of gravity: it was therefore proposed that the observed motions (see Figure 8.10) are made in order to reduce energy costs. This *determinants of gait* theory has recently been subjected to thorough analysis and empirical testing: it turns out that there is little evidence to suggest that people attempt to reduce energy costs by flattening the path of the center of gravity. Indeed, in some cases, the evidence suggests that flattening the path can increase energy cost, probably because doing so interferes with the strategy of exploiting the passive limb dynamics[32].

The results described in this section raise two important questions. First, *what makes a particular speed or stride rate or stride width more energetically costly than another?* Second, *how does a person or animal determine what movement pattern is the least energetically costly?* The second question will be addressed in section 8.2.9. Part of the answer to the first question has been hinted at already – it has to do with exploitation of the passive dynamics of the body. As an example, note that the minima in Figure 8.20 occur at intermediate speeds. You might imagine that your energy cost would be lower for a slower walk, but this is not the case. The reason comes in part from the fact that the passive dynamics of the legs have a natural periodicity. This is similar to the simple pendulum in a pendulum clock: the pendulum takes a particular amount of time – the period – to swing back and forth. The period is the same regardless of how hard a push the pendulum is given to make it swing. To make the pendulum take a longer or a shorter time to swing, you would have to apply forces so as to overcome its natural period, which would require additional energy. When walking, this reasoning applies to both the stance leg and the swing leg, since both act like pendulums. This indicates that the basic reasons for differences in energy efficiency are biomechanical.

8.2.8 Gait choices keep energy costs as low as possible

For getting around relatively slowly, we walk; to get around faster we trot (slow run), and when we want to go really fast, we sprint (fast run). The typical rates of energy expenditure for human walking and running at different speeds on a level surface are shown in Figure 8.22. The figure shows that at speeds below about 2.2 m/s, walking is cheaper than running in terms of energy expenditure; at greater speeds, running is cheaper than walking. If the principle of energy minimization applies, then we would expect that people would choose a running gait to go at speeds greater than about 2.2 m/s, and a walking gait to go slower. We

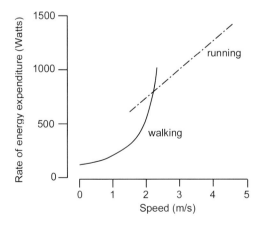

Figure 8.22: *Rate of energy expenditure as a function of speed for walking and running (based on data from Margaria, 1976).*

might also expect that if a person walks faster and faster – they might, for example, be walking on a motorized treadmill while the speed of the treadmill is gradually increasing – then there would be a spontaneous switch from walking to running when the speed reached about 2.2 m/s. Such a switch is called a **gait transition**. Empirical studies support the idea that people prefer to walk at speeds where it is energetically cheaper than running, and that spontaneous gait transitions between walking and running occur at speeds that are close to where the two graphs in Figure 8.22 cross one another. This provides further support for the hypothesis that the principle of energy minimization applies to human locomotion.

Studies of many animal species have yielded similar results to those with human participants. One particularly clear and famous study was done with ponies[33]. The ponies' rate of energy expenditure for walking, trotting and galloping gaits was measured on a motorized treadmill. The results are shown in panel A of Figure 8.23. Panel B plots the specific cost of transport calculated from the rate of energy expenditure, and shows that there are minimum values for the three gaits that occur at about 1.3 m/s, 3.0 m/s, and 6.2 m/s. Note that the minimum cost is about the same for all three gaits. When the ponies were free to choose their own speeds for walking, trotting and galloping, they tended to chose speeds very close to the values where the energy cost was smallest. Furthermore, when the speed of the treadmill was increased, the ponies would make gait transitions at approximately the speeds at which the curves in Figure 8.23 cross: from walk to trot (or vice-versa) at about 1.8 m/s, and from trot to gallop (or vice-versa) at about 4.5 m/s.

An interesting feature of human running is that unlike the trotting and galloping of ponies and other quadrupeds, the rate of energy expenditure increases linearly with speed (the straight line in Figure 8.22). As a consequence, there is no intermediate speed at which the cost of transport is at a minimum – for human running, the cost is more or less the same over a range of speeds from about 2.2 m/s to 5.6 m/s. It has been suggested that the lack of an optimal running speed could give people an advantage when chasing down large prey over long distances, as our ancestors would once have done[34]. Like ponies, large quadrupeds are likely to have a clear optimum speed; speeds that differ from the optimum will be relatively costly. People, in contrast, can run at a range of speeds without any change in their energy costs, and so are free to run in pursuit of their prey at any speed within this range, at least when there aren't any significant hills. By chasing at a speed that is costly and fatiguing for the prey being pursued, the early hunter might gain a significant advantage for pursuits over long distances.

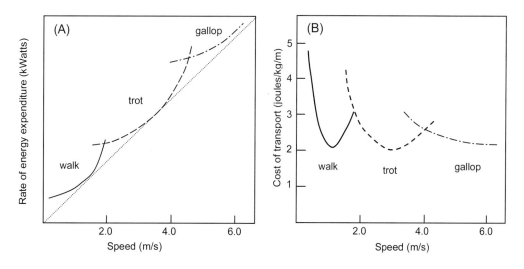

Figure 8.23: *Rate of energy expenditure (A) and the specific cost of transport (B) plotted as a function of speed for the three principal gaits of ponies and horses. Based on data reported by Hoyt and Taylor (1981).*

8.2.9 How does an animal determine the least costly mode of locomotion?

Given that animals and people walk and run in such a way that they incur close to the smallest energy cost possible, it is natural to ask how they achieve this. Perhaps animals have some way of measuring the metabolic energy that they consume when walking and running, and use these measurements to determine the style and speed that consumes the least. This would be a learning process: based on information obtained from many walks and runs, the animal discovers the least costly way to do it. The problem with this account is that it assumes animals have some way of directly measuring the energy cost of walking and running. There are receptors in the muscles and elsewhere that can, in principle, provide information about metabolic, ionic, thermal and mechanical stress[35]. This could provide a basis for estimating energy costs of motor activity through detection of its by-products, though there seems to be no direct evidence to support the idea[36]. It seems more likely that animals measure something else that is correlated with energy cost, such as effort and/or force transmitted by tendons and other connective tissues. Mechanoreceptors such as Golgi tendon organs can measure the muscle force transmitted via tendons to the skeleton, and the nervous system can keep track of the magnitude of command signals that drive muscular activity (see Chapter 3). This information could then be used to discover the manner of locomotion that minimizes a quantity like the total active muscle force exerted during a period of locomotion. Since the development of active muscle force is the major reason any motor behavior incurs an energy cost, minimizing a quantity like total active muscle force will also act to drive energy costs towards a minimum. At present, it is not yet known exactly how animals are able to discover what to do in order to keep energy costs close to the minimum possible[37]. Related issues are discussed in detail in Chapter 11.

8.3 Generation of Locomotor Patterns

8.3.1 Introduction

In this part of the chapter we will investigate how nervous systems generate locomotor muscle activation patterns. The following questions will be addressed:

▸ How is the alternating, bursting pattern of flexor-extensor muscle activation at each joint produced?
▸ How are the movements of the different joints of a single leg coordinated (*intra*limb coordination)?
▸ How are the movements of different legs coordinated (*inter*limb coordination)?

Most of the experiments that have tried to answer these questions involved animals rather than people. Therefore most of what we know about the neural control locomotion comes from animal studies.

8.3.2 A brain is not needed for locomotion

Many small, invertebrate animals like insects and spiders have a lot of legs – six or eight – but do not have enormous numbers of neurons. Indeed, many invertebrate species do not have a brain in the sense that vertebrate animals do. But we don't need to resort to invertebrates to find evidence that locomotor pattern generation can be achieved by relatively small-scale neural networks. A phenomenon that has been known about for possibly thousands of years is that a chicken will run around for some time after its head has been chopped off. There is a documented case of a chicken surviving for approximately eighteen months after its decapitation[38]. This chicken, known as 'Mike', became something of a celebrity in the south-western United States just after World War II. Although unable to feed himself, Mike was able to walk about, though presumably without knowing where he was going.

Mike and other headless chickens demonstrate that the neural circuits responsible for generating locomotor movement patterns are not located in the chicken's brain, but in its spinal cord. As we will see in this part of the chapter, locomotor patterns are generated by spinal circuits not only in birds, but also in mammals and probably in humans too. This has potentially important implications for people who have suffered trauma resulting in partial severance of the spinal cord. In these individuals, the legs are typically paralyzed and they cannot walk. If the circuits responsible for locomotor pattern generation are intact in these patients, it may be possible to activate them and restore the person's ability to walk, at least to some extent. We will return to this possibility in section 8.3.12.

8.3.3 Locomotor patterns are not produced by reflex chaining

In Chapter 5 we saw that spinal circuits are capable of generating complex patterns of movement in response to stimuli. Spinalized frogs, dogs, rats and cats are capable of complex reflex actions like withdrawal, wiping and scratching. It turns out that they are also capable of generating locomotor movement patterns. Sherrington proposed that locomotion could be explained using the reflex chaining principle: he suggested that somatosensory afference from the limbs was responsible for bringing about the transition from the stance phase and the swing phase – the **stance-to-swing transition** – and the transition from swing to stance[39]. The idea was that one phase of the movement cycle would be elicited by stimulation produced as a consequence of executing the other. It could work as follows: imagine that the swing phase of the left leg has begun, the left foot is off the ground, and the body is moving forwards pivoting about the right foot, which increases the extension of the right hip. Extension of the hip stretches the hip flexor muscles together with the associated tendons and ligaments. This stretch stimulates mechanoreceptors in the muscles and connective tissues. When this stimulation becomes strong enough, a flexion reflex response in the right leg is elicited, together with a crossed-extensor type response in the left leg. This switches the left leg into stance and the right leg into swing. As soon as the left foot touches the ground, mechanoreceptors in the sole of the foot are stimulated, and this stimulation elicits a reflex response called the extensor thrust response. As its name suggests, this response involves the leg extending so as to push against the ground; the reaction forces generated push the person or animal forward. The cycle then repeats itself.

Although a reflex chaining account of locomotor pattern generation may appear plausible at first glance, it was discovered early on that it is not correct. The account claims that afference is required to produce locomotion: without afferent feedback, none of the component reflex responses that are supposed to contribute to the locomotor cycle can be elicited. Thus, the idea should be simple to test: if afferent feedback is removed, then locomotor pattern generation should be impossible. Three basic methods have been used to remove movement-generated sensory feedback:

(1)   Deafferentation by cutting the dorsal spinal roots.
(2)   Muscle paralysis or motor nerve transection that prevents any movement from being produced.
(3)   Isolation of the spinal cord: the cord is surgically removed from an animal's body and kept alive in an artificial environment.

Regardless of the method used, the result is the same: locomotor pattern generation is possible without afferent feedback, conclusively demonstrating that reflex chaining cannot explain the generation of locomotor patterns.

8.3.4 Locomotor patterns can be produced in the absence of afferent feedback

The spinal neural networks of an animal that has been spinalized and had the dorsal roots cut (*dorsal rhizotomy*) are almost completely isolated from sensory input. No visual, auditory or olfactory information is transmitted into the spinal cord (in the spinal animal the cord has been cut close to the brainstem) and dorsal rhizotomy virtually eliminates all somatosensory input. Such animals – usually cats or rats – are unable to maintain upright posture, as you might expect, given the vital role of sensory information in postural control (Chapter 6). Nevertheless, if they are given artificial postural support, they are able, after some initial training, to walk and produce other gait patterns. This outcome strongly suggests that pattern generation is based on mechanisms within the spinal cord that can operate in the absence of sensory feedback.

Although the experiments in which animals underwent dorsal rhizotomy provide compelling evidence that locomotor patterns are produced by intrinsic spinal networks, the results are not completely conclusive, because not all somatosensory afferent input to the spinal cord is eliminated by this procedure[40]. A very small proportion of afferent axons enter the spinal cord via the ventral roots, though most of these innervate the viscera, not the muscles, joints or skin. Nevertheless, to be certain that locomotor pattern generation can proceed in the total absence of sensory input, a different method is needed. Two alternative methods have been devised – the prevention of movement either by paralysis or by isolation of the spinal cord (listed as methods 2 and 3 in the last section). The first of these can be used with adult mammals, but the use of spinal cord isolation is restricted to newborn mammals and some species of fish[41]. Use of either method means that there is no actual locomotion, and so there is no sensory feedback. Their use also means that neither movement nor muscle activity can be measured. Instead, neural activity is recorded directly from the relevant motor nerves using suitably placed electrodes. It has been found that the rhythmic bursting patterns of activity in these nerves are similar to the activity that would be recorded were the animal actually walking or running. For this reason, the animal (or spinal cord) is said to display **fictive locomotion** – although the animal is not actually locomoting, the nervous system is producing activation patterns in the motor nerves similar to those generated during actual locomotion[42].

Taken together, the results show that coordinated, rhythmic muscle activation patterns can be produced by spinal neural networks in the complete absence of sensory feedback. The patterns of muscle activation these circuits produce are similar to those observed during locomotion in intact animals. Of course, the fact that these networks can generate locomotor patterns without sensory feedback does not mean that sensory feedback does not play an important role in locomotion. Indeed, feedback is essential for adjusting locomotor patterns to different environmental conditions. The muscle activation patterns observed in deafferented animals and in fictive locomotion are more stereotyped than those observed in intact animals, because they are not subject to any adjustments.

8.3.5 Rhythm generators are building blocks of central pattern generators (CPGs)

Recall from Chapter 5 that a rhythm generator is a *neural network that can produce rhythmic bursts of output activity when excited by tonic input activity*. Such rhythm generators are basic components of the mechanisms responsible for locomotor pattern generation. In what follows, we will examine how rhythm generators can be combined to form neural mechanisms that generate locomotor patterns.

The neural mechanisms that generate locomotor movements are examples of networks called **central pattern generators** (CPGs). Such mechanisms are not exclusive to locomotion; the neural networks underlying production of other rhythmical behaviors such as breathing and scratching are also CPGs: the respiratory CPG and the scratch CPG, respectively. A CPG involved in locomotion is called a locomotor CPG:

CENTRAL PATTERN GENERATOR (LOCOMOTOR): A relatively complex (spinal) neural network capable of producing functional locomotor muscle activation patterns without any contribution from afferent feedback (although in normal circumstances, feedback does contribute to the locomotor pattern).

In all vertebrate animals, the locomotor CPG is located within the spinal cord.

In order to understand how individual rhythm generators contribute to a CPG, an intermediate level of organization can be introduced that will be referred to as the *CPG module*[43]:

CENTRAL PATTERN GENERATOR MODULE (LOCOMOTOR): A neural network capable of producing, without afferent feedback, rhythmic locomotor movements either in a single joint (e.g., flexion-extension of the knee) or in all the relevant joints of a single limb (e.g., flexion-extension of the hip, knee and ankle).

According to the definition, the locomotor movement pattern observed in a single leg might involve just one CPG module, or it might involve three – one for the ankle, one for the knee and one for the hip. Both possibilities will be discussed in more detail in the next section.

Each CPG module is built from rhythm generators. One of the simplest constructions was proposed for locomotion in the cockroach[44]. This module produces rhythmic flexion and extension movement in a single joint actuated by two muscles; it is shown in Figure 8.24. The circuit is composed of a rhythm generator and a population of inhibitory interneurons (represented as a single, black neuron in the figure) that inhibits activity in the extensor motorneuron pool. There is an external source of tonic activity that excites the rhythm generator, causing it to produce rhythmic bursts of output activity. The tonic activity also excites the extensor motorneuron pool. The rhythm generator is connected monosynaptically to the flexor MN pool and indirectly – via the population of inhibitory interneurons – to the extensor MN pool.

The result of the connectivity shown in Figure 8.24 is that when the rhythm generator produces a burst of activity, the flexor motorneurons are excited by the burst. Thus, the output activity in the flexor motorneuron pool closely resembles the input activity from the rhythm generator. A burst of rhythm generator activity also inhibits the extensor motorneuron pool (via the inhibitory interneurons): when the rhythm generator produces a burst, output activity from the extensor motorneuron pool is shut off. As the figure shows, the overall effect is that when the flexor muscle receives a burst of activation, the extensor muscle receives no activation, and vice-versa. Thus, a flexor contraction occurs together with relaxation of the extensor, followed by a contraction of the extensor together with a relaxation of the flexor, and so on. Alternative architectures have been suggested for mammalian CPG modules, as discussed next.

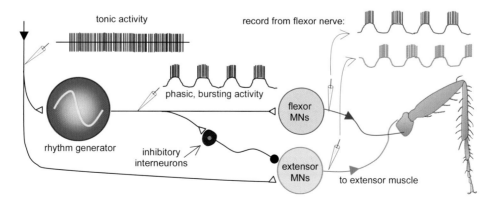

Figure 8.24: *Hypothetical CPG module in the cockroach.*

8.3.6 There are different models for mammalian CPG modules

As early as 1911, Graham Brown[45] proposed the **half-center model** for locomotor pattern generation by the mammalian spinal cord. The basic idea is shown in Figure 8.25. There are two populations of excitatory interneurons (INs), one associated with a flexor muscle's motorneuron pool (pink) and another with an extensor muscle's motorneuron pool (green). These two populations both receive tonic activation from an external source, such as the brain. Each interneuron population is a half-center, and they are mutually inhibitory by virtue of being coupled together via populations of inhibitory interneurons (purple). This circuit generates rhythmic activity as a consequence of fatigue processes within the half-centers. Thus, the coupled half-centers comprise a rhythm generator.

To see how the rhythm generating process might work, suppose that the excitatory interneurons in the half-center associated with the flexor MN pool are firing. This activity inhibits the extensor half-center and excites the flexor MNs. Firing of the excitatory interneurons fatigues them (the fatigue process) and their firing rate declines; as a result, inhibition of the extensor half-center declines. Once inhibition has declined sufficiently, the extensor half-center interneurons begin firing (the inhibition can no longer counteract the tonic excitation). Once they begin firing, inhibition of the flexor half-center is produced, shutting down activity in the fatigued neurons. The extensor half-center interneurons then continue firing and become fatigued as a result. At the same time, the interneurons in the flexor half-center are recovering from fatigue. Due to this fatigue and recovery cycle, activity alternates between the two half-centers, producing an alternating pattern of activation in the flexor and extensor muscles.

Although this original half-center model is simple and appealing, it does not fit with recent results from experiments with rats and other experimental animals in which inhibitory synaptic transmission was blocked by chemical agents. This blocking would have the effect of removing the inhibitory coupling between half-centers. According to the model, when there is no inhibitory coupling, there should be no rhythmical activity in either motorneuron pool. This is not what was observed in the experiments: it was found that rhythmic activation of flexor and extensor motorneurons can still be evoked when inhibitory synaptic transmission is completely blocked[46]. It has also been found that rhythmic activity can be evoked in the flexors independently of the extensors[47], which should not be possible according to the half-center model. This finding suggests that there must be two rhythm generators, one that drives the flexor muscles and one that drives the extensors.

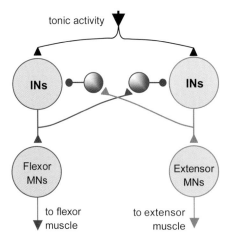

Figure 8.25: *Half-center model of a CPG module.*

Figure 8.26 shows the basic structure of more recent models that have two rhythm generators coupled in a mutually inhibitory fashion[48]. The role of the mutual inhibition is to ensure that activity alternates between flexors and extensors. To produce an alternating pattern of activity, when the rhythm generator connected to the flexor muscle produces a burst of activation, the one connected to the extensor muscle must be quiescent, and vice-versa. Suppose that the flexor rhythm generator produces the first burst of activity. This burst will inhibit the extensor generator, preventing activation of the extensor muscle. Once the flexor burst is over, the extensor generator is released from inhibition and becomes active, producing a burst of its own. Thus, an alternating, rhythmic pattern of flexor and extensor muscle activity is established that continues as long as tonic activation persists[49].

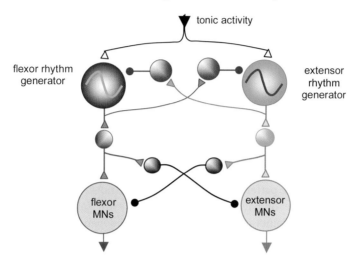

Figure 8.26: *Model of a CPG module involving two rhythm generators.*

In the original half-center model, rhythm generation is a property of the network, not of any of the individual neurons. In the model of Figure 8.26, rhythm generation could either be a network property, or it could depend on the intrinsic rhythm generating properties of neurons within the generators (pacemaker neurons). It is becoming clear that pacemaker type neurons are far more widespread in vertebrate rhythm generating circuits than was previously realized: the rhythm generators involved in mammalian locomotor pattern generation may involve populations of such neurons[50], but the exact cellular composition of these generators has yet to be elucidated.

8.3.7 Each leg is controlled by one or more CPG modules

According to the definition of CPG module given earlier, locomotor movement of the joints of a single leg are either driven by a single CPG module or by several, one for each joint. It is not yet known which of these two possible organizations is found in people and other mammals; both types are described in this section.

The idea that each leg joint that contributes to locomotion is driven by its own CPG module[51] is shown in Figure 8.27: there is one CPG module for the ankle joint (left), one for the knee (middle) and one for the hip (right), and each one has an extensor rhythm generator (green) and a flexor rhythm generator (red). The rhythm generators of these three CPG modules are coupled together. This is shown schematically by half-headed arrows, to indicate that signals go both ways – the coupling would actually be mediated by interneurons, which are not shown in the figure. It is the coupling between the CPG modules that allows them to work in a synchronous and coordinated fashion, so that the joints of the leg flex and extend with the correct phase relations.

The alternative model for a single leg is that there is only one CPG module which drives all the joints[52]. This model is illustrated in Figure 8.28, and shows a single rhythm generating network consisting of two mutually inhibitory rhythm generators whose outputs drive the three leg joints via pattern-forming networks – one for each joint. These networks have populations of excitatory interneurons (pink and green) and inhibitory interneurons (purple and black) interconnected in a fashion essentially identical to the connectivity of the CPG module shown

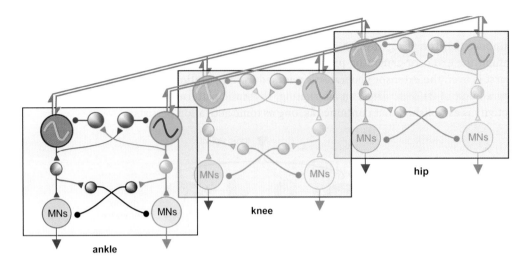

Figure 8.27: *A CPG module for one leg may be composed of three sub-modules, one for each joint.*

in Figure 8.27. However, the pattern-forming networks are not themselves capable of rhythm generation. The advantage of having separate networks to transmit rhythmic activity to the muscles of individual joints is that it allows some independence in the activity of the different joints. For example, the knee could be 'frozen out' by external inhibition selectively directed at the knee network, leaving the other two joints unaffected. This would produce a straight-leg, limping motion, and would be important to be able to do if the knee joint were damaged.

Experimental evidence for the existence of individual CPG modules for each leg has been obtained from spinal animals walking on split-belt treadmills. This evidence relies on the independent effects of afferent signals in the two limbs, and for this reason discussion is deferred until section 8.4.

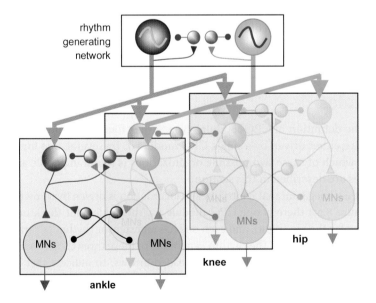

Figure 8.28: *CPG module for a single leg, composed of a single pair of rhythm generators that drive all the joints of the limb.*

8.3.8 Locomotor CPGs are built from interacting CPG modules

In the previous section we examined how a single-leg CPG module might be constructed from individual rhythm generators. Of course, leg locomotion in animals normally involves more than one leg: two, four, six, eight or more legs may be involved, depending on the animal. Coordination of the movements of two or more legs was referred to earlier as *interlimb coordination*. As mentioned in the last section, coordination between multiple CPGs or multiple rhythm generators can be achieved by coupling them together with either excitatory or inhibitory interconnections.

When people walk or run, the movements of the two legs follow an alternating, antiphase pattern. We have already seen that an antiphase coordination pattern of flexor and extensor muscle activation can be produced if there are two rhythm generators coupled together in a mutually inhibitory fashion. Thus, we might propose that antiphase coordination of the two legs could be produced if there were similar, mutual inhibitory coupling between the CPG modules associated with each leg. Note, however, that the effect of an inhibitory signal from one CPG or rhythm generator on another depends on when in the cycle the inhibition arrives. Since it takes time for signals to be transmitted from one place to another in the nervous system, an inhibitory signal from one CPG module could arrive too late to stop another CPG from bursting at the same time. Indeed, if the transmission time were sufficiently long, then it is possible that mutual inhibition could contribute to an in-phase coordination pattern. If the rhythm generating circuitry of one unit CPG is only a very short distance from that of another CPG module, then the transmission time could be very short. In this case, inhibitory coupling can produce the antiphase pattern.

Of course, the antiphase coordination pattern is not the only possibility for human locomotion; in-phase motion of the two legs is possible, and produces a jumping gait. To achieve an in-phase coordination pattern, the CPG modules need to be doing more or less the same thing at the same time, and this could be achieved by mutual excitatory coupling. Figure 8.29 shows a biped CPG composed of two CPG modules, one for each leg, that are coupled together by both inhibitory and excitatory interconnections. Each module has a complex internal structure, as described in section 8.3.7, but for simplicity they are represented as yin-yang type symbols.

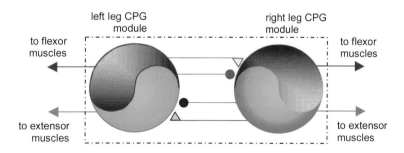

Figure 8.29: *A biped CPG composed of two coupled CPG modules.*

The more legs an animal has, the more CPG modules are involved. A quadruped like a cat or a dog would have four CPG modules. The two hindlimb CPG modules could be coupled like those in Figure 8.29, and the same would be true of the forelimb CPG modules. Couplings also exist between the forelimb CPG modules and the hindlimb CPGs to achieve the coordinated quadruped gait patterns described in 8.1.4. In this context it is important to remember that all four limbs are typically involved in human locomotion as well – not only do the legs move, the arms swing. Arm swinging is particularly significant in running, when the arms move in phase with the contralateral leg. There is some evidence to suggest that there are CPG modules associated with the human arms just as there are CPG modules associated with the forelimbs of quadrupeds[53]. This is perhaps to be expected, given that the first form of locomotion we are capable of is quadrupedal (crawling).

From the foregoing discussion we see that in order to understand how the complex, rhythmic patterns of muscle activation and movement that characterize locomotion are produced, three levels of organization are distinguished:

▸ **Level 1 – rhythm generator:** formed either from a population of pacemaker neurons, each with intrinsic rhythm generating properties, or from a network of interconnected neurons that are not individually capable of rhythm generation.
▸ **Level 2 – CPG module:** one or more rhythm generators, together with the circuitry that connects them to the muscles that actuate one or more joints of a single leg.
▸ **Level 3 – CPG:** the network of interconnected CPG modules that is responsible for movements in all the legs.

8.3.9 Spinal CPGs are activated by descending signals from the brain

We have discussed how spinal CPGs can generate locomotor patterns when they are stimulated in a sustained (tonic) fashion, but we have not yet discussed where such stimulation originates in the intact animal. In natural conditions, activation of a CPG will almost always issue from structures within the brain and descend to the CPG networks in the spinal cord. Descending activity can be produced artificially in an experimental animal, such as a cat, by electrically or chemically stimulating a number of different brain locations, including sites within the hindbrain such as the parapyramidal region of the medulla[54], sites in the midbrain (the **subthalamic locomotor region** and the **mesencephalic locomotor region**)[55], and sites in the hypothalamus and thalamus (the **diencephalic locomotor region**). These regions are rather circumscribed – you need to stimulate at the right location, otherwise the CPG will not be activated. These sites are examples of *locomotor regions*:

> **LOCOMOTOR REGION:** A circumscribed region of the brain containing neurons that when stimulated sufficiently strongly produce descending signals that activate the spinal locomotor CPG circuits and cause them to generate locomotor patterns.

The different locomotor regions are locations within descending *locomotor command pathways*, which can be defined as follows:

> **LOCOMOTOR COMMAND PATHWAY:** A pathway descending from the brain to the spinal CPG circuits that transmits signals for the initiation, termination, maintenance and control of locomotion.

Here we will restrict attention to the command pathway that includes the mesencephalic locomotor region (MLR). The MLR is a circumscribed part of the midbrain close to the inferior colliculus[56]. MLR neurons project to neurons in the pons and medulla that descend into the spinal cord along the reticulospinal tract, as shown in panel B of Figure 8.30. Stimulation of the MLR results in neural activity being transmitted down the reticulospinal tract to the spinal CPG. In the figure, the CPG is represented as a yin-yang symbol, but is distributed over many spinal segments. The axons descending through the reticulospinal tracts actually make synaptic connections with many neurons in different parts of the CPG, but this is too complex to show in the figure.

A group of Russian scientists discovered in the 1960s that electrical stimulation of the MLR in decerebrate cats could evoke locomotion[57]. The cats would begin walking on a treadmill, provided that the stimulation was sufficiently strong, and they would continue to do so as long as the stimulation was sustained – when the stimulation was turned off, the animal would stop walking. Panel A of Figure 8.30 shows a sagittal slice through the cat brain, with the cut used to prepare decerebrate animals marked as a dashed red line. The cut preserves connections between the MLR and the CPG, but disconnects the subthalamic locomotor region from the CPG. Stimulation of the MLR in intact animals has been found to have similar effects to stimulation in decerebrate animals[58].

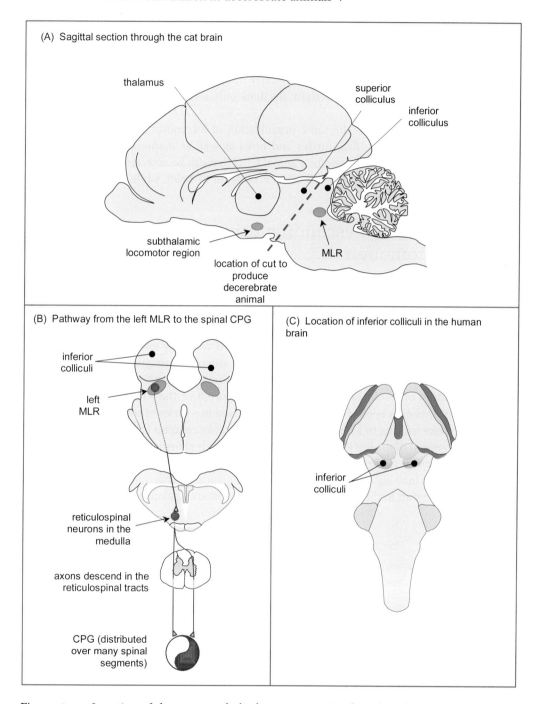

Figure 8.30: *Location of the mesencephalic locomotor region (MLR) and its connection to the locomotor CPG.*

There is evidence that a mesencephalic locomotor region is present in people close to the inferior colliculi (the location of the inferior colliculi in the human brainstem is shown in panel C of Figure 8.30). People with damage to this area of the midbrain suffer from astasia – an inability to walk or otherwise locomote – without showing any paralysis or any inability to perform other types of motor activity[59]. This suggests that the area is a critical part of the pathway involved in the voluntary initiation of locomotion. Presumably, signals from higher regions of the brain associated with voluntary control descend to the MLR and from there to the CPG.

It is known that the MLR receives excitatory inputs from the hypothalamus and the frontal cortex, and inhibitory inputs from the basal ganglia[60]: the excitatory inputs are the likely means by which voluntary and otherwise internally motivated locomotion is initiated[61]. The inhibitory inputs from the basal ganglia suppress activity in the MLR, and so are capable of preventing the accidental initiation of locomotion and also of rapidly terminating ongoing locomotion. The latter possibility suggests that there may be a specialized pathway for braking or terminating locomotion: MLR activity can be reduced or shut off by active inhibition, rather than simply by reducing excitation[62]. Active inhibition is useful for rapid termination of activity in a network where its activity declines only slowly after excitatory inputs are turned off[63].

It is interesting to note that the same organization of locomotor control is found in all vertebrate animals studied – fish, turtles and birds as well as mammals[64]. Locomotion in animals of all these types is governed by a spinal CPG that can be activated by stimulation of the MLR: MLR stimulation in a fish will cause it to begin to swim, while a bird will begin to walk or fly.

8.3.10 Increasing descending drive increases the speed of locomotion

Electrical stimulation of sufficient strength applied to the MLR will initiate locomotion in experimental animals. If this stimulation is maintained, the animal will continue to locomote for as long as stimulation persists. Both the speed of locomotion and the gait adopted by the animal have been shown to depend on stimulation strength. The basic finding is that the greater the stimulation strength, the faster the pace[65]. At relatively low stimulation strength, the animal walks, and walking speed increases as the stimulus strength is increased. As the stimulus strength is increased still further, the animal breaks into a trot and ultimately into a run. This pattern of results obtained is shown in Figure 8.31: the strength (i.e., voltage) of the electrical stimulation applied to the MLR is increased in a series of steps, from a low level sufficient to evoke walking to a high level sufficient to evoke running (galloping). The flexion-extension movement of the hip joints of the two hindlimbs is shown: it increases in frequency and the animal moves faster as the stimulation strength is increased. Initially, the two limbs move in antiphase (one leg flexes while the other extends), as is characteristic of walking and trotting. There is a shift to the in-phase pattern characteristic of galloping at the highest stimulus strength.

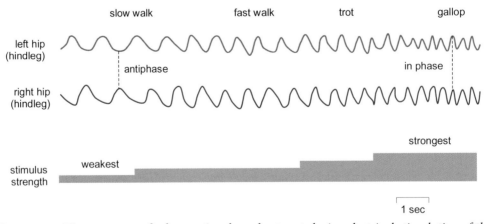

Figure 8.31: *Hip movement of a locomoting decerebrate cat during electrical stimulation of the MLR (illustrative, based on data reported by Shik, Severin, Orlovsky, 1966).*

The results shown in Figure 8.31 demonstrate that a single type of descending signal controls not only the initiation of locomotion, but also its speed and the gait pattern adopted. In other words, different signals for initiation, speed control, and gait switching are not needed – changes in the level of descending drive are sufficient for all three functions.

8.3.11 Descending signals are critical for effective locomotion

During locomotion in an intact animal, spinal circuits are being continuously regulated by signals transmitted down command pathways from the brain. These signals not only sustain locomotion and modulate its speed, but also play key roles in adapting the locomotor pattern so as to guide the animal through the environment, and in coordinating locomotion and posture so as to maintain dynamic balance. In fact, the brain plays at least five roles in locomotor control[66]:

(1)   Initiating and terminating CPG activity.
(2)   Controlling the level of CPG activation and hence the speed of locomotion and gait.
(3)   Adapting locomotion to the requirements of the task and environment.
(4)   Coordinating locomotor activity with concurrently executed activities.
(5)   Maintaining postural equilibrium during locomotion (dynamic balance).

The first and second of these roles have been discussed already (in sections 8.3.9 and 8.3.10). The third involves such things as guiding locomotion around and over obstacles, along paths and after prey. These functions are typically achieved using vision – though some animals use hearing, smell and touch (via whiskers, for example). A spinal animal cannot regulate locomotion using any of these senses, since no signals from the sensory organs can reach the spinal CPG. The guidance of locomotion by exteroceptive sensory information is the topic of Chapters 9 and 10. We will have very little to say about roles (4) and (5).

The above list does not necessarily include all the roles played by descending signals in locomotor control. For example, it has been found that there are differences between the locomotor pattern of spinal cats and that of intact cats: spinal cats exhibit some loss of synchronization of the flexor muscles acting at the different joints, which can result in dragging of the foot, asymmetrical stepping and some stumbling[67]. There is evidence that these deficits arise due to loss of descending signals from the cerebellum[68]. With extensive treadmill training, the deficits can be reduced. This reduction appears to be the result of spinal learning rather than spontaneous recovery or improved muscle strength[69].

8.3.12 A spinal CPG is the likely basis for locomotor pattern generation in people: evidence from spinal patients

It is impossible to use human participants in the type of experiments that have established the existence of spinal CPGs in experimental animals. For this reason, the sources of evidence for a locomotor CPG in the human spinal cord are necessarily indirect, but when they are taken together, the case is compelling. The evidence comes from two rather different sources: adults with spinal cord injuries and newborn infants. We will look at the first of these in this section and the second in the next section.

When people suffer spinal cord injury, a common result is some degree of paralysis – an inability to make voluntary movements. The degree of paralysis depends on the severity of the injury and its location. Spinal injuries typically cause the severance of the axons in descending tracts, which prevents higher levels of the nervous system from communicating with neurons in the spinal cord below the injury site. Such severance is typically only partial, and some descending tracts or parts of them remain intact. This is called *partial spinal cord injury (partial SCI)*. In some severe cases, the descending tracts are completely severed, at least as far as it is possible to tell. This is called *clinically complete spinal cord injury (complete SCI)*; here is the definition used in many studies[70]:

CLINICALLY COMPLETE SPINAL CORD INJURY/TRANSECTION (*complete SCI*): no sensory or motor function detectable below the level of the lesion, as assessed clinically using the *American Spinal Injury Association Scale*, and no sensory cortical evoked potentials (measured from scalp electrodes) recorded in response to stimulation of the lower leg.

An injury that results in complete spinal transection at the thoracic or cervical level has the same effect as the surgical procedure used to spinalize animals for use in experiments. A person with such an injury loses the ability to walk and is confined to a wheelchair. If the human locomotor CPG is spinally located, then like a spinal animal, a person with complete SCI could become able to walk, given the right conditions.

A spinalized mammal, such as a cat, requires training on a treadmill in order to recover a locomotor pattern adequate for sustained walking[71]. Once the pattern is recovered, the afferent excitation of the CPG produced by movement of the legs on the treadmill is sufficient to activate the CPG and sustain locomotion: the spinal cat can walk, trot and run to keep up with a motorized treadmill. These findings show that, for experimental animals at least, locomotor CPGs can be activated by movement-produced afferent feedback (possible pathways involved are discussed in the next part of the chapter). There have been several reports of success in training human patients with partial SCI to walk on treadmills when they are provided with some postural support[72]. However, since the transection is only partial, it is possible that supraspinal signals descending down the intact pathways are necessary for recovery of locomotor function in these patients: it is even possible that the locomotor pattern itself is generated at a supraspinal level. Results of studies with patients with complete SCI have shown that locomotor type muscle activation patterns can be produced by patients supported on treadmills, but manual assistance with stepping is needed initially, and even then the pattern cannot be sustained for many steps without continued assistance[73]. This suggests that the human spinal cord is capable of generating the basic locomotor pattern, but cannot sustain it in the absence of descending signals.

It could be argued that a spinal CPG is not involved in producing the patterns observed in complete SCI patients, but rather that the pattern is produced by movement-related afferent feedback, in a manner similar to Sherrington's original reflex chaining idea (see section 8.3.3). More evidence for the existence of a human spinal CPG is clearly desirable. One source comes from studies that have used epidural electrical stimulation of the lumbar spinal cord in complete SCI patients. Epidural stimulation involves applying an electrical stimulus to the outermost membrane surrounding the cord (the dura mater) at sufficient strength to stimulate the neurons beneath. It has been found that application of such stimulation at an appropriate frequency (between 30 and 40 Hz) at the level of the second lumbar vertebra is capable of evoking locomotor-like activity in complete SCI patients[74]. Repetitive, bursting patterns of EMG activity can be evoked in the leg muscles, together with cyclic movements of the hip and knee joints. Figure 8.32 illustrates this, showing knee joint motion and EMG activity in an extensor muscle group (quadriceps) and a flexor (gastrocnemius). Again, this evidence is not conclusive, since movement-related afferent feedback was still present and could have contributed to pattern generation. However, it is difficult to see how an account based entirely on movement-related feedback can explain all the experimental observations. If afferent feedback were responsible for pattern generation, then the role of the stimulation would be merely to get the movements going in the first place and to reinitiate them if the feedback stimulation is of insufficient strength to maintain the pattern. This does not appear to account for why the frequency of the stimulation is critical. The rhythmical pattern becomes less clear if the frequency drops below about 30 Hz, and cannot be elicited at all below about 10 Hz. Similarly, the cyclical pattern becomes less distinct at stimulation frequencies above 40 Hz, and cannot be elicited at all above about 110 Hz. Stimulation above about 110 Hz or below 10 Hz evokes tonic activity in the muscles.

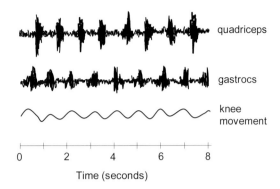

Figure 8.32: *Activity evoked by epidural stimulation in SCI. (Based on data reported in Gerasimenko, Roy, Edgerton, 2008.)*

8.3.13 A spinal CPG is the likely basis for locomotor pattern generation in people: evidence from young infants

The second source of evidence for a spinal CPG in people comes from young infants. In the first few weeks of life, an infant will display a behavior called the **stepping reflex**: if an infant is held upright with their feet touching the ground, the legs may make repeated stepping movements as if the infant were trying to walk. As already discussed in Chapter 6 in relation to the asymmetric tonic neck reflex, the spinal circuits can act somewhat more independently of the brain in the infant than in the adult. This is partly due to the fact that the descending tracts in the young infant are immature: myelination of the corticospinal tract, for example, is not complete until about two years of age[75]. The independence of the stepping reflex from cortical control is further evidenced by the finding that enancephalic infants – infants born without a cerebral cortex – also display the stepping reflex.

As described in more detail later in the chapter (section 8.4.3), the modulation of infant stepping by afferent signals closely resembles the modulation of stepping in the spinal cat by similarly evoked afference. This similarity suggests that similar mechanisms are involved, and in the cat, the existence of a spinal CPG is firmly established. One particularly interesting instance of this similarity relates to walking on a motorized, split-belt treadmill – a treadmill with two belts running side by side that can be independently driven. The two belts can be driven at different speeds: in order to step successfully under such conditions, the two legs need to step at different speeds so that the stepping of each leg matches the speed of its belt. Only by using afferent feedback from the moving limbs can this be achieved in a spinal animal. It has been found that human infants can successfully adapt their stepping reflex pattern so as to walk on a split-belt treadmill when the two belts move at different speeds[76]. The adaptations that infants make are essentially the same as the adaptations made by the hind legs of spinal cats, but very different from the adaptations observed in normal adult people when they perform the same task.

In summary, the reflex stepping patterns of young infants who are as yet unable to walk or even stand closely resemble the stepping patterns of the hind legs of spinal cats and other mammals. Since the latter involve a CPG, it seems reasonable to conclude that the infant reflex stepping is generated by a similar mechanism. Taken together, the evidence from spinal patients and young infants provides reasonably compelling evidence that the human spinal cord contains a locomotor CPG. Given that all other animal species that have been studied, including primates, posses spinal locomotor CPGs, it would be strange indeed to find that we humans did not also possess such a mechanism.

8.4 Sensory Influences on Locomotor Pattern Generation

8.4.1 Sensory signals are used to adapt locomotor patterns to suit the conditions

The circumstances in which a person or animal walks or runs will never be exactly the same on different occasions: the surface may be more or less slippery, softer or harder, there may be obstacles to avoid, inclines to ascend or descend, loads to carry. The ability of animals to adapt their locomotion to varied and changing conditions is something that clearly sets them apart from mechanical walking toys that execute stereotyped patterns of movement: such toys walk on smooth, hard surfaces without obstructions, but fail if these conditions are not met. The contrast with a living animal could hardly be more obvious.

An animal adapts its locomotion to different conditions using sensory information. A locomotor CPG is capable of pattern generation in the complete absence of sensory input, but this is not the normal situation. Normally there is sensory stimulation, some of which is produced by the act of locomotion itself – feedback activity. For example, as the joints of the legs flex and extend, somatosensory mechanoreceptors in the skin, joints and muscles are stimulated. When the feet make or break contact with the ground, mechanoreceptors within them are stimulated, signaling that a contact has been made or has been broken.

In a spinal animal, only somatosensory feedback can influence a CPG; in an intact animal, vision, hearing, smell and vestibular stimulation can influence a CPG, via signals transmitted along the descending pathways. When a person walks or runs, they typically rely on visual information to guide their locomotion: to control direction so that they go where they want and avoid obstacles, to determine where the feet should be placed when walking over rough ground, and to determine when to take a long stride or make a jump to cross a puddle or hurdle a stump.

The above examples illustrate the fact that normal locomotor patterns are the result of dynamic interactions between the CPG and sensory signals. When isolated from sensory inputs, a CPG produces a rather stereotyped pattern of muscle activation, but when sensory inputs are intact, the pattern has a richer and more varied structure that can hardly be described as stereotyped. In this part of the chapter, we will examine how sensory signals can modulate the activity of the CPG and adapt the locomotor pattern to different conditions. The focus will be on the effects of somatosensory afference; the use of vision to guide locomotion will be considered in Chapters 9 and 10.

8.4.2 Somatosensory afference affects the timing of the stance-to-swing transition

It has been found that spinal and decerebrate cats will walk on a motorized treadmill, and as the treadmill speed is increased or decreased, the animals will increase or decrease their walking speed to match the treadmill speed. In this case, walking speed changes without any change in descending drive. Just as with normal locomotion, as the speed of the treadmill increases, increased walking speed is achieved by decreasing the stance duration with little change in swing duration. If the speed of the treadmill is increased sufficiently, the animals will often make a transition to a galloping gait. This ability to keep pace with the treadmill provides strong evidence that sensory signals are modifying the activity of the locomotor CPG. Without sensory inputs and with no change in descending drive, CPG activity would be constant, and the animal would be unable to keep pace with the treadmill. Thus, the cat's ability to keep pace implies that sensory signals are modifying CPG activity.

The ability of spinal cats to keep pace with a motorized treadmill could be explained if somatosensory afference from the limbs affects the timing of the stance-to-swing transition. Delay of the stance-to-swing transition can increase the duration of the stance phase, whereas making an earlier transition can shorten its duration. When an animal walks on a motorized treadmill, the moving belt pulls the leg or legs that are in contact with the belt – the legs in the stance phase – backwards. This is shown in Figure 8.33: frames (1), (2) and (3) show three sequential positions of a cat's rear stance leg while walking on a motorized treadmill. The top of the belt is moving from right to left as indicated by the arrows. During stance, the leg supports some of the animal's weight. This support is greatest in mid-stance (frame 2), and then as the leg moves back and hip extension increases, the load decreases (frame 3). Thus, there are two important sensory consequences of motion of the leg backwards from mid-stance onwards: stimulation of load sensing receptors in the limb progressively decreases, and stimulation of receptors sensitive to hip extension progressively increases.

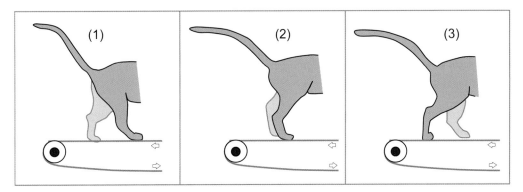

Figure 8.33: *Cat's hind legs during walking on a motorized treadmill. Arrows show direction of belt movement.*

There is now compelling evidence that the stance-to-swing transition in cats is influenced by sensory signals related to hip extension and limb loading[77]. Evidence that limb loading influences the transition comes from studies in which Golgi tendon organ (GTO) afferents were artificially stimulated during stance. GTOs respond to force in the tendons, and will be more active in extensor tendons when the leg is supporting the weight of the body. Artificial stimulation of extensor GTO afferents (type Ib afferents), particularly those of the ankle extensor tendons, has been found to extend the duration of the stance phase for as long as the stimulation persists[78]. This suggests that the afferent signals have an inhibitory effect on the flexor rhythm generator(s) of a leg's CPG module.

Figure 8.34 reproduces the CPG module circuit of Figure 8.26 and includes likely connections made by GTO (Ib) afferents with the rhythm generators[79]. When signals are transmitted along these afferents, the result is clear: the extensor rhythm generator activation is increased and the flexor rhythm generator is inhibited. The effect is to prevent the flexor rhythm generator from bursting, which in turn prevents the flexors from becoming active, so delaying the start of the swing phase. This can explain how a spinal or decerebrate cat can slow down so as to keep pace with a treadmill that is decreasing in speed. However, it is not sufficient to explain how the animal can keep pace when the treadmill speed increases. If the CPG is deafferented, its rate of bursting is determined by the level of descending drive: GTO signals can only slow the rate down, they cannot increase it beyond that determined by the descending drive. In order to explain how cats can keep pace with increasing treadmill speed when descending drive is constant, a signal that can shorten the stance phase is needed.

The other important sensory signal that is generated during the stance phase is due to the progressive extension of the hip. As the hip is extended and the hip flexors are stretched, muscle spindle receptors will be stimulated. Since hip flexor stretch increases towards the end of the stance phase, the activity of associated spindle afferents – particularly the type II afferents – could be used to facilitate the stance-to-swing transition. This would be achieved if the hip flexor spindle afferents had an excitatory effect on the flexor rhythm generator and

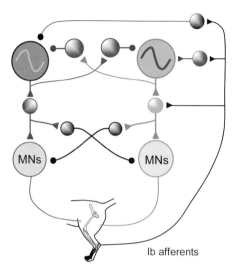

Ib afferents

Figure 8.34: *Connections of Golgi tendon organ (type Ib) afferents with the CPG module for one hind leg.*

an inhibitory effect on the extensor rhythm generator, as shown in Figure 8.35. It has been found that only when the hip is sufficiently extended does the sensory activity produced by flexor stretch become sufficient to trigger the transition from stance to swing[80]. The angle of hip extension required is similar to that at which the transition normally occurs.

The effects of spindle afferent signals can account for the ability of cats to keep pace with increasing speed of a motorized treadmill. As the treadmill moves faster, the hip is extended more quickly, and so the stretch-evoked activity in the hip flexor spindle afferents reaches the level needed to initiate the swing phase earlier. The result is a shorter stance phase and a quicker pace.

We have considered the effects of signals from GTO afferents related to limb loading and signals from hip flexor spindle afferents related to hip extension somewhat separately, but clearly these effects complement one another. As mentioned in relation to Figure 8.33, as the foot moves backwards relative to the cat's body, hip extension increases, and the load on the leg decreases. As a result, extensor GTO activity will decrease progressively and release the flexor rhythm generator from inhibition, while hip flexor spindle afferent activity will increase, exciting the flexor rhythm generator. The discussion has also focused on a single

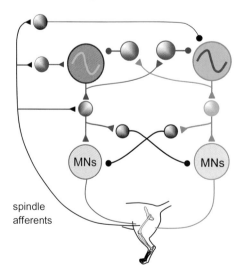

spindle afferents

Figure 8.35: *Connections of muscle spindle afferents with the CPG module for one hind leg.*

leg and its associated CPG module, which suggests that each leg can be affected somewhat independently of the others. In fact, it has been found that spinal cats can walk on split-belt motorized treadmills (see section 8.3.13) when the two belts are driven at different speeds. The left legs are on one belt and the right legs on the other, so if the belts are driven at different speeds, the left and right legs need to step at different rates to keep up with their belts. Intact, spinal and decerebrate cats all have no difficulty in walking in such circumstances[81] – the stance phase of the legs on the faster belt decreases relative to the stance phase of the legs on the slower belt.

8.4.3 How does somatosensory afference affect the timing of swing-to-stance transitions in human locomotion?

The results described in the last section, showing that the duration of the stance phase and the timing of the stance-to-swing transition can be strongly influenced by afferent signals, are the typical findings in spinal and decerebrate animals. In intact animals, these effects are much weaker, and may be absent altogether if stimulation is restricted to just one type of sensory receptor[82]. In human adults, the findings resemble those obtained from intact cats: for example, increased loading of the extensors during stance has been found to have little if any detectable effect on stance phase duration[83].

In adults, the locomotor CPG is affected by a variety of descending inputs relating to voluntary control, visual guidance, and the integration of the locomotor pattern with postural demands. These descending inputs may contribute to the timing of the stance phase and so reduce any apparent effects of an isolated source of somatosensory afference. In short, in the intact animal or person, a variety of different signals are likely to contribute to stance phase duration and the timing of the stance-to-swing transition; any one signal will make a relatively smaller contribution when it acts in concert with several other signals, and so its effects will be more difficult to observe in an experiment. When these other signals are reduced in number – as in the case of the spinal or decerebrate cat – the effects of any that remain should be relatively greater and easier to observe. Thus, the absence of detectable effects of somatosensory afferents on stance phase duration or stance-to-swing transitions does not mean that these signals make no contribution to stance phase timing. They may make a contribution, but one that is relatively minor when taken in the context of other factors. There is some evidence to support this idea from studies of stepping in human infants.

As mentioned in section 8.3.13, some descending pathways in the young infant are incompletely developed, permitting spinal mechanisms to act somewhat more autonomously in infants than in adults. Studies of infants less than a year old have shown that both limb loading and hip position provide sensory signals that can affect stance phase duration and the stance-to-swing transition in a manner very similar to that observed in spinal and decerebrate cats[84]. These results provide evidence that the neural machinery needed for somatosensory signals to affect the stance phase and onset of swing phase develops early in human beings, without the need for locomotor experience. The neural circuits are therefore likely to be present in adults, but their contribution to locomotor pattern generation is difficult to detect in adults given the other factors that also contribute.

8.4.4 Somatosensory afference affects the force developed for propulsion and load bearing

Effective locomotion requires that an animal develop sufficient propulsive force to move itself forwards and to maintain speed. More force needs to be applied to the ground to maintain speed when an animal goes uphill. Similarly, more force needs to be applied when the ground is spongy than when it is hard. Afferent signals can assist in the development of appropriate propulsive force by automatically adjusting extensor muscle activity as the terrain changes.

The connections made by GTO afferents with the CPG module circuitry shown in Figure 8.34 permit activity evoked in GTOs to increase extensor muscle activity, and so contribute to the development of propulsive force. Consider a cat walking on an incline, as shown in Figure 8.36. There are two relevant differences between this situation and walking on a horizontal surface. First, due to the line of action of the weight force relative to the cat's body, the maximum load on the stance legs occurs at a greater angle of hip extension than when the cat is walking on a level surface. Second, the hind legs of the cat must support more of the body's weight than the forelegs. This follows from the fact that the weight of the body acts vertically downwards at the cat's center of gravity, as shown in the figure. A result of the first of these differences is that peak activity in GTO afferents associated with the extensor muscles will occur at greater hip extension angles when walking uphill. Given the circuitry of Figure 8.34, the result will be a delay in the stance-to-swing transition and hence an extended stance phase. Thus, if the level of descending drive to the CPG remains constant, a cat will tend to walk more slowly uphill than on the level. The second difference means that when a cat walks uphill, the GTO organs in the extensor tendons of the rear stance leg are more strongly stimulated than those of the front stance leg, due to the greater load on the rear leg[85]. In the circuit of Figure 8.34, the effect of increased GTO activity in hind leg extensor tendons is that the extensor muscles develop more force. Thus, the GTO afferent connectivity helps ensure that the stance limbs develop sufficient force. This shows that afferent activity not only contributes to the timing of muscle activation during locomotion (section 8.3.2) but also to its amplitude.

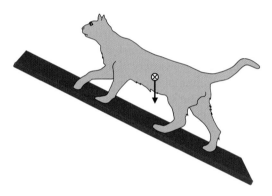

Figure 8.36: *Cat walking up an incline (⊗ = center of gravity).*

8.4.5 A stumbling corrective reaction occurs in response to mechanical stimulation produced by contact with obstacles

In natural environments, the ground over which we and other animals walk and run is often strewn with potential obstacles: small ones such as stones, twigs and branches, as well as larger ones like stumps and boulders. The smaller ones often go unnoticed until the foot or lower part of the leg collides with one, causing a trip or stumble. Such a contact has the potential to disrupt the locomotor step cycle and even to throw a person to the ground, so it is not surprising to find that there are reflexes that act to prevent this. The responses are known as **stumbling corrective reactions**[86].

One such reaction occurs during the swing phase of locomotion if the swing leg makes contact with a small obstacle. Consider the cat in Figure 8.37: it is walking along and there is a small obstruction in its path. If the cat does not see it, the left foreleg may collide with it during a swing phase of the locomotor cycle. The contact is likely to occur on the top of the paw or on the front of the lower leg. Such a contact stimulates cutaneous mechanoreceptors and elicits a flexor withdrawal type of response that lifts the foot up and over the obstacle. This is a stumbling corrective reaction, and can be considered to be a kind of withdrawal reflex response. However, the eliciting stimulus does not need to be aversive – a light touch is enough; even a puff of air can elicit the response from a cat.

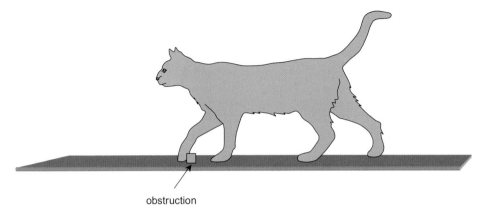

obstruction

Figure 8.37: *Walking cat approaching a small obstruction in the path of its left legs.*

An important feature of the stumbling corrective reflex is that it is subject to phase-dependent modulation during the step cycle. The response can be elicited during the swing phase, but if an identical stimulus is delivered to the same location of the foot or leg during the stance phase, no flexor withdrawal response is elicited. Indeed, a flexor withdrawal response to a stimulus applied to the top of the foot is essentially impossible in the stance phase – flexing the limb cannot withdraw the foot from the stimulus; it would only serve to move the foot into it. A stimulus applied to the top of the foot in the stance phase tends to enhance extensor activity in the stimulated leg, which is more or less the opposite of its effect in the swing phase. This is an example of the phenomenon of **reflex reversal**: a stimulus elicits one response in one context but the opposite response in another context. In the stumbling corrective withdrawal reflex, when the stimulus is applied during the swing phase, a flexor withdrawal response is elicited; when applied during the stance phase, an extensor response is elicited. Due to the fact that the context is defined by the different phases of locomotion, this phenomenon is called **phase-dependent reflex reversal**.

The stumbling corrective withdrawal reflex and its phase-dependent reversal can be observed in spinal cats, demonstrating that the neural mechanisms involved are located within the spinal cord. These mechanisms are discussed further in section 8.4.7; in the next section we consider phenomena in human walking similar to those described in the cat.

8.4.6 Stumbling corrective reactions are observed in human walking

It can be argued that avoiding tripping over obstacles is more important for a person walking on two legs than it is for an animal on four legs, because trips are much more likely to result in serious falls. Thus, we might expect to see withdrawal reactions in human walking that lift the stimulated foot up and over small obstacles, similar to those described in the last section. In one study, contact with an obstacle was produced by dropping a flat block onto the treadmill that experimental participants walked on[87]. The block obstructed the path of the left foot during the swing phase of the step cycle, as indicated in Figure 8.38. The drops could not be anticipated by participants, who only became aware of the object when they made contact with it with their foot. Although contact was restricted to the swing phase, the response elicited depended on when in swing it occurred. If contact occurred early in the swing phase, a flexor withdrawal type response was elicited: participants lifted their left foot up and over the obstacle. If contact occurred late in the swing phase, a quite different response was elicited: the foot would be rapidly put down on the treadmill belt (ground) so terminating the swing phase slightly early[88] (a placing response). The foot would then be brought over the obstacle on the next stride. If contact occurred in mid swing, the flexor withdrawal response was often elicited, but sometimes the placing response was elicited, which suggests that as the swing phase progresses, elicitation of the placing response becomes increasingly likely. Thus, there is an effective reversal of the response to the obstacle in later compared to early swing: lifting the foot early in swing, placing it down late in swing.

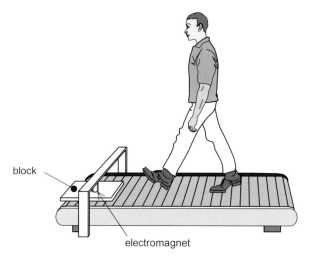

Figure 8.38: *Experimental apparatus for studying human responses to unexpected obstructions during locomotion. The obstacle (block) is held by an electromagnet; when the current to the magnet is turned off, the block falls onto the treadmill. (Based on Schillings, Van Wezel, Duysens, 1996.)*

Using real obstacles makes it difficult to precisely control the actual stimulation received, and difficult to study the effects of stimulation applied during the stance phase or to the sole of the foot. Using non-aversive electrical stimulation of nerves or skin can avoid these difficulties. The disadvantage of electrical stimulation is that it cannot reproduce the natural stimulation that occurs as a result of contact with a real object. Fortunately, in the cases where comparisons can be made, results obtained using electrical stimulation of the nerves do not appear to differ greatly from those obtained from direct contact with obstacles.

Different regions of the skin of the feet are innervated by various nerves, as shown in Figure 8.39. The plantar surface (sole) of the foot is primarily innervated by three branches of the posterior tibial nerve: the calcaneal branch, and the medial and lateral plantar nerves. The top of the foot is innervated by the peroneal nerve. The lateral and medial sides of the feet are innervated by the sural and saphenous nerves respectively. Brief, relatively low-intensity, non-noxious electrical stimulation of the superficial peroneal, tibial and sural nerves have been used in studies of reflex effects during human locomotion[89]. These stimuli produce feelings of brief pressure and tingling in the associated areas of the foot. We will consider stimulation of the superficial peroneal and tibial nerves in what follows. The major effects of stimulation are confined to the swing phase and stance-to-swing transition, with little effect during the stance phase; for this reason, we concentrate on swing and transition phases of the locomotor cycle.

Non-noxious electrical stimulation of the superficial peroneal nerve mimics mechanical stimulation of the top of the foot, and has been found to elicit responses similar to those obtained from studies using real obstacles[90]. A stimulus applied in the early to middle swing phase elicits a withdrawal type response in the stimulated limb that involves suppression of ankle dorsiflexion and an increased flexion of the knee. If the stimulus had resulted from actual object contact, these responses would have served to avoid tripping: increased knee flexion would lift the foot over an obstacle, while suppressing dorsiflexion allows the foot to passively plantarflex in response to mechanical obstruction.

Non-noxious stimulation of the posterior tibial nerve mimics cutaneous stimulation of the sole of the foot[91]. When applied at the stance-to-swing transition, the stimulus evokes an ankle dorsiflexion response, which would have the effect of moving the foot away from the source of a proximal mechanical stimulus. When the stimulus was applied during the swing phase, it continued to enhance ankle dorsiflexor muscle activity, and also knee flexor activity to some

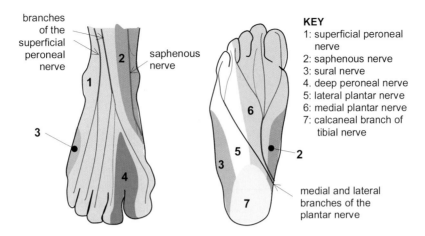

Figure 8.39: *Regions of the skin of the foot innervated by various nerves.*

extent. However, towards the end of the swing phase, the effect of the stimulus switched from dorsiflexion of the ankle to plantarflexion. The reason for this reflex reversal is probably that a non-noxious stimulus to the sole of the foot towards the end of the swing typically signals contact with the ground surface. In this situation, the appropriate response is to place the foot down so as to secure a firm contact with the ground, ready to take the weight of the body.

In summary, the results from human experiments using both real obstacles and non-noxious electrical stimuli produce results consistent with earlier experiments with cats. Cutaneous stimulation of the top (dorsum) of the foot in early to mid swing elicits a withdrawal response that tends to move the foot up and away from its location at the moment of stimulation. Stimulation later in swing can elicit a placing response (foot down), the opposite of withdrawal – an example of reflex reversal. Similarly functional effects have been observed in response to tibial nerve stimulation that mimics contacts of objects with the sole of the foot.

8.4.7 Phase dependent signals from the CPG modulate reflex excitability during locomotion

Stumbling corrective withdrawal reflexes are observed in spinal cats, showing that in these animals the mechanisms involved are located within the spinal cord. Phase dependent reflex modulation is also observed in spinal cats, showing that the modulation is also spinally mediated. There are two possible mechanisms that might be responsible: (1) the reflex pathways could be modulated by afferent signals generated by movement and muscle force development; (2) the pathways could be modulated by signals produced by the CPG modules. If the latter is the case, then reflex modulation effects should be observable during fictive locomotion. Recall from section 8.3.4 that the term *fictive locomotion* refers to the pattern of activity in the motor nerves produced when an animal's CPG is activated but the animal is paralyzed and no movement (or muscle activation) is possible. Cutaneous stimuli can be applied during different phases of the fictive locomotor cycle, and the effects show similar modulation to that observed during normal locomotion, including reflex reversal[92].

In the cat, the stumbling corrective withdrawal response evoked by cutaneous stimulation of the top of the foot involves disynaptic and trisynaptic pathways to the ipsilateral flexor motorneurons[93]. A diagram showing the excitatory components of proposed pathways mediating stumbling corrective withdrawal are shown in Figure 8.40[94]. The CPG module for the leg is shown as a yin-yang symbol. During the swing phase of locomotion, the CPG output is from the flexor rhythm generating component of the module (green). CPG output signals excite the flexor motorneurons of the leg and also a population of interneurons in the withdrawal reflex pathway. This excitation of the reflex pathway lowers its threshold, allowing flexor withdrawal responses to be elicited during the swing phase by non-noxious stimulation of the top of the foot. Such stimulation cannot evoke a response in the absence of additional excitation from the CPG.

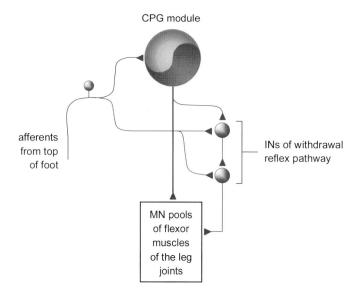

Figure 8.40: *Part of the spinal circuitry believed to underlie the stumbling corrective reaction.*

The circuit in Figure 8.40 can account for reflex reversal in a straightforward manner. During swing, the withdrawal reflex pathway involving non-nociceptive afferents from the top of the foot is potentiated, and so a cutaneous stimulus can elicit a withdrawal response. The effect of CPG module excitation by cutaneous afferent signals enhances flexion. During stance, the reflex pathway is not potentiated (there is no excitation from the extensor rhythm generator), and non-nociceptive cutaneous stimulation is unable to elicit withdrawal. The effect of CPG module excitation by cutaneous afferent signals is to enhance extension, the opposite response to that evoked in the swing phase. The simple type of spinal circuit shown in Figure 8.40 may be involved in the phasic modulation of stumbling corrective reflexes in human beings, but it is unlikely to be the only mechanism, as there is strong evidence in humans for the involvement of transcortical pathways[95].

References & Notes

[1] Digitigrade locomotion is often subdivided into two types: digitigrade proper, in which the animal walks on the whole digit (as in human tip-toe), and unguligrade, in which the animal walks only on the end of its digits (true tip-toe, as in ballet).

[2] See Inman, Ralston, Todd (1981).

[3] Huxham *et al.* (2006).

[4] See Enoka (2008).

[5] See Ivanenko, Poppele, Lacquaniti (2004); Cappellini *et al.* (2006).

[6] Winter, Yack (1987).

[7] See Zajac, Neptune, Kautz (2002, 2003).

[8] E.g., Enoka (2008), Winter (2009).

[9] See Anderson, Pandy (2001).

[10] See Alexander, Jayes (1980).

[11] Weber, Weber (1836).

[12] Basmajian (1976).

[13] See McMahon (1984).

[14] Kuo (2007).

[15] Kuo (2007); Kuo, Donelan (2009); McGeer (1992).

[16] Alexander (1984).

[17] $g = a_c = v^2/L$. Therefore, $g \times L = v^2$, and so $v = \sqrt{(g \times L)}$.

[18] Griffin, Tolani, Kram (1999).

[19] McGeer (1990).

[20] E.g., Collins *et al.* (2005).

[21] Collins, Wisse, Ruina (2001).

[22] McGeer (1992).

[23] McGeer (1993); Collins *et al.* (2005).

[24] Kuo (2002).

[25] Collins *et al.* (2005).

[26] Indirect tests have the advantage that they can find the energetically optimal gait at any speed without the need for extensive and elaborate empirical tests. For an interesting example see Srinivasan, Ruina (2006).

[27] E.g., Brockway (1987).

[28] Alexander (2002).

[29] Zarrugh, Radcliffe (1978).

[30] Donelan, Kram, Kuo (2001).

[31] Inman, Ralston, Todd (1981).

[32] See Kuo (2007); Kuo, Donelan (2009).

[33] Hoyt, Taylor (1981).

[34] Carrier (1984); Bramble, Lieberman (2004).

[35] Craig (2002); Kaufman *et al.* (2002).

[36] Marcora (2009).

[37] See Sparrow (2000).

[38] More information about Mike can be found at http://www.miketheheadlesschicken.org.

[39] Sherrington (1910).

[40] Grillner (1985).

[41] Grillner, Wallen (2002).

[42] E.g., Pearson, Rossignol (1991).

[43] There appears to be no generally used term for what is here called a CPG module. Grillner (1985) introduced the term 'unit CPG' to refer to networks that drive single joint-level degrees-of-freedom.

[44] Pearson (1976).

[45] Graham Brown (1911).

[46] See Kiehn (2006).

[47] Burke, Degtyarenko, Simon (2001).

[48] See McCrae, Rybak (2008).

[49] Various versions of the architecture shown in Figure 8.26 are possible, and some are more successful at accounting for the details of locomotor pattern generation than others (McCrae, Rybak, 2008).

[50] Arshavsky (2003).

[51] See Grillner (1985).

[52] See McCrae, Rybak (2008).

[53] Van Emmerick, Wagenaar, Van Wegen (1998); Zehr, Duysens (2004).

[54] See Jordan *et al.* (2008).

[55] See Whelan (1996).

[56] For the difficulties involved in giving a precise anatomical definition for the MLR, see Whelan (1996).

[57] Shik, Severin, Orlovsky (1966).

[58] Mori (1987).

[59] Masdeu *et al.* (1994); Hanna, Frank (1995).

[60] See Whelan (1996).

[61] See Takakusaki (2008).

[62] Grillner *et al.* (2005).

[63] See Roberts *et al.* (2008).

[64] For a review of the comparative neurobiology of locomotion see Stuart (2007).

[65] E.g., Shik, Severin, Orlovsky (1966).

[66] Orlovsky (1991).

[67] De Leon *et al.* (1999b).

[68] See Orlovsky (1991); Armstrong (1988).

[69] De Leon *et al.* (1999a).

[70] Harkema (2008).

[71] See Barbeau, Rossignol (1987).

[72] See Fouad, Pearson (2004); Harkema (2008).

[73] See Harkema (2008).

[74] See Gerasimenko, Roy, Edgerton (2008).

[75] Yakolev, Lecours (1967).

[76] Yang, Lamont, Pang (2005).

[77] See Pearson (2008).

[78] See Rossignol, Dubuc, Gossard (2006); Pearson (2008).

[79] See Rossignol, Dubuc, Gossard (2006).

[80] Grillner, Rossignol (1978).

[81] Kulagin, Shik (1970); Forssberg *et al.* (1980).

[82] See Pearson (2008).

[83] Stephens, Yang (1999).

[84] Pang, Yang (2000).

[85] Muscle activations during uphill and downhill walking differ in a number of respects from those observed for walking on the level (Pearson, 2000).

[86] Forssberg (1979).

[87] Schillings *et al.* (2000).

[88] Similar results using a slightly different type of obstruction protocol were reported in Eng, Winter and Patla (1994).

[89] See Rossignol, Dubuc, Gossard (2006); Zehr, Stein (1999).

[90] Zehr, Komiyama, Stein (1997).

[91] Electrical stimulation of the tibial nerve is also likely to evoke responses in muscle afferents, and as a consequence is not such a good mimic of cutaneous stimulation as electrical stimuli applied to either the superficial peroneal or the sural nerve. The latter mimics contact with the side of the foot (Zehr, Stein, 1999).

[92] See Rossignol, Dubuc, Gossard (2006).

[93] Quevedo, Katinka, McCrea (2005).

[94] See Quevedo, Katinka, McCrea (2005), Figure 8, page 2061.

[95] See Christensen *et al.* (2000).

CHAPTER 9

Getting Around: Visual Control of Locomotor Maneuvers

9.1 The Importance of Vision for Locomotion on Legs

9.1.1 Introduction: five roles for vision in the guidance of locomotion

Getting around in the world on legs involves steering along paths or towards specific locations, negotiating obstacles, adjusting to different surfaces and making changes in speed. These things are often achieved by making the necessary adjustments and maneuvers in an *anticipatory* fashion: we don't wait until we've made contact with an obstacle before stepping over it, and we don't wait until we've veered off the path before steering around a bend. In order to act in an anticipatory fashion, we need to be able to perceive the upcoming obstacle, bend or change in the surface. People normally do this using vision[1]: we look where we are going; we assess the ground ahead for obstacles, ledges, loose footings, curves and hills; and we use visual information to prepare and/or make appropriate adjustments and maneuvers. Five different roles for vision in the guidance of locomotion can be identified:

(1) **Detection** of hazards. Are there obstacles in the way? Is there a bend in the path?
(2) **Deciding** what maneuver to make. Visual perception can provide a basis for deciding what course of action to take.
(3) **Preparation** of a maneuver: determining how a maneuver will be executed; for example, determining how high the foot will be lifted when stepping over an obstacle, or how much thrust will be developed when jumping over a hurdle.
(4) **Initiation** of maneuvers: starting a maneuver at the right moment in time.
(5) **Adjustment** of the execution of maneuvers. If the maneuver is not achieving the desired outcome, this can be determined and corrective adjustments can be made.

Clearly, vision plays a crucial part in the guidance of locomotion. This suggests that it is important to look in the right places and at the right times to obtain the information needed for the five roles listed above. In this part of the chapter, we will consider where, when and for how long people look when negotiating their way through the environment. In subsequent parts, we will look at how people deal with different hazards, how decisions are made regarding what action to take, and what information is used.

9.1.2 People tend to look where they are going

The impression from everyday experience is that we look where we are going and scan the ground ahead for obstacles and other hazards when walking and running. If a person fixes their gaze on a particular location in a scene, then it is reasonable to infer that they did so in order to obtain some detailed information about the object or surface at that location. However, it is not possible to determine what that information is simply from the direction of gaze: what a person is looking at can only allow informed guesses concerning what information a person might be using. Nevertheless, knowing where people look and when they look provides a useful basis for understanding what it is important to see in order to guide locomotion.

In recent years, it has been possible to study where people look using head-mounted, lightweight, video-based eye-tracking equipment that allows the wearer to move about freely. The data obtained provides information about where in a scene a person's gaze is fixated, and for how long fixations last. Typical equipment is capable of measuring gaze direction to within about ±1°, and the duration of fixations can be estimated to within the time of one video frame (typically 33.33 ms)[2]. The spatial accuracy is good enough to tell you what a person is looking at, provided the thing is not too small or too far away: a 10-cm-wide object at a distance of 10 meters subtends a visual angle of just over ½°, so the measurements would be too imprecise to be certain whether or not a person was looking at that object.

Using this type of gaze-tracking equipment, it has been found that for the majority of the time, people's gaze points in the direction of travel as they walk along. If there are hazards such as obstacles, people tend to look at them before reaching them. For example, when walking along and stepping over a low obstacle (1, 15 or 30 cm tall), people were found to look at the obstacle as they approached it, but they made a few intermittent fixations rather than looking at it continuously[3] (see Figure 9.1 for a view of the layout in which people walked). Most fixations were made two or more steps before reaching the obstacle (during or before the step labeled 'step over minus 2' in Figure 9.1), and people never looked at the obstacle while actually stepping over it. It has been shown in other studies that seeing an obstacle only one or two steps in advance is sufficient for successful clearance of the obstacle[4].

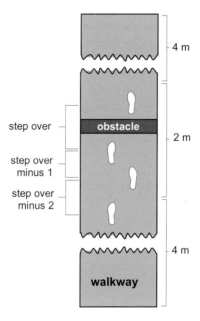

Figure 9.1: *Layout of an experiment reported by Patla and Vickers (1997).*

When walking over smooth, flat ground with few hazards, people gaze more or less straight ahead in the direction they are moving for much of the time[5], unless they have some specific reason for looking elsewhere. Given that people look at the ground when there are obstacles or hazards, and look more or less straight ahead when the ground is clear, we would expect that the number of fixations of the ground immediately ahead would increase as the number of potential hazards increases. This expectation has been confirmed in empirical studies. One study has looked at gaze behavior when people walk over a region of rough terrain composed of several uneven, lumpy, slippery and spongy areas[6]. The results showed that people looked much more often at this area of rough terrain than anywhere else (over 90% of all the fixations recorded were on this region). Participants would fixate on one location in the region and then on another, with most fixations lasting less than 400 ms. Many fixations were of a location that was subsequently stepped on; locations that participants preferred to avoid stepping on were seldom fixated. This suggests that a person quickly decides on a route through a rough region and then fixates upcoming locations on this route to guide him- or herself along it. As we will see in part 2 of the chapter, visual guidance of foot placement is important when walking or running over rough terrain.

9.1.3 People look ahead when turning

Everyday experience tells us that we look in the direction we are going not only when walking in a straight line, but also when walking or running along curved paths and when turning corners; empirical studies have confirmed this impression and provided quantitative detail[7].

The direction a person or an animal is going at any given moment of time is their **instantaneous heading direction**[8], often just called **heading**:

> **INSTANTANEOUS HEADING DIRECTION (HEADING):** The direction in which the body as a whole (indexed, for example, by the center of mass) is moving at a particular instant of time. The direction is measured with respect to a reference direction fixed with respect to the environment.

Any convenient reference direction could be used; obvious ones are the compass directions, which are clearly fixed (do not rotate) with respect to the environment.

Figure 9.2 shows the path that a person's center of gravity (CoG) might take as they walk a curved trajectory (viewed from above). In this figure, the heading at a point in time is the direction of the velocity vector at a point on the path. Four such vectors are shown as arrows, together with the position of the CoG (⊗). The heading at each point is the direction of the arrow. It is clear that the heading is changing continuously from moment to moment as the person walks along the curved path.

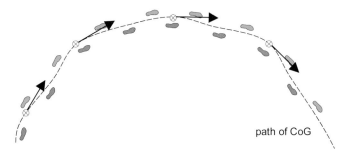

Figure 9.2: *Path of the CoG (⊗) while walking a curved path (dashed line). Arrows represent the velocity of the CoG, and the foot symbols represent footfall locations.*

When walking or running along curved paths, people tend to direct their gaze in the plane of the upcoming heading direction. In other words, people look in the direction they are about to turn, slightly before actually changing direction: gaze direction changes in anticipation of a change in the direction of locomotion. That people do this should come as no surprise – we need to see what is coming up. There are two basic situations that can be considered. First, the person makes a turn from one straight path to another. Second, the person follows a curved pathway. We will consider each of these.

(1)   **Making a turn to go in a new direction.** The person is initially progressing in one direction and then changes to another, new direction. When undertaking such a maneuver, people have been found to look in the new direction slightly in advance of actually making the turn. In one study[9], participants were required to turn to a new direction either 30° or 60° left or right of their initial direction of locomotion. The directions were marked by lines on the ground, and on the ground at the end of each pathway was a small light, as shown in Figure 9.3. The light was used to indicate to the participants which of the five possible routes they should take. In one condition, a light was illuminated from the start, and so the participant knew well in advance where they were required to go (advance knowledge condition). In the other condition, the participant did not know which of the five paths to take until they stepped on a pressure-sensitive mat which caused one of the lights to come on (cued condition). The mat was one step in front of the branch point, so that in the cued condition, participants had one stride to prepare and execute a change of direction. In fact, people made the direction change in one stride in both conditions.

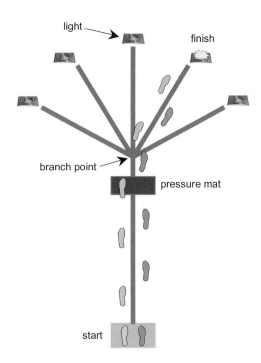

Figure 9.3: *Experimental layout used in a study by Hollands, Vickers, Patla (2002).*

People's gaze behavior was similar in the two conditions: during approach to the branch point people would fixate most of the time (about 70%) on environmental features that lay on or close to their heading direction, such as the pressure mat and the branch point. The rest of the time was largely spent either fixating possible future directions (in the cued condition), the known future direction (in the advance knowledge condition), or random points in the room. Prior to making the turn, people made a saccade to the new heading direction (usually to the light at the finish location), and almost simultaneously turned their heads so that they faced in the direction of the finish location (head reorientation tended to start about 20 ms later than the saccade).

(2)   **Following a curved path.** One study examined people's head and eye movements when they walked a path like that shown in panel A of Figure 9.4[10]. Two different curves were used: a sharp curve of radius 0.5 m, and a shallower curve of radius 2 m. It was found that as people walked the curved paths, their head and eyes moved so that they always looked ahead. The head moved smoothly, such that at each moment of time the person was facing slightly ahead (up to 25° ahead) of their heading direction. In contrast, the eyes moved saccadically, making a succession of brief fixations as the person walked round the curve. This behavior is illustrated in panel B of Figure 9.4 for the shallower curve. Head direction and gaze direction are plotted as a function of time from the first footfall to the last footfall (as indicated at the bottom of the graph). The head direction curve changes smoothly, whereas the gaze direction curve is stepped: each downward stroke in the stepped pattern corresponds to a saccade, and each horizontal stroke to a fixation. The eyes saccade successively to fixate points further ahead, and the head is always lagging behind. The head catches up with the eyes when the person has negotiated the bend and is walking along the final straight segment.

In the set-up shown in Figure 9.4, the person made three or three-and-a-half strides and about ten saccades. When the radius of the curve was 0.5 m, participants made 1.5 or so strides and two or three saccades[11]. Thus, the number of saccades increases the longer the curved path traversed. This is consistent with the results of the study described in the last section that employed the task shown in Figure 9.3, where there is no curved path as such. In this task, participants changed direction in just one stride, and typically made only one saccade.

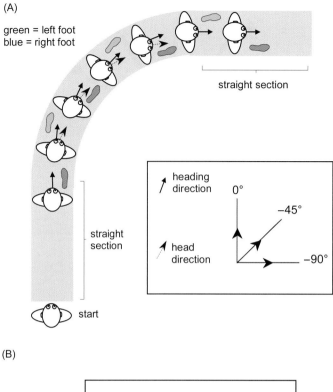

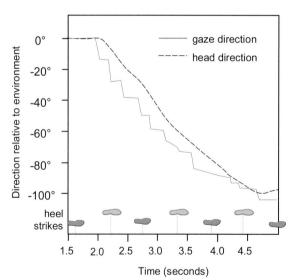

Figure 9.4: *Experimental layout (A) and results (B) from a study by Imai* et al. *(2001, data from Figure 6E).*

9.1.4 Continuous vision is not needed during locomotion

The results described in the previous section show that people look where they are going almost continuously, and spend relatively little time looking elsewhere. This does not mean, however, that continuous vision is required for the guidance of locomotion. It is easy to verify that continuous vision is not necessary: try walking along and closing your eyes. You will probably feel quite comfortable walking blind for several seconds, even if you need to turn a corner or avoid an obstacle.

The ability to prepare maneuvers in advance means that they can be executed without the need for continuous guidance by vision, so short periods without vision might be expected not to disrupt locomotion. The ability to go without visual guidance for short periods also means that vision can be intermittently used for other purposes, such as keeping an eye out for opponents or the ball in a game of soccer, reading road signs, reading a map and so on. People's ability to walk without continuous vision has been investigated in several studies in which participants were required to walk blind for some period of time – the **blind walking experimental protocol**. In the first systematic series of studies using this protocol, participants were required to walk a short obstacle course while blindfolded[12]. The course was nine meters from start to finish and contained up to a maximum of four obstacles, and participants were required to avoiding contacting them. Figure 9.5 shows the layout of a four-obstacle course; the dashed line shows the type of path that might be taken through the obstacles. At the start of an experimental trial, participants looked at the layout of the course; then they would be blindfolded and immediately attempt to walk to the end. They were able to successfully reach the end without contacting an obstacle on 70% of trials, and the number of obstacles did not significantly affect performance. Later studies have repeatedly confirmed that people are able to accurately negotiate obstacles and walk curved paths without visual guidance, provided that they can get information in advance[13].

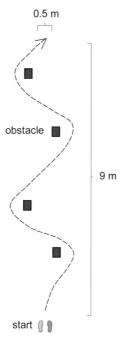

Figure 9.5: *Layout of obstacle course. Participants walk blindfolded from the start to the end of the course. A possible path is shown dashed.*

The nine meter distance between the start and finish of the walk is significant: it was found that people could walk blindfolded for up to eight or nine meters before becoming disoriented. This was shown quite clearly in experiments where people were asked to walk blindfolded to specific locations in the absence of any obstacles[14]. The locations were marked by visible targets on the floor. Participants viewed the scene from a standing start position for a few seconds, they then closed their eyes and immediately attempted to walk to a position alongside the target and stop. The graph in panel B of Figure 9.6 plots the results. The graph shows the average distance errors (circles) and the standard deviations (error bars) at each of seven target distances (mean of a group of participants). The distance error is the signed distance between the location of a mark on the foot and the target center when the person stopped, as indicated in panel A of Figure 9.6. The average distance error at each distance is quite small, indicating little tendency to overshoot or undershoot the target. At target distances of 9 m or less, the standard deviations were relatively small[15] (about 0.2 m). When the distance was greater than 9 m, the standard deviations increased nearly tenfold (to about 2 m). This dramatic increase in standard deviation indicates that participants lost track of where they were beyond about 9 m. Further investigation revealed that it is not the actual distance traveled that is responsible for the increased error; rather it is the time that elapses between loss of vision and stopping at the estimated target location (see next section).

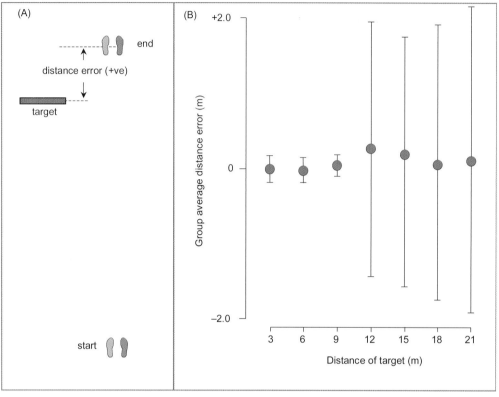

Figure 9.6: *Layout (A) and results (B) from a blind-walking experiment. Data in (B) from Figure 1A of Thomson (1983).*

Another type of experiment demonstrating that continuous vision is not needed for loco-motion involves participants voluntarily deciding when and for how long they need to look where they are going and at what is going on around them – the **visual sampling experimental protocol**[16]. This protocol resembles walking along while reading a newspaper: the person's vision is taken up with reading for much of the time, but they can look up and scan the scene ahead whenever they feel the need to. In experimental studies, experimental participants wear liquid crystal spectacles that can either be in an opaque state, in which the surroundings cannot be seen, or a transparent state. The spectacles can be switched between opaque and transparent by pressing a button. Participants hold the button in their hand and press it when they feel the need to view (visually sample) their surroundings; the spectacles remain transparent for as long as the button was pressed.

Studies using the visual sampling protocol found that people intermittently pressed the button so that they had periodic, brief views of their surroundings (visual samples) as they walked[17]. When there were no hazards or requirements to place a foot on a particular spot, the scene was visually sampled for only about 10% of the total time spent walking; the individual samples averaged between about 0.2 and 0.5 seconds, and so several seconds might elapse between one sample and the next. When there were hazards, or when the feet were required to be placed on particular spots, the time the scene was viewed increased to as much as 40% of the total time spent walking. All participants were found to increase the viewing time by increasing the number of samples; some participants also increased the duration of the samples.

The results described in this section clearly show that continuous viewing is not necessary in a variety of different locomotor tasks. These include walking to a visually specified location, stepping around or over obstacles, turning corners and placing the feet on visually defined locations. In these situations, people are able to perform adequately when vision is restricted to brief periods that occur in advance of performing the task or maneuver. This suggests that the visual information obtained during these periods is stored in some form and is subsequently used for control during performance of the task. We examine what form this storage might take in the next section.

9.1.5 Locomotion without continuous visual guidance implies a role for memory

In the previous section we discussed two situations in which visual information obtained in advance is used to subsequently guide locomotion when vision is prevented: the blind walking and visual sampling experimental protocols. The findings from both these protocols suggest that people are using some sort of memory of what they saw to determine what they should do during the subsequent blind period. Here we will briefly consider what types of memory are involved.

In the visual sampling protocol, when people stepped over an obstacle, they took a visual sample prior to doing so, but stepped over it blind. This is consistent with the results for gaze fixation studies described in section 9.1.2: people fixated an obstacle one or two steps in advance of reaching it, but looked elsewhere when actually stepping over it. The results suggest that we do not need to use vision to continuously guide the movements of the feet as they clear an obstacle. Instead, it appears that information obtained in advance is used to ensure that feet move appropriately for stepping over the obstacle. It has been proposed that visual information is used to prepare the steps appropriately for clearing the obstacle[18]. This preparation involves setting up a process that generates central commands for regulating the activity of the locomotor CPG so that the steps are long enough and high enough for the feet to clear the obstacle. A process of this sort is typically referred to as a **motor program**. This term must not be interpreted as meaning that the central commands exist in some stored form prior to being issued, or that their effects cannot be modified by sensory feedback. More appropriate conceptions of motor programs will be presented in Chapter 11. For present purposes, it is enough to be aware that the program embodies a working memory of the task-relevant visual information. This is not memory in the everyday sense, as it cannot be recalled in the way that a person's name can be recalled; rather, it is a kind of **procedural memory** that can only be demonstrated by actually executing the maneuver (see Chapter 14).

In the blind walking protocol, a person typically walks without vision for much longer than in the visual sampling protocol. It is possible that a program is prepared in advance based on the initial view of the scene, in a similar way to the program for stepping over an obstacle. However, there are other alternatives that can be proposed. For example, in the task where people look at a target on the ground some distance away and then walk blind to it and stop, it might be possible to estimate how many steps are needed to reach the target, and then count the steps during the walk and stop once the required number has been reached. In this case there is an explicit kind of memory of the distance: the person explicitly retains a memory of how many steps they thought would be required. However, this suggestion seems implausible given the sudden drop-off in precision that starts at 9 meters in Figure 9.6: why should a person's ability to walk accurately suddenly decline from about 9 m if a step-counting strategy were being used? A more plausible possibility is that the person forms a kind of visuo-spatial memory or mental image in which task-relevant features of the scene are represented. In effect, the person is obtaining information about the scene not by looking at the scene itself, but by consulting a memory of it – consulting the memory is analogous to looking at the scene[19]. This possibility seems intuitive: if you look around for a while and then close your eyes, you feel you know where things are and that you could walk to a specific location or guide yourself around for short periods based on a visuo-spatial memory.

Note that the existence of a visuo-spatial memory is not incompatible with the existence of a program. It is possible that people prepare a program for the whole walk in advance and also form a visual memory that can be used as a basis for making adjustments and corrections. The characteristics of the memory processes involved in blind walking are discussed next.

9.1.6 The memory is short term and has limited capacity

The increase in variable error observed for distances of 9 m or more (Figure 9.6) in target-directed blind walking tasks has been shown to be related to the time spent without vision – the **blind time** – rather than to distance as such. In the early studies it was found that if the blind time was less than 8 seconds, then the error was similar to that observed when full vision was available[20], regardless of the distance. For example, if a person covered 15 meters in less than 8 seconds – by walking fast or running – their variable distance error was about 20 cm, but if they walked normally and took longer than 8 seconds, the error was substantially greater. Conversely, when walking to a target 6 to 9 meters away, if a person delayed the start of their walk so that the blind time exceeded 8 seconds, the variable error was typically over 1 meter, whereas without the delay the error was less than 20 cm.

These results suggest that the memory involved in blind-walking tasks persists with negligible loss for about 8 seconds and then decays very rapidly. It seems rather strange that a loss of memory should occur so suddenly. There was another curious feature of the results: when distances less than 6 meters were studied, it was found that there was negligible drop-off in precision for blind times greater than 8 seconds (at least up to 12 or 13 seconds, which was as far as the study went[21]). This suggests that for distances of 6 meters or more, the visuo-spatial memory being used lasted about 8 seconds before decaying rapidly; for shorter distances, it lasted significantly longer, but for exactly how long is unclear.

It would be possible to speculate about why there is a rapid loss of memory after 8 seconds for distances of 6 meters or more, but not for shorter distances. For example, it might be that for short distances it is possible to prepare a program for the whole walk, whereas for longer distances this is not possible, and the person relies instead on a visuo-spatial memory[22]. However, before we get too carried away inventing explanations for these results, it is important to ask whether or not the data are sufficient to draw firm conclusions about the characteristics of the memory processes involved. Later studies suggest that the original data are not sufficient, since the precipitous decline in performance starting at about 8 seconds has not always been replicated[23]. Performance does decline, but there is evidence of decline prior to 8 seconds and of continuing decline long after 8 seconds[24]. One study that showed such an effect examined directional errors in blind walking. Participants were required to walk blind along a straight, narrow walkway (34.2 cm wide, 10 meters long)[25]. Participants stood and viewed the walkway for 10 seconds from the start position; vision was then occluded, and the participants remained standing for a period of time between 2 and 128 seconds (delay period) before starting to walk. Performance was quantified in terms of the distance traveled along the walkway without crossing the boundary on either side. The results are plotted in Figure 9.7, and show that there is a steady decline in the distance walked within the boundaries of the walkway as the delay period increased. There was no evidence for a sudden loss of orientation after 8 seconds.

Finally, the evidence suggests that the short-term memory involved in blind walking has limited capacity. As described earlier, people were found to be capable of walking blind through an obstacle course containing up to four obstacles (as in Figure 9.5). A capacity of up to four objects seems to be a general characteristic of visuo-spatial short-term memory and of short-term memory for other types of information[26]. It is possible to retain an accurate memory for the characteristics and locations of up to four objects, but when there are more than four, memory becomes progressively inaccurate. Further details can be found in the references[27].

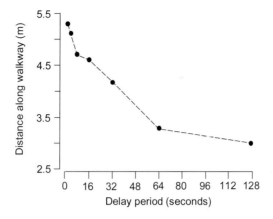

Figure 9.7: *Results from a blind walking task with initial delay periods between 2 and 128 seconds. (Data from Figure 3 of Tyrrell* et al., *1993).*

9.1.7 Continuous vision can play a role in adjusting locomotor movements

The ability to perform a maneuver without vision does not mean that when vision is present it plays no role in the control of that maneuver. As we saw in the last chapter, the basic locomotor pattern is produced by a CPG, and although the pattern can be generated in the complete absence of sensory feedback, it is normally modulated by such feedback. Somatosensory feedback is produced more or less continuously throughout the step cycle, and the evidence suggests that CPG activity is modulated by this afference. Likewise, although the step cycle can proceed without vision, when continuous vision is available it can be used to modulate movement during each stride.

What role does vision play in controlling movement during a step cycle? One role is to make adjustments to the path taken by the foot, to ensure that an obstacle is cleared or that the foot is placed in exactly the right spot. Imagine that you are trying to walk across a raging torrent by placing your feet on a series of small stepping stones. Accurate foot placement is crucial in such a situation, and it seems likely that you would keep looking at a stone right up to the moment you place your foot on it, so as to be able to adjust the path of the foot if needed. Experiments have shown that visual adjustments to the trajectory of the swing foot can improve the accuracy of foot placement[28].

Another use for continuous vision is to monitor for unexpected events or previously unnoticed hazards that could interfere with progress. If such events and hazards can be detected before collision, it may be possible to take evasive action. For example, another person or an animal might suddenly step into your path right in front of you; if you see a person step in front of you, then you may be able to take some evasive action. The ability to take evasive action depends on your having sufficient time to be able to initiate and complete the maneuver once you have detected the obstruction. As described earlier, when an obstacle or other hazard is seen early enough before it is reached, people plan an avoidance maneuver at least a step or two in advance. However, in situations when an unexpected hazard is detected within a stride of arrival, people can make some quite rapid adjustments[29] that may allow a collision to be avoided entirely or, if not, they can at least reduce the impact. This role of vision will be discussed further in section 9.2.

9.2 The Role of Vision in Guidance and Decision Making

9.2.1 Introduction

Looking where you are going allows you to see what is coming up and to prepare appropriate actions in advance. This is what people appear to do, as studies using the blind walking and visual sampling protocols demonstrate (see section 9.1.4). Planning a maneuver in advance means that a process internal to the nervous system is prepared that sends command signals to the locomotor CPG so that the maneuver is carried out appropriately. In section 9.1.5 this type of process was referred to as a *program*. Sticking with this terminology, we will say that a maneuver that is planned in advance is **pre-programmed**. This does not imply that the maneuver is normally carried out without any corrections or adjustments, like the program of a washing machine; it simply means that it is possible for the maneuver to be executed without any such corrections.

In this part of the chapter, we will examine some of the locomotor maneuvers people make in order to deal with cluttered terrain, and the role that is played by vision in both the preparation (pre-programming) and the correction/adjustment of these maneuvers. The maneuvers to be discussed are stepping over an obstacle, passing through a gap and ascending stairs.

9.2.2 Stepping over obstacles requires accurate placement and movement of the feet

Stepping or hurdling over an obstacle requires that one leg clears the obstacle first, followed by the other leg. The leg that clears the obstacle first is called the **leading leg**, and the leg that clears it second is the **trailing leg**. The size and shape of the obstacle will determine how the swing phase of each leg must be modified in order to clear it. The higher the obstacle, the higher the foot must be lifted; the 'longer' the obstacle, the greater the increase in step length needed. If the obstacle is both high and wide, the trailing knee can be flexed and raised high with the hip abducted, which is the technique adopted by hurdlers. In this section, the focus will be on stepping over relatively small obstacles while walking.

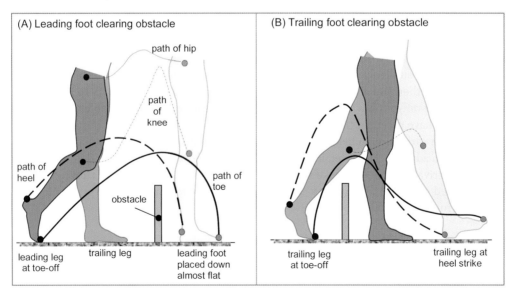

Figure 9.8: *Paths of hip, knee, heel and toe when stepping over a obstacle. Based on data reported by Patla and his colleagues (Patla, 1997).*

Panel A of Figure 9.8 shows the paths taken by the toes, heel, knee and hip of the leading leg when passing over a narrow obstacle about 30 cm high. For obstacles of this sort with heights between about 4 cm and 30 cm, the toes tend to clear the top of the obstacle by a margin of about 20 cm, irrespective of the obstacle's height[30]. This clearance is substantially greater than the maximum foot clearance over smooth, flat ground, which is typically less than 5 cm. Panel B of the figure shows the paths for the same locations on the trailing leg. The trailing foot is closer to the obstacle when the step over begins, and so the trailing foot is raised to its full clearance height more quickly than the leading foot (note the difference in the shape of the path of the toes and heel in panels A and B).

It is apparent from Figure 9.8 that the paths taken by the feet are such that a foot will clear the obstacle only if it starts from the right place. Figure 9.9 shows this explicitly for the path of the toes of the trailing foot from Figure 9.8B. In panel A of Figure 9.9, the foot is too far from the obstacle; as a result, the toes collide with the obstacle after reaching their highest point. In panel B, the foot is too close, and the toes collide with the obstacle before they reach the highest point. Thus, for a given path of the foot during the swing phase, an obstacle will only be successfully cleared if the foot is placed in the correct location prior to stepping over. This shows that stance foot placement and foot trajectory are mutually dependent determinants of successful obstacle clearance: in order for a particular foot path to clear the obstacle, the foot must start from the correct position.

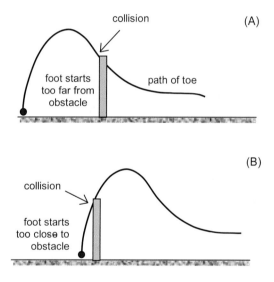

Figure 9.9: *Trailing leg toes will collide with an obstacle if the foot starts from too far away (A) or too close (B).*

Studies discussed in the first part of the chapter suggested that the stepping-over maneuver is prepared a step or two in advance, and can be executed without the need for continuous visual guidance. It was suggested that such preparation involves setting up a program that generates commands for adjusting the on-going step cycle. Such a program requires information about the height and length of the obstacle, so that the swing phase of both limbs can be adjusted so that the feet are raised high enough and the step is long enough to clear the obstacle. The height and length of the step of both the lead and trailing limbs depend on where the trailing foot is planted. This means that the location of trailing foot placement must be chosen in advance, and commands that determine the length of the step that moves the foot to the chosen location must be pre-programmed. Only vision can be used to choose such a location.

9.2.3 Two types of automatic, visually based adjustments to swing: pre-programmed reactions and feedback corrections

How does a person deal with the situation in which an obstacle suddenly appears in their path? This could happen if something falls or moves into the person's path, or if the obstacle was already there but had previously gone unnoticed. In one study, obstacles were unexpectedly placed in the path of experimental participants who were walking on a treadmill[31]. The apparatus used in the study was exactly the same as that shown in Figure 8.38 (previous chapter): an obstacle could be dropped on the treadmill in front of a participant's left foot, and to avoid it, they needed to step over it. The obstacle was a flat piece of board 40 cm long, 30 cm wide and 1.5 cm tall. The obstacle was dropped when the left leg was making the transition from stance to swing, either just before toe-off or just after toe-off. Thus, to avoid stepping on the obstacle or tripping on its edge, participants needed to adjust the step that had just started (or was just about to start).

Figure 9.10 shows a stride pattern diagram indicating the two possible times for an obstacle drop: just before and just after left toe-off (time runs from right to left across the page). The insert at the top right of the figure shows two possible adjustments that can be made to avoid the obstacle. A *long step adjustment* increases left leg step length (taking a long step) so the foot passes over the obstacle. A *short step adjustment* decreases left step length so that left heel strike is in front of the obstacle, which is then cleared by the other leg's subsequent step. Different participants had different preferences for the two types of adjustment: some only used the short step adjustment, some only used the long step adjustment, others would use both[32]. However, regardless of which adjustment was made, the latency of the first detectable change in the step made in response to the obstacle drop was about 120 milliseconds on average. It was subsequently found that people used peripheral vision to detect the obstacle drop – they did not need to look directly at the obstacle[33].

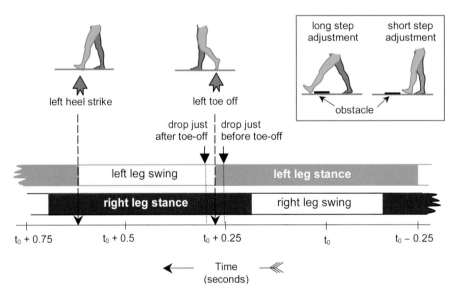

Figure 9.10: *Time line of the obstacle drop experiment, showing where in the step cycle the obstacle was dropped. Inset (top right) shows the long and short step adjustments made in response to the drop.*

The short latency of the adjustments, together with the tendency for people to prefer one or the other type, suggests that they might be prepared in advance and released automatically when the obstacle drop is visually detected. Such responses are examples of **pre-programmed reactions**, which are a kind of stimulus-elicited behavior that resemble the postural synergy reactions discussed in Chapter 7. Participants knew in advance what the obstacle would be (it was always the 40 × 30 × 1.5 cm board) and so could pre-program an appropriate reaction that could be triggered when needed. Visual detection of the obstacle drop produces the trigger signal.

When people do not know in advance how large the obstacle will be, preparation of a suitable reaction may not be possible. What do people do in these circumstances? One study suggests an answer[34]: the task was to step over an obstacle like that shown in Figure 9.8 which was directly in front of the participant. A second obstacle could appear behind the first one in an unpredictable fashion. Participants did not know in advance whether or not there would be a second obstacle on any given trial, and they could not be sure of its height – it could be either short or tall. If the second obstacle did appear, the required avoidance response was to increase the length of the step over the first, fixed obstacle so that the second obstacle would be cleared as well; the foot needed to be kept higher for the taller obstacle. It was found that people made a two-stage response to the appearance of the second obstacle. The first reaction had a latency of about 120 ms; it was of relatively large amplitude, and was the same regardless of the height of the second obstacle. Given the latency of the reaction, and its independence of obstacle height, this was probably a pre-programmed reaction elicited by the appearance of the obstacle. Shortly after this first response, smaller-amplitude adjustments of the foot trajectory were observed: these served to make the path of the foot appropriate for the height of the obstacle.

To summarize, when faced with a task in which an obstacle is likely to appear suddenly and require rapid modification of an on-going step, people can pre-program a reaction with short latency (120 ms) that is elicited by the visual appearance of the obstacle. Once elicited, the reaction can be corrected during execution if in error. A feedback control process is presumably responsible for these secondary corrections. Such a process can produce small adjustments to foot height to clear an obstacle, or small adjustments to foot direction to ensure accurate foot placement[35]. This process does not require that a pre-programmed reaction be elicited first – evidence suggests that it is active during normal strides as well[36]. Thus, there are two types of automatic adjustments to the swing phase that are made in response to the visual detection of sudden events or to errors in the swing foot trajectory: pre-programmed reactions triggered by detection of an event, and feedback-based error corrections.

9.2.4 How do people decide what maneuver to make to avoid an obstacle?

Some obstacles are easily stepped over; others are too large and must be circumnavigated. Typically, any obstacle that can be stepped over can also be circumnavigated. From our own experience, we know that we step over small obstacles rather than go around them, and that there are somewhat larger obstacles that we could step over, but we choose to go around them instead. The decision about what maneuver to make is made in advance and is based on our visual perception of the obstacle: we look at the obstacle and make a decision using the information we obtain. This leads to the following question: given an obstacle that could either be stepped over or circumnavigated, what factors determine whether a person will decide to go around it or step over it? It is likely that there are several factors that could contribute to the choice, such as the height of the obstacle, its length in the heading direction, the person's state of fatigue, how much of a hurry the person is in, whether they are carrying something or not, what clothes they are wearing, and presumably a variety of other things that depend on the person's goals and state of mind. In this section we will examine only the role of obstacle height.

The height of the obstacle is clearly a very important factor – if an obstacle is tall enough, it will be impossible to step over it. It is equally clear that a person with long legs can step over taller obstacles than a person with short legs, other things being equal. It is not the absolute height of an obstacle that matters, but the obstacle's height relative to the length of the person's legs. This suggests that people need to be able to estimate the height of an obstacle relative to the length of their legs in order to make a decision about whether to step over it or go around it. Another way of stating this is to say that people need to measure obstacle height in leg length units: for example, one obstacle might be one leg length tall, another half a leg length tall. We will call units of this kind **body-scaled units**.

An experimental study with participants of different leg lengths showed that on average, people chose to step over obstacles (vertical, flat boards like the obstacle in Figure 9.8) that were less than about 0.85 lower-leg lengths (sole of foot to knee) tall, and went around obstacles greater than 0.85 lower-leg lengths tall[37]. This suggests that people are able to visually estimate the height of the obstacle in body-scaled units and use a particular value of the body-scaled height to determine whether to step over it or go around it. In the experiment, this value was about 0.85. Thus, irrespective of how long a person's legs were, they chose to go around rather than step over the obstacle if its height was more than 0.85 of their lower leg length.

Why was the critical value 0.85? The experiment was unable to answer this question, but it may have had to do with energy cost. As discussed in Chapter 7, energy cost is an important determinant of locomotor behavior. In the case of obstacle avoidance, there will come a point at which the energy cost of lifting the legs up and over an obstacle exceeds the cost of going around it. It is possible that people choose to switch from stepping over to going around when the energy costs of the former exceed the costs of the latter. This has not been tested experimentally, though it predicts that the height at which people switch from stepping to going around an obstacle will be greater the further they have to go to get around it. This prediction corresponds to everyday experience.

The idea that a critical value of a perceived property of the environment, such as obstacle height, is used as the basis for deciding what maneuver to make during locomotor activity is an important one. It is discussed further in the next sections.

9.2.5 People can see whether or not steps are too steep to ascend

When walking or running, we often step from a lower level up to a higher level. Examples include stepping up onto a ledge or going up a flight of stairs. It is clear that some changes in level are too great to surmount by stepping, and we must either use our hands to help us climb up or find another route. This indicates that there is some critical ledge height or stair height at which a person will choose to switch from stepping to climbing, just as there is a critical obstacle height at which a person will switch from stepping over to going around (section 9.2.4). Here we will discuss an experimental study that sought to determine whether people are able to look at a flight of stairs and tell whether they are able to step up it or not[38].

We will call a set of stairs that can be ascended without use of the hands, a *steppable* set. Figure 9.11 shows a schematic of the maximum stair *riser height* (defined in the figure) a person can possibly step up onto. It would probably be extremely difficult to actually get up onto the next level from the position shown in the figure, but it would be impossible if the riser height were any greater. The riser height shown sets an absolute upper limit for stepping up in a person with legs of length L. This height is slightly less than the leg length. If the segments of both legs were vertical, then the riser height (R) would be equal to the leg length (L) less the difference between the length of the thigh (L_T) and the length of the lower leg (L_s). In shorthand, this can be written $R = L - (L_s - L_T)$ or, since $L = L_s + L_T$, $R = 2L_T$. This tells us that the maximum riser height that people can step up onto is less than about twice a person's thigh length ($2L_T$). This is the height that divides steppable sets of stairs from unsteppable sets, and it can be expressed in terms of total leg length: for the group of participants studied in the experiment, thigh length was about 0.44 of the total leg length, so the maximum steppable riser height was about 0.88 leg lengths. This is a body-scaled measure of the maximum riser height.

The experimental study attempted to answer the question, *can people visually perceive whether a set of stairs is steppable or unsteppable?* The analysis presented above suggests that if people can do this, then they should judge stairs to be steppable when the riser height is less than 0.88 of their leg length, and unsteppable when the riser height is greater. To test this experimentally, participants were shown photographic slides of sets of stairs that were identical except for differences in riser height (tread depth was always the same) and asked whether or not they would be able to step up them. There were five different riser heights: 20,

25, 30, 35 and 40 inches. The slides were presented in random order, with each set of stairs shown to participants five times. The results were expressed as the percentage of times each set of stairs was judged steppable: for example, if a person judged the set with a 25-inch riser height as steppable on four out of the five times it was presented, then the result would be 90% for this set.

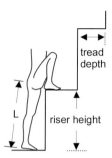

Figure 9.11: *Approximate leg position when stepping onto a stair with the maximum steppable riser height.*

The results are shown in Figure 9.12, plotted as a function of riser height in leg length units. The figure shows data from two subgroups of participants: a short group with an average height of 1.64 m (◆, leg length 76 cm), and a tall group whose average height was 1.90 m (○, leg length 91 cm). The riser height that would be judged steppable 50% of the time divides stairs more often judged steppable from those more often judged unsteppable. This value can be considered to correspond to a person's perceived critical riser height, and can be estimated from the plot in Figure 9.12, as indicated by the arrows. Accurate visual discrimination of steppable from unsteppable stairs implies that the 50% point should occur at 0.88 units along the horizontal axis. The actual values obtained were very close to this prediction: 0.89 for the tall group, and 0.88 for the short group. This outcome demonstrates that people can judge whether or not a set of stairs is steppable just by looking at them.

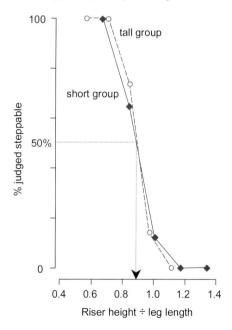

Figure 9.12: *Results from experiment reported by Warren (1984). See text for details.*

The ability to see whether stairs can be walked up or not is an example of a more general phenomenon: people are able to look at the terrain ahead and determine what it is possible to do and what it is not possible to do. This ability is essential for making appropriate choices between possible courses of action. The possibilities for action offered to a person (or animal) by objects and surfaces in the environment are called **affordances**[39]. The 'steppability' of a flight of stairs is an affordance: a steppable set of stairs is one that affords walking up, whereas an unsteppable set is one that does not. If a person can see what a set of stairs affords, then they can make the appropriate decision about what action to take in advance of reaching the first step.

There is, of course, more to making a decision about whether or not to do something than simply determining whether it is possible. In the case of ascending stairs, although a person could walk up a set of stairs with a riser height of 0.88 times their leg length, it is unlikely that they would attempt to do so unless there were no other choices – walking up such stairs would be extremely strenuous. As we saw from the results of the study discussed in the last section, although people were always able to step over the obstacle (the obstacle afforded stepping-over), they chose to go around it when its height exceeded 0.85 times their lower leg length. We suggested that the energy cost of the two alternative maneuvers might contribute to making the decision between them. In the next section, we examine the contribution of energy cost factors in determining people's preference for ascending one set of stairs rather than another.

9.2.6 People show a visual preference for stairs that can be ascended using the least energy

Given two flights of stairs that go up the same overall distance but have different riser heights, do people prefer one set over the other, and is their choice predictable from the energy cost of ascent? This question has been addressed in a study that involved two experiments[40]. The first experiment directly investigated the energy costs of walking up flights of stairs with different riser heights, by measuring participants' oxygen consumption as they ascended the stairs. The aim was to determine how riser height affects energy consumption, and whether there is a particular riser height for which the energy cost of ascent is less than that for other riser heights. The second experiment studied people's perception of the ease with which sets of stairs could be ascended. Participants were shown photographic slides displaying two sets of stairs with different riser heights but ascending to the same overall height (sets of stairs with shorter riser height had more steps), and asked to choose the set that they would prefer to walk up[41]. There were six different riser heights – 5, 6, 7, 8, 9 and 10 inches – all of which are easily steppable. The experiment aimed to determine whether people would choose the stairs with the lower energy cost (as determined in the first experiment) when shown two sets with different riser heights.

The participants in each experiment were divided into a short group and a tall group, and the results for the two groups are shown in Figure 9.13. Panel A shows the results from the first experiment, with energy cost (Joules/kg body weight/vertical meter climbed) plotted against riser height. For both the short and tall groups, there was an intermediate riser height where the energy consumption is at a minimum: 7.7 inches for the short group, and 9.5 inches for the tall group (marked by arrows in the figure). Expressed in body scaled units (riser height ÷ leg length), the optimal riser height was the same for the two groups, 0.26 leg lengths. Panel B shows the results from the second experiment: the proportion of times that stairs with a particular riser height were chosen is plotted against riser height. Stairs with riser heights closer to the optimal height were chosen more often by both short and tall participants. The tall group chose stairs with the 9-inch riser most frequently, and those with the 10-inch riser next most frequently. The short group chose the 7-inch riser most frequently, and the 8-inch riser the next most frequently. Thus, people did tend to choose the set of stairs that had an energy cost close to the minimum.

The first experiment demonstrates that the energy people expend when ascending stairs is at a minimum with an intermediate riser height of about 0.26 leg lengths. The results of the second experiment demonstrate that people visually perceive riser heights that are close to the least energetically costly height to be preferable for walking up. The ability to be able to visually perceive the likely energy cost associated with taking a particular route would allow us to make choices between potential routes before reaching the point where one or the other route must be taken.

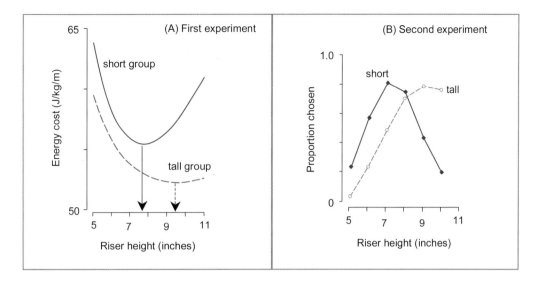

Figure 9.13: *Results from two experiments reported by Warren (1984). See text for details.*

The fact that people are able to perceive which stairs are energetically less costly to ascend than others raises the question: how are we able to do this? What information do we use to tell us which set of stairs is likely to use less energy to climb? Clearly, riser height information is necessary, but is not sufficient. We also need to associate some measure of energy cost with a given riser height. Note that the graphs shown in panel A of Figure 9.13 would allow you to do exactly this: if you pick a given riser height on the horizontal axis, you can go up to the curve and read off the energy cost associated with the chosen riser height. In order to obtain these graphs, the experiment had to be conducted. Is it likely that individuals have run similar 'experiments' that allow them to determine energy costs? Actually, the answer is 'yes': by going up and down different sets of stairs during their lifetimes, people can learn which need more effort to ascend, and so obtain some information about energy costs. Of course, the quality of this information will depend on the kind of stair climbing experience the person has had – the more stairs climbed, and the greater the variety of riser heights experienced, the more a person could learn. We would, therefore, expect that a person with more stair climbing experience would be better at making the discrimination required in the second experiment than one with less experience. This expectation has never been tested.

9.2.7 People can perceive whether or not a gap is passable

Progress through an environment frequently requires passing through gaps. Some gaps will be too narrow to squeeze through – *impassable* gaps; others will have plenty of room – *passable* gaps. 'Passability' is an affordance of a gap, and it depends on body size – a cat can squeeze through a much narrower gap than a person, and children can get through narrower gaps than adults. When approaching a gap, it is important to be able to determine in advance whether it is passable or not, and everyday experience tells us that we can do this quite effectively.

How someone passes through a gap depends on its width. If the gap is wide enough, a person can pass through without changing their speed or body orientation. Narrower gaps might cause a person to slow down to make sure that they don't bump into the sides, or to twist their trunks so as to pass through shoulder first. To pass through even narrower gaps, a person may need to stop and then squeeze themselves through. People's ability to visually perceive whether they can pass through a gap without turning the trunk has been studied experimentally[42]. One study consisted of two experiments designed to determine whether people would be able to visually discriminate between gaps that required rotation of the trunk from those that did not, and whether their perception would correspond to performance.

The first experiment of the study sought to determine how narrow a gap had to be in order that a person actually turned their trunk to pass through it. People were asked to walk through gaps of various widths and recorded on video so that the amount of turning could be estimated. The type of result obtained in this experiment is shown in Figure 9.14, where shoulder rotation angle is plotted against gap width. Rotation angle is defined as shown in the figure inset, and the data points are means from a group of participants with an average shoulder width of 40.4 cm. There is some shoulder rotation during normal walking, which was also observed in participants when they walked through the wider gaps, and which corresponds to the flat part of the curve. Thus, actual turning to pass through a narrower gap corresponds to the descending part of the curve, which shows that the degree of turning increased approximately linearly with decreasing gap width. The transition between the descending part of the curve and the flat part corresponds to the gap width that divides the two possible types of behavior: passing through without turning (flat part) or with turning (descending part). The critical gap width lies within the region marked with a gray bar, and was found to be greater for people who were wider across the shoulder, as would be expected. However, if measured in shoulder width units, the critical gap width was about the same regardless of a person's size – the value obtained in the experiment was about 1.3 shoulder widths.

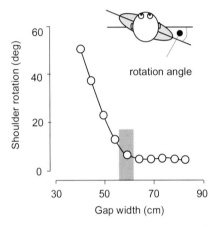

Figure 9.14: *Results from experiment reported by Warren and Whang (1987; data are from their Figure 2a). See text for details.*

The second experiment aimed to determine if people can visually perceive whether or not they would need to turn their shoulders in order to pass through a gap. Participants stood five meters from the gap and made judgments of whether or not they would be able to pass through without turning[43]. Participants fell into two groups: a large group with an average shoulder width of 47.7 cm, and a small group with an average shoulder width of 41.1 cm. The results are shown in Figure 9.15: the proportion of times a particular gap was judged to be impassable without a shoulder turn is plotted as a function of gap width in panel A, and as a function of gap width in units of shoulder width in panel B. The critical value of gap width (the 50% point) can be estimated from the graphs shown in the figure: it was greater for the large group than for the small group (55.5 and 45.5 cm, respectively), as would be expected. When gap width was expressed in shoulder width units, the difference between the two groups disappeared (Figure 9.15B), and the critical gap width was about 1.16 shoulder widths for both groups.

The results of the second experiment show that people were able to visually discriminate gaps that were passable-without-turning from those that were impassable-without-turning. Gaps less than or equal to a person's shoulder width were invariably perceived as impassable, and a critical value for making the decision was somewhat greater than shoulder width. However, the critical value obtained (1.16 shoulder widths) was slightly smaller than the value at which people actually turned their shoulders in the first experiment (1.3 shoulder widths). The authors of the study suggested that this difference might be attributable to the

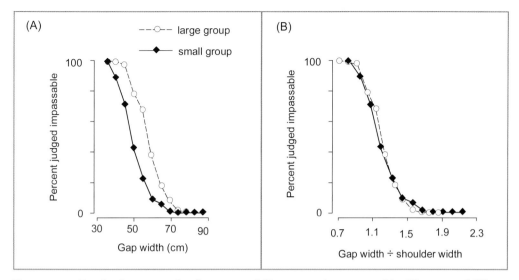

Figure 9.15: *Results from a study of gap-passability perception reported by Warren and Whang (1987; data are from their Figure 3). (A) Data plotted against gap width in standard units (cm). (B) Same data plotted against gap width in shoulder-width units.*

instructions given to participants in the second experiment, who were asked to state only whether it would be possible for them to pass through the gaps without turning. It would be possible to pass through a gap 1.16 shoulder widths wide without turning, though it is perhaps not what people would normally do[44].

9.3 Timing of Avoidance and Contact

9.3.1 Introduction: maneuvers need to be timed

When you are moving towards a flight of stairs, a doorway, an obstacle or some other hazard, it is not enough to decide what maneuver to make and then prepare a suitable program to control its execution – it is also important to execute that maneuver at the right time. For instance, when stepping up a ledge or over an obstacle, you must not wait too long or you will collide with it, and you must not start too soon or you risk completing the maneuver before you have arrived. You also need to know whether you have sufficient time to prepare and execute the maneuver (both of which take time). How do you know how long you have got before reaching a hazard? How do you determine the appropriate moment to start a maneuver? We will discuss possible answers to these questions in this part of the chapter.

9.3.2 Time to arrival is an important quantity

Consider, for example, the task of walking through a gap that requires a turn of the shoulders. The walker must not only determine that a shoulder turn is necessary and how large the turn should be; he or she also needs to determine when to begin turning, how long to take making the turn, and for how long to remain in the turned position. When should a person begin to turn? The task requires only that the shoulders be turned through the required angle by the time the person reaches the gap. However, it seems obvious that walking along with the shoulders turned is awkward (try it), so you probably do not want to remain turned for any longer than necessary. The shoulders only need to be turned while the person is actually passing through the gap. To keep to a minimum the time spent walking with turned shoulders, the person should start turning so that the turn is complete when the person reaches the gap, and they should start to straighten again as soon as they have passed through it.

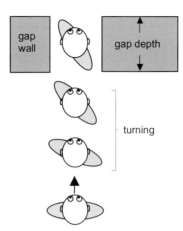

Figure 9.16: *Cartoon sequence showing a person approaching a narrow gap and turning so as to pass through.*

In Figure 9.16, the person needs to turn the shoulders through about 60° to pass through the gap. Suppose it takes a person 0.2 seconds to turn the shoulders through 60°. If the person is to complete the turn before they enter the gap, they need to start turning at least 0.2 seconds before reaching the gap. If they start turning more than 0.2 seconds prior to arriving, then they will spend some time walking along with their shoulders needlessly turned. If they start turning less than 0.2 seconds before arriving, then they will run the risk of bumping into the walls of the gap. The appropriate time to start turning is a little more than 0.2 seconds before arrival. Thus, timing the start of the turning maneuver is important: start too late and you run the risk of colliding with the walls; start too early and you may waste effort unnecessarily. To get the timing right, the person needs to know two things: first, how long it will take them to turn their shoulders through the required angle; second, the time remaining until they will reach the gap. The time remaining before you reach a particular place is called the **time to arrival**:

> **TIME TO ARRIVAL (TTA) of a moving thing at a designated place:** The time remaining before a specified point or part of a moving person, animal, vehicle or other object (the moving thing) reaches a designated spatial location or meets a specified line or boundary.

In cases where collision between two solid objects can occur, the time remaining until collision is usually referred to as the **time to collision** or the **time to contact (TTC)**:

> **TIME TO CONTACT (TTC) of one thing with another thing:** The time remaining before one thing collides with or makes contact with another thing. One or both of the things can be moving.

This term is also used when an object is moving towards a person and they wish to bring about a collision – the moving object might be a tennis ball, for example, and the person want to catch it in their hand or hit it with a racket, both catching and hitting being types of collision (see Chapter 12).

We have argued that TTA or TTC information of some sort is needed if maneuvers are to be initiated at an appropriate time. This raises two questions:

▸ *What information about TTA or TTC is used to time the initiation of a maneuver?*
▸ *How is the information used to initiate a maneuver?*

The answers to these questions are not known for certain, but there are some interesting ideas that we will discuss in what follows. First we will show that there is explicit TTA information available in the visual stimulus and that people and animals can make use of it. After that, we will discuss how the information might be used to time maneuver initiation. Finally, we will examine empirical studies that have attempted to determine what information is actually used to time various maneuvers.

9.3.3 Explicit information about time to arrival is visually available

As a person moves towards a location, their TTA with that location changes – it gets progressively shorter and shorter as the person approaches, until it reaches zero when they reach the location. The retinal images also change: images of objects move and change size; some things go out of view, while other things become visible (see Chapter 4). Thus, changes in TTA are associated with changes in the retinal images. If a retinal image quantity changes and those changes are in some way related to the change in TTA, then that image quantity carries some information about TTA. However, in order to provide reliable, accurate TTA information, the value of an image quantity at an instant of time should be perfectly correlated with the value of the TTA at that time. An image quantity that is perfectly correlated with the TTA will be said to provide **explicit** information about TTA. It has been shown that in certain conditions, explicit TTA information is available to a moving observer.

Sticking with the gap-passing example, suppose a one-eyed observer – we'll call him Cyclops – is approaching a gap in a wall. Cyclops is good for illustrative purposes: the single eye in the middle of his forehead simplifies the situation, so that we won't need any complex mathematics. Panel A of Figure 9.17 shows Cyclops at some moment during his approach to a gap with a width labelled W. At this moment he is moving with a speed V along a straight path (dashed line) and is a distance D from the gap: his TTA is his distance away divided by his speed of approach (=D/V).

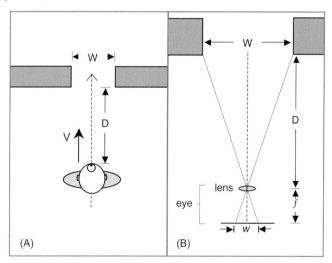

Figure 9.17: *(A) Cyclops (one-eyed man) approaches a gap in the wall. (B) Geometry of image formation in the horizontal plane.*

In Figure 9.17A, Cyclops is looking straight ahead, and the image formed on his retina contains the images of the wall segments on either side of the gap. Panel B shows a schematic of the geometry of image formation (horizontal cross-section, eye greatly enlarged). The imaging surface (retina) is shown flat and oriented perpendicular to the direction of Cyclop's motion. This simplifies the analysis but does not alter the basic conclusions to be drawn, despite the fact that a real retina is clearly not flat[45]. The lens has a focal length f, and only two image points are included: the images of the right and left edges of the gap. The distance between these images is the width of the gap's image (labeled w). There are two triangles in the figure, each with a vertex at the center of the lens: a large one in front of the lens, formed by the rays from the edges of the gap to the lens, with the gap itself as the base; and a small one behind the lens, with the image of the gap as its base. These triangles are similar (same angles), which means that the following relationship holds[46]:

$$D \times w = f \times W. \tag{9.1}$$

As Cyclops gets closer to the gap, the distance D decreases and the images of the gap edges get further apart on his retina, so w is getting larger (the image of the gap is expanding). The rate at which the distance is decreasing is equal to the speed with which Cyclops is approaching[47]; the rate at which w is growing is its rate of expansion, which we will denote by the symbol ε. The focal length of the lens does not change (f is constant), and neither does the gap width (W is constant).

We know that the rate of change of the right side of equation (9.1) must be equal to the rate of change of the left side. The right side is constant over time (both W and f are constant), and so has zero rate of change. This means that the rate of change of (D $\times$ w) must also be zero, but how can this be if both w and D are changing? The answer is that their rates of change cancel each other out. In fact, elementary differential calculus tells us that the rate of change of the left side of the equation is equal to (D $\times$ ε) $-$ ($w \times$ V), and so we can write[48],

$$(D \times \varepsilon) - (w \times V) = 0. \tag{9.2}$$

A little simple algebra shows that equation (9.2) can be written as follows:

$$D/V = w/\varepsilon \tag{9.3}$$

In words, equation (9.3) says that Cylcops' time to arrival at the gap (D/V) is equal to the size of the gap's image (w) divided by the rate at which the image is getting larger (expansion rate, ε). Thus, there is explicit information in the retinal image about time to arrival. This information is provided by the quantity w/ε. The **tau notation** is used to denote quantities of this sort[49]. This notation is as follows: if there is some time-varying stimulus quantity such as w, the tau function of the quantity at some moment of time is defined to be its value divided by its rate of change. So, for example, if the quantity is w, then the tau function of w – written $\tau(w)$ – is w/ε. Here is a definition:

> **The tau (τ) notation:** If z is a time-varying quantity and $\dot{z}$ is the rate of change of z with time, then $z/\dot{z}$ is the tau function of z and written as $\tau(z)$ (read 'tau of z') or just τ when there is no ambiguity; $\tau(z)$ can be called a **tau variable**.

Notice the TTA we have been dealing with is D/V, which is actually the TTA when the speed (V) is constant. If a person is slowing down (decelerating) or speeding up (accelerating), their TTA is not equal to D/V; it is either greater than D/V (if they are slowing) or less than D/V (if they are speeding up). We will say that when the speed is changing, D/V is a **first order approximation** to the true time to arrival. The tau variable $\tau(w)$ provides information about D/V, so if the person's speed is changing, it does not provide information about the actual time to arrival, but about the first order approximation.

Related analysis of the moving image to that presented here shows that tau variables can provide a moving observer with information about their time to arrival at – or more generally, the time they will pass by[50] – any visible object or feature in the fixed environment[51]. The fixed environment includes anything that does not change its physical size as the observer approaches it and that does not move around. Later we will consider what information is available when an object is not fixed but moving (Chapter 12).

Tau variables could be used for timing the start of locomotor maneuvers and to determine whether there is sufficient time to prepare a maneuver and execute it. In the following sections we consider whether people can make use of this information.

9.3.4 People can extract tau variables from retinal images and use them to estimate time to arrival

The existence of a source of information does not mean that people use it. There may, for example, be other sources of information that people use instead: perhaps the neural machinery of the visual system is unable to extract tau variables from retinal images, so some other source of TTA information is used. Thus, once a source of information has been identified, we need to answer two questions regarding its biological significance:

▶ Can the source of information be extracted by the perceptual system of interest, such as the human visual system?
▶ Is the source of information used in the planning and/or control of any particular actions?

There is good evidence that tau variables can be extracted from retinal images by the visual systems of several different species, including human beings[52], so they could be used in the control of timing (see below and Chapter 12). Nevertheless, there may be other sources of TTA information that a person could use.

It might have occurred to you that there is an alternative way of obtaining information about D/V: first make perceptual estimates of the distance (D) and the velocity (V), and then divide them. This has been traditionally suggested as the alternative to using tau variables, but is not generally considered to be plausible. There are several arguments against obtaining information about TTA this way. First, the method is roundabout and unnecessary: to obtain distance and velocity information involves measuring image size and image speed, but other things are required as well: for example, the information available in retinal images is typically insufficient – prior knowledge is typically needed as well. Why bother with these when image size and expansion rate are sufficient? Second, the method introduces more sources of error than measuring tau and is therefore likely to be less accurate[53]. Finally, it has been shown that people can visually estimate TTA or TTC when the stimulus contains no information about either distance or velocity, but when both image size and expansion rate are present[54]; this demonstrates, as noted earlier, that people are able to measure tau variables from the image and use them to make TTA and TTC estimates. It has never been shown that perception of distance and/or velocity are needed for estimating TTA[55], so we have no evidence that they are ever required. In summary, the idea that people obtain TTA information from independent estimates of distance and velocity is implausible and not supported by any evidence. The use of tau variables is much more plausible, and there is both human psychophysical evidence and neurophysiological evidence from other species[56] that these variables can be extracted from the stimulus.

9.3.5 How can TTA information be used to time maneuvers?

We have now seen that TTA information is available in the visual stimulus and can be extracted from retinal images. The next question to ask is *how exactly is such information used to time maneuvers?* We have already seen that it is critical to begin a pre-planned maneuver at an appropriate time: how could TTA information be used to do this?

Starting a pre-planned maneuver requires initiating the process of generating motor commands that drive execution. This requires an initiating signal of some sort, and starting a maneuver at the right time means that the signal must initiate command generation at the appropriate moment. This raises two questions:

▶ *When is the appropriate moment to initiate command generation?*
▶ *How is an initiating signal generated that can cause command generation to start at the right moment?*

Answers to these questions can be provided by considering once again the shoulder turning example. In section 9.3.2 we supposed that the turn was completed in 0.2 seconds. The turn should start a little earlier than 0.2 seconds prior to arrival, so as to give a margin of safety.

For illustrative purposes let's suppose that a TTA of 0.3 seconds is an appropriate time to start turning. How can the person ensure that they start turning at this time? One possibility is to use visual TTA information. As the person approaches the gap, vision provides an estimate of TTA that is continuously decreasing: at some point, the TTA estimate will be equal to the value that guarantees that the turn will start 0.3 seconds before reaching the gap – we will call this the **criterion value**. When this value is reached, command generation should be initiated.

What criterion value guarantees that the turn will begin at a TTA of 0.3 seconds? It is not 0.3 seconds, because it takes time to transmit signals from the retinas to the muscles – the eye-to-muscle transmission time. Therefore, the criterion value should be 0.3 seconds plus the eye-to-muscle transmission time. For example, if the transmission time is 0.2 seconds, the appropriate criterion TTA value is 0.5 seconds. This is illustrated in Figure 9.18, which shows a time line for the process, with time to arrival running from left to right starting at 0.5 seconds (the criterion value). Four different time periods are shown, each in a different color. The first period (blue) is the time it takes for TTA information in the stimulus to be extracted and cause command generation to be initiated. The second period (orange) is the time it takes for commands to be transmitted to the muscles and cause the shoulders to turn. The third period (pink) is the time taken to execute the shoulder turn. The final period (green) is the period during which the person walks with turned shoulders just prior to reaching the gap.

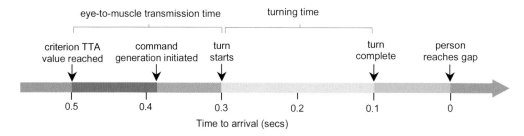

Figure 9.18: *Time line of events when turning the shoulders to pass through a gap.*

The process of initiating command generation according to the scheme in Figure 9.18 can be represented using a functional block diagram, as shown in Figure 9.19. The first block, labeled 'visual processing of TTA information', represents the process that extracts an estimate of TTA from the stimulus. The second block, labeled 'TTA = crit?', determines the moment that the TTA estimate provided by the first block reaches the criterion value: if criterion is reached, the block sends an initiating signal to the command generator (orange block). The time taken to transmit information from the left end to the right end in Figure 9.19 is the eye-to-muscle transmission time.

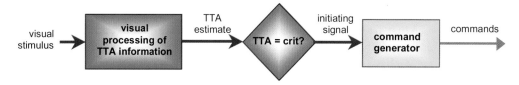

Figure 9.19: *Sequence of processes involved in initiating motor command generation using a criterion value of time to arrival (TTA).*

Initiating command generation when TTA reaches a criterion value of 0.5 seconds will work for any approach speed, but it will not work if the turning time is much greater than 0.2 seconds. Suppose the turning time were 0.4 seconds: using a 0.5 second TTA criterion would result in the turn starting 0.3 seconds prior to arrival, and so the turn would be complete 0.1 seconds after the person had reached the gap, so the person would probably bump into the walls. A turning time of less than 0.2 seconds is not as problematic, since it merely results in the person walking in the fully turned posture for slightly longer. In this example, a 0.5 second criterion works for turns that are completed in less than about 0.3 seconds. If the execution time is expected to exceed 0.3 seconds, then a different criterion value of TTA would be needed: *the appropriate criterion value depends on the duration of the maneuver to be executed.* In fact, according to the diagram above, if the turning time is T seconds, then the appropriate criterion value of TTA is equal to T plus the eye-to-muscle transmission time.

Notice that TTA reaching criterion is a stimulus event and it is this that gives rise to the signal that initiates the maneuver. This makes the maneuver a kind of stimulus-elicited behavior, though of a rather different type from those discussed in Chapter 5. Unlike the stimulus-elicited behaviors discussed earlier, the maneuver is prepared ahead of time and is only initiated when the stimulus event is detected. It is, therefore, a kind of pre-programmed maneuver.

Initiating command generation on the basis of a stimulus event, like TTA information reaching a criterion value, requires continuous extraction of TTA information so that the event is not missed. If the person were to look away or close their eyes, then they could miss it. We will refer to timing the onset of command generation when a stimulus event occurs as an example of **extrinsic timing**:

> **EXTRINSIC TIMING:** Determination of the time of occurrence of some characteristic of an action (such as its onset or termination) by a stimulus event.

Thus, the start of the turning maneuver in the example presented here is extrinsically timed. The alternative to extrinsic timing is called **intrinsic timing**:

> **INTRINSIC TIMING:** Determination of the time of occurrence of some feature or characteristic of an action (such as its onset or termination) by a process internal to the nervous system (e.g., the unfolding of a motor program, or a voluntary decision).

According to this definition, the timing of bursts of muscle activation generated by a CPG is intrinsic when the CPG is isolated from sensory inputs (see Chapter 7). When sensory inputs are present, there may be both intrinsic and extrinsic contributions to burst timing, so timing is not necessarily either intrinsic or extrinsic – it may be a bit of both.

9.3.6 Can maneuver intiation be intrinsically timed?

Extrinsic timing of initiation requires that TTA information is continuously extracted so that occurrence of the initiating stimulus event – TTA information reaching the criterion value – can be detected. We have seen, however, that continuous vision is not needed to perform some locomotor maneuvers. This raises the possibility that some maneuvers can be intrinsically timed.

Empirical evidence that a kind of intrinsic timing of locomotor maneuvers is possible comes from the results of studies using the **prediction-motion task**. This is an experimental task that typically involves participants looking at a computer-generated display that simulates either motion towards an object or else an approaching object. At some point during approach, the screen goes blank, and the person's task is to initiate a response at the moment they judge that they would have arrived at the object or that the object would have reached them (the arrival event). The time that elapses between the moment the display screen goes blank and the time of the arrival event will be referred to as the *occlusion period*. Figure 9.20 illustrates the sequence of events as they might take place when this task is performed.

The person's goal is to make the time of their response coincide with the time of the arrival event. The difference between the two times is therefore a measure of their timing error. In Figure 9.20, the person's response occurs earlier than the arrival event, and they are said to have made an **underestimation error**. If the response had occurred after the arrival event, they would have made an **overestimation error**.

The basic finding in studies of this task is that when the occlusion period is short (less than about 0.75 seconds), the constant and variable timing errors[57] are quite small, being on the order of tens of milliseconds. Both types of error increase as the duration of the occlusion period increases, and may be several seconds in magnitude for occlusion periods of eight to ten seconds[58]. For longer occlusion periods, the constant errors are invariably underestimation errors.

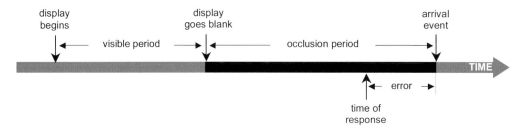

Figure 9.20: *Time line showing the sequence of events in a prediction-motion task.*

It is clear that the response in the prediction-motion task cannot be extrinsically timed in the manner described in the previous section, since TTA or TTC information is not available to initiate the response. Response initiation must, therefore, be intrinsically timed in some way. Intrinsic timing of an action does not necessarily mean that visual TTA or TTC information plays no role. One possibility that has been suggested to explain the timing of responses in prediction-motion tasks is that a neural process is used to count down TTA from the beginning of the occlusion period, and to initiate response command generation when a suitable point of the countdown is reached[59]. Such a process could involve the accumulation of output from a neural rhythm generator. The rhythm generator acts like a kind of neural clock, with each output burst corresponding to a 'tick'; the accumulated output is a count of the number of bursts (ticks) that have occurred, and so is a measure of elapsed time.

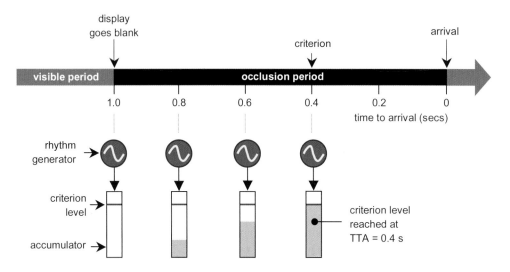

Figure 9.21: *Tick count model of response initiation in a prediction-motion task. The rhythm generator produces ticks (bursts of activity) like a clock, and the accumulator stores the ticks so that its level is proportional to the number of ticks, i.e., the time elapsed since accumulation began.*

Figure 9.21 shows how the process might work in a situation where the occlusion period is one second long and the criterion TTA value is 0.4 seconds. The TTA at the end of the visible period is one second: this is the last available estimate of TTA that can be obtained from the stimulus. The loss of the visual stimulus is the signal to activate a rhythm generator. The output of this rhythm generator is fed to an accumulator which simply stores up the rhythm generator outputs that it receives[60]. The accumulator starts off empty, and fills up as time goes by. The figure represents the accumulator as a kind of tank, and shows the amount of accumulated activation with gray infill. The level accumulated is shown at four points in time, 0.2 seconds apart, starting from the moment the display goes blank (accumulator empty). When the contents of the accumulator reach a preset level, a signal that initiates command generation is produced.

In order that command generating be correctly timed, the preset level in the accumulator must be reached when the TTA would have reached the criterion. Since the TTA criterion is 0.4 seconds, the preset level in the accumulator must correspond to a time elapsed following occlusion of 0.6 seconds (see Figure 9.21): i.e., the value of TTA when the display goes blank (1 second) minus the TTA criterion (0.4 seconds). Thus, although timing is intrinsic according to the definition given earlier, stimulus information plays a role: the perceived TTA when the display goes blank is used to determine the preset level of the accumulator.

Unfortunately, there is currently insufficient evidence to be able to say whether or not timing in prediction-motion type tasks involves a process of this sort[61]. It remains for future research to determine the answer. However, the description of such a process illustrates how timed responses could be initiated during an occlusion period, and so provides a concrete example of intrinsic timing.

9.3.7 Is explicit TTA information used for timing maneuver initiation?

So far we have seen that explicit information about TTA is visually available in the form of tau variables and that these variables can be extracted from the stimulus. We have also seen how TTA information could be used to time the initiation of maneuvers, in both extrinsic and intrinsic modes. However, we have not yet addressed what is perhaps the most important question: *Do people and other animals use explicit TTA information, such as that provided by tau variables, for timing the initiation of locomotor maneuvers?*

Although this question seems straightforward, it turns out to be very difficult to answer. Indeed, it is not known for sure what information is used to initiate locomotor maneuvers. A number of factors are responsible for the difficulties. There is empirical evidence that the following factors are relevant[62]:

(1)   Different maneuvers/actions may be initiated by different types of information.
(2)   The same maneuver may be initiated by different information under different conditions.
(3)   The information people use to initiate a maneuver may change with experience[63].

Given these complications, it is useful to ask the following questions:

▸ *What alternative types of information can be used to time the initiation of maneuvers?*
▸ *What determines the type of information that is used?*

Although explicit TTA information is perhaps the most obvious candidate for timing maneuver initiation, it is possible to use some other quantity that covaries with TTA instead. The most obvious alternative is the distance away: as a person moves towards a location or an object, the TTA decreases and so does their distance from it. When approaching at constant speed (V), the TTA is equal to the distance away (D) divided by the speed (V), which means that $D = V \times TTA$: D is directly proportional to TTA, with V the constant of proportionality. Thus, a criterion value of the perceived distance away might be used instead of a criterion TTA. People can perceive with a reasonable degree of accuracy how far things are away from them, as the results from studies of blind walking would suggest (section 9.1.4).

The disadvantage of using a criterion value of perceived distance is that a given criterion will work best for one particular speed of approach, but will not work so well for faster or slower speeds. We can use our earlier shoulder turning example to show why this is. In the example, a criterion TTA value of 0.5 seconds was appropriate for initiating a turn that takes 0.2 seconds. Suppose that the person approaches the gap at a comfortable walking pace of 1.2 m/s. At this speed, using a criterion distance of 0.6 meters from the gap is exactly equivalent to using a criterion TTA of 0.5 seconds. However, if the speed is a fast walk of 2.0 m/s, then a criterion distance of 0.6 meters is no good, as it would be equivalent to using a criterion TTA of 0.3 seconds. With an eye-to-muscle transmission time of 0.2 seconds, the turn would begin when the person was 0.1 seconds from the gap: they would only be about half way through the turn when they reached the gap. Thus, a specific criterion distance will only work well for one particular speed (1.2 m/s in our example). If the approach speed is greater, then the risk of colliding with the gap walls increases. In our example, using a criterion distance of 0.6 m would result in unavoidable collision for speeds of 3 m/s or more. At 3 m/s, the criterion distance is reached 0.6/3 = 0.2 seconds before arrival, which is the eye-to-muscle transmission time. The turn would therefore begin just as the gap is reached, which is no good at all.

What the above argument shows is that when the initiation of a pre-planned maneuver needs to be quite precisely timed, using a specific criterion distance is not adequate, because speed of locomotion is not always the same. However, when precise timing is not necessary, use of a criterion distance may be adequate. One relevant study looked at the initiation of anticipatory head rotation prior to turning to going around a corner marker (Figure 9.22, panel A)[64], an action that does not seem to require precise timing. People walked towards the corner marker at three different speeds (0.8, 1.2 and 1.6 m/s), and the time at which their head rotation began was recorded. The results are shown in panels B and C of Figure 9.22. Panel B plots participants' TTA at the corner line (dashed line in panel A) at the moment the head started to turn against walking speed. It is clear that the head would start to turn at a shorter TTA when walking speed was greater. Panel C shows how far away from the corner line participants were when they started to turn their heads: the distance away showed no systematic relationship with speed. The results are consistent with the head turn being initiated at a criterion distance from the corner line of about[65] 0.3 m.

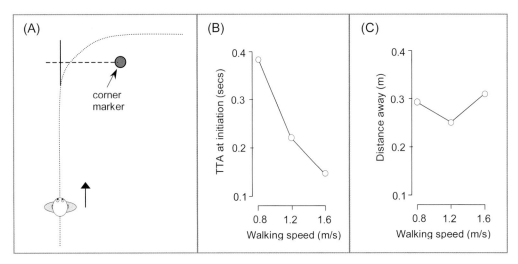

Figure 9.22: *Experimental task (A) and results (B) and (C) from a study reported by Prevost et al. (2002).*

It was also reported that people make head turning movements when they walked blind around the corner, in a manner that hardly differed from when they walked with full vision[66] (though the effect of speed of approach was not studied when participants walked blind). We have seen that in the blind walking protocol, people are likely to rely on a short-term, visuo-spatial memory representation of the scene. Such a memory contains spatial information such as distances, but does not contain any temporal information. Thus, it is logical to suppose that when people rely on such a memory for guidance, they use spatial information to determine when to initiate actions. The finding that head turns were initiated similarly with and without vision lends further support to the idea that distance rather than explicit TTA information is used to initiate this action.

In summary, the available data are consistent with the idea that when the moment at which a maneuver is initiated is not particularly critical, then initiation by explicit TTA information is not necessary, and something else may be used instead, such as distance away. When the moment of initiation is critical, then only explicit TTA information is adequate (discussed further in Chapter 12).

9.3.8 What information is used to time the initiation of actions when falling?

Deliberately falling under the action of gravity is a rather common occurrence during many types of locomotion. Deliberate falls occur, for example, when jumping or stepping down from a ledge. Landing on a hard surface from even a short drop of a few centimeters can be quite jarring if it is not properly controlled. We experience this when a foot makes contact with the ground after an unexpected step down from a stair or curb. If we fall a greater distance without controlling the landing, we risk very serious injury. This shows that reactions made following contact with the ground are not sufficient to protect us from the impact – we must prepare ourselves in advance, so as to absorb the force of impact in a way that avoids pain and injury. The actions taken to absorb the impact must be timed correctly – it's no good making them too late.

One of the first studies of the timing of controlled falls looked at diving into water. However, the divers were not people but northern gannets (*Morus bassanus*), a species of large seabird[67]. These birds make spectacular, high-speed dives into the sea when catching fish, starting from heights of as much as 30 meters above the surface. As shown in panel A of Figure 9.23, the birds retract their wings so that they enter the water in a streamlined posture. Wing retraction is necessary for two reasons: the streamlined posture allows the birds to penetrate deep enough to catch the fish, and it prevents damage to the wings that would occur if the bird struck the water at high speed with the wings extended. This means that wing retraction must be completed before the wings contact the water.

It is also important that the birds do not retract their wings too early, because in the streamlined posture they cannot control the direction of fall – they simply plummet like a falling arrow. Control of direction is important if the bird is to catch a fish. Indeed, wing retraction begins close to the moment of contact with the water. Thus, timing of wing retraction seems to be critical to the success of the dive: too late and the bird risks injuring its wings, too early and it risks missing the fish. How do the birds accurately time their wing retraction?

One possibility is that the birds extrinsically time the initiation of wing retraction using a criterion value of explicit TTC information. It was suggested that a tau variable could be used as the source of information about TTC with the surface of the sea[68]. The availability of a suitable tau variable is illustrated in panels B and C of Figure 9.23. The figure shows a gannet diving into the water (A and B) and a snapshot of the kind of image expansion pattern that arises when approaching a surface on a collision course (C). The lengths of the lines in the expansion pattern in panel C represent the speed with which points are moving in the image (points are moving slower near the center and faster at the edges). The orientation of the lines represents the direction points are moving in. The eye is looking directly at the point of contact, and this is the point at the center of the image in the figure: as the eye approaches, the image of the point of contact remains stationary and the images of all visible features seem to flow outwards from this point, which is called the *focus of radial outflow* (FRO; refer to Chapter 4 for more details). TTC of the eye with the surface of the water is given by the tau function of the retinal image distance between the FRO and any visible point[69]. Thus, a diving gannet has access to information about when its head will reach the water.

Since the bird is falling under gravity and so accelerating, the TTC information provided by tau will be a first order approximation to the true TTC (see section 9.3.3). This allows a prediction to be made concerning the timing of wing retraction if the bird is using one particular criterion value of tau to initiate the action. The prediction follows from the fact that the bird's speed as it approaches the water is greater the higher the point from which it started to dive. The greater the bird's speed when tau reaches the criterion, the closer the value of tau to the real TTC. For example, if the criterion tau value is 0.4 seconds and the bird's speed when criterion is reached is 10 m/s, then the true TTC is about 0.34 seconds – tau gives an error of only 0.06 seconds (15%). In contrast, if the bird's speed is only 1 m/s, then the true TTC is 0.2 seconds when tau is 0.4 seconds (a 100% error). Thus, if a bird initiates wing retraction using a specific criterion tau value, then the higher the start of the dive, the smaller the actual TTC will be at the moment the retraction begins. In fact, if retraction is initiated when a specific criterion value of tau is detected, then dive height and the actual TTC at the moment retraction starts should follow a curvilinear relationship. Analysis of films of gannets diving into the sea confirmed this prediction. The moment that wing retraction began could be estimated from the films, and so could the time between the start of retraction and contact with the water (i.e. the true TTC). The predictions were confirmed: the moment that wing retraction started did occur at shorter TTCs when the birds dived from greater heights, and the form of the relationship between dive height and TTC at retraction closely matched the expected relationship.

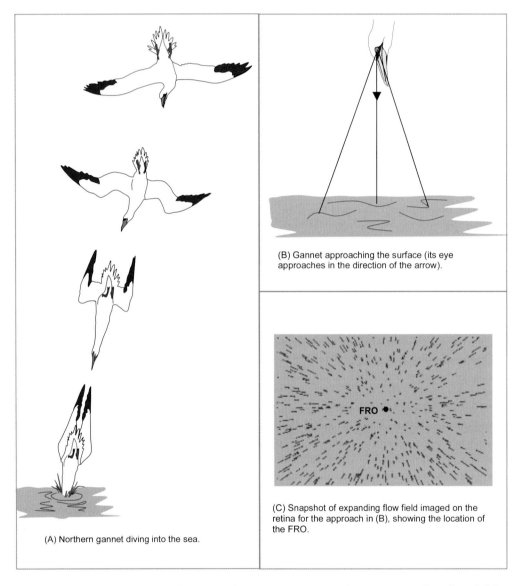

(B) Gannet approaching the surface (its eye approaches in the direction of the arrow).

(C) Snapshot of expanding flow field imaged on the retina for the approach in (B), showing the location of the FRO.

(A) Northern gannet diving into the sea.

Figure 9.23: *Northern gannet dives into the sea; as it approaches, an expanding flow field is imaged on its retinas.*

Unfortunately, though exciting and suggestive, these findings are not conclusive for two reasons. First, the range of dive heights in the study was too small to be able to rule out alternative explanations based on using a criterion distance above the water as a basis for initiating wing retraction[70]. Second, the assumption that the birds were using the same criterion value for initiation regardless of dive height has not been verified and remains hypothetical. Thus, firm conclusions regarding how gannets time their wing retraction must await future research.

Some people also dive from substantial heights into water, but no studies of the timing of actions taken in preparation for contact have been undertaken. However, almost everyone routinely steps down off ledges, curbs, stairs and other drop-offs when walking and running. As mentioned at the beginning of the section, actions need to be initiated prior to a foot making contact with the ground, so that the force of impact can be absorbed without pain or injury. Step- and jump-downs of this sort involve falls from short distances above the ground, rarely greater than a meter or so and usually much less. This means that tau variables are very unlikely to be useful for initiation of these actions: the shorter the drop, the lower the speeds reached, and consequently the less accurately tau approximates the true TTC. For example, a fall of 1 meter is completed in about 0.45 seconds: after falling for 0.1 seconds, the true TTC is 0.35 seconds, but the value of tau at this moment is 0.97 seconds – ground contact actually occurs 0.62 seconds earlier than tau predicts. Tau variables provide estimates of TTC that are too inaccurate to be of any use in initiating preparatory actions for the absorption of impact force when falling short distances under gravity[71]. Empirical work has confirmed that tau variables are not used to time the initiation of muscle activity made in preparation for landing from falls of up to 1.3 meters[72]. Indeed, step-downs from these heights can be accomplished reasonably well when people cannot see, though impact is absorbed more effectively when continuous vision is available[73]. It is likely that timing can be achieved on the basis of perceived drop height by virtue of the fact that the time it takes to fall a certain distance under gravity is determined by that distance, so if you know the distance, you know the time you will take to fall[74].

9.3.9 Explicit TTA information can be used for more than initiation

Explicit TTA and TTC information can be useful for purposes other than timing the initiation of maneuvers. For example, if you know your TTA, you can determine whether you have sufficient time to prepare and execute a particular maneuver, so TTA information is useful in making decisions about what course of action to take. In this section, we will look at how TTC information can be used to determine performance variables: specifically, the propulsive force applied to the ground during the stance phase when running over stepping stones.

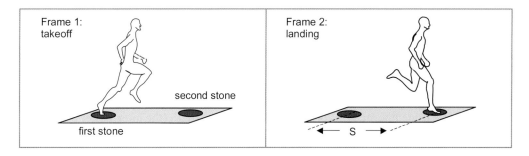

Figure 9.24: *Two-frame sequence of a person running over stepping stones.*

Imagine you are running over a series of stepping stones. Such a run amounts to a series of leaps or bounds from one stone to the next. In order for your foot to land on the next stone, your step length must be equal to the distance between the stones (labeled S in frame 2 of Figure 9.24). In principle, you could control step length by stretching the leg out more when you want to increase step length, and stretching it out less when you want to decrease step length. However, when you make contact with a stone, your landing leg must be in an appropriate posture (frame 2 of Figure 9.24): if the leg is too extended on landing, then it cannot easily flex to absorb the impact. Thus, controlling step length by varying the extent to which the leg is stretched forward is most appropriate for achieving small variations in step length. An alternative way of altering step length when running is to change the force with which you push off with the stance foot: the greater the push, the greater the step length. It was this method for controlling step length that was used by the participants in a study of stepping between visible targets when running[75].

In the study, participants ran at constant speed on a motorized treadmill equipped with a five-meter extension, so that they had a view of upcoming targets that they were required to step on (Figure 9.25). The force applied by the stance foot to the surface of the treadmill has a vertical component and a horizontal component. The reaction force from the treadmill on the foot provides propulsive thrust – the horizontal component propels the person forwards, the vertical component can propel the person upwards if large enough. Since participants ran at constant speed on the treadmill, the forward component of thrust was likely to be constant, and this was confirmed in the study. In order to change step length, participants altered the upward component. The total upward thrust developed during the stance phase is equal to the impulse of the vertical component of the reaction force: the impulse is equal to the average force multiplied by the total time for which force is developed[76].

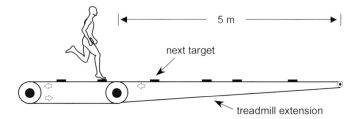

Figure 9.25: *Experimental set-up in experiment reported by Warren, Young, Lee (1986); see text for details.*

An important question to ask is, *how can vertical impulses be modulated so as to produce the step lengths needed to place the feet on the targets?* The vertical impulse determines the duration of the flight phase of each movement cycle when running (the flight phase is the period when both feet are off the ground) – the greater the impulse, the longer the duration of the flight phase. It is easy to see why this is so. Imagine throwing a ball straight up into the air; the harder you throw, the higher the ball goes up and the longer it stays up for – the duration of the ball flight is greater for more forceful throws. When a person is running at constant speed (or, as in the experiment, the person is staying in the same place and the treadmill belt is passing under them at constant speed), the distance traveled by the center of gravity during the flight phase is equal to the duration of the flight phase multiplied by the running speed. What this tells us is that the step length can be changed by altering the vertical impulse, because this changes the flight time.

The results of the study suggested that participants were controlling their step lengths primarily by modulating the vertical impulse. A particular vertical impulse leads to a particular flight time, and the flight time determines the step length. This means that instead of modulating the impulse using information about the required step length (the inter-target distance, S, Figure 9.24), the impulse could be modulated by information about the required flight time. The required flight time for the next step is the time taken to travel between the next two targets. This time is equal to the difference between the times to arrival at these targets: if the TTA at the next target is T1 and the TTA at the target after that is T2, then the required flight time is T2 − T1. These TTAs are given by visual tau variables, so if T1 is equal to τ_1 and T2 is equal to τ_2, then the required flight time is equal to $(\tau_2 - \tau_1)$. Thus, the vertical impulse of the next push-off needs to produce a flight time of $(\tau_2 - \tau_1)$. It is straightforward to show that this can be achieved if the vertical impulse is equal to $W \times (\tau_2 - \tau_1)$, where W is the person's weight[77]. In short, a person running over a series of stepping stones (foot placement targets) can step from one stone to the next by making the vertical impulse proportional to the visually derived quantity $(\tau_2 - \tau_1)$, with the constant of proportionality equal to their weight.

References & Notes

1 Blind people are also able to use echolocation, and sighted people can be trained to do so (Rosenblum, Gordon, Jarquin, 2000).

2 This kind of accuracy is achievable using eye trackers that are suitable for head mounting, like those of the Applied Science Laboratories (Bedford, MA, USA), used by A.E. Patla and colleagues in several studies described in this part of the chapter.

3 Patla, Vickers (1997).

4 Patla *et al.* (1991).

5 Patla, Vickers (1997, 2003).

6 Marigold, Patla (2007).

7 Grasso *et al.* (1998); Imai *et al.* (2001); Hollands, Vickers, Patla (2002).

8 The definition of heading given here is the one used in psychological and physiological research.

9 Hollands, Vickers, Patla (2002).

10 Imai *et al.* (2001).

11 Imai *et al.* (2001).

12 Thomson (1980).

13 E.g., Grasso *et al.* (1998).

14 Thomson (1980, 1983).

15 Similar to the constant error obtained in a full vision control condition in which participants were only prevented from seeing their feet when they reached the target location (Thomson, 1983).

16 Senders *et al.* (1967).

17 Patla *et al.* (1996).

18 Patla (1997).

19 Steenhuis, Goodale (1988).

20 Thomson (1983).

21 E.g., Thomson (1983); Elliott (1986). Presumably, there is an occlusion time that would affect accuracy at short distances, but no one has bothered to determine what it is.

22 Thomson's original proposal.

23 E.g., Steenhuis, Goodale (1988); Rieser *et al.* (1990).

24 Tyrrell *et al.* (1993).

25 Tyrrell *et al.* (1990).

26 Vogel, Woodman, Luck (2001); Cowan (2005).

27 See Cowan (2005).

28 Reynolds, Day (2005a).

29 Patla (1997); Weerdesteyn *et al.* (2004).

30 Mohagheghi, Moraes, Patla (2004).

31 Weerdesteyn *et al.* (2004).

32 Weerdesteyn *et al.* (2005).

33 Marigold *et al.* (2007).

34 Patla, Beuter, Prentice (1991).

35 See Reynolds, Day (2005a,b).

36 Reynolds, Day (2005a,b).

37 From an experiment reported in Patla (1997).

38 Warren (1984).

39 Gibson (1979).

40 Warren (1984), experiments 2 and 3.

41 Participants were asked to choose the set of stairs that they judged to be 'more comfortable ... to climb to the top' (Warren, 1984, page 697).

42 Warren, Whang (1987).

43 Participants also made judgments when walking towards the gap (from a distance of about 5 m), but the results did not differ.

44 It is quite possible that the true explanation for the difference is the other way around. Perhaps participants in the first experiment felt that there was an emphasis on avoiding any contact with the gap walls. As a consequence they may have behaved conservatively, producing a larger critical gap width than would be characteristic of their everyday behavior.

45 The shape of the imaging surface makes no difference to the basic argument, provided that it is smooth. However, there are some subtleties; see Tresilian (1991).

46 The similarity of the triangles means that the ratio W/D is equal to the ratio w/f.

47 In fact, the rate of change of D is –V.

48 Take the temporal derivative of both sides of equation (9.1).

49 This tau notation was introduced by D.N. Lee (Lee, Reddish, Rand, 1991). The mathematical argument showing that TTA information is available in images seems to have been first discovered by Sir Fred Hoyle, who presented it in a footnote in his science fiction novel *The Black Cloud*, published in 1957.

50 Sometimes called 'time to passage' (Kaiser, Mowafy, 1993).

[51] This was first shown in a restricted form in Lee (1974). A more general treatment was presented by Longuet-Higgins and Prazdny (1980).

[52] For evidence in humans see Regan, Hamstra (1993); Gray, Regan (1998).

[53] Tresilian (1991).

[54] E.g., Regan, Hamstra (1993).

[55] It has been shown that independent estimates of retinal distance (i.e., retinal size) and retinal velocity may be necessary for making some estimates of TTA (Smeets et al., 1996), but these are image quantities, not distances and velocities in the environment.

[56] E.g., Frost, Sun (2004).

[57] The constant timing error is the average of the timing errors on individual trials; the variable timing error is their standard deviation.

[58] E.g., Schiff, Detwiler (1979).

[59] E.g., DeLucia, Liddell (1998).

[60] This is a standard clock and counter type model of time estimation. Such models appear to be appropriate for estimation of longer intervals (on the order of seconds), but estimation of shorter intervals may involve different types of neural process (Karmarkar, Buonomano, 2007).

[61] There are various alternative possibilities for how intrinsic timing might be achieved (DeLucia, Liddell, 1998; Tresilian, 1995).

[62] See Tresilian (1999b).

[63] E.g., Smith et al. (2001).

[64] Prevost et al. (2002).

[65] The figure shows that the head started to turn when the distance was just under 0.3 m. The criterion distance would have to factor in the eye-to-muscle transmission time, and so would be a little over 0.3 m.

[66] Prevost et al. (2002); Grasso et al. (1998).

[67] Lee, Reddish (1981).

[68] Lee, Reddish (1981).

[69] The visible features on the water surface are likely to be wave crests or similar features that move. Since the motion of all such features will typically be coherent (the waves all tend to move in the same direction), the value of tau for all features in the image should be averaged to eliminate the effects of the coherent motion.

[70] The range of dive heights was between 0.5 and 4 meters (Wann, 1996).

[71] Many tau variables provide information about TTC with the eye, and so would be of no use for timing contacts between the feet and the ground.

[72] Santello, Mcdonagh, Challis (2001); Liebermann, Hoffman (2005).

[73] Santello, Mcdonagh, Challis (2001).

[74] For falls from rest, if the drop height is H, then the time taken to fall is equal to $\sqrt{2H/g}$, where g is the acceleration due to gravity.

[75] Warren, Young, Lee (1986).

[76] More properly, the impulse is the time integral of the force over the period for which the force is applied (the area under the force-time curve).

[77] Equation (5) in Warren, Young, Lee (1986).

10.1 Staying on Track by Correcting Errors

10.1.1 Introduction: path following, target acquisition and heading

When people move from one place to another, they often follow some sort of visible pathway: they might be hiking up a mountain path, running around an athletics track or driving along a road. We will refer to this as **locomotor path following**. In some situations there is no visible path to follow. For instance, you might be walking or running across an open field to reach a gate on the other side, or you might be paddling a canoe across a lake. Moving to a visible location in the absence of a marked path will be referred to as **locomotor target acquisition**. When path following, a person usually wants to avoid leaving the path – they need to stay on track. This requires sustained control of the direction of locomotion. The same is true in locomotor target acquisition: a person must steer so that they move towards the target location.

The direction in which a person moves through their environment during locomotor activity is the **heading direction**, or simply **heading**. The term applies regardless of how a person is moving – they could be walking, crawling, skiing, cycling, flying a plane or driving a motor vehicle[1]. In all the examples discussed in this chapter, the heading direction coincides with the direction in which the person or vehicle is 'pointing'. Pointing in this context is explained in Figure 10.1: a person points in the direction of the mid-sagittal plane of the pelvis (left), and a motor vehicle points in the direction of its long axis (right). We will refer to the direction that a person or vehicle points as the **pointing direction**. There are cases in which the heading direction is not the same as the pointing direction[2], but we will not encounter any of these in this chapter.

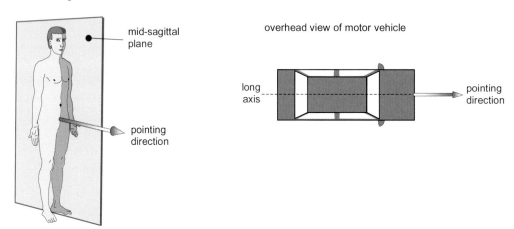

Figure 10.1: *Pointing direction for man and vehicle.*

This chapter is concerned with how people control their heading direction in both path-following and target acquisition tasks. In the first part of the chapter we will focus on the role of negative feedback control and how it has been studied in various tasks that require people to stay on track.

10.1.2 Feedback control can be used to stay on track

In order to use negative feedback control to stay on track, an error must be computed. The error needed is the **heading error**. Panel A of Figure 10.2 shows a situation in which a vehicle is on a straight section of road, but is heading towards the edge: it will leave the road if no corrective action is taken. The heading error (labeled β) is the angle between the direction of the road (dashed) and the heading direction. In general, heading error is the difference between the actual heading direction and the required heading direction, which in Figure 10.2 is the direction of the road:

> **HEADING ERROR:** The difference (at a given moment in time) between the actual heading direction and the required heading direction.

On a straight section of road, a heading error might be caused by a powerful gust of wind, or it might be the result of drift during a period of inattention. When driving along a winding road, heading errors can arise due to bends in the road, as shown in panel B of Figure 10.2. At the instant of time shown in the figure, the vehicle is heading along the line of the initial segment of road but has reached a point at the start of a curve. The road's direction at this point is shown by the dashed line (the tangent to the curve of the road at the vehicle's location); β is the heading error.

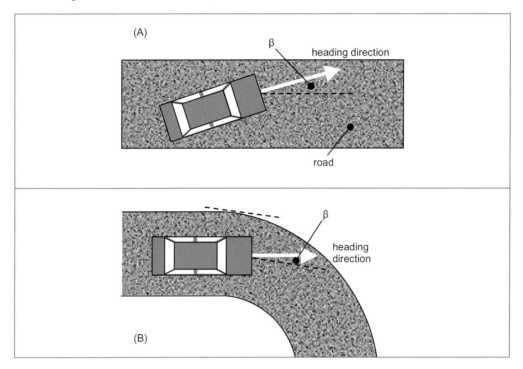

Figure 10.2: *Heading error (β) on a straight section of road (A) and upon entering a curve (B).*

The heading errors in Figure 10.2 can be eliminated by appropriate steering action, which could be achieved using feedback control based on heading error. This would involve the driver using sensory information about heading direction to obtain an estimate of the heading error. The error would then be used to determine how to turn the steering wheel – which direction, how far, and how fast – so as to eliminate the heading error. It is important to note, however, that feedback control of steering along a road does not require the computation of heading error. It is possible, for example, to use the distance from the edge of the road instead. A driver could steer so as not to get too close to the edges of the lane in which the vehicle is being driven. Figure 10.3 illustrates the idea: the driver tries to steer the vehicle so that it stays more than some (safe) distance, d, from the edges of the lane. In effect, the driver attempts to stay within a 'virtual' lane between the black lines. If any part of the vehicle is less than the distance d from a lane edge (has crossed the virtual edge), then there is an error, and a steering adjustment is made to bring the vehicle back inside the virtual lane. Such an error is called a **lateral position error**. There is evidence to suggest that when people drive they make steering adjustments in response to both heading errors and lateral position errors[3].

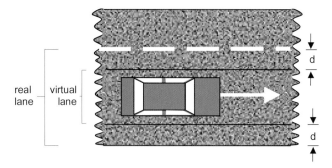

Figure 10.3: *A 'virtual lane' defined by a safe distance (d) between the vehicle and the lane edges.*

10.1.3 When staying on track, feedback control is known as compensatory control

In the context of continuous 'staying on track' tasks – or **tracking tasks** as they are usually called – the error-corrective, feedback mode of control is usually referred to as the **compensatory mode** of control:

> **COMPENSATORY CONTROL MODE:** The name given to the error-corrective, feedback mode of control when it is employed in a continuous tracking task.

The term is used because the person is compensating for errors by making corrective actions. There are three important questions we can ask about how people use the compensatory control mode to stay on track:

(1) What are the controlled variables in tasks that require staying on track or maintaining a course? For example, is heading the controlled variable? Or lateral position on the path? Or a combination of the two?

(2) What perceptual information do people use to obtain estimates of the controlled variables and/or the errors in these variables? For example, if heading is the controlled variable, how is it (and/or the heading error) perceived?

(3) How do people transform error estimates in control actions? For example, if a person driving a motor vehicle detects a heading error, what do they do with the error so as to obtain appropriate movements of the steering wheel?

We will address all these questions in what follows. Before doing so, we will briefly discuss why the compensatory mode is appropriate for correcting small, unexpected errors in heading (or lateral position), but less appropriate for large errors, such as those that could arise on entering a bend. The kind of control involved in steering around bends will be discussed later in the chapter (section 10.4).

10.1.4 The compensatory control mode is unsuitable for correcting large errors and for steering around curves

The error-corrective, compensatory control mode for staying on track has some disadvantages. It requires that the driver be constantly alert for errors: if the driver allows the errors to get too large, it will be impossible to correct them effectively. However, drivers perform a number of tasks other than steering, which are likely to interfere with sustained attention directed at the error-detection task; these include scanning the dashboard instruments, inspecting road signs, looking in rear view mirrors and adjusting the air conditioning or the sound system[4].

When approaching a bend in the road, large heading errors can develop quite quickly; these will be greater for a sharper curve. Only once the car has entered the bend does a heading error or a lateral position error occur. This must be corrected quickly, or the vehicle will go off the road. There are two difficulties: (1) making a rapid, large-amplitude steering correction can be dangerous, as the wheels may lose traction, resulting in a skid; (2) there will be a significant time delay between the development of an error and a change in the vehicle's heading, due to the time it takes the driver to compute and execute the corrective response. The delay has been estimated to be about 0.8 seconds[5], and drivers have been found to behave as if they have knowledge of this limitation[6].

Consider the second difficulty: when entering a bend in the road, is there enough time to correct the heading error once it has developed? The vehicle will start to change its direction of motion after at least 0.8 seconds, but by this time it will often be too late. Imagine driving along a winding country road at a moderate speed of 60 km/hr (about 37 mph): when the vehicle enters a bend, the distance from the front of the vehicle to the edge of the curve straight ahead (see Figure 10.2B) is likely to be less than ten meters. At 60 km/h it takes only about 0.6 seconds to cover this distance, and so the vehicle would leave the road before a corrective change of direction could be made. Thus, the error-corrective, compensatory mode of control is ineffective for steering around bends in the road, unless the bend is very gentle and the speed is low. Drivers must use a different mode of control when negotiating bends. This involves anticipation: a driver can see that there is a curve ahead, and act before a heading error has had a chance to develop. Anticipatory control of steering will be discussed in section 4 of this chapter.

10.1.5 Compensatory displays present only the error

In certain situations it may be impossible to perceive the direction you are going or where you want to go. Such situations may occur when sailing a boat in the open sea where no landmarks are visible, or when flying a plane through clouds, through fog, or above the cloud level. To assist the sailor or the pilot in these circumstances, various navigational aids have been developed to help the person stay on a desired course.

Some navigational aids do not present to the person the course to be followed or the vehicle's actual position, they present only the error: the difference between the actual position and the position the vehicle should be in if it is on course. No information is presented about the cause of the error. When only the error is presented, the navigator is obliged to control the vehicle's course in the compensatory (error-corrective) mode. A display that presents only the error is called a **compensatory display**:

> **COMPENSATORY DISPLAY:** A means by which feedback information about an error (difference between an actual state and a desired state of a system being controlled) is presented to a person.

A person who attempts to stay on track by using only a compensatory display is said to be carrying out a **compensatory tracking task**, a term that is to some extent self-explanatory:

> **COMPENSATORY TRACKING TASK:** A continuous control task in which a person attempts to keep an error as close as possible to zero. A display of the error itself is is presented to the person performing the task.

Compensatory tracking tasks have been extensively studied in laboratory experiments. A major aim was to discover the characteristics and limitations of people's performance in these tasks, so as to inform the design of aids for such things as flight control[7]. An example of such an aid that is used in some aircraft is the *zero* reader display, which presents the difference between the actual position of the aircraft and the flight path – it presents the positional error[8]. These displays can be used to control descent and landing when visibility is poor[9].

An example is shown in Figure 10.4: it consists of a small circle that is fixed in the middle of a screen, and two crosshairs. When the meeting point of the two crosshairs (the cross-point) is within the circle (panel A), then the aircraft is on the flight path (no error). If the cross-point falls outside the small circle, as in panel B, then the aircraft is not on the flight path (an error). The location of the cross-point relative to the circle indicates both the size and the direction of the error: in panel B, the position of the cross-point indicates that the plane is too high relative to the flight path (circle above cross-point) and is veering to the left of the flight path (circle to the left of cross-point). The greater the distance between the circle and the cross-point, the larger the error. To fly along the correct path, the pilot needs to move the steering yoke so as to keep the cross-point within the circle, or move it back to inside the circle if it moves outside it. The correct type of response to the error in Figure 10.4B is to push the yoke forward, so that the aircraft descends, and turn it to the right.

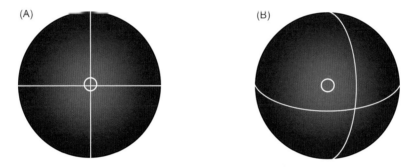

Figure 10.4: *Zero reader display. The small white circle represents the aircraft.*

10.1.6 In compensatory tracking tasks, the person is an element in a feedback control system

A schematic block diagram of a pilot following a flight path using a zero reader display is shown in Figure 10.5. The diagram shows that the pilot is an element in a negative feedback control system, in which the aircraft is the system being controlled, and the position error is computed as the difference between the actual position of the aircraft and that specified by the flight path. The error is then displayed on the zero reader display. The pilot watches the display and moves the yoke in response to errors. Thus, the pilot transforms the error into movements of the steering yoke.

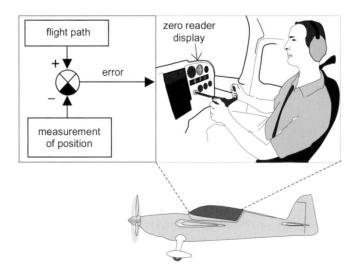

Figure 10.5: *The pilot as an element in a feedback control system.*

In the examples of negative feedback control that were described in previous chapters, the error was transformed into an input to the system under control (controlled system) by a relatively simple process. In Chapter 1 we described the simplest possible situation: the error (e) is transformed simply by multiplying it by some gain factor (k) so that the value of the controlling input is just the gain times the error (k × e). In the flight control system, the pilot needs to produce a control input that is not only of the right size, but also in the right direction – pushing the yoke forwards or backwards to make the plane go down or up, turning the yoke left or right to make the plane bank left or right. Furthermore, a pilot is a complex, sophisticated system who learns and predicts, takes time to process information, and has internal dynamics. As described later, a person can and does do more than just multiply the error by a gain factor.

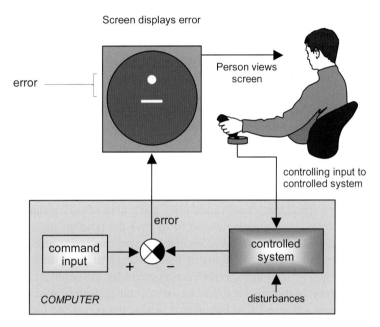

Figure 10.6: *Laboratory compensatory tracking task in which a person attempts to keep the dot over the bar by manipulating a joystick.*

It is clear from the definition of compensatory tracking that the controlled system does not need to be an aircraft, boat or other vehicle (real or simulated). The person is simply presented with an error, and they try to reduce the error to zero by manipulating a control device, which makes it easy to study performance on these tasks in the laboratory. Figure 10.6 shows a diagram of the typical laboratory compensatory tracking task. The person is presented with a display screen that contains a fixed mark (bar) and a movable mark (spot). If a computer display is used, the movable mark is referred to as the *cursor*. The task is to keep the spot over the bar by manipulating a control device such as a joystick. A computer simulates all the boxed elements in the figure: the controlled system, the disturbances, the comparator (⊗) and the *command input*. The command input is a specification of the desired output of the simulated controlled system – if the controlled system is a simulation of an aircraft, then the command input is a simulated flight course. The error is computed as the difference between the command input and the output of the simulated controlled system. The command input can be defined as follows:

> **COMMAND INPUT:** The path (track) or signal that a person attempts to make the output of the controlled system follow when performing a tracking task.

10.1.7 Do people use the compensatory control mode when performing compensatory tracking tasks?

In a compensatory tracking task, a person is not presented with the track they are attempting to follow (the command input) or with the response (output) of the system they are controlling. In such a task, the person appears to be restricted to attempting to correct the errors presented to them. However, a person does not necessarily have to act in the compensatory mode. For example, imagine that a person is piloting a motor boat over a completely calm, empty lake on windless day. They are required to steer the boat along a particular course by means of a compensatory display that gives a continuous presentation of the boat's positional error (the position of the boat relative to the required course). In such conditions, there are no disturbances that can unexpectedly alter the boat's heading (no waves, no gusts of wind). Errors will arise if the boat drifts off the course or if the course direction changes. The first time the person steers the boat along a particular course using only the error information presented, steering control will presumably be achieved in compensatory mode. However, if the person steers the same course several times, they can learn about the course from the error, which will vary in a predictable way. In fact, it has been shown that people can learn to predict how the error will vary when the same track is repeated in several trials, which allows the person to make anticipatory control actions. In this chapter we will focus on compensatory control.

When the error varies in an unpredictable way, a person has no option but to behave in compensatory mode[10]. Unpredictable error variation can easily be generated in an experimental compensatory tracking task. Panel A of Figure 10.7 shows one way of doing it: the command input is a signal that varies randomly – a segment of such a signal is shown in the command input block. An alternative would be to have the random signal input to the controlled system. This would simulate random disturbances corresponding to real-world situations: for example, landing a plane in fog by flying along a predetermined flight path using a zero-reader display, where unpredictable errors could be the result of gusts of wind and variations in air pressure that do not follow any particular pattern. A block diagram showing this situation is shown in panel B of Figure 10.7, where the command input is constant and the controlled system receives random disturbances[11].

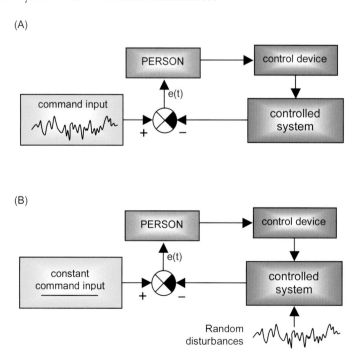

Figure 10.7: *Two ways of introducing random, unpredictable variation into the error signal in a compensatory tracking task.*

In situations where there are random errors, people have little choice other than to act in compensatory control mode and act as an element in a negative feedback control loop. The same is true in driving and other locomotor tasks where staying on track is subject to unpredictable disturbances of various sorts. Although there are typically other, anticipatory control processes operative in these tasks, the evidence shows that the compensatory mode is also continuously active, correcting for unexpected disturbances or driver errors[12]. Compensatory tracking tasks with random error signals have the advantage that the compensatory mode of control can be studied without the involvement of anticipatory modes of control; they have been extensively used for this purpose.

When operating in the compensatory mode, the person can be thought of as performing a sensorimotor transformation of the error perceived from the display into movements of the control device. The nature of this sensorimotor transformation has been found to depend on the type of control device and the nature of the system being controlled, as might be expected. However, the transformation has been found to have some interesting properties, as will be described in what follows.

10.1.8 Dynamic systems have various properties: system order

In a compensatory tracking task, a person will need practice in order to learn how the control device should be moved – how far, in what direction, and how fast – so as to reduce the error effectively[13]. Exactly what movements are needed depends on both the control device and the controlled system. As described in Chapter 1, we can consider the control device to be a component of the controlled system: the steering wheel (control device) can be considered to be part of the vehicle (controlled system), for example. In this section we will follow this convention.

A person must learn how to control a system. We don't simply get into a vehicle and start driving; we need an extended period of instruction and practice. During this period, we learn how to move the control device(s) so as to make the vehicle do what we want it to do. Such learning is often characterized as the formation of an internal model of the controlled system (discussed further in Chapter 15). In what follows, we will consider the behavior of skilled performers who have had plenty of practice.

Experiments have studied how performance, usually quantified by average error measures, depends on the properties of the controlled system[14]. These studies have provided information about how well people are able to control different types of controlled system and what type of control device give the best performance. In principle, the range of possible controlled system characteristics is enormously large. One particularly important characteristic is the **order** of the controlled system, which is specified by an integer – a system can be zero order, first order, second order, etc. The control device is called a *zero order control* if it is a component of a zero order controlled system, a *first order control* if it is a component of a first order controlled system, and so on. Order can be informally understood in terms of the type of output produced when a particular input is applied. We will consider zero, first and second order systems in turn (third and higher order systems are rather unusual).

▸ **Zero order controlled system:** a system in which the output is directly proportional to the input, so the output just follows the input. For example, if the input is a ramp, the output will be a ramp, as shown in panel A of Figure 10.8. A computer with a mouse is a first order controlled system. The output is the position of the cursor on the screen, which simply follows the displacement of the mouse on the pad. For this reason, zero order systems are also called **position control systems**: the output is a position which follows the displacement of the control device. A control device like a mouse is called a **zero order control** or a **position control**.

▸ **First order controlled system:** a system in which the speed at which the output changes is directly proportional to the input. For example, if the input is a step, the output will be a ramp, as shown in panel B of Figure 10.8. An automobile with an accelerator pedal is a first order controlled system[15]. A displacement of the pedal (an input) changes the speed of the vehicle, and as long as the pedal is displaced, the speed will continue to increase (until the forces of air and rolling resistance are sufficient to prevent any further increase). First order systems are also called **rate** or **velocity control systems**: the output is a velocity (or rate of change) that depends on the displacement of the control device. A control device like an accelerator is also called a **first order control** or a **velocity control**.

▸ **Second order controlled system:** a system in which the acceleration of the output is proportional to the input. For example, if the input is a step, the output is parabolically increasing, as shown in panel C of Figure 10.8. A motor vehicle with a steering wheel is a second order controlled system. A turn (angular displacement) of the wheel results in a continuous change in the direction in which the vehicle is heading (a change in direction is an acceleration). If you turn the wheel and hold it in the turned position, the heading direction will change continuously – the vehicle will go around in a circle. Second order systems are also called **acceleration control systems**. A control device like a steering wheel is also called a **second order control** or an **acceleration control**.

In the next section we will look briefly at the transformations carried out by skilled performers of compensatory tracking tasks, and how the transformation depends on the order of the controlled system.

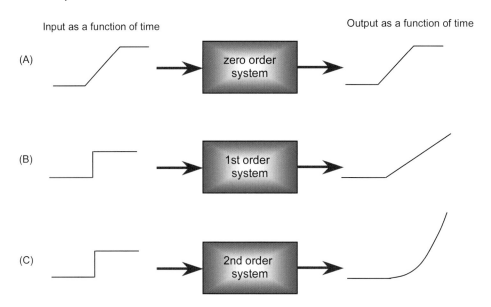

Figure 10.8: *Inputs (left) to zero, first and second order systems (middle) leading to different types of output (right).*

10.1.9 A person's transformation of error into movement of the control device depends on the system order

When operating in the compensatory mode, a person does more than simply scale the error to produce the control device input. We know, for example, that a person will introduce a time delay, due to the time it takes to transmit signals through the nervous system. In addition, the musculoskeletal system will introduce time lags, since movements and forces develop relatively slowly in response to neural inputs (see Chapter 2).

The data obtained from compensatory tracking experiments with unpredictable tracks or disturbances have been used to obtain a precise description of the transformation, from the error to movements of the control device, that people carry out when tracking in the compensatory mode[16]. As noted earlier, a skilled performer's transformation depends on the characteristics of the controlled system, such as its order: the performer learns to implement a transformation that is matched to the properties of this system. To understand the nature of the transformation that the person carries out and how it is matched to the properties of the controlled system, it is necessary to have some understanding of the use of Bode diagrams and Fourier analysis, and so the reader without this background may wish to skip the rest of this section.

Fourier analysis tells us that any signal likely to occur in the natural world can be represented as the sum of a number of distinct sinusoidal signals of different frequencies, amplitudes and phases – these are the frequency components of the signal. Thus, any signal can be considered as a function of time (the normal way) or as a function of frequency (Fourier's way). If the transformation from an input signal to an output signal is linear, then the output does not contain any frequency components that were not present in the input, though the phases and amplitudes of the components may be different. The Bode diagram is a graphical way of representing a linear input-output transformation. It consists of two plots: one represents how the amplitudes of the input frequency components are changed in the output; the other represents how the phases of the input components are changed in the output. The first of these is a graph of the gain of the transformation (output amplitude ÷ input amplitude) in logarithmic units against frequency (also in log units); the other part is a graph of the phase shift (output phase angle – input phase angle) against frequency.

It has been found[17] that for unpredictable tracks, a person performs an approximately linear transformation of the input (the error signal, e(t)) to produce their output (the movements of the control device, c(t)). This means that a Bode diagram can be used to represent the transformation. An example is shown in Figure 10.9 for data obtained from a person controlling a zero order system in a compensatory tracking experiment: panel A is the gain plot, and panel B is the phase plot. The gain plot (A) shows that frequency components greater than about 0.2 cycles per second are attenuated: the amplitude of the frequency components in the output is less than its amplitude in the input, and so the amplitude ratio (output amplitude ÷ input amplitude) is less than zero in logarithmic units. The attenuation increases with frequency, which is what we would expect – higher frequencies are more difficult to track than lower frequencies, because the signal changes more quickly; frequencies higher than 5 or 6 Hz are almost impossible to track[18]. The phase plot (B) shows that the frequency components in the output lag behind those in the input, since the phase shift is negative (input phase angles are greater than output phase angles). This means that the person introduces a time delay and/or a lag, as we would expect.

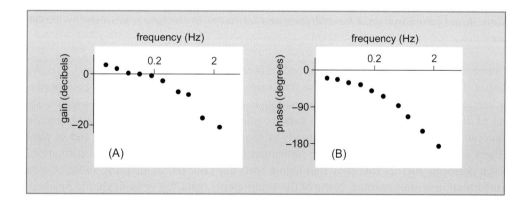

Figure 10.9: *Bode diagram for performance of a compensatory tracking task with a first order system. Based on original data from McRuer and Jex (1967), in the format provided by Wickens (1992).*

Figure 10.10 shows Bode diagrams for a person controlling a first order system (panel A) and a second order system (panel B) in a compensatory tracking experiment with random command inputs. Both diagrams represent the transformation from e(t) to c(t) being carried out by the person. Figures 10.9 and 10.10 show that the transformation is different when the order of the controlled system is different: the Bode diagram in panel (A) of Figure 10.10 is different from that in panel (B), and both are different from the diagram in Figure 10.9. In fact, the Bode diagrams can be interpreted as showing that when the controlled system is zero order, a person's transformation of the error signal closely approximates a constant gain together with a pure time delay and a lag (responsible for the attenuation of the higher frequencies). When the controlled system is first order, the transformation approximates a constant gain (of about one) with a time delay; a lag component is not evident, as there is no attenuation of higher frequencies (Figure 10.10A, top). When the controlled system is second order, the transformation is rather more complex. In particular, instead of lagging behind the input, frequency components between about 0.1 Hz and 1.0 Hz in the person's response are ahead of those in the input (phase shift > 0 in Figure 10.10B). This is a lead rather than a lag, and indicates that the person's response depends on the rate of change of the error.

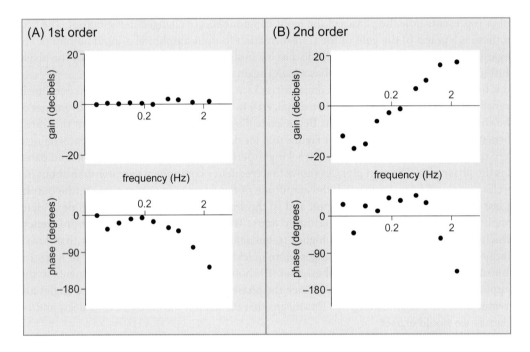

Figure 10.10: *Bode diagram for performance of a compensatory tracking task with a first order system. Based on original data from McRuer and Jex (1967), in the format provided by Wickens (1992).*

To summarize, the skilled performer's sensorimotor transformation from error, e(t), to movement of the control device, c(t), has the structure shown in Figure 10.11: it can be described mathematically as the product of a constant gain, a pure time delay, a lag and a lead[19]. This kind of description has been found to capture quite accurately the compensatory behavior of people driving cars along straight roads in the presence of disturbances[20], and of pilots in flight simulators[21]. It is important to remember that a description of the transformation a person performs such as that shown in Figure 10.11 does not tell us anything about how the transformation is implemented. None of the components (gain, lag or lead) should be identified with any physiological mechanism – the description tells us *what* the transformation is, not *how* it is done.

The experimental results show that when a skilled person is performing a continuous, compensatory tracking task, their learned sensorimotor transformation is approximately[22] linear and depends on the order of the controlled system. The dependency of the transformation on the controlled system means that the transformation embodies information about the controlled system. This is usually expressed by saying that the transformation incorporates an *internal model* of the controlled system (see Chapter 1). What exactly does changing the transformation from error to controlling input achieve? We discuss this in the next section.

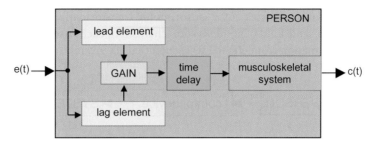

Figure 10.11: *A block diagram representation of the functional structure of a person when they are performing a compensatory tracking task.*

10.1.10 The whole system behaves as a good servomechanism

The skilled performer of a compensatory tracking task is able to keep the error relatively small. This, after all, is the goal of the task. Performance can be quantified by determining the average size of the error over a period of time spent on the task. At every moment of time, the error will have some value (possibly zero); an average error score takes measurements of error values at sequential moments in time and forms their average. Two commonly used average error scores are the **root mean square error** (RMSE for short) and the **mean absolute error** (MAE for short). To see how to calculate these errors, consider a very simple example: suppose an error was measured at three moments in time – say one, two and three seconds after starting the task – and the measured values were 2, 6 and –3 mm. Such errors might be measured from a display like that shown in Figure 10.6, where a positive error occurs when the moving spot (circle in Figure 10.6) is above the fixed mark (bar in Figure 10.6) and a negative error occurs when the spot is below it. The MAE is the average of the unsigned errors (all errors made positive), which is $(2 + 6 + 3)/3 = 3.67$ mm. The RMSE is the square root of the average of the squared errors, which is $\sqrt{[(2^2 + 6^2 + (-3)^2)/3]} = 4.04$ mm.

As you might expect, the more practice a person has with a tracking task, the smaller their error score. Figure 10.12 presents an example that shows the decline in MAE across a series of eight practice sessions on a compensatory task (sessions performed on consecutive days; each data point in the figure is the mean from 12 participants). The error scores have been scaled so that the error has a value of 100 if a participant does nothing.

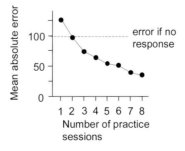

Figure 10.12: *Decline of mean absolute error in a compensatory tracking task over a series of sessions. Data are taken from Figure 9.4 in Poulton (1974).*

Once a person is performing at a high level of skill, their error score over a period of time can be quite small. It is at this stage that their performance has the characteristics described in the previous section (Figures 10.9, 10.10). The whole control system comprised of the person, the controlled system and the other elements in the loop behaves like a 'good' servomechanism. A good servomechanism is one that keeps the error acceptably small, responds sufficiently quickly and is stable. In fact, results of the kind presented in Figures 10.9 and 10.10 show that the behavior of the whole system is very similar regardless of the order of the controlled system: the skilled performer carries out a sensorimotor transformation that makes the whole system behave as the same kind of good servomechanism in each case. To put it another way, the person's transformation from e(t) to c(t) is such that the overall transformation from e(t) to y(t) shown here,

remains approximately the same despite changes in the properties of the controlled system[23]. This invariance is illustrated in Figure 10.13 using the Bode plot representation. In each cell, the upper graph is the gain plot and the lower graph is the phase plot. The column of plots on the left are Bode plots for zero, first and second order controlled systems: they present a graphical representation of the input-output transformation of the controlled system. The middle column presents Bode plots for the transformation carried out by the person; they are schematics of the plots of real data shown in Figures 10.9 and 10.10. The column on the right presents the Bode plots for the combination of person and controlled system acting together. If you add a controlled system plot (left) to the corresponding plot for the person (gain plot + gain plot; phase plot + phase plot), you end up with the plot for the person + controlled system (right). The transformation of this combined system that transforms the error, e(t), into the controlled system output, y(t), is similar for all orders of controlled system and displays the characteristics of a good servomechanism.

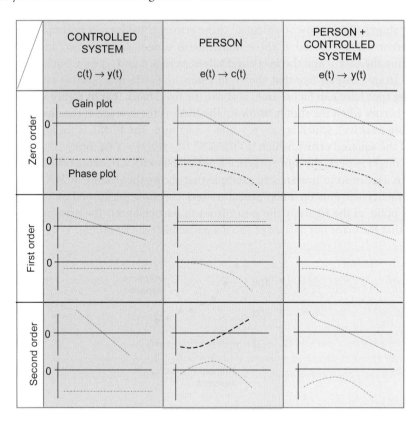

Figure 10.13: *Schematic Bode diagrams illustrating how people carry out different transformations of the error, e(t), to control actions, c(t) (middle), when controlling systems of different order (left) in such a way as to keep the overall system dynamics invariant (right). (Inspired by Figure 14.6 in Jagacinski and Flach, 2003.)*

10.1.11 Being able to see ahead when performing a tracking task is called preview

In a laboratory compensatory tracking task, the person is presented with a display of the error and cannot see the track itself. This permits a study of people's error-corrective control, since they only have access to error information and so cannot use anticipatory modes of control. However, in everyday tracking tasks like driving a motor vehicle along a road, it is always possible to see at least some part of the road ahead. As we will see in the next part of the chapter, people can obtain heading information and lateral road position information from their view of the road ahead and use this information to make corrective steering adjustments. Anticipatory steering control is also possible when the path ahead can be seen, and is certainly used to avoid obstacles (Chapter 9) and when following curved paths. However, when following a straight track in the absence of obstructions of any kind, people appear to use the compensatory mode of control.

In the literature on tracking, a view of the upcoming track is referred to as **preview**. A tracking task in which the track rather than the error is presented to the person is called a **pursuit tracking task**:

> **PURSUIT TRACKING TASK:** A continuous control task in which a person attempts to make a controlled system output follow a command input (the track).

In a locomotor pursuit tracking task, the controlled system output might be the direction of locomotion (heading); the command input might be the road, or it might be something that is being actively chased, such as a prey animal. There is a difference between chasing something and following a road or a pathway. When chasing something, you can see where it is, but you cannot be certain where it is going – it might make a sudden, unpredictable change in direction. When following a path, you can normally see the path for some distance ahead, and so can be certain of where the path is going. A path-following task in which you can see some of the path ahead is called a **pursuit tracking task with preview**. Driving along a road is a pursuit tracking task with preview.

10.1.12 How are error signals obtained for feedback control of everyday steering tasks?

Compensatory displays present the error directly to a person, but this is an artificial situation. The natural environment seldom does us the favor of displaying errors directly: a person needs to determine the error for themselves from the available stimulation. We have seen that there is evidence that people use heading error and road position error to control the direction of motion when driving along a road. A person must obtain the information needed to estimate these errors from retinal images of the scene, which raises the following question: *What perceptual information is it that people use to determine errors?* This question is addressed in relation to heading errors in the next section of this chapter. Once a heading error signal has been derived from the stimulus, it can be used to generate motor commands to the limbs. This process is considered further in section 3 of the chapter.

10.2 Perceiving That You Are Going in the Right Direction

10.2.1 Introduction

For the compensatory control of the direction of locomotion (heading), it is necessary to obtain information about the heading error, since the control process is one that corrects such errors. There are two ways in which heading error can be obtained:

(1)   Perceive heading (i.e., determine heading from stimulus information), and then form the heading error as the difference between the perceived heading and the desired heading.

(2)   Perceive heading error directly. In this case, heading is not perceived first and used to compute heading error; information about the error itself is extracted directly from the stimulus.

The first method has attracted the most attention. One early suggestion derived from the finding that the **focus of radial outflow** (FRO, see Chapter 4) specifies the eye's heading direction. If the location of the FRO in the image can be determined, then it is possible to perceive heading and hence determine heading error[24]. In this part of the chapter we will consider further the idea that heading is perceived by extracting the location of the FRO from retinal images. We will also describe other sources of stimulus information about both heading and heading error.

10.2.2 Retinal images contain several sources of heading-related information

Imagine that you are driving a motor vehicle down the middle of a straight stretch of clear road. You look at the road ahead, and the retinal images of points in the scene will move as a result of your motion along the road. If you are looking straight ahead and your eyes are not rotating (no eye movements), the image motion will exhibit a flow pattern like that shown in Figure 10.14. The figure shows an image of the scene ahead at a particular moment in time. The arrows are image velocity vectors, and they provide a representation of the image flow field: they represent the motion across the image plane of the points to which their tails are attached (see Chapter 4). The direction of an arrow represents the direction of motion, and the length of an arrow represents the speed of motion. The focus of radial outflow (FRO) is marked with a circle.

Figure 10.14: *The image flow pattern produced when driving down the middle of the road and looking in the direction of heading. The FRO (circle) lies in the heading direction.*

The FRO is a source of information about heading, since it lies in the direction in which the eye is moving: if a person can locate the FRO in an image, then they know in which direction they are going. However, it is not necessary to determine the location of the FRO in order to perceive heading. One alternative is to determine the location of the **locomotor flow line**[25]. This is the vertical line from the FRO to the lower boundary of the scene; in Figure 10.14, the solid lane-dividing line approximately coincides with the locomotor flow line.

Figure 10.15 shows a schematic image flow pattern similar to that in Figure 10.14 but showing only some image flow vectors, not the image itself. The FRO is again marked by a circle, and the locomotor flow line is shown as a dotted line. Notice from Figures 10.14 and 10.15 that points in the locomotor flow line are images of points in the environment over which the eye will pass if it continues to move in a straight line. This means that the locomotor flow line lies along the future path on the ground over which the person will move if they continue in their current direction. When the locomotor flow line is aligned with the desired travel path, such as the middle of the straight stretch of road in Figure 10.14, then you are heading in the right direction. If it is not aligned with the desired direction, then there is a heading error and a corrective steering action is needed. Likewise, there is an error if the locomotor flow line does not pass through the image of the target location towards which you want to move.

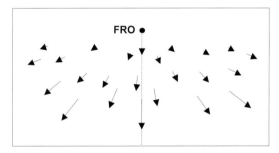

Figure 10.15: *The locomotor flow line (dashed) is a vertical line through the FRO.*

Figure 10.14 suggests a third type of heading information that is present when moving along a road or other visible pathway. The edges of a straight section of road project to an inverted V shape (∧) in the image. The image of each edge is at an angle to the image vertical (straight up the page in the figure). This angle is known as the **splay angle**[26], which is defined geometrically in Figure 10.16. Panel A shows an eye heading down the middle of a straight stretch of road. The eye is a height, H, above the ground, and a lateral distance, d, from the left edge of the road. Panel B shows the scene as imaged on the retina of the eye in panel A (turned the right way around so that it coincides with the view as seen by the eye). The splay angle of the left edge of the road is labeled σ – it is the angle as measured on the image plane (or the plane of the page) between the image of the road edge and any suitable vertical line in the image (the dotted line is one such line). The tangent of the splay angle is equal to the lateral distance divided by the eye height, which can be written as[27] $\tan \sigma = d/H$. Thus the splay angle depends on eye height and the eye's lateral position on the road.

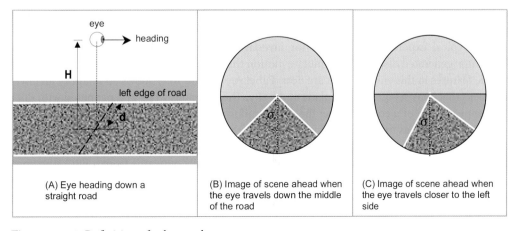

| (A) Eye heading down a straight road | (B) Image of scene ahead when the eye travels down the middle of the road | (C) Image of scene ahead when the eye travels closer to the left side |

Figure 10.16: *Definition of splay angle.*

If an eye moves straight along the road on a horizontal path then its height and lateral position do not change, so the splay angle is constant. However, if the splay angle is changing, then the eye is either moving up or down (a case we will not consider) or else it is moving towards one side of the road or the other. That the splay angle will change as you move closer to the side of the road is illustrated in panel C of Figure 10.16. The panel shows an image of the scene viewed by an eye positioned closer to the left edge than in Panel B, where the eye is in the center of the road. Thus, if the eye moves closer to the edge of the road, the splay angle decreases. If the splay angle is constant, heading is constant and is parallel to the edge of the road – you are heading down the road a constant distance from the edge. If splay angle is changing, then you are moving to one side of the road or the other. For example, if the splay angle in Figure 10.16B were getting smaller, then the eye would be moving towards the left side of the road[28]. This means that if the splay angle is changing, then there is a heading error (you are heading towards the edge of the road). The rate at which splay angle is changing over time is called the **splay rate**. In order to travel down a straight section of road, it is sufficient to steer so that the splay rate is kept at zero. In order to maintain lateral position on the road, the splay angle should be kept constant at a particular value, since different splay angles are associated with different lateral positions on the road (Figure 10.16). So you can steer straight down the road and maintain lateral position by making steering adjustments that act to keep the splay angle constant at a particular value.

To sum up, we have seen that images of the scene ahead may contain several sources of heading-related information:

▸ The **focus of radial outflow** (FRO): an image feature that lies in the visual direction in which the eye is heading. If the location of the FRO can be determined, then you know the direction in which you are heading.
▸ The **locomotor flow line**: another image feature that specifies heading. If you can find the locomotor flow line in the image, then you know the direction you are heading.
▸ The **splay rate**: the rate of change of splay angle, a feature of the image of straight roads and pathways with visible edges. If the splay angle is changing, then you are heading towards one edge of the path or the other. Thus, splay rate provides heading error information.

This is not an exhaustive list of the sources of visual information about heading and heading error. A few other sources have been identified, and some of these will be described later (section 10.2.6).

10.2.3 People can determine heading from image flow

The FRO and the locomotor flow line differ from splay angle information in two ways. First, they provide information about heading rather than heading error. Second, they do not require that any specific structure be present in the scene, whereas splay angle requires that road edges or similar straight line structures are present in the scene. This means the FRO and/or the locomotor flow line can be used to steer towards a visible goal location when there is no road or path, but splay angle cannot. In this section we will look at the question of whether people can perceive heading from the image flow in the absence of any marked pathway (no splay angle information).

The typical experimental method for investigating this issue is to present people with computer-generated displays that simulate motion through a fixed environment. Often the only visible features in this environment are dots. Panel A of Figure 10.17 shows an image of an environment that consists of a ground plane and a 'sky'. The ground is white and peppered with dots that appear to be of a constant size; the sky is uniformly white. The experimental participant, usually referred to as the **observer**, views a display that simulates what they would see through the front window of a vehicle that moves in a straight line through such an environment. This is represented in panel B: a flow pattern that expands radially outwards from a FRO (the lines attached to the dots indicate the paths followed by the dots as they move in the image). There are two tasks that the observer may be asked to perform so that their ability to perceive heading can be assessed: (1) a pointing task in which the observer indicates the perceived location in the scene towards which they appear to be moving; (2) a task in which a person indicates whether they are heading to the right or left of a probe line presented somewhere on the image (the probe line is not part of the scene and does not move).

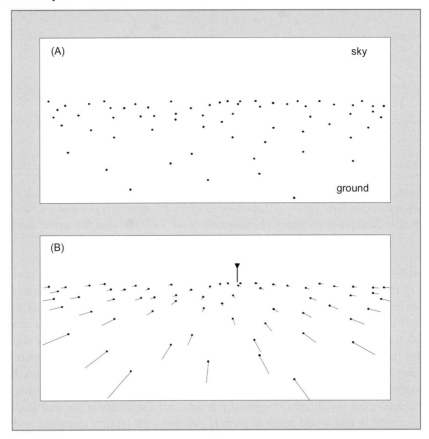

Figure 10.17: *(A) Simple environment consisting of a ground plane with dots. (B) Flow pattern produced by horizontal, straight line movement over the ground plane in (A). Also shown in (B) is a probe (line topped by a triangle), see text for explanation. (Based on Warren, Morris and Kalish, 1988.)*

The first experiments on heading perception used the (manual) pointing method in which the observer's task required them to point to the location of the FRO on the display screen[29]. Some example results from individual observers are shown in panels A and B of Figure 10.18: the FRO location is marked by a black circle, the center of the display screen is marked by a cross (these locations were not marked in the experiment), and the locations to which observers pointed are marked by diamonds. Observers showed relatively poor performance: the mean pointing errors typically lay between about 5° and 15° of visual angle (4.9° and 12.2° are the average errors in Figure 10.18A and B). This level of accuracy is not good enough for effective steering control, for which accuracy close to 1° or 2° is needed[30]. This might be taken to mean that steering control is not based on the type of heading information available to observers in the experiment (FRO and the locomotor flow line). However, no such conclusion is warranted, because the pointing method introduces certain biases – such as a tendency to point at the center of the display, which is particularly evident in panel B.

More recent experiments using the second method have shown that heading perception is accurate enough for effective steering control[31]. One of the first series of these more recent experiments[32] used scenes like that in Figure 10.17. The observer's task is to say whether or not they are heading to the left or to the right of the vertical probe line, which is in a fixed location. The closer the probe is to the true heading direction, the more difficult it is to say whether you are heading to left or right of it. Results from an experiment of this kind are shown in Figure 10.19. The dependent measure is the percentage of correct responses: the proportion of trials on which the heading was correctly judged as being to the left or right

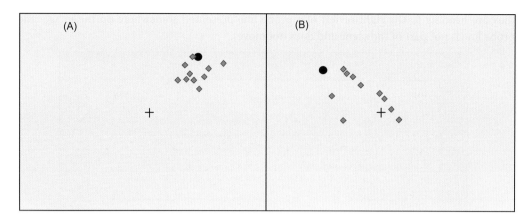

Figure 10.18: *Results from a heading perception experiment reported by Johnston, White, Cumming (1973, data from their Figure 2). Locations to which the observers pointed are shown as blue diamonds. For illustrative purposes, the locations of the FRO (●) and the screen center (+) are shown.*

of the probe, expressed as a percentage (50% is chance). The independent variable is the distance of the true heading from the probe (expressed as a visual angle). Results from two conditions are shown: one in which the ground plane was densely covered in dots, and one in which there were very few dots (only 10 in total). These results show that people can be quite good at determining the direction they are heading from displays like that in Figure 10.17, even when there are only a few visible features in the scene. The smallest difference between the position of the probe and the heading direction that can be reliably distinguished – the discrimination threshold – can be taken as the 75% correct point in the plots shown in Figure 10.19. The values for the threshold were about 0.65° for the dense scene and about 1.5° for the sparse scene. A real-world scene is densely covered with texture elements, and so these results suggest that people may be able to resolve their heading direction to within 1° of visual angle in everyday conditions, which is perfectly adequate for accurate steering.

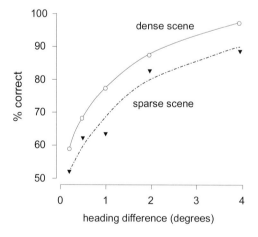

Figure 10.19: *Results from heading perception experiments. Panels A and B (Figure 10.18) are from a pointing experiment by Johnston, White, Cumming (1973, data from Figure 2). Panel C here shows data from an experiment by Warren, Morris, Kalish (1988, experiment 1).*

The fact that people were able to accurately determine where they are heading relative to the probe line tells us that they are able to extract heading-related information from the retinal image flow without the need for specific features like the edges of a road. Thus, we can conclude that splay angle information is not being used. However, we can neither determine exactly what information is used from these results nor how the information is extracted from the image. People might locate the position of the FRO and base their responses on that; alternatively, they might locate the locomotor flow line and use that instead[33]. A recent version of the pointing task has provided evidence that people are able to locate the FRO with reasonable accuracy. Experimental observers were required to make a saccadic eye movement to the location of the FRO[34]. Observers viewed computer-generated displays similar to that shown in Figure 10.17 and initially fixated a location some distance from the FRO. The task was to shift gaze from this initial location so as to look at the point towards which they appeared to be heading (the FRO). Observers were found to move their eyes to within about 3° of the true heading direction, which provides evidence that people can locate the FRO with a fair degree of accuracy. In the next section we briefly consider how heading information might be extracted from the image flow field.

10.2.4 How can the FRO be extracted from the image flow?

The focus of radial outflow (FRO) is a stationary point in the optic flow (see Chapter 3) and is only present in the retinal image when the eye is not rotating in its socket (no eye movement). In this section we will consider the problems associated with extracting the location of the FRO from the visual stimulus when the eye does not rotate (what happens when the eye rotates is discussed in the next section).

There are two basic problems that might be encountered. First, the FRO may lie at a location in the image where there are no visible features – in a region of 'empty' space. This is the case in Figure 10.17B, where the FRO lies in the 'sky' just above the horizon. When this is the case, it is clearly impossible to locate the FRO simply by identifying it with a point in the image flow that is not moving. When there is no visible point at the FRO, the FRO is said to be *implicit* in the image flow field. Second, even if there is a visible point at the location of the FRO, other points nearby will be moving so slowly that they too will appear stationary[35], so the FRO location cannot be precisely located simply by identifying a stationary point.

Both the two problems just described can be avoided by making use of the fact that all the image flow lines radiate out from the FRO. Figure 10.20 shows part of the flow pattern of Figure 10.17B with some of the flow lines extended back (dashed): the extended lines meet at the FRO. This simple fact can be used as the basis for computational procedures for finding the location of the FRO in image flow fields, and these have been successfully implemented using computers[36]. A variety of other methods have been proposed, and some of these have given rise to plausible models of the processing that takes place in the brain[37].

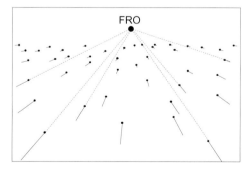

Figure 10.20: *The location of the FRO can be found by tracing back the flow lines.*

In Figure 10.20, the FRO is within the area of the image of the scene. It is possible for the FRO to be outside the image of the scene and still be implicit within it. Consider, for example, the flow field shown in panel A of Figure 10.21. This field is a part of the left half of the flow field shown in Figure 10.17B, and corresponds to viewing the scene through a circular window. The FRO lies outside the boundary of the window, but can clearly be located by extending the flow lines back, in the same manner as in Fig. 10.20. This situation has been studied experimentally, using a task in which observers pointed in the perceived heading direction[38] (see section 10.2.3). The FRO could be as far as 64° of visual angle beyond the boundary of the image displayed to observers. The results showed that people's accuracy in locating the FRO was similar regardless of whether or not it lay within the boundaries of the display (errors were about 5°, similar to those in other studies using the pointing task). Using a choice task similar to that used to obtain the data shown in Figure 10.19, it has been found that heading perception is more precise when the FRO lies within the display[39].

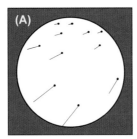 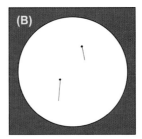

Figure 10.21: *Image flows in which the FRO is outside the viewing window.*

One final situation is worth considering, because it illustrates how some information about heading direction can be obtained without extracting the location of the FRO or finding the locomotor flow line. In the experiment described in section 10.2.3, where observers had to judge whether they were passing to the left or right of a probe line, it was found that it was still possible to perform the task with only two dots – a stimulus that hardly merits being described as a flow. Performance was significantly worse than with greater numbers of dots, but discrimination thresholds were still as low as 2.5°. Although it is possible to imagine tracing the two flow lines back to their meeting point in displays like that shown in Figure 10.20, there are other very simple cues to heading direction that a person could use. For example, in panel B of Figure 10.21 the point on the right is moving to the right and the one on the left is moving to the left. This means that the locomotor flow line must lie between them, because all points on the right of this line move to the right and all those on the left of it move to the left (Figure 10.15). If the two dots are both moving to the left, then the locomotor flow line is to the right of them; if they both move to the right, the locomotor flow line is on their left. This means that you can obtain some heading information just from the direction in which the dots move, and people can make use of information of this sort[40].

10.2.5 During eye movements, the image flow is the combination of two components

During normal locomotion, people do not typically keep their eyes steady for very long; they tend to look at different features in the environment and scan the path ahead for hazards (Chapter 9). If a person looks at some feature other than the FRO as they are moving along, they will generate a pursuit eye movement (or head and eye movement). When this happens, the point at which we are looking does not move on the retina, and so it is a stationary point on the retina (see Chapter 4). Thus, when we make a pursuit eye movement while moving through the environment, the image of the thing being looked at is stationary in the flow, and other visible points move away from it. The location that is looked at has similar characteristics to a FRO, which presents a potential difficulty[41]: if you rely on the FRO to determine your heading (or the locomotor flow line for that matter), how do you distinguish heading direction from the direction you are looking when the two are not the same?

Panel A of Figure 10.22 shows an example of a flow field pattern produced when making a pursuit eye movement during locomotion. The scene is the same as that shown in Figure 10.17A – a ground plane sparsely textured with dots. The motion pattern is due to translation through the scene in the same manner as that shown in Figure 10.17B, combined with a pursuit movement that maintains gaze on a particular feature on the ground plane (shown

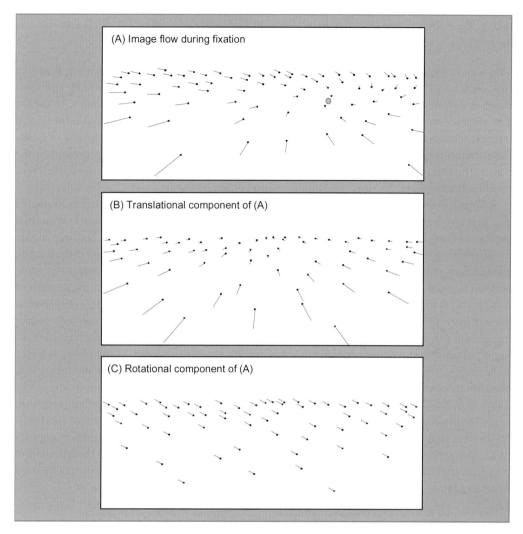

Figure 10.22: *Fixation of a stationary object (green circle) while moving through the environment results in an image flow field with a swirling motion (A). This is the sum of a component due to motion through the environment (B) and a component due to eye rotation (C). (Based on Warren, Morris and Kalish, 1988.)*

as a green circle). The dots move outwards from the fixated feature, but not radially outwards: the flow field has a motion pattern that seems to spiral out from the fixated feature[42]. Thus, the fixated point is a focus of outflow, but it is not a focus of *radial* outflow, and the fixated point does not coincide with the image location towards which the person is heading.

The flow field pattern shown in Figure 10.22A is a combination of two components. One component is due to locomotion through the environment; the other is due to the rotation of the eye relative to the environment that results from pursuit of the fixed feature. Panel B of Figure 10.22 shows the component due only to motion of the eye through the environment, and is exactly the same as the image flow pattern shown in Figure 10.17B. This component is called the **translational component** of the image flow, because it is due to *translational* motion of the eye through the environment[43]. Panel C shows the component due only to the pursuit eye movement, which is called the **rotational component** of the image flow. The flow pattern in panel A is simply the vector sum of the two components shown in panels B and C. Since the translational component of the flow pattern in panel B is the same as the flow pattern shown in Figure 10.17B, it contains the FRO and the locomotor flow line. The rotational component contains no information about a person's movement through the environment, because it is just the image motion produced by the eye movement.

10.2.6 Can people perceive heading when making pursuit eye movements?

One way to look at the problem of recovering heading information from an image flow like that shown in Figure 10.22A is to think of it as a process that involves removing the rotational component from the image flow to leave just the translational component[44]. In theory it is possible to remove the rotational component either by using extra-retinal information (somatosensory afference, vestibular afference and/or efference copy) about the eye or head-eye rotation responsible – the *extra-visual method* – or by using information present in the visual stimulus – the *visual method*[45]. Of course, these methods are not mutually exclusive: a combination of visual and non-visual information could be used.

A large number of studies have been conducted in an effort to determine how well people can perceive heading from image flow in the presence of eye rotations. Two experimental protocols have been used: the simulated eye-movement protocol, and the real eye-movement protocol[46]. In the simulation protocol, observers do not move their eyes; they fixate a stationary point in a visual display that simulates moving through an environment while making a pursuit eye movement. Panel A of Figure 10.23 presents a cartoon illustration of this protocol: the observer is shown fixating a stationary point (green circle) in a display that presents the flow pattern shown in Figure 10.22A. In this situation, the observer's retinal images are the same as they would be if they were moving through the dot scene and making a pursuit eye movement to maintain fixation on the green object. If people are able to accurately determine their heading direction when viewing displays of this sort, then it is possible to conclude that they are capable of discounting the rotational component of the image flow using visual information only (the visual method). Results have been mixed, with some studies finding performance accuracy too poor to support steering control[47], and others finding that performance accuracy was good enough[48]. The overall conclusion appears to be that people can perceive their heading reasonably accurately using the simulation protocol, indicating that extra-retinal information is not necessary[49], though it may be used when available.

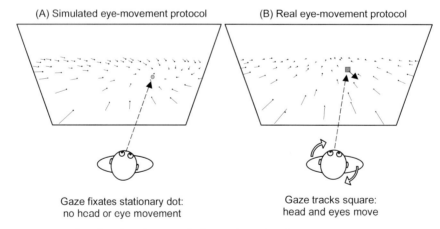

(A) Simulated eye-movement protocol

(B) Real eye-movement protocol

Gaze fixates stationary dot:
no head or eye movement

Gaze tracks square:
head and eyes move

Figure 10.23: *Simulated and real protocols for studying heading perception in the presence of eye rotation. Dashed line indicates gaze direction.*

In the real eye-movement protocol, observers are presented with a display simulating only translational motion through the scene, and are required to keep their gaze fixated on a particular feature as it moves in the display. This requires a pursuit movement of the eyes (or of the head and eyes), as illustrated in panel B of Figure 10.23, where the red square is the target feature. In this situation, the retinal image flow will be a combination of the motion in the display and the motion produced by the eye movement. Results using this protocol have shown the heading perception can be as accurate with pursuit eye movements as it is without them[50].

In sum, the answer to the question raised in the title of this section is, yes, people are able to perceive heading when they make pursuit eye movements. However, being able to do so is not strictly necessary for steering control. The fact that there is a swirling motion in the image flow when gaze pursues an image feature suggests a way to detect heading errors without perceiving heading. If you are heading in the direction you are looking, then the image flow has a radial pattern (Figure 10.17B). If you are not heading in the direction you are looking, then the flow has a swirling pattern (Figure 10.22A). Thus, if you look in the direction that you want to go and there is a swirling motion in the image flow, then there is an error – you are not heading in the direction you want to go. You should make steering adjustments that eliminate any swirl in the flow pattern[51]. The 'swirl' is actually a measure of the rate of change of heading error – **heading error rate** – which is zero if you are heading directly towards a stationary target.

10.2.7 Image motion is not needed for heading perception

All the sources of heading-related information described so far are contained within the retinal image flow. However, the image flow is not the only source of heading-related information. A source of information that does not involve image flow is suggested by the following observation: if you are driving along a road without skidding, your vehicle is 'pointing' in the direction in which it is heading: the vehicle's long axis lies in the heading direction. In these circumstances, perceiving heading is the same as perceiving the direction in which the vehicle is pointing. You can perceive the direction a vehicle is pointing when it is standing still, so image motion is not required to perceive heading using this method. Cues to pointing direction are provided by visible features both on the inside and outside of the vehicle (e.g., the center of the hood). A heading error exists when the long axis of the vehicle does not 'point' in the direction in which you want to go[52] (see Figure 10.2A).

Pointing direction when walking or running lies in the mid-sagittal plane of the pelvis (Figure 10.1). We are perceptually aware of the direction our bodies are facing, and it is easy to verify that people are able to indicate their pointing direction. This perceptual awareness is presumably based on somatosensory information (see Chapter 7). Thus, we could use pointing direction as a source of information about heading when walking or running. In the next part of the chapter we will discuss empirical evidence that people use information about pointing direction to control where they are heading.

10.2.8 There are many sources of heading-related information

So far in this section, we have described several different sources of sensory information about heading and/or heading error that are available to a person. By far the richest source of information is the image flow produced when the eye moves through the environment, but information about pointing direction can be obtained from somatosensory stimulation and/or static images. Table 10.1 lists all the sources of information described in the chapter that can provide information about heading error[53], and adds motion parallax as another source. For image flow sources to be available, the person must be able to see the road or terrain ahead. Thus, to use image flow information for path following, there must be preview. Preview is not needed to obtain pointing direction information.

Evidence presented in section 10.2.3 and section 10.2.5 shows that people are able to perceive heading from image flow without path-related cues like splay angle[54]. Evidence also exists to show that people can perceive splay angle and its rate of change for a straight section of marked path[55], which seems intuitive given the simple image geometry involved (Figure 10.16). We might expect that if a person can perceive heading or heading error, then they can control steering based on that perception. However, showing that people can make accurate perceptual judgments using a particular source of information does not demonstrate that people use that source of information to control steering. It is possible that a person can perceive heading or heading error using a certain source of information, but that they do not use that information to control steering. Thus, to determine what information people use to control steering it is necessary to study steering behavior. In the next part of the chapter we will examine what sources of information people actually use for the compensatory control of steering.

Table 10.1: *Different sources of heading-related information.*

Source of information	Stimulus	Information provided
Focus of radial outflow (FRO)	Image flow (translational component)	Heading
Locomotor flow line	Image flow (translational component)	Heading
Image flow 'swirl'	Image flow	Heading error rate (when you are looking where you want to go)
Splay rate	Image flow	Heading error
Motion parallax	Image motion and image flow	Heading error
Pointing direction	Somatosensory or visual stimulation (image flow not necessary)	Heading (under suitable conditions, e.g., no lateral skid or slide)

10.3 Perceptual Information and Compensatory Steering Control

10.3.1 Introduction

The compensatory (error-corrective) mode of control can be used for steering in two types of terrestrial locomotor task: (1) target acquisition tasks, in which the person moves over flat, uncluttered ground towards a stationary target; (2) straight-path-following tasks, in which the person moves along a straight (or gently curved) pathway. These tasks do not require anticipatory control for effective performance. A person could perform either task by correcting heading errors.

A path-following task requires not only that the person heads in the same direction as the path, but also that they stay on it. However, merely staying on the path is often not sufficient: people usually try not to get too close to the edges of the path or of their lane – an approximately central lateral position is commonly maintained. Figure 10.24 shows that simply correcting a heading error does not maintain a vehicle's lateral position on the road. The vehicle shown is initially traveling in the right direction (straight along the road and in lane, far left). A disturbance changes the vehicle's heading, causing a heading error and a change in lateral position. A steering adjustment is made that corrects the heading error, but the vehicle is no longer in the same lateral position – it is straddling the two lanes (far right).

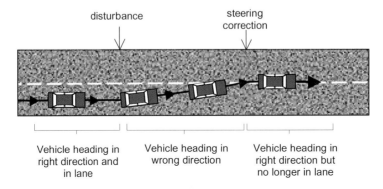

Figure 10.24: *Correcting heading errors does not maintain lane position.*

We have seen that there are a number of different sources of heading-related information in sensory stimulation (Table 10.1): any of these could be used as a basis for correcting heading errors. There are also a number of different sources of sensory information that could be used to correct lateral position errors. This raises the following questions:

(1)   How can the different sources of information be used to make corrective steering adjustments?
(2)   Which sources of information are people able to use for steering control?
(3)   When multiple sources of information are available, do people use just one or more than one of them?

These questions will be addressed in this part of the chapter.

10.3.2 How can heading information be used for steering to a visible target ?

In this section we will discuss how three sources of heading information – the FRO, locomotor flow line and pointing direction – might be used for compensatory steering control in target acquisition tasks. In later sections we will discuss evidence that they are used.

Perhaps the most influential idea was J.J. Gibson's suggestion about how the FRO could be used for steering towards a visible target[56]. Gibson noted that if the FRO lies within the image of the target object, then the person is heading directly towards the target (no heading error). Conversely, if the FRO lies outside the image of the target, then there is a heading error, and the person should change direction such that the FRO moves to inside the image. Figure 10.25 illustrates the idea in cartoon form. A cyclist is traveling over flat ground towards a wall and wants to pass through the gap on the right. In panel A, the cyclist is heading towards a point on the wall indicated by the white spot ($\bigcirc$). In the cyclist's retinal image of the scene, the FRO would be at the image of this point. The cyclist needs to steer to the right so that the FRO lies within the image of the gap in the wall. Panel B shows a moment during the steering adjustment, and panel C shows the cyclist after the adjustment has been completed – they are moving directly towards the gap, so the FRO is within the image of the gap (at the location of the white spot).

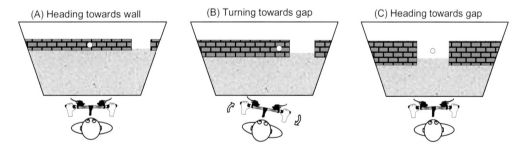

Figure 10.25: *Cartoon of a cyclist steering to pass through a gap in a wall. The white spot marks the location towards which the cyclist is heading.*

Gibson's suggestion is a negative feedback strategy for controlling heading, in which the heading error is the angular distance (visual angle) between the visual direction of the target and the FRO. The person needs to determine this error so that they can make a steering adjustment of appropriate amplitude in the right direction. The locomotor flow line and pointing direction can be used in a similar way – a heading error exists when the direction of the target does not coincide with the locomotor flow line or the pointing direction. This situation is illustrated in Figure 10.26 for the pointing direction. In the figure, only the target is visible, so that there is no visual information about heading, which could happen if a person walks in complete darkness towards a small light source; the only heading information available is somatosensory information about the pointing direction. A sequence of three frames is shown. In frame 1, the pointing direction and the egocentric direction of the light source do not coincide, and the angle between them (β) is the heading error. In frame 2, the person is in the process of turning so that the target and pointing directions coincide. In frame 3 the turn is complete, and the person is heading directly towards the light (the two directions coincide).

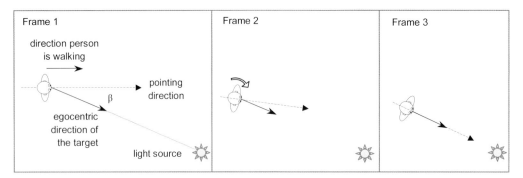

Figure 10.26: *Three frames of a cartoon movie of a person steering so as to head towards a visible target (light source).*

There is an alternative way of performing the target acquisition task shown in Figure 10.26, using the rate of change of the angle β instead of β itself. If the person in frame 1 continues to head in the direction shown rather than turning towards the target, then the target's egocentric direction will change, and hence the angle β will also change (it will get larger). This is shown in Figure 10.27. The egocentric direction of the target in frame 2 (β2) is greater than it is in frame 1 (β1). Thus, if the person is not heading towards the target, the egocentric direction of the target (β) will be changing as the person moves. If the person heads directly towards the target (Figure 10.26, frame 3), then its egocentric direction will remain constant. Thus, to steer towards a stationary target it is sufficient to move so that the rate of change of β is zero[57]. Since the angle β is heading error, the rate of change of β is the rate of change of the heading error. If you steer so that the rate of change of heading error is zero, then you must be heading straight for the target (provided the target is stationary[58]).

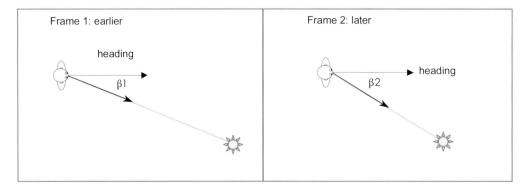

Figure 10.27: *As a person moves past a visible object, its egocentric direction changes.*

10.3.3 How can multiple sources of information be used for compensatory steering control?

There are two types of information that can be used for steering control when following a path: heading-related information that informs about heading (or heading error), and lateral position information that informs about the person's lateral position on the pathway. There are typically several different sources of heading-related information available (see Table 10.1). There are also likely to be several sources of lateral position information. Thus, we have two types of multiplicity:

(1)   Multiple sources of perceptual information about a particular quantity, such as heading.

(2)   Different quantities (e.g., heading, lateral position on a path, and rate of change of heading) that can be used to correct errors.

Consider the first type. When there are several different sources of stimulus information about a particular quantity, then the nervous system may extract all of them from the stimulus. For example, the nervous system may extract the FRO, the locomotor flow line, and the pointing direction to yield three different estimates of heading direction. These different estimates could then be combined together to provide an overall estimate that is more accurate than any one by itself. The overall estimate could then be used either to make perceptual judgments or to control steering.

Figure 10.28 shows a diagram that represents one version of this kind of idea. In the figure, perceptual processes extract two sources of heading information (e.g., the FRO and the locomotor flow line) to give two estimates of heading (H1 and H2) and one source of heading error information (e.g., splay rate) to give a heading error estimate (He). Error estimates are obtained from H1 and H2 by subtraction from the desired heading. The three heading error estimates are then combined together. There are several ways this combination could be done; a weighted average method is the simplest. With three error estimates, e1, e2, and e3, the normal average is calculated as (e1 + e2 + e3)/3. We can think of this as ⅓ e1 + ⅓ e2 + ⅓ e3: a weighted sum of the three errors, in which each has the weight ⅓. A weighted average is a weighted sum in which the weights can be different but all add up to one[59]. For example, a possible weighted average of the three errors is (⅛ e1 + ⅝ e2 + ¼ e3), since the weights add up to one (⅛ + ⅝ + ¼ = 1). The advantage of a weighted averaging method is that sources of information that are known to be more reliable or more accurate can be given greater weight than sources that are less reliable. If a source of information is too unreliable or inaccurate, it can be given a weight of zero.

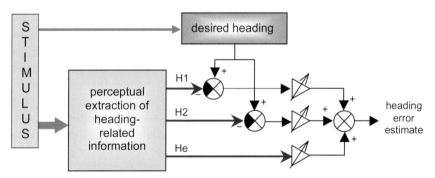

Figure 10.28: *Block diagram showing how different sources of heading-related information can be combined to give an overall heading error estimate.*

The triangular blocks in Figure 10.28 represent the weights given to the individual heading error estimates. The arrows running through the triangular blocks indicate that the weights are variable rather than fixed. This means that the weights can be adjusted in accordance with the reliability or accuracy of a given estimate of heading error. For instance, sources of heading-related information in the image flow are impoverished if the field of view is restricted or if there are few visible features in the environment (see sections 10.2.3 and 10.2.4): the accuracy of heading perception is better when the field of view is greater, and when the FRO lies within the visible part of the scene. Thus, the quality of image flow information is better when the field of view is greater and/or when there are more visible features, and so image flow information is likely to be weighted more heavily in these conditions. We will consider experimental evidence for these ideas later in this part of the chapter.

Now consider the second type of multiplicity. In this case it has been proposed that the perceived estimates of different quantities are used to make corrective steering adjustments via separate feedback loops[60]. The diagram in Figure 10.29 illustrates this idea for the case of heading and lateral position. The figure shows two feedback pathways – one for heading-related (HR) feedback information, shown in blue, and the other for lateral position (LP) feedback, shown in red. The blocks labeled H-error and LP-error transform the heading-related information and the lateral position information into estimates of the heading and lateral position errors respectively. The D-shaped blocks transform the error estimates into a command signal to the muscles; these commands simply add together in their effect on the muscles.

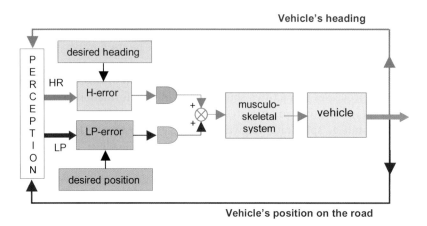

Figure 10.29: *Block diagram of two feedback loops that combine for the control of steering.*

10.3.4 Pointing direction information is used in steering control

That people can use pointing direction information is demonstrated by the fact that it is possible to walk towards small spots of light in complete darkness – it's easy to do, as the reader can verify. This is only possible if you can align your pointing direction with the perceived egocentric direction of the visible target. In normal situations, when image flow information is available, do people also use pointing direction information? This was tested in an experiment that used wedge prisms to alter the apparent egocentric direction of the target[61].

Wedge prisms are pieces of glass with a triangular cross-section (they are wedge-shaped) that refract light so that the direction of a ray is shifted, as shown in Figure 10.30. In the figure, a ray coming from an object that is straight ahead of the eye is refracted, so that it reaches the eye from a direction a few degrees to the right of straight ahead. The result is that the retinal image of the object is shifted, and the object appears to be slightly to the right of its true location: the prism alters the visually perceived direction of the object. The angular prismatic shift, labeled δ, is a characteristic of the particular prism involved: the thicker the wedge, the greater the shift.

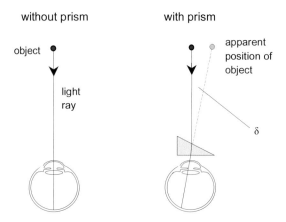

Figure 10.30: *A wedge prism displaces retinal images.*

People normally walk a straight path to a visible target if nothing gets in their way. The idea that people correct heading errors by aligning their pointing direction with the direction of the target predicts that people should follow a curved path to a visible target when wearing prisms. In contrast, the idea that people correct heading errors by moving so that the FRO is over the target's image predicts that prisms should have no effect on the path taken – people should follow a straight path regardless of whether prisms are worn (the use of other image flow sources makes the same prediction). To see why aligning the pointing direction with the egocentric direction of the target predicts a curved path, consider Figure 10.31. The person sees the target δ degrees to the right of its true position (panel A). They align their pointing direction in the apparent egocentric direction of the target (panel B) and walk towards the target's apparent position. As they get closer to the target the distance between the apparent position and the true position decreases, since the angular prismatic shift (δ) is constant (panel C). Thus, as the person gets nearer to the target, they need to keep adjusting their pointing direction so that it coincides with the apparent location of the target. This means that a person looking through prisms ends up following a curved path (panel D).

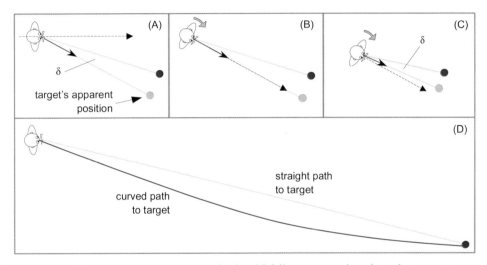

Figure 10.31: *When wearing prisms, people should follow a curved path to the target. In panels (A) – (C) the dashed arrow is the pointing direction and the solid arrow is the apparent direction of the target (circle). See text for details.*

As noted above, the use of image flow information to determine heading errors predicts that the path to the target should be unaffected by prisms, or at least only affected at the very beginning. If the person starts from a stationary position and begins walking towards the apparent direction of the target, then they will initially head in the wrong direction because they start to move to the target's apparent location. Once the person is under way, any image-flow-based method for correcting heading errors is unaffected by prisms, since the position of the FRO or locomotor flow line relative to the position of the target's image is unaffected by the prisms – all image features are shifted by the same amount. Thus, a strategy for regulating steering based only on image flow information predicts that the path people follow to a visible target will be the same when wearing prisms as it is without them, except at the beginning if the person starts from a stationary position.

The results of the experiment showed that people followed curved paths to a target when wearing wedge prisms, in the manner predicted by a steering control strategy based on aligning the body's pointing direction with the egocentric direction of the target. Without prisms, participants followed a straight path. These results are not what would be expected if people use only image flow information, which predicts straight line paths in both conditions. However, the results do not rule out a combination of image flow and pointing direction information.

10.3.5 Image flow is used in combination with pointing direction information to steer to a visible target

In the experiment described in the previous section showed that people use the body's pointing direction as information about heading. However, it is not possible to conclude from the results that people did not also use image flow information. Previous work had already shown that image flow cues could be used to control the direction of locomotion at walking speeds[62]. Thus, it is possible that people use a combination of pointing direction and image flow information to determine heading errors for correcting the direction of locomotion. As already discussed, when sources of information are combined, greater weight is given to the more salient sources. In the experiment described in the previous section, wearing prisms may have led to pointing direction information being weighted more heavily than image flow information, as prisms introduce optical distortions and restrict the field of view. This may result in people relying more on pointing direction information when wearing prisms[63].

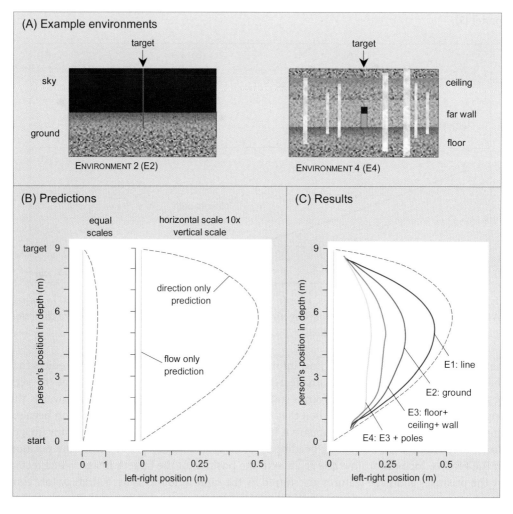

Figure 10.32: *Scene layout (left), predictions, and results (person's position in the environment relative to the start position) from an experiment by Warren* et al. *(2001, based on their Figure 3).*

The idea that the heading error estimate used for correcting the direction of locomotion is based on a weighted combination of both pointing direction and image flow cues was tested in an experiment using a similar logic to that described in section 10.3.4. The experiment was conducted in a computer-created interactive environment – a virtual environment – so that prism-like displacements could be introduced without the need for actual prisms[64]. It was proposed that the better the quality or quantity of image flow information, the greater its weighting in heading-error estimation and hence the greater its contribution to steering control. The quality of image flow information was manipulated by varying the richness of the virtual environment. Four environments were used in the experiment, from very simple to quite complex. The simplest (environment 1, E1) provided no image flow information, as only the target (vertical line) was visible. The next most complex (environment 2; E2, Figure 10.32A) included a ground plane that provided some flow information. The third most complex (environment 3, E3) provided more image flow information, as it had a textured floor, ceiling and far wall. The most complex (environment 4; E4, Figure 10.32A) was the same as E3 but included as poles at various distances. Participants could walk through the virtual environment as if it were the real world, and their task was to reach a target that appeared to be nine meters away – the red vertical line in E1 and E2, and a 'door' in E3 and E4.

Image flow and pointing direction cues to heading were dissociated in the experiment by introducing a prism-like displacement: if participants used only pointing direction information they would follow a curved path through the environment, whereas if they used only image flow information they would follow a straight path. These predictions are shown in panel B of Figure 10.32: the pointing-direction-only prediction is the dashed, blue line; the image-flow-only prediction is the straight, dotted line (the horizontal scale of the graph on the right of panel B has been expanded to accentuate the curvature of the direction only prediction). If both pointing direction and image flow information were used, the path followed would be intermediate between these two paths. If pointing direction information were weighted more heavily than image flow information, then the path would be expected to more closely resemble the curved path. If image flow information were weighted more heavily, the path would be expected to be closer to straight.

The results showed that participants followed straighter paths in the environments with richer and more salient image flow information. Panel C of Figure 10.32 shows the average paths followed by participants in the four environments (solid curves). When only the target was visible (E1), participants followed paths very close to that predicted if only pointing direction information about heading is used. When the image flow information was richer, the path was straighter, being straightest when the image flow information was richest (E4). These results confirm the hypothesis that image flow and pointing direction information are used in combination, with the contribution of image flow information being greater (weighted more heavily) when it is richer[65].

10.3.6 How can visual information be used for steering along a straight path?

As described earlier, following a straight path normally involves not only keeping the heading direction the same as the direction of the road, but also maintaining a lateral position. Heading information can be used to maintain lateral position, but not simply by keeping heading direction the same as the path direction – the heading direction needs to be kept aligned with a particular direction on the path. This is illustrated in Figure 10.33. Panel A shows an image of a straight road as might be seen by the driver of a vehicle, and superimposed on it is the flow pattern produced by heading directly down the middle, so that the driver is aligned with the central markings. The locomotor flow line is indicated by the thick red streamlines. The central road position could be maintained by keeping the locomotor flow line aligned with the central markings. The situation when the vehicle is heading off the left side of the road is shown in panel B. To restore the central position on the road, a steering adjustment is needed that not only aligns the locomotor flow line with the direction of the road, but also moves it back so that it overlays the center markings. In principle, any source of heading information could be used to maintain lateral position on a road. All that is required is that the person keep the heading aligned with some visually defined direction on the path (such as the center markings) that coincides with the desired lateral position.

There is also visual information that can be used to maintain lateral position but which does not involve the perception of heading. Splay angle is an example of such information: to maintain lateral position on the path, the splay angle should kept at a particular value (see section 10.2.2). Thus, lateral position on a path can be regulated using heading information or using information like the splay angle, or by using a combination of both. Research has demonstrated that splay angle information makes a major contribution to steering along straight paths, a contribution that can be substantially greater than that made by image flow information[66]. In the next section, an experiment will be described that provides an illustration of how lateral position can be maintained using a combination of splay and image flow information.

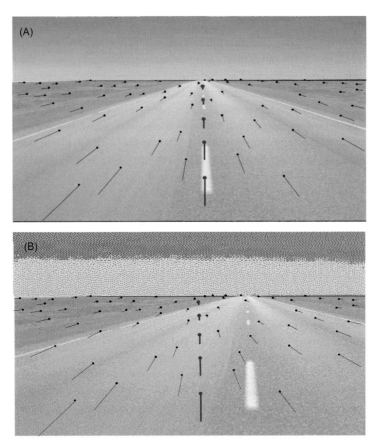

Figure 10.33: *Flow patterns when driving down the middle of a straight road (A) or heading off to the left (B).*

10.3.7 Multiple sources of information are used to maintain position on a straight pathway

In this section we will describe a study demonstrating that information sources are combined to regulate lateral position on a pathway. In this study, the task of participants was to steer down the center of a corridor in a computer-generated, virtual environment[67]. The corridor had textured walls and could be presented either with or without splay angle information, as shown in Figure 10.34. To maintain position in the middle of the corridor, it is sufficient to steer so that the splay angles on the left and right sides are kept equal. In other words, the splay angle difference (right splay angle – left splay angle) is an error signal: if it is not equal to zero, then you are not traveling down the middle of the corridor.

Another source of information that could be used, and which is particularly salient in a corridor or tunnel environment, is the speed of image flow. If you are heading down the middle of the corridor and looking straight ahead, then the flow speed in the images of the left and right walls will be the same. Thus, to maintain travel down the middle of the corridor, it is sufficient to steer so that the flow speeds are equal for the images of the left and right walls. In other words, the flow speed difference (right flow speed – left flow speed) is an error signal: if it is not equal to zero, then you are not traveling down the middle of the corridor[68].

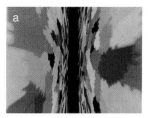

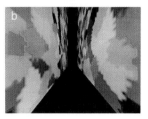

Figure 10.34: *Virtual corridors without splay information (a) and with it (b) used in an experiment by Duchon and Warren (2002, their Figure 2, © American Psychological Society.).*

The corridor study set out to determine whether people use both these sources of information – splay angle difference and flow speed difference – to steer down the middle of a straight corridor. To determine whether splay information contributed to steering control, a comparison was made between conditions in which splay information was absent (Figure 10.34a) with conditions in which it was present (Figure 10.34b). To determine whether image flow speed information contributed, the speed at which the two walls of the display moved were manipulated. This meant that the lateral position in the corridor at which the observer's image flow speed was the same on the two sides could be manipulated. The same effect could be generated in a real physical environment, rather than being computer generated, using the arrangement shown in panel A of Figure 10.35. Flexible canvas walls are wound on rollers that can be rotated by motors, allowing the walls to be moved forwards or backwards. If both walls are made to move by rotating the rollers at the same speed, as indicated in the figure, the person will have the illusion of moving forwards between them. If the right wall is made to move faster than the left, the image speed of features on the right wall will be greater than the image speed of features on the left wall for a person in the position shown in the figure. Under these circumstances, the person will have the illusion of being closer to the right wall than to the left. Thus, in order to have the impression of moving down the center of the path, the person should steer to the left until the speed of the images of features on the left and right walls are equal (flow speed difference is zero). In the experiment, the same effect was generated by computer, and the person walked on a treadmill.

If experimental participants used the flow speed difference to regulate steering, then when one wall in the display moves faster than the other, participants would be expected to move away from this wall to a position closer to the slower moving wall. Results of the experiment in which splay angle was absent from the display are shown in panel B of Figure 10.35. The plots show the path followed by the person in the virtual environment as they move down the corridor. There were three different wall motion conditions: (1) the left and right walls moved at the same speed (same condition); (2) the right wall moved 1.5 times faster than the left wall (1.5× condition); (3) the right wall moved twice as fast as the left wall (2× condition). In the 1.5× condition, the point at which the image flow speed is equal on the two sides is about 0.24 meters to the left of center. In the 2× condition, this point is about 0.4 meters to the left of center. Thus, we would expect people to move to roughly these lateral positions if they were steering, so as to eliminate any flow speed difference. The results were more or less as expected, demonstrating that participants were steering so as to keep the left and right flow speeds equal.

What is expected to happen when splay angle is added to the display? Left and right splay angles are equal when the person is in the center of the corridor, and this is unaffected by flow speed differences. It was expected that if splay angle difference information were used for steering control, then it would be used in combination with flow speed difference information. For example, the flow speed difference (ΔF) could be combined with splay angle difference (ΔS) as a weighted sum, to give an overall estimate (ΔE) of the error:

$$\Delta E = w_1 \Delta F + w_2 \Delta S \qquad\qquad\qquad\qquad (\mathbf{10.3.1})$$

where w_1 and w_2 are the weights. If people combine the information in this way, then when the lateral position at which ΔF is zero is different from the position in which ΔS is zero, people would be expected to move to a position intermediate between the two positions. If the weighting given to ΔS were equal to that given to ΔF, then the position to which people would move would be exactly halfway between the two positions. Panel C of Figure 10.35 shows the results obtained when splay angle was present: participants stayed much closer to the center of the corridor than they did when splay was absent – the effect of a difference in wall speed was reduced. This demonstrates that participants used splay and flow speed information in combination, and is consistent with the combination being a weighted sum. The fact that the participants steered close to the center when splay was present indicates that the splay angle difference was weighted more heavily than the flow speed difference: the authors of the study calculated that splay was weighted about 2¼ times as heavily as flow speed.

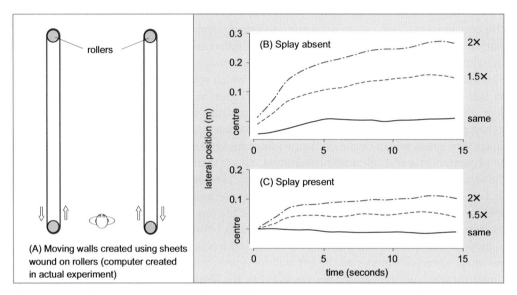

Figure 10.35: *Virtual corridor experiment. (A) A way of constructing a corridor with moving walls. (B, C) Results from an experiment by Duchon and Warren (2002, data from their Figure 4).*

10.3.8 Preview is important but not necessarily essential for steering along straight pathways

The sources of heading-related information in the image flow that have been described so far are all contained in the image of a scene ahead. Thus, use of these sources for steering control requires at least some preview (section 10.1.11). More accurate estimates of heading or heading error are likely to be possible when the preview is greater, at least up to a point. For example, if the FRO is used for estimating heading, more accurate estimates will be possible if preview is great enough to include the FRO.

Detection of lateral position error could be less dependent on preview. We saw in the previous section that splay angle and image flow speed information can be used to maintain position on a marked pathway. Perception of splay angle requires preview, and is more accurate the more of the road ahead you are able to see[69]. However, the person in Figure 10.35 could obtain image flow speed information from peripheral vision, so a peripheral view of relatively small sections of wall to the left and right might be all that is needed (though this has not been tested experimentally). Thus, in some conditions it may be possible to maintain lateral position on a pathway with little or no preview.

People are able to steer motor vehicles accurately enough to stay on relatively straight sections of road when driving in conditions that severely restrict preview, such as dense fog. On multi-lane highways, people often drive at high speeds in dense fog and have no trouble staying in lane or on the road[70]. Nevertheless, since more accurate heading and lateral position information is available when the preview distance is greater (up to a point), we would expect that restricting preview would have detrimental effects on compensatory steering performance. For example, errors would probably need to be greater before the driver notices them. The result would be that larger corrective adjustments would be needed, and so the path taken by the vehicle would be more erratic and would deviate more from a straight line. In the next section we will see what effects restricting preview has been found to have on steering control.

10.3.9 How does limiting preview affect steering control?

Several experimental studies have examined the effects of restricted preview on people's ability to steer a motor vehicle along a straight, unobstructed path. One study[71] used a set-up like that shown in Figure 10.36 in order to vary the driver's preview. The figure shows a side view of the vehicle with upper and lower sight screens; the screens obstruct part of the driver's vision. The upper screen was adjustable, so the far sight point (the farthest point visible to the driver) could be altered by moving the screen up or down. The inset shows the driver's view.

In the experiment, participants drove the vehicle along a straight stretch of wide, clear roadway without obstacles or other vehicles (actually a disused runway) at constant speeds of either 20 mph (32.3 km/h) or 30 mph (48.4 km/h). The lower sight screen was adjusted for drivers of different heights, such that the near sight distance was fixed at about 24 feet (7.3 m). The upper sight screen was moved into one of four different positions, so that the far sight distance was about 30 feet (9.14 m), 60 ft (18.29 m), 90 ft (27.43 m), or else 'unrestricted' (no upper sight screen). Since preview time is equal to preview distance ÷ speed, and occlusion time is the occlusion distance ÷ speed, both times were shorter at 30 mph (preview distance and occlusion distance are defined in Figure 10.36).

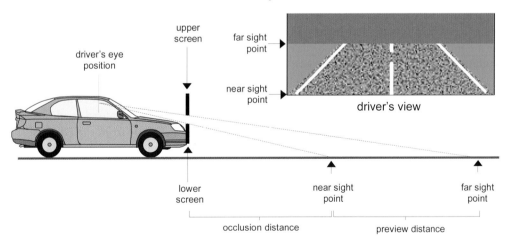

Figure 10.36: *Set-up for experiment in which vision of the road ahead was restricted to a gap between two screens.*

People were able to perform the task reasonably well in all conditions. Average steering accuracy during an experimental trial was quantified using three different root mean square (RMS) measures: RMS heading rate (rate of changes of heading angle), RMS heading angle and RMS lateral position error. The basic findings were the same for all three measures: performance was worse when the far sight distance was smaller. However, no difference in performance was detectable between the unrestricted condition and the 90 ft far sight condition. This suggests that being able to see 90 ft ahead is sufficient for accurate compensatory control of steering – being able to see further did not confer any detectable benefit. In fact, since the next furthest sight distance was 60 ft, it is possible that some distance between 60 and 90 ft permits a performance accuracy equivalent to unrestricted preview. It was estimated that a far sight distance of 70 ft (about 21.3 m) is the point beyond which no further improvements in steering accuracy can be detected, an estimate that has been confirmed by subsequent work[72]. It was also found that accuracy was unaffected by speed, suggesting that the preview time was always adequate[73].

In an additional experimental condition, the effect of restricting the preview window to a view through a narrow (⅛ inch ≈ 3 mm) slit was investigated. Participants were required to drive along a straight line marked on the road. Once again the near sight distance was 24 ft (7.3 m), though the far sight distance was less than four inches greater. Thus, the driver could see only a small segment of road less than four inches long (see Figure 10.37). Even under these severe restrictions, participants could steer effectively, with the overall accuracy measures taking values similar to those observed in the 30 ft preview condition in the main experiment. Steering was jerkier in the very restricted preview condition (more high frequency components), so the path followed by the vehicle was 'wigglier', but this did not reduce the average accuracy score taken over the whole run[74].

The results from the study described in this section, together with other studies[75], demonstrate that even with severe restrictions on preview, people can steer straight sections of road effectively. Performance is better with greater preview, but extending the preview distance beyond about 20 or 30 meters ahead does not appear to result in significant further improvements. Of course, all this applies only to driving along straight or gently curved roads and paths, where anticipatory control is not necessary. In real-world driving, anticipatory control is absolutely essential, because roads may have sharp bends and there are typically other road users, obstacles and intersections ahead.

10.3.10 Restricting preview affects the information used for compensatory control

In this part of the chapter we have seen that people use compensatory, error-corrective control when steering towards a visible target location (target acquisition task) and when following a straight path (path-following task). Evidence exists to show that people are able to use a number of different sources of stimulus information to detect and correct errors – both heading errors and lateral position errors.

Different sources of information are likely to be differently affected by restricted preview. Viewing through a narrow slit – the most restricted preview condition described in the previous section – eliminates almost all image flow information. However, lateral road position information may still be available, either from the road center line or from the edges of the road (if visible). In the set-up shown in Figure 10.36, the driver's view through the slit would have been something like that shown in Figure 10.37. Panel A shows a situation in which the road markings down the center line are visible, but the road edges are not: the driver is directly over the center line. To steer straight down the middle of the road, the driver needs to steer so as to keep the visible part of the center line in the position shown in the figure. Panel B shows a situation in which the road edge marking are visible, but there are no center markings: the driver is positioned in the middle of the road. To maintain this position on the road, the driver needs to steer so as to maintain the edge markings in the positions shown. As described in the last section, it is possible to maintain position on the road with the view

(A)   (B)

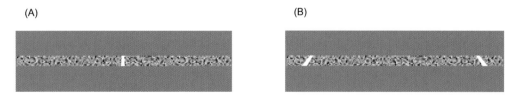

Figure 10.37: *Driver's view through a narrow slit when driving along a road with a center line but no edge markings (A) and with edge markings but no center line (B).*

shown in panel A. Other studies have shown that the position regulation task with only the edges visible is also possible when the preview window is very narrow[76]. Steering could be controlled in this task using the splay equalization method described in section 10.3.7.

Wider preview windows provide richer information than narrow ones. Image flow information is richer and easier to extract when the field of view is greater, and it is easier to detect the orientation of line segments (and hence splay angles) when the line segments are longer. Thus, compensatory control will be better when preview is greater. Preview is also essential for anticipatory control, as discussed in the next part of the chapter.

10.4 Cornering and Steering Along Winding Paths

10.4.1 Introduction

Although error-corrective, compensatory control is important, in everyday circumstances anticipation is essential. We need to anticipate intersections, gaps, bends and collisions. As discussed in Chapter 8, collision with obstacles during locomotion on foot can be avoided by the timely execution of a suitable pre-programmed maneuver, such as stepping over or steering around it. Effective execution of pre-programmed maneuvers requires anticipating that a collision will occur unless action is taken, advance preparation of the maneuver and initiation of that maneuver at the right moment prior to reaching the obstruction. Likewise, effective steering around a curve or turning a corner requires that the curve or corner be perceived in advance, so that suitable steering action can be taken before it is too late.

In everyday circumstances, the anticipation of curves and of collision with obstacles or other hazards requires preview, since vision is normally the only sense able to provide a person with information about what lies ahead. In this part of the chapter, we will consider how vision is used to control steering around curves.

10.4.2 Preview allows a winding track to be followed with little error

The ability to follow winding tracks when preview is available was first studied using laboratory pursuit tracking tasks. A simple version of such a task is shown in panel A of Figure 10.38. The task requires the person to trace along a wiggly line with a pen. The wiggly line is the track, and it is drawn on a roll of paper that is wound between two rollers. The paper moves from the person's left to right like a conveyor belt, as shown in the figure. The person can move the pen nib only in the narrow gap between two guide rails: they try to move the pen along the gap so that the line they draw on the paper follows the track. An adjustable screen obscures the person's view of the paper, so that they can only see the part of it that is in front of the screen (the preview window). When there is preview people can follow tracks quite closely, provided that there is sufficient preview time (the paper doesn't move too fast) and that the track does not wiggle too much (these two factors interact)[77]. This is illustrated at the top of panel B: the line the person draws (blue line) stays on or close to the track (black line). With little or no preview (bottom of panel B), the person is unable to keep the pen on the track: the shape of the person's response is similar to the shape of the track, but it is delayed – the response lags behind the track.

Without preview, the person is obliged to wait for an error to develop and then correct it (assuming that the wiggles in the track are unpredictable). Since responding to the error and correcting for it takes time, the response line lags behind the track. When preview is available, the movement of the pen that is needed to stay on track can be anticipated and the track followed without significant lag. It is as if the visible track tells you what you have to do to follow it – move left, move right, how far and how fast. Two questions then arise:

(1) What features of the track are perceived and used to determine the response?
(2) How is the response determined based on the perceived features of the track?

Before addressing these two questions for the case of steering a vehicle along a curved path, we will describe two possible anticipatory control modes that could be used to follow a winding path when preview is available.

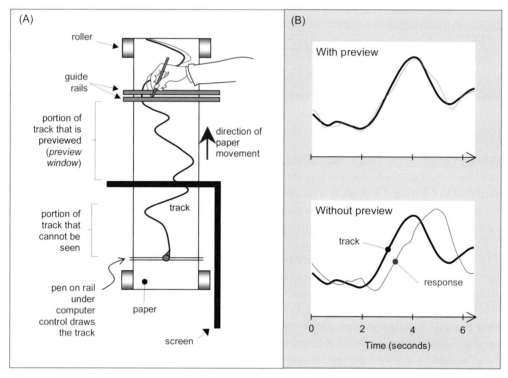

Figure 10.38: *(A) Tracking task in which the person attempts to keep the pen on the track (wiggly line). (B) Type of result obtained both with and without preview. (Not real data; based on Figures 3.1 and 3.4 in Poulton, 1974.)*

10.4.3 Two anticipatory control modes for path following

As described in Chapter 8, pre-programmed, locomotor maneuvers involve a type of anticipatory control. The process that generates the motor commands required to execute a maneuver is prepared in advance, using perceptual information obtained from preview of the scene ahead. Such maneuvers are learned responses to particular types of anticipated hazard, and are suitable only if the hazard has certain characteristics. For example, the stepping-over maneuver is only suitable if the hazard – an obstacle – is sufficiently small (is 'step-overable'). When the obstacle is 'step-overable', the maneuver is prepared so that it is suited to the particular size of the obstacle.

Since pre-programmed maneuvers are discrete actions, they are suited for negotiating spatially circumscribed hazards like obstacles, apertures and steps (see Chapter 8). They seem less well suited for negotiating winding tracks or paths such as those involved in pursuit tracking tasks, like that shown in Figure 10.38. A second anticipatory control mode has been proposed for tasks of this sort. In this mode, characteristics of the previewed track are transformed directly into motor commands in a continuous fashion. This will be referred to as the **pursuit control mode**[78]:

PURSUIT CONTROL MODE: In track following, a mode of control that involves the continuous transformation of characteristics of the track ahead (perceived from preview) into a command that steers the person/vehicle/effector along the track.

10.4.4 Desired path curvature could be used to steer a curved path

An early hypothesis was that road curvature is the perceived feature of a winding or curving road used to determine the steering response[79]. It was proposed that an automobile driver might perceive road curvature and move the steering wheel to a position that results in the curvature of the vehicle's path being appropriately matched to the curvature of the road.

The curvature of a circular arc can be quantified as the reciprocal of the radius of the circle, as indicated in panel A of Figure 10.39. In the figure, the vehicle is steering around a circular section of road along a circular path that is a constant distance (d) from the road's inside edge. The radius of the vehicle's path is denoted by the letter R. Denoting the curvature of the path by the letter C, we can write

$$C = 1/R \qquad\qquad\qquad (10.4.1)$$

The hypothesis proposes that the driver uses an estimate of curvature (C) to steer around the bend.

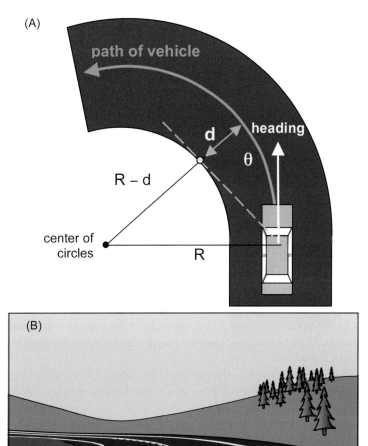

Figure 10.39: *(A) Overhead view of a vehicle entering a curve, defining geometrical quantities. (B) Driver's view when entering a curve.*

At the moment shown in panel A of Figure 10.39, the vehicle is heading in the direction indicated by the white arrow. The view that the driver has at this moment is something like that shown in panel B. A visible point on the inside edge of the road is marked in the figure with a yellow spot. The visual direction of this point – shown as a dashed line joining the point to the driver's position in panel A – is tangent to the inside edge of the road. For this reason the point is called the **tangent point**[80]. The angle between the visual direction of the tangent point and the direction of heading is labeled θ in panel A. The geometry of the situation shown in panel A means that the cosine of the angle θ is equal to the radius of the inside edge of the road (R – d) divided by the radius of the path (R): $\cos \theta = (R - d)/R$. Since $1/R$ is the path curvature (C), it is possible to write the following expression for curvature[81]:

$$C = (1 - \cos \theta)/d \tag{10.4.2}$$

This expression shows that the curvature of a path that goes around the bend a distance, d, from the inside edge can be determined by the driver prior to entering the bend, provided that the driver can perceive the angle θ. Perception of θ requires location of the tangent point – which seems simple enough in situations like that shown in Figure 10.39A – and perception of heading. The driver must also be able to perceive the distance of the vehicle from the inside edge. This is necessary because the driver must select a value of d for the path to be followed around the curve, and so needs to know if the car is the selected distance from the edge.

Once the curvature of the desired path has been determined, the driver must translate this into a movement of the steering wheel. How is this to be done? Figure 10.40 shows the geometry of a turn[82]. The car is moving along a circular path, and the radius of the path followed by the inside front wheels is denoted by the letter r. The car's wheelbase is W and the front wheels are rotated through an angle γ. To produce this angle of the wheels, the steering wheel is turned through an angle α, where $\alpha = n\gamma$. The number 'n' is called the **steering ratio**: a typical value for a modern family car is 12, meaning that one complete rotation of the steering wheel (360°) rotates the front wheels through $360/12 = 40°$. From the geometry shown in Figure 10.40, it is clear that $C = 1/r = [\sin (\alpha/n)]/W$. Thus, if the driver of the car wants to follow a circular path such that the inside front wheels maintain a constant distance from the inside edge of the road, then they should turn the steering wheel through an angle, α, given by the following equation:

$$\alpha = n \times \arcsin (CW) \tag{10.4.3}$$

with C given by equation (10.4.2) above. The steering ratio (n) and the wheelbase (W) are characteristics of the vehicle that the driver must learn about through experience, since they cannot be directly perceived.

A steering strategy that uses the curvature information provided by equation 10.4.2 and transforms it according to equation 10.4.3 works as follows:

(1)   The driver decides to steer the vehicle around an upcoming bend along a path that is some chosen distance (d) from the inside edge of the road. The chosen distance could simply be the same as the vehicle's distance from the edge as it approaches the bend; if not, then the driver must position the vehicle at the chosen distance before starting to steer around the bend.

(2)   Once a value for d is chosen, the curvature of the path to be steered (the desired curvature) is determined using equation 10.4.2 (implemented by an automatic perceptual process).

(3)   The desired curvature is translated into a motor command for moving the steering wheel through the angle determined by equation 10.4.3. The command should be issued before reaching the bend, so that the car starts to steer into the curve as soon as it reaches the bend. The appropriate timing could be achieved using visual information about time-to-arrival (TTA) with the curve (see Chapter 8).

(4)   At some point before exiting the bend, the driver must issue a command to move the steering wheel back into the center position. The command should be issued so that the car is heading straight along the road upon exiting the bend.

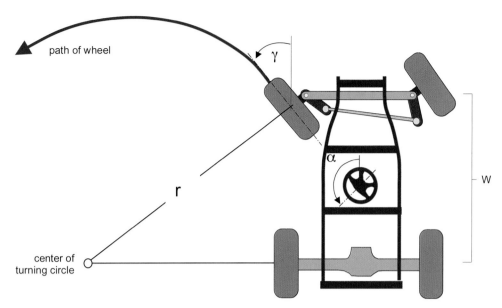

Figure 10.40: *Geometry of a vehicle turn.*

This steering strategy raises two questions. First, is motor command based on information obtained in advance, such that steering a bend is a pre-programmed maneuver, or is it formulated continuously using the pursuit mode? Second, is there any empirical evidence that people use the strategy for steering control? The first question is addressed in the next section.

10.4.5 Path curvature can be used in pre-programmed or pursuit mode

Steering a bend using the strategy described in the previous section could be effected using either pre-programmed or pursuit control modes. Consider the pre-programmed mode first[83]. The sequence of events (1) to (4) listed at the end of the previous section is shown diagrammatically in Figure 10.41, where the position of a vehicle on the road together with the angular position of the steering wheel is shown for eight moments in time. The turn could be implemented as a two-phase pre-programmed maneuver. Phase 1 involves determining the required path curvature in advance and using this to determine the angle to which the steering wheel needs to be moved (positions 1 to 6 in Figure 10.41). The steering wheel is held at this angle until the second phase begins. This phase moves the steering wheel back to the center position. Two phases are needed, because the whole curve cannot usually be seen on approach and so the driver cannot determine in advance when the steering wheel needs to be moved back to the center.

It seems plausible that steering around bends involves pre-programmed control, since all that is required to steer along a circular arc is that the steering wheel be moved to, and then held in, a fixed position. Empirical study has confirmed this simple intuition: people have been found to be able to steer around curves reasonably accurately without vision for short periods of up to about 1.5 seconds[84].

The pursuit mode has also been proposed as the means by which the steering command is generated when cornering[85]. The idea is that an estimate of required path curvature is continuously extracted from the stimulus (e.g., by means of equation 10.4.2) and transformed into a steering command signal. The result is that the steering wheel position continuously tracks the curvature of the road ahead, and so does the path followed by the vehicle (see below). The advantage of this mode over the pre-programmed mode is that the driver can steer smoothly along the road with continuous variations in curvature, as there is no need to continuously pre-program new maneuvers as the curvature changes. The observation that people can steer around corners for short periods without vision does not necessarily contradict the use of the

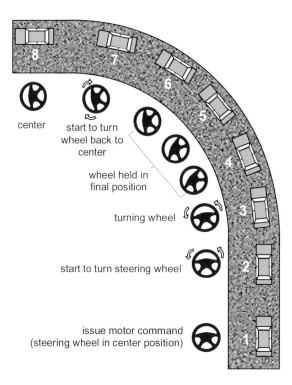

Figure 10.41: *Sequence of vehicle and steering wheel positions while negotiating a curve.*

pursuit mode. The person could continue to steer based on a memory (e.g., a mental image) of the road ahead, as has been suggested for negotiating obstacles in blind walking (Chapter 8). The question of how people are able to make their steering maneuvers at the right time in the pursuit mode has not been addressed empirically, and so we will not say anything more about it here. Some attempts have been made to determine whether people use perceived curvature to determine their steering responses; these are examined next.

10.4.6 Do people used perceived path curvature to steer a curved path?

It has been argued that evidence for the path curvature steering control strategy can be obtained from examining where people look when steering around curves. Specifically, looking at the tangent point on the inside edge of the road has been interpreted as evidence supporting the strategy[86], whereas not looking at it has been interpreted as evidence against[87]. However, such evidence could never be conclusive, either for or against, since it is not necessary to look at the tangent point in order to use equation 10.4.2 for estimating curvature, though it might conceivably assist in the extraction of the information from the stimulus (though this has not been demonstrated). Nevertheless, were it the case that people spent a significant proportion of time fixating the tangent point, then it would suggest that it was an important feature in the control of steering, consistent with the curvature steering strategy. Moreover, fixating the tangent point during approach to a curve but not so much when actually turning would be consistent with steering the curve in the pre-programming mode. Fixating the tangent point while turning as well as upon approach would be consistent with control in the pursuit mode.

There have been some reports that drivers do spend a significant amount of time fixating the tangent point prior to and during a turn[88]. One study found that drivers tended to first fixate the tangent point when they were about three seconds from the start of a bend, and would make repeated fixations throughout the remainder of the approach and during the turn itself[89]: during the last second of approach and the first second of the turn, the tangent point was fixated almost continuously (more than 70% of the time). Notably, drivers did not accurately follow the tangent point with a smooth pursuit eye movement; rather, they appeared to refixate the tangent point with a series of saccades.

Other studies have not found that fixations were predominantly directed at the tangent point. In these studies the tangent point was never fixated for more than about 20% of the time, and often for substantially less than this[90]. In one study, participants spent 80% of the time fixating locations around the center of the (single lane) road[91]. A further study found that people had a tendency to steer in the direction they were looking, such that if they were required to fixate the tangent point they tended to steer towards, it producing oversteer (steering too sharply for the bend); a requirement to fixate the outside edge of the road led to understeer (not steering sharply enough); only when they were required to fixate the center of the single land road did they steer around the curve without significant under- or oversteer[92].

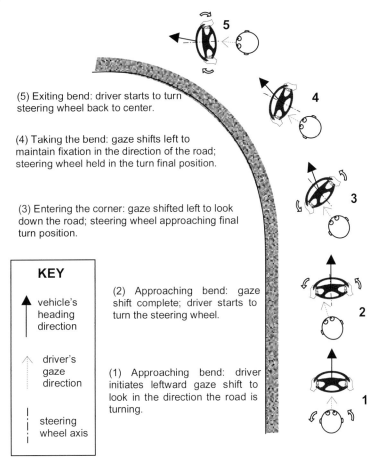

(5) Exiting bend: driver starts to turn steering wheel back to center.

(4) Taking the bend: gaze shifts left to maintain fixation in the direction of the road; steering wheel held in the turn final position.

(3) Entering the corner: gaze shifted left to look down the road; steering wheel approaching final turn position.

KEY

▲ vehicle's heading direction

↑ driver's gaze direction

| steering wheel axis

(2) Approaching bend: gaze shift complete; driver starts to turn the steering wheel.

(1) Approaching bend: driver initiates leftward gaze shift to look in the direction the road is turning.

Figure 10.42: *Sequence of gaze and heading directions while steering around a bend.*

Overall, the available empirical data do not consistently demonstrate tangent point fixation. What the data do show is that people have a strong tendency to look where they are intending to go when driving around a curve. They look in this direction both when they are approaching a bend and when they are steering around it, and make repeated refixations as they steer around. This is very similar to the kind of gaze behavior observed when going around a curve on foot, as described in Chapter 8 (section 8.1.3). A cartoon illustration of the driving situation is shown in Figure 10.42. The figure shows the driver's position at five moments in time, labeled 1 to 5. In position 1, the driver is approaching the bend and has initiated a saccadic gaze shift so as to look in the direction of the turn (arrows indicate direction of gaze shift). In position 2, the saccadic shift has been completed and the steering wheel is starting to be turned; gaze briefly pursues visible features in the new gaze direction. In position 3, a saccadic refixation of gaze has been made so that the driver is again looking in the direction the road is going; the steering wheel has nearly reached a position suitable for negotiating the curve. For a short period between 3 and 4, gaze pursues the visible feature in the gaze direction reached in 3. In position 4, a saccadic refixation has been made so that gaze is again pointing in the direction the road is going; the steering wheel is held in the position suitable for taking the corner. In position 5, the driver is preparing to exit the bend and has begun to turn the steering wheel back to the central position.

Overall, the data on gaze behavior does not tell us whether people use perceived curvature to determine their steering response. Unfortunately there are no published results that permit a firm conclusion regarding whether or not people use perceived curvature to determine their steering response when negotiating curved paths. Perceived curvature is not the only candidate for the perceptual information used to steer curved paths. An alternative hypothesis has recently been put forward and is described in the next section.

10.4.7 Cornering by steering towards viapoints

As described earlier, when you want to move towards a visible target somewhere ahead, you steer so that your heading direction coincides with the egocentric direction of the target. It has been suggested that people might negotiate curves by treating a point on the upcoming section of a curved path or road as a target to be steered towards[93]. Such a strategy for taking a curve is consistent with the gaze behavior described in the previous two sections: as a person progresses around the curve, they shift gaze from one target point to the next. The basic idea is illustrated in Figure 10.43. A two-frame sequence is shown. In frame 1 the driver is approaching the bend and is just about to start moving the steering wheel to steer towards the fixated location (✚). In frame 2 the driver is going around the bend; he or she has reached the location fixated in frame 1, and has shifted gaze to a new position further around the bend. Thus, as the car progresses around the curve, the driver fixates a sequence of target points or **viapoints** on the upcoming section of road and steers towards them in turn.

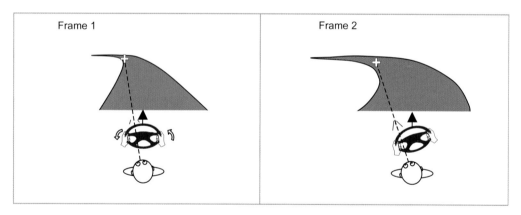

Figure 10.43: *Fixating a sequence of viapoints while steering around a curve.*

In section 10.3.2 we saw that the egocentric direction of a fixated target and the rate of change of this direction can be used to control steering towards the target. When the driver fixates the target so that the head is turned and the eyes are centered in their sockets, as shown in Figure 10.43, the target's egocentric direction is simply the angle of rotation of the head on the shoulders. This angular rotation is equal to the heading error, since when a driver is strapped into their seat, their pointing direction lies in the car's heading direction. As described in section 10.3.2, to move towards a visible target, the person could steer so as to reduce the target's egocentric direction to zero and/or to reduce the rate of change of target direction (heading error rate) to zero. There are, accordingly, three possibilities for how a person might steer around a bend using viapoints:

(1)   A driver could steer using a viapoint's egocentric direction as a heading error signal in a feedback control loop[94].

(2)   A driver could steer using the rate of change of a viapoint's direction as an error signal[95].

(3)   A driver could steer using a viapoint's egocentric direction as the error signal in one feedback loop and its rate of change in another feedback loop[96].

Simulation studies have shown that these three possibilities will all allow a person to successfully steer towards a visible target, but it appears that possibility three is the one that provides the best fit to empirical data[97].

Note that regardless of which possibility provides the best fit to the data, all three involve the error-correcting, compensatory control mode. Their success as accounts of steering around curves would, therefore, appear to contradict the assertion made in 10.1, that the compensatory mode is only suitable for steering along straight or gently curving paths. However, the fact that the driver steers towards a sequence of viapoints introduces an anticipatory component into the control process. The identification of a viapoint anticipates the need for a change in heading if the curve is to be negotiated smoothly and without error.

10.4.8 How do people steer curved paths?

In this part of the chapter we have discussed two strategies that people might use to steer around curved paths: the curvature matching (or tangent point) strategy and the viapoint strategy, both of which seem able to account for observed steering behavior. However, there are two reasons for thinking that the viapoint strategy is the more plausible candidate.

(1)   The viapoint strategy predicts that people will show a tendency to steer in the direction that they are looking.

Several studies have examined the effects of preventing people from using their normal gaze fixation pattern when cornering, by requiring them to fixate particular points[98]. The results show poorer steering performance when normal fixation behavior is prevented, and evidence for steering in the direction of gaze (see section 10.4.6). It is not clear what predictions the curvature matching strategy makes, though it does not appear to predict steering in the direction of gaze.

(2)   The viapoint strategy is more versatile and generic.

The curvature matching strategy is possible only when path-following, and only when the edge of the path is clear enough for the tangent point to be visible. In contrast, the viapoint strategy can be used whether there is a visible path or not. For example, it can be used to steer a slalom course, where the viapoints would be between the slalom gates: it has been shown that gaze behavior when negotiating a slalom course is consistent with use of a viapoint strategy, with gaze being directed from one gate to the next in a tight sequence[99]. More generally, the viapoint strategy can be used to steer a course through a cluttered environment by picking a series of points that take a person past obstacles and through gaps. In short, the viapoint strategy can be used whether there is a path or not, and is consistent with the gaze behavior observed in both situations.

The fact that the viapoint strategy provides a slightly better account of the available data on gaze behavior, and is more generic and flexible than the curvature matching strategy, does not allow us to conclude that people do not use curvature information to steer around corners. It is possible that both strategies are used. For instance, steering towards selected viapoints when path-following could be based on curvature up to the next viapoint rather than on making egocentric direction zero. Alternatively, curvature information could be used in combination with egocentric direction. Thus, the curvature matching and viapoint strategies do not represent mutually exclusive alternatives. Given the findings from target acquisition tasks and straight path-following tasks (see section 10.3), it is likely that people do not use just one type of information or one specific strategy, but are able to use a variety of different strategies and information sources. Only further research can provide the answers.

References & Notes

[1] In navigation and applied engineering, the term *heading* means 'the direction of the long axis of the vehicle'; the direction in which a vehicle moves is called the **course**. In the psychological literature, *heading* means the same as *course*, but there is no generally used term for the direction of a vehicle's long axis, so we have introduced the term *pointing direction*.

[2] For example, a yacht's pointing direction is defined by the fore–aft axis, but it will often be moving in a different direction.

[3] McRuer *et al.* (1975).

[4] See Hildreth *et al.* (2000).

[5] Land (1998).

[6] Godthelp (1988) conducted a study in which the drivers' task was to drive down a straight section of road and stay in lane. They were asked to delay making corrective maneuvers until the last possible moment that they felt that they could make the correction without leaving the lane. The drivers waited until the time to reach the lane boundary was about 1.5 seconds.

[7] Wickens, Hollands (1999).

[8] Poulton (1974).

[9] As technology has advanced, more sophisticated displays have been developed; see Jarrett (2005).

[10] Note that even a random signal has statistical properties that can be discovered through learning (mean, standard deviation, etc.).

[11] The two configurations shown in Figure 10.7 are not equivalent.

[12] McRuer *et al.* (1977).

[13] There are some systems which people cannot learn to control, regardless of how long they practice.

[14] Poulton (1974); Wickens, Hollands (1999).

[15] Technically it is a lagged first order control, because the speed of the car changes rather sluggishly in response to a change in the position of the pedal. All real-world systems, irrespective of their order, will have dynamic properties that introduce some lag (sluggishness).

[16] See McRuer *et al.* (1977).

[17] See Jagacinski, Flach (2003).

[18] See Poulton (1974). The random signals used in experimental studies usually have only low frequency components (they are low pass).

[19] McRuer, Jex (1967).

[20] McRuer *et al.* (1977).

[21] McRuer, Jex (1967).

[22] The linear description does not completely capture the transformation that a person implements (McRuer *et al.*, 1975).

[23] This finding is the basis for what is called the cross-over model of human compensatory tracking performance (McRuer *et al.*, 1977). For a textbook account see Jagacinski and Flach (2003).

[24] Gibson (1958).

[25] Lee, Lishman (1977).

[26] Flach *et al.* (1997).

[27] For details see Flach *et al.* (1997).

[28] The vanishing point (road vertex in the image) may also shift on the retina (Riemersma, 1981).

[29] Johnston, White, Cumming (1973).

[30] Cutting (1986).

[31] See Lappe, Bremmer, Van den Berg (1999).

[32] Warren, Morris, Kalish (1988).

[33] See Cutting (1996).

[34] Wilkie, Wann (2006).

[35] Cutting (1986, 1996).

[36] See Lawton (1983).

[37] See Britten (2008).

[38] Warren (1976).

[39] Crowell, Banks (1993).

[40] See Cutting *et al.* (1992).

[41] Regan, Beverley (1982).

[42] This is true provided that you are not headed directly for a vertical plane surface (like a wall). In this case, the flow pattern both with and without pursuit eye movement is radially expanding from a fixed point (Regan, Beverley, 1982).

[43] Longuet-Higgins, Prazdny (1980).

[44] It is important to recognize, however, that it is not necessary to filter out the rotational component in order to make heading judgments; see Wang and Cutting (2004).

[45] See Lappe *et al.* (1999).

[46] Warren, Hannon (1990).

[47] E.g., Banks *et al.* (1996).

[48] Warren, Hannon (1990).

[49] The problem with drawing firm conclusions from poor performance in studies using the simulation protocol is that keeping the eyes steady provides extra-retinal information that the eyes are not moving. This can lead people to confuse the stimulus presented with that produced when they are traveling on a curved path, as Banks *et al.* (1996) reported.

[50] See Lappe *et al.* (1999); Wilkie, Wann (2006).

[51] Wann, Swapp (2000). If you look at the point towards which you are heading, then the flow will be radial (no swirl), so you know when you are looking where you are heading.

[52] This does not apply at sea, where the direction of a boat's long axis is not necessarily the same as the heading direction.

[53] Wang, Cutting (2004).

[54] For details of path perception from image flow, see Li, Sweet, Stone (2006); Li, Cheng (2011).

[55] Riemersma (1981).

[56] Gibson (1958).

[57] Beall, Loomis (1996).

[58] If the target is moving, then it is possible for the rate of change of β to be zero, but for the person not to be heading towards the target.

[59] Technically this is a normalized weighted average.

[60] McRuer *et al.* (1977) showed that the position error feedback loop acts to maintain the vehicle's position on the road, and the heading error loop provides the damping needed for stability.

[61] Rushton *et al.* (1998).

[62] Cutting *et al.* (1992); Wang, Cutting (2004).

[63] Harris, Carre (2001).

[64] Warren *et al.* (2001).

[65] Li and Cheng (2010) reached similar conclusions.

[66] Beall, Loomis (1996); Li, Cheng (2010).

[67] Duchon, Warren (2002).

[68] Honeybees use this strategy when flying down tunnels (Srinivasan *et al.*, 1991).

[69] Riemersma (1981).

[70] Accidents occur because drivers cannot see far enough to make anticipatory avoidance maneuvers.

[71] McLean, Hoffman (1973).

[72] See Salvucci, Gray (2004).

[73] The variations in preview time and occlusion time did not have a detectable effect on performance. This does not imply that preview and occlusion time are unimportant, but only that in the conditions studied, they were always sufficiently long that their effect on performance could not be detected.

[74] A result also obtained by Land and Horwood (1995).

[75] Cloete, Wallis (2011); Land, Horwood (1995). Both studies involved simulations of roadways with gently curved as well as straight sections.

[76] Beall, Loomis (1996); Cloete, Wallis (2011); Land, Horwood (1995).

[77] Poulton (1974).

[78] McRuer *et al.* (1977). Pursuit tracking tasks can involve continuous control in which the track ahead is predicted rather than directly perceived. The definition given does not include such prediction.

[79] McRuer *et al.* (1977); Donges (1978).

[80] Land, Lee (1994).

[81] The curvature of the inside edge of the road (Cr = 1/[R − d]) can also be expressed as a function of θ and d: Cr = (sec θ − 1)/d. Land and Lee (1994) proposed that the driver should steer so that the vehicle follows a path of radius Cr. This will lead the driver to steer too sharply (oversteer).

[82] In Figure 10.40 the vehicle is assumed to be steering around the curve without skidding, and the front and rear wheels follow arcs of the same curvature. This is an ideal situation, and a vehicle that achieves it is said to have *neutral steering*. A real vehicle can only ever approximate neutral steering (Karnopp, Margolis, 2007).

[83] Donges (1978).

[84] Godthelp (1988).

[85] McRuer *et al.* (1977).

[86] Land, Lee (1994).

[87] Robertshaw, Wilkie (2008).

[88] Land, Lee (1994); Marple-Horvat *et al.* (2005).

[89] Land, Lee (1994). The statement that participants 'fixated the tangent point' means that they fixated points in the scene within a circular zone in the image, centered on the tangent point and with a radius of 2° of visual angle.

[90] Underwood *et al.* (1999); Wilkie, Wann (2003).

[91] Wilkie, Wann (2003).

[92] Robertshaw, Wilkie (2008).

[93] Salvucci, Gray (2004); Wann, Land (2000); Wilkie, Wann (2003); Wilson *et al.* (2007).

[94] Wilkie, Wann, Allison (2008).

[95] Wilkie, Wann (2003).

[96] Salvucci, Gray (2004); Wilkie, Wann, Allison (2008).

[97] Wilkie, Wann, Allison (2008).

[98] Marple-Horvat *et al.* (2005); Readinger *et al.* (2002); Wilkie, Wann, Allison (2008); Wilson, Chattington, Marple-Horvat (2008).

[99] Wilkie, Wann, Allison (2008).

CHAPTER 11

Programs and Pattern Generation in Voluntary Action

11.1 The Nature of Motor Programs

11.1.1 Introduction

The term **motor program** is widely used when referring to the processes that underlie the production of motor behavior. It is commonly used to refer to the generative processes underlying acquired behaviors, such as handwriting and serving in tennis, but it is not used exclusively in the context of learned behavior. Some authors use it as a general term and apply it to the processes underlying fundamental, genetically determined behaviors like locomotion, breathing, grooming and scratching[1]. The term has been a source of controversy[2] for two related reasons: its apparent implication that the processes that generate motor behavior are in some sense like programs that run on computers, and the lack of a generally accepted definition. Unfortunately, the term is used to mean quite different things by different authors, making controversy inevitable. In order to be useful, the term needs a definition that accurately reflects the workings of motor pattern generation. In this part of the chapter we will consider the nature of the internal processes that drive motor behavior, and arrive at a useful conception of the term *motor program*.

11.1.2 Voluntary action is prepared in advance of moving

A feature of behaviors that are generated by internal processes is that their basic characteristics are prepared in advance of execution. Some examples have been described in earlier chapters: pre-programmed maneuvers during locomotion in Chapter 9, and saccadic eye movements in Chapter 6. The latter provide a clear illustration of advance preparation. Saccades very quickly shift gaze from one direction to another, too quickly for their performance to be influenced by sensory stimulation arising during execution. This means that the amplitude and direction of the eyes' movements must be established prior to moving. Something similar is true for aimed movements of the limbs – the type of movements that are made when you reach out to touch or grasp something.

Studies of how people learn to deal with changes to the conditions that they normally experience have established that the direction and amplitude of aimed movements are prepared in advance of moving. For example, imagine using a computer with a digitizing tablet. When you move the stylus over the tablet, a cursor moves across the monitor screen. The normal arrangement is to set up the tablet so that when you move the stylus away from you (towards the screen), the cursor moves up the screen, and when you move it towards you (away from the screen) the cursor moves down the screen. The set-up is shown in panel A of Figure 11.1: the different colored arrows indicate the correspondence between movement of the stylus and movement of the cursor. A person who is well-practiced at using such a tablet and screen arrangement can quickly move the cursor between two locations on the screen by moving the stylus over the tablet. People typically move so that the thing being moved travels straight towards the target. Thus the cursor will move from a start location to a target location on the screen along an approximately straight path, as shown at the top of panel B.

Suppose that the arrangement is changed without the person's knowledge, and the correspondence between the screen directions and tablet directions is rotated through 90° counterclockwise. The result is that when the stylus is moved to the left, the cursor moves down; when the stylus is moved towards you, the cursor moves right; when the stylus moves right, the cursor moves up; and when the stylus moves away from you, the cursor moves left. If the person now attempts to move the cursor to a target location, they will start moving the stylus in the direction that would previously have been effective. The result is that the cursor does not move towards the target but in a perpendicular direction. Once the person sees that the cursor is moving in the wrong direction, they will make a correction, and a typical result is that the cursor spirals into the target as shown in panel B (bottom) of Figure 11.1. Corrections to movement direction typically occur between about 100 and 150 ms after the start of the movement. The fact that the initial movement is in the direction perpendicular to the target's direction clearly shows that the person establishes the movement direction in advance, based on their prior experience and (visual) information obtained prior to beginning the movement.

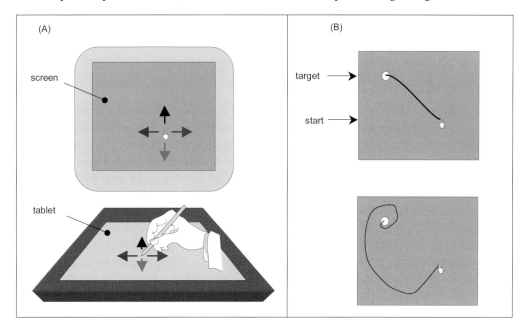

Figure 11.1: *Moving a stylus across a tablet moves a cursor over a monitor screen (not real data; see text for details).*

The observations just described, and others like them, show that performance characteristics such as movement direction and amplitude are established in advance of starting to move. Thus, many actions must involve prior planning or preparation. Evidence for advance preparation of maneuvers made during locomotion, such as stepping over an obstacle, was discussed in Chapter 9. Other evidence for advance preparation of voluntary actions comes from the anticipatory postural adjustments described in Chapter 7: only if the nervous system has planned an upcoming action in advance can appropriate postural adjustments be made in an anticipatory fashion. In order to account for observations of the kind we have been discussing, the concept of a motor program is usually invoked.

11.1.3 The traditional definition of motor program is problematic

An early and still influential definition of the motor program is formulated in terms of 'muscle commands' (control signals sent to individual muscles) that are prepared in advance and that can produce coordinated movement when sensory feedback is not available during execution[3]. Versions of this traditional definition are often found in textbooks[4]; one example is the following:

> [A] set of muscle commands that are structured before the motor acts begin and that can be sent to the muscles with the correct timing so that the entire sequence can be carried out in the absence of peripheral feedback[5].

In the definition, 'sequence' refers to the sequence of muscle contractions and/or bodily movements that comprise performance of the overall action; 'peripheral feedback' refers to sensory feedback about the behavior of the body parts that execute the action.

The definition does not explain where the commands come from; it simply states that they are structured in advance. The usual interpretation is that the commands are stored in some kind of memory from where they can be retrieved and sent to the muscles[6]. Thus, motor programs are conceived of as structured command sequences that pre-exist in memory: performance of an action involves retrieving the appropriate program and then running it. This conception implies that every different way of executing an action has a different stored program: reaching in one direction requires different commands from reaching in another direction, and so a different program is required for every possible direction. This and other difficulties with the idea that programs are stored command sequences are discussed next.

11.1.4 Commands for the muscles are not stored in advance

The idea that commands for the musculature exist in some kind of memory, from where they can be retrieved and sent to the muscles, does not describe the way in which commands are produced by the motor pattern generators described in earlier chapters. Locomotor CPGs (see Chapter 7) and brainstem saccade generators (see Chapter 6) do not store commands for the muscles: commands are generated on the fly once the generators are activated.

While it is possible that there are cases in which commands for the muscles are stored, there is no empirical evidence to establish that this is the case. The idea also fails to explain how the commands got into the memory in the first place. One possible answer is that they are generated by a mechanism like a CPG. An alternative answer is that they are memories of previous performances of the action. If they are produced by a pattern generator, then storage of the commands is a stage inserted between their generation and their being issued. This intermediate stage serves no explanatory purpose and its existence is not established by data.

The second answer amounts to a proposal that there is a unique program for every different way of executing every action: 100 different actions each executed in 100 different ways would require 10,000 distinct programs. Reaches in different directions would require different programs, and so would reaches over different distances. This seems rather implausible and leads to a **storage problem**[7]: is there sufficient capacity to store all the programs that would be needed for everyday living? The idea also fails to explain how people can produce movements that they have not produced previously (the **novelty problem**[8]). For example, if the programs for reaches in different directions are retrieved memories of commands issued in the past, then a person could only make initial movements in directions that they have previously moved[9]. Furthermore, since the mechanical action of a muscle will often depend on the relative positions of the body segments to which it is attached, the effect of a command will depend on segment positions. Similarly, the gravitational torque acting at a joint typically depends on the joint's angular position, and so a particular muscle force produced by a particular command can have different effects depending on joint position. The fact that the same command can have different effects in different conditions is referred to as **context conditioned variability**[10]. It means that a set of stored commands would only enable a person to move between body configurations that they have previously moved between, since different sets of muscle commands (programs) would be needed for different configurations.

It is difficult, if not impossible, to see how a control scheme based on sets of stored muscle commands could account for the observed flexibility of motor behavior, and no one has ever been able to provide such an account. It is more plausible to suppose that the same program is used for different executions of the same action, and that commands are generated on the fly, as we have already seen to be the case for locomotion and saccadic eye movements.

11.1.5 In exceptional circumstances, commands can be produced in the absence of sensory feedback

The traditional definition of motor program can be interpreted to mean that an action is controlled by a program 'only if it [can] be carried out uninfluenced by peripheral feedback'[11]. This is an extremely restrictive interpretation of the notion of a program. Even computer programs are not as limited as this: many require external inputs to complete their operations. It also seems to suggest that in behaviors generated by programs, sensory input has a limited role to play during execution. There are, however, some empirical findings that seem consistent with this interpretation. For example, we saw in Chapter 8 that the pattern of muscle activations and relaxations that produce locomotion can be generated in the absence of sensory input. Somewhat similar results have been obtained for reaching at visual targets by surgically deafferented animals (typically monkeys) and people who have been deafferented by pathological conditions. Both monkeys and people can recover the ability to make target-directed reaching movements, and they are able to make such movements even when they cannot see the moving limb during the reach (no visual feedback)[12]. Multi-joint aimed movements made by deafferented individuals tend to be clumsy and inaccurate, but single-joint movements can be executed with an accuracy similar to movements made by normally afferented individuals[13] (we will discuss these results further in section 11.2.8). These results show that it is possible for some behaviors to be executed in the absence of sensory feedback. However, the results do not demonstrate that these behaviors are executed without a contribution from sensory feedback in normal animals and people. Surgically deafferented animals are not able to perform the actions immediately after surgery: a period of adjustment is needed, during which they presumably learn how to adjust to the absence of feedback, and they are never able to restore the level of skill that they had prior to deafferentation (see below). Pathologically deafferented individuals are also clumsier and less skillful than normal individuals.

The picture that emerges from studies of motor performance in the absence of sensory feedback can be summarized by the following three points. (1) In the normal animal, the internally generated commands are suitable for producing behavior when sensory feedback is present. (2) If feedback is removed, the commands are no longer suitable for purpose, and the movements they generate will lack coordination and/or goal-directedness. (3) In order to recover the ability to execute goal-directed action, the animal must learn to modify the commands so that they are suited to generating behavior in the absence of sensory feedback. The next sections elaborate on points (1) and (2).

11.1.6 The term 'program' does not imply that afference is not necessary

Sensory signals are constantly fed to the motorneuron pools, particularly via muscle spindle afferent axons both directly (the monosynaptic stretch reflex pathway) or via interneurons. This means that a command signal arrives at a motor neuron pool along with a background of afferent input. Thus, a command cannot normally determine a muscle's activity – the activity at any moment is determined by the combination of afferent signals and command signals. For this reason, the more general term **motor command** is to be preferred over the term *muscle command*.

In Chapter 6 we discussed how central motor commands might interact with afferent signals from muscle spindle receptors to control the behavior of muscles. Two hypotheses were described: the follow-up servo hypothesis and the lambda (λ) equilibrium point hypothesis. Both are variations on the negative feedback control system architecture shown in Figure 11.2. In a system of this kind, the program element issues sequences of command signals. These are not sent directly to the controlled system (i.e., the muscle) but to intermediate elements (the comparator, $\otimes$, in Figure 11.2). The motor commands can be produced in the complete absence of sensory feedback, but they cannot generate appropriate behavior in these conditions. To see why, imagine that sensory feedback in the system in Figure 11.2 is stopped from reaching the comparator block ($\otimes$) by cutting through the connection at the point marked with an X. This is equivalent to deafferenting the system. The deafferented system cannot form an error (the difference between the required behavior of the controlled system and the actual behavior as measured by the sensor) – the comparator simply passes on the command signal unchanged[14]. The result is that the deafferented system cannot act to make the controlled system achieve the desired behavior specified by the command. Thus, according to the follow-up servo hypothesis and the λ-equilibrium point hypothesis, it is possible for an action to be governed by a motor program and for it not to be possible to carry out the program in the absence of sensory feedback, which contradicts the traditional definition.

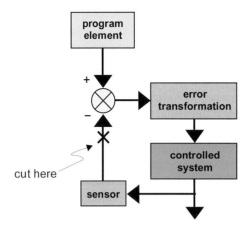

Figure 11.2: *Negative feedback control system that receives commands from a program.*

As described in section 11.1.5, monkeys and people can recover the ability to perform a variety of actions following deafferentation. If prior to deafferentation the commands are appropriate for controlling muscle-reflex systems, then after deafferentation the animal or patient must learn to produce commands appropriate for controlling muscles that lack stretch reflexes[15]. Empirical observations support this: for example, people with pathological conditions that lead to somatosensory deafferentation can recover the ability to perform a variety of behaviors, but they produce patterns of muscle activation that are very different from those of normal people, even when making the simplest, single-joint movements[16]. Of course, the fact that the ability to perform an action can be recovered following deafferentation provides evidence for a motor program of some kind. It does not provide evidence that the program, as it existed prior to deafferentation, could enable the action to be carried out in the absence of somatosensory feedback.

11.1.7 A motor program can be conceptualized as a procedure for generating commands

We have seen that the traditional definition of motor program does not provide an adequate characterization of the normal processes that underlie production of voluntary actions. In many cases, motor commands are not stored in advance, but are generated on the fly as the action unfolds. Clearly an alternative definition of 'motor program' is needed. One possible alternative would be to consider a motor program to be a sequence of commands generated by a motor pattern generator like a CPG. Under this conception, 'motor program' would just be an alternative term for 'command sequence'. A few authors have used the term in this way[17], but most adopt a different conception: the motor program is not a sequence of commands at all, but rather it is a procedure or formula for generating commands[18]. We will develop this second alternative.

A simple analogy illustrates some of the important differences between a program conceived of as a stored sequence of commands and one conceived of as a formula or procedure. Imagine a computing device that is capable of calculating the average of a set of numbers: you input the numbers and it outputs the average. If the device works like the traditional conception of a motor program, it would contain a store of values for the averages of different sets of numbers. You input a set of numbers, and the device searches through the store for the average value that goes with that set of numbers: a store of this kind is called a *look-up table*. Clearly, the device will only produce the correct average when it contains the stored value for the particular set of numbers that you gave it. Thus, to be useful, the device must store a very large number of programs (the *storage problem*, section 11.1.4). If you input a set of numbers that it does not have a stored value for, then it cannot provide you with the correct answer. This failure corresponds to the *novelty problem* faced by the traditional conception of a motor program. Now imagine a different device that implements the formula for calculating the average from a set of numbers: if we denote these numbers x_1, x_2, x_3, and so on, then the average of the set containing a total of N numbers is given by the formula $(x_1 + x_2 + ... + x_N)/N$. The device applies this formula to whatever set of numbers you give it, and will always produce the correct answer. A procedure is therefore much more flexible than a look-up table: it can deal with any input it is provided with, and does not face a storage problem. In motor terms, a program that implements a procedure is able to produce behavior appropriate for a wide range of conditions that have never been encountered before. The ability of a procedural program to deal with a range of conditions has prompted some authors to use the term **generalized motor program** to refer to programs that are implementations of procedures[19].

The conception of a motor program as a procedure is compatible with the operation of the pattern generators that produce commands for locomotion and saccadic eye movements. A motor pattern generator can be viewed as a mechanism that carries out a command generating procedure, so it is a mechanism that implements a motor program. This could be interpreted as a suggestion that a motor program is like the programs that run on digital computers: a motor program is a kind of software that 'runs' on the hardware of the nervous system. However, although an analogy can be drawn between motor programs and computer programs, it can be misleading, as discussed next.

11.1.8 Are motor programs like computer programs?

When people talk about computer programs they are almost always talking about programs for digital computers, the kind of computers that people use at home to surf the internet, play games and produce documents. A digital computer is a device that is capable of carrying out a potentially infinite number of different computational and data management tasks. It has a processor that is only capable of executing a small number of basic operations: it executes these at very high speed, and in any sequence that might be required. A program that runs on a computer is basically a set of instructions for carrying out a specific sequence of these operations in order to accomplish a task. For example, a program for computing the average of a set of numbers $\{x_1, x_2, ..., x_N\}$ input to the computer would comprise a set of instructions to carry out a sequence of processing operations that calculate $(x_1 + x_2 + ... + x_N)/N$. Programs are stored in a memory, from where they can be retrieved and then executed by the computer's processor. The memory and the processor are physically distinct structures and can be purchased separately at the computer store.

In many respects, the operation of a digital computer resembles cooking, which can provide a helpful metaphor[20]. The hardware for cooking comprises a kitchen and a cook. Recipes are the programs (software), and the recipe book is the memory in which they are stored. The raw ingredients are the inputs to the cooking process, and the outputs are cooked dishes (Figure 11.3). Recipes are sets of instructions written in terms of operations that the cook is capable of executing, such as 'measure 1 cup of flour', 'dice six carrots', 'continue stirring until smooth' and so forth. The cook reads the instructions from a recipe book and carries them out in the specified order. Thus, the cook is analogous to the processor in a digital computer; two cooks would be analogous to dual processors. A processor is essentially a device that is capable of executing any procedure that can be expressed as a sequence of the basic operations that it can perform; a cook is a person capable of cooking any dish that can be expressed as a recipe that involves carrying out a sequence of basic operations (stirring, dicing, chopping, mixing, etc.) that he or she is capable of.

The motor pattern generators that govern production of behaviors like locomotion operate in a manner quite different from digital computers. These mechanisms are special-purpose – they execute just one procedure or a few similar procedures, not many different procedures. There is no physical distinction between a memory in which the procedure is stored and a processor that carries out the procedure. Thus, motor pattern generators more closely resemble devices like the clockwork automata of Jacquet-Droz (see section 1.1.7) than computers. A clockwork automaton like the draughtsman (Chapter 1, Figure 1.4) does not consist of a memory component that passes instructions to another component that carries them out. The clockwork mechanism is constructed from certain cogs, cams and other components, linked together in such a way that the automaton makes particular movements. The 'memory' lies in the construction of the mechanism itself – the components from which it is made and the way they are put together. We can think of the clockwork mechanism as implementing a procedure or program, but there is no distinction between a memory and a processor as there is in a digital computer. As discussed in Chapter 1, clockwork mechanisms typically lack the flexibility needed to adjust behavior to suit different circumstances; such flexibility is a defining characteristic of goal-directed action. Biological motor programs achieve flexibility by adjusting their output using sensory information obtained both in advance of starting to move and during execution (see below).

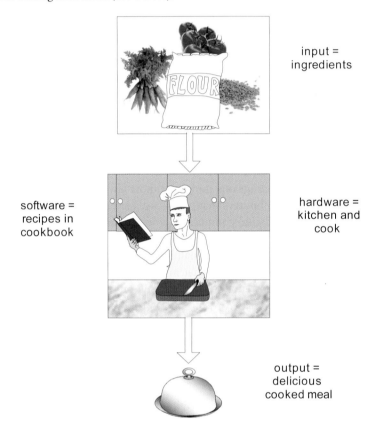

Figure 11.3: *Cooking is analogous to computing (see text for explanation).*

11.1.9 Are there different types of program?

It is possible that the pattern generating processes that underlie the production of acquired motor skills differ from those underlying genetically determined behaviors like locomotion. It has been suggested that the mechanisms that underlie production of at least some acquired skills possess an architecture similar to that of digital computers[21]; as one author puts it:

> First, the person must ... decide what program to run; the program must then be retrieved from memory and 'loaded' into a buffer (a temporary storage location) and readied to run[22].

This conception of a motor program clearly does not apply to the pattern generators described for locomotion or saccadic eye movements. However, these pattern generators produce only one pattern at any given time: you cannot make two different saccades at the same time, nor can you do two different walks at the same time. In contrast, you may be able to perform two instances of the same acquired skill simultaneously, or such that their execution overlaps to some extent. For example, you might reach out with the left and right hands so as to pick up two different objects simultaneously or in quick succession. It seems that such behavior requires two instantiations of a reach-to-grasp motor program, one to generate commands for the left arm and one for the right arm. This would be a bit like having two instantiations of a single application program running on your personal computer at the same time. If this is indeed what is happening, then the motor program could not be implemented as a hard-wired, pattern generating network. It would instead seem to need to be retrieved from a long-term memory structure and instantiated (loaded) into a network that carries out the program process (runs the program).

If two actions are performed concurrently, as in the reaching example in the previous paragraph, or in rapid sequence as in the case of key presses in typing or playing the piano, then it would seem that the programs responsible for the different acts must be executed either in parallel or sequentially. A process is needed to coordinate the recruitment of the motor programs so that the behaviors they produce occur at the correct time and/or in the correct order. As discussed in Chapter 13, skilled actions of this sort may be governed by high-level programs that coordinate the recruitment of the lower level programs that govern the components. Such high-level programs have been called **coordinated control programs**[23], or simply **control programs**. Some authors have argued that the term motor program should refer exclusively to these control programs[24], but we will not follow this usage.

The idea that some programs can have multiple instantiations and that high-level control programs govern complex behavior that is composed of multiple elements will be discussed in Chapter 13. This chapter will focus on programs for discrete actions. Next we will consider how programmed behavior can be tailored to fit the different conditions in which it might be executed.

11.1.10 Setting program parameters in advance allows behavior to be tailored to different conditions

We have seen that a motor program can be conceptualized as a kind of procedure or formula for generating the motor commands that govern production of an action. Thus, the same program is responsible for performance of the same action in different circumstances. In order for the program to generate commands that are suited to different circumstances, it must be supplied with information about what the circumstances are. Saccadic eye movements provide a straightforward example that will serve to illustrate some of the issues involved in generating commands to suit the circumstances.

Saccades are target-directed, aimed movements of the eyes. Consider the movement of one eye: to shift gaze to a new visible target, information about the retinal location of the target's image is fed to the brainstem saccade-generating mechanisms, which produce commands that cause the eye to rotate so that the image falls on the fovea. The retinal location of the target's image provides information about the direction and amplitude of the eye rotation needed. As described in Chapter 6, distinct brainstem mechanisms are responsible for horizontal and vertical saccades; oblique saccades are generated by simultaneous activity in both mechanisms (Figure 11.4 shows examples of these three types of saccade). The direction of a saccade is determined by the relative activation of the two mechanisms: a horizontal saccade is produced if only the horizontal generator is activated, a vertical saccade is produced if only the vertical generator is activated, and an oblique saccade at 45° to the horizontal is produced if the two generators are activated equally. Thus, information derived from the target's image must be used to activate the two generators in the appropriate ratio.

The saccadic eye movement example illustrates how flexibility of action can be achieved by the same mechanisms if they are supplied with sensory information about what movement is needed. Commands for saccades in different directions differ in the muscles to which the commands are sent; commands for saccades of different amplitudes differ in magnitude and duration. In other respects, the commands are similar: commands to the agonist muscles have the same burst-tonic pattern, for instance. The saccade-generating mechanisms can be considered as implementing a program for generating commands; the details of these commands can vary in particular ways, so as to produce saccades that differ in amplitude and/or direction.

The ways in which the commands can be varied so as to alter certain performance characteristics define what are called **parameters** of the motor program or simply **program parameters**. Different values of the parameters lead to behavior suited to different circumstances or requirements. Thus, the parameters of the saccade program correspond to the program variations that lead to the production of saccades that differ in amplitude and direction. Saccades are a very simple type of behavior, and the program has few parameters: the two that have been mentioned are the primary and perhaps the only parameters of the basic saccade program. The programs governing other behaviors may have several additional parameters. One obvious example is speed (or duration): unlike saccades, we can execute many movements that have the same amplitude faster or slower; we can move a finger ten centimeters at more or less any speed we want (up to some limit). Speed or duration and a variety of other parameters will be discussed later in the chapter.

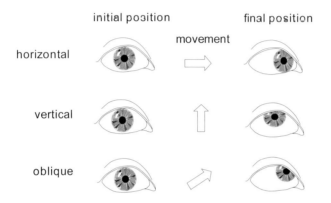

Figure 11.4: *Three possible directions for saccadic eye movements.*

11.1.11 Performance of programmed actions has invariant as well as variable features

The saccade program (or pattern generator) produces commands that have the same basic pattern regardless of the direction or amplitude of the saccade. A particular command pattern will tend to produce particular patterns in the movements and/or muscle activations that it gives rise to. The relationship between saccade commands and the eye movements they produce is particularly consistent and straightforward. The command pattern has a pulse-step form in the agonists (see Chapter 6) that leads to the characteristic saccadic movement – the eye smoothly and continuously progresses from its initial position to its new position, and its angular velocity profile possesses the characteristic bell shape. Figure 11.5 shows four saccadic movements with different amplitudes (between about 5° and 20°) that illustrate these characteristic features (eye position profiles on the left, velocity profiles on the right).

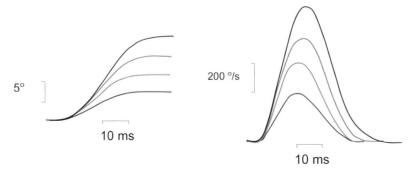

Figure 11.5: *Position and speed profiles of saccades of different amplitude (based on data obtained from a monkey, reported in Goossens, Van Opstal, 2006).*

Figure 11.5 illustrates the finding that the kinematic form of saccades is almost the same regardless of the amplitude or direction of the movement. Features of performance that are more or less the same whenever an individual person (or animal) performs an action are called **invariant features** or **invariant characteristics**:

> **INVARIANT FEATURE (OR CHARACTERISTIC)** of motor performance: A measurable aspect of an individual's performance of a motor action that is (almost) the same every time they execute the act, despite changes in other measurable characteristics. It does not change in a systematic way with changes in the conditions in which the act is executed.

Thus, an invariant feature remains the same while other things vary. For example, in the case of saccades, the direction, amplitude and peak speed of movement vary, but the kinematic pattern of movement illustrated in Figure 11.5 hardly changes and so is invariant. A characteristic of the movement kinematics (displacement, velocity, acceleration) that remains the same is often called a **kinematic invariant characteristic** or simply **kinematic invariant**. The invariant features of saccadic movements just described are examples of kinematic invariants. Note that although invariant characteristics are defined for individuals, it is typically found that the performance of different individuals possesses the same invariants.

Invariant and variable features can be identified in both stimulus driven and internally driven (program governed) behavior. In the latter case, many of the invariant characteristics will be a consequence of the structure of the program. In saccades, for example, the program generates a specific command pattern that is transformed into the characteristic movement pattern by the peripheral apparatus of the eyes: the extraocular muscles, the eyeball and associated soft tissues. Some variable features of performance will be associated with the parameters of the program: amplitude and direction are variable features of saccades and correspond to program parameters. Saccadic duration is also a variable characteristic of saccades, but it is not a distinct program parameter, since duration does not vary independently of amplitude (see section 4.4.3).

The invariant and variable features of performance can often provide important information about the organization of motor programs. How motor programs contribute to the invariant and variable features of performance is discussed in more detail later (section 11.2).

11.1.12 Programs can be altered before movement begins

As we have seen, aimed movements appear to be generated by a motor program with parameters that can be set in advance so that the working point moves directly to the target (see section 2.4.11 for a definition of *working point*). In the examples discussed so far, the parameters of the program are set based on information about the position of the target in space. It is possible that the position of the target may change during the period of time that elapses between the setting of the parameters and the start of the movement. Can the program be adjusted based on information about such a change in target position if the information is obtained prior to moving? This question has been addressed experimentally using a task in which participants are required to move their hand to a visible target as soon as they can after the target appears. The experiment involves two types of trial: *single-step* trials and *double-step* trials[25]. In a single-step trial, a target simply appears in some location and the person starts to move to it after a short time – their reaction time (RT). The location of the target is not known to the participant prior to its appearance, so they cannot accurately set the parameters of the program until the target appears. In a double-step trial, the target initially appears in one location, and after a short time (called the inter stimulus interval, ISI) it 'jumps' to a different location. This can be done by illuminating a target at one location (initial target position) and then illuminating an identical target at a different location while simultaneously switching off the target at the original location. In these trials, program parameters based on the initial target are not appropriate for moving to the new target location, and so some kind of correction is needed. Figure 11.6 shows a time line of events for a double-step trial in which the ISI is shorter than the reaction time, so the target jump occurs before movement begins.

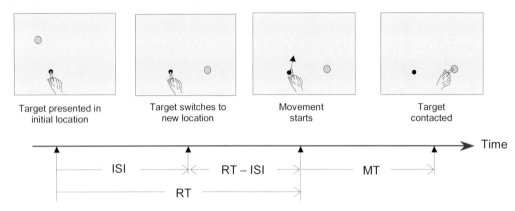

Figure 11.6: *Time line of events in double-step trials.*

Figure 11.7 shows some results obtained from a study that used ISIs between 25 and 100 ms, which was always less than the reaction time[26]. The participants moved their right index fingers from a start position (black circles in the figure) to the target stimulus 15 cm away (blue circles) with a movement time (MT) that averaged between about 150 and 200 ms. The figure shows some characteristic paths taken by the index finger to reach the target: panel A shows typical paths from single-step trials to two different targets, one to the right of the start position and one directly ahead. Panel B shows three typical paths from double-step trials in which the target was initially presented to the right of the start position and 'jumped' to the

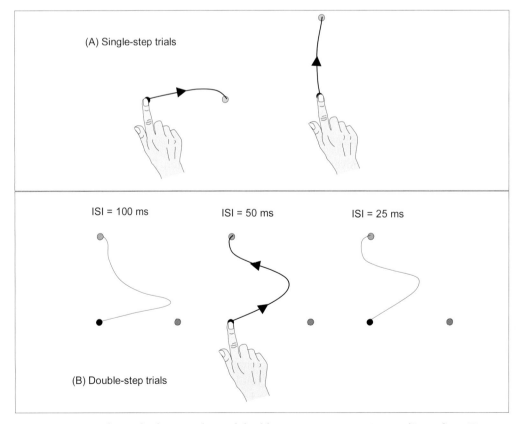

Figure 11.7: *Sample results from single- and double-step aiming experiment. (Data from Figure 2 of Van Sonderen, Denier van der Gon, Gielen, 1988.)*

directly ahead position. Paths from trials with ISIs of 25, 50 and 100 milliseconds are shown. These ISIs are all substantially less than the reaction times, which averaged between 250 and 350 milliseconds. The obvious feature of paths in panel B is that the movement starts off roughly in the direction of the initial target position and then changes direction towards the final target position.

At first glance, the paths shown in panel B of Figure 11.7 suggest that a feedback correction has been made after a person sees that they are moving in the wrong direction. However, this is not what is going on: two findings from the experiment provide evidence that the change in movement direction in double-step trials is not a feedback correction made after the movement has started, but is due to an adjustment to the program made prior to the start of the movement. First, the changes in movement direction evident in double-step trials (Figure 11.7B) occur too soon after the movement starts to be the result of visual feedback obtained during the movement. It is known that movements can be quite rapidly corrected by visual feedback during their execution: in upper limb movements the effects of feedback on an ongoing movement can be observed after a period no shorter than 100 ms, so it takes at least 100 ms for visual feedback to affect an ongoing movement (see Chapter 12). In the double-step task, the first major change in movement direction towards the final target position occurred within about 60 ms of movement onset, even in the longest ISI condition[27]. This is too short a time for the direction change to be a response to visual feedback obtained after the movement has started, so the adjustment that leads to the direction change must be based on information about the shift in target position obtained prior to movement onset.

The second source of evidence that adjustments take place prior to movement onset comes from the initial direction of the movement. The results showed that if the ISI in double-step trials was long (100 ms), the initial direction of the movement was towards the first target location and similar to the initial direction in single-step trials. If the ISI was shorter, the initial movement direction was deviated towards the target's final position. The effect is visible in Figure 11.7: the initial direction of the path in the 100 ms ISI double-step condition (panel B, left) is almost the same as the direction of movement in the corresponding single-step condition (panel A, left). In the 25 and 50 ms ISI conditions, the path's initial direction is further towards the location of the second target position. The same pattern has also been observed in experiments with monkeys performing a similar task[28]. Figure 11.8 shows some movement paths obtained in one such experiment that clearly shows the differences in initial movement direction on trials with different ISIs.

The results shown in Figure 11.7 show that the program is first parameterized based on the initial target position and that alterations are subsequently made based on the final target position. The alterations begin prior to the start of the movement when the ISI is less than 100 ms. Short ISIs correspond to a longer period of time between the moment the target jumps and the start of the movement (this is the time period equal to RT − ISI in Figure 11.6), which gives more time to alter the program before the movement starts. In the 100 ms ISI condition there was about 184 ms (284 − 100 ms) available to make alterations, which is too short a time for any effects to be evident when the movement starts; in the 25 ms ISI condition there was about 259 ms, which was long enough for effects to be evident. These findings suggest that the alteration process takes time to initiate and complete; it is not something that occurs instantaneously.

The results from experiments using double-step targets demonstrate that information about changes in the task situation that occur prior to movement can alter the motor program after the initial setting of the parameters. An obvious way in which the program could be altered would simply be to change the parameters from those appropriate for reaching the target in its initial location, to those appropriate for the final location. We will discuss possible mechanisms by which the program can be adjusted later.

11.1.13 Actions governed by motor programs can be adjusted by sensory feedback at peripheral and central levels

Setting the parameters of the motor program prior to moving is one way in which internally driven behavior can be made to suit the circumstances in which it is to be executed. Another way is to modify the execution of the behavior using sensory information that becomes available once the movement has started. Most voluntary actions are of sufficiently long duration that once they are under way, performance can, in principle, be influenced by sensory information in both the error-correcting, feedback mode and the anticipatory, feedforward mode. The feedback mode is briefly described here.

Feedback can operate at the peripheral level or at the central level. Feedback that acts at a peripheral level influences how the commands translate into muscle activation, but does not alter the commands themselves. Feedback that acts at a central level affects the commands. Figure 11.8 illustrates the distinction between these two levels in a system where a command generator (central program element) issues commands to a peripheral negative feedback loop. Signals from the sensor are delivered to the comparator block in the feedback loop and also to the central program element. The right side of the figure shows a simplified block-diagram representation of the elements involved in the control of an upper limb action such as a reach: central program circuits in the brain send command signals to spinal interneurons and motorneurons, which translate these commands into control signals to the muscles. Somatosensory afferents transmit sensory signals to the spinal circuits and also up the spinal cord (blue arrows) to the brain regions associated with the production of motor commands. The central program circuits also receive sensory feedback information from other sources such as the visual system (green arrows).

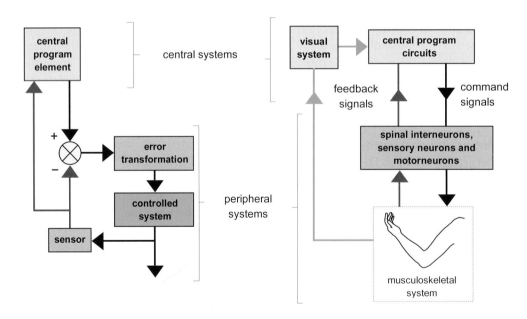

Figure 11.8: *Feedback can act at both central and peripheral levels; see text for explanation.*

Sensory feedback acting at the peripheral level can act to correct for small, transient disturbances that affect the body during performance and so make sure that the limbs move in the manner specified by the commands. Since this kind of feedback does not affect the commands themselves, it cannot correct for errors in the commands. Command errors will occur if the program parameters were not set correctly. For example, in the lower image in panel B of Figure 11.1, the initial direction of the aimed movement is not in the direction of the target, presumably because the setting of the program parameters was unable to take the 90° rotated relationship between movement of the stylus and movement of the cursor into account. In this situation, information about the error in movement direction cannot be obtained from somatosensory feedback, and so the feedback loops at the peripheral level cannot correct the error. The error can only be corrected if a person can see that the cursor is not moving towards the target. Visual information about the error can be used to make adjustments to the program so that the commands are appropriate for moving to the target.

11.1.14 The same basic motor pattern can be produced when executing acquired skills using different body parts

The genetically determined neural circuits that are responsible for generating motor commands for behaviors like locomotion, saccadic eye movements, breathing, chewing and swallowing are all closely tied to particular effector systems. The locomotor circuits send commands to the leg muscles; the saccade circuits send commands to the extraocular muscles; the chewing circuitry sends commands to the jaw muscles. The pattern-generating circuits that underlie many (but not all) of the animal behaviors described in previous chapters are similar: circuits that govern the production of modal action patterns such as courtship displays of birds, claw waving in fiddler crabs and egg retrieval in geese are all linked to specific groups of muscles so that particular body parts are moved. This can restrict the flexibility of the behavior: the fiddler crab cannot choose to wave his minor claw if he gets tired of waving his major one; the graylag goose cannot retrieve an egg with its foot or its wing.

Much of human voluntary behavior is very different from the examples just described. Rather than being restricted to using particular groups of muscles or a particular set of body parts, we are often able to use whatever muscles, body parts or tools happen to be suited to purpose. For example, if we wanted to retrieve an egg (move it closer to us), we could imagine doing it in many different ways: using one hand, both hands together, a foot, both feet, a stick or any other suitable item that happened to be nearby. Achieving the same outcome using different effectors is an example of motor equivalence (defined in Chapter 1). This enables us to do things in a very wide range of circumstances. Our flexibility in this respect is shared by very few other animal species. In many cases the flexibility is automatic and does not require us to reason out how to execute a task. Writing illustrates this automatic flexibility quite well.

As has been noted many times, most adults are capable of writing the same text using almost any set of effectors, including effectors that have never previously been used for writing. Figure 11.9 illustrates this: I have written the phrase 'motor equivalence'[29] using different effectors, from just the fingers and wrist of the dominant arm (panel A) to holding the pen clenched between the teeth (panel F). As might be expected, writing with different effectors produces differences in the quality of execution: I am right-handed, and it is clear that execution with the right hand (panel A) generated script that is more legible and less shaky than the other efforts. Writing with the right limb was also quicker than writing with the left or writing with the foot or head. Nevertheless, writing legible script is clearly possible with almost any set of effectors. What is notable, however, is not that the same words and letters can be written with different effectors, but that the style of the writing is recognizably similar. The features of the written text that characterize a person's writing when they use the usual effectors are preserved when they use other, unfamiliar effectors[30]. These characteristics are determined by the way in which a person moves the writing implement over the surface being written on: they are kinematic invariant characteristics of writing that give a person's writing its distinctive style. Other characteristics of writing production are not invariant: the joints used can vary, as can the joint motions, muscle activations and force-time patterns[31].

The ability to produce written text with characteristics of style that remain invariant over changes in the effectors demonstrates that there is something about the production process that is the same, regardless of the effectors that are used to write with[32]. Similar results have been reported for different types of voluntary action; the example of reaching is discussed in the next part of the chapter. These findings have led to the idea that the motor programs for acquired skills like handwriting and reaching are organized hierarchically. This idea is developed next.

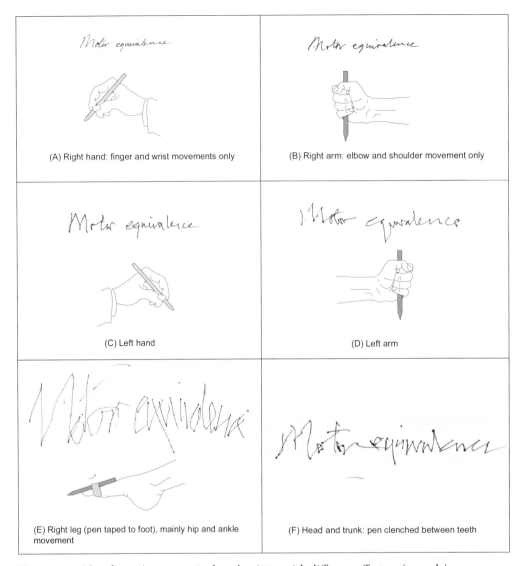

Figure 11.9: *The phrase 'motor equivalence' written with different effectors (to scale).*

11.1.15 Execution of the same action using different effectors involves the same program components

The results described in the last subsection suggest that there are components of the motor program that are the same, regardless of the muscles that are responsible for movement of the working point. Since these components are independent of which muscles are used, their neural mechanisms must lie in the brain and not in the spinal cord.

Further evidence for muscle independent components of motor programs comes from studies of central fatigue. Everyone knows that repeated performance of an action using the same muscles will eventually lead to these muscles becoming fatigued. It is probably less well known that repeatedly using neural circuitry can produce a similar effect – a kind of neural fatigue. This phenomenon can be exploited to determine whether performing an action with different effectors involves a common neural mechanism at a supraspinal level. Imagine, for example, writing a particular word or phrase over and over again with the same set of effectors. The muscles used would eventually get fatigued and the neural circuits underlying the production of writing could also get fatigued, both the peripheral circuits (motorneurons and associated spinal circuitry) and the circuits in the brain. If you switched to a different set of effectors once you had become tired, performance would not be affected by peripheral fatigue of the original effectors (muscle fatigue and any fatigue of the spinal circuits). However, if writing with different effectors involves common central components, then any fatigue in these components would persist, regardless of which effectors you switch to. No studies of writing using this method have been conducted, but one study has found evidence for central fatigue of common program components in handle-cranking and turning[33].

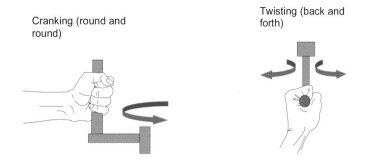

Cranking (round and round)

Twisting (back and forth)

Figure 11.10: *Cranking and twisting a handle (see text for explanation).*

In the study, participants first grasped a handle with one hand and either cranked it around and around as rapidly as possible for 30 seconds, or twisted it back and forth as rapidly as possible for 30 seconds (see Figure 11.10). The task was sufficiently strenuous to produce muscle fatigue. After the initial 30 seconds cranking or twisting with the first arm, participants immediately swapped to the other arm and performed either the cranking or twisting action for another 30 seconds. This meant that there were four possible sequences that participants could have performed in the study, as listed in Table 11.1. If there is a component to the cranking motor program that is the same for the two arms and is fatigued during the first 30 seconds, then performance should be worse (fewer cranks) when the cranking action is subsequently performed with the other hand. Conversely, if the twisting action is performed with the other hand after the cranking action, its performance should not be detrimentally affected by prior cranking. A similar result is expected if the twisting action is performed first and there are components of its motor program that are the same for both arms. Table 11.1 shows the results – the number of cranks performed in the second 30 seconds – obtained in the four conditions. The data are consistent with the idea that components of both the cranking program and the twisting program are the same for both arms: performance with the second arm was slightly worse (fewer cranks or twists) after the same task had been performed with the first arm than when the other task had been performed. Thus, the results of the study provide further evidence that performance with the left and right arms shares common program components[34]. What is the nature of these program components? This question is addressed next.

Table 11.1: *Experimental conditions and results from a cranking-twisting experiment.*

Action with first arm	Action with second arm	Average number of movements of second arm
cranking	cranking	106.7
twisting	cranking	111.2
twisting	twisting	165.0
cranking	twisting	167.4

11.1.16 Some programs have an effector-independent level of motor representation

The kinematic invariants of writing and reaching movements are defined for the working point. It is the pen nib that traces out written letters; it is the finger, hand or stylus that moves to a target location in a reaching movement (Figure 11.7). The working point's motion is produced by activating groups of muscles that rotate body segments about joints. For example, in panel B of Figure 11.9, the pen was moved by activating muscles that rotate the segments of the right arm about the shoulder and elbow joints. It has been found that when people repeat the same action several times with the same effectors, the motion of the working point is very much the same on each repetition, but the motions of the joints and the activations of the muscles are much more variable. Thus, there is a consistency in the motion of the working point that is not reflected in the motions of the joints and activations of the muscles. One of the first people to draw attention to this phenomenon was Nicolai Bernstein, in his studies of highly skilled actions by professional people[35] (see Chapter 1). Similar observations have subsequently been made in a variety of tasks, including handwriting[36] and reaching[37].

We have so far described three important observations that apply to a variety of acquired voluntary skills:

(1)   The same action can be performed with a wide range of different effectors. This means that the same outcome can be achieved using whatever muscles, body parts and sometimes tools happen to be suitable or available.

(2)   Not only can the same outcome be achieved using different effectors, but the working point of the effector system exhibits kinematic features that are the same (invariant) despite the use of different effectors.

(3)   Repeated execution of the same action using the same effectors is characterized by very similar motion of the working point, but variable motions of the joints and variable muscle activations.

These observations together indicate that the motor programs that underlie the production of skilled, voluntary actions involve some kind of 'representation' of a movement pattern for the working point. This movement pattern achieves the action's goal outcome. The representation of the movement pattern is independent of any particular effectors – muscles, limbs, body segments, tools – that might be used to execute the action. This effector-independent level of motor representation enables the nervous system to formulate some kind of 'instructions' for how the working point should move without specifying how the body segments should move or how the muscles should be activated. These 'instructions' must be 'translated' into control signals to the motor neuron pools of the muscles that will be used. This is the basic idea behind many explanatory accounts of how the brain organizes the control of actions that can be executed by different effectors[38]. Figure 11.11 shows a block diagram of the minimal structure of the motor program according to these accounts. The block labeled 'abstract pattern generator' is responsible for generating 'instructions' for how the working point should move. The word 'abstract' is used to emphasize that the pattern generator output specifies how the working point should move, but does not specify how the joints should move or how the muscles should be activated. The abstract pattern generator requires information about the behavioral goal in order to produce an output. For example, in a reaching task, information about the target to be reached for is needed in order to specify how the working point should move there.

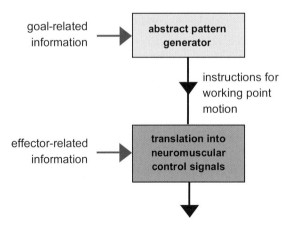

Figure 11.11: *Block diagram of the basic structure of a motor program for skilled, voluntary actions (see text for explanation).*

The second, lower block in Figure 11.11 receives the output signals from the abstract pattern generator and converts them into command signals to the motor neuron pools of the muscles that will move the body. This process requires information about the effectors to be used for executing the act, as indicated in the figure. The structure of the diagram illustrates in a simple way the hierarchical structure of the motor program: a high-level block (the abstract pattern generator) instructs a lower level block (the translation block).

The block diagram in Figure 11.11 represents only the simplest outline of how motor programs for well-learned, voluntary skills are believed to be structured. We have not considered exactly what the two blocks are doing: what kind of instructions does the higher level block send to the lower level block? How does it generate these instructions? How does the lower level block covert the input it receives into command signals to spinal circuits? We will consider possible answers to these questions later in the chapter. It is also important to recognize that not all well-learned skills are likely to have a hierarchical structure with an effector-independent level. Some skills, such as speaking, can only be performed with one set of effectors.

11.1.17 What is a motor program?

We have discussed several characteristics of behavior that are not consistent with the traditional definition of a motor program. The main conclusions can be summarized as follows:

(1)   The nervous system does not store sequences of commands that can be sent to motor neuron pools and associated spinal circuitry.

(2)   It is not motor command sequences that are 'stored' in the nervous system, but sets of procedures or rules for generating commands. Thus, a motor program is better conceived of as a 'stored set of rules'[39].

(3)   The conceptual distinction between rules or procedures for generating commands and the neural circuitry that embodies and implements these procedures is the reason for using the term *program*: the program is the set of rules, the neural circuitry is the physical embodiment of these rules. In the case of a locomotor CPG, the neural circuits in the spinal cord constitute the CPG itself; the principles and procedures that govern production of motor commands constitute the locomotor program.

(4)   In some cases, the set of rules or procedures that constitute a motor program are not stored in one structure or region of the nervous system and then transferred to other regions to be executed. Rather, the procedures are embodied in the structure of the neural circuits that execute them. This may not be true for all motor programs.

(5)   The motor patterns actually produced when performing an action are the result of a complex interplay between commands generated by pattern generators, sensory feedback processes, and the mechanical properties of the body and environment.

(6)   The programs for many, but probably not all, well-learned skills have a hierarchical structure with at least two levels: a higher, effector-independent level, and a lower level that converts the output of the higher level into the commands that are sent to the motor neuron pools and associated interneurons.

(7)   A distinction can be drawn between the programs that govern discrete actions and the *control programs* that coordinate the recruitment of discrete programs to form compound actions – actions in which an overall goal is achieved by means of several discrete component actions, executed in sequence or concurrently.

The term 'motor program' provides a convenient way of referring to the processes underlying the production of internally generated motor behaviors, provided that it is not taken to imply that these processes share the characteristics of other types of program, such as those that run on digital computers.

11.2 Program Structures for Aimed Movement

11.2.1 Introduction: target-directed aiming

A very simple kind of task is to move an arm in order that a working point, such as a finger or stylus, is brought into contact with (or positioned so that it points at) a specified object or location called the **target**. Contacting or otherwise reaching a target is called **target acquisition**. Many different variants can be imagined, from moving a stylus or finger so that its tip makes contact with the target, to manipulating a computer interface device such as a mouse to bring a cursor to a target location on the screen.

When the task involves moving a working point from a fixed starting position to a target that is not moving, it will be referred to as a **(discrete) target-directed aiming task** or simply **aiming task**; the movements made when executing the task will be referred to as **aimed (or aiming) movements**. Depending on the precise nature of the task, aimed limb movements may also be referred to as *reaching movements*, *point-to-point reaching movements* or *pointing movements*. The latter term is used when the working point is positioned so that it points at the target rather than making contact with it.

Aimed movements are one of the three most widely studied types of movement in motor neuroscience; the others are eye movements and locomotor movements. Unlike many tasks that people are able to perform, aiming tasks can be executed by some animal species, notably monkeys. As a result, our understanding of how nervous systems generate and control aiming movements is substantially better developed than is our understanding of most other kinds of movement. In this part of the chapter we will discuss some of what is known about the generation of aimed movements, and consider what the motor programs for such movements involve. We will consider aiming tasks in which target acquisition is easy, in the sense that it requires little accuracy. The effects of different accuracy requirements are discussed in Chapter 12.

11.2.2 Planar aimed movements are those in which the working point moves in two dimensions

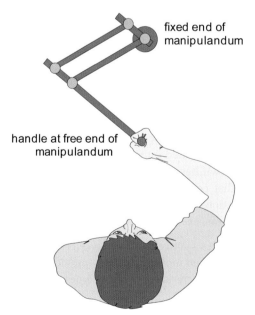

Figure 11.12: *Example of a manipulandum that constrains the hand to move in a plane.*

A widely studied class of aimed movement involves moving a working point in a plane: for example, moving a finger tip or stylus across a flat surface. Such movements are called **planar aimed movements**. Another way of constraining the hand to move in a plane is to have the experimental participant grasp the handle of a manipulandum made of rigid segments linked together at hinge joints, as shown in Figure 11.12. In the figure, the joints between the linked segments only allow the handle of the manipulandum to be moved in the plane of the page[40].

A typical aiming task using an apparatus like that shown in Figure 11.12 requires participants to move the manipulandum so that the handle is directly above a marked target area (see Figure 11.14): the handle is the working point. The arm movement will typically involve motions about the shoulder, elbow and wrist joints. When more than one joint is involved, the movement is referred to as a **multi-joint aimed movement**. When motion is restricted to a single joint, the task is called a *single-joint aiming task*.

11.2.3 Working point motion in unobstructed aimed movements exhibits kinematic invariants

In multi-joint aiming tasks, the working point can typically be moved between the start and target positions along an indefinitely large number of differently shaped paths. For instance, in the planar aiming task shown in Figure 11.13 you could choose to move between the start and target locations along any one of the four paths drawn in the figure. The stylus tip could be moved along a chosen path in a variety of different ways – it could be slowed down and speeded up, or moved forwards and backwards along the path in almost any way you might wish. However, unless there is some particular reason to do otherwise, when people and monkeys make planar aimed movements the working point follows a roughly straight or gently curved path, and the tangential speed profile (see Chapter 2) closely resembles the bell-shaped profiles that characterize saccadic eye movements (Figure 11.5) and other single-joint movements[41]. Sharp deviations from straightness are only observed when a person corrects for an error in movement direction.

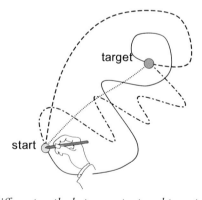

Figure 11.13: *Four different paths between start and target.*

Figure 11.14 reproduces some results from an individual participant in a study of planar aimed movements (panel A)[42]. Participants moved in a horizontal plane between six different targets (crosses labeled 1 to 6 in panel A) by means of rotations about the elbow and shoulder joints (the wrist was fixed by a splint). Panel B shows example paths of the hand of a typical participant (red lines) as they moved in sequence from target 1 to 4 to 2 to 6 to 5 to 1 to 3 and finally to target 6 (the arrows indicate the direction of movement along the paths). Panel C shows individual movements from target 1 to 4 and from target 2 to 5. The paths of the working point (hand) are roughly straight or very gently curved. This is true regardless of the direction, amplitude or starting point of the movement.

The top row in panel D of Figure 11.14 shows tangential speed profiles of the hand's movement along its path for movements between three different pairs of targets: these show the bell-shape that is characteristic of aimed movements that have little demand for end-point accuracy. The lower two rows of panel D show the elbow angle (green curves) and shoulder angle (blue curves) profiles and the angular velocity profiles for the three movements. In order to move the hand along a straight path, the motion of the two joints must be properly coordinated. The figure shows that the joints start and stop moving at almost exactly the same time – their movements are temporally coordinated – and the exact pattern of joint motion differs when moving between different pairs of targets. During the movement from target 1 to target 4, the elbow extends and the shoulder flexes. During the movement between

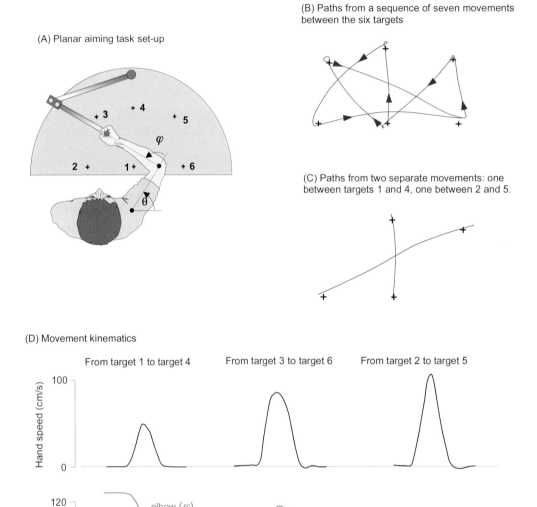

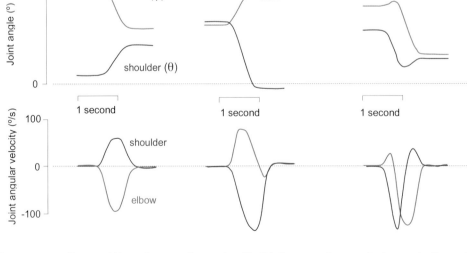

Figure 11.14: *Set-up (A) and example results (B–D) from a planar aiming task. Data from Morasso (1981, subject 1).*

targets 3 and 5, the elbow flexes and then extends a little (a reversal of direction); the shoulder extends. During the movement between targets 2 and 5, the elbow extends briefly and then flexes; the shoulder extends and briefly flexes at the end of the movement. Thus, the pattern of joint movement is different when moving between different pairs of targets, but the pattern of working point movement is very similar.

Figure 11.14 illustrates the general finding that for unobstructed, low-accuracy, multi-joint, planar aiming movements, the working point follows a straight or gently curved path with a bell-shaped speed profile. These two features are kinematic invariants of planar aimed movements: they are observed despite changes in other aspects of performance, such as the direction of movement, the distance moved[43], the initial posture of the reaching limb, the speed with which the movement is executed[44], the particular joints and muscles that contribute to the working point's motion[45], whether a body part, tool[46] or manipulandum handle serves as the working point, the orientation of the limb with respect to gravity[47], and whether or not any mass is being moved in addition to that of the limb[48]. When the working point needs to be positioned accurately, the speed profile is typically asymmetrical and there is often evidence of feedback corrections; these features will be described in Chapter 12.

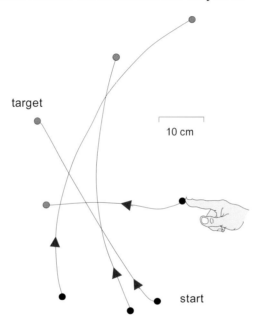

Figure 11.15: *Paths followed by the working point (finger tip) during unobstructed aimed movements in the vertical plane. Data from Figure 4 in Atkeson, Hollerbach (1985).*

The kinematic invariants of planar aimed movements have been also been observed when movements are made in three dimensions. For example, if a person moves their hand to a target somewhere nearby without any external constraints on how they can move – no obstacles and no restriction to move in a plane – it has been found that the hand follows a roughly straight or gently curving path with a bell-shaped speed profile[49]. Some example paths of the finger for movements from four different start locations (black circles) to four different targets (blue circles) are shown in Figure 11.15. In these examples, the finger moved in a vertical plane (the plane of the page in the figure). One feature of the paths shown in Figure 11.15 is that some are more curved than others, an observation that is discussed in more detail next.

11.2.4 Working point paths are not strictly invariant

The shape of the paths followed by the working point in unobstructed aimed movements is almost always gently curved or nearly straight. The literature tends to emphasize straightness, but curved paths seem to have been much more widely reported[50], and in some studies systematic variations in curvature have been found. Figures 11.14 and 11.15 illustrate this: the paths of movements made laterally across the body (e.g., from target 2 to 6 in Figure 11.14) and those made up or down the body (Figure 11.15) tend to show a bow-like shape that is curved outward from the body. This contrasts with the paths of movements made radially outwards or inwards, which are much straighter. These variations in path curvature with movement direction have been found in most studies[51]. Figure 11.16 presents a clear example. The experimental task is shown in panel A: participants moved their index finger from a start location directly in front of them to four different target locations (blue circles in the figure labeled 1–4) that were 30 cm from the start location and arranged at 20° intervals on the circumference of a circle. Panel B shows the paths of the index finger of one participant as they moved to the targets (other participants were similar). These paths suggest that path curvature was greater when the movement was more lateral (left to right across the body)[52]. This was a general finding as shown in panel C, which presents a plot of a measure of path curvature[53] for the four targets (average of all the experimental participants).

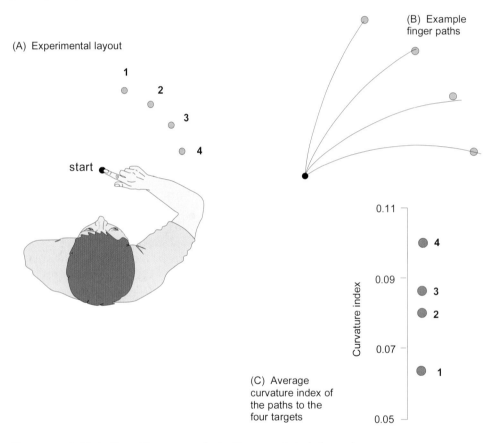

Figure 11.16: *Data from Figures 2 and 3 in Desmurget* et al. *(1997a).*

The fact that such systematic variations in curvature exist means that the shape of the working point path is not truly invariant. If the shape were truly invariant it should show no systematic variations over changes in the conditions in which the movement is executed. Nevertheless, the approximately invariant shape of the path of the working point is often treated as if it were a true invariant, and this has generated many ideas about the rules and principles used in the generation of aimed movements, as discussed in what follows.

11.2.5 Invariant characteristics provide clues about the rules implemented by motor programs

The kinematic invariants of multi-joint aimed movements are not essential for achieving the task goal (e.g., contact with the target), nor are they necessary consequences of the biomechanical or physiological properties of the body. This suggests that the kinematic invariants reflect the operation of the rules and principles that govern the motor command generating processes. For this reason, the invariants can provide clues concerning the contents of motor programs. However, it is important to note that not all invariant characteristics reflect the operation of generative rules. For example, the working point in single degree-of-freedom, single-joint aimed movements will always follow a roughly circular arc, because all points on a body segment that rotates about the joint move in a circle. In this case, the invariant path shape is an inevitable consequence of the biomechanical properties of the body and does not depend on the process of command generation[54]. Invariant characteristics that are a consequence of the mechanical properties of the musculoskeletal system cannot inform us about the contents of the motor program[55]. Invariants of this sort cannot typically be changed by deciding to do something different – you cannot decide to make a single-joint movement in such a way that the working point moves in a straight line, for instance. Only those invariants that could be different, like the working point paths of multi-joint aimed movements, can provide clues concerning the contents of motor programs.

The fact that people spontaneously produce gently curved or straight working point paths indicates that path shape is specified in some way by the underlying motor program. Similarly, the fact that the working point moves continuously towards the target (no direction reversals) with a smooth increase and decrease in speed (bell-shaped profile) suggests that the program specifies the motion along the path. The program may specify these characteristics explicitly at a level of representation that is independent of the effector system. Alternatively, they might emerge as a consequence of specifying other characteristics of performance, such as joint angular motions[56] or joint torques[57]. One important clue concerning which of these alternatives is more likely is the observation that the joint motions show a more variable, less consistent pattern than does the motion of the working point. Joint motions sometimes show reversals of motion direction but sometimes do not (Figure 11.14), and generally show more variability over repeated executions[58]. These findings suggest that the nervous system generates whatever joint motions and muscle forces are needed to move the working point along a trajectory with the kinematic invariant characteristics described above. This conclusion is further evidenced by the finding that these invariants are still observed in working point motion regardless of whether a reaching or pointing movement is actually performed. For example, if the working point is a cursor on a computer screen, the cursor motion will exhibit the kinematic invariants of aimed movements if it is moved by manipulating a joystick, or by exerting force with the arm but not actually moving the limb at all[59].

The observations described above support the idea that the motor program specifies the trajectory of the working point at an effector-independent (high) level. According to this idea, the output of the effector-independent level of the program carries information about the working point trajectory; the output is transmitted to lower levels of the program hierarchy, where it is used to generate commands that cause the working point to move as specified. Of course, if it is the case that the working point trajectory is specified by a high level of the motor program, it remains to be explained why the specified trajectory has the invariant characteristics we have described. This question will be addressed later in the chapter; first we will consider further the evidence supporting the idea that trajectories of aimed movements are specified by a high level of the motor program.

11.2.6 The specification of a trajectory is referred to as 'planning'

The idea that the motor program specifies trajectories for effectors is referred to in the research literature as **trajectory planning**[60]. The structure that generates the information that specifies a trajectory is called a **trajectory planner**[61], or alternatively a **trajectory generator** (the term we will use). Trajectory planning is said to be spatial or to take place in *external space* or *working-point space* if the trajectory of the working point through the environment is specified. Thus, **spatial trajectory planning** is the process of specifying the trajectory of the working point through the environment. An alternative is the specification of the trajectories for the various joints comprising the effector system, a strategy known as **joint-space trajectory planning**[62].

It is important to be clear about the use of the words 'planning' and 'planner' in this context. In everyday language, the word *planning* suggests the preparation of a plan or blueprint that is completed before being sent to the next stage of a process. For example, an architect draws up a set of plans for a building, and only when these are complete are they sent to the building firm that does the construction work. This could be a very misleading analogy for the generation of aimed movements. As we will see later, the trajectory planner is likely to operate in the same way as the pattern generators for saccades and locomotion described in previous chapters: trajectory information is generated according to a set of rules or principles, and is continuously transmitted to lower levels as it is being generated. In other words, a complete plan is not created first and then transmitted: a trajectory planner does not necessarily create a trajectory plan. Thus, the terms 'planning' and 'planner' have the potential to mislead, so it is necessary to be careful when using them. *Trajectory planning* can be defined as follows:

> **TRAJECTORY PLANNING:** The (internal) process of specifying a trajectory for a working point (or a set of trajectories for a system of joints). The process does not necessarily result in the production of an explicit plan, as the word 'planning' might seem to imply.

An alternative to trajectory planning is provided by what is called the **final position control hypothesis**, which was originally proposed to explain the results of experiments performed on monkeys[63], but was later supported by studies with human participants[64]. According to this hypothesis, the program only specifies the final position of the working point[65] needed to acquire the target; movement trajectories are not specified at any level of the motor program, but rather they emerge as a consequence of the properties of the skeletomuscular system and spinal reflexes. However, the available data do not support the final position control hypothesis, as discussed next.

11.2.7 Final position control is not supported by empirical evidence

If the effector system is following a specified (planned) trajectory, then the system would be expected to return to the specified trajectory following an unexpected disturbance[66]. In contrast, if the program simply establishes a final configuration of the effectors (final position control), then a disturbance will not lead to the limb being returned to a specified trajectory, since no such trajectory exists. An experiment that tested these alternatives was conducted using monkeys, and employed a single-joint, aimed movement task[67]. The monkeys were strapped into an upright seated position similar to that of the person shown in Figure 11.12. The upper arms were held in a fixed position and their forearms were strapped into a manipulandum that allowed flexion and extension of the elbow joint (see Figure 11.21). The monkeys' task was to move the forearm from a starting position so that it pointed at a visible target (long axis of the forearm pointing at the target region). The targets were small lights, and the monkeys were trained to move to point at them as soon as one was illuminated. The monkey could see the target but was unable to see its arm.

Two conditions in the experiment are of interest. (1) *Assisting-torque-pulse condition* (performed by normal monkeys): a motor applied a brief torque to the arm immediately after it started to move towards the target; the torque was in the direction of the movement, and so had the effect of accelerating the limb towards the target more quickly than it would otherwise do. (2) *Holding-at-target condition* (performed by deafferented monkeys): shortly before the target was illuminated, the torque motor would move the arm quickly to the target location and hold it there for a short time after the monkey had activated its muscles in its attempt to move to the target.

If the final position control hypothesis were correct, then it would be expected that in the assisting-torque-pulse condition, the arm would accelerate more quickly during the torque pulse and would then continue more slowly towards the target after the pulse ended. In the holding-at-target condition, the final position control hypothesis would predict that the monkey would hardly move at all when the holding torque was turned off. In this condition the monkey would have no way of knowing that its arm had been moved (because the animals in this condition were deafferented), and so when the target was illuminated, the hypothesis predicts that the animal would issue a motor command that establishes a new equilibrium position for the limb where it points at the target. If the limb were already in this position, then once the holding torque was turned off, the arm would simply stay pointing at the target (or possibly move slightly if the motor command had established an equilibrium position slightly different from the holding position). The results of the experiment showed that the animals' behavior did not conform to the predictions of the final position control hypothesis. Figure 11.17 presents representative joint angle profiles from three conditions. Panel A is from a control condition in which no additional torques were applied. Panel B is from the assisting-torque-pulse condition. Panel C is from the holding-at-target condition. The joint angle profile in panel A is typical of single-joint aimed movements (see Chapter 2): the forearm segment rotates continuously in the direction of the target (amplitude ≈ 60°). In panel B, the torque pulse makes the forearm move towards the target more quickly than in panel A, but once the torque pulse ends, the forearm changes direction and rotates back towards its start position before continuing to the target. In panel C, the limb is moved and held at the target angle before the target is presented. Once the holding torque is turned off, the limb does not remain at the target location, but moves back towards its initial start position before returning back to the target position.

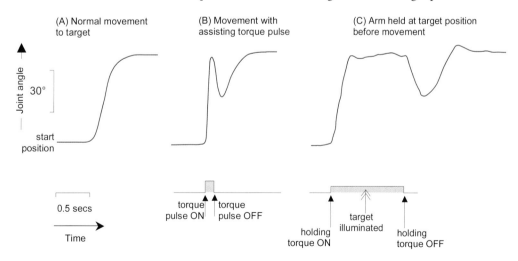

Figure 11.17: *Representative results from an experiment that tested the final position control hypothesis (see text for explanation). Data from Figures 5 and 6 in Bizzi* et al. *(1984).*

Clearly, the results obtained in the assisting-torque-pulse and holding-at-target conditions are not consistent with the final position control hypothesis. The results are instead consistent with the idea that the motor command continuously drives the forearm segment from the start to the target. If the arm receives an external push (assisting torque pulse) towards the target, then once the push stops, the limb moves to the position specified by the motor command at that time. A similar interpretation applies in the holding-at-target condition shown in the figure: when the holding torque was released, the arm moved back towards the starting position, since the command was still progressing towards its final level. The longer the limb is held at the target position, the less backward motion of the limb would be expected on release, since the command would be closer to its final level. This result was also observed in the experiment[68].

Figure 11.18 shows a schematic illustration of the difference between the final position control hypothesis (panel A) and one version of the idea that the command continuously drives the limb to the target position (panel B). In the final position control hypothesis, the command that specifies joint position changes from a level associated with the starting position to a level associated with the target position. Limb movement begins shortly after the command shifts (due to delays in transmitting command signals through the nervous system and the sluggish contractile response of the muscles to neural input). In the continuous drive case (panel B), the command level shifts continuously from the level associated with the start position to the level associated with the target position. The shift is sufficiently slow that the command is still shifting after the movement has started. The faster the command shifts, the more quickly the limb would be expected to move. Thus, the instantaneous shift that characterizes final position control could be viewed as a limiting case of the continuous command shift idea[69]. This highlights another deficiency of the final position control hypothesis: there is no simple or obvious way in which the speed of the movement can be programmed, so the scheme offers no principled explanation for how a person can decide to move quickly or slowly to the target[70].

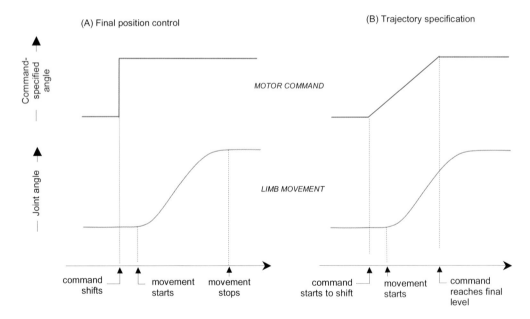

Figure 11.18: *Difference between the final position control hypothesis (A) and the continuous command shift (B) that characterizes trajectory planning models (for a single-joint movement; see text for explanation).*

The single-joint aimed movement experiment described in the foregoing paragraphs demonstrates that the final position control hypothesis is not generally correct for aimed limb movements[71]. The alternative idea of a continuously shifting command that specifies how the limb should move (trajectory planning) provides a plausible account of the results and is also able to provide an account of the control of multi-joint aimed movements[72]. As mentioned earlier, the trajectory planner could specify the movement in joint space or in external, environmental space. We next consider which of these alternatives best accounts for observed behavior.

11.2.8 Adaptation experiments provide evidence for spatial trajectory planning

Intuitively, it seems that spatial trajectory planning is a more likely strategy than joint-space planning, because the working point must move through the environment to reach a target, and may need to negotiate obstacles or pass through particular locations on its way there. It seems more natural to plan a trajectory for the working point when such environmental constraints exist. Furthermore, it is the spatial trajectory of the working point that possesses invariant features; the trajectories of the joints are typically more variable than the working point trajectory. However, some studies have reported invariant characteristics in joint motions[73] and as described in section 11.2.4, working point trajectories are not strictly invariant. It has been argued that a better account of these results is provided by the idea that the trajectory is planned in joint space[74]. However, studies that have employed an adaptation protocol provide strong evidence in favor of spatial planning.

The type of adaptation experiments that support spatial planning involve either an alteration of the force environment through which a person moves their hand, or alteration of the visual feedback from the moving limb (Figure 11.1). When the person first moves within the altered environment, their working point trajectory can differ substantially from those normally produced; in particular, the kinematic invariants are no longer present. As the person practices moving to targets within the altered environment, the normal form of the working point trajectories is re-established: the kinematic invariants of the working point trajectory are restored. Results from an example study[75] are shown in Figure 11.19. Participants performed a planar aiming task using a manipulandum of the sort shown in Figure 11.12. The starting position was the center of a circle of radius 10 cm, on which a series of targets were arrayed as shown in Figure 11.19. When participants were able to freely move the manipulandum without experiencing any applied force, they moved directly from the start location to the target along roughly straight paths, as shown in panel B of the figure (the movements shown were executed without visual feedback). In a subsequent series of trials, force was applied to the handle by means of motors attached to the joints of the manipulandum. The force was proportional to the speed with which the participant moved and was applied at an angle to the direction of movement; this produced something called a *viscous force field*. Panel A illustrates the forces that would be applied to the manipulandum handle if it moved along a straight path to the target with a bell-shaped speed profile. Each arrow represents a force vector: the length of an arrow corresponds to the relative magnitude of the force, and its direction corresponds to the direction of the force.

When participants first experienced the force field, their movements were strongly affected by the applied forces. As shown in panel C of Figure 11.19, the forces drove the hand away from its normal, roughly straight path (movements shown were executed without visual feedback). The participants then practiced moving to the targets in the force field with visual feedback available for several hundred trials: the *training phase* of the experiment. During the training phase, the participants' hand paths became progressively straighter the longer they practiced; by the end of the training phase, the paths were similar to those produced at the beginning of the experiment when there was no force field. Panel D shows the average paths from a number of test trials performed during the final stages of the training phase (these trials were performed without visual feedback): these paths are similar to those shown in panel A. Not only does the path become straighter as the person learns to move in the force field – referred to as adaptation to the force field (see Part III for further discussion) – but the tangential speed profile becomes progressively more bell-shaped as well. As discussed in section 11.2.3, the single-peaked, bell-shaped profile is characteristic of aimed movements in normal conditions. On first exposure to the viscous force field, a multi-peaked profile is observed like the one shown in panel E of Figure 11.19. By the final stages of the training phase, the single-peaked form has been restored (panel F).

The results in Figure 11.19 show that as a person practices making aimed movements in the altered conditions, their working point paths become straighter and the velocity profiles become more bell-shaped. Finally, after a sufficient amount of practice, the kinematic invariants observed in normal conditions are restored. These results suggest that the nervous system not only has the goal of getting the working point to the target, but also has a secondary goal that leads to a working point trajectory with the kinematic invariants we have

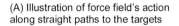

(A) Illustration of force field's action along straight paths to the targets

(B) Paths of free movements to the eight targets (no force field)

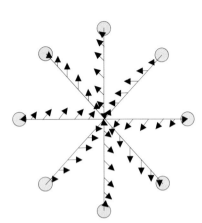

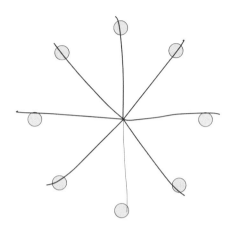

(C) Example paths from a participant when first experiencing the force field

(D) Average paths from test trials performed during the final stages of the training phase

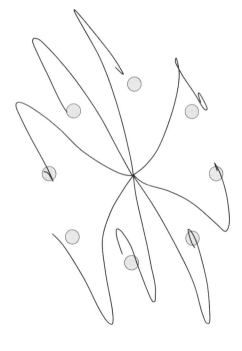

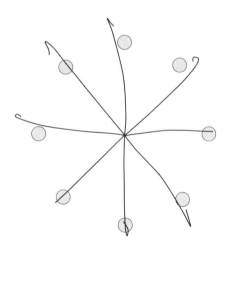

(E) Typical speed profile of a movement when first exposed to the force field

(F) Typical speed profile of a movement during the final stages of the training phase

Figure 11.19: *Study of people's ability to move in the novel force field shown in panel A (see text for details). Data from Figures 6, 7 and 10 of Shadmehr, Mussa-Ivaldi (1994).*

described (see section 11.2.10 for a discussion of what the secondary goal might be). When the conditions change so that the motor program normally used is no longer able to achieve this secondary goal, the person learns to modify the program so that the kinematic invariants of working point motion are re-established. It has been demonstrated that this learning can be driven by perceptual feedback, particularly visual feedback, about the trajectory of the working point[76]. In one study, when participants moved a finger to a visible target, they saw a cursor move through a virtual environment, but could not see their finger or arm[77]. The visually perceived spatial location of the cursor at any time could either be made to coincide with the true location of the finger or to deviate from the true location. For a series of trials, the cursor position on the screen was made to differ slightly from the true location of the finger while the movement was being executed (but not at the start or end of the movement). The effect of this manipulation was that the cursor moved along a path slightly more curved than the true movement of the finger. If the path normally followed by the working point is a secondary goal in the aiming task, then we might expect that people will learn to move so that the curvature of the visible cursor path is reduced. This expectation is based on the general finding that vision dominates kinesthesis (see Chapter 3). In order to achieve a less curved cursor path, the path followed by the finger would have to be more curved than normal. The results of the study confirmed the expectation. Prior to practicing in the distorted condition, the paths of participants' finger movements were quite straight. After a few practice trials in the distorted condition, participants had adapted their behavior so that the visible cursor moved along a roughly straight path, but the unseen finger moved along a curved path. Figure 11.20 presents a schematic illustration of the experimental protocol and the main finding just described (the distortion of the cursor path is exaggerated for illustrative purposes[78]).

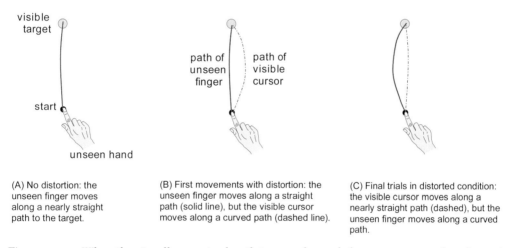

(A) No distortion: the unseen finger moves along a nearly straight path to the target.

(B) First movements with distortion: the unseen finger moves along a straight path (solid line), but the visible cursor moves along a curved path (dashed line).

(C) Final trials in distorted condition: the visible cursor moves along a nearly straight path (dashed), but the unseen finger moves along a curved path.

Figure 11.20: *When the visually perceived path is curved, people learn to move so that the path appears straight (see text for explanation).*

The results from adaptation studies have led to a partial consensus that the motor program for aimed movements involves a process that plans the trajectory for the working point somewhat independently of the effectors that will be used to move it (spatial trajectory planning). In order to specify a trajectory for a working point, the planning process requires information not only about the end point of the trajectory (the target), but also about the starting point. The next section describes the empirical evidence that information about the initial position is important in aiming movements.

11.2.9 Information about the initial position of the limb is important for accurate aiming

If the nervous system is to specify a path for the working point from an initial location to a target location, the trajectory generator needs information about the location of the target and of the working point. Information about the working point's location could be obtained visually or kinesthetically (the latter will only work if the working point is a body part or hand-held tool). In section 11.1.5 we briefly mentioned experimental studies in which deafferented monkeys were found to be able to make accurate aiming movements when they could see the target but not their limb. In these studies the animals could neither see nor feel where the limb was, so their accurate performance seems to contradict the idea that information about the working point's location is needed to plan a trajectory. However, as we will see, there is no contradiction.

In one classic study[79], monkeys were trained to make single-joint aimed movements to targets arrayed at 5° intervals on a circle centered at the elbow joint in a set-up like that shown in Figure 11.21, panel A. The monkey was strapped into a chair and the upper arm was held in a fixed position. The task was to extend the elbow from a starting location so that the forearm pointed at the location of an illuminated target: in Figure 11.21(A) the forearm is pointing at the central, illuminated target, as indicated by the dashed line. The task was performed in the dark, so the monkey could see the illuminated target, but could not see its arm. After training, the monkeys were deafferented and tested again following recovery. If the set-up in the post-deafferentation test session was identical to that used in the training session, the monkeys were able to point accurately at the targets.

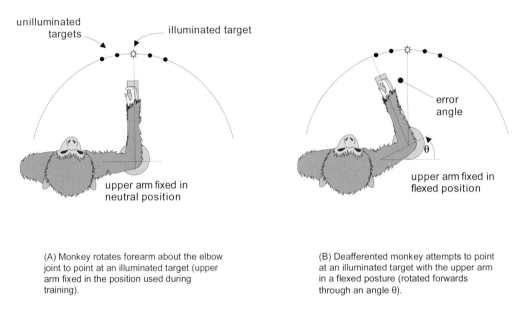

(A) Monkey rotates forearm about the elbow joint to point at an illuminated target (upper arm fixed in the position used during training).

(B) Deafferented monkey attempts to point at an illuminated target with the upper arm in a flexed posture (rotated forwards through an angle θ).

Figure 11.21: *Experimental set-up used in a study of the ability of monkeys to flex or extend the elbow so that the forearm pointed at an illuminated target (see text for explanation).*

At first glance, the results just described seem to suggest that the monkeys were able to point accurately without any information about the starting location of the limb. However, a slight modification of the experimental conditions showed that this was not the case. Panel B of Figure 11.21 shows another condition tested after deafferentation, but not practiced by the monkeys during the training session: the upper arm was fixed in a flexed position (rotated forwards through an angle θ). With the upper arm in this position, the monkeys were no longer able to point accurately at the targets: the monkeys made systematic errors, as indicated in panel B. The figure suggests what was happening. When the deafferented monkey is tested in conditions identical to those experienced during training, each target is associated with a particular elbow joint angle. For example, the central target in panel A is associated with an angle of 90°. When it saw the target, the deafferented animal was able to move its elbow joint to the angle required. If it did the same thing when the shoulder was flexed, the forearm would end up pointing in the wrong direction. This is what is shown in panel B: the monkey sees that the central target is illuminated and has moved the forearm to the angular position appropriate for the trained condition (90°). However, because the shoulder is in a flexed position, this elbow angle is no longer appropriate. Thus, the deafferented animal remembers which elbow angles were appropriate in the training stage and is able to reproduce them in the test phase, but it is unable to adjust its elbow position when the shoulder is in a different position. In contrast, normal monkeys were able to learn very quickly to adjust their forearm positions when the shoulder position was altered.

The results described above demonstrate that information about the starting position of the limb is needed to program an accurate aiming movement, even for single-joint movements. Similar results for multi-joint aiming movements have been reported in studies of patients who have been deafferented as a result of pathology and are unable to aim accurately when they cannot see their limbs[80]. When a deafferented patient is provided with visual information about the initial location of their arm, multi-joint aimed movements made with that arm are substantially more accurate than movements prior to which no visual information about initial arm position is available (i.e., when participants did not see their limb while reaching)[81]. The same kind of experiment can be conducted with normal people[82]. A typical experiment compares two conditions: in one condition, participants are able to see their hand immediately before reaching but not during the reach (condition A); in the other condition, they do not see their hand at all (condition B). When performance in the two conditions is compared, it is usually found that people are more accurate in condition A than in condition B[83]. Thus, when a person has both visual and proprioceptive information about the initial position of the hand (condition A), their aiming movements are more accurate than when only proprioceptive information is available (condition B).

In the experiments just described, the person or monkey not only has information about the working point's initial position, but also has information about the initial state of the effector system. That the information about the working point's location is critical is obvious when you consider the task of moving a cursor to a target location on a computer screen by manipulating a mouse: if you do not know the initial position of the cursor, then it is impossible to move it to a target, since you have no idea how far or in which direction to move the mouse. To move the cursor to a target, you must first locate the cursor position on the screen. Figure 11.22 shows an experimental method that demonstrates the importance of correctly locating the position of the working point for making accurate reaching movements. The participant's task is to move the finger tip of the unseen hand to an illuminated visible target (they cannot see any part of their reaching limb). There were two conditions in the experiment[84]. In the control condition (Figure 11.22(A)), a light emitting diode (LED) on the finger tip was illuminated prior to moving and was extinguished when the aiming movement began. In the 'displaced' condition (Figure 11.22(B)), the finger-tip LED was made to appear to the right of the felt position of the finger using prisms (see Chapter 10, section 10.3.4 for an explanation of the displacing effects of prisms); the target was seen in its true location.

If the person uses visual information about the finger tip's initial position to determine its trajectory to the target, then it would be expected that the trajectory generator would specify a path between the visually perceived LED position to the target in both conditions. In the control condition, movement along the specified path would take the finger tip to the target (blue line in Figure 11.22(A)). In the displaced condition, movement along a path from the visually perceived initial position to the target (dashed line in Figure 11.22(B)) would result in the finger following the path shown as a solid line. As a result, the finger tip would end up displaced to the left of the target – a systematic aiming error in the x-direction. These errors were observed in the experiment: the average results from the participants are shown in panel C of Figure 11.22, where the systematic error is represented by the difference between the control condition (circles) and the displaced condition (triangles).

The results described in this subsection add further weight to the idea that the nervous system specifies a working point trajectory from a start position to the target. This idea raises a number of questions; we will address the following in the remainder of the chapter:

(1)   Why does the specified working point trajectory have the invariant characteristics observed in experiments (straight or gently curved paths, bell-shaped speed profiles)?

(2)   How does the working point trajectory planning process operate? What is the nature of the information about the working point trajectory that is transmitted to lower levels of the motor program?

(3)   How do the lower levels generate appropriate motor commands in response to the input from the higher level?

(4)   Working point trajectory planning is not completely independent of the effectors, since the initial position of the working point is needed. Does any other effector-related information make a contribution to the trajectory planning process?

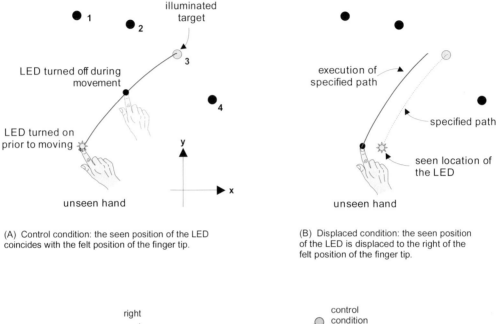

(A) Control condition: the seen position of the LED coincides with the felt position of the finger tip.

(B) Displaced condition: the seen position of the LED is displaced to the right of the felt position of the finger tip.

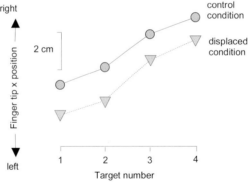

(C) Results (data from Rossetti, Desmurget, Prablanc, 1995).

Figure 11.22: *Experimental conditions and results from a study of reaching with an unseen hand to visible targets (see text for details).*

11.2.10 Why does working point motion exhibit the observed kinematic invariants?

The existence of invariant performance characteristics that can be attributed to the operation of neural pattern generating mechanisms raises the question: why these particular invariant characteristics? Why do the pattern generating mechanisms that produce the commands for aimed movements act to drive the working point along a roughly straight path with a bell-shaped speed profile? Is there something about these trajectories that make them preferable over other possible trajectories?

One way to approach these questions is to adopt the hypothesis that the control processes of the nervous system have one, or possibly more, performance objectives in addition to the primary task goals. These additional objectives can be expressed in terms of costs that the control processes attempt to minimize[85]. The basic idea is that the system attempts to produce movements that incur the smallest possible cost while meeting the primary task goals. An example was discussed in Chapter 8, where we examined the hypothesis that the nervous system has the objective of generating locomotor behavior with the smallest possible energy cost. Is something similar true of other types of behavior such as aiming?

Several hypotheses have been put forward regarding what cost the nervous system is trying to minimize in the production of aimed movements. Before discussing these, we will briefly outline the methods used to the test these hypotheses. As explained in Chapter 7, there are two basic methods: the direct and indirect methods. The indirect method has been used in studies of aimed movement; it involves using mathematical models to determine the movement pattern with the smallest cost and then comparing the movement pattern(s) actually produced with those derived mathematically. If the mathematically derived patterns that minimize a particular cost match those actually observed, then we have some evidence that minimizing that cost is an objective of the control process.

A particularly influential idea is that the nervous system is concerned with producing movements that show as little jerkiness as possible[86]. A movement appears jerky if its velocity changes abruptly and frequently. The rate of change of acceleration provides a quantitative measure of jerkiness; as a consequence, the rate at which acceleration changes over time is called **jerk**. Like acceleration and velocity, jerk is a variable quantity and is defined at every instant of time during a movement. The **jerk cost** of a particular movement is a measure of the total jerk during the entire movement[87]. A low value of the jerk cost means that the movement is smooth, and so a movement that incurs the smallest possible jerk cost – the minimum jerk movement – is also the smoothest possible movement. Thus, the idea that a secondary objective of the nervous system in the production of aimed movements is to make the jerk cost as small as possible can also be expressed as follows:

> 'Generate the smoothest motion to bring the [working point] from the initial position to the final position in a given time.' [88]

It is relatively straightforward to show that the working point trajectory that meets this objective – the minimum jerk motion – takes the form of a straight line with a bell-shaped speed profile[89]. Thus, when people make aimed movements, the trajectory of the working point closely approximates the minimum jerk trajectory. This suggests that minimizing jerk may be a secondary task objective, an idea that we will refer to as the **minimum jerk hypothesis** for aimed movement.

The minimum jerk hypothesis is supported by additional analysis and data. For example, when people have to move around an obstacle or pass through a particular location in order to reach a target, the working point typically follows a curved path, and the tangential speed profile typically has two or more peaks. A movement in which a person passes through a specific location on their way to a target location is called a **viapoint** movement. An example of a planar viapoint movement is shown in panel A of Figure 11.23: the task is to move the pen over the page from the start to the target by way of the viapoint. The minimum jerk trajectory for this kind of movement can be derived mathematically, and the correspondence between real trajectories and the minimum jerk trajectory is typically very close. In addition, analyses have shown that jerk minimization produces working point trajectories that match real movements more closely than minimization of other cost functions[90].

Note that the minimum jerk hypothesis involves learning: the nervous system must learn how to make movements that minimize jerk. Thus, minimum jerk movements are characteristic of skilled performance, which is smooth and graceful[91]. Unskilled performance is expected to be much jerkier and to become progressively less so with more practice and experience. This conforms to everyday experience and has been confirmed quantitatively in empirical studies for reaching and for other types of behavior such as handwriting[92]. In order to learn to produce movements that minimize jerk, it must be possible for the nervous system to obtain feedback information about how jerky movements are. This information is needed to drive the learning process. Sensory information about the jerkiness of movement can, in principle, be obtained from proprioceptive afference or vision[93].

(A) Planar viapoint movement from start to target

(B) Type of tangential speed profile associated with viapoint movements like that in (A)

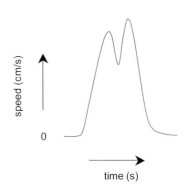

Figure 11.23: *A planar viapoint movement is a movement in a plane from one location to another via an intermediate point. Movements via one intermediate point often have bimodal (two-peaked) speed profiles.*

The minimum jerk hypothesis has been very influential, and provides a straightforward example of how minimizing a cost can account for why particular movement patterns are observed. However, it suffers from a number of problems, as discussed next.

11.2.11 The minimum jerk hypothesis suffers from three problems

In section 11.2.10, we asked why it is that working point motion in unconstrained aimed movement displays the observed kinematic invariants. The answer provided by the minimum jerk hypothesis is that the nervous system has the secondary objective of producing working point motions that are as smooth as possible. This raises another question: why should the secondary objective be to make the working point motion as smooth as possible? In effect, the minimum jerk hypothesis changes the question, 'why the kinematic invariants?' into the question 'why make movements as smooth as possible?'

The idea that a secondary objective in locomotor behavior is to keep metabolic energy costs as low as possible makes evolutionary sense. Animals that use their muscles efficiently and use little energy can keep going for longer and can survive on less food than they would if they were less efficient. This enhances their chances of survival and hence their reproductive success. Thus, it is easy to imagine that natural selection would favor animals that have the secondary objective of energy minimization built into their nervous systems. It is also possible to imagine that the same logic would apply to reaching: many primates spend long periods foraging for foods such as fruits, insects, leaves and other plant material, and in doing so repeatedly make aimed movements of the upper limbs to reach for the food and return it to the mouth[94]. Efficient use of the muscles involved in reaching would be advantageous to these animals, and models of aimed movements that minimize energy costs have been successfully developed[95].

The advantages of minimizing energy are fairly clear, but the advantages of minimizing the jerk of the working point are not so obvious. Thus, the first problem with the minimum jerk hypothesis is that it does not explain why the nervous system should care about minimizing the jerkiness of the working point motion. One early suggestion was that minimum jerk movements might have the effect of minimizing the wear and tear on the joints and muscles[96]. Wear and tear is something that accrues gradually over long periods of use; the tiny amount of wear and tear caused by a single movement cannot be sensed directly. In contrast, jerk is present in every movement, and information about it can, at least in principle, be obtained from the sensory systems. In short, minimizing jerk may be a means for minimizing wear and tear. Unfortunately, this idea has two significant shortcomings. First, there is no evidence that minimizing jerk is better for reducing wear and tear than is minimizing a number of other possible costs[97]. Second, although it is plausible that a minimum jerk motion of a single-joint movement reduces wear and tear, it is not so plausible to suggest that a minimum jerk motion of the working point in a multi-joint movement does so – it is the joints and muscles that accrue the wear and tear, not the working point[98]. Another possibility is that minimizing jerk serves as a proxy for energy minimization: minimum jerk movements turn out to be very similar to those that minimize energy costs, and so from a practical perspective, minimizing jerk does the same job. However, there are other costs that could equally well serve as energy cost proxies[99].

A second problem with the minimum jerk hypothesis is that it predicts straight-line working point paths for unconstrained aimed movements[100]. However, as we have seen, working point paths show systematic curvature and are seldom straight. If the objective is to produce minimum jerk movements, why are observed movements often curved? The minimum jerk hypothesis cannot provide an answer to this question without additional hypotheses concerning the cause(s) of the curvature. Two basic ways of accounting for the curvature have been proposed:

(1)   The processes involved in transforming the centrally specified trajectory into actual movements of the body do not result in an accurate production of the specified trajectory (assumed to be straight); the actual movement is curved[101].

(2)   The specified trajectories are those that are perceived to be straight (or to have minimum jerk). However, perceptions can be erroneous and some movements that are perceived to be straight are in reality slightly curved[102]. In this case, the actual trajectory matches the specified trajectory, which corresponds to the perceptually straight trajectory.

Neither of these attempted 'fixes' for the minimum jerk hypothesis are very satisfactory. The first fix asserts that the trajectory generator specifies a straight, minimum jerk trajectory, but the lower level mechanisms fail to accurately implement the specified trajectory. This might be plausible if curved paths were seldom observed, but the available data show that a substantial proportion of actual movement paths are curved to some degree. If the objective is to minimize the jerk of actual trajectories, it would be expected that the nervous system would learn to generate commands that result in the production of a minimum jerk movement. The fact that this does not happen casts considerable doubt on the minimum jerk idea. How the learning process could lead to the formation of a system that specifies straight paths but generates curved ones has never been explained, and experimental data do not support the idea[103]. The second fix is perhaps more plausible, but is contradicted by a number of empirical results[104]: for instance, it fails to explain how people are able to produce perfectly straight paths when instructed to do so (see section 11.2.14), a result that is also difficult to explain if curved movements arise due to a failure of the lower level mechanisms to produce a specified straight path.

The third and final problem with the minimum jerk hypothesis is that minimizing other costs can provide an equally good fit to the available data, and for certain sets of data, minimizing other costs can provide a better fit[105]. It is not even obvious that the nervous system should be concerned with minimizing just one cost: perhaps several different costs might be relevant, with some being more important for certain tasks than others[106]. For example, when lifting and moving a full cup of hot coffee, smoothness of movement is important if spillage is to be avoided, and so a minimum jerk movement would be useful[107]. Minimizing effort[108] might be more appropriate for repeated aiming movements or when moving a heavy load. Minimizing the uncertainty concerning where the working point will end up (minimizing a terminal position error cost)[109] would be appropriate when the working point needs to be accurately positioned.

It is notable that many of the different possible costs that have been considered all predict similar working point trajectories, trajectories that closely resemble those actually produced[110]. The trajectories that minimize terminal error costs are very similar to those that minimize jerk costs, which in turn are very similar to those that minimize effort or energy costs. This makes it difficult to determine what cost(s) the nervous system uses, if indeed it uses any. The invariant characteristics of aimed movements demonstrate that there is some kind of secondary objective (or objectives) involved in aimed movement production. The idea that these objectives can be conceptualized in terms of costs that are to be minimized has been influential and fruitful, but has not yet yielded any firm conclusions. All we can really say at this point is that the system may be minimizing something, but we do not yet know what it is.

11.2.12 A planned trajectory is not precomputed and stored

So far we have discussed evidence that the nervous system specifies the trajectory of the working point in aimed movements. What kind of process is involved? One possibility is succinctly described in the following quote:

> ... when you decide to make a movement, your CNS computes a minimum-jerk trajectory ... your CNS stores this trajectory somewhere and plays it out like a tape. At each instant of time, the tape provides the desired state of the limb – its location, velocity, and acceleration[111].

This statement refers explicitly to the minimum jerk idea, but could equally apply to any rules or principles by which a trajectory might be computed. The key characteristics of the process can be summarized in terms of a functional block diagram, as shown in Figure 11.24. This view of trajectory planning is based on an analogy with artificial devices, not on any evidence about how the nervous system works, and several authors have strongly criticized this view of trajectory planning, on grounds of both plausibility and empirical evidence[112].

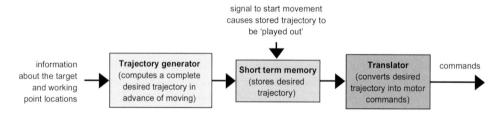

Figure 11.24: *Block diagram of the processes hypothetically underlying trajectory generation.*

The alternative view is that the trajectory generator does not pre-compute a desired trajectory for the working point, but generates trajectory information on the fly. The trajectory information constitutes a command signal that specifies the working point's position over time. As the command signal is generated, it is transmitted directly to the lower level processes that convert it into commands to the muscles, so there is no short term storage of a complete trajectory. There are a number of different ways in which such a process might work[113], but the models that have been proposed involve a similar basic principle: a feedback mechanism is used to generate the trajectory command signal. These models derive from ideas first put forward to explain the production of saccadic eye movements (described in Chapter 6, see section 6.2.4) and work in a very similar way[114], though they are typically more complex and can be difficult to understand. We will first consider a simplified version in order to illustrate the basic idea.

Figure 11.25 shows a block diagram representation of the simplified, feedback trajectory generator. It consists of two components: the position command circuit, and a 'differencing circuit' that computes an error as the difference between the desired position of the working point in external space (the target position) and the position as specified by the command signal (the feedback signal). Thus, the feedback signal is within the trajectory generator itself (internal feedback). In order for this mechanism to successfully drive the error to zero, the position command circuit must function as an integrator: over time it must continuously sum up the error input to form the command output[115]. This process continuously updates the position command signal, causing it to shift from its initial value to a final value where the error is zero and the updating process stops. The working point position specified by this final value is, of course, the target position. The continuous shift of the commanded working point position constitutes a specification of the working point trajectory[116].

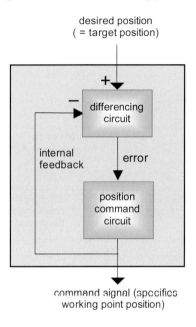

Figure 11.25: *A simplified model of a command trajectory generator.*

The description of the feedback trajectory generator given here provides a rough idea about how the motor program for aimed movement could generate trajectory information without formulating a complete trajectory plan in advance. Such a trajectory generation process is compatible with the idea that the nervous system has the secondary objective of producing movements that minimize some cost such as jerk, energy, effort or error. For example, learning processes could adjust the way in which the trajectory generator operates so that it produces commands that lead to movements that minimize a cost[117].

The following questions concerning feedback trajectory generation will be addressed in subsequent sections of the chapter:

(1)   How does the trajectory generator produce a command that specifies both the direction and the amplitude of the working point movement?

(2)   How does the generator produce commands for working point trajectories that possess the invariant characteristics of aimed movements?

(3)   How is working point trajectory information transformed into command signals for individual muscles?

(4)   How does the generator produce commands for movements of different speeds?

11.2.13 Working point position error is a difference vector

The spatial difference between the positions of the working point and the target is a vector quantity: it has a magnitude (the distance between the working point and target) and a direction (the direction of the target from the working point). In panel A of Figure 11.26, this vector is represented by a directed line segment (an 'arrow') that joins the working point to the target. It is equal to the vector difference between the position vector of the target (**T**) and the position vector of the working point (**W**), which are shown in Figure 11.26 as dashed line segments that start from an origin. This vector difference is written **T** − **W** and is usually referred to as a **difference vector** in the literature on aimed movement[118], rather than an error vector. This terminology avoids any confusion with errors of aiming (see Chapter 12). There is evidence that the nervous system uses an estimate of the difference vector to generate commands for aimed movements[119], and this idea is consistent with the results described in section 11.2.9.

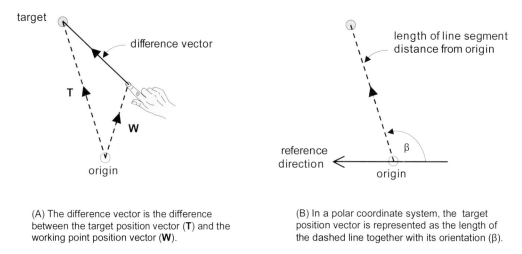

(A) The difference vector is the difference between the target position vector (**T**) and the working point position vector (**W**).

(B) In a polar coordinate system, the target position vector is represented as the length of the dashed line together with its orientation (β).

Figure 11.26: *Different position vectors; see text for explanation.*

The differencing circuit of the trajectory generator in Figure 11.25 can compute the difference vector if information about the position vector **T** is input as the desired position, and the output of the position command circuit specifies the vector **W**. To compute the difference vector accurately, **T** and **W** must be represented in the same coordinate system, which means the same origin and the same set of reference directions. For example, panel B of Figure 11.26 shows that the target position vector can be represented in a polar coordinate system defined by the origin, and reference direction as the distance of the target from the origin (the length of the dashed line) and the angular orientation of the line relative to a reference direction (β). Since target information is typically acquired visually, we might suppose that the origin corresponds to the visual egocenter, but exactly what coordinate system is being used and where the origin is located are questions that must be resolved empirically[120].

The simple trajectory generation circuit shown in Figure 11.25 will act to continuously shift the specified working point position in the direction of the difference vector, and so the commanded path of the working point will be a straight line. Thus, like the minimum jerk hypothesis, our simplified model of a trajectory generator does not explain why actual working point paths are often curved. We will consider how this shortcoming can be dealt with in what follows.

11.2.14 Inverse kinematics refers to the translation from working point trajectory commands into motions for individual joints

A working point trajectory specified by the trajectory generator must be transformed into command signals for individual muscles. It is usually proposed that this transformation proceeds in a series of stages. Most models agree that working point trajectories that are specified in external (working point) space are first transformed into trajectories for the different joints of the effector system. Such a transformation is referred to as an **inverse kinematics transformation**.

In order to illustrate what is needed in order to carry out an inverse kinematic transformation, consider a two-joint planar aiming task similar to that discussed earlier, in which the person grasps a handle and moves it in a horizontal plane from one location to another. Suppose that the wrist and trunk are held fixed so that only the shoulder and elbow joint angles can change. Under these conditions, the arm has only two degrees-of-freedom of movement: elbow flexion-extension (one d.o.f.) and shoulder flexion-extension (second d.o.f.). In panel A of Figure 11.27, the hand is shown in two locations: a start location where a movement begins, and a finish location where it ends. At the start, the shoulder angle is θ_s and the elbow angle is ϕ_s. At the finish, the two angles are θ_f and ϕ_f. In both positions, the values of the two angles uniquely specify the configuration of the arm, so when the hand is in the start location the joint angles must be θ_s and ϕ_s.

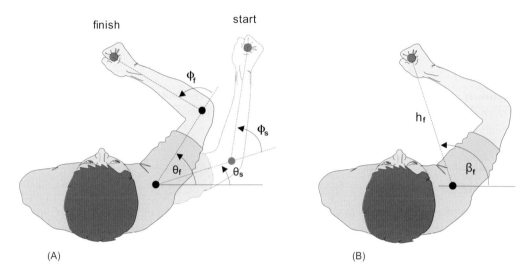

Figure 11.27: *The configuration of the arm in a planar aiming task is described by the elbow and shoulder angles (A). The position of the hand (working point) can be described in a body-centered coordinate system such as the polar coordinate system in (B).*

In the planar aiming task, the hand's position in the plane (working point space) has two degrees-of-freedom of movement – it is free to move forwards and backwards (one d.o.f.) and from side to side (second d.o.f.). This means that the hand's position can be completely described by two coordinates. In panel B of Figure 11.27, the hand's finish position in a polar coordinate system (origin at the shoulder joint) is specified by the angle β_f and the distance from the shoulder to the hand (h_f). These coordinates provide a specification of the position of the hand in the plane. The inverse kinematic transformation from the hand position in working point space to the arm configuration (joint space) can be expressed as the transformation from the polar coordinates of the hand to the joint angular coordinates of the arm. So, for example, the inverse kinematic transformation of the finish position converts the polar coordinates (h_f, β_f) into the angular coordinates (θ_f, ϕ_f). This requires some trigonometry and knowledge of the lengths of the segments of the arm, but is a relatively simple computation. It is somewhat more involved mathematically to transform motions of the hand in working point space into motions of the joints (joint space motion), but the computation poses no particular difficulties[121]. Figure 11.28 gives a pictorial summary of what has been said so far. The left of the figure shows the path of the hand through the environment (in working point space) from the start to the finish location (as in Figure 11.27); the graph on the right shows the corresponding path of the arm through joint space from the start position (θ_s, ϕ_s) to the finish (θ_f, ϕ_f). The inverse kinematics transformation (block arrow) converts a description of the hand's path (or trajectory) in working point space into the corresponding joint space description. In order to carry out an inverse kinematics transformation, the nervous system requires knowledge of the lengths of the segments of the effector system (forearm and upper arm in Figure 11.27). Knowledge of this type is usually referred to as an **internal model** of the effectors.

   In general, when the number of degrees-of-freedom of the working point is equal to the number of degrees-of-freedom of the effector system, the inverse kinematics transformation is usually straightforward. Normally, however, the effector system has more degrees-of-freedom than the working point, and this complicates matters, as described next.

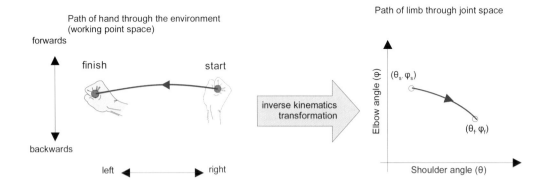

Figure 11.28: *The inverse kinematic transformation takes the motion of the working point in external space and transforms it into a set of joint motions (a motion through joint space).*

11.2.15 An abundance of d.o.f.s provides flexibility but requires choice

Imagine a planar aiming task in which the working point is the tip of the index finger, where the wrist joint is free to move in radio-ulnar deviation and the metacarpophalangeal joint of the finger is free to move in adduction-abduction. In this situation the working point has two degrees-of-freedom since it is free to move in the plane, but the effector system has four degrees-of-freedom: flexion-extension of the shoulder and elbow, together with the motions of the wrist and finger just mentioned. When the effector system has more degrees-of-freedom than the working point, there may be infinitely many possible configurations of the effectors associated with a single location of the working point. Figure 11.29 illustrates this: it shows three different configurations of the arm that achieve the same spatial location of the finger tip. This is easy to demonstrate practically: place your finger tip in contact with something – you will find that you can move your arm into different configurations while keeping your finger tip in the same place. In these circumstances the effector system is said to have **excess** or **redundant degrees-of-freedom** – degrees-of-freedom that are not necessary for task performance.

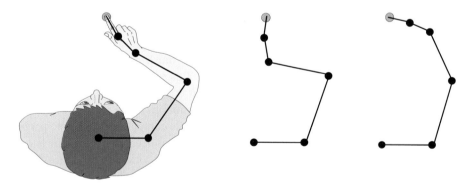

Figure 11.29: *Three different configurations of the right arm in which the finger tip is in the same place.*

A system with excess d.o.f.s can perform a given task in different ways, which gives it flexibility. A system without excess d.o.f.s is limited in how it can perform a task, and can be easily thwarted: if a task can only be done in one way and that way is blocked, then there are no other options. A system with excess d.o.f.s is not limited in this way. For this reason, excess d.o.f.s can be a considerable asset, but the terms 'excess' and 'redundant' seem to imply that there are too many d.o.f.s and it would be better to have fewer. In fact, for adaptive, goal-directed behavior, it is better to have 'excess' d.o.f.s. Some authors have emphasized this by using the term *abundance*[122] and argue that it is more appropriate to say that the human body has **abundant d.o.f.s** than it is to say that it has redundant d.o.f.s.

Having the flexibility to perform a task in lots of different ways gives you a choice, but you need some means of making that choice. This is the same kind of issue that we discussed previously in connection with planning a trajectory for the working point. In the context of inverse kinematics, the process of choosing a particular joint space trajectory from the numerous possibilities that produce the same working point trajectory is usually referred to as *resolving redundancy* at the joint level. We can imagine various rules or criteria that the nervous system might use to resolve joint-level redundancy. It might, for example, find the joint space trajectory that minimizes a cost, such as jerk or effort (see section 11.2.10). Alternatively, it could constrain joint velocities so that the velocity of one joint was determined by the velocity of another[123]. An example of such a constraint would be to keep the ratio of the joint angular velocities constant during the movement, something that has been observed in aimed arm movements[124]. Another alternative is simply to choose to fix a joint so that its angle does not change during the movement: this eliminates the degrees-of-freedom associated with that joint[125].

11.2.16 Is there a stagewise transformation from planned trajectory to motor commands?

The discussion so far suggests that the motor program for aimed movement might have a functional architecture that can be summarized in block diagram terms, as shown in Figure 11.30. The trajectory generator outputs a command signal that specifies the working point trajectory; the inverse kinematics transformation is carried out by the second block, which outputs a specification of the joint trajectories for the effector system. The third block converts the joint trajectories into motor commands that are sent to spinal motorneurons and interneurons. Exactly what the third block needs to do will depend on what the neuromuscular control variable is. At present the nature of the neuromuscular control variable – or possibly variables – is uncertain: in Chapter 6 we discussed the possibility that it is the muscle length at which tonic stretch reflex recruitment of motor units begins (denoted λ; see section 6.4 for details), but this is just one of several possibilities. We will briefly return to this issue later (see section 11.2.17).

Figure 11.30: *Transformation of the output of a working point trajectory generator into motor commands.*

The sequence of transformations shown in Figure 11.30 follows in a logical way from our discussion so far. However, as noted in section 11.2.14, there is no direct experimental evidence that motor commands are generated by a sequence of stages like this. Several authors have argued that such a strict sequence of transformations has difficulty accounting for the flexibility of human performance and for the results from some empirical studies[126] (discussed below). An alternative approach is to develop models where the distinctions between the different stages are not clear-cut, but are blurred or absent altogether[127]: the distinction between the inverse kinematics and the generation of motor commands could be blurred, or the distinction between working point trajectory generation and inverse kinematics could be blurred. An example of the latter type of model will be briefly described in what follows.

Figure 11.31 shows a block diagram of a feedback-type trajectory generator[128]. It takes information about the location of the target as input, and outputs motor commands specifying angular trajectories for the joints of an effector system. However, the joint trajectory commands are not derived from a specification of the working point trajectory by an inverse kinematic transformation – there is no position command circuit that computes a working point trajectory command, as there is in Figure 11.26. What happens instead is that the spatial difference vector (DV) is derived as described earlier (see section 11.2.13) and transformed directly into a specification of the joint angular motions that will move the working point to the target (the block labeled 'translation to joint velocities'). These are subsequently transformed by an integrating process into commands that continuously specify the joint angles. Note that internal feedback of the joint angle command signal must be transformed into a signal that specifies the working point location before the difference vector can be computed. This is called a **forward kinematics transformation**. Rather than take a working point position and give the configuration of the joints that achieves it (inverse kinematics), the forward kinematics transformation takes a joint configuration and gives the associated working point position. Like the inverse transformation, the forward kinematics transformation requires knowledge of the effector system (an internal model).

An additional feature of the trajectory generator in Figure 11.31 is the presence of an input signal called a 'GO signal'. The circular block in the diagram is a multiplier: it multiplies the joint velocity signal by the GO signal. This means that if there is no GO signal (that is, if the signal is equal to zero), then there will be no input to the integration block and hence no output motor command. The GO signal is needed in order for motor commands to be generated and so it serves to initiate movement production, which is why it is called a GO signal. Not only does this signal serve to initiate motor command production, it also determines the speed with which the command shifts to its final level and hence the speed of the movement. The magnitude of the GO signal affects the speed with which the feedback circuit drives the difference vector to zero: the larger the magnitude of the GO signal, the faster this happens, and so the faster the commands shift to their final values. So the GO signal is, as its name suggests, an initiating signal, but it also determines the speed with which the movement is executed.

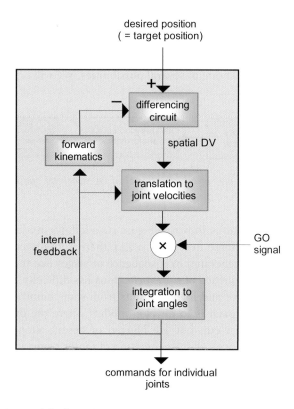

Figure 11.31: *Alternative model of a trajectory generator.*

Models that posit strictly distinct stages – i.e., working point trajectory generation stage, inverse kinematics stage, motor command computation stage – have the advantage that they are easier to understand. For example, if working point trajectory generation is independent of the effector system (and so followed by a distinct inverse kinematic transformation), then it is easy to see how a working point trajectory with the same kinematic characteristics can be executed with different sets of effectors. However, there is empirical evidence to suggest that working point trajectory planning is not completely independent of the effector system. For example, consider moving the index finger tip between the start and target locations in a horizontal plane, as shown in Figure 11.32. Moving the finger tip along a straight path (blue line) feels rather awkward and uncomfortable. Moving along a curved path (dashed line) feels more comfortable. As described earlier, when people move between locations like those in Figure 11.32, they tend to follow curved paths and not straight ones (see section 11.2.4). Experimental studies have shown that although people can move the working point along a straight path when making a movement like that shown in the figure, they prefer to move along a curved path like that shown as a dashed line[129]. Furthermore, the curvature of the working point path has been found to depend on the arm's configuration in the starting position[130].

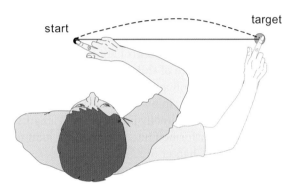

Figure 11.32: *People prefer to make this planar movement to the target along a curved path (dashed).*

The findings described in the previous paragraph, together with results from other studies[131], show that the working point trajectory depends on the effector system. This means that working point trajectory planning is unlikely to be completely independent of the effectors. Models like that shown in Figure 11.31, in which working point trajectory planning and joint level motion command generation are integrated, provide more satisfactory accounts of the available data than models in which the stages are separate. In the next section, we will consider how motor commands that are sent to the motorneuron pools and associated circuitry are produced.

11.2.17 Generation of motor commands may involve implicit rather than explicit inverse dynamics

In order to make the joints rotate in a specified manner, signals must be sent to the muscles spanning those joints so that they develop appropriate patterns of contractile force. This suggests that once the joint motions needed to move the working point to the target have been determined, the next step is to compute the muscle forces needed to produce the joint motions. The transformation from a set of joint motions into the forces required to produce those motions is called an **inverse dynamics transformation**. This transformation requires knowledge about the physical properties of the effectors, such as their lengths and moments of inertia; about the laws of mechanics that describe how forces and motions are related; and about the orientation of the limb segments with respect to gravity[132].

Several accounts of how the nervous system formulates motor commands propose that the process involves an explicit inverse dynamics transformation[133]. A neural process that implements an explicit inverse dynamics transformation takes the specified joint motions as inputs, and outputs commands that specify the forces (or torques) that are required to produce those joint motions. In block diagram terms, such an explicit transformation is represented like this:

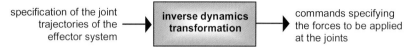

specification of the joint trajectories of the effector system → **inverse dynamics transformation** → commands specifying the forces to be applied at the joints

As we saw in Chapter 1, the process that implements a transformation of this kind is called an *inverse model*; it tells you what inputs you need to apply to a system (the effector system within a specific force environment) in order to get a desired output (motions of the joints). The better the internal model, the more accurate the computed force/torque commands, and the more closely the motions of the effector system will match those specified.

What has been said so far supposes that the motor commands specify force. This is sometimes called the **force-control hypothesis**[134]. Force control of multi-joint aimed movements requires an inverse dynamics transformation to convert specification of joint trajectories into force commands. It seems logical, even necessary, that the nervous system carries out an explicit inverse dynamics transformation. However, if motor commands that descend to motorneurons do not specify force, but specify muscle length instead[135], then an explicit inverse dynamics transformation is not required. Given that there is no direct evidence that the nervous system carries out explicit inverse dynamics transformations[136], alternative models that do not assume force control are equally valid. Models based on the λ-equilibrium point (λ-EP) hypothesis are of this alternative type. As described in Chapter 6, the λ-EP hypothesis proposes that commands are formulated in terms of muscle's threshold lengths for motorneuron recruitment. In models based on this idea, the specification of the joint motions are transformed either directly into threshold lengths for the contributing muscles, or else they are initially transformed into intermediate joint level commands (e.g., the r- and c-commands described in Chapter 6)[137].

Motor commands formulated in positional or muscle length terms do not make an inverse dynamics transformation unnecessary. In order that the commands result in movements that follow the specified trajectory, they must somehow take into account the dynamical properties of the effectors, the effects of gravity and the laws of mechanics (see Chapter 6 for simple examples). Although no explicit inverse dynamic transformation is required and no explicit internal model of the effector system dynamics need be involved, the formulation of the commands must use knowledge of dynamics and gravity. For example, it is possible to imagine a hypothetical robot that moves limb segments about joints using servo-motors with almost instantaneous feedback (no feedback loop delay)[138]. These motors can be fed commands specifying joint trajectories, and the servo-motors ensure that the joints follow the commanded trajectory by almost instantaneously generating torques that eliminate the difference between the actual trajectory and the commanded trajectory. Such a robot does not implement an explicit inverse dynamics transformation, but knowledge of the dynamical properties of the effectors and the force environment is embodied implicitly in the feedback gains of the servo-motors (see Chapter 1). Thus, even if a system does not explicitly compute an inverse transformation, it can still be considered to carry out such a transformation *implicitly*. According to the λ-EP hypothesis, therefore, a kind of inverse dynamics transformation must be implicitly carried out by the process that formulates the motor commands[139].

Robotics engineers came up with the strategy of transforming a representation of a working point trajectory into commands for a set of motors via a sequence of stages[140]. The engineers wanted to design a controller for a mechanical arm that would enable movement of the end-effector (working point) along a specified trajectory from an initial location to a target location. The stage-wise strategy provides a tractable means for achieving this by dividing a difficult overall problem up into a sequence of much simpler, solvable problems:

(1)   What trajectory should the working point follow?
(2)   How should the individual limb segments rotate about the joints so as to achieve that trajectory?

(3)   What forces or torques should the motors develop at the joints so as to make them move as required?

Each of these problems can be solved separately from the others, and the solutions can be executed as a strict sequence of stages. Each stage performs a specific transformation from one representation of a required movement into another representation. The advantage of this scheme is precisely that it decomposes a very difficult overall problem into a sequence of much simpler sub-problems. This provides an easily understandable framework for robotic control and, by analogy, biological movement control. However, ease of understanding and engineering convenience are hardly reliable guides to deciphering how biological movement control actually works. We have seen that there is neither direct empirical evidence nor a biological basis for a strict sequence of stages in which an inverse kinematics stage is followed by an inverse dynamics stage. It seems more likely that the process is more integrated and that inverse transformations occur implicitly rather than explicitly.

11.2.18 Is there a role for muscle synergies?

In Chapter 6 we discussed evidence that muscle synergies (groups of muscles linked together by low-level neural circuits) are recruited by higher level mechanisms in the production of some voluntary actions. We have not considered whether or not the recruitment of such circuits occurs during voluntary aimed movements, with the exception of saccadic eye movements (see Chapter 6). Some researchers have suggested that the recruitment of muscle synergies could be useful, since the number of command signals that higher levels of the control hierarchy need to generate is reduced[141] if they are formulated for groups of muscles rather than for the individual motorneuron pools. The recruitment of muscle synergies rather than individual muscles can also reduce the redundancy of the effector system at the muscle level[142]. Unfortunately, little empirical research has been conducted into the role of muscle synergies – in the sense of linkages implemented by low level (spinal) circuits – in reaching, or into how the recruitment of the circuitry might fit into the trajectory generation processes described earlier (sections 11.2.12 and 11.2.16). Thus, the exact roles for such circuits, if any, in aimed movements remain to be determined[143].

11.2.19 Conclusion: a 'motor program' for aimed movement

In this second part of the chapter we have described some of the characteristics of aimed movements and some ideas concerning how the motor program that generates these movements is organized. We saw that the data support the idea that aimed movement programs involve a top level of motor representation that is, at least to some degree, independent of the particular effectors that will be used to execute the action. At this level, the program represents the action in terms of the working point's required movement through the environment.

Some early, robotics-inspired theories proposed that the nervous system first plans a whole trajectory for the working point, and then passes this plan to lower levels of the program to be translated into motor commands. According to these theories, a complete 'desired trajectory' is established in advance and then played out 'like a tape' (see section 11.2.12). This view of the aiming program closely resembles the traditional conception of motor programs, in which a stored set of commands is retrieved from memory and played out like a tape. In the first part of the chapter we argued that this conception of motor programs is misguided. Theories that propose a pre-planned, desired trajectory have great difficulty providing a coherent account of the characteristics of working point motion observed in the performance of aimed movements. Typically, the theories propose that the desired working point trajectory is straight, and go on to propose reasons for why the straight-line plan fails to be executed. This is contrived and unsatisfactory; an alternative is needed.

The most widely accepted alternative view proposes that the motor program more closely resembles the pattern generators responsible for the production of behaviors like locomotion and saccadic eye movements. The program is a process that generates commands on the fly, according to a set of rules or principles – there is no pre-planned, desired trajectory. Theoretical models of this process typically work in a negative feedback fashion to generate a continuous specification of the direction and speed of working point motion. This specification must be transformed into command signals to the muscles, a process that may be carried out by one or more subsequent stages: the number of distinct stages varies between models, as there is no clear empirical evidence concerning how many such stages exist.

The negative feedback trajectory generator models shown in Figures 11.25 and 11.31 represent two possible ways of organizing the process that generates commands for aimed movements. Neither of the block diagrams shown possesses a means by which sensory information about the location of the working point can influence the generated commands: the block diagrams represent the model in the open-loop situation in which sensory feedback from the effector system is unavailable. In normal conditions, sensory information about working point location can influence aimed movement performance. It is relatively straightforward to augment the block diagram of Figure 11.31 so that computation of the difference vector can incorporate visual and proprioceptive information about the working point location. Figure 11.33 shows a possible augmentation that achieves this[144]. The forward kinematics block now represents a process that transforms feedback information about the configuration of the effectors – both internal and afferent feedback – into an estimate of the working point's location over time. The multimodal integration block combines the estimate of working point position provided by the forward kinematics block with information about the seen position of the working point (if available). If neither proprioceptive nor visual information is available, the system reduces to that shown in Figure 11.31. Simulation studies of models like that shown in Figure 11.33 have shown that they are capable of generating movements that closely resemble those observed in experimental studies of aiming[145]; they can deal effectively with changing conditions and alterations to the effector system, such as immobile joints and use of a hand-held stick or pointer[146].

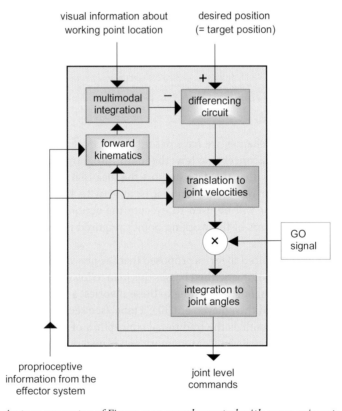

Figure 11.33: *Trajectory generator of Figure 11.31 supplemented with sensory inputs.*

The pattern generator shown in Figure 11.33 generates commands when it is supplied with various input signals that can be considered to set the parameters of the program (see 11.1.10).

The GO signal, for example, determines the overall speed of the movement as well as initiating the process of generating descending motor commands. The target position input, together with information about the initial position of the working point, determine the direction of the movement and, indirectly, its amplitude. Not shown in Figures 11.31 and 11.33 are signals that determine which actual effector system and working point will be used to perform the task. These signals must somehow ensure that the blocks that depend on the characteristics of the effectors (those implementing forward and inverse kinematics transformations and inverse dynamics, if present) are appropriate for the effector system that is selected. The process by which this occurs has not been addressed systematically in simulation studies of these models.

In the first part of this chapter, we argued that motor programs are not stored sets of commands that can be played out like a tape, as the traditional conception proposes. They are more appropriately conceived of as pattern generating processes that produce commands on the fly, based on a set of rules or principles. The program is to be viewed as a distributed neural mechanism that is governed by these rules and that generates commands when activated. Exactly how this all works is currently unknown, even for simple aimed movements, though there are several promising theoretical models. We have discussed one class of models in which commands are generated by an internal feedback process that drives a difference vector to zero. These models are quite unlike models based on traditional motor program ideas, and closely resemble the pattern generating mechanisms discussed in previous chapters.

References & Notes

1 Grillner *et al.* (2005); Kupfermann, Weiss (2001).

2 Summers, Anson (2009).

3 Keele (1968).

4 E.g., Purves *et al.* (2008).

5 Brooks (1986), p. 7.

6 Summers, Anson (2009); Schmidt, Lee (2011); Rosenbaum (2009).

7 Schmidt, Lee (2011).

8 Schmidt, Lee (2011).

9 See Schmidt, Lee (2011).

10 Turvey, Fitch, Tuller (1982).

11 Jeannerod (1988).

12 See Jeannerod (1988) for review.

13 Polit, Bizzi (1979).

14 The situation is rather more complex than this, according to the λ-equilibrium point hypothesis: see Chapter 6 for details.

15 See Berkinblit, Feldman, Fukson (1986); Latash (1993).

16 Sanes *et al.* (1985); Forget, Lamarre (1987).

17 Van Sonderen, Denier van der Gon (1990); Ivanenko, Poppele, Lacquaniti (2006).

18 Proposed in the 1930s by N. Bernstein (Latash, 2008a).

19 See Schmidt, Lee (2011).

20 See Harel, Feldman (2004).

21 E.g., Rosenbaum (2009); Schmidt, Lee (2011).

22 Schmidt (1982), p. 225.

23 Introduced by M. Arbib, this term applies to the process that controls the recruitment of low-level programs ('schemas') in any type of action that is composed of several more elementary components; see Arbib (1989).

24 Keele, Cohen, Ivry (1990) define a motor program to be, 'the representation of the orders of actions rather than their elementary movements . . . a plan' (p. 78).

25 Soechting, Lacquaniti (1983); Flash, Henis (1991).

26 Van Sonderen, Denier van der Gon, Gielen (1988).

27 Van Sonderen, Gielen, Denier van der Gon (1989).

28 Georgopoulos, Kalaska, Massey (1981).

29 Following Lashley (1942).

30 E.g., Castiello, Stelmach (1993); Teulings, Thomassen, Van Galen (1986); Wright (1990, 1993).

31 Teulings, Thomassen, Van Galen (1986).

32 Wright (1990); Wing (2000). The similarity of the written text is not alone sufficient to establish the use of a common production process: it is possible that some instances are produced by the normal writing program, while others are produced by copying programs (Latash, 1993).

33 Rosenbaum (1977).

34 This is a valid conclusion only if nothing other than the central program is the same when performing a task with the left and right arms. If there are other things that are the same, these may have been fatigued during the first 30 seconds and be responsible for the results.

35 Chapter 2 in Bernstein (1967).

36 Teulings, Thomassen, Van Galen (1986).

37 Georgopoulos (1986).

38 E.g., Hollerbach (1982); Saltzman (1979); Bullock, Grossberg, Guenther (1993).

39 Gottlieb (1993).

40 Flash, Hogan (1985); Morasso (1981).

41 Abend, Bizzi, Morasso (1982); Georgopoulos, Kalaska, Massey (1981); Morasso (1981); Soechting, Lacquaniti (1981).

42 Morasso (1981).

43 Gordon, Ghilardi, Ghez (1994).

44 Flash, Hollerbach (1982); Boessenkool, Nijhof, Erkelens (1998).

45 For example, working point motion remains the same regardless of whether the trunk contributes to the motion or not (Adamovich *et al.*, 2001). For similarities and differences in aiming with the left and right arms, see Sainburg, Kalakanis (2000).

46 Lacquaniti, Soechting, Terzuolo (1982).

47 Soechting, Lacquaniti (1983); Atkeson, Hollerbach (1985).

48 Atkeson, Hollerbach (1985); Bock (1990).

49 Atkeson, Hollerbach (1985); Morasso (1983); Biess, Liebermann, Flash (2007).

50 E.g., Wadman, Denier van der Gon, Derksen (1980); Flash (1987); Atkeson, Hollerbach (1985).

51 Haggard, Richardson (1996); Hollerbach, Atkeson (1987); Osu *et al.* (1997); Papaxanthis, Pozzo, Schieppati (2003).

[52] Desmurget *et al.* (1997a) found that the curvature was much reduced, and the variations in curvature with direction all but disappeared when participants were required to slide a 'cursor' across the table top rather than move the finger tip freely to the target.

[53] Introduced by Atkeson, Hollerbach (1985).

[54] See also Charles, Hogan (2010).

[55] It can be difficult to determine whether an observed invariant is a necessary consequence of the musculosketal dynamics or is due to a central program; see, e.g., Gribble, Ostry (1996).

[56] See Atkeson, Hollerbach (1985); Soechting, Lacquaniti (1981).

[57] Uno, Kawato, Suzuki (1989).

[58] Haggard, Hutchinson, Stein (1995).

[59] E.g., Shemmell *et al.* (2005).

[60] Hollerbach (1982); Shadmehr, Wise (2005).

[61] Kawato (1999); Nishii, Taniai (2009).

[62] Atkeson, Hollerbach (1985); Hollerbach, Atkeson (1987).

[63] Polit, Bizzi (1979).

[64] Kelso (1977); Schmidt, McGown (1980).

[65] Or the final limb configuration.

[66] Provided that the movement is slow enough that the commands that cause the limb to move along the specified trajectory are not completed by the time the limb has had time to show a response to the disturbance.

[67] Bizzi *et al.* (1984).

[68] Bizzi *et al.* (1984).

[69] Instantaneous shifts do not necessarily produce the fastest movements (Latash, 1993).

[70] Bullock, Grossberg (1988).

[71] Some studies suggest a similar shift of the command during multi-joint aimed movements in humans (Won, Hogan, 1995; Ghafouri, Feldman, 2001).

[72] Bullock, Grossberg, Guenther (1993); Flash, Hogan (1985); Shadmehr, Wise (2005).

[73] Soechting, Laquaniti (1981); Lacquaniti, Soechting, Terzuolo (1986).

[74] Atkeson, Hollerbach (1985); Desmurget *et al.* (1998); Soechting, Lacquaniti (1981).

[75] Shadmehr, Mussa-Ivaldi (1994).

[76] Flanagan, Rao (1995); Wolpert, Ghahramani, Jordan (1995).

[77] Wolpert, Ghahramani, Jordan (1995).

[78] The distortion was too small for the participants to be consciously aware of it.

[79] Polit, Bizzi (1979).

[80] See Jeannerod (1988); Desmurget *et al.* (1998).

[81] Ghez, Gordon, Ghilardi (1995).

[82] Prablanc *et al.* (1979).

[83] Prablanc *et al.* (1979); Elliott (1988); Rossetti *et al.* (1994); Desmurget *et al.* (1997b).

[84] Rossetti, Desmurget, Prablanc (1995).

[85] Nelson (1983); Campos, Calado (2009).

[86] Flash, Hogan (1985).

[87] The jerk cost of a planar movement can be defined to be $\frac{1}{2} \int [(da_x/dt)^2 + (da_y/dt)^2]$ dt, where a_x and a_y are the x and y components of the acceleration, and the integral is evaluated over the total duration of the movement (Flash, Hogan, 1985).

[88] Flash, Hogan (1985), p. 1689.

[89] Flash, Hogan (1985).

[90] Nelson (1983); Richardson, Flash (2002). See Flash, Hogan (1995) for original minimum jerk analysis of viapoint movements.

[91] Hogan, Flash (1987).

[92] Wann (1987).

[93] Wann, Nimmo-Smith, Wing (1988).

[94] See Hohmann, Robbins, Boesch (2006).

[95] Alexander (1997).

[96] Hogan (1984).

[97] Such as joint torque change (Uno, Kawato, Suzuki, 1989) or effort (Hasan, 1986).

[98] There have been some attempts to apply the minimum jerk idea to joint-space planning so that it applies to the joint level trajectories (Flanagan, Ostry, 1990).

[99] E.g., effort, torque change, or minimum motor command change (Kawato, 1992).

[100] Curved paths are predicted for viapoint movements. However, the shape of the predicted path is invariant with respect to rotation within the workspace (only the relative positions of the start, target and viapoints matter). This prediction has not been upheld in experiments (Todorov, Jordan, 1998; Uno, Kawato, Suzuki, 1989).

[101] Flash (1987).

[102] Wolpert, Ghahramani, Jordan (1994); Wann, Nimmo-Smith, Wing (1988).

[103] Osu *et al.* (1997); Boessenkool, Nijhof, Erkelens (1998).

[104] Boessenkool, Nijhof, Erkelens (1998); Desmurget *et al.* (1997a).

[105] Minimizing the joint torque change cost, for example, generates gently curved paths without additional 'fixes' (Osu *et al.*, 1997; Uno, Kawato, Suzuki, 1989).

[106] Seif-Naraghi, Winters (1990).

[107] Alexander (1997).

[108] Hasan (1986).

[109] Harris, Wolpert (1998).

[110] Regardless of whether the costs are defined in joint space (e.g., Uno, Kawato, Suzuki, 1989; Osu *et al.*, 1997) or in environmental space (Richardson, Flash, 2002).

[111] Shadmehr, Wise (2005), p. 353.

[112] Cisek (2005); Shadmehr, Wise (2005); Todorov (2004).

[113] Bullock, Grossberg, Guenther (1993); Hoff, Arbib (1993); Saltzman, Kelso (1987).

[114] Similar to displacement models of saccade generation (see section 6.2.4).

[115] Bullock, Grossberg, Guenther (1993).

[116] The feedback trajectory generator imposes a spring-like dynamic in an internal representation of working point space (cf. Saltzman, Kelso, 1987).

[117] Alternatively, the trajectory generator could explicitly minimize a cost, such as jerk (Hoff, Arbib, 1993).

[118] See Shadmehr, Wise (2005).

[119] Bock, Eckmiller (1986); Bullock, Grossberg, Guenther (1993); Shadmehr, Wise (2005).

[120] Shadmehr and Wise (2005) conclude that the coordinate system involved is centered on the point in the visual field that the eyes are fixating.

[121] See Saltzman (1979); Whitney (1972).

[122] Latash (2008a).

[123] See Saltzman (1979).

[124] Soechting, Laquaniti (1981); Lacquaniti, Soechting, Terzuolo (1986).

[125] See Saltzman (1979).

[126] See Cisek (2005); Todorov (2004).

[127] E.g., Goodman, Gottlieb (1995).

[128] Based on Bullock, Grossberg, Guenther (1993).

[129] Cruse, Bruwer (1987); Desmurget *et al.* (1997a).

[130] Cruse, Bruwer (1987).

[131] E.g., Sabes, Jordan, Wolpert (1998).

[132] Inverse dynamics is computationally complex; see Saltzman (1979).

[133] See Shadmehr, Wise (2005).

[134] Latash (2008b); Ostry, Feldman (2003).

[135] See Ostry, Feldman (2003).

[136] There is evidence that inverse dynamics transformations are carried out (Shadmehr, Wise, 2005), but nothing to tell us whether the transformation is implicit or explicit.

[137] See Feldman, Levin (1995); Flanagan, Ostry, Feldman (1993).

[138] Shadmehr, Wise (2005).

[139] The λ-EP hypothesis and related ideas (Flash, 1987) propose that the viscoelastic properties of reflexive muscles serve to reduce the amount of detailed knowledge that is needed to formulate motor commands.

[140] Hollerbach (1982); Saltzman (1979).

[141] See Saltzman (1979); Tuller, Turvey, Fitch (1982).

[142] Saltzman (1979).

[143] See Tresch, Jarc (2009).

[144] Based on Figure 1 of Bullock, Grossberg, Guenther (1993).

[145] Bullock, Grossberg, Guenther (1993); Bullock, Cisek, Grossberg (1998); Micci-Barreca, Guenther (2001).

[146] Bullock, Grossberg, Guenther (1993).

12.1 Accuracy of Movements Aimed at Visible Targets

12.1.1 Introduction: accuracy requirements of visual targets

In the previous chapter we discussed some of the performance characteristics of manual aimed movements in which a working point is moved to a target location. The focus was on tasks that did not require accurate terminal positioning of the working point. In many everyday manual aiming tasks, being accurate does matter. Examples include pressing a light switch, inserting a key into a keyhole and moving a cursor to an icon on a computer screen. In each case, the task requires that the working point – finger tip, key, cursor – is positioned accurately enough to achieve the desired outcome.

The accuracy with which the working point needs to be positioned depends on the size of the target region. In general, a large target will require less accurate positioning than a small target. Although this might seem obvious, there are situations in which it is not the case. Figure 12.1 shows three different targets. Imagine that you are required to make contact with the target region (shaded blue in each case) with the tip of the stylus shown at the bottom of the figure. Target 2 has a convoluted shape but a larger area than target 1: making contact with target 2 requires more accurate positioning than target 1. Target 3 is square with a hole in the middle; its area is about the same as target 1, but contacting it requires more accurate positioning of the stylus. In this chapter we will not deal with targets with holes or with unusual, convoluted shapes; only movements aimed at 'solid' targets without gaps and holes will be considered.

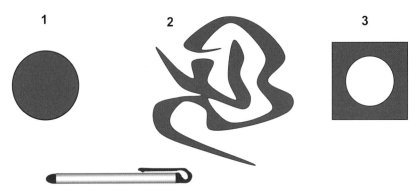

Figure 12.1: *Three different two-dimensional targets and a stylus.*

In this part of the chapter, we will consider how to quantitatively describe the accuracy of movements aimed at targets that are visually specified: that is, information about their size, distance, and direction is available through vision, but not through any other sensory system. We will describe some of the factors that limit people's ability to be accurate. Accuracy is easiest to quantify in one-dimensional aimed movement tasks and we will begin with a discussion of these.

12.1.2 Performance accuracy can be quantified using constant and variable errors

When performing an aimed movement task, the working point may be free to move through three-dimensional space, or may be constrained to move in only one or two dimensions. Accuracy in one-dimensional (1-D) aimed movement tasks is easiest to quantify and understand.

Any single-joint aimed movement task that involves one degree-of-freedom of motion, such as elbow flexion-extension (see Figure 11.21), is a 1-D aimed movement task. Figure 12.2 shows two other examples. The task in panel A requires a person to slide a pointer along a straight track so that it ends up within the target zone (shaded blue). In panel B, the task is to turn the knob so that the pointer moves to a desired target zone[1], such as the 4 mark or between the 7 and 8 marks.

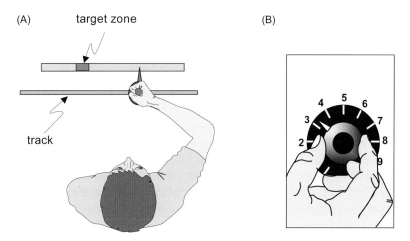

Figure 12.2: *One-dimensional aiming tasks (see text for details).*

If people are given unlimited time and are permitted to see what they are doing, then they are able to position a pointer in tasks like those shown in Figure 12.2 very accurately. A normal person with good vision is able to align the tip of a pointer with a target that is only as wide as a human hair when making adjustments on a sliding vernier scale, like those found on micrometer calipers. If people have little time or are unable to see what they are doing once they have started, then they are much less accurate.

Consider the task in panel A of Figure 12.2: imagine closing your eyes as soon as you start to move, so that you are unable to see what you are doing (no visual feedback). If you perform the task in this way, you might finish with the pointer inside the target zone or you might not. Making just one attempt does not give a very good picture of your ability to be accurate, since the outcome is subject to a number of random factors. A better picture can be obtained by repeating the task several times. Figure 12.3 shows the outcomes of an imaginary experiment in which three people made ten attempts to move the pointer into a 6-cm-wide target zone without visual feedback; each final position of the pointer is marked by a white circle. The results from the three people are labeled person 1, person 2 and person 3 in the figure. One way to quantify performance would simply be to count the number of times the pointer was successfully positioned within the target zone ('hits') and the number of times it was not ('misses'). Person 1 had three misses and seven hits; person 2 had six misses and four hits, and so did person 3.

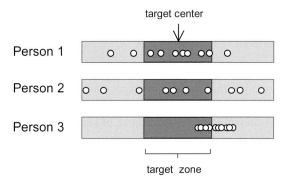

Figure 12.3: *Final positions of the pointer (white circles) in one-dimensional aiming task of Figure 12.2A. (Not real data.)*

Although persons 2 and 3 had the same number of hits and misses, their performance is clearly very different. Person 2's attempts are widely spread out, whereas person 3's are tightly bunched together. We would normally say that person 2's performance was rather inconsistent or imprecise, whereas person 3 was much more consistent (or precise). In addition, person 3's attempts are all to the right of the center of the target zone, whereas person 2's are equally distributed on either side of the center. To capture these differences, another way of quantifying performance is needed. A standard method is to measure the distance of each attempt from the target center and compute the average (arithmetic mean) and the standard deviation of the results. The average is a measure of the central tendency of the data, and the standard deviation is a measure of spread. An example should help to make the idea concrete.

Table 12.1 lists the distances (in centimeters) from the target center for the ten attempts for each of the three people in Figure 12.3. Positive numbers are used for positions to the left of the target center; negative numbers are used for positions to the right of the target center. On average, persons 1 and 2 were very close to the center of the target: the averages of the numbers in Table 12.1 are +0.29 cm for person 1 (slightly to the left of center) and −0.1 cm for person 2 (slightly to the right of center). Person 3 was 3.37 cm to the right of center on average. The standard deviation of the numbers in Table 12.1 provides a measure of the spread of the data points about the average positions: the standard deviations are 3.16, 5.26 and 1.05 cm for persons 1, 2 and 3 respectively.

It is usual to refer to the distances from some nominally perfect outcome – the center of the target in our example – as *errors*, though the person has not strictly made an error unless the pointer falls outside the target zone. In this context, the average of the errors is called the **constant error statistic** or, more simply, the **constant error (CE)** (an alternative term is **systematic error**[2], but its use is uncommon in the study of motor behavior). The standard deviation of the errors is called the **variable error** (**VE**). These two quantities can be defined as follows for a one-dimensional aiming task:

> **CONSTANT ERROR (CE)** (in a series of repeated trials of an aimed movement task): the arithmetic mean of the distances between terminal positions of the working point and a position that defines (nominally or actually) perfectly accurate performance. If there are N trials and the terminal position on trial i is x_i, then the distance between x_i and the perfect performance point (P) is $(x_i - P)$. Thus, the CE can be calculated using the following equation:
>
> $$CE = [(x_1 - P) + (x_2 - P) + \ldots + (x_N - P)]/N = \Sigma(x_i - P)/N$$

> **VARIABLE ERROR (VE)** (in a series of repeated trials of an aimed movement task): the standard deviation of the distances between terminal positions of the working point and the position that defines perfectly accurate performance (P). The VE can be calculated using the following equation:
>
> $$VE = \sqrt{\{[(x_1 - CE)^2 + (x_2 - CE)^2 + \ldots + (x_N - CE)^2]/N\}} = \sqrt{[\Sigma(x_i - CE)^2/N]}$$
>
> For small values of N, it is usual to replace N by (N − 1) in the above equation.

These definitions are valid provided that the errors are normally distributed. The notion of normally distributed errors is illustrated in Figure 12.4. Suppose that person 2's errors are normally distributed and that they made a large number of repeated attempts to move the pointer into the target. The middle panel of Figure 12.3 shows the results from the first ten attempts. These can be plotted as a histogram, using the method shown in panel A of Figure 12.4, in which a series of eleven 'bins' two centimeters wide have been constructed. The number of attempts that fall into each bin have been counted, as shown in the figure, and these counts are plotted as a histogram at the bottom of panel A. Panel B shows the same thing as panel A, but for the first 40 attempts. As more and more attempts are included, the distribution of errors gets progressively more symmetrical about the central bin, until the histogram looks something like that shown in panel C.

Table 12.1: *Distances from the target center of the data points in Figure 12.3.*

Person 1	Person 2	Person 3
−4.3	−7.5	−4.8
−2.9	−5.2	−4.5
−2.2	−4.8	−4.2
−1.0	−2.8	−4.0
−0.5	−0.7	−3.7
+0.3	+0.5	−3.3
+1.5	+1.2	−2.9
+2.2	+3.3	−2.5
+3.8	+6.8	−2.1
+6.0	+8.2	−1.7

The data plotted in the histogram shown in Figure 12.4C show the characteristic shape of the *normal curve*, which has been drawn in the figure. The normal curve is sometimes referred to as the 'bell curve', and can be thought of as the continuous curve formed when the bins forming the histogram are infinitesimally thin. The normal curve is completely determined by two parameters, the position of the peak and its width. These parameters correspond to the mean and the standard deviation of the distribution respectively. Thus, a set of normally distributed error data can be completely described by its mean (CE) and its standard deviation (VE) provided there are a sufficiently large number of data points. In the study of aimed movement, it is typically found that errors are approximately normally distributed, and so it is appropriate to use the CE and the VE to describe error data.

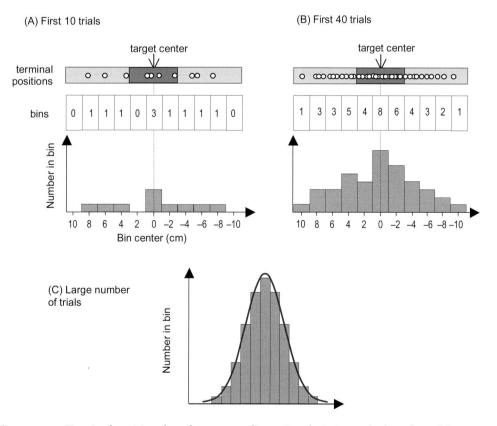

Figure 12.4: *Terminal position data from a one-dimensional aiming task plotted as a histogram.*

12.1.3 CE is a measure of bias, VE is a measure of precision

The constant and variable errors are both measures of the accuracy of a person's performance over a series of trials. In a single trial, the error itself gives a measure of accuracy, but it does not provide a realistic picture of a person's capabilities. The CE and VE calculated from the errors obtained from a series of trials gives a much more realistic picture.

The CE is a measure of how far the center of the error distribution is from the location that defines zero error (perfect performance). A CE of zero means that the distribution is centered on the zero error location. This does not necessarily mean that performance was accurate; in fact, it could be very poor. For example, person 2 in Figure 12.3 has a CE very close to zero, but they missed the target more often than they hit it. What the CE tells you is whether or not the person has a systematic tendency to overshoot or undershoot the zero error position, and how large this tendency is. A systematic tendency to undershoot or overshoot is called a **bias**: a person with a CE that is zero or very close to zero is **unbiased**. In Figure 12.3, person 1 has a small positive bias (tendency to overshoot), person 2 is close to being unbiased, and person 3 has a relatively large negative bias (tendency to undershoot).

The VE is a measure of how scattered the data points are. A VE of zero means that all the data points are the same. This does not necessarily mean that the person was accurate in the sense that they were able to hit the target – all their attempts may have missed; it means that the person consistently reached the same location. Thus, in an aiming task, VE is a measure of the consistency of aiming, a feature of performance that is often called **precision**. In Figure 12.3, person 3 is biased but relatively precise (consistent), whereas person 2 is imprecise despite being unbiased.

12.1.4 In two dimensions, constant and variable errors each have two components

The CE and VE as defined in 12.1.2 are appropriate for describing accuracy in 1-D target-directed aiming tasks. However, many real-world aiming tasks require accuracy in two or sometimes three dimensions. Planar aimed movement tasks like those discussed in Chapter 11 are 2-D tasks. An example of the error distributions obtained in a planar aiming task is shown in Figure 12.5. The task itself is shown in panel A: participants in the experiment slid a rectangular pointing device similar to a computer mouse over a flat tablet so as to move a cursor across a monitor screen; the aim was to position the cursor inside a circular target[3]. There were 16 possible targets and all of them are shown together on the screen in panel A; in the experiment, only one target and the start position would be visible during a trial. During the movement, the cursor could not be seen moving across the screen (no visual feedback), but the target remained visible.

Panel B shows the distributions of the final cursor positions – the cursor end points – for movements aimed at the six targets in the top right quadrant of the screen (all data is from the same person). As with the 1-D example discussed earlier, the end points are distributed around the target, and the person often missed. A quantitative description of accuracy in the 2-D task requires measures of both bias and precision; how can these be provided?

As with the 1-D case, it is straightforward to calculate the average position of the end points. An example is shown in Figure 12.6: a number of cursor end points are shown (open circles) together with their average location (blue square). We can see from the figure that the average position does not coincide with the target center, indicating that the person was biased. In the example shown, the person tended to overshoot the target center and to aim slightly to the left of the line that connects the start location to the target center (the *target axis*). In order to describe the bias, therefore, we need a way to represent both the overshoot and the off-axis aim. One obvious way to do this is to consider the constant error as the vector (directed line segment) that connects the target center to the average location of the end points. This vector can be resolved into a component in the direction of the target axis and a component perpendicular to the target axis, as shown at the bottom of Figure 12.6. The

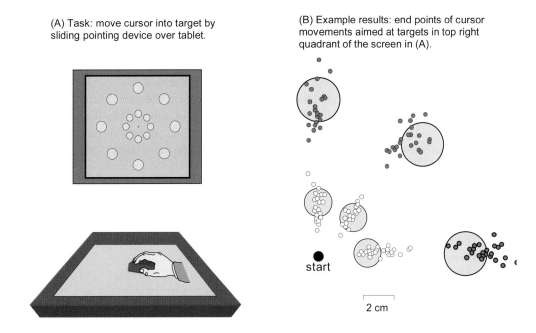

(A) Task: move cursor into target by sliding pointing device over tablet.

(B) Example results: end points of cursor movements aimed at targets in top right quadrant of the screen in (A).

start

2 cm

Figure 12.5: *Computer-based aimed movement task and example results. Data from Gordon, Ghilardi, Ghez (1994a).*

signed lengths of these components are the two components of the constant error[4]: a distance component that can be referred to as the **constant error of distance** (CE_D), and a lateral component that can be referred to as the **constant error of aim** (CE_A) (the sign indicates whether there is an overshoot or undershoot, and whether the aim is to the left or right of the target axis).

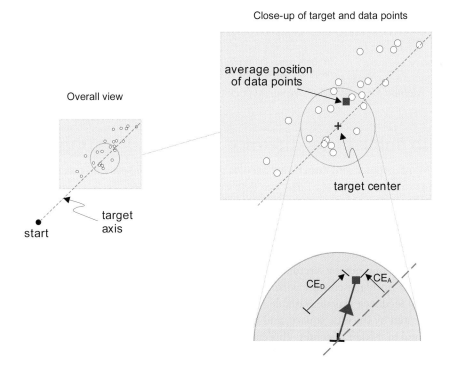

Close-up of target and data points

average position of data points

target center

Overall view

target axis

start

CE_D CE_A

Figure 12.6: *Definition of the constant error in the 2-D aiming task of Figure 12.5.*

How should a 2-D variable error be calculated? A method[5] that follows the definition given for the 1-D case but which provides a two-component variable error is illustrated in Figure 12.7. Panel A reproduces the top left panel of Figure 12.6, and adds a line called the reach axis, which passes through the start position and the average location of the data points (blue square). The two components of the VE are the standard deviation of the data points as measured along the reach axis, and the standard deviation as measured along the axis perpendicular to the reach axis. For consistency with the terminology introduced for the constant error, these components can be called the **variable error of distance** (VE_D) and the **variable error of aim** (VE_A) respectively. Panel B shows how VE_D can be calculated: the data points are moved onto the reach axis by shifting them perpendicularly (as indicated by the arrows); the SD of the points in panel B is then calculated as the mean of their squared distances from the average location (exactly as for the 1-D case). Panel C shows the same things for VE_A: it is the standard deviation of the data points along the line perpendicular to the reach axis.

In summary:

(1) Accuracy in a planar aimed movement task has a distance (or amplitude) component and a directional component.

(2) The distance component of the constant error (CE_D) and of the variable error (VE_D) are measures of the distance accuracy of aiming.

(3) The perpendicular component of the constant error (CE_A in Figure 12.6) and of the variable error (VE_A) can be considered to be measures of the directional accuracy of aiming.

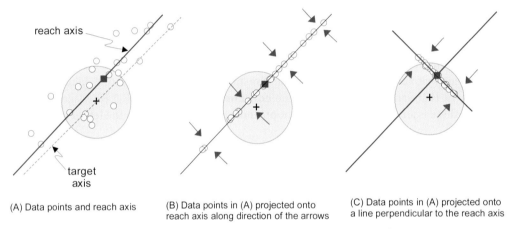

(A) Data points and reach axis

(B) Data points in (A) projected onto reach axis along direction of the arrows

(C) Data points in (A) projected onto a line perpendicular to the reach axis

Figure 12.7: *Method for calculating the variable error in a 2-D aiming task.*

12.1.5 In some tasks distance accuracy is unimportant

The measures of distance and directional accuracy described in the previous section are suitable for planar aimed movement tasks like that shown in Figure 12.5, where accurate performance depends on moving the right distance in the right direction[6]. When hammering a nail or pressing a button, accuracy in distance is relatively unimportant; it is directional accuracy that matters. In such tasks, the target is two dimensional (the nail head or button), but a slightly different description of accuracy is needed. An example is shown in Figure 12.8: the task is to reach out and press a circular button with the index finger (panel A). Panel B shows where the finger tip made contact with the target or mounting surface on a series of trials in which visual feedback was unavailable (not real data). The average location of the contact points is indicated by the blue square, and the target center by a cross. There is a bias to aim slightly high and to the left of center. This can easily be quantified by giving the horizontal (X) and vertical (Y) distances of the average location from the target center, which yields a two-component constant error (CE_x, CE_y). In the figure, CE_x is about two cm left (−2 cm) and CE_y is about 1.5 cm high (+1.5 cm). The variable error can be defined in a corresponding way, VE_x being the standard deviation in the horizontal direction and VE_y the standard deviation in the vertical direction. In this example, CE_x and VE_x quantify the horizontal directional accuracy of aiming, while CE_y and VE_y quantify the vertical directional accuracy.

(A) Task: press the target area
with the tip of the index finger

(B) Contact points of finger with
target/background (circles)

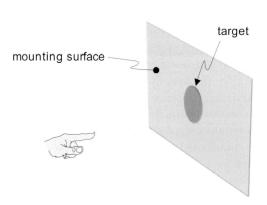
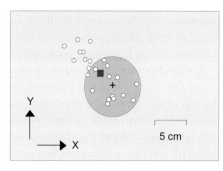

Figure 12.8: *A two-dimensional aiming task (A) in which distance accuracy is not necessarily important. B) Contact points (white circles) and their average location (blue square) (not real data).*

Although the two-component constant and variable errors that have been described in this section often provide useful quantitative descriptions of accuracy in 2-D aiming tasks, they do not always capture everything about performance accuracy that is of interest. One potentially important feature of the data that is missed is the orientation of a set of data points. Figure 12.9 illustrates what this means using two sets of (imaginary) data points that might have been obtained in a series of trials in a task like that shown in Figure 12.8A. The cloud of data points in Figure 12.9A look as if they are spread out along the dashed line – the cloud is said to be *oriented* along the direction of the dashed line. The cloud of points in panel B are not oriented; they are spread out more or less equally in all directions. Neither the constant nor variable errors defined with respect to the horizontal (X) and vertical (Y) directions capture the presence or absence of orientation in the two clouds of data points shown in Figure 12.9. What is needed is a method for reliably determining the orientation of a cloud of data points. A standard statistical method called *principal component analysis* does exactly this job, and is used for characterizing the orientation of error distributions when such a characterization is needed[7]. Once the primary orientation of the data points has been determined (dashed line in Figure 12.9A), the variable error along this direction and the perpendicular direction can be computed (see Figure 12.7) to give a two-component VE.

(A) A cloud of end points that are
oriented along a particular direction

(B) A cloud of end points that are not
oriented in any particular direction

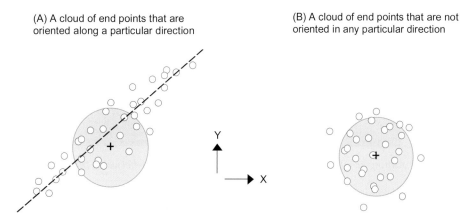

Figure 12.9: *Possible distributions of contact points in a task like that in Figure 12.8A.*

12.1.6 What causes bias and lack of precision?

As Figure 12.5 shows, people display significant inaccuracy when they make planar aimed movements without visual feedback from the working point. There may be a bias to over-shoot or undershoot, or to aim to one side or the other, and performance will show limited precision. What factors are responsible for biases and limited precision?

A rifle-shooting example aids in identifying various sources of error. Imagine that you are trying to hit a target with a projectile fired from a rifle. You look through a sight mounted on the top of the barrel, and move the rifle so that the target appears in the center of the sight, between the cross-hairs, as shown in Figure 12.10. In this figure, the target is a tin can sitting on a fence, and the middle of the can is right between the cross-hairs. You pull the trigger but fail to hit the can: a variety of factors could have contributed to this outcome. These factors can be roughly divided into two types: (1) those that have different effects on performance on different attempts; (2) those that have a similar effect on every attempt.

Consider factors of the first type. One of these is physiological tremor: it is impossible to hold a gun perfectly steady, since there will always be some shaking of the body. This tremor is often so slight that it is imperceptible, but the barrel of the gun may only need to be displaced by a fraction of a degree for the target to be missed. The effect of tremor will vary from one attempt to another, and so it has an effect on the consistency of performance (variable error) without introducing a bias. Similarly, breathing and the beating of the heart can disturb postural stability (Chapter 7), and hence affect our ability to hold a rifle steady. These factors will affect consistency but are unlikely to produce a bias. Other things can have effects on some attempts but not others, including momentary lapses of concentration, distracting effects of events in the environment (people talking, a car backfiring), and external disturbances such as a gust of wind. All these factors have semi-random effects on performance and are generally referred to as **noise**. Noise can be of internal origin – random fluctuations in the firing of neurons or motor units, for example – or of external origin, such as unpredictable disturbances produced by gusts of winds or other events in the environment. Noise that has an internal origin is often called **intrinsic noise**. Noise primarily results in variability over repeated attempts, and so its effects are manifested in the variable error.

Figure 12.10: *Aiming a rifle by positioning the target (tin can) between the cross-hairs of a telescopic sight.*

Now consider factors of the second type that have similar effects on different attempts. In rifle shooting, one such factor is misalignment of the sight on the gun barrel. In order for the bullet to be shot in the direction of the object between the cross-hairs, the sight must be very precisely aligned with the barrel. If the sight points in a different direction from the barrel, then the shot will be off-target in the direction of the barrel. A very small misalignment can easily lead to a missed shot. For example, suppose the target is 50 meters away and the sight misalignment is one tenth of a degree to the left of the line of the barrel. This will cause the shot to be about 9 cm off to the right of the target center. A typical tin can is less than 9 cm wide. The effect of such a misalignment will be the same on every attempt, and so it will lead to a bias to shoot wide of the target.

The shooting example shows that variable error arises due to the effects of random disturbances and fluctuations (noise), whereas constant error (bias) can arise if structural characteristics of the system (e.g., sight-barrel alignment) are not properly taken into account. Consider in more detail what is going on in the case of sight-barrel misalignment. The alignment of the sight with respect to the barrel is a structural characteristic of the gun. If the shooter does not know that the sight is not perfectly aligned with the barrel, then they will assume that the gun is properly aimed when the center of the cross-hairs is within the target, as shown in panel A of Figure 12.11. The sight and barrel are misaligned by about 10° and the barrel points off to the right when the target is sighted, as indicated by the dashed line. The shooter can learn to compensate for the error by aiming about 10° to the left, as shown in panel B of Figure 12.11. In other words, if the shooter learns what the misalignment is, then they can make a compensatory adjustment for it. In Chapter 1 we noted that knowledge about the characteristics of a system that is being controlled is often referred to as an *internal model* of that system. In the shooting example, the shooter's knowledge concerning the alignment of the sight on the barrel is part of their internal model of the rifle. If they do not know that the sight is misaligned and aim as if it were properly aligned, then they can be said to have an erroneous internal model. In general, an erroneous internal model will give rise to biases in performance. As discussed in Chapter 11, the generation of aimed movements involves transformations that incorporate internal models of the structural and mechanical characteristics of the body (e.g., forward and inverse kinematic transformations, inverse dynamics transformations). If these internal models are approximate or inaccurate, then there will be systematic effects on performance that will manifest themselves in the constant error[8]. This has led to a body of research that attempts to deduce the approximations or inaccuracies of internal models by studying the pattern of errors obtained for aimed movements executed without visual feedback: a discussion of these matters, however, is beyond the scope of this text[9].

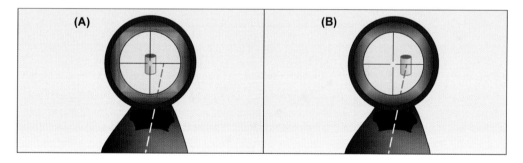

Figure 12.11: *Aiming at a target (tin can) through a misaligned sight. (A) The target is centered in the sight, but the barrel is not pointing at it (dashed line). (B) The barrel is pointing at the target when the target is off-center in the sight.*

12.1.7 What task factors influence accuracy?

The bias and precision of aimed movement can be affected by factors such as the conditions in which the task is performed, the instructions a person is given, and/or the motivation that they have to perform well. Probably the most important factor influencing the accuracy of movements aimed at visible targets is the quality and availability of visual information. This includes visual information about the size and location of the target and visual feedback information. If visual information is unavailable (visually open-loop conditions), the accuracy of performance is limited by how accurately the target's location can be perceived and used to program the movement: if you don't know exactly where the target is, then you cannot be very accurate. If visual information is available and a person has unlimited time, then accuracy is normally limited only by physiological tremor and the person's ability to visually detect whether there is an error or not. The role of vision in aimed movement control will be discussed in more detail later in the chapter.

Another factor that is generally considered to be an important determinant of accuracy is the average speed with which a person executes the movement. Speed may be determined by task constraints (e.g., the person only has a certain amount of time to reach the target), instructions given by the experimenter, or a person's choice. The proverb 'haste makes waste' succinctly summarizes the idea that if you try to do something quickly, you will inevitably make mistakes. The consensus is that movements executed quickly are less accurate than those executed more slowly[10]. One reason for this is that if a movement is executed very quickly, there is too little time to act on visual feedback information and make corrections to the movement. Another possibility is that faster movements are intrinsically less accurate, regardless of feedback. This possibility is considered further in sections 12.1.9–11.

The last factor we will discuss is experimental design. It has been found that the way in which an experimental study is conducted can be responsible for certain patterns of constant error[11]. One such pattern is known as the **range effect** or **contraction bias**. This can occur in experiments in which each participant is required to make aimed movements (without visual feedback) to each of a number of targets at different distances from the start location[12]. The distances of the targets lie within the range defined by the nearest and farthest targets. In such studies, the contraction bias is a systematic tendency to overshoot nearer targets and undershoot the more distant targets, while being unbiased when aiming at targets in the middle of the range[13]. If the constant error is plotted against target distance in a 1-D aiming task, the contraction bias produces a pattern like that shown in Figure 12.12. A possible explanation for the contraction bias is that participants learn about the distribution of targets (the target range) during the course of the experiment, and if uncertain about the precise distance to reach, they tend to move to the more likely location (given their knowledge of the range) – on any given trial the target is less likely to be at the extreme of the range than in the middle[14]. The contraction bias (and other biases that arise due to features of the experimental design[15]) must be taken into account when explaining the pattern of results[16].

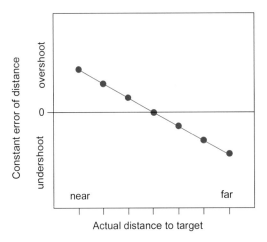

Figure 12.12: *Illustration of the pattern of constant errors produced by a contraction bias in a 1-D aiming task (not real data).*

12.1.8 It is important to maintain a clear distinction between movement time and movement speed

When someone says that they executed an aimed movement task quickly, they may be talking about the speed of the movement, or they may be talking about the time taken. These two things are, of course, closely related, but they are clearly not the same. The time taken to execute an aimed movement is well defined: it is the time taken to move from the start position to the target (the movement time, MT). The meaning of 'speed of movement' is not so obvious, since speed varies as movement progresses: an aimed movement is slow at the beginning and at the end, but faster in the middle. When people refer to the speed of an aimed movement, they often mean the average speed. The average speed is closely related to MT: if S is the distance traveled by the working point, then the average speed of the movement is equal to S ÷ MT. Thus it is possible for a movement with a high average speed to have a relatively long MT (when the distance is large) and for a movement with a low average speed to have a short MT (when the distance is small). For this reason it is necessary to be clear whether you are talking about movement speed or movement time when discussing accuracy.

12.1.9 Early studies suggested that speed has little effect on accuracy in visually open-loop conditions

One of the earliest and most influential experimental studies of the accuracy of aimed movement was conducted by R.S. Woodworth towards the end of the nineteenth century[17]. One of Woodworth's inspirations for his studies were his observations of the speed and accuracy with which construction workers were able to hammer piles into the ground. The workers repeatedly swung long-handled hammers from an overhead position down onto the top of the pile – Woodworth estimated that the distance traveled by the hammer-head was over 1.5 meters. He counted 4000 strikes with only one miss. The hammer-head and the top of the pile were both 4 cm in diameter, so errors of more than 4 cm off-center would produce a miss. Given a miss rate of 1 in 4000, he estimated that the average error must have had a magnitude of less than 1 cm.

Woodworth devised an experimental task that allowed him to measure the accuracy of aimed movements executed at different speeds. The task required participants to move a pencil repeatedly back and forth through a slit. The back and forth movements had to be made in time with a metronome, so the faster the metronome, the more quickly the movements had to be executed. The goal was to move the pencil a target distance; the error was computed as the difference between distance actually moved and the target distance (i.e., a distance error), but the sign of the difference was ignored. The average of these unsigned differences yields an overall error statistic called the *absolute error*. Figure 12.13 shows the absolute error results Woodworth obtained when participants executed movements with vision (eyes open) and without vision (eyes closed). The units on the horizontal axis are 'movements per minute': the average speed of the slowest movements (20/min) was about 5 cm/s and each took about 1.5 seconds; the average speed of the fastest (200/min) was about 50 cm/s and each took about 150 milliseconds[18] (the average distance moved was between 13 and 14 cm). The results showed several things:

(1)   Accuracy with eyes open is generally better than with eyes closed.
(2)   The advantageous effects of visual feedback decline systematically with increases in speed, and appear to be absent at the very fastest speeds.
(3)   People were quite accurate with their eyes closed (absolute error less than 5 mm).
(4)   Speed of execution had little or no effect on accuracy in the eyes-closed condition.

These findings suggest that moving quickly is not itself a significant cause of inaccuracy; rather, it is the reduction in the time available to make corrections based on visual feedback that is responsible (kinesthetic feedback was available in both conditions).

In Woodworth's study, visual information during the movement to the target was removed by asking participants to close their eyes; they opened them again during the return movement. Woodworth had no way of knowing to what extent his participants obeyed the instructions, and could not measure when his participants opened and closed their eyes. A better controlled replication has been reported in which participants performed similar back-and-forth aimed movements in time with a metronome[19]. Participants made repetitive movements with a stylus from a home position to a target (a cross marked on a sheet of paper); the home and target locations were instrumented so that the lights went out when the stylus left the home position, and came back on again when it made contact with the target. MTs were in the range 0.35 for the fastest movements to 1.5 seconds for the slowest. Variable errors of both distance and aim were measured and showed very little variation with movement speed, averaging between about 6 and 7.5 mm for VEs of distance and between 5 and 6.8 mm for VEs of aim[20]. The largest errors were observed for the slowest and fastest movements, and the smallest for movements executed at an intermediate pace.

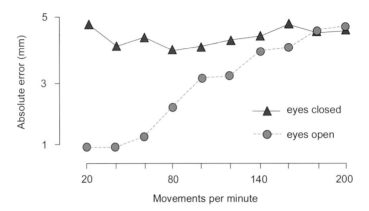

Figure 12.13: *Results from Woodworth's repetitive aiming experiment (data points are the averages of four participants). Data from Woodworth (1899), Fig. 3.*

The findings described in this section suggest that movements that are executed faster are not intrinsically less accurate than those executed more slowly. This would mean that the reason for the lower accuracy of faster movements observed in daily life is due to there being less time to make visually based corrections. However, the results from many later studies have challenged these conclusions, as discussed next.

12.1.10 Does movement speed affect accuracy?

Most studies of aimed movements conducted since the 1960s have used discrete aiming tasks in which each trial in an experiment consists of a single movement to a target. One strategy for studying the effect of the speed of execution on movement accuracy using discrete movements has been to employ a specially designed task. The task requires participants to attempt to make contact with a visible target with a movement that lasts a particular length of time. This time is specified in advance by the experimenter and will be referred to as the **required movement time**. In effect, this kind of task requires that participants match their MT to required MT, and is called a **time-matching task**:

> **TIME-MATCHING TASK:** an aimed movement task that requires a person to move to a stationary target with a movement of a pre-specified duration (the *required* MT). Thus, the task has a spatial goal (contact the target) and a temporal goal (execute a movement of the required duration).

Of course, if you asked a person to move to a target with a required MT of 175 milliseconds, they could hardly be expected to comply with your instruction. In order to do it, people must be trained. The training involves a session in which people execute movements and are given feedback about their actual movement times[21]. A sequence of between 30 to 50 practice trials is usually sufficient to enable people to reproduce the required MT to within about ±10%. We will consider the temporal aspect of time-matching tasks in more detail in section 4 of this chapter. Here we will focus on how these tasks have been used to study how the spatial accuracy of aimed movement depends on the speed of execution.

One particularly influential study[22] involved training people to make aimed movements with required MTs of 140, 170 and 200 ms. Movements were executed with full vision, but the short MTs meant that there was very limited opportunity to make visually based corrections. The task was to move a hand-held stylus from a start location to a point target (dot) marked on a sheet of paper lying flat on a table, as shown in panel A of Figure 12.14. Targets were located at three different distances (10, 20 and 30 cm) from the start location, which led to movements with nine different average speeds (3 distances × 3 required MTs). As the figure shows, the task is executed by lifting the stylus off the start location and bringing it down onto the target. Panel B shows the acceleration profile of such a movement. The spike in the deceleration phase occurred when the stylus struck the table, indicating that the stylus was moving quite quickly when it made contact. The position of the first contact of the stylus with the target sheet was recorded, from which the error (distance from the target point) could be measured. From these measurements, the variable errors of aim (VE_A) and of distance (VE_D) were computed. The results are shown in panel C of Figure 12.14.

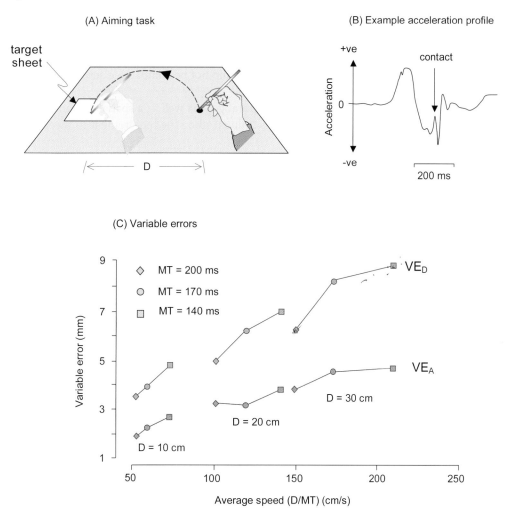

Figure 12.14: *Results from a study of an aimed movement task in which participants attempted to move a specified distance in a specified MT (200, 170 or 140 ms). Data from Schmidt et al. (1979).*

The results in panel C show that variable errors were greater when the average speed was greater, regardless of whether the greater speed was due to moving a greater distance in the same time, or due to moving the same distance in a shorter time. Similar results have been obtained in a number of subsequent studies[23]. Given the short MTs, the data in Figure 12.14C seem to provide a clear demonstration that faster movements are less accurate, even when there is little or no opportunity to make corrections. This supports the idea that faster movements are intrinsically less accurate than slower ones. However, the findings do not firmly establish that faster movements are less accurate, for the following reasons.

(1)   Average speed was, in part, confounded with distance to the target (D): the larger VEs to more distant targets may either have been an effect of speed or an effect of distance.

(2)   The height to which the stylus was lifted off the table was not measured, so actual average speed and distance moved were not measured. In Figure 12.14A, the distance moved is the length of the dashed path, which is greater than the horizontal distance (D) to the target. The average speed was calculated as D divided by MT, but the true average speed is the path length divided by MT. Since the true average speed was not measured, the true relationship between movement speed and accuracy was not accurately determined[24].

(3)   MTs of 170 and 200 ms are long enough for sensory information (both visual and kinesthetic) to influence the movement, and so it is possible that the greater accuracy of longer-duration movements was a result of corrective adjustments.

(4)   Participants moved the stylus down onto the target and the impact stopped the movement. The impact occurred at some point during the deceleration phase of the movement (Figure 12.14B), but at what point was not recorded. If the point in the deceleration phase at which impact occurred was different for different MTs or distances, then the variability of impact points (the VEs) would not be comparable across movements executed at different speeds[25].

(5)   The time-matching task involves a temporal goal as well as a spatial one and it is not known whether the spatial accuracy is influenced by the requirement to meet a temporal goal.

A set of experiments without the problems described in the last two paragraphs examined the accuracy of open loop aiming under instructions to move at different speeds[26]. Participants reached to the remembered locations of targets in the dark (visually open-loop aiming). In one study they reached at a normal speed (i.e., without specific instruction) and under three speed instructions: slower than normal, faster than normal, and as fast as possible[27]. These instructions produced movements that had peak speeds ranging from about 0.5 m/s to 4.5 m/s and MTs ranging from less than 200 ms to nearly two seconds. It was found that speed of execution had no detectable effect on either constant or variable error[28]. In sum, when other possible factors are excluded, it seems that the effect of speed on accuracy can be very small[29].

12.1.11 Movement distance affects variable errors in visually open-loop conditions

Although movement speed has a negligible effect on terminal accuracy in visually open-loop conditions, the distance moved does tend to have an effect: the greater the distance moved, the lower the accuracy achieved. In this section we will consider the effect of distance on variable errors.

Variable errors are typically found to be greater when the distance to the target is greater[30], but there are some subtleties. Figure 12.15 shows some results from an experiment conducted using the task set-up shown in Figure 12.5A. Participants aimed to move a cursor into five targets at different distances (2.4, 4.8, 9.6, 19.2 and 33.6 cm) from a start point. The target centers all lay on an (invisible) line oriented at 30° to the horizontal (the target axis): in panel A of Figure 12.15, the target centers are marked by crosses. On any given trial in the experiment, only one target would appear on the screen. The ovals in panel A are a statistical characterization of the end-point distributions produced by one participant (95% of all end-points fall within the oval). The ovals clearly increase in size perpendicular to the target axis – they are fatter for the more distant targets – indicating that VE_A increases with distance. VE_D was also found to increase with distance, but the effect was smaller than for VE_A. Note that an error in the direction of aiming is an angular error, and will therefore lead to a greater spatial error as distance increases. This is illustrated in panel B of Figure 12.15: a straight-line movement path (solid line) with an angular error of ε degrees produces a lateral error of E_a, E_b and E_c to targets a, b and c respectively. The variable error of aim (VE_A) will therefore be larger for more distant targets for a given angular variability. Does this account for the increase in VE_A with distance?

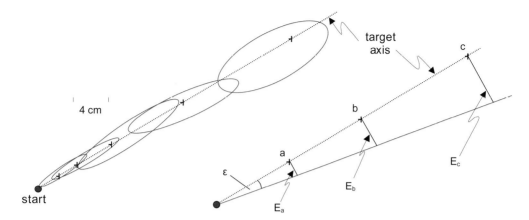

Figure 12.15: *Aiming to targets (centers marked by crosses) located at different distances from the start location. Left: ellipses represent the distribution of end-points (from Gordon et al., 1994a, Figure 6). Right: a straight movement (blue line) with an aiming error of ε° leads to progressively larger lateral errors (E) with distance.*

Since the tangent of the angular error (ε) is simply the lateral error (E) divided by the target distance, expressing the variable error of aim as a proportion of the distance (VE_A/D) provides an approximate way of assessing whether the angular error is the same for targets at different distances or greater for more distant ones. Figure 12.16 shows both VE_A and VE_D as a proportion of the target distance (proportional VE) plotted against the average distance moved (data points are the averages from six participants; the distance scale is logarithmic). The figure clearly shows that the proportional variable error of aim (VE_A/D) was hardly affected by movement distance, which indicates that the angular variable error was almost the same regardless of target distance[31] (i.e., the increase in VE_A was due almost entirely to the effect shown in Figure 12.15B). Figure 12.16 also shows that the proportional variable error of distance (VE_D/D) was smaller when the participants moved further (more distant targets). Given that VE_D increased slightly with distance, the decline of VE_D/D means that larger movement distances lead to progressively smaller and smaller increases in VE_D.

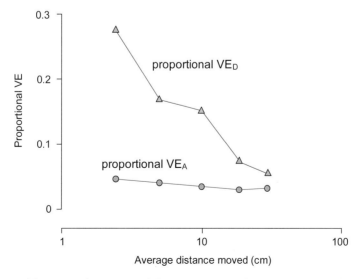

Figure 12.16: *Variable errors of aiming and distance expressed as a proportion of target distance. Data from Gordon, Ghilardi, Ghez (1994a).*

12.1.12 Summary

In this part of the chapter we have considered how to characterize the spatial accuracy of aimed movement and discussed some of the factors that lead to error in visually open-loop conditions. Visual information can be used to correct errors; without it, error is inevitable and people show various biases (quantified by the constant error) and are imprecise (quantified by the variable error).

The speed of execution might be thought to have a strong effect on the precision of visually open-loop aiming, but turns out to have only a weak effect, and in some studies the effect was either absent or too small to detect. The time taken to execute the movement (something strongly correlated with the speed of execution) has a powerful effect on accuracy when vision is available (see Figure 12.13). The basic reason for this is easy to understand: if you can see that your movement is in error, then you can correct the error if you have sufficient time to do so. For instance, if you want to poke the end of a length of cotton thread through the eye of a needle, then you might require anything from a few seconds to a few minutes depending on your dexterity and experience.

When vision is available, you can correct errors if you need to, provided that you have enough time. This means that a sensible strategy would be to give yourself more time when you need to be more accurate, which can be thought of as sacrificing speed for accuracy, since you can give yourself more time by decreasing the average speed of your movement. Conversely, if you want to be quick, then you must sacrifice accuracy for speed.

Some have argued that the main reason for reducing speed when accuracy is needed is not to give yourself more time, but to avoid the inaccuracies associated with fast movements[32]. It is widely held that faster movements are intrinsically less accurate than slower ones. This view is supported by findings showing that the variability of large-amplitude muscle forces and neural signals is greater than that of low-amplitude forces and signals[33]. The idea is that faster movements involve larger-amplitude forces and control signals, which results in greater variability in movement outcome. However, the effect of speed on spatial variable error appears to be rather small, and so may not be a significant factor in determining how quickly to move in order to achieve a desired level of accuracy. Sacrifice of speed (or time) for accuracy is the topic of the next part of the chapter.

12.2 The Speed-Accuracy Trade-Off

12.2.1 Introduction: trading speed for accuracy

It is a matter of everyday experience that we take longer and move more slowly when we need to be accurate than we do when accuracy is not a concern. This is not something imposed upon us by the task: we could choose to move very quickly to a target that requires a high degree of accuracy and so risk making an error. For this reason, the tendency to take longer (move slower) should be thought of as a **strategy** that people adopt. In the context of aimed movement, a strategy can be thought of as a 'set of rules'[34] used by a person to determine how a task is executed in a particular context. A person need not be consciously aware of adopting a strategy, it may be something that occurs automatically as part of meeting the task goals.

The strategy of taking longer to make a movement (and so decreasing its average speed) when greater accuracy is required is an example of a speed-accuracy trade-off that we will refer to as the **spatial speed-accuracy trade-off**. The reason for including the word *spatial* is to emphasize that the trade-off concerns getting the working point to a particular spatial location (the target). A typical definition of *trade-off* is: 'an exchange of one thing in return for another, especially relinquishment of one benefit or advantage for another regarded as more desirable'[35]. In aimed movement, either speed or accuracy may be beneficial, but if you want to be accurate you must relinquish speed, because as we saw in 12.1 your accuracy is limited when you move faster and have less time. We will adopt the following definition:

> **SPATIAL SPEED-ACCURACY TRADE-OFF:** the strategy of decreasing average speed (and so increasing movement time) in order to achieve greater (spatial) end-point accuracy. Speed is given up in exchange for more accurate performance. (*Applies to movements aimed at stationary targets.*)

It should be pointed out that many authors use the term *trade-off* to describe speed-accuracy relationships in which there is no possibility for a strategic exchange of speed for accuracy[36]. One such relationship is that shown in Figure 12.14: the data were obtained from people whose movements were prescribed – they were required to move specific distances in specific times – and their accuracy was measured. The participants did not have the opportunity to exchange speed for accuracy. If the term 'trade-off' is to have any useful meaning, then it cannot be applied to speed-accuracy relationships in which there is no exchange of speed for accuracy (or vice-versa). Experimental results of the form shown in Figure 12.14 will be referred to as **speed-accuracy relationships**.

In this part of the chapter we will discuss empirical studies of how people trade off speed for accuracy in aimed movements and consider how the trade-off can be quantified. We will be particularly concerned with the quantitative description of the speed-accuracy trade-off proposed by Paul Fitts and widely known as Fitts' law.

12.2.2 The spatial speed-accuracy trade-off in some aiming tasks is described by Fitts' law

In the 1950s and 60s, Paul Fitts reported the results of several landmark studies that investigated the speed-accuracy trade-off in aimed movement. His first study used a task in which participants moved a hand-held stylus from one flat target to another and back again in a repetitive manner[37]. The task is sometimes called the *reciprocal tapping task* because participants alternately tap the targets with the tip of the stylus. The task layout is shown in panel A of Figure 12.17. Participants were instructed to repetitively contact one target and then the other *as fast as possible but without making errors* (i.e., without missing the target) for 20 seconds. The instruction means that you should make as *many movements as you can in the time available.* The instructions specifically stress both speed (as fast as possible) and accuracy (make few errors). The acceptable level of accuracy is usually that people miss the target on less than 5% of occasions. The instructions require people to trade speed for accuracy so that they can achieve this level of accuracy.

Fitts studied how the average time taken to make a movement between the two targets (average MT) depended on the width of the targets (W, the two targets had equal widths) and the inter-target distance, D (Figure 12.17A). The width of the target constrained the distance accuracy of the movement; the length of the target did not vary, and was sufficiently large that it placed no constraint on the directional accuracy of the movement. This arrangement meant that only distance accuracy mattered, making the task similar to a one-dimensional aiming task. In Fitts' study there were four different target widths (W = 0.25, 0.50, 1.00 and 2.00 inches) and four different inter-target distances (2, 4, 8 and 16 inches). It would be expected from the spatial speed-accuracy trade-off that MT would be greater when the target width was smaller. This was exactly the result obtained, as shown in Figure 12.17B, which plots the average MT against target width for each of the inter-target distances (data points for the same inter-target distance are connected together by lines). The figure clearly shows that average MT was longer when the targets were narrower. It also shows that when the targets were further apart, MTs were longer (people took longer when going further).

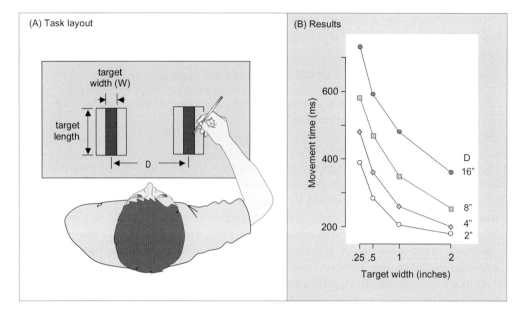

Figure 12.17: *Fitts' reciprocal aiming task and results for different values of target width (W) and distance (D). Data from Fitts (1954), 1 oz stylus.*

In Figure 12.17B, neither the relationship between MT and distance nor that between MT and width are proportional. Fitts found that MT varied in proportion to the logarithms of the width and distance: $MT \propto \log_2 D$ and $MT \propto -\log_2 W$ (2 is the base of the logarithm[38]). These two relationships can be combined[39] to give $MT \propto \log_2(D/W)$. If MT is proportional to $\log_2(D/W)$, then plotting MT against $\log_2(D/W)$ should result in all the data points falling on the same straight line. Figure 12.18 shows the data plotted in this way: $\log_2(2D/W)$ is used so that the value of the logarithm does not fall below zero[40]. To a good approximation, the data points do all fall on the same straight line. Thus, MT is approximately proportional to $\log_2(2D/W)$ and we can write the relationship as follows:

$$MT = a + b \log_2(2D/W) \tag{12.1}$$

where a is the point where the straight line through the data points in Figure 12.18 intersects the movement time axis (the intercept) and b is the slope of the line. $\log_2(2D/W)$ is usually called the **index of difficulty** (**ID**) because an aiming task is deemed to be more difficult if it takes longer to execute. Figure 12.18 shows that MT is greater for larger values of $\log_2(2D/W)$, so it provides a measure (or index) of the difficulty of the task.

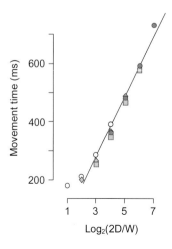

Figure 12.18: *Data from Figure 12.17B plotted against the index of difficulty.*

The value of the intercept (a) is the MT when the ID is zero: it corresponds to a sort of minimum movement time, which could be zero. The slope, b, tells you by how much MT increases per unit increase in the ID (ID itself is dimensionless). These two parameters are found to be different for different people, different sets of data, and different experimental set-ups. For Fitts' original data set (Figure 12.18), the intercept is 12.8 milliseconds and the slope is 94.7 milliseconds/unit ID. In another study using the same task[41], the data were well described by equation 12.1 with a = −105 ms and b = 106 ms.

Equation 12.1 is known as **Fitts' law** because it has been found to provide a good description of the results of a very large number of different experiments (discussed in next section). It is important not to confuse Fitts' law with the spatial speed-accuracy trade-off itself: Fitts' law is a quantitative description of the trade-off that tells you how MT increases as the accuracy requirements become more stringent.

12.2.3 Fitts' law describes the results from many different studies

A very large number of studies have been conducted investigating the generality of Fitts' law, and these have used a wide variety of different aiming tasks. Fitts himself used not only the reciprocal tapping task (Figure 12.17) but also a washer transfer task, a pin transfer task (inserting thin rods into holes)[42], and a discrete aiming task[43]. The washer transfer task involved repetitively moving washers (discs with holes in the middle) from one peg to another using the apparatus shown in Figure 12.19. The instruction was again to perform the task as *quickly and accurately as possible*. The distance, D, in this task is the distance between the centers of the two pegs, as shown in the figure. The diameters of the peg and the washer hole jointly determine the accuracy with which the participant must position the washer as it is placed over the peg. Fitts used the clearance between the peg and washer (= radius of washer hole minus radius of peg) as the analog of target width in this task. With D and W defined as shown in Figure 12.19, Fitts found that MT was again approximately proportional to $\log_2(2D/W)$ (equation 12.1).

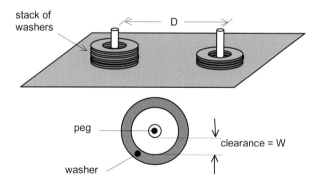

Figure 12.19: *Washer transfer task.*

In all the tasks he studied, Fitts found that the results were well described by equation 12.1. Many subsequent studies have confirmed this finding, using a variety of different tasks. These include tasks that require accuracy in only one dimension, like Fitts' original task (Figure 12.17) and tasks involving rotation about a single joint or rotation of a handle[44]; and also tasks that require accuracy in two dimensions, such as the washer transfer task. Most studies involve aiming movements executed with the arm, but some have involved moving the head, a leg or individual fingers, and Fitts' law has been found to describe the results quite well[45]. The law has also been found to hold for tasks in which cursors were moved to targets on a screen by manipulating a variety of computer interface devices such as joysticks, track-balls, touchpads and mice[46]. Lastly, most studies have instructed participants to be *as fast and as accurate as possible*: when performed under this instruction the task is sometimes called the **time minimization task**[47]. However, Fitts' law does not only apply under such instructions; it has also been found to apply when no explicit instruction concerning speed is given: the data still tend to follow Fitts' law.

It seems, therefore, that Fitts' law provides a general description of the speed-accuracy trade-off in aiming tasks regardless of (i) whether the task is repetitive or discrete, (ii) whether the task requires accuracy in one or two dimensions and (iii) what effectors are used. Despite giving a good overall description of group average data, two important things need to be appreciated. First, Fitts' law is a description and nothing more – it offers no explanation for why people perform the way that they do. Second, as we will see in what follows, the description provided by Fitts' law is rarely as accurate as has been claimed, and in several cases the data clearly contradict the law in the sense that *there are systematic features of the MT data reported in many experiments that the law fails to describe*. These features are discussed next.

12.2.4 Fitts' law does not always provide a good description of performance

In Figure 12.18 you can see that not all the data points lie on the straight line. The points at low values of the ID lie above the line. This pattern is characteristic of most experiments that have included small values of the ID: the data points tend to fall on a J-shaped curve when plotted against the ID, not on a straight line. Another departure from Fitts' law that has been reported in many studies is that MTs at different distances tend to fall not on the same line when plotted against the index of difficulty, but on separate lines[48]. This is not an obvious feature of Fitts' original data (Figure 12.18) but is clearly shown by the data in Figure 12.20: the data in panel A come from one study, those in panel B from another. In both studies there were four different distances (D), and the data for these are shown using different symbols connected by lines. The figure clearly shows that the data from the different distances do not all fall on the same straight line; they fall on curves rather than straight lines. These features of the data are not consistent with Fitts' law.

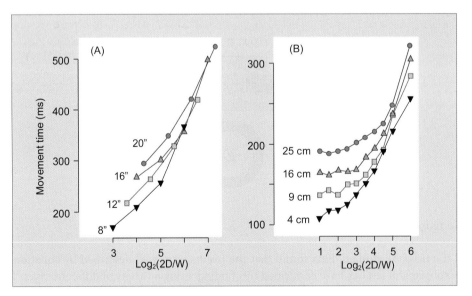

Figure 12.20: *Results from two studies of the dependency of MT on target distance and width. (A) Data from Kerr and Langolf (1977). (B) Data from Gan and Hoffman (1988).*

According to Fitts' law, MT should be the same when the ID is the same regardless of what combination of target width and distance is used to produce that ID. Figure 12.20 shows that this is not always the case: sometimes the MT can be different for the same ID produced by different combinations of D and W. Specifically, *for a given ID, a narrow-target and short-distance combination tends to produce a longer MT than a wide-target–long-distance combination.*

The failures of Fitts' law to capture the features of the data described in this section might be due to the law being an approximation to the true relationship between MT and the task parameters (distance and target width). We will return to this idea later (section 12.2.8). Alternatively, the law might accurately represent the true relationship, but there is something that has been left out that needs to be taken into account. There are a few things that do not appear in the Fitts' law equation but might be expected to have an effect on performance. One of these is the size of the working 'point' with which target contact is made, as discussed next.

12.2.5 Fitts' law is sometimes improved by taking into account the size of the pointer

Making contact with a target with something small like the tip of a pen demands more accuracy than contacting it with something large, like a fly swatter. Fly swatters have a large area precisely because it would be difficult to hit something as small as a fly with something small. Figure 12.21 represents the situation in which a target (rectangle) is contacted by the end of a pointing device (circle). In the figure, the location of the circle represents where the end of the pointer was when it contacted the target. In panel A of the figure, the pointer landed with its end wholly within the boundary of the target. In B, the pointer landed so that only its right edge contacted the target. In C, only the left edge of the pointer contacted the target. If both B and C are accepted as hits, then the end of the pointer can fall within a region of width W + P and still hit the target. In effect, the target width has been increased by the diameter of the pointer. This suggests that Fitts' law should be modified as follows:

$$MT = a + b \log_2(2D/[W + P])$$
(**12.2**)

This modification was tested experimentally[49] using a discrete aiming task. It was found that use of a larger pointer (the index finger) produced shorter MTs than a smaller pointer (stylus with a sharp point). The data obtained when the finger was used were not well described by the standard form of Fitts' law (equation 12.1), as shown in panel A of Figure 12.22. There were five different target widths (from 2 to 18 mm) and three different distances: the data for different target widths fall on different lines, contrary to Fitts' law. Panel B shows the same data plotted as a function of $\log_2(2D/[W + P])$. The data come much closer to falling on the same straight line in panel B, consistent with the modified form of Fitts' law (equation 12.2). This shows that when a pointing device with a large end-point is used, Fitts' law needs to be modified in the manner described by equation 12.2.

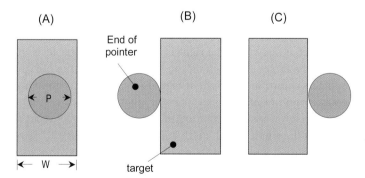

Figure 12.21: *Contact configurations between the end of a pointer (red) and a target (blue).*

Although taking pointer size into account can allow Fitts' law to give a better fit to the data in Figure 12.22, many studies in which the data points do not fall on a straight line when plotted as a function of the Fitts' index of difficulty were conducted with a stylus with a small point. In these cases, taking the diameter of the pointer tip into account makes little difference.

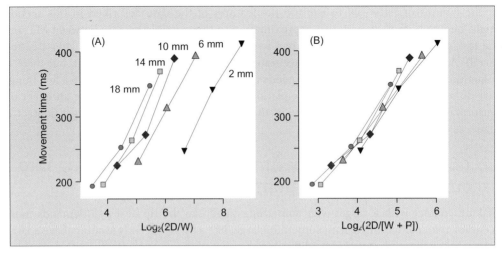

Figure 12.22: *Movement time data from a discrete aiming task to targets of width 2, 6, 10, 14 and 18 mm plotted against Fitts' ID (A) and a modified ID that takes pointer size into account (B). Data from Hoffman and Sheikh (1991).*

12.2.6 Fitts' law might be improved by using the effective target width and effective distance

Fitts' law relates MT to two physical variables that describe the task situation: distance and target width. A problem with these variables is that they do not necessarily describe the distance a person actually moves or the accuracy that is actually achieved. Figure 12.23A shows a Fitts-type discrete aiming task in which the target has a width, W, and its center is a distance, D, from the start point. A person does not move the stylus tip through a distance D, however. In Fitts' experiments, the stylus leaves the table and follows a path like one of those illustrated in Figure 12.23B. The distance traveled by the stylus depends on how high it is lifted: path 1 in the figure is clearly much shorter in length than path 2. Even the horizontal (X) distance traveled by the stylus tip is not equal to D, since the stylus can land anywhere within the target area, so it can be between D − ½W and D + ½W.

Not only does the distance, D, not represent the distance actually moved, the size of the target does not represent the accuracy achieved. If a person makes many movements to a target, the contact locations might be distributed over the whole width of the target, or they might be bunched together. Figure 12.24 illustrates these two outcomes. When the contact points are all bunched together (Figure 12.24 right), the person might just as well have been aiming to hit a smaller target – they are being more accurate than they need to be. A person who contacts the target as shown on the right is achieving a greater level of accuracy than a person who contacts the target as shown on the left. In addition, the horizontal (X) distance moved for the contacts shown on the right of Figure 12.24 is slightly greater than the distance moved for the contacts on the left.

To summarize, a person whose distribution of target hits looks like that shown on the left of Figure 12.24 is using the whole target width and moves on average a horizontal distance D. A person whose distribution looks like that on the right is effectively hitting a target of width ½ W and moving an average distance of D + ¼ W. Considerations like these suggest that a proper description of how MT depends on accuracy constraints (target size) and distance requires the use of measures of the actual accuracy achieved and the actual distance moved. What measures of these would be appropriate?

It has been found that the contact points in studies of aiming tasks that use the time mini-mization paradigm are normally distributed across the width of the target[50] (they conform to the normal distribution, see Figure 12.4). Since the X-positions of the hit points are normally distributed, they can be well described by their mean (average) and standard deviation. The horizontal distance of the average from the start location can be used as a measure of the horizontal distance a person actually moved. This is sometimes called the **effective target distance**[51], D_e.

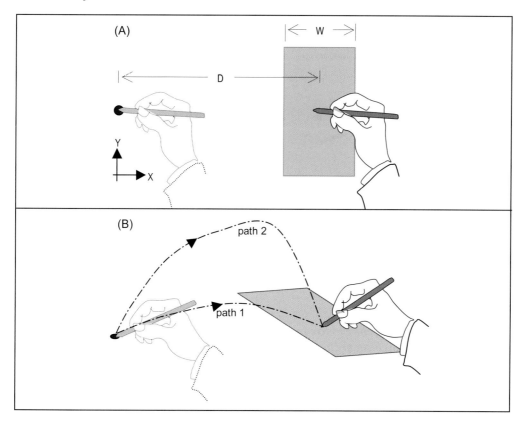

Figure 12.23: *(A) Aiming to contact a target of width W a distance D from the start location. (B) The stylus tip could follow many paths, such as paths 1 and 2.*

The standard deviation of the X-positions of the hit points has been used to define an **effective target width**, W_e. As stated in section 12.2.2, the usual requirement in studies of Fitts' law is to make fewer than 5% errors, which means that at least 95% of hits must land within the target. In a normal distribution, 95% of the distribution lies within ±1.96 standard deviations of the mean, as shown schematically in Figure 12.25. For this reason, 2 × 1.96 (= 3.92) SDs has been used as a measure of the effective width of the target[52]. In Figure 12.25, 3.92 SDs is wider than the target itself, and so the effective target width is greater than the width of the actual target (3.92 SDs > W) and the error rate will be greater than 5%.

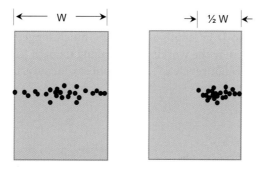

Figure 12.24: *Two possible distributions of contact points of movements aimed at a target (rectangle).*

If effective target distance (D_e) and effective target width (W_e) are used instead of actual distance (D) and width (W), the Fitts' law equation becomes

$$MT = a + b \log_2(2D_e/W_e).$$

(12.3)

This adjustment to Fitts' law can sometimes describe experimental results better than Fitts' original version. The improvement tends to be small[53], particularly for distance: replacing D with D_e tends to make very little difference, though perhaps it would be better to use the total distance moved (the length of the path taken by the working point, see Figure 12.23)[54] rather than D_e.

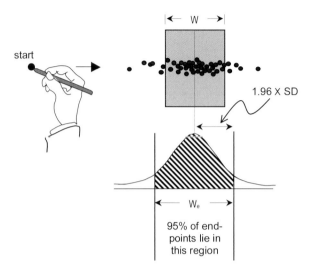

Figure 12.25: *Definition of the effective target width (W_e) as the region in which 95% of the endpoints of the aimed movement are located (see text for details).*

Of course, both the effective target distance and the effective size must be derived from performance; they are not properties of the task situation like the actual distance and width of the target. Thus, Fitts' law formulated in terms of D_e and W_e (equation 12.3) cannot be used to predict performance, and so loses its practical significance.

12.2.7 How well does Fitts' law apply in two dimensions?

In Fitts' law (equation 12.1) the distance (D) and target width (W) are measured along the same spatial dimension. Thus, D and W are one-dimensional descriptions of the task and they are clearly appropriate when the working point moves in one dimension, as in the single-joint aiming task shown in Figure 12.21 or the task shown in Figure 12.15. However, in many studies the working point is free to move in two or three dimensions (see Figures 12.16, 12.19, 12.20 and 12.23). In these circumstances it is not clear that D and W are appropriate descriptions of the task. In the last section, we saw that in Fitts' original task, the working point was free to move in three dimensions. As a result, the working point follows a path that is not equal to D in length and may be much longer (Figure 12.23). Whether the actual distance traveled by the working point along its path (the path length) would be more appropriate than D is not yet clear – we cannot say for sure, because this has not been studied in experiments.

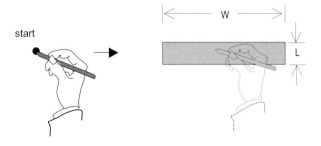

Figure 12.26: *Moving to contact a target that is wider than it is long (W > L).*

In Fitts' original task and many that have followed, the length of the target was large enough that it would not have been expected to influence performance; only the width was relevant. Outside the laboratory, this seldom applies: targets that you might wish to aim at, switches and buttons for example, are rarely much longer than they are wide. Figure 12.26 shows a target that is wider than it is long. It seems reasonable to suppose that MT would be affected more by the length than by the width when aiming at this target.

Figure 12.27 shows the results of a study that included targets that were wider than they were long (i.e., like that in Figure 12.26). The experiment involved a single distance (320 mm), three different target widths (10, 20 and 40 mm) and seven different lengths (1, 2, 5, 10, 20, 40 and 200 mm). Panel A shows the average movement times for the group of participants plotted against target length. At each of the three widths, MTs were shorter when the target was longer, and the MT was shorter for the wider targets. The figure shows that when the target was relatively long (20 mm or more), it had little or no effect on MT, regardless of the width of the target. At shorter lengths (less than 20 mm) there was an effect on MT: MT was greater when the target was shorter. This is the kind of effect we would expect – people take longer when moving to smaller targets.

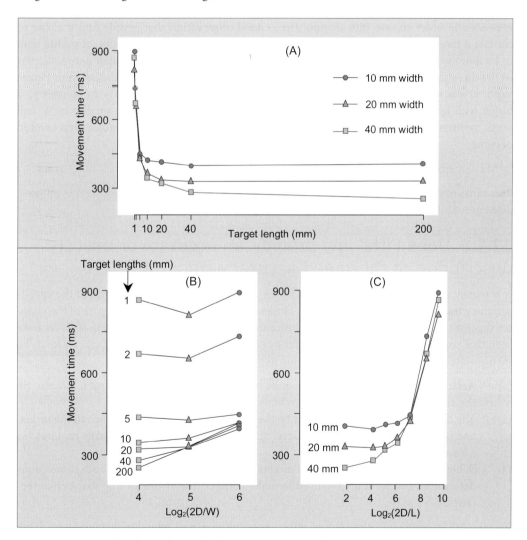

Figure 12.27: *Results of a study in which participants aimed to contact rectangular targets with a stylus tip. Both the width and the length of the target were varied (see text for details). Data from Hoffman and Sheikh (1994).*

Do the data shown in Figure 12.27 conform to Fitts' law? In order to answer this question, the data can be plotted against a Fitts-type index of difficulty computed either for target width or for target length. The ID for width is $\log_2(2D/W)$, the ID for length is $\log_2(2D/L)$. Panel B of

Figure 12.27 shows the data plotted as a function of the width ID. Panel C shows the data plotted as a function of the length ID. Interpretation of panels B and C requires a little thought and attention. The plot in panel B can be used to assess whether Fitts' law holds in its original form (where the ID is $\log_2[2D/W]$) irrespective of how long the target is. If the law holds, then the MT should increase linearly with changes in ID. This is roughly the case for values of L greater than 20 mm. For values less than 20 mm, MT does not increase linearly with Fitts' ID. The plot in panel C can be used to assess whether Fitts' law holds when the ID is modified to depend on target length rather than width (ID = $\log_2(2D/L)$). If the law holds in this modified form, then the MT should increase linearly with changes in the new ID. From the figure we can see that this appears to be true when the length is small (less than 10 mm, ID > 6) but is not true at the longer lengths (ID ≤ 6). These observations can be summarized as follows:

▸ When the length is relatively large, the data follow Fitts' law for width (ID = $\log_2[2D/W]$).
▸ When the length is relatively small, the data follow Fitts' law for length (ID = $\log_2[2D/L]$).

Results of this sort have suggested that Fitts' law can be extended to two-dimensional rectangular targets in a simple way: compute ID using whichever of W or L is the smaller[55]. The notation for this is *min[W, L]*, which just means 'the smaller of W and L'. A small modification is needed in order to take into account the general observation that people find it easier to contact a target that has a small length than one that has a small width: contact points tend to be more spread out along the direction of motion (towards the target) than perpendicular to the direction of motion (see, e.g., Figure 12.5). On the basis of the results shown in Figure 12.27, it was suggested[56] that a target with a width of one unit was as easy to contact as a target with length 0.75 units, and so Fitts' law should be applied with the smaller of W and 0.75L, written *min[W, 0.75L]*. Thus, Fitts' law for a two-dimensional rectangular target would become,

$$\text{MT} = a + b \, \text{Log}_2(2D/(min[W, 0.75L])). \tag{12.4}$$

This same basic idea also seems to work for targets with other simple shapes, such as ellipses, diamonds and triangles[57].

12.2.8 Does Fitts' law provide an accurate or useful description of the speed-accuracy trade-off?

It is widely accepted that Fitts' law provides an accurate and useful description of the speed-accuracy trade-off in aimed movement[58]. However, the data reviewed in this part of the chapter suggest that the description can be inaccurate and may not be particularly useful. We have seen that some of the inaccuracies arise for one or another of three reasons that can easily be incorporated into the law without changing its form; these are:

(1) Accuracy required by the task depends not only on the size of the target, but also on the size of the working point.
(2) The distance people move may not be the same as the horizontal distance to the target, and people may achieve a greater level of accuracy than the target actually requires (or a lower level).
(3) When aiming at two-dimensional targets, the size of the target along both dimensions determines the accuracy required to make contact with it (for simple shapes like rectangles).

To take (2) into account, the idea of effective target size and effective distance have been introduced; to take (3) into account, the dimension that places the greater constraint on accuracy can be used in the law. With these adjustments incorporated, Fitts' law becomes:

$$\text{MT} = a + b \, \text{Log}_2(2D_e/(min[W_e, 0.75 \, L_e])). \tag{12.5}$$

We can imagine incorporating working point size as well, in the manner described in 12.2.5. However, these adjustments cannot accommodate two widely reported failures of Fitts' law. First, Fitts' law proposes that distance (D) and size (W or L) do not have independent effects on performance and so can be combined together in a single ID. It has been repeatedly reported that distance and size have separable effects[59]. To accommodate these findings, equation 12.5 can be modified to read:

$$MT = a + b \, Log_2(D_e) - c \, Log_2(min[W_e, \textit{0.75} \, L_e]) \qquad\qquad \textbf{(12.6)}$$

where c is a positive constant. If b and c are the same, equation 12.6 reduces to equation 12.5. However, equation 12.6 is unable to account for the finding that Fitts' law does not hold at small values of the ID. It has been proposed either that the logarithmic relationship between MT and the task variables (W and D) does not hold at small values, or that the law holds but that small and large values should be treated separately[60]. The latter idea is illustrated in Figure 12.28. The figure reproduces the data points from the 9 cm distance in Figure 12.20B and divides them into two groups: data points for which the ID is greater than 3 (blue squares), and those for which it is 3 or less (green squares). The standard version of Fitts' law gives a good fit to both sets of points taken separately (straight lines), but not to all the points taken together.

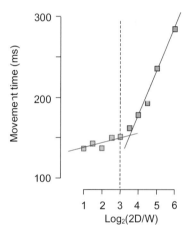

Figure 12.28: *Data from a study in which participants aimed at differently size targets 9cm distant (see text for details). Data from Gan and Hoffman (1988).*

While all these adjustments to Fitts' original description of the speed-accuracy trade-off can provide an accurate fit to the data from almost all the studies that have been published, the purpose of making these adjustments should be questioned. The adjustments are made in order to better describe the data; they do not provide a better understanding of the mechanisms responsible for the trade-off. An adjustment like that illustrated in Figure 12.28 is a particularly obvious case: there is no theoretical reason for dividing the data points into two sets; it is done simply to get the law to fit the data. Furthermore, the adjusted law (equation 12.6) seems to be of little practical significance, since it does not allow us to make quantitative predictions of what people will do. There are two reasons for this. First, effective target sizes and distances are measures of performance, and so cannot be used as a basis for predicting performance. Second, the parameters of the law (e.g., a, b, c in equation 12.6, and the value that divides low and high IDs as in Figure 12.28) depend on the individual and the task – different values are needed to describe the data from different people, different tasks and different effectors – and so cannot be used as a basis for quantitative prediction.

Another way of approaching the speed-accuracy trade-off is to attempt to determine what processes are responsible for the differences in the time taken when aiming at targets of different sizes and at different distances. Various models have been developed that attempt to do this; some of these are discussed in the next part of the chapter.

12.3 Effects of Accuracy Requirements on Movement Kinematics

12.3.1 Introduction

In the previous part of the chapter we saw that people take longer to complete an aimed movement when they have to be more accurate and when they need to move further. What has not yet been described is how execution differs between movements that require accuracy and those that do not. In this part of the chapter we will describe some of the effects that accuracy has on the execution of movement and consider what these tell us about the mechanisms responsible for the increase in movement time observed when accuracy requirements increase.

12.3.2 Accurate movements often show an extended deceleration phase

In Chapter 11 we saw that aimed movements that have little requirement for end-point accuracy are characterized by smooth, 'bell-shaped' speed profiles. When end-point accuracy is required, the movements tend to be executed a little differently. In particular, the speed profile tends to be more asymmetric, with a deceleration phase that is of longer duration than the acceleration phase[61]. In addition, although the acceleration phase is typically smooth, the deceleration phase often shows irregularities.

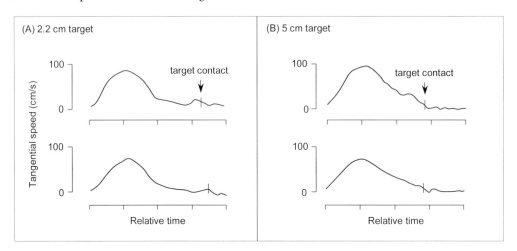

Figure 12.29: *Example speed profiles for movements aimed at two differently sized targets. Relative time was computed as [100× MT × (peak speed)]/(distance moved)]. Data from Soechting (1984), Fig. 2.*

Figure 12.29 shows some example speed profiles (of the index finger) from an individual participant in an experiment that used a task similar to that shown in Figure 12.8A. Participants reached out over a distance of about 35 cm to vertically oriented targets in front of them; the targets were circular depressions either 2.2 (panel A) or 5 cm (panel B) in diameter, into which participants had to move their index fingers to lightly depress a plate that actuated a switch (the short vertical lines in the figure indicate the moment the target plate was depressed). The figure shows that the deceleration phase of the movement to both targets was longer than the acceleration phase, and that this is more pronounced for the smaller target. For the participant shown, MTs were about 30% greater for reaches to the smaller target than to the larger one. The example speed profiles in Figure 12.29 are typical for those obtained when there is soft (low speed) contact or slow arrival at the target in both 1-D and 2-D aiming tasks. Hard (high speed) contacts are discussed later (12.3.4).

12.3.3 Both average and peak speed are lower when greater accuracy is required

Not only does the acceleration phase tend to be longer when greater spatial accuracy is required, but the average speed and the peak speed also tend to be lower. That the average speed is lower follows directly from the fact that MTs are longer. A longer MT does not necessarily imply that peak speed is lower, but it is often found to be lower (though the differences can be quite small or even nonexistent[62]). A typical set of results is shown in Figure 12.30. Panel A shows the experimental task: a 1-D aiming task in which participants made elbow flexion movements to targets of different angular sizes (3°, 6°, 9° and 12°) over difference angular distances (18°, 36° and 72°). Panel B shows the peak speeds plotted against target size for the three different distances. The plots clearly show that peak speed is lower when the target is smaller and so requires greater spatial accuracy. It is also clear that the greater the distance, the greater the peak speed (discussed in Chapter 2 and Chapter 11). Similar results have been obtained in 2-D aiming tasks[63].

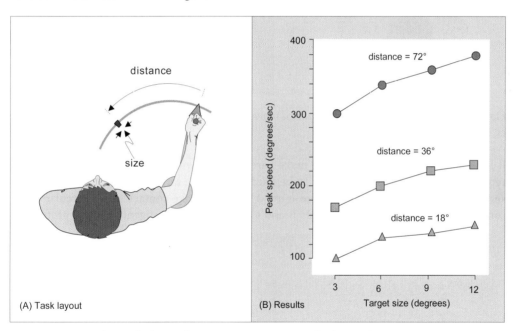

Figure 12.30: *Peak speed of aimed movements are greater for larger distances and targets. Data from Corcos, Gottlieb, Agarwal (1988), Fig. 3.*

12.3.4 People make harder contacts with larger targets

The tasks that have been considered so far in this part of the chapter involve either a soft contact with the target or no physical contact at all (e.g., Figure 12.30). An everyday example of a task without physical contact with a target is moving a cursor to an icon on a computer screen by manipulating a mouse. Many aimed movement tasks involve hard contacts: they are *hitting tasks*. Hammering a nail is an everyday example. Whether hitting moving or stationary targets, people have been found to make contact with the target close to the moment of peak speed, and so there is little or no deceleration phase[64]. We will return to hitting tasks later in the chapter; here we will discuss hard contacts in tasks that do not require hitting.

In many tasks that do not require that the target be hit, people hit it nonetheless. Figure 12.31 shows an example of this behavior. Two tangential speed profiles are plotted in panel B. One profile is from a task in which the participant was asked to reach out and grasp a disc between the index finger and thumb (a soft-contact task), the other is from a task in which the participants was instructed to use the index finger to touch the target (pointing task). In both tasks the participants were told to be as fast and accurate as possible. The profiles have been normalized in time so that the units are percent of the total time (both end at 100%), which obscures the fact that the reach-to-grasp movement took longer. The plots clearly show the following: (i) when reaching to grasping the target, the hand slowed down to a stop at the moment of contact, and there is a long deceleration phase. (ii) When pointing to the target, the index finger made a hard contact with the target, and there is only a very short deceleration phase (in the figure, contact occurred just after peak speed). The force of contact rapidly slowed the finger to a stop (not shown in the figure).

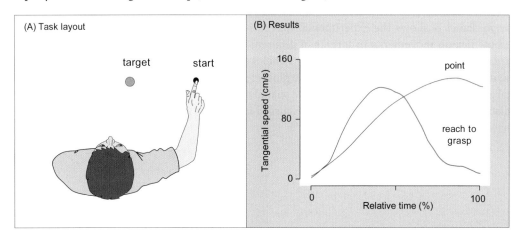

Figure 12.31: *Hard and soft contact in aimed movement (see text for details). Data from Marteniuk et al. (1987), Fig. 1.*

It has been found that when people make hard contacts with targets in the absence of any requirement to do so, contact tends to be harder when the target is larger[65]. An example is shown in Figure 12.32: the task was to move a stylus to make contact with a circular target some distance away (panel A). Panels B and C shows average tangential speed profiles for

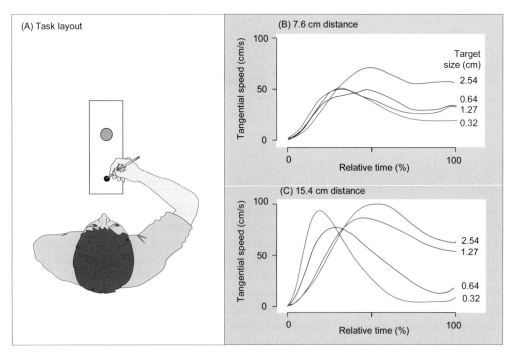

Figure 12.32: *Contact with smaller targets is softer (lower speed) than contact with larger targets. Data from MacKenzie et al. (1987).*

movements over a short distance (B) and a longer distance (C) to different sized targets (diameters = 0.32, 0.64, 1.27 and 2.54 cm). The profiles have been normalized in time, which obscures the fact that movements to smaller targets took longer. What the plots clearly show is that the speed at the end of the movement, when the stylus made contact with the target, was greater when the target was larger. This means that the larger targets were hit harder (at higher speed).

12.3.5 The speed profile may have multiple peaks in the deceleration phase

When end-point accuracy is required, the deceleration phase of the speed profile is not only extended in duration relative to the acceleration phase, but it may also be irregular, with one or more smaller peaks[66]. Some of the speed profiles in Figure 12.29 show evidence of this. Figure 12.33 shows an example from a task in which people were asked to move a short rod and insert the end of it into a hole 9.5 mm in diameter (the target). This speed profile has a main (highest) peak and at least two smaller, secondary peaks. This pattern is often interpreted as a main movement (the main peak) that brings the working point into the vicinity of the target, followed by submovements (the secondary peaks): these are smaller movements superimposed at the end of the main movement that bring the working point accurately to the target. This interpretation is supported by the finding that the greater the end-point accuracy required (the smaller the target), the greater the likelihood of secondary peaks[67]. These submovements are usually thought of as being made in response to visual feedback[68], in which case they represent discrete feedback-based corrections to the main movement. However, care needs to be taken when interpreting secondary peaks, as discussed next.

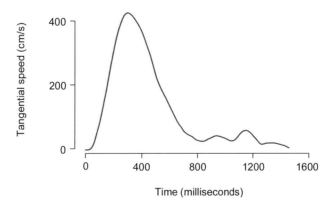

Figure 12.33: *Speed profile with multiple peaks in the deceleration phase. Data from Milner (1992), Fig. 4.*

12.3.6 Secondary peaks can be produced by various mechanisms

Although secondary peaks in the speed profile have often been interpreted as corrective submovements, they can arise due to factors other than feedback-based correction. For instance, since speed is the magnitude of the velocity and always positive, then movement back towards a target following an overshoot will appear as a secondary peak. Thus, if there is oscillatory movement about the target involving overshoot, then undershoot, and so on, a series of secondary peaks will be visible in the speed profile. Oscillations of this kind can arise due to the visco-elastic properties of the peripheral neuromechanics (see Chapters 1 and 2), and so have nothing to do with the execution of corrective submovements. Terminal oscillations do seem to occur, particularly in single-joint aiming movements[69], but they are not particularly associated with smaller targets or with slower movements (in fact, they are more likely to occur in rapid movements). However, this does not imply that secondary peaks in slow movements can be interpreted as feedback-based corrections, since there are at least two other ways in which secondary peaks can arise.

First, secondary peaks may be associated with the production of slow movement. It has been observed that when people are requested to produce a movement that is slower than the movement that they would prefer to produce, secondary peaks can arise[70]. An example of such a movement is shown in Figure 12.34: the task was to insert the end of a small rod (9.5 mm diameter) into a relatively large hole (50.5 mm diameter). The participant was instructed to make the movement slowly so that it would take about a second, about twice the MT of movements to these targets at a self-selected speed. It has been suggested that the slow approach to the target often observed in aiming tasks that require soft contact is affected by factors such as motor noise and tremor, which can produce secondary peaks[71].

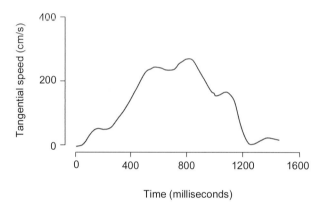

Figure 12.34: *Multiple peaks in the speed profile of an aimed movement executed more slowly than normal. Data from Milner (1992), Fig. 5.*

Second, secondary peaks can emerge when movements are curved due to mechanisms that have nothing to do with adjustments based on sensory information (see section 11.2.9). In many studies of the effects of end-point accuracy requirements on the performance of aimed movement, the path followed by the working point is strongly curved. This is particularly the case for studies in which the start point and target both lie on a table top and the working point is lifted off the table and brought down again onto the target (e.g., Figures 12.14 and 12.23). This source of secondary peaks does not necessarily predict that such peaks will be more likely when greater terminal accuracy is required, but its contribution to the peaks observed is unknown.

The fact that secondary peaks can arise due to factors other than corrections, means that the presence of secondary peaks (or other fluctuations in the deceleration phase of the speed profile) cannot be taken as evidence of corrections. It is also possible for corrections to take place without producing secondary peaks[72]. This means that if secondary peaks are absent, we cannot conclude that there were no corrections.

12.3.7 The two-component hypothesis

Based on results like those shown in Figure 12.13, Woodworth put forward a simple account of aimed movement control that will be referred to as the **two-component hypothesis**. The proposal is simply that aimed movements involve two phases (or components): an initial phase that moves the working point into the vicinity of the target, and a homing-in phase that brings the working point into contact with the target. Woodworth proposed that the initial phase involved a net force impulse that propels the working point towards the target and is entirely under central control: it is produced by a program and is not affected by feedback. The second phase involves visual feedback control; visual information about the relative position of the working point and the target is used to make corrective adjustments to the movement so that the target is contacted.

Woodworth's two-component hypothesis has formed the basis for many subsequent and more formal models of aimed movement production and control[73]. These models use two basic mechanisms to account for why movements take longer when the target is smaller:

(1)   Movements to smaller targets involve more corrective submovements; each submovement adds to the time taken to complete the movement (and so lowers the average speed of the whole act).

(2)   Movements to smaller targets are executed in such a way that they take longer (the average speed is lower), irrespective of whether additional submovements occur or not.

The difference between the type of speed profiles produced by these two mechanisms is illustrated in Figure 12.35.

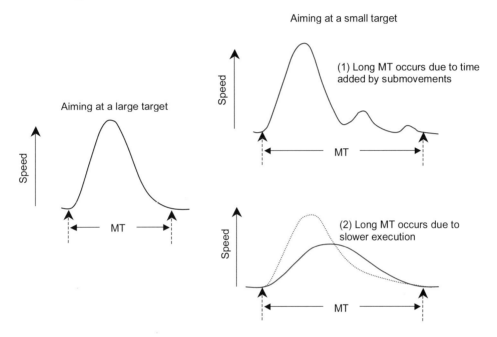

Figure 12.35: *Two ways in which longer MTs to small targets might be produced (illustrative). When aiming at large targets (left), a bell-shaped speed profile is produced without evidence of submovements. Longer MTs can be produced either as a result of time added by submovements (top right) or to slower execution (bottom right). Slower execution can involve increased asymmetry of the speed profile (dotted line) or not (solid).*

There are two types of model based on these mechanisms. One type is based on the first mechanism, and proposes that movement to a target is composed of a sequence of submovements, each being a feedback-based correction to the previous one[74]. Models of this type are called **iterative correction models**. It has been shown that two of these models lead directly to a Fitts' law type relationship between MT and target width[75]. However, these models have been found to be unable to produce realistic kinematic characteristics[76]. They also fail to account for results showing that Fitts' law holds regardless of whether visual feedback is available or not[77]. Consequently, models of this type are no longer considered to provide viable accounts of aimed movement control.

The other type of model incorporates both mechanisms. One influential model of this kind is the **optimized submovement model**[78]. It proposes that aimed movements consist of one or more submovements; each submovement is governed by a program that runs unaffected by sensory feedback. Movements that require little terminal accuracy will typically consist of only one submovement, termed the *primary submovement*. Movements that require terminal accuracy (small targets) will typically involve one or more *secondary submovements* that correct errors in the primary submovement. It differs from iterative correction models by proposing that the duration and hence the speed of each submovement is pre-planned so as to achieve an optimal trade-off between speed and accuracy. Submovements with short MTs (high average speeds) are assumed to be intrinsically less accurate than slower ones (see section 12.1.12). Achieving a moderate level of accuracy might be done either by means of a relatively slow primary submovement, or by a relatively fast primary submovement followed by a corrective secondary submovement. The model supposes that the nervous system chooses the option that achieves the required accuracy in the least time: if the duration of the slow primary submovement is less than that of the sequence of a fast primary submovement followed by a correction, then the slow primary submovement option would be chosen.

The optimized submovement model is problematic because it supposes that execution of the submovements is not influenced by sensory information, so corrections can only be made by executing secondary submovements. It follows that corrections should be observable as secondary peaks in the speed profile, as shown in Figure 12.35 (top right). This raises two problems. First, as discussed in section 12.3.6, it is difficult, if not impossible, to determine whether a secondary peak represents a corrective submovement or not. Second, there is evidence to suggest that on-going movements can be adjusted in a graded, continuous fashion, contrary to the model[79].

Although there is substantial evidence that people do make corrective submovements, models of movement control that restrict the role of sensory information obtained during movement execution to the preparation and initiation of such submovements are no longer considered to be adequate.

12.3.8 The initial phase of an aimed movement is not ballistic

Models based on the two-component hypothesis derive from the traditional conception of a motor program as a set of motor commands that are completely pre-established prior to moving. If the commands are pre-established, then corrections for any errors cannot be generated until sufficient time has elapsed for the error to be detected, for it to be transformed into commands for a corrective submovement, and for these commands to be transmitted to the muscles. Woodworth's data (Figure 12.13) and other early estimates[80] indicated that the time required for corrections based on visual information is greater than 200 milliseconds. These estimates are consistent with the two-component hypothesis, since they imply that no correction can be made until the movement is underway.

More recent estimates indicate that an on-going aimed movement can be influenced by visual information in under 150 milliseconds[81]; estimates from different experiments vary, the shortest being about 100 milliseconds[82] (more details are provided in the next section). These latencies, together with data showing that corrective adjustments can be smoothly integrated into an ongoing movement (see section 12.3.6), have led to the rejection of models that involve sequences of submovements, but they do not contradict the basic idea of the two-component hypothesis[83]. However, all versions of the two-component hypothesis propose that the initial phase of an aimed movement (the primary submovement) is pre-programmed and cannot be influenced by visual information for at least 100 milliseconds after the movement starts. This is consistent with the outdated view of a motor program as a pre-established set of commands, but is not wholly consistent with the operation of the type of motor command generation process described in Chapter 11. This process involves a trajectory generator (Figure 11.34) that continuously transforms input representations of the target location and the working point location into signals that specify motions of the effector system that will take the working point to the target. The target and working point representations derive, in part, from sensory information (see Figure 11.33). Thus, if the target location changes or the location of the working point changes, sensory information about these changes can alter the input representations of the trajectory generator and hence its output.

Changes to the input representations of the trajectory generator can, in principle, occur at any time. In particular, a change to an input representation could occur at any time before the movement has started. If such a change occurred a short time in advance, then we might expect to see an adjustment to the movement trajectory within 100 ms of movement onset.

In fact, amendments within 100 ms of movement onset have been observed in experiments in which target position was changed just prior to the start of the movement, as described in Chapter 11 (Figure 11.7 presents some results from these experiments). Thus, the notion of an initial phase of aimed movement that is the result of an immutable, pre-computed program that cannot be influenced by sensory information for at least 100 milliseconds does not fit the experimental data. This presents some difficulties for the two-component hypothesis, as there does not seem to be an empirical basis for distinguishing between an initial ballistic component and a subsequent component that is controlled by sensory information. There does, however, appear to be a distinction between automatic, unconscious amendments to an on-going movement and intentional corrective submovements that we are aware of intending to make. Automatic trajectory amendments are discussed in the next section.

12.3.9 Short-latency, unconscious adjustments are made in response to visual perturbations

Early estimates of how long it takes for visual information to affect the execution of an on-going movement were based on how long a movement needed to last before visual information led to a detectable effect on accuracy. For example, the data of Woodworth (Figure 12.13) suggest that vision was having an influence when participants were making movements at a rate of less than about 150 to 160 movements a minute (when the two sets of data begin to diverge), which corresponds to an MT to the target of about 200 milliseconds[84]. This method provides an estimate of the time taken for any visually based adjustments to influence movement accuracy; for the adjustments to have any effect on accuracy, they must have been at least partially completed. Thus, the method does not provide an estimate of the *latency* of corrective adjustments. The latency is the time between the visual stimulus that evokes the adjustment and the onset of the adjustment, i.e., before the adjustment has been executed.

The latency of visually based adjustments can be estimated by making visual perturbations and measuring performance to determine when execution begins to change in response to these perturbations. The perturbations are usually sudden changes in the location of the target or in the visual location of the working point. Note that in the case of a change in target location, any corrective response is not, strictly speaking, a feedback-based correction, since information about the person's behavioral output is not being fed back. The latency estimates that have been obtained from perturbation studies lie in a range from about 100 ms to about 300 ms. These differences occur due to a number of different factors, including the way in which the onset of the corrective response is measured, the type of perturbation and the kind of correction that is made. For example, in a series of studies of reaching to grasp a target object, perturbations were made to object location[85] and to object size[86]. To grasp the target, participants needed to make corrective adjustments to the direction of the reaching movement in response to the position perturbations, and adjustments to the grasp aperture formed by the fingers and thumb in response to size perturbations, as shown in Figure 12.36. The latency of adjustments to position changes was about 100 ms; the latency of adjustments to size changes was over 300 ms. This large difference in latency suggests that the difference is due to the operation of different central mechanisms with different processing times[87]. It has also been found that corrections to perturbations that require changing movement direction (e.g., Figure 12.36A) have a shorter latency (by about 20 to 30 milliseconds) than corrections to perturbations that require adjustments to movement amplitude[88].

The short latency of corrective adjustments to the direction and amplitude of aimed movements suggests that they are not mediated by conscious intentions. This has been demonstrated experimentally by arranging for the perturbation to occur while the eyes made a saccade[89]. The basic idea is shown in panel A of Figure 12.37. The participant directs their gaze at the fixation point and then one of the targets is illuminated, indicating that the person should move their finger to it. The task is to move as quickly as possible to the target as soon as it appears. The person's response starts with a saccade to the target followed by the arm movement (for larger-amplitude saccades, the hand starts to move before the saccade is

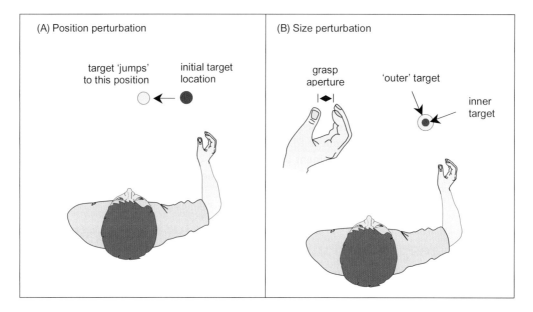

Figure 12.36: *Perturbations to object size and position during a reach-to-grasp task. (A) Target at the initial location is illuminated at the start of a trial. During the movement, the illumination of the initial target is turned off and a target at a new position is illuminated (target appears to jump instantaneously between the two locations). (B) Target is composed of an inner and outer part that can be separately illuminated, so that it can appear small (inner) or larger (outer). Shifting illumination from the inner to the outer target produces an instantaneous change in target size.*

complete). On some trials, the initially illuminated target is turned off during the saccade and a different target is illuminated. In the experiments, participants were unaware that the target position had been changed, but they nevertheless made corrections to their arm movements. Panel B of Figure 12.37 shows example finger paths from an unperturbed trial to target 2, a trail where the target switched from 2 to 1 during the saccade, and a trial where it switched from 2 to 3. The participants were not only unaware of the target switch, but also of the fact that they had corrected their movements.

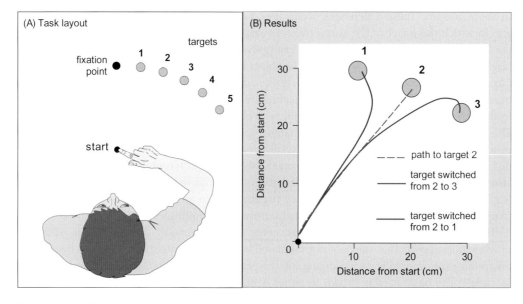

Figure 12.37: *Experiment demonstrating rapid, unconscious adjustment to aimed movement in response to changes in target position made during saccades. (A) Based on Prablanc and Martin (1992), Fig.1. (B) Data from Prablanc and Martin (1992).*

Subsequent experiments have shown that the unconscious, short-latency corrective adjustments are mediated by circuits in the posterior parietal cortex[90]. This finding is consistent with the idea that visual information about target position is transmitted to the trajectory generator along the dorsal stream of visual processing (see section 4.2.11), the stream that is associated with visuomotor control (see sections 4.2.12 and 4.2.13).

12.4 Aiming to Reach a Particular Place at a Particular Time

12.4.1 Introduction

Some tasks require that you be at a particular place at a particular time – catching a bus, for example. To catch a bus you must be at the bus stop (a particular place) when the bus arrives (a particular time). You can think of the bus stop as a spatial target and the time of the bus's arrival as a temporal target. The temporal target is not very demanding: you have to get to the stop before the bus leaves; if you arrive well in advance of the bus you just have to wait. Other tasks are different and demand preeise and accurate timing. Hitting moving targets are the best examples of such tasks: accurate timing is essential when playing strokes in racket sports like tennis and squash, as well as in games such as baseball. In this part of the chapter we will consider tasks that require temporal accuracy. We will begin with further discussion of the *time-matching task* (see section 12.1.10).

12.4.2 In time-matching tasks you try to move to a specified place in a specified time

The time-matching aiming task requires a person to move a working point from a start location to a target location in a pre-specified time, the *required MT*. The task may require that the working point stop at the target location (e.g., Figure 12.14) or it may not; here we will concentrate on tasks that do not require stopping at the target. Since there is no requirement to stop at the target, people typically just keep on moving (they move through or hit the target). This means that the working point definitely reaches the target. The majority of studies of this kind have used one-dimensional aiming tasks that either involve movement about a single joint, like the task in Figure 12.30A, or involve moving a slider along a track (see Figure 12.2), but with a single line defining the target (e.g., Figure 12.39A).

The temporal goal in such a task is that the target location be reached after the pre-specified time has elapsed. Figure 12.38 shows the time line of events in a time-matching task and defines the error. The goal is to make the duration of the movement (actual MT) equal to the required MT. In the figure, the actual MT is less than the required MT and so there is a **time-matching error**, defined as follows:

Time-matching error = [actual MT] – [required MT]

Thus, when the actual MT is less than the required MT, the working point arrived at the target location too early, and the time-matching error is negative. If the actual MT is greater than the required MT, the working point arrived too late, and the time-matching error is positive.

In a typical experiment, participants are first trained to make movements with the required MTs. Once they have learned to do this (see section 12.1.10), they perform a series of trials without feedback concerning their temporal accuracy, and the time-matching errors are measured over the series. The measured errors are usually summarized using the mean and the standard deviation. The mean time-matching error is the **constant time-matching**

error (abbreviated $C_{TM}E$); the standard deviation of the temporal errors is the **variable time-matching error** ($V_{TM}E$). The $C_{TM}E$ tells us whether or not there was a bias to reach the target earlier or later than required (temporal bias). The $V_{TM}E$ tells us about the spread of the matching errors (temporal precision).

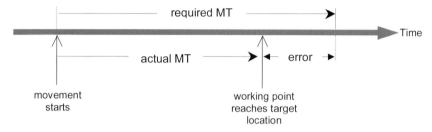

Figure 12.38: *Time line for the time-matching task; see text for details*

12.4.3 Variable time-matching errors are smaller for briefer, faster movements

A consistent finding in time-matching tasks is that the variable time-matching error ($V_{TM}E$) depends on the required MT: the longer the required MT, the greater the error. A typical set of results is shown in Figure 12.39. Panel A shows the type of task used: participants moved a slider along a track, with the goal of making the duration of the movement from the start location to the target line equal to the required MT. The participants made movements over two different distances (5 and 15 cm) and the required MTs were 100, 500 and 1000 milliseconds. Panel B shows the variable errors for the two distances plotted against the required MT: for both distances, $V_{TM}E$ increases in approximate proportion[91] to required MT. The relationship is such that the variable error is about 10% of the required MT (in Figure 12.39, the error lies between 8.6% and 14.9% of the required MT). These results clearly show that people are able to produce shorter MTs much more consistently than longer MTs, a key finding that has been found in many other studies[92] and will be returned to later.

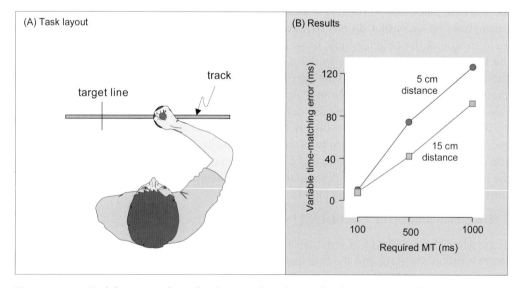

Figure 12.39: *Task layout and results showing the relationship between variable time-matching error and required MT. Data are averages of a group of participants, from Newell* et al. *(1979).*

The results in Figure 12.39(B) also show that the error is larger when the distance is smaller, which is consistent with the error being inversely proportional to the average speed of the movement. The average speed is approximately equal to distance covered divided by the required MT, so an inverse proportional relationship would mean that $V_{TM}E \propto$ [required MT]/ distance. If this relationship holds, then for a given distance, $V_{TM}E$ should increase in proportion to the required MT, which is approximately true for both distances in Figure 12.39B. In addition, the slope of the relationship should be larger when the distance is smaller, which is also true of the data shown in the figure. Thus, the pattern of data is suggestive of an inverse proportional relationship between $V_{TM}E$ and average speed. To test whether the relationship holds, we can apply similar logic to that applied by Paul Fitts to the data shown in Figure 12.17B, and plot the data in Figure 12.39B against [required MT]/D: if all the data points fall on the same straight line, then the relationship holds. Figure 12.40 plots the data in this way, and clearly shows that the data points do not all lie on the same straight line.

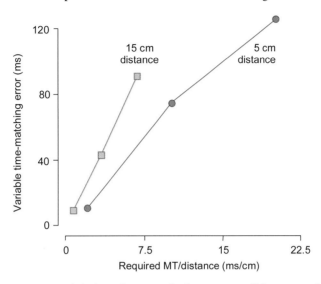

Figure 12.40: *Data in Figure 12.39(B) plotted against the 'average speed' (= required MT/distance).*

What relationship between error, required MT and distance can account for the pattern shown in Figures 12.39B and 12.40? An answer is suggested by the results of a more extensive experiment[93] that involved many more required MTs and distances than that shown in Figure 12.39. The task was a single-joint aiming task like that shown in Figure 12.30(A): participants made elbow flexion movements to a target line with required MTs of 100, 125, 150 and 400 ms. Angular distances from the start position to the target line were 1°, 2°, 3.5°, 5° and 10° for required MTs of 100 and 125 ms; 1°, 2°, 5°, 10°, 20° and 50° for required MTs of 150 ms; and 2°, 5°, 10°, 50° and 100° for required MTs of 400 ms. These conditions yielded average angular speeds from about 2.5°/second to about 333°/second. The variable time-matching errors were found to follow the pattern shown in Figure 12.41.

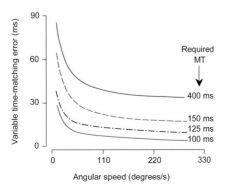

Figure 12.41: *Pattern of variable time-matching error as a function of angular speed for four different required MTs (illustrative, based on data reported by Newell* et al., *1993).*

The figure clearly shows two effects. (1) For each required MT, the variable error is smaller at higher speeds (the shape of the curve is consistent with an inverse proportional relationship between speed and error). (2) The curves for different required MTs are ordered such that the errors are always greater when the required MT is larger (consistent with a proportional relationship between MT and error). Taken together, these two effects suggest that the variable error is proportional to MT as well as being inversely proportional to the average speed; i.e., $V_{TM}E \propto$ required MT and $V_{TM}E \propto$ [required MT]/distance. If the constants of proportionality are denoted 'b' and 'c', then the data suggest a relationship of the following form:

$$V_{TM}E = a + MT_{req}(b + c/D) \tag{12.7}$$

where a, b and c are constants and MT_{req} is the required MT.

If the relationship described by equation 12.7 holds, then plotting the data in Figure 12.39B against $MT_{req}(b + c/D)$, with suitable chosen values for b and c, should result in all the data points falling on the same straight line. Figure 12.42 shows such a plot (with b = 1 and c = 4). The data points lie close to the same straight line, confirming the relationship described by equation 12.7.

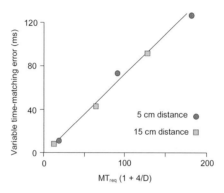

Figure 12.42: *Variable time-matching error data from Figure 12.39 plotted against a function of the required MT (MT$_{req}$, in seconds) and distance (D, in meters) see text for explanation.*

12.4.4 Constant time-matching errors show little variation over changes in MT and speed

In contrast with variable errors, constant time-matching errors ($C_{TM}E$) have been found to be relatively small (except at very low speeds) and to vary much less with changes in the required MT and movement speed[94]. Most studies have found that the constant error is slightly positive (bias to arrive late) and remains fairly constant over changes in the speed and brevity of movement. For example, in one study[95] it was found that the constant error was positive and less than 10 milliseconds for elbow flexion movements made at speeds greater than about 20°/s. The error was unaffected by speed but it was found that shorter MTs were associated with smaller errors: for example, for an MT of 400 ms, the constant error was about 10 ms, but was only about 2 ms for an MT of 100 ms.

12.4.5 If you want to be temporally accurate, be quick

The results described so far in this part of the chapter show that when people attempt to make movements of a particular duration (required MT), they are able to do it more reliably and consistently when the MT is short and when the speed is high. People are able to achieve greater temporal precision when they make brief, fast movements. The results suggest, therefore, a strategy for achieving temporal accuracy: when greater temporal accuracy is needed, make a briefer and faster movement. Such a strategy does not represent a speed-accuracy trade-off, since speed is not being exchanged for accuracy.

Results obtained using the time-matching task cannot tell us whether people adopt the strategy just described, since the task does not impose different temporal accuracy requirements. In order to determine whether people adopt the strategy or not, we need to use a task that does impose requirements for temporal accuracy. Using such a task, we can then change the accuracy requirements and observe how people respond to these changes. This is the basic method used in studies of the spatial speed-accuracy trade-off discussed previously in this chapter: these studies involved changing the spatial accuracy requirements of the task. Such changes are easy to make – simply use targets of different sizes (greater accuracy is needed to contact a smaller target). How can changes in temporal accuracy requirements be made? To do this, we need a task that requires temporal accuracy. Tasks that involve the interception of a moving target require temporal accuracy, as discussed next.

12.4.6 Intercepting a moving target requires temporal accuracy

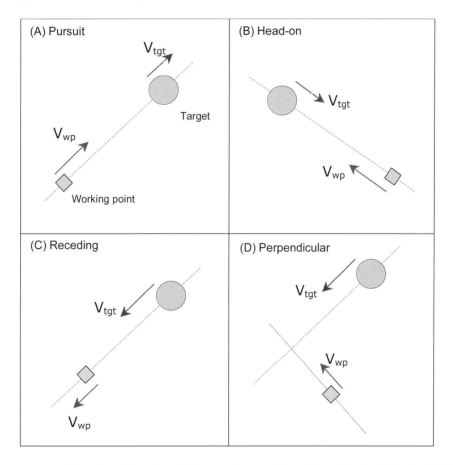

Figure 12.43: *Four two-dimensional interception configurations. Dashed line is the line of approach; V_{wp} is the working point's velocity; V_{tgt} is the target's velocity (arrows represent the velocity vectors). (A) Pursuit: contact requires that $V_{wp} > V_{tgt}$. (B) Head on: velocities in opposite directions. (C) Receding: contact requires $V_{wp} < V_{tgt}$. (D) Perpendicular: paths of target and working point at 90°.*

Tasks in which the goal is to make contact with a moving target – interception tasks – require temporal accuracy. Catching and hitting balls in sports like baseball, tennis and squash are examples. Making contact requires that the working point and the target be at the same place at the same time. Interceptive tasks fall into two basic categories:

(1)   **capture tasks:** the goal is not merely to make contact with the target but to capture it as well. This usually involves bringing the moving object to rest, and so the momentum of the moving object is absorbed. Catching a ball is an example.

(2)   **hitting tasks:** the goal is to make contact with the moving target and to transfer momentum from the working point (e.g., racket head or bat) to the target.

In both types of tasks, the working point and the target must approach one another in order for contact to occur. Figure 12.43 illustrates four basic approach configurations (combinations of these configurations are possible[96]). Capture of a moving target might involve any of these configurations. Hitting, however, cannot be effected in the receding configuration (C): you don't hit the target, the target hits you. Hitting is usually effected in either the head-on configuration (B) or the perpendicular configuration (D).

In what follows, we will focus exclusively on hitting tasks. The perpendicular configuration for hitting allows us to define the temporal accuracy needed for successful interception independently of the strategy adopted by the performer. In the perpendicular configuration, the point at which interception is made – the **interception point** – is at the junction of the paths of the target and the working point. This point is the same regardless of how fast the target or the working point move, which is not true in any of the other configurations. In order to intercept the target in the perpendicular configuration, the working point must arrive at the interception point at the same time as the target. How can the temporal accuracy be defined for the perpendicular configuration? This is discussed next.

12.4.7 Temporal accuracy is defined by the time window

In the perpendicular approach configuration, it is possible for the working point to contact the target only for a specific period of time. This short period of time can be precisely defined. Panel A of Figure 12.44 shows an interceptive task that has a perpendicular approach configuration. The person moves a bat (the working point) along a track that is perpendicular to the track along which the target moves. Both the target and the bat move in the horizontal plane. The goal of the task is to strike the target with the bat. Panel B defines the task variables. The target is rectangular, with length L, and moves with a constant speed, V. The bat is also rectangular, with width W, and starts a distance D from the target track.

The bat can make contact with the target only when the target is in line with the path of the bat. When the target moves, the target is in line for a period of time that we will refer to as the task's **time window**[97]. Successful contact with the moving target requires that the bat reaches the path of the target within the boundaries of this window; in a similar way, successful contact with a stationary target requires that the working point lands within the spatial boundaries of the target. Thus, the time window can be considered to be a measure of the moving target's temporal size (how big it is in time): a larger time window means that the target is temporally bigger and requires less temporal accuracy.

The boundaries of the time window are defined by the earliest and latest moments when it is possible for the bat to strike the target. These moments are shown in Figure 12.45. The earliest time at which the target could be hit is when the leading edge of the target reaches the location at which it can just be touched by the right edge of the bat (panel A). If the bat arrives any earlier, the target will be missed. The latest time at which the target could be hit is when the trailing edge of the target reaches the location at which it can just be touched by the left edge of the bat (panel B). If it the bat arrives any later, the target will be missed. The time taken for the target to travel between the locations shown in panels A and B of Figure 12.45 is the time window. Since the distance traveled is (L + W) and the target moves at a speed V, the time taken to travel between them is (L + W)/V, or in words:

Time window = [target length + bat width]/(target speed)   **(12.8)**

The time window quantifies the temporal accuracy demanded of a hitting task executed in the perpendicular configuration.

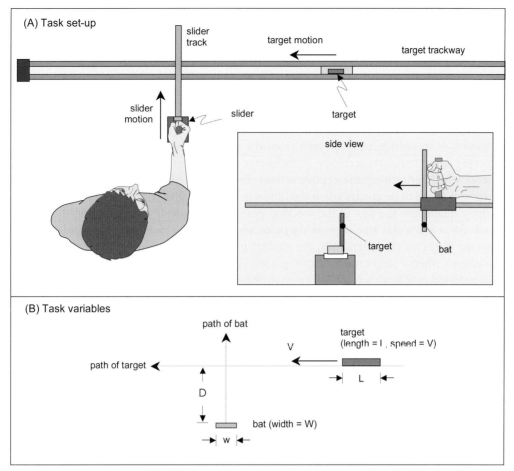

Figure 12.44: *A hitting task with a perpendicular approach configuration. (A) Task layout in plan view and side view. The target passes beneath the slider track and the bat extends below the track so that it is able to contact the target. (B) Definition of task variables.*

In order to clearly define a time window, the person must be constrained: they must be able to move the working point (bat) only along a fixed, straight path. If they are free to move along any path they choose, then it is not possible to precisely define a time window. This is because the time window depends on the relative velocity of the working point and target along the direction of target motion. In the perpendicular configuration, the working point does not move in the direction of target motion, only perpendicular to it, and so the relative velocity we are interested in is just the velocity of the target. If you can move in any way you choose, then you can move the working point in the same direction as the target. For example, if the

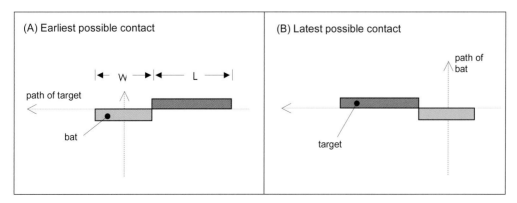

Figure 12.45: *Earliest and latest moments when contact between bat and target is possible in the task shown in Figure 12.44.*

target were moving slowly enough, you would be able to move the working point – your hand perhaps – along with it, so that the target and your hand move together at the same speed in the same direction. In this case, the relative velocity of hand and target would be zero. In these circumstances, the concept of the time window is not applicable.

12.4.8 Is people's performance of interceptions influenced by the time window?

As discussed in section 12.4.5, results from the time-matching task suggest a strategy for achieving better temporal accuracy: make briefer and faster movements. If people adopt this strategy when performing interceptive actions, then we would expect MT to be shorter and movement speed to be greater when the time window is smaller. The time window is defined by three quantities: the size of the working point, the length of the target and the target's speed. For a particular size of working point and target, the time window will be shorter when the target moves faster. Thus, the strategy predicts that people will make briefer, faster movements when a target moves more quickly. A number of studies of interceptive actions have reported exactly this result[98]. However, these studies often do not provide strong support for use of the strategy, for two reasons. First, it is not clear that the speed effect is of the type the strategy predicts (we return to this in the next section). Second, the design of the studies confounded the speed of the targets with the time for which they were seen.

A faster target takes less time than a slow target to move between two points. Thus, if the start point and the interception point are fixed, then faster targets will take less time to move between them. This occurs in ball sports, where the distance that the ball covers is roughly the same each time, but the ball can move at different speeds. For example, in baseball, the pitcher and batter stand in roughly prescribed locations so that the distance between them is always roughly the same (Figure 12.46), so a faster ball takes less time to reach the batter: a fastball thrown at 40 m/s takes about 430 milliseconds, whereas a knuckleball thrown at 30 m/s takes about 570 milliseconds. This means that the batter has less time to view the moving ball and execute the swing when the pitcher throws a faster ball. Thus, we might expect people to swing the bat faster (shorter swing times) when the pitched ball moves faster, and there is evidence that batters behave in this way[99].

In many experimental studies of interception, targets moved at different speeds over the same distance, so the faster-moving targets were seen for shorter periods of time[100]. In these studies, shorter MTs to intercept the faster targets could be either an effect of the speed or an effect of the shorter viewing time. It is known that people make briefer, faster interceptive movements when the viewing time is shorter, irrespective of the speed of the target[101]. Thus, before we can conclude that people make briefer, faster movements when the time window is narrower, we need to exclude the possibility that they are simply making briefer movements because the viewing time is shorter.

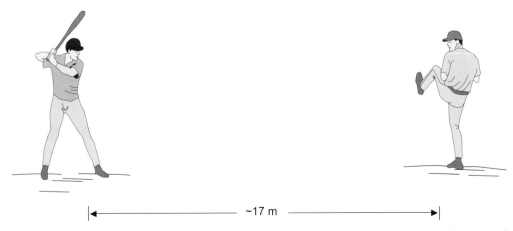

|←——————————— ~17 m ———————————→|

Figure 12.46: *In a baseball game, the pitcher throws the ball at the batter from a distance of about 17 meters.*

12.4.9 When the time window is narrower, people make briefer movements

In order to test the hypothesis that people make briefer, faster movements when greater temporal accuracy is required (smaller time window), we need an experiment that has the following three features:

(1)   The time window can be defined independently of how the participant executes their movement. Such a task is shown in Figure 12.44.

(2)   The time window can be changed by altering the values of the quantities that define it: the speed and length of the target, and the bat width (equation 12.8).

(3)   Changes in the time window are not confounded with changes in other factors that could influence the brevity and speed of movement. For example, changes in target speed should not be confounded with changes in target viewing time (see previous section).

Figure 12.47 shows the results of an experiment with these three features. The task (panel A) was the same as that shown in Figure 12.44. Different time windows were produced by using four different target lengths (4, 7.5, 11 and 14 cm)[102] and four different speeds (100, 142, 180 and 220 cm/s); the bat width (0.5 cm) was not changed, and the distance from the start location to the interception point was 22 cm (as indicated in the figure). The time taken for the target to move from the position it was first seen to the interception point was the same (1.6 secs) regardless of target speed[103].

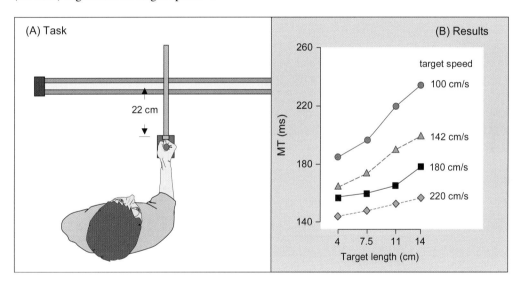

Figure 12.47: *Task layout and results of an experiment that examined the effect of target speed and target length on performance of movements made to intercept a moving object. Data from Tresilian and Houseman (2005).*

Panel B of Figure 12.47 shows the average MTs from the group of participants for all sixteen target distance/target length combinations. MT is here defined to be the time between the start of the movement and the moment the bat made contact with the target (or in the case of a miss, with the interception point). The figure shows two obvious effects:

(1)   An effect of target length: MT was greater when the target was longer.

(2)   An effect of target speed: MT was greater when the target moved more slowly.

Both these effects are what would be expected if MT varied in direct proportion to the time window: MT ∝ [target length + bat width]/(target speed). If this proportional relationship holds, then for a particular speed and bat width, MT should increase in direct proportion to increases in target length: the figure shows that MT does increase in approximate proportion to target length. The slope of the relationship should also be steeper for slower-moving targets. This is also the case for the results shown in the figure: the increase in MT with target length is greater at the slower target speeds.

The results shown in Figure 12.47 confirm the expectation that when the time window is smaller, people make briefer movements. They also suggest that MT varies in direct proportion to the time window. This possibility can be evaluated more directly by plotting the MTs against the time window: if a directly proportional relationship holds, then all the data points should fall on the same straight line (see sections 12.2.2 and 12.4.3). Panel A of Figure 12.48 shows the MT data from Figure 12.47 plotted against the time window. Panel B shows the data from a second experiment that was identical to the one described except that the width of the bat was changed (bat widths = 4, 7.5, 11 and 14 cm)[104] and the target always stayed the same (0.5 cm long). The graphs in both panels are similar: data points do not all fall on the same straight line, but on separate straight lines, one for each speed, though in each graph the slopes of the lines are similar. This pattern indicates that MT is proportional to the time window (as data points fall on straight lines with similar slopes) and also inversely proportional to the speed, i.e., $MT \propto (L + W)/V$ and $MT \propto 1/V$ (V is speed, L is length and W is width). Thus, the relationship between MT and the task variables (L, W and V) is described by the following equation:

$$MT = a + b(L + W)/V + c/V \tag{12.9}$$

where a, b and c are constant parameters. This relationship means that if the data shown in Figure 12.48 are plotted against $(b(L + W)/V + c/V)$ with suitably chosen values for b and c, then all the points should fall on the same straight line (cf. Figure 12.18): Figure 12.49 confirms this expectation for the data shown in Figure 12.48B.

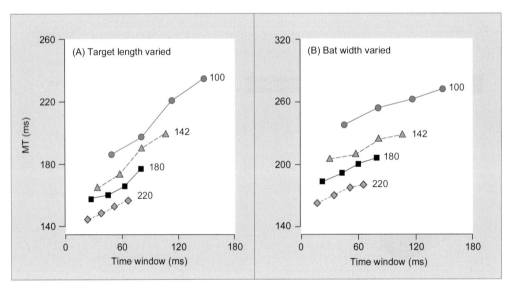

Figure 12.48: *MT data plotted against the time window. (A) Data from Tresilian and House-man (2005). (B) Data from an experiment identical to that reported in Tresilian and Houseman (2005) except that target length was held constant and bat width varied (Tresilian, Plooy, 2006).*

Of course, there is a limit to how fast a person can move, so someone cannot continue to move more and more quickly as the time window gets smaller and smaller. Similarly, as the time window gets larger and larger, we would not expect a person to move more and more slowly indefinitely. These limits were evidently not reached in the experiments described in this section.

The results discussed in this section show that people respond to requirements for greater temporal accuracy (a smaller time window) by making briefer movements. Given that the distance moved was not changed, briefer movements were faster. In fact, it was found that participants hit the target close to the moment of peak speed, and peak speed was greater, when the MT was shorter[105]. This meant that they hit the smaller, faster targets harder than the larger slower ones. These findings raise two further questions:

(1)   Do people actually achieve better temporal accuracy in interceptive tasks by moving faster? This question is addressed in the next section.

(2)   Why do people not always move as fast as they can, so as to achieve the best temporal accuracy regardless of the time window?

The answer to the second question probably has to do with the physical effort involved in moving as fast as possible. Faster movements require more effort, and as described in chapters 8 and 11, people move in such a way that effort is kept as low as possible. Thus, if the required temporal accuracy does not require people to move as fast as possible, then they move more slowly and so expend less effort. It has been found that even if people are instructed to hit a moving target as hard as they can (equivalent to moving as fast as possible), they still move more slowly to slower-moving targets[106].

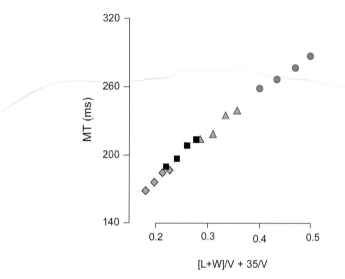

Figure 12.49: *MT data from panel B of Figure 12.48 plotted against b(L+W)/V + c/V with b = 1 and c = 35. Different symbols represent different speeds, as in Figure 12.48.*

12.4.10 People are more temporally accurate when the time window is smaller

Measurement of the temporal error in the interceptive task of Figure 12.44 requires that we identify what constitutes zero error or a 'perfect hit'. Striking the middle of the target with the middle of the bat is a natural way to define a perfect hit where the error is zero: the bat-target contact configuration is shown as case (1) in panel A of Figure 12.50. Case (2) reproduces the contact configuration shown in Figure 12.45A: the bat arrives before the target reaches the position shown in case (1), and the time difference between the two configurations is the temporal error. Since the configuration in case (2) occurs before the configuration in (1), the bat arrives too early for a perfect hit, and the error is considered negative; for the case shown, the error is equal to $-(L + W)/2V$. Case (3) is where the trailing edge of the target is just contacted by the left-hand edge of the bat. In this case, the bat arrives too late for a perfect hit, and the temporal error is positive; in the case shown, it is equal to $+(L + W)/2V$. The arithmetic mean of the temporal errors for a sequence of trials is the **temporal constant error**, and the standard deviation is the **temporal variable error**.

The constant temporal error has been found to be small and to change very little with changes to the time window[107], which is consistent with the results from the time-matching task described earlier (see section 12.4.4). The temporal VE has been found to be larger when the MT is longer[108]. Panel B of Figure 12.50 shows mean temporal VEs from an experiment in which target speed and bat width were varied (the same experiment from which the data in Figure 12.48B were obtained). The graph shows that shorter MTs are associated with smaller

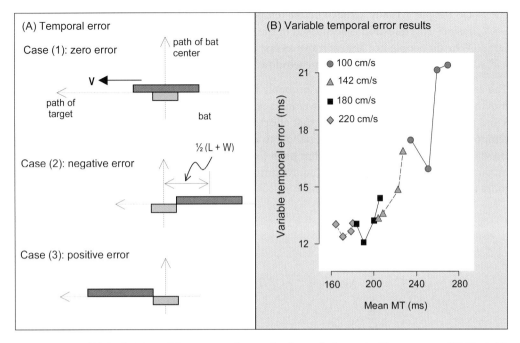

Figure 12.50: *(A) Definition of the temporal error in the task shown in Figure 12.44. (B) Variable temporal errors plotted against the mean MT for four different target speeds. Data from Tresilian and Plooy (2006).*

variable errors: people achieved greater temporal accuracy when they made briefer movements. Since the MT was longer when the time window was larger, it follows that temporal VE was smaller when the time window was smaller.

12.4.11 Interceptive MT changes very little in response to different spatial accuracy requirements

We have seen that when an interceptive hitting task requires greater temporal accuracy, people make briefer and faster movements. This was demonstrated in a task that required temporal accuracy but did not require spatial aiming accuracy, since the interception point was fixed. Most interceptive hitting tasks require some degree of spatial accuracy. Baseball batting provides a good example. It has been estimated that a firm strike of a baseball with the sweet spot of the bat demands that the bat swing be spatially accurate to within about ±1.5 cm: not more than 1.5 cm above or below the path of the center of the ball[109], and such that the sweet spot is not more than 1.5 cm to the left or right of the ball's center[110]. A temporal accuracy of better than ±10 ms (i.e., within a 20 ms time window) is also needed[111]. Hitting a home run off a fastball in the professional game may demand a temporal accuracy of ±2.5 ms (5 ms time window)[112].

The need to be both spatially and temporally accurate appears to place conflicting demands on the batter's motor system. We have seen that better temporal accuracy is achieved by making briefer, faster movements, and that better spatial accuracy is achieved by making slower movements. How do people achieve spatial and temporal accuracy simultaneously? The answer to this question may depend on the type of interceptive task being considered[113]. In what follows we will consider only rapidly executed hitting tasks like baseball batting, and laboratory tasks like that in Figure 12.44.

Hitting movements in baseball, tennis and ping-pong must typically be executed very rapidly, partly because the goal is to hit the ball hard. In addition, there is very little time available to make the hit: a pitched baseball typically travels from pitcher to batter in under half a second (see section 12.4.8). It is not surprising, therefore, to find that baseball batters swing the bat very rapidly: the end of a baseball bat may reach speeds of over 35 m/s at the moment of contact[114], and the time taken from the start of the swing to ball contact is typically less than 200 ms in professional players[115]. In fact, better batters swing faster: professional batters swing faster than amateurs, and the batters with the highest batting averages tend to have the fastest swings[116]. These observations suggest that in hitting tasks, people may not adopt the usual strategy of making slower movements to achieve greater spatial accuracy. What do people actually do?

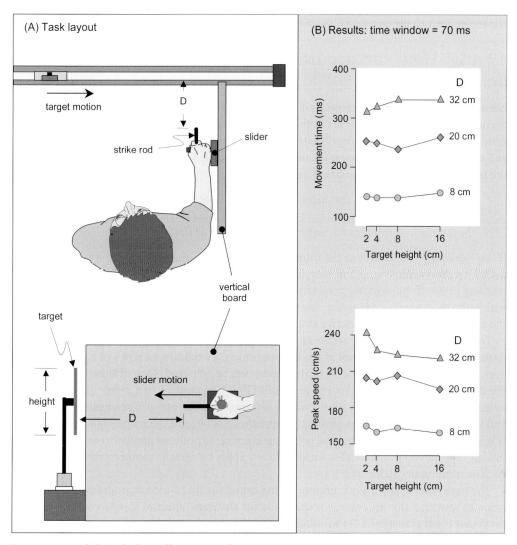

Figure 12.51: *(A) Task that allows spatial accuracy requirements to be manipulated independently of temporal accuracy requirements: plan view (top) and side view (bottom). (B) Mean movement time and peak speed data from Tresilian, Plooy, Carroll (2004).*

There have been very few studies of how people respond to variations in the requirements for spatial accuracy when intercepting moving objects. Only one study[117] has examined how people respond to changes in spatial accuracy requirements independently of changes in the temporal accuracy requirements (the time window). The study employed the task as shown in panel A of Figure 12.51. The performer grasps the handle of a slider that can be moved over the surface of a vertical board. The goal is to hit the target with the tip of the strike rod. The vertical size (height) of the target places a constraint on spatial (aiming) accuracy, but does not affect the time window. The length of the target constrains temporal accuracy, as in the task described earlier (Figure 12.44), but does not constrain spatial accuracy. Four different target heights were used (2, 4, 8 and 16 cm) and three different distances (D). Panel B shows results from a condition in which the target was 7 cm long and moved at 114 cm/s, which gave a 70 ms time window. The mean MT data from the group of participants (top) clearly does not show the Fitts' law pattern: there was no detectable effect of target height on MT (in fact, the 2 cm target was associated with slightly shorter MTs than the 16 cm target). Peak speed data are shown at the bottom of panel B: there was a small tendency to reach higher peak speeds when the targets were shorter, which meant that participants hit smaller targets harder.

The results shown in Figure 12.51 provide preliminary evidence that people do not make slower interceptive movements when greater spatial accuracy is required. This suggests that people do not employ the strategy of slowing down so as to allow more opportunity for making corrections to the ongoing movement (see section 12.4.14).

12.4.12 How can accurate timing of interceptive actions be achieved?

Contact between a moving target and an intercepting effector (or working point) can only occur if the target and effector are at the same place at the same time. Thus, there is a spatial condition for successful interception (the target and working point must be at the same place) and a temporal condition (they must be there at the same time). For a given place of contact, the temporal condition can be stated as follows:

> **Temporal condition for interception:** *The time remaining before the intercepting effector (working point) reaches the interception location (its time to arrival, TTA) must be less than or equal to the target's time to arrival at that location.*

If the working point arrives at the interception point first, then its TTA is less than the target's TTA, and it must stop and wait for the target to arrive. In this case, the target hits the working point. If the working point is to hit the target, then the two TTAs must be equal (to within the time window). How can the execution of a hitting movement be controlled so that the working point and target arrive at an interception location simultaneously?

To make a working point arrive at an interception point at the same time as a moving target requires accurate control of movement timing. Two different types of hypothesis have been proposed to explain how accurate timing can be achieved. One of these proposes that the duration of interceptive movements (the MT) is a parameter of a motor program that is prepared in advance. This hypothesis will be referred to as the **pre-programming hypothesis** and will be described here; the alternative hypothesis is beyond the scope of our discussion[118]. It is important to recognize that the pre-programming hypothesis applies to rapidly executed hitting-type interceptions, and is known not to apply to certain capture-type interceptions such as running to catch a ball[119].

The basic idea of the pre-programming hypothesis is that a motor program is established prior to moving. The program is responsible for the generation of motor commands for a movement that transports the working point to the interception location in a specific time. Thus, the time taken to move the working point to the interception location is encoded in the program; we will refer to this time as the **pre-programmed MT**. Such a program should not be conceived as a set of pre-established motor commands, but as a parameterization of a trajectory generator: when the trajectory generation process is initiated, motor commands are produced that drive the working point to the interception location in the pre-programmed MT.

Given that the MT is pre-programmed, the temporal condition for interception can be met by starting the movement at the right time. At the moment the movement starts, the working point's TTA with the interception location is equal to the pre-programmed MT (assuming that execution follows the program). Thus, to make a successful interception the working point should start moving when the target's TTA with the interception location is equal to the pre-programmed MT. In order for this to happen, the command generation process needs to be initiated slightly before the target's TTA is equal to the pre-programmed MT, so as to take into account the time it takes to transmit commands to the muscles (the command transmission time) and for the muscles to begin to produce contractile force in response to the commands (the electromechanical delay). Figure 12.52 shows a time line for this sequence of events. There is a temporal error if the time at which the working point reaches the interception location differs from the time of arrival of the target. In the figure, the working point arrives early, and so the error shown is negative. Successful interception

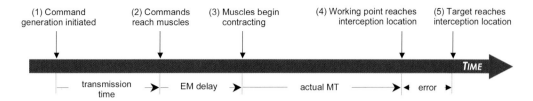

Figure 12.52: *Time line for an interceptive task; see text for explanation (EM delay = electro-mechanical delay).*

requires that the error is less than ½ the time window; how can timing be controlled so as to achieve this? We address this question next.

12.4.13 Interceptive timing requires accurate preparation and precisely timed initiation

From the discussion presented in the last section, we see there are two key components to achieving accurate timing according to the pre-programming hypothesis:

(1)   The movement needs to be executed such that the actual MT is close to the pre-programmed MT.

(2)   Motor command generation must be initiated at the right moment: initiate too soon and the working point will arrive at the interception location before the target (negative temporal error); initiate too late and the working point will arrive after the target (positive error).

To accomplish the first of these, the program needs to be properly prepared and organized so that the MT can be accurately produced. When a high degree of temporal accuracy is required (small time window), it is important that the MT be precisely encoded in the program and the movement executed so that the actual MT is close to the pre-programmed MT.

   We have seen that people can execute short MTs more consistently than longer ones, and that they produce shorter MTs when the time window is smaller. These findings imply that when the temporal accuracy requirements are tight, people pre-program a short MT. A short MT also means that there is more time before the movement starts. Thus, a shorter MT is not only executed more consistently, it also gives you more time to view the moving target and to prepare the program prior to starting the movement. In summary, short MTs provide at least two advantages over longer ones: short MTs can be more consistently executed, and they take up less of the available time and so extend the period for which the target can be viewed and the program prepared. It is known that the preparation of motor programs is a time-consuming process, and if it is not complete when a movement is initiated, then performance will be inaccurate[120]. Furthermore, a longer viewing time allows more accurate information to be obtained about the target's motion[121]. Thus, the longer the start of movement can be delayed, the more accurately the program can be prepared.

   Being able to precisely execute a movement of pre-programmed duration will not result in successful interception unless the command generation process is initiated at the right moment. A period of time equal to the command transmission time + the electromechanical delay + the pre-programmed MT elapses between the initiation of command generation and the working point reaching the interception location (Figure 12.52). To ensure that the working point and the target reach the interception location simultaneously, command generation should be initiated when the target's TTA is equal to this period of time. Thus, an estimate of the target's TTA with the interception location is needed: people must be able to perceive the target's TTA. When the perceived value of the TTA reaches a specific criterion value, motor command generation should be initiated (as discussed in Chapter 9, section 9.3.5). In effect, a criterion value of the target's perceived TTA is used to trigger the command generator. This criterion value must, of course, be matched to the value of the pre-programmed MT. To be precise, the criterion value (TTA_{crit}) is given by,

$$\text{TTA}_{crit} = (\text{pre-programmed MT}) + (\text{motor delay}) + (\text{perceptual processing time})$$

where the motor delay is the command transmission time plus the electromechanical delay, and the perceptual processing time is the time taken to extract TTA information from sensory stimulation and transmit it to the command generator.

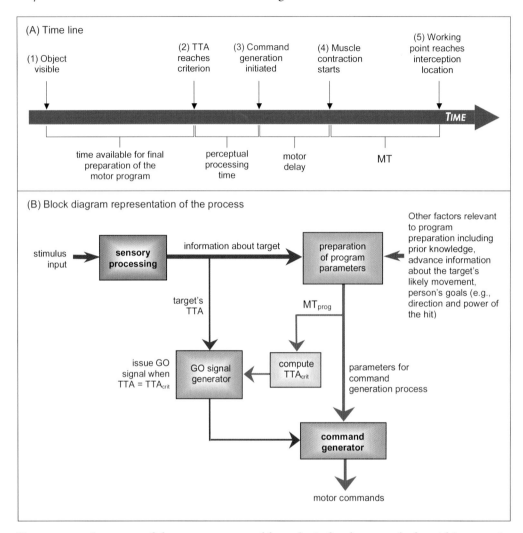

Figure 12.53: *Summary of the pre-programmed hypothesis for the control of rapid interceptive action. (A) Temporal order of events showing periods occupied by various processes. (B) Block diagram representation of the processes involved (MT_prog = pre-programmed MT; TTA_crit = criterion value of target's TTA).*

In summary, the pre-programming hypothesis proposes that a motor command generator is prepared prior to moving, so that it is ready to produce commands for a movement that will reach a chosen interception location in a specific time (the pre-programmed MT). Command generation is triggered when the perceived value of the target's TTA reaches a criterion value that is matched to the pre-programmed MT. Figure 12.53 provides a pictorial representation of the hypothesis: panel A shows a time line of the events involved, and panel B shows a block diagram of the processes involved.

12.4.14 Visual information plays several roles in the control of interceptive action

The block diagram in Figure 12.53B shows that visual information plays at least two roles in interceptive movement production. It is used to prepare the program, and it is used to trigger a GO signal that initiates command generation. Program preparation involves setting the parameters for command generation so that the working point will get to the right place (the interception location) in a specified time (the pre-programmed MT). Since MT in the task shown in Figure 12.44 depends on the time window (see section 12.4.11), perceptual information about target size and speed is presumably being used to pre-program MT. The interception location must also be perceived, which means that it must be possible to perceive where the target is going. In the case of the task in Figure 12.44, the path of the target is simply the track-way along which it moves, and the interception location is determined by the configuration of the apparatus. In most real-world interceptive tasks the target's path

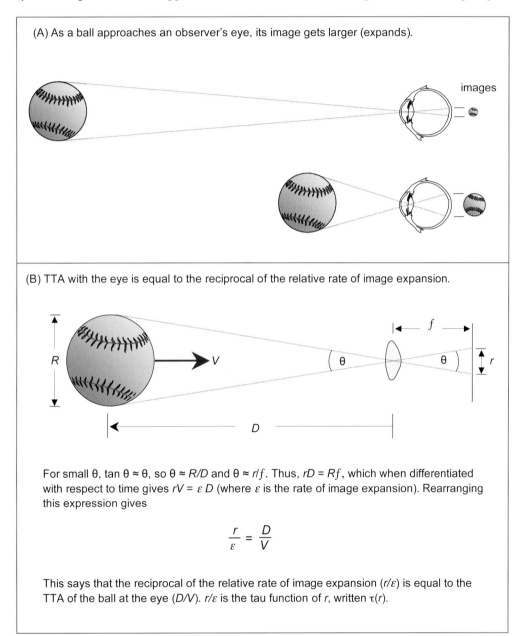

(A) As a ball approaches an observer's eye, its image gets larger (expands).

images

(B) TTA with the eye is equal to the reciprocal of the relative rate of image expansion.

R V θ f θ r

D

For small θ, tan $\theta \approx \theta$, so $\theta \approx R/D$ and $\theta \approx r/f$. Thus, $rD = Rf$, which when differentiated with respect to time gives $rV = \varepsilon D$ (where ε is the rate of image expansion). Rearranging this expression gives

$$\frac{r}{\varepsilon} = \frac{D}{V}$$

This says that the reciprocal of the relative rate of image expansion (r/ε) is equal to the TTA of the ball at the eye (D/V). r/ε is the tau function of r, written $\tau(r)$.

Figure 12.54: *Time to arrival information is available from the expanding image of an approaching ball.*

is not visible; information about where the target is going must be extracted from the visual stimulus[122] so that a suitable interception location can be chosen. A discussion of how people perceive where a moving object is going is beyond the scope of this text.

In Figure 12.53B, the GO signal is triggered when the perceived value of the target's TTA reaches its criterion value. We discussed the perception of TTA in Chapter 9, where the focus was restricted to TTA of a moving observer with a stationary object or environmental feature. If an object is moving directly towards a stationary observer, then the tau function (see section 9.3.3 for definition) of the object's retinal image size provides information about the object's TTA with the observer, as explained in Figure 12.54. This information provides a basis for release of the GO signal and so can correctly time the start of the movement[123]. It has been shown that the smaller the value of TTA, the more precisely its value can be extracted from retinal images[124]. Since a shorter pre-programmed MT is associated with a smaller criterion value of the target's TTA, movements with shorter MTs will tend to be initiated by more precise TTA estimates. This represents another advantage of shorter MTs over longer ones for achieving precisely timed interceptions.

Finally, it should be noted that while it is possible for sensory information to be used to adjust or correct the execution of an interceptive hitting action, its role is limited, due to the brevity and forcefulness of such acts. Average MTs in the experiments described in section 12.4.9 were all less than 270 ms, and some were less than 150 ms; swing times of professional baseball batters are typically[125] between 150 and 200 ms. Accurate timing can be achieved with brief, fast movements, but it would seem to come at the cost of reduced spatial accuracy, due to the limited opportunity for corrective adjustment. However, as we have seen, speed of execution has only a small effect on spatial accuracy: it is possible that the longer preparation time that is available when the MT is shorter could allow more accurate pre-programming of a movement's spatial parameters. Furthermore, there is some evidence that movements executed at near maximum speed are more spatially accurate than movements executed slightly more slowly[126]. Thus, if an interception needs to be executed quickly, the best way to achieve a high degree of both spatial and temporal accuracy is to make the briefest, fastest movement possible.

References & Notes

[1] The classic study is Carter (1978).

[2] Kirkup, Frenkel (2006).

[3] Gordon, Ghilardi, Ghez (1994a).

[4] For discussion see Hancock, Butler, Fischman (1995).

[5] Gordon, Ghilardi, Ghez (1994a).

[6] For extension to 3-dimensions see McIntyre, Stratta, Lacquaniti (1997).

[7] See, e.g., Morrison (2004).

[8] The effects can also be manifested in the orientation of the set of end points (Gordon *et al.*, 1994b; McIntyre *et al.*, 2000).

[9] See Flanders, Helms-Tillery, Soechting (1992); McIntyre, Stratta, Lacquaniti (1997); Soechting, Flanders (1989).

[10] Schmidt, Lee (2011).

[11] Poulton (1979).

[12] Poulton (1973, 1974, 1979).

[13] Fitts (1951). The effect also occurs with eye movements (Kapoula, 1985).

[14] This explanation predicts that the more uncertain the person is about the targets' distances, the greater the contraction bias, which is the result obtained experimentally (Tresilian, Mon-Williams, Kelly, 1999).

[15] Poulton (1979).

[16] Worringham, Dennis (1992).

[17] Woodworth (1899).

[18] Schmidt, Lee (2011).

[19] Beggs *et al.* (1972); Howarth, Beggs (1985).

[20] Beggs *et al.* (1972); speed had no detectable effect on CEs.

[21] Schmidt *et al.* (1979).

[22] Schmidt *et al.* (1979).

[23] E.g., Zelaznik *et al.* (1988).

[24] Wright and Meyer (1983) found that VED increased with speed in a single d.o.f. task that did not suffer from the problem described here. The effect was small: more than doubling average speed (10 cm/s to 24.3 cm/s) only increased VED by 1 mm.

[25] But see Wright, Meyer (1983).

[26] Adamovich *et al.* (1994, 1999); Latash, Gottlieb (1990).

[27] Adamovich *et al.* (1994).

[28] Spatial variability depends on where in the trajectory it is measured; see Gutman *et al.* (1993).

[29] Fast movements can sometimes be more accurate than slower ones (Beggs *et al.*, 1972; Schmidt, Sherwood, 1982).

[30] Prablanc *et al.* (1979); Jeannerod (1988).

[31] See also Khan *et al.* (2004).

[32] E.g., Harris, Wolpert (1998).

[33] Jones, Hamilton, Wolpert (2002); Schmidt *et al.* (1979).

[34] Corcos, Gottlieb, Agarwal (1988); Gottlieb, Corcos, Agarwal (1989b).

[35] From http://www.thefreedictionary.com.

[36] E.g., Schmidt, Lee (2011).

[37] Fitts (1954).

[38] Fitts used base two for theoretical reasons.

[39] Assuming the same constant of proportionality for both.

[40] If D is less than ½ W, then the targets overlap by more than half their width – there is really just one target.

[41] Langolf, Chaffin, Foulke (1976).

[42] Fitts (1954).

[43] Fitts, Peterson (1964).

[44] E.g., Corcos, Gottlieb, Agarwal (1988); Crossman, Goodeve (1983); Wright, Meyer (1983).

[45] Individual fingers (Langolf, Chaffin, Foulke, 1976); head movements (Andres, Hartung, 1989); leg movements (Drury, 1975).

[46] Zhai (2004).

[47] Meyer *et al.* (1990).

[48] Bainbridge, Sanders (1972); Duarte, Latash (2007); Jagacinski *et al.* (1980); MacKenzie, Graham (1997); Sheridan (1979); Welford (1968).

[49] Hoffman, Sheikh (1991).

[50] E.g., Crossman, Goodeve (1983); Fitts, Radford (1966).

[51] Soukoreff, MacKenzie (2004).

[52] Crossman (1960).

[53] Soukoreff, MacKenzie (2004); Zhai, Kong, Ren (2004).

[54] Jaric *et al.* (1999).

[55] E.g., MacKenzie, Buxton (1992).

[56] Hoffman, Sheikh (1991).

[57] Sheikh, Hoffman (1994); Bohan *et al.* (2003).

[58] See Rosenbaum (2009); Schmidt, Lee (2011).

[59] See note 49.

[60] Gan, Hoffman (1988); Hoffman, Sheikh (1994).

[61] See Plamondon, Alimi (1997); Elliot *et al.* (2010).

[62] MacKenzie *et al.* (1987).

[63] E.g., MacKenzie *et al.* (1987).

[64] E.g., Tresilian, Plooy, Carroll (2004).

[65] E.g., MacKenzie *et al.* (1987); Soechting (1984); Worringham (1987).

[66] MacKenzie *et al.* (1987); Meyer *et al.* (1990).

[67] Meyer *et al.* (1988, 1990).

[68] See Elliott, Helsen, Chua (2001).

[69] Corcos, Gottlieb, Agarwal (1988).

[70] E.g., Doeringer, Hogan (1998); Milner (1992).

[71] Fradet, Lee, Dounskaia (2008); Wisleder, Dounskaia (2007). These authors suggested, for example, that larger levels of co-contraction in aimed movements that require end-point accuracy (Gribble *et al.*, 2003) could lead to more motor noise (Harris, Wolpert, 1998; Schmidt *et al.*, 1979) and hence larger fluctuations in the trajectory as the target is approached.

[72] See, e.g., Elliott, Binstead, Heath (1999); Saunders, Knill (2004).

[73] See Elliott, Helsen, Chua (2001).

[74] E.g., Crossman, Goodeve (1983).

[75] Crossman, Goodeve (1983); Keele (1968).

[76] Jagacinski *et al.* (1980). For review see Elliott *et al.* (2010).

[77] E.g., Wallace, Newell (1993); Wu, Yang, Honda (2010).

[78] Meyer *et al.* (1990).

[79] For review see Elliott *et al.* (2010).

[80] E.g., Keele, Posner (1968).

[81] E.g., Brenner, Smeets (1997); Prablanc, Martin (1992); Saunders, Knill (2003, 2004).

[82] E.g., Paulignan *et al.* (1991b).

[83] Elliott *et al.* (2010).

[84] Each movement went to the target and back, MT to the target = 60/(2 × 150) (Carlton, 1992).

[85] Paulignan *et al.* (1991b).

[86] Paulignan *et al.* (1991a).

[87] Paulignan *et al.* (1991a), but see Smeets, Brenner (1999).

[88] E.g., Saunders, Knill (2004), who used perturbations of visually perceived working point location.

[89] Goodale, Pelisson, Prablanc (1986); Pelisson *et al.* (1986); Prablanc, Martin (1992). Note that Bridgeman, Kirch and Sperling (1981) had earlier demonstrated unconscious corrections using a different method.

[90] Desmurget *et al.* (1999).

[91] The relationship may not be exactly proportional (Newell, Carlton, Kim, 1994).

[92] See Newell, Carlton, Kim (1994).

[93] Newell *et al.* (1993).

[94] $C_{TM}E$ is typically around 3% of the required MT (Newell *et al.*, 1993; Newell, Carlton, Kim, 1994).

[95] Newell *et al.* (1993).

[96] See Tresilian (2005).

[97] After McLeod, McGlaughlin, Nimmo-Smith (1985).

[98] E.g., Bairstow (1987); Brenner, Smeets, De Lussanet (1998); Brouwer, Brenner, Smeets (2000); Van Donkelaar, Lee, Gellman (1992).

[99] Gray (2002); Ranganathan, Carlton (2007).

[100] See Mason, Carnahan (1999).

[101] E.g., Laurent, Montagne, Savelsbergh (1994); Mason, Carnahan (1999); Tresilian, Houseman (2005).

[102] To the nearest millimeter.

[103] The distance over which the target was seen to move was longer at higher speeds.

[104] Tresilian, Plooy (2006).

[105] See Tresilian, Houseman (2005); Tresilian, Plooy (2006).

[106] Brenner, Smeets, De Lussanet (1998); Brouwer, Brenner, Smeets (2000).

[107] Tresilian, Plooy (2006); Tresilian, Plooy, Marinovic (2009).

[108] Schmidt (1969); Tresilian, Oliver, Carroll (2003).

[109] Watts, Bahill (2000).

[110] Regan (1992, 1997).

[111] Watts, Bahill (2000).

[112] Regan (1992, 1997).

[113] See Tresilian (2005); Tresilian, Plooy, Marinovic (2009).

114 Welch *et al.* (1995).

115 Hubbard, Seng (1954); Watts, Bahill (2000).

116 Breen (1967); Watts, Bahill (2000).

117 Tresilian, Plooy, Carroll (2004).

118 The alternative proposes that MT, amplitude and direction are not prepared, but result from a continuous sensorimotor transformation (e.g., Dessing *et al.*, 2002, 2005).

119 See Tresilian (2005) for a discussion of the scope of the hypothesis. See Zago *et al.* (2009) for a wide-ranging review.

120 See, e.g., Ghez *et al.* (1997); Marinovic, Plooy, Tresilian (2008).

121 See, e.g., Bahill, Karnavas (1993); Regan (1997).

122 For discussion of how this might be done, see, e.g., Bahill, Karnavas (1993); Regan, Gray (2000).

123 For discussion of the limitations of tau functions see Tresilian (1999b).

124 Gray, Regan (1998); the precision of the estimates is about 2% of the TTA.

125 Hubbard, Seng (1954); Watts, Bahill (2000).

126 See note 29.

CHAPTER 13

Sequences and Series

13.1 A Combinatorial Approach to Serial Action

13.1.1 Introduction: complex actions are built from simpler elements

Most people agree that complex behaviors are built from a limited number of simpler behavioral elements that are somehow linked together[1]. The behavioral elements can be linked to form sequences, or they can be linked in parallel so that they are performed concurrently. Some tasks, such as typing, require that behavioral elements (keystrokes) be performed in sequence; a task like playing a piece of music on the piano will require both sequential and concurrent performance of elements. A fundamental qualifying characteristic of a behavioral element is that *it can appear as a component of different complex actions*. We will take the view that the elemental components of complex actions are themselves goal-directed actions[2] – elemental actions (see Chapter 1).

In this part of the chapter we will describe the characteristics of complex actions and their elemental components, and consider the nature of the generative processes that underlie the production of these behaviors. The discussion will be based on the hypothesis that the generation of complex acts involves the recruitment of distinct production elements (e.g., motor programs) that are responsible for generating the elemental components. This provides a flexible way of producing complex behavior: use a small number of mechanisms, each of which produces relatively simple behaviors, and combine these in different ways, rather like a limited alphabet of letters can be used to form complex structures like written words and sentences. This is another example of the combinatorial approach introduced in Chapter 5.

A variety of terms can be found in the literature that refer to the elements from which complex actions are constructed: examples include *motor schemas*, *action units*, *movemes*, *movement quanta*, *functional synergies* and *motor primitives*[3]. No generally accepted terminology yet exists, and the various terms are used in slightly different ways by different authors: sometimes the terms refer to behavioral elements (e.g., elemental actions), while sometimes they refer to production elements (e.g., motor programs). Given that it is important to distinguish behavioral elements from production elements, we will use the terms *elemental action* and *elemental program* for behavioral and production elements respectively.

It seems obvious that a sequential act can be executed by voluntarily performing each element in the sequence, one after the other. When we make a cup of coffee, for instance, we perform a sequence of individual acts such as turning a faucet and picking up a cup. We will typically be consciously aware of voluntarily choosing to perform each one of these acts. However, many complex actions do not involve conscious activation of components. It is acts of this sort that we will be concerned with in this chapter.

13.1.2 Program combination may be the basis for complex action

If complex acts can be decomposed into a limited number of parts that occur in different acts, then those parts are likely to be elemental behavioral components generated by distinct production elements. For example, spoken language can be decomposed into sequences of a relatively small number of phonemes that can each appear in many different spoken words. The different phonemes can be considered to be generated by the activity of different production elements (see section 13.2). Thus, it can be proposed that if behavior can be decomposed into elemental parts, then there are distinct mechanisms of production responsible for generating the parts. We will refer to this idea as the **program combination hypothesis**, since the production elements may be considered to be programs of some sort:

> **PROGRAM COMBINATION HYPOTHESIS:** Complex acts that can be divided up into simpler, elemental components are generated by control processes that recruit distinct motor programs (or program instantiations) that are responsible for generating the individual components.

13.1.3 Practice results in increased speed and fluency

Individual motor programs can be recruited into a sequential act either volitionally or by automatic, subconscious processes. Volitional recruitment tends to result in sequences with distinct pauses between one component and the next, due to the time it takes to voluntarily initiate an action once the previous one has been completed. The result is that the sequence proceeds relatively slowly and lacks fluency since the components do not run smoothly, one into the next. This kind of behavior is characteristic of people in their first attempts at sequential skills such as typing and playing musical instruments. It occurs if a person is following a set of memorized verbal instructions or reading them. A classic example is of the beginner driver when first shifting gear in a vehicle with a manual transmission[4]. The beginner is given verbal instructions about how to shift gears; these are expressed in terms of actions that they already know how to perform. The instructions might specify the following sequence of actions:

(1) take foot off accelerator pedal;
(2) depress clutch pedal;
(3) move gear stick out of gear into neutral position;
(4) shift stick into required gear position;
(5) slowly release clutch pedal;
(6) depress accelerator pedal.

The beginner executes each of these actions in the remembered order, volitionally initiating the next element in the sequence once the previous one has been completed. The process demands continuous attention; the beginner may need to look at the gear stick while moving it, and they find it very disruptive to perform other voluntary behaviors at the same time, such as holding a conversation with a passenger, reading road signs or negotiating a turn.

The behavior of the experienced driver is very different from that of the beginner: they execute a gear change much more quickly, fluently and consistently than a beginner, and without having to recall a set of instructions or think about the individual steps involved. Execution does not demand the expert driver's continuous attention; they are able to do other things such as hold a conversation and watch the road while changing gears. The performance differences are summarized in Table 13.1. We will consider the learning processes that are responsible for these changes in performance in Chapter 15.

Table 13.1: *Differences in the performance of novices and experts.*

Performance characteristic	Unfamiliar/unpracticed sequence (novice performance)	Highly practiced sequence (expert performance)
Speed	Relatively slow; cannot be executed rapidly.	Can be executed rapidly (or slowly if necessary).
Fluency	Not fluent; may be periods of inaction between elements.	Fluent; elements run smoothly and seamlessly together.
Consistency	More likely to omit an element or perform elements out of sequence. Performance lacks a consistent timing pattern.	Less likely to make errors of omission or sequence. Performance possesses a consistent timing pattern.
Dual tasking	Difficult or impossible to concurrently perform a second task that makes cognitive demands (e.g., talking).	Possible to concurrently perform a second task without significant degradation of performance.

13.1.4 The expert's performance involves automatic control; the novice's involves cognitive control

The beginner's execution of a sequential act is described as being **cognitively controlled**, a term that refers to the attention or mental effort that is involved[5]. The performance of an expert is described as being **automatic**, because execution can proceed without attention and mental effort. It appears that as skill is acquired, production of a sequence is transferred to a level of control that is below the level of conscious awareness. The individual elements are sequenced by a subconscious process that is much quicker than the slow, volitional process employed by the novice. Cognitively controlled and automatic sequencing involve different types of process that are usually considered to be carried out by two distinct systems[6]:

> (a) ... a cognitive system which plans and represents (symbolically) a goal structure of action, and (b) ... a motor system which organizes movements appropriate to the goal[7].

This idea has been termed the **dual-processor model**[8], since it involves two processing systems. The cognitive system is a high-level process that is consciously accessible and involves mental effort; the motor system is not consciously accessible and operates without mental effort. According to the program combination hypothesis, both these systems can recruit and coordinate the motor programs that generate the behavioral elements of the complex act.

The idea that expert and novice performance differ in the role played by cognitive processing, and that practice leads to automatic sequencing, has been appreciated for a long time, as the following quote from 1906 illustrates:

> At the outset each step of the performance is separately and distinctly the object of attention and effort; and as practice proceeds and expertness is gained ... the separate portions thereof become fused into larger units, which in turn make a constantly diminishing demand upon consciousness[9].

Fusion into 'larger units' refers to the transition to automatic sequencing of a series of elements so that the whole series proceeds as if it were a single element (unit). Larger units that are formed from the combination of several more elemental units are sometimes referred to as **motor chunks**[10]. The mechanism underlying the production of a motor chunk can be recruited by a single signal from the cognitive system in the same way as an elemental program. Thus, a chunk may play the role of an elemental program in another chunk. In other words, the components of chunks can themselves be chunks. In fact, for a chunk to qualify as a behavioral element in its own right, it must be possible for it to be recruited as a component of more complex actions. It is then possible for chunks to be formed with components that are chunks, and for these component chunks to have other chunks as their components, and so on.

13.1.5 There are at least two ways in which automatic sequencing could be achieved

We have suggested that expert performance of serial acts involves the automatic sequencing of production elements (elemental programs). How is this automatic sequencing achieved? There are two basic possibilities:

(1) **Response chaining:** activity of one production element generates a signal that activates the next element in the sequence.
(2) **Programmed sequencing:** a control program recruits the elements in the sequence in a specific order.

Response chaining comes in two varieties, which we will call *sensory feedback chaining* and *internal chaining* (sometimes called *associative chaining*[11]). Feedback chaining was described in Chapter 5 in the context of reflex action: sensory feedback produced by executing one response serves as the eliciting stimulus for the following response, and so on. During the first half of the 20th century, feedback chaining was thought to be the mechanism underlying a wide variety of sequential behavior including speech[12]. It later became clear that locomotion and other complex behavioral acts, such as grooming, are not chains of reflex responses but are produced by pattern generators (see Chapter 8). These findings and other arguments led to feedback chaining being abandoned as an explanatory principle, as one theorist concluded:

> The ... chaining hypothesis, contending that a movement sequence is assembled by the response-produced stimuli of each segment becoming the cue for the next ... is dead in both animal and human learning[13].

We will discuss some further arguments against feedback chaining later (section 13.1.9) and conclude that although it cannot account for the sequencing of behavioral elements that occur in rapid succession, it is a viable concept in certain cases (see also section 5.5.7). Thus, it is not a question of either feedback chaining or some other method of sequencing; rather, the method used to control sequencing is likely to depend on the type of sequence concerned.

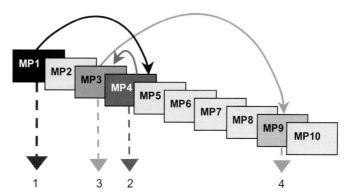

Figure 13.1: *A pictorial representation of an internal chaining scheme in which connections between elemental production units (motor programs MPs) underlie the sequencing of behavioral elements (see text for explanation).*

Internal chaining is an alternative method that does away with the need for sensory feedback. The basic idea is that activation of one elemental program not only results in the generation of motor commands, but also in a signal[14] that activates the next elemental program in the sequence, and so on[15]. This means that the elemental programs of the sequence are linked together by interconnections, as suggested by the schematic in Figure 13.1. The figure shows ten blocks (MP1, ... , MP10) that represent different elemental motor programs. Four are linked together, so that MP1 triggers MP4, which triggers MP3, which triggers MP9, leading to the execution of the associated behavioral elements in that sequence (the color of the program blocks represents their order of recruitment: the darker the color, the earlier the program is recruited). We will discuss the problems with internal chaining later (section 13.1.9).

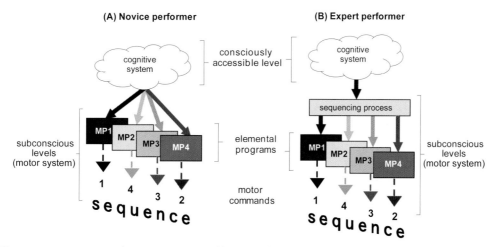

Figure 13.2: *A pictorial representation of how production of a behavioral sequence in a novice may differ from production by an expert.*

The second basic method for sequencing elemental programs proposes that there is a higher-level sequencing mechanism or control program. This idea is different from the voluntary sequencing that is characteristic of a novice, in that the sequencing mechanism works automatically. Figure 13.2 shows a pictorial representation of the distinction. Panel A shows how sequencing can be conceived in the novice: a cognitive system that holds sequence information in working memory is responsible for sequencing. This system sends activating signals to the motor programs governing the component actions in sequence, so that they issue motor commands in a particular order (1, 2, 3, 4). The color of the connecting arrows and blocks represents the temporal order of activation – a darker color represents an earlier time. Panel B shows how the process might be organized in the expert. Here, cognitive processes send only one signal, which activates a subconscious sequencing process.

13.1.6 The existence of behavioral elements does not imply elemental programs

The discussion of sequencing presented so far has been based on the program combination hypothesis: the observable elements of a serial behavior are each generated by a distinct production element (motor program). While this idea seems almost incontrovertible for the novice who is consciously aware of making a decision to perform each element in a sequence, it might not be true for the expert: a motor chunk may be generated by a mechanism that cannot be meaningfully divided into component programs[16]. In other words, learning might result not in the formation of a process that automatically coordinates the activity of elemental motor programs (as shown in panel B of Figure 13.2), but in the formation of an entirely new motor program that does not consist of elementary components but is an elemental program in its own right. This alternative can be represented pictorially as shown in Figure 13.3. Novice performance is generated as before (panel A of Figure 13.3 reproduces panel A of Figure 13.2); expert performance results in the formation of a new elemental program (dark block in panel B).

The alternative possibility is plausible in cases where individual component acts used in practice do not occur in the highly skilled act. The elements that occur initially may simply serve as a scaffold on which to erect the skilled action: once skill is acquired, the scaffold is no longer present. A possible example is making a turn when skiing. When people start learning to turn in downhill skiing, they typically do so by the cognitively controlled execution of a sequence of simpler actions explained to them by an instructor. To make a left turn, these might be as follows: (1) form a snowplow (point the tips of the skis inwards to form a 'V' shape); (2) angle the inside edge of the right ski into the slope while turning it slightly further to the left; (3) transfer body weight to the right ski; (4) as the turn is made, allow the uphill (left) ski to move so as to become parallel with the right ski. A skillful downhill skier does not form a snowplow, but keeps the skis almost parallel throughout the turn, and there is no reason to suppose that the other elements executed by the beginner are present in an expert's turns, which are executed as smooth, single acts.

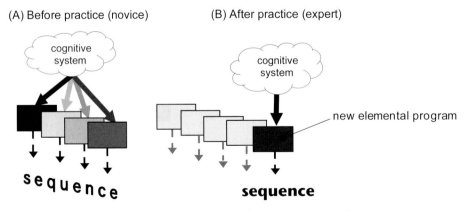

Figure 13.3: *Alternative conception of the difference between expert and novice performance, in which the expert develops a new elemental program.*

In section 13.1.1 we drew an analogy between the combinatorial approach and alphabetic writing systems, in which the same set of elements (the letters of the alphabet) are used to write all the different words in a language. There is an alternative type of writing system, termed *logographic*, in which each word is represented by a distinct little picture (pictogram or hieroglyph) or other complex symbol[17]. We can think of the alternative conception of how complex motor acts are produced as analogous to a logographic writing system: each complex action or motor chunk (analogous to a word) is written as a distinct hieroglyph (analogous to a complex but unitary motor program).

Given that there are these two alternative conceptions for how the production mechanisms of complex actions are organized, how can we determine from empirical observations of skilled performance whether or not elemental programs are being recruited? It might be possible to divide performance into behavioral elements, but this is not a demonstration that the behavioral elements are generated by component programs. For example, when people draw smooth, well-learned shapes such as figure eights, the motion of the working point (pen tip) is continuous but can be analyzed into a series of segments using particular criteria[18]. These segments have the characteristics of behavioral elements, but it has been shown that working point motion can display a segmented structure and yet can be generated by a process that does not have any components[19]. Thus, the existence of behaviorally identifiable components does not necessarily mean that there are corresponding component programs.

Note that it is not the case that the two conceptions shown in panel B of Figures 13.2 and 13.3 represent mutually exclusive hypotheses regarding how the motor system is organized. It could be that in some cases the acquisition of automaticity and skill is associated with the development of a control program (Figure 13.2B), whereas in other cases it is associated with the development of a new elemental program (Figure 13.3B).

In summary, the existence of behaviorally identifiable components does not establish the existence of corresponding elements of control (elemental programs). This is, in part, why we referred to the program combination idea as an hypothesis in section 13.1.2. In the remainder of the chapter, we will examine how this hypothesis applies to various types of serial behavior.

13.1.7 How can chunks be identified?

To qualify as a behavioral unit, a chunk must appear in different behavioral contexts[20] – preceded by different acts and followed by different acts on different occasions. It is not sufficient merely to observe that the same sequence of components can be performed in different contexts. There are two reasons for this: first, the sequence could have been entirely or partially cognitively controlled in some contexts. Second, the same elements can be components of different chunks, so if the same sequence of elements E_1,E_2,E_3 is observed in two contexts – such as E_4,E_1,E_2,E_3,E_5 and E_6,E_1,E_2,E_3,E_7 – it is not necessarily the case that E_1,E_2,E_3 form a chunk. For example, it might be that E_4,E_1,E_2 form a chunk in the first sequence and E_2,E_3,E_7 in the second. We need some way to determine which sequences of elements in an ongoing stream of behavior constitute chunks, and where the chunks begin and end.

The production of a motor chunk is governed by an automatic, subconscious process – a kind of control program. This suggests that performance might exhibit invariant characteristics – features of performance that remain very similar despite changes in the context in which the chunk appears. Since the control program is assumed to be responsible for the temporal sequencing of component elements, invariant characteristics would be expected to be observed in the timing of these components: in other words, the sequencing of components is expected to exhibit an invariant temporal pattern (the consistent timing pattern referred to in Table 13.1).

Of course, there are cases in which a temporal structure is imposed by the task itself. Playing a piece of music is the most obvious example: the individual notes in the sequence not only need to be executed in the right order, but also with the correct timing, so that the performance has the right rhythm. However, in other cases, such as handwriting and typing, the task itself imposes no particular timing requirements. In these tasks, an invariant temporal pattern is not expected to be observed if a sequence of elements is performed under cognitive control[21].

Studies of expert touch-typists have provided evidence for invariant temporal patterns in the typing of common short words and commonly encountered sequences of two or three letters such as 'th' and 'ing'. In one series of studies, skilled typists typed various texts in which certain words and letter sequences appeared in different contexts (i.e., preceded and followed by different words or letters)[22]. An example of the kind of result obtained is shown in Figure 13.4: typists typed textual material that contained 27 instances of the word 'trouble'. Panel A shows the times at which each key was struck (circles) for 15 of these instances in the order that they were typed by one individual typist (key presses of the different instances are shown in different shades). The figure shows that some instances of the word were typed more quickly than others: for example, instance 13 was typed most quickly, taking about 850 milliseconds, whereas instance 7 was took the longest time to type (just over 1200 milliseconds). Panel B shows the instances ordered by the time taken, with the shortest time at the top (instance 13) and the longest at the bottom (instance 7).

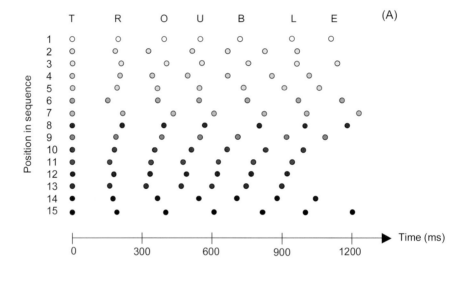

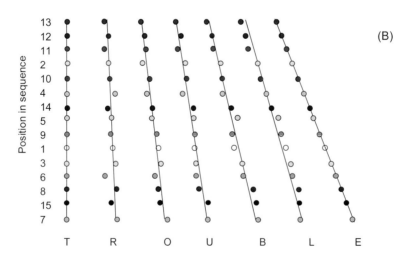

Figure 13.4: *(A) Temporal occurrence of keystrokes (circles) when typing the word 'trouble' (15 different instances in the order of performance). (B) Data shown in A ordered according to the total time taken to type the word; the vertical spacing between sequences is proportional to the difference in the total time taken to type the sequences. (Data from Terzuolo and Viviani, 1979.)*

Panel B of Figure 13.4 reveals that there is a temporal structure to the way in which the typist typed the word. Although the intervals between keystrokes differ in the different instances of the typed word, the relative durations of the intervals is similar in all instances. For example, the duration of the first interval (between the T and R keystrokes) is about 160 ms in instance 7 and 210 ms in instance 13: instance 13 is about 50 ms or 30% longer than instance 7. The subsequent intervals – between R and O, O and U, and so on – are all greater in instance 13 by a similar proportion (about 30%). This means that the intervals between keystrokes take a similar proportion of the total time in both instance 7 and instance 13, though the actual durations of the intervals differ. An alternative way of expressing this is to say that the ratios of subsequent pairs of intervals are almost the same in the different instances: the ratio of the T-R interval to the R-O interval is the same in the two instances, the ratio of the R-O interval and O-U interval is the same, and so on.

When the actual durations differ but the proportional times are very similar (or, equivalently, the ratios of subsequent pairs of intervals are similar), we say that there is variable *absolute timing* but invariant **relative timing**. The pattern in 13.4B shows that the word 'trouble' was typed with invariant relative timing, a finding that can also be represented by plotting the data points against proportional (relative) time, rather than against actual time. This is done in Figure 13.5: panel A shows the data from Figure 13.4 plotted in relative time units[23], and clearly illustrates that the keystrokes occur at almost the same relative times in all instances. Examples of the relative timing patterns of four other words typed by another typist are shown in panel B. It was also found that the relative timing patterns remained unchanged when weights were attached to the fingers[24]. As we will see in Chapter 15, as people acquire skill in sequential behaviors like typing, they develop characteristic, invariant timing patterns for short, well-practiced sequences. These timing patterns are intrinsic to the skilled performance: people find it difficult to execute a well-practiced sequence with a timing pattern different from that acquired during practice[25]. On the basis of these findings, it may be proposed that the sequences with these characteristics are motor chunks produced by an automatic process such as a control program.

Some authors have criticized the notion that invariant relative timing is a fundamental characteristic of skilled serial actions[26] and have doubted its usefulness as a criterion for identifying motor chunks. However, the criticisms miss the mark for at least two reasons. First, strictly invariant relative timing is not predicted (the examples shown in Figures 13.4 and 13.5 are not strictly invariant), due to the presence of noise in the motor system and the possibility of execution being influenced by sensory feedback[27]. Second, invariant relative timing is not likely to be observed in all serial motor chunks. Invariant timing patterns do not necessarily have to involve simple proportional scaling of all the intervals within a sequence of events (i.e., invariant relative timing): it may be that the pattern involves some more complex, non-proportional relationship between the intervals. Indeed, not all serial acts exhibit evidence of invariant relative timing[28].

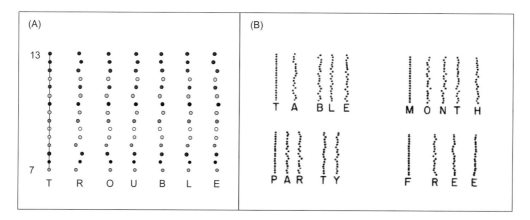

Figure 13.5: *Invariant relative timing patterns in typing are revealed when keystrokes are plotted on a relative time scale (horizontal). (A) Data from Figure 13.4. (B) Extract from Terzuolo and Viviani (1980), Figure 7.*

Regardless of the exact nature of the temporal pattern, temporal characteristics of performance can provide useful empirical criteria for the identification of motor chunks. Invariant relative timing is one such criterion, which if met provides evidence that a sequence forms a chunk. Two further criteria are as follows[29]:

(1)   *Correlation of chunk component durations.* The times to execute the elements within a chunk should be related to each other – if one element takes longer, the others should take longer as well. This will lead to the durations of elements within a chunk being correlated with one another over repeated executions. No such correlation is expected between the same elements if they do not appear within the same chunk[30].

(2)   *Temporal grouping.* Times between the onset of one element and the next are shorter when the elements occur within a chunk than when they occur in two different (but sequentially executed) chunks. In key-pressing tasks such as typing, this means that inter-keystroke intervals are shorter within chunks than between successive chunks[31] (or within unfamiliar sequences).

Another feature often observed in the performance motor chunks (though it is not necessarily exclusive to chunks) is that execution of the elements overlap with one another. This will tend to shorten the time intervals between sequential events such as keystrokes (item 2 in the above list). Overlap of execution is discussed next.

13.1.8 The execution of elements may overlap in serial motor chunks

Motor chunks that involve sequences of elemental components – serial motor chunks – are typically executed in a fluid manner, with apparently seamless transitions between elements. Seamless transitions can be produced if execution of the elements may overlap, such that the execution of one element begins while execution of the previous one is still in progress. For example, finger movements in a sequence of letters typed by skilled typists typically overlap one another, so that the movement to type the next letter is underway before the previous movement is complete[32]. In some cases, moving a finger in preparation to strike a key can occur before the previous letter has been typed. For example, when typing the word 'epic', a typist may start moving the finger that will ultimately strike the 'i' key before either the 'e' or the 'p' key has been struck (note that the 'i' and 'p' keys are struck by fingers on the right hand, whereas the 'e' key is struck by a finger on the left hand). It is even possible for the finger that will type the 'i' to make preparatory movements before the fingers that type the 'e' and the 'p' begin to move. This is illustrated in Figure 13.6, where the periods of time for which movements of the fingers occurred for each letter are represented by horizontal bars; the longer the bar, the longer the time for which the finger was in motion.

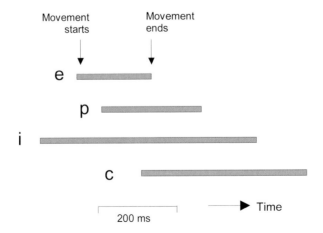

Figure 13.6: *Durations of finger movements when typing an instance of the word 'epic'. Data from Figure 2.9 in Rosenbaum (2009).*

The overlap of execution observed in skilled typing is found in a number of other types of behavior: the experienced driver, for instance, may begin to depress the clutch with one foot while the other foot is still executing the movement that releases the accelerator. Overlap will be discussed in more detail in part 4 of this chapter, together with other types of interaction between adjacent behavioral elements in a sequence. We will consider next some problems associated with the program combination hypothesis.

13.1.9 Can response chaining account for the sequencing of elements in motor chunks?

We have seen that there are two basic accounts of how sequencing of elemental programs is organized to form a motor chunk: response chaining, and programmed sequencing. These accounts should not be viewed as alternative hypotheses regarding how the motor system as a whole organizes sequencing. It is quite possible that sequencing in some acts is achieved using chaining and in others it is governed by a program.

As noted in section 13.1.5, some authors have concluded that the hypothesis of sensory feedback chaining is dead. However, such conclusions are premature. In some situations, it may be important that a particular act in a sequence begin only after the previous one has been successfully completed – it is often essential in cooking. That an act has been successfully completed can only be conclusively determined from sensory feedback, so elicitation of one act based on feedback from the preceding act can be a sensible sequencing strategy. We will describe one case in which feedback chaining is operative later (section 13.1.11). Nevertheless, it is clear that there are some important sequential behaviors in which feedback chaining is not a viable sequencing strategy. These include linguistic behaviors – speaking, typing, writing and signing – and playing musical instruments. There are four basic problems with feedback chaining accounts of these behaviors[33]: (1) there is too little time for feedback from the execution of one element to trigger the next; (2) some sequences can be executed (in part) without feedback; (3) there is no obvious way of dealing with cases in which an element appears more than once in a sequence but is preceded by different elements; (4) there seems to be no means by which a sequence can be sped up and slowed down with relative timing remaining invariant. The first three problems will be briefly discussed in this section.

Consider the first problem: in some sequential actions the elements are too brief and sequences are executed too rapidly for it to be possible that feedback from one element triggers the next. For example, highly skilled typists can produce keystrokes at rates approaching 1000 a minute, about 17 every second[34]. Even if we assume that feedback from very early in the execution of a keystroke is used to trigger the next, this rate is too quick for feedback chaining to be plausible. Assuming that keystroke programs are instantiated in the brain, it would be expected to take at least 80 milliseconds for a stroke to be initiated by feedback from the previous stroke[35], which would correspond to an upper limit of about 12.5 keystrokes per second. In addition, we have seen that finger movements for keystrokes can overlap, so that movement to execute one stroke may start only a few milliseconds after movements to execute the previous one have started. In some cases, a movement may start before the movements for preceding strokes have started, as is the case for the movement for the 'i' keystroke in Figure 13.6. The only way that chaining could account for this is by supposing that a keystroke is triggered not by feedback from the preceding keystroke, but by execution of whatever strokes happen to start early enough. So, for instance, typing the word 'epic' in Figure 13.6 might begin by initiating the 'i' keystroke; then as the finger starts moving, sensory feedback is generated that triggers the 'e' keystroke, and then a little later the 'p' keystroke (which occurs too soon to be initiated by feedback from execution of the 'e' keystroke). Accounts of this type are obviously very contrived (they are invented purely to fit the theory to the data) and the feedback would have no functional role beyond triggering subsequent elements (it is not being used as a check for successful completion of previous elements). In addition, there is no experimental data that supports such accounts.

The second problem for feedback chaining is that some sequences can be executed, at least initially, without sensory input of any kind being present during execution[36]. After only a few elements the fingers fail to reach their targets, and the sequence breaks down[37]. However, this seems to be due to the inability to make corrective adjustments, so that errors accumulate[38], rather than to a failure to trigger subsequent elements. Nevertheless, it is evident that some serial actions can be partially executed in the absence of sensory feedback, and so response chaining cannot be the mechanism responsible for sequencing.

The third problem relates to how a chaining mechanism can account for the recruitment of the same element in different contexts. For example, imagine typing the word 'every' in which the letter 'e' is followed by a 'v' and by an 'r'. A simple feedback chaining account would predict that 'e' would always be followed by the same letter. In order to account for cases like these, the feedback chaining theory would either need to invoke an additional mechanism, or else resort to contrived explanations like those discussed above in relation to the first problem with chaining.

These problems with feedback chaining have led to it being abandoned as a plausible account of rapidly executed sequences in skilled linguistic acts or in musical performance[39]. Of course, the first two of the problems described above do not apply to internal chaining in which a signal generated by one elemental program triggers the next (as in Figure 13.1). The third problem, however, does apply to internal chaining. There have been several attempts to get around it, but none of them are considered satisfactory[40]. Much more plausible accounts of element sequencing in language production have been constructed based on the idea that sequence order is established by a process at a higher level to that of the elemental programs (or production units) themselves, i.e., a sequencing process or control program (Figure 13.2B).

The fact that response chaining is unable to provide a satisfactory account of some types of serial act does not imply that there are no serial acts for which chaining is the sequencing mechanism. In fact, there are some cases in which sensory information arising from execution of one element in a sequence appears to be necessary for production of subsequent elements. One such act is described next.

13.1.10 Lane-changing is a two-phase maneuver

Changing lanes when driving a motor vehicle is a commonly executed maneuver. The path followed by the vehicle along the road during a lane change is shown on the left of Figure 13.7 (arrows to indicate the direction of travel). The middle of the figure shows the position of the

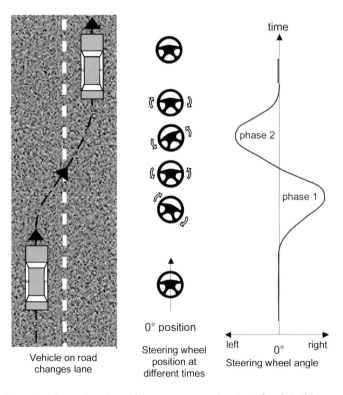

Figure 13.7: *Changing lanes is a two-phase maneuver (see text for details).*

steering wheel at different times; the zero position is adopted during straight line driving. The steering wheel angle as a function of time (angle-time graph) is shown on the right of the figure. The angle-time graph shows that steering wheel movement involves two 'phases': a movement to the right and back to the center (phase 1) followed by a movement to the left and back to the center again (phase 2).

Most people are unaware that lane-changing involves a two-phase (biphasic) movement of the steering wheel, though they are quite capable of executing the maneuver in a skillful fashion. When people are asked what kind of steering wheel movement is required to make a lane-change maneuver, they typically say that only the first phase is needed – a turn to the right and back to the center, as in in Figure 13.7 – and omit the second phase[41]. This is an example of the memory underlying motor skill being *implicit*, which is to say that a person can demonstrate their knowledge through doing (a person can competently execute a lane change), but is not able to consciously retrieve information from memory concerning what exactly it is that they actually do.

It is possible that the lane change is a motor chunk comprised of two behavioral elements corresponding to the two phases. If this is the case, we can ask whether the second element is initiated by a signal from a governing control program, or whether feedback arising from execution of the first element serves as the trigger.

13.1.11 Visual feedback triggers the second phase of the lane-change maneuver

If execution of the two phases of the lane-change is governed by a program, then it should be possible to execute the entire maneuver in the absence of vision. This was tested in a study that used a fixed-base driving simulator[42] (see Figure 13.8A). A participant's task in the experiment was to steer along a straight section of road with four lanes, two in each direction. The road passed through a tunnel. Speed was constant and not under the participant's control. Upon entering the tunnel, visibility rapidly declined until the scene was no longer visible. At this point, no visual information about heading direction or the road was available, and it was as if the person were driving in complete darkness (the visual display was blank). As soon as the display was completely blank, a visual cue was presented to the participants indicating that they should change from the lane they were in to the other lane on their side of the highway, and then continue straight down the road in the new lane. A trial ended when the participant indicated that they were in the new lane and heading straight down the road (though they could not actually see that this was the case, as they were still in the tunnel). In short, participants were required to execute a lane change maneuver without being able to obtain visual feedback about the execution.

If a lane change maneuver is pre-programmed as a whole unit, then it would be expected that both phases of the maneuver would be performed even though participants were driving without being able to see the scene ahead of them. However, the participants did not execute both phases of the maneuver; only the first phase was executed, and the second was typically absent. The effect of omitting the second phase is to change heading direction, as shown in panel B of Figure 13.8. This part of the figure shows the paths taken by the driver through the virtual environment for lane changes from the left lane to the right lane (blue) and vice versa (red). As the paths show, the driver crosses into the other lane (the first phase of the maneuver) but fails to straighten up (the second phase). When the second phase is omitted, the car heads straight off the road (or straight into the tunnel wall).

These findings show that people can execute the first phase of the maneuver without vision, but that they do not produce the second phase unless they can see where they are going[43]. Thus, initiation of the second phase requires feedback from execution of the first phase. The experiment suggests that the feedback information required is visual, and more recent work has confirmed that a brief view of the scene ahead is all that is needed to initiate the second phase[44]. However, it is possible that the second phase could also be initiated by somatosensory or vestibular information. The somatosensory and vestibular systems are stimulated during real lane-change maneuvers but are not stimulated in a fixed-based driving simulator, since

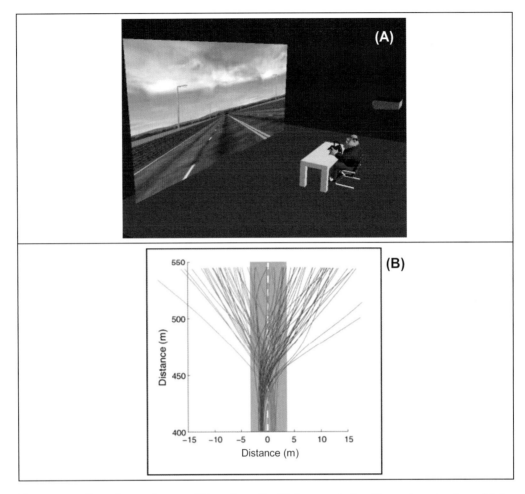

Figure 13.8: *Experimental set-up (A) and results (B) from a study of lane changing in a driving simulation. (A) Courtesy of Guy Wallis. (B) Reproduced from* Current Biology, *12,* Wallis *et al. An unexpected role for visual feedback in vehicle steering control. 295–299. Copyright (2002), with permission from Elsevier.*

the person is not subject to any real accelerations. When the same task as described above was performed in a motion-based driving simulator, which tilted participants as if their vehicle was subject to the lateral (centripetal) accelerations that would be present when driving a real car along curved paths, the results were almost identical to those obtained in the fixed-based simulator[45]. This result confirms that visual feedback information provides the signal that triggers the second phase of the lane-change.

13.1.12 Sensory information can play several roles in the production of motor chunks

We have seen that sensory feedback from earlier elements is not used to trigger later elements in some voluntary serial acts, whereas it is in some others. Feedback triggering is useful when execution of one element should only occur once the previous element has been successfully completed – it is not appropriate, for instance, to execute the second phase of a lane change until the first phase has moved you into the new lane. Thus, it is not the case that feedback chaining and programmed sequencing are mutually exclusive alternative accounts of how the motor system is organized; they are different methods for sequencing that are appropriate in different circumstances.

In cases where sequencing is governed by a program of some kind, sensory information can contribute to control of the behavior. As discussed in the context of locomotion (Chapter 8), although sequencing of the step cycle is governed by a central pattern generator (CPG), sensory information obtained during execution plays a vital role in adapting movement to the conditions and correcting errors. The locomotor CPG produces rhythmical signals and distributes them to the appropriate motor neuron pools and associated circuitry, and is thus responsible for producing the basic pattern of the locomotor movement cycle. Nevertheless, it would be impossible to adapt the locomotor movement cycle to the environment or to correct for slips or stumbles without sensory information, which is continuously being fed into the CPG circuitry. Sensory information plays a similar role during the execution of rapid sequences in speaking[46] and typing[47].

It is also important to note that even if sequencing is governed by a program, sensory feedback can still play a role in sequencing. Locomotion provides examples: we saw in Chapter 8 that feedback from the legs can play a role in initiating the switch from the stance phase to the swing phase, and can also delay the switch that would otherwise be initiated by the CPG.

13.2 Speech Production

13.2.1 Introduction

Linguistic acts may be the most frequently and skillfully executed of all sequential human motor behaviors, and are probably the most thoroughly researched. People produce language for long periods every day, starting from an age of about one-and-a-half years. We speak or use sign language, we write or type, sometimes for hours at a time. Whatever the form of a linguistic act – spoken, typed, written, signed – it can be segmented into distinct behavioral elements, though the movements involved are often executed as a continuous stream without distinct boundaries between elements.

A great deal of research has been conducted on all different kinds of language production with a view to understanding the neural processes responsible. The combinatorial approach is commonly adopted[48], which means that the production processes are conceived as being composed of distinct elements (e.g., elemental programs) responsible for the production of the behavioral elements[49]. To apply the approach, we need to identify behavioral elements and then try to understand how the mechanisms that produce these elements are organized so as to produce sequences. In this part of the chapter we will look at the segmentation of continuous streams of speech into behavioral elements (speech sounds), and consider how the combinatorial approach can be applied to speech production; similar issues for handwriting will be discussed in section 3 of the chapter.

13.2.2 Production of linguistic acts requires the coordinated activity of large numbers of muscles

Execution of linguistic acts involves the coordinated activity of many muscles and fine control over numerous moving parts. Skilled writing, typing, and signing involve coordinated movements of the joints of several fingers, and of one or both arms; a large number of different muscles are directly involved (see Chapter 2). Speaking is similar: all the sounds we make when we speak occur as the result of muscular contractions and relaxations. About one hundred different muscles cooperate in the production of speech. This includes the intercostal muscles of the chest, diaphragm and abdomen that control the flow of air into and out of the lungs, and the muscles of the vocal tract, as listed below.

Figure 13.9 shows a mid-sagittal cross-section of the human head and neck to show the location of various structures of the vocal tract, which consists of the larynx, the pharynx, the mouth and lips (oral cavity) and the nasal cavity[50]. The parts of the vocal tract involved in the production of different sounds are referred to as **speech articulators**. Speech articulators do not necessarily move while a person is speaking. For example, the alveolar ridge does not move, but it counts as an articulator because it is an important piece of anatomy in the production of various sounds. Likewise, the top front teeth do not move, but they count as a speech articulator because the tongue must make contact with them to produce the 'th'-sound in words like *thought* and *thank*.

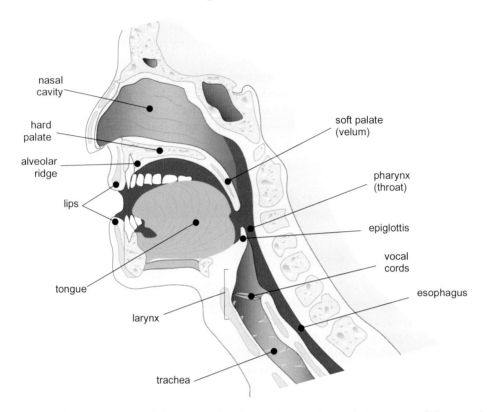

Figure 13.9: *Sagittal section of the human head, showing anatomical structures of the mouth, nose and throat.*

The muscles involved in speech are those that are used to force air from the lungs and those involved in moving the active articulators. The muscles that move the active articulators are:

(1)   Muscles of the velum (soft palate): there are three that act to lower the velum (depressors), two that act to raise it (elevators) and a muscle that tightens (tenses) it.

(2)   Muscles that move the lips: rounding the lips, protruding them (pouting), raising and lowering them and bringing them together (closing the mouth) involve six different muscles. There are also muscles that lower the corners of the mouth (as when making a sad face, ☹) or raise them (as when smiling, ☺).

(3)   Muscles of the jaw: there are eight muscles that move the jaw.

(4)   Muscles of the tongue: there are four muscles within the tongue body (intrinsic muscles), and four others that move the tongue but are external to it (extrinsic muscles).

(5)   The muscles of the pharynx (throat): there are at least three of these, and when they contract they narrow the pharynx (pharyngeal constrictors).

(6)   The extrinsic and intrinsic muscles of the larynx ('voice box'): there are eight intrinsic muscles and another twelve muscles that are external to the larynx. The external muscles either act to raise it (elevators) or lower it (depressors), and some also have effects on other articulators involved in speaking.

This list indicates that production of the rapid sequences of sounds that make up spoken words and sentences requires fast, precise and coordinated control over many component parts that are actuated by a large number of distinct muscles. Handwriting, typing and signing may not require coordinated control over quite as many muscles as speaking, but they nevertheless represent masterful feats of fine motor control.

13.2.3 Continuous speech can be segmented into individual speech sounds

At first glance, the basic behavioral elements from which linguistic acts are composed might appear fairly clear cut: the behavioral elements in typing are keystrokes, the behavioral elements in speaking are individual speech sounds, the behavioral elements in handwriting are individual written letters. In the case of typing and speech, these may be the fundamental elements of behavior: individual keystrokes and speech sounds cannot be meaningfully divided into smaller elemental components (handwriting is discussed in the next part of the chapter).

In all types of linguistic act, the individual behavioral elements in a motor chunk typically run seamlessly together in a continuous stream. In handwriting, this is particularly clear in the case of a written word when the word is formed by a continuous line drawn with the pen. Sound is usually produced continuously when individual words are uttered, and often when uttering whole sentences – there are normally no silent moments during the utterance of words, and seldom are there moments of silence between words during normal conversational speech. The continuous line drawn by the pen or the continuous stream of sound issuing from the mouth can be segmented into identifiable, distinct elements. When we look at handwritten words we can (usually) discern the individual letters; when we listen to continuous speech we can hear strings of more or less distinct, individual sounds that roughly correspond to letters. That continuous streams of speech can be divided into elemental sound segments (distinct speech sounds) is relatively uncontroversial and is the foundation of phonetics. However, there are no easily identifiable and readily defined acoustic boundaries between different speech sounds: for present purposes, we will simply assume that this division can be carried out in a principled, unambiguous way and yields valid elemental segments of the acoustic speech signal[51].

Consider uttering the English word *peek*. The utterance constitutes a single syllable, but can be segmented into three speech sounds: a 'p'-sound, an 'e'-sound and a 'k'-sound. These speech sounds count as behavioral elements of speech, for they appear in many different utterances where they are preceded and followed by different sounds. For example, utterance of the words *cool*, *keen*, *cat*, *skull* and *look* all involve utterance of a 'k'-sound. In each case the 'k'-sounds occur in the context of other speech sounds: we will refer to this as the **linguistic context**. The linguistic context of the 'k'-sound is different in these different words: the 'k'-sound in *cool* is preceded by silence (if the word is spoken in isolation) and followed by an 'oo'-sound, the 'k'-sound in *skull* is preceded by an 's'-sound and followed by an 'uh'-sound. A spoken syllable may also appear in different linguistic contexts (it may be a part of many different words), but it is a chunk, not an element, since it can be further segmented into component sounds.

The idea that a given type of speech sound such as a 'k'-sound can be segmented out of a continuous vocal stream and appear in many different linguistic contexts is what it means to say that the sound is a behavioral element of speech production. It seems to be incontrovertibly true – you can hear 'k'-sounds in the utterances of thousands of different words. However, it turns out that when a particular person produces a 'k'-sound in different contexts, the acoustic properties of the sounds that they produce are slightly different. A listener will normally recognize these slightly different sounds as instances of the same type of sound (a 'k'-type sound). The speech sound types mentioned in the previous paragraph are examples of **phonemes**, and acoustic variants of a phoneme are called **allophones**. These concepts are discussed further in the next section.

13.2.4 Speech sounds vary with linguistic context

Different people may utter the same speech sound slightly differently as a consequence of their individual experience and biomechanics. We will not be concerned with the differences between individual speakers, but rather with the differences in the utterances of speech sounds by the same speaker in different contexts. As noted earlier, there are often detectable differences in the qualities of a particular type of speech sound when it is uttered by the same person in different linguistic contexts. For example, when a person utters the word *keen*, the 'k'-sound is normally produced with a puff of air called *aspiration* and the 'k'-sound is said to be *aspirated*. The 'k'-sounds in *skull* and *look* are normally produced without aspiration. Phoneticists identify at least five different variations in the way the 'k'-sound is uttered in British received pronunciation[52]. Although these variations are acoustically slightly different, they are all obviously 'k'-sounds – they are variants of the same **phoneme** in English. The shorthand notation for the 'k' phoneme is /k/; the forward slashes indicate that it is the phoneme we are referring to and not a letter or a particular utterance of a speech sound.

A phoneme may be defined to be *a speech sound type that can determine differences in the meaning of utterances*. This means that if you exchange one phoneme for another one, the meaning of the utterance will (usually) change[53]. For example, utterance of the word *keen* begins with an aspirated 'k'-sound; if the 'k'-sound is replaced with a 's'-sound (a different phoneme) the word *seen* is produced, which has a different meaning. Replacing the aspirated 'k'-sound with an unaspirated one (same phoneme) does not change the meaning – the word *keen* is still uttered (though it might sound a little funny).

It is important to recognize that a phoneme is a speech sound type, which is a conceptual entity, not a particular utterance. A given phoneme can take many different forms: it can have different acoustic properties and/or be produced by different movements of the speech articulators. The phoneme is defined by the characteristics that all its different variants have in common[54]. Acoustic variants of a phoneme are called **allophones** of that phoneme. Any given language (or dialect) will have a relatively small number of phonemes – English spoken in British received pronunciation has about 47 phonemes[55] – but will have very much larger number of acoustically distinguishable speech sounds, because each phoneme can have numerous allophones. Note that a speech sound that is an allophone of one phoneme in a certain language may not be an allophone of that phoneme in a different language[56]. For example, in the Icelandic language, aspirated and unaspirated 'k'-sounds are instances of different phonemes (exchanging them can alter the meaning of the utterance), whereas in English they are allophones of /k/.

Variation in how a person utters a phoneme in different linguistic contexts is often a consequence of the way in which the speech articulators need to move in order to produce the different speech sounds in quick succession so that they run together in a continuous stream. In what follows, we will provide an outline of how speech sounds are produced, before discussing the processes responsible for the effects of linguistic context on phoneme production.

13.2.5 The larynx produces sounds that are amplified and modified as they pass through the upper vocal tract

The variety of possible speech sounds and associated movements of the active articulators is quite complex; there is an associated technical vocabulary that is extensive and difficult to come to grips with[57]. A full discussion would go too far beyond the current discussion, but some basic facts will be useful.

Vowels and vowel-like sounds, as well as sung notes, are produced by vibrations of the vocal cords as air escapes past them. The process is similar to that involved in blowing a raspberry, in which air escapes past the lips, causing them to vibrate and produce a buzzing sound. The vocal cords sit in the larynx (Figure 13.9), also known as the voicebox because it is the region where sounds of different pitch and volume are produced. When breathing in and out the cords are abducted (Figure 13.10A) and there is an opening between them (open glottis), allowing air to flow freely through the larynx. When using the voice to sing or make a vowel sound, the cords are adducted and the glottis is closed (Figure 13.10B). Figure 13.10 shows a view from the back of the mouth down into the larynx. When air is forced from the lungs and the cords are adducted (panel B), pressure builds up behind them. The cords are flexible bands, and with sufficient pressure they open slightly and a puff of air is released, which reduces the pressure immediately behind them so that the cords spring back to the closed position. Pressure builds up again and the open-close cycle is repeated. This cycle happens very quickly, fast enough for many hundreds of cycles to occur every second – the vocal cords vibrate. This vibration is largely responsible for the fundamental frequencies of vowel sounds and sung notes. The principal way in which notes or vowels of different fundamental frequencies are produced is by altering the tension in the cords: the greater the tension, the higher the pitch of the sound produced[58]. The same principle applies to blowing raspberries: the tighter the lips, the higher the frequency of the 'buzz'.

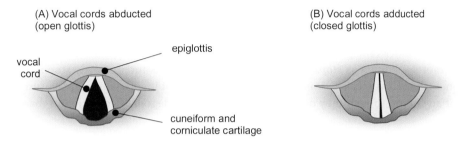

Figure 13.10: *The view looking down the throat at the vocal cords.*

The sounds generated in the larynx are shaped by the articulators in the parts of the vocal tract above the larynx. The tubes and cavities of the supralaryngeal vocal tract have particular characteristics that tend to resonate at some frequencies but not at others, which results in the attenuation of some sound frequencies but not others. This means that the upper vocal tract acts as a filter of the sounds produced in the larynx; some sounds pass through relatively unaffected, while others do not. The conception that has just been outlined is called the **source-filter model** of speech sound production[59], and is represented in block diagram form in Figure 13.11.

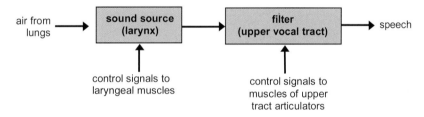

Figure 13.11: *Block diagram of the source-filter model of speech sound production*

Figure 13.11 indicates that the sound produced by the larynx (its output) is largely controlled by means of muscles that actuate the vocal cords; the filtering characteristics of the upper vocal tract are controlled by means of muscles that actuate the upper tract articulators (pharynx, tongue, velum, lips and jaw). These movements produce narrowing (or widening) of the vocal tract at particular locations. Narrowing is usually called *constriction* in this context, and the moveable articulators most frequently involved are the tongue, lips and jaw. Movement of the velum also produces a particular kind of constriction – it narrows or blocks the pharyngeal passage into the nasal cavity. Thus, there are three fundamental ways in which movements of the speech articulators can influence the kinds of vocal sounds that a person produces:

(1)   Adducting and tensioning the vocal cords to produce sounds of different fundamental frequencies.

(2)   Lowering or raising the velum to allow air into the nasal cavity and out through the nose.

(3)   Constricting the vocal tract either partially or completely, which modifies the sound in various ways depending on the nature of the constriction.

Some examples of movements involved in making particular speech sounds are described next.

13.2.6 Utterance of consonant sounds can involve complete closure of the vocal tract

To produce different vowel sounds, the vocal cords are adducted and the supralaryngeal articulators, particularly the tongue and lips, move so as to alter the shape of the vocal tract and produce different degrees of constriction, but the tract is never completely closed, so air can always escape through the mouth. To produce consonants, the tract may be momentarily completely closed: to make a 'b'-sound, 'm'-sound or 'p'-sound the lips must close; to make a 't'-sound or a 'k'-sound the tongue makes contact with the hard palate and momentarily blocks the passage of air. Consonant sounds that involve the complete closure of the tract are known as *stops*, because the passage of air is momentarily stopped. Other consonant sounds such as 'f'-sounds and 'sh'-sounds do not involve complete closure of the tract at any point, though they do involve a much greater degree of constriction than vowel sounds.

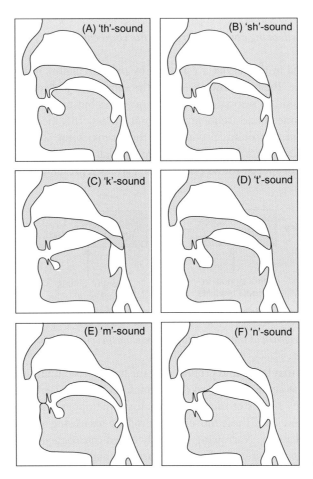

Figure 13.12: *Postures of the speech articulators when articulating different consonant sounds.*

The primary location at which the vocal tract is constricted when a consonant sound is produced is called the **place of articulation** of the sound. Some examples are shown in Figure 13.12, which shows postures of the speech articulators in cross-section (passages through which air can pass are unshaded). Panels A and B show postures for producing 'th'- and 'sh'-sounds where the vocal tract is constricted by moving the tongue to the palate. These constrictions do not block the vocal tract: in both cases there is a small gap through which air can pass. When making a 'th'-sound, as when uttering the words *think* or *thank*, air escapes between the tip of the tongue and the back of the upper front teeth; the sound is said to have a *dental* articulation. To make 'sh'-sounds, the gap is between the tongue tip and the *alveolar* ridge; the sound has an alveolar articulation. Panels C to F show postures where the vocal tract is completely closed so that air cannot escape through the mouth. To make 'k'-sounds, the back of the tongue contacts the roof of the mouth at the velum (velar articulation, panel C); alveolar articulation is used to produce 't'-sounds (panel D). Production of 'm'- and 'n'-sounds involves closure of the tract so that air cannot escape through the mouth, but the velum is depressed so air can pass into the nasal cavity and out through the nose. Production of 'm'-sounds involves lip closure (panel E, bilabial articulation); alveolar articulation is used to produce 'n'-sounds (panel F).

13.2.7 Production of a speech sound is influenced by the sounds that precede it and follow it

Since different speech sounds are produced by different movements and postures of the speech articulators, we can safely assume that acoustically different variants of the same phoneme (allophones) are the result of variation in the movements and/or postures of the articulators[60]. Such variation of articulator movement and posture has been demonstrated to occur when the same phoneme is uttered in different linguistic contexts[61].

Most of the systematic variations in articulator movements and postures that occur when a phoneme is uttered in different contexts can be attributed to the fact that it is being articulated in a rapid, continuous sequence with other speech sounds. The movements and postures produced during the utterance of a particular phoneme are influenced by the articulation of neighboring sounds in the sequence. A straightforward example is provided by the utterance of the 'a'-sound by an English speaker when it is followed by an 'm'-sound or an 'n'-sound, which occurs when speaking words such as *hammer* or *and*. When an 'a'-sound is uttered in isolation or in contexts where there are no 'm'- or 'n'-sounds nearby, the velum is raised and the nasopharynx is closed (as it is in panels A–D of Figure 13.12). In contrast, when it is followed by an 'm'- or 'n'-sound, an 'a'-sound will typically be articulated with the velum lowered. As indicated in panels E and F of Figure 13.12, lowering of the velum is required for proper utterance of 'm'- and 'n'-sounds.

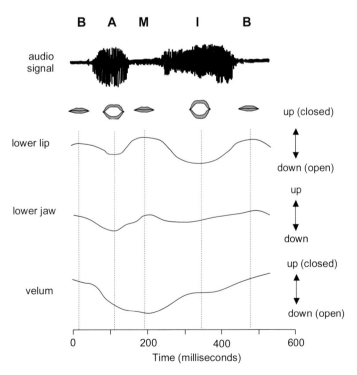

Figure 13.13: *Acoustic signal and vertical movements of selected speech articulators during an utterance of /bamib/. Based on data presented in Figure 1 of Saltzman and Munhall (1989), originally reported by R.A. Krakow.*

Figure 13.13 shows how lowering of the velum associated with production of an 'm'-sound occurs during articulation of a preceding 'a'-sound when an English speaker utters the nonsense word *bamib* as part of the phrase, 'it's a *bamib* sid'. The figure shows records of the sound being made by a person (audio signal, top), together with the vertical position of selected speech articulators (lower lip, lower jaw and velum) as functions of time. The audio signal shows the vowel utterances as two distinct sound bursts (above the 'A' and the 'I') that have a greater intensity than the sound produced when making the 'b'-sound or the 'm'-sound. The lips are apart (mouth open) while the vowels are being uttered, and briefly come together to articulate the consonant sounds. The figure shows that downward movement of the velum begins when the 'a'-sound starts to be uttered (beginning of the first burst in the audio signal) and continues to move down throughout the 'a'-sound's utterance. The fact that the nasopharynx is open during utterance of the 'a'-sound means that air can escape through the nose. This affects the acoustic quality of the sound – it gives it a nasal quality (the sort of sound quality you get when you hum with your lips tightly shut). Such an 'a'-sound is said to be *nasalized*; it is a nasal allophone of the particular 'a'-sound phoneme[62] that the person uttered.

In the foregoing example, the articulation of the 'a'-sound was influenced by the 'm'-sound that follows it. Figure 13.13 also provides an example of articulation of a speech sound being influenced by the sound that precedes it: the articulation of the 'i'-sound is influenced by the preceding 'm'-sound. When 'i'-sounds are uttered in isolation or in linguistic contexts without nasal consonants, the nasopharynx is closed (velum raised). Inspection of Figure 13.13 shows that the velum is moving upwards throughout the utterance of the 'i'-sound, and so the nasopharynx is at least partially open for almost the whole time this sound is being produced. As a result, the 'i'-sound is nasalized.

The influence that articulation of one phoneme has on the articulation of other phonemes in the same utterance is referred to as **coarticulation**:

> **COARTICULATION (SPEECH):** the influence of the linguistic context on the movements and postures of the speech articulators during the production of a particular speech sound type (phoneme). The influence of adjacent (or nearby) phonemes on each other's articulation.

Note that although the term is suggestive of concurrent or overlapping articulation of two or more speech sounds, concurrent execution per se does not constitute coarticulation[63]. Only if articulation of one phoneme affects the articulation of another is there coarticulation. Thus, if the articulation of two phonemes overlaps in time but the overlap has no effect either on the articulatory movements made or on the sounds uttered[64], then there is no coarticulation. As discussed later (section 13.2.9), concurrent articulation of phonemes usually results in coarticulation.

Two varieties of coarticulation are sometimes distinguished, *anticipatory coarticulation* and *carry-over coarticulation*. Anticipatory coarticulation refers to the situation in which an upcoming phoneme has an influence on one or more of the phonemes that precede it in a sequence: the influence of the /m/ phoneme on articulation of the preceding 'a'-sound in Figure 13.13 is an example. Carry-over coarticulation refers to the situation in which a phoneme influences one or more of those that follow it in a sequence: the influence of the /m/ phoneme on articulation of the following 'i'-sound in Figure 13.13 is an example.

The lowering of the velum during the production of the 'a'-sound in Figure 13.13 is a coarticulation of the 'a'- and 'm'-sounds. In this example, movement of an articulator that is usually immobile during the utterance of an 'a'-sound does move during its utterance when an 'm'-sound follows. In other cases, coarticulation of two phonemes can involve an articulator that must move in order to articulate either one of them. For example, consider uttering the English words *key* and *core* that both have /k/ as their initial phoneme. Articulation of the subsequent vowel phonemes – the 'e' phoneme in key (written /iː/ in the international phonetic alphabet) and the 'o' phoneme in *core* (written /ɔː/) – involve moving the tongue into different positions: the back of the tongue moves up to produce a smaller gap between the tongue body and the palate to articulate /ɔ:/, the front of the tongue is moved up to articulate /i:/. The back of the tongue makes contact with the velum when articulating the initial /k/ (see Figure 13.12C), but the place of contact is typically different in utterances of *key* and *core*: it is influenced by how the tongue must subsequently move to articulate the vowel. When the front of the tongue must be raised to articulate the /i:/ in *key*, the place of articulation of the preceding /k/ occurs further forward (closer to the teeth); when the back of the tongue must be raised to articulate /ɔ:/, the preceding /k/ is articulated further back[65]. It seems as if the tongue reaches 'a compromise with the demands of an adjacent articulation'[66]. This is sometimes referred to as *blending* of articulations[67].

Coarticulation is the rule rather than the exception in speech; there are very few cases in which adjacent speech sounds in a sequence show no signs of coarticulation[68]. Even if evidence of coarticulation is not present in the acoustic signal, it will be present in the articulatory movements themselves. In the two sections that follow, we will address the following two questions: (1) can coarticulation be observed in serial acts other than speech? (2) What processes underlie observed coarticulations?

13.2.8 Coarticulation is not only observed in speech

As discussed in section 1 of the chapter, sequential acts may involve overlapping execution of elements. For example, Figure 13.6 shows that the movements made to press different keys while typing can occur concurrently: in the figure, the movements made to strike the four letters keys when typing 'epic' all overlap with one another. However, we would not call such concurrent execution coarticulation unless the execution of one movement had some kind of measurable effect on the execution of the others. Such measurable effects have been found to be relatively rare in typing[69] and other keyboarding activities such as piano playing[70]: movements of individual fingers involved in making a particular keystroke only rarely show any signs of being influenced by other keystrokes in the sequence. In speech production and sign language, however, such effects are quite common[71]. Measureable effects of one element on the next are also found in handwriting[72]; for example, the shape and timing of a written letter has been found to depend on the letter that precedes it[73]. Similar effects have also been reported in sequential target-directed aiming movements in which people move from one target to the next in a specified sequence[74]. A general definition of coarticulation may thus be given that applies to any serial act[75] (including speech):

> **COARTICULATION (GENERAL):** the influence of the 'movement context' on the movements being made when executing a particular behavioral element within a sequence. The influence of adjacent behavioral elements on each other's execution.

13.2.9 What is responsible for coarticulation?

The examples of coarticulation given earlier strongly suggest that the phenomenon is the result of an overlapping execution of two or more behavioral elements. For instance, during the utterance of the 'a'- and 'm'-sounds shown in Figure 13.13, it looks as if velar lowering is part of the articulation of the 'm'-sound that overlaps with articulation of the 'a'-sound. In speech production, coarticulation and overlap are often treated as if they were more or less the same thing, with coarticulation occuring because 'the movements of different articulators for the production of successive phonetic segments overlap in time and interact with one another'[76].

The combinatorial approach to speech production asserts that each behavioral element (phoneme) is generated by a production element of some kind (e.g., an elemental program): speech acts are built by combining production elements together to form chunks (such as syllables) and ultimately meaningful sentences and statements. Speaking an individual word or syllable involves coordinating the activation of the appropriate production elements in the correct order and with the right timing. From this point of view, it is the behavioral outputs of different production elements that overlap: articulatory activity generated by one production element occurs at the same time as articulatory activity generated by others. This is sometimes referred to as **coproduction**[77]. For example, the 'm'- and 'a'-sounds in an utterance of *bamib* (Figure 13.13) would each be produced as a consequence of activating a specific production element. The 'm'-phoneme production element is responsible for velar lowering, since this is an essential component of producing the 'm'-sound but not the 'a'-sound. Thus, velar lowering during articulation of the 'a'-sound is due to overlap of the production (coproduction) of the 'a'- and 'm'-sounds.

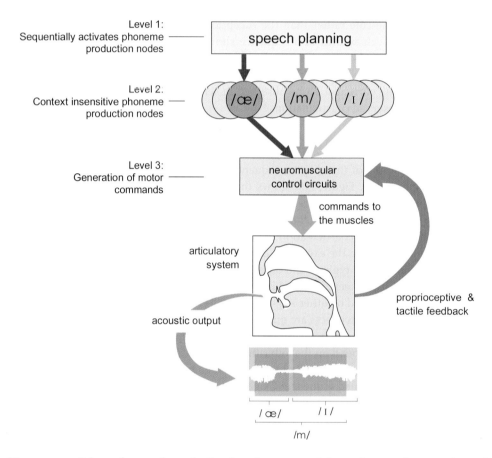

Figure 13.14: *Scheme for speech production based on sequential recruitment of context-insensitive phonemic production nodes (see text for explanation).*

According to the coproduction view just described, coarticulation arises due to overlap in the activity of two or more phonemic production elements[78]. These elements are responsible for the production of particular phonemes – whenever a particular phoneme needs to be produced, its production element is activated. The output of these production elements is not sensitive to the linguistic context – their output is the same regardless of the context. Thus, coarticulation is not a consequence of differences in the outputs of the phonemic production elements themselves, but occurs at the levels of the motor system that implement the commands they issue. Figure 13.14 illustrates the kind of control architecture involved in this account of coarticulation: the system is shown producing the sequence of phonemes /æ/, then /m/, and then /ɪ/, as might occur during an utterance of the nonsense word *bamib*[79]. Three different levels or layers of neural control are shown. The top level is labeled speech planning; it is responsible for specifying the sequence of phonemes in the utterance, and its output is a temporal sequence of activation signals for the next level (it corresponds to the sequencing process in Figure 13.2). The second (middle) level consists of phonemic production elements (or nodes), one for each phoneme in the speaker's repertoire. Activation signals from the top level activate first the /æ/ element, then the /m/ element, and lastly the

/ɪ/ element. The timing of these activation signals is crucial if articulation of the phonemes is to overlap: the /m/ element must be activated, while the /æ/ element is in the process of producing its output so that the output of the /m/ element overlaps with the output of the /æ/ element. The production elements send output signals to the lowest level of the control system (neuromuscular control circuits), which produce command signals for the muscles of the vocal tract. At the bottom are shown schematics of the articulators and the acoustic signal uttered by the speaker. Differently formatted zones overlie the acoustic signal to give a rough indication of the overlapping articulation: the time during which /æ/ is articulated is shaded orange; the period of /ɪ/ articulation is shaded green.

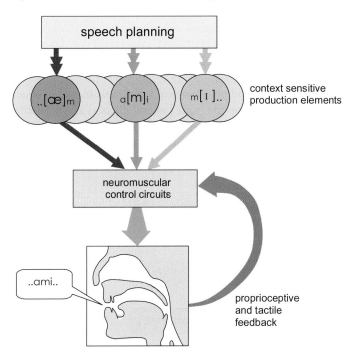

Figure 13.15: *Scheme for speech production based on sequential recruitment of context-sensitive phonemic production nodes (see text for explanation).*

From a combinatorial perspective, coproduction of the behavioral elements provides an obvious explanation for coarticulation. However, it is not necessarily the case that coarticulation is the result of coproduction. For example, it is possible to imagine that production elements are parameterized differently according to the sequence in which they appear, and that it is this difference in parameterization that allows them to run together smoothly and produce what appears to be overlap but is not[80]. There are various ways in which this might be organized; one simple possibility will be described for illustrative purposes[81]. Consider again the sequential production of an 'a'-sound and an 'm'-sound when uttering *bamib*. It might be that the velum moves downwards while the 'a'-sound is being uttered because the production element that generates 'a'-sounds is parameterized differently so that it produces velar lowering. This is done because the speech planning system 'knows' that an 'm'-sound is to be produced next, and adjusts the 'a'-sound program in a way that facilitates production of the 'm'-sound so as to achieve a smooth transition. According to an account of this kind, there is no overlap in the production of 'a'- and 'm'-sounds in the sense of overlapping outputs of the 'a'- and 'm'-sound production elements. Figure 13.15 illustrates the kind of control architecture that could be operative in this account of coarticulation. The levels of control are the same as those in Figure 13.14 except that the phonemic production elements are no longer context-insensitive; they are parameterized so as to produce outputs that are appropriate for the context. The /æ/ production element is parameterized so as to produce a nasal allophone of the phoneme (denoted [æ]$_m$) in anticipation of the /m/ that is to follow. The /m/ production element is parameterized so as to produce an allophone (denoted $_a$[m]$_i$) suited to the context provided by the preceding /æ/ and following /I/ and similarly for the /I/ production element. These parameterizations are provided by the speech planning level, as indicated by the double arrows, which represent the fact that in this account the signals both activate and parameterize the phonemic production elements.

It is also possible for phoneme production elements to be context-insensitive, but for coarticulation to arise not because of overlap of phoneme articulation but as a result of the processes that transform the output of the production elements into motor commands (the processes that take place in the blocks labeled 'neuromuscular control circuits' in Figures 13.14 and 13.15). A model in which coarticulation effects can be produced in this way is outlined next.

13.2.10 Phonemic production elements feed into a speech trajectory generator

A particularly well-developed and physiologically plausible model of speech production will be discussed here. It is is based on the same general ideas as the model trajectory generator for reaching described in Chapter 11. There are two different versions of this speech production model, an early version[82] and a later version[83]. We will provide a basic outline of the earlier version, since it is slightly simpler and easier to understand.

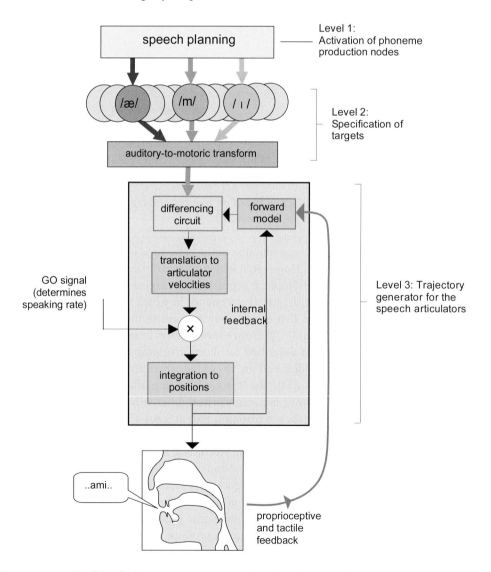

Figure 13.16: *Model of phoneme sequence production incorporating a trajectory generator for the articulators.*

Figure 13.16 shows a block diagram[84] representing the essential components of the model. There are three main levels, which are similar to those in Figure 13.14. Level 3 is a speech articulator trajectory generator that works in basically the same way as the reaching trajectory generator described in Chapter 11. The reaching trajectory generator (Figure 11.31) receives a specification of a target, and outputs commands for moving a limb so that its working point reaches the target. Likewise, the speech trajectory generator receives specifications of speech sound (phonemic) targets and transforms these into commands to the muscles that actuate the speech articulators. Phonemic targets that are input to the trajectory generator are represented as sets of vocal tract constrictions needed to produce instances of the phonemes. Thus, the targets are specifications of the vocal tract shapes or configurations associated with production of particular speech sounds (phonemes): if the target vocal tract shape is achieved, an instance of the associated phoneme will be produced. The initial stage of the trajectory generator forms a 'difference vector' by subtracting an estimate of the current configuration of the vocal tract (obtained from information in sensory and internal feedback signals) from the target configuration.

Targets are generated by the Level 2 components shown in Figure 13.16. There are two layers in Level 2. The first layer consists of phonemic production nodes (one for each phoneme in the speaker's repertoire). These nodes represent phonemes in terms of variables that encode perceived qualities of speech sounds such as their frequency characteristics and other features that give them their perceptual distinctiveness. The second layer – the auditory-to-motoric transformation – transforms the auditory representation of phonemes into the vocal tract constriction representations that serve as targets for the speech trajectory generator. It is possible to imagine a simpler, single-layer structure for Level 2 in which the phonemic production nodes represent phonemes as tract constriction targets, which makes an auditory representation of phonemes unnecessary. Some authors have explicitly argued that speech production only involves tract constriction representations of phonemes[85]. The representation of phonemic targets in speech production has become a major topic in recent years, and there are reasons for supposing that phonemes are represented auditorily within the speech production mechanism, but the details are too complex to discuss here[86].

Simulations of the model shown in Figure 13.16 have shown that it is able to reproduce a wide range of phenomena observed in normal human speech, including coarticulation and motor equivalence. Since the model shown involves a single trajectory generator into which sequences of phonemic targets are fed, true overlap of speech sound articulation of the type discussed earlier with reference to Figure 13.14 is unlikely to occur. Overlap of articulation can occur in the model due to the sluggish dynamics of the speech articulators themselves (produces carry-over coarticulation), but the model does not account for anticipatory coarticulation in terms of overlap[87]. In this respect it contrasts with some other models, in which the main mechanism underlying anticipatory coarticulation is overlapping articulation; these models assume that there are distinct programs for each phoneme that can be activated in parallel[88]. Coarticulation in the model shown in Figure 13.16 is discussed next.

13.2.11 Sources of coarticulation in a trajectory generation model of speech production

As might be expected, the movements of the articulators needed to reach a specific target configuration are different for different initial configurations. This is obvious in the example shown in Figure 13.17. Panel A shows a sequence of three frames illustrating characteristic constrictions associated with an utterance of the phoneme sequence /kɐt/ (the word *cut*)[89]; panel B shows constrictions associated with an utterance of the sequence /tɐk/ (the word *tuck*). An 'uh'-sound (instance of the phoneme /ɐ/) appears in both utterances. To produce the constriction needed to articulate this sound, the tongue must move differently depending on the articulation involved in producing the preceding sound ('k'-sound or 't'-sound); the arrows in the first frame of each panel indicate the primary movement of the tongue. The speech trajectory generator of Figure 13.16 produces different movements for the /k/ to /ɐ/ transition and the /t/ to /ɐ/ transition because it forms motor commands that act to drive the articulators from their initial configurations (associated with articulating /t/ or /k/) to their target configurations (for articulating /ɐ/).

According to the definition of coarticulation given earlier, we should view the differences in tongue movements needed to make the /k/ to /ɐ/ transition and the /t/ to /ɐ/ transition as instances of coarticulation. Although this is not a very interesting kind of coarticulation, it does illustrate the fact that the speech articulators can reach the same tract configuration by means of different movements – a kind of motor equivalence. Of more interest in the present context are cases in which the configurations actually achieved are different in different linguistic environments, such as was the case for the articulation of /k/ when it appears in utterances of the words *key* and *core* as discussed in section 13.2.7. The model can generate coarticulation of this sort as a consequence of the way in which the phonemic targets are conceived.

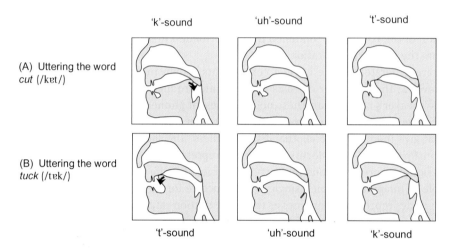

Figure 13.17: *Sequence of postures when uttering the words* cut *(A) and* tuck *(B).*

So far, we have not been very precise about the representation of phonemic targets. Consider the concept of a target configuration of the vocal tract. A number of variables that describe the vocal tract have been identified as important for defining phonemic targets[90]; in the model, these include: (i) lip aperture (the size of the gap between the lips); (ii) tongue tip height (vertical distance of the tongue tip from the upper jaw); (iii) tongue body height (vertical distance of the body of the tongue from the upper jaw); (iv) tongue tip horizontal position (forwards-backwards position of the tongue tip); (v) tongue body horizontal position. A complete target configuration would specify values for these five variables along with several others that are also included in the model[91]. However, the values do not need to be specified exactly: a range of values for each variable is typically compatible with the production of a particular speech sound type (phoneme). Thus, vocal tract configuration targets can be specified as ranges of values for the different variables rather than specific, single values for each. The tract configuration target for a phoneme can be considered to be a list of value ranges for each tract variable. A pictorial representation of this type of target specification is shown in Figure 13.18 for /k/. To keep things simple, only two vocal tract variables are considered – tongue body height (TBH) and tongue body horizontal position (TBP)[92]. This allows us to represent the target graphically as a rectangular region in a two-dimensional space, where one dimension corresponds to TBH and the other to TBP. The /k/ target is specified as a TBH range and a TBP range, and is shown as a shaded rectangular region in the figure. A 'k'-sound is produced provided that the tongue's position lies somewhere within the target region; its exact position does not matter.

Targets specified as regions within articulatory configuration 'space' can give rise to coarticulation in a way that differs from the coarticulatory mechanisms already discussed. Figure 13.19 provides a pictorial illustration for an example in which /k/ is articulated in two different contexts. In panel A, /k/ is articulated after the articulation of /i/ such as might occur when saying the work *leak* (the 'e'-sound in *leak* is an instance of the phoneme /i/). The tongue configuration for making the utterance of /i/ is shown as a blue circle: when uttering

/i/ the tongue body tends to be positioned moderately high, but relatively far back in the mouth. In panel B, /k/ is articulated following an articulation of /u/ such as might occur when saying the word *Luke* (the 'u'-sound in *Luke* is an instance of /u/). The tongue configuration for making the utterance of /u/ is again shown as a blue circle: when uttering /u/, the tongue body tends to be positioned moderately high, but relatively far forward in the mouth. The trajectory generator drives the tongue from the initial configurations to different final configurations within the /k/ target, as indicated by the arrows: further back in the target in panel A, further forward in B. The result is that the place of articulation of /k/ (the contact between the tongue and palate) is different in the two utterances.

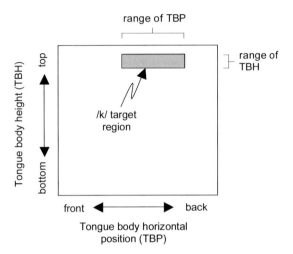

Figure 13.18: *Phonemic targets are specified by ranges of tract variables, and so correspond to regions (volumes) in tract configuration space; see text for explanation.*

The example shown in Figure 13.19 is an instance of carry-over articulation – utterance of a speech sound influences the articulation of a subsequent sound in a sequence (see 13.2.7) – but it is not due to overlapping articulations of two sequential phonemes. The model can also generate anticipatory coarticulation, by modification of the configuration target for an upcoming phoneme so that it is appropriate for the preceding linguistic context. Such modifications are achieved by enlarging or shrinking the target along one or more dimensions, making corresponding changes in specified ranges of the tract variable(s)[93]. This is a variation on the idea of parameterizing phonemic production nodes so that the target specified is the one best suited to the utterance being produced (see section 13.2.9 and Figure 13.15)[94].

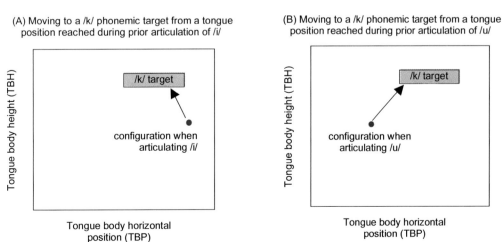

Figure 13.19: *Approaching a /k/ phoneme target from two different initial tongue configurations; see text for explanation. (Based on Figure 12 in Guenther, 1995.)*

13.2.12 Speech production is a hierarchical process

In this part of the chapter we have discussed speech production from the point of view of the combinatorial approach. The approach is particularly well suited to speech, which divides up very naturally into behavioral elements, many of which are common to all spoken languages. There is currently no theory of speech production that is not combinatorial, and it is very hard to imagine how such a theory might be constructed. The model of speech production outlined in the foregoing sections comprises a hierarchy of levels, and includes a level of control in which there are individual production elements (nodes) responsible for each behavioral element (phoneme) in a speaker's repertoire. These nodes specify targets for a speech articulator trajectory generator (next level down in the hierarchy) that produces motor commands that drive the articulators to the targets. The model exhibits both carry-over and anticipatory coarticulation and displays motor equivalent speech production – generates instances of the same speech sound using different articulatory movements and tract configurations – as well as several other phenonema of speech production, such as rapid compensation for disturbances[95].

We have not discussed how the phonemic production nodes themselves are activated in the right order and with the right timing to produce meaningful utterances. In Figures 13.14–13.16, the top level of the hierarchy – the block labeled *speech planning* – is responsible for these functions and for formulating plans for uttering words, statements and other acts of linguistic communication. This block represents an array of complex processes that cooperate to generate sequences of signals that activate the production nodes. These processes are likely to include some of the most complex activities carried out by the human brain, and go far beyond the domain of motor control – they fall into the domain of psycholinguistics. The generally accepted view seems to be that the subprocesses of speech planning are themselves organized in a hierarchical fashion, but we will not attempt a discussion of these theoretical ideas here: a discussion of the lowest level of the planning hierarchy that outputs signals to the production nodes can be found in some of the literature already cited[96].

13.3 Writing and Drawing

13.3.1 Introduction

People are able to move a working point along paths that have a seemingly endless variety of shapes. This is particularly evident in drawing and writing, where the working point is usually the point of a pen or pencil, with which we can draw a vast array of different curves, forms and letters. We can produce the same form in different sizes, at different speeds and using different effectors. As briefly discussed in Chapter 11, it is possible to write using a wide variety of different effectors, even if you have never written with them before. These abilities suggest that the nervous system represents the shapes of letters and figures in an abstract form that does not specify size, speed of production or the body parts to be used. This raises two important questions:

(1)   What is the nature of the internal representations of letters and other figures?
(2)   How are these representations transformed into motor commands that cause the working point to move so as to trace out a figure or write letters and words?

In this part of the chapter we will describe some of the performance characteristics of writing and drawing and consider answers to the questions just raised. As we will see, most people who have studied the control processes involved in writing and drawing have adopted a combinatorial approach. They have tried to understand continuous, complex movement patterns as sequences of elemental components, in much the same way that speech production can be understood in terms of sequences of elemental sound-types (phonemes) and typewriting as sequences of keystrokes. The ability to write and draw with similar performance invariants using different effectors (see section 11.1.14) implies that the elemental components involved in handwriting and drawing are encoded by the nervous system in an effector-independent manner (i.e., in working point coordinates).

In speech and typewriting the identity of the elemental components is uncontroversial, perhaps because it is easy to identify the elemental components as individual, goal-directed actions – the production of a sound type or the striking of a key. In handwriting and drawing, it turns out to be less simple. We might propose that the elemental actions in handwriting correspond to the production of individual letters (when the written language employs an alphabet). Written letters certainly have characteristics that we might expect of elemental components: they are recognizable in the script, the same letter can appear in different words, and letters can be written individually. However, it might be that the elemental actions are not letters at all, but smaller elements (strokes) from which the letters are composed. Most accounts of how writing and drawing is generated propose the existence of elemental strokes that are segments of a continuous trajectory, and that do not achieve any goal independent of the production of the segment itself. As a result, there is no consensus concerning what the elements are, or if they exist at all[97]. We will consider such elemental segments and the evidence for their existence in this part of the chapter.

13.3.2 The kinematics of letter writing exhibits invariant patterns

When people write letters, words and numerals the primary goal is to draw a particular shape on the writing surface, and so the working point must follow a particular path. How the working point actually moves along this path does not matter as far as the overall goal is concerned: there are infinitely many possible ways in which the working point could move along any given path. As with target-directed aiming movements, it has been found that people spontaneously move the working point in particular ways that display certain lawful regularities.

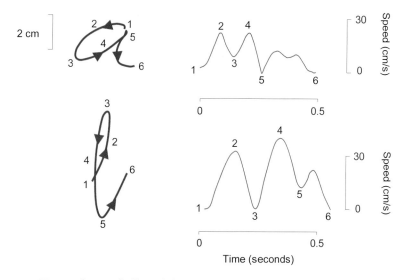

Figure 13.20: *Written letters (left) and the tangential speed of the penpoint as they were written. Data from Viviani and Terzuolo (1982b).*

Figure 13.20 shows two examples of letters written by individual participants in one series of studies[98]. The written letters themselves are shown on the left of the figure; they correspond to the path traversed by the penpoint (the arrows indicate the penpoint's direction of motion). As the penpoint traverses its path to draw the letter, its speed increases and decreases. This is clear from the tangential speed profiles of the penpoint shown on the right of the figure. The numbers next to locations on the letter correspond to those next to locations on the tangential speed profile: for the letter 'a', number 1 is the point where the pen first makes contact with the paper, and point 6 is where the pen leaves the paper. Inspection of the figure reveals that the locations of the letter where the path is most tightly curved (points 3 and 5 on both letters) are points at which the tangential speed is lowest (minima in the speed profile). Conversely, the speed is greatest (maxima in the speed profile) where the path is straightest (points 2 and 4 on both letters). The relationship between path curvature and tangential speed is described further in the next section.

A person can write the same letter at different speeds and with different systems of effectors, and can produce letters of a wide range of sizes. As discussed in section 11.1.14, the form of the written letter remains approximately the same (invariant) across these kinds of variations in production: written letters retain the characteristic style of the writer, despite changes in writing size, speed, and effectors[99]. Some examples are shown in Figure 13.21. Panel A shows the tangential speed profiles obtained from a person who wrote the letter 'a' five times; the person was instructed to write the same sized letter at different speeds. In the figure, the different speeds are ordered from the quickest (top) to the slowest (bottom), which clearly shows that the temporal pattern of peaks and valleys in the speed profile is preserved over changes in speed. More precisely, the relative timing of the peaks and valleys is approximately the same in all five cases: the five profiles look like squeezed or stretched versions of one another.

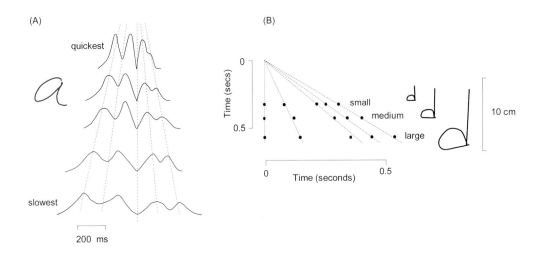

Figure 13.21: *Kinematic patterns of pen motion when writing letters shows invariant relative timing; see text for explanation. Data from Figures 4 and 6 in Viviani and Terzuolo (1980).*

Panel B of Figure 13.21 illustrates invariant relative timing when the same letter is written in different sizes. The same person wrote the letter 'd' three times: a large, medium, and small sized letter, as shown on the right. The largest letter took longer to complete than the medium letter, which took longer than the smallest. The different sized letters also involved different joints – the smallest letter was written using movements of finger and wrist joints, whereas the largest letter involved elbow and shoulder joint motion. The time of occurrence of various kinematic landmarks – tops of peaks and bottoms of valleys – were derived from the speed profiles for the letters, and the times of five of these are shown on the left side of panel B (filled circles), showing the same five landmarks for each sized letter. The plot shows that the relative timing of the landmarks is approximately the same for the different sized letters. These examples and others like them[100] suggest that not only is a person's handwriting of a similar shape and form when written at different speeds, with different sizes and with different effectors, but also that the penpoint's movement is similar: the speed profile has a similar pattern of peaks and troughs, with similar relative timing.

The results described above are for single letters, but similar results have been obtained for written words and syllables[101]. Letters are seldom written in isolation, but appear within words and phrases; that is, they appear in different (written) linguistic contexts. When a person writes the same letter as an element in different words, it is recognizably the same letter (assuming the person can write legibly). A person's style of writing individual letters is preserved across changes in linguistic context[102], and there are some data to suggest that the kinematic patterns of the tangential speed profiles of individual letters are preserved when the letters appear within words[103].

13.3.3 Writing and drawing at different sizes has a relatively small effect on movement time

When people are asked to write the same text or to draw the same figure with different sizes, they move the working point faster (greater average and peak speeds) when they write or draw larger. The result is that the proportional increase in the time taken to complete the movement (movement time, MT) is smaller than the proportional increase in size. For example, if the size is doubled (100% increase), an increase in MT of less than 10% is typical. In Figure 13.21B, the largest letter is about three and a half times the size of the smallest. In contrast, the MTs are about 0.43 seconds for the smallest letter and about 0.55 seconds for the largest, an increase of just over one quarter: a 350% increase in writing size is associated with an increase in time of less than 30%.

There seems to be no general relationship between changes in size (or trajectory length) and changes in MT. Different figures and words, different levels of practice, different effectors and different task demands all seem to affect the relationship between MT and size[104]. Some studies have reported very little change in MT across quite large changes in size. For example, in one study a 600% increase in size was associated with an increase in MT of only about 5%[105]. Other studies have reported much larger effects. One of the largest was obtained in a study of writing the letters 'l' and 'e' in the string 'ele' within different linguistic contexts[106]: the letters were written in two sizes, one 27% larger than the other, and there was a 24% difference in MT.

The general rule is that larger-amplitude writing and drawing movement are executed at greater speed, so that increases in MT are relatively smaller than the increases in path length. This finding has been rather confusingly called the *isochrony principle*[107] – the term *isochrony* comes from the Greek meaning 'same time'. This term is not really appropriate, since the movement times for differently sized movements are not the same. It has been suggested that the relatively small increases in MT observed for large changes in size may be a manifestation of the speed-accuracy trade-off in writing and drawing[108]. The speed-accuracy trade-off was discussed in Chapter 12.

13.3.4 Speed and curvature are tightly coupled in drawing and writing movements

As mentioned earlier, Figure 13.20 suggests that there is a consistent relationship between the speed with which a path is traversed and the curvature of the path. The working point moves faster when the curvature is low, and slower when the curvature is high[109]. The same behavior is observed in aimed movements that require passing through viapoints or moving around obstacles. An example of a planar viapoint movement is shown in Figure 13.22: panel A shows the path taken by the working point when a person was instructed to pass through a viapoint on the way to target point. The main feature of the path is that it has two low-curvature (roughly straight) regions and a high-curvature region in the vicinity of the viapoint, which is typical of such movements[110]. Panel B shows the tangential speed profile for the movement; it has two peaks separated by a minimum. The minimum occurs near the viapoint, where the path is most sharply curved; the peaks are the maximum speeds reached while traversing the relatively straight sections of the path. This behavior is superficially like that observed when people drive, skate, cycle or run: movement slows down when negotiating curves.

(A) Viapoint movement to target

(B) Tangential speed profile for movement in (A)

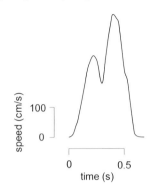

Figure 13.22: *A planar viapoint movement and its tangential speed profile (based on data reported in Bullock* et al., *1999).*

Figure 13.23 illustrates the phenomenon for the same letter 'a' shown in Figure 13.20. Panel A shows how curvature can be given a numerical value at any point on a curve drawn on a plane surface. Intuitively, the idea is to draw the circle that passes through a given point on the curve and most closely approximates the curve in the neighborhood of that point[111]. Two such circles are shown in the figure; they are drawn through a point where the curved line (blue) is tightly curved (P1) and through a point where it is not so tightly curved (P2). The radius of such a circle is the **radius of curvature** of the curved line at the associated point, so the radius of curvature at point P2 in panel A is R. The **curvature** at a point is defined to be the reciprocal of the radius of curvature, so the curvature at point P2 is 1/R. The larger the radius of curvature, the smaller the curvature (the less curved the line is); for a straight line the curvature is zero (the radius of curvature is infinite). Thus the value of the curvature is greater at point P1 than at point P2, which is as you would expect. Panel B shows a plot of the tangential speed of the penpoint as it drew a letter 'a' (top), and a plot of the radius of curvature (1/curvature) of the path of the pen at each moment in time (each moment in time corresponds to a unique point on the letter 'a').

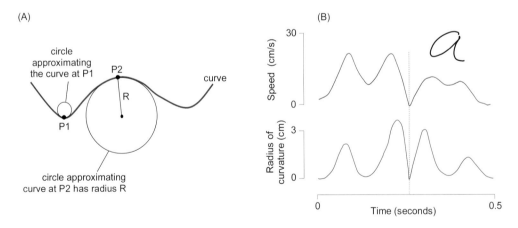

Figure 13.23: *Radius of curvature co-varies with the speed of the working point. (A) Definition of the radius of curvature; see text for details. (B) Tangential speed and radius of curvature profiles for a letter 'a' (data from Viviani and Terzuolo, 1982b).*

Figure 13.23B shows that as the person wrote the letter, the speed of the penpoint increased as the radius of curvature increased (curvature decreased) and decreased as the radius of curvature decreased (curvature increased). The peaks and valleys in the two profiles correspond closely in time. This type of co-variation of speed and curvature has been observed in studies of handwritten letters and words[112], hand-drawn geometrical figures, spirals and scribbles[113], and drawings of a variety of specified shapes made by tracing around templates[114] or passing through viapoints[115]. An example from a study in which participants repeatedly traced a specified shape formed of two ellipses, a small one inside a larger one, is shown in Figure 13.24. The right of the figure shows the paths followed by a participant as they traced around the figure five times with a stylus. The left of the figure displays plots of the tangential speed of the stylus tip (top) and the radius of curvature (bottom) as the paths on the right were traced out.

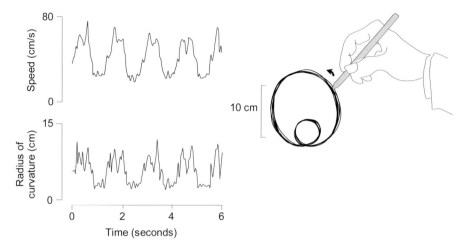

Figure 13.24: *Tangential speed and radius of curvature when repeatedly tracing a double ellipse (right). Data from Figure 1 of Viviani and McCollum (1983).*

13.3.5 The one-third power law describes the speed-curvature relationship

The relationship between the tangential speed of the working point and the radius of curvature of the path when writing or drawing has been quantified as a power law relationship of the following form:

$$V = G \times R^{\beta} \tag{13.1}$$

which states that the tangential speed (V) is proportional to the radius of curvature (R) raised to a power (β), with G being the constant of proportionality (called the *gain factor*)[116]. Since the curvature (κ) is equal to 1/R, equation (13.1) can also be written,

$$V = G \times \kappa^{-\beta} \tag{13.2}$$

The value of the gain factor (G) tends to be different for different shapes, for different people, and when a figure is drawn at different speeds. In contrast, the value of the exponent, β, has been reported to be about 1/3 (the cube root) regardless of shape, speed or the individual[117]. This is not only the case for movements of a working point over a plane surface, as in drawing and writing, but also for movements in 3-D space (drawing or scribbling in the air)[118]. For this reason, the relationship described by equations (13.1) and (13.2) can be called the **one-third power law**[119]. In the literature, it is also known as the **two-thirds power law** because of the way in which it was first expressed (in terms of the angular speed of the working point rather than the tangential speed; see section 13.3.7)[120]. Thus, the two-thirds and one-third forms are two different ways of formulating the same law – they are two names for the same thing[121].

Although the one-third power law is called a 'law' it is really more of a rough rule of thumb. Across different types of drawing and writing tasks and different individuals, the average value of the exponent comes out to be around 1/3, but the values for different tasks range from less than 0.25 to nearly one[122]. Thus, the value of 1/3 represents a rough average rather than precise and unvarying characteristic of movement. What is clear, however, is that there is a rather tight relationship between speed and curvature in drawing, writing and tracing movements that is well described by a power law (equations 13.1 and 13.2).

13.3.6 What is the origin of the one-third power law?

The one-third power law provides a good description of people's movements in a wide variety of different tasks, including tongue movements during speech[123]. Thus, it is a descriptive or empirical regularity, not an explanatory construct; it can be viewed as a kind of approximate invariant of motor performance, similar to the invariants of reaching described in Chapter 11. As discussed in section 11.2.5, performance invariants can provide clues regarding the content of motor programs, but in some cases they can arise as consequences of the biomechanical properties of the musculoskeletal system.

It has been a matter of debate whether the one-third power law is encoded in the central commands or is a consequence of biomechanical factors[124]. Some authors have preferred the former interpretation, based on demonstrations that the law is a consequence of the application of optimality principles at the level of trajectory planning (see section 11.2). For example, it has been shown that the law can arise as a consequence of minimizing jerk[125] and minimizing end-point variance[126]. It has also been shown that the law can arise from the operation of the kind of trajectory generator discussed in Chapter 11 (see section 11.2.17)[127], as well as other types of trajectory generation principles[128]. Thus, the one-third power law may be encoded in the motor commands themselves, rather than emerging as a consequence of the way in which the biomechanical periphery responds to these commands in the process of movement execution. Evidence supporting this view is provided by electrophysiological studies of the firing patterns of neurons in the motor and premotor cortex of monkeys: the firing patterns of populations of such neurons during the execution of drawing movements have been found to carry information about movement that incorporates the one-third power law[129]. These findings are consistent with the one-third power law being encoded in the motor commands. There can be little doubt, however, that the biomechanical properties of the muscles and limbs have a significant influence on the kinematic characteristics of movement, and so it is possible that the one-third power law arises as a consequence of both the central commands and the peripheral biomechanics[130]. Regardless of the relative contributions, the power law seems to emerge from principles that we have already discussed, and so it does not require any additional concepts or control processes to account for it.

13.3.7 Complex working point trajectories can be segmented into sequences of simpler elements

As mentioned in the introduction to this part of the chapter, the combinatorial approach has been popular as a means for understanding the production of elaborate working point trajectories such as those shown in Figures 13.20–13.23. This approach proposes that the trajectories observed in handwriting and drawing are composed of sequences of elemental segments generated by distinct production units.

If a continuous drawing or handwriting trajectory is composed of sequences of elemental segments, then it must be possible to identify these segments unequivocally. A relatively straightforward way of segmenting handwriting, for example, is simply to divide the trajectory at the points of maximum curvature (or, equivalently, the minima in the speed profile). This method would segment the letters 'a' and 'l' in Figure 13.20 into three segments each: a segment between points 1 and 3, another between points 3 and 5, and the last between points 5 and 6. An example of this segmentation procedure applied to the handwritten letter string *eyleyl* is shown in Figure 13.25: each circle marks a point of maximum curvature (minimum speed), and pairs of points define individual segments. The string is therefore divided into 16 segments, one between points 0 and 1, the next between 1 and 2, the next between 2 and 3, and so on. A number of possible means for identifying segments similar to this simple method have been proposed[131]. However, there is no generally accepted way of identifying trajectory segments that corresponds to the outputs of production units, and there is no evidence to suggest that the segments shown in Figure 13.25 correspond to elements of the production process. In what follows, we will describe a method for segmenting continuous trajectories based on the one-third power law, which has been claimed to provide the most compelling evidence for segmented control of continuous trajectories[132].

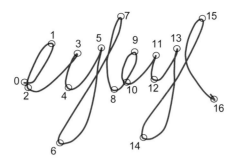

Figure 13.25: *The handwritten letter string* eyleyl *can be resolved into a sequence of 16 segments by treating the points of maximum curvature (inside the circles labeled 1 to 16) as the boundaries between neighboring segments. (Data from Wright, 1993.)*

The one-third power law as expressed by equations (13.1) and (13.2) is a relationship between the speed of movement (V) and the curvature (or radius of curvature) that has two parameters: the power (β), which has been found to be about 1/3, and the proportionality (or gain) factor (G). As mentioned, the power does not vary very much, but the gain factor varies systematically, and is different for different shaped paths and speeds of execution. The gain factor has been found to be different for different pieces of a continuous working point path; to put it another way, continuous paths have been found to be made up of several segments, each with a different value for gain factor. Figure 13.26 presents an example from one study[133]. Panel A shows a spiral figure drawn by a participant in the study; it also indicates how the angular position (ϕ) of the penpoint at an instant of time can be defined. The rate of change over time of this angular position is the angular velocity of the penpoint. Panel B plots the magnitude of the angular velocity against path curvature (κ) raised to 2/3 power ($\kappa^{2/3}$). If the power law is expressed in terms of the angular velocity rather than the tangential speed, the power comes out as 2/3 rather than 1/3 (see section 13.3.5). According to the law, if angular

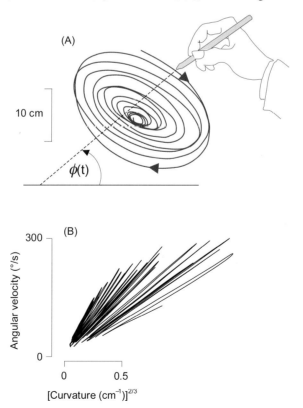

Figure 13.26: *A spiral drawn by an experimental participant (A) and the magnitude of the angular speed of the pen as the spiral was traversed, plotted against curvature²ᐟ³ (B). Data from Lacquaniti, Terzuolo, Viviani (1983), Figure 9.*

velocity is plotted against the 2/3 power of the curvature, the result will be a straight line with a slope equal to the gain factor. Panel B shows this to be the case, but also shows that there are a variety of different slopes. In fact, each straight line in the graph corresponds (approximately) to one of the loops of the spiral: as the spiral gets tighter and tighter towards the center, the slope of the line decreases (so the largest loops are associated with the steepest lines). This means that the one-third power law holds for every loop of the spiral, but that the gain factor is different for each loop, though constant throughout each loop.

The results shown in Figure 13.26 suggest a possible way to divide a continuous trajectory into a sequence of segments: define a segment to be a piece of the path where the one-third power law holds with a constant value of the gain factor. This idea has been investigated for scribbling and drawing elliptical shapes of various kinds[134]. Figure 13.27 presents a simple example from an experiment in which participants repeatedly traced out a double-ellipse figure (one complete tracing is shown on the left) with a continuous motion of the stylus. The graph on the right of the figure plots the tangential speed of the stylus tip against the radius of curvature of the figure (raised to the 1/3 power, $R^{1/3}$) for a continuous sequence of tracings around the figure. If the drawing motion obeys the one-third power law ($V = G\ R^{1/3}$), then a plot of *tangential speed* against $R^{1/3}$ will be a straight line with a slope equal to the gain factor. The graph on the right of Figure 13.27 shows that this is the case for repeated tracings of the double ellipse figure: there are two approximately straight lines with different slopes that both intercept the vertical axis close to zero. The upper line (1) corresponds to several movements around the outer (larger) ellipse; the lower line (2) corresponds to several movements around the inner ellipse.

The results shown in Figure 13.27 show that the double ellipse can be resolved into two segments for which the one-third power law holds – the gain factor is constant for each segment (the two lines are straight) and different for the two segments (the lines have different slopes). The two segments correspond to the inner and outer ellipses of the figure. Similar segmentation has been observed for more complex figures and for scribbling[135]. It has been proposed that the behavioral segments identified using the one-third power law (or closely related criteria[136]) reflect an underlying segmentation of the control process[137]. Before considering what kind of segmented control might be involved in drawing and handwriting, we will briefly consider whether the existence of behaviorally identifiable segments is evidence for segments of control.

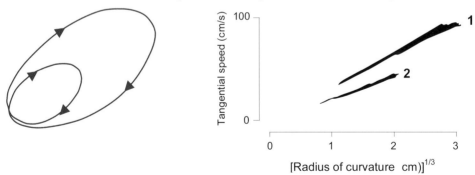

Figure 13.27: *Path traced by a stylus, and the tangential speed of the stylus tip plotted against radius of curvature to the 1/3 power. Data from Figures 1A and 2A of Viviani and Cenzato (1985).*

13.3.8 The existence of behavioral segments does not imply segmented control

If a continuous trajectory can be resolved into a sequence of segments, then it is possible that the trajectory is generated by a process that is itself segmented (segmented control): distinct units of production might be responsible for generating the segments of the trajectory. However, empirical segmentation of a trajectory using a method like that described in section 13.3.7 can only provide evidence for segmented control if non-segmented control processes can be conclusively ruled out. In other words, it is necessary to demonstrate that a continuous control process cannot produce trajectories that can be resolved into segments using the chosen method.

Several studies have shown that continuous control mechanisms are able to generate trajectories that can be resolved into segments. For example, one study showed that if the nervous system preplans a minimum jerk trajectory for a complete figure (e.g., that shown in Figure 13.27) and subsequently plays out the plan in a continuous fashion – a continuous, non-segmented mode of control – the executed trajectory is resolvable into segments for which the one-third power law holds (approximately) with a constant value of the gain factor[138]. This result demonstrates that the ability to resolve a trajectory into segments using the power law method does not establish that the underlying control process is segmented. Empirical studies have also provided evidence to suggest that segmentation of trajectories does not imply that they are produced by a segmented control process[139].

Thus, the short answer to the question 'does the existence of behavioral segments imply segmented control?' is 'no, not necessarily', because continuous, unsegmented production and control processes generate trajectories that can be resolved into segments. The situation is further complicated by the fact that the answer to the converse question – does segmented control imply the existence of observable, behavioral segments? – also appears to be 'no, not necessarily'. In other words, a failure to be able to resolve a trajectory into segments does not necessarily imply that control is continuous and unsegmented. This can happen if the outputs of the elemental production units (programs) overlap in time, which results in overlap in the execution of the elements. The overlap in execution obscures the boundaries between one element and the next, so that they cannot be observed in the trajectory[140]. In this case, it could happen that production is segmented but the observed motion appears to be continuous and unsegmented. Additional evidence is needed to determine whether or not the process of movement generation involves elements of production.

To summarize, the existence of behavioral trajectory segments is neither a necessary nor a sufficient condition for segmented control. It is not necessary because segmented control can generate trajectories that appear to be continuous and unsegmented. It is not sufficient because unsegmented control processes are able to generate trajectories that can be resolved into behavioral segments.

Alternative criteria for identifying trajectory segments that correspond to the output of elemental units of control (elemental programs) have recently been proposed. One idea is that if a segment is generated by a production element, then once production has been started, it cannot be voluntarily terminated, but must run to completion. Thus, a movement element produced by an element of production can be defined as a trajectory segment 'that cannot be intentionally stopped before its completion'[141], and so could potentially be identified by means of experimental procedures that require people to try to stop ongoing performance when signaled to do so[142]. Unfortunately, there is no evidence to demonstrate that movements that can be voluntarily terminated before completion – such as target-directed aiming movements – are not elemental actions. In addition, there is no method that can unequivocally determine whether a movement that cannot be volitionally terminated once started is an element or a chunk, since a chunk can behave like an element (see section 13.1.4).

A different approach has been adopted in studies of handwriting. Handwritten text is hypothesized to be composed of sequences of elements that are simpler than letters[143]. These elements are not normally identified by applying a segmentation criterion (such as the one-third power law criterion or the maximum curvature criterion discussed in section 13.3.7), but by making proposals concerning what the elemental segments might be and then using modeling to demonstrate the sufficiency of the proposed elements for the generation of handwriting. Handwriting models are discussed next.

13.3.9 Most models of handwriting propose the existence of elemental strokes

Many theoretical accounts of how handwriting is generated propose that the elemental units are not letters but smaller segments called **strokes**, which are generated by distinct production elements[144]. These accounts all propose that there are only a very few different types of strokes, though the exact number varies: some propose only one or two types of stroke, while others have five or more. Well-practiced sequences of strokes form motor chunks that might be single letters, strings of commonly co-occurring letters (e.g., 'ing' or 'th'), or frequently written words and signatures[145]. A program for a chunk specifies the sequence of strokes, together with other characteristics such as their orientation and size (exactly what other characteristics are specified differs for different models).

Most models suggest that the production mechanisms in drawing and writing are organized in a similar way to those described in section 13.2 for speech production: there are production units for each of the behavioral elements (strokes), and these feed into a trajectory generator or trajectory generators (see below). The units themselves are activated in the appropriate order with an appropriate timing by superordinate control programs. Two different ways in which stroke information is encoded have been proposed:

(1)   As complete specifications of the working point path (or trajectory) for each stroke[146].

(2)   As appropriately timed sequences of discrete spatial targets[147].

One version of the first way of encoding stroke information proposed a set of five elemental strokes[148]: straight line, oval, 'u'-shape, loop and 'hook' stroke (these are shown inside the stroke production units in Figure 13.29). The set of strokes is not unique, so the idea is compatible with different people using slightly different sets of basic strokes, and with the possibility that different people's basic stroke sets contain different numbers of strokes (at least five seem to be needed[149], but an individual's stroke set could contain six or seven strokes or possibly more). To form a given letter, the strokes are strung together and can appear in different orientations, sizes and positions.

The second way of encoding strokes is in terms of spatial targets, which are sent in sequence to a trajectory generator. In this type of scheme, the timing of the sequence is critical for the production of smoothly curved strokes. For example, imagine a hook stroke encoded as a sequence of two spatial targets relative to a starting location, as shown in panel A of Figure 13.28. If the targets are fed into the trajectory generator such that the second is fed in after the working point has reached the first, then the result would be a sequence of roughly straight segments, as shown in panel B. In order to produce a curvilinear stroke, the second target must be fed into the trajectory generator while the commands that drive the working point to the first target are still being generated, so the first target serves as a viapoint through which the path passes on its way to the second target (see Chapter 11). Correctly timing the input of the targets to the trajectory generator produces the required curvilinear hook stroke (panel C).

(A) Graphical representation of the internal encoding of a stroke as a sequence of two targets.

(B) Stroke produced if second target is fed to trajectory generator too late.

(C) Stroke produced if the two targets are issued at the correct time.

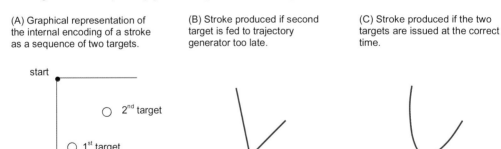

Figure 13.28: *A stroke encoded as a sequence of targets requires that the targets be fed to the trajectory generator with the correct timing, in order that the working point be driven along a curvilinear path.*

The basic structure of a model of the type just described closely resembles the structure of the speech production model shown in Figure 13.14. Figure 13.29 shows a simplified picture of the kind of model architecture involved in a handwriting model that uses a set of five elemental strokes described above. Each stroke is encoded by a production unit (or elemental program), perhaps as a timed sequence of targets. The outputs of these units are fed into a trajectory generator that generates commands for the muscles of the effectors used for writing. The sequencing of individual strokes is controlled by a higher level 'writing planner' that activates the stroke units in the required sequence and with the correct timing so as to generate the desired written text. In the figure, the first four units from the left are activated in the sequence 1, 2, 3, 4 (color denotes order in the sequence, with darker colors denoting earlier activation). The result of this sequence of activations is that the pen writes 'ul' (as shown). Models of this type that employ the feedback trajectory generators proposed for reaching and speech[150] (Figures 11.33 and 13.16) are able to successfully simulate many features of human handwriting, including relative timing invariance of kinematic events (e.g., Figure 13.21), invariance of letter shape over changes in writing size and speed, coarticulation effects (see section 13.2.8), and the relationship between path curvature and tangential speed (Figure 13.23).

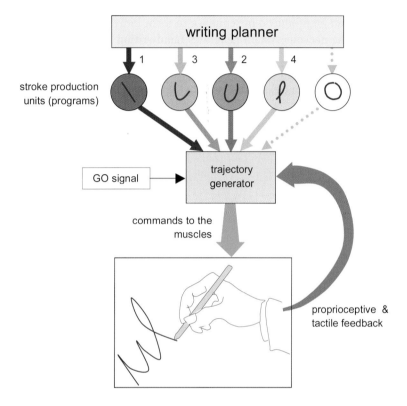

Figure 13.29: *Basic architecture of stroke-based models of handwriting that incorporate a general-purpose trajectory generator.*

Although various models of the types that have been discussed in this section can produce convincing simulations of handwriting that display many of the characteristics of real handwriting, there is currently no empirical data that allows us to determine exactly how handwriting is generated by the nervous system. Indeed, it is not even clear whether the nervous system uses a stroke-based method for generating handwriting. Non-stroke-based models exist that are also capable of generating realistic cursive script; one such model is outlined next.

13.3.10 Writing may be generated by oscillatory mechanisms

Although stroke-based models are by far the most dominant type in handwriting research, it is not firmly established that the nervous system works this way. For this reason, it is important to recognize that other possibilities exist. One such possibility is the oscillation model of handwriting[151]. The basic idea of this model is that handwriting is generated using two cyclical processes; one moves the working point (e.g., penpoint) up and down on the writing surface, and the other moves it left and right. Each process on its own simply results in the repetitive drawing of a line in one place, as shown in panel A of Figure 13.30. Superimposing a constant left-to-right motion of the pen on these oscillations produces extended, repeating patterns. For example, if a constant left-right motion is superimposed on an up-down oscillation, the pen moves across the page and traces out a sine wave pattern, as shown in panel B. Combining all three motions (up-down oscillation, left-right oscillation, and movement across the page) generates more complex repeating patterns, which can exhibit loops, humps and cusps, as shown in panel C of the figure. The exact type of loop, hump or cusp shape produced depends, in part, on the phase relationship between the up-down and left-right oscillations. The height of the shape depends on the amplitude of the up-down oscillation. Controlling the amplitudes, phases and frequencies of the oscillations will change the pattern drawn by the working point. By controlling these characteristics of the oscillations, it is possible to generate realistic-looking cursive script, as loops, cusps and humps of different shapes and sizes that can be produced in sequence to form individual letters[152]. Thus, it can be hypothesized that the nervous system generates handwriting by modulating the activity of two rhythm generators that are responsible for the up-down and left-right motion of the working point. The motor program in this scheme would be a specification of the amplitudes, phase-relationships, and frequencies of the two rhythm generators needed to produce the required letters and words.

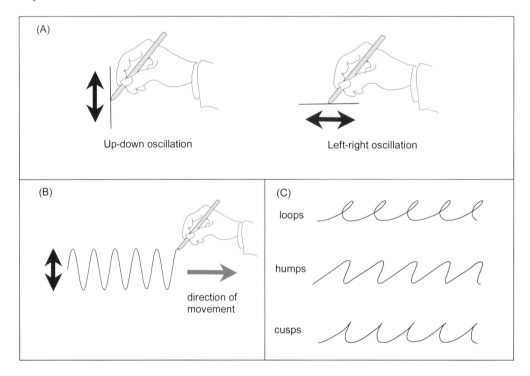

Figure 13.30: *Oscillation theory of handwriting; see text for explanation. (Panel C based on examples from Figure 1 of Hollerbach, 1981.)*

At the time of writing, it is not known exactly how the human nervous system generates writing and drawing movements. A number of sophisticated models have been developed that can successfully reproduce many of the basic features of handwriting. Most of these models are stroke-based and propose the existence of elemental writing units from which letters and words are constructed. In such models, the strokes are encoded in spatial coordinates of some form. The oscillation theory proposes instead that stroke and letter shapes are encoded in terms of the relative amplitudes, phases, and frequencies of two oscillatory processes, but the encoding is still made up of sequences of elemental components. Whatever the nature of the encoding, all models propose that there are higher-level programs that encode sequences of elements to be generated by lower-level production processes. In these terms, spatial encoding models and oscillation models are both examples of the combinatorial approach.

References & Notes

[1] See Flash, Hochner (2005); Sternberg, Knoll, Turock (1990).

[2] E.g., Reed (1982a).

[3] See Degallier, Ijspeert (2010); Flash, Hochner (2005); Giszter, Patil, Hart (2007).

[4] MacKay (1982); Schmidt, Lee (2011).

[5] A term from psychology for processes that require thought and/or attention (e.g., Ashcraft, Radvansky, 2010).

[6] MacKay (1982); Pew (1966); Verwey (2001).

[7] Shaffer (1991), p. 372.

[8] Verwey (2001).

[9] Jastrow (1906), p. 42. See also Bryan, Harter (1897).

[10] The term 'chunk' has been in common use in psychology since the 1950s; see Ivry (1996); Verwey (2001).

[11] For review see Rhodes *et al.* (2004).

[12] E.g., Watson (1920).

[13] Adams (1984), p. 20.

[14] This could be an efference copy signal.

[15] This seems to imply that the signal from one element excites the next. However, an alternative scheme in which execution of one element releases the next from inhibition is also possible (see Rosenbaum, 2009; Rumelhart, Norman, 1982).

[16] Kelso, Saltzman, Tuller (1986); Goodman, Kelso (1980).

[17] Ancient Egyptian and several eastern languages, such as Chinese, use logograms. Chinese is not purely logographic, as it employs other principles that resemble the alphabetic system.

[18] See Soechting, Terzuolo (1987).

[19] Sternad, Schaal (1999).

[20] Sternberg, Knoll, Turock (1990); Verwey (2001).

[21] E.g., Sternberg *et al.* (1990).

[22] Terzuolo, Viviani (1979); Terzuolo, Viviani (1980).

[23] The easiest way to compute relative time would be to express each interval as a proportion of the total duration of the typed word. Terzuolo and Viviani used a more sophisticated method that they describe as follows: '[e]ach instance was ... transformed either by increasing or decreasing its actual duration in such a way that: (a) the average across all instances of the time of occurrence of each event in the sequence is the same before and after the transformation; (b) the variance of the time of occurrence across all instances and for each event of the sequence is the least' (Terzuolo, Viviani, 1980, p. 1089).

[24] Terzuolo, Viviani (1980).

[25] Summers (1975); Schmidt, Lee (2011).

[26] E.g., Gentner (1982, 1987).

[27] It is possible for the control program to display strictly invariant relative timing of elemental program activation, and for performance of the sequence to lack invariant relative timing due to the presence of randomness in the neuromechanical system (Heuer, 1988, 1991).

[28] See Schmidt, Lee (2011).

[29] Sternberg, Knoll, Turock (1990).

[30] Young, Schmidt (1990); Benecke *et al.* (1986).

[31] See Verwey (2001).

[32] Gentner (1983); Soechting, Flanders (1992); Teulings (1996).

[33] Lashley (1951).

[34] According to *Guinness World Records*, the world record typing rate is 200 words a minute, which corresponds to 1000 or more individual keystrokes.

[35] The time would be expected to be at least as long (if not longer) than the latency of long loop reflexes, which typically exceed 80 milliseconds (Chapter 5).

[36] Gordon, Soechting (1995); Rosenbaum (2009).

[37] Gordon, Soechting (1995); Terzuolo, Viviani (1980).

[38] Breakdown of sequencing has been reported in a deafferented patient who was required to repeat touching his thumb pad with each finger tip in turn without looking. He could sustain the sequence for a short period, but errors accrued gradually, and after about 30 seconds he was unable to make the finger tips meet the thumb (Rothwell *et al.*, 1982).

[39] See Rosenbaum (2009).

[40] See Rhodes *et al.* (2004); Rosenbaum (2009).

[41] Wallis, Chatziastros, Bulthoff (2002).

[42] Wallis, Chatziastros, Bulthoff (2002), experiment 1.

[43] If people are made aware that they have not straightened up to drive down the new

lane, they can learn to produce the second phase even in the absence of vision (Wallis, Chatziastros, Bulthoff, 2002).

[44] Wallis *et al.* (2007).

[45] Wallis *et al.* (2007).

[46] Abbs, Gracco, Cole (1984); Gracco, Abbs (1985); Gracco, Abbs (1989).

[47] Terzuolo, Viviani (1980).

[48] See Fowler (2007); Fowler (2003); Teulings (1996).

[49] Kelso, Saltzman, Tuller (1986) present an alternative view.

[50] Clark, Yallop and Fletcher (2007) include the trachea and lungs as part of the vocal tract.

[51] See Clark, Yallop, Fletcher (2007).

[52] Lass (1984).

[53] Changing the phoneme does not always change the meaning, as there are sometimes alternative pronunications of the same word. For example, the English word *have* can be pronounced with a 'v'-sound (an allophone of /v/) or with an 'f'-sound (an allophone of /f/).

[54] It turns out to be difficult to say exactly what common properties define phonemes (Fowler, 2007).

[55] Wells (1990).

[56] See Clark, Yallop, Fletcher (2007).

[57] See Clark, Yallop, Fletcher (2007)

[58] See Hewlett, Beck (2006).

[59] Hewlett, Beck (2006).

[60] Characteristics of vowel sounds can also change if the gas being expelled from the lungs is different from normal. Breathing helium, for example, results in significant changes in the acoustic characteristics of vowels and other voiced sounds.

[61] See Clark, Yallop, Fletcher (2007); Fowler (2003, 2007).

[62] This was presumably the 'a'-sound phoneme that also appears in words like *bat* and *black*, which is written /æ/ using the international phonetic alphabet. There are other 'a'-sound phonemes in English: for instance, the 'a'-sound produced when uttering words like *father* or *arm* sounds different from the 'a'-sound in *bat* and is an instance of another phoneme.

[63] The term is used rather inconsistently in the literature (Clark *et al.*, 2007). Many authors explicitly define coarticulation in terms of overlap, e.g., Fowler (1996); Farnetani, Racesans (2010); Raphael, Borden, Harris (2007).

[64] This may never actually occur in speech production.

[65] See Clark, Yallop, Fletcher (2007).

[66] Clark, Yallop, Fletcher (2007), p. 86.

[67] Hewlett, Beck (2006).

[68] See Clark *et al.* (2007).

[69] Soechting, Flanders (1992).

[70] Engel, Flanders, Soechting (1997).

[71] For a study of coarticulation in sign language see Jerde, Soechting, Flanders (2003).

[72] See Teulings (1996).

[73] Wing, Nimmo-Smith, Eldridge (1983).

[74] Bullock *et al.* (1999); Rand, Stelmach (2000); Sidaway, Sekiya, Fairweather (1995); Sosnik *et al.* (2004).

[75] E.g., Soechting, Flanders (1992); Jerde, Soechting, Flanders (2003).

[76] Farnetani, Racesans (2010), p. 316.

[77] Fowler, Saltzman (1993).

[78] The task dynamic model of speech production (Saltzman, Munhall, 1989; Fowler, Saltzman, 1993) is a model that attributes most instances of coarticulation to overlapping production of adjacent or nearby phonemes.

[79] Assuming that the 'a'-sound is an instance of the /æ/ phoneme (the type of 'a'-sound that English speakers utter when they say a word like *bat* or *paddle*) and the 'i'-sound is an instance of the /I/ phoneme.

[80] E.g., Daniloff, Hammarberg (1973).

[81] The idea described here is introduced for illustrative purposes and is based loosely on Wickelgren (1969), who actually proposed (rather implausibly) that every possible allophone had a distinct production node, rather than having parameterizable phonemic production nodes.

[82] The DIVA model (Guenther, 1994, 1995).

[83] The later version (Guenther, Hampson, Johnson, 1998; Bohland, Bullock, Guenther, 2010) differs from the earlier version in that the 'difference vector' (or 'direction vector') is formed in an auditory space (in the early model it is formed in a tract constriction space). The development enables the model to explain a broader range of findings, but is too complex to describe here.

[84] The figure is based on the neural mapping style diagram presented in Guenther (1995, Figure 2) and the block diagram form presented in Micci-Barreca and Guenther (2001).

[85] Fowler, Saltzman (1993); Browman, Goldstein (1992).

[86] See Guenther, Hampson, Johnson (1998); Tourville, Guenther (2011).

[87] Although it would be possible to build in the sort of partial overlap that is produced by altering the temporal sequence of constrictions specified in the phonemic target in the manner similar to that proposed by Whalen (1990).

[88] The task dynamic model of Saltzman and Munhall (1989) has this character, though the units of production are not called programs.

[89] /ɐ/, the 'uh'-sound phoneme, is also written /ʌ/.

[90] See Browman and Goldstein (1992); Saltzman, Munhall (1989); Guenther, Hampson, Johnson (1998).

[91] Model implementations employed either 11 or 16 different variables (Guenther, 1994, 1995).

[92] This example is loosely based on one presented in Guenther (1995).

[93] For details see Guenther (1995). For how the same process works for auditorily specified targets, see Guenther, Hampson, Johnson (1998).

[94] It is important to note that it is very difficult to distinguish empirically between centrally planned coarticulation (as described in the text) and coarticulation that arises due to peripheral, unplanned interactions between the articulations of adjacent phonemes (Ostry, Gribble, Gracco, 1996).

[95] See Guenther (1994, 1995); Tourville, Guenther (2011).

[96] Bohland, Bullock, Gunther (2010); Rhodes *et al.* (2004).

[97] See, for example, Degallier, Ijspeert (2010); Richardson, Flash (2002); Sternad, Schaal (1999).

[98] Viviani, Terzuolo (1982b).

[99] Wright (1993).

[100] E.g., Hollerbach (1981); Viviani, Terzuolo (1980, 1982b).

[101] See Teulings (1996).

[102] See Wing (2000).

[103] Viviani, Terzuolo (1980, 1983).

[104] See Wright (1993).

[105] Though this result was obtained in only one person (Denier van der Gon, Thuring, 1965).

[106] Wing (1980).

[107] Viviani, Terzuolo (1983).

[108] Viviani, Cenzato (1985).

[109] An observation first made by Jack (1895).

[110] See also Abend, Bizzi, Morasso (1982); Bullock *et al.* (1999).

[111] For mathematical treatment see, e.g., Simmons (1995).

[112] Viviani, Terzuolo (1980, 1983); Laquaniti (1989).

[113] Lacquaniti, Terzuolo, Viviani (1983)

[114] Viviani, Cenzato (1985); Viviani, Flash (1995).

[115] Wann, Nimmo-Smith, Wing (1988).

[116] The data can be better fit by a slightly different 'law' in which R in equation 11.1 is replaced by $R/[1 + \alpha R]$, where α is another parameter that is constant over strokes or segments of a path (Viviani, Schneider, 1991).

[117] Viviani, Flash (1995).

[118] In 3-D space a trajectory can 'twist' as well as curve. This 'twist' is called the *torsion*; see Simmons (1995). The power law must be modified to incorporate this additional degree-of-freedom; see Maoz, Berthoz, Flash (2009); Pollick *et al.* (2009).

[119] See Gribble, Ostry (1996).

[120] The relationship between angular speed (A) and curvature is: $A = g\,\kappa^{2/3}$, hence two-thirds power law (Lacquaniti, Terzuolo, Viviani 1983).

[121] It has recently been shown that the one-third power law is also equivalent to moving with constant equi-affine speed, a concept we will not attempt to explain here (see Flash, Handzel, 2007; Pollick *et al.*, 2009).

[122] For various examples in which the exponent differs markedly from a value of 1/3, see Lacquaniti, Terzuolo, Viviani (1983); Schaal, Sternad (2001); Teulings (1996); Viviani, McCollum (1983); Wann, Nimmo-Smith, Wing (1988).

[123] Perrier, Fuchs (2007).

[124] Gribble, Ostry (1996); Maoz, Berthoz, Flash (2009); Schaal, Sternad (2001).

[125] Richardson, Flash (2002); Viviani, Flash (1995); Wann, Nimmo-Smith, Wing (1988).

[126] Harris, Wolpert (1998).

[127] See Bullock, Grossberg (1988); Bullock *et al.* (1993, 1999).

128 Plamondon, Guerfali (1998b); Woch, Plamondon (2004).

129 Schwartz (1994); Schwartz, Moran (2000).

130 See Pellizzer, Zesiger (2009).

131 See, for example, Hollerbach (1981); Krebs *et al.* (1999); Morasso, Mussa-Ivaldi, Ruggiero (1983); Wright (1993).

132 Richardson, Flash (2002).

133 Lacquaniti, Terzuolo, Viviani (1983).

134 See Lacquaniti, Terzuolo, Viviani (1983); Viviani, Cenzato (1985). See also Polyakov *et al.* (2009a), who studied scribbling in monkeys and found that the movement trajectories could be resolved into sequences of parabolic segments; these can be considered to be equivalent to segments that obey the one-third power law with a constant gain factor.

135 See, e.g., Viviani and Flash (1995) and the studies of Polyakov *et al.* (2009a,b), who segmented trajectories in a slightly different way.

136 Polyakov *et al.* (2009a).

137 Viviani, Cenzato (1985); Polyakov *et al.* (2009a).

138 Richardson, Flash (2002).

139 Sternad, Schaal (1999).

140 Morasso, Mussa-Ivaldi (1982).

141 Polyakov *et al.* (2009a), p. 1.

142 Sosnik, Shemesh, Abeles (2007).

143 E.g., Bullock, Grossberg, Mannes (1993); Djioua, Plamondon (2009); Edelman, Flash (1987); Morasso, Mussa-Ivaldi (1982); Morasso, Sanguineti (1993); Plamondon, Djioua (2006); Teulings (1996); Wada *et al.* (2005).

144 See previous note.

145 See Teulings (1996).

146 Morasso, Mussa-Ivaldi (1982).

147 Morasso, Sanguinetti (1993); Plamondon, Privitera (1996); Plamondon, Guerfali (1998b).

148 Edelman, Flash (1987).

149 According to Edelman and Flash (1987), though they offer no proof.

150 E.g., Bullock, Grossberg, Mannes (1993); Grossberg, Paine (2000).

151 Hollerbach (1981).

152 A variety of examples are presented in Hollerbach (1981).

PART **III**

SENSORIMOTOR LEARNING

CHAPTER 14

Introduction to Sensorimotor Learning

14.1 Learning and Memory

14.1.1 Introduction

In everyday language, 'learning' is frequently used to refer to the process of acquiring factual knowledge about a subject area. This knowledge is said to reside in *memory*, and each item of knowledge in the memory may itself be referred to as a *memory*. For example, we might learn that Ouagadougou is the capital city of Burkina Faso, a country in West Africa. Learning this fact means storing it in memory, which is a kind of fact container in the brain. When it is stored, we say that we have a memory of it (or a *memory trace*). If someone later asks, 'What is the capital of Burkina Faso?', we may be able to retrieve the information from memory and answer 'Ouagadougou'. This usage of the terms *learning* and *memory* is intuitive and corresponds to how they are used in everyday language. However, it only describes one type of learning and the associated memory. There are other cases to which this description does not seem to be applicable. One such case is the formation of what are called *autobiographical memories* – memories of things that we did or that happened to us. For instance, if a person had sushi for lunch on Thursday and has a memory of having done so, then that memory is autobiographical. However, to say that they learned that they had sushi for lunch on Thursday does not correspond to everyday usage. Thus, there appear to be circumstances in which memories are formed but the process of their formation is not learning as commonly understood.

There also cases in which learning takes place (i.e., knowledge of some form is acquired), but it does not result in the formation of memories that can be recalled and verbalized. This is the type of learning that produces improvements in a person's facility for doing something, or enables them to do something that they could not previously do. Learning to ride a bicycle is an example: the result is the ability to ride a bicycle, which is something that cannot be recalled and described in words. Nevertheless, some kind of memory is presumably formed, since a person who can ride a bicycle possesses the knowledge of how to ride a bicycle.

In this chapter and the next, we will be concerned exclusively with the kind of learning that results in changes in sensorimotor behavior – changes in facility and technique, changes in how stimulation is responded to, and changes in what can be done (acquisition of new behaviors). This kind of learning is often referred to as *motor learning*[1], a term which implicitly suggests that the mechanisms of behavior can be neatly divided into sensory parts and motor parts and that the learning takes place in the latter. We have emphasized throughout this book that the sensory and the motor form an integrated system, and that treating one without the other can be an inappropriate simplification. In fact, improvements in motor performance can occur if the accuracy or capability of the sensory systems improves, though such improvements themselves are usually classed as the outcome of sensory or perceptual learning. For these reasons, we will use the term **sensorimotor learning**. The following statement describes sensorimotor learning quite well: 'a process by which an organism benefits from experience so that its future behavior is better adapted to its environment'[2].

In order to understand sensorimotor learning and the kind(s) of memory it produces, we will need to have a clear idea about what counts as learning and what does not. We will also need to be clear about the different kinds of memory that can be formed. These matters will be discussed in the first part of this chapter, beginning with further information about the distinction between the different types of memory mentioned above.

14.1.2 There are different types of memory

In the previous section an intuitive distinction was drawn between factual knowledge and the kind of knowledge possessed by someone who knows how to do something, such as ride a bicycle. If someone knows that something is the case or that something happened, then they can tell you – they can verbally declare the contents of their memory. In contrast, a person cannot verbally declare the knowledge that enables them to ride a bicycle – they cannot explain how they were able to contract and relax the large number of different muscles needed to keep balanced on the bicycle and moving forwards. This difference is captured in the terms **declarative memory** and **non-declarative memory**[3], both of which are used to refer to storage of information over the long term rather than for short periods:

> **DECLARATIVE MEMORY:** A form of memory that involves the (conscious) recollection of experiences and facts. These recollections can be communicated to someone else either verbally or by some other means (they can be declared).
>
> **NON-DECLARATIVE MEMORY:** A form of memory that does not involve conscious recollection and that cannot be described or expressed verbally (cannot be declared). The existence of the memory is expressed through performance (e.g., of a motor act).

The distinction described by these terms relates only to whether or not the contents of memory can be consciously recollected and described: it is not meant to imply that all declarative memories are of the same type, or that all non-declarative memories are of the same type. In fact, there is evidence for different subtypes of both forms of memory[4]: we will encounter different forms of non-declarative memory in this chapter.

Other terms that relate to the distinction are frequently encountered. For example, the term **explicit memory** refers to memory that involves the 'conscious recollection of previous experiences'[5] and is often used as a synonym for declarative memory; the term **implicit memory** is used as a synonym for non-declarative memory[6]. Another term that is widely used to refer to the type of non-declarative memory associated with acquired motor skill is *procedural memory*[7]. We will not use this term because it is potentially a source of confusion. There are two reasons for this: (1) in some cases there is no clear sense in which what is learned can be characterized as a procedure[8]; (2) a declarative memory of a procedure is not a procedural memory, so if you can remember and describe the sequence of actions needed for changing gears in a motor vehicle, you have a memory of a procedure but you don't necessarily have a procedural memory. A skilled driver who knows how to change gears is likely to have two different memories associated with changing gears: a declarative memory of the procedure, and a non-declarative memory that underlies actually changing gear. To avoid confusion, we will use the term **sensorimotor memory** to refer to the type(s) of non-declarative memory underlying performance of sensorimotor behaviors.

Further evidence for the distinction between declarative and sensorimotor memory comes from what some authors have referred to as a paradox, noting that '[e]xperts spend years acquiring knowledge about their skill, which they use very effectively to support their performance, but they have little explicit access to that knowledge'[9]. Skilled typists provide a good example of this. A skilled typist who is capable of accurately typing over 100 words a minute clearly knows where the different letter keys are located on the keyboard, yet they may not have the ability to access this knowledge consciously. Skilled typists have been found to be no better than novices at describing where particular letters are located on the keyboard. A different example was briefly described in Chapter 13: experienced drivers who regularly change lanes do not have explicit knowledge of the movements of the steering wheel that are needed to make a lane change (see section 13.1.10).

14.1.3 Declarative and sensorimotor memory involve different regions of the brain

The first direct evidence that declarative and non-declarative, sensorimotor memory involve different parts of the nervous system came from studies of people with amnesia. To many people the term *amnesia* means memory loss, usually memory loss that occurs as the result of traumatic head injury or heavy drinking. Amnesia has often featured in the movies, where the problem typically involves the loss of memory for events in the person's past; frequently the person has forgotten who they are (loss of identity) and exhibits changes in personality as a result[10]. This 'movie amnesia' does not accurately characterize the kind of memory loss that is typically observed in real people with amnesia[11].

In the real world, amnesia due to brain injury is rather different. There is often partial inability to recall events that occurred prior to the damage (termed *retrograde amnesia*), but loss of identity is not common, and associated personality changes are very rare indeed. A type of memory loss seldom exhibited by movie amnesics is **anterograde amnesia** – a serious impairment of the ability to form memories of things that occurred after the brain was damaged[12]. It is anterograde amnesia that we will consider here.

The anterograde amnesic can remember facts acquired prior to the damage and can recall life events that occurred prior to the damage, but he or she cannot remember anything experienced after the damage. They can hold some things in mind for a few seconds, but usually for no more than a minute or so. Thus, they are considered to have an intact short-term working memory that allows them to hold a limited number of things in mind, but a severely impaired ability to form new long-term memories. Several patients exhibiting this form of amnesia have been studied in detail[13]; the most famous of these was Henry Molaison (known as HM in published studies), who was studied for over fifty years until his death in 2008. HM suffered from very severe epilepsy, for which he received brain surgery when he was 27 years old (in 1953). The surgery was drastic, and involved removing the medial parts of the temporal lobe (including the hippocampus) on both sides of the brain. The hippocampus is a folded 'terminal' part of the cerebral cortex that lies close to the midbrain; its location in the human brain is shown in Figure 14.1.

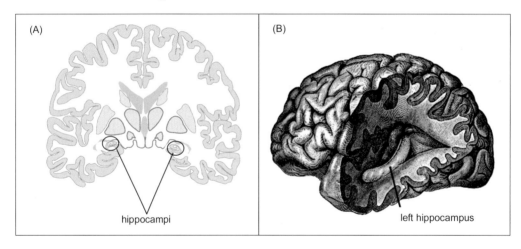

Figure 14.1: *Location of the hippocampus in the human brain. (A) Coronal section. (B) Cutaway of the temporal and parietal lobes to expose the hippocampus (shaded blue), from the 20th edition of* Gray's Anatomy of the Human Body *(1918).*

HM's surgery successfully dealt with his epilepsy, and had little or no detectable effect on his personality, perceptual ability or intelligence. However, it left him unable to form new memories of events in his life and of new facts. He was described as forgetting the events in his daily life almost as fast as they occurred[14], and many years after the surgery it was reported that he 'does not know where he lives, who cares for him, or where he ate his last meal'[15]. However, this inability to remember was found to be largely confined to declarative memory, as he was able to develop skill in a variety of motor tasks, and to retain what he had learned for many months or years. An example of his ability to develop motor skill and retain it over several days is shown in Figure 14.2. The task was to move a pen around a star shape, keeping the pen within the gap between the inner and outer stars, as shown in panel A. This had to be done when the star, the pen and the hand could only be seen in a mirror (mirror tracing task). Performance was scored as the number of times the pen crossed the lines of either the inner or outer star (each crossing of the line from inside the gap to outside it was scored as an error). HM attempted to draw around the star without crossing the lines ten times using his right (dominant) hand on each of three consecutive days. The results are shown in panel B of Figure 14.2. On the first attempt on day 1, he made 29 errors; by day 3 he made no more than four errors on any of his ten attempts. Thus, HM was able to improve performance of the mirror tracing task and retain the improvement over an extended period, though he had no recollection on either day 2 or day 3 of ever having performed the task before.

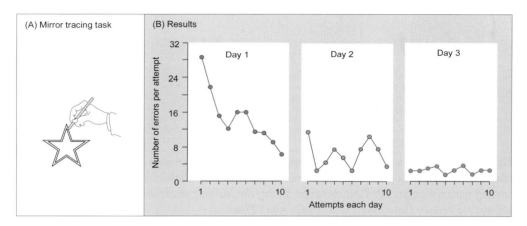

Figure 14.2: *Mirror tracing experiment in patient HM. (A) Task: trace around the star pattern between the lines. (B) Number of errors per attempt on three consecutive days. Data from Milner (1962).*

Findings of the sort just described are not unique to HM – they have been replicated in many other patients who suffer from anterograde amnesia[16]. One such patient, known as Boswell, suffered a loss of neural tissue similar to but more extensive than HM and has 'one of the most severe impairments ever reported for learning of all types of declarative knowledge'[17]. Figure 14.3 shows the results from a study of learning and retention of performance on a pursuit rotor task in this patient, compared with a group of six normal control participants. The task, shown in panel A, required the participants to try to keep a stylus in continuous contact with a metal disc attached to a turntable that made thirty complete revolutions every minute. Performance on each attempt (trial) was scored as the total time for which the stylus remained in contact with the target. The initial training phase consisted of five trials of thirty seconds each. Following this, two retention tests were administered to determine whether the participants remembered what they had learned during the training phase. The first test was administered twenty minutes after the training phase; the second test was administered two years later. Panel B shows the results: during the training phase, performance improved over the five trials, and Boswell's performance was indistinguishable from that of the control participants (the average performance of the controls is shown). In the retention tests, Boswell performed slightly better than the average of the controls, showing clear evidence of retaining the skill acquired during the training phase over a period of two years. Although Boswell learned and retained the ability to perform the pursuit rotor task similarly to or better than the controls, he was unable to remember having performed the task or anything about it at any stage following the training phase. This contrasted with the control participants, who were able to recall the task and having practiced it. Note that remembering what task you have carried out, or what action you have performed, or what movement(s) you have made, are all declarative memories.

The results from patients HM and Boswell described in this section show a clear dissociation between declarative memory and sensorimotor memory[18]. The patients can acquire and retain sensorimotor skill but fail to explicitly recall ever having performed the task before. The structures damaged or removed in patients who show this dissociation implicate the medial temporal lobe of the cerebral cortex (which includes the hippocampus and nearby regions such as the entorhinal cortex and perirhinal cortex) in the process of forming long-term declarative memories. However, these structures are not necessary for the formation of sensorimotor memories. Other parts of the brain are evidently involved in the formation of these memories.

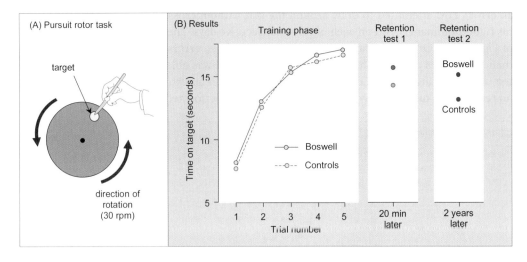

Figure 14.3: *Pursuit rotor experiment comparing the performance of an amnesic patient (Boswell, blue symbols) and the average of six normal controls (red symbols). (A) Task: keep the stylus in contact with the target. (B) Time on target during the training phase and the two retention tests; see text for details. Data from Tranel* et al. *(1994), Figure 1.*

14.1.4 What is the nature of the sensorimotor memory formed as performance progressively improves?

Declarative memory is often thought of as a kind of long-term storage facility or set of storage facilities. At least two such facilities are generally distinguished, one for facts – called *semantic memory* – and another for experienced events, places and situations – called *episodic* or *autobiographical memory*[19]. Individual memories within these stores can be recalled into consciousness by a retrieval process, enabling a person to verbally describe (declare) remembered facts and past experiences. This conception closely resembles the way in which memory is organized in a digital computer: there is a hard disk that serves as a long-term storage facility; items can be retrieved from the hard disk and moved into a 'working memory', where they are available for use by an application program. For example, word-processed documents are stored as files on the hard drive, and when the user wishes to read them or edit them, they can be retrieved from the hard drive into RAM (working memory) and displayed ready for editing or reading.

The conception of memory as a store from which items can be retrieved and held in a working memory (or 'consciousness') probably influenced early views of motor programs as stored sets of commands. As described in Chapter 11, motor programs cannot, in general, be understood as stored sets of commands, and so the notion of memory as a storage facility is unlikely to be an appropriate metaphor for the type of sensorimotor memory that underlies the improvement of performance over repeated attempts (Figures 14.2 and 14.3). A different way of thinking about memory is needed.

In previous chapters, we discussed in detail the kinds of mechanisms responsible for the production of motor behavior. As a result of practice and experience, these mechanisms are altered (specific examples will be discussed later). These alterations result in changes in performance of the associated behaviors. Changes in performance can take a variety of different forms that are usually considered to be improvements: for example, it may become less error prone (as in Figure 14.2), more economical (require less effort and/or consume less energy), and/or quicker. These performance changes are improvements because the task goals are met more effectively and/or more efficiently. We can imagine that these performance improvements are made possible by adjustments to the way in which pattern generating mechanisms and motor programs produce motor commands and/or how they are affected by sensory information.

In Chapter 11, the clockwork automaton known as the Draughtsman (described in Chapter 1) was used as a metaphor for explaining why motor programs are not like computer programs. It can also help provide alternative ways of thinking about sensorimotor memory. Imagine that a basic motor program or a pattern generator is analogous to the clockwork mechanism within the Draughtsman that enables him to generate drawings (see Figure 1.4B). We can imagine that Monsieur Jacquet-Droz, who constructed the Draughtsman, spent time refining the positions and shapes of the cogs, cams, levers and other components of the clockwork mechanism so that the drawings produced were as he wanted them. This process of adjustment and refinement is analogous to the process of motor learning that leads to improvements in motor performance. The actual changes to the mechanism are analogous to sensorimotor memories (another example is discussed in the next section).

14.1.5 Performance of a feedback controller can be improved by adjusting its parameters

Chapter 1 provided an intuitive introduction to the theory of feedback control and discussed how the transformation from the error to the controlling input to the system being controlled must incorporate information about the latter system if control is to be effective. This is sometimes expressed by saying that this transformation incorporates a kind of internal model of the controlled system. In the simplest kind of proportional feedback control system, the error transformation is a multiplication of the error by a gain factor. In order to achieve effective control, the value of the gain factor needs to be 'correct'. As discussed in Chapter 1, the correct value depends on the nature of the controlled system (the correct value thus incorporates information about the controlled system, and can be viewed as a kind of crude internal model[20]). To get an artificial proportional feedback controller to work properly (i.e., get the controlled system to produce the required output), an engineer needs to set the gain to the correct value, a process sometimes referred to as *tuning*. Such tuning could proceed through trial and error: try a value for the gain and then test the system to see if it works – if not, try another value, and so on. In this example, the process of tuning is analogous to learning, and the value of the gain that results from the tuning process is a kind of memory.

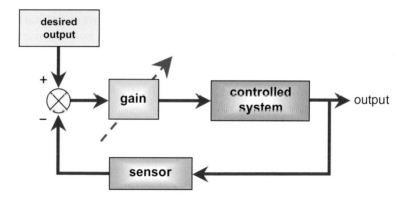

Figure 14.4: *Block diagram of a negative feedback control system with an adjustable gain (indicated by the dashed arrow through the gain block).*

Figure 14.4 shows a block diagram of a simple negative feedback control system and indicates an adjustable gain using a dashed arrow that passes through the gain block. This representation draws attention to the fact that in this example, the structure of the control system is fixed (the blocks themselves and the way they are interconnected). Tuning consists of adjusting the parameters of particular blocks (just the gain block in our example). Some sensorimotor learning can be usefully viewed as a process that tunes or adjusts existing mechanisms (we will discuss examples later in the chapter), but not all. For example, adjusting a mechanism to make it function more effectively cannot account for the acquisition of new behaviors. Acquisition of a new behavior or of a new technique for doing something requires new mechanisms (programs). To represent such cases in block diagram form, we would need to allow structural changes, such as new interconnections between existing blocks and/or the introduction of new blocks. We will discuss the acquisition of new behaviors in Chapter 15; for the remainder of this chapter we will mainly be concerned with the refinement and adjustment of existing behavior.

14.1.6 What questions about learning do we want to answer?

The main questions that we will address in this chapter and the next regarding sensorimotor learning are as follows:

(1)   If performance changes as a result of practice or other experience, how can we determine whether the changes are produced by learning?

(2)   What conditions are needed for learning? What factors enhance and facilitate the learning process? What factors impede learning or are otherwise detrimental?

(3)   If performance improves as a result of experience, how are these improvements actually achieved? What changes in movements and forces enable goals to be achieved more effectively and efficiently? What changes take place in the processing of information and the production of motor commands?

(4)   What exactly is learned as the result of practice and experience? What knowledge or information can be considered to have been acquired?

(5)   What is (or are) the mechanism(s) of learning? How exactly is experience and practice able to change the way behavior is produced? In the examples given in the previous two sections, the processes of adjustment, refinement and tuning were carried out by a craftsman or engineer. How are analogous processes carried out within the nervous system?

These are all difficult questions to give definitive answers to. In the remainder of this chapter we will examine some of the issues that arise when attempting to answer them, and discuss the nature of the answers that have been given. In the next section we will look at the first question, which arises in the study of sensorimotor learning because performance can change due to factors other than learning. If we cannot be certain whether or not learning has taken place, then we cannot hope to discover how learning works or how it can be facilitated or impeded.

14.1.7 Factors other than learning can change how behaviors are performed

We all think we know what learning is, but it has proven to be very difficult to define. The difficulty has led many authors to abandon any attempt to provide a complete definition[21], and the definitions that have been provided are often not very enlightening[22]. Nevertheless, we do need to identify the defining characteristics of learning if we are to distinguish it from other processes that change behavior, though no attempt will be made to provide a definition as such.

One important feature of learning that is not shared by other factors that can produce behavioral changes is that it involves the acquisition of information or knowledge. This is obvious for the learning of facts or learning a language but, as described earlier, it is also true of sensorimotor learning. Some other factors that can change behavior and that might do so during the course of a practice session or as the result of some sensory experience are listed below:

(a)   **Muscle fatigue:** when you practice doing something, your muscles may become tired; the longer or more intense the practice, the more fatigued the muscles are likely to be.

(b)   **Central fatigue:** neural factors contribute to fatigue, and we may feel physically fatigued even though our muscles have not been used, as sometimes occurs when we are ill. Repeated performance (practice) may lead to changes within the nervous system that are associated with fatigue rather than learning[23].

(c)   **Arousal:** a person's state of alertness or arousal can increase or decrease during a practice session (decreases may be associated with fatigue).

(d)   **Motivation:** related to alertness and arousal is motivation – a person may be more or less motivated to carry out a task, and their level of motivation may change over the course of a practice session. The less motivation a person has to perform well, the less well they are likely to perform.

(e)   **Mood:** a person's performance can be affected by their mood (happy, depressed, bored, anxious, etc.), though these effects might be due (in part) to the effect of mood on motivation and arousal.

None of these factors involve the acquisition of knowledge from practice or experience. However, in some cases variations in these factors can lead to changes in performance that are similar to the effects of learning. For example, an increase in fatigue over the course of a practice session is likely to lead to a decline in the speed and/or forcefulness of execution. Normally, of course, learning does not result in a decline in speed and forcefulness, but there are exceptions: the process of learning can be associated with a decline in response speed and forcefulness when a person is in the process of learning not to do something. A kind of learning known as *habituation* is of this kind – it results in a progressive decline in the vigor of stimulus-elicited behavior. Habituation is discussed in more detail in section 2 of this chapter.

When learning and fatigue both lead to the same type of effect on performance over the course of a training session, it is impossible to say which of them is responsible for the observed change in behavior: it might all be due to learning, all to fatigue or, more likely, some combination of the two. In order to study learning we need some means for the effects of learning to be distinguished from the effects of fatigue. An obvious difference between learning and fatigue is that fatigue wears off during a period of rest, whereas the effects of learning do not usually wear off. Learning has specific, accumulative effects that normally last longer than the effects of fatigue.

Like fatigue, the other factors on the above list have transient effects on performance (though these effects can be either improvements or declines in performance). Thus, learning is potentially distinguishable from the other factors because it has specific, longer lasting effects. However, practice can have long lasting effects that are not due to learning. Imagine spending a period of time performing a particular action over and over again. Such periods are characteristic of practice sessions, but they are also characteristic of exercise sessions. Whether we call repetition of an action practicing or exercising depends on what we are trying to achieve. If we are trying to improve technique or skill, then it's practice; if we are trying to improve fitness, strength or flexibility, then it's exercise.

Improvements in fitness, strength and flexibility are due, in part, to physiological changes in the musculoskeletal and cardiovascular systems. For example, strength gains result from increases in the size of muscle fibers (hypertrophy), changes of some type I fibers to type II (the latter type generate more force than the former), and possibly also an increase in the number of fibers (hyperplasia)[24]. These changes are accumulative and relatively long lasting but are not the result of learning. However, they can have similar effects. It turns out, for example, that at least some of the improvements in strength that occur as a result of lifting weights and other forms of resistance training are due to learning. Training leads to improved technique – people learn how to activate and control their muscles so as to produce more force or to fatigue less quickly[25]. Conversely, improvements that appear to be due to learning may be due to strength gains. Imagine a person shoots one hundred arrows at a target every other day for two weeks. On the first day, performance is very poor; most of the arrows don't even reach the target, let alone stick in it. On the last day, however, performance is much better; all the arrows shot stick in the target, and perhaps one or two are within the bull's-eye. This performance improvement might be due to learning, but increases in muscular strength could be a major factor: if the person was initially too weak to pull back the bow string, then they would be unable to shoot effectively. Over the two weeks of training, however, their muscles could have strengthened sufficiently to enable them to shoot more accurately.

In this section we have seen that the effects of learning on performance can be mixed up with the effects of other things. Thus, it is not always possible to attribute changes in performance exclusively to learning, because of the presence of other factors that might have contributed to the observed changes. This can create difficulties when studying habituation (where learning and fatigue have similar effects on performance) and when trying to determine the factors that facilitate and impede learning. In the latter case, it is often necessary to assess how much learning has taken place during a practice or training session. How can we make this assessment if the effects of learning are confounded with the effects of other factors? In the following sections, we will see how this question can be answered.

14.1.8 Performance changes during practice are not reliable indicators of learning

Sensorimotor learning is not something that is directly measurable; we can only measure the effects that learning has on behavior and, in some cases, its effects on the nervous system. In studies of sensorimotor learning, it is usual to measure the quality of performance over a sequence of attempts at carrying out a task. Figures 14.2 and 14.3 provide examples: in each graph a measure of performance quality is plotted on the vertical axis, and trial or attempt number is plotted on the horizontal axis. In the day 1 panel of Figure 14.2 and the training phase panel of Figure 14.3, performance quality improves systematically as the number of trials completed increases. It is reasonable to attribute such improvements to learning, though they could perhaps be the result of a gradual increase in motivation or alertness. One way to determine whether the improvements were due to learning or to some other factor is to administer a re-test some time after completion of the initial training phase. The idea is that during the period of time between the end of the training phase and the re-test, a person's state of fatigue, arousal and motivation will have had a chance to return to their normal levels (or for a group of participants, the average levels of these variables for the group will be the same at the beginning of the re-test as they were at the beginning of the training phase). The re-test is usually called a **retention test**, because it provides a measure of the extent to which improvements made during the training phase are retained over the interval of time between the training phase and the re-test (the **retention interval**).

An examination administered to students at the end of a course of academic study is often a kind of retention test, designed to determine how much the students have learned or what they have learned. Retention tests administered in studies of sensorimotor learning are not administered to determine what or how much has been learned, but to evaluate the effects of learning on some measure of performance.

The results shown in Figure 14.3 indicate that learning took place, because performance in the retention tests was superior to performance at the beginning of the training phase: the participants learned something during the training phase that enabled them to perform better at a later time. In the figure, performance at the end of the training phase was slightly better than it was in the first retention test, which suggests that something has been lost during the retention interval. This type of result is quite often obtained (we will return to it in section 14.1.10), but not always. Figure 14.5 shows some results from a pursuit rotor experiment in which performance at the beginning of the retention test was better than at the end of the training phase. Data from three different groups of participants who were trained under different conditions are shown: Group (i), Group (ii) and Group (iii). These results are worth discussing in more detail.

The figure shows that over the 21 trials of the training phase, there was very little improvement in the performance of Group (i), but more in the other groups. This might be taken to mean that Group (i) learned very little, but the retention test suggests otherwise, since performance is substantially better in the retention test than at the end of the training phase. The nature of the conditions suggests an explanation. Participants in Group (i) performed one trial after another with no rest in between. Group (ii) participants were given 30 seconds' rest between trials, and Group (iii) were given 60 seconds' rest. The participants in Group (i) were therefore more likely to get progressively fatigued than those in the other groups, and fatigue can impair performance and prevent people from performing at the level that they are capable of. The substantially better performance in the retention test supports this interpretation: participants rested for five minutes after the training phase, during which time at least some of the effects of fatigue would have worn off. Being less fatigued in the retention test, participants were better able to demonstrate the skill that they had acquired during the training phase. Thus, participants in Group (i) did learn during the training phase, but it was only in the retention test that they were able to demonstrate that they had learned.

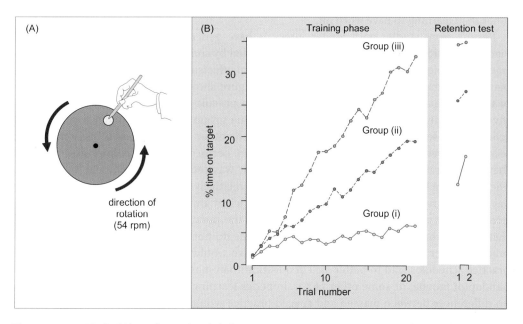

Figure 14.5: *Task (A) and results (B) from an experiment comparing the performance of three groups of 25 participants who trained under three different conditions. The target was 5 inches from the center of rotation. Data points are the averages from 25 participants (Bourne, Archer, 1956).*

Although the fatigue explanation can account for the pattern of results shown in Figure 14.5, it is speculative, because there is no independent evidence for the presence of fatigue. Fatigue was not measured in the study, and so we do not actually know whether the participants in Group (i) were more fatigued than those in the other groups, nor do we know to what extent the hypothetical fatigue wore off during the five-minute retention interval. However, it is difficult to see what alternative there is to the general idea of the fatigue explanation: performance was affected by some factor during the training phase that prevented the participants from demonstrating their level of skill, but once the effects of this factor had worn off, participants were able to demonstrate their skill. The factor could be fatigue or something else such as motivation; we cannot say for sure[26]. Whatever the factor is, it is difficult to see how the results can be accounted for in any other way.

The results from the retention test (Figure 14.5) suggest that allowing short breaks between practice trials results in more effective learning, and the longer the break (up to 60 seconds at least), the more beneficial the effect. However, if the retention test is to assess learning, the effects of other factors that may have accrued during the training phase should not be present in the retention test. In the experiment of Figure 14.5, the retention interval was only five minutes, which may not have been long enough for the effects of other factors, such as fatigue, to wear off. Performance in the retention test may have been contaminated by these effects, and the contamination would be expected to be greater for groups with shorter inter-trial breaks. It is possible, therefore, that if the retention interval had been longer, performance in the retention trials would have been similar in the three groups. This possibility is considered next.

14.1.9 Spaced practice typically leads to larger performance gains than massed practice

In the literature[27], when the break between practice trials is short (a few seconds or less), practice is said to be **massed**; when the break is more than a few seconds, practice is said to be **spaced** (or *distributed*). The retention test results in Figure 14.5 suggest that massing practice impedes learning. However, to conclude that people are able to learn more effectively when practice is spaced, the retention interval needs to be long enough for the effects of factors other than learning to have worn off.

Results from studies with longer intervals have generally reproduced the findings in Figure 14.5, which suggests that learning is impeded by short inter-trial intervals[28]. An illustrative example of results showing the detrimental effects of massing practice over a longer period of training is shown in Figure 14.6. The figure shows average data from two groups of ten participants who performed 15 trials on a pursuit rotor task each day for ten days (five consecutive days in each of two weeks). One group performed under a spaced trial schedule (65-second breaks between trials) and the other under a massed trial schedule (5 seconds between trials). During each daily session, performance clearly improved more for the spaced practice group, and the improvement was retained from one day to the next. The difference between the groups on day 1 was relatively small, but it was much larger by day 5. These results show that not allowing sufficient time between trials (massing practice) impedes the acquisition of skill, at least in the pursuit rotor task. The implication is that people who practice under a massed schedule do not learn as effectively as those who practice under a spaced schedule[29]. Of course, we would only expect to find that spaced practice schedules lead to better skill acquisition than massed schedules for tasks in which buildup of fatigue, or some other factor, impedes learning. In the absence of such a factor, no differences between massed and spaced practice would be expected. The failure to find differences in some discrete tasks such as placing pegs in holes[30] may have been because there was no factor impeding learning. Unfortunately, without the ability to independently measure these putative factors, it is impossible to directly evaluate whether they are responsible or not. This may account for why research on massed and spaced practice schedules is no longer undertaken[31].

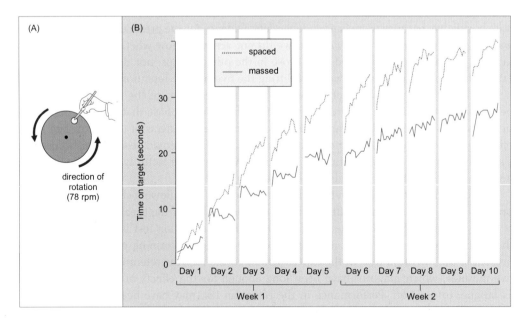

Figure 14.6: *Task (A) and results (B) from an experiment comparing the performance of two groups of 10 participants who performed under a massed (blue) or a spaced (red, dotted) training schedule. The target was 5 inches from the center of rotation. Data from Kimble and Shatel (1952).*

14.1.10 Warm-up decrement is found in most sensorimotor learning studies

Figures 14.3 and 14.6 show evidence of a phenomenon that is frequently observed in studies of sensorimotor learning: performance at the end of a practice session is better than performance in a subsequent retention test or at the beginning of the next practice session[32]. In Figure 14.6, the effect is present for the spaced practice group throughout and for the massed practice group only in week 2: performance at the beginning of one day's session was always worse than performance at the end of the practice on the previous day. Performance is typically found to quickly return to the level achieved at the end of the previous session – only two or three trials were needed in the study shown in Figure 14.6; performance improvements then proceed more slowly.

One obvious reason for the performance loss is that something learned during practice has been forgotten over the interval between one session and the next. However, the rapid restoration of performance during the first two or three trials following the interval suggests that the effect may not be due to forgetting[33]. The argument is that if the effect were due to forgetting, then what was lost would need to be re-learnt in order to restore the earlier level of performance, which does not account for why the level of performance is restored so quickly. This argument is weak, since relearning may be quicker than the original learning[34]. An alternative account of the effect does not appeal to forgetting; it proposes instead that there is a need to 'warm up' before being able to fully demonstrate the skill acquired during earlier practice[35]. This alternative account has led to the effect being called **warm-up decrement**:

> **WARM-UP DECREMENT:** A drop in the level of performance observed in the execution of task following a break or rest period (performance is worse upon resuming the task than it was at the end of a prior practice session). Upon resumption, the level of performance is very quickly restored to the level attained at the end of the practice session.

The kind of 'warm-up' thought to be involved is not warm-up of the limbs and muscles that a person might undertake before exercise, but a kind of warm-up that takes place within the nervous system. It has been suggested that it might involve re-establishing a postural set (see Chapter 7, section 7.5.2) that is best suited for supporting the task that is being practiced[36]. Alternatively, it might be associated with activating and parameterizing the motor program governing performance of the focal task. Either way, the idea is that the performance decrement is due to the loss of some kind of preparatory state (set) that needs to be established if a person is to perform at the level they are capable of. The 'warm-up' process is thought to involve re-establishing the preparatory state that was lost during the retention interval. This idea has intuitive appeal, but it has yet to be conclusively demonstrated that the rapid restoration in performance over the first few trials in retention tests or subsequent practice sessions is due to re-establishing an internal state rather than to learning[37]. Thus, although the term *warm-up decrement* is used to refer to the effect, it is not known for certain whether it has anything to do with 'warming up', nor has it been conclusively established that the decrement is due to loss of 'set' and not to loss of skill (i.e., forgetting). During learning over several distinct sessions, the decrement seen at the beginning of one session relative to the end of the prior session could be due to loss of skill (a failure to fully consolidate the motor memory[38]). There is ample evidence, however, that even highly skilled professional athletes, whose motor memories are presumably firmly established, need a period of warm-up not only for their muscles and ligaments but for their brains[39]. Players of ball sports, for example, need a warm-up period to 'get their eye in'.

Although warm-up decrement is very often observed – according to some authors it 'has been found in nearly every motor task that has been studied'[40] – there are circumstances in which the opposite effect occurs. Figure 14.5 shows examples, as does the performance of the massed practice group in week 1 in Figure 14.6. A possible explanation is that during the retention interval (Figure 14.5) or the interval between sessions (Figure 14.6), two types of loss are occurring: the loss of task-related internal state (set) and the loss of fatigue. The loss of set leads to poorer performance after the interval, whereas loss of fatigue enables better performance. If the loss of set outweighs the loss of fatigue, then warm-up decrement is observed (performance is worse after the interval). If the loss of fatigue outweighs the loss of set, then the opposite effect is observed (performance is better after the interval).

14.1.11 Measuring performance is not the same as measuring learning

In order to draw reliable conclusions concerning the relative effectiveness of learning under different practice conditions, it is necessary to be able to measure the effects of learning on performance in a way that is uncontaminated by other factors that may have accumulated during practice. As already discussed, one way to do this is to assess performance after the effects of the other factors have worn off (warm-up decrement need not be a problem when assessing the relative effectiveness of learning if the effect is similar in the different conditions). However, we have not yet discussed how performance should be evaluated.

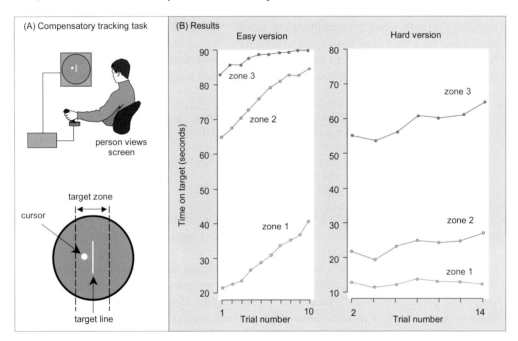

Figure 14.7: *Results from a study in which participants performed a sequence of trials on a compensatory tracking task (A); one group performed an easy version of the task, and another a harder version. Three different target zones were used for scoring performance. Data from Bahrick, Fitts, Briggs (1957).*

Measures of error and percentage of time on target evaluate the extent to which performance achieves a primary task goal: the primary goal in the pursuit rotor task, for example, is to maintain contact with the target throughout the trial (100% of the time). If performance meets the criterion, then performance is effectively perfect (100% of time on target, zero error). If performance meets the criterion, then any further improvements in performance that may occur cannot be measured – the measure is blind to any further improvement. In such circumstances, we say that the measure is not **sensitive** to any changes in performance that occur once criterion is reached. The insensitivity of evaluative performance measures can lead to problems of interpretation. Figure 14.7 presents an example that was designed to illustrate these problems[41]. Two groups of participants performed a series of 90-second trials on a compensatory tracking task (see Chapter 10, section 10.1.5) in which they attempted to keep a cursor (white dot in Figure 14.7A) over a vertical line by manipulating a control lever. One group performed an easy version of the task; the other performed a more difficult version (the difficulty was determined by the function that transformed movements of the control lever into movement of the cursor on the screen). Performance was scored as the amount of time for which the cursor was in a target zone ('time on target') around the vertical target line, as indicated at the bottom of Figure 14.7, panel A. Three different target zones were used: zone 1 was small (0.5 cm wide), zone 2 was wider (1.5 cm), and zone 3 was the widest (3.1 cm). Thus, the same performance was scored in three different ways. Panel B shows the results obtained using the three zones.

The different ways of scoring performance led to very different sets of data and suggest rather different interpretations of what was occurring during trials. Consider the results from the easy version of the task. Scored using the large target zone (zone 3), the data suggest that there was very little performance improvement over the ten trials, which might be taken to means that the participants were not learning very much or very effectively. However, we can see from the scores using the smaller target zones (1 and 2) that there were in fact substantial performance gains. Clearly the scoring using zone 3 was insensitive to the performance improvements that were occurring over the trial sequence. The data exhibit what is known as a **ceiling effect**: performance starts close to the best possible performance score (90 seconds is the perfect score in Figure 14.7), which acts as a limit (or ceiling) – scores cannot be any better. There is, therefore, very little room for improvement, and once the ceiling is reached, no further improvements can be detected. Ceiling effects typically occur when the criterion that defines the performance measure is very easy to meet and a person can achieve it with little practice.

Now consider the results from the harder version of the tracking task (Figure 14.7B, graph on right). In this case, data obtained when scoring using the larger target zones (2 and 3) provided evidence of performance improvement over trials. In contrast, when scoring using zone 1, there was no evidence of improvement. The absence of improvement might be taken to mean that no task-relevant learning took place, but such a conclusion is clearly contradicted by the results obtained when larger target zones were used. In this case, scoring using zone 1 was insensitive to the performance improvements that were occurring over the trial sequence. The data exhibit what is known as a **floor effect**[42]: performance starts at a very poor level (so there is plenty of room for improvement) but fails to show any improvement. Floor effects typically occur when the criterion that defines the performance measure is very difficult to achieve.

The examples shown in Figure 14.7 clearly show that if a measure of performance fails to change as a result of practice, we cannot conclude that no task-related learning took place. This is true for any measure of performance that we might choose. If the performance measure does not change, the most that we can hope to conclude is that learning had a negligible effect on that performance measure under the conditions studied. Such a conclusion is warranted provided that performance is not contaminated by any of the other factors discussed earlier (section 14.1.7), so a retention test is also needed (see section 14.1.8). If a performance measure does show an improvement that persists in a retention test, then we can conclude that learning did have an effect on that measure of performance in the conditions of the study. We cannot, however, conclude anything about the amount learned, since we have only assessed learning using one particular measure of performance – other measures may change differently.

In summary, we cannot measure learning as such; we can only measure the effects of learning on measures of performance. Measurements of the effects of learning on particular aspects of performance can be used to determine what factors, such as practice schedules, facilitate learning to improve those aspects, and which impede such learning. However, we cannot conclude anything about the effects of learning on aspects of performance that were not measured, and we cannot conclude anything about what was learnt or how much was learnt. Thus, we can provide answers to questions of the second type listed in section 14.1.6 using this kind of methodology, but we cannot answer questions of the third, fourth or fifth type. As discussed in section 14.1.14, learning can affect many different aspects of performance, and we can never hope to measure them all.

14.1.12 Improvements in performance show a characteristic trend called the 'law of practice'

Unless there is a floor or ceiling effect, it is normally found that performance improves systematically over trials in a practice or training session (e.g., Figures 14.3, 14.5, 14.7) or over a series of sessions (Figure 14.7). The pattern of improvement (once it starts) has a characteristic form: it is rapid at first, and becomes slower and slower as the amount of practice increases. This pattern may not be particularly obvious in graphical presentations when the practice period is short or there are few trials (as in Figures 14.5 and 14.7), but it is typically very obvious for long practice periods or larger numbers of trials. Two classic examples are shown in Figure 14.8. Panel A shows selected results from one of the earliest studies of mirror tracing[43]. Participants traced around the star pattern 20 times with one minute breaks between trials: the performance score (= 1000/[T + E]) combines the number of errors (E) and the time taken (T), and the graph shows that it increased with practice. The top graph in panel A plots this score against the trial number (an index of the amount of practice); the bottom graph plots the same data on logarithmic scales. Panel B shows results from a study of workers in a cigar factory who rolled cigars using a specialized, hand-operated machine[44]. The index of practice in this case is the number of cigars rolled, and the performance score is the time taken to roll a cigar (the cycle time of the machine). In this case, the factory workers produced large numbers of cigars over a period of several years: after seven years, an individual worker may have produced as many as ten million (10^7) cigars.

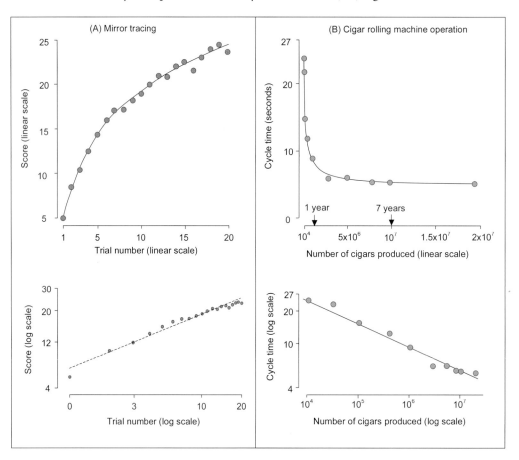

Figure 14.8: *Results from two studies of performance change with practice. Top graphs show data plotted on linear scales; bottom graphs show the same data plotted on logarithmic scales. (A) Data from Snoddy (1926), Figure 2. (B) Data from Crossman (1959).*

The results in Figure 14.8 clearly show the characteristic pattern of improvement: early in practice, performance improves rapidly as the amount of practice increases (the curve is steeper on the left side of the graph); later in practice, the improvements accrue more slowly (the curve is less steep on the right side). In panel B, for example, there are rapid gains in cigar rolling speed in the first year (after which time a typical worker will have rolled nearly a million cigars), but only a very small additional improvement over the next 6 or more years (after which time a worker may have rolled nearly 20 million cigars). By this stage, the speed at which workers are rolling cigars is close to the limit of the rolling machine (about 5 or 6 seconds). The pattern is represented by the curved lines in the graphs at the top of Figure 14.8 – called **performance curves** – and can be quite well described by an equation of the form,

$$P = \beta A^\gamma \tag{14.1}$$

where P is the measure of performance, A is the measure of the amount of practice (e.g., number of trials); β and γ are parameters (the parameter β corresponds to the performance score on the first attempt, i.e., before there has been any practice). This is sometimes called the **power law of practice** (or simply the *law of practice*) because it is a power function (A is raised to the power γ) and has been found to describe quite accurately the data from a large number of different studies using different tasks, measures of performance and practice schedules[45].

The graph of equation 14.1 is a curve when plotted using ordinary linear coordinate scales, but is a straight line when the scales are logarithmic, as shown in the bottom graphs in Figure 14.8. This is because when you take logarithms of both sides of equation 14.1 you get a straight line with a slope γ: $\mathrm{Log}(P) = \mathrm{Log}(\beta A^\gamma)$ can be written

$$\mathrm{Log}(P) = \gamma\, \mathrm{Log}(A) + \mathrm{Log}(\beta) \tag{14.2}$$

which has the form $Y = mX + c$, which is the equation of a straight line[46]. This way of plotting the data provides a convenient way of assessing whether the data follow a power law: if they do, then they should fall on a straight line.

There exists a continuing controversy concerning what type of equation provides the best description of how performance changes as a function of the amount of practice (the power function is one of several possibilities)[47]. Such controversy arises for two basic reasons: (1) different theories of how learning produces performance improvements make slightly different predictions concerning the shape of the performance curve[48], and (2) the performance curves of individual people can differ substantially from the curve obtained by averaging data from a group of people[49]. Performance curves typically incorporate the effects of other processes that accrue with practice, such as fatigue (over short periods) and changes in the muscles and connective tissues (over long periods), as well as the effects of learning (see section 14.1.7). Although the overall shape of the curve provides a rough indication of the gains in performance due to learning, the fact that it is likely to be contaminated by the effects of other factors means that the precise shape of the curve cannot be reliably used to assess theories of learning[50]. Thus, determining exactly what equation best describes the available data is unlikely to be of any great significance.

What seems to be generally true is that on average, and provided that floor and ceiling effects are avoided, performance improves roughly according to a power function – quickly early on, and more slowly later. Although this description applies to data averaged over a number of participants (100 in the case of the data shown in Figure 14.8A), such averaging tends to mask individual differences in the shape of the performance curve, and may produce a curve that is not representative of any individual person[51]. Nevertheless, performance curves of individuals often show the same overall form as the group average curves shown in Figure 14.8, though they tend to fluctuate up and down and so they are not as smooth (e.g., the day 1 graph in Figure 14.2B). However, there is a type of exception that is of potential significance: the existence of performance **plateaus** in the performance curves of individuals. Plateaus are flat sections of the performance curve – periods of practice during which no improvement is observed. A brief discussion follows.

14.1.13 Performance curves of individuals sometimes contain plateaus

Plateaus have been reported occasionally since the earliest systematic studies of performance improvements with practice. One of the earliest reported examples is reproduced in panel A of Figure 14.9. It comes from a study of telegraphers, whose tasks were to translate telegraphic messages from Morse code into English (receiving), and to send messages in Morse code from text written in English (sending)[52]. The telegraphers' performance was tested every week for several months, during which time they had accrued many hours of practice in both sending and receiving messages. The receiving performance curves of individual telegraphers frequently exhibited plateaus like that shown in Figure 14.9A, though the performance curves for sending did not show reliable evidence of plateaus. Subsequent studies of a variety of motor tasks have sometimes reported plateaus and sometimes not[53]. An example is shown in panel B of Figure 14.9. It comes from a participant in a study of performance on a three-dimensional tracking task that involved 105 practice trials each day for ten consecutive days[54] (averages of each day's trials are shown plotted against practice day).

Plateaus are observed during periods of extended practice distributed over many days, weeks or months. Since they are not observed in all participants and have sometimes not been observed at all, they are very difficult to study and interpret. Most modern studies of sensorimotor learning involve relatively short practice sessions conducted on a single day or over only a few days, and so are not well suited to the investigation of plateau phenomena[55]. Even in the more extended studies, the lack of consistency in finding plateaus and the frequent failure to do so has led to the conclusion that they are likely to be a result of temporary periods during which there is a lack of motivation due to discouragement, boredom or some other factor[56]. Only in a few individuals are such periods likely to last long enough to produce identifiable plateaus such as the one in Figure 14.9A, which lasted over two months. However, such interpretations of plateaus are speculative, as there is no evidence concerning whether or not there were any temporary losses of motivation, and consequently no evidence that plateaus occurred during periods of diminished motivation. It remains possible, therefore, that plateaus are a result of the learning process.

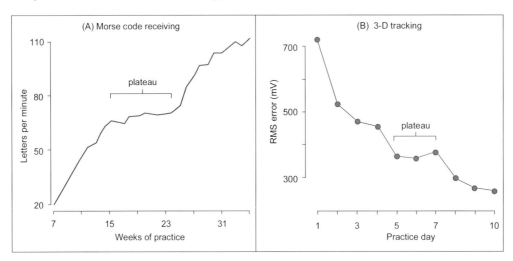

Figure 14.9: *Plateaus in performance curves of individual participants. (A) Data from Bryan and Harter (1899). (B) Data from Franks and Wilberg (1982).*

Plateaus in performance curves might arise as a result of learning in several ways. Two prominent possibilities are (1) a stage-like development of hierarchical structures, or (2) insight or discovery. The authors of the study from which the results shown in Figure 14.9A are taken suggested a version of the first possibility[57]. The idea was that learning to interpret Morse code proceeded by first learning to recognize the codes for individual letters – the telegrapher learns to recognize the pattern of dots and dashes that represents a letter as a single unit, without having to pay attention to the individual elements (a perceptual *chunk*[58]; see Chapter 13, section 13.1.4). Once the letter code patterns can be recognized, the telegrapher can learn to recognize sequences of letter codes that form syllables and words, without having to pay attention to the individual letter patterns themselves (higher-order chunks). According to this conception, plateaus arise because higher-order chunks cannot be formed until the lower-order chunks from which they are built have already been established. For example, the form of the curve in Figure 14.9A might be explained by suggesting that the part of the curve up until the end of the plateau corresponds to learning to recognize the code patterns of individual letters (letter chunks): as recognition relies less and less on attending to the individual dots and dashes, the number of letters per minute that can be decoded increases. The plateau would then be a ceiling effect due to the person closing in on the fastest performance possible based on letter chunks. Once the letter chunks have been established, higher-order syllable and word patterns can be learned, enabling the rapid recognition of longer letter sequences and faster decoding of messages. Thus, a new phase of learning is enabled, and the plateau ends. Clearly the same basic idea can be used to explain plateaus in the learning of a serial sensorimotor skill like typewriting[59], which is believed to involve the formation of motor chunks (see Chapter 13, sections 13.1.4–13.1.8).

The second possibility is based on the idea that rapid gains in performance can be achieved if a person discovers a new and more effective method or technique for achieving the goal of the task[60]. Such a discovery might occur as the result of some kind of insight on the part of the learner, whether from watching how someone else does it, by instruction from a teacher, or by chance. Plateaus can then arise due to one method of performing the task approaching a ceiling, followed by the discovery of a new, better method or technique, at which point performance improves quickly as the new method is adopted.

The two possibilities discussed here do not exhaust the possible mechanisms by which plateaus in performance curves can arise as a result of learning, but there is not space here to discuss other possibilities[61]. It is important to note again that we cannot draw firm conclusions about what is happening when a measure of performance does not change over the course of a period of practice, unless we have measured those things that are thought to be responsible (e.g., motivation, or quantities that describe technique or provide an index of chunking). Without such measures, it is impossible to state conclusively whether plateaus arise due to learning processes or due to motivational processes.

14.1.14 Learning can produce changes in many different aspects of performance

Assessment of performance is most obviously done by measuring it relative to the goal of the task. If the goal of the task is to maintain contact with a target for as long as possible, as in the pursuit rotor task (Figures 14.3, 14.5, 14.6) or compensatory tracking task (Figure 14.7), then a 'time on target' measure seems appropriate, since it is directly related to the task goal. Likewise, in the mirror tracing task (Figure 14.2), the number of times the pen moves outside the lines (error number) seems appropriate, since the goal is to trace between the lines. However, the following should be obvious:

(1)   Behavior may change as a result of learning in ways that are not assessed by time-on-target scores or error scores (or any other individual performance measure). For example, in the mirror tracing task, the time taken to trace around the star shape will probably get shorter as a person's skill improves, but this change is clearly not captured by an error score.

(2)   Changes in measures of performance that relate to goal-outcome cannot inform us about how the changes were produced. For example, if a person's ability to stay on or close to the target in a tracking task improves with practice, we have no idea what enabled the person to perform better.

These two observations are related. Achieving the goal of any motor task involves moving limb segments, activating muscles, using sensory information to plan and adjust movement, and possibly other things as well. Improvements in the ability to achieve the task goal must, therefore, be brought about by making changes to how the limbs move, and/or how the muscles are activated, and/or how and what sensory information is used in planning and control. Unless we measure these things, we cannot determine exactly how improvements in overall performance – such as a reduction in the size or number of errors – were achieved. The basic idea here is that overall performance, as assessed by a measure like error or time on target, is the outcome of a complex process. Measurement of the changes in overall performance cannot tell us about how this process itself was adjusted or modified to produce the performance changes.

One way to begin addressing these issues is to obtain a complete description of performance on each practice trial, rather than just one overall goal-related measure such as error. To do this we would need to measure the movement kinematics (of the working point and of all the contributing segments), the activation patterns of the contributing muscles, and possibly the muscle torques and other kinetic variables. An example of such an approach is described next.

14.1.15 Practice can affect even the simplest kinds of movement

Figure 14.10 shows some results from a study of a single-joint, target-directed aiming task that required participants to flex the elbow from a fixed starting position through an angle of about 54° so as to move a cursor on a screen into a target zone[62]. The task is shown in panel A (the width of the zone on the screen corresponded to an angular target of 3°). The participants were instructed to perform the task as fast as possible and undertook seven practice sessions, one every other day (so they had a day's rest between sessions). In each session they performed 200 trials. Since the task involved only elbow flexion, the only movement that needed to be measured was the elbow flexion movement (angle, angular velocity and angular acceleration were measured). EMG was recorded from the primary agonist (biceps brachii) and the antagonist (triceps brachii). The left side of panel B shows the average elbow joint kinematics and average, rectified EMGs from one participant from sessions 1, 2 and 4. The right side of panel B shows four selected performance measures from the same participant across all seven practice sessions – the average maximum speed, the standard deviation of the maximum speed, the final elbow joint position and the SD of the final position. The results from all the participants showed the same pattern of change exhibited by the individual whose results are shown in the figure.

The results show that performance changes systematically with practice, even in a simple elbow flexion task. This was evident in both the kinematic and EMG profiles (Figure 14.10B, left) and the descriptive variables (Figure 14.10B, right). The former did not change their form to any great extent – the velocity profiles, for example, retained their characteristic bell-shape over sessions (see Chapter 11) – but they did change in height and width (duration). Thus, the kinematic and EMG measures allow us to see in what ways the movements change and in what ways they remain the same (invariant) during practice. Given that the task instructions required participants to move as fast as possible, it is perhaps not surprising to find that the maximum speed reached during the movement increased over sessions (and the movement time decreased, not shown in Figure 14.10); maximum speed also became progressively more consistent (standard deviation decreased over sessions). On average, the movement ended within the target zone and the constant error remained small in all sessions; the variable error decreased over sessions. This means that participants learned how to increase the speed of their movements without sacrificing accuracy.

The results in Figure 14.10 clearly give a much more complete picture of what changes (and what does not) over the practice sessions than would any single measure related to the task goals such as maximum speed or error. Such a picture allows us to determine what changes in muscle activations and movements are associated with overall performance gains. A complete picture of how all aspects of execution are affected by practice also allows us to determine whether or not performance changes are taking place during periods when an overall performance measure is not changing. However, providing a complete description is practical only for very simple, constrained acts like single-joint aiming movements. When multi-joint movements are involved, the number of variables that would need to be measured increases, and in many cases it would be almost impossible to record EMG activity from all the contributing muscles. For this reason, complete descriptions of how performance changes with practice are seldom attempted.

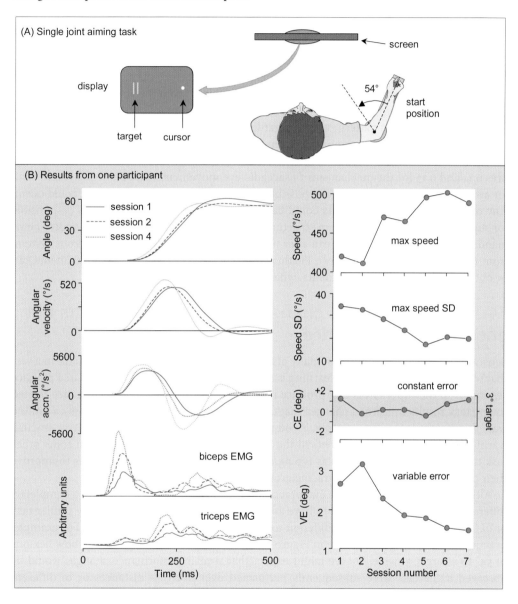

Figure 14.10: *Aiming task (A) and results of a single participant (B) from a study of the effects of practice on a range of measures. Data from Corcos* et al. *(1993), participant 5.*

It should also be noted that artificially constraining a person's movement to one joint is likely to limit the type of learning that can occur. For example, it has been noted a number of times that in the early stages of learning a new skill, such as skiing, people tend to hold themselves rigid by co-contracting antagonist muscles at various joints. This is often referred to as **freezing joint level degrees-of-freedom**[63]. As learning progresses and a person acquires more skill, the person becomes progressively less rigid[64], and previously 'frozen' joints may come to play a functional role in performance[65]. This gives the person more flexibility since the more degrees-of-freedom are involved in performance, the wider the range of possibilities for moving differently to achieve the task goal. It may also allow a person to generate more power: for example, when throwing a discus, the novice uses only the arm, whereas the skilled athlete uses their whole body, spinning around several times before releasing the disc.

Changes in task execution that can be attributed to learning must be the result of changes to the control mechanisms that are responsible for generating muscle forces and movement. These changes cannot be measured directly in humans, and in most cases the mechanisms themselves are not fully understood. Nevertheless, we can draw some inferences about the kinds of changes that might be taking place. For example, in Figure 14.10, the movement and muscle activation patterns do not change with practice: the kinematic and EMG profiles have the same basic form early and late in practice. These patterns are characteristic of single-joint aimed movements. The kinematics of such movements were discussed in Chapters 2 and 11; the EMG pattern is characterized by a two-burst sequence in the agonist and a single burst in the antagonist that begins after the first agonist burst, but before the second – the so-called **triphasic EMG pattern** for rapid single-joint movements[66]. From this it is reasonable to infer that the motor program has not been changed as a result of practice, since it is responsible for generating the basic pattern, which is hardly altered. We must suppose instead that the program has been refined in some way. Given that the program mechanisms for aimed movements have a relatively complex structure with multiple functional components (see, e.g., Figures 6.11 and 6.13 for the mechanisms of saccadic eye movements, and Figures 11.9 and 11.34 for arm movements), there are many possible adjustments and refinements that could occur. Any of the functional components could be adjusted, as could the mechanisms responsible for supplying inputs to the program structures or the spinal circuits that receive motor commands: it is known that learning can alter neural circuits at all levels of the nervous system, from the spinal cord to the cortex[67]. Further information about the type of adjustments can be obtained from transfer experiments, which are described next.

14.1.16 Performance changes transfer to situations not encountered in practice

Sensorimotor learning differs from many of the other factors that affect performance in a way that we have not mentioned yet: learning is *specific* either to the task performed in a practice session or to the experiences that produce it. This means that experience or practice related to one task results in learned changes that do not carry over (or carry over in only a limited way) to different tasks. For example, if you practice a particular task such as mirror tracing, learning will produce improvements in the performance of that task, but not in some other task that was not practiced, such as typing or playing the piano. No one expects to improve their piano playing by practicing tracing around shapes in a mirror.

Although we would not expect that practicing one task would have effects on a completely different task, we might expect it to have an effect on the performance of a very similar task or of the same task in conditions different to those experienced during practice. For example, practice of the aiming task shown in Figure 14.10 was only done for right arm elbow flexions of 54° to a target 3° wide, but we might expect that similar performance changes would be observed if the task were subsequently performed over different distances or to different sized targets, or perhaps with the left elbow. The authors of the study tested this expectation for the case of distances not encountered during practice[68]. Two days before the sequence of seven practice sessions began, participants were tested making elbow flexions over five angular distances – 18°, 36°, 54°, 72° and 90° (the pre-test phase of the experiment). They were tested at these distances again two days after the final practice session (the post-test phase of the experiment). Sample results from the pre- and post-test phases are presented in Figure 14.11. These results clearly show that the changes observed at the practiced distance (54°) were also observed at the unpracticed distances: movements over the unpracticed distances in the post-test phase were faster (panels A and B), more consistent (panel C) and more precise (panel D) than in the pre-test phase.

The example just described illustrates the fact that the specificity of learning is not all-or-nothing: the effects of learning can carry over to new conditions not encountered in practice. When this happens, the learning is said to **transfer** or **generalize** to the new conditions. The latter term is usually restricted to carry-over within the same task: so, for example, the learning that took place when practicing 54° elbow flexion movements (Figure 14.10) generalized to the unpracticed distances (Figure 14.11). The term *transfer* is more widely used: it can refer to carry-over both within a task (in which case it is an alternative term to *generalize*) and between tasks, and it can be either positive or negative. For example, if practicing mirror tracing was found to lead to improvements in piano playing, we would say that there was a **positive transfer** effect of mirror tracing on piano playing. If it led to impairment of piano playing, we would say that there was a **negative transfer** effect.

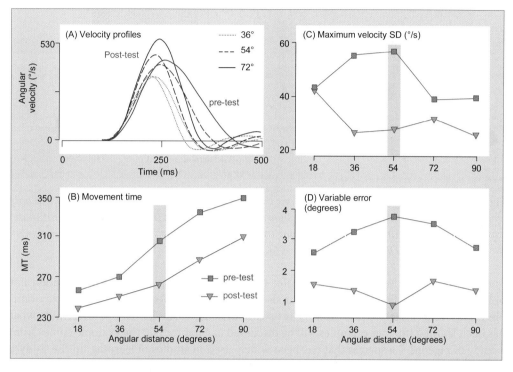

Figure 14.11: *Results from before (pre-test, blue) and after (post-test, red) a series of seven practice sessions making elbow flexion movements over 54° (practiced distance is highlighted). Panel A shows selected data from one participant. Panels B–D show average data from a group of five participants. Data from Jaric et al. (1993).*

A test of performance that occurs after a practice session or series of practice sessions is often called a **transfer test** if performance of the practiced task is evaluated either in conditions not encountered during practice or in a different task. The post-test phase of the single-joint aiming task described earlier (Figure 14.11) is an example of a transfer test. The term *retention test* (see section 14.1.8) is used if the task and conditions are the same as those encountered during practice.

As mentioned at the beginning of this section, we do not expect transfer between very different tasks like mirror tracing and piano playing, but we might expect generalization of learned effects within a particular task. As described in Chapter 11, the motor programs responsible for the production of learned skills such as writing and reaching are best thought of as rules or procedures for generating motor commands. This conception solves the problem of how to produce movements suited to different circumstances that have never before been encountered (the 'novelty problem'). Thus, a capacity for generalization to new conditions is a basic characteristic of a motor program. It does not follow from this that refinement of an existing motor program that occurs when practicing under a restricted set of conditions (such as those of Figure 14.10A) should necessarily generalize to other conditions. The degree of generalization will depend on what exactly is being refined by the learning process. As described in Chapter 11, many motor programs appear to involve an effector-independent level of representation. If this level is refined or adjusted as a result of practice with one set of effectors (e.g., the right arm), then performance changes should transfer to other effectors (e.g., the left arm). In contrast, if the program were refined at an effector-dependent level (e.g., refinement or adjustment of an internal model of the right arm), then performance changes should not transfer to other effectors.

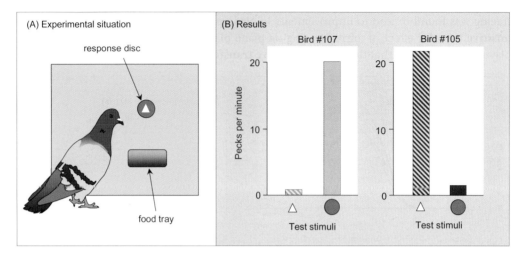

Figure 14.12: *Results from a study of pigeons trained to peck a response key for food reward only when it was illuminated with the pattern shown in (A). (B) Results (number of pecks per minute) from two birds (lab numbers given) following training when the disc was illuminated as shown on the horizontal axis. (Data from Reynolds, 1961.)*

The examples just given show that transfer tests can, in principle, provide information not only about the specificity of learning, but also about what has been learned. A simple example will serve to illustrate how transfer tests can, in some cases, be used to determine what has been learned (further examples will be discussed in Chapter 15). The example comes from a study of pigeons – a species that has been widely used in studies of learning. In the study[69], food pellets were delivered to pigeons when they pecked at a circular response disc, but only when the disc was illuminated with a pattern that consisted of a white triangle on a red background (Figure 14.12A). When the disc was not illuminated, no food was delivered when it was pecked. By the end of a training session in which food was delivered in this way, pigeons learned to peck at the disc when it was illuminated, and not to bother when it was not illuminated. Once this pecking behavior was established, it is possible to ask what the pigeons had learned to peck at. Had they learned to peck at a white triangle on a red background? Perhaps only the background was relevant to the pigeon, or perhaps only the triangle. The way to find out is to use a transfer test: after the training period, illuminate the response disk with a white triangle only or with a red disc only, and see if the pigeons peck it or not. The results of such tests on two different pigeons are shown in panel B of Figure 14.12. One pigeon pecked when the disc was illuminated with the white triangle alone, but not when only the red background was present. The other pigeon did the opposite. This example illustrates two things. First, transfer tests can be used to answer questions about what has been learned. Second, different individuals may learn different things when given the same training experiences.

14.1.17 What is sensorimotor learning for?

Sensorimotor learning can be thought of as a process (or set of processes) by which animals acquire, from practice and other experience, information about their environments and about themselves. The information is retained within the nervous system in the structure of the mechanisms that generate behavior, not as retrievable memories (see section 14.1.4). Sensorimotor learning is, in effect, a process of refining and adjusting existing mechanisms and of assembling new ones. It seems from this conception that the function of learning may be either to improve an animal's ability to perform an established behavior, or to allow the animal to acquire the ability to do something new. These two functions together comprise what is widely referred to as **skill acquisition**:

> **SKILL ACQUISITION:** (1) The process of improving, through learning, the proficiency (skillfulness) with which a particular type of motor task can be performed. *Acquisition of the ability to perform with skill.*
>
> (2) The process of acquiring, through learning, either the ability to carry out a motor task that could not previously be carried out, or a new and superior technique for carrying out a task that could already be carried out. *Acquisition of a new motor skill.*

It has been noted that 'many discussions of motor learning concentrate exclusively on ... skill acquisition'[70]. However, sensorimotor learning can produce other outcomes in addition to the acquisition of skill. Here is a (partial) list of ways in which behavior can be changed by learning that may be overlooked if one concentrates exclusively on skill acquisition (as defined above):

(1)   Learning not to perform a behavior. For example, responding to a stimulus may be important or beneficial in some situations, but in others it simply wastes time and effort. Learning not to respond in the latter situations is useful, as it saves times and energy. This type of learning is discussed in the next part of the chapter.

(2)   Learning to make appropriate choices about what to do, or to select an appropriate course of action for a particular set of circumstances.

(3)   Retaining (or regaining) an existing level of skill when conditions change (no new level of skill or new behavior is acquired). The process of re-establishing skill in changed conditions is referred to as *sensorimotor adaptation*. It is discussed further in Chapter 15.

(4)   Learning to learn. Just as you can improve your ability to do something like play the piano by doing it (practicing), you can improve your ability to learn by doing it. In other words, whenever you learn you are practicing learning. This can be viewed as a special kind of skill acquisition, 'the acquisition of learning skills as a result of practice'[71].

All of these types of learning lead to improvements in the ability to act effectively in changing environments. It is sometimes helpful to think of learning processes as processes that solve problems posed by tasks[72]. In Chapter 1 we saw that a motor task gives rise to a motor problem, and that a motor action can be viewed as a solution to the problem. For example, if the task is to tie shoelaces, then the problem is how to contract muscles and move the body in such a way that the laces get tied. Learning to tie your shoelaces is the process of finding a solution to this motor problem. This is an instructive way to think about sensorimotor learning, as it emphasizes that learning is a process (or processes) for finding solutions to problems, and hence that we cannot hope to understand learning unless we know what the problems are. In other words, in order to understand why behavior changes in the way that it does, we need to understand the problems that the sensorimotor system is solving. This idea also provides a simple and novel definition of sensorimotor learning, which it will be useful to remember (though no claim is made for its completeness):

> **SENSORIMOTOR LEARNING:** The process of finding solutions to (sensori)motor problems.

In the next part of the chapter we will see how many of the ideas that we have discussed so far apply to some of the simplest forms of sensorimotor learning.

14.2 Experience Changes Elicited Behavior: Learning Not to Respond

14.2.1 Introduction

In many situations, responses elicited by stimuli achieve useful outcomes, but in some situations a response can be a waste of time and effort, or can disrupt other, more important activities. Consider, as an example, the startle and orienting reflexes: these reflex responses can be elicited by a sudden loud noise. The startle response terminates ongoing behavior and readies an animal for action; the orienting response moves the animal's sensory organs so that they are best positioned to determine the cause of the noise. Often such responses are important, as a sudden noise is likely to have been caused by something that requires some action to be taken: the crack of a stick as it is broken by an approaching predator, a falling rock, or fruit hitting the ground. However, the noise may sometimes be of little significance – it is not accompanied by anything harmful nor anything beneficial to the animal – in which case responding to it wastes time and effort and disrupts other activities. Not responding to such stimulation provides a simple means for achieving more efficient and effective behavior: more efficient because effort is not wasted making unnecessary responses; more effective because the animal is free to respond to significant stimuli without interference. It would be beneficial, therefore, for an animal to respond to stimulation that is caused by something significant but not to respond to stimuli that are of no particular significance. This poses a problem that can be solved by learning. From its experience of different stimuli, an animal can learn which to respond to and which to ignore. In this part of the chapter we examine how stimulus-elicited behavior changes as a result of exposure to stimuli that have little or no significance. As we will see, study of this simple type of learning in simple organisms has allowed researchers to unravel its neural mechanisms.

14.2.2 Response vigor declines with repeated elicitation if the stimulus has no significance

If a stimulus is of no particular significance to an animal then, whenever it occurs, nothing of any particular interest or significance accompanies its occurrence. There is no need to respond to such a stimulus: how can an animal learn not to respond? The learning problem involves discovering that the occurrence of the stimulus is not associated with anything of significance. How can this be done?

Evidence that a stimulus is not associated with anything significant can be obtained from repeated observations that when the stimulus occurs, nothing of significance accompanies its occurrence. The more often this happens, the better the evidence. It might be expected, therefore, that if an animal is repeatedly exposed to a stimulus that is not associated with anything significant, then the strength or vigor of the responses will decline over repeated occurrences. This is what typically happens. Indeed, it has been found to happen in every species of animal that has been studied, ranging from invertebrates like worms and flies to human beings[73]. The startle reflex provides an everyday example. If someone bursts a balloon behind you, then you will most likely jump or flinch. This is the involuntary *startle response*. The first time a person unexpectedly hears a balloon pop, they typically react with a relatively vigorous startle response. If another balloon pops soon afterwards, the response will be less vigorous. After hearing several in succession, the person may not respond at all.

Figure 14.13 shows an example of how the vigor of the startle response declines over repeated elicitations by a stimulus that is not associated with anything significant. Laboratory rats were startled by loud (92 dB), high-pitched (10 kHz) tones of two seconds duration, and their responses were measured by pressure sensors in the floor of the cage[74]. The experiment consisted of three phases. In the first phase, the rats were exposed to only one tone stimulus each day for 11 consecutive days. The results are shown in the left graph in panel B of the figure: the startle response was most vigorous on the first presentation, and subsequently declined over the next ten days, but was still present on day 11. The second phase of the experiment occurred on the 12th day, when the animals were exposed to 300 tone stimuli with only one second between them. The results are shown in the middle graph of panel B: by the end of the sequence of stimuli, the rats were showing little or no startle response. The third phase started on the 13th day and consisted of three stimulus presentations, one per day on three consecutive days. Notice that on day 13, the vigor of the response is much greater than it was at the end of the previous day's session.

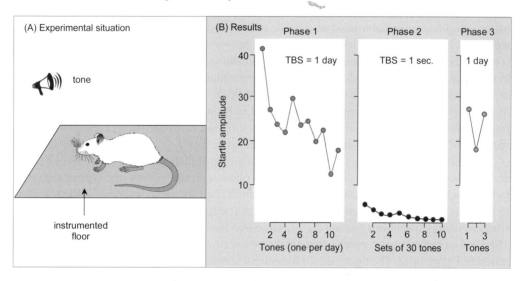

Figure 14.13: *Results of a study of decline in startle response amplitude over repeated elicitations. Results show average startle amplitude (arbitrary units) for the group of experimental animals for three sessions with time between stimuli (TBS) as indicated. Data from Leaton (1976).*

The results shown in Figure 14.13 illustrate some phenomena that frequently occur when animals (and people) are repeatedly exposed to stimuli. Phase 1 of the experiment shows that the decline in response vigor can persist for at least a day. A decline in response vigor that persists for a day or more and is due to learning is called a **long-term habituation effect**. Phases 2 and 3 together show that the decline in responsiveness produced in phase 2 failed to last until the next day: on day 13, response vigor had returned to the level it was towards the end of phase 1. Note the similarity of these results to the results of studies of massed and distributed practice described earlier. In Figure 14.13, phase 1 involved distributed training, and phase 2 involved massed training. The results suggest that the effects of distributed training are retained better than the effects of massed training. A decline in response vigor that only persists for minutes or hours and that is due to learning is called a **short-term habituation effect**. The restoration of response vigor following a period without stimulus presentations is called **spontaneous recovery**. The learning process that produces habituation effects is, as might be expected, called an **habituation process** or simply **habituation**:

> **HABITUATION (PROCESS):** A learning process that leads to the reduction of the vigor (strength) of an animal's behavioral response to a stimulus over repeated presentations of that stimulus. It occurs when the stimulus has no significance for the animal (i.e., it is not associated with anything either harmful or beneficial).

14.2.3 How can short-term habituation be distinguished from muscle fatigue?

Identification of short-term habituation effects is complicated by the fact that short-lived reductions of response vigor can be produced by fatigue as well as by learning (see section 14.1.7). There is nothing in Figure 14.13 that allows us to say that the decline in responsiveness observed in phase 2 of the experiment was not due to fatigue. The rats were presented with 300 stimuli, one after the other, so some fatigue would seem inevitable. How can we determine whether short-term habituation contributed to a reduction of response vigor that persists for a short time?

Habituation is the process of learning not to respond to a stimulus that is of no significance. It would be expected, therefore, that the learning would apply only to the non-significant stimulus and not to other stimuli. For example, if your startle and orienting responses to a balloon pop had been habituated as a result of repeated exposure to popping balloons, you would not expect to be habituated to other loud noises such as gunshots. This kind of result is what is typically found, namely that habituation shows **stimulus-specificity**: the reduction in the vigor of a response produced by repeated presentation of a particular stimulus has little or no effect on the vigor of that response when it is elicited by a sufficiently different stimulus[75]. Muscle fatigue, in contrast, is not expected to be stimulus-specific. If tired muscles are responsible for reduced response vigor, then eliciting the response using a different type of stimulus will have no effect – the muscles are still tired.

The difference in stimulus-specificity suggests a way of distinguishing short-term habituation effects from the effects of muscle fatigue. Following training with one type of stimulus, switch to a different type of stimulus that is known to elicit the same response. If the response to the new stimulus is not reduced in vigor, then the reduction of vigor to the first type of stimulus cannot have been due to fatigue and so was likely to have been an habituation effect. The kind of experimental results that might be obtained using such a procedure are illustrated in Figure 14.14. The figure shows hypothetical results from an experiment in which the startle response is repeatedly elicited by a tone (auditory stimulus) during a training phase. After the training phase, a visual stimulus (bright flash of light) is presented (the pre-test is used to establish the vigor of the startle response elicited by this stimulus). The figure shows the case in which training with the auditory stimulus does not affect the vigor of a subsequent response to the visual stimulus – the decline in vigor is specific to the auditory stimulus. This is consistent with an habituation effect but not with muscle fatigue, because muscle fatigue would affect the production of the response regardless of the stimulus used to elicit it.

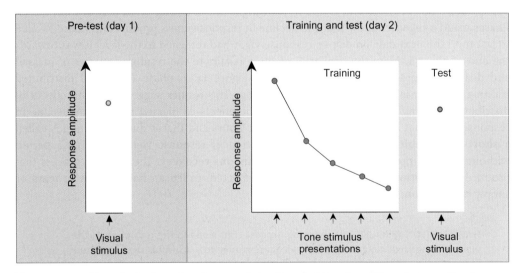

Figure 14.14: *Hypothetical results characteristic of an habituation effect. A tone stimulus was presented repeatedly during a training session and followed shortly afterwards by a visual stimulus (test).*

Unfortunately, the failure of the training with an auditory stimulus to affect the vigor of the response to the visual stimulus does not conclusively establish that training produced an habituation effect. It is possible that training with tone stimuli produced fatigue of the auditory sensory receptors. This fatigue would reduce the vigor of the response elicited by auditory stimuli, but would not affect its vigor when elicited by visual stimuli. Thus, the pattern of results in Figure 14.14 is consistent with training producing fatigue of the auditory receptors (sensory fatigue). We consider how short-term habituation effects can be distinguished from the effects of sensory fatigue next.

14.2.4 How can short-term habituation be distinguished from sensory fatigue?

The simplest way to distinguish short-term habituation is by means of a phenomenon called **dishabituation**. This is a kind of 'un-doing' of habituation that is produced by aversive, arousing or particularly intense stimuli. Figure 14.15 presents hypothetical results from an experiment that demonstrates the effect[76]. The experiment begins with a training session similar to phase 2 of the experiment in Figure 14.13: a series of presentations of an innocuous stimulus are used to repeatedly elicit a startle response and follow one after the other in quick succession. Immediately after this session, an aversive stimulus (e.g., painful electric shock) is administered. A test phase, in which the original innocuous stimulus is presented, follows after only a few seconds' delay. The figure shows that the startle response at the beginning of the test phase is as vigorous as it was at the beginning of the training phase. This restoration of response vigor is the result of dishabituation – the 'wiping out' of the habituation effect developed during the training session. It is not spontaneous recovery, since only a few seconds have elapsed since the end of the training session; and it cannot be explained by fatigue of any kind, because fatigue cannot be 'wiped out' simply by presenting an aversive stimulus. Dishabituation is thought to be due to a process called *sensitization*, which is discussed further in section 14.2.6.

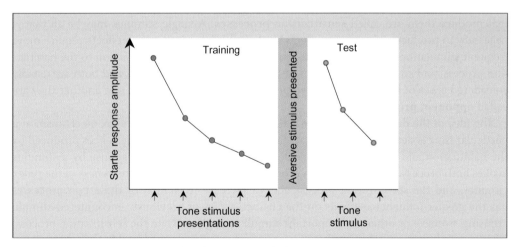

Figure 14.15: *Hypothetical results illustrating dishabituation: the restoration of response vigor following presentation of an aversive stimulus.*

14.2.5 Repetition of a stimulus does not always produce habituation effects

We have emphasized that habituation of elicited behavior occurs when the eliciting stimulus is of no significance – the animal learns from experience that the stimulus has no significance and learns not to waste time and effort responding to it. If the stimulus does have significance, then repeatedly using it to elicit a response does not typically produce habituation effects. For example, repeatedly eliciting the vestibulo-ocular reflex (VOR) response does not normally result in habituation: you can swivel your head all day long, and counter-rotational eye movements will be reflexively evoked with no detectable decline in their speed or amplitude (the gain remains stable). The same is true for a variety of other reflexes, including the pupiliary light reflex and the vestibulocollic reflex, which function almost continuously throughout the day without any noticeable decline in their responsiveness.

It may be that responsiveness habituates when there is nothing to sustain it. The VOR provides an example. When the environment is illuminated and there is visual stimulation, the VOR does not habituate, as described above. However, when the VOR is repeatedly elicited in complete darkness (no visual stimulation), it does habituate[77]. The purpose of the VOR is to keep the images steady on the retinas so that it is possible to see clearly. In complete darkness, there are no retinal images, and so the VOR has no beneficial outcome – in the absence of such an outcome, it habituates. When there is a beneficial outcome (stable images), the VOR does not habituate, implying that there is a process sustaining it.

The process that sustains the VOR is an associative process: in illuminated conditions the VOR is associated with a particular outcome (stable images). We will return to associative processes later in this chapter and in Chapter 15. Here we will discuss a simpler kind of sustaining process that does not require that the reflex response be associated with any outcome; it arises due to the arousing or aversive properties of the stimulus itself (i.e., not due to the stimulus or the response it elicits being associated with any other stimulus or any particular outcome). This *non-associative* process is discussed next in the context of the *dual process theory*.

14.2.6 Dual process theory proposes that behavioral change is due to two opposing processes

If a person or an animal is exposed to a painful or otherwise aversive stimulus, the vigor of subsequently elicited defensive and orienting responses may be increased relative to their levels prior to the noxious stimulus. This type of effect can also be produced using stimuli that are particularly intense or arousing rather than aversive. Increases in responsiveness following aversive or arousing stimuli are called **sensitization effects**, and the processes that produce them are called **sensitization processes**. A single stimulus may be all that is necessary to produce a short-term effect, but long-lasting sensitization effects require more frequent stimulation. The sensitization process acts in the opposite direction to the habituation process, and so undoes the effects of habituation (and vice-versa), and both are usually considered types of learning. When two processes act in opposition to one another they are called **opponent processes**.

The idea of the dual process theory is that the responsiveness of a reflex mechanism at a particular time is determined (in part at least) by the effects of past experiences produced by the habituation and sensitization processes[78]. Elicitation of a reflex response by a stimulus evokes both processes: the habituation process acts to reduce the responsiveness of the reflex circuitry, and the sensitization process acts to increase it. Which of these two processes has the greater influence depends on the characteristics of previously encountered stimuli: arousing, aversive or otherwise important stimuli strongly activate the sensitization process, whereas weaker, innocuous or otherwise unimportant stimuli only weakly activate it. Thus, any eliciting stimulus will activate the habituation process and cause the reflex circuits to become less responsive, and will also activate the sensitization process, which has the opposite effect. Several outcomes are possible, depending on the relative influence of the two processes:

(1)   If the stimulus is innocuous and unimportant, the habituation process will be activated, but the sensitization process will be activated only weakly, if at all. The habituation process has the stronger effect, which will result in a progressive decline in the responsiveness of the reflex circuitry over repeated stimulus presentations and a corresponding decline in response vigor (habituation effect).

(2)   If the stimulus is of significance, but neither aversive nor arousing, then both processes will be activated and it is possible for them to cancel each other. This will result in

no change in the responsiveness of the reflex circuitry, and so the response vigor will remain the same over repeated elicitation.

(3) If the stimulus is aversive or arousing, the sensitization process will have a greater effect on the responsiveness of the reflex circuitry than the habituation process. This will result in an increase in responsiveness of the reflex circuitry and a corresponding increase in response vigor (sensitization effect).

These examples illustrate that changes in the vigor of a reflex response over repeated elicitations are the result of the combined effects of the habituation and sensitization processes – the dual process theory proposes that both processes normally contribute to observed changes in response vigor.

To see how dual process theory accounts for empirical observations, we will consider the results shown in panel A of Figure 14.16. The experiment involved habituating the flexion withdrawal reflex in the left hind limb of spinal cats by repeatedly administering small, single-pulse electric shocks to the skin of the foot at a rate of 2 per second for a period of 6 minutes. The vigor of the response is measured as the percentage of a baseline amplitude of the response to the stimulus estimated from previously administered control trials. The results show an initial increase in response vigor above baseline, after which vigor declines progressively as more stimuli are administered. Such initial increases in response vigor are often observed during habituation to mildly aversive stimuli[79]. Panel B shows a hypothetical account of the results in panel A based on the dual process theory. The dashed curve (red) shows the effect on response vigor of the sensitization process: the data would follow this curve if there were no habituation process. The dot-dashed curve (green) shows the effect of the habituation process on response vigor: the data would follow this curve if there were no sensitization process. The solid blue curve is the curve actually observed in the experiment (it is a smooth curve drawn through the data points in panel A): it is the sum of the effects of the sensitization and habituation processes. The initial 'hump' in the data curve is accounted for by proposing that initially the sensitization process has a stronger effect than the habituation process.

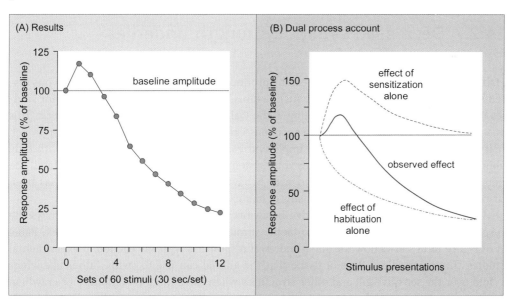

Figure 14.16: *(A) Results of a study of flexion withdrawal habituation in the spinal cat (data from Groves, Thompson, 1970). (B) Dual process theory account of the pattern of data in panel A.*

The dual process theory can be considered to solve the problem of learning not to respond as follows. If a stimulus has no significance to the animal, the sensitization process is not activated (or hardly activated), so the habituation process (which is always active to some extent) gradually reduces the responsiveness of the reflex circuitry. If the stimulus is significant, the sensitization process is activated and opposes the action of the habituation process.

As a result, responsiveness can be maintained or even increased (sensitization) if the stimulus is sufficiently aversive. The theory is able to explain a number of phenomena that have been observed in studies of habituation and sensitization, and is widely accepted[80], though it is not the only successful theory[81]. It was originally proposed that the two processes occur in different neural circuits: the habituation process was hypothesized to occur entirely within the reflex pathway, whereas the sensitization process was hypothesized to be the result of an external influence on the reflex pathway. Studies of habituation and sensitization in animals with very simple nervous systems have shown that in some cases at least, these hypotheses appear to be correct; some of these studies are discussed in the next section. Figure 14.17 shows a schematic illustration of the sites of habituation, sensitization and the fatigue effects discussed earlier.

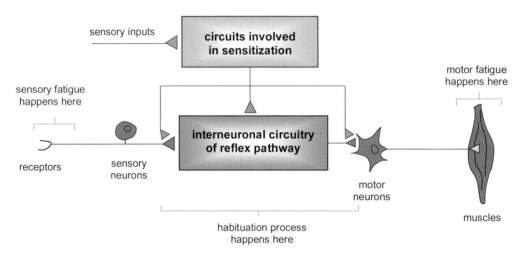

Figure 14.17: *Schematic circuit illustrating the loci of different processes underlying behavioral change.*

14.2.7 Decreased synaptic strength underlies habituation effects

Habituation and sensitization effects can be produced in simple organisms with nervous systems that consist of few neurons. One such organism that has been extensively used for studies of the physiological basis of learning is the California Seahare, *Aplysia californica*. This is a large species of sea slug – adult specimens can weigh over 30 kilograms and approach half a meter in length – that has a simple and easily accessible nervous system with only about 20,000 neurons. The simple nervous system makes it possible to study in detail the neurophysiological changes associated with behavioral changes, and a great deal has been discovered about the cellular mechanisms of habituation and sensitization[82].

Aplysia possess a variety of reflexive behaviors; one of the most studied withdraws the respiratory organ (gill) in response to tactile stimulation – the gill-withdrawal reflex. Panel A of Figure 14.18 shows how the gill-withdrawal response is typically elicited in experimental studies. The parapodia – flaps of tissue that the animal can use to swim, rather like wings – fold over the sensitive gill and other structures when the animal is stationary or crawling. In the figure, the parapodia are pinned back to expose these structures: the gill, the mantle shelf and the siphon. Withdrawal of the gill can be elicited by weak tactile stimulation, such as that provided by a jet of water, to the skin of the siphon (shown), to the mantle shelf, or to the gill itself. The drawing on the left shows the gill in an unretracted state and a small jet of water (stimulus) being directed at the siphon. The drawing on the right shows the withdrawal response: the siphon retracts slightly and the gill has shrunk substantially. Panel B shows the basic reflex arcs that underlie the gill-withdrawal reflex: the reflex pathway involves a population of between about 20 and 30 mechanosensory neurons that innervate the skin of the siphon, and a population of about 6 motor neurons that innervate the muscle of the gill[83].

Both short-term and long-term habituation effects can be produced in *Aplysia* and evidence of both is present in the data shown in panel C of Figure 14.18. The data in the figure come from an experiment in which animals were stimulated with jets of water each lasting 0.8 seconds. The animals received 10 stimuli in succession, with an interval of 30 seconds between them, for four consecutive days (training). They then received a retention session after a delay of eight days[84]. The response magnitude was measured as the duration of the gill withdrawal. A substantial reduction in the response was produced in the first training session (day 1), but the effect was not retained until the session on day 2 (it was predominantly a short-term effect). Over sessions, however, a substantial habituation effect developed that was largely retained until the retention session eight days later (long-term effect). The short-term effect has been found to last less than an hour, whereas the long-term effect can persist for 3 weeks or more[85]. Development of the long-term effect requires a training protocol like that shown in Figure 14.18C: several sessions in which stimuli are presented in quick succession, separated by several hours.

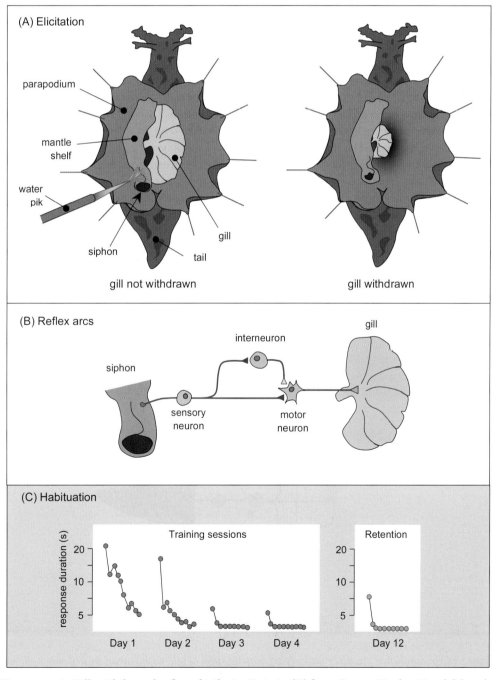

Figure 14.18: *Gill-withdrawal reflex of* Aplysia. *Data in (C) from Carew, Pinsker, Kandel (1972).*

Both short-term and long-term habituation effects are due to loss of effectiveness of synaptic connections within the reflex pathway. The changes are largely confined to the synaptic connections of the sensory neurons with the interneurons and motor neurons (the synapses shaded dark blue in Figure 14.18B)[86]. The short-term effect has been found to be due to a reduction in the amount of neurotransmitter released by the synaptic terminals of the sensory neurons, and so does not involve changes in the postsynaptic cells (interneurons and motorneurons). The long-term effect involves changes to the synaptic terminals of the sensory neurons and to the postsynaptic cell, and can involve the loss of some synapses[87] (see Figure 14.20). In both cases, the sensory neurons have less excitatory effect on the postsynaptic neurons, which results in less activation of the motor neurons and a smaller response. A great deal is known about the cellular mechanisms that produce these changes, though they are not yet completely understood; a discussion is beyond the scope of this text[88].

Changes in synaptic strength are the main results of learning processes within the nervous system: all forms of learning appear to involve changing the strength of connections between neurons[89]. The changes themselves constitute the neural basis of memory. Thus, the changes in synaptic strength within *Aplysia*'s gill-withdrawal reflex pathway can be considered to be a kind of memory – the kind that is best viewed as a refinement or adjustment of the mechanisms underlying the production of behavior (see 14.1.4). Synaptic strength can either go up or down. A reduction of synaptic strength (as in habituation) is called **synaptic depression**, and when it persists for a long period of time (hours or more) it is called **long-term synaptic depression**.

Which synapses are reduced in strength by habituation processes has been found to differ in different reflexes and different species. As we have seen, in *Aplysia*'s gill-withdrawal reflex, the synapses between the sensory neurons and the motor neurons and interneurons are weakened. In constrast, the strength of the synapses between sensory neurons and interneurons does not appear to change in habituation of the flexor withdrawal reflex in the cat (there are no monosynaptic connections with motor neurons in this case)[90].

14.2.8 Increased synaptic strength underlies sensitization effects

Sensitization of *Aplysia*'s gill-withdrawal reflex can be produced by applying aversive electric shocks to the skin of the animal more or less anywhere on its body. A single shock produces a sensitization effect that lasts less than an hour; five or more shocks produces long-term sensitization effects that can last days or even weeks[91]. Figure 14.19 shows a simplified representation

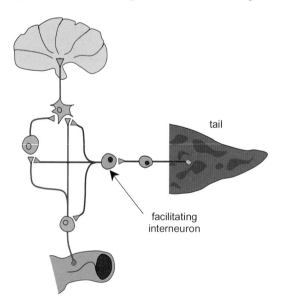

Figure 14.19: *Simplified circuitry underlying sensitization of gill-withdrawal by tail shock. Based on Kandel (2000), Figure 63-3A.*

of the neural circuitry involved in sensitization of the reflex when the shock is delivered to the skin of the animal's tail. The arcs of the gill-withdrawal reflex shown in Figure 14.18B are reproduced (elements shaded blue) and neurons external to the reflex arcs are also shown (shaded red). The latter comprise a sensory neuron that innervates the skin of the tail and a facilitating interneuron that makes synaptic connections with the sensory neuron in the reflex arc: notably there are connections with the synaptic terminals of the sensory neuron. A shock to the tail excites the sensory receptors, and action potentials are transmitted via the facilitating interneurons to the sensory neurons that innervate the siphon. The excitation of the sensory neurons by the facilitating interneurons following tail shock increases the strength of the synaptic connections between the sensory neurons and the motor neurons and interneurons, an effect called **synaptic facilitation**. This effect persists for some time after the shock, and underlies the behavioral sensitization effects. The increase of synaptic strength in sensitization is opposite to the decrease in strength in habituation, and is consistent with the dual process theory described in section 14.2.6 (compare Figures 14.17 and 14.19).

Short-term sensitization effects are mediated by short-term facilitation, which involves increased release of neurotransmitter from the synaptic terminals of the sensory neurons. Long-term sensitization effects are mediated by changes in the postsynaptic neurons as well as the sensory neurons[92]. Both long-term sensitization and habituation effects have been found to involve not only changes within existing synaptic terminals and the postsynaptic synaptic sites, but also the growth of new synaptic terminals[93] and the development of corresponding synaptic sites in the postsynaptic cells. The types of structural change in the terminal neurites of the sensory neurons that occur during sensitization and habituation in *Aplysia* are shown in Figure 14.20. The biochemical and gene transcription processes that underlie the changes in the synaptic connectivity are quite well understood, at least in outline, but are beyond the scope of the present discussion[94].

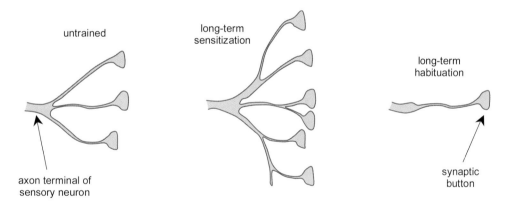

Figure 14.20: *Growth and loss of synaptic terminals in long-term sensitization and habituation in* Aplysia. *Based on Bailey and Chen (1988).*

14.2.9 The type of learning that produces habituation and sensitization effects is called non-associative learning

The type of learning that is responsible for the habituation effects described in this part of the chapter is a process that reduces the excitability of reflex pathways to stimulation that is of little or no significance. According to the dual process theory, when a stimulus is arousing or aversive, reflex excitability can be maintained (or increased) by the sensitization process. Stimuli of no significance that are neither arousing nor aversive activate the habituation process but do not activate the sensitization process; as a result the reflex pathways become progressively less excitable over repetitions of these stimuli. In effect, the animal is learning that the stimuli are not associated with anything of importance. The kind of learning involved is referred to as **non-associative learning**, learning that occurs when a stimulus is not associated with anything else. Both habituation processes and sensitization processes are considered to be types of non-associative learning.

When an animal learns that something is associated with something else the process is called **associative learning**. It is possible for associative learning to be responsible for progressive decline in reflex response vigor over repeated stimulation. An example is provided by the progressive reduction of the strength of the stretch reflex response in the gastrocnemius muscle of a standing person when the stretch stimulus is produced by tilts of the surface on which the person stands[95]. The experimental set-up is shown in panel A of Figure 14.21: the participant stands on a level platform, which can be tilted either backwards (toes up) or forwards (toes down). In the figure, the platform tilts backwards, which stretches the calf muscles and elicits a stretch reflex response in these muscles. The experiment involved a series of four such tilts of the platform (6°/s for 300 milliseconds) delivered unexpectedly, with random times between them of between 15 and 60 seconds. Panel B shows example results from one participant for the sequence of four trials (1, 2, 3 and 4): the plots on the left show the rectified EMG responses to the tilt-induced stretch in the gastrocnemius muscle of one leg; the plots on the right show the body sway measured at the hip.

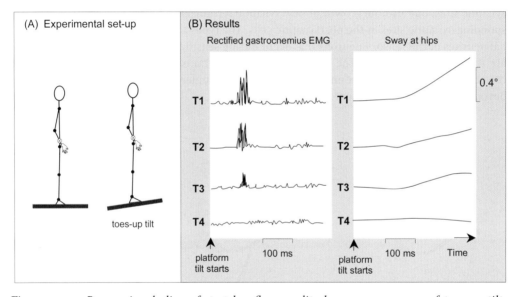

Figure 14.21: *Progressive decline of stretch reflex amplitude over a sequence of toes-up tilts of the support platform (T1 to T4) and associated decrease in body sway. Based on data from Nashner (1976).*

The decline in the stretch reflex response over a series of repeated stretches of the gastrocnemius muscle looks very much like an habituation effect, but there are two reasons for thinking that it is not. First, four stretches of a muscle has not been found to be sufficient to induce any significant habituation of the stretch reflex, which shows negligible declines in amplitude if stretch stimuli are spaced at intervals greater than five seconds[96]. Second, the reflex response has a destabilizing effect on posture: stretch elicits a contraction of the gastrocnemius that pulls on the femur, tending to flex the knee, which topples the person backwards. This contrasts with the stabilizing effect of the stretch reflex when the platform shifts forwards or backwards (see Chapter 7). Suppression of the reflex response in gastrocnemius is therefore beneficial when the muscle is stretched by platform tilts. The beneficial effect is illustrated in the figure: a reduction in body sway is associated with the decline in amplitude of the reflex response. These facts lead to the conclusion that the reduction of the stretch reflex response amplitude in Figure 14.21 is not an habituation effect, because the person is not learning that the stretch stimulus is associated with nothing. The effect is more properly interpreted as the result of an associative learning process: the person learns to suppress the reflex as it is associated with an undesirable outcome – a destabilization of upright posture.

In summary, we have seen that a person or animal can learn not to produce a response to a stimulus for at least two reasons (there may be others[97]): (1) because the stimulus is of no interest or significance, and responding to it would be a waste of time and effort; (2) because responding to the stimulus produces some aversive or otherwise undesirable outcome. Learning not to respond for the first reason is habituation, and the learning process involved is likely to be non-associative. Learning not to respond for the second reason is not habituation; it is a kind of associative learning. Associative learning is discussed in the next part of the chapter and in Chapter 15.

14.3 Experience Changes Elicited Behavior: Learning to Anticipate

14.3.1 Introduction: anticipation and conditioning

As discussed in Chapter 5, animals and people are born with a variety of reflexes and other types of stimulus-elicited behavior. In these behaviors the response is elicited by particular types of stimulation, but not by other types. For instance, withdrawal responses are normally elicited by tactile contact with a noxious stimulus. Likewise, responses that an animal produces when eating and digesting (ingestive reflexes) – such as salivation and the production of stomach acid – are normally elicited by orosensory contact with the food: smelling it, tasting it or feeling it in the mouth. In these examples, the animal simply reacts to something once it makes contact with it. In many cases like these, the animal could derive some advantage if it were able to anticipate contact. In the case of withdrawal, if contact could be anticipated, withdrawal could be elicited before contact was made. It would be advantageous to do this whenever contact would be damaging. For instance, contact with a hot surface will elicit withdrawal, but although withdrawal reactions have a short latency, there may still be sufficient time for the hot surface to burn the skin before withdrawal begins. In the case of feeding, an animal will gain an advantage from eating quickly if it is competing with others for the food: feeding can proceed more quickly and effectively if an animal is ready and salivating before the food arrives.

In situations such as those just described, anticipatory responding would be possible if there were stimulus events that reliably occurred before the skin contacted the noxious object or before the food arrived. Such stimulus events would signal imminent contact or the arrival of food – they carry information about upcoming contact or food arrival. If the animal were able to learn to use this information, it could reduce the chance of damaging contact, or gain an advantage in feeding by being ready for rapid ingestion when the food arrives. One way to make use of such information would be to respond to the stimuli that predict contact or food arrival. As first discovered by Ivan Pavlov, animals learn to do this: an animal that repeatedly hears a bell ringing immediately prior to being exposed to food stimuli will come to salivate and produce stomach acid when it hears the bell ring. Before being exposed to this relationship between the bell and food, it would only salivate and produce acid in response to the food itself. The animal has learned to respond to the bell in a new way, and the response prepares the animal for the arrival of the food – it is an anticipatory response.

The kind of learned anticipatory responding just described involves the modification of stimulus-elicited behaviors, particularly reflexes. The animal learns to modify its behavior such that an existing kind of response (e.g., withdrawal, salivation) comes to be elicited by a type of stimulus that did not originally elicit it. The training procedures used to study this kind of learning in the laboratory are called **classical** or **Pavlovian conditioning** procedures.

Training an animal using one of these procedures is simply called (Pavlovian) **conditioning**. The kind of learning involved is an instance of *associative learning* because the animal learns about the association between the two types of stimuli involved (see next section). In this part of the chapter we will discuss what has been found out about learning and its neural mechanisms from studies of Pavlovian conditioning.

14.3.2 Pavlovian conditioning procedures involve pairing two stimuli

The basic Pavlovian conditioning procedure is very simple. It involves a stimulus-elicited behavior and two types of stimulus. One of these is the eliciting stimulus for the behavior; it elicits the behavior before any training takes place, The other is a stimulus that does not elicit the behavior prior to training. For example, if the stimulus-elicited behavior were a withdrawal reflex, the eliciting stimulus might be an electric shock to the skin, and the other stimulus might be a bell ring. The eliciting stimulus and the behavioral response are referred to as the **unconditional stimulus** and the **unconditional response** in the context of Pavlovian conditioning, because the ability of the stimulus to elicit the response is not conditional on training (note that the word *unconditioned* is commonly used instead of *unconditional*):

> **UNCONDITIONAL STIMULUS (US):** A stimulus that elicits a particular response from an animal prior to training (usually the eliciting stimulus of a reflex).
>
> **UNCONDITIONAL RESPONSE (UR):** A response elicited by the unconditional stimulus prior to training (usually a reflex response).

Thus, when studying the conditioning of the withdrawal reflex, the US is an aversive stimulus to the skin and the UR is the withdrawal response elicited by the US.

The other stimulus is called the **conditional stimulus**, and the response that it comes to elicit as a result of the training procedure is called the **conditional response** (note that the word *conditioned* is commonly used instead of *conditional*):

> **CONDITIONAL STIMULUS (CS):** A stimulus that is paired with the US during training and that does not elicit the same response as the US.
>
> **CONDITIONAL RESPONSE (CR):** A response elicited by the conditional stimulus after training.

These terms are used because the elicitation of the CR by the CS is *conditional* on the training procedure. The CR and the UR may be the same response, or at least very similar, but as we will see later, this is not necessarily the case: in some cases the two responses are very different from one another.

During a training session, the two stimuli are repeatedly presented as a pair. The most common pairings are shown in Figure 14.22. The pairings in panel A are the most effective at producing conditional responses. Training with the pairing at the top of panel A is called **delay conditioning**: the CS starts first and the US starts while the CS is still on-going, so the two stimuli overlap in time. The time that elapses between the start of the CS and the start of the US is called the **delay interval**. The US and CS often terminate at the same time (as shown), but in some cases the US may terminate either before or after the CS. Training with the stimulus pairing shown at the bottom of panel A is called **trace conditioning**: a period of time called the **trace interval** between the end of the CS and the start of the US distinguishes this stimulus pairing from the pairing in delay conditioning.

The pairings in panel B of Figure 14.22 tend to be ineffective at producing conditional response. Training with the pairing at the top of panel B is called **simultaneous conditioning**: the CS and the US start at the same time and usually end at the same time. Training with the pairing at the top of panel B is called **backward conditioning**: the US starts before the CS.

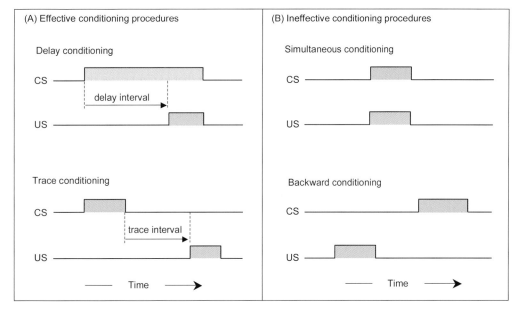

Figure 14.22: *US-CS pairings in various types of Pavlovian conditioning procedure.*

14.3.3 Training often leads to the acquisition of a conditional response

Most studies of Pavlovian conditioning have used food-related elicited behaviors such as salivation, or defensive elicited behaviors like withdrawal[98]. One reason for using these behaviors is that they can be repeatedly elicited without habituating, as the conditioning procedures require, provided that the animal can be kept motivated to respond. To motivate an animal to produce food-related behaviors, it is sufficient to keep the animal hungry; to motivate an animal to withdraw, the eliciting stimulus must have aversive qualities (see section 14.2.6). A behavior that has been extensively studied is the reflex eye-blink response elicited by irritation to the eye. Animals and people will blink in response to a puff of air directed at the eye (see Chapter 5, section 5.1.2) or to a weak electric shock to the eyelid, and they will do so repeatedly without significant habituation. In some animals, such as the rabbit, these stimuli elicit a blink of the *nictitating membrane*, sometimes called the third eyelid. We will refer to all blinks as *eye-blinks* regardless of the eyelid involved. Although eye-blink conditioning seems somewhat contrived and far removed from real-world situations, it has proved to be a useful tool for unraveling the neural mechanisms of learning[99] and in the study of some neurological disorders such as Alzheimer's disease, autism, fetal alchohol syndrome and obsessive compulsive disorders[100].

In eye-blink conditioning, a puff of air or a shock to the eyelid is the US that evokes blinks (URs) without training. The CS could be a tone or some other stimulus that does not normally elicit blinks. After training using a delay or trace conditioning procedure, animals and people can acquire conditional eye-blink responses (CRs): they blink in response to the CS. Figure 14.23 shows a schematic of the experimental procedure typical of studies of eye-blink conditioning using the delay conditioning procedure. Training consists of a sequence of CS-US pairings in which the US starts after the CS. On the first trial, the animal blinks in response to the US, but late in practice the animal starts to blink before the US occurs, apparently in response to the CS. Once training is complete, it is usual to test for CRs by presenting the CS without the US (bottom). Test trials are not strictly necessary if responses to the CS can be indentified in experimental trials. If the animal blinks and the blink was elicited by the CS (criteria for elicitation are discussed in section 5.1.2), it is likely to be a CR, but additional evidence may be needed to draw this conclusion, as discussed below.

If the CS comes to elicit blinks in the test trials after training, then it is likely that the animal has learned to respond to the CS as a result of its relationship with the US. How can we be sure that the CR occurs because of a learned association between the CS and US? This may seem like a strange question, but it is possible for responses to be elicited by the CS after training for other reasons. One reason results from the fact that in most cases the US is arousing or aversive. This avoids habituation, but may result in sensitization. When sensitization occurs an animal becomes more likely to respond to stimuli that were previously ineffective in eliciting responses. Thus, it could happen that exposure to the US sensitizes the animal, making it more likely to respond to the CS not because it has learned that the CS is associated with the US, but simply because it is sensitized. This is called **pseudo-conditioning**. In order to exclude the possibility that responses to the CS acquired as a result of training are due to sensitization, it is usual to run experiments with two groups of participants. One group is trained using the CS-US pairing – the *experimental group.* The other group – the *control group* – is exposed to the same number of CSs and USs, but they are not presented together: usually the CSs are presented without the US in one block of trials, and the USs are presented without the CS in another block of trials. Thus, the experimental group experiences a reliable relationship between the CS and the US, but the control group experiences no relationship between the two types of stimuli. If the experimental group comes to respond to the CS but the control group does not, then it can be concluded that the experimental group has learned about the CS-US relationship. However, if both groups come to respond to the CS, then it cannot be concluded that the experimental group have learned about the relationship (it might be pseudo-conditioning).

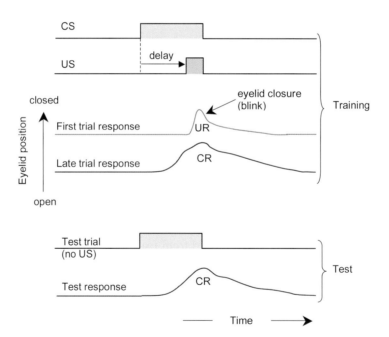

Figure 14.23: *Training and test trials in eye-blink condition using a delay procedure. Illustrative, based on Yeo and Hesslow (1998), Box 1.*

Figure 14.24 shows some results from an eye-blink conditioning experiment conducted on domestic rabbits using a delay procedure with an air-puff US and a tone CS (panel A). The experimental group received 70 conditioning trials per day for eight consecutive days. The control group received a block of 70 tone stimuli and a separate block of 70 air puffs on each day. Panel B plots the proportion of trials on which the CS elicited a blink on each training day for both groups. The figure shows that as training of the experimental group progressed, the likelihood that presentation of the CS would elicit a blink response increased; by the 8th day, a CS elicited a blink on about 90% of trials. The control group showed no tendency for the likelihood that the tone stimulus (CS) would elicit a blink to increase over sessions: a blink hardly ever followed a tone stimulus on any of the 8 days. The lack of any change in the control group indicates that the experimental group learned to respond to the CS as a result of its being paired with the US. Is this kind of learned response anticipatory or not? We address this question next.

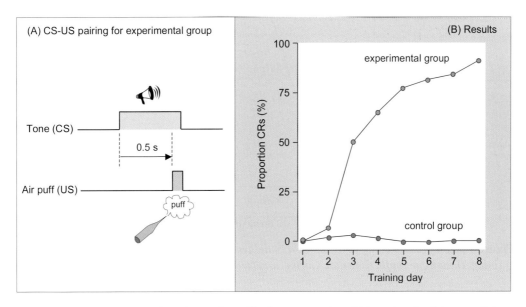

Figure 14.24: *Acquisition of conditional eye-blink responses in rabbits using the delay conditioning procedure. The control group received the same number of CSs and USs as the experimental group, but unpaired. Data from Schneiderman and Gormezano (1964).*

14.3.4 Conditional eye-blink responses are anticipatory

Evidence supports the idea that eye-blink CRs acquired in delay conditioning procedures (e.g., Figure 14.24) are anticipatory of the US. In delay conditioning, the CS starts before the US, and so the onset of the CS signals that a US is coming up. Given that the delay interval is the same on all trials in most experiments, the CS not only signals that a CS is coming up, but also when it will occur. Thus, if the CRs acquired during training are anticipatory, we might expect two things: first, that CRs will only be acquired if CS is predictive of the occurrence of the US, which is the case if the CS comes first and the US follows later, but not if the US comes first. Second, a blink elicited by the CS will be executed in such a way that maximum eyelid closure occurs at the time the US is presented. Both of these expectations have been confirmed in experiments.

Figure 14.25 shows the results from a set of experiments in which seven different groups of rabbits were trained with different intervals between the start of the CS (a tone) and the start of the US (brief shock to the eyelid)[101]. The interval ranged from −50 to 800 milliseconds. The data are from test trials administered after a series of daily training sessions. An interval of −50 ms means that the US came before the CS, a backward conditioning procedure (Figure 14.22B). An interval of 0 ms means that the CS and US started at the same time, a simultaneous conditioning procedure (Figure 14.22B). For intervals greater than zero, the procedure was delay conditioning. The graph in Figure 14.25 clearly shows that CRs were not acquired in simultaneous[102] and backward conditioning (0 and −50 ms delays): these are procedures in which the CS does not predict the occurrence of the US. For delays greater than zero, CRs are acquired, but to an extent that depends on the delay interval. A delay of 50 ms is almost as ineffective as simultaneous or backward conditioning. The most effective delay studied was 200 ms. Longer delays lead to less effective acquisition of conditional responding. This pattern is typical of delay conditioning of a variety of different behaviors, not only eye-blinks, though the most and least effective delays vary with the type of behavior[103]. In eye-blink conditioning with the delay procedure, if the delay interval is longer than about 4 or 5 seconds, CRs are not acquired[104]. Similar results have been obtained using the trace conditioning procedure, but CRs are not acquired if the trace interval is longer than about 2 seconds[105].

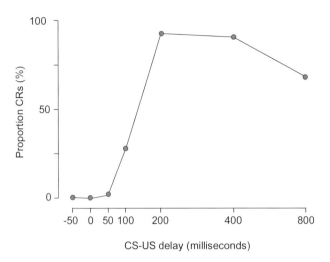

Figure 14.25: *Effectiveness of different CS-US delays at producing conditioned eye-blinks after training. Data from Smith, Coleman, Gormezano (1969).*

Confirmation of the second expectation is illustrated in Figure 14.26, which shows results from a study in which rabbits were trained using a delay conditioning procedure: one group were trained with a delay interval of 200 ms, another group were trained with a delay interval of 700 ms. Panel A shows the progressive acquisition of CRs over the five daily sessions of training for the two groups: acquisition for the 200 ms group proceeded more quickly than that of the 700 ms group. Panel B shows the averaged eyelid position profiles for CRs elicited on test trials after days 1, 3 and 5 of training. As can be seen, peak eyelid closure occurs close to the time at which the US was presented in training trials: 700 ms (top) or 200 ms (bottom) after the CS. This has been the general finding in experiments with both delay and trace conditioning procedures[106]. Two other features of the learned responses can be noted from the figure. First, as training progresses, the CR increases in amplitude (the eyelid moves further over the eyeball) suggesting that the strength of the CR increases with training. Second, there is little change in the latency of the blink: the animal does not learn to delay starting to blink following the CS; rather, it learns to slow down the movement of the eyelid so that maximum closure occurs at the time of the US.

The results shown in Figures 14.25 and 14.26 demonstrate that the responses to the CS (CRs) acquired by training on a conditioning procedure are anticipatory: they are not acquired unless the CS is predictive of an upcoming US (Figure 14.25) and they are executed in such a way that the time of maximum eyelid closure occurs at about the time at which the US occurs. These findings show that a behavior which appears to be very simple is capable of being changed by learning in quite a complex way. This is illustrated further by the results of experiments in which animal-training sessions comprise CS-US pairings with two different intervals between the CS and the US. Figure 14.27 shows an averaged eyelid position profile for the CRs acquired after training with this type of mixed-delay procedure[107]: during training, half the trials had a delay of 200 ms and half a delay of 700 ms in a random sequence. The kind of blink elicited by the CS is unlike normal blinks in that it shows two peaks: the eyelid closes, then opens slightly, closes again and finally opens agains. The peak eyelid closures occur at about 200 ms and 700 ms after the start of the CS, the times at which the US was presented during training. This pattern of response is consistent with the predictability of the US: in training, the trial sequence was random, so the animals were unable to predict whether the US will occur 200 or 700 ms after the start of the CS. It seems, therefore, that both possibilities were being covered by producing a double-blink with two peak closures coinciding with the two possible times of CS delivery. Similar findings have been reported with other animals using the trace rather than the delay conditioning procedure[108].

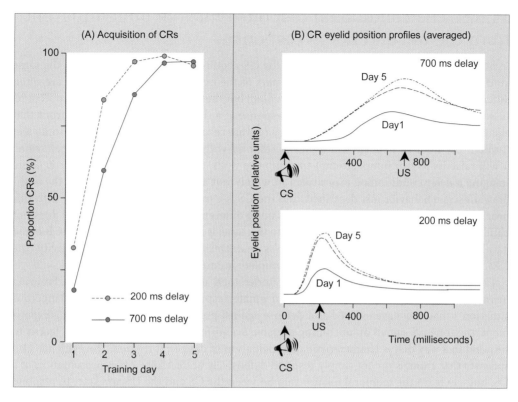

Figure 14.26: *Acquisition of conditional eye-blink responses in two groups of rabbits using delay conditioning procedures. (A) Group average percentage of CRs elicited in test trials (CR only) on each training day. (B) Average eyelid position on test trials (days 1, 3 and 5). Data from Coleman and Gormezano (1971).*

The eyelid position profiles in Figures 14.26 and 14.27 show that the execution of the blink CRs depends on the delay interval(s). These blinks also differ from blinks elicited by the US in that the eyelid moves more slowly and usually does not move as far. These differences illustrate the more general finding, that CRs often differ from the UR elicited by the US. In many cases these differences are quite subtle, and the type of response is the same: both the CR and the UR in eye-blink conditioning are blinks, albeit executed slightly differently. There are cases, however, in which the CR and the UR are different types of action; we discuss such cases next.

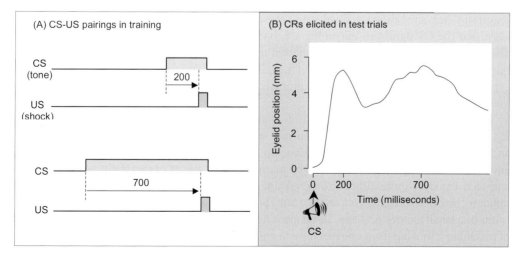

Figure 14.27: *Double-peaked blink CRs are acquired when animals are trained with two different delay intervals. Data in (B) from Millenson, Kehoe, Gormezano (1977).*

14.3.5 The conditional response may be quite different from the unconditional response

In many studies of Pavlovian conditioning, the CR acquired as a result of training is the same kind of response elicited by the US at the start of the experiment (the UR). There are often differences in the way the responses are executed, but they achieve the same type of outcome. In some cases, however, the conditional response is a different type of response from that elicited by the US. For example, a laboratory rat that receives a mild electric shock to its feet through the floor of its cage will typically respond with withdrawal and escape behaviors: it will raise its feet or jump, attempt to climb the walls, or run out if the cage door is open. Imagine a delay conditioning experiment in which foot shock is the US, the UR is the withdrawal/escape behavior just described, and the CS is a tone. As a result of training with this procedure, the animal acquires a CR that is quite different from the UR: the animal does not climb, jump, lift its feet or run in response to the tone; it freezes[109]. In this case, the CR could hardly be more different from the UR: one is characterized by vigorous motor activity (the UR), the other is characterized by almost complete immobility (the CR).

Freezing in response to the CS can be understood in terms of anticipation[110]. Freezing in rats and a variety of other animals is an innate response to certain types of dangerous situation[111] that may have evolved as a defense against predation. In the conditioning experiment, the tone CS signals an upcoming aversive event (foot shock), and the animal learns to respond in a way that is characteristic of anticipation of danger: it freezes. The evidence also suggests that animals do not simply respond defensively or 'fearfully' upon presentation of a CS, but can learn the temporal relationship between the CS and the US and start to respond defensively as the time of the US approaches[112]. This can be advantageous, particularly for longer CS-US delays, since defensive behavior interrupts other behaviors such as feeding: if the animal can predict when a dangerous event will occur, it can continue feeding for longer[113].

14.3.6 Pavlovian conditioning provides a method for studying how animals learn to behave in an anticipatory manner

The findings that we have discussed so far demonstrate that the CRs acquired as a result of training with Pavlovian conditioning procedures are anticipatory: the animal or person learns to respond to the CS in a manner that anticipates the US. Clearly, in order to learn to respond in anticipation of the US, the CS must carry information about an upcoming occurrence of the US. This is exactly what the CS does in the conditioning procedures that are effective at producing CRs: the delay and trace conditioning procedures (Figure 14.22A). The CRs acquired when animals are trained using these procedures show that the animals not only learn that the CS signals an upcoming US, but that they also learn when the US will occur. The animal can learn to use the information provided by the CS to produce an appropriate response at the appropriate moment[114]. Thus, Pavlovian conditioning procedures provide an experimental tool for the study of how animals and people learn to behave in an anticipatory manner.

The learning problem in the acquisition of anticipatory responding amounts to determining the predictive relationship between one stimulus event (the CS) and another (the US) and using information about this relationship in the production of behavior. In the natural environment, it is likely that there will be many stimulus events occurring at any given time, and so it could be quite difficult to determine what predicts what. To illustrate the kind of difficulty involved, imagine yourself in a busy place that you are unfamiliar with, a production room in a small factory perhaps. There are a number of people in the room operating pieces of machinery, moving from one machine to another, and so forth. Every so often, the electric lights in the room flicker and dim for a few moments before returning to normal brightness. The problem is to determine what causes this from observations of what is going on in the room. This is a kind of search problem: there are numerous events occurring all the time, and we need to find the one that causes the lights to flicker. To do this, we might first recognize that not all events occurring in the room are possible causes, and so can be ruled out. A list of events that can probably be excluded as candidate causes is as follows:

(i)   Events that occur after the effect (flickering lights): the cause always comes before the effect.
(ii)   Events that occur too long before the effect: causes produce their effects after particular periods of time have elapsed (the exact time depends on what causes and effects we are dealing with).
(iii) Events that we already know cannot be causes: for example, someone scratching their ear or taking a sip of coffee does not cause lights to flicker.

Excluding these events narrows down the search for the cause. The second thing we could do is to pay particular attention to events that we already know to be likely causes of flickering lights, such as power drains due to the operation of a piece of heavy machinery.

An animal in a Pavlovian conditioning experiment faces a similar kind of problem if it is to acquire a CR: it must discover which stimulus predicts the US. Imagine the animal in a large, busy laboratory, where many experiments are being conducted. There are lots of noises – footsteps and voices of experimenters, opening and closing of doors, vocalizations of the other animals, the bells and lights of other experiments (this is a very badly run laboratory). If the animal's learning processes are to discover what predicts the US, then they could (i) ignore all events that occur after the US; (ii) ignore events that occurred too long before the US; (iii) ignore events that it is familiar with and that have not previously been associated with the US; (iv) be biased towards events likely to be causes of the US. Is there any evidence that the learning processes involved in the acquisition of CRs employ these heuristics?

The results described in earlier sections are consistent with the idea that the learning mechanisms are insensitive to stimuli that occur after the US (since CRs are not acquired in backward conditioning) and insensitive to stimuli that occur too soon before the US (since CRs are not acquired if the CS-US interval is long[115]). More direct evidence will be encountered in the next section, where the mechanisms of Pavlovian conditioning are discussed.

A number of phenomena discovered in studies of Pavlovian conditioning show that it is more difficult for animals to acquire CRs to types of stimuli that are familiar from past experience. It has been found, for example, that animals acquire conditional responses to novel stimuli more quickly and reliably than to familiar ones. A direct demonstration is provided by the *CS-pre-exposure effect*[116]. This effect is obtained in experiments that use the training procedure shown in Table 14.1. In phase 1, the experimental group is pre-exposed to a stimulus that will be used as the CS in phase 2. The control group is not pre-exposed to this stimulus. The result is that in phase 2, the control group acquire a CR to the CS (which is new to them); the experimental group may acquire a CR to the CS (which is familiar to them), but acquisition is slower and less reliable than in the control group. This finding has been obtained in both animals and people, and demonstrates that it is more difficult to learn to respond in a new way to familiar stimuli than to novel ones[117].

Finally, it appears that genetic inheritance predisposes animals to acquire CRs when a US is paired with some types of CS, but not when it is paired with others. This is likely, because the causal structure of the world is such that predictive relationships between stimuli are not arbitrary: some stimuli are more likely to be related to one another than are others, hence 'repeated generations have faced a stable world that makes it likely that a particular individual will have to learn some associations rather than others ... it would be surprising if biases had not developed favoring the learning of certain associations'[118]. Thus, animals are predisposed to acquire a CR only when trained with certain types of CSs. An example is provided by the acquisition of fear-related responses to CSs in humans and primates when the CS was paired with an aversive US (usually an electric shock). Fear-related responses include distress, increased heart-rate and increased skin conductance (due to sweating). Experimental studies have shown that the acquisition of fear-related CRs proceeds more rapidly and reliably when the CS is 'fear-relevant' than when it is not[119]. 'Fear-relevant' stimuli included pictures of snakes or spiders; fear-irrelevant stimuli include pictures of flowers and mushrooms. It seems

Table 14.1: *Two-phase experimental design used to demonstrate the CS-pre-exposure effect.*

	Phase 1	Phase 2
Experimental Group	⎍ CS only	CS ⎍ US ⎍
Control Group	No stimulus presentations	CS ⎍ US ⎍

likely that evolution has predisposed us to be more likely to associate aversive consequences with snakes and spiders than with flowers, so that 'fear conditioning occurs most readily in situations that provide recurrent survival threats in mammalian evolution'[120].

In this section we have seen that the ability to learn to respond in an anticipatory fashion requires the use of learning mechanisms that are able to determine what stimulus events are predictive of others. Discovering predictive relationships between stimuli is aided by four heuristics and these seem to be embodied in the mechanisms involved in learning anticipatory responses. Of course, this does not explain how these mechanisms actually work or how they embody the heuristics. Many theories have been put forward about how learning mechanisms work, but a full discussion is beyond the scope of this text[121].

14.3.7 Acquisition of conditional responses is possible in simple neural circuits

Pavlovian conditioning experiments were originally used to study learning in mammals, including humans, and birds – rats, pigeons, rabbits, dogs and cats being popular species for study. However, simple invertebrate species also learn to produce CRs when trained using Pavlovian conditioning procedures: examples include snails, fruit flies, leeches, *Aplysia*, and the tiny roundworm *Caenorhabditis elegans*, which has a nervous system comprising only about 300 neurons[122]. Clearly a complex nervous system is not needed for this kind of associative learning. Study of Pavlovian conditioning in simple organisms allows researchers to investigate the cellular mechanisms that underlie behavioral changes. We will briefly discuss one simple example here: the Pavlovian conditioning of the gill-withdrawal reflex in *Aplysia*.

The type of conditioning procedure used in the studies of *Aplysia* differs slightly from those described earlier, in that the CS was not completely neutral. The procedure is illustrated in panel A of Figure 14.28. The US was an electric shock to the tail, a stimulus that elicits a strong, vigorous withdrawal of the gill (the UR). Two conditional stimuli were used[123]. One was a light tactile stimulus (tickle) to the mantle shelf (CS1); the other was a tickle of the siphon (CS2). Both these stimuli elicited weak gill-withdrawal responses prior to training. The conditioning procedure paired the stimulus to the mantle shelf (CS1) with the tail shock US (delay conditioning with a delay interval of less than half a second, see panel A). The stimulus to the siphon (CS2) served as control, as it was not paired with the US: these stimuli were presented on their own during the relatively long intervals between CS1-US pairings (see panel A).

After training using this conditioning procedure, animals responded to CS1 (mantle shelf tickle) with a strong, vigorous gill-withdrawal (prior to training it elicited only weak withdrawal). In contrast, the response to CS2 was not affected by the training. This established that the more vigorous response to CS1 was not simply due to sensitization by the US (see section 14.2.8): sensitization would have produced the same change in the response to both CS1 and CS2. Moreover, the effect of training on the response to CS1 was greater than the sensitization effect on the gill-withdrawal response to mantle-shelf tickling produced by tail shock. It can be concluded, therefore, that the vigorous response to CS1 was a conditional response (CR) acquired as a result of the training. As with other behaviors, acquisition of the CR was found to occur only if CS1 started before the US with a short delay interval (about half a second or less).

Panel B of Figure 14.28 shows results that illustrate some of the changes that occur at the cellular level. Intracellular recordings were made from sensory neurons stimulated by the two CS stimuli: sensory neurons stimulated by touching the mantle shelf (SN1) and neurons stimulated by touching the siphon (SN2). Recordings were also made from motor neurons that innervate the gill. The insets in the figure show typical membrane potentials recorded from theses neurons in response to CS1 and CS2 before training and one hour after training. The top two insets show potentials recorded from SN1 and a motor neuron following stimulation to the mantle shelf (CS1). SN1 responds similarly before and after training, but the change in the motor neuron's membrane potential is much larger after than it was before, consistent with the more vigorous gill-withdrawal response. The bottom two inserts show the potentials recorded from SN2 and the motor neuron following stimulation to the siphon (SN2). Neither the change in potential in SN2 nor in the motor neuron are larger after training than before; if anything, the change in the potential in the motor neuron is slightly smaller after training. These findings mean that the synaptic connections between SN1 and the motor neuron were strengthened as a result of training, but the strength of the connections between SN2 and the motor neuron were not.

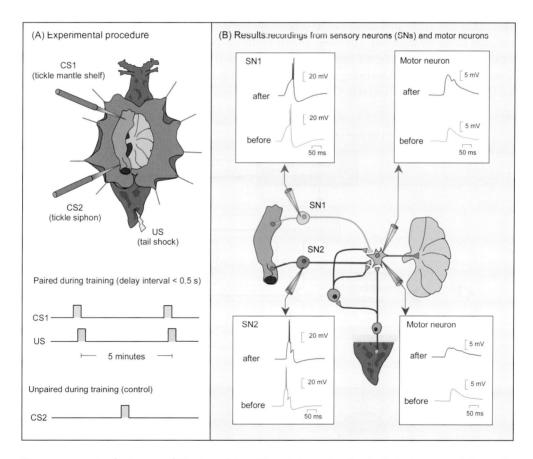

Figure 14.28: *Pavlovian conditioning of the gill-withdrawal reflex in* Aplysia; *see text for explanation. Based on Hawkins* et al. *(1983), Figure 1.*

The results described so far show that pairing of the CS and the US was necessary to produce a CR, and that the CR was mediated by a strengthening of the synaptic connections between the sensory neurons stimulated by the CS and the motor neurons associated with the response. Specifically, CR acquisition required that the CS occurred slightly before the US. At the cellular level, presentation of CS1 causes the sensory neurons (SN1) to fire and causes their synapses with the motorneurons to release neurotransmitter (refer to the circuit in Figure 14.28B). Immediately after this, the US causes the sensory neurons innervating the tail to fire, which results in presynaptic excitation of the SN1-motor neuron synapses via the facilitating interneurons. Thus, pairing of CS1 and the US results in activity in the SN1-motor neuron synapses, followed very shortly afterwards by additional activity in these same synapses. This sequential activity in these synapses causes their strength to be increased (synaptic facilitation), but only if the CS comes first and the delay before the US is presented is not more than about half a second. The biochemical mechanisms underlying these changes in synaptic strength have been worked out in some detail, but are beyond the scope of this text[124].

14.3.8 Acquisition of CRs in mammals is mediated by circuits that encompass many brain structures

In the previous section we saw that conditional responses can be acquired as a result of training with Pavlovian procedures even in animals with very simple nervous systems. Consequently, the circuitry involved in learning is relatively simple in these animals and is quite well understood. In contrast, the circuitry involved in the acquisition of eye-blink CRs in mammals is quite complex, and incorporates neurons in many different brain structures. The circuitry underlying acquisition of eye-blink CRs using the delay conditioning procedure involves the cerebellum and other structures in the brainstem. Figure 14.29 shows a block-diagram representation of the basic circuit. The components of the air-puff, eye-blink reflex itself are located at the bottom left of the figure (enclosed by dashed box). The other components are involved in one way or another in learning and producing CRs; these are not only involved in learning eye-blink CRs, but other discrete CRs as well (such as limb withdrawal)[125].

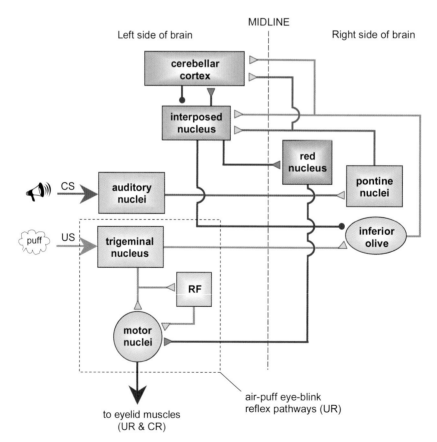

Figure 14.29: *Block diagram representation of brainstem structures involved in delay conditioning of eye-blinks (circuitry for stimuli applied to left eye and left ear only). RF = reticular formation. Based on Figures 1 and 4 in Thompson and Steinmetz (2009).*

In the circuit shown in Figure 14.29, the reflexive eye-blink response to an air-puff (the UR) is produced by the air-puff eye-blink reflex pathways. The CR is produced by the circuit that transmits auditory stimulus information to the cerebellum via nuclei in the pons (pontine nuclei); eye-blink motor commands are transmitted to the eyelid muscle motor neurons via the red nucleus. Thus, the production of the CR involves a completely different circuit than production of the UR, unlike production of the gill-withdrawal CR in *Aplysia* discussed in the last section. Learning to produce eye-blink CRs does not, therefore, change synaptic strengths within the reflex pathways; rather, it involves changing synaptic strengths within the pontine-cerebellar-red-nucleus pathway. Evidence suggests that the changes in synaptic strength occur in the cortex of the cerebellum[126]. These changes appear to be reductions in synaptic strength that can persist for long periods – *long-term synaptic depression* (LTD); such changes can be considered to constitute the memory formed by the learning process. These findings were some of the first that implicated the cerebellum as a site of sensorimotor learning. Subsequent research has shown that the cerebellum is involved in other types of sensorimotor learning[127].

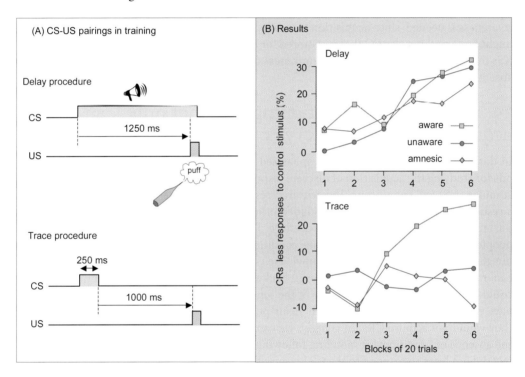

Figure 14.30: *Acquisition of conditional eye-blink responses in normal participants and amnesic patients during training with delay and trace procedures. Data in (B) from Clark and Squire (1998).*

It turns out that the circuitry shown in Figure 14.29 is necessary and sufficient for the acquisition of CRs using delay conditioning procedures, but is not sufficient for acquisition when trace conditioning procedures with relatively long delays (>1 second in humans[128]) are used. Acquisition of CRs in trace conditioning with sufficiently long trace delays requires the hippocampus and other forebrain structures in addition to brainstem structures. These structures seem to be required to bridge longer temporal gaps between the end of the CS and the start of the US[129]. In humans, damage to the hippocampus would be expected to impair acquisition of eye-blink CRs in trace conditioning, but not in delay conditioning. As discussed in section 14.1.3, hippocampal damage leads to anterograde amnesia, and so we might expect to find that amnesics are impaired in CR acquisition in trace conditioning. Figure 14.30 shows experimental results that confirm this expectation. The experiment involved training amnesic patients and normal participants using a delay procedure with a delay interval of 1250 ms, and a trace procedure with a trace interval of 1000 ms (panel A); training took place while the participants watched a silent movie. Immediately after the training sessions, participants completed a questionnaire that included questions about their awareness of the CS-US relationship (e.g., is the statement 'I believe the tone predicted when the air puff would come' true or false?). Participants who scored above chance when answering these questions were classified as *aware* of the CS-US relationship; those who scored at chance were classified as *unaware*. All the amnesic patients were classified as unaware, as they could not remember the stimuli, let alone the relationship between them. Some of the normal participants were also classified as unaware. This classification led to three groups of participants: amnesics, normal aware, and normal unaware.

The results for the three groups are shown in panel B of Figure 14.30. All three groups gradually acquired CRs when trained using the delay procedure, which shows that neither an intact hippocampus nor having conscious knowledge of the CS-US relationship is necessary for learning. In contrast, only the aware group of normal participants acquired CRs when the trace procedure was used. This finding is consistent with the idea that an intact hippocampus and conscious awareness of the CS-US relationship are needed for the acquisition of CRs in trace conditioning[130]. Note that this result does not conclusively demonstrate that such awareness is needed, since acquisition was only found to be correlated with awareness. There might be something else (X) that is required for both awareness and for CR acquisition: if this X is missing or damaged, then both awareness of the relationship and CR acquisition will be absent.

14.3.9 Pavlovian conditioning does not only lead to the acquisition of anticipatory conditional responding

In this part of the chapter we have emphasized Pavlovian conditioning procedures as methods for studying the acquisition of discrete responses to stimuli (CSs) that signal that another stimulus (US) will soon occur. The acquired responses (CRs) are anticipatory of the US. As a result of this emphasis, we have excluded other types of learning that may be taking place during training on a conditioning procedure. For example, we saw in the last section that people trained using the delay and trace conditioning procedures may acquire eye-blink CRs, but they may also acquire explicit knowledge concerning the tone/air-puff relationship. We can imagine that someone trained using a backward or simultaneous conditioning procedure could also acquire explicit knowledge of the tone/air-puff relationship – after all, they would have experienced many trials in which an air-puff and tone occurred together – even though they would not acquire CRs. In general, we cannot conclude that nothing was learned from the absence of conditional responding following training: we can only conclude that the subject did not learn to respond to the CS because this is the only type of learning we have tested for. Thus, if we do not measure in some way an animal's knowledge of a CS-US relationship, then we cannot conclude that it has not acquired knowledge of it.

Our emphasis on the acquisition of discrete, anticipatory conditional responses means that we have not discussed all the kinds of things that can be learned as a result of training on Pavlovian conditioning procedures. Discussion of all the types of knowledge that can be acquired as a result of Pavlovian conditioning procedures is beyond the scope of this text[131].

References & Notes

[1] E.g., Magill (2010); Schmidt, Lee (2011); Shadmehr, Wise (2005).

[2] Rescorla (1988), p. 329.

[3] E.g., Squire (2004).

[4] Squire (2004); Ashcraft, Radvansky (2010).

[5] Graf, Schacter (1985), p. 501.

[6] E.g., Ashcraft, Radvansky (2010).

[7] E.g., Schacter, Wagner, Buckner (2000).

[8] Habituation and Pavlovian conditioning are often classified as resulting in the formation of procedural memories (e.g., Bear, Connors, Paradiso, 2007), but these are not memories of procedures.

[9] Lui, Crump, Logan (2010), p. 474.

[10] A survey of the US public showed that most people (83%) believe that amnesia involves loss of identity (Simons, Chabris, 2011).

[11] Baxendale (2004).

[12] There have been movies that feature anterograde amnesiacs; *Memento* (2000) is one example.

[13] Corkin (2002); Spiers, Maguire, Burgess (2001); Tranel *et al.* (1994).

[14] Scoville, Milner (1957).

[15] Corkin (1984), p. 255.

[16] See Shadmehr, Brandt, Corkin (1998).

[17] Tranel *et al.* (1994), p. 165.

[18] The dissociation is not as well established for the kinds of non-declarative memory that underlie cognitive skills (Reder, Park, Kieffaber, 2009).

[19] E.g., Squire (2004); Ashcraft, Radvansky (2010).

[20] Goodwin, Graebe, Salgado *et al.* (2006).

[21] E.g., Kling (1971); Shadmehr, Wise (2005).

[22] Shadmehr, Wise (2005). Many definitions state that learning is a 'change in behavior' (e.g., Kling, 1971). I have never been able to make much sense of this.

[23] Enoka (2008) presents a review of the mechanisms of fatigue.

[24] See Enoka (2008).

[25] Carroll *et al.* (2011) discuss the neural changes produced by strength training.

[26] Hull (1943) devised a theory based on two hypothetical (and unobservable) factors internal to the nervous system: reactive and conditioned inhibition. Reactive inhibition was assumed to dissipate during rest in a similar way to fatigue. Hull's theory is no longer accepted (see Adams, 1987).

[27] E.g., Kling (1971); Magill (2010).

[28] See Schmidt, Lee (2011).

[29] Other interpretations are possible. Hull (1943) proposed that learners develop *conditioned inhibition* (learned tendency not to perform the behavior, see Irion, 1966), in massed schedules, but there is no evidence for this (Adams, 1987).

[30] Carron (1969); see also Lee, Genovese (1989).

[31] Schmidt and Lee (2011) describe the decline in this area of research.

[32] See Adams (1961); Ammons (1947); Newell, Liu, Meyer-Kress (2001).

[33] Adams (1961); Postman (1971).

[34] The rapid reacquisition is sometimes called 'savings' in this context (Krakauer, Shadmehr, 2006).

[35] See Adams (1961).

[36] Ammons (1947).

[37] See Adams (1961); Nacson, Schmidt (1971); Schmidt, Lee (2011).

[38] See Krakauer, Shadmehr (2006).

[39] See e.g., Ajemian *et al.* (2010).

[40] Schmidt, Lee (2011), p. 477.

[41] Bahrick, Fitts, Briggs (1957).

[42] Note that the terms *ceiling effect* and *floor effect* do not imply that the ceiling is at the top of the graph and that performance scores approach it from below (as for the easy task in Figure 14.7), or that the floor is at the bottom of the graph. If the measure of performance in Figure 14.7 were not time on target, but time off target (i.e., 90 seconds minus time on target), then the ceiling would be zero (always on target) and the scores would approach from above.

[43] Snoddy (1926).

[44] Crossman (1959).

[45] Newell, Rosenbloom (1981); Ivry (1996).

[46] Y is Log(P), m is γ, X is Log(A) and c is Log(β).

[47] See Heathcote, Brown, Mewhort (2000); Mazur, Hastie (1978); Newell, Liu, Meyer-Kress (2001).

[48] E.g., Mazur, Hastie (1978).

[49] Estes (1956); Kling (1971); Heathcote, Brown, Mewhort (2000); Adi-Japha et al. (2008).

[50] See Schmidt, Lee (2011).

[51] See note 49.

[52] Bryan, Harter (1897, 1899).

[53] Adams (1987); McGeoch (1927).

[54] Franks, Wilberg (1982).

[55] See Newell et al. (2001).

[56] Adams (1987); Keller (1958); Magill (2010).

[57] Bryan, Harter (1899).

[58] See Ivry (1996).

[59] E.g., Book (1925).

[60] Step-like performance curves in which there are rapid changes in behavior have been found in studies of animal learning (e.g., Gallistel, Fairhurst, Balsam, 2004) and during infant development where skill acquisition is sometimes stage-wise (Adolph, Vereijken, Denny, 1998; Adolph et al., 2008).

[61] See, e.g., Newell, Liu, Meyer-Kress (2001).

[62] Corcos et al. (1993)

[63] After Bernstein (1967).

[64] E.g., Gribble et al. (2003); Osu et al. (2002).

[65] E.g., Bernstein (1967); Vereijken et al. (1992).

[66] Typical of arm movements (Sternad, Corcos, 2001), but not eye movements (Chapter 6).

[67] See Feldman (2009); Wolpaw (2007).

[68] Jaric et al. (1993).

[69] Reynolds (1961).

[70] Shadmehr, Wise (2005), p. 40.

[71] Postman (1971), p. 1040. For a recent discussion related specifically to sensorimotor learning, see Braun, Mehring, Wolpert (2010).

[72] For a similar view of animal learning see Johnston (1981).

[73] Christofferson (1997).

[74] Leaton (1976).

[75] See Domjan (2010).

[76] For experimental examples and discussion see Groves, Thompson (1970).

[77] Baloh, Henn, Jäger (1982).

[78] Groves, Thompson (1970).

[79] See Groves, Thompson (1970).

[80] Domjan (2010); Prescott (1998).

[81] See, e.g., Schöner, Thelen (2006).

[82] See Kandel (2009) and Glanzman (2009) for overviews.

[83] Kandel (2000).

[84] A retention test on the fifth day was also administered (Carew, Pinsker, Kandel, 1972), but is not shown in Figure 14.18.

[85] Kandel (2000, 2009).

[86] Kandel (2000).

[87] See Glanzman (2009).

[88] For review see Glanzman (2009, 2010).

[89] E.g., Kandel (2009).

[90] Groves, Thompson (1970); Kandel (2000).

[91] Kandel (2000).

[92] Glanzman (2010).

[93] Bailey, Chen (1988).

[94] See Glanzman (2009, 2010) for reviews.

[95] Nashner (1976).

[96] E.g., Rothwell et al. (1986). See also Jackson, Gutierrez, Kaminski (2009).

[97] E.g., conditioned inhibition (see Domjan, 2010).

[98] See Domjan (2010).

[99] Thompson, Steinmetz (2009); Yeo, Hesslow (1998).

[100] See, e.g., Steinmetz, Tracy, Green (2001).

[101] Similar findings have been reported for eye-blink conditioning in humans and other animal species (Gormezano, 1966).

[102] In some more complex types of behavior, such as escape, simultaneous conditioning procedures can lead to the acquisition of conditional responding (e.g., Esmoris-Arranz, Pardo-Vasquez, Vasquez-Garcia, 2003).

[103] Rescorla (1988).

[104] Gormezano (1966).

[105] Kehoe, Cool, Gormezano (1991); Solomon et al. (1986).

[106] See Gormezano (1966); Yeo, Hesslow (1998).

[107] Millenson, Kehoe, Gormezano (1977).

[108] E.g., Moore, Choi (1997).

[109] E.g., Bolles, Collier (1976); Esmoris-Arranz, Pardo-Vasquez, Vasquez-Garcia (2003).

[110] See, e.g., Balsam, Gallistel (2009); Esmoris-Arranz, Pardo-Vasquez, Vasquez-Garcia (2003).

[111] Bolles (1970).

[112] See, e.g., Balsam, Gallistel (2009).

[113] For an example, see LaBarbera, Church (1974).

[114] For reviews see Balsam, Gallistel (2009); Balsam *et al.* (2010).

[115] What counts as too long depends on the kind of behavior concerned. For some other behaviors, delays of minutes or hours can lead to the acquisition of CRs (see Domjan, 2010).

[116] Also called *latent inhibition* (Lubow, Moore, 1959).

[117] See Domjan (2010) for review.

[118] Rescorla (1988), p. 348.

[119] See Öhman, Mineka (2001).

[120] Mineka, Öhman (2002), p. 928.

[121] See Domjan (2010) for an introduction.

[122] See Steinmetz, Kim, Thompson (2003).

[123] Carew, Hawkins, Kandel *et al.* (1983); Hawkins *et al.* (1983).

[124] See Kandel (2000); Roberts, Glanzman (2003).

[125] Thompson, Steinmetz (2009); Yeo, Hesslow (1998).

[126] See Thompson, Steinmetz (2009) for review.

[127] For reviews see e.g., Bloedel (2004); Carey (2011); Shadmehr, Krakauer (2008).

[128] Clark, Squire (1998).

[129] Woodruff-Pak, Disterhoft (2008).

[130] It does not demonstrate that the memory underlying the CR is a declarative one, as some have suggested (Purves *et al.*, 2008, p. 403).

[131] For introductions to the field see Domjan (2005, 2010).

CHAPTER 15

Learning by Doing

15.1 Learning from Consequences

15.1.1 Introduction: learning by trial and error

People and animals are able to learn how to do things by interacting with their environments and observing the consequences of those interactions, a fact well expressed in the following quotation:

> The idea that we learn by interacting with our environment is probably the first to occur to us when we think about the nature of learning. When an infant plays ... it has no ... teacher, but it does have a direct sensorimotor connection to its environment. Exercising this connection produces a wealth of information about cause and effect, about the consequences of actions, and about what to do in order to achieve goals.[1]

In the absence of instruction, you have to discover how to achieve a desirable outcome by doing different things and using your senses to determine whether or not the outcome occurs. This is the essence of *learning by trial and error*. Some things that you try will be unsuccessful (error), others may be successful: you discard the unsuccessful ones and retain the successful. There are two basic methods by which the things to be tried out might be generated:

(1) *The intelligent method*: try to determine through reasoning which variant of a behavior in your existing repertoire is able to solve the problem of how to achieve the desired outcome.

(2) *The unintelligent method*: try out variations of the behaviors in your repertoire that are in some way related to the problem; you might hit on a solution by chance.

The learning process uses information about success or failure – *evaluative feedback* information – to develop the tendency to perform the successful behavior(s) and not to perform the unsuccessful ones. Various ideas about what this process might involve will be discussed in this part of the chapter.

15.1.2 An example of learning by trial and error

Edward Thorndike's early studies of how animals learned to escape from puzzle boxes provide straightforward examples of learning from consequences. A hungry animal, usually a domestic cat, was placed inside a box with a morsel of food outside. In order to reach the food, the cat had to escape from the box. Escape required a specific action or series of actions. Panel A of Figure 15.1 shows two of Thorndike's boxes. Box A required that the cat pull down on a loop, which released a catch and allowed the door to fall open. Box K required three actions to release the catches holding the door closed: depress a treadle, pull on a string and push up or down on a bar. When first put in a puzzle box, cats would engage in what appeared to be species-typical, escape-related behaviors. Thorndike observed that a cat

> ... tries to squeeze through any opening; it claws and bites at the bars or wire; it thrusts its paws out through any opening and claws at everything it reaches ... [it] seems to strive instinctively to escape from confinement ... it will claw and bite and squeeze incessantly[2].

These behaviors would not lead to escape unless, by accident, they resulted in the effective action. Note that the animal does not have to learn how to perform a new kind of action: it already has the ability to pull on loops, push down on bars and depress treadles. If escape required something that the animal could not already do, then it would not do it by chance.

Thorndike would put an animal in a box and measure how long it took it to escape (a trial) and then, after a short time, he would put the animal back in the box and make the same measurement. He would run the animal through many such trials. Panel B of Figure

15.1 shows some characteristic results: the graphs plot the time taken to escape for each of a sequence of trials. The top graph shows the times for one cat to escape from box K for a sequence of 117 trials conducted over 7 days. The bottom graph shows the times for another cat to escape from box A for a sequence of 21 trials over 2 days. Both graphs show a trend for the animals to take less time to escape as the number of trials increases. The animal in box A took about 160 seconds to escape on its first trial, after about 15 trials the time was down to 5 or 6 seconds. Over repeated trials the animal would engage less and less in ineffective behavior and come to perform the effective action (or actions) soon after being put in the box. Thus, animals learned to execute the effective action as a result of their repeated experiences in the box. How did the animals do this? Thorndike's answer is discussed next.

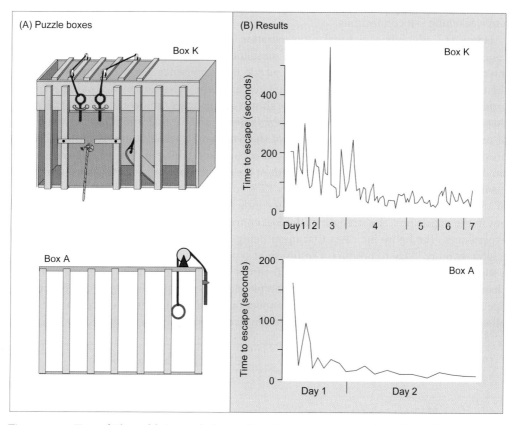

Figure 15.1: *Two of Thorndike's puzzle boxes (Box K and Box A, based on Thorndike, 1898) and the times taken to escape over a sequence of trials carried out on consecutive days (see text for details). Data from Thorndike (1898), Figures 2 and 10.*

15.1.3 What is learned and how? Thorndike's answers

Thorndike wondered how animals learned to perform the effective action and to stop performing ineffective ones. The answer he gave is expressed in what he called the **law of effect**, which states:

> Of several responses made to the same situation, those which are accompanied or closely followed by satisfaction to the animal will, other things being equal, be more firmly connected with the situation, so that, when it recurs, they will be more likely to recur ... those which are accompanied or closely followed by discomfort to the animal will, other things being equal, have their connections with that situation weakened, so that, when it recurs, they will be less likely to occur[3].

In the puzzle box, an effective action is closely followed by satisfying outcomes: door opening and food. The satisfaction strengthens the 'connection' between the action and the situation, and so the animal is more likely to carry out that action when it finds itself in the same situation. Ineffective actions are followed by frustration at being trapped and hungry ('discomfort'), and their connection to the situation is weakened.

The Law of Effect is an hypothesis that incorporates Thorndike's conviction that animals do not have any understanding of the consequences of their actions. A cat that has learned to pull the loop in box A does not pull the loop in order to get out; it does so because learning has established a strong connection between loop pulling and the stimulation present when in the box. This stimulation elicits the loop-pulling action by virtue of the connection. The kind of connection involved is called a **stimulus-response (S-R) connection**[4]. According to the Law of Effect, the consequences of actions only play a role in learning as a result of the internal states of 'satisfaction' or 'discomfort' they produce. These states respectively strengthen and weaken S-R connections, which makes learning a process of strengthening and weakening S-R connections.

Figure 15.2 presents a pictorial representation of how the Law of Effect might change connection strengths. Panel A shows a simplified block-diagram representation of the internal mechanisms of behavior prior to puzzle-box experience. Sensory stimulation from the confining puzzle-box environment elicits escape-type behaviors by activating response production circuits: three such circuits are shown in the figure, and could represent circuits that generate scratching, pulling and squeezing behaviors. Mutual inhibition between pairs of response circuits means that only one of the pair can be active at any given time, which prevents response interference such as could occur if scratching and squeezing were active simultaneously (see Chapter 5). The strength of the connections between the sensory mechanisms and the response-generating circuits (S-R connections) are indicated by the thickness of the connecting line: thicker, darker lines indicate stronger connections. Prior to being put in the puzzle box, the strength of the S-R connections depends on the animal's previous experiences. The figure indicates that upon being first put into the puzzle box, the animal is slightly more likely to produce a response of type 2 than either of the others, since it has a slightly stronger S-R connection. Panel B shows how the strength of the connections has changed as a result of repeated trials in the puzzle box: a response of type 1 is effective at opening the door to the box, and its S-R connection has been strengthened; responses of the other types are ineffective, and their connection strengths have been weakened.

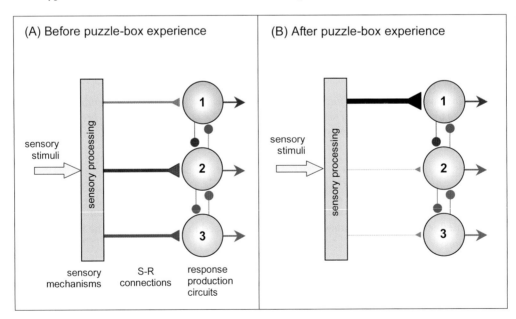

Figure 15.2: *Representation of response production mechanisms before and after repeated puzzle-box experience, according to the Law of Effect: mutually inhibitory response production circuits are activated by stimuli to different extents, depending on the strength of the S-R connections (thicker, darker lines = stronger connections). The response generated by circuit 1 is effective; the other responses are ineffective.*

15.1.4 Animals acquire knowledge about the consequences of their actions

Our subjective experience is that we perform learned behaviors with the intention of achieving some desired outcome (goal). Our goals seem to play a causal role in the production of behavior: they somehow provide the impetus or motive to produce behavior. It is difficult to imagine that it could be otherwise. If we saw a cat immediately reach up and pull on the loop and escape from puzzle box A (Figure 15.1), then it would be natural to assume that the cat pulled on the loop in order to escape: the pull was motivated by the cat's desire to escape.

For Thorndike, goals, desires and other internal states that cannot be measured were not acceptable in scientific explanations, so he avoided attributing a causal role to goals and desires. According to him, sensory stimulation is the causal agent in the elicitation of behavior, learned or not. Although some have agreed with Thorndike (even for human behavior[5]), others have invoked internal states to explain the production of behavior. Nowadays it is almost universally accepted that internal states can serve as the causes of behavior. In previous chapters we described voluntary actions as those evoked by activation that derives from some kind of intent or other internal motive state. We were not concerned with the nature of such states, only with their functional role in activating the mechanisms that generate behavior. As discussed in Chapter 6, many behaviors can be elicited either by a stimulus or by a volitional signal. The main example was that of saccadic eye movements: these movements are generated by circuits in the brainstem that can be activated either by signals evoked directly by stimuli (reflex saccades) or by signals generated in the cerebral cortex (voluntary saccades).

The view that internal motive states can play a causal role in evoking behavior does not mean that learned behavior cannot be stimulus-elicited. It may be that in animals such as cats, learned behaviors are stimulus-elicited, as Thorndike proposed. Is there evidence to suggest that desirable outcomes play a role in the production of behavior? A method often used to find out is based on the following logic. If an animal learns to perform a particular action in order to achieve a particular outcome, then the animal will no longer perform that action when the outcome is no longer desirable. In contrast, if the animal acquires a S-R connection, then the desirability of the outcome should have little effect on whether or not the animal performs the action (see Chapter 1, section 1.1.7). The following hypothetical example illustrates how this might work for a cat in a puzzle box: "if a dog is waiting outside the box, such that opening the door is no longer a desirable outcome for the cat, according to the S-R theory the cat will nevertheless perform the sequence of actions that will lead to the door opening, while [the action-outcome] theory deems that the cat will refrain from this behavior[6]." Experiments based on this logic have supported the idea that animals do learn about the association between actions and their consequences[7]. Exactly what role this knowledge plays in the production of behavior cannot be determined from these experiments; various ideas have been proposed[8], and one possibility is discussed in the next section.

The modern consensus is that experience can change the strength of S-R connections, and that it can also result in the acquisition of knowledge about actions and their consequences, knowledge that can play a causal role in the production of behavior[9]. Learned behaviors that are elicited by stimuli, without desired outcomes playing any causal role in their production, are often referred to as **habitual behaviors** or **habits**[10]. As discussed in Chapter 1, behaviors of this sort are typically goal-directed, but not in the sense of being directed by an explicit internal representation of the goal. Some interesting evidence that supports the existence of stimulus-response connections in well-learned human behavior is discussed next.

15.1.5 Frontal syndromes reveal that learned human action involves S-R connections

Although we are usually aware of having the intention to perform learned behaviors, there are some situations in which well-learned actions are performed without any conscious intent. An example of such behavior is described in the following quotation:

> I recently went into a room ... where I work and found myself making a pulling movement with my left hand in the air. Somewhat puzzled, I realized that the cord that controlled the light switch had been removed, but that the act of passing through the door ... together with the requirement ... for light had triggered a [program] for activating the switch in that particular room[11].

It is difficult to study acts like these, since they seldom occur, and the conditions in which they happen are unlikely to be easily reproduced in a laboratory. There are, however, other types of behavior that are not initiated by intentions but are amenable to empirical study. Interceptive actions are one type. We usually think of interceptive acts like hitting or catching a moving object as intentional, but such acts are unlikely to be evoked by a voluntary signal because of the need for precise timing in relation to the moving object. As discussed in Chapter 12, interceptive acts are thought to be initiated by a stimulus event: specifically, the value of the moving target's perceived time-to-arrival reaching a predetermined criterion (see sections 9.3.5 and 12.4.13). The role of intention is not to initiate an interceptive action, but to activate the production mechanisms so that they are ready to begin generating commands when the appropriate stimulus event occurs. This accounts for why some interceptions that occur in fast racket sports like tennis or badminton are often referred to as 'reflexive'. These acts are not, strictly speaking, reflexes (see Chapter 5), but like reflexes they are stimulus-elicited[12].

Another class of behavior not initiated by acts of will (or conscious intent) occurs in individuals who have suffered certain types of damage to their frontal lobes. One example of this class characterizes a condition known as **anarchic hand syndrome**, which has been described as follows:

> The ... movements of one hand are apparently directed towards a goal and are smoothly executed, yet are unintended ... The patients are aware of their bizarre and potentially hazardous behavior but cannot inhibit it[13].

The involuntary movements of the affected limb are not random or uncontrolled, but goal-directed: the hand may grab things, press switches, do up buttons on shirts and jackets, pick things up, open and close doors and turn the pages of a book[14]. In some cases the affected limb opposes intended actions carried out by the unaffected limb[15]. It is typical for patients to describe their affected limb as having a mind of its own or of being disobedient[16], and they may resort to restraining it using their unaffected hand. The patients have normal sensation in the affected limb, and they are well aware that the limb is their own[17].

Anarchic hand syndrome typically results from unilateral lesions of the supplementary motor area (SMA)[18] and/or nearby regions of frontal cortex such as the pre-SMA and the rostral cingulate cortex[19]. Damage to these areas in both hemispheres is associated with a phenomenon called **utilization behavior**[20]. This involves the spontaneous performance of object-appropriate actions when the person sees an object, regardless of time, context or ownership. For example, the patient may be visiting the neurologist and see on the doctor's desk a toothbrush or a comb, and will reach out, grasp it and begin executing the object-appropriate activity – brushing teeth or combing hair. The patient is typically unable to comply with instructions not to carry out such actions. Unlike patients with anarchic hand syndrome, patients who exhibit utilization behavior do not report that their behavior is unwanted or unwilled and usually do not realize that their behavior is inappropriate. The following quotation describes the behavior of a particular patient[21]:

> ... while being tested, he spotted an apple and a knife on a corner of the testing desk. He peeled the apple and ate it. The examiner asked why he was eating the apple. He replied: 'Well...it was there.' 'Are you hungry?' 'No. Well, a bit.' 'Have you not just finished eating?' 'Yes.' 'Is this apple yours?' 'No.' 'And whose apple is it?' 'Yours, I think.' 'So why are you eating it?' 'Because it is here.'[22]

Both anarchic hand syndrome and utilization behavior appear to occur when well-learned sensorimotor behaviors are released from volitional control and can be elicited involuntarily by appropriate environmental stimuli (objects such as apples, pens, combs, toothbrushes, cups, knives and so forth)[23]. In order for this to happen, there must be sensorimotor connections that can activate the pattern-generating mechanisms responsible for producing the behaviors. The connections that transmit sensory information to the pattern-generating mechanisms are most likely mediated by the parietal cortex. As we have seen, visual information transmitted along the dorsal stream can have rapid effects on motor behavior that a person may be unaware of (see sections 4.2.13 and 12.3.9). The idea is that visual (or other sensory inputs) are transmitted directly to parietal lobe systems that are capable of initiating command generation. The parietal systems and/or the command generators themselves are normally under inhibitory control by frontal lobe structures, but damage to these structures removes or reduces the inhibition, and it becomes possible for suitable stimuli to involuntarily elicit behaviors that are normally executed voluntarily. This suggests a functional architecture for well-learned human motor skills that incorporates connections similar to those shown in Figure 15.2. Several models of the processes underlying the selection and initiation of human action incorporate direct sensorimotor connections together with other systems that modulate and/or control the activity of these linkages[24].

In summary, much well-learned human behavior incorporates sensorimotor connections overlaid by an intentional system (or systems) mediated by the frontal cortex[25]. These intentional processes can either release sensorimotor linkages from inhibition and so allow stimuli to elicit behavior, or directly activate pattern generating mechanisms. Thus, initiation of well-learned behaviors may be organized in a similar manner to that of the genetically determined behaviors like saccadic eye movements and locomotion, discussed in earlier chapters (see sections 6.2 and 8.3). This does not imply, of course, that the sensorimotor connections are established in the manner proposed by Thorndike in his Law of Effect. However, it does show that Thorndike's proposal is not as counterintuitive as it may seem when applied to human behavior.

15.1.6 Behavior can have reinforcing or punishing consequences

Although in many cases there is more to learning by trial and error than is expressed in the Law of Effect, the law incorporates some basic ideas that have stood the test of time. One important basic idea is that (perceived) behavioral consequences evoke an internal signal (or state) that acts to strengthen connections within the nervous system. Thorndike called the internal state 'satisfaction'. A satisfying or otherwise rewarding consequence of a behavior is usually called a **reinforcer**, and obtaining a reinforcer is called **reinforcement**[26]:

> **REINFORCER:** Something that is capable either of increasing the likelihood that the behavior that produced it will be performed again, or of otherwise increasing the strength of that behavior (also called **reward**).
>
> **REINFORCEMENT:** The delivery of a reinforcer to (or the acquisition of a reinforcer by) an animal or person.

These definitions are *behavioral* in the sense that they do not make reference to feelings of pleasure, satisfaction or enjoyment that reinforcement may evoke. The term **reward** is often used instead of *reinforcer* (it can also be used instead of reinforcement), but some authors feel that it carries connotations of subjective feelings of satisfaction or enjoyment, and so avoid it (we will use *reward* interchangeably with *reinforcer* whenever the usage improves readability). A reinforcer might be something like a tasty morsel of food, or it might be the termination of an aversive situation (such as release from being confined in a puzzle box)[27]. The distinction between these is usually expressed by calling those of the first type **positive reinforcers** because something is added (presented or obtained), and calling those of the second type **negative reinforcers** because something is subtracted (removed or terminated).

The opposite of reinforcement is **punishment**. Intuitively, punishment corresponds to the delivery of a painful or otherwise aversive stimulus, though we can define it without reference to pain or discomfort: punishment is the delivery of something that decreases the likelihood that a behavior will be performed again (or otherwise weakens the behavior). This definition avoids reference to subjective states, and is also consistent with painful stimulation being reinforcing (e.g., for a masochist). The term *punisher* is sometimes used to refer to the punishing stimulus. As with reinforcement, positive and negative types of punishment can be distinguished. **Positive punishment** is the delivery of a punishing stimulus. **Negative punishment** refers to the removal or loss of something desirable, or to the prevention of access to something desirable. Table 15.1 summarizes reinforcement and punishment.

At first glance, the way in which reward and punishment act to change behavior may seem very simple: 'give a subject something good for doing something, and it does it more; give a subject something unpleasant and it will stop what it was doing'[28]. This much every dog-owner knows, but it leaves unanswered the following question: how does the subject know what behavior the 'something good' was given for and what behavior the 'something unpleasant' was given for? More generally, how does an animal discover relationships between behaviors and consequences? We discuss this question after a brief account of the experimental method used to study learning from reinforcement and punishment.

Table 15.1: *Relationships between behavior and consequences (reinforcing or punishing).*

Reinforcement	Positive	BEHAVIOR ——produces——▶ REINFORCER	
	Negative	BEHAVIOR ——eliminates——◆ PUNISHING STIMULUS	
Punishment	Positive	BEHAVIOR ——produces——▶ PUNISHING STIMULUS	
	Negative	BEHAVIOR ——eliminates or prevents——◆ REWARDING STIMULUS	

15.1.7 Instrumental conditioning procedures are used to study learning from consequences

The experimental study of what animals and people learn to do as a result of the rewarding and punishing consequences of their behavior involves the use of **instrumental conditioning procedures** (also called *operant conditioning procedures*). The term *instrumental* is used because a behavior is instrumental in producing certain consequences. The following terminology is used:

(1)   *Instrumental conditioning procedure*: the training procedure (see below).
(2)   *Instrumental conditioning*: the process of training with an instrumental conditioning procedure.
(3)   *Instrumental learning*: the type of learning involved.

Instrumental conditioning procedures involve making the delivery of a reinforcer or punisher conditional on the trainee performing a particular action, and can involve any of the four relationships in Table 15.1. For example, if a rat (trainee) presses a lever (action), then a food pellet (reinforcer) is delivered. This is a positive reinforcement procedure in which delivery of a food pellet is a consequence of pressing the lever. Negative reinforcement procedures are often referred to as escape or avoidance procedures, depending on whether a behavior allows an animal to escape from an aversive situation or to avoid punishment, respectively. Thorndike's puzzle-box experiments involved an escape procedure, but he also included positive reinforcement in the form of food outside the box.

Use of instrumental conditioning procedures in experiments allows investigators to determine whether animals or people can discover what to do so as to obtain reinforcers or avoid punishment. The literature in this area is vast; we will only discuss as much as is necessary to introduce concepts useful for understanding sensorimotor learning.

15.1.8 The time between an action and its reinforcement has a powerful effect on learning

In Thorndike's studies, when a cat performed the effective action, the door opened almost immediately. Thus, reward very quickly followed the effective action. It seems intuitively obvious that the temporal relationship between an action and reinforcement is the key to discovering what actions are effective. This is incorporated into the Law of Effect: of all the actions that the animal executes, only 'those which are accompanied or closely followed by' reinforcement are actually reinforced. This makes ecological sense because when an animal engages in motor behavior (exerts forces and moves its body), the biologically relevant effects caused by that behavior often occur immediately or very soon after it is executed.

Thorndike's basic idea was that reinforcement acts to strengthen only those actions that were performed immediately prior to the occurrence of the reward. In any search to discover which actions were responsible for important outcomes, this narrows down the number of candidates substantially: animals normally engage in continuous streams of activity, so the longer the interval over which a search is conducted, the more candidates there will be.

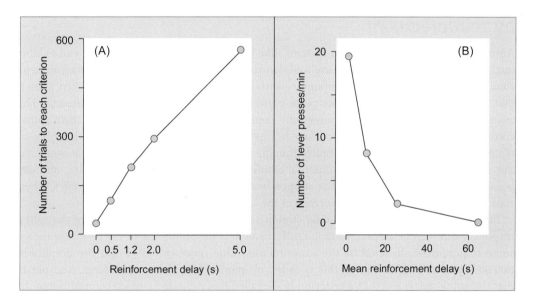

Figure 15.3: *The effect of reinforcement delay on learning in instrumental conditioning experiments. (A) Data from a maze-learning experiment (Grice, 1948). (B) Data from a lever-pressing experiment (Dickinson, Watt, Griffiths, 1994).*

Whether rewards act only on actions performed in a short interval of time prior to their occurrence can be easily tested in instrumental conditioning experiments, by varying the delay between performance of an action and delivery of the reinforcer. The consensus[29] is that the delay has a strong influence on whether or not an animal will learn about the relationship between the action and the reinforcer: the longer the delay, the less effectively the animal learns. The same is true for punishment[30]. Figure 15.3 shows the results from two experiments that demonstrate the effect of reinforcement delay on learning. Panel A shows the results from an experiment in which hungry rats were placed in a 'maze' with two corridors (one on the left and one on the right). One corridor was painted black, the other white (switched from trial to trial); the white corridor had food at the end. The rats were rewarded if they reached the food, and so had to learn to choose the white corridor. The graph in the figure plots the number of trials that the rats needed before they were choosing the correct corridor on 75% of trials (the criterion). A delay of only 5 seconds in the presentation of the reward made a dramatic difference: rats needed fewer than 30 trials to reach criterion if rewards were presented immediately, but needed nearly 600 trials when the delay was 5 seconds. Panel B of the figure shows results from a study in which hungry rats had to learn to press a lever if they were to obtain food pellets. The delay between the lever press and pellet delivery varied from 2 seconds to 64 seconds. The graph in panel B shows that delay had a large effect on the acquisition of lever pressing; lever pressing was not acquired at all when the delay was 64 seconds.

The finding that animals only learn about the relationship between a behavior and its consequences if these occur shortly after the behavior has been executed (the shorter the time the better) implies that there is some kind of short-term memory involved. This is what might be expected: in order to learn from the consequences of its actions, the animal must remember what it has recently done if it is to strengthen (or weaken) the behavior that produced those consequences. Reinforcement, therefore, acts on memories of recently performed actions. Such a memory could simply be the effects of recent activity in the pattern-generating mechanisms responsible for the production of an action. Whatever the nature of the memory, it evidently declines quickly (within a matter of seconds), though the most important factor producing decay in the memory for a particular behavior may not be time per se but performance of other activities[31].

15.1.9 Simple reflex behavior can be modified by reinforcement

Animals with very simple nervous systems, like the sea slug *Aplysia californica*, can exhibit instrumental learning[32]. Even the tiny roundworm *Caenorhabditis elegans*, with its 300 neurons, seems to be capable of rudimentary instrumental learning[33]. It has also been shown that instrumental learning can take place entirely within the spinal cord of mammals. For example, leg flexion can be instrumentally conditioned in rats that have had their spinal cords surgically disconnected from their brains[34]. However, most instrumental learning in mammals appears to involve the brain, though spinal circuits can be involved as well[35]. In this section we will consider instrumental conditioning of the spinal stretch reflex, and the possible mechanisms underlying the suppression of the gastrocnemius stretch reflex when standing on a tilting surface, as described in the last chapter.

Instrumental conditioning of spinal stretch reflex amplitude involves eliciting the reflex response, and then delivering positive reinforcement if the amplitude of the response meets some requirement specified by the experimenter. One requirement is that the amplitude exceed a pre-set criterion level; this is called up-mode (↑-mode) conditioning. Another is that the amplitude is less than a criterion level, called down-mode (↓-mode) conditioning. In successful ↑-mode conditioning, the subject learns to increase the excitability of the reflex; in successful ↓-mode conditioning, they learn to decrease its excitability. Successful conditioning has been demonstrated in a variety of mammalian species, including humans[36].

In most conditioning experiments, responses are elicited from the stretch reflex circuits associated with a particular muscle by electrically stimulating the nerve that innervates that muscle. A very brief (about 1 millisecond) pulse of electrical stimulation is used, and the intensity is carefully chosen so that the type Ia spindle afferents are preferentially depolarized[37]. The result is that a brief volley of action potentials is transmitted along the Ia afferent axons to the spinal cord. This is very similar to the effect of tapping the muscle tendon and, like the tendon tap, the electrical stimulus evokes a response from the muscle, primarily via the monosynaptic stretch reflex pathway (see Chapter 5). Elicitation of a response from the spinal stretch reflex pathways using electrical stimulation is referred to as **Hoffman's reflex** or **H-reflex** for short[38]. It is standard usage to refer to the response itself as the H-reflex.

Panel A of Figure 15.4 shows a schematic of the basic set-up for eliciting and recording H-reflexes from a rat's soleus. A stimulator applies the electrical stimulus to the tibial nerve, and the H-reflex it evokes in the muscle is recorded using EMG electrodes. Panel B shows selected results from two groups of rats: one group subjected to the ↑-mode procedure, the other to the ↓-mode procedure. The reinforcer (food pellet) was delivered 200 milliseconds after a 'correct' response. The baseline amplitude of the H-reflex was determined during an initial ten-day period prior to the start of the conditioning procedure, which was conducted over the following 40 days.

The results in Figure 15.4B clearly show that the ↑-mode group learned to increase the H-reflex amplitude, and the ↓-mode group learned to decrease the amplitude. These effects have been found to be specific to the muscle that determines the reward[39]. Detailed analysis has shown that the change in reflex amplitude consists of two phases, an initial phase and a late phase[40] (these phases are not evident in the figure). The initial phase involves a small but relatively rapid change that occurs during the first day or so of conditioning. The late phase involves a more gradual change over the following weeks.

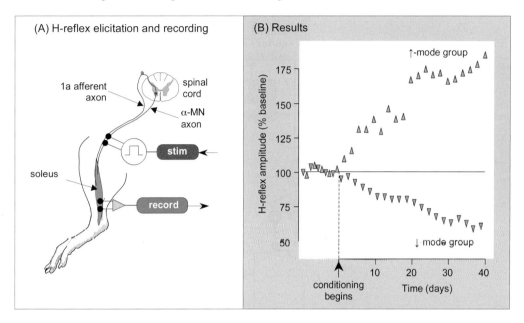

Figure 15.4: *Instrumental conditioning of the H-reflex. (A) Schematic of the set-up for eliciting and recording H-reflexes from the rat's soleus. (B) Selected data from Wolpaw (1997), Fig. 2B; see text for details.*

It would be expected that supraspinal structures are involved in the changes in reflex amplitude, because it is in the brain that reinforcement is perceived. In line with this expectation, it has also been shown that the corticospinal tract is essential for the observed changes, which indicates that signals that suppress or potentiate the reflex pathway are transmitted down the corticospinal tract. The cerebral cortex (from where the corticospinal tract arises), the cerebellum, and the basal ganglia have been found to be the critical brain structures involved[41]. Figure 15.5 presents a partial and simplified picture of some of the structures and pathways involved (rat nervous system). The initial phase of conditioning that occurs during the first day or so is probably the result of signals descending via the corticospinal tract that either potentiate or suppress the reflex pathway. As conditioning progresses, there are changes in the strength of synapses within the spinal circuits, notably the synapses with the α-MNs that are within the reflex pathways. This is demonstrated by disconnecting the brain from the spinal cord and showing that the learned changes in reflex excitability are not abolished. Following this procedure, the decreased excitability of stretch reflex pathways produced by ↓-mode conditioning do gradually decay away, showing that continued supraspinal input is required to maintain the learned effect[42].

It has been suggested that the mechanisms that underlie changes in the excitability of spinal stretch reflex circuitry, resulting from the type of instrumental conditioning procedure described above, may also be involved in learned changes to stretch reflex excitability that occur due to life experiences. Many studies have shown that 'spinal reflexes are affected by the nature, intensity and duration of past physical activity and by specific training regimens. [Spinal stretch reflexes] and H-reflexes are different in athletes and non-athletes and among different kinds of athletes.'[43] It is plausible that similar learning processes are involved in decreasing the amplitude of the stretch reflex response in gastrocnemius to unexpected tilts of the support platform (refer to Figure 14.21). When the platform tilts such that the toes are rotated up (dorsiflexion), the reflex response evoked in gastrocnemius is destabilizing to upright posture and increases postural sway. This increased sway is an undesirable consequence of the reflex response (equivalent to punishment of the response). If the reflex is suppressed, then the punishment is reduced or eliminated. The decline in reflex amplitude that occurs over a few trials indicates that the person's nervous system quickly discovers the means to suppress the reflex. It is possible that the mechanism is similar to that involved in the early phase of suppression of the H-reflex in ↓-mode conditioning.

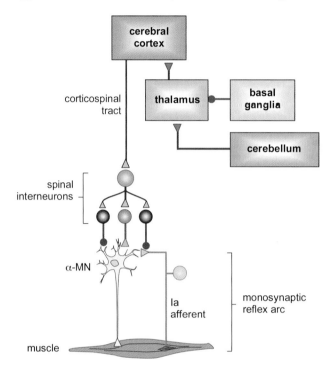

Figure 15.5: *Part of the circuitry involved in the instrumental conditioning of the H-reflex in rats (based on Wolpaw, 2007).*

It is not known exactly how people and animals can learn to suppress the action of the spinal stretch reflex in response to rewarding or punishing stimuli. Acquisition of stretch reflex suppression occurs within only a few trials in the tilting platform situation, but in the H-reflex conditioning experiments, acquisition takes many more trials, and the reflex is only about 50% suppressed after 40 days of training (Figure 15.4B). Since the reflex is part of the system of mechanisms that preserve upright posture (see Chapter 7), the rapid learning in the platform experiments suggests that central modulation of the stretch reflex is something that the nervous system is likely to try out in situations where there are threats to postural stability. In the H-reflex conditioning procedures, the connection between changing reflex excitability and reinforcement is arbitrarily imposed by the experimenter.

15.1.10 Does the law of effect apply to human skill acquisition?

Many years after his pioneering studies of learning in cats, Thorndike attempted to test the validity of his Law of Effect in human motor learning[44]. The task he used was very simple: people were instructed to draw straight lines of specified lengths without being able to see what they were doing. During training, some of the participants were given verbal feedback about the outcome of their actions (participants never saw the lines that they drew). Results from a study that used Thorndike's task are shown in Figure 15.6. Four groups of participants were instructed to draw lines three inches in length while blindfolded (panel A), and were given different types of feedback about their performance after each attempt. One group was told how much longer or shorter their drawn lines were (in ⅛-inch units) than the target length of 3 inches (precise outcome feedback); a second group were told 'right' if the drawn line was within ⅛ inch of the target length and 'wrong' if not (right-wrong outcome feedback). The third and fourth groups were control groups that received no information about their performance: one group was told nothing, while the other received nonsense syllables after each attempt (nonsense feedback). The training phase consisted of 100 attempts; the results in Figure 15.6B show the average absolute error[45] for blocks of 10 trials. Following training, a retention test was conducted which was the same as training except that no outcome feedback was given (the test was not performed by the no-feedback control group). The results clearly show that people's performance improved during the training phase if they were given informative feedback, and these performance gains were preserved in the retention test. Without feedback, no performance improvement took place.

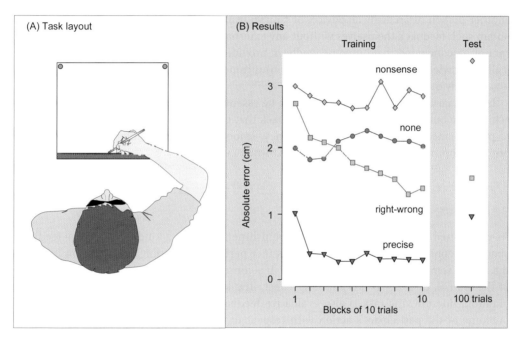

Figure 15.6: *Blindfolded line drawing. (A) Task (see text for details). (B) Results from four groups receiving different types of feedback in a training phase and retention test (data from Trowbridge and Cason, 1932).*

Consider the right-wrong outcome feedback condition that was also used by Thorndike. He likened the task to the cat in the puzzle box: repeated attempts at drawing lines would be followed either by satisfaction ('right') or dissatisfaction ('wrong'). He supposed that the instruction (e.g., 'Draw a 3-inch line') was an essential component of the stimulus that led to the line-drawing response. Whatever was done to draw a line that results in 'right' would have its connection to the instruction strengthened (with connection weakened if 'wrong' was the result). Over many repeated attempts, people would gradually become better at drawing lines of the required length. Presumably, what participants were doing in this task was trying out different values for the parameters for the line-drawing motor program, retaining those values that led to 'right', and discarding those that led to 'wrong'. Although the language of the Law of Effect seems rather antiquated nowadays, Thorndike's basic idea provides a possible account of how people improved in the task with right-wrong outcome feedback. However, we do not yet understand how reward and punishment function in sensorimotor learning of the type involved in the line-drawing task or in skill acquisition more generally[46].

Thorndike's ideas cannot explain in any obvious way why the precise feedback group were able to improve so much more quickly than the right-wrong group (they were performing better within the first 10 trials than the right-wrong group after 100 trials). We will return to this point in section 15.1.12.

15.1.11 Outcome feedback is important for motor learning

Suppose a person's goal is to achieve a particular result, such as drawing a 3-inch line. It would seem that improving at such a task requires some kind of feedback information about whether or not the goal was achieved when an attempt was made. Experiments have repeatedly confirmed this common-sense expectation[47]. The results in Figure 15.6 provide an example: when there was no outcome feedback, performance did not improve. In these experiments, participants could only obtain outcome feedback from the experimenter. Without this feedback, there was no reliable way for the participants to determine whether or not they had achieved the required outcome or to determine how close they were to achieving it. It seems clear, therefore, that feedback about outcome achievement is needed to improve the ability to achieve that outcome over repeated attempts. Such feedback does not need to be supplied by another person or an artificial device, of course: in normal conditions, a person can usually obtain such feedback themselves without any external aid. Thus, contrary to some claims[48], it cannot be concluded that outcome feedback provided by another person or artificial device (called knowledge of results; see next section) is important for sensorimotor learning, unless it is the only outcome feedback available.

In summary, outcome feedback seems to be essential for learning to improve the ability to achieve the outcome. More generally, feedback that provides information about some aspect of performance, such as its energy efficiency, smoothness or gracefulness, is necessary to produce improvements in that aspect of performance.

15.1.12 Outcome feedback can have directive as well as selective effects

As mentioned earlier, reinforcement and punishment provide a kind of evaluative feedback about the consequences that an action has in a particular situation (the situation in which the reinforcement/punishment is received). If a consequence meets a goal or satisfies a drive of the animal, then it has a reinforcing effect. The kind of verbal feedback provided in the blindfold line-drawing task is also evaluative feedback, as it provides an evaluation of the outcome of the participant's action with respect to the goal of the task. Any kind of error feedback is evaluative feedback. According to the Law of Effect, no error (or a small error) is satisfying, whereas a large error is dissatisfying and connection strengths are altered accordingly. It should be noted that terms such as *satisfaction, reward, discomfort* and so forth, are potentially misleading, as they imply subjective feelings of some kind. No 'feelings' are actually needed for learning to occur; all that is needed is an evaluation of outcomes with respect to the goal. Such an evaluation can be used to select effective actions and discard ineffective ones in a system that is capable of generating a range of actions to try out[49].

The evaluative feedback provided in the line-drawing experiments is used because it is delivered by, and hence completely under the control of, the experimenter. Feedback of this kind is called either **extrinsic feedback** or **augmented feedback**, and can be delivered by a person or by an artificial device: it is feedback added by an external agent to the feedback a person normally obtains by sensing or observing their own behavior and its consequences (*intrinsic feedback*). Extrinsic feedback about the outcome of an action is called **knowledge of results (KR)**:

> **KNOWLEDGE OF RESULTS (KR):** Extrinsic feedback about the outcome of an action delivered to a person either by another person or by a device. It is usually an error score or another measure of 'correctness'.

KR allows the experimenter to control evaluative feedback about the outcome of actions, just as the delivery of reinforcers and punishers is under experimental control in instrumental conditioning experiments. Thus, KR allows investigation of how the type, quality, frequency and timing of outcome feedback affect learning and performance (provided that intrinsic outcome feedback is not available).

Thorndike proposed that KR acts like reinforcement/punishment, and that learning from KR involved strengthening the connection between situational stimuli (e.g., instructions) and whatever led to rewarding KR (e.g., 'right' or a high score). This is a selective effect: feedback is used to select between alternative actions. It quickly became clear, however, that the effect of KR can involve more than selection. Within a few years of Thorndike's line-drawing experiments, Elwell and Grindley observed that in an aiming task, 'if a subject missed ... he tried, next time, to correct for his error by altering his response in the appropriate direction'[50]. This was possible because the KR provided information about the direction and size of the error, information which could be used to adjust a motor program so that the error is smaller on the next attempt. Elwell and Grindley obtained evidence that people can use the information in this way, and concluded that one way in which KR leads to improvement is 'by setting up a tendency to correct, in the appropriate direction, any unsuccessful actions'[51]; they referred to this as the *directive effect* of KR. The difference between the effects of precise KR and right-wrong KR shown in Figure 15.6 is probably due to the fact that only the precise KR provided information about how the program should be adjusted in order to improve the outcome.

Elwell and Grindley also recognized that KR can have motivating effects that can improve performance during acquisition and enhance the learning process[52] – the more motivated someone is to learn, the more effective their learning will be: they wrote that KR leads to improvement 'by setting up a conscious attitude or mood conducive to accurate performance'[53]. The motivating effects of KR are beyond the scope of our discussion[54].

15.1.13 Delaying outcome feedback does not necessarily impair learning

KR experiments have generally examined similar issues, regarding the role of behavioral outcomes in learning, to those examined in instrumental conditioning experiments. One example is the effect of a delay between completion of an act and delivery of feedback. As described in section 15.1.8, the reinforcement delay in instrumental conditioning has a powerful effect on learning: the shorter the delay, the better the animal learns. The result in KR experiments is quite different: it has been repeatedly found that there is little or no consistent effect of KR delay on learning, at least for delays up to a few minutes in length[55] (a few seconds can have dramatic effects in instrumental conditioning experiments, as shown in Figure 15.3). In a few cases it has even been found that delaying KR can be more beneficial than providing it immediately on completion of a task or a movement[56]. An example is shown in Figure 15.7. The task (panel A) was a simulated interceptive task: participants rotated a manipulandum such that a light-emitting diode (LED) at its end reached a target position at the same moment that an LED at the target position was illuminated[57] – a kind of simulated 'strike' of the target LED with the manipulandum LED. The target LED was one of a series of LEDs that were illuminated in strict sequence. This gave an impression of a moving light and allowed participants to anticipate when the target LED would be illuminated. KR about the quality of performance was given in the form of a score that combined the spatial error (distance of manipulandum LED from the target LED when it was illuminated) and the speed of the manipulandum – high scores were obtained if the error was small and the speed was high. The task was to improve the score over repeated attempts (training trials). Panel B shows selected results from two groups of participants; one group received KR 0.2 seconds after the target LED was illuminated, and the other received KR after a delay of 3.2 seconds. No KR was delivered to either group in the retention tests. The results shown illustrate the basic finding of the study: performance of the group with the longer delay was better (higher score), both during acquisition and in a retention test conducted two days later.

Clearly, the results obtained in studies of KR-delay are very different from those obtained in studies of reinforcement delay (Figure 15.3). There are several differences between the two types of experiment that might account for the discrepant results[58]:

(1) Participants in KR experiments know what act the KR relates to, and once they have completed the action, they stop and wait for KR. This is not the case in instrumental conditioning experiments. In fact, in 'delayed reinforcement experiments ... everything is done to avoid defining the moment of occurrence of the [target] response, and the question of major interest is the effect of subsequent [reinforcement] when behavior has continued to flow past the [target] response'[59].

(2) KR has a directive effect, but reinforcement and punishment do not. A long KR delay does not necessarily interfere with the directive use of KR, provided that the person can remember what it was that they did. Thus, we might expect the KR delay to be detrimental only if it is sufficiently long for a person to forget how they performed the act to which it relates.

(3) In instrumental conditioning, the subject's goal is typically to obtain reinforcement (or avoid punishment), whereas in KR experiments, a person's goal is not to obtain KR (KR is given regardless of what the participant does).

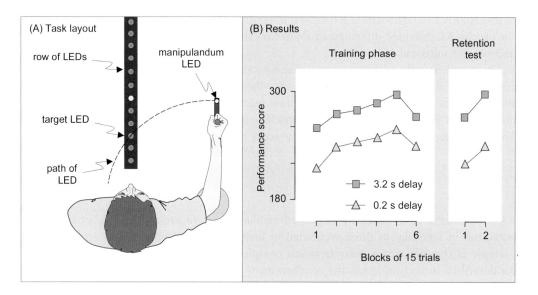

Figure 15.7: *Task and results from simulated interception experiment with two KR delays. (A) Task: participants attempted to move a manipulandum so that an LED at its end reached a target location at the same time that an LED at that location was illuminated. (B) Average results from two groups of participants with different KR delays. Selected data from Swinnen et al. (1990), Fig. 4.*

The first and third of these differences relate to the fact that in instrumental conditioning experiments, subjects need to discover what action caused delivery of a reinforcer (or punisher). In this process, reinforcement and punishment have a selective effect; as discussed in section 15.1.8, animals may have a built-in tendency to select only actions performed in the immediate past. If a task were constructed in which the directive effect of KR were less important than the selective effect, then we might expect to obtain results similar to those obtained in instrumental conditioning experiments. One study has attempted to do this and reported the expected result: when the selective effect of KR was important, participants performed better in both acquisition and retention when KR was presented immediately rather than after a delay[60].

Interestingly, it has been found that delaying intrinsic feedback about outcome (pointing error) in prism adaptation (see section 15.2.4 for explanation) can significantly impair learning: the amount of adaptation to the prismatic displacement was found to be greater when the delay was shorter, being greatest at zero delay[61]. In the experiment, the outcome feedback had a demonstrable directive effect. Thus, it appears that a delay can in some cases impair people's ability to exploit the directive properties of outcome feedback. Why the results from prism adaptation should be different from those in studies like that shown in Figure 15.7 is unclear, but it appears that there may be at least two types of process operating in prism adaptation: strategic (cognitive) processes that are relatively unaffected by delay, and unconscious, automatic processes that are affected by delay (see section 15.2.5). Increasing delay impairs the latter type of process but spares the former.

15.1.14 Care must be taken when making claims about learning

On the basis of results like those shown in Figure 15.7, it has been claimed that shorter KR delays 'degrade' learning[62] (similar claims regarding the effects of frequent KR are discussed in the next section). What such a claim means is unclear: the results in the figure indicate that learning how to achieve a higher score was more effective when the KR-delay was longer. It could perhaps be said that learning with a short KR-delay was 'degraded' relative to learning with the longer delay, but this is just another way of saying that learning was more effective with the longer delay. To use the pejorative term 'degraded' is misleading.

It should also be noted that the use of the term 'learning' is potentially misleading, because learning per se cannot be measured. As discussed in Chapter 14, the learning process can change many aspects of how a task is performed. Figure 15.7 shows only the change in the score. The learning that took place during the training phase of the experiment may have involved changes in other things such as the efficiency of the movement, the muscles and joints involved in moving the manipulandum, and the ability to extract relevant information from the visual stimulus. Since none of these were measured, it is impossible to say anything about whether or not the KR-delay affected any changes that may have taken place due to learning: shorter KR delays may have led to better learning on some measures. All that can be said is that the data in Figure 15.7 suggest that learning how to achieve a higher score was more effective when the KR-delay was longer, which is quite different from claiming that short KR-delays degrade learning.

15.1.15 Frequent KR is not detrimental to learning

Given that an animal in an instrumental conditioning experiment is faced with the problem of discovering what behavior leads to reinforcement or punishment, it is not surprising to find that animals learn more quickly if reinforcement (or punishment) follows every execution of the target behavior. It seems likely that a similar result would be obtained in KR experiments: people will learn more quickly and effectively if KR is provided after every attempt at performing a task. However, this result is not what has been obtained. A typical set of results is shown in Figure 15.8.

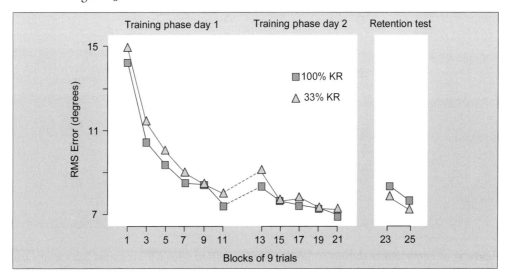

Figure 15.8: *Performance during acquisition and retention of a movement pattern with 100% and 33% knowledge of results (KR). Selected data from Winstein and Schmidt (1990), Figure 2.*

The task required participants to grasp a manipulandum similar to that shown in Figure 15.7, and move it back and forth four times in a specified pattern. KR was given as a score that represented the deviation of the pattern produced by the participant from the target pattern; perfect performance received a score of zero. Two groups of participants performed 198 training trials over two days and received different amounts of KR: one group received KR after every trial (100% KR group), the other received KR on only one in three trials (33% KR group). Ten minutes after the final training trial, participants performed a retention test. The graphs in Figure 15.8 show that there was very little difference between the two groups; only during the first training day was there any indication that the 100% KR group performed better.

The kind of results shown in Figure 15.8 are typical of studies that have investigated the effects of KR frequency on learning a motor skill: providing KR on every attempt does not lead to significantly better learning than providing it less frequently[63]. In addition, several studies have found that performance in retention tests was actually better when KR was not presented after every attempt. Two examples are shown in Figure 15.9. Panel A shows results

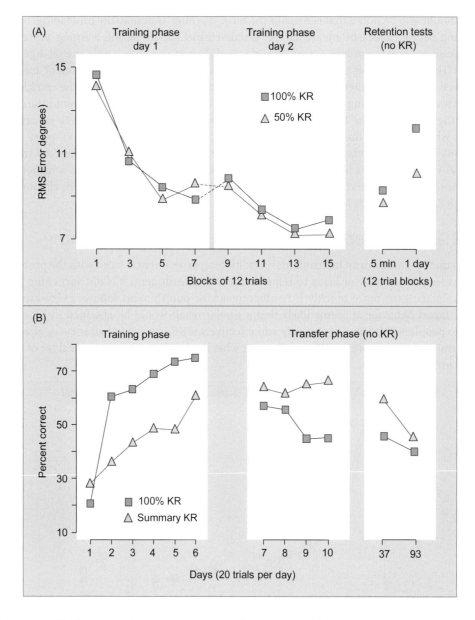

Figure 15.9: *Performance during acquisition and retention with KR presented after every trial (100% KR) or only after certain trials (see text for details). (A) Selected data from Winstein and Schmidt (1990), Figure 3. (B) Selected data from Lavery (1962).*

from a study that used the same task as the study presented in Figure 15.8. Of two groups, one received KR on every trial (100%); the other received KR on half the trials (50%). During the training phase of the experiment, performance of the two groups was very similar, but in the retention tests, performance of the 50% group was superior.

Panel B of Figure 15.9 shows the results from a study in which KR was presented after every trial (100%) to one group of participants, and only after each block of 20 trials to another group (summary KR). In the latter case, KR was presented about performance of all 20 trials in the block. Participants performed several variants of a task that required a ball to be propelled up a track to reach a target (Figure 15.9 shows the results from all the task variants combined). The results in panel B are relatively clear cut: throughout the training phase of the experiment, performance in the 100% KR group was superior to the summary KR group. In the subsequent no-KR phase of the experiment (called the transfer phase), performance of the group previously trained with summary KR was consistently superior to the group who had been training with 100% KR.

The results shown in Figure 15.9 and other similar results have been interpreted as showing that providing KR after every trial is detrimental to learning. The idea is that during training, the superior performance shown by people who received KR on every trial is not due to learning but due to some other temporary effect of KR, such as increased motivation. When participants are subsequently tested without KR, the relatively poorer performance of people who received more KR during training is due to their having learned less. This interpretation is unwarranted for two reasons:

(1)   The no-KR situation differs more from the training conditions for the 100% KR groups than for the other groups who performed some trials without KR during training. It cannot be concluded, therefore, that the 100% KR group learned less, as they may have learned differently. (Note that in the retention tests in Figure 15.8, KR was presented on some trials, and performance of the 100% KR group in retention trials was not inferior to the 33% KR group.)

(2)   The 100% KR group would have learned to expect KR, and its absence in the transfer or retention trials may have been frustrating or demotivating. This could lead to a decline in performance in the transfer test, not because the 100% KR group learned less, but due to the effects of frustration/demotivation in the test trials[64].

In summary, the results from studies of the effects of KR frequency and summary KR do not show that more outcome feedback is detrimental to learning per se, as has sometimes been claimed. The results suggest that participants learn differently depending on how frequently the feedback is delivered. This is an example of the **principle of specificity of learning**: what is learned depends on the particular task performed and the conditions in which it is performed – it is specific to the training experience. The effects of learning may transfer or generalize to other situations not encountered in training, but the extent to which this occurs must be examined in further experiments. Of course, what you may want is for the learned behavior to generalize across as many situations as possible. Thus, if you want behavior learned with KR to generalize to no-KR conditions, then it would be better to include no-KR trials in the training sessions. Generalization of learning to new conditions is discussed further in the next part of the chapter.

15.2 Sensorimotor Adaptation

15.2.1 Introduction

When someone executes a well-learned action in circumstances that are different from those they have previously encountered, then a period of familiarization with these new circumstances will typically be needed before the person can perform as well as they had previously been able to. During this period, the person learns how to adjust execution of the act so that it is effective in the new circumstances. An example was described in Chapter 11: a person who is familiar with using a stylus and tablet to move a cursor on a computer screen attempts to use a system that is arranged slightly differently from those they had used previously (refer to Figure 11.1). In the new arrangement, moving the stylus away from the body and towards the screen does not cause the cursor to move up the screen; it causes it to move from right to left across the screen (the normal stylus-cursor relationship has been rotated through +90°). This kind of alteration to the normal situation is called a **visuomotor rotation**. Upon first encountering such a rotation, a person's ability to move the cursor where they want is impaired; given time to practice, their performance is restored to its previous level. Once the person's level of performance has been restored, they are said to have **adapted** to the new circumstances. The process of learning how to change performance so that it is effective in new circumstances is called **sensorimotor adaptation**.

Sensorimotor adaptation is the term used to describe the process of learning to re-establish an existing level of skill in new conditions or when circumstances change. For this reason, adaptation may be distinguished from skill acquisition[65]: skill acquisition refers to improving skill level or adding to the motor repertoire (Chapter 14), while in adaptation no new ability is acquired and no higher skill level is attained (though improvements in adaptability may be possible and an ability to switch between multiple adaptive states may be acquired). This should not be taken to imply that the learning processes involved are different, only that the outcome of learning is different. Of course, the learning processes may be different, but this is something that would have to be established empirically.

The kind of adaptation that we will discuss can also be distinguished from the adjustments made to restore performance when some part of the motor system is damaged or lost due to injury or disease. In such cases, if performance is to be restored to the level exhibited prior to the damage, then the person or animal must learn to compensate. Compensation for loss or damage may involve substitution of an intact system for the damaged subsystem. Substitution of this kind is distinct from adaptation.

Adaptation occurs in both genetically determined, reflexive behaviors and learned, voluntary behaviors. In this part of the chapter we discuss examples of adaptation in both types of behavior, but provide only a sketch of some of the basic phenomena. The literature on the subject is extensive, and even selected portions of it would require book-length treatments to be comprehensive.

15.2.2 The vestibulo-ocular reflex adapts when image motion results from head movement

The circuitry responsible for the production of much reflexive behavior in mammals is laid down during fetal development and is operative at birth. Nevertheless, such behaviors are typically not fixed, but can be modified by experience. In Chapter 14 we discussed two types of learned change that can occur in some reflexive behaviors: decline in responsiveness to innocuous stimuli (habituation), and an acquired capability to respond to stimuli that predict the occurrence of the normal eliciting stimuli (Pavlovian conditioning). A third type of change occurs in a number of different reflexes; it acts to maintain function when a reflex must operate in new conditions. Such changes are examples of sensorimotor adaptation, which occurs in reflexes that do not readily habituate, such as the vestibulo-ocular reflex and the pupiliary reflex.

As described in detail in Chapters 4 and 5, the rotational vestibulo-ocular reflex (r-VOR) acts to keep the retinal images steady as the head jiggles around, by producing counter-rotational eye movements. If the head rotates and the eyes do not counter-rotate, the image moves as a whole across the retina (called **retinal image slip**)[66]. When the r-VOR is operating correctly, head rotations are exactly compensated for by counter-rotational eye-movements and there is no retinal slip. Conversely, if there is retinal slip, then the r-VOR is operating incorrectly. Thus, retinal slip serves as an error signal indicating that adjustment of the r-VOR mechanisms is required. There are mechanisms that maintain the r-VOR in correct adjustment by using uncompensated retinal image slip to adjust the r-VOR circuits in such a way that the jiggle is reduced[67]. This is a learning process that uses feedback about the effectiveness of the mechanisms to adjust their operation; it keeps the r-VOR working effectively despite changes due to growth, aging and disease. The learning process allows the r-VOR to adapt to changes in the circumstances in which it must operate, and is a type of sensorimotor adaptation that is sometimes referred to as *calibration*.

Adaptation of the r-VOR is usually studied by optically changing the relationship between head rotations and retinal image motion in such a way that the r-VOR is no longer able to compensate and retinal image slip occurs. One extreme example of this method involved participants wearing reversing prisms (Dove prisms) in glasses frames[68]. When someone wears reversing prisms in an appropriate orientation, the retinal images are left-right inverted, so written text appears to be mirror writing. The direction of image motion produced by head movement is also reversed. If the r-VOR were inactive, a leftward rotation of the head would cause the whole image to move across the retina in the direction indicated on the left of Figure 15.10A. The r-VOR prevents this image motion by counter-rotating the eyes to the right, as shown on the right of Figure 15.10A. When the person wears left-right inverting prisms, the image moves in the opposite direction from normal (Figure 15.10B, left). The r-VOR does not compensate for this motion, it doubles it (Figure 15.10B, right).

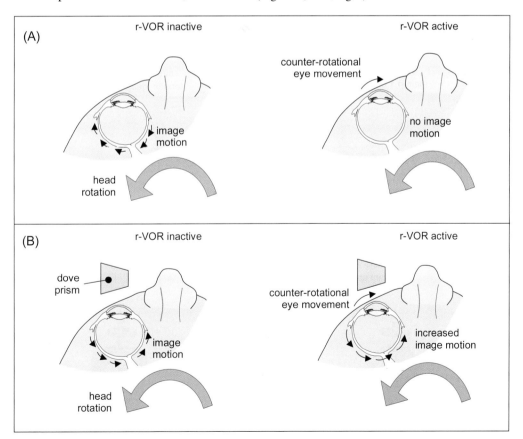

Figure 15.10: *Effect of horizontal r-VOR with (B) and without (A) inverting prisms; see text for explanation.*

Wearing inverting prisms results in changes to the gain of the r-VOR; these changes are assessed using the following experimental protocol:

(1) **Pre-test phase:** gain is measured in the dark (see section 4.3.10) prior to wearing prisms.
(2) **Exposure** or **training phase:** prisms are worn for a period of time in normal illumination, with the head free to move.
(3) **Post-test phase:** gain is measured again without prisms in the dark.

It has been found that after just a few minutes of wearing inverting prisms, the value of the r-VOR's gain declines[69]; it continues to do so over a period of days, down to 25% or less of its pre-test value of about 1.0. This gain reduction does not enable the r-VOR to compensate for head movement, and people are observed to make strategic changes in their pattern of head movement and saccadic movements to help keep the images stable[70]. Prolonged exposure of several weeks results in reversal of the direction of the r-VOR and an increase in its gain, so that it once again acts to keep the retinal images stable as the head turns[71]. Less extreme changes in the r-VOR are required to keep the retinal images stable when a person wears magnifying or minifying lenses in glasses, as discussed next.

15.2.3 Changes in the gain of the VOR restore image stability

Wearing magnifying or minifying glasses changes the normal relationship between head movement and retinal image motion. Magnifying lenses increase the speed of image motion, and minifying lenses decrease it. Thus, the speed of the counter-rotational eye movements generated by the normally effective r-VOR will be too slow when magnifying lenses are put on (gain too low); with minifying lenses, the eye movements are too fast (gain too high). In order to restore the effectiveness of the r-VOR, the gain needs to be increased when magnifying lenses are worn and decreased when minifying lenses are worn. As might be expected given the results described in the previous section, people, monkeys and other species show the appropriate adaptive changes in the gain of the r-VOR[72].

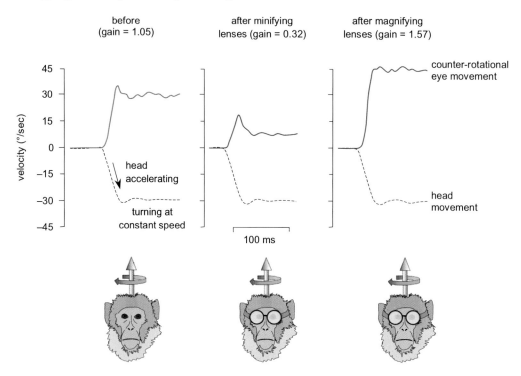

Figure 15.11: *Adaptive changes to the gain of the horizontal component of the r-VOR in monkeys. Counter-rotational eye movements (solid lines) in response to a rightward turn of the head (dashed lines) evoked prior to lens exposure (before) and after either magnifying or minifying lenses. (Based on data reported in Lisberger, 1988.)*

Figure 15.11 shows plots of the velocity of counter-rotational eye movements evoked by a turn of the head to the right before and after monkeys were exposed to magnifying and minifying lenses. The magnifying lenses doubled the image size (2×), the minifying lenses reduced it to ¼ of its normal size (0.25×). The head movement shown in the figure involved a rapid acceleration followed by a rotation at a constant speed of about 30°/s. Prior to exposure, the speed of the evoked eye movements was approximately equal and opposite to the speed of the head (gain = 1.05). After several days wearing the magnifying lenses, the gain increased (to 1.57 in the example shown, and to as high as 1.8 in some subjects); with 2× lenses, the gain required for perfect compensation is 2.0. After several days wearing the minifying lenses, the gain decreased (to 0.32 in the example shown and to as low as 0.3 in some subjects); with 0.25× lenses, the optimal gain is 0.25. Similar results have been obtained with people[73]. The gain of the r-VOR can be considered to embody information about the relationship between head movement and image motion; it is a kind of internal model (see Chapter 1).

In order for adaptation of the r-VOR to take place, the subject needs to be exposed to simultaneous head rotations and retinal image slip. If the head is held stationary or if there is no structured visual input (e.g., eyes closed or lights out), then no adaptation occurs. Evidently, the co-occurrence of image slip and head rotation stimulates adaptive neural mechanisms that cause the gain of the r-VOR to change in such a way that the slip is gradually eliminated. Therefore, we would expect 'the information that guides learning in the VOR to be carried in the correlation between two or more neural signals'[74]. These include the visual signal that carries information about retinal slip (the 'error' signal) and signals from the vestibular system that carry head movement information.

It has been found that the cerebellum is an essential element in the adaptation of the r-VOR: without connections to and from the cerebellum, the r-VOR still operates, but no adaptive changes take place[75]. Figure 15.12 shows a block diagram of some of the major elements in the neural circuits that mediate the r-VOR and its adaptation. Changes in synaptic strengths in the cerebellar loop are clearly involved in adaptation of the r-VOR, though it is possible that changes also occur in the reflex pathways themselves. Detailed modeling studies have been conducted in an effort to discover how the adaptive changes to the circuits are produced and what is the role of changes at different sites within the circuits, but these studies are beyond the scope of our discussion[76].

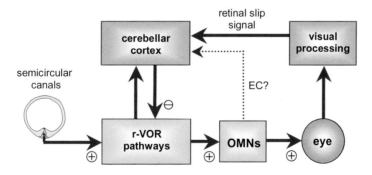

Figure 15.12: *Block diagram of major functional elements mediating the horizontal r-VOR and its adaptation. A hypothetical efference copy signal (EC?) is shown dotted (see Porrill, Dean, 2008). Excitatory pathways are marked ⊕, inhibitory pathways are marked ⊖; unmarked pathways may involve both. OMNs = oculomotor neurons.*

15.2.4 Spatially directed behavior adapts to shifts of the visual field produced by prisms

Study of sensorimotor adaptation in voluntary behaviors has focused on target-directed aiming of one kind or another, though studies of how people adapt to new dynamic properties in tracking tasks have also been investigated (see part 1 of Chapter 10). In studies of aimed movement, experimental participants are required to move in conditions that are altered either by imposing unfamiliar force fields (see section 11.2.8 for an example) or by introducing a **sensorimotor discordance**. We have already encountered two examples of sensorimotor discordance: that introduced when a person wears wedge prism glasses (see section 10.3.4) and that produced by a visuomotor rotation (see section 15.2.1). We will focus on **prism adaptation:** adaptation to the sensorimotor discordance produced when wearing wedge prisms.

Wedge prisms mounted in glasses frames and worn over the eyes, as shown in Figure 15.13, displace the retinal images either to the right or to the left depending on whether the thick ends (bases) of the wedges are, respectively, on the left (as shown in the figure) or on the right. The displacing effect is explained in Chapter 10 (refer to Figure 10.30; see also Figure 15.17, panels A and B). Figure 15.13 shows a variant of the most common experimental task used to study prism adaptation: a person points to a visible target with an index finger, but is only able to see their finger when it reaches its terminal position. Thus, the person only sees their pointing error and so cannot use vision to correct their movement as they attempt to move their finger to the target. This is sometimes called the **terminal display** experimental protocol[77]. If the person is able to see the movement of their pointing limb towards the target, it is called a **concurrent display** protocol.

Use of a concurrent display means that participants can correct their movements using visual feedback, and so they are able, in principle, to point accurately to a visible target. Use of a terminal display does not permit such corrections, and so a participant's terminal pointing errors can be measured. The protocol has been described as follows:

> Prism adaptation is commonly studied by having a person put on goggles bearing wedge prisms that laterally displace the visual field, for example, in the [rightward] direction. The person then interacts with the environment, for example, by pointing toward visual targets. Initially, the person makes pointing errors to the [right] of a target, but errors disappear in a dozen or so pointing trials, depending upon exposure conditions[78].

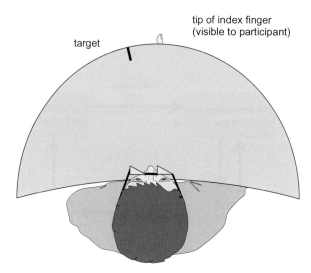

Figure 15.13: *Typical set-up for a terminal display prism adaptation experiment. Seen through the prisms, the target appears to be further to the right than its true position, and the person initially points to the apparent position.*

Figure 15.14 shows the typical pattern of results obtained in studies that used a terminal display protocol. The figure shows the results of an imaginary experiment in which the prisms displaced the images by 12° to the right and the target was 50 centimeters from the eyes in the transverse plane (it would appear to be 10.6 cm to the left of its true position). The experiment uses the standard pre-test–training–post-test design, in which participants perform the training trials with prisms and the pre- and post-test trials without prisms. In such conditions pointing is typically quite accurate (as is the case in the pre-test phase in the figure). When first exposed to the prisms, people point to the optically displaced location of the target rather than its actual location and so make errors. The magnitude of the error decreases over the course of thirty trials or so and a pre-test level of performance is re-established: people adapt to the prisms. In the post-test phase the prisms are removed, and people initially make large errors in the opposite direction to those made at the beginning of the training phase. This is referred to as an **after-effect** of prism adaptation. Since it is in the opposite direction to the initial effect of the prisms, it is sometimes referred to as a **negative after-effect**. The after-effect gradually declines as people point without prisms and pointing accuracy is restored to its pre-test level.

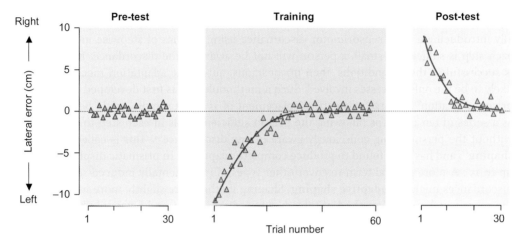

Figure 15.14: *Typical pattern of results obtained in terminal display prism adaptation experiments in which the participant attempts to bring a pointer into contact with a target (imaginary data).*

The results shown in Figure 15.14 are characteristic of those from studies that used a terminal display protocol. Use of a concurrent protocol may allow a person to correct their errors as they move to the target, and so terminal errors are not produced during the training phase. After-effects can be tested for in a post-test phase that does not allow a person to see the moving limb. After-effects are typically obtained with concurrent displays, provided that the starting position of the pointing limb is not visible in the training phase. If the starting point is visible, then after-effects may be absent[79]. In the absence of both after-effects and gradual error reduction during training, it may be argued that no adaptation has taken place (see next section).

15.2.5 Both unconscious adaptive processes and cognitive strategies may contribute to sensorimotor adaptation

Most prism adaptation experiments involve the use of fairly powerful prisms that displace the image by between about 6° and 20°. This means that a target 40 cm from the eyes would appear to be displaced to the right or left of its true position by between 4 cm and 15 cm: people are well aware of their pointing errors in such circumstances. As many authors have noted, conscious awareness of the discordance 'raises the possibility of the [participants] compensating in a "cognitive" manner ... and making corrective adjustments for the distortion without undergoing any fundamental ... sensory-motor, or motor change'[80]. For example, a person might point to targets in the set-up shown in Figure 15.13 and notice that they were consistently off to the right by, say, 6 cm, and think to themselves, 'I am consistently pointing off to the right by 6 cms, so if I deliberately point 6 cms to the left of where I normally would, then I'll be accurate'. This would be a cognitive strategy that involves no change to the underlying sensorimotor mechanisms.

Both cognitive strategies and unconscious, automatic processes of change in the underlying mechanisms can contribute to sensorimotor adaptation. Experimental studies of adaptation to visuomotor rotations[81] have shown that both processes can be operative during adaptation. It has been suggested that two features of sensorimotor adaptation indicate that a change to the underlying mechanisms is taking place[82]: (1) the incremental (trial by trial) nature of the change observed during the training phase, which indicates that participants are not simply noticing the size of their error and making a conscious correction for it. (2) The presence of substantial after-effects that incrementally decline over trials in the post-test phase. If a person simply made a conscious decision to compensate for their error, then it would be expected that when normal conditions were restored the person would no longer apply the correction. Of course, even if these two features are present in the data, we cannot exclude the possibility that cognitive strategies were also involved, as both types of process normally operate in prism adaptation.

It is possible to prevent participants using cognitive error correcting strategies by gradually introducing a large sensorimotor discordance using a series of stepwise increments. If each step is sufficiently small, a person will not be aware of the discordance. If adaptation is successful in these conditions, then unconscious, automatic adaptation mechanisms are likely to be the only processes involved. Such a methodology was first developed in studies of prism adaptation[83]. A large prismatic displacement of 15°, for example, could be introduced as a series of ten 1.5° steps (allowing the person sufficient trials in each step to adapt to it), without the person being consciously aware of any discordance[84]. This is called **prismatic shaping**[85], and has been found to produce complete adaptation to prismatic displacements of up to 15°. A more general term to cover other types of incrementally induced sensorimotor discordances might be **adaptive shaping**. Shaping methods are slightly more involved than the more usual 'sudden' method of introducing a discordance, and have only been used in a few studies[86]. The general finding is that adaptation proceeds effectively and without the participants being aware that they have been subjected to a discordance.

15.2.6 Prism adaptation exhibits partial generalization

Prism adaptation has been studied for over 100 years[87], and in that time many different hypotheses about the nature of the changes that underlie the observed behavioral pattern of adaptation (e.g., Figure 15.14) have been put forward[88]. One hypothesis is that adaptation is due to a change in the sensed angular positions of the eyes in the head[89]. We will consider this idea and use it to illustrate the concept of *generalization* in sensorimotor learning.

Pointing accurately at a visible target requires information about the direction of the target relative to the body – the *bodycentric* direction of the target. As discussed in section 3.1.18, the bodycentric direction of a visible target cannot be determined from the retinal images; it requires information about the angular position of the eyes in the head and of the head on the shoulders. Thus, a person could correct for the displacing effects of prisms by changing the sense of eye position in the head by an amount equal but opposite to the angular displacement of the retinal images introduced by the prisms. For example, if the prisms displace the retinal images 10° to the right, then a change in the sense of eye position of 10° to the left will correct for the prism displacement.

The hypothesis that the sensed position of the eye in the head can change amounts to a proposal that adaptation leads to the correct perception of the bodycentric direction of visible points. If this is true, then it should apply to visible points in all directions, not just to those encountered during the training phase of an experiment. The set-up and results from one study[90] that investigated whether or not this happens are shown in Figure 15.15. Panel A of the figure shows a schematic of the experimental set-up. Participants sat in a dark room, with one eye covered and the head held in a fixed position. Nothing could be seen except a visible target (light-emitting diode, LED) and the task was to point at the target with the index finger so that the viewing eye, finger tip and target lay on the same line, as shown in the figure. In the pre-test phase, participants attempted to point at targets located on a circular arc from 25° left of center (0°) to 25° right of center, and received no visual feedback about accuracy. In the training phase, an 11.3° displacing prism was placed over the viewing eye, and participants attempted to point at a target located straight in front of them. If they pointed at the true location of the target, then an LED on their finger tip would be illuminated. Panel B of Figure

15.15 shows a person pointing at the target's displaced position: the finger is not pointing at the target's actual location, and so the finger LED is not illuminated. Panel C shows a person pointing at the target's actual location, and so the finger LED is illuminated and lies on the line joining the viewing eye to the target's displaced position. The task required participants to adapt so that they pointed at the target's actual location (panel C). At the start of the training phase, participants would point at the displaced position of the target (panel B), but they slowly adapted over the course of the training phase, so that by the end of it they were pointing at the actual target location (panel C) with reasonable accuracy. To do this, they had to discover how to point so that the finger LED was illuminated.

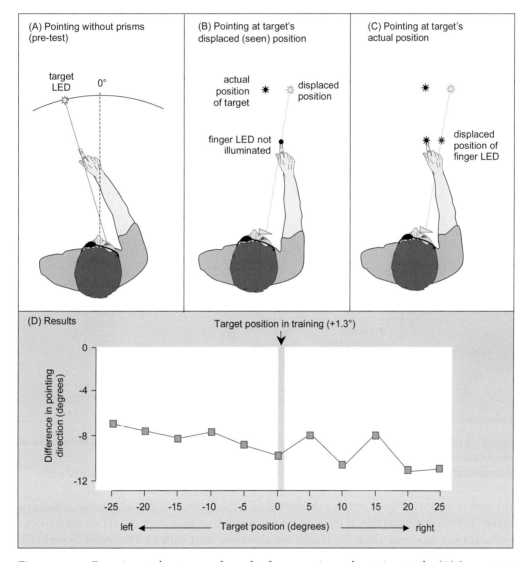

Figure 15.15: *Experimental set-up and results from a prism adaptation study. (A) In pre-test, participants pointed to illuminated target LEDs in complete darkness (the targets were 111.8 cm from the eyes). (B) During adaptation, participants viewed the target through a prism that displaced it to the right. If pointing was inaccurate, the LED on the pointing finger was not illuminated. (C) When pointing was accurate, the finger LED was illuminated. (D) Data selected from Bedford (1989), Fig 3. See text for explanation.*

A post-test phase similar to the pre-test phase was conducted after the training phase: the prism was removed, and participants pointed to various targets over the same 50° range as in the pre-test. If the sensed position of the eye has changed, then we would expect to see similar after-effects of the adaptation induced by training at all the post-test targets. This is an example of what is usually called **generalization** of learning (for further discussion, see section 15.2.8).

The results presented in panel D of Figure 15.15 show that the effects of training generalized to all the target locations tested. The measure of performance is the difference between where participants pointed in the pre- and post-test phases (post-test minus pre-test). This is a measure of the after-effect of adaptation. If there was no after-effect, then pointing would be the same in pre- and post-tests, and the measure would be zero. If there is a negative after-effect, then pointing in the post-test should be to the left of the actual location of the targets, and the measure will be negative. The graph shows that there was a negative after-effect at all target locations tested, which means that the effects of adaptation generalized across locations. The graph also shows that the measure did not vary systematically across the target locations: the effects generalized similarly to locations more distant from the trained location ($\pm25°$) and to those nearby ($\pm5°$). Figure 15.16 shows what the results might have looked like if the adaptation had been restricted to the trained location (no generalization, panel A) and if generalization had been restricted to target locations near to the trained location (limited generalization, panel B).

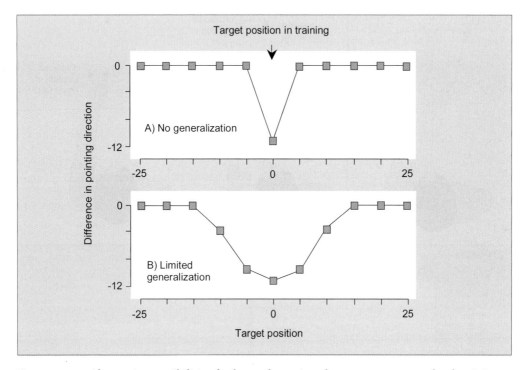

Figure 15.16: *Alternative possibilities for how adaptation that occurs as a result of training at one location (arrow) might generalize to new locations. (A) No generalization to locations not experienced in training. (B) Generalization to nearby locations, but not to more distant ones.*

The results shown in Figure 15.15 are consistent with the hypothesis that adaptation is due to a change in the sensed position of the eye(s) in the head. They do not establish that the hypothesis is correct, however, since the results are also consistent with an alternative hypothesis: that adaptation is due to a change in the kinesthetically sensed position of the pointing limb[91]. This alternative hypothesis is discussed in the next section.

15.2.7 Prism adaptation may be mediated by changes throughout the sensorimotor system

The idea that adaptation changes the kinesthetically sensed (felt) position of the pointing limb is called the **felt-position hypothesis**, and has been described as follows:

> 'If a person's eyes are closed when he first puts on displacing prisms, he is surprised when he opens his eyes and looks at his hand. Because the prisms shift its visual image, his hand does not appear to be where he felt it was ... the subject comes to feel that his arm is where he saw it through prisms[92].'

To see what this means, refer to Figure 15.17, which shows a hypothetical experimental situation in which a person points in the dark to an illuminated target while looking through prisms. Once the pointing movement is complete, the lights come on, and the person can see (through the prisms) where their hand is. Panels A and B show the situation at the start of the training phase, before any adaptation has taken place, so the felt position of the hand is the same as the actual position of the hand. In panel A, the person sees the target displaced from its actual position, and points to this location with their unseen hand (they do not point to the target's true location, but to its displaced position as seen through the prisms, so their pointing is in error). When the lights are turned on (panel B), the person sees their hand in a displaced position to the right of its actual position – they see that they have made a pointing error. At the end of the training phase, the person has adapted, and the situation according to the felt-position hypothesis is shown in panels C and D. In panel C, the person points with their unseen hand to the target; the hand actually moves to the true position of the target, but it is felt to move to the seen (i.e., displaced) position of the target. When the lights are turned on, the hand is seen and felt to be pointing at the target's seen position. Thus, there is no change in where the target is seen to be, only in where the hand is felt to be.

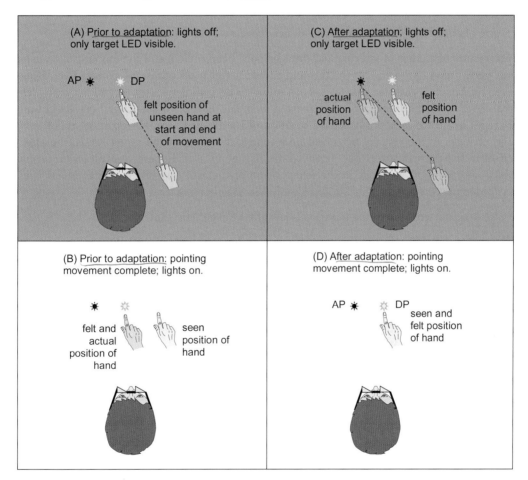

Figure 15.17: *Prism adaptation according to the felt-position hypothesis (see text for explanation). Felt positions of the hand are shown in blue, actual positions in pink (in panel A, the felt and actual positions are the same). AP = actual position of target; DP = displaced position of target.*

The felt-position hypothesis is consistent with the finding that adaptation generalizes to locations not encountered in training (e.g., Figure 15.15 panel D): if the arm's felt position has shifted, this shift would be expected to be applied when attempting to point at a target, regardless of its direction. However, the original version of the felt-position hypothesis differs from hypotheses that propose that the visual perception of direction has changed (e.g., the hypothesis that the sensed eye position changes) because it predicts that adaptation effects should be exhibited only by the arm used in training (the trained arm). The usual way of expressing this is to say that adaptation is predicted not to **transfer** to untrained limbs (the other arm or the legs). In contrast, a change in the visual perception of direction predicts that the effects will be observed regardless of the limb used: the learning is predicted to transfer to the untrained limbs.

Many prism adaptation experiments have studied the **intermanual transfer** of the effects of training (transfer to the arm not used in training). One protocol that can be used to assess intermanual transfer involves a pre-test phase in which participants point at visible targets without prisms with both their left and their right arms, a training phase in which only one arm is used to point, and a post-test phase similar to the pre-test phase. The post-test phase measures the after-effects in both the trained and the untrained arm. The extent to which the effects of training transfer to the untrained arm can be assessed using a variety of different methods. One method is to use a measure such as the ratio of the after-effect in the untrained arm to the after-effect in the trained arm:

$$\text{percent intermanual transfer} = \frac{(\text{size of after-effect in untrained arm})}{(\text{size of after-effect in trained arm})} \times 100$$

where the size of the after-effect is calculated as:

size of after-effect = (pre-test performance score) − (post-test performance score)

The results of studies of intermanual transfer have been mixed, and the amount of transfer has been found to depend on the training and post-test procedures and conditions[93]. However, intermanual transfer has never been found to be complete[94] (100%) and is usually less than 50%. These findings can be interpreted to mean that prism adaptation results in both changes in the kinesthetically sensed position of the trained arm (felt-position hypothesis) and changes in the visually perceived bodycentric direction of the target. Thus, the after-effect in the trained arm is due partly to the change in visually perceived direction (visual shift) and partly to a change in the felt position of the arm (kinesthetic shift). It has been proposed that these two contributions simply add together[95] so that,

size of after-effect in trained arm = visual shift + kinesthetic shift

The size of the after-effect in the untrained arm is due to the visual shift alone. The additivity of the two kinds of change has been tested by using independent measures of the visual and kinesthetic shifts and determining whether or not the pointing after-effect is equal to the sum of the measures of the two shifts[96]. An independent measure of the visual shift can be obtained by determining the change in what appears to be visually 'straight ahead' before and after the training phase; a measure of the kinesthetic shift can be obtained by asking a person to point to what feels to be straight ahead[97].

Overall, it appears that adaptive changes can take place throughout the sensorimotor systems involved in the task. The extent to which the adaptive changes affect different components of the system has been found to depend on the conditions in which training takes place, and on the type of training undertaken[98]. For example, in one study[99], the left arm was trained with a prism that displaced images to the left, and the right arm was trained with a prism that displaced images to the right. The fact that the two arms could be successfully adapted to the different displacements indicates that transfer between arms was not interfering with performance. Thus, the site of the adaptation would not have been in the eye-head kinesthetic system, but separately in the kinesthetic systems of the individual arms. It has also been found that the site of adaptation in different people can be different, even if everything else is the same[100]. A full discussion of how the nature of the adaptive changes depends on the individual and the conditions of training is beyond the scope of this text.

15.2.8 Transfer of learned changes is often limited

As discussed in the last chapter (section 14.1.16) the terms 'generalize' and 'transfer' are often used interchangeably. However, the usage in the literature is not completely consistent. For example, the terms have been defined as follows: 'Generalization of motor learning refers to our ability to apply what has been learned in one context to other contexts. When generalization is beneficial, it is termed transfer, and when it is detrimental, it is termed interference.'[101] 'Transfer' and 'interference', as used in this quotation, are more commonly referred to as positive and negative transfer, respectively (see section 14.1.16). Some authors have defined transfer such that it applies only to cases in which people are trained on one task and tested on another. For example, a person might train at the task of performing a tennis serve and then be tested on their performance of the volleyball serve. Transfer is then defined to be 'the gain (or loss) in the capability for performance in one task as a result of practice or experience on some other task.'[102] The term *transfer* is most commonly used when the carry-over is from one task to another – called **intertask transfer** – or from one limb to another, called **interlimb transfer** (intermanual transfer is an example). **Intralimb** or **interjoint transfer** is also possible, in which training using one joint of a limb carries over to another joint not utilized in training[103].

The extent to which learning transfers (or generalizes) to situations and tasks different from those encountered in training is important both from a practical point of view and a theoretical one. For example, when learning to play a musical instrument or a particular sport, a student typically practices drills or exercises. The 'instructor usually does not ... care whether the student can perform these drills, per se, well; rather [they] assume that, by practicing them, the student will learn something that will transfer to [tasks] of primary interest'[104], such as playing pieces of music, or playing an opponent in a sport. Inter-task transfer is usually found to be small and positive[105]. This is another way of saying that the learning is specific to the task and conditions of training or practice[106].

From a theoretical perspective, transfer and generalization are important because they provide insight into what has changed as a result of learning or what has been learned. As discussed in the previous two sections, different hypotheses concerning the nature of the changes that underlie prism adaptation make different predictions concerning the type and extent of transfer or generalization that should occur (see also section 14.1.16). It has been proposed that generalization and transfer of prism adaptation depends on the extent to which a shift (or realignment) in the visually perceived bodycentric direction of visible targets has taken place during the training phase[107] (presumably these shifts are a result of changes in the eye-head kinesthetic system, as discussed in section 15.2.7). Transfer will be limited if little or no visual realignment has taken place. Table 15.2 lists some examples of studies in which transfer was found to be limited: adaptation in these studies may have involved changes in effector-specific kinesthetic systems or other forms of sensorimotor learning[108].

Table 15.2: *Examples in which prism adaptation shows limited or no detectable transfer to a different action or to different conditions of execution.*

Trained action/conditions	Transfer action/conditions	Extent of transfer
Throwing ball at a target using an overhand action	Throwing ball at a target using an underhand action	None or very small in the majority of participants[109]
Pointing to visible targets using slow movements	Pointing to visible targets using fast movements	None or very small[110]
Pointing to visible targets using fast movements	Pointing to visible targets using slow movements	None or very small[111]
Catching balls with weights attached to the catching arm	Catching balls with different weights attached to the catching arm	Reduced relative to the weights experienced in training[112]
Pointing to visible targets with the limb starting in a particular posture	Pointing to visible targets with the limb starting in a different posture	Reduced; less transfer the greater the difference between starting postures encountered in training and post-test[113]
Pointing to visible targets using one hand with the wrist joint free to move but other joints of the arm (and trunk) fixed	Pointing with the forearm using elbow and shoulder joints (transfer of learning from distal joints to proximal ones)	None or very small[114]

In summary, adaptation to displacing prisms is straightforward to demonstrate and may seem to be a relatively simple process, but it turns out to be complex, involving different processes and different sites of adaptive change in the nervous system. Despite over 100 years of research, it is still not properly understood why different training procedures recruit different adaptive processes, and what determines the sites of adaptive change[115].

15.3 Automaticity and Sequence Learning

15.3.1 Introduction: stages of learning in skill acquisition

When a person first starts to deliberately learn to do something new, they are typically aware not only of their lack of skill and proficiency, but also of the concentration and mental effort needed to achieve a useful outcome. Once a person has developed a degree of expertise, their skill increases, but performance also requires less mental effort and concentration (see section 1 of Chapter 13). Observations of this sort have led to the idea that the deliberate learning of new behaviors has at least two stages[116]. A beginner is at an initial stage, characterized by performance that is slow, hesitant, error prone and under conscious control; the overall goal may not be achieved (failure). Performance of a more experienced person exhibits greater fluency, rarely ends in failure and requires less conscious effort: they are thought to have made a transition to a different stage of the learning process.

Perhaps the most influential description of the stages of learning posits a three-stage sequence[117]: the **cognitive stage**, the **fixation stage**[118], and the **autonomous stage**. The cognitive stage is the beginner's stage and is characterized by the involvement of cognitive activity, as its name implies. We have already described four ways in which cognitive, intentional processes can be involved in performance:

(1)   Reasoning: figuring out an effective way to achieve a desired outcome (see section 15.1.1).

(2)   Decision making and volitional initiation: deciding what to do and when to do it, and initiating actions when needed (see sections 13.1.3 and 15.1.5).

(3)   Paying conscious attention to important aspects of performance and the outcome (see sections 13.1.3 and 13.1.4).

(4)   Holding in working memory a description of the procedure (possibly verbal) for achieving the desired outcome. Such a description could be an ordered sequence of subtasks (see 13.1.3), such as those involved in changing gear.

During the cognitive stage, some or all of these processes may be involved. During this stage, a person might arrive at an effective way to achieve the task goal by a gradual process of successively closer and closer approximations. When learning a sequential act, the person becomes familiar with the sequence, can remember it, and is less reliant on exteroceptive senses (like vision) for determining if and when each element is complete. Thus, during the cognitive phase the learner establishes a method or procedure for achieving the task goal, and the improvements 'can be thought of as verbal-cognitive in nature'[119] rather than involving changes to the sensorimotor mechanisms themselves.

Once a method has been established, further practice results in changes to the sensorimotor mechanisms that gradually reduce the need for any cognitive control. In sequential acts, this involves the formation of motor chunks – motor programs that govern well-practiced sequences so that the individual elements no longer need to be intentionally initiated (see sections 13.1.4 and 13.1.5). Once performance is released from cognitive control, it is said to be automatic (section 13.1.4). During the fixation stage, there is a gradual change from cognitive control to automaticity; once automaticity is established, the autonomous stage begins, during which gradual refinement of efficiency and technique can still occur. Figure 15.18

summarizes the learning process according to the three-stage account in a manner that is supposed to show that the boundaries between stages are not sharp but fuzzy and overlapping, so that one stage blends into the next. It should be noted that the stages are not confined to the complete beginner: even someone experienced at a particular skill, such as typing or playing the piano, will go through these stages when adding a new motor chunk to their repertoire.

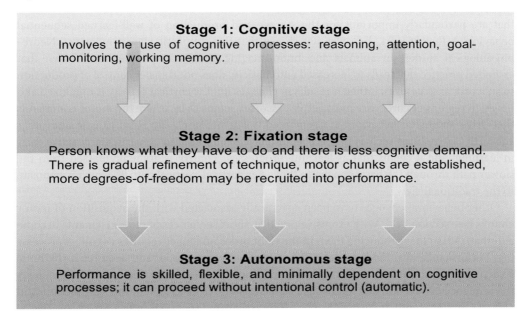

Figure 15.18: *The three-stage description of skill acquisition.*

The three-stage description is most frequently applied to skill acquisition (as defined in section 14.1.17), though it may apply equally well to any type of sensorimotor learning in which the person is aware of the goal of the task and is trying to improve their performance. This part of the chapter will briefly discuss some of what happens when a person makes the transition from cognitive-controlled to automatic performance of short sequences of simple elements such as key-presses (i.e., during the formation of motor chunks). In the cases to be discussed, the person is always aware of the sequence that they are attempting to produce[120].

15.3.2 What changes as a sequence becomes automatic?

Some of the differences between automatic and cognitively controlled behavior were discussed in Chapter 13 (see section 13.1.3). One important difference concerns the extent to which performance is resistant to interference from a concurrently executed task. As described in section 7.4.8, if performance on task A is worse when another task (B) is performed at the same time, then task B is said to interfere with task A. This is called *dual-task interference*. Two tasks would be expected to interfere with one another to the extent that they rely on the same mechanisms and processes. For example, you would expect eating and speaking to interfere, because they both rely on the orofacial articulators. Similarly, if two tasks involve the same cognitive process or mechanism, they would be expected to interfere with one another when executed concurrently, provided that the process has insufficient capacity to meet the demands of both tasks simultaneously. Working memory, for example, is known to have limited capacity (see section 9.1.6). Thus, if a novice driver, who needs to hold in working memory the sequence of acts needed to change gears, were required to change gears at the same time as carrying out an additional working memory task, it would be expected that performance on one or both tasks would be impaired.

It has been found that the more practiced a person is at a particular task, the less performance is affected by concurrent performance of a second, cognitive task. The extent to which a task is resistant to dual-task interference depends on the nature of the secondary task, but the overall consensus is that dual-task interference declines with practice, indicating an increase in automaticity (by definition)[121].

It used to be thought that cognitively controlled behavior relies on processes carried out in the cerebral cortex, whereas automatic behaviors, being less reliant on cognition, were produced by subcortical mechanisms. From this perspective, 'novel behaviors are mediated primarily in cortex and ... development of automaticity is a process of transferring control to subcortical structures'[122]. The basal ganglia have been identified as the subcortical structures that are particularly important for the storage and production of well-learned sequential behaviors[123]. Recent work, however, has shown that this simplistic view is incorrect. Neurophysiological studies in animals and brain-imaging studies in people have shown that extended practice that leads to increased automaticity does not transfer control of production to subcortical structures; rather, it results in changes in how cortical activity is organized and in which regions of cortex are most active[124]. Cortex seems to be where the motor commands that drive automatic behaviors are generated[125]. Furthermore, the basal ganglia and other subcortical structures such as the cerebellum have been found to be particularly active early in learning, and it seems that as learning progresses, 'control is gradually passed from the slower path through the basal ganglia to the faster cortical-cortical path'[126], which is opposite to the traditional view.

Other behavioral changes have been specifically associated with the acquisition of motor chunks (see section 13.1). With extensive practice, short sequences of motor elements become automatized, so that producing them in the right order no longer requires cognitive processing. Performance also tends to get quicker and less error prone, and acquires a rhythmic structure, as described in section 13.1.7. In addition, there may be changes in how quickly the sequence can be initiated following a signal to start, as described in the next section, and changes in the extent to which elements are co-articulated (see section 15.3.4).

15.3.3 The response complexity effect on reaction time can be eliminated with practice

It has been repeatedly found that if people are asked to execute a motor sequence as soon as possible following the presentation of an imperative stimulus, then the reaction time (RT) is greater the more elements there are in the sequence[127]. This is usually referred to as the **response complexity effect** on RT, where the 'complexity' refers to the number of distinct elements in the response sequence[128]. Figure 15.19 shows a typical set of results. Experienced typists were asked to type short sequences of keystrokes consisting of 2, 3, 4 and 5 elements

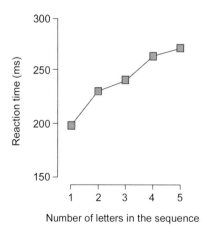

Figure 15.19: *Increase in reaction time with sequence length. Mean data from a group of competent typists, from Sternberg et al. (1978).*

(a single-element 'sequence' was also included). The sequences were unfamiliar and therefore not well-practiced, and the experiment did not allow the participants to perform any particular sequence repeatedly (so avoiding practice of any sequence during the experimental session). The participant was presented with a sequence that they had to hold in working memory until an imperative stimulus signaled that they should type the sequence as quickly as possible. The plot shows the average RTs (times between the imperative stimulus and the start of the first keystroke) plotted against sequence length: the longer the sequence, the greater the RT.

The response complexity effect on RT (Figure 15.19) has been found to disappear with extended practice with particular sequences. The data shown in Figure 15.19 were obtained from typists who were experienced but were not familiar with the particular sequences that they were required to type in the experiment. With practice, the response complexity effect gradually decreases. Typical sets of results are shown in Figure 15.20. Panels A and B show results from a study in which participants practiced pressing a single key to produce morse-code type sequences – short keypresses to give a dot ('dit'), longer presses to produce a dash ('dah'). Keypresses were executed as soon as possible following an imperative stimulus, and were either four elements sequences (dit-dah-dah-dit or dah-dit-dit-dah), or single presses (dit or dah). The response complexity effect is evident in the data from the first few days of practice (160 trials/day): the RT for the 4-keypress sequences was longer than the RT for the single keypress. The difference in RT gradually declined over the eight practice days, and was absent on the last day (panel B plots the differences of the RTs in panel A). Panels C and D show similar results from a study in which participants typed sequences of characters on a standard QWERTY keyboard. Fifteen sessions of 168 trials were conducted. Data from sequences of 2 and 6 characters are shown: RT was longer for the 6-character sequences, but the difference declined gradually over sessions, and was almost absent in the last two sessions.

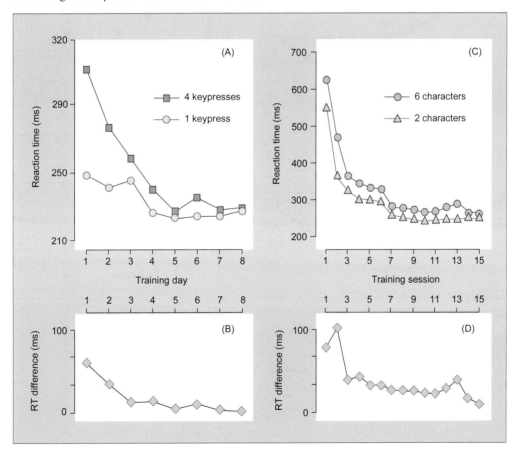

Figure 15.20: *Reduction of the response complexity effect on RT with practice. Each lower plot shows the difference in the RTs from the two conditions in the plot above it. (A) and (B) Mean data from 10 participants (Klapp, 1995, Table 1). (C) and (D) Mean data from 18 participants (Verwey, 1999). (See text for details.)*

Figure 15.20 shows that with extended practice, the time taken to initiate a response following an imperative stimulus (the RT) is independent of the number of elements in the response. This result has been taken to indicate the formation of a motor chunk: once a chunk is formed, it behaves like an element, and the RT should be much the same regardless of the nature of the element concerned[129].

15.3.4 Practice results in the blending together of elements in a sequence

As briefly described in Chapter 13, extended practice of sequential behaviors like typing, drawing, writing and speaking leads to increases in speed, fluency and efficiency of execution. These changes are usually associated with increased coarticulation of elements: increases in the influence one element has on other elements in the sequence, and the extent to which their performance overlaps (section 13.2.8). Most studies of these changes have compared the performance of experts with that of novices, rather than documenting the changes as they occur during extended periods of practice. One exception examined the changes in performance of an aimed movement task that required participants to move a stylus between four visible targets (crosses) in sequence, as fast and as accurately as possible[130]. Participants practiced with one of three configurations of targets for a series of between 5 and 15 sessions (one per day) each of 400 trials. Figure 15.21 shows some typical results from one participant in the study, who practiced moving sequentially between targets 1, 2, 3 and 4, and then back

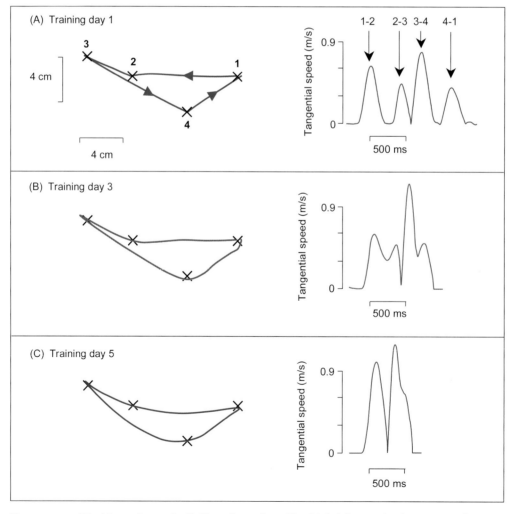

Figure 15.21: *Working point paths (left) and speed profiles (right) for moving in sequence between targets (crosses). Movements between targets were in the order 1→ 2 → 3 → 4 → 1; see text for details. Data selected from Sosnik et al. (2004), Fig. 3.*

to 1. Data are shown from the sessions on the first, third and fifth days of training, with working point paths on the left of the figure, speed profiles on the right. On day 1 (panel A), the participant made approximately straight-line movements between one target and the next, and each movement had a characteristic bell-shaped speed profile (see Chapter 11). The stylus came to a stop at each target, and paused briefly on targets 2 and 4; the whole sequence was executed in about 1.5 seconds. On day 3, the sequence was executed much more quickly (total time about 1 second), and there are no longer stops or pauses at targets 2 and 4. On day 5, the sequence is executed as two curved movement segments: one from target 1 to 3 via 2, the other from 3 to 1 via 4. The sequence took less than half the time taken on day 1.

Figure 15.21 provides an illustration of how a sequence initially executed as a series of distinct elements comes to be executed quite differently after a period of extended practice. The individual elements have somehow been blended together into what appear to be two chunks[131]. In terms of the ideas introduced in Chapters 11 and 13, a sequencing program has been constructed that specifies a series of targets for a trajectory generator in quick succession, so that the next target is specified before the commands generated in response to the previous target have been completed[132] (see section 13.3.9).

References & Notes

[1] Sutton, Barto (1998), p. 3.

[2] Thorndike (1898), p. 13.

[3] Thorndike (1911), p. 244.

[4] Or an *S-R association*.

[5] Skinner (1938).

[6] Staddon, Niv (2008).

[7] E.g., Colwill, Rescorla (1985); Dickinson (1994).

[8] See Domjan (2010).

[9] Dickinson (1994); Domjan (2010).

[10] See Ashby, Turner, Horvitz (2010); Yin, Knowlton (2006).

[11] Shallice (1982), pp. 199–200.

[12] This may also account for the almost normal execution of interceptive acts in Parkinson's Disease and related disorders (Majsak *et al.*, 1998).

[13] Della Salla (2005), p. 606.

[14] Parkin (1996).

[15] Biran *et al.* (2006); Parkin (1996).

[16] Similar types of experience can be evoked in normal people (Cheyne, Carriere, Smilek, 2009).

[17] In *alien hand syndrome*, the patient denies ownership of the affected limb (Marchetti, Della Salla, 1998). Anarchic and alien hand syndromes are often not distinguished (e.g., Biran *et al.*, 2006; Scepkowski, Cronin-Golomb, 2003).

[18] Della Sala, Marchetti, Spinnler (1994).

[19] Scepkowski, Cronin-Golomb (2003).

[20] Lhermitte (1983); Boccardi *et al.* (2002).

[21] With a bilateral SMA lesion (Boccardi *et al.*, 2002).

[22] Della Salla (2005), p. 608.

[23] Lhermitte (1983); Shallice *et al.* (1989).

[24] See, e.g., Arbib (1989); Shallice (1982). For a broader perspective see Moors, De Houwer (2006); Wood, Neal (2007).

[25] See also Woodworth (1918).

[26] Following historical usage (see Kling, Schrier, 1971).

[27] A behavior can be a reinforcer.

[28] Wynne (1994), p. 156.

[29] It took a long time to reach this consensus (see Kling, Schrier, 1971).

[30] Domjan (2010).

[31] E.g., Killeen (1994).

[32] Brembs *et al.* (2002).

[33] E.g., Zariwala *et al.* (2003).

[34] Grau *et al.* (2006).

[35] Wolpaw (2010).

[36] Wolpaw (1997).

[37] The largest α-MN axons will also be depolarized; Latash (2008a) gives a textbook account.

[38] After Paul Hoffman, who first described it; Latash (2008a) gives a textbook account.

[39] Wolpaw (1997).

[40] Wolpaw (1997, 2007).

[41] These findings are well established for $\downarrow$-mode conditioning; the picture for $\uparrow$-mode conditioning is less clear cut (Wolpaw, 1997, 2007).

[42] See Wolpaw (2007, 2010).

[43] Wolpaw (2007), p. 161.

[44] Thorndike (1927).

[45] Average of the magnitudes of the differences between the drawn and target lengths.

[46] See Wolpert, Diedrichsen, Flanagan (2011).

[47] Schmidt, Lee (2011).

[48] E.g., Schmidt, Lee (2011) claim that KR is 'the single most important variable for motor learning', p. 427.

[49] See Dayan, Niv (2008); Sutton, Barto (1998); Wolpert *et al.* (2011).

[50] Elwell, Grindley (1938), p. 51.

[51] Elwell, Grindley (1938), p. 39.

[52] Also true of reinforcement and punishment (Kling, Schrier, 1971).

[53] Elwell, Grindley (1938), p. 39.

[54] For review and data see Lewthwaite, Wulf (2010).

[55] See Kling, Schrier (1971).

[56] Kling, Schrier (1971); Schmidt, Lee (2011).

[57] The required movement involved two phases (Swinnen *et al.*, 1990).

[58] These possibilities do not account for the better performance with the longer delay found by Swinnen *et al.* (1990).

59 Kling, Schrier (1971), p. 687.

60 Liebermann, Vogel, Nisbet (2008); see also Held, Efstathiou, Greene (1966).

61 Kitazawa, Kohno, Uka (1995); see also Tanaka, Homma, Imamizu (2011).

62 Swinnen *et al.* (1990); Schmidt, Lee (2011).

63 Schmidt, Lee (2011) provide a detailed review.

64 A version of this idea may explain reduction of responding in instrumental conditioning experiments when reinforcement is removed (Rescorla, 2001).

65 Shadmehr, Wise (2005).

66 A rotational image flow (see section 4.1.12).

67 This is part of a more complex picture; see Leigh, Zee (2006); Schubert, Zee (2010).

68 Gonshor, Melvill Jones (1976a,b).

69 Gonshor, Melvill Jones (1976a).

70 Bloomberg, Melvill Jones, Segal (1991).

71 Gonshor, Melvill Jones (1976b).

72 Miles, Fuller (1974); Schubert, Zee (2010).

73 Gauthier, Robinson (1975); Schubert, Zee (2010).

74 Raymond, Lisberger (1998), p. 9112.

75 Du Lac *et al.* (1995).

76 See Porrill, Dean (2008); Tabata, Yamamoto, Kawato (2002).

77 Howard (1968).

78 Redding, Wallace (2006a), p. 1006.

79 Redding, Wallace (1996, 2001), consistent with the difference vector model of aimed movements described in Chapter 11.

80 Dewar (1971), p. 155.

81 Mazzoni, Krakauer (2006); Taylor, Ivry (2011); Werner, Bock (2007).

82 Mazzoni, Krakauer (2006).

83 Howard (1968). It can be most easily accomplished using a Risley rotary prism (Keeler, Singh, Dua, 2010).

84 Dewar (1971); Howard (1968).

85 Howard (1968).

86 Magnification/minification has been introduced incrementally in studies of VOR adaptation (Schubert, Della Santina, Shelhamer, 2008) and visuomotor rotations have also been introduced incrementally (e.g., Kagerer, Contreras-Vidal, Stelmach, 1996).

87 Helmholtz (1925).

88 See, e.g., Harris (1965); Howard (1982).

89 See Howard (1982).

90 Bedford (1989).

91 Harris (1965).

92 Harris (1965), p. 421.

93 See, e.g., Howard (1982); Redding, Wallace (2009).

94 Howard (1982).

95 E.g., Harris (1965).

96 Wilkinson (1971).

97 E.g., Uhlarik, Canon (1971); Redding, Wallace (2006a).

98 See, Howard (1982); Martin *et al.* (2002); Redding, Wallace (2006b).

99 Prablanc, Tzavaras, Jeannerod (1975).

100 Templeton, Howard, Wilkinson (1974).

101 Krakauer *et al.* (2006), p. 1.

102 Schmidt, Lee (2011), p. 465.

103 See Putterman, Robert, Bregman (1969) for an example. For a more recent study see Krakauer *et al.* (2006).

104 Schmidt, Lee (2011), p. 481.

105 See Schmidt, Lee (2011) for review. Cases of negative transfer are rare and often difficult to interpret.

106 Note that 'learning to learn' can be considered to be a kind of positive transfer, in which learning one task, or in one context, aids the learning of another task or learning in another context.

107 E.g., Bedford (1999); Redding, Wallace (2006a,b).

108 Redding, Wallace (1996); see also Baraduc, Wolpert (2002).

109 Martin *et al.* (1996); Field, Shipley and Cunningham (1999) reported a similar result for ball catching.

110 Baily (1972).

111 Kitazawa, Kimura, Uka (1997), but not Baily (1972).

112 Fernandez-Ruiz *et al.* (2000).

113 Baraduc, Wolpert (2002).

114 Putterman, Robert, Bregman (1969).

115 For review see Redding, Wallace (2006b). For a more theoretical overview that links to other types of sensorimotor learning, see Krakauer, Mazzoni (2011).

116 E.g., Snoddy (1926); Adams (1971).

[117] Fitts, Posner (1967).

[118] Schmidt, Lee (2011); also called the *associative stage* or the *refining stage* (Anderson, 1995; Fitts, Posner, 1967).

[119] Schmidt, Lee (2011), p. 431.

[120] Learning about sequences can take place without the person being aware that there is a sequence. This is usually studied in serial reaction time tasks in which people do not learn to perform a specific sequence, they acquire information about the sequence. See Keele *et al.* (2003) and Abrahamse *et al.* (2010) for reviews.

[121] There is insufficient space to review the findings here. For overviews see Ivry (1996); Moors, De Houwer (2006); Wood, Neal (2007).

[122] Ashby, Turner, Horvitz (2010), p. 208.

[123] Doyon *et al.* (2009).

[124] E.g., Wu, Chan, Hallett (2008). See Ashby, Turner, Horvitz (2010) for review.

[125] See Bullock, Cisek, Grossberg (1998) for a neurophysiologically inspired model of the cortical generation of reaching movements.

[126] Ashby, Turner, Horvitz (2010), p. 212. Desmurget and Turner (2010) showed that the basal ganglia are not responsible for storing the programs for well-learned behaviors and are not essential for producing well-learned sequences.

[127] This effect was apparently first reported by F.N. Freeman in 1907 (Rhodes *et al.*, 2004) and later by Henry and Rogers (1960). More recent work has separated the sequence effects from the effects of other variables such as movement duration (longer MTs are associated with greater RTs; Klapp, Erwin, 1976), movement amplitude, and accuracy (RT is greater when the Fitts' index of difficulty is greater; Fitts, Peterson, 1964).

[128] Henry (1980); Rhodes *et al.* (2004).

[129] This is not necessarily true for choice RT. For discussion see Klapp (1996); Verwey (1999).

[130] Sosnik *et al.* (2004).

[131] Sosnik *et al.* (2004) provided further evidence for chunks by demonstrating that they transferred to novel target configurations.

[132] Sosnik *et al.* (2004) offer an alternative account.

References

A.

Abbs, J.H., Gracco, V.L., Cole, K.J. (1984) Control of multimovement coordination: Sensorimotor mechanisms in speech motor programming. *J. Mot. Behav.*, 16, 195–231.

Abend, W., Bizzi, E., Morasso, P. (1982) Human arm trajectory formation. *Brain*, 105, 331–348.

Abrahamse, E.L., Jimenez, L., Verwey, W.B., Clegg, B.A. (2010) Representing serial action and perception. *Psychon. Bull. Rev.*, 17, 603–623.

Adamovich, S.V., Archambault, P.S., Ghafouri, M., Levin, M.F., Poizner, H., Feldman, A.G. (2001) Hand trajectory invariance in reaching movements involving the trunk. *Exp. Brain Res.*, 138, 288–303.

Adamovich, S.V., Berkinblit, M., Fookson, O., Poizner, H. (1999) Pointing in 3D space to remembered targets, II: Effects of movement speed toward kinesthetically defined targets. *Exp. Brain Res.*, 125, 200–210.

Adamovich, S.V., Berkinblit, M., Smetani, B., Fookson, O., Poizner, H. (1994) Influence of movement speed on accuracy of pointing to memorized targets in 3D space. *Neurosci. Lett.*, 172, 171–174.

Adams, J.A. (1961) The second facet of forgetting: A review of warm-up decrement. *Psychol. Bull.*, 58, 257–273.

Adams, J.A. (1971) A closed-loop theory of motor learning. *J. Mot. Behav.*, 3, 111–150.

Adams, J.A. (1984) Learning of movement sequences. *Psychol. Bull.*, 96, 3–28.

Adams, J.A. (1987) Historical review and appraisal of research on the learning, retention, and transfer of human motor skills. *Psychol. Bull.*, 101, 41–47.

Adi-Japha, E., Karni, A., Parnes, A., Loewenschuss, I., Vakil, E. (2008) A shift in task routines during the learning of a motor skill: Group-averaged data may mask critical phases in the individuals' acquisition of skilled performance. *J. Exp. Psychol. Learn. Mem. Cogn.*, 34, 1544–1551.

Adkin, A.L., Frank, J.S., Carpenter, M.G., Peysar, G.W. (2000) Postural control is scaled to level of postural threat. *Gait Posture*, 12, 87–93.

Adolph, K.E., Robinson, S.R., Young, J.E., Gill-Avarez, F. (2008) What is the shape of developmental change? *Psychol. Rev.*, 115, 527–543.

Adolph, K.E., Vereijken, B., Denny, M.A. (1998) Learning to crawl. *Child Dev.*, 69, 1299–1312.

Ajemian, R., D'Ausilio, A., Moorman, H., Bizzi, E. (2010) Why professional athletes need a prolonged period of warm-up and other peculiarities of human motor learning. *J. Mot. Behav.*, 42, 381–388.

Alexander, R.M. (1984) Walking and running. *Am. Scientist*, 72, 348–354.

Alexander, R.M. (1997) A minimum energy cost hypothesis for human arm trajectories. *Biol. Cybern.*, 76, 97–105.

Alexander, R.M. (2002) Energetics and optimization of human walking and running. *Am. J. Hum. Biol.*, 14, 641–648.

Alexander, R.M., Jayes, A.S. (1980) Fourier analysis of forces exerted in walking and running. *J. Biomech.*, 13, 383–390.

Alexandrov, A.V., Frolov, A.A., Horak, F.B., Carlson-Kuhta, P., Park, S. (2005) Feedback equilibrium control during human standing. *Biol. Cybern.*, 93, 309–322.

Al-Falahe, N.A., Nagaoka, M., Vallbo, A.B. (1997) Response profiles of human muscle afferents during active finger movements. *Brain*, 113, 325–346.

Allen, T.J., Proske, U. (2006) Effect of muscle fatigue on the sense of limb position and movement. *Exp. Brain Res.*, 170, 30–38.

Ammons, R.B. (1947) Acquisition of motor skill: I. Quantitative analysis and theoretical formulation. *Psychol. Rev.*, 54, 263–281.

Anderson, F.C., Pandy, M.G. (2001) Contributions of individual muscles to support during normal gait. *Gait Posture*, 13, 292–293.

Anderson, J.R. (1995) *Cognitive Psychology and Its Implications* (4th edition). New York: W.H. Freeman.

Andersson, G., Magnusson, M. (2002) Neck muscle vibration causes short-latency electromyographic activation of lower leg muscles in postural reactions of the standing human. *Acta Otolaryngol.*, 122, 284–288.

Andres, R.O., Hartung, K.J. (1989) Predictions of head movement time using Fitts' Law. *Hum. Factors*, 31, 703–713.

Angelaki, D. (2004) Eyes on target: What neurons must do for the vestibular-ocular reflex during linear motion. *J. Neurophysiol.*, 92, 20–35.

Aniss, A.M., Diener, H.C., Hore, J., Burke, D., Gandevia, S.C. (1990) Behavior of human muscle receptors when reliant on proprioceptive feedback during standing. *J. Neurophysiol.*, 64, 661–670.

Anstis, S.M. (1998) Picturing peripheral acuity. *Perception*, 27, 817–825.

Aramaki, Y., Nozaki, D., Masani, K., Sato, T., Nakazawa, K., Yano, H. (2001) Reciprocal angular acceleration of the ankle and hip joints during quiet standing in humans. *Exp. Brain Res.*, 136, 463–473.

Arbib, M.A. (1989) *The Metaphorical Brain 2: Neural Networks and Beyond*. New York: Wiley.

Armel, K.C., Ramachandran, V.S. (2003) Projecting sensations to external objects: Evidence from skin conductance response. *Proc. Roy. Soc. Lond. B*, 270, 1499–1506.

Armstrong, D.M. (1988) The supraspinal control of mammalian locomotion. *J. Physiol.*, 405, 1–37.

Arshavsky, Y. (2003) Cellular and network properties in the functioning of the nervous system: From central pattern generators to cognition. *Brain Res. Rev.*, 41, 229–267.

Aruin, A.S., Latash, M.L. (1995) The role of motor action in anticipatory postural adjustments studied with self-induced and externally triggered perturbations. *Exp. Brain Res.*, 106, 291–300.

Aruin, A.S., Latash, M.L. (1996) Anticipatory postural adjustments during self-initiated perturbations of different magnitude triggered by a standard motor action. *Electroencephalogr. Clin. Neurophysiol.*, 101, 497–503.

Aruin, A.S., Shiratori, T., Latash, M.L. (2001) The role of action in postural preparation for loading and unloading in standing subjects. *Exp. Brain Res.*, 138, 458–466.

Asai, Y., Tasaka, Y., Nomura, K., Nomura, T., Casadio, M., Morasso, P. (2009) A model of postural control in quiet standing: Robust compensation of delay-induced instability using intermittent activation of feedback control. *PLoS ONE*, 4(7), e6169.

Asanuma, H. (1981) The pyramidal tract. In V.B. Brooks (ed.) *Handbook of Physiology: Section 1. The Nervous System*, vol. II: *Motor Control*, 703–733. Bethesda, MD: American Physiological Society.

Asch, S.E., Witkin, H.A. (1948) Studies in space orientation: II. Perception of the upright with displaced visual fields and with body tilted. *J. Exp. Psychol.*, 38, 455–477.

Ashby, F.G. (2011) *Statistical Analysis of FMRI Data*. Cambridge, MA: MIT Press.

Ashby, F.G., Turner, B.O., Horvitz, J.C. (2010) Cortical and basal ganglia contributions to habit learning and automaticity. *Trends Cogn. Sci.*, 14, 208–215.

Ashcraft, M.H., Radvansky, G.A. (2010) *Cognition* (5th edition). Upper Saddle River, NJ: Pearson Education.

Atkeson, C.G., Hollerbach, J.M. (1985) Kinematic features of unrestrained vertical arm movements. *J. Neurosci.*, 5, 2318–2330.

Attwell, D., Laughlin, S.B. (2001) An energy budget for signaling in the grey matter of the brain. *J. Cereb. Blood Flow Metab.*, 21, 1133–1145.

Azzopardi, P., Cowey, A. (1993) Preferential representation of the fovea in the primary visual cortex. *Nature*, 361, 719–721.

B.

Bach-y-Rita, P. (1972) *Brain Mechanisms in Sensory Substitution*. New York: Academic Press.

Bach-y-Rita, P. (2004) Tactile sensory substitution studies. *Ann. N.Y. Acad. Sci.*, 1013, 83–91.

Baerends, G.P., Blokzijl, G.J., Kruijt, J.P. (1982) The processing of heterogeneous information on egg features inducing the retrieval response. *Behavior*, 82, 212–224.

Bahill, A.T., Adler, D., Stark, L. (1975) Most naturally occurring saccades have magnitudes of 15 degrees or less. *Invest. Ophthalmol.*, 14, 468–469.

Bahill, A.T., Ciuffreda, K.J., Kenyon, R., Stark, L. (1976) Dynamic and static violations of Hering's law of equal innervation. *Am. J. Optom. Physiol. Opt.*, 53, 786–796.

Bahill, A.T., Karnavas, W.J. (1993) The perceptual illusion of baseball's rising fastball and breaking curveball. *J. Exp. Psychol. Hum. Percept. Perform.*, 19, 3–14.

Bahrick, H.P., Fitts, P.M., Briggs, G.E. (1957) Learning curves – facts or artefacts? *Psychol. Bull.*, 54, 256–268.

Bailey, C.H., Chen, M. (1988) Long-term memory in *Aplysia* modulates the total number of varicosities of single identified sensory neurons. *Proc. Natl. Acad. Sci. USA*, 85, 2373–2377.

Baily, J.S. (1972) Adaptation to prisms: Do proprioceptive changes mediate adapted behaviour with ballistic arm movements? *Quart. J. Exp. Psychol.*, 24, 8–20.

Bainbridge, L., Sanders, M. (1972) The generality of Fitts's law. *J. Exp. Psychol.*, 96, 130–133.

Bairstow, P. (1987) Analysis of hand movement to moving targets. *Hum. Mov. Sci.*, 6, 205–231.

Baker, C.L., Braddick, O.J. (1985) Eccentricity-dependent scaling of the limits of short-range motion perception. *Vision Res.*, 25, 803–812.

Baloh, R.W., Henn, V., Jäger, J. (1982) Habituation of the human vestibulo-ocular reflex with low-frequency harmonic acceleration. *Am. J. Otolaryngol.*, 3, 235–241.

Balsam, P.D., Drew, M.R., Gallistel, C.R. (2010) Time and associative learning. *Comp. Cogn. Behav. Rev.*, 5, 1–22.

Balsam, P.D., Gallistel, C.R. (2009) Temporal maps and informativeness in associative learning. *Trends Neurosci.*, 32, 73–78.

Banks, M.S., Ehrlich, S.M., Backus, B.T., Crowell, J.A. (1996) Estimating heading during real and simulated eye movements. *Vision Res.*, 36, 431–443.

Banta, C. (1995) *Seeing is Believing? Haunted Shacks, Mystery Spots, and Other Delightful Phenomena*. Agoura Hills, CA: Funhouse Press.

Baraduc, P., Wolpert, D.M. (2002) Adaptation to a visuomotor shift depends on the starting posture. *J. Neurophysiol.*, 88, 973–981.

Baratta, R.V., Solomonow, M., Best, R., D'Ambrosia, R. (1993) Isotonic length/force models of nine different skeletal muscles. *Med. Biol. Eng. Comput.*, 31, 449–458.

Barbeau, H., Rossignol, S. (1987) Recovery of locomotion after chronic spinalization in the adult cat. *Brain Res.*, 412, 84–95.

Barlow, G.W. (1977) Modal action patterns. In T.A. Sebeok (ed.) *How Animals Communicate* (pp. 98–134). Bloomington, IN: Indiana University Press.

Barnes, G.R. (2008) Cognitive processes involved in smooth pursuit eye movements. *Brain Cogn.*, 68, 309–326.

Bartlett, F.C. (1932) *Remembering: A Study in Experimental and Social Psychology*. New York: Cambridge University Press.

Barto, A.G., Fagg, A.H., Sitkoff, N., Houk, J.C. (1999) A cerebellar model of timing and prediction in the control of reaching. *Neural. Comput.*, 11, 565–594.

Bartolami, S.B., Pierobon, A., DiZio, P., Lackner, J.R. (2006a) Localization of the subjective vertical during roll, pitch and recumbent yaw body tilt. *Exp. Brain Res.*, 173, 364–373.

Bartolami, S.B., Roca, S., Daros, S., DiZio, P., Lackner, J.R. (2006b) Mechanisms of human static spatial orientation. *Exp. Brain Res.*, 173, 374–388.

Basmajian, J.V. (1976) The human bicycle. In P.V. Komi (ed.) *Biomechanics*, vol. 5-A. Baltimore, MD: University Park Press.

Basmajian, J.V., DeLuca, C. (1985) *Muscles Alive: Their Functions Revealed by Electromyography* (5th edition). Philadelphia: Lippincott Williams & Wilkins.

Baud-Bovy, G., Viviani, P. (1998) Pointing to kinaesthetic targets in space. *J. Neurosci.*, 18, 1528–1545.

Baxendale, S. (2004) Memories aren't made of this: Amnesia at the movies. *Br. Med. J.*, 329, 1480–1483.

Beall, A.C., Loomis, J.M. (1996) Visual control of steering without course information. *Perception*, 25, 481–494.

Bear, M.F., Connors, B.W., Paradiso, M.A. (2007) *Neuroscience: Exploring the Brain* (3rd edition). Philadelphia: Lippincott Williams & Wilkins.

Becker, W. (1991) Saccades. In R.H.S. Carpenter (ed.) *Eye Movements: Vision and Visual Dysfunction*, vol. 8 (pp. 95–137). New York: Macmillan.

Bedford, F.L. (1989) Constraints on learning new mappings between perceptual dimensions. *J. Exp. Psychol. Hum. Percept. Perf.*, 15, 232–248.

Bedford, F.L. (1999) Keeping perception accurate. *Trends Cogn. Sci.*, 3, 4–11.

Beggs, W.D.A., Andrew, J.A., Baker, M.L., Dove, S.R., Fairclough, I., Howarth, C.I. (1972) The accuracy of non-visual aiming. *Quart. J. Exp. Psychol.*, 24, 515–523.

Belenkii, V.Y., Gurfinkel, V.S., Paltsev, Y.I. (1967) Elements of control of voluntary movements. *Biofizika*, 12, 135–141.

Benecke, R., Rothwell, J.C., Day, B.L., Dick, J.P., Marsden, C.D. (1986) Motor strategies involved in the performance of sequential movements. *Exp. Brain Res.*, 63, 585–595.

Berkinblit, M.B., Feldman, A.G., Fukson, O. (1986) Adaptability of innate motor patterns and motor control mechanisms. *Behav. Brain Sci.*, 9, 585–638.

Bernstein, N.A. (1967) *The Co-ordination and Regulation of Movements*. Oxford: Pergamon Press.

Berson, D.M. (2003) Strange vision: Ganglion cells as circadian photoreceptors. *Trends Neurosci.*, 26, 314–320.

Berthoz, A., Lacour, M., Soechting, J.F., Vidal, P.P. (1979) The role of vision in the control of posture during linear motion. *Prog. Brain Res.*, 50, 197–210.

Biess, A., Liebermann, D.G., Flash, T. (2007) A computational model for redundant human three-dimensional pointing movements: Integration of independent spatial and temporal motor plans simplifies movement dynamics. *J. Neurosci.*, 27, 3045–3064.

Binder, M.D., Kroin, J.S., Moore, G.P., Stuart, D.G. (1977) The response of Golgi tendon organs to single motor unit contractions. *J. Physiol.*, 271, 337–349.

Biran, I., Giovannetti, T., Buxbaum, L., Chatterjee, A. (2006) The alien hand syndrome: What makes the alien hand alien? *Cogn. Neuropsychol.*, 23, 563–582.

Bizzi, E., Accornero, N., Chapel, W., Hogan, N. (1984) Posture control and trajectory formation during arm movement. *J. Neurosci.*, 4, 2738–2744.

Bizzi, E., Hogan, N., Mussa-Ivaldi, F.A., Giszter, S. (1992) Does the nervous system use equilibrium-point control to guide single and multiple joint movements? *Behav. Brain Sci.*, 15, 603–613.

Bizzi, E., Tresch, M.C., Saltiel, P., D'Avella, A. (2000) New perspectives on spinal motor systems. *Nat. Rev. Neurosci.*, 1, 101–108.

Blanchard, P., Devaney, R.L., Hall, G.R. (2011) *Differential Equations* (4th edition). Pacific Grove, CA: Brooks-Cole.

Bloedel, J.R. (2004) Task-dependent role of the cerebellum in motor learning. *Prog. Brain Res.*, 143, 319–329.

Bloem, B.R., Allum, J.H., Carpenter, M.G., Verschuuren, J.J., Honegger, F. (2002) Triggering of balance corrections and compensatory strategies in a patient with total leg proprioceptive loss. *Exp. Brain Res.*, 142, 91–107.

Bloomberg, J., Melvill Jones, G., Segal, B. (1991) Adaptive plasticity in the gaze stabilizing synergy of slow and saccadic eye movements. *Exp. Brain Res.*, 84, 35–46.

Boccardi, E., Della Sala, S., Motto, C., Spinnler, H. (2002) Utilisation behaviour consequent to bilateral SMA softening. *Cortex*, 38, 289–308.

Bock, O. (1990) Load compensation in human goal-directed arm movements. *Behav. Brain Res.*, 41, 167–177.

Bock, O., Eckmiller, R. (1986) Goal-directed arm movements in the absence of visual guidance: Evidence for amplitude rather than position control. *Exp. Brain Res.*, 62, 451–458.

Bockisch, C.J., Straumann, D., Haslwanter, T. (2005) Human 3-D aVOR with and without otolith stimulation. *Exp. Brain Res.*, 161, 358–367.

Boessenkool, J.J., Nijhof, E.J., Erkelens, C.J. (1998) A comparison of curvatures of left and right hand movements in a simple pointing task. *Exp. Brain Res.*, 120, 369–376.

Bohan, M., Longstaff, M.G., Van Gemmert, A.W., Rand, M.K., Stelmach, G.E. (2003) Differential effects of target height and width on 2D pointing movement duration and kinematics. *Motor Control*, 7, 278–289.

Bohland, J.W., Bullock, D., Guenther, F.H. (2010) Neural representations and mechanisms for the performance of simple speech sequences. *J. Cog. Neurosci.*, 22, 1504–1529.

Bolles, R.C. (1970) Species-specific defence reactions and avoidance learning. *Psychol. Rev.*, 77, 32–48.

Bolles, R.C., Collier, A.C. (1976) The effect of predictive cues on freezing in rats. *Animal Learn. Behav.*, 4, 6–8.

Book, W.F. (1925) *The Psychology of Skill*. New York: Gregg.

Bottaro, A., Casadio, M., Morasso, P., Sanguineti, V. (2005) Body sway during quiet standing: Is it the residual chattering of an intermittent stabilization process? *Hum. Mov. Sci.*, 24, 588–615.

Botvinick, M., Cohen, J. (1998) Rubber hands 'feel' touch that eyes see. *Nature*, 391, 756.

Bourne, L.E., Archer, E.J. (1956) Time continuously on target as a function of distribution of practice. *J. Exp. Psychol.*, 51, 25–33.

Bramble, D.M., Lieberman, D.E. (2004) Endurance running and the evolution of *Homo. Nature*, 432, 345–352.

Brandt, T., Dichgans, J., Koenig, E. (1973) Differential effects of central versus peripheral vision on egocentric and exocentric motion perception. *Exp. Brain Res.*, 16, 476–491.

Brandt, T., Wist, E.R., Dichgans, J. (1975) Foreground and background in dynamic spatial orientation. *Percept. Psychophys.*, 17, 497–503.

Braun, D.A., Mehring, C., Wolpert, D.M. (2010) Structure learning in action. *Behav. Brain Res.*, 206, 157–165.

Breen, J.L. (1967) What makes a good hitter? *J. Health Phys. Educ. Recr.*, 38, 36–39.

Brembs, B., Lorenzetti, F.D., Reyes, F.D., Baxter, D.A., Byrne, J.H. (2002) Operant reward learning in Aplysia: Neuronal correlates and mechanisms. *Science*, 296, 1706–1709.

Brenner, E., Smeets, J.B.J. (1997) Fast responses of the human hand to changes in target position. *J. Mot. Behav.*, 29, 297–310.

Brenner, E., Smeets, J.B.J., De Lussanet, M. (1998) Hitting moving targets: Continuous control of the acceleration of the hand on the basis of the target's velocity. *Exp. Brain Res.*, 122, 467–474.

Bridgeman, B., Kirch, M., Sperling, A. (1981) Segregation of cognitive and motor aspects of visual information using induced motion. *Percept. Psychophys.*, 29, 336–342.

Britten, K.H. (2008) Mechanisms of self-motion perception. *Annu. Rev. Neurosci.*, 31, 389–410.

Brockway, J.M. (1987) Derivation of formulae used to calculate energy expenditure in man. *Hum. Nutr. Clin. Nutr.* 41, 463–471

Brooks, V.B. (1986) *The Neural Basis of Motor Control*. New York: Oxford University Press.

Brouwer, A.-M., Brenner, E., Smeets, J.B.J. (2000) Hitting moving objects: The dependency of hand velocity on the speed of the target. *Exp. Brain Res.*, 133, 242–248.

Browman, C., Goldstein, L. (1992) Articulatory phonology: An overview. *Phonetica*, 49, 155–180.

Brown, P., Rothwell, J.C., Thompson, P.D., Britton, T.C., Day, B.L., Marsden, C.D. (1991) New observations on the normal auditory startle reflex in man. *Brain*, 114, 1891–1902.

Bruce, V., Green, P.R., Georgeson, M.A. (2003) *Visual Perception: Physiology, Psychology and Ecology*. Hove, UK: Psychology Press.

Bryan, W.L., Harter, N. (1897) Studies in the physiology and psychology of the telegraphic language. *Psychol. Rev.*, 4, 27–53.

Bryan, W.L., Harter, N. (1899) Studies on the telegraphic language: The acquisition of a hierarchy of habits. *Psychol. Rev.*, 6, 345–375.

Buchanan, J.J., Horak, F. (1999) Emergence of postural patterns as a function of vision and translation frequency. *J. Neurophysiol.*, 81, 2325–2339.

Bullock, D., Bongers, R.M., Lankhorst, M., Beek, P.J. (1999) A vector-integration-to-endpoint model for performance of viapoint movements. *Neural Netw.*, 12, 1–29.

Bullock, D., Cisek, P., Grossberg, S. (1998) Cortical networks for the control of voluntary arm movements under variable force conditions. *Cereb. Cortex*, 8, 48–62.

Bullock, D., Grossberg, S. (1988) Neural dynamics of planned arm movements: Emergent invariants and speed-accuracy properties during trajectory formation. *Psychol. Rev.*, 95, 49–90.

Bullock, D., Grossberg, S. (1991) Adaptive neural networks for control of movement trajectories invariant under speed and force rescaling. *Hum. Mov. Sci.*, 10, 3–53.

Bullock, D., Grossberg, S., Guenther, F.H. (1993) A self-organizing neural model of motor equivalent reaching and tool use by a multijoint arm. *J. Cog. Neurosci.*, 5, 408–435.

Bullock, D., Grossberg, S., Mannes, C. (1993) A neural network for cursive script production. *Biol. Cybern.*, 70, 15–28.

Burgess, P.R., Clark, F.J. (1969) Characteristics of knee joint receptors in the cat. *J. Physiol.*, 203, 317–333.

Burke, D., Gandevia, S.C., Macefield, G. (1988) Responses to passive movement of receptors in joint, skin and muscle of the human hand. *J. Physiol.*, 402, 347–361.

Burke, R.E., Degtyarenko, A.M., Simon, E.S. (2001) Patterns of locomotor drive to motoneurons and last-order interneurons: Clues to the structure of the CPG. *J. Neurophysiol.*, 86, 447–462.

Burke, R.E., Levine, D.N., Tsairis, P., Zajac, F.E. (1973) Physiological types and histochemical profiles in motor units of the cat gastrocnemius. *J. Physiol.*, 234, 723–748.

Burton, G., Turvey, M.T. (1990) Perceiving the lengths of rods that are held but not wielded. *Ecol. Psychol.*, 2, 295–324.

Burton, H. (2002) Cerebral cortical regions devoted to the somatosensory system: Results from brain imaging studies in humans. In R.J. Nelson (ed.), *The Somatosensory System: Deciphering the Brain's Own Body Image*. New York: CRC Press.

C.

Campos, F.M.M.O., Calado, J.M.F. (2009) Approaches to human arm movement control: A review. *Annu. Rev. Control*, 33, 69–77.

Cappellini, G., Ivanenko, Y.P., Poppele, R.E., Lacquaniti, F. (2006) Motor patterns in human walking and running. *J. Neurophysiol.*, 95, 3426–3437.

Carello, C., Fitzpatrick, P., Turvey, M.T. (1992) Haptic probing: Perceiving the length of a probe and the distance of a surface probed. *Percept. Psychophys.*, 51, 580–598.

Carew, T.J., Hawkins, R.D., Kandel, E.R. (1983) Differential classical conditioning of a defensive withdrawal reflex in Aplysia Californica. *Science*, 219, 397–400.

Carew, T.J., Pinsker, H.M., Kandel, E.R. (1972) Long-term habituation of a defensive withdrawal reflex in Aplysia. *Science*, 175, 451–454.

Carey, M.R. (2011) Synaptic mechanisms of sensorimotor learning in the cerebellum. *Curr. Opin. Neurobiol.*, 21, 609–615.

Carlton, L.G. (1981) Processing visual feedback information for movement control. *J. Exp. Psychol. Hum. Percept. Perform.*, 7, 1019–1030.

Carlton, L.G. (1992) Visual processing time and the control of movement. In L. Proteau, D. Elliott (eds) *Vision and Motor Control* (pp. 3–31). Amsterdam: Elsevier.

Carpenter, R.H.S. (1998) *Movements of the Eyes* (2nd edition). Cambridge University Press.

Carpenter, R.H.S. (2003) *Neurophysiology* (4th edition). London: Arnold.

Carrier, D.R. (1984) The energetic paradox of human running and hominid evolution. *Curr. Anthropol.*, 25, 483–495.

Carriot, J., DiZio, P., Nougier, V. (2008) Vertical frames of reference and control of body orientation. *Neurophysiol. Clin.*, 38, 423–437.

Carroll, T.J., Selvanayagam, V.S., Riek, S., Semmler, J.G. (2011) Neural adaptations to strength training: Moving beyond transcranial magnetic stimulation and reflex studies. *Acta Physiol.* (Oxf.), 202, 119–140.

Carron, A.V. (1969) Performance and learning in a discrete motor task under massed vs. distributed practice. *Res. Quart.*, 40, 481–489.

Carson, R.G., Riek, S., Shahbazpour, N. (2002) Central and peripheral mediation of human force sensation following eccentric or concentric contractions. *J. Physiol.*, 539, 913–925.

Carter, R.C. (1978) Knobology Underwater. *Hum. Factors*, 20, 641–647.

Casadio, M., Morasso, P., Sanguineti, V. (2005) Direct measurement of ankle stiffness during quiet standing: Implications for control modelling and clinical applications. *Gait Posture*, 21, 410–424.

Castiello, U., Stelmach, G.E. (1993) Generalized representation of handwriting: Evidence of effector independence. *Acta Psychol.*, 82, 53–68.

Cavanagh, P.R., Kram, R. (1989) Stride length in distance running: velocity, body dimensions, and added mass effects. *Med. Sci. Sports Exerc.*, 21, 467–479.

Chan, T.C. (1994) Haptic perception of partial-rod lengths with the rod held stationary or wielded. *Percept. Psychophys.*, 55, 551–561.

Charles, S.K., Hogan, N. (2010) The curvature and variability of wrist and arm movements. *Exp. Brain Res.*, 203, 63–73.

Cheyne, J., Carriere, J., Smilek, D. (2009) Absent minds and absent agents: Attention-lapse induced alienation of agency. *Conscious. Cogn.*, 18, 481–493.

Christensen, L.O., Petersen, N., Andersen, J.B., Sinkjaer, T., Nielsen, J. (2000) Evidence for transcortical reflex pathways in the lower limb of man. *Prog. Neurobiol.*, 62, 251–272.

Christoffersen, G.R. (1997) Habituation: Events in the history of its characterization and linkage to synaptic depression. A new proposed kinetic criterion for its identification. *Prog. Neurobiol.*, 53, 45–66.

Cisek, P. (2005) Neural representations of motor plans, desired trajectories, and controlled objects. *Cogn. Process.*, 6, 15–24.

Clark, F.J., Burgess, R.C., Chapin, J.W., Lipscomb, W.T. (1985) Role of intramuscular receptors in the awareness of limb position. *J. Neurophysiol.*, 54, 1529–1540.

Clark, F.J., Horch, K.W., Bach, S.M., Larson, G.F. (1979) Contributions of cutaneous and joint receptors to static knee position sense in man. *J. Neurophysiol.*, 42, 877–888.

Clark, J.E, Yallop, C., Fletcher, J. (2007) *An Introduction to Phonetics and Phonology* (3rd edition). London: Blackwell.

Clark, R.E., Squire, L.R. (1998) Classical conditioning and brain systems: The role of awareness. *Science*, 280, 77–81.

Clarke, J. (1994) SQUIDs. *Scientific American*, 271, 46–53.

Clément, G., Bukley, A.P. (eds) (2007) *Artificial Gravity* (Space Technology Library, vol. 20). Berlin: Springer-Verlag.

Clément, G., Moore, S.T., Raphan, T., Cohen, B. (2001) Perception of tilt (somatogravic illusion) in response to sustained linear acceleration during space flight. *Exp. Brain Res.*, 138, 410–418.

Clément, G., Reschke, M.F. (2008) *Neuroscience in Space*. Berlin: Springer-Verlag.

Cloete, S., Wallis, G. (2011) Visuomotor control of steering: The artefact of the matter. *Exp. Brain Res.*, 208, 475–489.

Cole, J.D., Sedgwick, E.M. (1992) The perceptions of force and of movement in a man without large myelinated sensory afferents below the neck. *J. Physiol.*, 449, 503–515.

Coleman, S.R., Gormezano, I. (1971) Classical conditioning of the rabbit's (*Oryctolagus cuniculus*) nictitating membrane response under symmetrical CS–US interval shifts. *J. Comp. Physiol. Psychol.*, 77, 447–455.

Collewijn, H., Kowler, E. (2008) The significance of microsaccades for vision and oculomotor control. *J. Vision*, 8(14), a20.

Collins, C.J.S., Barnes, G.R. (1999) Independent control of head gaze movements during head-free pursuit in humans. *J. Physiol.*, 515, 299–314.

Collins, D.F., Refshauge, K.M., Todd, G., Gandevia, S.C. (2005) Cutaneous receptors contribute to kinesthesia at the index finger, elbow, and knee. *J. Neurophysiol.*, 94, 1699–1706.

Collins, J.J., De Luca, C.J. (1995) The effects of visual input on open-loop and closed-loop postural mechanisms. *Exp. Brain Res.*, 103, 151–163.

Collins, S.H., Ruina, A.L., Tedrake, R., Wisse, M. (2005) Efficient bipedal robots based on passive-dynamic walkers. *Science*, 307, 1082–1085.

Collins, S.H., Wisse, M., Ruina, A.L. (2001) A 3-D passive dynamic walking robot with two legs and knees. *Int. J. Robotics Res.*, 20, 607–615.

Colwill, R.M., Rescorla, R.A. (1985) Postconditioning devaluation of a reinforcer affects instrumental responding. *J. Exp. Psychol. Anim. Behav. Process.*, 11, 120–132.

Conforto, S., Schmid, M., Camomilla, V., D'Allessio, T., Cappozo, A. (2001) Hemodynamics as a possible internal mechanical disturbance to balance. *Gait Posture*, 14, 28–35.

Corcos, D.M., Gottlieb, G.L., Agarwal, G.C. (1988) Accuracy constraints upon rapid elbow movements. *J. Mot. Behav.*, 20, 255–272.

Corcos, D.M., Jaric, S., Agarwal, G.C., Gottlieb, G.L. (1993) Principles for learning single joint movements: I. Enhanced performance by practice. *Exp. Brain Res.*, 94, 499–513.

Cordo, P.J., Nashner, L.M. (1982) Properties of postural adjustments associated with rapid arm movements. *J. Neurophysiol.*, 47, 287–302.

Corkin, S. (1984) Lasting consequences of bilateral medial temporal lobectomy: Clinical course and experimental findings in HM. *Sem. Neurol.*, 4, 249–259.

Corkin, S. (2002) What's new with amnesic patient HM? *Nat. Rev. Neurosci.*, 3, 153–160.

Cornsweet, T. (1956) Determinants of stimuli for involuntary drifts and saccadic eye movements. *J. Opt. Soc. Am. B*, 46, 987–993.

Correia, M.J., Hixson, W.C., Niven, J.I. (1968) On predictive equations for subjective judgments of vertical and horizon in a force field. *Acta Otolaryngol. Suppl.*, 230, 1–20.

Coury, B.G. (1999) Water level control for the toilet tank: A historical perspective. In W.S. Levine (ed.) *Control System Applications* (pp. 3–13). New York: CRC Press.

Cowan, N. (2005) *Working Memory Capacity*. Hove, UK: Psychology Press.

Cowey, A. (2009) The blindsight saga. *Exp. Brain Res.*, 200, 3–24.

Cowey, A. (2010) How does blindsight arise? *Curr. Biol.*, 20, R702–R704.

Crago, A., Houk, J.C., Rymer, Z.W. (1982) Sampling of total muscle force by tendon organs. *J. Neurophysiol.*, 47, 1069–1083.

Craig, A.D. (2002) How do you feel? Interoception: the sense of the physiological condition of the body. *Nat. Rev. Neurosci.*, 3, 655–666.

Craske, B. (1977) Perception of impossible limb positions induced by tendon vibration. *Science*, 196, 71–73.

Crawford, J. (1952) Living without a balancing mechanism. *N. Engl. J. Med.*, 246, 458–460.

Crawford, J.D., Medendorp, W.P., Marotta, J.J. (2004) Spatial transformations for eye-hand coordination. *J. Neurophysiol.*, 92, 10–19.

Creath, R., Kiemel, T., Horak, F., Peterka, R., Jeka, J. (2005) A unified view of quiet and perturbed stance: Simultaneous co-existing modes. *Neurosci. Lett.*, 377, 75–80.

Crossman, E.F.R.W. (1959) A theory of the acquisition of speed skill. *Ergonomics*, 2, 153–166.

Crossman, E.F.R.W. (1960) The information capacity of the human motor system in pursuit tracking. *Quart. J. Exp. Psychol.*, 12, 1–16.

Crossman, E.F.R.W., Goodeve, P.J. (1963/1983) Feedback control of hand movement and Fitts' law. *Quart. J. Exp. Psychol.*, 35A, 251–278.

Crowe, A., Matthews, P.C.B. (1964) The effects of stimulation of static and dynamic fusimotor fibres on the response to stretching of the primary endings of muscle spindles. *J. Physiol.*, 174, 109–131.

Crowell, J.A., Banks, M.S. (1993) Perceiving heading with different retinal regions and types of optical flow. *Percept. Psychophys.*, 53, 325–337.

Cruse, H., Bruwer, M. (1987) The human arm as a redundant manipulator: The control of path and joint angles. *Biol. Cybern.*, 57, 137–144.

Curtoys, I.S. (1999) The delay of the oculogravic illusion. *Brain Res. Bull.*, 40, 407–412.

Cutting, J.E. (1986) *Perception with an eye for motion*. Cambridge, MA: MIT Press.

Cutting, J.E. (1996) Wayfinding from multiple sources of local information in retinal flow. *J. Exp. Psychol. Hum. Percept. Perform.*, 22, 1299–1313.

Cutting, J.E., Springer, K., Braren, P., Johnson, S. (1992) Wayfinding on foot from retinal, not optical flow. *J. Exp. Psychol. Gen.*, 121, 41–72.

D.

Dacey, D.M., Liao, H.W., Peterson, B.B., Robinson, F.R., Smith, V.C., Pokorny, J., Yau, K.W., Gamlin, P.D. (2005) Melanopsin-expressing ganglion cells in primate retina signal colour and irradiance and project to the LGN. *Nature*, 433, 749–754.

Dancause, N., Taylor, M.D., Plautz, E.J., Radel, J.D., Whittaker, T., Nudo, R.J., Feldman, A.G. (2007) A stretch reflex in extraocular muscles of species purportedly lacking muscle spindles. *Exp. Brain Res.*, 180, 15–21.

Daniloff, R., Hammarberg, R. (1973) On defining coarticulation. *J. Phonetics*, 1, 239–248.

Darling, W.G. (1991) Perception of forearm angles in three-dimensional space. *Exp. Brain Res.*, 87, 445–456.

Darling, W.G., Hondzinski, J.M. (1999) Kinesthetic perceptions of earth- and body-fixed axes. *Exp. Brain Res.*, 126, 417–430.

Day, B.L., Cole, J.D. (2002) Vestibular evoked postural responses in the absence of somatosensory information. *Brain*, 125, 2081–2088.

Day, B.L., Guerraz, M. (2007) Feedforward *versus* feedback modulation of human vestibular-evoked balance responses by visual self-motion information. *J. Physiol.*, 582, 153–161.

Day, B.L., Steiger, M.J., Thompson, P.D., Marsden, C.D. (1993) Effect of vision and stance width on human body motion when standing: Implications for afferent control of lateral sway. *J. Physiol.*, 469, 479–499.

Dayan, P., Niv., Y. (2008) Reinforcement learning: The good, the bad and the ugly. *Curr. Opin. Neurobiol.*, 18, 185–196.

Degallier, S., Ijspeert, A. (2010) Modeling discrete and rhythmic movements through motor primitives: A review. *Biol. Cybern.*,103, 319–338.

Della Salla, S. (2005) The anarchic hand. *Psychologist*, 18, 606–609.

Della Sala, S., Marchetti, C., Spinnler, H. (1994) The anarchic hand: A frontomesial sign. In F. Boller, J.Grafman (eds) *Handbook of Neuropsychology*, vol. 9 (pp. 233–255). Amsterdam: Elsevier.

Delcomyn, F. (1998) *Foundations of Neurobiology*. New York: W.H. Freeman.

De Leon, R.D., Hodgson, J.A., Roy, R.R., Edgerton, V.R. (1999a) Retention of hindlimb stepping ability in adult spinal cats after the cessation of step training. *J. Neurophysiol.*, 81, 85–94.

De Leon, R.D., London, N.J., Roy, R.R., Edgerton, V.R. (1999b) Failure analysis of stepping in adult spinal cats. *Prog. Brain Res.*, 123, 341–348.

DeLucia, P.R., Liddell, G.W. (1998) Cognitive motion extrapolation and cognitive clocking in judgments of time to contact. *J. Exp. Psychol. Hum. Percept. Perform.*, 24, 901–914.

Denier van der Gon, J.J., Thuring, J.P. (1965) The guiding of human writing movements. *Kybernetik*, 2, 145–148.

Desmurget, M., Epstein, C.M., Turner, R.S., Prablanc, C., Alexander, G.E., Grafton, S.T. (1999) Role of the posterior parietal cortex in updating reaching movements to a visual target. *Nat. Neurosci.*, 2, 563–567.

Desmurget, M., Jordan, M., Prablanc, C., Jeannerod, M. (1997a) Constrained and unconstrained movements involve different control strategies. *J. Neurophysiol.*, 77, 1644–1650.

Desmurget, M., Pelisson, D., Rossetti, Y., Prablanc, C. (1998) From eye to hand: Planning goal-directed movements. *Neurosci. Biobehav. Rev.*, 22, 761–788.

Desmurget, M., Rossetti, Y., Jordan, M., Meckler, C., Prablanc, C. (1997b) Viewing the hand prior to movement improves accuracy of pointing performed toward the unseen contralateral hand. *Exp. Brain Res.*, 115, 180–186.

Desmurget, M., Turner, R.S. (2010) Motor sequences and the basal ganglia: Kinematics not habits. *J. Neurosci.*, 30, 7685–7690.

DeSperati, C., Viviani, P. (1997) The relationship between curvature and velocity in two-dimensional smooth pursuit eye movements. *J. Neurosci.*, 17, 3932–3945.

Dessing, J.C., Bullock, D., Peper, C.L., Beek, P.J. (2002) Prospective control of manual interceptive actions: Comparative simulations of extant and new model constructs. *Neural Netw.*, 14, 163–179.

Dessing, J.C., Peper, C.L., Bullock, D., Beek, P.J. (2005) How position, velocity, and temporal information combine in the prospective control of catching: Data and model. *J. Cogn. Neurosci.*, 17, 668–686.

Deutsch, H., Kilani, H., Moustafa, E., Hamilton, N., Herbert, J.P. (1987) Effect of head-neck position on elbow flexor muscle torque position. *Phys. Ther.*, 67, 517–521.

Dewar, R. (1971) Adaptation to displaced vision: Variations on the 'prismatic-shaping' technique. *Percept. Psychophys.*, 9, 155–157.

Dickinson, A. (1994) Instrumental conditioning. In N.J. Mackintosh (ed.) *Animal Learning and Conditioning* (pp. 45–79). New York: Academic Press.

Dickinson, A., Balleine, B. (1994) Motivational control of goal-directed action. *Anim. Learn. Behav.*, 22, 1–18.

Dickinson, A., Watt, A., Griffiths, W.J.H. (1994) Free-operant acquisition with delayed reinforcement. *Quart. J. Exp. Psychol. B*, 45, 241–258.

Diener, H., Horak, F.B., Nashner, L.M. (1988) Influence of stimulus parameters on human postural responses. *J. Neurophysiol.*, 59, 1888–1905.

Dieterich, M., Brandt, T. (2008) Functional brain imaging of peripheral and central vestibular disorders. *Brain*, 131, 2538–2552.

Dietz, V., Trippel, M., Horstmann, G.A. (1991) Significance of proprioceptive and vestibulo-spinal reflexes in the control of stance and gait. In A.E. Patla (ed.) *Adaptability of Human Gait* (pp. 37–52). Amsterdam: Elsevier.

Dijkstra, T.M.H., Gielen, C.C.A.M., Melis, B.J.M. (1992) Postural responses to stationary and moving scenes as a function of distance to the scene. *Hum. Mov. Sci.*, 1, 195–203.

Dijkstra, T.M.H., Schöner, G., Gielen, C.C.A.M. (1994) Temporal stability of the action-perception cycle for postural control in a moving visual environment. *Exp. Brain Res.*, 97, 477–486.

Dixon, D. (1981) *After Man: A Zoology of the Future*. New York: St Martin's Press.

Djioua, M., Plamondon, R. (2009) A new algorithm and system for the characterization of handwriting strokes with delta-lognormal parameters. *IEEE Transactions on Pattern Analysis, Machine Intelligence*, 31, 2060–2072.

Doeringer, J.A., Hogan, N. (1998) Intermittency in preplanned elbow movements persists in the absence of visual feedback. *J. Neurosci.*, 80, 1787–1799.

Domjan, M. (2005) Pavlovian conditioning: A functional perspective. *Annu. Rev. Psychol.*, 56, 179–206.

Domjan, M. (2010) *The Principles of Learning and Behavior* (6th edition). Belmont, CA: Wadsworth, Cengage Learning.

Donelan, J.M., Kram, R., Kuo, A.D. (2001) Mechanical and metabolic determinants of the preferred step width in human walking. *Proc. Roy. Soc. Lond. B*, 268, 1985–1992.

Donges, E. (1978) A two-level model of driver steering behavior. *Hum. Factors*, 20, 691–707.

Dorf, R.C., Bishop, R.H. (2008) *Modern Control Systems* (11th edition). New York: Prentice Hall.

Doyon, J., Bellec, P., Amsel, R., Penhune, V., Monchi, O., Carrier, J., Lehéricy, S., Benali, H. (2009) Contributions of the basal ganglia and functionally related structures to motor learning. *Behav. Brain Res.*, 199, 61–75.

Drury, C.G. (1975) Application of Fitts' Law to foot pedal design. *Hum. Factors*, 17, 368–373.

Duarte, M., Latash, M.L. (2007) Effects of postural task requirements on the speed-accuracy trade-off. *Exp. Brain Res.*, 180, 457–467.

Dubrovsky, A.S., Cullen, K.E. (2002) Gaze-, eye-, and head-movement dynamics during closed- and open-loop gaze pursuit. *J. Neurophysiol.*, 87, 859–875.

Duchon, A.P., Warren, W.H. (2002) A visual equalization strategy for locomotor control. *Psychol. Sci.*, 13, 272–278.

Du Lac, S., Raymond, J.L., Sejnowski, T.J., Lisberger, S.G. (1995) Learning and memory in the vestibulo-ocular reflex. *Annu. Rev. Neurosci.*, 18, 409–441.

Dutia, M.B., Hunter, M.J. (1985) The sagittal vestibulocollic reflex and its interaction with neck proprioceptive afferents in the decerebrate cat. *J. Physiol.*, 359, 17–29.

E.

Ebenholtz, S.M. (2003) *Oculomotor Systems and Perception*. Cambridge University Press.

Edelman, S., Flash, T. (1987) A model of handwriting. *Biol. Cybern.*, 57, 25–36.

Edin, B.B. (2001) Cutaneous afferents provide information about knee joint movements in humans. *J. Physiol.*, 531, 289–297.

Edin, B.B., Johansson, N. (1995) Skin strain patterns provide kinaesthetic information to the central nervous system. *J. Physiol.*, 487, 243–251.

Edwards, A.S. (1946) Body sway and vision. *J. Exp. Psychol.*, 36, 526–535.

Edwards, W.H. (2010) *Motor Learning and Control: From Theory to Practice*. Pacific Grove, CA: Brooks-Cole.

Ehrsson, H.H., Weich, K., Weiskopf, N., Dolan, R.J., Passingham, R.E. (2007) Threatening a rubber hand that you feel is yours elicits a cortical anxiety response. *Proc. Natl. Acad. Sci. USA*, 104, 9828–9833.

Eimer, M., Schlaghecken, F. (1998) Effects of masked stimuli on motor activation: Behavioral and electrophysiological evidence. *J. Exp. Psychol. Hum. Percept. Perform.*, 24, 1737–1747.

Einstein, A. (1920) *Relativity: The Special and the General Theory* (translated by R.W. Lawson). London: Methuen.

Eklund, G. (1972) General features of vibration-induced effects on balance. *Ups. J. Med. Sci.*, 77, 112–124.

Elliott, D. (1986) Continuous visual information may be important after all: A failure to replicate Thomson (1983). *J. Exp. Psychol. Hum. Percept. Perform.*, 12, 388–391.

Elliott, D. (1988) The influence of visual target and limb information on manual aiming. *Can. J. Psychol.*, 42, 57–68.

Elliott, D., Binsted, G., Heath, M. (1999) The control of goal-directed limb movements: Correcting errors in the trajectory. *Hum. Mov. Sci.*, 18, 121–136.

Elliott, D., Hansen, S., Grierson, L.E., Lyons, J., Bennett, S.J., Hayes, S.J. (2010) Goal-directed aiming: Two components but multiple processes. *Psychol. Bull.*, 136, 1023–1044.

Elliott, D., Helsen, W.F., Chua, R. (2001) A century later: Woodworth's (1899) two-component model of goal-directed aiming. *Psychol. Bull.*, 127, 342–357.

Elwell, J.L., Grindley, G.C. (1938) The effect of knowledge of results on learning and performance. I. A co-ordinated movement of the two hands. *Br. J. Psychol.*, 29, 39–54.

Eng, J.J., Winter, D.A., Patla, A.E. (1994) Strategies for recovery from a trip in early and late swing during human walking. *Exp. Brain Res.*, 102, 339–349.

Engel, K.C., Flanders, M., Soechting, J.F. (1997) Anticipatory and sequential motor control in piano playing. *Exp. Brain Res.*, 113, 189–199.

Enoka, R. (2008) *Neuromechanics of Human Movement* (4th edition). Champaign, IL: Human Kinetics.

Enright, J.T. (1996) Slow-velocity asymmetrical convergence: A decisive failure of Hering's Law. *Vision Res.*, 36, 3667–3684.

Erkelens, C.J., Regan, D. (1986) Human ocular vergence movements induced by changing size and disparity. *J. Physiol.*, 379, 145–169.

Erkelens, C.J., Steinman, R.M., Collewijn, H. (1989a) Ocular vergence under natural conditions. II: Gaze shifts between real targets differing in distance and direction. *Proc. Roy. Soc. Lond. B*, 236, 441–465.

Erkelens, C.J., Van der Steen, J., Steinman, R.M., Collewijn, H. (1989b) Ocular vergence under natural conditions. I: Continuous changes in target distance along the median plane. *Proc. Roy. Soc. Lond. B*, 236, 417–440.

Esmoris-Arranz, F.J., Pardo-Vazquez, J.L., Vazquez-Garcia, G.A. (2003) Differential effects of forward or simultaneous conditioned stimulus-unconditioned stimulus intervals on the defensive behavior system of the Norway rat (*Rattus norvegicus*). *J. Exp. Psychol. Anim. Behav. Proc.*, 29, 334–340.

Estes, W.K. (1956) The problem of inference from curves based on group data. *Psychol. Bull.*, 53, 134–140.

F.

Farnetani, E., Racesans, D. (2010) Coarticulation and connected speech processes. In W.J. Hardcastle, J. Laver, F.E. Gibbon (eds) *The Handbook of Phonetic Sciences* (2nd edition). Oxford: Blackwell.

Fasold, O., von Brevern, M., Kuhberg, M., Ploner, C., Villringer, A., Lempert, T., Rudiger, W. (2002) Human vestibular cortex as identified with caloric stimulation in functional magnetic resonance imaging. *NeuroImage*, 17, 1384–1393.

Feldman, A.G. (1980a) Superposition of motor programs I – rhythmic forearm movements in man. *Neuroscience*, 5, 81–90.

Feldman, A.G. (1980b) Superposition of motor programs II – rapid forearm flexion in man. *Neuroscience*, 5, 91–95.

Feldman, A.G. (1986) Once more on the equilibrium point hypothesis (lambda model) for motor control. *J. Mot. Behav.*, 18, 17–54.

Feldman, A.G., Adamovich, S.V., Ostry, D.J., Flanagan, J.R. (1990) The origins of electromyograms – explanations based on the equilibrium point hypothesis. In J.M. Winters, S.L.-Y. Woo (eds) *Multiple Muscle Systems. Biomechanics and Movement Organization*. New York: Springer-Verlag.

Feldman, A.G., Latash, M.L. (1982) Afferent and efferent components of joint position sense: Interpretation of kinaesthetic illusions. *Biol. Cybern.*, 42, 205–214.

Feldman, A.G., Latash, M.L. (2005) Testing hypotheses and the advancement of science: Recent attempts to falsify the equilibrium point hypothesis. *Exp. Brain Res.*, 161, 91–103.

Feldman, A.G., Levin, M.F. (1995) The origin and use of positional frames of reference in motor control. *Behav. Brain Sci.*, 18, 723–744.

Feldman, A.G., Levin, M.F. (2009) The equilibrium-point hypothesis – past, present and future. *Adv. Exp. Med. Biol.*, 629, 699–726.

Feldman, A.G., Orlovsky, G.N. (1972) The influence of different descending systems on the tonic stretch reflex in the cat. *Exp. Neurol.*, 37, 481–494.

Feldman, D.E. (2009) Synaptic mechanisms for plasticity in neocortex. *Annu. Rev. Neurosci.*, 32, 33–55.

Fernandez-Ruiz, J., Hall-Haro, C., Diaz, R., Mischner, J., Vergara, P., Lopez-Garcia, J.C. (2000) Learning motor synergies makes use of information on muscular load. *Learn. Mem.*, 7, 193–198.

Ferrell, W.R., Gandevia, S.C., McCloskey, D.I. (1987) The role of joint receptors in human kinaesthesia when intramuscular receptors cannot contribute. *J. Physiol.*, 386, 63–71.

Feynman, R.P., Leighton, R.B., Sands, M. (1970) *The Feynman Lectures on Physics*, vol. 1. Addison Wesley.

Field, D.P., Shipley, T.F., Cunningham, D.W. (1999) Prism adaptation to dynamic events. *Percept. Psychophys.*, 61, 161–176.

Fincham, E.F. (1951) The accommodation reflex and its stimulus. *Br. J. Ophthalmol.*, 35, 381–393.

Findlay, J.M., Gilchrist, I.D. (2003) *Active Vision: The Psychology of Looking and Seeing*. New York: Oxford University Press.

Fitts, P.M. (1951) Engineering psychology and equipment design. In S.S. Stevens (ed.) *Handbook of Experimental Psychology*. New York: Wiley.

Fitts, P.M. (1954) The information capacity of the human motor system in controlling the amplitude of movement. *J. Exp. Psychol.*, 47, 381–391.

Fitts, P.M., Peterson, J.R. (1964) Information capacity of discrete motor responses. *J. Exp. Psychol.*, 67, 103–112.

Fitts, P.M., Posner, M. (1967) *Human Performance*. Belmont, CA: Brooks-Cole.

Fitts, P.M., Radford, B.K. (1966) Information capacity of discrete motor responses under different cognitive sets. *J. Exp. Psychol.*, 71, 475–482.

Fitzpatrick, R.C., Day, B.L. (2004) Probing the human vestibular system with galvanic stimulation. *J. Appl. Physiol.*, 96, 2301–2316.

Fitzpatrick, R.C., Gandevia, S. (2005) Paradoxical muscle contractions and the neural control of movement and balance. *J. Physiol.*, 564, 2.

Fitzpatrick, R.C., McCloskey, D.I. (1994) Proprioceptive, visual and vestibular thresholds for the perception of sway during standing in humans. *J. Physiol.*, 478, 173–186.

Fitzpatrick, R.C., Rogers, D.K., McCloskey, D.I. (1994) Stable human standing with lower-limb muscle afferents providing the only sensory input. *J. Physiol.*, 480, 395–403.

Fitzpatrick, R.C., Taylor, J.L., McCloskey, D.I. (1992) Ankle stiffness of standing humans in response to imperceptible perturbation: Reflex and task dependent components. *J. Physiol.*, 454, 533–537.

Flach, J.M., Warren, R., Kelly, L., Stanard, T. (1997) Perception and control of altitude: Splay and depression angles. *J. Exp. Psychol. Hum. Percept. Perform.*, 23, 1764–1782.

Flanagan, J.R., Ostry, D.J. (1990) Trajectories of human multi-joint arm movements: Evidence of joint level planning. In V. Hayward, O. Khatib (eds) *Experimental Robotics 1* (pp. 594–613). London: Springer-Verlag.

Flanagan, J.R., Ostry, D.J., Feldman, A.G. (1993) Control of trajectory modifications in target directed reaching. *J. Mot. Behav.*, 25, 140–152.

Flanagan, J.R., Rao, A.K. (1995) Trajectory adaptation to a nonlinear visuomotor transformation: Evidence for motion planning in visually perceived space. *J. Neurophysiol.*, 74, 2174–2178.

Flanders, M., Helms-Tillery, S.I., Soechting, J.F. (1992) Early stages in a sensorimotor transformation. *Behav. Brain Sci.*, 15, 309–320.

Flanders, M., Soechting, J.F. (1992) Kinematics of typing: Parallel control of the two hands. *J. Neurophysiol.*, 67, 1264–1274.

Flash, T. (1987) The control of hand equilibrium trajectories in multi-joint arm movements. *Biol. Cybern.*, 57, 257–274.

Flash, T., Handzel, A. (2007) Affine differential geometry analysis of human arm movements. *Biol. Cybern.*, 96, 577–601.

Flash, T., Henis, E. (1991) Arm trajectory modifications during reaching towards visual targets. *J. Cog. Neurosci.*, 3, 220–230.

Flash, T., Hochner, B. (2005) Motor primitives in vertebrates and invertebrates. *Curr. Opin. Neurobiol.*, 15, 660–666.

Flash, T., Hogan, N. (1985) The coordination of arm movements: An experimentally confirmed mathematical model. *J. Neurosci.*, 5, 1688–1703.

Flash, T., Hollerbach, J.M. (1982) Dynamic interactions between limb segments during planar arm movements. *Biol. Cybern.*, 44, 67–77.

Flynn, J.P. (1972) Patterning mechanisms, patterned reflexes, and attack behavior in cats. *Nebraska Symposium on Motivation*, 20, 125–153.

Foley, J.M. (1980) Binocular distance perception. *Psychol. Rev.*, 87, 411–434.

Forget, R., Lamarre, Y. (1987) Rapid elbow flexion in the absence of proprioceptive and cutaneous feedback. *Hum. Neurobiol.*, 6, 27–37.

Forssberg, H. (1979) Stumbling corrective reaction: A phase-dependent compensatory reaction during locomotion. *J. Neurophysiol.*, 42, 936–953.

Forssberg, H., Grillner, S., Halbertsma, J., Rossignol, S. (1980) The locomotion of the low spinal cat. II: Interlimb coordination. *Acta Physiol. Scand.*, 108, 283–295.

Fouad, K., Pearson, K. (2004) Restoring walking after spinal cord injury. *Prog. Neurobiol.*, 73, 107–126.

Fowler, C.A. (1996) Speaking. In H. Heuer, S.W. Keele (eds) *Handbook of Perception and Action vol. 2: Motor Skills*. Hillsdale NJ: Lawrence Erlbaum.

Fowler, C.A. (2003) Speech production and perception. In A.F. Healy, R.W. Proctor (eds) *Handbook of Psychology, vol. 4: Experimental Psychology* (pp. 237–268). New York: Wiley.

Fowler, C.A. (2007) Speech production. In M.G. Gaskell (ed.) *The Oxford Handbook of Psycholinguistics* (pp. 489–501). New York: Oxford University Press.

Fowler, C.A., Saltzman, E.L. (1993) Coordination and coarticulation in speech production. *Lang. Speech*, 36, 171–195.

Fradet, L., Lee, G., Dounskaia, N. (2008) Origins of submovements during pointing movements. *Acta Psychol.*, 129, 91–100.

Fraenkel, G.S., Gunn, D.L. (1940) *The Orientation of Animals*. New York: Oxford University Press.

Fraizer, E.V., Mitra, S. (2008) Methodological and interpretive issues in posture-cognition dual-tasking in upright stance. *Gait Posture*, 27, 271–279.

Franks, I.M., Wilberg, R.B. (1982) The generation of movement patterns during the acquisition of a pursuit tracking skill. *Hum. Mov. Sci.*, 1, 251–272.

Fredericks, C.A., Giolli, R.A., Blanks, R.H., Sadun, A.A. (1988) The human accessory optic system. *Brain Res.*, 454, 116–122.

Freedman, E.G. (2008) Coordination of the eyes and head during visual orienting. *Exp. Brain Res.*, 190, 369–387.

Frost, B.J., Sun, H. (2004) The biological bases of time-to-collision computation. In H. Hecht, G.J.P. Savelsbergh (eds) *Time-to-Contact*. Amsterdam: Elsevier.

Fuentes, C.T., Bastian, A.J. (2010) Where is your arm? Variations in proprioception across space and tasks. *J. Neurophysiol.*, 103, 164–171.

Fukuda, T. (1961) Studies on human dynamic postures from the viewpoint of postural reflexes. *Acta Oto-Laryngol., Suppl.*, 161, 1–52.

Fukushima, K. (1997) Corticovestibular interactions: Anatomy, electrophysiology, and functional considerations. *Exp. Brain Res.*, 117, 1–16.

Fuller, J.H. (1992) Head movement propensity. *Exp. Brain Res.*, 92, 152–164.

G.

Gage, W.H., Winter, D.A., Frank, J.S., Adkin, A.L. (2004) Kinematic and kinetic validity of the inverted pendulum model in quiet standing. *Gait Posture*, 19, 124–132.

Gallistel, C.R. (1980) *The Organization of Action: A New Synthesis*. Hillsdale, NJ: Lawrence Erlbaum.

Gallistel, C.R., Fairhurst, S., Balsam, P. (2004) The learning curve: Implications of a quantitative analysis. *Proc. Natl. Acad. Sci. USA*, 101, 13124–13131.

Gambra, E., Wang, Y., Yuan, J., Kruger, P.B., Marcos, S. (2010) Dynamic accommodation with simulated targets blurred with high order aberrations. *Vision Res.*, 50, 1922–1927.

Gan, K.-C., Hoffman, E.R. (1988) Geometrical conditions for ballistic and visually controlled movements. *Ergonomics*, 31, 829–839.

Gancarz, G., Grossberg, S. (1998) A neural model of the saccade generator in the reticular formation. *Neural Netw.*, 11, 1159–1174.

Gandevia, S.C. (1987) Roles for perceived motor commands in motor control. *Trends Neurosci.*, 10, 81–85.

Gandevia, S.C. (1996) Kinaesthesia: Roles for afferent signals and motor commands. In L.B. Rowell, T.J. Sheperd (eds) *Handbook of Physiology*, section 12, Exercise: Regulation and integration of multiple systems (pp. 128–172). New York: Oxford University Press.

Gandevia, S.C., Burke, D. (1992) Does the nervous system depend on kinaesthetic information to control natural limb movements? *Behav. Brain Sci.*, 15, 614–632.

Gandevia, S.C., Hall, L.A., McCloskey, D.I., Potter, K.E. (1983) Proprioceptive sensation at the terminal joint of the middle finger. *J. Physiol.*, 335, 507–517.

Gandevia, S.C., McCloskey, D.I. (1976) Joint sense, muscle sense, and their combination as position sense measured at the distal interphalangeal joint on the middle finger. *J. Physiol.*, 260, 387–407.

Gandevia, S.C., McCloskey, D.I. (1977) Sensations of heaviness. *Brain*, 100, 345–354.

Gandevia, S.C., Smith, J., Crawford, M., Proske, U., Taylor, J.L. (2006) Motor commands contribute to human position sense. *J. Physiol.*, 571, 703–710.

Gatev, P., Thomas, S., Kepple, T., Hallett, M. (1999) Feedforward ankle strategy of balance during quiet stance in adults. *J. Physiol.*, 514, 915–928.

Gauthier, G., Robinson, D.A. (1975) Adaptation of the human vestibuloocular reflex to magnifying lenses. *Brain Res.*, 92, 331–335.

Gawthrop, P., Loram, I., Lakie, M., Gollee, H. (2011) Intermittent control: A computational theory of human control. *Biol. Cybern.*, 104, 31–51.

Gerasimenko, Y., Roy, R.R., Edgerton, V.R. (2008) Epidural stimulation: Comparison of the spinal circuits that generate and control locomotion in rats, cats and humans. *Exp. Neurol.*, 209, 417–425.

Gentner, D.R. (1982) Evidence against a central control model of timing in typing. *J. Exp. Psychol. Hum. Percept. Perform.*, 6, 793–810.

Gentner, D.R. (1983) The acquisition of typewriting skill. *Acta Psychol.*, 54, 233–284.

Gentner, D.R. (1987) Timing of skilled motor performance: Tests of the proportional duration model. *Psychol. Rev.*, 94, 255–276.

Georgopoulos, A.P. (1986) On reaching. *Annu. Rev. Neurosci.*, 9, 147–170.

Georgopoulos, A.P., Kalaska, J.F., Massey, J.T. (1981) Spatial trajectories and reaction times of aimed movements: Effects of practice, uncertainty and change in target location. *J. Neurophysiol.*, 46, 725–743.

Ghafouri, M., Feldman, A.G. (2001) The timing of control signals underlying fast point-to-point arm movements. *Exp. Brain Res.*, 137, 411–423.

Ghez, C., Favilla, M., Ghilardi, M.F., Gordon, J., Bermejo, R., Pullman, S. (1997) Discrete and continuous planning of hand movements and isometric force trajectories. *Exp. Brain Res.*, 115, 217–233.

Ghez, C., Gordon, J., Ghilardi, M.F. (1995) Impairments of reaching movements in patients without proprioception, II: Effects of visual information on accuracy. *J. Neurophysiol.*, 73, 361–372.

Gibson, J.J. (1958) Visually controlled locomotion and visual orientation in animals. *Br. J. Psychol.*, 49, 182–194.

Gibson, J.J. (1962) Observations on active touch. *Psychol. Rev.*, 69, 6, 477–491.

Gibson, J.J. (1966) *The Senses Considered as Perceptual Systems*. Boston: Houghton Mifflin.

Gibson, J.J. (1979) *The Ecological Approach to Visual Perception*. Boston: Houghton Mifflin.

Giszter, S., Patil, V., Hart, C. (2007) Primitives, premotor drives, and pattern generation: A combined computational and neuroethological perspective. *Prog. Brain Res.*, 165, 323–346.

Glanzman, D.L. (2009) Habituation in Aplysia: The Cheshire Cat of neurobiology. *Neurobiol. Learn. Mem.*, 92, 147–154.

Glanzman, D.L. (2010) Common mechanisms of synaptic plasticity in vertebrates and invertebrates. *Curr. Biol.*, 20, R31–R36.

Glaser, J.S. (1999) *Neuro-Ophthalmology* (3rd edition). Philadelphia: Lippincott Williams, Wilkins.

Godthelp, H. (1988) The limits of path error-neglecting in straight lane driving. *Ergonomics*, 31, 609–619.

Goldberg, J.M., Cullen, K.E. (2011) Vestibular control of the head: Possible functions of the vestibulocollic reflex. *Exp. Brain Res.*, 210, 331–345.

Goldberg, J.M., Fernandez, C. (1971) Physiology of peripheral neurons innervating semicircular canals of the squirrel monkey, I. Resting discharge and response to constant angular accelerations. *J. Neurophysiol.*, 34, 635–660.

Gonshor, A., Melvill Jones, G. (1976a) Short-term adaptive changes in the human vestibulo-ocular reflex arc. *J. Physiol.*, 256, 361–379.

Gonshor, A., Melvill Jones, G. (1976b) Extreme vestibulo-ocular adaptation induced by prolonged optical reversal of vision. *J. Physiol.*, 256, 381–414.

Goodale, M.A., Milner, A.D. (1992) Separate visual pathways for perception and action. *Trends Neurosci.*, 15, 20 25.

Goodale, M.A., Milner, A.D., Jakobson, L.S., Carey, D.P. (1991) A neurological dissociation between perceiving objects and grasping them. *Nature*, 349, 154–156.

Goodale, M.A., Pelisson, D., Prablanc, C. (1986) Large adjustments in visually guided reaching do not depend on vision of the hand or perception of target displacement. *Nature*, 320, 748–750.

Goodman, D., Kelso, J.A.S. (1980) Are movements prepared in parts? Not under compatible (naturalized) conditions. *J. Exp. Psychol. Gen.*, 109, 475–495.

Goodman, S.R., Gottlieb, G.L. (1995) Analysis of kinematic invariances of multijoint reaching movement. *Biol. Cybern.*, 73, 311–322.

Goodwin, G.C., Graebe, S.F., Salgado, M.E. (2006) *Control System Design*. New York: Prentice Hall.

Goodwin, G.M., McCloskey, D.I., Matthews, P.C.B. (1972) The contribution of muscle afferents to kinaesthesia shown by vibration induced illusions of movement and by the effects of paralysing joint afferents. *Brain*, 95, 705–748.

Goossens, H.H.L.M., Van Opstal, A.J. (2006) Dynamic ensemble coding of saccades in monkey superior colliculus. *J. Neurophysiol.*, 95, 2326–2341.

Gordon, A.M., Soechting, J.F. (1995) Use of tactile afferent information in sequential finger movements. *Exp. Brain Res.*, 107, 281–292.

Gordon, J., Ghilardi, M.F., Ghez, C. (1994a) Accuracy of planar reaching movements, I: Independence of direction and extent variability. *Exp. Brain Res.*, 99, 97–111.

Gordon, J., Ghilardi, M.F., Cooper, S.E., Ghez, C. (1994b) Accuracy of planar reaching movements, II: Systematic extent errors resulting from intertial anisotropy. *Exp. Brain Res.*, 99, 112–130.

Gormezano, I. (1966) Classical conditioning. In J.B. Sidowski (ed.), *Experimental Methods and Instrumentation in Psychology* (pp. 385–420). New York: McGraw-Hill.

Gottlieb, G.L. (1993) A computational model of the simplest motor program. *J. Mot. Behav.*, 25, 153–161.

Gottlieb, G.L., Corcos, D.M., Agarwal, G.C. (1989a) Organizing principles for single-joint movements, I: A speed insensitive strategy. *J. Neurophysiol.*, 62, 342–357.

Gottlieb, G.L., Corcos, D.M., Agarwal, G.C. (1989b) Strategies for the control of voluntary movement with one mechanical degree of freedom. *Behav. Brain Sci.*, 12, 189–250.

Gracco, V.L., Abbs, J.H. (1985) Dynamic control of perioral system during speech: Kinematic analysis of autogenic and nonautogenic sensorimotor processes. *J. Neurophysiol.*, 54, 418–432.

Gracco, V.L., Abbs, J.H. (1989) Sensorimotor characteristics of speech motor sequences. *Exp. Brain Res.*, 75, 586–598.

Graf, P., Schacter, D.L. (1985) Implicit and explicit memory for new associations in normal and amnesic subjects. *J. Exp. Psychol. Learn. Mem. Cogn.*, 11, 501–518.

Graham Brown, T.G. (1911) The intrinsic factors in the act of progression in the mammal. *Proc. Roy. Soc. Lond. B*, 84, 308–319.

Granit, R. (1970) *The Basis of Motor Control.* London: Academic Press.

Grasso, R., Prevost, P., Ivanenko, Y.P., Berthoz, A. (1998) Eye-head coordination for the steering of locomotion in humans: An anticipatory synergy. *Neurosci. Lett.*, 253, 115–118.

Grau, J.W., Crown, E.D., Ferguson, A.R., Washburn, S.N., Hook, M., Miranda, R.C. (2006) Instrumental learning within the spinal cord: Underlying mechanisms and implications for recovery after injury. *Behav. Cogn. Neurosci. Rev.*, 5, 1–48.

Gray, R. (2002) Behavior of college baseball players in a virtual batting task. *J. Exp. Psychol. Hum. Perc. Perform.*, 28, 1131–1148.

Gray, R., Regan, D. (1998) Accuracy of estimating time to collision using binocular and monocular information. *Vision Res.*, 38, 499–512.

Graybiel, A. (1952) Oculogravic illusion. *AMA Arch. Ophthalmol.*, 48, 605–615.

Graziano, M.S.A. (2006) The organization of behavioural repertoire in motor cortex. *Annu. Rev. Neurosci.*, 29, 105–134.

Graziano, M.S.A. (2010) Ethologically relevant movements mapped onto the motor cortex. In M.A. Platt, A. Ghazanfar (eds), *Primate Neuroethology* (pp. 454–470). New York: Oxford University Press.

Graziano, M.S.A., Aflalo, T.N. (2007) Mapping behavioral repertoire onto the cortex. *Neuron*, 56, 239–251.

Green, A.M., Angelaki, D.E. (2010a) Multisensory integration: Resolving sensory ambiguities to build novel representations. *Curr. Opin. Neurobiol.*, 20, 353–360.

Green, A.M., Angelaki, D.E. (2010b) Internal models and neural computation in the vestibular system. *Exp. Brain Res.*, 200, 197–222.

Gribble, P.L., Mullin, L.I., Cothros, N., Mattar, A. (2003) Role of cocontraction in arm movement accuracy. *J. Neurophysiol.*, 89, 2396–2405.

Gribble, P.L., Ostry, D. (1996) Origins of the power law relation between movement velocity and curvature: Modeling the effects of muscle mechanics and limb dynamics. *J. Neurophysiol.*, 76, 2853–2860.

Grice, G.R. (1948) The relation of secondary reinforcement to delayed reward in visual discrimination learning. *J. Exp. Psychol.*, 38, 1–16.

Griffin, T.M., Tolani, N.A., Kram, R. (1999) Walking in simulated reduced gravity: Mechanical energy fluctuations and exchange. *J. Appl. Physiol.*, 86, 383–390.

Grigg, P., Finerman, G.A., Riley, L.H. (1973) Joint-position sense after total hip replacement. *J. Bone Joint Surg. Am.*, 55, 1016–1025.

Grillner, S. (1985) Neurobiological bases of rhythmic motor acts in vertebrates. *Science*, 228, 143–149.

Grillner, S., Hellgren, J., Ménard, A., Saitoh, K., Wikström, M.A. (2005) Mechanisms for selection of basic motor programs – roles for the striatum and pallidum. *Trends Neurosci.*, 28, 364–370.

Grillner, S., Rossignol, S. (1978) On the initiation of the swing phase of locomotion in chronic spinal cats. *Brain Res.*, 146, 269–277.

Grillner, S., Wallen, P. (2002) Cellular bases of a vertebrate locomotion system – steering, intersegmental and segmental coordination and sensory control. *Brain Res. Rev.*, 40, 92–106.

Grohmann, J. (1939) Modifikation order Funktionsreifung? Ein Betrag zur Klärung der wechselseitigen Beziehungen zwischen Instinkthandlung und Erfahrung. *Zeitschrift für Tierpsychologie*, 2, 132–144.

Grossberg, S., Paine, R.W. (2000) A neural model of corticocerebellar interactions during attentive imitation and predictive learning of sequential handwriting movements. *Neural Netw.*, 13, 999–1046.

Grossman, G.E., Leigh, R.J., Abel, L.A., Lanska, D.J., Thurstone, S.E. (1988) Frequency and velocity of rotational head perturbations during locomotion. *Exp. Brain Res.*, 70, 470–476.

Grossman, G.E., Leigh, R.J., Bruce, E.N., Huebner, W.P., Lanska, D.J. (1989) Performance of the human vestibulo-ocular reflex during locomotion. *J. Neurophysiol.*, 62, 264–272.

Groves, P.M., Thompson, R.F. (1970) Habituation: A dual process theory. *Psychol. Rev.*, 77, 419–450.

Guenther, F.H. (1994) A neural network model of speech acquisition and motor equivalent speech production. *Biol. Cybern.*, 72, 43–53.

Guenther, F.H. (1995) Speech sound acquisition, coarticulation, and rate effects in a neural network model of speech production. *Psychol. Rev.*, 102, 594–621.

Guenther, F.H., Hampson, M., Johnson, D. (1998) A theoretical investigation of reference frames for the planning of speech movements. *Psychol. Rev.*, 105, 611–633.

Guest, E.A. (1947) *Collected Verse of Edgar A. Guest.* Chicago, Reilly & Lee Co.

Guldin, W.O., Grusser, O.J. (1998) Is there a vestibular cortex? *Trends Neurosci.*, 21, 254–259.

Gurfinkel, V.S., Ivanenko, Y.P., Levik, Y.S., Babakova, I.A. (1995) Kinesthetic reference for human orthograde posture. *Neuroscience*, 68, 229–243.

Guthrie, B.L., Porter, J.D., Sparks, D.L. (1983) Corollary discharge provides accurate eye position information to the oculomotor system. *Science*, 221, 1193–1195.

Gutman, S.R., Latash, M.L., Almeida, G., Gottlieb, G.L. (1993) Kinematic description of variability of fast movements: Analytical and experimental approaches. *Biol. Cybern.*, 69, 485–492.

H.

Haggard, P.N., Hutchinson, K., Stein, J. (1995) Patterns of coordinated multijoint movement. *Exp. Brain Res.*, 107, 254–266

Haggard, P.N., Newman, C., Blundell, J., Andrew, H. (2000) The perceived position of the hand in space. *Percept. Psychophys.*, 68, 363–377.

Haggard, P.N., Richardson, J. (1996) Spatial patterns in the control of human arm movement. *J. Exp. Psychol. Hum. Percept. Perform.*, 22, 42–62.

Hamman, R.G., Mekjavic, I., Mallinson, A., Longridge, N.S. (1992) Training effects during repeated therapy sessions of balance training using visual feedback. *Arch. Phys. Med. Rehabil.*, 73, 738–744.

Hancock, G.R., Butler, M.S., Fischman, M.G. (1995) On the problem of two-dimensional error scores: Measures and analyses of accuracy, bias, and consistency. *J. Mot. Behav.*, 27, 241–250.

Hanna, J.P., Frank, J.I. (1995) Automatic stepping in the pontomedullary stage of central herniation. *Neurology*, 45, 985–986.

Harel, D., Feldman, Y. (2004) *Algorithmics: The Spirit of Computing* (3rd edition). Harlow, UK: Addison Wesley.

Harkema, S.J. (2008) Plasticity of interneuronal networks of the functionally isolated human spinal cord. *Brain Res. Rev.*, 57, 255–264.

Harris, A.J., Duxson, M.J., Butler, J.E., Hodges, P.W., Taylor, J.L., Gandevia, S.C. (2005) Muscle fiber and motor unit behavior in the longest human skeletal muscle. *J. Neurosci.*, 25, 8528–8533.

Harris, C.H. (1965) Perceptual adaptation to inverted, reversed and displaced vision. *Psychol. Rev.*, 72, 419–444.

Harris, C.M., Wolpert, D.M. (1998) Signal dependent noise determines motor planning. *Nature*, 394, 780–784.

Harris, M.G., Carre, G. (2001) Is optic flow used to guide walking while wearing a displacing prism? *Perception*, 30, 811–818.

Hasan, Z. (1986) Optimized movement trajectories and joint stiffness in unperturbed, inertially loaded movements. *Biol. Cybern.*, 53, 373–382.

Hashemi, R., Bradley, W.G., Lisanti, C.J. (2010) *MRI: The Basics.* Philadelphia: Lippincott, Williams, Wilkins.

Hawkins, R.D., Abrams, T.W., Carew, T.J., Kandel, E.R. (1983) A cellular mechanism of classical conditioning in Aplysia: Activity-dependent amplification of presynaptic facilitation. *Science*, 219, 400–405.

Heathcote, A., Brown, S., Mewhort, D.J. (2000) The power law repealed: The case for an exponential law of practice. Psychon. *Bull. Rev.* 7, 185–207.

Held, R., Efstathiou, A., Greene, M. (1966) Adaptation to displaced and delayed visual feedback from the hand. *J. Exp. Psychol.*, 72, 887–891.

Hellebrandt, E. (1938) Standing as a geotropic reflex. The mechanism of the asynchronous rotation of motor units. *Am. J. Physiol.*, 121, 471–474.

Hellebrandt, F.A., Houtz, S.J., Partridge, M.J., Walters, C. (1956) Tonic reflexes in exercises of stress in man. *Am. J. Phys. Med.*, 35, 144–159.

Helmholtz, H. von (1925) *Treatise on Physiological Optics*, vol. III (3rd edition, translated by J.P.C. Southall). Optical Society of America.

Helms Tillery, S.I., Flanders, M., Soechting, J.F. (1991) A coordinate system for the synthesis of visual and kinaesthetic information. *J. Neurosci.*, 11, 770–778.

Henneman, E. (1979) Functional organization of motoneuron pools: The size principle. In H. Asanuma, V.J. Wilson (eds) *Integration in the Nervous System* (pp. 13–25). Tokyo: Igaku-Shoin.

Henry, F.M. (1980) Use of simple reaction time in motor programming studies: A reply to Klapp, Wyatt, and Lingo. *J. Mot. Behav.*, 12, 163–168.

Henry, F.M., Rogers, D.E. (1960) Increased response latency for complicated movements and a memory drum theory of neuromotor reaction. *Res. Quart.*, 31, 448–458.

Heuer, H. (1988) Testing the invariance of relative timing: comment on Gentner (1987). *Psychol. Rev.*, 95, 552–558.

Heuer, H. (1991) Invariant relative timing in motor program theory. In J. Fagard, P.H. Wolff (eds) *The Development of Timing Control and Temporal Organization in Coordinated Action*, 37–68. Amsterdam: Elsevier.

Hewlett, N., Beck, J.M. (2006) *An Introduction to the Science of Phonetics.* Hillsdale, NJ: Lawrence Erlbaum.

Hildreth, E.C., Beusmans, J.M., Boer, E.R., Royden, C.S. (2000) From vision to action: Experiments and models of steering control during driving. *J. Exp. Psychol. Hum. Percept. Perform.*, 26, 1106–1132.

Hirasaki, E., Moore, S.T., Raphan, T., Cohen, B. (1999) Effects of walking velocity on vertical head and body movements during locomotion. *Exp. Brain Res.*, 127, 117–130.

Hodges, P.W., Gurfinkel, V.S., Brumagne, S., Smith, T.C., Cordo, P. (2002) Coexistence of stability and mobility in postural control: Evidence from postural compensation for respiration. *Exp. Brain Res.*, 144, 293–302.

Hoff, B., Arbib, M.A. (1993) Models of trajectory formation and temporal interaction of reach and grasp. *J. Mot. Behav.*, 25, 175–192.

Hoffman, E.R., Sheikh, I.H. (1991) Finger width corrections in Fitts' law: Implications for speed-accuracy research. *J. Mot. Behav.*, 23, 259–262.

Hoffman, E.R., Sheikh, I.H. (1994) Effect of varying target height in a Fitts movement task. *Ergonomics*, 37, 1071–1088.

Hogan, N. (1984) An organizing principle for a class of voluntary movements. *J. Neurosci.*, 4, 2745–2754.

Hogan, N., Flash, T. (1987) Moving gracefully: Quantitative theories of motor coordination. *Trends Neurosci.*, 10, 170–174.

Hogan, N., Sternad, D. (2007) On rhythmic and discrete movements: Reflections, definitions and implications for motor control. *Exp. Brain Res.*, 181, 13–30.

Hohmann, G., Robbins, M.M., Boesch, C. (eds) (2006) *Feeding Ecology in Apes and Other Primates: Ecological, Physiological and Behavioral Aspects.* Cambridge University Press.

Hollands, M.A., Vickers, J.N., Patla, A.E. (2002) 'Look where you're going!' Gaze behaviour associated with maintaining and changing the direction of locomotion. *Exp. Brain Res.*, 143, 221–230.

Hollerbach, J.M. (1981) An oscillation theory of handwriting. *Biol. Cybern.*, 39, 139–156.

Hollerbach, J.M. (1982) Computers, brains and the control of movement. *Trends Neurosci.*, 5, 189–192.

Hollerbach, J.M., Atkeson, C.G. (1987) Deducing planning variables from experimental arm trajectories: pitfalls and possibilities. *Biol. Cybern.*, 56, 279–292.

Horak, F.B. (2010) Postural compensation for vestibular loss. *Restor. Neurol. Neurosci.*, 28, 57–68.

Horak, F.B., MacPherson, J.M. (1996) Postural orientation and equilibrium. In L.B. Rowell, J.T. Shepherd (eds) *Handbook of Physiology*, section 12, Exercise: regulation and integration of multiple systems (pp. 255–292). New York: Oxford University Press.

Horak, F.B., Nashner, L.M. (1986) Central programming of postural movements: Adaptation to altered support-surface configurations. *J. Neurophysiol.*, 55, 1369–1381.

Horlings, C.G.C., Carpenter, M.G., Honegger, F., Allum, J.J. (2009) Vestibular and proprioceptive contributions to human balance corrections. *Ann. N.Y. Acad. Sci.*, 1164, 1–12.

Houk, J.C. (1979) Regulation of stiffness by skeletomotor reflexes. *Annu. Rev. Physiol.*, 41, 99–114.

How, M.J., Zeil, J., Hemmi, J.M. (2009) Variability of a dynamic visual signal: The fiddler crab claw-waving display. *J. Comp. Physiol.* A, 195, 55–67.

Howard, I.P. (1968) Displacing the optical array. In S.J. Freedman (ed.), *The Neuropsychology of Spatially Oriented Behavior* (pp. 19–36). Homewood, IL: Dorsey Press.

Howard, I.P. (1982) *Human Visual Orientation.* New York: Wiley.

Howard, I.P., Hu, G. (2001) Visually induced reorientation illusions. *Perception*, 30, 583–600.

Howard, I.P., Rogers, B.J. (2008) *Seeing in Depth.* New York: Oxford University Press.

Howard, I.P., Templeton, W. (1966) *Human Spatial Orientation.* New York: Wiley.

Howarth, C.I., Beggs, W.D.A. (1985) The control of simple movements by multisensory information. In H. Heuer, U. Kleinbeck, K.H. Schmidt (eds), *Motor Behavior: Programming, Control and Acquisition* (pp. 121–151). Berlin: Springer-Verlag.

Hoyt, D.F., Taylor, C.R. (1981) Gait and energetics of locomotion in horses. *Nature*, 292, 239–240.

Hsu, W., Scholz, J.P., Schoner, G., Jeka, J.J., Kiemel, T. (2007) Control and estimation of posture during quiet stance depends on multijoint coordination. *J. Neurophysiol.*, 97, 3024–3035.

Hubbard, A.W., Seng, C.N. (1954) Visual movements of batters. *Research Quart.*, 25, 48–57.

Hughes, A. (1972) A schematic eye for the rabbit. *Vision Res.*, 12, 123–138.

Hull, C.L. (1943) *Principles of Behavior: An Introduction to Behavior Theory.* New York: Appleton Press.

Hung, G.K., Ciuffreda, K.J. (2002) Models of saccade-vergence interactions. In G.K. Hung, K.J. Ciuffreda (eds) *Models of the Visual System* (pp. 441–464). Berlin: Springer Verlag.

Hung, G.K., Ciuffreda, K.J., Semmlow, J.L., Horng, J. (1994) Vergence eye movements under natural viewing conditions. *Invest. Ophthalmol. Vis. Sci.*, 35, 3486–3492.

Hunter, I.W., Kearney, R.E. (1981) Respiratory components of human postural sway. *Neurosci. Lett.*, 25, 155–159.

Huntley, G.W., Jones, E.G. (1991) Relationship of intrinsic connections to forelimb movement representations in monkey motor cortex: A correlative anatomic and physiological study. *J. Neurophysiol.*, 66, 390–413.

Huxham, F., Gong, J., Baker, R., Morris, M., Iansek, R. (2006) Defining spatial parameters for non-linear walking. *Gait Posture*, 23, 159–163.

I.

Imai, T., Moore, S.T., Raphan, T., Cohen, B. (2001) Interaction of the body, head and eyes during walking and turning. *Exp. Brain Res.*, 136, 1–18.

Inman, V.T., Ralston, H.J., Todd, F. (1981) *Human Walking.* Baltimore: Williams & Wilkins.

Irion, A.L. (1966) A brief history of research on the acquisition of skill. In E.A. Bilodeau (ed.) *Acquisition of Skill.* New York: Academic Press.

Isa, T., Sparks, D.L. (2006) Microcircuit of the superior colliculus: A neuronal machine that determines timing and endpoint of saccadic eye movements. In S. Grillner, A.M. Graybiel (eds) *Microcircuits: The Interface between Neurons and Global Brain Function* (pp. 5–34). Cambridge, MA: MIT Press.

Ivanenko, Y.P., Poppele, R.E., Lacquaniti, F. (2004) Five basic muscle activation patterns account for muscle activity during human locomotion. *J. Physiol.*, 556, 267–283.

Ivanenko, Y.P., Poppele, R.E., Lacquaniti, F. (2006) Motor control programs and walking. *Neuroscientist,* 12, 339–348.

Ivry, R. (1996) Representational issues in motor learning: Phenomena and theory. In Heuer, H., Keele, S.W. (eds) *Handbook of Perception and Action*, vol. 2: *Motor Skills*. Hillsdale, NJ: Lawrence Erlbaum.

Izhikevich, E.M. (2007) *Dynamical Systems in Neuroscience*. Cambridge, MA: MIT Press.

J.

Jack, W.R. (1895) On the analysis of voluntary muscular movement by certain new instruments. *J. Anat. Physiol.*, 29, 473–478.

Jackson, N.D., Gutierrez, G.M., Kaminski, T.W. (2009) The effect of fatigue and habituation on the stretch reflex of the ankle musculature. *J. Electromyogr. Kinesiol.*, 19, 75–84.

Jagacinski, R.J., Flach, J.M. (2003) *Control Theory for Humans. Hillsdale*, NJ: Lawrence Erlbaum.

Jagacinski, R.J., Repperger, D.W., Moran, M.S., Ward, S.L., Glass, B. (1980) Fitts' law and the microstructure of rapid discrete movements. *J. Exp. Psychol. Hum. Percept. Perform.*, 6, 309–320.

James, T.W., Culham, J., Humphrey, G.K., Milner, A.D., Goodale, M.A. (2003) Ventral occipital lesions impair object recognition but not object-directed grasping: An fMRI study. *Brain*, 126, 2463–2475.

Jarchow, T., Mast, F.W. (1999) The effect of water immersion on postural and visual orientation. *Aviat. Space Environ. Med.*, 70, 879–886.

Jaric, S., Corcos, D.M, Agarwal, G.C., Gottlieb, G.L. (1993) Principles for learning single joint movements, II: Generalizing a learning behavior. *Exp. Brain Res.*, 94, 514–521.

Jaric, S., Ferreira, S.M., Tortoza, C., Marconi, N.F., Almeida, G.L. (1999) Effects of displacement and trajectory length on the variability pattern of reaching movements. *J. Mot. Behav.*, 31, 303–308.

Jarrett, D.N. (2005) *Cockpit Engineering*. Ashfield Publishing.

Jastrow, J. (1906) *The Subconscious*. Boston: Houghton-Mifflin.

Jeannerod, M. (1988) *The Neural and Behavioral Organization of Goal-Directed Movements*. New York: Oxford University Press.

Jeannerod, M., Decety, J., Michel, F. (1994) Impairment of grasping movements following a bilateral posterior parietal lesion. *Neuropsychologia*, 32, 369–380.

Jeka, J.J. (1997) Light touch contact as a balance aid. *Phys. Ther.*, 77, 476–487.

Jeka, J.J., Lackner, J.R. (1994) Fingertip contact influences human postural control. *Exp. Brain Res.*, 100, 495–502.

Jeka, J.J., Schöner, G., Dijkstra, T., Ribeiro, P., Lackner, J.R. (1997) Coupling of fingertip somatosensory information to head and body sway. *Exp. Brain Res.*, 113, 475–483.

Jerde, T.E., Soechting, J.F., Flanders, M. (2003) Coarticulation in fluent fingerspelling. *J. Neurosci.*, 23, 2383–2393.

Johansson, G. (1977) Studies on visual perception of locomotion. *Perception*, 6, 365–376.

Johansson, R., Magnusson, M. (1991) Human postural dynamics. *Biomed. Eng.*, 18, 413–437.

Johansson, R.S., Flanagan, J.R. (2009) Coding and use of tactile signals from the fingertips in object manipulation tasks. *Nat. Rev. Neurosci.*, 10, 345–359

Johansson, R.S., Vallbo, A.B. (1983) Tactile sensory coding in the glabrous skin of the human hand. *Trends Neurosci.*, 6, 27–32.

Johnston, I.R., White, G.R., Cumming, R.W. (1973) The role of optical expansion patterns in locomotor control. *Am. J. Psychol.*, 86, 311–324.

Johnston, K., Everling, S. (2008) Neurophysiology and neuroanatomy of reflexive and voluntary saccades in non-human primates. *Brain Cogn.*, 68, 271–283.

Johnston, T.D. (1981) Contrasting approaches to a theory of learning. *Behav. Brain Sci.*, 4, 125–173.

Jones, K.E., Hamilton, A.F., Wolpert, D.M. (2002) Sources of signal-dependent noise during isometric force production. *J. Neurophysiol.*, 88, 1533–1544.

Jones, L.A. (1988) Motor illusions: What do they reveal about proprioception? *Psychol. Bull.*, 103, 72–86.

Jones, L.A., Lederman, S.J. (2006) *Human Hand Function*. New York: Oxford University Press.

Jordan, L.M., Liu, J., Hedlund, P.B., Akay, T., Pearson, K. (2008) Descending command systems for the initiation of locomotion in mammals. *Brain Res. Rev.*, 57, 183–191.

Jordan, M.I. (1996) Computational aspects of motor control and motor learning. In H. Heuer, S. Keele (eds) *Handbook of Perception and Action*, vol. 2. New York: Academic Press.

K.

Kaas, J.H., Lyon, D.C. (2007) Pulvinar contributions to the dorsal and ventral streams of visual processing in primates. *Brain Res. Rev.*, 55, 285–296.

Kagerer, F.A., Contreras-Vidal, J.L., Stelmach, G.E. (1997) Adaptation to gradual as compared with sudden visuomotor distortions. *Exp. Brain Res.*, 115, 557–561.

Kaiser, M.K., Mowafy, L. (1993) Optical specification of time-to-passage: Observers' sensitivity to global tau. *J. Exp. Psychol. Hum. Percept. Perform.*, 19, 1028–1040.

Kalman, R.E., Falb, P.L., Arbib, M.A. (1969) *Topics in Mathematical System Theory*. New York: McGraw-Hill.

Kandel, E.R. (2000) Cellular mechanisms of learning and the biological basis of individuality. In Kandel, Schwartz, Jessel (2000), pp. 1248–1279.

Kandel, E.R. (2009) The biology of memory: A forty-year perspective. *J. Neurosci.*, 29, 12748–12756.

Kandel, E.R., Schwartz, J.H., Jessell, T.M. (2000) *Principles of Neural Science* (4th edition). New York: McGraw-Hill.

Kapoula, Z. (1985) Evidence for a range effect in the saccadic system. *Vision Res.*, 25, 1155–1157.

Karmarkar, U.R., Buonomano, D.V. (2007) Timing in the absence of clocks: Encoding time in neural network states. *Neuron*, 53, 427–438.

Karnath, H.O., Perenin, M.T. (2005) Cortical control of visually guided reaching: Evidence from patients with optic ataxia. *Cereb. Cortex*, 15, 1561–1569.

Karnath, H.O., Ruter, J., Mandler, A., Himmelbach, M. (2009) The anatomy of object recognition-visual form agnosia caused by medial occipitotemporal stroke. *J. Neurosci.*, 29, 5854–5862.

Karnopp, D., Margolis, D.L. (2007) *Engineering Applications of Dynamics.* New York: Wiley.

Katz, B. (1950) Depolarization of sensory nerve terminal and the initiation of impulses in the muscle spindle. *J. Physiol.*, 111, 261–282.

Kaufman, M.P., Hayes, S.G., Adreani, C.M., Pickar, J.G. (2002) Discharge properties of group III and IV muscle afferents. *Adv. Exp. Med. Biol.*, 508, 25–32.

Kavounoudias, A., Roll, R., Roll, J.P. (1998) The plantar sole is a 'dynamometric map' for human balance control. *NeuroReport*, 9, 3247–3252.

Kavounoudias, A., Roll, R., Roll, J.P. (1999) Specific whole body shifts induced by frequency-modulated vibrations of human plantar soles. *Neurosci. Lett.*, 266, 181–184.

Kavounoudias, A., Roll, R., Roll, J.P. (2001) Foot sole and ankle muscle inputs contribute jointly to human erect posture regulation. *J. Physiol.*, 532, 869–878.

Kawato, M. (1992) Optimization and learning in neural networks for formation and control of coordinated movement. In Meyer, D.E., Kornblum, S. (eds) *Attention and performance XIV* (pp. 821–849). Cambridge, MA: MIT Press.

Kawato, M. (1999) Internal models for motor control and trajectory planning. *Curr. Opin. Neurobiol.*, 9, 718–727.

Keele, S.W. (1968) Movement control in skilled motor performance. *Psychol. Bull.*, 70, 387–403.

Keele, S.W., Cohen, A., Ivry, R. (1990) Motor programs: Concepts and issues. In M. Jeannerod (ed.). *Attention and performance XIII* (pp. 77–110). Hillsdale, NJ: Erlbaum.

Keele, S.W., Ivry, R.B., Hazeltine, E., Mayr, U., Heuer, H. (2003) The cognitive and neural architecture of sequence representations. *Psychol. Rev.*, 110, 316–339.

Keele, S.W., Posner, M.I. (1968) Processing visual feedback in rapid movements. *J. Exp. Psychol.*, 77, 155–158.

Keeley, R., Singh, A.D., Dua, H.S. (2010) Doubling up: Two prisms, two names, two countries. *Br. J. Opthalmol.*, 94, 1419–1420.

Kehoe, E.J., Cool, V., Gormezano, I. (1991) Trace conditioning of the rabbit's nictitating membrane response as a function of CS-US interstimulus interval and trials per session. *Learn. Motiv.*, 22, 269–290.

Keller, E.L., Robinson, D.A. (1971) Absence of a stretch reflex in extraocular muscles of the monkey. *J. Neurophysiol.*, 34, 908–921.

Keller, F.S. (1958) The phantom plateau. *J. Exp. Anal. Behav.*, 1, 1–13.

Kelso, J.A.S. (1977) Motor control mechanisms underlying human movement reproduction. *J. Exp. Psychol. Hum. Percept. Perform.*, 3, 529–543.

Kelso, J.A.S., Holt, K.G., Flatt, A.E. (1980) The role of proprioception in the perception and control of human movement: Towards a theoretical reassessment. *Percept. Psychophys.*, 28, 45–52.

Kelso, J.A.S., Saltzman, E., Tuller, B. (1986) The dynamical perspective on speech production: Data and theory. *J. Phonetics*, 14, 29–59.

Kelso, J.A.S., Schöner, G., Scholz, J.P., Haken, H. (1987) Phase-locked modes, phase transitions and component oscillators in biological motion. *Physica Scripta*, 35, 79–87.

Kelton, I.W., Wright, R.D. (1949) The mechanisms of easy standing by man. *Aus. J. Exp. Biol. Med.*, 27, 505–516.

Kerr, B., Condon, S.M., McDonald, L.A. (1985) Cognitive spatial processing and the regulation of posture. *J. Exp. Psychol. Hum. Percept. Perform.*, 11, 617–622.

Kerr, B.A., Langolf, G.D. (1977) Speed of aiming movements. *Quart. J. Exp. Psychol.*, 29, 475–481.

Keshner, E.A. (2003) Head-trunk coordination during linear anterior-posterior translations. *J. Neurophysiol.*, 89, 1891–1901.

Keshner, E.A., Peterson, B.W. (1988) Motor control strategies underlying head stabilization and voluntary head movements in humans and cats. In O. Pompeiano, J.H.J. Allum (eds) *Vestibulospinal Control of Posture and Movement: Prog. Brain Res.* (pp. 329–339). Amsterdam: Elsevier Science Publishers BV.

Kiehn, O. (2006) Locomotor circuits in the mammalian spinal cord. *Annu. Rev. Neurosci.*, 29, 279–306.

Killeen, P.R. (1994) Mathematical principles of reinforcement. *Behav. Brain Sci.*, 17, 105–135.

Kimble, G.A., Shatel, R.B. (1952) The relationship between two kinds of inhibition and the amount of practice. *J. Exp. Psychol.*, 44, 355–359.

King, W.M., Zhou, W. (2000) New ideas about binocular coordination of eye movements: Is there a chameleon in the primate family tree? *Anat. Record*, 261, 153–161.

Kingma, I., Van der Langenberg, R., Beek, P.J. (2004) Which mechanical invariants are associated with the perception of length and heaviness of a nonvisible handheld rod? Testing the inertia tensor hypothesis. *J. Exp. Psychol. Hum. Percept. Perform.*, 30, 346–354.

Kirkup, L., Frenkel, R.B. (2006) *An Introduction to Uncertainty in Measurement.* Cambridge University Press.

Kitaharra, M., Uno, R. (1967) Equilibrium and vertigo in a tilted environment. *Annals of Otolaryngology*, 76, 166–178.

Kitazawa, S., Kimura, T., Uka, T. (1997) Prism adaptation of reaching movements: Specificity for the velocity of reaching. *J. Neurosci.*, 17, 1481–1492.

Kitazawa, S., Kohno, T., Uka, T. (1995) Effects of delayed visual information on the rate and amount of prism adaptation in the human. *J. Neurosci.*, 15, 7644–7652.

Klapp, S.T. (1995) Motor response programming during simple and choice reaction time: The role of practice. *J. Exp. Psychol. Hum. Percept. Perf.*, 21, 1015–1027.

Klapp, S.T. (1996) Reaction time analysis of central motor control. In H. Zelaznik (ed.), *Advances in Motor Learning and Control*. Champaign, IL: Human Kinetics Press.

Klapp, S.T., Erwin, C.I. (1976) Relation between programming time and duration of the response being programmed. *J. Exp. Psychol. Hum. Percept. Perf.*, 2, 591–598.

Kling, J.W. (1971) Learning: Introductory survey. In J.W. Kling, L.A. Riggs (eds) *Woodworth & Schlossberg's Experimental Psychology* (3rd edition). New York: Holt, Rinehart & Winston.

Kling, J.W., Schrier, A.M. (1971) Positive reinforcement. In J.W. Kling, L.A. Riggs (eds) *Woodworth & Schlossberg's Experimental Psychology* (3rd edition). New York: Holt, Rinehart & Winston.

Koenderink, J.J. (1986) Optic flow. *Vision Res.*, 26, 161–79.

Kono, R., Poukens, V., Demer, J.L. (2002) Quantitative analysis of the structure of the human extraocular muscle pulley system. *Invest. Ophthalmol. Vis. Sci.*, 43, 2923–2932.

Krakauer, J.W., Mazzoni, P. (2011) Human sensorimotor learning: Adaptation, skill, and beyond. *Curr. Opin. Neurobiol.*, 21, 636–644.

Krakauer, J.W., Mazzoni, P., Ghazizadeh, A., Ravindran, R., Shadmehr, R. (2006) Generalization of motor learning depends on the history of prior action. *PLoS Biol.*, 4(10), e316.

Krakauer, J.W., Shadmehr, R. (2006) Consolidation of motor memory. *Trends Neurosci.*, 29, 58–64.

Krebs, H.I., Aisen, M.L., Volpe, B.T., Hogan, N. (1999) Quantization of continuous arm movements in humans with brain injury. *Proc. Natl. Acad. Sci. USA*, 96, 4645–4649.

Krishnan, V., Aruin, A.S., Latash, M.L. (2011) Two stages and three components of the postural preparation to action. *Exp. Brain Res.*, 212, 47–63.

Kugler, P.N., Kelso, J.A.S., Turvey, M.T. (1982) On the control and coordination of naturally developing systems. In J.A.S. Kelso, J.E. Clark (eds), *The Development of Movement Control and Coordination*. New York: Wiley.

Kugler, P.N., Turvey, M.T. (1987) *Information, Natural Law and the Self-Assembly of Rhythmic Movement*. Hillsdale, NJ: Lawrence Erlbaum.

Kulagin, A.S., Shik, M.L. (1970) Interaction of symmetrical limbs during controlled locomotion. *Biofizika*, 15, 171–178.

Kuo, A.D. (2002) Energetics of actively powered locomotion using the simplest walking model. *J. Biomech. Eng.*, 124, 113–120.

Kuo, A.D. (2007) The six determinants of gait and the inverted pendulum analogy: A dynamic walking perspective. *Hum. Mov. Sci.*, 26, 617–656.

Kuo, A.D., Donelan, J.M. (2009) Dynamic principles of gait and their clinical implications. *Phys. Ther.*, 90, 157–174.

Kupfermann, I., Weiss, K.R. (2001) Motor program selection in simple model systems. *Curr. Opin. Neurobiol.*, 11, 673–677.

L.

LaBarbera, J.D., Church, R.M. (1974) Magnitude of fear as a function of the expected time to an aversive event. *Anim. Learn. Behav.*, 2, 199–202.

Lackner, J.R. (1988) Some proprioceptive influences on the perceptual representation of body shape and orientation. *Brain*, 111, 281–297.

Lackner, J.R., Levine, M.S. (1979) Changes in apparent body orientation and sensory localization induced by vibration of postural muscles: Vibratory myesthetic illusions. *Aviat. Space Environ. Med.*, 50, 346–354.

Lackner, J.R., Rabin, E., DiZio, P. (2001) Stabilization of posture by precision touch of the index finger with rigid and flexible filaments. *Exp. Brain Res.*, 139, 454–464.

Lacquaniti, F. (1989) Central representations of human limb movement as revealed by studies of drawing and handwriting. *Trends Neurosci.*, 12, 287–291.

Lacquaniti, F., Soechting, J.F., Terzuolo, C.A. (1982) Some factors pertinent to the organization and control of arm movements. *Brain Res.*, 252, 394–397.

Lacquaniti, F., Soechting, J.F., Terzuolo, C.A. (1986) Path constraints on point-to-point arm movements in three-dimensional space. *Neuroscience*, 17, 313–324.

Lacquaniti, F., Terzuolo, C.A., Viviani, P. (1983) The law relating the kinematic and figural aspects of drawing movements. *Acta Psychol.*, 54, 115–130.

Land, M.F. (1998) The visual control of steering. In L.R. Harris, M. Jenkin (eds) *Vision and Action*. Cambridge, UK: Cambridge University Press.

Land, M.F. (2004) The coordination of rotations of the eyes, head and trunk in saccadic turns produced in natural situations. *Exp. Brain Res.*, 159, 151–160.

Land, M.F., Horwood, J. (1995) Which parts of the road guide steering. *Nature*, 377, 339–340.

Land, M.F., Lee, D.N. (1994) Where do we look when we steer? *Nature*, 369, 742–744.

Land, M.F., Mennie, N., Rusted, J. (1999) The roles of vision and eye movements in the control of activities of everyday living. *Perception*, 28, 1311–1328.

Langolf, G.D., Chaffin, D.B., Foulke, J.A. (1976) An investigation of Fitts' law using a wide range of movement amplitudes. *J. Mot. Behav.*, 8, 113–128.

Lappe, M., Bremmer, F., Van den Berg, A. (1999) Perception of self motion from visual flow. *Trends Cogn. Sci.*, 3, 329–336.

Lashley, K.S. (1930) Basic neural mechanisms in behaviour. *Psychol. Rev.*, 37, 1–24.

Lashley, K.S. (1942) The problem of cerebral organization in vision. In J. Cattell (ed.) *Biological Symposia vol. VII. Visual Mechanisms*, pp. 301–322. Lancaster PA: Jacques Cattell Press.

Lashley, K.S. (1951) The problem of serial order in behavior. In L.A. Jeffress (ed.) *Cerebral mechanisms in behavior* (pp. 112–131). New York: Wiley.

Lass, R. (1984) *Phonology: An Introduction to Basic Concepts.* Cambridge UK: Cambridge University Press.

Latash, M.L. (1993) *Control of Human Movement.* Champaign, IL: Human Kinetics.

Latash, M.L. (2008a) *The Neurophysiological Basis of Movement* (2nd edition). Champaign, IL: Human Kinetics.

Latash, M.L. (2008b) *Synergy.* New York: Oxford University Press.

Latash, M.L., Gottlieb, G.L. (1990) Equilibrium point hypothesis and variability of the amplitude, speed and time of single-joint movements. *Biofizika*, 35, 870–874.

Latash, M.L., Scholz, J.F., Danion, F., Schoner. G. (2001) Structure of motor variability in marginally redundant multifinger force production tasks. *Exp. Brain Res.*, 141, 153–165.

Laurens, J., Droulez, J. (2007) Bayesian processing of vestibular information. *Biol. Cybern.*, 96, 389–404.

Laurent, M., Montagne, G., Savelsbergh, G.J.P. (1994) The control and coordination of one-handed catching: The effect of temporal constraints. *Exp. Brain Res.*, 101, 314–322.

Laurutis, V.P., Robinson, D.A. (1986) The vestibulo-ocular reflex during human saccadic eye movements. *J. Physiol.*, 373, 209–233.

Lavery, J.J. (1962) Retention of simple motor skills as a function of knowledge of results. *Can. J. Psychol.*, 16, 300–311.

Lawton, D.T. (1983) Processing translational motion sequences. *Comput. Graph. Image Process.*, 22, 116–144.

Leaton, R.N. (1976) Long-term retention of the habituation of lick suppression and startle response produced by a single auditory stimulus. *J. Exp. Psychol. Anim. Beh. Process.*, 2, 248–259.

Lederman, S.J., Ganeshan, S., Ellis, R.E. (1996) Effortful touch with minimum movement: Revisited. *J. Exp. Psychol. Hum. Percept. Perform.*, 22, 851–868.

Lederman, S.J., Klatzky, R.L. (1987) Hand movements: A window into haptic object recognition. *Cogn. Psychol.*, 19, 342–368.

Lederman, S.J., Klatzky, R.L. (2009) Haptic perception: A tutorial. *Percept. Psychophys.*, 71, 1439–1459.

Lee, D.N. (1974) Visual information during locomotion. In R.B. MacLeod, H.L. Pick, Jnr (eds), *Perception: Essays in Honor of James J. Gibson* (pp. 250–267). Ithaca, NY: Cornell University Press.

Lee, D.N., Aronson, E. (1974) Visual proprioceptive control of standing in human infants. *Percept. Psychophys.*, 15, 529–532.

Lee, D.N., Lishman, J.R. (1975) Visual proprioceptive control of stance. *J. Hum. Mov. Stud.*, 1, 87–95.

Lee, D.N., Lishman, J.R. (1977) Visual control of locomotion. *Scand. J. Psychol.*, 18, 224–230.

Lee, D.N., Reddish, P.E. (1981) Plummeting gannets: A paradigm of ecological optics. *Nature*, 293.

Lee, D.N., Reddish, P.E., Rand, D.T. (1991) Aerial docking by hummingbirds. *Naturwissenschaften*, 78, 526–527.

Lee, P.H., Helms, M.C., Augustine, G.J., Hall, W.C. (1997) Role of intrinsic synaptic circuitry in collicular sensorimotor integration. *Proc. Natl. Acad. Sci. USA*, 94, 13299–13304.

Lee, T.D., Genovese, E.D. (1989) Distribution of practice in motor skill acquisition: Different effects for discrete and continuous tasks. *Res. Quart. Ex. Sport*, 60, 59–65.

Leigh, R.J., Zee, D.S. (2006) *The Neurology of Eye Movements* (4th edition). New York: Oxford University Press.

Lemon, R.N. (2008) Descending pathways in motor control. *Annu. Rev. Neurosci.*, 31, 195–218.

Levangie, P.K., Norkin, C.C. (2001) *Joint Structure and Function: A Comprehensive Analysis.* Sydney: MacLennan & Petty.

Lewthwaite, R., Wulf, G. (2010) Social-comparative feedback affects motor skill learning. *Quart. J. Exp. Psychol.*, 63, 738–749.

Lhermitte, F. (1983) 'Utilisation behaviour' and its relation to lesions of the frontal lobes. *Brain*, 106, 237–255.

Li, L., Cheng, J.C.K. (2010) Relative contributions of optic flow, bearing, and splay angle information to lane keeping. *J. Vision*, 10(11), pii: 16.

Li, L., Cheng, J.C.K. (2011) Perceiving path from optic flow. *J. Vision*, 11(1), pii: 22.

Li, L., Sweet, B.T., Stone, L.S. (2006) Humans can perceive heading without visual path information. *J. Vision*, 6, 874–881.

Liao, K., Walker, M.F., Joshi, A., Reschke, M., Strupp, M., Leigh, R.J. (2009) The human vertical translational vestibulo-ocular reflex: Normal and abnormal responses. *Ann. N. Y. Acad. Sci.*, 1164, 68–75.

Libet, B. (1985) Unconscious cerebral initiative and the role of conscious will in voluntary action. *Behav. Brain Sci.*, 8, 529–566.

Liddell, E.G.T., Sherrington, C.S. (1924) Reflexes in response to stretch (myotatic reflexes). *Proc. Roy. Soc. Lond. B*, 96, 212–242.

Liebermann, D.A., Vogel, A.C.M., Nisbet, J. (2008) Why do the effects of delaying reinforcement in animals and delaying feedback in humans differ? A working memory analysis. *Quart. J. Exp. Psychol.*, 61, 194–202.

Liebermann, D.G., Hoffman, J.R. (2005) Timing of preparatory landing responses as a function of availability of optic flow information. *J. Electromyogr. Kinesiol.*, 15, 120–130.

Lisberger, S.G. (1988) The neural basis for learning of simple motor skills. *Science*, 242, 728–735.

Lobel, E., Kahane, P., Leonards, U., Grosbras, M.-H., Lehéricy, S., LeBihan, D., Berthoz, A. (2001) Localization of human frontal eye fields: Anatomical and functional findings of functional magnetic resonance imaging and intracerebral electrical stimulation. *J. Neurosurg.*, 95, 804–815.

Loeb, G.E., Gans, C. (1986) *Electromyography for Experimentalists*. Chicago: University of Chicago Press.

Longuet-Higgins, H.C., Prazdny, K. (1980) The interpretation of a moving retinal image. *Proc. Roy. Soc. Lond. B*, 208, 385–397.

Loomis, J., Lederman, S.J. (1986) Tactile perception. In K. Boff, L. Kaufman, J. Thomas (eds) *Handbook of Human Perception and Performance* (pp. 31.01–31.04). New York: Wiley.

Loram, I.D., Lakie, M. (2002) Direct measurement of human ankle stiffness during quiet standing: The intrinsic mechanical stiffness is insufficient for stability. *J. Physiol.*, 545, 1041–1053.

Loram, I.D., Magnaris, C.N., Lakie, M. (2005a) Active, non-spring-like muscle movements in human postural sway: How might paradoxical changes in muscle length be produced? *J. Physiol.*, 564, 281–293.

Loram, I.D., Magnaris, C.N., Lakie, M. (2005b) Human postural sway results from frequent, ballistic bias impulses by soleus and gastrocnemius. *J. Physiol.*, 564, 295–311.

Loram, I.D., Magnaris, C.N., Lakie, M. (2007) The passive, human calf muscles in relation to standing: The non-linear decrease from short range to long range stiffness. *J. Physiol.*, 584, 661–675.

Lorenz, K.Z. (1950) The comparative method in studying innate behavior patterns. In *Physiological mechanisms in animal behavior; Symposium of the Society of Experimental Biology*, 4, pp. 221–268. Cambridge University Press.

Lorenz, K.Z., Tinbergen, N. (1939) Taxis und Instinkthandlung in der Eirollbewegung der Graugans. *Zeitschrift für Tierpsychologie*, 2, 1–29.

Lubow, R.E., Moore, A.U. (1959) Latent inhibition: The effect of non-reinforced preexposure to the conditioned stimulus. *J. Comp. Physiol. Psychol.*, 52, 415–419.

Lui, X., Crump, M.J., Logan, G.D. (2010) Do you know where your fingers have been? Explicit knowledge of the spatial layout of the keyboard in skilled typists. *Mem. Cogn.*, 38, 474–484.

Lund, S., Broberg, C. (1983) Effects of different head positions on postural sway in man induced by a reproducible vestibular error signal. *Acta Physiol. Scand.*, 117, 307–309.

M.

MacIntosh, B.R., Gardiner, P.F., McComas, A.J. (2006) *Skeletal Muscle: Form and Function* (2nd edition). Champaign, IL: Human Kinetics.

MacKay, D.G. (1982) The problems of flexibility, fluency and speed-accuracy trade-off in skilled behavior. *Psychol. Rev.*, 89, 483–506.

MacKenzie, C.L., Graham, E.D. (1997) Separating A and W effects: Pointing to targets on computer displays. *Behav. Brain Sci.*, 20, 316–317.

MacKenzie, C.L., Marteniuk, R.G., Dugas, C., Liske, D., Eickmeier, B. (1987) Three-dimensional movement trajectories in Fitts' task: Implications for control. *Quart. J. Exp. Psychol. A*, 39, 629–647.

MacKenzie, I.S., Buxton, W. (1992) Extending Fitts' law to two-dimensional tasks. Proceedings of the CHI 1992 Conference on Hum. Factors in Computing Systems, ACM, New York, pp. 219–226.

Magill, R.A. (2010) *Motor Learning: Concepts and Applications* (9th edition). New York: McGraw-Hill.

Maier, J.X., Groh, J.M. (2009) Multisensory guidance of orienting behavior. *Hearing Res.*, 258, 106–112.

Majsak, M.J., Kaminski, T., Gentile, A.M., Flanagan, J.R. (1998) The reaching movements of patients with Parkinson's disease under self-determined maximal speed and visually cued conditions. *Brain*, 121, 755–766.

Maoz, U., Berthoz, A., Flash, T. (2009) Complex unconstrained three-dimensional hand movement and constant equi-affine speed. *J. Neurophysiol.*, 101, 1002–1015.

Marchetti, C., Della Salla, S. (1998) Disentangling the alien and anarchic hand. *Cogn. Neuropsychiat.*, 3, 191–207.

Marcora, S. (2009) Perception of effort during exercise is independent of afferent feedback from skeletal muscles, heart and lungs. *J. Appl. Physiol.*, 106, 2060–2062.

Margaria, R. (1938) Sulla fisiologia e specialmente sul consumo energetico della marcia e della corsa a varie velocità ed inclinazioni del terreno. *Atti. Accad. Naz. Lincei Memorie, serie VI*, 7, 299–368.

Margaria, R. (1976) *Biomechanics and Energetics of Muscular Exercise*. Oxford, UK: Oxford University Press.

Marigold, D.S., Patla, A.E. (2007) Gaze fixation patterns for negotiating complex ground terrain. *Neuroscience*, 144, 302–313.

Marigold, D.S., Weerdesteyn, V., Patla, A.E., Duysens, J. (2007) Keep looking ahead? Re-direction of visual fixation does not always occur during an unpredictable obstacle avoidance task. *Exp. Brain Res.*, 176, 32–42.

Marinovic, W., Plooy, A., Tresilian, J.R. (2008) The time course of amplitude specification in brief interceptive actions. *Exp. Brain Res.*, 188, 275–288.

Marple-Horvat, D.E., Chattington, M., Anglesea, M., Ashford, D.G., Wilson. M., Keil, D. (2005) Prevention of coordinated eye movements and steering impairs driving performance. *Exp. Brain Res.*, 163, 411–420.

Marr, D.C. (1982) *Vision*. New York: W.H. Freeman.

Marteniuk, R.G., MacKenzie, C.L., Jeannerod, M., Athenes, S., Dugas, C. (1987) Constraints on human arm movement trajectories. *Can. J. Psychol.*, 41, 365–378.

Martin, T.A., Keating, J.G., Goodkin, H.P., Bastian, A.J., Thach, W.T. (1996) Throwing while looking through prisms, II: Specificity and storage of multiple gaze-throw calibrations. *Brain*, 119, 1199–1211.

Martin, T.A., Norris, S.A., Greger, B.E., Thach, W.T. (2002) Dynamic coordination of body parts during prism adaptation. *J. Neurophysiol.*, 88, 1685–1694.

Masdeu, J.C., Alampur, U., Cavaliere, R., Tavoulareas, G. (1994) Astasia and gait failure with damage of the ponto-mesencephalic locomotor region. *Ann. Neurol.*, 35, 619–621.

Mason, A.H., Carnahan, H. (1999) Target viewing time and velocity effects on prehension. *Exp. Brain Res.*, 127, 83–94.

Masseck, O.A., Hoffmann, K.P. (2009) Comparative neurobiology of the optokinetic reflex. *Ann. N. Y. Acad. Sci.*, 1164, 430–439.

Massion, J. (1998) Postural control systems in developmental perspective. *Neurosci. Biobehav. Rev.*, 22, 465–472.

Matthews, P.C.B. (1959a) A study of certain factors influencing the stretch reflex of the decerebrate cat. *J. Physiol.*, 147, 547–564.

Matthews, P.C.B. (1959b) The dependence of tension upon extension in the stretch reflex of the soleus of the decerebrate cat. *J. Physiol.*, 47, 521–546.

Matthews, P.C.B. (1959c) Muscle spindles: Their messages and their fusimotor supply. In V.B. Brooks (ed.) *Handbook of Physiology*, section 1. The nervous system, vol. ii: Motor control (pp. 189–228). Bethesda, MD: American Physiological Society.

Maxwell, J.S., Schor, C.M. (2006) The coordination of binocular eye movements: Vertical and torsional alignment. *Vision Res.*, 46, 3537–3548.

Mazur, J.E., Hastie, R. (1978) Learning as accumulation: A re-examination of the learning curve. *Psychol. Bull.*, 85, 1256–1274.

Mazzoni, P., Krakauer, J.W. (2006) An implicit plan overrides an explicit strategy during visuomotor adaptation. *J. Neurosci.*, 26, 3642–3645.

McCloskey, D.I., Ebeling, P., Goodwin, G.M. (1974) Estimation of weights and tensions and apparent involvement of a 'sense of effort'. *Exp. Neurol.*, 42, 220–232.

McCloskey, D.I., Torda, T.A. (1975) Corollary motor discharges and kinaesthesia. *Brain Res.*, 100, 467–470.

McCrae, D.A., Rybak, I.A. (2008) Organization of mammalian locomotor rhythm and pattern generation. *Brain Res. Rev.*, 57, 134–146.

McDowell, J.E., Dyckman, K.A., Austin, B., Clementz, B.A. (2008) Neurophysiology and neuroanatomy of reflexive and volitional saccades: Evidence from studies of humans. *Brain Cogn.*, 68, 255–270.

McGeer, T. (1990) Passive dynamic walking. *Int. J. Robotics Res.*, 9, 68–82.

McGeer, T. (1992) Principles of walking and running. In R.M. Alexander (ed.) *Advances in Comparative and Environmental Physiology*, vol. 11: *Mechanics of Animal Locomotion*. Berlin: Springer-Verlag.

McGeer, T. (1993) Dynamics and control of bipedal locomotion. *J. Theor. Biol.*, 163, 277–314.

McIlroy, W., Maki, B. (1993) Do anticipatory adjustments precede compensatory stepping reactions evoked by perturbation? *Neurosci. Lett.*, 164, 199–202.

McIlroy, W., Maki, B. (1999) The control of lateral stability during rapid stepping reactions evoked by antero-posterior perturbation: Does anticipatory control play a role? *Gait Posture*, 9, 190–198.

Mcintosh, R.D., Schenk, T. (2009) Two visual streams for perception and action: Current trends. *Neuropsychologia*, 47, 1391–1396.

McIntyre, J., Stratta, F., Lacquaniti, F. (1997) Viewer-centered frame of reference for pointing to memorized targets in three-dimensional space. *J. Neurophysiol.*, 78, 1601–1618.

McIntyre, J., Stratta, F., Droulez, J., Lacquaniti, F. (2000) Analysis of pointing errors reveals properties of data representations and coordinate transformations within the central nervous system. *Neural. Comput.*, 12, 2823–2855.

McLean, J.R., Hoffman, E.R. (1973) The effects of restricted preview on driver steering control and performance. *Hum. Factors*, 15, 421–430.

McLeod, P., McGlaughlin, C., Nimmo-Smith, I. (1985) Information encapsulation and automaticity: Evidence from the control of finely timed actions. In J. Long, A.D. Baddeley (eds) *Attention and Performance IX* (pp. 391–406). Hillsdale, NJ: Lawrence Erlbaum.

McMahon, T.A. (1984) *Muscles, Reflexes and Locomotion*. Princeton, NJ: Princeton University Press.

McRuer, D.T., Allen, R.W., Weir, D.H., Klein, R. (1977) New results in driver steering control models. *Hum. Factors*, 19, 381–397.

McRuer, D.T., Jex, H.R. (1967) A review of quasi-linear pilot models. *IEEE Trans. Hum. Factors*, 8, 231–249.

McRuer, D.T., Weir, D.H., Jex, H.R., Magdaleno, R.E., Allen, R.W. (1975) Measurement of driver-vehicle multiloop response properties with a single disturbance input. *IEEE Trans. Syst. Man Cybern.*, 5, 490–497.

Mena-Segovia, J., Bolam, J.P., Magill, P.J. (2004) Pedunculopontine nucleus and basal ganglia: Distant relatives or part of the same family? *Trends Neurosci.*, 27, 585–588.

Mendell, L.M., Henneman, E. (1971) Terminals of single 1a fibers: Location, density, and distribution within a pool of 300 homonymous motorneurons. *J. Neurophysiol.*, 34, 171–187.

Merton, P.A. (1953) Speculations on the servo-control of movement. In G.E.W. Wolstenholme (ed.) *The Spinal Cord*. London: Churchill (pp. 247–255).

Meyer, C.H., Lasker, A.G., Robinson, D.A. (1985) The upper limit of human smooth pursuit velocity. *Vision Res.*, 25, 561–563.

Meyer, D.E., Abrams, R.A., Kornblum, S., Wright, C.E., Smith, J.E. (1988) Optimality in human motor performance: Ideal control of rapid aimed movements. *Psychol. Rev.*, 95, 340–370.

Meyer, D.E., Smith, J.E., Kornblum, S., Abrams, R.A., Wright, C.E. (1990) Speed-accuracy tradeoffs in aimed movements: Toward a theory of rapid voluntary action. In M. Jeannerod (ed.) *Attention and Performance XIII: Motor Representation and Control* (pp. 173–226). Hillsdale, NJ: Lawrence Erlbaum Associates.

Mian, O.S., Dakin, C.J., Blouin, J.S., Fitzpatrick, R.C., Day, B.L. (2010) Lack of otolith involvement in balance responses evoked by mastoid electrical stimulation. *J. Physiol.*, 588, 4441–4451.

Micci-Barreca, D., Guenther, F.H. (2001) A modelling study of potential sources of curvature in human reaching movements. *J. Mot. Behav.*, 33, 387–400.

Miles, F.A. (1998) The neural processing of 3-D visual information: Evidence from eye movements. *Eur. J. Neurosci.*, 10, 811–822.

Miles, F.A., Fuller, J.H. (1974) Adaptive plasticity in the vestibulo-ocular responses of the rhesus monkey. *Brain Res.*, 80, 512–516.

Millenson, J.R., Kehoe, E.J., Gormezano, I. (1977) Classical conditioning of the rabbit's nictitating membrane response under fixed and mixed CS-US intervals. *Learn. Motiv.*, 8, 351–366.

Miller, E.F., Fregly, A.R., Graybiel, A. (1968) Visual horizontal perception in relation to otolith function. *Am. J. Psychol.*, 81, 488–496.

Miller, J.M. (2007) Understanding and misunderstanding extraocular muscle pulleys. *J. Vision*, 10, 1–15.

Milner, A.D., Goodale, M.A. (2006) *The Visual Brain in Action* (2nd edition). Oxford University Press.

Milner, B. (1962) Les troubles de la mémoire accompagnant les lésions hippocampiques bilatérales. *Physiologie de l'Hippocampe, Colloques Internationaux*, 107, 257–272.

Milner, B., Squire, L.R., Kandel, E.R. (1998) Cognitive neuroscience and the study of memory. *Neuron*, 20, 445–468.

Milner, T.E. (1992) A model for the generation of movements requiring endpoint precision. *Neuroscience*, 49, 487–496.

Mineka, S., Öhman, A. (2002) Phobias and preparedness: The selective, automatic, and encapsulated nature of fear. *Biol. Psychiatry*, 52, 927–937.

Mittelstaedt, H. (1983) A new solution to the problem of the subjective vertical. *Naturwissenschaften.*, 70, 272–281.

Mittelstaedt, H. (1996) Somatic graviception. *Biol. Psychol.*, 42, 53–74.

Mittelstaedt, H. (1998) Origin and processing of postural information. *Neurosci. Biobehav. Rev.*, 22, 473–478.

Mohagheghi, A., Moraes, R., Patla, A.E. (2004) The effects of distant and on-line visual information on the control of approach phase and step over an obstacle during locomotion. *Exp. Brain Res.*, 155, 459–468.

Monster, A.W., Chan, H.C. (1977) Isometric force production by motor units of extensor digitorum communis muscle in man. *J. Neurophysiol.*, 40, 1432–1443.

Mon-Williams, M.A, Tresilian, J.R. (2000) Ordinal depth information from accommodation? *Ergonomics*, 43, 391–404.

Moore, J.W., Choi, J.S. (1997) Conditioned response timing and integration in the cerebellum. *Learn. Mem.*, 4, 116–129.

Moore, S.T., Hirasaki, E., Cohen, B., Raphan, T. (1999) Effect of viewing distance on the generation of vertical eye movements during locomotion. *Exp. Brain Res.*, 129, 347–361.

Moors, A., De Houwer, J. (2006) Automaticity: A theoretical and conceptual analysis. *Psychol. Bull.*, 132, 297–326.

Morasso, P. (1981) Spatial control of arm movements. *Exp. Brain Res.*, 42, 223–227.

Morasso, P. (1983) Three dimensional arm trajectories. *Biol. Cybern.*, 48, 1–8.

Morasso, P., Mussa-Ivaldi, F.A. (1982) Trajectory formation and handwriting: A computational model. *Biol. Cybern.*, 45, 131–142.

Morasso, P., Mussa-Ivaldi, F.A., Ruggiero, C. (1983) How a discontinuous mechanism can produce continuous patterns in trajectory formation and handwriting. *Acta Psychol.*, 54, 83–142.

Morasso, P., Sanguineti, V. (1993) Neurocomputing aspects in modelling cursive handwriting. *Acta Psychol.*, 82, 213–235.

Morasso, P., Schieppati, M. (1999) Can muscle stiffness alone stabilize upright standing? *J. Neurophysiol.*, 82, 1622–1626.

Mori, S. (1987) Integration of posture and locomotion in acute decerebrate cats and in awake, free moving cats. *Prog. Neurobiol.*, 28, 161–196.

Mori, S. (2007) *Introduction to Diffusion Tensor Imaging*. Amsterdam: Elsevier.

Morrison, D.F. (2004) *Multivariate statistical methods* (4th edition). New York: McGraw-Hill.

Moschovakis, A.K. (1995) Are laws that govern behaviour embedded in the structure of the CNS? The case of Hering's Law. *Vision Res.*, 35, 3207–3216.

Moschovakis, A.K., Kitama, T., Dalezios, Y., Petit, J., Brandi, A., Grantyn, A.A. (1998) An anatomical substrate for the spatiotemporal transformation. *J. Neurosci.*, 18, 10219–10229.

Moschovakis, A.K., Scudder, C.A., Highstein, S.M. (1996) The microscopic anatomy and physiology of the mammalian saccadic system. *Prog. Neurobiol.*, 50, 133–254.

Moses, R.A. (ed.) (1975) *Adler's Physiology of the Eye* (5th edition). C.V. Mosby Co.

Mountcastle, V.B. (2005) *The Sensory Hand: Neural Mechanisms of Somatic Sensation*. Cambridge, MA: MIT Press.

Mountcastle, V.B., LaMotte, R.H., Carli, G. (1972) Detection thresholds for stimuli in humans and monkeys: Comparison with threshold events in mechanoreceptive afferent nerve fibers innervating the monkey hand. *J. Neurophysiol.*, 35, 122–136.

Mountcastle, V.B., Talbot, W.H., Kornhuber, H.H. (1966) The neural transformation of mechanical stimuli delivered to the monkey's hand. In A.V.S. de Reuck, J. Knight (eds) *Ciba Foundation Symposium: Touch, Heat and Pain* (pp. 325–351). London: Churchill.

Munoz, D.P., Schall, J.D. (2003) Concurrent, distributed control of saccade initiation in the frontal eye field and superior colliculus. In W.T. Hall, A. Moschovakis (eds) *The Superior Colliculus: New Approaches for Studying Sensorimotor Integration* (pp. 55–82). New York: CRC Press.

N.

Nacson, J., Schmidt, R.A. (1971) The activity set hypothesis for warm-up decrement. *J. Mot. Behav.*, 3, 1–15.

Nagai, M., Isida, M., Saitoh, J., Hirata, Y., Natori, H., Wada, M. (2009) Characteristics of the control of standing posture during pregnancy. *Neurosci. Lett.*, 462, 130–134.

Nagasaki, H. (1989) Asymmetric velocity and acceleration profiles of human arm movements. *Exp. Brain Res.*, 74, 319–326.

Nakazawa, K., Kawashima, N., Obata, H., Yamanaka, K., Nozaki, D., Akai, M. (2003) Facilitation of both stretch reflex and corticospinal pathways of the tabialis anterior muscle during standing in humans. *Neurosci. Lett.*, 338, 53–56.

Nardone, A., Tarantola, J., Miscio, G., Pisano, F., Schenone, A., Schieppati, M. (2000) Loss of large-diameter spindle afferent fibres is not detrimental to the control of body sway during upright stance: Evidence from neuropathy. *Exp. Brain Res.*, 135, 155–162.

Nashner, L.M. (1976) Adapting reflexes controlling the human posture. *Exp. Brain Res.*, 26, 59–72.

Nashner, L.M. (1977) Fixed patterns of rapid postural responses among leg muscles during stance. *Exp. Brain Res.*, 30, 13–24.

Nashner, L.M. (1983) Analysis of movement control in man using the movable platform. *Adv. Neurol.*, 39, 607–619.

Nashner, L.M., Berthoz, A. (1978) Visual contribution to rapid motor responses during postural control. *Brain Res.*, 150, 403–407.

Nashner, L.M., McCollum, G. (1985) The organization of human postural movements: A formal basis and experimental synthesis. *Behav. Brain Sci.*, 8, 135–172.

Neilson, P.D., Andrews, G., Guitar, B.E., Quinn, P.T. (1979) Tonic stretch reflexes in lip, tongue and jaw muscles. *Brain Res.*, 178, 311–327.

Nelson, W.L. (1983) Physical principles for economies of skilled movements. *Biol. Cybern.*, 46, 135–147.

Newell, A., Rosenbloom, P.S. (1981) Mechanisms of skill acquisition and the law of practice. In J.R. Anderson (ed.), *Cognitive Skills and Their Acquisition* (pp. 1–55). Hillsdale, NJ: Erlbaum.

Newell, K.M., Carlton, L.G., Kim, S. (1994) Time and space-time movement accuracy. *Hum. Perform.*, 7, 1–21.

Newell, K.M., Carlton, L.G., Kim, S., Chung, C.-H. (1993) Space-time accuracy of rapid movements. *J. Mot. Behav.*, 25, 8–20.

Newell, K.M., Hoshizaki, L.E., Carlton, M.J., Halbert, J.A. (1979) Movement time and velocity as determinants of movement timing accuracy. *J. Mot. Behav.*, 11, 49–58.

Newell, K.M., Liu, Y., Mayer-Kress, G. (2001) Time scales in motor learning and development. *Psychol. Rev.*, 108, 57–82.

Nidermeyer, E., Lopes da Silva, F. (2005) *Electroencephalography: Basic Principles, Clinical Applications and Related Fields* (5th edition). Philadelphia: Lippincott, Williams, Wilkins.

Nilsson, J., Thorstensson, A., Halbertsma, J. (1985) Changes in leg movements and muscle activity with speed of locomotion and mode of progression in humans. *Acta Physiol. Scand.*, 123, 457–475.

Nishamaru, H., Restrepo, C.E., Ryge, J., Yanagawa, Y., Kiehn, O. (2005) Mammalian motoneurons corelease glutamate and acetylcholine at central synapses. *Proc. Natl. Acad. Sci. USA*, 102, 5245–5249.

Nishii, J., Taniai, Y. (2009) Evaluation of trajectory planning models for arm reaching movements based on energy cost. *Neural. Comput.*, 21, 2634–2647.

Novacheck, T.F. (1998) Biomechanics of running. *Gait Posture*, 7, 77–95.

Nunez, P.L. (2002) EEG. In V.S. Ramachandran (ed.) *Encyclopedia of the Human Brain* (pp. 169–179). La Jolla: Academic Press.

O.

Öhman, A., Mineka, S. (2001) Fear, phobias, and preparedness: Towards an evolved module of fear and fear learning. *Psychol. Rev.*, 108, 483–522.

Oie, K.S., Kiemel, T., Jeka, J.J. (2002) Multisensory fusion: Simultaneous re-weighting of vision and touch for the control of human posture. *Cogn. Brain Res.*, 14, 164–176.

Ono, H. (1983) The combination of version and vergence. In C. Schor, K.J. Ciuffreda (eds) *Vergence Eye Movements: Basic and Clinical Aspects* (pp. 373–400). Boston: Butterworths.

Orlovsky, G.N. (1991) Cerebellum and locomotion. In M. Shimamura, S. Grillner, V.R. Edgerton (eds) *Neurobiological Basis of Human Locomotion* (pp. 187–199). Tokyo: Japan Scientific Societies Press.

Østerberg, G. (1935) Topography of the layer of rods and cones in the human retina. *Acta Ophthalmol.*, 6, 1–103.

Ostry, D.J., Feldman, A.G. (2003) A critical evaluation of the force control hypothesis in motor control. *Exp. Brain Res.*, 153, 275–288.

Ostry, D.J., Gribble, P.L., Gracco, V.L. (1996) Coarticulation of jaw movements in speech production: Is context sensitivity in speech kinematics centrally planned? *J. Neurosci.*, 16, 1570–1579.

Osu, R., Franklin, D.W., Kato, H., Gomi, H., Domen, K., Yoshioka, T., Kawato, M. (2002) Short- and long-term changes in joint co-contraction associated with motor learning as revealed from surface EMG. *J. Neurophysiol.*, 88, 991–1004.

Osu, R., Uno, Y., Koike, Y., Kawato, M. (1997) Possible explanations for trajectory curvature in multijoint arm movements. *J. Exp. Psychol. Hum. Percept. Perform.*, 23, 890–913.

P.

Paillard, J. (1991) *Brain and Space*. Oxford: Oxford University Press.

Paillard, J., Brouchon, M. (1968) Active and passive movement in the calibration of position sense. In S.J. Freedman (ed.), *The Neuropsychology of Spatially Oriented Behavior* (pp. 35–55). Homewood, IL: Dorsey.

Pang, M.Y., Yang, J.F. (2000) The initiation of the swing phase in human infant stepping: Importance of hip position and leg loading. *J. Physiol.*, 528, 389–404.

Papaxanthis, C., Pozzo, P., Schieppati, M. (2003) Trajectories of arm pointing movements on the sagittal plane vary with both direction and speed. *Exp. Brain Res.*, 148, 498–503.

Park, S., Horak, F.B., Kuo, A.D. (2004) Postural feedback responses scale with biomechanical constraints in human standing. *Exp. Brain Res.*, 154, 417–427.

Parkin, A.J. (1996) The alien hand. In P.W. Halliga, J.C. Marshall (eds) *Method in Madness: Case Studies in Cognitive Neuropsychiatry* (pp. 173–183). Hove, UK: Psychology Press.

Pascual-Leone, A., Walsh, V., Rothwell, J.C. (2000) Transcranial magnetic stimulation in cognitive neuroscience: Virtual lesion, chronometry, and functional connectivity. *Curr. Opin. Neurobiol.*, 10, 232–237.

Pastor, M., Day, B.L., Marsden, C.D. (1993) Vestibular induced postural responses in Parkinson's disease. *Brain*, 116, 1177–1190.

Patla, A.E. (1997) Understanding the roles of vision in the control of human locomotion. *Gait Posture*, 5, 54–69.

Patla, A.E., Adkin, A., Martin, C., Holden, R., Prentice, S. (1996) Characteristics of voluntary visual sampling of the environment for safe locomotion over different terrains. *Exp. Brain Res.*, 112, 513–522.

Patla, A.E., Beuter, A., Prentice, S. (1991) A two stage correction of limb trajectory to avoid obstacles during stepping. *Neuroscience Research Communications*, 8, 153–159.

Patla, A.E., Prentice, S., Robinson, C., Neufeld, J. (1991) Visual control of locomotion: Strategies for changing direction and for going over obstacles. *J. Exp. Psychol. Hum. Percept. Perform.*, 17, 603–634.

Patla, A.E., Vickers, J.N. (1997) Where and when do we look as we approach and step over an obstacle in the travel path? *Neuroreport*, 8, 3661–3665.

Patla, A.E., Vickers, J.N. (2003) How far ahead do we look when required to step on specific locations in the travel path during locomotion? *Exp. Brain Res.*, 148, 133–138.

Paul, A.C. (2001) Muscle length affects the architecture and pattern of innervation differently in leg muscles of mouse, guinea pig and rabbit compared to those of human and monkey muscles. *Anat. Record*, 262, 301–309.

Paulignan, Y., Jeannerod, M., MacKenzie, C., Marteniuk, R. (1991a) Selective perturbation of visual input during prehension movements, 2: The effects of changing object size. *Exp. Brain Res.*, 87, 407–420.

Paulignan, Y., MacKenzie, C., Marteniuk, R., Jeannerod, M. (1991b) Selective perturbation of visual input during prehension movements, 1: The effects of changing object position. *Exp. Brain Res.*, 83, 502–512.

Paulus, W.M., Staube, A., Brandt, T. (1984) Visual stabilization of posture: Physiological stimulus characteristics and clinical aspects. *Brain*, 107, 1143–1163.

Pavani, F., Spence, C., Driver, J. (2000) Visual capture of touch: Out-of-the-body experiences with rubber gloves. *Psychol. Sci.*, 11, 353–359.

Pearson, K.G. (1976) The control of walking. *Scientific American*, 235, 72–86.

Pearson, K.G. (2000) Neural adaptation in the generation of rhythmic behavior. *Annu. Rev. Physiol.*, 62, 723–753.

Pearson, K.G. (2008) Role of sensory feedback in the control of stance duration in walking cats. *Brain Res. Rev.*, 57, 222–227.

Pearson, K.G., Rossignol, S. (1991) Fictive motor patterns in chronic spinal cats. *J. Neurophysiol.*, 66, 1874–1887.

Pelisson, D., Prablanc, C., Goodale, M.A., Jeannerod, M. (1986) Visual control of reaching movement without vision of the limb, II: Evidence of fast unconscious processes correcting the trajectory of the hand to the final position of a double-step stimulus. *Exp. Brain Res.*, 62, 303–311.

Pelisson, D., Prablanc, C., Urquizar, C. (1988) Vestibuloocular reflex inhibition and gaze saccade control characteristics during eye-head orientation in humans. *J. Neurophysiol.*, 75, 309–319.

Pellizzer, G., Zesiger, P. (2009) Hypothesis regarding the transformation of the intended direction of movement during the production of graphic trajectories: A study of drawing movements in 8- to 12-year-old children. *Cortex*, 45, 356–367.

Penfield, W., Boldrey, E. (1937) Somatic motor and sensory representation in the cerebral cortex of man as studied by electrical stimulation. *Brain*, 60, 389–443.

Penfield, W., Rasmussen, T. (1950) *The Cerebral Cortex of Man*. New York: Macmillan.

Perrier, P., Fuchs, S. (2007) Speed-curvature relations in speech production challenge the 1/3 power law. *J. Neurophysiol.*, 100, 1171–1183.

Peterka, R.J. (2002) Sensorimotor integration in human postural control. *J. Neurophysiol.*, 88, 1097–1118.

Peterka, R.J., Loughlin, P.J. (2004) Dynamic regulation of sensorimotor integration in human postural control. *J. Neurophysiol.*, 91, 410–423.

Petkova, V.I., Ehrsson, H.H. (2008) If I were you: Perceptual illusion of body swapping. *PLoS ONE*, 3(12), e3832.

Petkova, V.I., Ehrsson, H.H. (2010) Body self-perception. In *McGraw-Hill 2010 Yearbook of Science, Technology* (pp. 50–53). New York: McGraw-Hill Professional.

Pierrot-Deseilligny, E., Burke, D. (2005) *The Circuitry of the Human Spinal Cord*. Cambridge UK: Cambridge University Press.

Pinter, I.J., van Swigchem, R., van Soest, A.J., Rozendaal, L.A. (2008) The dynamics of postural sway cannot be captured using a one-segment inverted pendulum model: A PCA on segment rotations during unperturbed stance. *J. Neurophysiol.*, 100, 3197–3208.

Pisella, L., Sergio, L., Blangero, A., Torchin, H., Vighetto, A., Rossetti, Y. (2009) Optic ataxia and the function of the dorsal stream: Contribution to perception and action. *Neuropsychologia*, 47, 3033–3044.

Plamondon, R., Alimi, A.M. (1997) Speed/accuracy trade-offs in target-directed movements. *Behav. Brain Sci.*, 20, 279–349.

Plamondon, R., Djioua, M. (2006) A multi-level representation paradigm for handwriting stroke generation. *Hum. Mov. Sci.*, 25, 586–607.

Plamondon, R., Guerfali, W. (1998a) The 2/3 power law: When and why? *Acta Psychol.*, 100, 85–96.

Plamondon, R., Guerfali, W. (1998b) The generation of handwriting with delta-lognormal synergies. *Biol. Cybern.*, 78, 119–132.

Plamondon, R., Privitera, C.M. (1996) A neural model for generating and learning a rapid movement sequence. *Biol. Cybern.*, 74, 117–130.

Polit, A., Bizzi, E. (1979) Characteristics of the motor programs underlying arm movements in monkeys. *J. Neurophysiol.*, 42, 183–194.

Pollick, F.E., Maoz, U., Handzel, A.A., Giblin, P.J., Sapiro, G., Flash, T. (2009) Three-dimensional arm movements at constant equi-affine speed. *Cortex*, 45, 325–339.

Polyakov, F., Drori, R., Ben-Shaul, Y., Abeles, M., Flash, T. (2009a) A compact representation of drawing movements with sequences of parabolic primitives. *PLoS Comput. Biol.*, 5(7), e1000427.

Polyakov, F., Stark, E., Drori, R., Abeles, M., Flash, T. (2009b) Parabolic movement primitives and cortical states: Merging optimality with geometric invariance. *Biol. Cybern.*, 100, 159–184.

Pope, D.S. (2000) Testing function of fiddler crab claw waving by manipulating social context. *Behav. Ecol. Sociobiol.*, 47, 432–437.

Porrill, J., Dean, P. (2008) Silent synapses, LTP, and the indirect parallel-fibre pathway: Computational consequences of optimal cerebellar noise-processing. *PLoS Comput. Biol.*, 4(5), e1000085.

Postman, L. (1971) Transfer, interference and forgetting. In J.W. Kling, L.A. Riggs (eds) *Woodworth & Schlossberg's Experimental Psychology* (3rd edition). New York: Holt, Rinehart & Winston.

Postuma, R.B., Lang, A.E. (2003) Hemiballism: Revisiting a classic disorder. *Lancet Neurology*, 2, 661–668.

Poulton, E.C. (1973) Unwanted range effects from using within-subjects experimental designs. *Psychol. Bull.*, 80, 113–121.

Poulton, E.C. (1974) *Tracking Skill and Manual Control*. New York: Academic Press.

Poulton, E.C. (1979) Range effects and asymmetric transfer in studies of motor skill. In C.H. Nadeau *et al.* (eds) *Psychology of Motor Behavior and Sport*. Champaign, IL: Human Kinetics.

Powers, W.T. (1973) *Behavior: The Control of Perception*. Aldine Transaction Press.

Prablanc, C., Echallier, J.F., Komilis, E., Jeannerod, M. (1979) Optimal response of eye and hand motor systems in pointing at a visual target, I: Spatio-temporal characteristics of eye and hand movements and their relationship when varying the amount of visual information. *Biol. Cybern.*, 35, 113–124.

Prablanc, C., Martin, O. (1992) Automatic control during hand reaching at undetected two-dimensional target displacements. *J. Neurophysiol.*, 67, 455–469.

Prablanc, C., Tzavaras, A., Jeannerod, M. (1975) Adaptation of the two arms to opposite prism displacements. *Quart. J. Exp. Psychol.*, 27, 667–671.

Prescott, S.A. (1998) Interactions between suppression and facilitation within neural networks: Updating the dual-process theory of plasticity. *Learn. Mem.*, 5, 446–466.

Previc, F.H., Ercoline, W.R. (2004) *Spatial Disorientation in Aviation*. Reston, VA: American Institute of Aeronautics, Astronautics Inc.

Prevost, P., Ivanenko, Y., Grasso, R., Berthoz, A. (2002) Spatial invariance in anticipatory orienting behaviour during human navigation. *Neurosci. Lett.*, 339, 243–247.

Priest, H.F., Cutting, J.E. (1985) Visual flow and direction of locomotion. *Science*, 227, 1063–1064.

Prochazka, A. (1996) Proprioceptive feedback and movement regulation. In L.B. Rowell, T.J. Sheperd (eds) *Handbook of Physiology*, section 12, Exercise: Regulation and integration of multiple systems (pp. 89–127). New York: Oxford University Press.

Proske, U., Gandevia, S.C. (2009) The kinaesthetic senses. *J. Physiol.*, 587, 4139–4146.

Proske, U., Morgan, D.L., Gregory, J.E. (1993) Thixotropy in skeletal muscle and in muscle spindles: A review. *Prog. Neurobiol.*, 41, 705–721.

Purves, D., Brannon, E.M., Cabeza, R., Huettel, S.A., LaBar, K.S., Platt, M.L., Woldorff, M.G. (2008) *Principles of Cognitive Neuroscience*. Sunderland, MA: Sinauer Associates.

Putterman, A.H., Robert, A.L., Bregman, A.S. (1969) Adaptation of the wrist to displacing prisms. *Psychon. Sci.*, 16, 79–80.

Q.

Quevedo, J., Katinka, S., McCrea, D.A. (2005) Intracellular analysis of reflex pathways underlying the stumbling correction reaction during fictive locomotion in the cat. *J. Neurophysiol.*, 94, 2053–2062.

R.

Rack, P.M.H., Westbury, D.R. (1969) The effects of length and stimulus rate on tension in the isometric cat soleus muscle. *J. Physiol.*, 204, 443–460.

Ramenzoni, V.C., Riley, M.A., Shockley, K., Chiu, C.Y.P. (2007) Postural responses to specific types of working memory tasks. *Gait Posture*, 25, 368–373.

Rand, M.K., Stelmach, G.E. (2000) Segment interdependency and difficulty in two-stroke sequences. *Exp. Brain Res.*, 134, 228–236.

Ranganathan, R., Carlton, L.G. (2007) Perception-action coupling and anticipatory performance in baseball batting. *J. Mot. Behav.*, 39, 369–380.

Raphael, L.J, Borden, G.J., Harris, K.S. (2007) *Speech Science Primer: Physiology, Acoustics, and Perception of Speech* (5th edition). Philadelphia: Lippincott, Williams, Wilkins.

Rathelot, J.-A., Strick, P.L. (2006) Muscle representation in the macaque motor cortex: An anatomical perspective. *Proc. Natl. Acad. Sci. USA*, 103, 8257–8262.

Raymond, J.L., Lisberger, S.G. (1998) Neural learning rules for the vestibulo-ocular reflex. *J. Neurosci.*, 18, 9112–9129.

Readinger, W.O., Chatziastros, A., Cunningham, D.W., Bülthoff, H.H., Cutting, J.E. (2002) Gaze-eccentricity effects on road position and steering. *J. Exp. Psychol. Appl.*, 8, 247–258.

Redding, G.M., Wallace, B. (1996) Adaptive spatial alignment and strategic perceptual-motor control. *J. Exp. Psychol. Hum. Percept. Perform.*, 22, 379–394.

Redding, G.M., Wallace, B. (2001) Calibration and alignment are separable: Evidence from prism adaptation. *J. Mot. Behav.*, 33, 401–412.

Redding, G.M., Wallace, B. (2006a) Generalization of prism adaptation. *J. Exp. Psychol. Hum. Percept. Perform.*, 32, 1006–1022.

Redding, G.M., Wallace, B. (2006b) Prism adaptation and unilateral neglect: Review and analysis. *Neuropsychologia*, 44, 1–20.

Redding, G.M., Wallace, B. (2009) Asymmetric visual prism adaptation and intermanual transfer. *J. Mot. Behav.*, 41, 83–94.

Reder, L.M., Park, H., Kieffaber, P.D. (2009) Memory systems do not divide on consciousness: Re-interpreting memory in terms of activation and binding. *Psychol. Bull.*, 135, 23–49.

Reed, E.S. (1982a) An outline of a theory of action systems. *J. Mot. Behav.*, 14, 98–134.

Reed, E.S. (1982b) Darwin's earthworms: A case study in evolutionary psychology. *Behaviorism*, 10, 165–185.

Reed, E.S. (1988) Applying the theory of action systems to the study of motor skills. In O.G. Meijer, K. Roth (eds) *Complex Movement Behavior: The Motor-Action Controversy* (pp. 45–86). New York: Elsevier, North Holland.

Regan, D. (1992) Visual judgments and misjudgments in cricket, and the art of flight. *Perception*, 21, 91–115.

Regan, D. (1997) Visual factors in hitting and catching. *J. Sports Sci.*, 15, 533–58.

Regan, D., Beverley, K.I. (1982) How do we avoid confounding the direction we are looking and the direction we are moving? *Science*, 215, 194–196.

Regan, D., Gray, R. (2000) Visually guided collision avoidance and collision achievement. *Trends Cog. Sci.*, 4, 99–107.

Regan, D., Hamstra, S. (1993) Dissociation of discrimination thresholds for time-to-contact and rate of angular expansion. *Vision Res.*, 33, 447–462.

Reinhard, J., Trauzettel-Klosinski, S. (2003) Nasotemporal overlap of retinal ganglion cells in humans: A functional study. *Invest. Ophthalmol. Vis. Sci.*, 44, 1568–1572.

Reiter, L.A., Ison, J.R. (1977) Inhibition of the human eyeblink reflex: An evaluation of the sensitivity of the Wendt-Yerkes method for threshold detection. *J. Exp. Psychol. Hum. Percept. Perform.*, 3, 325–336.

Rescorla, R.A. (1988) Behavioral studies of Pavlovian conditioning. *Annu. Rev. Neurosci.*, 11, 329–352.

Rescorla, R.A. (2001) Experimental extinction. In R.R. Mowrer, S.B. Klein (eds) *Contemporary Learning Theories* (pp. 119–154). Hillsdale, NJ: Erlbaum.

Reynolds, G.S. (1961) Attention in the pigeon. *J. Exp. Anal. Behav.*, 4, 203–208.

Reynolds, R.F., Day, B.L. (2005a) Visual guidance of the human foot during a step. *J. Physiol.*, 569, 677–684.

Reynolds, R.F., Day, B.L. (2005b) Rapid visuo-motor processes drive the leg regardless of balance constraints. *Curr. Biol.*, 15, R48–R49.

Rhodes, B.J., Bullock, D., Verwey, W.B, Averbeck, B., Page, M.P.A. (2004) Learning and production of movement sequences: Behavioral, neurophysiological, and modeling perspectives. *Hum. Mov. Sci.*, 23, 699–746.

Richardson, M., Flash, T. (2002) Comparing smooth arm movements with the two-thirds power law and the related segmented-control hypothesis. *J. Neurosci.*, 22, 8201–8211.

Riemersma, J.B.J. (1981) Visual control during straight road driving. *Acta Psychol.*, 48, 215–225.

Rieser, J.J., Ashmead, D.H., Talor, C.R., Youngquist, G.A. (1990) Visual perception and the guidance of locomotion without vision to previously seen targets. *Perception*, 19, 675–689.

Riley, M.A., Mitra, S., Stoffregen, T.A., Turvey, M.T. (1997) Influences of body lean and vision on postural fluctuations in stance. *Motor Control*, 1, 229–246.

Roberts, A., Li, W.-C., Soffe, S.R., Wolf, E. (2008) Origin of excitatory drive to a spinal locomotor network. *Brain Res. Rev.*, 57, 22–28.

Roberts, A.C., Glanzman, D.L. (2003) Learning in Aplysia: Looking at synaptic plasticity from both sides. *Trends Neurosci.*, 26, 662–670.

Roberts, T.D.M. (1978) *The Neurophysiology of Postural Mechanisms*. London: Butterworths.

Roberts, T.D.M. (1995) Understanding Balance: *The Mechanics of Posture and Locomotion*. London: Chapman, Hall.

Robertshaw, K.D., Wilkie, R.M. (2008) Does gaze influence steering around a bend? *J. Vision*, 8, 1–13.

Robinson, D.A. (1972) Eye movements evoked by collicular stimulation in the alert monkey. *Vision Res.*, 12, 1795–1808.

Robinson, D.A. (1975) Oculomotor control signals. In G. Lennerstrand, P. Bach-y-Rita (eds), *Basic Mechanisms of Ocular Motility and their Clinical Implications* (pp. 337–374). Oxford: Pergamon.

Rodieck, R.W. (1998) *The First Steps in Seeing*. Sunderland, MA: Sinauer Associates.

Rogers, B., Graham, M. (1979) Motion parallax as an independent cue for depth perception. *Perception*, 8, 125–134.

Roll, J.P., Albert, F., Thyrion, C., Ribot-Ciscar, E., Bergenheim, M., Mattei, B. (2009) Inducing any virtual two-dimensional movement in humans by applying muscle tendon vibration. *J. Neurophysiol.*, 101, 816–823.

Roll, J.P., Gilhodes, J.C., Roll, R., Harlay, F. (1996) Are proprioceptive sensory inputs combined into a 'Gestalt'? In T. Inui, J.L. McClelland (eds) *Attention and Performance XVI: Information Integration in Perception and Communication* (pp. 291–314). Cambridge, MA: MIT Press.

Roll, J.P., Roll, R. (1988) From eye to foot: A proprioceptive chain involved in postural control. In B. Amblard, A. Berthoz, F. Clarac (eds), *Posture and Gait: Development, Adaptation and Modulation* (pp. 155–164). Amsterdam: Elsevier.

Roll, J.P., Vedel, J.P., Ribot, E. (1989) Alteration of proprioceptive messages induced by tendon vibration in man: A microneurographic study. *Exp. Brain Res.*, 76, 213–222.

Rosen, R. (1985) *Anticipatory Systems*. Oxford: Pergamon Press.

Rosenbaum, D.A. (1977) Selective adaptation of 'command neurons' in the human motor system. *Neuropsychologia*, 15, 81–91.

Rosenbaum, D.A. (2009) *Human Motor Control* (2nd edition). New York: Academic Press.

Rosenbaum, D.A., Cohen, R.G., Jax, S.A., Weiss, D.J., Van der Wel, R. (2007) The problem of serial order in behavior: Lashley's legacy. *Hum. Mov. Sci.*, 26, 525–554.

Rosenblum, L.D., Gordon, M.S., Jarquin, L. (2000) Echolocation by moving and stationary listeners. *Ecological Psychol.*, 12, 181–206.

Rossetti, Y., Desmurget, M., Prablanc, C. (1995) Vectorial coding of movement: Vision, proprioception or both? *J. Neurophysiol.*, 74, 457–463.

Rossetti, Y., Stelmach, G.E., Desmurget, M., Prablanc, C., Jeannerod, M. (1994) The effect of viewing the static hand prior to movement onset on pointing kinematics and accuracy. *Exp. Brain Res.*, 101, 323–330.

Rossignol, S., Dubuc, R., Gossard, J.P. (2006) Dynamic sensorimotor interactions in locomotion. *Physiol. Rev.*, 86, 89–154.

Rothwell, J.C., Day, B.L., Berardelli, A., Marsden, C.A. (1986) Habituation and conditioning of the human long latency stretch reflex. *Exp. Brain Res.*, 63, 197–204.

Rothwell, J.C., Traub, M.M., Day, B.L., Obseso, J.A., Thomas, P.K., Marsden, C.A. (1982) Manual motor performance in a deafferented man. *Brain*, 205, 515–542.

Roy, J.E., Cullen, K.E. (1998) A neural correlate for vestibulo-ocular reflex suppression during voluntary eye-head gaze shifts. *Nat. Neurosci.*, 1, 404–410.

Rozendaal, L.A., van Soest, A.J. (2008) Stabilization of a multi-segment model of bipedal standing by local joint control overestimates the required ankle stiffness. *Gait Posture*, 28, 525–527.

Rucci, M., Iovin, R., Poletti, M., Santini, F. (2007) Miniature eye movements enhance fine spatial detail. *Nature*, 447, 852–855.

Rumelhart, D.E., Norman, D.A. (1982) Simulating a skilled typist: A study of skilled cognitive-motor performance. *Cognitive Sci.*, 6, 1–36.

Runge, C.F., Shupert, C.L., Horak, F.B., Zajac, F.E. (1999) Postural strategies defined by joint torques. *Gait Posture*, 10, 161–170.

Rushton, S.K., Harris, J.M., Lloyd, M., Wann, J.P. (1998) Guidance of locomotion on foot uses perceived target location rather than optic flow. *Curr. Biol.*, 8, 1191–1194.

Ruskell, G.L. (1999) Extraocular muscle proprioceptors and proprioception. *Prog. Retin. Eye Res.*, 18, 269–291.

Ruxton, G.D., Speed, M.P., Kelly, D.J. (2004) What, if anything, is the adaptive function of countershading? *Animal Behav.*, 68, 445–451.

S.

Sabes, P.N., Jordan, M.I., Wolpert, D.M. (1998) The role of inertial sensitivity in motor planning. *J. Neurosci.*, 18, 5948–5957.

Sadeghi, S.G., Chacron, M.J., Taylor, M.C., Cullen, K.E. (2007) Neural variability, detection thresholds, and information transmission in the vestibular system. *J. Neurosci.*, 27, 771–781.

Sadeghi, S.G., Goldberg, J.M., Minor, L.B., Cullen, K.E. (2009) Efferent-mediated responses in vestibular nerve afferents of the alert macaque. *J. Neurophysiol.*, 10, 988–1001.

Sainburg, R.L., Kalakanis, D. (2000) Differences in control of limb dynamics during dominant and nondominant arm reaching. *J. Neurophysiol.*, 83, 2661–2675.

Saltzman, E.L. (1979) Levels of sensorimotor representation. *J. Math. Psychol.*, 20, 91–163.

Saltzman, E.L., Kelso, J.A.S. (1987) Skilled actions: A task dynamic approach. *Psychol. Rev.*, 94, 84–106.

Saltzman, E.L., Munhall, K. (1989) A dynamical approach to gestural patterning in speech production. *Ecological Psychol.*, 1, 333–382.

Salvucci, D.D., Gray, R. (2004) A two-point visual control model of steering. *Perception*, 33, 1233–1248.

Sanes, J.N., Mauritz, K.H., Dalakas, M.C., Evarts, E.V. (1985) Motor control in humans with large-fiber sensory neuropathy. *Hum. Neurobiol.*, 4, 101–114.

Santello, M., McDonagh, M.J.N., Challis, J.H. (2001) Visual and non-visual control of landing movements in humans. *J. Physiol.*, 571, 313–327.

Saunders, J.A., Knill, D.C. (2003) Humans use continuous visual feedback from the hand to control fast reaching movements. *Exp. Brain Res.*, 152, 341–352.

Saunders, J.A., Knill, D.C. (2004) Visual feedback control of hand movements. *J. Neurosci.*, 24, 3223–3234.

Scepkowski, L.A., Cronin-Golomb, A. (2003) The alien hand: Cases, categorizations, and anatomical correlates. *Behav. Cogn. Neurosci. Rev.*, 2, 261–277.

Schaal, S., Sternad, D. (2001) Origins and violations of the 2/3 power law in rhythmic three-dimensional arm movements. *Exp. Brain Res.*, 136, 60–72.

Schacter, D.L., Wagner, A.D., Buckner, R.L. (2000) Memory systems of 1999. In E. Tulving, F.I.M. Craik (eds) *Oxford Handbook of Memory* (pp. 627–643). New York: Oxford University Press.

Schall, J.D. (2002) The neural selection and control of saccades by the frontal eye field. *Phil. Trans. Roy. Soc. Lond. B*, 357, 1073–1082.

Schieber, M.H. (2001) Constraints on somatotopic organization in the primary motor cortex. *J. Neurophysiol.*, 86, 2125–2143.

Schiff, W., Detwiler, M.L. (1979) Information used in judging impending collision. *Perception*, 8, 647–658.

Schiller, P.H., Stryker, M. (1972) Single-unit recording and stimulation in superior colliculus of the alert rhesus monkey. *J. Neurophysiol.*, 35, 915–924.

Schillings, A.M., Van Wezel, B.M.H., Duysens, J. (1996) Mechanically induced stumbling during human treadmill walking. *J. Neurosci. Methods*, 67, 11–17.

Schillings, A.M., Van Wezel, B.M.H., Mulder, T.H., Duysens, J. (2000) Muscular responses and movement strategies during stumbling over obstacles. *J. Neurophysiol.*, 83, 2093–2102.

Schmid, M.C., Panagiotaropoulos, T., Augath, M.A., Logothetis, N.K., Smirnakis, S.M. (2009) Visually driven activation in macaque areas V2 and V3 without input from the primary visual cortex. *PLoS ONE*, 4(5), e5527.

Schmidt, R.A. (1969) Movement time as a determiner of timing accuracy. *J. Exp. Psychol.*, 79, 43–47.

Schmidt, R.A. (1982) The schema concept. In J.A.S. Kelso (ed.) *Human Motor Behavior: An Introduction*. Hillsdale, NJ: Lawrence Erlbaum.

Schmidt, R.A., Lee, T.D. (2011) *Motor Control and Learning: A Behavioral Emphasis* (5th edition). Champaign, IL: Human Kinetics.

Schmidt, R.A., McGown, C. (1980) Terminal accuracy of unexpectedly loaded rapid movements: Evidence for a mass-spring mechanism in programming. *J. Mot. Behav.*, 12, 149–161.

Schmidt, R.A., Sherwood, D.E. (1982) An inverted-U relation between spatial error and force requirements in rapid limb movements: Further evidence for the impulse-variability model. *J. Exp. Psychol. Hum. Percept. Perform.*, 8, 158–170.

Schmidt, R.A., Zelaznik, H., Hawkins, B., Frank, J., Quinn, J.T. (1979) Motor-output variability: A theory for the accuracy of rapid motor acts. *Psychol. Rev.*, 86, 415–451.

Schneiderman, N., Gormezano, I. (1964) Conditioning of the nictitating membrane of the rabbit as a function of the CS-US interval. *J. Comp. Physiol. Psychol.*, 57, 188–195.

Scholz, J.P., Kelso, J.A.S., Schöner, G. (1987) Nonequilibrium phase transitions in coordinated biological motion: Critical slowing down and switching time. *Physics Lett. A*, 123, 390–394.

Scholz, J.P., Schöner, G., Hsu, W.L., Jeka, J.J., Horak, F., Martin, V. (2007) Motor equivalent control of the center of mass in response to support surface perturbations. *Exp. Brain Res.*, 180, 163–179.

Schöne, H. (1964) On the role of gravity in human spatial orientation. *Aerospace Medicine*, 35, 764–772.

Schöne, H. (1984) *Spatial Orientation: The Spatial Control of Behavior in Animals and Man*. Princeton, NJ: Princeton University Press.

Schöne, H., Wade, N.J. (1971) The influence of force magnitude on the perception of body position, II: Effect of body posture. *Br. J. Psychol.*, 62, 347–352.

Schöner, G., Thelen, E. (2006) Using dynamic field theory to rethink infant habituation. *Psychol. Rev.*, 113, 273–299.

Schouenborg, J. (2002) Modular organization and spinal somatosensory imprinting. *Brain Res. Rev.*, 40, 80–91.

Schouenborg, J. (2008) Action-based sensory encoding in spinal sensorimotor circuits. *Brain Res. Rev.*, 57, 111–117.

Schreiber, K., Crawford, J.D., Fetter, M., Tweed, D. (2001) The motor side of depth vision. *Nature*, 410, 819–822.

Schroeder, C.E., Wilson, D.A., Radman, T., Scharfman, H., Lakatos, P. (2010) Dynamics of active sensing and perceptual selection. *Curr. Opin. Neurobiol.*, 20, 172–176.

Schubert, M.C., Della Santina, C.C., Shelhamer, M. (2008) Incremental angular vestibulo-ocular reflex adaptation to active head rotation. *Exp. Brain Res.*, 191, 435–446.

Schubert, M.C., Zee, D.S. (2010) Saccade and vestibular ocular motor adaptation. *Restor. Neurol. Neurosci.*, 28, 9–18.

Schwartz, A. (1994) Direct cortical representation of drawing. *Science*, 265, 540–542.

Schwartz, A., Moran, D. (2000) Arm trajectory and representation of movement processing in motor cortical activity. *Eur. J. Neurosci.*, 12, 1851–1856.

Scoville, W.B., Milner, B. (1957) Loss of recent memory after bilateral hippocampal lesions. *J. Neurol. Neurosurg. Psychiat.*, 20, 11–21.

Scudder, C.A., Kaneko, C.R., Fuchs, A.F. (2002) The brainstem burst generator for saccadic eye movements: A modern synthesis. *Exp. Brain Res.*, 142, 439–462.

Searle, J.R. (1983) *Intentionality.* Cambridge University Press.

Seif-Naraghi, A.H., Winters, J.M. (1990) Optimized strategies for scaling goal-directed dynamic limb movements. In J.M. Winters, S.L.-Y. Woo (eds) *Multiple Muscle Systems. Biomechanics and Movement Organization* (pp. 312–334). New York: Springer-Verlag.

Semmlow, J.L., Yuan, W., Alvarez, T.L. (1998) Evidence for separate control of slow version and vergence movements: Support for Hering's Law. *Vision Res.*, 38, 1145–1152.

Senders, J.W., Kristofferson, A.B., Levison, W.H., Dietrich, C.W., Ward, J.L. (1967) The attentional demand of automobile driving. *Highway Res. Record*, 195, 15–32.

Shadmehr, R., Brandt, J., Corkin, S. (1998) Time-dependent motor memory processes in amnesic subjects. *J. Neurophysiol.*, 80, 1590–1597.

Shadmehr, R., Krakauer, J.W. (2008) A computational neuroanatomy for motor control. *Exp. Brain Res.*, 185, 359–381.

Shadmehr, R., Mussa-Ivaldi, F.A. (1994) Adaptive representation of dynamics during learning of a motor task. *J. Neurosci.*, 14, 3208–3224.

Shadmehr, R., Wise, S.P. (2005) *The Computational Neurobiology of Reaching and Pointing.* Cambridge, MA: MIT Press.

Shaffer, L.H. (1991) Cognition and motor programming. In J. Requin, G.E. Stelmach (eds), *Tutorials in Motor Neuroscience* (pp. 371–383). Dordrecht: Kluwer.

Shallice, T. (1982) Specific impairments of planning. *Phil. Trans. Roy. Soc. Lond. B*, 298, 199–209.

Shallice, T., Burgess, P.W., Schon, F., Baxter, D.M. (1989) The origins of utilization behaviour. *Brain*, 112, 1587–1598.

Sheikh, I.H., Hoffman, E.R. (1994) Effect of target shape on movement time in a Fitts task. *Ergonomics*, 37, 1533–1547.

Shemmell, J., Forner, M., Tresilian, J.R., Riek, S., Carson, R.G. (2005) Neuromuscular adaptation during skill acquisition on a two degree-of-freedom target acquisition task: Isometric torque production. *J. Neurophysiol.*, 94, 3046–3057.

Sheridan, M.R. (1979) A reappraisal of Fitts' law. *J. Mot. Behav.*, 11, 179–188.

Sherrington, C.S. (1906/1947) *The Integrative Action of the Nervous System.* New Haven: Yale University Press.

Sherrington, C.S. (1910) Flexor-reflex of the limb, crossed extension reflex, and reflex stepping and standing. *J. Physiol.*, 40, 28–121.

Sherrington, C.S. (1913) Reflex inhibition as a factor in the co-ordination of movements and postures. *Quart. J. Exp. Physiol.*, 6, 251–310.

Shik, M.L., Severin, F.V., Orlovsky, G.N. (1966) Control of walking and running by means of electric stimulation of the midbrain. *Biofizika*, 11, 659–666.

Shimamura, A.P., Prinzmetal, W. (1999) The Mystery Spot illusion and its relation to other visual illusions. *Psychol. Sci.*, 10, 501–507.

Shimojo, S. (2008) Self and world: Large scale installations at science museums. *Spat. Vis.*, 21, 337–346.

Shimojo, S., Shams, L. (2001) Sensory modalities are not separate modalities: Plasticity and interactions. *Curr. Opin. Neurobiol.*, 11, 505–509.

Shimono, K., Higashiyama, A., Tam, W.J. (2001) Location of the egocenter in kinesthetic space. *J. Exp. Psychol. Hum. Percept. Perform.*, 27, 848–861.

Shumway-Cook, A., Woollacott, M. (2011) *Motor Control: Translating Research into Clinical Practice* (4th edition). Philadelphia: Lippincott, Williams, Wilkins.

Sidaway, B., Sekiya, H., Fairweather, M. (1995) Movement variability as a function of directional accuracy demand in programmed serial aiming response. *J. Mot. Behav.*, 27, 67–76.

Simmons, G.F. (1995) *Calculus with Analytic Geometry* (2nd edition). New York: McGraw-Hill.

Simons, D.J., Chabris, C.J. (2011) What people believe about how memory works: A representative survey of the U.S. population. *PLoS ONE*, 6(8), e22757.

Sincich, L.C., Park, K.F., Wohlgemuth, M.J., Horton, J.C. (2004) Bypassing V1: A direct geniculate input to area MT. *Nat. Neurosci.*, 7, 1123–1128.

Skavenski, A.A., Hansen, R., Steinman, R.M., Winterson, B.J. (1979) Quality of retinal image stabilization during small natural and artificial body rotations in man. *Vision Res.*, 19, 675–683.

Skinner, B.F. (1938) *The Behavior of Organisms.* New York: Appleton-Century-Crofts.

Smeets, J.B.J., Brenner, E. (1999) A new view on grasping. *Motor Contol*, 3, 237–271.

Smeets, J.B.J., Brenner, E., Trebuchet, S., Mestre, D.R. (1996) Is judging time-to-contact based on 'tau'? *Perception*, 25, 583–590.

Smith, J.L., Crawford, M., Proske, U., Taylor, J.L., Gandevia, S.C. (2009) Signals of motor command bias joint position sense in the presence of feedback from proprioceptors. *J. Appl. Physiol.*, 106, 950–958.

Smith, J.W. (1957) The forces operating at the human ankle joint during standing. *J. Anat.*, 91, 545–564.

Smith, M.C., Coleman, S.R., Gormezano, I. (1969) Classical conditioning of the rabbit's nictitating membrane response at backward, simultaneous, and forward CS-US intervals. *J. Comp. Physiol. Psychol.*, 69, 226–231.

Smith, M.R.H., Flach, J.M., Dittman, S.M., Stanard, T. (2001) Monocular optical constraints on collision control. *J. Exp. Psychol. Hum. Percept. Perform.*, 27, 395–410.

Smythies, J.R. (1996) A note on the concept of the visual field in neurology, psychology, and visual neuroscience. *Perception*, 25, 369–371.

Snoddy, G.S. (1926) Learning and stability: A psychophysical analysis of a case of motor learning with clinical applications. *J. Appl. Psychol.*, 10, 1–36.

Soechting, J.F. (1982) Does position sense at the elbow reflect a sense of elbow joint angle or one of limb orientation? *Brain Res.*, 248, 392–395.

Soechting, J.F. (1984) Effect of target size on spatial and temporal characteristics of a pointing movement in man. *Exp. Brain Res.*, 54, 121–132.

Soechting, J.F., Flanders, M. (1989) Errors in pointing are due to approximations in sensorimotor transformations. *J. Neurophysiol.*, 62, 595–608.

Soechting, J.F., Flanders, M. (1992) Oganization of sequential typing movements. *J. Neurophysiol.*, 67, 1275–1290.

Soechting, J.F., Lacquaniti, F. (1981) Invariant characteristics of a pointing movement in man. *J. Neurosci.*, 1, 710–720.

Soechting, J.F., Lacquaniti, F. (1983) Modification of trajectory of a pointing movement in response to a change in target location. *J. Neurophysiol.*, 49, 548–564.

Soechting, J.F., Ross, B. (1984) Psychophysical determination of coordinate representation of human arm orientation. *Neuroscience*, 13, 595–604.

Soechting, J.F., Terzuolo, C.A. (1987) Organization of arm movements: Motion is segmented. *Neuroscience*, 23, 39–51.

Solomon, H.Y., Turvey, M.T. (1988) Haptically perceiving the distances reachable with hand-held rods. *J. Exp. Psychol. Hum. Percept. Perform.*, 14, 404–427.

Solomon, P.R., Vander Schaaf, E.R., Thompson, R.F., Weisz, D.J. (1986) Hippocampus and trace conditioning of the rabbit's classically conditioned nictitating membrane response. *Behav. Neurosci.*, 100, 729–744.

Sosnik, R., Hauptmann, B., Karni, A., Flash, T. (2004) When practice leads to co-articulation: The evolution of geometrically defined movement primitives. *Exp. Brain Res.*, 156, 422–438.

Sosnik, R., Shemesh, M., Abeles, M. (2007) The point of no return in planar hand movements: An indication of the existence of high level motion primitives. *Cogn. Neurodyn.*, 1, 341–358.

Soukoreff, R.W., MacKenzie, I.S. (2004) Towards a standard for pointing device evaluation: Perspectives on 27 years of Fitts' law research in HCI. *Int. J. Hum. Comput. Stud.*, 61, 751–789.

Sparks, D.L. (1986) The neural translation of sensory signals into commands for the control of saccadic eye movements: The role of the primate superior colliculus. *Physiol. Rev.*, 66, 118–171.

Sparks, D.L. (2002) The brainstem control of saccadic eye movements. *Nat. Rev. Neurosci.*, 3, 952–964.

Sparks, D.L., Nelson, J.S. (1987) Sensory and motor maps in the mammalian superior colliculus. *Trends Neurosci.*, 10, 312–317.

Sparrow, W.A. (2000, ed.) *Energetics of Human Activity*. Champaign IL: Human Kinetics.

Spiers, H.J., Maguire, E.A., Burgess, N. (2001) Hippocampal amnesia. *Neurocase*, 7, 357–382.

Squire, L.R. (2004) Memory systems of the brain: A brief history and current perspective. *Neurobiol. Learn. Mem.*, 82, 171–177.

Squire, L.R., Bloom, F.E., Spitzer, N.C., du Lac, S., Ghosh, A., Berg, D. (2008) *Fundamental Neuroscience* (3rd edition). London: Academic Press.

Srinivasan, M., Ruina, A. (2006) Computer optimization of a minimal biped model discovers walking and running. *Nature*, 439, 72–75.

Srinivasan, M.V., Lehrer, M., Kirchner, W., Zhang, S.W. (1991) Range perception through apparent image speed in freely flying honeybees. *Visual Neurosci.*, 6, 519–535.

Staddon, J.E.R., Niv, Y. (2008) Operant conditioning. *Scholarpedia*, 3(9), 2318.

Steenhuis, R.E., Goodale, M.A. (1988) The effects of time and distance on accuracy of target-directed locomotion: Does an accurate short-term memory for spatial location exist? *J. Mot. Behav.*, 20, 399–415.

Steinmetz, J.E., Kim, J., Thompson, R.F. (2003) Biological models of associative learning. In M. Gallagher, R.J. Nelson (eds) *Handbook of Psychology* vol. 3: *Biological Psychology*. Hoboken, NJ: John Wiley & Sons.

Steinmetz, J.E., Tracy, J.A., Green, J.T. (2001) Classical eyeblink conditioning: Clinical models and applications. *Integ. Physiol. Behav. Sci.*, 36, 220–238.

Stephens, M.J., Yang, J.F. (1999) Loading during the stance phase of walking in humans increases the extensor EMG amplitude but does not change the duration of the step cycle. *Exp. Brain Res.*, 124, 363–370.

Sternad, D., Corcos, D. (2001) Effect of task and instruction on patterns of muscle activation: Wachholder and beyond. *Motor Control*, 5, 307–336.

Sternad, D., Schaal, S. (1999) Segmentation of endpoint trajectories does not imply segmented control. *Exp. Brain Res.*, 124, 118–136.

Sternberg, S., Knoll, R.L., Turock, D.L. (1990) Hierarchical control in the execution of action sequences: Tests of two invariance principles. In M. Jeannerod (ed.) *Attention and Performance XIII* (pp. 3–35). Hillsdale, NJ: Lawrence Erlbaum.

Sternberg, S., Monsell, S., Knoll, R.L., Wright, C.E. (1978) The latency and duration of rapid movement sequences: Comparisons of speech and typewriting. In G.E. Stelmach (ed.), *Information Processing in Motor Control and Learning* (pp. 117–152). New York: Academic Press.

Stoffregen, T.A. (1986) The role of optical velocity in the control of stance. *Percept. Psychophys.*, 39, 355–360.

Stuart, D.G. (2007) Reflections on integrative and comparative movement neuroscience. *Integr. Comp. Biol.*, 47, 482–504.

Stuart, G., Spruston, N., Sakmann, B., Hausser, M. (1997) Action potential initiation and backpropagation in neurons of the mammalian nervous system. *Trends Neurosci.*, 20, 125–131.

Sturm, R., Nigg, B., Koller, E.A. (1980) The impact of cardiac activity on triaxially recorded endogenous microvibrations of the body. *Eur. J. Appl. Physiol. Occup. Physiol.*, 44, 83–96.

Sturnieks, D.L., Wright, J.R., Fitzpatrick, R.C. (2007) Detection of simultaneous movement at two human arm joints. *J. Physiol.*, 585, 833–842.

Summers, J.J. (1975) The role of timing in motor program representation. *J. Mot. Behav.*, 7, 229–241.

Summers, J.J., Anson, J.G. (2009) Current status of the motor program: Revisited. *Hum. Mov. Sci.*, 28, 566–577.

Sutton, R.S., Barto, A.G. (1998) *Reinforcement Learning: An Introduction.* Cambridge, MA: MIT Press.

Swinnen, S.P., Schmidt, R.A., Nicholson, D.E., Shapiro, D.C. (1990) Information feedback for motor acquisition: Instantaneous knowledge of results degrades learning. *J. Exp. Psychol. Learn. Mem. Cogn.*, 16, 706–716.

T.

Tabata, H., Yamamoto, K., Kawato, M. (2002) Computational study on monkey VOR adaptation and smooth pursuit based on the parallel control-pathway theory. *J. Neurophysiol.*, 87, 2176–2189.

Takakusaki, K. (2008) Forebrain control of locomotor behaviors. *Brain Res. Rev.*, 57, 192–198.

Talbot, W.H., Darian-Smith, I., Kornhuber, H.H., Mountcastle, V.B. (1968) The sense of flutter-vibration: Comparison of the human capacity with response patterns of mechanoreceptive afferents from the monkey hand. *J. Neurophysiol.*, 31, 301–334.

Tanaka, H., Homma, K., Imamizu, H. (2011) Physical delay but not subjective delay determines learning rate in prism adaptation. *Exp. Brain Res.*, 208, 257–268.

Tastevin, J. (1937) En partant de l'experience d'Aristotle. *L'Encéphale*, 1, 57–84.

Taylor, J.A., Ivry, R.B. (2011) Flexible cognitive strategies during motor learning. *PLoS Comput. Biol.*, 7(3), e1001096.

Teasdale, N., Schmidt, R.A. (1991) Deceleration requirements and the control of pointing movements. *J. Mot. Behav.*, 23, 131–138.

Templeton, W.B., Howard, I.P., Wilkinson, D.A. (1974) Additivity of components of prismatic adaptation. *Percept. Psychophys.*, 15, 249–257.

Terzuolo, C.A., Viviani, P. (1979) About the central representation of learned motor patterns. In R. Talbot, D.R. Humphrey (eds) *Posture and Movement: Perspectives for Integrating Neurophysiological Research in Sensory-Motor Systems* (pp. 113–121). New York: Raven Press.

Terzuolo, C.A., Viviani, P. (1980) Determinants and characteristics of motor patterns used for typing. *Neuroscience*, 5, 1085–1103.

Teulings, H.L. (1996) Handwriting movement control. In H. Heuer, S.W. Keele (eds) *Handbook of Perception and Action*, vol. 2: Motor Skills (pp. 561–613). New York: Academic Press.

Teulings, H.L., Thomassen, A., Van Galen, G.P. (1986) Invariants in handwriting: The information contained in a motor program. In H.S. Kao, G.P. van Galen, R. Hoosian (eds), *Graphonomics: Contemporary Research in Handwriting* (pp. 305–315). Amsterdam: Elsevier.

Thayer, A.H. (1896) The law which underlies protective coloration. *Auk*, 13, 124–129.

Thomas, D.P., Whitney, R.J. (1959) Postural movements during normal standing in man. *J. Anat.*, 93, 524–539.

Thompson, R.F., Steinmetz, J.E. (2009) The role of the cerebellum in classical conditioning of discrete behavioral responses. *Neuroscience*, 162, 732–755.

Thomson, J.A. (1980) How do we use visual information to control locomotion? *Trends Neurosci.*, 3, 247–250.

Thomson, J.A. (1983) Is continuous visual monitoring necessary in visually guided locomotion? *J. Exp. Psychol. Hum. Percept. Perform.*, 9, 427–443.

Thorndike, E.L. (1898) Animal intelligence: An experimental study of the associative processes in animals. *Psychol. Rev., Monograph Suppl.*, 2, no. 8.

Thorndike, E.L. (1911) *Animal intelligence.* New York: Macmillan.

Thorndike, E.L. (1927) The law of effect. *Am. J. Psychol.*, 39, 212–222.

Ting, L.H., McKay, J.L. (2007) Neuromechanics of muscle synergies for posture and movement. *Curr. Opin. Neurobiol.*, 17, 622–628.

Todorov, E. (2004) Optimality principles in sensorimotor control. *Nat. Neurosci.*, 7, 907–915.

Todorov, E., Jordan, M.I. (1998) Smoothness maximization along a predefined path accurately predicts the speed profiles of complex arm movements. *J. Neurophysiol.*, 80, 696–714.

Todorov, E., Jordan, M.I. (2002) Optimal feedback control as a theory of motor coordination. *Nat. Neurosci.*, 5, 1126–1235.

Tokizane, T., Murao, M., Ogata, T., Kondo, T. (1951) Electromyographic studies on tonic neck, lumbar and labyrinthine reflexes in normal persons. *Jap. J. Physiol.*, 2, 130–146.

Tolman, E.C. (1925) Purpose and cognition: The determiners of animal learning. *Psychol. Rev.*, 32, 285–297.

Tonolli, I., Aurenty, R., Lee, R.G., Viallet, F., Massion, J. (2000) Lateral leg raising in patients with Parkinson's disease: Influence of equilibrium constraint. *Movement Disorders*, 15, 850–861.

Tootell, R.B., Hadjikhani, N.K., Mendola, J.D., Marrett, S., Dale, A.M.(1998) From retinotopy to recognition: fMRI in human visual cortex. *Trends Cogn. Sci.*, 2, 174–183.

Torres-Oviedo, G., Ting, L.H. (2007) Muscle synergies characterizing human postural responses. *J. Neurophysiol.*, 98, 2144–2156.

Torres-Oviedo, G., Ting, L.H. (2010) Subject-specific muscle synergies in human balance control are consistent across different biomechanical contexts. *J. Neurophysiol.*, 103, 3084–3098.

Torrey, C.C. (1985) Visual flow and direction of locomotion. *Science*, 4690, 1063–1065.

Tourville, J.A., Guenther, F.H. (2011) The DIVA model: A neural theory of speech acquisition and production. *Lang. Cogn. Process.*, 26, 952–981.

Tranel, D., Damasio, A.R., Damasio, H., Brandt, J.P. (1994) Sensorimotor skill learning in amnesia: Additional evidence for the neural basis of nondeclarative memory. *Learn. Mem*, 1, 165–179.

Travis, R.C. (1945) An experimental analysis of dynamic and static equilibrium. *J. Exp. Psychol.*, 35, 216–234.

Tresch, M.C., Jarc, A. (2009) The case for and against muscle synergies. *Curr. Opin. Neurobiol.*, 19, 601–607.

Tresilian, J.R. (1991) Empirical and theoretical issues in the perception of time-to-contact. *J. Exp. Psychol. Hum. Percept. Perform.*, 17, 865–876.

Tresilian, J.R. (1995) Perceptual and cognitive processes in time-to-contact estimation: Analysis of prediction-motion and relative judgment tasks. *Percept. Psychophys.*, 57, 231–245.

Tresilian, J.R. (1999a) Retaining the equilibrium-point hypothesis as an abstract description of the neuromuscular system. *Motor Control*, 3, 67–89.

Tresilian, J.R. (1999b) Visually timed action: Time out for tau? *Trends Cogn. Sci.*, 3, 301–310.

Tresilian, J.R. (2005) Hitting moving targets: Perception and action in the timing of fast interceptions. *Percept. Psychophys.*, 67, 129–149.

Tresilian, J.R., Houseman, J.H. (2005) Systematic variation in performance of an interceptive action with changes in the temporal constraints. *Quart. J. Exp. Psychol.*, A58, 447–466.

Tresilian, J.R., Mon-Williams, M., Kelly, B. (1999) Increasing confidence in vergence as a cue to distance. *Proc. Roy. Soc. Lond. B*, 266, 39–44.

Tresilian, J.R., Oliver, J., Carroll, T.J. (2003) Temporal precision of interceptive action: Differential effects of target speed and size. *Exp. Brain Res.*, 148, 425–438.

Tresilian, J.R., Plooy, A.M. (2006) Systematic changes in the duration and precision of interception in response to variations of amplitude and effector size. *Exp. Brain Res.*, 171, 421–435.

Tresilian, J.R., Plooy, A.M., Carroll, T.J. (2004) Constraints on the spatio-temporal accuracy of interceptive action: effects of target size on hitting a moving target. *Exp. Brain Res.*, 155, 509–526.

Tresilian, J.R., Plooy, A.M., Marinovic, W. (2009) Manual interception in two dimensions: Performance and space-time accuracy. *Brain Res.*, 1250, 202–217.

Trousselard, M., Barraud, P.A., Nougier, V., Raphel, C., Cian, C. (2004) Contribution of tactile and interoceptive cues to the perception of the direction of gravity. *Cogn. Brain Res.*, 20, 355–362.

Trousselard, M., Cian, C., Nougier, V., Pla, S., Raphel, C. (2003) Contribution of somaesthetic cues to the perception of body orientation and subjective visual vertical. *Percept. Psychophys.*, 65, 1179–1187.

Trowbridge, M.H., Cason, H. (1932) An experimental study of Thorndike's theory of learning. *J. Gen. Psychol.*, 7, 245–260.

Tuller, B., Turvey, M.T., Fitch, H.L. (1982) The Bernstein perspective, II: The concept of muscle linkage or coordinative structure. In Kelso, J.A.S. (ed.) *Human Motor Behavior: An Introduction*. Hillsdale, NJ: Lawrence Erlbaum.

Turner, R.S., Desmurget, M. (2010) Basal ganglia contributions to motor control: A vigorous tutor. *Curr. Opin. Neurobiol.*, 20, 704–716.

Turvey, M.T. (1996) Dynamic touch. *Am. Psychologist*, 51, 1134–1152.

Turvey, M.T., Carello, C. (1995) Dynamic touch. In W. Epstein, S. Rogers (eds), *Handbook of perception and cognition*, vol. 5, *Perception of space and motion* (pp. 401–490). San Diego: Academic Press.

Turvey, M.T., Fitch, H.L., Tuller, B. (1982) The Bernstein perspective: I. The problems of degrees of freedom and context conditioned variability. In J.A.S. Kelso (ed.) *Human Motor Behavior: An Introduction* (pp. 239–252). Hillsdale, NJ: Lawrence Erlbaum.

Tweed, D. (2003) *Microcosms of the Brain: What Sensorimotor Systems Reveal about the Mind*. Oxford University Press.

Tyrrell, R.A., Rudolph, T., Eggers, B.G., Leibowitz, H.W. (1993) Evidence for the persistence of visual guidance information. *Percept. Psychophys.*, 54, 431–438.

U.

Uchino, Y. (2004) Role of cross-striolar and commissural inhibition in the vestibulocollic reflex. *Prog. Brain Res.*, 143, 403–409.

Uhlarik, J.J., Canon, L.K. (1971) Influence of concurrent and terminal exposure conditions on the nature of perceptual adaptation. *J. Exp. Psychol.*, 9, 233–239.

Underwood, G., Chapman, P., Crundall, D., Cooper, S., Wallen, R. (1999) The visual control of steering and driving: Where do we look when negotiating curves? In A.G. Gale, I.D. Brown, C.M. Haslegrave, S.P. Taylor (eds) *Vision in Vehicles VII*. Oxford: Elsevier.

Ungerleider, L.G., Mishkin, M. (1982) Two cortical visual systems. In D.J. Ingle, M.A. Goodale, R.J.W. Mansfield (eds) *Analysis of Visual Behavior* (pp. 549–586). Cambridge, MA: MIT Press.

Uno, Y., Kawato, M., Suzuki, R. (1989) Formation and control of optimal trajectory in human multi-joint arm movement: Minimum torque-change model. *Biol. Cybern.*, 61, 89–101.

V.

Valbo, Å.B. (1971) Muscle spindle response at the onset of isometric voluntary contractions in man: Time difference between fusimotor and skeletomotor effects. *J. Physiol.*, 219, 405–431.

Van Asten, N.J.C., Gielen, C.C.A.M., Denier van der Gon, J.J. (1988) Postural adjustments induced by simulated motion of differently structured environments. *Exp. Brain Res.*, 73, 371–383.

Van der Langenberg, R., Kingma, I., Beek, P.J. (2008) The perception of limb orientation depends upon the center of mass. *J. Exp. Psychol. Hum. Percept. Perform.*, 34, 624–639.

Van Donkelaar, P., Lee, R.G., Gellman, R.S. (1992) Control strategies in directing the hand at moving targets. *Exp. Brain Res.*, 91, 151–161.

Van Emmerick, R.E., Wagenaar, R.C., Van Wegen, E.E. (1998) Interlimb coupling patterns in human locomotion: Are we bipeds or quadrupeds? *Ann. N.Y. Acad. Sci.*, 860, 539–542.

Van Essen, D.C. (2005) Corticocortical and thalamocortical information flow in the primate visual system. *Prog. Brain Res.*, 149, 173–185.

Van Sonderen, J.F., Denier van der Gon, J.J. (1990) A simulation study of a programme generator for centrally programmed fast two-joint arm movements: Responses to single- and double-step target displacements. *Biol. Cybern.*, 63, 35–44.

Van Sonderen, J.F., Denier van der Gon, J.J., Gielen, C.C.A.M. (1988) Conditions determining early modification of motor programmes in response to changes in target direction. *Exp. Brain Res.*, 71, 320–328.

Van Sonderen, J.F., Gielen, C.C.A.M., Denier van der Gon, J.J. (1989) Motor programmes for goal-directed movements are continuously adjusted according to changes in target location. *Exp. Brain Res.*, 78, 139–146.

Vereijken, B., van Emmerik, R.E.A., Whiting, H.T.A., Newell, K.M. (1992) Free(z)ing degrees of freedom in skill acquisition. *J. Mot. Behav.*, 24, 133–142.

Verwey, W.B. (1996) Buffer loading and chunking in sequential keypressing. *J. Exp. Psychol. Hum. Percept. Perform.*, 22, 544–562.

Verwey, W.B. (1999) Evidence for a multi-stage model of practice in a sequential movement task. *J. Exp. Psychol. Hum. Percept. Perform.*, 25, 1693–1708.

Verwey, W.B. (2001) Concatenating familiar movement sequences: The versatile cognitive processor. *Acta Psychol.*, 106, 69–95.

Viviani, P., Cenzato, M. (1985) Segmentation and coupling in complex movements. *J. Exp. Psychol. Hum. Percept. Perform.*, 6, 828–845.

Viviani, P., Flash, T. (1995) Minimum-jerk, two-thirds power law, and isochrony: Converging approaches to movement planning. *J. Exp. Psychol. Hum. Percept. Perform.*, 21, 32–53.

Viviani, P., McCollum, G. (1983) The relationship between linear extent and velocity in drawing movements. *Neuroscience*, 10, 211–218.

Viviani, P., Schneider, R. (1991) A developmental study of the relation between geometry and kinematics in drawing movements. *J. Exp. Psychol. Hum. Percept. Perform.*, 17, 198–218.

Viviani, P., Terzuolo, C.A. (1980) Space-time invariance in learned motor skills. In G.E. Stelmach, J. Requin (eds) *Tutorials in Motor Behavior*. Amsterdam: North Holland (pp. 525–533).

Viviani, P., Terzuolo, C.A. (1982a) On the relation between word-specific patterns and the central control model of typing: A reply to Gentner. *J. Exp. Psychol. Hum. Percept. Perform.*, 8, 811–813.

Viviani, P., Terzuolo, C.A. (1982b) Trajectory determines movement dynamics. *Neuroscience*, 7, 431–437.

Viviani, P., Terzuolo, C.A. (1983) The organization of movement in handwriting and typing. In B. Butterworth (ed.) *Language Production*, vol. 2 (pp. 103–146). London: Academic Press.

Vogel, E.K., Woodman, G.F., Luck, S.J. (2001) Storage of features, conjunctions and objects in visual working memory. *J. Exp. Psychol. Hum. Percept. Perform.*, 27, 92–114.

Vogel, S. (2003) *Comparative Biomechanics: Life's Physical World*. Princeton, NJ: Princeton University Press.

Von Holst, E., Mittelstadt, H. (1950/1973) 'Der Reafferenzprinzip' (The reafference principle), reprinted in R. Martin (translator), *The Behavioural Physiology of Animals and Man: The Collected Papers of Erich von Holst*. Coral Gables, FL: University of Miami Press.

W.

Wada, M., Kawahara, H., Shimada, S., Miyazaki, T., Baba, H. (2002) Joint proprioception before and after total knee arthroplasty. *Clin. Orthop. Relat. Res.*, 403, 161–167.

Wada, M., Sunaga, N., Nagai, M. (2001) Anxiety affects the postural sway of the antero-posterior axis in college students. *Neurosci. Lett.*, 302, 157–159.

Wada, Y., Kawato, M. (1995) A theory for cursive handwriting based on the minimization principle. *Biol. Cybern.*, 73, 3–13.

Wada, Y., Koike, Y., Vatikiotis-Bateson, M., Kawato, A. (2005) Computational model for cursive handwriting based on the minimization principle. In J.D. Cowan, G. Tesauro, J. Alspector (eds) *Advances in Neuronal Information Processing Systems 6* (NIPS6) (pp. 727–737). San Francisco: Morgan Kaufmann.

Wade, N.J., Schöne, H. (1971) The influence of force magnitude on the perception of body position, I: Effect of head posture. *Br. J. Psychol.*, 62, 157–163.

Wadman, W.J., Denier van der Gon, J.J., Derksen, D. (1980) Muscle activation patterns for fast goal-directed arm movements. *J. Hum. Mov. Stud.*, 6, 19–37.

Wallace, S.A., Newell, K.M. (1983) Visual control of discrete aiming movements. *Quart. J. Exp. Psychol. A*, 35, 311–321.

Waller, A.D. (1891) The sense of effort: An objective study. *Brain*, 14, 179–249.

Wallis, G., Chatziastros, A., Bulthoff, H. (2002) An unexpected role for visual feedback in vehicle steering control. *Curr. Biol.*, 12, 295–299.

Wallis, G., Chatziastros, A., Tresilian, J., Tomasevic, N. (2007) The role of visual and non-visual feedback in a vehicle steering task. *J. Exp. Psychol. Hum. Percept. Perform.*, 33, 1127–1144.

Walsh, L.D., Moseley, G.L., Taylor, J.L., Gandevia, S.C. (2011) Proprioceptive signals contribute to the sense of body ownership. *J. Physiol.*, 589, 3009–3021.

Wang, R.F., Cutting, J.E. (2004) Eye movements and an object-based model of heading perception. In L. Vaina, S. Beardsley, S. Rushton (eds) *Optic flow and beyond* (pp. 61–78). Dordrecht: Kluwer Academic Press.

Wann, J.P. (1987) Trends in the refinement and optimization of fine motor trajectories: Observations from an analysis of the handwriting of primary-school children. *J. Mot. Behav.*, 19, 13–37.

Wann, J.P. (1996) Anticipating arrival: Is the tau margin a specious theory? *J. Exp. Psychol. Hum. Percept. Perform.*, 22, 1031–1048.

Wann, J.P., Mon-Williams, M., Rushton, K. (1998) Postural control and co-ordination disorders: The swinging room revisited. *Hum. Mov. Sci.*, 17, 491–513.

Wann, J.P., Nimmo-Smith, I., Wing, A.M. (1988) Relation between velocity and curvature in movement: Equivalence and divergence between a power law and a minimum-jerk model. *J. Exp. Psychol. Hum. Percept. Perform.*, 14, 622–637.

Wann, J.P., Swapp, D.K. (2000) Why you should look where you are going. *Nat. Neurosci.*, 3, 647–648.

Ward, J. (2010) *The Student's Guide to Cognitive Neuroscience*. Hove, UK: Psychology Press.

Wark, B., Lundstrom, B.N., Fairhall, A. (2007) Sensory adaptation. *Curr. Opin. Neurobiol.*, 17, 423–429.

Warren, R. (1976) The perception of egomotion. *J. Exp. Psychol. Hum. Percept. Perform.*, 2, 448–456.

Warren, W.H. (1984) Perceiving affordances: Visual guidance of stair climbing. *J. Exp. Psychol. Hum. Percept. Perform.*, 10, 683–703.

Warren, W.H., Hannon, D.J. (1990) Eye movements and optical flow. *J. Opt. Soc. Am. A*, 7, 160–169.

Warren, W.H., Kay, B.A., Zosh, W.D., Duchon, A.P., Sahuc, S. (2001) Optic flow is used to control human walking. *Nat. Neurosci.*, 4, 213–216.

Warren, W.H., Morris, M., Kalish, M.L. (1988) Perception of translational heading from optical flow. *J. Exp. Psychol. Hum. Percept. Perform.*, 14, 646–660.

Warren, W.H., Whang, S. (1987) Visual guidance of walking through apertures: Body-scaled information for affordances. *J. Exp. Psychol. Hum. Percept. Perform.*, 13, 371–383.

Warren, W.H., Young, D.S., Lee, D.N. (1986) Visual control of step length during running over irregular terrain. *J. Exp. Psychol. Hum. Percept. Perform.*, 12, 259–266.

Watson, J.B. (1920) Is thinking merely the action of the language mechanisms? *Br. J. Psychol.*, 11, 86–104.

Watson, J.S. (2005) The elementary nature of purposive behavior: Evolving minimal neural structures that display intrinsic intentionality. *Evol. Psychol.*, 3, 24–48.

Watts, R.G., Bahill, A.T. (2000) *Keep Your Eye on the Ball: Curve Balls, Knuckleballs, and Fallacies of Baseball*. New York: W.H. Freeman.

Weber, W., Weber, E. (1836) *Mechanik der Menschlichen Gehwerkzauge* (Mechanics of human locomotion). Göttingen: Dieterich.

Weerdesteyn, V., Nienhuis, B., Hampsink, B., Duysens, J. (2004) Gait adjustments in response to an obstacle are faster than voluntary reactions. *Hum. Mov. Sci.*, 23, 351–363.

Weerdesteyn, V., Nienhuis, B., Mulder, T., Duysens, J. (2005) Older women strongly prefer stride lengthening to shortening in avoiding obstacles. *Exp. Brain Res.*, 161, 39–46.

Weiskrantz, L., Warrington, E.K., Sanders, M.D., Marshall, J. (1974) Visual capacity in the hemianopic field following a restricted occipital ablation. *Brain*, 97, 709–728.

Welch, C.M., Banks, S.A., Cook, F., Draovitch, P. (1995) Hitting a baseball: a biomechanical description. *J. Orth. Sports Phys. Ther.*, 22, 193–201.

Welford, A.T. (1968) *Fundamentals of Skill*. London: Methuen.

Wells, J.C. (1990) *Longman Pronunciation Dictionary*. London: Longman.

Werner, S., Bock, O. (2007) Effects of variable practice and declarative knowledge on sensorimotor adaptation to rotated visual feedback. *Exp. Brain Res.*, 178, 554–559.

Whalen, D.H. (1990) Coarticulation is largely planned. *J. Phonetics*, 18, 3–35.

Whelan, P.J. (1996) Control of locomotion in the decerebrate cat. *Prog. Neurobiol.*, 49, 418–515.

White, B.W., Saunders, F., Scadden, L., Bach-y-Rita, P., Collins, C.C. (1970) Seeing with the skin. *Percept. Psychophys.*, 7, 23–27.

Whitney, D.E. (1972) The mathematics of coordinated control of prosthetic arms and manipulators. *ASME J. Dynamic Systems, Measurement & Control*, 94, 303–309.

Whittlesey, S.N., Van Emmerik, R.E., Hamill, J. (2000) The swing phase of human walking is not a passive movement. *Motor Control*, 4, 273–292.

Wickelgren, W.A. (1969) Context-sensitive coding, associative memory, and serial order in (speech) behavior. *Psychol. Rev.*, 76, 1–15.

Wickens, C.D., Hollands, J.G. (1999) *Engineering Psychology and Human Performance* (3rd edition). New York: Prentice Hall.

Wickens, C.D., Lee, J., Lui, Y.D., Gordon-Becker, S. (2003) *An Introduction to Human Factors Engineering*. Pearson Education.

Wiener, N. (1948/1961) *Cybernetics: or Control and Communication in the Animal and the Machine*. Cambridge, MA: MIT Press.

Wilkie, R.M., Wann, J.P. (2003) Controlling steering and judging heading: Retinal flow, visual direction and extra-retinal information. *J. Exp. Psychol. Hum. Percept. Perform.*, 29, 363–378.

Wilkie, R.M., Wann, J.P. (2006) Judgments of path, not heading, guide locomotion. *J. Exp. Psychol. Hum. Percept. Perform.*, 32, 88–96.

Wilkie, R.M., Wann, J.P., Allison, R.S. (2008) Active gaze, visual look-ahead and locomotor control. *J. Exp. Psychol. Hum. Percept. Perform.*, 34, 1150–1164.

Wilkinson, D.A. (1971) Visual-motor control loop: A linear system? *J. Exp. Psychol.*, 89, 250–257.

Wilson, M., Chattington, M., Marple-Horvat, D.E. (2008) Eye movements drive steering: Reduced eye movement distribution impairs steering and driving. *J. Mot. Behav.*, 40, 190–202.

Wilson, M., Stephenson, S., Chattington, M., Marple-Horvat, D.E. (2007) Eye movements coordinated with steering benefit performance even when vision is denied. *Exp. Brain Res.*, 176, 397–412.

Wilson, V.J., Bolton, P.S., Goto, T., Schor, R.H., Yamagata, Y., Yates, B.J. (1992) Spatial transformation in the vertical vestibulocollic reflex. *Ann. N.Y. Acad. Sci.*, 656, 500–506.

Wilson, V.J., Melvill Jones, G. (1979) *Mammalian Vestibular Physiology.* New York: Plenum Press.

Wilson, V.J., Schor, R.H. (1999) The neural substrate of the vestibulocollic reflex: What needs to be learned. *Exp. Brain Res.*, 129, 483–493.

Windhorst, U. (1994) Shaping static elbow torque-angle relationships by spinal cord circuits: A theoretical study. *Neuroscience*, 59, 713–727.

Windhorst, U. (2007) Muscle proprioceptive feedback and spinal networks. *Brain Res. Bull.*, 73, 155–202.

Wing, A.M. (1980) The height of handwriting. *Acta Psychol.*, 46, 141–151.

Wing, A.M. (2000) Mechanisms of motor equivalence in handwriting. *Curr. Biol.*, 10, R245–R248.

Wing, A.M., Nimmo-Smith, I., Eldridge, M.A. (1983) The consistency of cursive letter formation as a function of position in the word. *Acta Psychol.*, 54, 197–204.

Winstein, C.J, Schmidt, R.A. (1990) Reduced frequency of knowledge of results enhances motor skill learning. *J. Exp. Psychol. Learn. Mem. Cogn.*, 16, 677–691.

Winter, D.A. (1995) Human posture and balance during standing and walking. *Gait Posture*, 3, 193–214.

Winter, D.A. (2009) *Biomechanics and motor control of human movement* (4th edition). New York: Wiley.

Winter, D.A., Patla, A.E., Prince, F., Ishac, M.G., Gielo-Perczak, K. (1998) Stiffness control of balance in quiet standing. *J. Neurophysiol.*, 80, 1211–1221.

Winter, D.A., Patla, A.E., Rietdyk, S., Ishac, M.G. (2001) Ankle muscle stiffness in the control of balance during quiet standing. *J. Neurophysiol.*, 85, 2630–2633.

Winter, D.A., Prince, F., Frank, J.S., Powell, C., Zabjek, K.F. (1996) Unified theory regarding A/P and M/L balance in quiet stance. *J. Neurophysiol.*, 175, 2334–2343.

Winter, D.A., Yack, H.J. (1987) EMG profiles during normal human walking: Stride-to-stride and inter-subject variability. *Electroencephalogr. Clin. Neurophysiol.*, 67, 402–411.

Winterson, B.J., Collewijn, H. (1976) Microsaccades during finely guided visuomotor tasks. *Vision Res.*, 16, 1387–1390.

Wisleder, D., Dounskaia, N. (2007) The role of different submovement types during pointing to a target. *Exp. Brain Res.*, 176, 132–149.

Witkin, H.A. (1949) Perception of body position and the position of the visual field. *Psychological Monographs*, 6 (7), 1–63.

Witkin, H.A., Wapner, S.S. (1950) Large oscillating visual displays increase postural instability. *Am. J. Psychol.*, 63, 385–392.

Woch, A., Plamondon, R. (2004) Using the framework of the kinematic theory for the definition of a movement primitive. *Motor Control*, 8, 547–557.

Wolfe, J.M., Kluender, K.R., Levi, D.M., Bartoshuk, L.M., Herz, R.S., Klatzky, R.L., Lederman, S.J., Merfeld, D.M. (2011) *Sensation and Perception* (3rd edition). Sunderland, MA: Sinauer Associates.

Wolpaw, J.R. (1997) The complex structure of a simple memory. *Trends Neurosci.*, 20, 588–594.

Wolpaw, J.R. (2007) Spinal cord plasticity in acquisition and maintenance of motor skills. *Acta Physiol. (Oxf.)*, 189, 155–169.

Wolpaw, J.R. (2010) What can the spinal cord teach us about learning and memory? *Neuroscientist*, 16, 532–49.

Wolpert, D.M., Diedrichsen, J., Flanagan, J.R. (2011) Principles of sensorimotor learning. *Nat. Rev. Neurosci.*, 12, 739–751.

Wolpert, D.M., Ghahramani, Z., Jordan, M.I. (1994) Perceptual distortion contributes to the curvature of human reaching movements. *Exp. Brain Res.*, 98, 153–156.

Wolpert, D.M., Ghahramani, Z., Jordan, M.I. (1995) Are arm trajectories planned in kinematic or dynamic coordinates? An adaptation study. *Exp. Brain Res.*, 103, 460–470.

Won, J., Hogan, N. (1995) Stability properties of human reaching movements. *Exp. Brain Res.*, 107, 125–136.

Wong, S.C.P., Frost, B.J. (1978) Subjective motion and acceleration induced by the movement of the observer's entire visual field. *Percept. Psychophys.*, 24, 115–120.

Wood, R.W. (1895) The 'haunted swing' illusion. *Psychol. Rev.*, 2, 277–278.

Wood, W., Neal, D.T. (2007) A new look at habits and the habit-goal interface. *Psych. Rev.*, 114, 843–863.

Woodruff-Pak, D.S., Disterhoft, J.F. (2008) Where is the trace in trace conditioning? *Trends Neurosci.*, 31, 105–112.

Woods, T.M., Reganzone, G.H. (2004) Cross-model interactions evidenced by the ventriloquism effect in humans and monkeys. In G. Calvert, C. Spence, B.E. Stein (eds) *The Handbook of Multisensory Processes* (pp. 35–48). Cambridge, MA: MIT Press.

Woodworth, R.S. (1899) The accuracy of voluntary movement. *Psychol. Rev.*, 3 (Suppl. 13), 1–119.

Woodworth, R.S. (1918) *Dynamic Psychology.* New York: Columbia University Press.

Worringham, C.J. (1987) *Spatial variability and impact force in aiming movements.* Unpublished doctoral dissertation, University of Wisconsin, Madison.

Worringham, C.J., Dennis, R.G. (1992) Distance errors – pointing at the range effect. *Behav. Brain Sci.*, 15, 352–353.

Worringham, C.J., Stelmach, G.E., Martin, Z.E. (1987) Limb segment inclination sense in proprioception. *Exp. Brain Res.*, 66, 653–658.

Wright, C.E. (1990) Generalized motor programs: Reexamining claims of effector independence in writing. In M. Jeannerod (ed.) *Attention and Performance XIII* (pp. 294–320). Hillsdale, NJ: Erlbaum.

Wright, C.E. (1993) Evaluating the special role of time in the control of handwriting. *Acta Psychol.*, 82, 5–52.

Wright, C.E., Meyer, D.E. (1983) Conditions for a linear speed-accuracy trade-off in aimed movements. *Quart. J. Exp. Psychol. A*, 35, 279–296.

Wu, J., Yang, J., Honda, T. (2010) Fitts' law holds for pointing movements under conditions of restricted visual feedback. *Hum. Mov. Sci.*, 29, 882–892.

Wu, T., Chan, P., Hallett, M. (2008) Modifications of the interactions in the motor networks when a movement becomes automatic. *J. Physiol.*, 586, 4295–4304.

Wulf, G., Mercer, J., McNevin, N., Guadagnoli, M.A. (2004) Reciprocal influences of attentional focus on postural and suprapostural task performance. *J. Mot. Behav.*, 36, 189–199.

Wynne, C.D.L. (1994) The return of the reinforcement theorists. *Behav. Brain Sci.*, 17, 156.

Y.

Yakolev, P.I., Lecours, A.R. (1967) The myelogenetic cycles of regional maturation of the brain. In A. Minkowski (ed.), *Regional Development of the Brain in Early Life* (pp. 3–70). Oxford: Blackwell.

Yang, J.F., Lamont, E.V., Pang, M.Y. (2005) Split-belt treadmill stepping in infants suggests autonomous pattern generators for the left and right leg in humans. *J. Neurosci.*, 25, 6869–6876.

Yang, Q., Le, T., Kapoula, Z. (2009) Aging effects on the visually driven part of vergence movements. *Invest. Ophthalmol. Vis. Sci.*, 50, 1145–1151.

Yeo, C.H., Hesslow, G. (1998) Cerebellum and conditioned reflexes. *Trends Cogn. Sci.*, 2, 322–330.

Yin, H.H., Knowlton, B.J. (2006) The role of the basal ganglia in habit formation. *Nat. Rev. Neurosci.*, 7, 464–476.

Young, D.E., Schmidt, R.A. (1990) Units of motor behaviour: Modifications with practice and feedback. In M. Jeannerod (ed.) *Attention and Performance XIII* (pp. 763–795). Hillsdale, NJ: Lawrence Erlbaum.

Young, L.R. (1999) Artificial gravity considerations for a Mars exploration mission. *Ann. N.Y. Acad. Sci.*, 871, 367–378.

Young, L.R. (2003) Spatial orientation. In P.S. Tsang, M.A. Vidulich (eds) *Principles and Practice of Aviation Psychology*. Hillsdale, NJ: Lawrence Erlbaum.

Z.

Zago, M., McIntyre, J., Senot, P., Lacquaniti, F. (2009) Visuo-motor coordination and internal models for object interception. *Exp. Brain Res.*, 192, 571–604.

Zajac, F.E., Neptune, R.R., Kautz, S.A. (2002) Biomechanics and muscle coordination of human walking, Part I: Introduction to concepts, power transfer, dynamics and simulations. *Gait Posture*, 16, 215–232.

Zajac, F.E., Neptune, R.R., Kautz, S.A. (2003) Biomechanics and muscle coordination of human walking, Part II: Lessons from dynamical simulations and clinical populations. *Gait Posture*, 17, 1–17.

Zariwala, H.A., Miller, A.C., Faumont, S., Lockery, S.R. (2003) Step response analysis of thermotaxis in *Caenorhabditis elegans*. *J. Neurosci.*, 23, 4369–4377.

Zarrugh, M.Y., Radcliffe, C.W. (1978) Predicting metabolic cost of walking. *Eur. J. Appl. Physiol.*, 38, 215–223.

Zee, D.S., Optican, L.M., Cook, J.D., Robinson, D.A., Engel, W.K. (1976) Slow saccades in spinocerebellar degeneration. *Archives of Neurology*, 33, 243–251.

Zee, D.S., Robinson, D.A. (1979) Velocity characteristics of normal human saccades. In H.S. Thompson, R. Daroff, J.S. Glaser, M.D. Sanders (eds) *Topics in Neuro-Ophthalmology*. Baltimore, MD: Williams and Wilkins.

Zehr, E.P., Duysens, J. (2004) Regulation of arm and leg movement during human locomotion. *Neuroscientist*, 10, 347–361.

Zehr, E.P., Komiyama, T., Stein, R.B. (1997) Cutaneous reflexes during human gait: Electromyographic and kinematic responses to electrical stimulation. *J. Neurophysiol.*, 77, 3311–3325.

Zehr, E.P., Stein, R.B. (1999) What functions do reflexes serve during human locomotion? *Prog. Neurobiol.*, 58, 185–205.

Zelaznik, H.N., Mone, S., McCabe, G.P., Thaman, C. (1988) Role of temporal and spatial precision in determining the nature of the speed-accuracy trade-off in aimed hand movements. *J. Exp. Psychol. Hum. Percept. Perform.*, 14, 221–230.

Zelaznik, H.N., Schmidt, R.A., Gielen, C.C.A.M. (1986) Kinematic properties of rapid aimed hand movements. *J. Mot. Behav.*, 18, 353–372.

Zhai, S. (2004) Characterizing computer input with Fitts' law parameters: The information and non-informational aspects of pointing. *Int. J. Hum. Comput. Stud.*, 61, 785–804.

Zhai, S., Kong, J., Ren, X. (2004) Speed-accuracy tradeoff in Fitts' law tasks: On the equivalency of actual and nominal pointing precision. *Int. J. Hum. Comput. Stud.*, 61, 823–856.

Zhang, Y., Kiemel, T., Jeka, J. (2007) The influence of sensory information on two-component coordination during quiet stance. *Gait Posture*, 26, 263–271.

Zhou, W., King, W.M. (1998) Premotor commands encode monocular eye movements. *Nature*, 393, 692–695.

Ziemann, U. (2010) TMS in cognitive neuroscience: Virtual lesion and beyond. *Cortex*, 46, 124–127.

Index